Contemporary
Literary Criticism

Guide to Gale Literary Criticism Series

For criticism on	You need these Gale series
Authors now living or who died after December 31, 1959	*CONTEMPORARY LITERARY CRITICISM (CLC)*
Authors who died between 1900 and 1959	*TWENTIETH-CENTURY LITERARY CRITICISM (TCLC)*
Authors who died between 1800 and 1899	*NINETEENTH-CENTURY LITERATURE CRITICISM (NCLC)*
Authors who died between 1400 and 1799	*LITERATURE CRITICISM FROM 1400 TO 1800 (LC)* *SHAKESPEAREAN CRITICISM (SC)*
Authors who died before 1400	*CLASSICAL AND MEDIEVAL LITERATURE CRITICISM (CMLC)*
Authors of books for children and young adults	*CHILDREN'S LITERATURE REVIEW (CLR)*
Black writers of the past two hundred years	*BLACK LITERATURE CRITICISM (BLC)*
Short story writers	*SHORT STORY CRITICISM (SSC)*
Poets	*POETRY CRITICISM (PC)*
Dramatists	*DRAMA CRITICISM (DC)*
Major authors from the Renaissance to the present	*WORLD LITERATURE CRITICISM, 1500 TO THE PRESENT (WLC)*

For criticism on visual artists since 1850, see

MODERN ARTS CRITICISM (MAC)

ISSN 0091-3421

Volume 77

Contemporary Literary Criticism

Excerpts from Criticism of the Works
of Today's Novelists, Poets, Playwrights,
Short Story Writers, Scriptwriters, and
Other Creative Writers

James P. Draper
EDITOR

Jennifer Brostrom
Jennifer Gariepy
Christopher Giroux
Drew Kalasky
Marie Lazzari
Thomas Ligotti
Kyung-Sun Lim
Dan Marowski
Brigham Narins
Sean René Pollock
Janet Witalec
ASSOCIATE EDITORS

Gale Research Inc. • *DETROIT* • *WASHINGTON, D.C.* • *LONDON*

STAFF

James P. Draper, *Editor*

Jennifer Brostrom, Jennifer Gariepy, Christopher Giroux, Drew Kalasky, Marie Lazzari, Thomas Ligotti, Kyung-Sun Lim, Dan Marowski, Brigham Narins, Sean René Pollock, Janet Witalec, *Associate Editors*

Jeffery Chapman, Joseph Cislo, Ted Mouw, Lynn M. Spampinato, *Assistant Editors*

Jeanne A. Gough, *Permissions & Production Manager*
Linda M. Pugliese, *Production Supervisor*
Donna Craft, Paul Lewon, Maureen Puhl, Camille P. Robinson, Sheila Walencewicz, *Editorial Associates*
Elizabeth Anne Valliere, *Editorial Assistant*

Sandra C. Davis, *Permissions Supervisor (Text)*
Maria L. Franklin, Josephine M. Keene, Michele Lonoconus, Shalice Shah, Denise Singleton, Kimberly F. Smilay, *Permissions Associates*
Jennifer A. Arnold, Brandy C. Merritt, *Permissions Assistants*

Margaret A. Chamberlain, *Permissions Supervisor (Pictures)*
Pamela A. Hayes, Keith Reed, *Permissions Associates*
Susan Brohman, Arlene Johnson, Barbara A. Wallace, *Permissions Assistants*

Victoria B. Cariappa, *Research Manager*
Maureen Richards, *Research Supervisor*
Robert S. Lazich, Mary Beth McElmeel, Donna Melnychenko, Tamara C. Nott, *Editorial Associates*
Karen Farrelly, Kelly Hill, Julie Leonard, Stefanie Scarlett, *Editorial Assistants*

Mary Beth Trimper, *Production Director*
Shanna Heilveil, *Production Assistant*

Cynthia Baldwin, *Art Director*
C. J. Jonik, *Desktop Publisher*
Willie F. Mathis, *Camera Operator*

Library of Congress Catalog Card Number 76-38938
ISBN 0-8103-4983-3
ISSN 0091-3421

Printed in the United States of America
Published simultaneously in the United Kingdom
by Gale Research International Limited
(An affiliated company of Gale Research Inc.)
10 9 8 7 6 5 4 3 2 1

The trademark **ITP** is used under license.

Contents

Preface vii

Acknowledgments xi

Preface

A Comprehensive Information Source on Contemporary Literature

Named "one of the twenty-five most distinguished reference titles published during the past twenty-five years" by *Reference Quarterly*, the *Contemporary Literary Criticism (CLC)* series provides readers with critical commentary and general information on more than 2,000 authors now living or who died after December 31, 1959. Previous to the publication of the first volume of *CLC* in 1973, there was no ongoing digest monitoring scholarly and popular sources of critical opinion and explication of modern literature. *CLC*, therefore, has fulfilled an essential need, particularly since the complexity and variety of contemporary literature makes the function of criticism especially important to today's reader.

Scope of the Series

CLC presents significant passages from published criticism of works by creative writers. Since many of the authors covered by *CLC* inspire continual critical commentary, writers are often represented in more than one volume. There is, of course, no duplication of reprinted criticism.

Authors are selected for inclusion for a variety of reasons, among them the publication or dramatic production of a critically acclaimed new work, the reception of a major literary award, revival of interest in past writings, or the adaptation of a literary work to film or television.

Attention is also given to several other groups of writers—authors of considerable public interest—about whose work criticism is often difficult to locate. These include mystery and science fiction writers, literary and social critics, foreign writers, and authors who represent particular ethnic groups within the United States.

Format of the Book

Each *CLC* volume contains about 500 individual excerpts taken from hundreds of book review periodicals, general magazines, scholarly journals, monographs, and books. Entries include critical evaluations spanning from the beginning of an author's career to the most current commentary. Interviews, feature articles, and other published writings that offer insight into the author's works are also presented. Students, teachers, librarians, and researchers will find that the generous excerpts and supplementary material in *CLC* provide them with vital information required to write a term paper, analyze a poem, or lead a book discussion group. In addition, complete bibliographical citations note the original source and all of the information necessary for a term paper footnote or bibliography.

Features

A *CLC* author entry consists of the following elements:

- The **Author Heading** cites the author's name in the form under which the author has most commonly published, followed by birth date, and death date when applicable. Uncertainty as to a birth or death date is indicated by a question mark.

- A **Portrait** of the author is included when available.

- A brief **Biographical and Critical Introduction** to the author and his or her work precedes the excerpted criticism. The first line of the introduction provides the author's full name, pseudonyms (if applicable), nationality, and a listing of genres in which the author has written. Previous volumes of *CLC* in which the author has been featured are also listed in the introduction.

- A list of **Principal Works** notes the most important works by the author.

- The **Excerpted Criticism** represents various kinds of critical writing, ranging in form from the brief review to the scholarly exegesis. Essays are selected by the editors to reflect the spectrum of opinion about a specific work or about an author's literary career in general. The excerpts are presented chronologically, adding a useful perspective to the entry. All titles by the author featured in the entry are printed in boldface type, which enables the reader to easily identify the works being discussed. Publication information (such as publisher names and book prices) and parenthetical numerical references (such as footnotes or page and line references to specific editions of a work) have been deleted at the editor's discretion to provide smoother reading of the text.

- Critical essays are prefaced by **Explanatory Notes** as an additional aid to readers. These notes may provide several types of valuable information, including: the reputation of the critic, the importance of the work of criticism, the commentator's approach to the author's work, the purpose of the criticism, and changes in critical trends regarding the author.

- A complete **Bibliographical Citation** designed to help the user find the original essay or book follows each excerpt.

- A concise **Further Reading** section appears at the end of entries on authors for whom a significant amount of criticism exists in addition to the pieces reprinted in *CLC*. Cross-references to other useful sources published by Gale Research in which the author has appeared are also included: *Children's Literature Review, Contemporary Authors, Something about the Author, Dictionary of Literary Biography, Drama Criticism, Poetry Criticism, Short Story Criticism, Contemporary Authors Autobiography Series,* and *Something about the Author Autobiography Series.*

Other Features

CLC also includes the following features:

- An **Acknowledgments** section lists the copyright holders who have granted permission to reprint material in this volume of *CLC*. It does not, however, list every book or periodical reprinted or consulted during the preparation of the volume.

- A **Cumulative Author Index** lists all the authors who have appeared in the various literary criticism series published by Gale Research, with cross-references to Gale's biographical and autobiographical series. A full listing of the series referenced there appears on the first page of the indexes of this volume. Readers will welcome this cumulated author index as a useful tool for locating an author within the various series. The index, which lists birth and death dates when available, will be particularly valuable for those authors who are identified with a certain period but whose death dates cause them to be placed in another, or for those authors whose careers span two periods. For example, Ernest Hemingway is found in *CLC,* yet a writer often associated with him, F. Scott Fitzgerald, is found in *Twentieth-Century Literary Criticism.*

■ A **Cumulative Nationality Index** alphabetically lists all authors featured in *CLC* by nationality, followed by numbers corresponding to the volumes in which the authors appear.

■ A **Title Index** alphabetically lists all titles reviewed in the current volume of *CLC.* Listings are followed by the author's name and the corresponding page numbers where the titles are discussed. English translations of foreign titles and variations of titles are cross-referenced to the title under which a work was originally published. Titles of novels, novellas, dramas, films, record albums, and poetry, short story, and essay collections are printed in italics, while all individual poems, short stories, essays, and songs are printed in roman type within quotation marks; when published separately (e.g., T. S. Eliot's poem *The Waste Land*), the titles of long poems are printed in italics.

■ In response to numerous suggestions from librarians, Gale has also produced a **Special Paperbound Edition** of the *CLC* title index. This annual cumulation, which alphabetically lists all titles reviewed in the series, is available to all customers and is published with the first volume of *CLC* issued in each calendar year. Additional copies of the index are available upon request. Librarians and patrons will welcome this separate index: it saves shelf space, is easy to use, and is recyclable upon receipt of the following year's cumulation.

Citing *Contemporary Literary Criticism*

When writing papers, students who quote directly from any volume in the Literary Criticism Series may use the following general forms to footnote reprinted criticism. The first example pertains to material drawn from periodicals, the second to material reprinted in books:

[1]Anne Tyler, "Manic Monologue," *The New Republic* 200 (April 17, 1989), 44-6; excerpted and reprinted in *Contemporary Literary Criticism,* Vol. 58, ed. Roger Matuz (Detroit: Gale Research Inc., 1990), p. 325.

[2]Patrick Reilly, *The Literature of Guilt: From 'Gulliver' to Golding* (University of Iowa Press, 1988); excerpted and reprinted in *Contemporary Literary Criticism,* Vol. 58, ed. Roger Matuz (Detroit: Gale Research Inc., 1990), pp. 206-12.

Suggestions Are Welcome

The editor hopes that readers will find *CLC* a useful reference tool and welcomes comments about the work. Send comments and suggestions to: Editor, *Contemporary Literary Criticism,* Gale Research Inc., Penobscot Building, Detroit, MI 48226-4094.

Acknowledgments

The editors wish to thank the copyright holders of the excerpted criticism included in this volume, the permissions managers of many book and magazine publishing companies for assisting us in securing reprint rights, and Anthony Bogucki for assistance with copyright research. We are also grateful to the staffs of the Detroit Public Library, the Library of Congress, the University of Detroit Library, Wayne State University Purdy/Kresge Library Complex, and the University of Michigan Libraries for making their resources available to us. Following is a list of the copyright holders who have granted us permission to reprint material in this volume of *CLC.* Every effort has been made to trace copyright, but if omissions have been made, please let us know.

COPYRIGHTED EXCERPTS IN *CLC*, VOLUME 77, WERE REPRINTED FROM THE FOLLOWING PERIODICALS:

America, v. 126, January 8, 1972. © 1972. All rights reserved. Reprinted with permission of American Press, Inc., 106 West 56th Street, New York, NY 10019.—*The American Poetry Review,* v. 21, May-June, 1992. Copyright © by World Poetry, Inc./ v. 17, September-October, 1988 for "The Last Man" by Susan Stewart. Copyright © 1988 by World Poetry, Inc. Reprinted by permission of the author.—*Arizona Quarterly,* v. 42, Spring, 1986 for "The Voices of Misery and Despair in the Fiction of James Alan McPherson" by William Domnarski. Copyright © 1986 by Arizona Board of Regents. Reprinted by permission of the publisher and the author.—*The Atlantic Monthly,* v. 242, December, 1978 for "On Becoming an American Writer" by James Alan McPherson. Copyright 1978 by The Atlantic Monthly Company, Boston, MA. Reprinted by permission of Bramdt & Bramdt Literary Agents, Inc.—*Ball State University Forum,* v. XXV, Autumn, 1984. © 1984 Ball State University. Reprinted by permission of the publisher.—*Belles Lettres: A Review of Books by Women,* v. 4, Summer, 1989. Reprinted by permission of the publisher.—*Biography,* v. 15, Summer, 1992. © 1992 by the Biographical Research Center. All rights reserved. Reprinted by permission of the publisher. *Black American Literature Forum,* v. 24, Summer, 1990 for "Singing the Black Mother: Maya Angelou and Autobiographical Continuity" by Mary Jane Lupton. Copyright © 1990 by the author. Reprinted by permission of the author.—*Book World—The Washington Post,* September 29, 1991 for "Mysteries and Magnolias" by Joan Aiken. © 1991, *The Washington Post.* Reprinted by permission of the author./ January 31, 1982; January 21, 1990; June 2, 1991; January 3, 1993. © 1982, 1990, 1991, 1993, *The Washington Post.* All reprinted by permission of the publisher.—*boundary 2,* v. XII, Winter, 1984. Copyright © *boundary 2,* 1984. Reprinted by permission of the publisher.—*Callaloo,* v. 9, Fall, 1986. Copyright © 1986 by Charles H. Rowell. All rights reserved. Reprinted by permission of the publisher.—*The CEA Critic,* v. 50, Winter, 1987-Summer, 1988. Copyright © 1988 by the College English Association, Inc. Reprinted by permission of the publisher.—*Chasqui,* v. XX, May, 1991. Reprinted by permission of the publisher.—*The Christian Science Monitor,* June 2, 1988 for "Latin America Seen through the Eyes of Contemporary Writers" by Majorie Agosin. © 1988 The Christian Science Publishing Society. All rights reserved. Reprinted by permission of the author.—*CLA Journal,* v. XXII, June, 1979; v. XXVI, December, 1982. Copyright, 1979, 1982 by The College Language Association. Both used by permission of The College Language Association.—*College Literature,* vs. 19 & 20, October, 1992 & February, 1993. Copyright © 1993 by West Chester University. Reprinted by permission of the publisher.—*Commentary,* v. 65, April, 1978 for "Staging England's Decline" by Peter Shaw. Copyright © 1978 by the American Jewish Committee. All rights reserved. Reprinted by permission of the publisher and the author.—*Commonweal,* v. XCVI, March 24, 1972. Copyright © 1972 Commonweal Publishing Co., Inc. Reprinted by permission of Commonweal Foundation.—*Conjunctions,* v. 9, 1986. Copyright © 1986 *Conjunctions.* All rights reserved. Reprinted by permission of the publisher.—*Critical Inquiry,* v. 16, Summer, 1990 for "Kristeva and Poetry as Shattered Signification" by Calvin Bedient. Copyright © 1990 by The University of Chicago. Reprinted by permission of the publisher and the author.—*Diacritics,* v IV, Fall, 1974. Copyright © Diacritics, Inc., 1974. Reprinted by permission of the publisher.—*Discourse: A Review of the Liberal Arts,* v. 13, Fall-Winter, 1990-91 for "An Interview with Julia Kristeva: Cultural Strangeness and the Subject in Crisis" by Suzanne Clark and

permission of the publisher.—*Popular Music & Society,* v. V, 1977. Copyright © 1977 by R. Serge Denisoff. Reprinted by permission of the publisher.—*The Progressive,* v. 39, February, 1975. Copyright © 1975, The Progressive, Inc. Reprinted by permission from *The Progressive,* Madison, WI 53703.—*Renascence,* v. XL, Fall, 1987. © copyright, 1987, Marquette University Press. Reprinted by permission of the publisher.—*Salmagundi,* ns. 82 & 83, Spring, 1989. Copyright © 1989 by Skidmore College. Reprinted by permission of the publisher.—*San Francisco Review of Books,* Spring, 1989. Copyright © by the *San Francisco Review of Books* 1989. Reprinted by permission of the publisher.—*The Saturday Review,* New York, v. LII, May 21, 1969; v. LIV, October 30, 1971. © 1969, 1971 *Saturday Review,* magazine.—*Sight and Sound,* v. 53, Spring, 1984 for an excerpt by Alan Bennett. Copyright © 1984 by The British Film Institute. Reprinted by permission of the Peters, Fraser & Dunlop Group Ltd./ v. 48, Spring, 1979. Copyright © 1979 by The British Film Institute. Reprinted by permission of the publisher.—*Signs,* v. 7, Autumn, 1981 for "Introduction to Julia Kristeva's 'Women's Time'" by Alice Jardine. © 1981 by The University of Chicago. All rights reserved. Reprinted by permission of the publisher and the author./ v. 9, Autumn, 1983. © 1983 by The University of Chicago. All rights reserved. Reprinted by permission of the publisher.—*South Atlantic Bulletin,* v. XLII, May, 1977. Copyright © 1977 by South Atlantic Modern Language Association. Reprinted by permission of the publisher.—*The Spectator,* v. 260, April 2, 1988. © 1988 by *The Spectator.* Reprinted by permission of *The Spectator.*—*Studies in American Fiction,* v. 1, Autumn, 1973. Copyright © 1973 Northeastern University. Reprinted by permission of the publisher.—*Studies in Short Fiction,* v. 25, Fall, 1988. Copyright 1988 by Newberry College. Reprinted by permission of the publisher.—*Sub-Stance,* ns. 37-38, 1983. Copyright © Sub-Stance, Inc. 1983. Reprinted by permission of the publisher.—*The Times,* London, November 27, 1978; September 6, 1986. © Times Newspapers Limited 1978, 1986. Both reproduced from *The Times,* London by permission. *The Times Literary Supplement,* n. 3805, February 7, 1975; n. 4627, December 16, 1991. © The Times Supplements Limited 1975, 1991./ n. 3637, November 12, 1971; n. 4344, July 4, 1986; n. 4598, May 17, 1991; n. 4639, February 28, 1992. © The Times Supplements Limited 1971, 1986, 1991, 1992. All reproduced from *The Times Literary Supplement* by permission.—*The Village Voice,* v. XXXV, January 30, 1990 for "False Alarm" by Christine Schwartz. Copyright © News Group Publications, Inc., 1990. Reprinted by permission of *the Village Voice* and the author.—*The Washington Post,* January 21, 1993. © 1993, Washington Post Co. Reprinted with permission of the publisher.—*The Women's Review of Books,* v. IV, July-August, 1987 for "Strong beyond All Definitions..." by Angela Davis. Copyright © 1987. All rights reserved. Reprinted by permission of the author.

COPYRIGHTED EXCERPTS IN *CLC*, VOLUME 77, WERE REPRINTED FROM THE FOLLOWING BOOKS:

Beer, John. From "The Undying Worm," in *E. M. Forster A Passage to India: A Casebook.* Edited by Malcolm Bradbury. Macmillan and Co. Ltd., 1970. Selection and editorial matter © Malcolm Bradbury 1970. Reprinted by permission of the author.—Bloom, Harold. From an introduction to *John Ashbery: Modern Critical Views.* Edited by Harold Bloom. Chelsea House Publishers, 1985. Introduction © 1985 by Harold Bloom. All rights reserved. Reprinted by permission of the author.—Bradbury, Malcolm. From *Aspects of E. M. Forster.* Arnold, 1969. © Edward Arnold (Publishers) Ltd. 1969. Reprinted by permission of the author.—Das, Bikram K. From "A Stylistic Analysis of the Speech of the Indian Characters in Forster's 'A Passage to India'," in *Focus on Forster's "A Passage to India:" Indian Essays in Criticism.* Edited by V. A. Shahane. Orient Longman, 1975. © this edition, Orient Longman Ltd., 1975. Reprinted by permission of the publisher.—Day, Aidan. From *Jokerman: Reading the Lyrics of Bob Dylan.* Blackwell, 1988. Copyright © Aidan Day 1988. All rights reserved. Reprinted by permission of Basil Blackwell Limited.—Gray, Michael. From *Song & Dance Man: The Art of Bob Dylan.* Hart-Davis, MacGibbon, 1972. Copyright © 1972 by Michael Gray. All rights reserved.—Herdman, John. From *Voice Without Restraint: A Study of Bob Dylan's Lyrics and Their Background.* Delilah Books, 1982. © copyright critical text John Herdman 1981. Critical text © copyright John Herdman, 1982. All rights reserved.—Kuykendall, Eléanor H. From "Questions for Julia Kristeva's Ethics of Linguistics," in *The Thinking Muse: Feminism and Modern French Philosophy.* Edited by Jeffner Allen and Iris Marion Young. Indiana University Press, 1989. © 1989 by Indiana University Press. All rights reserved. Reprinted by permission of the publisher and the author.—Lechte, John. From *Julia Kristeva.* Routledge, 1990. © 1990 John Lechte. All rights reserved. Reprinted by permission of the publisher.—McPherson, James Alan. From *Elbow Room.* Little, Brown and Company, 1977. Copyright © 1972, 1973, 1974, 1977 by James Alan McPherson. All rights reserved.—Neubauer, Carol E. From "Maya Angelou: Self and a Song of Freedom in the Southern Tradition," in *Southern Women Writers: The New Generation.* Edited by Tonette Bond Inge. University of Alabama Press, 1990. Copyright © 1990 by The University of Alabama Press. All rights reserved. Reprinted by permission of the publisher.—O'Neal, Sondra. From "Reconstruction of the Composite Self: New Images of Black Women in Maya Angelou's Continuing Autobiography," in *Black Women Writers (1950-1980): A Critical Evaluation.* Edited by Mari Evans. Anchor Press/Doubleday, 1984. Copyright © 1983 by Mari Evans. All rights reserved. Used by permission of Doubleday, a division of Bantam Doubleday Dell Publishing, Inc.—Parry, Benita. From "The Politics of Representation in 'A Passage to India'," in *A Passage to India: Essays in Interpretation.* Edited by John Beer. The Macmillan Press Ltd., 1985. © John Beer 1985. All rights reserved. Reprinted by permission of Macmillan, London and Baskingstoke.—Sahni, Chaman L. From "The Marabar Caves in the Light of Indian Thought," in *Focus on Forster's "A Passage to India:" Indian Essays in Criticism.* Edited by V. A. Shahane. Orient Longman, 1975. © this edition Orient Longman Ltd., 1975. Reprinted by permission of the publisher.—Scobie, Stephen. From *Alias Bob Dylan.* Red Deer College Press, 1991. Copyright © 1991 Stephen Scobie. All rights reserved. Reprinted by permission of the publisher.—Williams, Paul. From *Bob Dylan Performing Artist: The Middle Years, 1974-1986.* Underwood-Miller, 1992. Copyright © 1992 by Paul Williams. All rights reserved. Reprinted by permission of the author.

PHOTOGRAPHS AND ILLUSTRATIONS APPEARING IN *CLC*, VOLUME 77, WERE RECEIVED FROM THE FOLLOWING SOURCES:

Tim Richmond/Katz Pictures: **p. 1**; © Jerry Bauer: **pp. 39, 132, 260, 297**; Photograph by Merk Gerson: **p. 81**; © Roy Lewis 1974: **p. 107**; AP/Wide World Photos: **pp. 158, 194**; Collection Particulière: **p. 280**; Photograph by Linda Dawn Hammond, Montreál: **p. 340**; Information Services, University of South Carolina: **p. 349**.

Maya Angelou

1928-

(Born Marguerite Johnson) American autobiographer, poet, scriptwriter, playwright, nonfiction writer, composer, and editor.

The following entry contains coverage of Angelou's career through 1993. For further information on Angelou's life and career, see *CLC,* Volumes 12, 35, and 64.

INTRODUCTION

Hailed as one of the great voices of contemporary African-American literature, Angelou is best known for *I Know Why the Caged Bird Sings,* the first in her series of five autobiographical books. In addition to her prose, Angelou has written poetry, performed as a singer and dancer, composed musical scores, and written, directed, and acted in plays and films. Angelou's literary works have generated critical and popular interest in part because they depict her triumph over formidable social obstacles and her struggle to achieve a sense of identity and self-acceptance. Critics have praised her dynamic prose style, poignant humor, and illumination of African-American history and consciousness through her portrayal of personal experiences. Angelou has stated: "I speak to the black experience but I am always talking about the human condition—about what we can endure, dream, fail at and still survive."

Angelou has described the art of autobiography as a means for a writer to go back to the past and recover through imagination and invention what has been lost. She began producing her autobiographical works after friends, among them such notable writers as James Baldwin and Jules Feiffer, suggested she write about her childhood spent between rural, segregated Stamps, Arkansas, where her pious grandmother ran a general store, and St. Louis, Missouri, where her worldly, glamorous mother lived. *I Know Why the Caged Bird Sings,* which became a great critical and commercial success, chronicles Angelou's life up to age sixteen, providing a child's perspective on a perplexing and repressive world of adults. This volume contains the gruesome account of how Angelou, at the age of eight, was raped by her mother's lover. Angelou refused to speak for five years following the attack, believing that she had killed her assailant—who was murdered several days later—simply by speaking his name. Much critical discussion has focused on the correlation between language, speech, and identity evidenced by Angelou's suppression and eventual recovery of her own voice. *I Know Why the Caged Bird Sings* concludes with Angelou's attempts as a single, teen-aged mother to nurture and protect her newborn son. In addition to creating a trenchant account of a girl's coming-of-age, this work

also affords insights into the social and political tensions pervading the 1930s.

The next four volumes of Angelou's autobiography—*Gather Together in My Name, Singin' and Swingin' and Gettin' Merry Like Christmas, The Heart of a Woman,* and *All God's Children Need Traveling Shoes*—continue to trace her psychological, spiritual, and political odyssey as she emerges from a disturbing and oppressive childhood to become a prominent figure in contemporary American literature. Angelou's quest for self-identity and emotional fulfillment continues to result in such extraordinary experiences as her encounters with Malcolm X and Dr. Martin Luther King, Jr. Angelou also describes her involvement with the civil rights and feminist movements in the United States and in Africa, her developing relationship with her son, and the hardships associated with lower-class American life. Although some critics fault these volumes for lacking moral complexity and universality, others praise Angelou's narrative skills and her impassioned responses to the challenges in her life.

All God's Children Need Traveling Shoes, Angelou's fifth autobiographical installment, is distinctive in its examination of black America's intellectual and emotional connections with post-colonial Africa. In this work Angelou describes her four-year stay in Ghana where she worked as a free-lance writer and editor. The overriding theme in this volume is the search for "home," or what Patrice Gaines-Carter terms "a place or condition of belonging." Angelou finds much to venerate about Africa, but gradually realizes that although she has cultural ties to the land of her ancestors, she is nevertheless distinctly American and in many ways isolated from traditional African society. Angelou observes: "If home was not what we had expected, nevermind, our need for belonging allowed us to ignore the obvious." Wanda Coleman mirrored the general critical opinion of *All God's Children Need Traveling Shoes* when she stated that Angelou's work is "an important document drawing much needed attention to the hidden history of a people both African and American."

Angelou's poetry, in which she combines terse lyrics with jazz rhythms, addresses social and political issues relevant to African-Americans and challenges the validity of traditional American values and myths. In "America," for example, she rejects the notion that justice is available to all Americans, citing such deep-rooted problems as racism and poverty. Angelou directed national attention to humanitarian concerns with her poem "On the Pulse of Morning," which she recited at the 1993 inauguration of President Bill Clinton. In this poem, Angelou calls for recognition of the human failings pervading American history and a renewed national commitment to unity and social improvement.

PRINCIPAL WORKS

Cabaret for Freedom [with Godfrey Cambridge] (drama) 1960

The Least of These (drama) 1966

Black, Blues, Black (television series) 1968

I Know Why the Caged Bird Sings (autobiography) 1970

Just Give Me a Cool Drink of Water 'fore I Diiie (poetry) 1971

Georgia, Georgia (screenplay) 1972

Ajax [adaptor; from the drama *Ajax* by Sophocles] (drama) 1974

All Day Long (screenplay) 1974

Gather Together in My Name (autobiography) 1974

Assignment America (television series) 1975

Oh Pray My Wings Are Gonna Fit Me Well (poetry) 1975

And Still I Rise (drama) 1976

"The Inheritors" (television script) 1976

"The Legacy" (television script) 1976

Singin' and Swingin' and Gettin' Merry Like Christmas (autobiography) 1976

And Still I Rise (poetry) 1978

The Heart of a Woman (autobiography) 1981

"Sister, Sister" (television script) 1982

Shaker, Why Don't You Sing? (poetry) 1983

All God's Children Need Traveling Shoes (autobiography) 1986

Now Sheba Sings the Song (poetry) 1987

I Shall Not Be Moved (poetry) 1990

"On the Pulse of Morning" (poem) 1993

CRITICISM

Sondra O'Neale (essay date 1984)

[*In the following essay on Angelou's autobiographies, O'Neale discusses the author's exploration of collective black identity and her subversion of common myths about black women.*]

The Black woman is America's favorite unconfessed symbol. She is the nation's archetype for unwed mothers, welfare checks, and food stamps. Her round, smiling face bordered by the proverbial red bandanna is the requisite sales image for synthetic pancakes and frozen waffles "just like Mammy use to make." Only her knowledgeable smile of expertise can authenticate the flavor of corporately fried chicken. When sciolists have need to politicize reactionary measures, they usually fabricate self-serving perceptions of "universal" Black women: ostensibly trading poverty vouchers for mink-strewn Cadillacs, or hugging domestic accouterments in poses of beneficent penury, or shaking a firm bodice as a prostituting Lilith, who offers the most exquisite forbidden sex—all cosmologically craved images of a remote, ambivalent Mother Earth. Regardless of which polemic prevails, these mirrors of the same perverted icon provide the greatest reservoir of exploitable and subconsciously desired meaning in American culture.

That said, if the larger society does not know who Black women are, only who it wants them to be; if even Black men as scholars and thinkers writing in this century could not "free" the images of Black women in the national psyche, it remained for Black women to accomplish the task themselves. Thus the emergence of Black feminine expression in drama, poetry, and fiction during the seventies was long overdue. Because ebon women occupy so much space on the bottom rung in American polls of economy, opportunity, and Eurocultural measurements of femininity, some of these new writers know that for Black liberation art must do more than serve its own form, that fictional conceptions of depth and integrity are needed to reveal the Black women's identity, and that ethnic women readers are bereft of role models who can inspire a way of escape.

Although Black writers have used autobiography to achieve these ends since the days of slavery, few use the genre today. One who employs only the tools of fiction but not its "make-believe" form to remold these perceptions, one who has made her life her message and whose message to all aspiring Black women is the reconstruction of her experiential "self," is Maya Angelou. With the wide public and critical reception of *I Know Why the Caged Bird*

Sings in the early seventies, Angelou bridged the gap between life and art, a step that is essential if Black women are to be deservedly credited with the mammoth and creative feat of noneffacing survival. Critics could not dismiss her work as so much "folksy" propaganda because her narrative was held together by controlled techniques of artistic fiction as well as by a historic-sociological study of Black feminine images seldom if ever viewed in American literature.

No Black women in the world of Angelou's books are losers. She is the third generation of brilliantly resourceful females, who conquered oppression's stereotypical maladies without conforming to its expectations of behavior. Thus, reflecting what Western critics are discovering is the focal point of laudable autobiographical literature, the creative thread which weaves Angelou's tapestry is not herself as central subject; it is rather a purposeful composite of a multifaceted "I" who is: (1) an indivisible offspring of those dauntless familial women about whom she writes; (2) an archetypal "self" demonstrating the trials, rejections, and endurances which so many Black women share; and (3) a representative of that collective obsidian army which stepped out of three hundred years of molding history and redirected its own destiny. The process of her autobiography is not a singular statement of individual egotism but an exultant explorative revelation that she *is* because her life is an inextricable part of the misunderstood reality of who Black people and Black women truly are. That "self" is the model which she holds before Black women and that is the unheralded chronicle of actualization which she wants to include in the canon of Black American literature.

In *Caged Bird,* one gets a rare literary glimpse of those glamorous chignoned Black women of the twenties and thirties who, refusing to bury their beauty beneath maid trays in segregated Hollywood films or New York's budding but racist fashion industry, adapted their alluring qualities to the exciting, lucrative streetlife that thrived in the Jazz Age during the first third of this century. Buzzing with undertones of settlement of the Black urban North and West, these were the days of open gambling, speakeasies, and political bossism. Angelou's mother and maternal grandmother grandly supported their families in these St. Louis and San Francisco environments in ways that cannot be viewed as disreputable because they were among the few tools afforded Black folk for urban survival. But other than nostalgic mention of performing headliners such as Duke Ellington or Billie Holiday, one does not get a sense of Black life in literary or historic reconstructions of the era. Truthful assessment would show that most Blacks were not poor waifs lining soup kitchen doors during the Depression or, because they were denied jobs in the early years of the war effort, pining away in secondary involvement. The landscape in *Caged Bird* is not that of boardinghouse living among middle-class whites as depicted through eyes of nineteenth-century Howellian boredom, but rather that of colorful and adventurous group living in San Francisco's Fillmore district during the shipbuilding years of World War II.

From her moneyed stepfather, Daddy Clidell, Angelou received a basic ghetto education:

> He owned apartment buildings and, later, pool halls, and was famous for being the rarity "a man of honor." He didn't suffer, as many "honest men" do, from the detestable righteousness that diminishes their virtue. He knew cards and men's hearts. So during the age when Mother was exposing us to certain facts of life, like personal hygiene, proper posture, table manners, good restaurants and tipping practices, Daddy Clidell taught me to play poker, blackjack, tonk and high, low, Jick, Jack and the Game. He wore expensively tailored suits and a large yellow diamond stickpin. Except for the jewelry, he was a conservative dresser and carried himself with the unconscious pomp of a man of secure means.
> [*I Know Why the Caged Bird Sings*]

Through Clidell she "was introduced to the most colorful characters in the Black underground." And from men with names like "Stonewall Jimmy, Just Black, Cool Clyde, Tight Coat and Red Leg," she heard of the many Brer Rabbit con games which they hustled on Mr. Charlie. Angelou the narrator, detached from Angelou the child, who absorbed from this parlor banter a Black history unavailable in formal education, is able to philosophize and again structure role models:

> When he finished, more triumphant stories rainbowed around the room riding the shoulders of laughter. By all accounts those storytellers, born Black and male before the turn of the twentieth century, should have been ground into useless dust. Instead they used their intelligence to pry open the door of rejection and not only became wealthy but got some revenge in the bargain. It wasn't possible for me to regard them as criminals or be anything but proud of their achievements.

> The needs of a society determine its ethics, and in the Black American ghettos the hero is that man who is offered only the crumbs from his country's table but by ingenuity and courage is able to take for himself a Lucullan feast.
> [*I Know Why the Caged Bird Sings*]

That same sense of historical but undiscovered Black life is seen in the panorama of the now four-volume autobiography. Whether from vivid recollection of fond fellowships in rural schools contrasted with the bitter remembrance of a segregated system designed to animalize Black students that one finds in *Caged Bird,* or from the startling reminiscences of Black entertainers who managed to evade Hitlerism and form enclaves of Black performers in Europe during the war years (e.g., Josephine Baker, Bernard Hassel, Mabel Mercer, "Brickie" Bricktop, Nancy Holloway, and Gordon Heath) that one finds in *Singin' and Swingin' and Gettin' Merry Like Christmas,* or from the poignant view of a Northern perch in both the creative (the Harlem Writers Guild) and the political (Northern Coordinator for the SCLC) thought and action of the Civil Rights Movement, as well as the annexing gravitation to African liberation (protest demonstrations at the UN following Lumumba's death) that one finds in her latest work, *The Heart of a Woman*—Angelou's message is one blending chorus: Black people and Black women do not just endure, they triumph with a will of collective consciousness that Western experience cannot extinguish.

If there is one enduring misrepresentation in American literature it is the Black Southern matriarch. When Blacks appeared first in James Fenimore Cooper's novel *The Spy,* the Black woman was silent, postforty, corpulent, and in the kitchen. Cooper's contemporary, Washington Irving, duplicated that perspective, and for much of the period that followed, white American authors more or less kept her in that state. By modern times, given characters such as Faulkner's Molly and Dilsey, the images of nonmulatto Southern Black women had still not progressed. When seen at all they were powerless pawns related only to contexts of white aspirations. But Angelou's depiction of her paternal Grandmother Annie Henderson is a singular repudiation of that refraction. While Mrs. Henderson is dependent on no one, the entire Stamps community is at times totally dependent upon her, not as a pietous but impotent weeping post but as a materially resourceful entrepreneur. When explaining that her family heritage precludes acceptance of welfare, Angelou describes Mrs. Henderson's self-sufficiency:

> And welfare was absolutely forbidden. My pride had been starched by a family who assumed unlimited authority in its own affairs. A grandmother, who raised me, my brother and her two own sons, owned a general merchandise store. She had begun her business in the early 1900's in Stamps, Arkansas, by selling meat pies to saw men in a lumber mill, then racing across town in time to feed workers in a cotton-gin mill four miles away.
> [*Singin' and Swingin' and Gettin' Merry Like Christmas*]

Through frugal but nonarrogant management of her finances under the meddlesome eye of jealous and avaricious whites, Mrs. Henderson not only stalwartly provides for her crippled son and two robust grandchildren, she feeds the Black community during the Depression *and* helps keep the white economy from collapse. Angelou aptly contrasts gratitude and its absence from both segments. While holding the reluctant hand of her granddaughter Maya, who was suffering from a painful abcessed tooth, Grandmother Henderson endured contemptuous rejection from the town's white dentist: "Annie, my policy is I'd rather stick my hand in a dog's mouth than in a nigger's." She reminded him:

> "I wouldn't press on you like this for myself but I can't take No. Not for my grandbaby. When you come to borrow my money you didn't have to beg. You asked me, and I lent it. Now, it wasn't my policy. I ain't no moneylender, but you stood to lose this building and I tried to help you out."
> [*I Know Why the Caged Bird Sings*]

No matter that the lordly Black woman saved him from ruin when the power structure to which he belonged would not, he still refused to pull her granddaughter's tooth. The author neither supports nor condemns her

grandmother's traditional Christian forbearance. What she does do is illustrate alternative views of a Southern Black woman who would not be subjugated by such unconscionable oppression—essential visions of a "composite self."

Another facet of the unknown Southern Black woman is her majestic octoroon maternal grandmother, Mrs. Baxter, who ruled a ghetto borough in Prohibition-era St. Louis:

> . . . the fact that she was a precinct captain compounded her power and gave her the leverage to deal with even the lowest crook without fear. She had pull with the police department, so the men in their flashy suits and fleshy scars sat with church-like decorum and waited to ask favors from her. If Grandmother raised the heat off their gambling parlors, or said the word that reduced the bail of a friend waiting in jail, they knew what would be expected of them. Come election, they were to bring in the votes from their neighborhood. She most often got them leniency, and they always brought in the vote.
> [*I Know Why the Caged Bird Sings*]

The only change is the urban setting, but the self-reliant woman in control of her environment is the atypical contribution which Angelou makes as a corrective to images of Black women. That the medium is not fiction serves the interest of young readers, who can learn to do likewise.

By far the role model which Angelou presents as having the greatest impact on her own life is her mother, Vivian Baxter, whose quintessence could only be shown by her actions for "to describe my mother would be to write about a hurricane in its perfect power. Or the climbing, falling colors of a rainbow" [*I Know Why the Caged Bird Sings*]. With firm velveted command often braced with creative violence, Vivian obviated life's obstacles with anything but sentimentality and she reared Maya to do the same: "She supported us efficiently with humor and imagination. . . . With all her jollity, Vivian Baxter had no mercy. . . . 'Sympathy' is next to 'shit' in the dictionary, and I can't even read" [*I Know Why the Caged Bird Sings*]. That meant she refused Maya psychological and, after Guy's birth, financial dependence:

> By no amount of agile exercising of a wishful imagination could my mother have been called lenient. Generous she was; indulgent, never. Kind, yes; permissive, never. In her world, people she accepted paddled their own canoes, pulled their own weight, put their own shoulders to their own plows and pushed like hell. . . .
> [*Gather Together in My Name*]

But through the four books, Vivian is Angelou's certain rock, an invincible resource from which the mystique of exultant Black feminine character is molded. Tough, a rarefied beauty, Vivian effectively challenged any stereotypical expectations with which the white world or Black men attempted to constrict her being. Her instructions to Angelou are mindful of the pitiful words in Zora Neale Hurston's novel: "The Black woman is the mule of the world," but Vivian insisted that not one ebon sister has to accept that warrant:

"People will take advantage of you if you let them. Especially Negro women. Everybody, his brother and his dog, thinks he can walk a road in a colored woman's behind. But you remember this, now. Your mother raised you. You're full-grown. Let them catch it like they find it. If you haven't been trained at home to their liking tell them to get to stepping." Here a whisper of delight crawled over her face. "Stepping. But not on you."

"You hear me?"

"Yes, Mother. I hear you."
                            [*Gather Together in My Name*]

At a time in life when most women were expected to surrender in place, to Maya's astonishment, Vivian put her age back fifteen years and took on the merchant marine "because they told me Negro women couldn't get in the union. . . . I told them 'You want to bet?' I'll put my foot in that door up to my hip until women of every color can walk over my foot, get in that union, get aboard a ship and go to sea" [*The Heart of a Woman*]. This is the essence of Angelou's composite: Black progress has been attained in this country not only because of the leadership of Black men but also because of the unsung spirit of noncompliant Black women. This is the revelation she intends the careful portrayals of major women in her life to celebrate.

The process of [Angelou's] autobiography is not a singular statement of individual egotism but an exultant explorative revelation that she *is* because her life is an inextricable part of the misunderstood reality of who Black people and Black women truly are.

—Sondra O'Neale

Finally the most elusive identity in the accumulative "self " is Angelou. One sees her only through the eyes with which she views the world. Attempts at self-description in the opus are rare. As a child and teenager Angelou was inexorably lonely (". . . I was surrounded, as I had been all my life, by strangers" [*I Know Why the Caged Bird Sings*]. But to describe her as filled with self-loathing as one of the few critical examinations of her work [Regina Blackburn's "In Search of the Black Female Self " in *Women's Autobiography: Essays in Criticism,* 1980] has done is inaccurate: " . . . Maya Angelou expresses the most severe self-hatred derived from her appearance. Beaten down by massive self-loathing and self-shame, she felt her appearance was too offensive to merit any kind of true affection from others." The critic concludes, "Angelou's conception of self caused her to be self-limiting and to lack self-assertion and self-acceptance." The young Angelou of *Caged Bird* could be more poignantly described as in the throes of probing self-discovery, deliberation common to adolescence. A child who was searching for

inward panacea, to withstand real—not imagined—rejection, disappointment, and even onslaught from an adult world, the young Angelou had few refuges, among them her brother Bailey and her world of books. In the end, self-education through literature and the arts gave her the additional fortitude and intellectual acumen to be a Baxter-Henderson woman of her own generation.

When the adult Angelou faced the world, the humble requirements of Stamps, Arkansas, the speakeasies of St. Louis, and the shipyard boardinghouses of San Francisco had passed away. Through art she could preserve the tenacious women who survived the crucibles those eras intended but aside from will and determination she could not extract dependable techniques from their experiences. Hence the conclusions of Angelou herself as role model for this present age: if Black women are to "paddle their own canoes" in postindustrial society they must do it through force of intellect. Her own experiential development as traced thus far in the latest work, *The Heart of a Woman,* teaches that no option—marriage, entertainment, any dependent existence—is as much a lasting or consummate reservoir. "I made the decision to quit show business. Give up the skintight dresses and manicured smiles. The false concern over sentimental lyrics. I would never again work to make people smile inanely and would take on the responsibility of making them think" [*The Heart of a Woman*]. That decision is her passport to irrevocable freedom to which the definitiveness of the autobiography attests. Angelou, the developing character, had sounded the vastness of a lifetime of loneliness and ascended as Angelou the writer. Art became an assertive statement for three generations of an evolving self.

Unlike her poetry, which is a continuation of traditional oral expression in Afro-American literature, Angelou's prose follows classic technique in nonpoetic Western forms. The material in each book while chronologically marking her life is nonetheless arranged in loosely structured plot sequences which are skillfully controlled. In *Caged Bird* the tenuous psyche of a gangly, sensitive, withdrawn child is traumatically jarred by rape, a treacherous act from which neither the reader nor the protagonist has recovered by the book's end. All else is cathartic: her uncles' justified revenge upon the rapist, her years of readjustment in a closed world of speechlessness despite the warm nurturing of her grandmother, her granduncle, her beloved brother Bailey, and the Stamps community; a second reunion with her vivacious mother; even her absurdly unlucky pregnancy at the end does not assuage the reader's anticipatory wonder: isn't the act of rape by a trusted adult so assaultive upon an eight-year-old's life that it leaves a wound which can never be healed? Such reader interest in a character's future is the craft from which quality fiction is made. Few autobiographers however have the verve to seize the drama of such a moment, using one specific incident to control the book but with an underlining implication that the incident will not control a life.

The denouement in *Gather Together in My Name* is again sexual: the older, crafty, experienced man lasciviously preying upon the young, vulnerable, and, for all her exposure by that time, naïve woman. While foreshadowing apprehension guided the reader to the central action in the first work, Maya presses the evolvement in *Gather Together* through a limited first-person narrator who seems to know less of the villain's intention than is obvious to the reader. Thrice removed from the action, the reader sees that L. D. Tolbrook is nothing but a slick pimp, that his seductive sexual refusals can only lead to a calamitous end; that his please-turn-these-few-tricks-for-me-baby-so-I-can-get-out-of-an-urgent-jam line is an ancient inducement for susceptible females, but Maya the actor in the tragedy cannot. She is too much in love. Maya, the author, through whose eyes we see a younger, foolish "self," so painstakingly details the girl's descent into the brothel that Black women, all women, have enough vicarious example to avoid the trap. Again, through using the "self" as role model, not only is Maya able to instruct and inspire the reader but the sacrifice of personal disclosure authenticates the autobiography's integral depth.

Just as the title of *Gather Together* is taken from a New Testament injunction for the travailing soul to pray and commune while waiting patiently for deliverance and the *Caged Bird* title is taken from a poem by the beloved Paul Laurence Dunbar, who gave call to Angelou's nascent creativity, the title of the third work, *Singin' and Swingin' and Gettin' Merry Like Christmas,* is a folkloric title symbolic of the author's long-deserved ascent to success and fulfillment. This volume's plot and tone are lifted above adroit reenactments of that native humor so effective in relieving constant struggle in Black life which is holistically balanced in the first two books. The buoyancy is constant because Maya (who had theretofore been called Marguerite or Ritie all her life) the singer, Maya the dancer, Maya the actress, had shed the fearful image of "typical" unwed Black mother with a dead-end destiny. She knew she was more than that. But the racist and sexist society—which had relegated her to dishwasher, short-order cook, barmaid, chauffeur, and counter clerk; which had denied her entrance into secure employment and higher education in the armed services; and which programmed her into a familiar void when the crush of changing modernity even eradicated the avenues which partially liberated her foremothers—seemed invincible. The culmination of her show business climb is a dual invitation: either to replace Eartha Kitt in the Broadway production of *New Faces* or to join the star-studded cast of *Porgy and Bess,* which began a world tour in 1954. From that climax the settings shift to such faraway places as Rome, Venice, Paris, Yugoslavia, Alexandria, Cairo, Athens, and Milan; and the narrator, character, and reader view life from glorious vistas auspiciously removed from the world of that dejected girl in Stamps, Arkansas.

The step from star, producer, and writer for the benefit show *Cabaret for Freedom* to being northern coordinator for the Southern Christian Leadership Conference provides the focus for her latest excursus, *The Heart of a Woman.* Here also, as with each of the previous installments, the work ends with abrupt suspense. In this way dramatic technique not only centralizes each work, it also makes the series narrative a collective whole. In *Caged Bird* the shock-effect ending is the rash conception of her

son when in the concluding action of the book she initiates an emotionless affair to see if the word "lesbian" fits her self-description. With a lofty rhetoric which wisdom hindsights she articulates the anguish of a benumbed pregnant sixteen-year-old:

> . . . For eons, it seemed, I had accepted my plight as the hapless, put-upon victim of fate and the Furies, but this time I had to face the fact that I had brought my new catastrophe upon myself. How was I to blame the innocent man whom I had lured into making love to me? In order to be profoundly dishonest, a person must have one of two qualities: either he is unscrupulously ambitious, or he is unswervingly egocentric. He must believe that for his ends to be served all things and people can justifiably be shifted about, or that he is the center not only of his own world but of the worlds which others inhabit. I had neither element in my personality, so I hefted the burden of pregnancy at sixteen onto my own shoulders where it belonged. Admittedly, I staggered under the weight.
>   [*I Know Why the Caged Bird Sings*]

And, after viewing a boyfriend's confessed addiction to heroin, she ends *Gather Together* with an initiate's faith: "The next day I took the clothes, my bags and Guy back to Mother's. I had no idea what I was going to make of my life, but I had given a promise and found my innocence. I swore I'd never lose it again" [*Gather Together*].

Both of these passages are lucid philosophical treatments of life's vicissitudes but the test of superior autobiography is the language and structure of those mundane, though essential, ordinary moments in life. One of the forms that Angelou uses to guide the reader past these apparent surfaces is precise analogy. When describing one of her daddy's girlfriends, the language is not only symbolic but portends their mutual jealousy:

> Dolores lived there with him and kept the house clean with the orderliness of a coffin. Artificial flowers reposed waxily in glass vases. She was on close terms with her washing machine and ironing board. Her hairdresser could count on absolute fidelity and punctuality. In a word, but for intrusions her life would have been perfect. And then I came along.
>   [*I Know Why the Caged Bird Sings*]

When variously citing the notable absences of men in her life, tone and symbolism are delicately synthesized: "I could moan some salty songs. I had been living with empty arms and rocks in my bed" [*The Heart of a Woman*]; "Indeed no men at all seemed attracted to me. . . . No, husbands were rarer than common garden variety unicorns" [*Singin' and Swingin' and Gettin' Merry Like Christmas*]; and "Charles had taken that journey and left me all alone. I was one emotional runny sore" [*Gather Together*].

Another aspect of style which prevents ponderous plodding in the narrative is Angelou's avoidance of a monolithic Black language. As first-person narrator, she does not disavow an erudition cultivated from childhood through early exposure to and constant reading of such Western masters as Dostoyevsky, Chekhov, Gorky, Dickens, Dunbar, Du Bois, Shakespeare, Kipling, Poe, Alger, Thackeray, James Weldon Johnson, and even the Beowulf poet. Through direct dialogue the reader gleans that Maya is perfectly capable of more expected ghetto expressiveness but such is saved for appropriate moments of high drama such as when a Brooklyn gang threatens to murder her son Guy:

> "I understand that you are the head of the Savages and you have an arrangement with my son. I also understand that the police are afraid of you. Well, I came 'round to make you aware of something. If my son comes home with a black eye or a torn shirt, I won't call the police."

> His attention followed my hand to my purse. "I will come over here and shoot Susie's grandmother first, then her mother, then I'll blow away that sweet little baby. You understand what I'm saying? If the Savages so much as touch my son, I will then find your house and kill everything that moves, including the rats and cockroaches."

> I showed the borrowed pistol, then slid it back into my purse. For a second, none of the family moved and my plans had not gone beyond the speech, so I just kept my hand in the purse, fondling my security. Jerry spoke, "O.K., I understand. But for a mother, I must say you're a mean motherfucker."

> [*The Heart of a Woman*]

In addition to sparse use of street vernacular, she also does not overburden Black communicants with clumsy versions of homespun Black speech. From Arkansas to Europe, from San Francisco to New York, the only imitative affectation is of her uncle Willie's stuttering, "You know . . . how, uh, children are . . . th-th-these days . . . "; her father's corrective pauses of "er," which reaffirms his pretentious mask, "So er this is Daddy's er little man? Boy, anybody tell you errer that you er look like me?"; and the light badinage of customers in Grandma Henderson's store, "Sister, I'll have two cans of sardines. I'm gonna work so fast today I'm gonna make you look like you standing still. Just gimme a coupla them fat peanut paddies." The choice not to let imitations of known variables in Black speech dominate expressiveness is reinforcement of a major premise in the works: the nativistic humanness and potential of Black identity.

The four-volume autobiography effectively banishes several stereotypical myths about Black women which had remained unanswered in national literature. Angelou casts a new mold of Mother Earth—a Black woman who repositions herself in the universe so that she chooses the primary objects of her service. And ultimately that object may even be herself. Self-reconstruction of the "I" is a demanding, complex literary mode which not only exercises tested rudiments of fiction but also departs from the more accepted form of biography. Just as in fiction, the biographer can imagine or improvise a character's motives; but the autobiographer is the one narrator who really knows the truth—as well, that is, as any of us can truly know ourselves. In divulging that truth Angelou reveals a new total-

ity of archetypal Black woman: a composite self that corrects omissions in national history and provides seldom-seen role models for cultural criteria. (pp. 25-35)

> *Sondra O'Neale, "Reconstruction of the Composite Self: New Images of Black Women in Maya Angelou's Continuing Autobiography," in* Black Women Writers (1950-1980): A Critical Evaluation, *edited by Mari Evans, Anchor Press/Doubleday, 1984, pp. 25-37.*

Mary Jane Lupton (essay date Summer 1990)

[*In the following essay, Lupton discusses unifying stylistic and thematic elements in Angelou's autobiographies.*]

> Now my problem I have is I love life, I love living life and I love the art of living, so I try to live my life as a poetic adventure, everything I do from the way I keep my house, cook, make my husband happy, or welcome my friends, raise my son; everything is part of a large canvas I am creating, I am living beneath.

This energetic statement from [an] interview with Maya Angelou [in *Black Scholar,* January-February, 1977] merely hints at the variety of roles and experiences which sweep through what is presently her five-volume autobiographical series: *I Know Why the Caged Bird Sings* (1970), *Gather Together in My Name* (1974), *Singin' and Swingin' and Gettin' Merry Like Christmas* (1976), *The Heart of a Woman* (1981), and *All God's Children Need Traveling Shoes* (1986). It is fitting that Angelou, so adept at metaphor, should compare her "poetic adventure" to the act of painting: " . . . everything is part of a large canvas I am creating, I am living beneath." Like an unfinished painting, the autobiographical series is an ongoing creation, in a form that rejects the finality of a restricting frame. Its continuity is achieved through characters who enter the picture, leave, and reappear, and through certain interlaced themes—self-acceptance, race, men, work, separation, sexuality, motherhood. All the while Angelou lives "beneath," recording the minutest of details in a constantly shifting environment and giving attention to the "mundane, though essential, ordinary moments of life" [Sondra O'Neale in *Black Women Writers (1950-1980): A Critical Evaluation,* 1984].

I Know Why the Caged Bird Sings is the first and most highly praised volume in the series. It begins with the humiliations of childhood and ends with the birth of a child. At its publication, critics, not anticipating a series, readily appreciated the clearly developed narrative form. In 1973, for example, Sidonie Smith discussed the "sense of an ending" in *Caged Bird* as it relates to Angelou's acceptance of Black womanhood [in "The Song of a Caged Bird: Maya Angelou's Quest after Self-Acceptance," *Southern Humanities Review,* Vol. 7, 1973]: "With the birth of her child Maya is herself born into a mature engagement with the forces of life." But with the introduction in 1974 of Angelou's second autobiographical volume, *Gather Together in My Name,* the tight structure appeared to crumble; childhood experiences were replaced by episodes which a number of critics consider disjointed or bizarre. Selwyn Cudjoe, for instance, noted the shift from the "intense solidity and moral center" in *Caged Bird* to the "conditions of *alienation* and *fragmentation*" in *Gather Together,* conditions which affect its organization and its quality, making it "conspicuously weak." Lynn Z. Bloom [in *Dictionary of Literary Biography,* Vol. 38] found the sequel "less satisfactory" because the narrator "abandons or jeopardizes the maturity, honesty, and intuitive good judgment toward which she had been moving in *Caged Bird.*" Crucial to Bloom's judgment is her concept of movement *toward,* which insinuates the achievement of an ending.

The narrator, as authentic recorder of the life, indeed changes during the second volume, as does the book's structure; the later volumes abandon the tighter form of *Caged Bird* for an episodic series of adventures whose so-called "fragments" are reflections of the kind of chaos found in actual living. In altering the narrative structure, Angelou shifts the emphasis from herself as an isolated consciousness to herself as a Black woman participating in diverse experiences among a diverse class of peoples. As the world of experience widens, so does the canvas.

What distinguishes, then, Angelou's autobiographical method from more conventional autobiographical forms is her very denial of closure. The reader of autobiography expects a beginning, a middle, and an end—as occurs in *Caged Bird.* She or he also expects a central experience, as we indeed are given in the extraordinary rape sequence of *Caged Bird.* But Angelou, by continuing her narrative, denies the form and its history, creating from each ending a new beginning, relocating the center to some luminous place in a volume yet to be. Stretching the autobiographical canvas, she moves forward: from being a child; to being a mother; to leaving the child; to having the child, in the fifth volume, achieve his independence. Nor would I be so unwise as to call the fifth volume the end. For Maya Angelou, now a grandmother, has already published a moving, first-person account in *Woman's Day* of the four years of anguish surrounding the maternal kidnapping of her grandson Colin.

Throughout the more episodic volumes, the theme of motherhood remains a unifying element, with Momma Henderson being Angelou's link with the Black folk tradition—as George Kent, Elizabeth Schultz, and other critics have mentioned. Since traditional solidity of development is absent, one must sometimes search through three or four books to trace Vivian Baxter's changing lovers, Maya Angelou's ambivalence towards motherhood, or her son Guy's various reactions to his non-traditional upbringing. Nonetheless, the volumes are intricately related through a number of essential elements: the ambivalent autobiographical voice, the flexibility of structure to echo the life process, the intertextual commentary on character and theme, and the use of certain recurring patterns to establish both continuity and continuation. I have isolated the mother-child pattern as a way of approaching the complexity of Angelou's methods. One could as well select other kinds of interconnected themes: the absent and/or substitute father, the use of food as a psycho-sexual sym-

bol, the dramatic/symbolic use of images of staring or gazing, and other motifs which establish continuity within and among the volumes.

Stephen Butterfield says of *Caged Bird* [in his *Black Autobiography in America,* 1974]: "Continuity is achieved by the contact of mother and child, the sense of life begetting life that happens automatically in spite of all confusion—perhaps also because of it." The consistent yet changing connection for Maya Angelou through the four subsequent narratives is that same contact of mother and child—with herself and her son Guy; with herself and her own mother, Vivian Baxter; with herself and her paternal grandmother; and, finally, with the child-mother in herself.

Moreover, in extending the traditional one-volume form, Angelou has metaphorically mothered another book. The "sense of life begetting life" at the end of *Caged Bird* can no longer signal the conclusion of the narrative. The autobiographical moment has been reopened and expanded; Guy's birth can now be seen symbolically as the birth of another text. In a 1975 interview with Carol Benson [in the January issue of *Writer's Digest*], Angelou uses such a birthing metaphor in describing the writing of *Gather Together:* "If you have a child, it takes nine months. It took me three-and-a-half years to write *Gather Together,* so I couldn't just drop it." This statement makes emphatic what in the autobiographies are much more elusive comparisons between creative work and motherhood; after a three-and-a-half-year pregnancy she gives birth to *Gather Together,* indicating that she must have planned the conception of the second volume shortly after the 1970 delivery of *Caged Bird.*

Each of the five volumes explores, both literally and metaphorically, the significance of motherhood. I will examine this theme from two specific perspectives: first, Angelou's relationship to her mother and to mother substitutes, especially to Momma Henderson; second, Angelou's relationship to her son as she struggles to define her own role as mother/artist. Throughout the volumes Angelou moves backwards and forwards, from connection to conflict. This dialectic of Black mother-daughterhood, introduced in the childhood narrative, enlarges and contracts during the series, finding its fullest expression in *Singin' and Swingin' and Gettin' Merry Like Christmas.*

In flux, in defiance of chronological time, the mother-child configuration forms the basic pattern against which other relationships are measured and around which episodes and volumes begin or end. Motherhood also provides the series with a literary unity, as Angelou shifts positions—from mother to granddaughter to child—in a non-ending text that, through its repetitions of maternal motifs, provides an ironic comment on her own sense of identity. For Angelou, despite her insistence on mother love, is trapped in the conflicts between working and mothering, independence and nurturing—conflicts that echo her ambivalence towards her mother, Vivian Baxter, and her apparent sanctification of Grandmother Henderson, the major adult figure in *Caged Bird.*

Annie Henderson is a solid, God-fearing, economically independent woman whose general store in Stamps, Arkansas, is the "lay center of activities in town," much as Annie is the moral center of the family. According to Mildred A. Hill-Lubin [in *Ngambika: Studies of Women in African Literature,* 1986], the grandmother, both in Africa and in America, "has been a significant force in the stability and the continuity of the Black family and the community." Hill-Lubin selects Annie Henderson as her primary example of the strong grandmother in African-American literature—the traditional preserver of the family, the source of folk wisdom, and the instiller of values within the Black community. Throughout *Caged Bird* Maya has ambivalent feelings for this awesome woman, whose values of self-determination and personal dignity gradually chip away at Maya's dreadful sense of being "shit color." As a self-made woman, Annie Henderson has the economic power to lend money to whites; as a practical Black woman, however, she is convinced that whites cannot be directly confronted: "If she had been asked and had chosen to answer the question of whether she was cowardly or not, she would have said that she was a realist." To survive in a racist society, Momma Henderson has had to develop a realistic strategy of submission that Maya finds unacceptable. Maya, in her need to re-image her grandmother, creates a metaphor that places Momma's power above any apparent submissiveness: Momma "did an excellent job of sagging from her waist down, but from the waist up she seemed to be pulling for the top of the oak tree across the road."

There are numerous episodes, both in *Caged Bird* and *Gather Together,* which involve the conflict between Maya and her grandmother over how to deal with racism. When taunted by three "powhitetrash" girls, Momma quietly sings a hymn; Maya, enraged, would like to have a rifle. Or, when humiliated by a white dentist who'd rather put his "hand in a dog's mouth than in a nigger's," Annie is passive; Maya subsequently invents a fantasy in which Momma runs the dentist out of town. In the italicized dream text, Maya endows her grandmother with superhuman powers; Momma magically changes the dentist's nurse into a bag of chicken seed. In reality the grandmother has been defeated and humiliated, her only reward a mere ten dollars in interest for a loan she had made to the dentist. In Maya's fantasy Momma's *"eyes were blazing like live coals and her arms had doubled themselves in length"*; in actuality she "looked tired."

This richly textured passage is rendered from the perspective of an imaginative child who re-creates her grandmother—but in a language that ironically transforms Annie Henderson from a Southern Black storekeeper into an eloquent heroine from a romantic novel: *"Her tongue had thinned and the words rolled off well enunciated."* Instead of the silent "nigra" of the actual experience, Momma Henderson is now the articulate defender of her granddaughter against the stuttering dentist. Momma Henderson orders the *"contemptuous scoundrel"* to leave Stamps *"now and herewith."* The narrator eventually lets Momma speak normally, then comments: " *(She could afford to slip into the vernacular because she had such eloquent command of English.)"*

This fantasy is the narrator's way of dealing with her ambivalence towards Momma Henderson—a woman who throughout *Caged Bird* represents to Maya both strength and weakness, both generosity and punishment, both affection and the denial of affection. Here her defender is *"ten feet tall with eight-foot arms,"* quite capable, to recall the former tree image, of reaching the top of an oak from across the road. Momma's physical transformation in the dream text also recalls an earlier description: "I saw only her power and strength. She was taller than any woman in my personal world, and her hands were so large they could span my head from ear to ear." In the dentist fantasy, Maya eliminates all of Momma Henderson's "negative" traits—submissiveness, severity, religiosity, sternness, down-home speech. It would seem that Maya is so shattered by her grandmother's reaction to Dentist Lincoln, so destroyed by her illusions of Annie Henderson's power in relationship to white people, that she compensates by reversing the true situation and having the salivating dentist be the target of Momma's wrath. Significantly, this transformation occurs immediately before Momma Henderson tells Maya and Bailey that they are going to California. Its position in the text gives it the impression of finality. Any negative attitudes become submerged, only to surface later, in *Gather Together,* as aspects of Angelou's own ambiguity towards race, power, and identity.

In *Caged Bird* Momma Henderson had hit Maya with a switch for unknowingly taking the Lord's name in vain, "like white folks do." Similarly, in *Gather Together* Annie slaps her granddaughter after Maya, on a visit to Stamps, verbally assaults two white saleswomen. In a clash with Momma Henderson that is both painful and final, Maya argues for "the principle of the thing," and Momma slaps her. Surely, Momma's slap is well intended; she wishes to protect Maya from "lunatic cracker boys" and men in white sheets, from all of the insanity of racial prejudice. The "new" Maya, who has been to the city and found a sense of independence, is caught in the clash between her recently acquired "principles" and Momma's fixed ideology. Thus the slap—but also the intention behind it—will remain in Maya's memory long after the mature Angelou has been separated from Annie Henderson's supervision. Momma makes Maya and the baby leave Stamps, again as a precaution: "Momma's intent to protect me had caused her to hit me in the face, a thing she had never done, and to send me away to where she thought I'd be safe." Maya departs on the train, never to see her grandmother again.

In the third volume Angelou, her marriage falling apart, is recuperating from a difficult appendectomy. When she tells her husband Tosh that she wants to go to Stamps until she is well, he breaks the news that Annie Henderson died the day after Angelou's operation. In recording her reaction to her grandmother's death, Angelou's style shifts from its generally more conversational tone and becomes intense, religious, emotional:

> Ah, Momma. I had never looked at death before, peered into its yawning chasm for the face of the beloved. For days my mind staggered out of balance. I reeled on a precipice of knowledge that even if I were rich enough to travel all over

the world, I would never find Momma. If I were as good as God's angels and as pure as the Mother of Christ, I could never have Momma's rough slow hands pat my cheek or braid my hair.

Death to the young is more than that undiscovered country; despite its inevitability, it is a place having reality only in song or in other people's grief.

[Singin' and Swingin']

This moving farewell, so atypical of Angelou's more worldly autobiographical style, emerges directly from a suppressed religious experience which Angelou narrates earlier in the same text—a "secret crawl through neighborhood churches." These visits, done without her white husband's knowledge, culminate in Angelou's being saved at the Evening Star Baptist Church. During her purification, Angelou cries for her family: "For my fatherless son, who was growing up with a man who would never, could never, understand his need for manhood; for my mother, whom I admired but didn't understand; for my brother, whose disappointment with life was drawing him relentlessly into the clutches of death; and, finally, I cried for myself, long and loudly." Annie Henderson is strangely absent from this list of family for whom Angelou cries during the short-lived conversion. But only a few pages later, Angelou remembers her grandmother's profound importance, in the elegiac passage on Momma's death.

In this passage Angelou creates a funeral song which relies on the Black gospel tradition, on the language of Bible stories, and on certain formative literary texts. Words like *chasm, precipice, angels,* and *beloved* have Sunday School overtones, a kind of vocabulary Angelou more typically employs for humorous effects, as in the well-known portrait of Sister Monroe (*Caged Bird*). The gospel motif, so dominant in the passage, seems directly related to Angelou's rediscovery of the Black spiritual: "The spirituals and gospel songs were sweeter than sugar. I wanted to keep my mouth full of them and the sounds of my people singing fell like sweet oil in my ears" (*Singing' and Swingin'*). During her conversion experience Angelou lies on the floor while four women march round her singing, "Soon one morning when death comes walking in my room"; in another spiritual the singers prepare for the "walk to Jerusalem." These and similar hymns about death had been significant elements of the "folk religious tradition" of Momma Henderson. Now, for a brief time, they become part of the mature Angelou's experience. That their revival is almost immediately followed by the death of Momma Henderson accounts, to a large extent, for Angelou's intensely religious narrative.

Angelou's singing of the Black grandmother in this passage contains other refrains from the past, most notably her desire to have "Momma's rough slow hands pat my cheek." These are the same hands that slapped Maya for having talked back to the white saleswomen—an event that was physically to separate grandmother and granddaughter (*Gather Together*). That final slap, softened here, becomes a loving pat on the cheek akin to a moment in *Caged Bird* in which Maya describes her grandmother's love as a touch of the hand: "Just the gentle pressure of her rough hand conveyed her own concern and assurance

to me." Angelou's tone throughout the elegy is an attempt, through religion, to reconcile her ambivalence towards Momma Henderson by sharing her traditions. Angelou wishes to be "as good as God's angels" and as "pure as the Mother of Christ," metaphors which seem to represent Angelou's effort to close off the chasm between herself and Momma Henderson through the use of a common language, the language of the church-going grandmother.

As Momma Henderson, the revered grandmother, recedes from the narrative, Angelou's natural mother gains prominence. By the third volume Maya Angelou and Vivian Baxter have established a closeness that somewhat compensates for Maya's having been sent off to Stamps as a child, a situation so painful that Maya had imagined her mother dead:

I could cry anytime I wanted by picturing my mother (I didn't quite know what she looked like) lying in her coffin. . . . The face was brown, like a big O, and since I couldn't fill in the features I printed M O T H E R across the O, and tears would fall down my cheeks like warm milk.

(Caged Bird)

Like Maya's fantasy of her grandmother and Dentist Lincoln, the above passage is an imaginative revision of reality, Maya's way to control the frustrations produced by Vivian's rejection. The images of the dream text invoke romance fiction and Amazonian strength. Here the images concern, first, the artist who fills in the empty canvas (the O) with print; second, the mother-like child who cries tears of "warm milk" in sympathy for her imagined dead mother. These interlaced metaphors of writing and nurturance appear frequently in the continuing text, as Angelou explores her relationships with mothers and children.

> Like an unfinished painting, [Angelou's] autobiographical series is an ongoing creation, in a form that rejects the finality of a restricting frame.
>
> —*Mary Jane Lupton*

When Maya is eight years old, she and Bailey visit their mother in St. Louis, where Maya discovers her exquisite beauty: "To describe my mother would be to write about a hurricane in its perfect power. Or the climbing, falling colors of a rainbow. . . . She was too beautiful to have children" (*Caged Bird*). Ironically, this mother "too beautiful to have children" is to a large degree responsible for her own child's brutal rape. Vivian's beauty attracts a lover, Mr. Freeman, who is constantly in the house waiting for a woman who is not there, and he "uses Angelou as an extension of her mother" to satisfy his sexual urges [Stephanie A. Demetrakopoulos, in *Women's Autobiography: Essays in Criticism,* 1980]. It could also be suggested that Vivian uses Maya, somehow knowing that in her own absence Maya will keep her lover amused. When Maya becomes ill, Vivian responds in a motherly manner: making broth, cooking Cream of Wheat, taking Maya's temperature, calling a doctor. After she discovers the rape, Vivian sends Maya to a hospital, bringing her flowers and candy (*Caged Bird*).

It is Grandmother Baxter, however, who sees to it that the rapist is punished; after the trial a policeman comes to the house and informs an unsurprised Mrs. Baxter that Freeman has been kicked to death. Mrs. Baxter is a political figure in St. Louis, a precinct captain and gambler whose light skin and "six mean children" bring her both power and respect. Like Momma Henderson, Grandmother Baxter is a source of strength for Maya. Both grandmothers are "strong, independent[,] skillful women who are able to manage their families and to insure their survival in a segregated and hostile society" [Mildred A. Hill-Lublin, in *Ngambika: Studies of Women in African Literature*, 1986].

Despite their positive influence, however, Maya has ambivalent feelings towards her powerful grandmothers. Maya feels guilty for having lied at the trial, a guilt compounded when she learns of Grandmother Baxter's part in Freeman's murder. To stop the "poison" in her breath, Maya retreats into a "perfect personal silence" which neither of the Baxter women can penetrate, and which Maya breaks only for Bailey. The disastrous St. Louis sequence stops abruptly, without transition: "We were on the train going back to Stamps . . . ". Thus, the end of the visit to Grandmother Baxter parallels chapter one of *Caged Bird;* a train moves from an urban center to rural Arkansas and to the protection of Annie Henderson.

Back at her grandmother's general store, Maya meets Mrs. Bertha Flowers, "the aristocrat of Black Stamps." This unambivalently positive mother figure helps Maya to recover her oral language through the written text—reading *A Tale of Two Cities.* In a series of sharp contrasts, the narrator conveys Maya's divided feelings between the sophisticated mother figure, Mrs. Flowers, and her more provincial grandmother. Mrs. Flowers wears gloves, whereas Mrs. Henderson has rough hands. Mrs. Flowers admires white male writers, whereas Annie Henderson will not tolerate them. And in a set of contrasts that occurs almost simultaneously in the text, the literary Mrs. Flowers rewards Maya's language with sweets, whereas the religious grandmother punishes Maya's spoken words ("by the way") without making any effort to explain her anger. In an earlier passage, however, the narrator merges these basic oppositions into a dynamic interaction between two Black women: "I heard the soft-voiced Mrs. Flowers and the textured voice of my grandmother merging and melting. They were interrupted from time to time by giggles that must have come from Mrs. Flowers (Momma never giggled in her life). Then she was gone." These contrasts appear following Maya's failed relationship with Vivian Baxter. They are indications of the split mother—the absent natural mother, the gentle Mrs. Flowers, the forceful Annie Henderson—whose divisions Angelou must articulate if she is to find her own autobiographical voice.

Although most critics have seen a wholeness in Maya's personality at the conclusion of *Caged Bird,* a few have observed this division of self, which Demetrakopoulos relates to Maya's conflicts about the mother: She "splits the feminine archetype of her mother's cold Venus and her grandmother's primal warm sheltering Demeter aspects." The Jungian metaphors may jar in this African-American context, but I agree with Demetrakopoulos that at the end of *Caged Bird* the narrator is split. She is a mother who is herself a child; a daughter torn by her notions of mother love; an uncertain Black teenager hardly capable of the heavy burden of closure placed on her by Sidonie Smith, Stephen Butterfield, Selwyn Cudjoe, and other critics.

Nor is this split mended when Angelou gives birth to *Gather Together.* Here she introduces herself by way of contradictions: "I was seventeen, very old, embarrassingly young, with a son of two months, and I still lived with my mother and stepfather." Vivian Baxter intermittently takes care of Guy while his young mother works as a cook or shopkeeper. When Momma Henderson forces Maya and her son to leave Stamps, they go immediately to the security of Vivian's fourteen-room house in San Francisco. One gets a strong sense throughout *Gather Together* of Maya's dependence on her mother. Angelou admires her mother for her self-reliance, her encouragement, and her casual approach to sexuality. She also continues to be captivated by Vivian's beauty, by her "snappy-fingered, head-tossing elegance" (*Singin' and Swingin'*). On the other hand, she recognizes Vivian Baxter's flaws: "Her own mind was misted by the knowledge of a failing marriage, and the slipping away of the huge sums of money which she had enjoyed and thought her due" (*Gather Together*).

As for her son, Angelou reveals similar contradictory feelings. After quitting a job to be with Guy, Angelou writes: "A baby's love for his mother is probably the sweetest emotion we can savor" (*Gather Together*). In a more depressed mood, however, she comments that her child's disposition had "lost its magic to make me happy." What Angelou does in these instances is to articulate her feelings as they convey the reality of her experiences, even though some of these negative emotions might not represent her best side.

The most dramatic mother-child episode in *Gather Together* occurs while Angelou is working as a prostitute. She leaves Guy with her sitter, Big Mary. Returning for Guy after several days, she learns that her son has been kidnapped. Angelou finally recovers her child, unharmed; at that moment she realizes that they are both separate individuals and that Guy is not merely a "beautiful appendage of myself." Angelou's awareness of the inevitable separation of mother and child, expressed here for the first time, is a theme that she will continue to explore through the remaining autobiographical volumes.

Gather Together closes with Angelou's and Guy's returning to the protection of Vivian Baxter, following Angelou's glimpse at the horrors of heroin addiction: "I had no idea what I was going to make of my life, but I had given a promise and found my innocence. I swore I'd never lose it again." In its tableau of mother, child, and grandmother, this concluding paragraph directly parallels the ending of *Caged Bird.*

In the next volume, *Singin' and Swingin'*, the closeness between mother and daughter continues. As she matures, Angelou becomes more in control of her feelings and more objective in her assessment of Vivian Baxter's personality. Additionally, the separation of egos that Angelou perceived after locating her kidnapped son would extend to the mother-daughter and grandmother-granddaughter relationships as well. But *Singin' and Swingin' and Gettin' Merry Like Christmas* is, despite its joyful title, a mesh of conflicts—many of them existing within the autobiographical self; many of them involving separations which, although consciously chosen, become unbearable. A number of ambiguities appear throughout the book, especially as they concern the mother-child pattern which is to dominate this and the subsequent texts.

The underlying drama in *Singin' and Swingin'* is played out between Angelou, the single parent of a young son, and Angelou, the actress who chooses to leave that son with Vivian Baxter in order to tour Europe with the company of *Porgy and Bess*. Angelou is keenly aware that putting Guy in the care of his grandmother is an echo of her own child-mother experience:

> The past revisited. My mother had left me with
> my grandmother for years and I knew the pain
> of parting. My mother, like me, had had her mo-
> tivations, her needs. I did not relish visiting the
> same anguish on my son, and she, years later,
> told me how painful our separation was to her.
> But I had to work and I had to be good. I would
> make it up to my son and one day would take
> him to all the places I was going to see.

Angelou's feelings are compounded by the fact that, as a young, Black, single mother, she alone is finally responsible for giving her child a sense of stability. In identifying the conflict between working and mothering, Angelou offers a universalized representation of the turmoil which may arise when a woman attempts to fulfill both roles.

Angelou suffers considerably on the European tour. In some instances her longings for Guy make her sleep fitfully or make her distracted—as when she sees some young Italian boys with "pale-gold complexions" who remind her of her son. When she is paged at a Paris train station, Angelou fears that something dreadful has happened to Guy, and she blames herself: "I knew I shouldn't have left my son. There was a telegram waiting for me to say he had been hurt somehow. Or had run away from home. Or had caught an awful disease." On other occasions she speaks quite directly of her guilt: "I sent my dollars home to pay for Clyde's [Guy's] keep and to assuage my guilt at being away from him."

Of the many examples in *Singin' and Swingin'* which address this conflict, I have selected one particular passage to illustrate the ways in which Angelou articulates her ambivalence about mothering. While she is in Paris, Angelou earns extra money by singing in a nightclub and decides to send the money home rather than spend it on a room with a private bath: "Mom could buy something wonderful for Clyde every other week and tell him I'd sent it. Then perhaps he would forgive my absence." The narrator shows no qualms about lying to her son; Vivian could "tell

him I'd sent it." Additionally, she makes no connection between her efforts to buy forgiveness and the anger she felt as a child when her absent mother, the same "Mom" of the above passage, sent Maya a tea set and a doll with yellow hair for Christmas: "Bailey and I tore the stuffing out of the doll the day after Christmas, but he warned me that I had to keep the tea set in good condition because any day or night she might come riding up" (*Caged Bird*). Liliane K. Arensberg interprets the tea cups as "symbols of a white world beyond Maya's reach of everyday experience," whereas the torn doll "serves as an effigy of her mother by virtue of being female and a gift." Although I agree with Arensberg's interpretation, I tend to read the gifts as metaphors for Maya's divided self. The preserved tea set, the torn doll—what better signifiers could there be for the split feelings of the abandoned child, who destroys one gift to show anger but saves the other in anticipation of the mother's return? I would also suggest that the seemingly inappropriate title *Singin' and Swingin' and Gettin' Merry Like Christmas* may be intended to signal the reader back to the very unmerry Christmas of *Caged Bird.*

In the Paris sequence the narrator seems to have suppressed, in her role as *mother,* some of the anguish she had experienced during childhood—although in the passage previously cited (*Singin' and Swingin'*), she recognizes the similarities between her own "pains of parting" and her son's. Angelou refers to this separation from her son so frequently in the text that he becomes a substantial part of the narrative, the source of Angelou's guilt but also the major factor in the development of dramatic tension. Angelou, in this most complex of the autobiographies, is richly and honestly rendering the split in her own psyche between being a "good" mother (being at home) and being a "bad" mother (selfishly staying in Europe). The narrator pretends to herself that her son wants a gift, thus prolonging the admission that he really wants his mother—as Maya had wanted hers.

To arrive at this interpretation the reader must move back and forth among the texts, perceiving parallels in order to decipher the narrator's motivations. The frequent references in *Singin' and Swingin'* to separation and to guilt give one considerable access to the narrator's complex personality; at the same time, these references demand to be read against and with the entire series—intertextuality in its strictest sense.

Angelou returns from Europe to find her son suffering from a skin disease that is an overt expression of his loneliness. In a promise that recalls the last lines of *Gather Together* (never again to lose her innocence), Angelou vows to Guy: "I swear to you, I'll never leave you again. If I go, you'll go with me or I won't go" (*Singin' and Swingin'*). She takes Guy with her to Hawaii, where she has a singing engagement. *Singin' and Swingin'* closes in a sentence which highlights, through its three nouns, the underlying tensions of the book: "Although I was not a great *singer* I was his *mother,* and he was my wonderful, dependently independent *son*" (emphasis added). Dialectical in phrasing, this statement not only functions to close the first three books but also opens itself to the mother-son patterns of the future volumes: fluctuations between dependence and independence.

In *The Heart of a Woman* the tension between mothering and working continues, but to a lesser extent. Guy is now living with his mother and not with Vivian Baxter. But Angelou, despite her earlier vow, does occasionally leave her son. During a night club engagement in Chicago, Angelou trusts Guy to the care of her friend John Killens. One night Killens phones from Brooklyn and informs her that "there's been some trouble." In a moment of panic that recalls her fears at the Paris train station (*Gather Together*), Angelou again imagines that Guy has been injured, stolen, "struck by an errant bus, hit by a car out of control."

Angelou confronts these fears in the Brooklyn adventure, the most dramatic episode of *The Heart of a Woman.* Unlike the internal conflicts of *Gather Together,* this one operates outside of the narrator, showing Maya Angelou as a strong, aggressive Black mother rather than a mother torn by self-doubt. While Angelou was in Chicago, Guy had gotten in trouble with a Brooklyn street gang. In order to protect her son, she confronts Jerry, the gang leader, and threatens to shoot his entire family if Guy is harmed. Jerry's response is an ironic comment on the motherhood theme of the autobiographies: "O.K., I understand. But for a mother, I must say you're a mean motherfucker." Powerful, protective of her son, Angelou has become in this episode a reincarnation of Momma Henderson.

Unfortunately, no mother or grandmother or guardian angel, no matter how strong, can keep children forever from danger. Near the end of *The Heart of a Woman,* Guy is seriously injured in a car accident. In a condensed, tormented autobiographical passage, Angelou gazes at the face of her unconscious son and summarizes their life together:

> He was born to me when I was seventeen. I had taken him away from my mother's house when he was two years old, and except for a year I spent in Europe without him, and a month when he was stolen by a deranged woman, we had spent our lives together. My grown life lay stretched before me, stiff as a pine board, in a strange country, blood caked on his face and clotted on his clothes.

Guy gradually recovers, moving, during the process of physical healing, toward a position of greater independence from his mother.

But Angelou, too, moves towards a separateness, much as she had predicted in *Gather Together.* In *The Heart of a Woman* the texture of Angelou's life changes significantly. She travels a lot, seeing far less of Vivian—although she does write to her mother from Ghana asking for financial help after Guy's accident. She strengthens her public identity, becoming a coordinator in the Civil Rights Movement and a professionally recognized dancer and actress. She also, for the first time in the autobiographies, begins her account of self as writer. Angelou attends a writer's workshop; publishes a short story; becomes friends with John Killens, Rosa Guy, Paule Marshall, and other Black novelists. Most important, writing forces her into a con-

scious maturity: "If I wanted to write, I had to be willing to develop a kind of concentration found mostly in people awaiting execution. I had to learn technique and surrender my ignorance." By extension, the rich ambivalence of *Singin' and Swingin'* could only have been achieved by a writer who had abandoned "ignorance" for a conscious self-exploration.

Paradoxically, the independent writer/mother establishes this "kind of concentration" in maternal solitude. *Singin' and Swingin'* had ended with mother and son reunited, both dependent and independent. *The Heart of a Woman* ends in separation. Guy, now a student at the University of Ghana, is moving to a dormitory. In the last two paragraphs we find Angelou alone:

> I closed the door and held my breath. Waiting for the wave of emotion to surge over me, knock me down, take my breath away. Nothing happened. I didn't feel bereft or desolate. I didn't feel lonely or abandoned.

> I sat down, still waiting. The first thought that came to me, perfectly formed and promising, was "At last, I'll be able to eat the whole breast of a roast chicken by myself."

Angelou's reaction to having "closed the door" on her son is, like so many of her feelings in this complicated relationship, ambivalent. The language of the passage is initially charged with negativity: "Nothing happened. I didn't feel. . . . I didn't feel. . . ." The son she had loved through all of "our lives together" is gone. Angelou sits waiting for something dreadful to happen to herself—as she had earlier imagined Guy's being stolen or being hit by a bus. But the narrator counters this negative attitude with a note of irony in which she reverses the biological assumption of the mother as she-who-nourishes: She can now have the "whole breast" to herself.

The family chicken dinner is a recurring motif in the autobiographical series. Recall the marvelous scene from *Caged Bird* in which Maya and Bailey watch Reverend Howard Thomas gobble down Momma Henderson's chicken dinner: "He ate the biggest, brownest and best parts of the chicken at every Sunday meal." Now there is no competition. Angelou has the best part, the breast, to herself. On the negative side, Angelou is left, at the end of the fourth volume, in isolation; the last word of *The Heart of a Woman* is "myself." But the negativity is outweighed by the more "promising" aspects of being alone, the word *promising* an echo of the resolutions of *Gather Together* and *Singin' and Swingin',* which end in vows of innocence and of commitment. The "perfectly formed" thought at the end of *The Heart of a Woman* is Angelou's realization of a new "myself," of a woman no longer primarily defined as granddaughter or daughter or mother—a woman free to choose herself.

All God's Children Need Traveling Shoes opens by going back in time to Angelou the mother, who anxiously waits at the hospital following Guy's car accident. In an image that parodies the well-fed mother of *The Heart of a Woman,* Angelou compares her anxiety over Guy to being eaten up:

July and August of 1962 stretched out like fat men yawning after a sumptuous dinner. They had every right to gloat, for they had eaten me up. Gobbled me down. Consumed my spirit, not in a wild rush, but slowly, with the obscene patience of certain victors. I became a shadow walking in the white hot streets, and a dark spectre in the hospital.

The months of helplessly waiting for Guy to heal are like fat, stuffed men, a description that evokes memories of Reverend Thomas, who ate Momma Henderson's chicken, and of Mr. Freeman, who ate in Vivian Baxter's kitchen and raped her daughter. Guy's accident has an effect similar to the rape; Angelou retreats into silence. She is a "shadow," a "dark spectre," a Black mother silenced by the fear of her son's possible death.

Guy does recover. Their relationship, which like the autobiographical form itself is constantly in flux, moves once again from dependence to independence, climaxing in a scene in which Angelou learns that her son is having an affair with an American woman a year older than herself. Angelou at first threatens to strike him, but Guy merely pats her head and says: "Yes, little mother. I'm sure you will." Shortly afterwards Angelou travels to Germany to perform in Genet's *The Blacks.* Guy meets her return flight and takes her home to a dinner of fried chicken he has cooked for her. Then, asserting his independence, he announces that he has "plans for dinner."

Reading between the texts, we see Angelou alone again before a plate of chicken, as she was at the conclusion of *The Heart of a Woman.* In the *Traveling Shoes* episode, however, the conflicting feelings of love and resentment are more directly stated:

> He's gone. My lovely little boy is gone and will never return. That big confident strange man has done away with my little boy, and he has the gall to say he loves me. How can he love me? He doesn't know me, and I sure as hell don't know him.

In this passage Angelou authentically faces and records the confusions of seeing one's child achieve selfhood, universalizing the pain a mother experiences when her "boy" is transformed into a "big confident strange man" who refuses to be his mother's "beautiful appendage" (*Gather Together*).

Yet through much of the fifth volume, Angelou continues to separate herself from Guy and to form new relationships. She shares experiences with other women, including her two roommates; she befriends an African boy named Koko; she enjoys her contacts with the colony of Black American writers and artists living in Ghana; and she continues her sexual involvements with men. The love affair which seems most vital in *Traveling Shoes,* however, is with Africa herself. In her travels through West Africa Angelou discovers certain connections between her own traditions and those of her African ancestors. She takes great satisfaction in her heritage when she is mistaken for a Bambara woman. Among African women she discovers strong mother figures, most notably Patience Aduah, whose custom of giving away food by the campfire evokes

memories of Momma Henderson's having shared her table with Black American travelers denied rooms in hotels or seats in restaurants during the era of segregation in much of America (*Traveling Shoes*). Through her identification with Africa, Angelou reaffirms the meaning of motherhood.

Although captivated by the oral traditions of Mother Africa, Angelou chooses to leave, at the conclusion of *Traveling Shoes,* in order to return to the rhythms of Southern Black churches, the rhythms of her grandmother. In so doing, however, she must also leave her son. The final scene in the book is at the Accra airport. Angelou is saying farewell to her friends and, most specifically, to Guy, who "stood, looking like a young lord of summer, straight, sure among his Ghanaian companions." Through this suggestion of Guy as an African prince, Angelou roots him in the culture of West Africa.

If we look at the closure of *Traveling Shoes* on a literal level, then Angelou's son is a college student, staying on to complete his degree. But if we accept a grander interpretation, Guy has become, through his interaction with the Ghanaians, a "young lord" of Africa, given back to the Mother Continent freely, not lost, like so many other children, in mid-passage or in slavery. Angelou lovingly accepts the separation, knowing that "someone like me and certainly related to me" will be forming new bonds between himself and Mother Africa. Guy is making an essentially free choice that centuries of Black creativity in America have helped make possible: "Through the centuries of despair and dislocation we had been creative, because we faced down death by daring to hope."

As in the four earlier autobiographies, this one closes with the mother-son configuration. But in the final, puzzling line of *Traveling Shoes* Angelou swings the focus away from Guy and towards the edge of the canvas: "I could nearly hear the old ones chuckling." In this spiritual call to her ancestors Angelou imaginatively connects herself to the Ketans and the Ghanaians, to the people placed in chains, to all of God's children who had "never completely left Africa." Ironically, the narrator herself has not completely left Africa either. The rhythmic prose that concludes the fifth volume is an anticipated departure to a new world, with the narrator still at the airport. As in the other volumes, the closure is thus another opening into the next narrative journey. (pp. 257-74)

Mary Jane Lupton, "Singing the Black Mother: Maya Angelou and Autobiographical Continuity," in Black American Literature Forum, *Vol. 24, No. 2, Summer, 1990, pp. 257-76.*

Maya Angelou with George Plimpton   (interview date Fall 1990)

[*Plimpton is an American nonfiction writer, editor, and author of children's books. In the brief passage below, he discusses Angelou's life and career. In the interview that follows, Angelou discusses the writing process and autobiographical literature.*]

Maya Angelou described herself in 1972 as "a born loser—had to be: from a broken family, raped at eight, unwed mother at sixteen." Yet in her sixty-two years Angelou has achieved prominence as an author, poet, conductor, actor, singer, songwriter, playwright and film director. She is perhaps best known for the autobiographical series which she began in 1970 with *I Know Why the Caged Bird Sings.* The book was an immediate critical and popular success and was nominated for the National Book Award. James Baldwin hailed it as part of "the beginning of a new era in the minds and hearts of all black men and women, liberating the reader into life simply because Maya Angelou confronts her own life with such moving wonder, such a luminous dignity." In this first autobiography, Angelou depicts her experience of growing up in the segregated Southern town of Stamps, Arkansas. Angelou was born April 4, 1928 in St. Louis, Missouri, but her divorced parents, Bailey Johnson, a doorman and later a naval clinician, and Vivian Baxter Johnson, sent her to live with her grandmother in Stamps. There, she attended and graduated from Lafayette County Training School. At thirteen, she went to San Francisco to live with her mother. She graduated from Mission High School at sixteen, and gave birth to her son, Guy Johnson two months later.

In *Gather Together in My Name* (1974) Angelou recounts the next four years of her life as a single mother with a young child. She worked as a Creole cook, a waitress, and an inexperienced madam for two lesbian prostitutes. *Singin' and Swingin' and Gettin' Merry Like Christmas* (1976), chronicles Angelou's life into the 1950s. *The Heart of a Woman* (1981), and *All God's Children Need Traveling Shoes* (1986), tell of Angelou's journey to Africa and her return to the United States, as well as her involvement in the civil rights movement.

Angelou's first volume of poetry, *Just Give Me a Cool Drink of Water 'for I Diiie* (1971), was nominated for the Pulitzer Prize. Her other collections include *Oh Pray My Wings Are Gonna Fit Me Well* (1975), and *And Still I Rise* (1978), poetry which often hinges on the complexities of race relations from an involved personal viewpoint. In 1960 and 1961 she worked for Martin Luther King, Jr., as a coordinator for the Southern Christian Leadership Conference.

Throughout her life, Angelou has been involved in the performing arts. She has studied theater with Frank Silvera and Gene Frankel and her roles in *Look Away* (1973), and as Nyo Boto, the grandmother in *Roots* (1977), earned Angelou Tony nominations. She has studied dance with Martha Graham, Pearl Primus and Ann Halprin; as the première danseuse in a State Department-sponsored production of *Porgy and Bess,* Angelou toured twenty-two countries in Europe and Africa. She has also composed music, some of which has been recorded by B. B. King. Working in film and television, Angelou was the first black woman to have an original screenplay produced (*Georgia, Georgia,* 1971), and was also the first black American woman film director.

Angelou lived for five years in Africa, becoming associate editor of the *Arab Observer,* and editor of *African Review,*

and an administrator at the University of Ghana. She has held positions at several universities in the United States, including California State University and Wichita State University. She was a Yale University Chubb Fellow in 1970, was a Rockefeller Scholar in Italy (1975) and has received honorary degrees from Smith College (1975), Mills College (1975), and Lawrence University (1976). She currently resides in Winston-Salem, North Carolina, where she is Reynolds Professor of American Studies at Wake Forest University.

This interview was conducted on the stage of the YMHA on Manhattan's upper East Side. A large audience, predominantly women, was on hand, filling indeed every seat, with standees in the back . . . a testament to Maya Angelou's drawing-power. Close to the stage was a small contingent of black women dressed in the white robes of the Black Muslim order. Her presence dominated the proceedings. Many of her remarks drew fervid applause, especially those which reflected her views on racial problems, the need to persevere, and "courage." She is an extraordinary performer and has a powerful stage presence. Many of the answers seemed as much directed to the audience as to the interviewer so that when Maya Angelou concluded the evening by reading aloud from her work—again to a rapt audience—it seemed a logical extension of a planned entertainment.

. . . . .

[Plimpton]: *You once told me that you write lying on a made-up bed with a bottle of sherry, a dictionary,* Roget's Thesaurus, *yellow pads, an ashtray and a Bible. What's the function of the Bible?*

[Angelou]: The language of all the interpretations, the translations, of the Judaic Bible and the Christian Bible, is musical, just wonderful. I read the Bible to myself; I'll take any translation, any edition, and read it aloud, just to hear the language, hear the rhythm, and remind myself how beautiful English is. Though I do manage to mumble around in about seven or eight languages, English remains the most beautiful of languages. It will do anything.

Do you read it to get inspired to pick up your own pen?

For melody. For content also. I'm working at trying to be a Christian, and that's serious business. It's like trying to be a good Jew, a good Muslim, a good Buddhist, a good Shintoist, a good Zoroastrian, a good friend, a good lover, a good mother, a good buddy: it's serious business. It's not something where you think, "Oh, I've got it done. I did it all day, hot-diggety." The truth is, all day long you try to do it, try to be it, and then in the evening, if you're honest and have a little courage, you look at yourself and say, "Hmm. I only blew it eighty-six times. Not bad." I'm trying to be a Christian, and the Bible helps me to remind myself what I'm about.

Do you transfer that melody to your own prose? Do you think your prose has that particular ring that one associates with the King James version?

I want to hear how English sounds; how Edna St. Vincent Millay heard English. I want to hear it, so I read it aloud. It is not so that I can then imitate it. It is to remind me what a glorious language it is. Then, I try to be particular, and even original. It's a little like reading Gerald Manley Hopkins or Paul Laurence Dunbar, or James Weldon Johnson.

And is the bottle of sherry for the end of the day, or to fuel the imagination?

I might have it at 6:15 A.M. just as soon as I get in, but usually it's about eleven o'clock when I'll have a glass of sherry.

When you are refreshed by the Bible and the sherry, how do you start a day's work?

I have kept a hotel room in every town I've ever lived in. I rent a hotel room for a few months, leave my home at six and try to be at work by 6:30. To write, I lie across the bed, so that this elbow is absolutely encrusted at the end, just so rough with callouses. I never allow the hotel people to change the bed, because I never sleep there. I stay until 12:30 or 1:30 in the afternoon, and then I go home and try to breathe; I look at the work around five; I have an orderly dinner: proper, quiet, lovely dinner; and then I go back to work the next morning. Sometimes in hotels I'll go into the room, and there'll be a note on the floor which says, "Dear Miss Angelou, let us change the sheets. We think they are moldy." But I only allow them to come in and empty wastebaskets. I insist that all things are taken off the walls. I don't want anything in there. I go into the room, and I feel as if all my beliefs are suspended. Nothing holds me to anything. No milkmaids, no flowers, nothing. I just want to *feel* and then when I start to work I'll remember. I'll read something, maybe the Psalms, maybe, again, something from Mr. Dunbar, James Weldon Johnson. And I'll remember how beautiful, how pliable the language is, how it will lend itself. If you pull it, it says, "Okay." I remember that, and I start to write. Nathaniel Hawthorne says, "Easy reading is damn hard writing." I try to pull the language in to such a sharpness that it jumps off the page. It must look easy, but it takes me forever to get it to look so easy. Of course, there are those critics—New York critics as a rule—who say, "Well, Maya Angelou has a new book out and, of course, it's good but then she's a natural writer." Those are the ones I want to grab by the throat and wrestle to the floor because it takes me forever to get it to sing. I *work* at the language. On an evening like this, looking out at the auditorium, if I had to write this evening from my point of view, I'd see the rust-red used worn velvet seats, and the lightness where people's backs have rubbed against the back of the seat so that it's a light orange; then, the beautiful colors of the people's faces, the white, pink-white, beige-white, light beige and brown and tan—I would have to look at all that, at all those faces and the way they sit on top of their necks. When I would end up writing after four hours or five hours in my room, it might sound like: "It was a rat that sat on a mat. That's that. Not a cat." But I would continue to play with it and pull at it and say, "I love you. Come to me. I love you." It might take me two or three weeks just to describe what I'm seeing now.

How do you know when it's what you want?

I know when it's the best I can do. It may not be the best there is. Another writer may do it much better. But I know when it's the best I can do. I know that one of the great arts that the writer develops is the art of saying, "No. No, I'm finished. Bye." And leaving it alone. I will not write it into the ground. I will not write the life out of it. I won't do that.

How much revising is involved?

I write in the morning, and then go home about midday and take a shower, because writing, as you know, is very hard work, so you have to do a double ablution. Then I go out and shop—I'm a serious cook—and pretend to be normal. I play sane: "Good morning! Fine, thank you. And you?" And I go home. I prepare dinner for myself and if I have houseguests, I do the candles and the pretty music and all that. Then, after all the dishes are moved away, I read what I wrote that morning. And more often than not, if I've done nine pages I may be able to save two and half, or three. That's the cruelest time you know, to really admit that it doesn't work. And to blue pencil it. When I finish maybe fifty pages, and read them—fifty acceptable pages—it's not too bad. I've had the same editor since 1967. Many times he has said to me over the years, or asked me, "Why would you use a semi-colon instead of a colon?" And many times over the years I have said to him things like: "I will never speak to you again. Forever. Goodbye. That is it. Thank you very much." And I leave. Then I read the piece and I think of his suggestions. I send him a telegram that says, "OK, so you're right. So what? Don't ever mention this to me again. If you do, I will never speak to you again." About two years ago I was visiting him and his wife in the Hamptons. I was at the end of a dining room table with a sit-down dinner of about fourteen people. Way at the end I said to someone, "I sent him telegrams over the years." From the other end of the table he said, "And I've kept every one!" Brute! But the editing, one's own editing, before the editor sees it, is the most important.

The five autobiographical books follow each other in chronological order. When you started writing **I Know Why the Caged Bird Sings** *did you know that you would move on from that? It almost works line by line into the second volume.*

I know, but I didn't really mean to. I thought I was going to write **Caged Bird** and that would be it and I would go back to playwriting and writing scripts for television. Autobiography is awfully seductive; it's wonderful. Once I got into it I realized I was following a tradition established by Frederick Douglas—the slave narrative—speaking in the first-person singular talking about the first-person plural, always saying "I" meaning "we." And what a responsibility. Trying to work with that form, the autobiographical mode, to change it, to make it bigger, richer, finer, and more inclusive in the twentieth century has been a great challenge for me. I've written five now, and I really hope—the works are required reading in many universities and colleges in the United States—that people *read* my work. The greatest compliment I receive is when people walk up to me on the street or in airports and say, "Miss Angelou, I *wrote* your book last year and I really—I mean I *read* . . ." That is it: that the person has come into the books so seriously, so completely, that he or she, black or white, male or female, feels, "That's my story. I told it. I'm making it up on the spot." That's the great compliment. I didn't expect, originally, that I was going to continue with the form. I thought I was going to write a little book and it would be fine, and I would go on back to poetry, write a little music.

What about the genesis of the first book? Who were the people who helped you shape those sentences that leap off the page?

Oh well, they started years and years before I ever wrote, when I was very young. I loved the black American minister. I loved the melody of the voice, and the imagery, so rich, and almost impossible. The minister in my church in Arkansas, when I was very young, would use phrases such as "God stepped out, the sun over his right shoulder, the moon nestling in the palm of his hand." I mean, I just loved it, and I loved the black poets, and I loved Shakespeare, and Edgar Allan Poe, and I liked Matthew Arnold a lot, still do. Being mute for a number of years, I read, and memorized, and all those people have had tremendous influence . . . in the first book, and even in the most recent book.

Mute?

I was raped when I was very young. I told my brother the name of the person who had done it. Within a few days the man was killed. In my child's mind—seven and a half years old—I thought my voice had killed him. So I stopped talking for five years. Of course I've written about this in *Caged Bird.*

When did you decide you were going to be a writer? Was there a moment when you suddenly said "This is what I wish to do for the rest of my life?"

Well, I had written a television series for PBS, and I was going out to California. I thought I was a poet and playwright. That was what I was going to do the rest of my life. Or become famous as a real estate broker. This sounds like namedropping, and it really is—but James Baldwin took me over to dinner with Jules and Judy Feiffer one evening. All three of them are great talkers. They went on with their stories and I had to fight for the right to play it good. I had to insert myself to tell some stories too. Well, the next day, Judy Feiffer called Bob Loomis, an editor at Random House, and suggested that if he could get me to write an autobiography, he'd have something. So he phoned me and I said, "No, under no circumstances; I certainly will not do such a thing." So I went out to California to produce this series on African and black American culture. Loomis called me out there about three times. Each time I said no. Then he talked to James Baldwin. Jimmy gave him a ploy which always works with me—though I'm not proud to say that. The next time he called, he said, "Well, Miss Angelou. I won't bother you again. It's just as well that you don't attempt to write this book, because to write autobiography as literature is almost impossible." I said, "What are you talking about? I'll do it." I'm not proud about this button which can be pushed and I will immediately jump.

Do you select a dominant theme for each book?

I try to remember times in my life, incidents in which there was the dominating theme of cruelty, or kindness, or generosity, or envy, or happiness, glee . . . perhaps four incidents in the period I'm going to write about. Then I select, the one which lends itself best to my device and which I can write as drama without falling into melodrama.

Did you write for a particular audience?

I thought early on if I could write a book for black girls it would be good, because there were so few books for a black girl to read that said "This is how it is to grow up." Then, I thought "I'd better, you know, enlarge that group, the market group that I'm trying to reach." I decided to write for black boys, and then white girls, and then white boys.

But what I try to keep in mind mostly is my craft. That's what I really try for; I try to allow myself to be impelled by my art—if that doesn't sound too pompous and weird—accept the impulse, and then try my best to have a command of the craft. If I'm feeling depressed, and losing my control, then I think about the reader. But that is very rare—to think about the reader when the work is going on.

So you don't keep a particular reader in mind when you sit down in that hotel room and begin to compose or write. It's yourself.

It's myself . . . and my reader. I would be a liar, a hypocrite, or a fool—and I'm not any of those—to say that I don't write for the reader. I do. But for the reader who hears, who really will work at it, going behind what I seem to say. So I write for myself and that reader who will pay the dues. There's a phrase in West Africa, in Ghana; it's called "deep talk." For instance, there's a saying: "The trouble for the thief is not how to steal the chief's bugle, but where to blow it." Now, on the face of it, one understands that. But when you really think about it, it takes you deeper. In West Africa they call that "deep talk." I'd like to think I write "deep talk." When you read me, you should be able to say "Gosh, that's pretty. That's lovely. That's nice. Maybe there's something else? Better read it again." Years ago I read a man named Machado de Assis who wrote a book called *Dom Casmro: Epitaph of a Small Winner.* Machado de Assis is a South American writer—black mother, Portuguese father—writing in 1865, say. I thought the book was very nice. Then I went back and read the book and said, "Hmm. I didn't realize all that was in that book." Then I read it again, and again, and I came to the conclusion that what Machado de Assis had done for me was almost a trick: he had beckoned me onto the beach to watch a sunset. And I had watched the sunset with pleasure. When I turned around to come back in I found that the tide had come in over my head. That's when I decided to write. I would write so that the reader says, "That's so nice. Oh boy, that's pretty. Let me read that again." I think that's why *Caged Bird* is in its twenty-first printing in hardcover and its twenty-ninth in paper. All my books are still in print, in hardback as well as paper, because people go back and say, "Let me read that. Did she *really* say that?"

The books are episodic, aren't they? Almost as if you had put together a string of short stories. I wondered if, as an autobiographer, you ever fiddled with the truth to make the story better.

Well, sometimes. I love the phrase "fiddle with." It's so English. Sometimes I make a character from a composite of three or four people, because the essence in any one person is not sufficiently strong to be written about. Essentially though, the work is true though sometimes I fiddle with the facts. Many of the people I've written about are alive today, and I have them to face. I wrote about an ex-husband—he's an African—in *The Heart of a Woman.* Before I did, I called him in Dar-es-Salaam and said, "I'm going to write about some of our years together." He said, "Now before you ask, I want you to know that I shall sign my release, because I know you will not lie. However, I am sure I shall argue with you about your interpretation of the truth."

Did he enjoy his portrait finally, or did you argue about it?

Well, he didn't argue, but I was kind, too.

I would guess this would make it very easy for you to move from autobiography into novel, where you can do anything you want with your characters.

Yes, but for me, fiction is not the sweetest form. I really am trying to do something with autobiography now. It has caught me. I'm using the first-person singular, and trying to make that the first-person plural, so that anybody can read the work and say, "Hmm, that's the truth, yes, *uh-huh,*" and live in the work. It's a large ambitious dream. But I love the form.

Aren't the extraordinary events of your life very hard for the rest of us to identify with?

Oh my God, I've lived a very simple life! You can say, "Oh yes, at thirteen this happened to me, and at fourteen . . . " But those are facts. But the facts can obscure the truth, what it really felt like. Every human being has paid the earth to grow up. Most people don't grow up. It's too damn difficult. What happens is most people get older. That's the truth of it. They honor their credit cards, they find parking spaces, they marry, they have the nerve to have children, but they don't grow up. Not really. They get older. But to grow up costs the earth, the *earth.* It means you take responsibility for the time you take up, for the space you occupy. It's serious business. And you find out what it costs us to love and to lose, to dare and to fail. And maybe even more, to succeed. What it costs, in truth. Not superficial costs—anybody can have that—I mean in truth. That's what I write. What it really is like. I'm just telling a very simple story.

Aren't you tempted to lie? Novelists lie, don't they?

I don't know about lying for novelists. I look at some of the great novelists, and I think the reason they are great is that they're telling the truth. The fact is they're using made-up names, made-up people, made-up places and made-up times, but they're telling the truth about the human being—what we are capable of, what makes us lose, laugh, weep, fall down and gnash our teeth and wring our hands and kill each other and love each other.

James Baldwin, along with a lot of writers in this series, said that "when you're writing you're trying to find out something you didn't know." When you write do you search for something that you didn't know about yourself or about us?

Yes. When I'm writing, I am trying to find out who I am, who we are, what we're capable of, how we feel, how we lose and stand up, and go on from darkness into darkness. I'm trying for that. But I'm also trying for the language. I'm trying to see how it can really sound. I really love language. I love it for what it does for us, how it allows us to explain the pain and the glory, the nuances and the delicacies of our existence. And then it allows us to laugh, allows us to show wit. Real wit is shown in language. We need language.

Baldwin also said that his family urged him not to become a writer. His father felt that there was a white monopoly in publishing. Did you ever have any of those feelings: that you were going up against something that was really immensely difficult for a black writer?

Yes, but I didn't find it so just in writing. I've found it so in all the things I've attempted. In the shape of American society, the white male is on top, then the white female, and then the black male, and at the bottom is the black woman. So that's been always so. That is nothing new. It doesn't mean that it doesn't shock me, shake me up. . . .

I can understand that in various social stratifications, but why in art?

Well, unfortunately, racism is pervasive. It doesn't stop at the university gate, or at the ballet stage. I knew great black dancers, male and female, who were told early on that they were not shaped, physically, for ballet. Today, we see very few black ballet dancers. Unfortunately, in the theater and in film, racism and sexism stand at the door. I'm the first black female director in Hollywood; in order to direct, I went to Sweden and took a course in cinematography so I would understand what the camera would do. Though I had written a screen play, and even composed the score, I wasn't allowed to direct it. They brought in a young Swedish director who hadn't even shaken a black person's hand before. The film was *Georgia, Georgia* with Diane Sands. People either loathed it or complimented me. Both were wrong, because it was not what I wanted, not what I would have done if I had been allowed to direct it. So I thought, well, what I guess I'd better do is be ten times as prepared. That is not new. I wish it was. In every case I know I have to be ten times more prepared than my white counterpart.

Even as a writer where . . .

Absolutely.

Yet a manuscript is what arrives at the editor's desk, not a person, not a body.

Yes. I must have such control of my tools, of words, that I can make this sentence leap off the page. I have to have my writing so polished that it doesn't look polished at all.

I want a reader, especially an editor, to be a half-hour into my book before he realizes it's reading he's doing.

But isn't that the goal of every person who sits down at a typewriter?

Absolutely. Yes. It's possible to be overly sensitive, to carry a bit of paranoia along with you. But I don't think that's a bad thing. It keeps you sharp, keeps you on your toes.

Is there a thread one can see through the five autobiographies? It seems to me that one prevailing theme is the love of your child.

Yes, well, that's true. I think that that's a particular. I suppose, if I'm lucky, the particular is seen in the general. There is, I hope, a thesis in my work: we may encounter many defeats, but we must not be defeated. That sounds goody two-shoes, I know, but I believe that a diamond is the result of extreme pressure and time. Less time is crystal. Less than that is coal. Less than that is fossilized leaves. Less than that it's just plain dirt. In all my work, in the movies I write, the lyrics, the poetry, the prose, the essays, I am saying that we may encounter many defeats—maybe it's imperative that we encounter the defeats—but we are much stronger than we appear to be, and maybe much better than we allow ourselves to be. Human beings are more alike than unalike. There's no real mystique. Every human being, every Jew, Christian, back-slider, Muslim, Shintoist, Zen Buddhist, atheist, agnostic, every human being wants a nice place to live, a good place for the children to go to school, healthy children, somebody to love, the courage, the unmitigated gall to accept love in return, someplace to party on Saturday or Sunday night, and someplace to perpetuate that God. There's no mystique. None. And if I'm right in my work, that's what my work says.

Have you been back to Stamps, Arkansas?

About 1970, Bill Moyers, Willie Morris and I were at some affair. Judith Moyers as well—I think she was the instigator. We may have had two or three scotches, or seven or eight. Willie Morris was then with *Harper's* magazine. The suggestion came up: "Why don't we all go back South." Willie Morris was from Yazoo, Mississippi. Bill Moyers is from Marshall, Texas, which is just a hop, skip, and a jump—about as far as you can throw a chitterling—from Stamps, my hometown. Sometime in the middle of the night there was this idea: "Why don't Bill Moyers and Maya Angelou go to Yazoo, Mississippi, to visit Willie Morris? Then why don't Willie Morris and Maya Angelou go to Marshall, Texas, to visit Bill Moyers?" I said, "Great." I was agreeing with both. Then they said Willie Morris and Bill Moyers would go to Stamps, Arkansas to visit Maya Angelou, and I said, "No way, José. I'm not going back to that little town with two white men! I will not do it!" Well, after a while Bill Moyers called me—he was doing a series on "creativity"—and he said, "Maya, come on, let's go to Stamps." I said, "No way." He continued, "I want to talk about creativity." I said, "You know, I don't want to know where it resides." I really don't, and I still don't. One of the problems in the West is that people are too busy putting things under microscopes and so

forth. Creativity is greater than the sum of its parts. All I want to know is that creativity is there. I want to know that I can put my hand behind my back like Tom Thumb and pull out a plum. Anyway, Moyers went on and on and so did Judith and before I knew it, I found myself in Stamps, Arkansas. Stamps, Arkansas! With Bill Moyers, in front of my grandmother's door. My God! We drove out of town: me with Bill and Judith. Back of us was the crew, a New York crew, you know, very "Right, dig where I'm comin' from, like, get it on," and so forth. We got about three miles outside of Stamps and I said, "Stop the car. Let the car behind us pull up. Get those people in with you and I'll take their car." I suddenly was taken back to being twelve years old in a southern, tiny town where my grandmother told me, "Sistah, never be on a country road with any white boys." I was two hundred years older than black pepper, but I said, "Stop the car." I did. I got out of the car. And I knew these guys—certainly Bill. Bill Moyers is a friend and brother-friend to me; we care for each other. But dragons, fears, the grotesques of childhood always must be confronted at childhood's door. Any other place is esoteric and has nothing to do with the great fear that is laid upon one as a child. So anyway, we did Bill Moyers's show. And it seems to be a very popular program, and it's the first of the "creativity" programs. . . .

Did going back assuage those childhood fears?

They are there like griffins hanging off the sides of old and tired European buildings.

It hadn't changed?

No, worse if anything.

But it was forty years before you went back to the South, to North Carolina. Was that because of a fear of finding griffins everywhere, Stamps being a typical community of the South?

Well, I've never felt the need to prove anything to an audience. I'm always concerned about who I am to me first, to myself and God. I really am. I didn't go south because I didn't want to pull up whatever clout I had, because that's boring, that's not real, not true; that doesn't tell me anything. If I had known I was afraid, I would have gone earlier. I just thought I'd find the South really unpleasant. I have moved south now. I *live* there.

Perhaps writing the autobiographies, finding out about yourself, would have made it much easier to go back.

I know many think that writing sort of "clears the air." It doesn't do that at all. If you are going to write autobiography, don't expect that it will clear anything up. It makes it more clear to you, but it doesn't alleviate anything. You simply know it better, you have names for people.

*There's a part in **Caged Bird** where you and your brother want to do a scene from* The Merchant of Venice, *and you don't dare do it because your grandmother would find out that Shakespeare was not only deceased but white.*

I don't think she'd have minded if she'd known he was deceased. I tried to pacify her—My mother knew Shakespeare, but my grandmother was raising us. When I told her I wanted to recite—it was actually Portia's speech—Mama said to me, "Now sistah, what are you goin' to render?" The phrase was so fetching. The phrase was: "Now, little mistress Marguerite will render her rendition." Mama said, "Now, sistah, what are you goin' to render?" I said, "Mama, I'm going to render a piece written by William Shakespeare." My grandmother asked me, "Now, sistah, who is this very William Shakespeare?" I had to tell her that he was white, it was going to come out. Somebody would let it out. So I told Mama, "Mama, he's white, but he's dead." Then I said, "He's been dead for centuries," thinking she'd forgive him because of this little idiosyncracy. She said, "No Ma'am, little mistress you will not. No Ma'am, little mistress you will not." So I rendered James Weldon Johnson, Paul Laurence Dunbar, Countee Cullen, Langston Hughes.

Were books allowed in the house?

None of those books were in the house; they were in the school. I'd bring them home from school, and my brother gave me Edgar Allan Poe because he knew I loved him. I loved him so much I called him "EAP." But as I said, I had a problem when I was young: from the time I was seven and a half to the time I was twelve and a half I was a mute. I could speak, but I didn't speak for five years, and I was what was called a "volunteer mute." But I read and I memorized just masses—I don't know if one is born with photographic memory, but I think you can develop it. I just have that.

What is the significance of the title, **All God's Children Need Traveling Shoes?**

I never agreed, even as a young person, with the Thomas Wolfe title *You Can't Go Home Again.* Instinctively I didn't. But the truth is, you can never *leave* home. You take it with you; it's under your fingernails; it's in the hair follicles; it's in the way you smile; it's in the ride of your hips, in the passage of your breasts; it's all there, no matter where you go. You can take on the affectations and the postures of other places, and even learn to speak their ways. But the truth is, home is between your teeth. Everybody's always looking for it: Jews go to Israel; black-Americans and Africans in the Diaspora go to Africa; Europeans, Anglo-Saxons go to England and Ireland; people of Germanic background go to Germany. It's a very queer quest. We can kid ourselves; we can tell ourselves, "Oh yes, honey, I live in Tel Aviv, actually. . . ." The truth is a stubborn fact. So this book is about trying to go home.

If you had to endow a writer with the most necessary pieces of equipment, other than, of course, yellow legal pads, what would these be?

Ears. Ears. To hear the language. But there's no one piece of equipment that is most necessary. Courage, first.

Did you ever feel that you could not get your work published? Would you have continued to write if Random House had returned your manuscript?

I didn't think it was going to be very easy, but I knew I was going to do something. The real reason black people exist at all today is because there's a resistance to a larger society that says, "You can't do it. You can't survive. And if you survive, you certainly can't thrive. And if you thrive, you can't thrive with any passion or compassion or humor or style." There's a saying, a song which says, "Don't you let nobody turn you 'round, turn you 'round, turn you 'round. Don't you let nobody turn you 'round." Well, I've always believed that. So knowing that, knowing that nobody could turn me 'round, if I didn't publish, well, I would design this theater we're sitting in. Yes. Why not? Some human being did it. I agree with Terence. Terence said, *"Homo sum: humani nihil a me alienum puto."* I am a human being. Nothing human can be alien to me. When you look up Terence in the encyclopedia, you see beside his name, in italics: "Sold to a Roman senator, freed by that Senator." He became the most popular playwright in Rome. Six of his plays and that statement have come down to us from 154 B.C. This man, not born white, not born free, without any chance of every receiving citizenship, said, "I am a human being. Nothing human can be alien to me." Well, I believe that. I ingested that, internalized that at about thirteen or twelve. I believed if I set my mind to it, maybe I wouldn't be published, but I would write a great piece of music, or do something about becoming a real friend. Yes, I would do something wonderful. It might be with my next door neighbor, my gentleman friend, with my lover, but it would be wonderful as far as I could do it. So I never have been very concerned about the world telling me how successful I am. I don't need that.

You mentioned courage . . .

. . . the most important of all the virtues. Without that virtue you can't practice any other virtue with consistency.

What do you think of white writers who have written of the black experience: Faulkner's The Sound and the Fury, *or William Styron's* Confessions of Nat Turner?

Well, sometimes I am disappointed—more often than not. That's unfair, because I'm not suggesting the writer is lying about what he or she sees. It's my disappointment, really, in that he or she doesn't see more deeply, more carefully. I enjoy seeing Peter O'Toole or Michael Caine enact the role of an upper-class person in England. There the working class has had to study the upper-class, has been obliged to do so, to lift themselves out of their positions. Well, black Americans have had to study white Americans. For centuries under slavery, the smile or the grimace on a white man's face, or the flow of a hand on a white woman could inform a black person: "You're about to be sold, or flogged." So we have studied the white American, where the white American has not been obliged to study us. So often it is as if the writer is looking through a glass darkly. And I'm always a little—not a little—saddened by that poor vision.

And you can pick it up in an instant if you . . .

Yes, yes. There are some who delight and inform. It's so much better, you see, for me, when a writer like Edna St. Vincent Millay speaks so deeply about her concern for herself, and does not offer us any altruisms. Then when I look through her eyes at how she sees a black or an Asian my heart is lightened. But many of the other writers disappoint me.

What is the best part of writing for you?

Well, I could say the end. But when the language lends itself to me, when it comes and submits, when it surrenders and says "I am yours, darling"—that's the best part.

You don't skip around when you write?

No, I may skip around in revision, just to see what connections I can find.

Is most of the effort made in putting the words down onto the paper, or is it in revision?

Some work flows, and you know, you can catch three days. It's like . . . I think the word in sailing is "scudding"—you know, three days of just scudding. Other days it's just awful—plodding and backing up, trying to take out all the ands, ifs, tos, fors, buts, wherefores, therefores, howevers; you know, all those.

And then, finally, you write "The End" and there it is; you have a little bit of sherry.

A lot of sherry then. (pp. 145-67)

> Maya Angelou and George Plimpton, "The Art of Fiction CXIX: Maya Angelou," in The Paris Review, *Vol. 32, No. 116, Fall, 1990, pp. 145-67.*

Carol E. Neubauer   (essay date 1990)

[*In the following essay, Neubauer provides an overview of Angelou's life and career and discusses the principal themes in her poetry.*]

Within the last fifteen years, Maya Angelou has become one of the best-known black writers in the United States. Her reputation rests firmly on her prolific career as an autobiographer, poet, dancer-singer, actress, producer, director, scriptwriter, political activist, and editor. Throughout her life, she has identified with the South, and she calls Stamps, Arkansas, where she spent ten years of her childhood, her home.

Maya Angelou was born Marguerite Annie Johnson on 4 April 1928 in St. Louis to Vivian Baxter and Bailey Johnson, a civilian dietitian for the U.S. Navy. At age three, when her parents' marriage ended in divorce, she was sent, along with her brother, Bailey, from Long Beach to Stamps to be cared for by their paternal grandmother, Mrs. Annie Henderson. During the next ten years, a time of severe economic depression and intense racial bigotry in the South, she spent nearly all of her time either in school, at the daily meetings of the Colored Methodist Episcopal Church, or at her grandmother's general merchandise store. In 1940, she graduated with top honors from the Lafayette County Training School and soon thereafter returned to her mother, who lived in the San Francisco-Oakland area at that time. There she continued her education at George Washington High School under the direction of her beloved Miss Kirwin. At the same time, she attended evening classes at the California Labor School, where she received a scholarship to study drama and dance. A few weeks after she received her high school diploma, she gave birth to her son, Guy Bailey Johnson.

Her career as a professional entertainer began on the West Coast, where she performed as a dancer-singer at the Purple Onion in the early 1950s. While working in this popular cabaret, she was spotted by members of the *Porgy and Bess* cast and invited to audition for the chorus. Upon her return from the play's 1954-55 tour of Europe and Africa, she continued to perform at nightclubs throughout the United States, acquiring valuable experience that would eventually lead her into new avenues of professional work.

In 1959, Angelou and her son moved to New York, where she soon joined the Harlem Writers Guild at the invitation of John Killens. Together with Godfrey Cambridge, she produced, directed, and starred in *Cabaret for Freedom* to raise funds for the Southern Christian Leadership Conference. Following the close of the highly successful show, she accepted the position of Northern coordinator for the SCLC at the request of Dr. Martin Luther King, Jr.

Her work in theater landed her the role of the White Queen in Genet's *The Blacks,* directed by Gene Frankel at St. Mark's Playhouse. For this production, she joined a cast of stars—Roscoe Lee Brown, Godfrey Cambridge, James Earl Jones, and Cicely Tyson. In 1974, she adapted Sophocles' *Ajax* for its premiere at the Mark Taper Forum in Los Angeles. Original screenplays to her credit include the film version of **Georgia, Georgia** and the television productions of **I Know Why the Caged Bird Sings** and **The Sisters.** She also authored and produced a television series on African traditions inherent in American culture and played the role of Kunte Kinte's grandmother in *Roots.* For PBS programming, she served as a guest interviewer on *Assignment America* and most recently appeared in a special series on creativity hosted by Bill Moyers, which featured a return visit to Stamps.

Among her other honors, Maya Angelou was appointed to the Commission of International Women's Year by former President Carter. In 1975, *Ladies' Home Journal* named her Woman of the Year in communications. A trustee of the American Film Institute, she is also one of the few women members of the Directors Guild. In recent years, she has received more than a dozen honorary degrees, including one from the University of Arkansas located near her childhood home. Fluent in seven languages, she has worked as the editor of the *Arab Observer* in Cairo and the *African Review* in Ghana. In December 1981, Angelou accepted a lifetime appointment as the first Reynolds Professor of American Studies at Wake Forest University in Winston-Salem, where she lectures on literature and popular culture. In 1983, Women in Communications presented her with the Matrix Award in the field of books.

Her personal life has been anything but smooth. As a young mother, Angelou had to endure painful periods of separation from her son while she worked at more than one job to support them. Often her ventures into show business would take her far from home, and she would put Guy in the care of her mother or baby-sitters. When she was twenty-one years old, she married Tosh Angelos, a sailor of Greek-American ancestry, but their marriage ended after three years. While working in New York, she met and later married Vusumzi Make, a black South African activist who traveled extensively raising money to end apartheid. They divided their time between New York and Cairo, but after a few years their marriage deteriorated. In 1973, Angelou married Paul du Feu, a carpenter and construction worker she had met in London. They lived together on the West Coast during most of their seven-year marriage.

Although she is rarely called a regional writer, Maya Angelou is frequently identified with the new generation of Southern writers. She has always called the South her home, and recently, after much deliberation, she settled in North Carolina, ending an absence of more than thirty years. Her autobiographies and poetry are rich with references to her childhood home in Arkansas and to the South in general. For Angelou, as for many black American writers, the South has become a powerfully evocative metaphor for the history of racial bigotry and social inequality, for brutal inhumanity and final failure. Yet the South also represents a life-affirming force energized by a somewhat spiritual bond to the land itself. It is a region where generations of black families have sacrificed their brightest dreams for a better future; yet it is here that ties to forebears whose very blood has nourished the soil are most vibrant and resilient. Stamps, Arkansas, in the 1930s was not a place where a black child could grow up freely or reach her full intellectual and social potential, but the town was nevertheless the home of Angelou's grandmother, who came to stand for all the courage and stability she ever knew as a child.

Her literary reputation is based on the publication of five volumes of autobiography (*I Know Why the Caged Bird Sings, Gather Together in My Name, Singin' and Swingin' and Gettin' Merry Like Christmas, The Heart of a Woman,* and *All God's Children Need Traveling Shoes*) and five volumes of poetry (*Just Give Me a Cool Drink of Water 'fore I Diiie, Oh Pray My Wings Are Gonna Fit Me Well, And Still I Rise, Shaker, Why Don't You Sing?* and *Now Sheba Sings the Song*). In the twenty years of her publishing history, she has developed a rapport with her audiences who await each new work as a continuation of an ongoing dialogue with the author. Beginning with *Caged Bird* in 1970, her works have received wide critical acclaim and have been praised for reaching universal truths while examining the complicated life of one individual. The broad appeal of her autobiographies and poetry is evidenced in the numerous college anthologies that include portions of her work and in the popularity of the television adaptation of *Caged Bird.* In years to come, Angelou's voice, already recognized as one of the most original and versatile, will be measured by the standards of great American writers of our time.

In her first volume of autobiography, *I Know Why the Caged Bird Sings* (1970), Maya Angelou calls displacement the most important loss in her childhood, because she is separated from her mother and father at age three and never fully regains a sense of security and belonging. Her displacement from her family is not only an emotional handicap but is compounded by an equally unsettling sense of racial and geographic displacement. Her parents frequently move Angelou and her brother, Bailey, from St. Louis to Arkansas to the West Coast. As young children

in Stamps in the 1930s, racial prejudice severely limits their lives. Within the first pages, she sums up this demoralizing period of alienation: "If growing up is painful for the Southern Black girl, being aware of her displacement is the rust on the razor that threatens the throat." The pain of her continual rejection comes not only from the displacement itself, but even more poignantly, from the child's acute understanding of prejudice. A smooth, clean razor would be enough of a threat, but a rusty, jagged one leaves no doubt in the victim's mind.

In *Caged Bird,* Angelou recounts many explosive incidents of the racial discrimination she experienced as a child. In the 1930s, Stamps was a fully segregated town. Marguerite and Bailey, however, are welcomed by a grandmother who is not only devoted to them but, as owner of the Wm. Johnson General Merchandise Store, is highly successful and independent. Momma is their most constant source of love and strength. "I saw only her power and strength. She was taller than any woman in my personal world, and her hands were so large they could span my head from ear to ear." As powerful as her grandmother's presence seems to Marguerite, Momma uses her strength solely to guide and protect her family but not to confront the white community directly. Momma's resilient power usually reassures Marguerite, but one of the child's most difficult lessons teaches her that racial prejudice in Stamps can effectively circumscribe and even defeat her grandmother's protective influence.

In fact, it is only in the autobiographical narrative that Momma's personality begins to loom larger than life and provides Angelou's memories of childhood with a sense of personal dignity and meaning. On one occasion, for example, Momma takes Marguerite to the local dentist to be treated for a severe toothache. The dentist, who is ironically named Lincoln, refuses to treat the child, even though he is indebted to Momma for a loan she extended to him during the depression: "'Annie, my policy is I'd rather stick my hand in a dog's mouth than in a nigger's.'" As a silent witness to this scene, Marguerite suffers not only from the pain of her two decayed teeth, which have been reduced to tiny enamel bits by the avenging "Angel of the candy counter," but also from the utter humiliation of the dentist's bigotry as well: "It seemed terribly unfair to have a toothache and a headache and have to bear at the same time the heavy burden of Blackness."

In an alternate version of the confrontation, which Angelou deliberately fantasizes and then italicizes to emphasize its invention, Momma asks Marguerite to wait for her outside the dentist's office. As the door closes, the frightened child imagines her grandmother becoming "ten feet tall with eight-foot arms." Without mincing words, Momma instructs Lincoln to "'leave Stamps by sundown'" and "'never again practice dentistry'": "'When you get settled in your next place, you will be a vegetarian caring for dogs with the mange, cats with the cholera and cows with the epizootic. Is that clear?'" The poetic justice in Momma's superhuman power is perfect; the racist dentist who refused to treat her ailing granddaughter will in the future be restricted to treating the dogs he prefers to "niggers." After a trip to the black dentist in Texarkana,

Momma and Marguerite return to Stamps, where we learn the "real" version of the story by overhearing a conversation between Momma and Uncle Willie. In spite of her prodigious powers, all that Momma accomplishes in Dr. Lincoln's office is to demand ten dollars as unpaid interest on the loan to pay for their bus trip to Texarkana.

In the child's imagined version, fantasy comes into play as the recounted scene ventures into the unreal or the impossible. Momma becomes a sort of superwoman of enormous proportions ("ten feet tall with eight-foot arms") and comes to the helpless child's rescue. In this alternate vision, Angelou switches to fantasy to suggest the depth of the child's humiliation and the residue of pain even after her two bad teeth have been pulled. Fantasy, finally, is used to demonstrate the undiminished strength of the character of Momma. Summarizing the complete anecdote, Angelou attests, "I preferred, much preferred, my version." Carefully selected elements of fiction and fantasy in the scene involving Dr. Lincoln and her childhood hero, Momma, partially compensate for the racial displacement that she experiences as a child.

When Angelou is thirteen, she and Bailey leave the repressive atmosphere of Stamps to join their mother. During these years, she continues to look for a place in life that will dissolve her sense of displacement. By the time she and Bailey are in their early teens, they have criss-crossed the western half of the country traveling between their parents' separate homes and their grandmother's in Stamps. Her sense of geographic displacement alone would be enough to upset any child's security, since the life-styles of her father in southern California and her mother in St. Louis and later in San Francisco represent worlds completely different and even foreign to the pace of life in the rural South. Each time the children move, a different set of relatives or another of their parents' lovers greets them, and they never feel a part of a stable family group, except when they are in Stamps at the general store with Momma and Uncle Willie.

Once settled in San Francisco in the early 1940s, Angelou enrolls at George Washington High School and the California Labor School, where she studies dance and drama in evening classes. She excels in both schools, and her teachers quickly recognize her intelligence and talent. Later she breaks the color barrier by becoming the first black female conductor on the San Francisco streetcars. Just months before her high school graduation, she engages in a onetime sexual encounter to prove her sexuality to herself and becomes pregnant. *Caged Bird,* however, ends on a note of awakening with the birth of her son and the beginning of a significant measure of strength and confidence in her ability to succeed and find her place in life. As autobiographer, Angelou uses the theme of displacement to unify the first volume of her life story as well as to suggest her long-term determination to create security and permanency in her life.

Between the conclusion of *Caged Bird* and the beginning of Angelou's second volume of autobiography, *Gather Together in My Name* (1974), there is virtually no break in the narrative. As the first ends with the birth of her son, the second starts when Guy is only a few months old. As a whole, *Gather Together* tells the story of his first three years and focuses on a young single mother's struggle to achieve respect, love, and a sense of self-worth. Her battle to win financial independence and the devotion of a faithful man could hardly have been easy in the years immediately following World War II, when racial discrimination, unemployment, and McCarthyism were all on the rise. In spite of her initial optimism, which is, incidentally, shared by many members of the post-war black community who fervently believed that "race prejudice was dead. A mistake made by a young country. Something to be forgiven as an unpleasant act committed by an intoxicated friend," Angelou soon realizes that her dreams for a better America are still too fragile to survive. But worst of all is the burden of guilt that rests on the shoulders of the seventeen-year-old mother who desperately believes that she must assume full adult responsibility. Fortunately, her mother encourages her to set high goals, to maintain her sense of dignity and self-worth, and to work hard to succeed. Her mother's words come back to her throughout her life: "Anything worth doing is worth doing well," and "be the best of anything you get into."

Like many young women who came of age in the postwar era, Angelou easily imagines herself moving into a life modeled on *Good Housekeeping* and *Better Homes and Gardens.* She describes herself as both a "product of Hollywood upbringing" and her own "romanticism" and continually envisions herself smoothly slipping into the role guaranteed by popular culture. Whenever she meets a man who might potentially fulfill her dream, she anticipates the enviable comfort of "settling down." The scenario is always the same: "I would always wear pretty aprons and my son would play in the Little League. My husband would come home (he looked like Curly) and smoke his pipe in the den as I made cookies for the Scouts meeting," or "We would live quietly in a pretty little house and I'd have another child, a girl, and the two children (whom he'd love equally) would climb over his knees and I would make three layer caramel cakes in my electric kitchen until they went off to college." These glamorous dreams, of course, never quite materialize, but Angelou maintains a hopeful outlook and a determination to support and protect herself and her infant son. Her primary motivation during these early years of motherhood is to spare her son the insecurity and rejection she faced as a child. During these years, Angelou even works as an absentee madam and a prostitute, in hopes of achieving a regular family life and easing her unabiding sense of guilt over not being able to provide herself and her son with financial and familial security.

Yet Angelou understands that the hurdles she has to cross on her road to success are often higher than those set by her own expectations and standards of performance. Although she spends the first years of her son's life in California, both in the Bay Area and in San Diego, she often faces racial discrimination reminiscent of her childhood experiences in the South. At one point in *Gather Together,* when she suspects that her thriving business as a madam of a two-prostitute house will soon be uncovered by the police, Angelou returns to Stamps with her son, hoping to find the same comfort and protection she had known as a child. Specifically, she seeks her grandmother's "protective embrace" and her "courage" as well as the "shield of anonymity," but she soon realizes that the South is not ready to welcome her and that she has "outgrown" its "childhood protection." The five years she has spent in school and working in California have broadened her horizons and convinced her of her right to be accepted on the basis of her character and intelligence. But the South to which she returns is unchanged: "The town was halved by railroad tracks, the swift Red River and racial prejudice, . . . " and "above all, the atmosphere was pressed down with the smell of old fears, and hates, and guilt."

Not long after her arrival in Stamps, Angelou comes face to face with the double standards of racial discrimination during an unpleasant confrontation with a salesclerk in the white-owned general merchandise store. Although she attempts to explain to her grandmother why she refused to accept the clerk's humiliating insults, Momma warns her that her "principles" are all too flimsy a protection against the unrestrained contempt of bigotry: " 'You think 'cause you've been to California these crazy people won't kill you? You think them lunatic cracker boys won't try to catch you in the road and violate you? You think because of your all-fired principle some of the men won't feel like putting their white sheets on and riding over here to stir up trouble? You do, you're wrong.' " That same day, her grandmother sends her back to California where she and her son are somewhat more distanced from the lingering hatred of the South. Not until the filming of a segment for Bill Moyer's PBS series on creativity thirty years later does Angelou return to her childhood home.

Upon her return to the Bay Area and to her mother's home, she is more determined than ever to achieve independence and win the respect of others. Leaving her son in the care of baby-sitters, she works long hours first as a dancer and entertainer and then as a short-order cook in Stockton. But as is often the case, the reality of her situation falls far below her ideal, and Angelou eventually turns to marijuana as a temporary consolation: "The pot had been important when I was alone and lonely, when my present was dull and the future uncertain." During this period, she also falls in love with an older man who is a professional gambler supported by prostitution. When his luck fails him, Angelou agrees to help him pay his debt by becoming a prostitute herself. She makes this sacrifice fully believing that after her man has regained his financial security, he will marry her and provide her with the fulfillment of her romantic dream. Rationalizing her decision, she compares prostitution to marriage: "There are married women who are more whorish than a street prostitute because they have sold their bodies for marriage licenses, and there are some women who sleep with men for money who have great integrity because they are doing it for a purpose." But once again her dreams are disappointed, and she finds herself on her own at the end.

The second volume of her autobiography ends just before she decides to settle down with a man she pictures as an "ideal husband," who is in fact a heroin addict and gambler. Before it is too late, Angelou learns that she is on the verge of embracing disaster and defeat. At the end, she regains her innocence through the lessons of a compassionate drug addict: "I had walked the precipice and seen it all; and at the critical moment, one man's generosity pushed me safely away from the edge. . . . I had given a promise and found my innocence. I swore I'd never lose it again." With these words, ready to accept the challenge of life anew, Angelou brings the second volume of her life story to a close. In *Gather Together in My Name,* a title inspired by the Gospel of Matthew (18:20), she asks her family and readers to gather around her and bear witness to her past.

The third volume of Maya Angelou's autobiography, *Singin' and Swingin' and Gettin' Merry Like Christmas* (1976) concentrates on the early years of her career as a professional dancer and singer, her related experience with racial prejudice, and with the guilt suffered through separation from her young son. During her childhood, her love for music grows through her almost daily attendance at the Colored Methodist Episcopal Church in Stamps and through her dance classes in California. Music in fact is her closest companion and source of moral support during her first few months back in the San Francisco area. She calls music her "refuge" during this period of her life and welcomes its protective embrace, into which she could "crawl into the spaces between the notes and curl [her] back to loneliness." Without losing any time, she secures a job in sales and inventory at the Melrose Record Shop on Fillmore, which at the time served as a meeting place for musicians and music lovers of all description. In addition to earning enough money to quit her two previous jobs and bring her son home from the baby-sitter's in the evenings and on Sundays, Angelou also gains valuable exposure to the newest releases in blues and jazz and to an expansive circle of eccentric people.

Her sales position at the record shop is her first step into the world of entertainment. Her hours behind the cashier counter studying catalogs and helping customers make their selections bring her an easy familiarity with the newest stars and songs. Relying on her dance lessons and her trusted memory of popular lyrics, she later auditions for a position as a dancer at the Garden of Allah, where she is eventually hired as the first black show girl. Unlike the three white women who are also featured in the nightly show, Angelou is not required to strip but rather earns her audience's attention on the basis of her dance routines alone. All of the dancers, however, are instructed to supplement their regular salary by selling B-grade drinks and bottles of champagne on commission to interested customers. At first reluctant to put herself at the mercy of fawning, flirtatious spectators, she soon learns to sell more drinks than any of the others, simply by giving away the house secret on the composition of the ginger ale and Seven-Up cocktails and the details of the commission scale. But her success evokes the jealousy of the other women, and soon her first venture into professional entertainment comes to an end.

Through contacts established during her work at the Garden of Allah, Angelou auditions for an opening at the Purple Onion, a North Beach cabaret where she soon replaces

Jorie Remus and shares the nightly bill with Phyllis Diller. After lessons with her drama coach, Lloyd Clark, who, incidentally, is responsible for coining her stage name, Maya Angelou, she polishes her style as an interpretative dancer and perfects a series of calypso songs that eventually comprise her regular act at the cabaret. Although the audience at the Purple Onion has never been entertained by a performer like Angelou, she quickly becomes extremely popular and gains much wider exposure than she did as a dancer at the Garden of Allah. Many professional stars and talent scouts, visiting San Francisco from New York and Chicago, drop in at the Purple Onion and some eventually invite her to audition for their shows. In 1954, for example, Leonard Sillman brought his Broadway hit *New Faces of 1953* to the Bay Area. When she learns through friends that Sillman needed a replacement for Eartha Kitt, who would be leaving for an engagement in Las Vegas, she jumps at the chance to work with a cast of talented performers. Even though she is invited to join the show, the management at the Purple Onion refuses to release her from her contract. Her first real show business break, therefore, does not come until after she goes to New York to try out for a new Broadway show called *House of Flowers,* starring Pearl Bailey and directed by Saint Subber. While there she is unexpectedly asked to join the company of *Porgy and Bess* in the role of Ruby, just as the troupe is finishing up its engagement in Montreal and embarking on its first European tour. She accepts, thereby launching her international career as a dancer-singer.

As her professional career in entertainment develops, Angelou worries about her responsibility to care for her young son and provide him with a secure family life. In *Singin' and Swingin',* she continues to trace her pursuit of romantic ideals in the face of loneliness and disappointment. While working in the Melrose Record Shop, she meets Tosh Angelos, a sailor of Greek-American heritage, and later marries him. Her first impression of marriage could not have been more idealistic:

> At last I was a housewife, legally a member of that enviable tribe of consumers whom security made fat as butter and who under no circumstances considered living by bread alone, because their husbands brought home the bacon. I had a son, a father for him, a husband and a pretty home for us to live in. My life began to resemble a *Good Housekeeping* advertisement. I cooked well-balanced meals and molded fabulous jello desserts. My floors were dangerous with daily applications of wax and our furniture slick with polish.

Unfortunately, after a year, Tosh and she begin to argue and recognize that their different attitudes stand in the way of true compatibility and trust. Her "Eden"-like homelife and "cocoon of safety" begin to smother her sense of integrity and independence. In her autobiography, she describes this difficult period as a time in which she felt a "sense of loss," which "suffused [her] until [she] was suffocating within the vapors." When their marriage ends, Angelou again looks for a way to give her young child a stable home and a permanent sense of family security. Understandably, her son temporarily distrusts her and

wonders whether she will stop loving him and leave him behind to be cared for by others.

Before she marries Tosh, she seriously questions the nature of inter-racial marriage and is advised by others, including her mother, to examine the relationship carefully. Throughout *Singin' and Swingin',* she studies her attitude toward white people and explains her growing familiarity with their life-styles and their acceptance of her as an equal within the world of entertainment. When she first meets her future Greek-American husband, she suspects that her racial heritage precludes the possibility of any kind of permanent relationship. Her Southern childhood is too close, too vibrant in her memory: "I would never forget the slavery tales, or my Southern past, where all whites, including the poor and ignorant, had the right to speak rudely to and even physically abuse any Negro they met. I knew the ugliness of white prejudice." Although she discounts her suspicion in her dealings with Tosh Angelos, her deeply rooted fears stay close to the surface as she comes to associate with a large number of white artists and entertainers during her career as a dancer: "I knew you could never tell about white people. Negroes had survived centuries of inhuman treatment and retained their humanity by hoping for the best from their pale-skinned oppressors but at the same time being prepared for the worst." Later, during her role as Ruby in *Porgy and Bess,* which played throughout Europe, the Middle East, and North Africa, she observes the double standards of white people who readily accept black Americans in Europe, because they are fascinated by their exotic foreignness, but who are equally quick to discriminate against other people of color. In North Africa, she witnesses yet another version of racial bigotry in the way members of the Arab elite mistreat their African servants, "not realizing that auction blocks and whipping posts were too recent in our history for us [black Americans] to be comfortable around slavish servants."

While in Rome, Angelou decides to cut short her engagement with *Porgy and Bess,* not because she has witnessed the complexities of racial prejudice but rather because she realizes that her son has suffered during her extended absence. Throughout her European tour, she carries the burden of guilt, which comes to characterize her early years of motherhood. Although she recognizes the pattern of abandonment emerging in her son's life as it had in her own, she often sees no alternative than to accept a job and, with it, the pain of separation. Finally, upon learning that her son has developed a severe and seemingly untreatable rash in her absence, she decides to return to San Francisco. Once there, she assumes full responsibility for "ruining [her] beautiful son by neglect" and for the "devastation to his mind and body." Shortly after her return, Guy recovers, and together they reach a new level of trust and mutual dependence based on the understanding that their separation is now over for good. *Singin' and Swingin'* comes to a close as mother and son settle into a Hawaiian beach resort where she has just opened a new engagement at a nightclub. She achieves a longed for peace of mind as she comes to treasure her "wonderful, dependently independent son."

In *The Heart of a Woman* (1980), the fourth in the autobiographical series, Maya Angelou continues the account of her son's youth and, in the process, repeatedly returns to the story of her childhood. The references to her childhood serve partly to create a textual link for readers who might be unfamiliar with the earlier volumes and partly to emphasize the suggestive similarities between her childhood and her son's. Her overwhelming sense of displacement and instability is, ironically, her son's burden too. In a brief flashback in the second chapter, she reminds us of the displacement that characterized her youth and links this aspect of her past with her son's present attitude. When Guy is fourteen, Angelou decides to move to New York. She does not bring Guy to the East until she has found a place for them to live, and when he arrives after a one-month separation, he initially resists her attempts to make a new home for them:

> The air between us [Angelou and Guy] was burdened with his aloof scorn. I understood him too well.
>
> When I was three my parents divorced in Long Beach, California, and sent me and my four-year-old brother, unescorted, to our paternal grandmother. We wore wrist tags which informed anyone concerned that we were Marguerite and Bailey Johnson, en route to Mrs. Annie Henderson in Stamps, Arkansas.
>
> Except for disastrous and mercifully brief encounters with each of them when I was seven, we didn't see our parents again until I was thirteen.

From this and similar encounters with Guy, Angelou learns that the continual displacement of her own childhood is something she cannot prevent from recurring in her son's life.

In New York, Angelou begins to work as the Northern coordinator of the Southern Christian Leadership Conference and devotes most of her time to raising funds, boosting membership, and organizing volunteer labor, both in the office and in the neighborhoods. Throughout *Heart of a Woman,* she expands her own narrative by including anecdotes about well-known entertainers and political figures. Her account of a visit with Martin Luther King, Jr., at her SCLC office is just one example of this autobiographical technique. When Dr. King pays his first visit to the New York office during her tenure, she does not have advance notice of his presence and rushes into her office one day after lunch to find him sitting at her desk. They begin to talk about her background and eventually focus their comments on her brother, Bailey:

> "Come on, take your seat back and tell me about yourself."
>
> . . . When I mentioned my brother Bailey, he asked what he was doing now.
>
> The question stopped me. He was friendly and understanding, but if I told him my brother was in prison, I couldn't be sure how long his understanding would last. I could lose my job. Even more important, I might lose his respect. Birds

of a feather and all that, but I took a chance and told him Bailey was in Sing Sing.

> He dropped his head and looked at his hands.
>
> . . . "I understand. Disappointment drives our young men to some desperate lengths." Sympathy and sadness kept his voice low. "That's why we must fight and win. We must save the Baileys of the world. And Maya, never stop loving him. Never give up on him. Never deny him. And remember, he is freer than those who hold him behind bars."

Angelou appreciates King's sympathy and of course shares his hope that their work will make the world more fair and free. She recognizes the undeniable effects of displacement on Bailey's life and fervently hopes that her own son will be spared any further humiliation and rejection.

From time to time, Angelou sees marriage as the answer to her own sense of dislocation and fully envisions a perfect future with various prospective husbands. While in New York, she meets Vusumzi Make, a black South African freedom fighter, and imagines that he will provide her with the same domestic security she had hoped would develop from other relationships: "I was getting a husband, and a part of that gift was having someone to share responsibility and guilt." Yet her hopes are even more idealistic than usual, inasmuch as she imagines herself participating in the liberation of South Africa as Vus Make's wife: "With my courage added to his own, he would succeed in bringing the ignominious white rule in South Africa to an end. If I didn't already have the qualities he needed, then I would just develop them. Infatuation made me believe in my ability to create myself into my lover's desire." In reality, Angelou is only willing to go so far in re-creating herself to meet her husband's desires and is all too soon frustrated with her role as Make's wife. He does not want her to work but is unable on his own to support his expensive tastes as well as his family. They are evicted from their New York apartment just before they leave for Egypt and soon face similar problems in Cairo. Their marriage dissolves after some months, despite Angelou's efforts to contribute to their financial assets by working as editor of the *Arab Observer.* In *Heart of a Woman,* she underscores the illusory nature of her fantasy about marriage to show how her perspective has shifted over the years and how much understanding she has gained about life in general. Re-creating these fantasies in her autobiography is a subtle form of truth telling and a way to present hard-earned insights about her life to her readers.

A second type of fantasy in *Heart of a Woman* is borne out in reality rather than in illusion, as is the case with her expectations of marriage. One of the most important uses of the second kind of fantasy involves a sequence that demonstrates how much she fears for Guy's safety throughout his youth. A few days after mother and son arrive in Accra, where they move when her marriage with Vus Make deteriorates, some friends invite them to a picnic. Although his mother declines, Guy immediately accepts the invitation in a show of independence. On the way home from the day's outing, her son is seriously injured in an automobile accident. Even though he has had very little experience driving, his intoxicated host asks Guy to drive. When their return is delayed, Angelou is terrified by her recurring fear for Guy's safety. Later, in the Korle Bu emergency ward, her familiar fantasy about harm endangering her son's life moves to the level of reality, as she relates the vulnerability she feels in her role as mother with full responsibility for the well-being of her only child. In a new country, estranged from her husband and with no immediate prospects for employment, she possesses very little control over her life or her son's safety. After the accident in Ghana, Guy is not only fighting for independence from his mother but also for life itself. The conclusion of *Heart of a Woman,* nevertheless, announces a new beginning for Angelou and hope for her future relationship with Guy.

Her most recent autobiography, *All God's Children Need Traveling Shoes* (1986), has swept Angelou to new heights of critical and popular acclaim. Her life story resumes exactly where it ended chronologically and geographically in *The Heart of a Woman,* with Guy's recovery from his automobile accident in Accra. Although only portions of two earlier volumes of her autobiographical narrative occur in Africa, her latest addition to the series takes place almost exclusively in Ghana. In *All God's Children Need Traveling Shoes,* however, Angelou focuses primarily on the story of her and many other black Americans' attempts in the early 1960s to return to the ancestral home in Africa. As in her four previous autobiographies, she explores the theme of displacement and the difficulties involved in creating a home for oneself, one's family, and one's people.

In choosing to live in Ghana following the deterioration of her marriage to Vus Make, Angelou hopes to find a place where she and her son can make a home for themselves, free at last from the racial bigotry she has faced throughout the United States, Europe, and parts of the Middle East. While Guy is recuperating from his injuries, she carefully evaluates her assets and concludes that since his birth, her only home has been wherever she and her son are together: "we had been each other's home and center for seventeen years. He could die if he wanted to and go off to wherever dead folks go, but I, I would be left without a home." Her initial expectations, therefore, for feeling at ease and settling down in West Africa are, understandably, considerable: "We had come home, and if home was not what we had expected, never mind, our need for belonging allowed us to ignore the obvious and to create real places or even illusory places, befitting our imagination." Unfortunately, the Ghanian people do not readily accept Angelou, her son, and most of the black American community in Accra, and they unexpectedly find themselves isolated and often ignored.

Taken as a whole, *All God's Children Need Traveling Shoes* recounts the sequence of events that gradually brings the autobiographer closer to an understanding and eventually to an acceptance of the seemingly unbreachable distance between the Ghanians and the black American expatriates. Within the first few weeks of her stay in Ghana, Angelou suspects that she has mistakenly fol-

lowed the misdirected footsteps of other black Americans who "had not come home, but had left one familiar place of painful memory for another strange place with none." In time, she understands that their alienation is most likely based on the fact that they, unlike the Ghanians, are the descendants of African slaves, who painfully bear the knowledge that " 'not all slaves were stolen, nor were all slave dealers European.' " No one in the expatriate group can feel fully at ease in Africa as long as they carry the haunting suspicion that "African slavery stemmed mostly from tribal exploitation" and not solely from European colonial imperialism.

Angelou, nevertheless, perseveres; she eventually settles into lasting friendships with both Americans and Africans and finds work through her talents as a journalist and a performer. With her professional and personal contacts, she meets many African political activists, as well as diplomats and artists from around the world. These acquaintances, in addition to a brief tour in Berlin and Venice with the original St. Mark's Playhouse company of Genet's *The Blacks,* enlarge Angelou's perspective on racial complexities and help her locate a place in Africa where she can live, albeit temporarily, at peace.

In *All God's Children Need Traveling Shoes,* Angelou continually reminds the reader that the quest for a place to call home is virtually endemic to the human condition. During her time in Ghana, she comes to understand that the search is seldom successful, regardless of the political or social circumstances involved. Toward the end of her personal narrative, Angelou sums up her conclusions about the struggle to find or create a home: "If the heart of Africa still remained allusive, my search for it had brought me closer to understanding myself and other human beings. The ache for home lives in all of us, the safe place where we can go as we are and not be questioned." In a 1984 interview conducted during the period when she was completing an earlier draft of *All God's Children Need Traveling Shoes,* Angelou voices the same illuminating insight:

> [*Neubauer*]: *How far will the fifth volume go?*
>
> [Angelou]: Actually, it's a new kind. It's really quite a new voice. I'm looking at the black American resident, me and the other black American residents in Ghana, and trying to see all the magic of the eternal quest of human beings to go home again. That is maybe what life is anyway. To return to the Creator. All of that naivete, the innocence of trying to. That awful rowing towards God, whatever it is. Whether it's to return to your village or the lover you lost or the youth that some people want to return to or the beauty that some want to return to.
>
> *Writing autobiography frequently involves this quest to return to the past, to the home. Sometimes, if the home can't be found, if it can't be located again, then that home or that love or that family, whatever has been lost, is recreated or invented.*
>
> Yes, of course. That's it! That's what I'm seeing in this trek back to Africa. That in so many cases that idealized home of course is non-existent. In

so many cases some black Americans created it on the spot. On the spot. And I did too. Created something, looked, seemed like what we have idealized very far from reality.

Whatever vision of home Angelou creates for herself and her son in Ghana, she discovers a heightened sense of self-awareness and independence. By the end of her stay in West Africa, she has a renewed image of herself as a woman, lover, mother, writer, performer, and political activist. In her state of fortified strength, she decides to leave Africa and return to the country of her birth, however disturbing the memories of slavery and the reality of racial hatred. In fact, Angelou ends her sojourn in foreign lands to commit herself to Malcolm X's struggle for racial equality and social justice in the United States, by planning to work as an office coordinator for the Organization of Afro-American Unity. She has finally freed herself from the illusion of claiming an ancestral home in Africa. Ironically perhaps, with the writing of **All God's Children Need Traveling Shoes** and the brilliant clarity of the autobiographical present, "this trek back to Africa," Maya Angelou also decides to return to the South, and for the first time since her youth, make her home there. Although she has learned that "the idealized home of course is nonexistent," she leaves her readers to suspect that her traveling shoes are never really out of sight; if nothing else, we will soon find ourselves following her paths of autobiographical discovery once again.

Most of the thirty-eight poems in Maya Angelou's **Just Give Me a Cool Drink of Water 'fore I Diiie** (1971) appeared several years earlier in a collection called **The Poetry of Maya Angelou**. Among these are some of her best known pieces, such as **"Miss Scarlett, Mr. Rhett and Other Latter Day Saints"** and **"Harlem Hopscotch."** The volume is divided into two parts; the first deals with love, its joy and inevitable sorrow, and the second with the trials of the black race. Taken as a whole, the poems cover a wide range of settings from Harlem streets to Southern churches to abandoned African coasts. These poems contain a certain power, which stems from the strong metric control that finds its way into the terse lines characteristic of her poetry. Not a word is wasted, not a beat lost. Angelou's poetic voice speaks with a sure confidence that dares return to even the most painful memories to capture the first signs of loss or hate.

The first twenty poems of **Cool Drink** describe the whole gamut of love, from the first moment of passionate discovery to the first suspicion of painful loss. One poem, in fact, is entitled **"The Gamut"** and in its sonnet form moves from "velvet soft" dawn when "my true love approaches" to the "deathly quiet" of night when "my true love is leaving." Two poems, **"To a Husband"** and **"After,"** however, celebrate the joyous fulfillment of love. In the first, Angelou suggests that her husband is a symbol of African strength and beauty and that through his almost majestic presence she can sense the former riches of the exploited continent. To capture his vibrant spirit, she retreats to Africa's original splendor and conjures up images as ancient as "Pharoah's tomb":

> You're Africa to me

At brightest dawn.
The congo's green and
Copper's brackish hue . . .

In this one man, she sees the vital strength of an entire race: "A continent to build / With Black Man's brawn." His sacrifice, reminiscent of generations of unacknowledged labor, inspires her love and her commitment to the African cause. **"After"** also speaks of the love between woman and man but is far more tender and passionate. The scene is the lovers' bed when "no sound falls / from the moaning sky" and "no scowl wrinkles / the evening pool." Here, as in **"To a Husband,"** love is seen as strong and sustaining, even jubilant in its harmonious union, its peaceful calm. Even "the stars lean down / A stony brilliance" in recognition of their love. And yet there is a certain absent emptiness in the quiet that hints of future loss.

In the second section, Angelou turns her attention to the lives of black people in America from the the time of slavery to the rebellious 1960s. Her themes deal broadly with the painful anguish suffered by blacks forced into submission, with guilt over accepting too much, and with protest and basic survival.

"No No No No" is a poem about the rejection of American myths that promise justice for all but only guarantee freedom for a few. The powerfully cadenced stanzas in turn decry the immorality of American involvement in Vietnam,

> while crackling babies
> in napalm coats
> stretch mouths to receive
> burning tears . . .

as well as the insincere invitation of the Statue of Liberty, which welcomes immigrants who crossed "over the sinuous cemetery / of my many brothers," and the inadequate apologies offered by white liberals. The first stanza ends with the refrain that titles the complete collection of poems, "JUST GIVE ME A COOL DRINK OF WATER 'FORE I DIIIE." In the second half of the poem, the speaker identifies with those who suffered humiliation

> on the back porches
> of forever
> in the kitchens and fields
> of rejections

and boldly cautions that the dreams and hopes of a better tomorrow have vanished. Even pity, the last defense against inhumanity, is spent.

Two poems that embody the poet's confident determination that conditions must improve for the black race are **"Times-Square-Shoeshine Composition"** and **"Harlem Hopscotch."** Both ring with a lively, invincible beat that carries defeated figures into at least momentary triumph. **"Times-Square"** tells the story of a shoeshine man who claims to be an unequaled master at his trade. He cleans and shines shoes to a vibrant rhythm that sustains his spirit in spite of humiliating circumstances. When a would-be customer offers him twenty-five cents instead of the requested thirty-five cents, the shoeshine man refuses the job and flatly renounces the insulting attempt to minimize the value of his trade. Fully appreciating his own expertise, the vendor proudly instructs his potential Times Square patron to give his measly quarter to his daughter, sister, or mamma, for they clearly need it more than he does. Denying the charge that he is a "greedy bigot," the shoeshine man simply admits that he is a striving "capitalist," trying to be successful in a city owned by the super rich.

Moving uptown, **"Harlem Hopscotch"** celebrates the sheer strength necessary for survival. The rhythm of this powerful poem echoes the beat of feet, first hopping, then suspended in air, and finally landing in the appropriate square. To live in a world measured by such blunt announcements as "food is gone" and "the rent is due," people need to be extremely energetic and resilient. Compounding the pressures of hunger, poverty, and unemployment is the racial bigotry that consistently discriminates against people of color. Life itself has become a brutal game of hopscotch, a series of desperate yet hopeful leaps, landing but never pausing long: "In the air, now both feet down. / Since you black, don't stick around." Yet in the final analysis, the words that bring the poem and the complete collection to a close triumphantly announce the poet's victory: "Both feet flat, the game is done. / They think I lost. I think I won." These poems in their sensitive treatment of both love and black identity are the poet's own defense against the incredible odds in the game of life.

Within four years of the publication of *Just Give Me a Cool Drink 'fore I Diiie,* Maya Angelou completed a second volume of poetry, *Oh Pray My Wings Are Gonna Fit Me Well* (1975). By the time of its release, her reputation as a poet who transforms much of the pain and disappointment of life into lively verse had been established. During the 1970s, her reading public grew accustomed to seeing her poems printed in *Cosmopolitan.* Angelou had become recognized not only as a spokesperson for blacks and women, but also for all people who are committed to raising the moral standards of living in the United States. The poems collected in *My Wings,* indeed, appear at the end of the Vietnam era and in some important ways exceed the scope of her first volume. Many question traditional American values and urge people to make an honest appraisal of the demoralizing rift between the ideal and the real. Along with poems about love and the oppression of black people, the poet adds several that directly challenge Americans to reexamine their lives and to strive to reach the potential richness that has been compromised by self-interest since the beginnings of the country.

One of the most moving poems in *My Wings* is entitled **"Alone,"** in which carefully measured verses describe the general alienation of people in the twentieth century. **"Alone"** is not directed at any one particular sector of society but rather is focused on the human condition in general. No one, the poet cautions, can live in this world alone. This message punctuates the end of the three major stanzas and also serves as a separate refrain between each and at the close of the poem:

> Alone, all alone
> Nobody, but nobody
> Can make it out here alone.

Angelou begins by looking within herself and discovering that her soul is without a home. Moving from an inward glimpse to an outward sweep, she recognizes that even millionaires suffer from this modern malaise and live lonely lives with "hearts of stone." Finally, she warns her readers to listen carefully and change the direction of their lives:

> Storm clouds are gathering
> The wind is gonna blow
> The race of man is suffering.

For its own survival, the human race must break down barriers and rescue one another from loneliness. The only cure, the poet predicts, is to acknowledge common interests and work toward common goals.

A poem entitled **"America"** is no less penetrating in its account of the country's problems. Again Angelou pleads with the American people to "discover this country" and realize its full potential. In its two-hundred-year history, "the gold of her promise / has never been mined." The promise of justice for all has not been kept and in spite of "her crops of abundance / the fruit and the grain," many citizens live below the poverty line and never have enough food to feed their families. Similarly, racial bigotry has denied generations of Americans their full dignity and natural rights, while depriving them of the opportunity to contribute freely to the nation's strength. At the close of the poem, Angelou calls for the end of "legends untrue," which are perpetrated through history to "entrap" America's children. The only hope for the country is to discard these false myths once and for all and to guarantee that all people benefit from democratic principles.

In one poem, **"Southeast Arkansia,"** the poet shifts her attention from the general condition of humanity to the plight of black people in America. The setting of this tightly structured poem is the locale where Angelou spent most of her childhood. At the end of the three stanzas, she poses a question concerning the responsibility and guilt involved in the exploitation of the slaves. Presumably, the white men most immediately involved have never answered for their inhumane treatment of "bartered flesh and broken bones." The poet doubts that they have ever even paused to "ponder" or "wonder" about their proclivity to value profit more than human life.

Any discussion of *My Wings* that did not address the poems written about the nature of love would be necessarily incomplete. The entire volume is dedicated to Paul du Feu, Angelou's husband from 1973 to 1980. One very brief poem, **"Passing Time,"** speaks of a love that is finely balanced and delicately counterpoised. This love stretches over time, blanketing both the beginning and end of a day: "Your skin like dawn / Mine like dusk." Together is reached a certain harmony that carries the lovers through the day, perfectly complementing each other's spirit. Equally economical in form is the poem **"Greyday,"** which in nine short lines compares a lonely lover to Christ. While she is separated from her man, "the day hangs heavy / loose and grey." The woman feels as if she is wearing "a crown of thorns" and "a shirt of hair." Alone, she suffers in her solitude and mourns that

> No one knows
> my lonely heart
> when we're apart.

Such is love in the world of *My Wings;* when all is going well, love sustains and inspires, but when love fades, loneliness and pain have free rein.

As the title of Maya Angelou's third volume of poetry, ***And Still I Rise*** (1978), suggests, this collection contains a hopeful determination to rise above discouraging defeat. These poems are inspired and spoken by a confident voice of strength that recognizes its own power and will no longer be pushed into passivity. The book consists of thirty-two poems, which are divided into three sections, "Touch Me, Life, Not Softly," "Traveling," and "And Still I Rise." Two poems, **"Phenomenal Woman"** and **"Just for a Time"** appeared in *Cosmopolitan* in 1978. Taken as a whole, this series of poems covers a broader range of subjects than the earlier two volumes and shifts smoothly from issues such as springtime and aging to sexual awakening, drug addition, and Christian salvation. The familiar themes of love and its inevitable loneliness and the oppressive climate of the South are still central concerns. But even more striking than the poet's careful treatment of these subjects is her attention to the nature of woman and the importance of family.

One of the best poems in this collection is **"Phenomenal Woman,"** which captures the essence of womanhood and at the same time describes the many talents of the poet herself. As is characteristic of Angelou's poetic style, the lines are terse and forcefully, albeit irregularly, rhymed. The words themselves are short, often monosyllabic, and collectively create an even, provocative rhythm that resounds with underlying confidence. In four different stanzas, a woman explains her special graces that make her stand out in a crowd and attract the attention of both men and women, although she is not, by her own admission, "cut or built to suit a fashion model's size." One by one, she enumerates her gifts, from "the span of my hips" to "the curl of my lips," from "the flash of my teeth" to "the joy in my feet." Yet her attraction is not purely physical; men seek her for her "inner mystery," "the grace of [her] style," and "the need for [her] care." Together each alluring part adds up to a phenomenal woman who need not "bow" her head but can walk tall with a quiet pride that beckons those in her presence.

Similar to **"Phenomenal Woman"** in its economical form, strong rhyme scheme, and forceful rhythm is **"Woman Work."** The two poems also bear a thematic resemblance in their praise of woman's vitality. Although **"Woman Work"** does not concern the physical appeal of woman, as **"Phenomenal Woman"** does, it delivers a corresponding litany of the endless cycle of chores in a woman's typical day. In the first stanza, the long list unravels itself in forcefully rhymed couplets:

> I've got the children to tend
> The clothes to mend
> The floor to mop
> The food to shop
> Then the chicken to fry
> Then baby to dry.

Following the complete category of tasks, the poet adds

four shorter stanzas, which reveal the source of woman's strength. This woman claims the sunshine, rain, and dew as well as storms, wind, and snow as her own. The dew cools her brow, the wind lifts her "across the sky," the snow covers her "with white / Cold icy kisses," all bringing her rest and eventually the strength to continue. For her, there is no other source of solace and consolation than nature and its powerful elements.

In two poems, **"Willie"** and **"Kin,"** Angelou turns her attention from woman to her family. **"Willie"** tells the story of her paternal uncle, with whom she and her brother, Bailey, lived during their childhood in Stamps, Arkansas. This man, although "crippled and limping, always walking lame," knows the secret of survival. For years, he suffers humiliation and loneliness, both as a result of his physical affliction and his color. Yet from him, the child learns about the hidden richness of life and later follows his example to overcome seemingly insurmountable hardships. Willie's undying message echoes throughout the poem: "I may cry and I will die, / But my spirit is the soul of every spring" and "my spirit is the surge of open seas." Although he cannot personally change the inhumane way people treat their brothers and sisters, Willie's spirit will always be around; for, as he says, "I am the time," and his inspiration lives on beyond him.

As in **"Willie,"** the setting of **"Kin"** is the South, particularly Arkansas, and the subject is family. This powerful poem is dedicated to Bailey and is based on the painful separation of brother and sister during their adult years. As children, Marguerite and Bailey were constant companions and buffered each other somewhat from the continual awareness of what it meant to grow up black in the South. Then, she writes, "We were entwined in red rings / Of blood and loneliness. . . ." Now, distanced by time and Bailey's involvement with drugs, the poet is left

> . . . to force strangers
> Into brother molds, exacting
> Taxations they never
> Owed or could pay.

Meanwhile, her brother slips further and further away and fights

> . . . to die, thinking
> In destruction lies the seed
> Of birth. . . .

Although she cannot reach him in his "regions of terror," Angelou sinks through memory to "silent walks in Southern woods" and an "Arkansas twilight" and is willing to concede that her brother "may be right."

But ultimately, the poet challenges her readers to fight against the insipid invitation of destruction and death. Throughout ***And Still I Rise,*** the strong, steady rhythm of her poetic voice beckons whoever will listen to transcend beyond the level of demoralizing defeat and to grasp life on its own terms. The single strongest affirmation of life is the title poem, **"And Still I Rise."** In the face of "bitter, twisted lies," "hatefulness," and "history's shame," the poet promises not to surrender. Silently, she absorbs the power of the sun and moon and becomes a "black ocean, leaping and wide, / Welling and swelling I bear in the tide." Her inner resources, "oil wells," "gold mines," and "diamonds," nourish her strength and sustain her courage. Her spirit will soar as she transforms "the gifts that my ancestors gave" into poetry, and herself into "the dream and the hope of the slave." Through all of her verse, Angelou reaches out to touch the lives of others and to offer them hope and confidence in place of humiliation and despair.

Her fourth volume of verse, *Shaker, Why Don't You Sing?* (1983), is dedicated to her son, Guy Johnson, and her grandson, Colin Ashanti Murphy Johnson. As do her three previous collections of poems, *Shaker* celebrates the power to struggle against lost love, defeated dreams, and threatened freedom, and to survive. Her poetic voice resonates with the control and confidence that have become characteristic of Angelou's work in general and of her determination that "life loves the person who dares to live it." The vibrant tone of these poems moves gracefully from the promise of potential strength to the humor of light satire, at all times bearing witness to a spirit that soars and sings in spite of repeated disappointment. Perhaps even more than in her earlier poems, Angelou forcefully captures the loneliness of love and the sacrifice of slavery without surrendering to defeat or despair.

More than half of the twenty-eight poems in *Shaker* concern the subject of love between woman and man, and of these, most deal with the pain, loss, and loneliness that typically characterize unrequited love. In many of these poems, a woman awakens at sunrise, with or without her lover by her side, wondering how much longer their dying relationship will limp along before its failure will be openly acknowledged. An underlying issue in these poignant poems about love is deception—not so much the intricate fabrication of lies to cover up infidelity but rather the unvoiced acquiescence to fading and failing love. In **"The Lie,"** for example, a woman protects herself from humiliation when her lover threatens to leave her by holding back her anger and pretending to be unmoved, even eager to see her man go:

> I hold curses, in my mouth,
> which could flood your path, sear
> bottomless chasms in your road.

Deception is her only defense:

> I keep, behind my lips,
> invectives capable of tearing
> the septum from your
> nostrils and the skin from your back.

Similarly, in the very brief poem **"Prelude to a Parting,"** a woman lying in bed beside her lover senses the imminent end when he draws away from her touch. Yet neither will acknowledge "the tacit fact" or face the "awful fear of losing," knowing, as they do without speaking, that nothing will "cause / a fleeing love / to stay."

Not all of the love poems in this collection suggest deception or dishonesty, but most describe the seemingly inevitable loss of love. The title poem, **"Shaker, Why Don't You Sing?,"** belongs to this second group. A woman, "evicted from sleep's mute palace" and lying awake alone in bed, remembers the "perfect harmonies" and the "insis-

tent / rhythm" of a lost love. Her life fills with silence now that love has withdrawn its music, its "chanteys" that "hummed / [her] life alive." Now she rests "somewhere / between the unsung notes of night" and passionately asks love to return its song to her life: "O Shaker, why don't you sing?" This mournful apostrophe to love serves as a refrain in an unsung song and, in its second utterance, brings the poem to a close unanswered.

The same determined voice comes through in a number of other poems that relate unabiding anguish over the oppression of the black race. Several of these poems deal specifically with the inhumane treatment of the slaves in the South. **"A Georgia Song,"** for example, in its beautifully lyrical cadences, recalls the unforgotten memories of slavery, which linger like "odors of Southern cities" and the "great green / Smell of fresh sweat. / In Southern fields." Angelou deftly recounts the "ancient / Wrongs" and describes a South broken by injustice and sorrow. Now, "dusty / Flags droop their unbearable / Sadness." Yet the poet calls for a new dream to rise up from the rich soil of Georgia and replace the "liquid notes of / Sorrow songs" with "a new song. A song / Of Southern peace." Although the memories of "ancient / Wrongs" can never be forgotten, the poem invites a renewal of Southern dreams and peace.

Perhaps the most powerful poem in this collection is **"Caged Bird,"** which inevitably brings Angelou's audience full circle with her best-known autobiography, *I Know Why the Caged Bird Sings.* This poem tells the story of a free bird and a caged bird. The free bird floats leisurely on "trade winds soft through the sighing trees" and even "dares to claim the sky." He feeds on "fat worms waiting on a dawn-bright lawn" and soars to "name the sky his own." Unlike his unbound brother, the caged bird leads a life of confinement that sorely inhibits his need to fly and sing. Trapped by the unyielding bars of his cage, the bird can only lift his voice in protest against his imprisonment and the "grave of dreams" on which he perches. Appearing both in the middle and end of the poem, this stanza serves as a dual refrain:

> The caged bird sings
> with a fearful trill
> of things unknown
> but longed for still
> and his tune is heard
> on the distant hill
> for the caged bird
> sings of freedom.

Although he sings of "things unknown," the bird's song of freedom is heard even as far as the "distant hill." His song is his protest, his only alternative to submission and entrapment. Angelou knows why the caged bird and all oppressed beings must sing. Her poems in *Shaker, Why Don't You Sing?* imply that as long as such melodies are sung and heard, hope and strength will overcome defeated dreams.

At the end of *All God's Children Need Traveling Shoes,* Angelou hints at her association with Tom Feelings, a young black American artist who lived in Ghana during the early 1960s. Angelou cites Malcolm X's introduction of this newcomer to the black American expatriate com- munity: " 'A young painter named Tom Feelings is com- ing to Ghana. Do everything you can for him. I am count- ing on you.' " By introducing Feelings at the conclusion of her latest autobiography, she subtly sets the scene for her most recent publication, ***Now Sheba Sings the Song*** (1987), a single poem, illustrated by eighty-two of Feel- ings's drawings of black women, sketched throughout the world over a period of twenty-five years. Together the poem and the sepia-toned drawings royally celebrate the universal majesty of the black woman. In his introduction to the book, Feelings credits Angelou as the "someone who shared a similar experience [with the women he drew], someone who traveled, opened up, took in, and mentally recorded everything observed. And most impor- tant of all, it [his collaborator] had to be someone whose *center* is woman." Angelou's poem, in turn, glorifies the spiritual, physical, emotional, and intellectual powers of black women or what Feelings calls "Africa's beauty, strength, and dignity [which are] wherever the Black woman is." Angelou affirms the black woman's "love of good and God and Life" and beckons "he who is daring and brave" to meet the open challenge of the radiant Queen of Sheba. Maya Angelou's songs, like Sheba's, testi- fy to the creative powers inherent in the works of today's Southern women writers. (pp. 114-41)

> *Carol E. Neubauer, "Maya Angelou: Self and a Song of Freedom in the Southern Tradition,"* in Southern Women Writers: The New Gen- eration, *edited by Tonette Bond Inge, The University of Alabama Press, 1990, pp. 114-42.*

Mary Vermillion (essay date Summer 1992)

[*In the following excerpt, Vermillion discusses Angelou's representation of rape and depiction of the black female body in* I Know Why the Caged Bird Sings.]

[In ***I Know Why the Caged Bird Sings***] Angelou first con- nects her rape [at age eight] with the suffering of the poor. "The act of rape on an eight-year-old body," she writes, "is a matter of the needle giving because the camel can't." In this description, Angelou subtly links her rapist with the wealthy man whom Jesus warned would have a diffi- cult time getting into heaven, and she reinforces this link by alluding to Jesus's words in her ironic description of a black revival congregation's sentiments: "The Lord loved the poor and hated those cast high in the world. Hadn't He Himself said it would be easier for a camel to go through the eye of a needle than for a rich man to enter heaven?" As she continues to imagine the congregation's thoughts, Angelou makes the connection between her rape and the plight of the poor in class society more racially ex- plicit, and, like Jacobs, she also demonstrates that privi- leging a future world over the present perpetuates black oppression:

> They [the congregation] basked in the righteous- ness of the poor and the exclusiveness of the downtrodden. Let the white folks have their money and power and segregation and sarcasm and big houses and schools and lawns like car-

pets, and books, and mostly—mostly—let them have their whiteness.

With the image of the camel and the needle, Angelou transforms her rape into a symbol of the racism and soma- tophobia that afflict Maya and her race throughout much of *Caged Bird.*

Rape in Angelou's text, however, primarily represents the black girl's difficulties in controlling, understanding, and respecting both her body and her words in a somatophobic society that sees "sweet little white girls" as "everybody's dream of what was right with the world." Angelou con- nects white definitions of beauty with rape by linking Maya's rape with her first sight of her mother, Vivian Bax- ter. Angelou's description of Vivian echoes that of the ghost-like whites who baffle young Maya. Vivian has "even white teeth and her fresh-butter color looked see- through clean." Maya and her brother, Bailey, later deter- mine that Vivian resembles a white movie star. Angelou writes that her mother's beauty "literally assailed" Maya and twice observes that she was "struck dumb." This as- sault by her mother's beauty anticipates the physical as- sault by Mr. Freeman, her mother's boyfriend, and Maya's muteness upon meeting her mother foreshadows her silence after the rape. With this parallel Angelou indi- cates that both rape and the dominant white culture's defi- nitions of beauty disempower the black woman's body and self-expression.

Angelou further demonstrates the intimate connection be- tween the violation of Maya's body and the devaluation of her words by depicting her self-imposed silence after Freeman's rape trial. Freeman's pleading looks in the courtroom, along with Maya's own shame, compel her to lie, and after she learns that her uncles have murdered Freeman, she believes that her courtroom lie is responsible for his death. Angelou describes the emotions that silence Maya:

> I could feel the evilness flowing through my body and waiting, pent up, to rush off my tongue if I tried to open my mouth. I clamped my teeth shut, I'd hold it in. If it escaped, wouldn't it flood the world and all the innocent people?

Angelou's use of flood imagery in this crucial passage en- ables her to link Maya's inability to control her body and her words. Throughout the text Maya's failure to keep her bodily functions "pent up" signals the domination of her body by others. The autobiography's opening scene merges her inability to control her appearance, words, and bodily functions. Wanting to look like a "sweet little white girl," Maya is embarrassed about her own appearance and cannot remember the words of the Easter poem she re- cites. With her escape from the church, Angelou implicit- ly associates Maya's inability to rule her bladder with her inability to speak:

> I stumbled and started to say something, or maybe to scream, but a green persimmon, or it could have been a lemon, caught me between the legs and squeezed. I tasted the sour on my tongue and felt it in the back of my mouth. Then before I reached the door, the sting was burning down my legs and into my Sunday socks. I tried

to hold, to squeeze it back, to keep it from speed-
ing.

Maya's squeezing back in this passage anticipates her
stopping the flood of her words after the rape, and Angelou also connects this opening scene of urination with
one of Freeman's means of silencing Maya. After ejaculat-
ing on a mattress, he tells her that she has wet the bed, and
with this lie, he denies her knowledge about her own body
and confounds her ability to make a coherent story out of
his actions.

This inability to create a story about her body pervades the
remainder of **Caged Bird** as Maya struggles to cope with
her emerging womanhood. Angelou, however, is not content to let the mute, sexually abused, wishing-to-be-white
Maya represent the black female body in her text. Instead,
she begins to reembody Maya by critiquing her admiration
for white literary discourse. An early point at which Angelou foregrounds this critique is in Maya's meeting with
Mrs. Bertha Flowers. Presenting this older black woman
as the direct opposite of young Maya, Angelou stresses
that Flowers magnificently rules both her words and her
body. Indeed Flower's bodily control seems almost supernatural: "She had the grace of control to appear warm in
the coldest weather, and on the Arkansas summer days it
seemed she had a private breeze which swirled around,
cooling her." She makes Maya proud to be black, and
Maya claims that Flowers is more beautiful and "just as
refined as whitefolks in movies and books." Although
Maya begins to respect and admire the black female body,
white heroines still provide her standard for beauty, and
Angelou pokes fun at the literary discourse that whitens
Maya's view of Bertha Flowers and womanhood:

> She [Flowers] appealed to me because she was
> like people I had never met personally. Like
> women in English novels who walked the moors
> (whatever they were) with their loyal dogs rac-
> ing at a respectful distance. Like the women who
> sat in front of roaring fireplaces, drinking tea in-
> cessantly from silver trays full of scones and
> crumpets. Women who walked over the 'heath'
> and read morocco-bound books.

This humorous passage demonstrates that Maya's self-
perception remains dangerously regulated by white culture. Angelou treats such regulation less comically when
Flowers breaks Maya's self-imposed silence by asking her
to read aloud. The first words Maya speaks after her long
spell of muteness are those of Charles Dickens.

Angelou dramatizes the danger that a borrowed voice
poses to Maya in her description of Maya's relationship
with Viola Cullinan. Maya makes fun of this white
woman, whose kitchen she briefly works in, until she discovers that Cullinan's husband has two daughters by a
black woman. Then Maya—in a gesture of sisterhood and
empathy that is never returned by Cullinan—pities her
employer and decides to write a "tragic ballad" "on being
white, fat, old and without children." Such a ballad
would, of course, completely exclude Maya's own experience: black, thin, young, and (near the end of her autobiography) with child. Through Maya's speculation that
Cullinan walks around with no organs and drinks alcohol

to keep herself "embalmed," Angelou implies that Maya's
potential poetic identification with Cullinan nearly negates her own body. Cullinan's empty insides echo Maya's
own perception of herself after the rape as a "gutless doll"
she had earlier ripped to pieces.

Angelou's most complex and subtle examination of
Maya's attachment to white literary discourse occurs
when she lists as one of her accomplishments the memori-
zation of Shakespeare's *The Rape of Lucrece*. Christine
Froula maintains that Maya's feat of memory suggests the
potential erasure of black female reality by white male literary discourse [in "The Daughter's Seduction: Sexual Violence and Literary History," *Signs,* 1986.] More specifically, I believe, Angelou's reference to *Lucrece* subtly indicates that Maya's propensity for the verbal and the literary
leads her to ignore her own corporeality. After their rapes
both Maya and Lucrece turn to representations of suffering women. Maya reads about Lucrece, and Lucrece, finding a painting of the fall of Troy, views Hecuba's mourning the destruction of her city and husband, King Priam.
Unlike Lucrece, Maya seeks strength not from pictorial
representations of female bodies, but from print, and this
preference for the verbal over the pictorial suggests her
tendency to privilege literature over her own physical reality. Lucrece decides to speak for the mute sufferers in the
painting, and Shakespeare writes, "She lends them words,
and she their looks doth borrow." Maya's situation is an
inversion of Lucrece's lending of words and borrowing of
looks. The once mute Maya can borrow Lucrece's words,
but she must somehow lend these words her own "looks"
if she does not wish Shakespeare's equation of Lucrece's
virtue and whiteness to degrade her own blackness. In remembering *The Rape of Lucrece* Maya must also remember or reconstruct her own body.

One of the ways that she accomplishes this is by celebrating the bodies of other black women. In the only story
Maya creates within **Caged Bird,** she augments her grandmother's physical and verbal powers. After a white dentist
refuses to treat Maya because she is black, Maya imagines
her grandmother ten feet tall, arms doubling in length. As
this fantasy grandmother orders the dentist out of town
and commands him to quit practicing dentistry, her
words, too, metamorphose: "Her tongue had thinned and
the words rolled off well enunciated. Well enunciated and
sharp like little claps of thunder." With Maya's brief fantasy, Angelou demonstrates how her own autobiography
functions. Maya's story, which empowers her grandmother's body and speech, attacks the dentist's derogatory behavior; Angelou's autobiography, which celebrates
Maya's body and words, critiques the rape and racial oppression she suffers.

Maya finds, however, that her body and words exist uneasily together. While in the early part of the narrative Maya
depends heavily on literature, in the text's final San Francisco section, all words, particularly those packaged as literature, fail to account for her adolescent body's changes.
Reading Radclyffe Hall's *The Well of Loneliness* (1928)
leads Maya to mistakenly interpret these changes as signals that she is becoming a lesbian. When Maya confronts
her mother with this fear, Angelou further demonstrates

the inability of the verbal to explain the physical. Vivian's requiring Maya to read aloud the dictionary definition of the word "vulva" echoes strangely Flowers's asking Maya to read aloud from Dickens. Unlike Dickens's prose, however, Noah Webster's and Vivian's words lose their soothing power as soon as Maya is confronted with a stronger physical reality—her own admiration for her girlfriend's fully developed breasts. This scene in which Maya shifts her attention from words to bodies paves the way for Angelou's concluding celebration of the black female body.

Seeking physical rather than verbal knowledge of her sexuality, Maya determines to have sex with one of "the most eligible young men in the neighborhood." Their encounter, which "is unredeemed by shared tenderness," leaves sixteen-year-old Maya pregnant and alone. The young man quits talking to her in her fourth month, and Maya's brother, who is overseas, advises her not to tell her parents until she graduates from high school. Yet it would be wrong to see Maya's motherhood as "a tragic way to end the book and begin life as an adult" [Stephanie A. Demetrakopoulos in *Women's Autobiography: Essays in Criticism*, 1980]. While Angelou portrays the pain and confusion resulting from Maya's pregnancy, she places a far greater emphasis on her newfound autonomy. Even Maya's naive style of seduction accentuates her feminist stance. She asks the young man, "Would you like to have a sexual intercourse with me?" In posing this straightforward question, Maya claims control of her body and her identity for the first time in the text. . . . Angelou celebrates Maya's encounter with the young man. She accentuates Maya's reclamation of her body and volition by ironically alluding to the violation she suffered as an eight year old. "Thanks to Mr. Freeman nine years before," asserts Angelou, "I had had no pain of entry to endure."

By detailing how the pregnant Maya copes with her isolation, Angelou pays further tribute to Maya's increased autonomy and acceptance of her own body. Beginning to reject the literary myths that led her to deny her own agency, Maya accepts complete responsibility for her pregnancy: "For eons, it seemed, I had accepted my plight as the hapless, put-upon victim of fate and the Furies, but this time I had to face the fact that I had brought my new catastrophe upon myself." This acceptance of responsibility also leads Maya to a greater acceptance of her own body's powers:

> I had a baby. He was beautiful and mine. Totally mine. No one had bought him for me. No one had helped me endure the sickly gray months. I had had help in the child's conception, but no one could deny that I had had an immaculate pregnancy.

Angelou's use of the word "immaculate" not only challenges racist stereotypes that associate black women with illicit sexuality, but it also suggests that Maya has shed her earlier conceptions of her body as "dirty like mud" and "shit-colored." Because the eight-year-old Maya perceives her own mother as looking like the "Virgin Mary," the word "immaculate" also indicates that the teenage Maya begins to see in herself the power and beauty she sees in Vivian.

Maya's lack of confidence in her body briefly returns, however, in the autobiography's final paragraphs. Vivian's suggestion that Maya sleep with her child accentuates her worry that she is too clumsy to handle a baby. Vivian banishes this fear by waking Maya and showing her the baby sleeping under a tent that Maya unconsciously formed with her body and a blanket. "See," Vivian whispers, "you don't have to think about doing the right thing. If you're for the right thing then you do it without thinking." Presenting the mother/child bond as a symbol of Maya's newfound autonomy, this closing scene reverses her earlier privileging of the verbal over the physical and celebrates the harmonious interaction of her body and will. (pp. 250-56)

> *Mary Vermillion, "Reembodying the Self: Representations of Rape in 'Incidents in the Life of a Slave Girl' and 'I Know Why the Caged Bird Sings',"* in Biography, *Vol. 15, No. 3, Summer, 1992, pp. 243-60.*

Catherine S. Manegold   (essay date 20 January 1993)

[*In the following essay based on an interview, Angelou recalls several experiences that significantly influenced her writing. She also discusses "On the Pulse of Morning," the poem commissioned for President Clinton's inauguration.*]

It was one of those Southern winter days just short of raining when the sky is so gray that it blurs the horizon and seems to fuse with the grayness on the ground. The humidity hung thick as mist and had worked its way into Maya Angelou's already aching joints. "My arthritis is bad today," she said by way of greeting. "Let's have some wine."

And so she called in that deep, rich voice of hers down to her niece for a bottle of Chafeau Ste. Michelle, a 1990 chardonnay, "and a straw!" and then wrestled—"No, I don't need help"—with the pain in her fingers to extract its cork. Moving into a sun room that had no sun that day but was, instead, a wraparound reminder of the heaviness of the afternoon, she folded her six-foot, 64-year-old frame into a chair of mint-green crushed velvet, poured the wine, stretched her legs and tried to hide her irritation with the pain in her body.

Today, at the inauguration, she will stand shoulder to shoulder with the new President [Bill Clinton], ignoring whatever pain lingers, to read a poem written for the occasion. She will be the first poet since Robert Frost spoke at the inauguration of John F. Kennedy to apply verse to a moment of political change and read it at the inauguration. For weeks she has been padding about in her bedroom in her trim brick house in Winston-Salem, reading aloud from the voices that have formed her language and her politics—Frederick Douglass, Patrick Henry, Thomas Paine—trying "to see, to remember, the power of words, their power to move, to cause people to move."

Alone in that house, at odd hours of the day and night, her voice has been the only sound, reciting words that have caught the nation's history and its hope, seeking "the lyricism possible when one is talking about the country," its wars and triumphs and the pain it sometimes bears.

She quotes from a memory filled with the rhythms and cadences of other writers. Frances Harper, whom she has been rereading lately, wrote of slavery without polemic, and Ms. Angelou saluted that in the dim afternoon, pulling a passage from her memory:

"The sale began," she said, as though she herself had seen it, back in 1850. "Young girls were there." She closed her eyes. "And mothers stood with streaming eyes and saw their dearest children sold. And heeded those, their bitter cries, as tyrants bartered them for gold."

She wore black, head to toe, that afternoon. Black sweater. Black pants. Black sheer stockings that did not hide black feet that looked as if they had climbed a mountain barefoot, a dancer's feet, tough and covered with calluses, a physical testimony to those years when she would dance, "Young and mad!" wildly, far into the night, with Alvin Alley, neither of them wearing much to impede the moment. A dancer's feet that have jumped and kicked and slammed against the floor, feet that have borne the bruises that are rough service to that art.

So we began with no beginning at all, really, as though this ambling conversation were something that had somehow started earlier, part of an endless round of storytelling and recollection. Winding her long fingers around a glass of chardonnay, she spoke, first, of life's "grand teachable moments" when one is struck by either truth or possibility. "My mother, who was very precious to me, died a year ago," she said.

> When I was 20 I had gone over to her big house, a 14-room house, in San Francisco. I had gone over there and we had had a good afternoon, two or three hours, and we walked out of the house and down the hill. And we were at the very bottom of the hill and she knew I wouldn't take a ride from her, that I would take the streetcar, that I had to own myself. And she said, "You know, baby, I think you are the greatest woman I have ever met."

Ms. Angelou laughed, seeing her big, bony self at the age of 20, already with a son in tow, towering over her mother, thinking nothing much about the future. She was stunned by the comment and by what her mother said next: that she had a rare combination of intelligence and kindness. The two kissed, then moved apart. But in that brief exchange something in her life had changed.

> I watched her, with the light, go to the other corner and I crossed to get the No. 22 streetcar and I sat there and I remember everything, the color of the light, the wooden seats, and I remember thinking: "She's very intelligent and she's too mean to lie. So, just suppose she's right? Suppose I really am somebody?" And it was the first time I ever remember being on the earth as opposed to a part of the earth. I was aware, at that moment, of being on a ball.

She stopped, self-conscious, then shifted to dispel an intensity she still could feel. "It was one of those moments when the sky rolled back and TA-DA, TATA!" She laughed, loud-

ly, almost singing the sound, as she does at times to illustrate a thought for which language temporarily fails her. "It's almost as if at times like that, the whole earth holds its breath."

She could not resist the memory. It is, she said, those times when the everyday slips away and the simplest things take on a cast that fixes them forever in the mind, a face, a comment, a moment, those times when life seems surely bigger than it has been, times "that are really the essence and the origin of poetry," she said, "because whether one knows it or not, one goes to those watersheds, those times when you are moved, to write."

Ms. Angelou, whose name ends with a long "oh" and whose assistants will correct anyone who gets that wrong, is not a woman of classical beauty. Her features are broad, like chunks of clay collected roughly on a frame. Her hands are large, her mouth a cut of red across her face. Even her laugh seems big. But she has the innate and compelling grace of a woman who has constructed a full life, one lived without concession or false excuse.

She has married and divorced. She will not say how many times. People, she said, tend to find a certain capriciousness in the frequency. "They honor the coward who stays in a murderous and abusive relationship," she said. "They herald that as something wonderous. But in every marriage I went with everything I had. Humor. Intelligence. Honesty. Faithfulness. Good appetites for everything. But if it didn't work, I never stayed."

Now she lives alone, far from her son, Guy Johnson, and grandson, Colin, in California. Yet, as the Reynolds professor of American studies at Wake Forest University in Winston-Salem, she has, she said, "a large umbrella." She continued: "A lot of people stand under it. A lot of young blacks and whites and students and some plain, some tall, some very, very smart and some slow."

She is good at collecting people, she said, using everything she can to pull them in.

> I will dance. I will tell a story. I will pinch and I will pat and I will hug. It's asking: Trust me and I'll trust you. I will dare! I will dare to pry myself loose from my ignorance. It was given to me by my *mother*. But I will try to pry loose. It was given to me by my *father*, but I will try to get it off.

Though she holds 50 honorary degrees and has written three books of popular, plain-spoken poetry, she is best known for her volumes of autobiographical fiction. She is also in great demand on the lecture circuit, making about 80 appearances a year, at a standard fee of $15,000.

Her own learning came mostly in life, not libraries. And her love of the human voice, of which she speaks again and again over several hours of desultory conversation, was deepened, perhaps, when she lost her own, an event that forms the core of her most celebrated novel, ***I Know Why the Caged Bird Sings.***

She was born in 1928 in St. Louis, then moved to California. She was 3½ when her parents separated, and that year her mother, a splashy, bejeweled owner of hotels and bars, shipped her off by train, with her older brother, to Stamps, Ark., to live with her father's mother. She lived there four years and then went back to her mother's house in San Francisco. "I was raped by her boyfriend," she said with the directness of someone who knows both the cost and the lessons learned. "I was 7½."

The man was beaten to death a short time later. Though the killing was not related to the assault, Ms. Angelou said she believed that she was responsible.

"I thought he was killed because I spoke his name," she said. "That was the only logic I was able to employ. So I thought if I spoke, anybody might die. I just might open my mouth and—*Prrraaaaaa*—I could see whole roads of people dying. But after a while it didn't matter why I didn't speak. It was just accepted."

Instead, in the five years that she was mute, until an older friend in Arkansas eased her out of that self-imposed isolation, she listened and, developed a voice and style that seem peculiarly unlinked to region, race, history or circumstance, something endlessly changeable and uniquely hers.

> Language. I loved it. And for a long time I would think of myself, of my whole body, as an ear, and that I could just go into a room and I could just absorb sound, just *schlouuuup*. I never did find a voice I didn't find wonderful and beautiful. Because I really like the way we talk. I find it wonderful.

Her own accent is indecipherable, her voice a swoop, a lingering vowel, an octave dropped for emphasis. She sings and chuckles and plays with sound as she talks, telling stories as though she were playing a piano, using every croak and sensuous riff her voice can conjure. In the South, where she has lived 11 years, she said she finds language "more languorous, sweeter, softer" and the imagery more intense. And so she stays and talks to herself there, spinning stories and repeating tales.

Often, there is no one there to hear. She wakes at 4 A.M. daily and is off to work in a nearby hotel room that she keeps because at home "every room is filled with paintings, memories and every excuse to be lackadaisical or to be distracted." She added: "Every excuse. And there goes my great idea." On good days she works until almost noon. But lately, in the hubbub preceding the Inauguration, she has had to stop earlier to deal with reporters and other demands of this turn in the nation's spotlight.

In the afternoon as she juggles these duties she battles her arthritis and frets about a word, a faux pas, a moment of embarrassment in front of the entire nation. She has hoped, she said, to capture something fundamental in her inaugural poem. "In all my work, what I try to say is that as human beings we are more alike than we are unalike," she said. "It may be that Mr. Clinton asked me to write the inaugural poem because he understood that I am the kind of person who really does bring people together."

Still, she worries. And she pleads, unabashedly, for prayers. "I ask everybody to pray for me all the time," she said.

Pray. Pray. Pray. Just send me some good energies. Last night I said to this group of hundreds of people, I said: "Pray for me, please, for the inaugural poem. Not in general. Pray for me by name. Say: 'Lord! Help Maya Angelou.' Don't just say 'Lord, help six-foot tall black ladies or poets or anything like that. Lord. Help Maya Angelou. Please!'"

She drifted, from there, to a parable from the Bible, an account of her childhood and musings on the English language, tumbling naturally from one theme to the next. She spoke of friends and long, slow dinners and a house full of buddies, all with doctoral degrees, helping her to lay the rugs in her immaculately kept home. She stood, stiffly, to show pictures of her mother and grandmother and speak of their histories and charms.

But finally the light dimmed and the airport taxi came and there was a plane to catch and the spell, that eternal spell of sharing stories, was broken. She rose and cautiously tested a movement here, another there, like the dancer that she was. She pronounced herself much improved. At the door, she waved and laughed and reminded an addled visitor to get her bags.

In the gathering darkness on the way back to the airport, it was hard to shake that image of Maya Angelou in Washington, up on that stage, all the while hoping that somewhere someone would be praying: "Lord! Help Maya Angelou."

Though she hardly seemed to need it. (pp. C1, C8)

Catherine S. Manegold, "A Wordsmith at Her Inaugural Anvil," in The New York Times, *January 20, 1993, pp. C1, C8.*

Maya Angelou   (poem date 20 January 1993)

[*Below is Angelou's poem "On the Pulse of Morning," which she delivered at President Clinton's inaugural ceremony on 20 January 1993. In this work she acknowledges the injustices pervading American history and expresses hope for social change.*]

A Rock, A River, A Tree
Hosts to species long since departed,
Marked the mastodon.
The dinosaur, who left dry tokens
Of their sojourn here
On our planet floor,
Any broad alarm of their hastening doom
Is lost in the gloom of dust and ages.

But today, the Rock cries out to us, clearly,
  forcefully,
Come, you may stand upon my
Back and face your distant destiny,
But seek no haven in my shadow.
I will give you no hiding place down here.

You, created only a little lower than
The angels, have crouched too long in
The bruising darkness,
Have lain too long
Face down in ignorance.
Your mouths spilling words

Armed for slaughter.
The Rock cries out to us today, you may stand
    on me,
But do not hide your face.

Across the wall of the world,
A River sings a beautiful song,
It says, come rest here by my side.

Each of you a bordered country,
Delicate and strangely made proud,
Yet thrusting perpetually under siege.
Your armed struggles for profit
Have left collars of waste upon
My shore, currents of debris upon my breast.
Yet, today I call you to my riverside,
If you will study war no more. Come,
Clad in peace and I will sing the songs
The Creator gave to me when I and the
Tree and the Rock were one.
Before cynicism was a bloody sear across your
Brow and when you yet knew you still
Knew nothing.
The River sings and sings on.

There is a true yearning to respond to
The singing River and the wise Rock.
So say the Asian, the Hispanic, the Jew
The African, the Native American, the Sioux,
The Catholic, the Muslim, the French, the
    Greek
The Irish, the Rabbi, the Priest, the Sheikh,
The Gay, the Straight, the Preacher,
The privileged, the homeless, the Teacher.
They all hear
The speaking of the Tree.

They hear the first and last of every Tree
Speak to humankind today. Come to me, here
    beside the River.
Plant yourself beside me, here beside the River.

Each of you, descendant of some passed
On traveller, has been paid for.
You, who gave me my first name, you
Pawnee, Apache, Seneca, you
Cherokee Nation, who rested with me, then
Forced on bloody feet, left me to the employ-
    ment of
Other seekers—desperate for gain,
Starving for gold.
You, the Turk, the Arab, the Swede, the Ger-
    man, the Eskimo, the Scot,
You the Ashanti, the Yoruba, the Kru, bought
Sold, stolen, arriving on a nightmare
Praying for a dream.
Here, root yourselves beside me.
I am that Tree planted by the River,
Which will not be moved.
I, the Rock, I the River, I the Tree
I am yours—your Passages have been paid.
Lift up your faces, you have a piercing need
For this bright morning dawning for you.
History, despite its wrenching pain,
Cannot be unlived, but if faced
With courage, need not be lived again.

Lift up your eyes upon
This day breaking for you.
Give birth again

To the dream.

Women, children, men,
Take it into the palms of your hands.
Mold it into the shape of your most
Private need. Sculpt it into
The image of your most public self.
Lift up your hearts
Each new hour holds new chances
For new beginnings.
Do not be wedded forever
To fear, yoked eternally
To brutishness.

The horizon leans forward,
Offering you space to place new steps of change.
Here, on the pulse of this fine day
You may have the courage
To look up and out and upon me, the
Rock, the River, the Tree, your country.
No less to Midas than the mendicant.
No less to you now than the mastodon then.

Here on the pulse of this new day
You may have the grace to look up and out
And into your sister's eyes, and into
Your brother's face, your country
And say simply
Very simply
With hope
Good morning.

Maya Angelou, in a poem in The Washington
Post, *January 21, 1993, p. A25.*

FURTHER READING

Arensberg, Liliane K. "Death as Metaphor of Self in *I Know
Why the Caged Bird Sings.*" *CLA Journal* XX, No. 2 (December 1976): 273-91.

  Examines the relationship between self and the interpretation of experience in *I Know Why the Caged Bird
  Sings.*

Danahay, Martin A. "Breaking the Silence: Symbolic Violence and the Teaching of Contemporary 'Ethnic' Autobiography." *College Literature* 18, No. 3 (October 1991): 64-79.

  Discusses the significance of language and speech in relation to socialization in several autobiographies, including Angelou's *I Know Why the Caged Bird Sings,* Maxine Hong Kingston's *The Woman Warrior,* and Richard
  Rodriguez's *Hunger of Memory.*

Demetrakopoulos, Stephanie A. "The Metaphysics of
Matrilinearism in Women's Autobiography: Studies of
Mead's *Blackberry Winter,* Hellman's *Pentimento,* Angelou's
I Know Why the Caged Bird Sings, and Kingston's *The
Woman Warrior,*" in *Women's Autobiography: Essays in Crit-
icism* edited by Estelle C. Jelinek, pp. 180-205. Bloomington:
Indiana University Press, 1980.

  Faults Angelou's presentation of matriarchal elements
  in *I Know Why the Caged Bird Sings.*

Elliot, Jeffrey M., ed. *Conversations with Maya Angelou.* Jackson: University Press of Mississippi, 1989, 246 p.

Collection of reprinted interviews with Angelou.

Fox-Genovese, Elizabeth. "Myth and History: Discourse of Origins in Zora Neale Hurston and Maya Angelou." *Black American Literature Forum* 24, No. 2 (Summer 1990): 221-35.

Discusses the relationship between Southern history and the development of personal identity explored in Hurston's *Dust Tracks* and Angelou's *I Know Why the Caged Bird Sings.*

Froula, Christine. "The Daughter's Seduction: Sexual Violence and Literary History." *Signs* 11, No. 4 (Summer 1986): 621-44.

Considers *I Know Why the Caged Bird Sings* in the context of a discussion on sexual abuse in literature.

Kent, George E. "Maya Angelou's *I Know Why the Caged Bird Sings* and Black Autobiographical Tradition." *Kansas Quarterly* 7, No. 3 (Summer 1985): 72-8.

Asserts that *I Know Why the Caged Bird Sings* holds a unique place within the black autobiographical tradition.

Mackethan, Lucinda H. "Mother Wit: Humor in Afro-American Women's Autobiography." *Studies in American Humor* 4, Nos. 1-2 (Spring-Summer 1985): 51-61.

Discusses Angelou's use of humor in *I Know Why the Caged Bird Sings.*

McMurry, Myra K. "Role-Playing as Art in Maya Angelou's *Caged Bird.*" *South Atlantic Bulletin* XLI, No. 2 (May 1976): 106-11.

Discusses the themes of identity and repression in *I Know Why the Caged Bird Sings.*

Molotsky, Irvin. "Poet of the South for the Inauguration." *The New York Times* (5 December 1992): L8.

Feature article in which Angelou discusses her political views and the poem she wrote for President Clinton's inauguration.

Washington, Carla. "Maya Angelou's Angelic Aura." *The Christian Century* 105, No. 3 (23 November 1988): 1031-32.

Explores Angelou's spirituality as evidenced in her poetry and autobiographies.

Additional coverage of Angelou's life and career is contained in the following sources published by Gale Research: *Black Literary Criticism,* Vol. 1; *Black Writers; Contemporary Authors,* Vols. 65-68; *Contemporary Authors New Revision Series,* Vol. 19; *Contemporary Literary Criticism,* Vols. 12, 35, 64; *Dictionary of Literary Biography,* Vol. 38; *Major 20th-Century Writers;* and *Something about the Author,* Vol. 49.

John Ashbery

1927-

(Full name John Lawrence Ashbery; also wrote under the pseudonym Jonas Berry) American poet, critic, editor, novelist, dramatist, and translator.

This entry presents criticism on Ashbery's works from 1984 through 1992. For further information on his life and works, see *CLC*, Volumes 2, 3, 4, 6, 9, 13, 15, 25, and 41.

INTRODUCTION

Ashbery is considered one of the most influential and controversial contemporary American poets. Much of his verse features long, conversational passages in which he experiments with syntactical structure and perspective, producing poems that seem accessible yet resist interpretation. Roberta Berke commented: "In Ashbery's poems there are constant echoes of other secret dimensions, like chambers resounding behind hollow panels of an old mansion rumored to contain secret passages (which our guide emphatically denies exist). Ashbery both hunts for these secrets and tries to conceal them." Although some critics fault Ashbery's works for obscurity and lack of thematic depth, many regard him as an innovator whose works incorporate randomness, invention, and improvisation to explore the complex and elusive relationships between existence, time, and perception.

Ashbery became interested in writing while a student at Harvard University. During the 1950s, he won a scholarship to study in France. Ashbery lived there for ten years, supporting himself by working as a poet and translator and by writing art criticism for the Paris edition of *The New York Herald Tribune*. Painting, which first attracted Ashbery when he was in his teens, has had a lasting influence on his approach to writing poetry. He once stated: "I attempt to use words abstractly, as an artist uses paint." Ashbery received immediate critical recognition with the publication of his first volume *Some Trees* in 1956; early in his career he was frequently linked by critics to the avant-garde "New York School" of poetry which included such surrealist and abstract impressionist poets as Frank O'Hara and Kenneth Koch. Although many critics rejected the experimental nature of Ashbery's works during the 1960s, his *Self-Portrait in a Convex Mirror*, published in 1975, won the Pulitzer Prize, the National Book Award, and the National Book Critics Circle Prize, and is widely regarded as a masterpiece in the realm of contemporary poetry. The volume established Ashbery as a highly original poet whose works subvert traditional concepts of structure, content, and theme. Ashbery's recent works, including *April Galleons* and his book-length poem *Flow Chart*, have continued to demonstrate his sense of humor and his penchant for bizarre juxtapositions of words and phrases and experimentation with poetic form.

Critics frequently note the influence of visual art and film in Ashbery's verse, observing that Ashbery's experience as an art critic has instilled him with a sensitivity to the interrelatedness of visual and verbal artistic mediums. The abstract expressionist movement in modern painting, which stresses nonrepresentational methods of picturing reality, is a particularly important presence in his poems, which are often viewed as "verbal canvases." In *The Tennis Court Oath*, for example, Ashbery intermingles disjointed words and phrases to create the impression of the multiple and shifting details of visual perception. The influence of film is apparent in Ashbery's celebrated *Self-Portrait in a Convex Mirror*, which incorporates poetic techniques that create the effect of crosscuts, flashbacks, montages, and fade-outs. Although some critics have faulted the seemingly rambling and disconnected quality of these works, supporters of Ashbery's art assert that Ashbery's poetry reflects the open-ended and multifarious quality of sensory perception. In an essay Ashbery commented: "Why shouldn't a painting tell a story, or not tell it, as it sees fit? Why should poetry be intellectual and nonsensory, or the reverse? Our eyes, minds, and feelings do not exist in isolated compartments but are part of each other, constantly crosscutting, consulting and reinforcing each other."

Throughout his career Ashbery has experimented with a diverse range of poetic forms. Often considered one of his most difficult works, *The Tennis Court Oath* presents disjointed and surrealistic poems that have been likened to visual collages. A more restrained use of language characterizes *Three Poems,* in which Ashbery's stream-of-consciousness technique conveys subtle transformations of mood, tone, and image. "Litany," the long poem included in Ashbery's critically-acclaimed volume *As We Know: Poems,* offers another example of poetic experimentation in its presentation of two columns of verse that function, according to Ashbery, as "simultaneous but independent monologues." Ashbery turned to traditional poetic structure in *A Wave,* the winner of the Lenore Marshall/Nation Poetry Prize. The volume, which utilizes such conventional forms as the sonnet and the masque, received praise for its use of distinctly American idioms to explore elusive aspects of experience—the title poem, for example, is a meditation on love, death, and transformation that fluctuates between mysterious and ordinary images and emotions, personal and universal concerns, and objective and subjective perception.

Critics often emphasize Ashbery's continuing interest in the complex relationships between perception, reality, and the process of creating art. His self-reflexive poem "Self-Portrait in a Convex Mirror," for example, was inspired by Francesco Parmigianino's self-portrait of the same title. In this work Ashbery juxtaposes observations based on Parmigianino's painting with images of himself at work on the poem. The nature of perception and the human psyche is also a prominent motif in *April Galleons,* in which Ashbery employs a characteristically disjointed style to explore the complex relationship between language, consciousness, and knowledge; this motif also extends to *Selected Poems,* in which he addresses the private and inarticulated aspects of emotional experience. Also representative of Ashbery's poetic process is his 1991 work *Flow Chart,* a book-length poem that encompasses an expansive range of subject matter in a ruminating, trance-like style. Many reviewers have asserted that *Flow Chart* addresses the complexity of human experience and reveals Ashbery's concern with contemporary moral consciousness despite its characteristically farcical tone.

Ashbery is considered a prominent and influential figure in the mainstream of American poetry and is among the most highly honored poets of his generation. Howard Wamsley asserted: "The chances are very good that he will dominate the last third of the century as Yeats . . . dominated the first." Although his poetry is occasionally faulted for obscurity, many critics argue that traditional critical approaches often lead to misinterpretations of Ashbery's works, which are concerned with the process of creating art rather than the final product. Harold Bloom, for example, views the disjointed quality of Ashbery's verse as an element of his originality and maintains that Ashbery is a revolutionary figure in the American Romantic literary tradition that includes Walt Whitman and Wallace Stevens. Helen Vendler commented: "Ashbery is, above all, a poet of the moral life, but his means are the means of farce: pratfalls, absurd scenarios, preposterous coincidences, a Chaplinesque wistfulness, and—

something often absent in farce—a hatful of colored scarves of language."

PRINCIPAL WORKS

The Heroes (drama) 1952
Turandot and Other Poems (poetry) 1953
The Compromise (drama) 1956
Some Trees (poetry) 1956
The Poems (poetry) 1960
The Tennis Court Oath (poetry) 1962
The Philosopher (drama) 1964
Rivers and Mountains (poetry) 1966
Selected Poems (poetry) 1967
Sunrise in Suburbia (poetry) 1968
Fragment (poetry) 1969
A Nest of Ninnies [with James Schuyler] (novel) 1969
Three Madrigals (poetry) 1969
The Double Dream of Spring (poetry) 1970
The New Spirit (poetry) 1970
Three Poems (poetry) [with Joe Brainard] 1972
Self-Portrait in a Convex Mirror (poetry) 1975
The Vermont Notebook (poetry) 1975
Houseboat Days (poetry) 1977
*Three Plays (drama) 1978
As We Know: Poems (poetry) 1979
Shadow Train: Fifty Lyrics (poetry) 1981
A Wave (poetry) 1984
Selected Poems (poetry) 1985
April Galleons (poetry) 1987
Flow Chart (poetry) 1991
Hotel Lautreamont (poetry) 1992

*This work contains *The Heroes, The Compromise,* and *The Philosopher.*

CRITICISM

John Ashbery with John Koethe   (interview date 1982)

[*In the following interview, conducted on 3 April 1982, Ashbery discusses significant influences on the development of his career as well as his views on contemporary poetry and the craft of writing.*]

[*John Koethe*]: *When you first started writing poetry, or when you were writing in the fifties, there seemed to be a very different poetry scene than there is now—something you could call an academic establishment, with which you didn't ally yourself. Could you describe the way you saw poetry then and the way the poetry world strikes you now, since it seems to be somewhat different?*

[John Ashbery]: Actually, I did identify a lot with much of the poetry then that would be considered academic, I suppose. I admired a number of poets like Delmore Schwartz, for instance, as well as a lot of lesser known people who have appeared in the Oscar Williams Anthology every year. And I've always felt that is a period that's been rather overlooked. There were a lot of very interesting poets then. Maybe it was just because I began reading contemporary poetry at that time. But somehow the thirties and forties in American poetry are kind of blank, unlike the twenties, with Cummings, Eliot and so on. Many of the poets I read when I first became aware of modern poetry have not had any lasting influence. My earliest poetic efforts were trying to sound like these forties poets without having any real sense. Schwartz was one of my models, and one of my first poetry "crushes" was Muriel Rukeyser. I liked a lot of women poets then, such as Jean Garrigue and Ruth Hershberger. It was thrilling when I finally got to New York and met Jean Garrigue.

What was it then that made people like you, Frank O'Hara, and Kenneth Koch more comfortable with people in the music and art worlds than with people in university or literary circles?

I think around 1950, with the rise of Robert Lowell, everything became much more codified and academicized. It seems that the fifties were stricter and more structured than the forties and thirties. Randall Jarrell said in an essay I once read that "in this post-Auden climate, it seems that a coat hanger could write a marvelous poem about the delights and torments of being a college professor."

How does the poetry world strike you today? It seems much more diffuse, much more eclectic than it was in the fifties. Has this had any effect on the way you conceive of what it is you are doing in relation to other writers?

Not so much. Once I started writing the way I do, I lost interest in following contemporary poetry and now only read it occasionally when a student—Benjamin Sloane, for instance—presents me with a poem. And I don't keep up anymore in the way I felt I had to when I was first writing. There are a few people whose work I follow with interest: James Tate, Sandra MacPherson, Elizabeth Bishop (who is now dead). But I no longer feel I have to keep in contact and touch every base in order to figure out what I'm doing, because I've already figured it out and for better or worse, I'm doing it. What I'm doing doesn't really have much relation to what I read.

In the early sixties, you were thought of as the quintessential avant-garde poet. Do you think of yourself that way, or did you then? Do you have any conception of what the avant-garde is now? And did you then?

No. And in the early sixties, I don't think my poetry was being read at all, and I don't think I was considered the quintessential avant-garde poet.

Let us roll the scene back several hundred years. What sorts of poets—pre-twentieth century poets—interest you, since you seem to read earlier poets more extensively than do many contemporary poets?

When I decided to write poetry, I really didn't get much out of poetry of the past and was only turned on by con-

temporary poets. Gradually I've become more *retardataire* and don't read so much modern poetry. The poetry of the past, which seemed like museum exhibits to me when I first read it, doesn't anymore. This week my favorite poets are Tennyson and Suckling. Next week, who knows? When I was in high school and even college, the poets we read in classes were Longfellow, Tennyson, Browning, and if you were lucky, you got up to Robert Frost. Today everybody is thoroughly modern. They read *me* in high schools. But I didn't understand the poetry of the past. It didn't affect me the way contemporary poetry written at the present moment had. It took a long time for this to happen.

How does poetry of the present or past affect you? Does it stimulate you to write your own works or is there a certain thing it does to you that you find pleasant and enjoyable?

I think both probably. I get envious of the successful forms of the past, like those of Spenser or Donne. It may be a kind of reaction that has set in, as with De Chirico who renounced all of modern art and went back to paint like Rubens and Rembrandt.

It sounds as though your conception of poetry is a rather static one—not one that is constantly progressing and changing but, relatively speaking, always with us.

Well, I suppose so, but I also read a lot of things that aren't poetry that I find very useful, like seed catalogues, high school yearbooks, cereal boxes.

How do you conceive of poetry in relation to writing in general? Is there some distinction in your mind between the two or is it all more or less continuous? What are you doing when you're writing poetry that you wouldn't be doing if you were, say, writing an essay?

I like the situation of trying to communicate something to somebody even in the crudest forms of yellow journalism. I get carried away and start to cry when I read some article in a tabloid newspaper about a woman who accidentally flushed her baby down the toilet or something like that. This seems like real life.

When you are writing poetry, do you have someone in mind to whom you are trying to communicate something?

I do, but it's no particular person. I suppose it's probably me. I desperately want to communicate something to someone but I don't know who that person is. So, I'll have to do until someone better comes along.

Have you ever written any sort of love poetry or poetry directed towards a particular individual?

Not really. I write off of particular individuals, let's say. When I decided to write **Three Poems,** I couldn't figure out what to write, so I asked my psychoanalyst, who is sort of unconventional and unorthodox—I suppose they all are—what should I do? I would really like to write this long poem and have it be very interesting and full of information and political goodies, but I don't have anything to say. And he said, "Well, let's see, what could you do? Why don't you try thinking about people who have meant a lot to you in your life and then instead of writing about them, write about what you feel when you think about them?"

So I did. I thought about various people whom I was in love with and my dead brother and my parents, and so on.

Is there any discernible connection between what you wrote while thinking about these people and the people themselves?

Sort of. I won't tell you what it is.

You mentioned Elizabeth Bishop as one of your favorite poets but I don't believe you've ever, with a few exceptions, written poems which are primarily descriptive of places or locations, though locations seem to mean a lot to you in your poems. Is naturalistic poetry something that you've ever thought of doing or plan to do?

No. I like Bishop's poetry because it's so unlike mine. I read to be entertained and to discover someone who doesn't resemble me in the least. I find her poetry terribly exciting because she can describe something perfectly and not draw any moral from it, and she doesn't have to at that point.

Would you talk about the various things that have influenced your conception of poetry—for example the climate of opinion that you encountered when you were living in France for those ten years? What sort of effect did it have on the way you perceived your own poetry and, say, American poetry?

The intellectual climate didn't rub off on me very much. I had a horror of French intellectuals which remains with me to this very day. And the idea that you could explain everything and *then* do it is, I think, an appalling notion. Basically, what was valuable for me when I was living in France was being totally out of touch with American poetry and feeling totally lost and knowing what I was going to do and not getting any input whatever from what was happening in France.

Your book **The Tennis Court Oath** *was mostly written while you were in France. You've said that you don't feel terribly close to it anymore, but would you talk about what you had in mind when you were writing it?*

I was kind of scrounging around to find some new way of writing that would appeal to me because I was already satisfied with *Some Trees* but didn't want to go on writing in that way, whatever that way is. It was mainly a question of grouping for different things, knowing what I didn't want to do and not really knowing what I did want to do. I suppose it was rather valuable being cut off from everything. Also, at that time people started to become interested in my poetry but I didn't know it for years—that might have been good too. If I had been living in New York and someone had told me that I had just written a terrific poem, I might have been conditioned by it to go on writing in the same way. But, there I was rather isolated and enjoying the life in France very much.

Do you stop and cast about and try to do something different periodically? It sounds as though you were doing that with **Three Poems.**

Yes, I'm always trying to do that and don't succeed very often, the main reason being that I continue to be the same person.

What is it that you don't like about **The Tennis Court Oath** *now, or why don't you feel as close to it as you once did?*

Those poems were more in the line of sketches that I thought I would recycle into something more finished. Most of the poems in that work seem somewhat tentative and experimental. There are some poems though in that book where I felt I actually had succeeded in writing in a new way that was satisfactory to me, such as **"They Dream Only of America"** and **"How Long Will I Be Able To. . . ."**

Is **"Idaho"** *the first sort of mixed prose and verse you wrote? I don't recall anything before that.*

I think so. But then, for reasons I never understood, I abandoned that way of writing which, in fact, fulfilled my specifications for what I wanted to do and it got lost in things like **"Europe"** and **"Measles"** and those other peculiar poems. I don't know quite what happened.

Many of those who are interested in your poetry seem to be interested in it in connection with theoretical ideas, particularly French theoretical ideas, like those of Jacques Derrida. Do you ever read works by such theorists, or do their views influence you secondhand, or do you ever use them in any way?

No. I think I'm very good subject matter for people who are trying to elaborate new theories of criticism. Perhaps it would be better for me if I didn't know anything about them because then I might consciously try to write stuff that would fit their theories.

One constant theme in your poetry is a certain puzzlement about the point of writing poetry and about what will become of poetry, as in the moving part at the end of **"Syringa"** *when it all disappears onto microfilm.*

I suppose so . . . yes. Occasionally, people ask me why I write poetry, which is a question I've never been able to answer satisfactorily. And my answers have usually been considered arrogant, since people respond with such statements as: "he knows perfectly well why he wants to write poetry, he's just not saying why." I suppose one reason is that I can't do anything else satisfactorily, for myself at least. It comforts me, in a way, to try to explain things to myself as I wander down life's weary path, as it were.

A lot of your work is concerned with time in various ways, such as the passage of time.

Yes. I read Proust at an early age and got involved with the problem of time, and for many years I thought I was writing poetry about nothing, that my poetry didn't have any subject matter. Having reached a fairly advanced age, it seems to me that the subject in my poetry is actually time and getting older—a subject that was not available to me when I was young. And probably, that is mostly what people think about.

Your poetry certainly isn't religious poetry, but there does at times seem to be a certain religious tone to it, or at least an insinuation of concern with things like everlasting life and salvation. Do you have any religious influences in your background, and interest in or fascination with religion?

Yes, though I don't really know much about it. I had a church upbringing and I'm still basically religious but in a way that is satisfactory to me and probably not to God.

Everything seems to be sort of transcendental, a kind of shadow of something else. I read a very beautiful passage in Borges recently about how certain things in life—landscapes, remarks made by strangers, whatever—had a significance that we should have been aware of when it happened but weren't. That seems to be basically what I feel about religion: that somehow we miss the boat at every possible moment. There is always the prospect of grace, but we shouldn't count on it too much.

There are two other general aspects of your poetry which I like very much and want to ask you about. Even though your poems aren't love poems, they often seem to be poems with sex as their unofficial subject. At the very least there's a certain eroticism to the language, which tends to be sensuous in many ways. Are you conscious of this at all?

No. I sometimes throw in a little sex just because you ought to have as many things as possible in a poem. There might be a lot of suppressed or sublimated eroticism in my poetry because, as I say, I write off of people whom I'm thinking about. Some of them are people to whom I'm sexually attracted. But I try to keep that quiet, not out of prudery, but just because it seems there are more important things, though I don't yet know what they are.

Another very distinctive aspect of your poetry is that it is informed by an active, suppressed sense of humor. It is not at all somber and solemn, though it's also usually not straightforwardly funny. What sorts of things do you find funny both in writing and in your life?

Practically everything, I would think. I include humor just as I include somberness and tragedy and sex and whatever else, just because it's something that crops up every day and you should try to make your poem as representative as possible. My poetry is not totally funny, but there is a lot of humor in it which, actually, most people don't get—for example, the line in the Popeye sestina—"If this is all we need fear from spinach, then I don't mind so much"—which no one has ever laughed at, and I think it's terribly funny. Spinach is a sort of atomic force in Popeye. We're supposed to be really scared of what will happen if Popeye ingests spinach, but it turns out that it really doesn't matter that much for the moment as the power of spinach is in abeyance and we can go around leading our lives in an ordinary fashion. As for comic writers or artists who appeal to me, I suppose Ronald Firbank would be considered a comic artist. I think he is much more than that, but I love the humor in his work. I like James Wolcott's articles on TV in the *Village Voice*. George Ade, an Indiana writer, is one of my favorites. He's sort of a humorous proto-Ring Lardner writer of the early 1900s who wrote *Fables in Sland and More Fables in Sland*. Once he was traveling in the Mediterranean with a friend who prided himself on his knowledge of Middle Eastern languages and a toothless old beggar came up to them mumbling something, and the friend was very embarrassed because he couldn't understand what the man was saying despite his knowledge of Middle Eastern languages, and Ade

said, "Don't worry, he was probably speaking Gum-Arabic."

In light of your accommodating and catholic view of what you can put into poetry, is there anything you don't like or find unacceptable in your poems or other people's poems?

Politics. Only for the reason that I don't know of any political poetry that isn't boring. Presumably, somebody will come along and write a political poem that will be absolutely beautiful and mesmerizing, but I've not yet had this experience. Too much sex is also a no-no, just because we think about it all the time, and therefore we don't need to have our knowledge refreshed.

Of course, the same is true of time, as you've said.

I don't think about it all the time; it thinks about me, I would say.

What about compositional techniques or forms that you haven't used yet?

I don't much like sonnets.

But you just wrote a whole book of them.

They're sixteen lines long, however. And I've never written a Pindaric ode although I've asked my students to try (nobody would do it). Heroic couplets don't appeal to me terribly. But I think these are all things that I would like to do just because I don't see any way of doing them at the present time.

What do you have in mind before you write? Do you usually decide that you're going to do some writing during a certain period of the day and then find out what you have to write about, or do you carry around ideas with you until you are ready to use them?

Well, I wait until I have some time when I can write. Usually I've been puzzling over a remark I overheard someone say that doesn't make any sense and I'm wondering exactly what they meant, or I might have seen some object that pleases me such as a store window—these are just little bits of odds and ends that I then summon when I start writing a poem.

Let me ask you about "Litany." Did you have it in mind to write a poem of that sort when you started it? How did you go about writing it day to day?

With a lot of my long poems, I can't remember what I was thinking about before I started writing them and "Litany" is one of them. It seemed to me that I'd been doing it for a while before I realized that I was writing two-column poems. When I was writing "Litany," I wrote one column from the beginning of the page to the end of the page one day, and another column another day, and so on and so forth. I like the idea of two separate voices and of trying to monitor them both at the same time because it's something that happens every day: someone is telling you something very important and at the same time, you're hearing someone at the other end of the room saying something that you'd like to clue into.

You've written poems alternating between voices as far back as I've known your work. There's a poem called "Eclogue" in **Some Trees** *which switches back and forth, and there is also "Fantasia on The Nut-Browne Maid." Do you have any sense of what the difference is between these voices? Is there any general way of characterizing this polarity?*

Well, I hear voices. . . . I don't have any idea of what my own voice is, if indeed I have one, and I'm usually listening rather than talking and what I hear somehow gets written down.

How did you go about writing the poems in **Shadow Train**? *Did you have it in mind to write a fifty-poem sequence?*

Yes, I think I did. Again, that was an artificial concept that was loose enough to let me do what I wanted and strict enough to bring me to the task each time I wanted to do it. I did the same thing with **"Fragment"** actually. That's fifty ten-line stanzas and I decided that I would do two of them each time I sat down to write and not do any more or less. **"Fragment"** took about six months to write but of writing every once in a while. *Shadow Train* took about nine months of irregular periods of writing.

More than most poets, you've written long poems periodically. In a way, you've revived the long poem. Are there any kinds of long poems that you would like to write in the future? You've written long prose and sequence poems, and you've written a continuous meditation, **Self-Portrait in a Convex Mirror.**

I would like to do more but I haven't figured out what form they're going to take yet—in fact I prefer to do that after I've already begun. But I like the idea of writing something that takes a great deal of time because your mind changes while you are doing it and the reader isn't aware at what point you left off and put it aside for two months and then came back; there aren't any seams. The long poem seems to gain a kind of richness from being written by not different poets, but a poet who is different each time.

Self-Portrait in a Convex Mirror, *which expanded your readership, appears philosophically more continuous than some of your poems, in the sense of carrying an argument through to the end. Do you want to do that again, or is that something you wanted to do just one time?*

I guess it's something that I wanted to do just that one time and I think its continuity is actually very specious. It seems to have fooled a lot of people. I think if it were examined closely, it would be found to be just as "incoherent" as my more notorious long poems. It's not a poem that I particularly like—it seems too serious.

Creative writing as a subject open to everyone is a recent development in American education. Since the mid-seventies, you've been teaching poetry. What is your experience of teaching poetry and what sorts of techniques do you find work? Do you think it's a good idea on the whole since it's not something that you ever learned when you were young? Do you think there is any danger that creative writing classes "professionalize" poetry in a way that discourages experimentation?

Teaching creative writing is a very good idea for me because I couldn't make a living otherwise. I don't really

know how it works although it does seem to work. I've noticed that the work of certain poets gets better during the course of the year, but I don't know how that works. I actually did take a poetry writing course when I was an undergraduate, before such things really existed, and I was so pleased to be noticed once in a while by Theodore Spencer, the poet who was teaching the class. It did a lot for me though the assignments he gave weren't really very interesting or provocative. I think it's very valuable for me to act just the way I am and not pretend to be any smarter or nicer than I actually am and to really be quite silly every now and then. This destroys the artificial barrier between me and the students. They realize that not only am I not any smarter, I'm really not a better person than they are. But I think a lot of poets use creative writing classes for ego trips and invent all sorts of artificial disciplines and act professional. That's not something I do. My classes are really on a sort of low conversational level. Yet I think that the more demotic the discussion becomes, the better it is for all of us.

One final area: the difference between written and spoken poetry, and the idea of poetry as something you read on the page as opposed to something you read aloud. Many people think it makes a great deal of difference how you conceive of poetry—as something to be heard or something to be read. Do you think it makes much difference, and do you tend to conceive of your own work as primarily something to be read on the page rather than heard?

I, myself, enjoy reading it rather than hearing it read. On the other hand, the input for my poetry seems to come from colloquial talk and the inaccurate ways we present our ideas to other people and yet succeed in doing so despite our sloppiness. On the other hand, I don't really like to hear it, I would rather see it. I can hear it better when I see it. I seldom go to poetry readings, and I don't like performance poetry. The word "performance" reminds me of a line in *Hebdomeros* by De Chirico. I forget exactly what it is that sets off the hero at that particular point. I think it is the idea of eating oysters, or strawberries and cream. The line is: "It made him flee like Orestes pursued by the Furies." The word "performance" has a similar effect on me. (pp. 178-86)

John Ashbery and John Koethe, in an interview in Sub-Stance, *Nos. 37-38, 1983, pp. 178-86.*

Brooke Horvath   (essay date Autumn 1984)

[*In the following essay, Horvath discusses the role of memory and the past in Ashbery's poetry, using examples from the collection* Houseboat Days.]

This essay offers an introductory reading of John Ashbery's poetry as it relates to memory and tradition, with the intent to make more accessible a poet often faulted for excessive obscurity and to account in passing for certain features of his poetics often regarded as faults. I use here poems from *Houseboat Days* because this book, representative of his work in general, is Ashbery's most readable and enjoyable work to date.

Ashbery's best work uses memory to construct tolerable

worlds in which the poet can feel at home. Though this may be a practice endemic in modern poetry (one thinks, immediately, of Whitman and Stevens), Ashbery seems to be among those who believe that any received tradition is bound to fail, that any given form of order succumbs before the unrelatedness of the stuff of life as it plunges "unchecked through the sluices / Of the days" (**"The Other Tradition"**). Thus, any pattern or tradition imposed upon experience to render it livable must necessarily be personal. If Ashbery's fictive worlds do not constitute our reality, that is not their function. Likewise, if his "results" are, at times, almost incomprehensibly private, that, too, is part of the point: for Ashbery seems to be showing how each of us must construct his own pleasing, habitable world that will, through memory's transformative power, render experience meaningful and time harmless. The poems, then, become illustrations of the possibility of living sanely and happily, not exemplums for how to live. In **"Fantasia on 'The Nut-Brown Maid,' "** Ashbery writes, "Life is a living picture." And like a composed picture, life is finally what one chooses to include, how one chooses to see. In **"Collective Dawns"** he says, "You can have whatever you want. / Own it, I mean. In the sense / Of twisting it to you, through long, spiralling afternoons."

However, beyond the transcending of what may be a rather boring or trivial reality through the creation of dream landscapes manufactured from one's past, time remains a problem. Ashbery's poems ask how to compose a livable reality—hence, how to define the self—from the flux of disjunctive and often trivial and unintelligible events that emerge from a dubious future only to fade away into a past recalled fitfully, if at all. The past, as Marjorie Perloff has demonstrated [in "Tangled Versions of Truth," *The American Poetry Review,* Vol. 7, September/October, 1978] with regard to certain poems in ***Houseboat Days,*** is problematic because it is so sporadically remembered, punctured throughout with forgotten spaces and stitched together with the threads of fiction:

> . . . progress occurs through re-inventing
> These words from a dim recollection of them,
> In violating that space in such a way as
> To leave it intact
>
> (**"Blue Sonata"**)

Throughout **"Blue Sonata,"** the poet argues that the past is always our destiny, because it is always through the past that we define ourselves and prepare to meet the future: we exist in an interpretation, violating the world "in such a way as / To leave it intact." Only through violation of the space in which we exist can this space become meaningful, coherent, inhabitable. And this is why, after all, we do belong here: it is each of us, in his own way, who creates the world. "Our understanding . . . is justified," because it orders the sighs of time.

If the past is problematic, the present, which is the sum of the past "re-invented" and "re-imagined" (**"Blue Sonata"**), is consequently even more so. Too frequently, we are the victims of time, although we fancy ourselves in control. As we read in **"Syringa,"** Ashbery's retelling of the Orpheus and Eurydice myth, "it isn't enough / To just go on singing," to move uncritically through time. Still, even

to define our lives as we move through time may not be enough, for when the song is engulfed in blackness, "The singer / Must then pass out of sight, not even relieved / Of the evil burthen of words." **"Saying It to Keep It from Happening"** tells us, "—it's time / That counts, and how deeply you have invested in it, / Crossing the street of an event, as though coming out of it were / The same as making it happen." Like Nietzsche, Ashbery suggests the discomfiting possibility that finally man is more spoken than speaking. Time, he goes on to say, "is a long field, and we know only the far end of it, / Not the part we presumably had to go through to get there": the present is the most we can really know of time, not the past we went through to arrive at today.

This paradoxical problem—a familiarity with the past as prerequisite for composing a livable present, yet the belief that the present only, and not the past, is knowable—is compounded, because the present is always slipping into the future, a movement not necessarily ameliorative. **"Collective Dawns"** informs us that "Life is getting cheaper / In some senses": "people go around with a fragment of a smile / Missing from their faces," while "The sunset jabs down, angled in a way it couldn't have / Been before." The poet finds the future a continual threat: as "He" tells "She" in **"Fantasia on 'The Nut-Brown Maid,' "** "You are like someone whose face was photographed in a crowd scene once and then gradually retreated from people's memories, and from life as well." If the future does not get much play in Ashbery's work, its imminence is a constant source of anxiety:

> . . . Meanwhile this tent is silence
> Itself. Its walls are opaque, so as not to see
> The road; a pleasant, half-heard melody climbs
>   to its ceiling—
> Not peace, but rest the doctor ordered.
> Tomorrow . . .
>
> (**"Business Personals"**)

The thought of tomorrow trails off in implication. A tranquility sufficient for today has been achieved, but tomorrow, who knows? This same mistrust of futurity is voiced elsewhere. In **"Valentine"** the poet speaks of the way the "different parts" of a string quartet

> . . . are always meddling with each other,
> Pestering each other, getting in each other's way
> So as to withdraw skillfully at the end, leaving—
>   what?
> A new kind of emptiness, maybe bathed in freshness,
> Maybe not. Maybe just a new kind of emptiness.

The problem is the familiar one of determining what it means to be; that is, how to avoid being caught up in change, confusion, and forgetfulness, in simply living one's life to arrive at "a new kind of emptiness"—in a word, to avoid what we masochistically like to call the modern condition or tradition (although anti-tradition is perhaps a better word). In **"The Lament upon the Waters,"** Ashbery writes, "The problem isn't how to proceed / But is one of being: whether this was, and whose / It shall be." It is a question of dealing with the present, of defining ourselves against our pasts in order to discover to whom our lives belong.

[Poetry] for Ashbery seems to be a means of incorporating the anxiety over tomorrow, the randomness and disappointment of today, and the regret for failing yesterdays into livable space.

—*Brooke Horvath*

Furthermore, the individual is alone in his predicament, because experience is necessarily private. This theme, too, is well-known, and Ashbery gave it succinct statement upon receiving the National Book Award for *Self-Portrait in a Convex Mirror* (a title that captures the difficulty of gaining a clear and accurate view even of oneself by reference to some outer "reality"): "For as long as I have been publishing poetry, it has been criticized as 'difficult' and 'private,' though I never meant for it to be. At least, I wanted its privateness to suggest the ways in which all of us are private and alone."

However, a solution is offered, for if time is in large part beyond our control, as are events, and things as they are are finally not enough, we can imaginatively take control of reality and re-see it in personal terms:

> If it isn't enough, take the idea
> Inherent in the day, armloads of wheat and flowers
> Lying around flat on handtrucks, if maybe it
>   means more
> In pertaining to you, yet what is is what happens
>   in the end
> As though you cared
> **("Saying It to Keep It from Happening")**

"The event," the poem concludes, "it's both there / And not there, like washing or sawdust in the sunlight, / At the back of the mind, where we live now." Our careful seeing is the creative "look of force" that transforms the insufficient "idea / Inherent in the day" and creates a world that is "both there / And not there": "not there" because it is only the mind's creation, yet "there" because without this act of creative seeing the world does not exist for the individual—it lacks interest and substance and so does not penetrate to "the back of the mind, where we live now." And it does not much matter what engages our attention (or forms the subject of our poem), as long as we care for it and make it a part of us: "what is is what happens in the end / As though you cared." The answer, for Ashbery at least, is to persuade oneself that what one has (including those shored fragments reflected in the convex mirror of memory) is significant and what one has always wanted. Ashbery takes the teacups and T-shirts, failed affairs and lost opportunities, painful events and impossible fantasies, bits of the past and nonsense of today and transforms them all into a pleasing world he finds sensible and livable. Thus the chaos of the present is ordered, the past captured and defined, and the future's uncertainty cancelled, because whatever may come will undergo an imaginative change as it moves through today into yesterday. And through

this recreative act, the isolation of the self is escaped (cf. **"Valentine"**), because in recollection our love is always returned, communion attained. No matter what has happened or may happen, Ashbery as much as says through these poems, it will be all right once I am finished with it:

> Not what we see but how we see it matters; all's
> Alike, the same, and we greet him who announces
> The change as we would greet the change itself.
> All life is but a figment
> **("Daffy Duck in Hollywood")**

Our songs of yesterday, of which the poet's are exemplary, are necessary, if the floating heart would not drift senselessly. Yet unlike a modernist like Gass, Ashbery would have us remember that our songs, our memory-dreams, are fictive renderings, creating our reality by ordering and informing some *other* reality, our reality taking precedence over this other reality only because it is the pattern we find comprehensible and safe, and to which we choose to subscribe. Grace Schulman argues [in "To Create the Self," *Twentieth Century Literature,* Vol. 23, October, 1977] that Ashbery's work consists of meditations through which the soul strives toward unity by dramatizing "the belief in the power of art to reveal a continuous present and to cut through the limiting divisions of days, hours, and years," for she sees his efforts as "a medium for knowing a hidden objective reality and revealing its beauty." On the other hand, it can be argued that Ashbery's effort is toward creating rather than revealing the present by creating a past, a tradition or pattern of thought, that serves to interpret the present:

> To be able to write the history of our time, starting with today,
> It would be necessary to model all these unimportant details
> So as to be able to include them; otherwise the narrative
> Would have that flat, sandpapered look the sky gets
> Out in the middle west toward the end of summer
>
> **("Pyrography")**

The importance of the everyday is here set paradoxically against the suggestion a few lines later that we go about our business "in spite of everything": "Therefore, since we have to do our business / In spite of things, why not make it in spite of everything?" I take this to mean that one's private world is at once conjured from the everyday details that fill life, and yet a gesture distinct from any objective reality. Thus, **"All Kinds of Caresses"** ends with praise for the mental gestures that become us: "Our gestures have taken us farther into the day / Than tomorrow will understand. / They live us."

The solution Ashbery offers accounts for the quality of his poems. The domestic and ordinary predominate because he realizes that the props and settings of life are most often common and homey. For the same reason, his language is often colloquial, flat, clichéd, and sometimes vulgar. The creation of fictive worlds from a past that he recognizes is never lost, though hard to know "exactly," explains his fascination with the pleasing fictions about him:

movies, comics, romance literature, myth. His sense of staging or dramatizing life accounts for the metaphor of the theater that runs throughout his work. Again, the creation of dream worlds must yield poems that operate according to the logic of dreams rather than the logic of the rhetoric class. And to see this clarifies, in part, Ashbery's peculiar voice, meandering syntax, and juxtaposition of seemingly unrelated objects and events.

It is this world-transforming power of memory that saves us, finally, from the isolation that Auden called our entrapment in "the cell of the self." Left to construct a place tolerable to himself, how can the individual relate to others? This self-expressive function of memory is necessary; however, as Georges Gusdorf, for example, argues [in *La Parole,* 1963], we purchase self-expression at the cost of greater self-isolation. Perhaps this is why Ashbery spends too much time apparently addressing himself or some hoped-for, unspecified other. Yet **"Valentine,"** a love poem in verse and prose to a friend who is not present and never visits, suggests an answer. After analyzing this friendship, expressing regret for its shortcomings, and hoping for its healthier future growth, the poet concludes his recollections by returning to the present moment of the poem's composition:

> These things I write for you and you only.
> Do not judge them too harshly. Temper the wind,
> As he [that is, the poet] was saying, They are infant things
> That may grow up to be children, perhaps—who knows?—
> Even adults some day, but now they exist only in the blindness
> Of your love for me and are the proof of it.
> . . . . . .
>   I am the inhabitable one.
> But my back is as a door to you, now open, now shut,
> And your kisses are as dreams, or an elixir
> Of radium, or flowers of some kind.
> Remember about what I told you.

Is the poem addressed to some unnamed friend, the reader, or the poet himself? All three readings are possible and none lacks problems. Still, what is clear is that communion of some sort has been achieved or seen as possible and the isolation of the self dissolved in the calming solution of memory, in which everything can become (if we know our business) more to our liking. It is this desire for communion that may explain, too, the poems' difficulty: they are poetic acts calculated to detain the reader, to keep him from immediately understanding and so deserting the poet.

In **"What Is Poetry,"** Ashbery recalls school discussions in which the meaning of a poem was all that counted; he concludes that it was what was left after this intellectual gleaning that constituted a poem's charm for him:

> . . . . In school
> All thought got combed out:
> What was left was like a field.
> Shut your eyes and you can feel it for miles around.

> Now open them on a thin vertical path.
> It might give us—what?—some flowers soon?

Poetry, then, for Ashbery seems to be a means of incorporating the anxiety over tomorrow, the randomness and disappointment of today, and the regret for failing yesterdays into livable space. **"The Thief of Poetry"** concludes:

> you come back so seldom
> but it's all right
> . . . .
> The dream you lost
> firm in its day
> reassured and remembered.

Beyond any extractable meanings, it is the dream of life, always in danger of being lost, that the poem can give us, persuade us is true, along with a few flowers, perhaps, with which to decorate the rooms of memory, where we live now. (pp. 55-61)

> *Brooke Horvath, "Dwelling in Persuasion: John Ashbery's Dream of Life," in* Ball State University Forum, *Vol. XXV, No. 4, Autumn, 1984, pp. 55-62.*

David Rigsbee   (essay date 1984)

[*In the following essay, Rigsbee responds to charges that Ashbery's poetry is obscure.*]

Reaction to John Ashbery's poetry has ranged from the grandiose ["It is likely that he will come to dominate the second half of this century just as Yeats dominated the first."] to the contemptuously dismissive ["garbage"]. Among the older literary establishment schooled in the New Criticism, "Ashbery" has become a metonymy for all that is suspect in American poetry: Lack of discernible structure, lack of clear referentiality, lack of subject. Similar suspicions have been held against Ashbery from other outposts on the literary horizon: the acolytes of Pound, the West Coast poets, the town gang, the parochial poets of the so-called "deep image." I am exaggerating, of course, but not by much. The fact that hostility to Ashbery is so geographically and culturally widespread testifies to his vitality as an upsetter of all the varieties of *status quo* in which American poetry is currently sequestered.

I remember several incidents from my own experience that served to indicate to me the ambiguous regard with which Ashbery's poetry is held. When I was a scruffy undergraduate at Chapel Hill, I once walked into my poetry workshop bearing a just-bought copy of **The Double Dream of Spring.** My teacher, the poet Carolyn Kizer, glanced at my book and asked, "You *like* him?" And followed with the more ominous and unanswerable, "*What* do you like about him?" A few years later at a poetry festival, I happened to ask Stanley Kunitz in a general sort of way if he "liked" Ashbery. "Yes," he said, adding with the good-natured laughter of one who has seen much, "but his poems are so *boring*!" I could add to this the way a genuinely disgruntled Donald Davie shouldered his way out of a symposium on John Ashbery's poetry at the MLA convention in 1977. At this meeting, a panel of speakers ranging in enthusiasm from full partisanship (Marjorie Perloff) to qualified approval (myself) had managed to mystify the Ashbery case to the point where it was not clear who was more obscure: Ashbery or his friendly exegetes.

The question of obscurity, indeed of some kind of willful literary fraud, clings to Ashbery still. What I propose to do here is to address my remarks to this question of obscurity, to break it down into its specific component questions, and to attempt to answer these briefly in turn, using **"Self-Portrait in a Convex Mirror,"** as my primary point of departure. As I see it, the charge of unnecessary obscurity fall into three categories: 1) anti-lyricism/lack of subject matter or subject instability; 2) shifting pronouns; and 3) excessive self-referentiality.

The charges that Ashbery's poems are not "lyrical" presuppose a critical consensus about the nature of lyricism that is fundamentally historical. And indeed, the strain of lyrical, subject-oriented, essentially elegiac poetry is the predominate groove of the English poetic genius and comprises much of the syllabus of poetic literacy from the Tudor period right down to the Twentieth Century. The lyric poem, as we have come to appreciate and understand it, depicts a so-called "privileged moment" of insight and underwrites a notion that such moments (while in fact imaginative reenactments) not only sum up but displace other possible moments according to a historically-grounded scale of accepted values—Petrarchan love conventions, for example, proceed from a shared vision of the world.

But where today do we have a "shared vision of the world?" And in what sort of commonality might we ground a lyricism? I do not mean to suggest that the lyricism of, say, Keats, is no longer viable, only that it becomes increasingly more difficult to, as it were, pass the insights. Reinforcing the old varieties is one way, as these are taken for granted, and this has in fact dominated the poetries of a good many of our best contemporary poets, ranging from Denise Levertov and David Ignatow all the way to Maxine Kumin and Howard Nemerov. But there is now an ascending feeling that we, in a sense, "Know all that." As Ashbery puts it:

> My poetry is often criticized for a failure to communicate, but I take issue with this; my intention is to communicate and my feeling is that a poem that communicates something that's already known to the reader is not really communicating anything to him and in fact shows a lack of respect for him.

Consequently, the mission of poetry shifts from a subject-oriented one to a, so to say, "poetically-oriented" one. This is not to suggest that the skeptics of the "old lyricism" are themselves devoid of subject matter, but as Ashbery, again, explains,

> I feel that subject matter is, might well be, some tributary part of a poem; because I think when there is a poem—take a poem of the past, for instance, a poem by Hardy or [Matthew Arnold's] "Dover Beach," or something like that where the meaning is perfectly clear, the subject matter is common knowledge and it's the other things that get included into the poem that raise it to

the level of poetry. I suppose one might say really that subject matter is a kind of structure which gets transformed in the process of the poem's being written. . . .

This shift, moreover, tends to free poetry from the old burden of morally-bound signification, by which I mean that language moves toward being a thing-in-itself, relatively autonomous, and distanced from the adulterated language of daily use—language that leftist critics, for instance, identify with "false consciousness," the surrender of discourse itself to the requirements of the *status quo*. In noticing this shift, we also begin to notice the political character of Ashbery's work—the subtle, inside moves that are implicitly critical of much contemporary discourse. A typical send-up occurs in the notorious poem, **"Decoy,"** which begins,

> We hold these truths to be self-evident:
> That ostracism, both political and social
> Has its place in the 20th Century scheme of
>   things . . .

We might also notice that Ashbery generously punctures his *own* discourse in **"Self-Portrait"** in a later poem called **"Daffy Duck in Hollywood,"** in which Daffy exclaims,

> I scarce dare approach me mug's attenuated
> Reflection in your hubcap. . . .

Parmigianino—or perhaps Ashbery—reduced to the quackings of a cartoon duck.

If we accept the assertion that the lyric poem in English (and American) is itself a convention, with its rules of what is or is not acceptable, with its monumentalizing, if you will, of past moments of insight, we can begin to understand the need of a consciousness like Ashbery's which is (as he says in 1. 396 of **"Self-Portrait"**)

> Always creating into his present . . .

to formulate a more inclusive method of poetic expression. Again, as he writes in **"Self Portrait"** (ll. 414-422):

> We don't need paintings or
> Doggerel written by mature poets when
> The explosion is so precise, so fine.
> Is there any point even in acknowledging
> The existence of all that? Does it
> Exist? Certainly the leisure to
> Indulge stately pastimes doesn't
> Anymore. Today has no margins, the event ar-
>   rives
> Flush with its edges.

We might do well to disgress here for a moment to consider that the need for inclusiveness was not always paramount to Ashbery's aesthetic. Like Beckett, he once engaged in a "leaving-out business" asking "What can I leave out and still have a poem?" The result was the disastrously boring elliptical experiments of **The Tennis Court Oath,** a book that, more than any other, spawned the sad rumor of Ashbery's unintelligibility. Clearly, for a poet of sensibility and nuance, the method of surrealistic pastiche was not the way to go.

Neither, meanwhile, were the old Romantic notions of transcendence. And this reminds me of a naughty anecdote. An old Emeritus professor of my acquaintance, a Wordsworth scholar, sat through the honors examination of a senior English major, who in turn persisted in yammering on and on about transcendence in the lyrics of Wordsworth. Finally the old professor turned to the student (actually turned *on* the student) and with the voice of doom told him what he could do with his transcendence. Even Wordsworthians realize that all is not well in the search for transcendent values:

> Longing to be free, outside, but it (the soul) must stay
> Posing in this place. It must move
> As little as possible. This is what the portrait says.
> But there is in that gaze a combination
> Of tenderness, amusement, and regret, so powerful
> In its restraint that one cannot look for long.
> The secret is too plain. The pity of it smarts,
> Makes hot tears spurt: that the soul is not a soul,
> Has no secret, is small, and it fits
> Its hollow perfectly. . . .
> ["Self-Portrait" ll. 37-46]

. . . . .

A great many well-meaning readers of Ashbery become unhinged by his pronouns that have no discoverable antecedents. On this point, Ashbery himself is disarmingly candid:

> The personal pronouns in my work very often seem to be like variables in an equation. "You" can be myself or it can be another person, someone whom I'm addressing, and so can "he" and "she" for that matter "we"; sometimes one has to deduce from the rest of the sentence what is being meant and my point is also that it doesn't really matter very much, that we are somehow all aspects of a consciousness giving rise to the poem and the fact of addressing someone, myself or someone else, is what's the important thing at that particular moment rather than the particular person involved. I guess I don't have a very strong sense of my own identity, and I find it very easy to move from one person in the sense of a pronoun to another and this again helps to produce a kind of polyphony in my poetry which I again feel is a means toward greater naturalism.

. . . . .

The charge that Ashbery's poems are ultimately self-referential is analogous to the charge of self-referentiality of modern abstract art, a charge that, to my mind, has been adequately met. When one comes right down to it, no language text can be ultimately self-referential for the simple fact that words have their context in the world. The burden of inclusiveness, of trying "to get it all in" sometimes gives one the impression of self-referentiality, but the fact is that if, as he says, "the event arrives flush with its edges," and if the project is to communicate a sense of this, one can easily feel intimidated—there is a code, the key to which is apparently missing. By the same token—and moving on to the next dimension—one can feel lost

in the present tense. As he says in line 151 of **"Self-Portrait"**:

> Tomorrow is easy, but today is uncharted

One is not surprised that Ashbery wishes to commune with a self-portrait of the past. If the past is brought to the present, by a quick ratio we realize that the inner is made manifest on the surface:

> Your eyes proclaim
> That everything is surface. The surface is what's there.
> And nothing can exist except what's there.
> (ll.80-83)

Thus the surface is to space as the present is to time, and the inner psychic state of the city, indeed of America, is made manifest in what the city, New York, is for the poet in 1974: a slum. This intolerable state of affairs, this anxiety, resonates through the poem's landscape.

Finally, one should mention that interpretation presupposes a set of critical tools. Most of the current criticism of Ashbery falls short of taking an account of his inclusiveness for the reason that his output and range have so far exceeded the tools available—one might say the vocabulary available—for adequate criticism. Every poet creates the audience by which he is understood, or as Ashbery puts it in **"The New Spirit"**:

> In you I fall apart, and outwardly am a single fragment, a puzzle to itself. But we must learn to live in others, no matter how abortive or unfriendly their cold, piecemeal renderings of us: they *create* us.
> (pp. 49-53)

David Rigsbee, "Some Notes on the Obscurity of John Ashbery," in Penbroke Magazine, *No. 16, 1984, pp. 49-53.*

Harold Bloom   (essay date 1985)

[*Bloom is one of the most prominent American critics and literary theorists. In* The Anxiety of Influence *(1973), he advanced a theory called revisionism that is based on a perceived authorial urge for individuality of literary voice and vision. Bloom claims that in order to overcome the influence of earlier literary figures, each author deliberately revises, or "misreads," texts, imposing interpretations that conform to his or her own personal philosophy. Thus, there is no single reading of any text, but multiple readings by authors and critics who understand a work in ways that allow them to assert their own individuality or vision. Bloom is an ardent supporter of Ashbery, whom he views as a literary descendant of Wallace Stevens. The following essay, written as the introduction to the collection of critical essays* John Ashbery, *is derived from his works* The Anxiety of Influence *and* A Map of Misreading *(1975). Here, he discusses the relationship between Ashbery's poetry and the works of Wallace Stevens, and considers Ashbery's relationship to the American literary tradition.*]

In the exquisite squalors of Tennyson's *The Holy Grail,* as Percival rides out on his ruinous quest, we can experience the hallucination of believing that the Laureate is overly influenced by *The Waste Land,* for Eliot too became a master at reversing the *apophrades.* Or, in our present moment, the achievement of John Ashbery in his powerful poem **"Fragment"** (in his volume *The Double Dream of Spring*) is to return us to Stevens, somewhat uneasily to discover that at moments Stevens sounds rather too much like Ashbery, an accomplishment I might not have thought possible.

The strangeness added to beauty by the positive *apophrades* is of that kind whose best expositor was Pater. Perhaps all Romantic style, at its heights, depends upon a successful manifestation of the dead in the garments of the living, as though the dead poets were given a suppler freedom than they had found for themselves. Contrast the Stevens of "Le Monocle de Mon Oncle" with the **"Fragment"** of John Ashbery, the most legitimate of the sons of Stevens:

> Like a dull scholar, I behold, in love,
> An ancient aspect touching a new mind.
> It comes, it blooms, it bears its fruit and dies.
> This trivial trope reveals a way of truth.
> Our bloom is gone. We are the fruit thereof.
> Two golden gourds distended on our vines,
> Into the autumn weather, splashed with frost,
> Distorted by hale fatness, turned grotesque.
> We hang like warty squashes, streaked and
>   rayed,
> The laughing sky will see the two of us,
> Washed into rinds by rotting winter rains.
>   (—"Le Monocle," VIII)

> Like the blood orange we have a single
> Vocabulary all heart and all skin and can see
> Through the dust of incisions the central perim-
>   eter
> Our imaginations orbit. Other words,
> Old ways are but the trappings and appurte-
>   nances
> Meant to install change around us like a grotto.
> There is nothing laughable
> In this. To isolate the kernel of
> Our imbalance and at the same time back up
>   carefully
> Its tulip head whole, an imagined good.
>   (—"Fragment," XIII)

An older view of influence would remark that the second of these stanzas "derives" from the first, but an awareness of the revisionary ratio of *apophrades* unveils Ashbery's relative triumph in his involuntary match with the dead. This particular strain, while it matters, is not central to Stevens, but is the greatness of Ashbery whenever, with terrible difficulty, he can win free to it. When I read "Le Monocle de Mon Oncle" now, in isolation from other poems by Stevens, I am compelled to hear Ashbery's voice, for this mode has been captured by him, inescapably and perhaps forever. When I read **"Fragment,"** I tend not to be aware of Stevens, for his presence has been rendered benign. In early Ashbery, amid the promise and splendors of his first volume, *Some Trees,* the massive dominance of Stevens could not be evaded, though a *clinamen* away from the master had already been evidenced:

> The young man places a bird-house

> Against the blue sea. He walks away
> And it remains. Now other

> Men appear, but they live in boxes.
> The sea protects them like a wall.
> The gods worship a line-drawing

> Of a woman, in the shadow of the sea
> Which goes on writing. Are there
> Collisions, communications on the shore

> Or did all secrets vanish when
> The woman left? Is the bird mentioned
> In the waves' minutes, or did the land advance?
>   (—**"Le livre est sur la table,"** II)

This is the mode of "The Man with the Blue Guitar," and urgently attempts to swerve away from a vision whose severity it cannot bear:

> Slowly the ivy on the stones
> Becomes the stones. Women become

> The cities, children become the fields
> And men in waves become the sea.

> It is the chord that falsifies.
> The sea returns upon the men,

> The fields entrap the children, brick
> Is a weed and all the flies are caught,

> Wingless and withered, but living alive.
> The discord merely magnifies.

> Deeper within the belly's dark,
> Of time, time grows upon the rock.
>   (—"The Man with the Blue Guitar," XI)

The early Ashbery poem implies that there are "collisions, communications" among us, even in confrontation of the sea, a universe of sense that asserts its power over our minds. But the parent-poem, though it will resolve itself in a similar quasi-comfort, harasses the poet and his readers with the intenser realization that "the discord merely magnifies," when our "collisions, communications" sound out against the greater rhythms of the sea. Where the early Ashbery attempted vainly to soften his poetic father, the mature Ashbery of **"Fragment"** subverts and even captures the precursor even as he appears to accept him more fully. The ephebe may still not be mentioned in the father's minutes, but his own vision has advanced. Stevens hesitated almost always until his last phase, unable firmly to adhere to or reject the High Romantic insistence that the power of the poet's mind could triumph over the universe of death, or the estranged object-world. It is not every day, he says in his "Adagia," that the world arranges itself in a poem. His nobly desperate disciple, Ashbery, has dared the dialectic of misprision so as to implore the world daily to arrange itself into a poem:

> But what could I make of this? Glaze
> Of many identical foreclosures wrested from
> The operative hand, like a judgment but still
> The atmosphere of seeing? That two people
>   could
> Collide in this dusk means that the time of
> Shapelessly foraging had come undone: the
>   space was
> Magnificent and dry. On flat evenings

In the months ahead, she would remember that
   that
Anomaly had spoken to her, words like disjointed beaches
Brown under the advancing signs of the air.

This, the last stanza of **"Fragment,"** returns Ashbery full circle to his early **"Le livre est sur la table."** There are "collisions, communications on the shore" but these "collide in this dusk." "Did the land advance?" of the early poem is answered partly negatively, by the brown, disjointed beaches, but partly also by "the advancing signs of the air." Elsewhere in **"Fragment,"** Ashbery writes: "Thus reasoned the ancestor, and everything / Happened as he had foretold, but in a funny kind of way." The strength of the positive *apophrades* gives this quester the hard wisdom of the proverbial poem he rightly calls **"Soonest Mended,"** which ends by:

> . . . learning to accept
> The charity of the hard moments as they are
>   doled out,
> For this is action, this not being sure, this care-
>   less
> Preparing, sowing the seeds crooked in the fur-
>   row,
> Making ready to forget, and always coming back
> To the mooring of starting out, that day so long
>   ago.

Here Ashbery has achieved one of the mysteries of poetic style, but only through the individuation of misprision.

Another misprision is a haunting lyric of belatedness, Ashbery's recent **"As You Came from the Holy Land,"** where the parodistic first-line/title repeats the opening of a bitter ballad of lost love attributed to Ralegh, one of whose stanzas lingers throughout Ashbery's gentler poem:

> I have lovde her all my youth,
>   Butt now ould, as you see,
> Love lykes not the fallyng frute
>   From the wythered tree.

"Her" is the personal past in Ashbery's elegy for the self:

> of western New York state
> were the graves all right in their bushings
> was there a note of panic in the late August air
> because the old man had peed in his pants again
> was there turning away from the late afternoon
>   glare
> as though it too could be wished away . . .
> was any of this present
> and how could this be
> the magic solution to what you are in now
> whatever has held you motionless
> like this so long through the dark season
> until now the women come out in navy blue
> and the worms come out of the compost to die
> it is the end of any season
>
> you reading there so accurately
> sitting not wanting to be disturbed
> as you came from that holy land
> what other signs of earth's dependency were
>   upon you
> what fixed sign at the crossroads
> what lethargy in the avenues

> where all is said in a whisper . . .
> what tone of voice among the hedges
> what tone under the apple trees
> the numbered land stretches away
> and your house is built in tomorrow
> but surely not before the examination
> of what is right and will befall
> not before the census
> and the writing down of names
>
> remember you are free to wander away
> as from other times other scenes that were tak-
>   ing place
> the history of someone who came too late
> the time is ripe now and the adage
> is hatching as the seasons change and tremble
> it is finally as though that thing of monstrous in-
>   terest
> were happening in the sky
> but the sun is setting and prevents you from see-
>   ing it
> out of night the token emerges
> its leaves like birds alighting all at once under a
>   tree
> taken up and shaken again . . .
> put down in weak rage
> knowing as the brain does it can never come
>   about
> not here not yesterday in the past
> only in the gap of today filling itself
> as emptiness is distributed
> in the idea of what time it is
> when that time is already past

Ashbery, probably because of his direct descent from Stevens, tends like Stevens to follow rather precisely the crisis-poem paradigm that I have traced in my map of misreading. This model, Wordsworthian-Whitmanian, never restores as much representational meaning as it continually curtails or withdraws, as I have observed earlier. Ashbery's resource has been to make a music of the poignance of withdrawal. So, in this poem, the "end of any season" that concludes the first stanza is deliberately too partial a synecdoche to compensate for the pervasive absences of the ironies throughout the stanza. Ashbery's turnings-against-the-self are wistful and inconclusive, and he rarely allows a psychic reversal any completeness. His origins, in the holy land of western New York state, are presented here and elsewhere in his work with an incurious rigidity that seems to have no particular design on the poet himself, characteristically addressed as "you." The next stanza emphasizes Ashbery's usual metonymic defense of isolation (as opposed to the Stevensian undoing or the Whitmanian regression), by which signs and impulses become detached from one another, with the catalog or census completing itself in the reductive "writing down of names," in which "down" takes on surprising difference and force. The third stanza, one of Ashbery's most radiant, marks the poem's *daemonization,* the American Counter-Sublime in which Ashbery, like Stevens, is so extraordinarily at home. Ashbery's mingled strength and weakness, indeed his deliberate pathos, is that he knowingly begins where [Byron's] Childe Roland ended, "free to wander away" yet always seeing himself as living "the history of someone who came too late" while sensing that "the time is ripe now." Studying his own habitual expression in his prose *Three Poems,* he had compared himself explicitly to Childe Roland at the Dark Tower. Here also, his Sublime sense that a Stevensian reality is happening in the war of the sky against the mind is necessarily obscured by a sunset akin to Roland's "last red leer."

Ashbery's finest achievement, to date, is his heroic and perpetual self-defeat, which is of a kind appropriate to conclude this book, since such self-defeat pioneers in undoing the mode of transumption that Stevens helped revive. Ashbery's allusiveness is transumptive rather than conspicuous, but he employs it against itself, as though determined to make of his lateness a desperate cheerfulness. In the final stanza of **"As You Came from the Holy Land,"** the most characteristic of Shelleyan-Stevensian metaphors, the fiction of the leaves, is duly revealed as a failure ("taken up and shaken again / put down in weak rage"); but the metalepsis substituted for it is almost a hyperbole of failure, as presence and the present fall together "in the gap of today filling itself / as emptiness is distributed." The two lines ending the poem would be an outrageous parody of the transumptive mode if their sad dignity were not so intense. Ashbery, too noble and poetically intelligent to subside into a parodist of time's revenges, flickers on "like a great shadow's last embellishment."

Ashbery is that American anomaly, an antithetical Transcendentalist, bearer of an influx of the Newness that he cannot know himself.

—*Harold Bloom*

Ashbery has been misunderstood because of his association with the "New York School" of Kenneth Koch, Frank O'Hara and other comedians of the spirit, but also because of the dissociative phase of his work as represented by much of a peculiar volume, *The Tennis Court Oath.* But the poet of *The Double Dream of Spring* and the prose *Three Poems* is again the Stevensian meditator of the early *Some Trees.* No other American poet has labored quite so intensely to exorcise all the demons of discursiveness, and no contemporary American poet is so impressively at one with himself in expounding a discursive wisdom. Like his master, Stevens, Ashbery is essentially a ruminative poet, turning a few subjects over and over, knowing always that what counts is the mythology of self, blotched out beyond unblotching.

Ashbery's various styles have suggested affinities to composer-theorists like Cage and Cowell, to painters of the school of Kline and Pollock, and to an assortment of French bards like Roussel, Reverdy and even Michaux. But the best of Ashbery, from the early *Some Trees* on through **"A Last World"** and **"The Skaters"** to the wonderful culminations of his great book, *The Double Dream of Spring* and the recent *Three Poems,* shows a clear descent from the major American tradition that began in

Emerson. Even as his poetic father is Stevens, Ashbery's largest ancestor is Whitman, and it is the Whitmanian strain in Stevens that found Ashbery. I would guess that Ashbery, like Stevens, turned to French poetry as a deliberate evasion of continuities, a desperate quest for freedom from the burden of poetic influence. The beautiful group called "French Poems" in *The Double Dream of Spring* were written in French and then translated into English, Ashbery notes, "with the idea of avoiding customary word-patterns and associations." This looks at first like the characteristic quarrel with discursiveness that is endemic in modern verse, but a deeper familiarity with the "French Poems" will evoke powerful associations with Stevens at his most central, the seer of "Credences of Summer":

> And it does seem that all the force of
> The cosmic temperature lives in the form of contacts
> That no intervention could resolve,
> Even that of a creator returned to the desolate
> Scene of this first experiment: this microcosm.

> . . . and then it's so natural
> That we experience almost no feeling
> Except a certain lightness which matches
> The recent closed ambiance which is, besides
> Full of attentions for us. Thus, lightness and wealth.

> But the existence of all these things and especially
> The amazing fullness of their number must be
> For us a source of unforgettable questions:
> Such as: whence does all this come? and again:
> Shall I some day be a part of all this fullness?

The poet of these stanzas is necessarily a man who must have absorbed "Credences of Summer" when he was young, perhaps even as a Harvard undergraduate. Every strong poet's development is a typology of evasions, a complex misprision of his precursor. Ashbery's true precursor is the composite father, Whitman-Stevens, and the whole body to date of Ashbery's work manifests nearly every possible revisionary ratio in regard to so formidable an American ancestry. Though the disjunctiveness of so much of Ashbery suggests his usual critical placement with the boisterousness of Koch or the random poignances of O'Hara, he seems most himself when most ruefully and intensely Transcendental, the almost involuntary celebrator "of that *invisible light* which spatters the silence / Of our everyday festivities." Ashbery is a kind of invalid of American Orphism, perpetually convalescing from the strenuous worship of that dread Orphic trinity of draining gods: Eros, Dionysus, Ananke, who preside over the Native Strain of our poetry.

I propose to track Ashbery back to his origins in another essay, but here I have space only to investigate some poems of his major phase, as it seems developing in his two most recent books. To enter at this point a judgment of current American poets now entering their imaginative maturity, Ashbery and A. R. Ammons are to me the indispensable figures, two already fully achieved artists who are likely to develop into worthy rivals of Frost, Stevens, Pound, Williams, Eliot, Crane, and Warren. Merwin,

James Wright, Merrill, perhaps Snyder in the school of Williams and Pound, perhaps James Dickey of a somewhat older generation (if he yet returns to the strength of earlier work) are candidates also. Yet all prophecy is dangerous here; there are recent poems by Howard, Hollander, Kinnell, Pack, Feinman, Hecht, Strand, Rich, Snodgrass, among others, which are as powerful as all but the very best of Ammons, Ashbery, Wright. Other critics and readers would nominate quite different groupings, as we evidently enter a time of singular wealth in contemporary verse.

Ashbery's poetry is haunted by the image of transparence, but this comes to him, from the start, as "a puzzling light," or carried by beings who are "as dirty handmaidens / To some transparent witch." Against Transcendental influx, Ashbery knows the wisdom of what he calls "learning to accept / The charity of the hard moments as they are doled out," and knows also that: "One can never change the core of things, and light burns you the harder for it." Burned by a visionary flame beyond accommodation (one can contrast Kinnell's too-easy invocations of such fire), Ashbery gently plays with Orphic influx ("Light bounced off the ends / Of the small gray waves to tell / Them in the observatory / About the great drama that was being won."). Between Emerson and Whitman, the seers of this tradition, and Ashbery, Ammons and other legatees, there comes the mediating figure of Stevens:

> My house has changed a little in the sun.
> The fragrance of the magnolias comes close,
> False flick, false form, but falseness close to kin.
>
> It must be visible or invisible,
> Invisible or visible or both;
> A seeing and unseeing in the eye.

These are hardly the accents of transport, yet Stevens does stand precariously, in the renewed light. But even the skepticism is Emerson's own; his greatest single visionary oration is "Experience," a text upon which Dickinson, Stevens and Ashbery always seem to be writing commentaries:

> Thus inevitably does the universe wear our color, and every object fall successively into the subject itself. The subject exists, the subject enlarges; all things sooner or later fall into place. As I am, so I see; use what language we will, we can never say anything but what we are. . . . And we cannot say too little of our constitutional necessity of seeing things under private aspects, or saturated with our humors. And yet is the God the native of these bleak rocks. . . . We must hold hard to this poverty, however scandalous, and by more vigorous self-recoveries, after the sallies of action, possess our axis more firmly. . . .

The Old Transcendentalism in America, like the New, hardly distinguishes itself from a visionary skepticism, and makes no assertions without compensatory qualifications. Still, we tend to remember Emerson for his transparencies, and not the opaquenesses that more frequently haunted him and his immediate disciples. I suspect that this is because of Emerson's *confidence*, no matter where

he places his emphases. When Stevens attains to a rare transparence, he generally *sees* very little more than is customary, but he *feels* a greater peace, and this peace reduces to a confidence in the momentary capability of his own imagination. Transcendentalism, in its American formulation, centers upon Emerson's stance of Self-Reliance, which is primarily a denial of the anxiety of influence. Like Nietzsche, who admired him for it, Emerson refuses to allow us to believe we must be latecomers. In a gnomic quatrain introducing his major essay on self-reliance, Emerson manifested a shamanistic intensity still evident in his descendents:

> Cast the bantling on the rocks,
> Suckle him with the she-wolf's teat,
> Wintered with the hawk and fox,
> Power and speed be hands and feet.

This is splendid, but Emerson had no more been such a bantling than any of my contemporaries are, unless one wants the delightful absurdity of seeing Wordsworth or Coleridge as a she-wolf. "Do not seek yourself outside yourself" is yet another motto to "Self-Reliance," and there is one more, from Beaumont and Fletcher, assuring us that the soul of an honest man:

> Commands all light, all influence, all fate
> Nothing to him falls early or too late.

These are all wonderful idealisms. Whitman, who had been simmering, read "Self-Reliance" and was brought to the boil of the 1855 "Song of Myself." Ashbery, by temperament and choice, always seems to keep simmering, but whether he took impetus from Whitman, Stevens or even the French partisans of poetic Newness, he has worked largely and overtly in this Emersonian spirit. Unfortunately, like Merwin and Merwin's precursor, Pound, Ashbery truly absorbed from the Emerson-Whitman tradition the poet's over-idealizing tendency to lie to himself, against his origins and against experience. American poets since Emerson are all antithetical completions of one another, which means mostly that they develop into grotesque truncations of what they might have been. Where British poets swerve away from their spiritual fathers, ours attempt to rescue their supposedly benighted sires. American bards, like Democritus, deny the swerve, so as to save divination, holding on to the Fate that might make them liberating gods. Epicurus affirmed the swerve, ruining divination, and all poetry since is caught between the two. Emerson, though close to Democritus, wants even divination to be a mode of Self-Reliance. That is, he genuinely shares the Orphic belief that the poet is already divine, and realizes more of this divinity in writing his poems. Lucretian poets like Shelley who find freedom by swerving away from fathers (Wordsworth and Milton, for Shelley) do not believe in divination, and do not worship an Orphic Necessity as the final form of divinity. Orphic poets, particularly American or Emersonian Orphics, worship four gods only: Ananke, Eros, Dionysus and—most of all surely—themselves. They are therefore peculiarly resistant to the idea of poetic influence, for divination—to them—means primarily an apprehension of their own possible sublimity, the gods they are in process of becoming. The gentle Ashbery, despite all his quite genuine and hard-won wisdom, is as much in this tradition as those spheral men, Emerson, Whitman, Thoreau, and that sublime egoist, Stevens, or the American Wordsworth.

The Double Dream of Spring has a limpidly beautiful poem called **"Clouds,"** which begins:

> All this time he had only been waiting,
> Not even thinking, as many had supposed.
> Now sleep wound down to him its promise of
>   dazzling peace
> And he stood up to assume that imagination.
>
> There were others in the forest as close as he
> To caring about the silent outcome, but they had
>   gotten lost
> In the shadows of dreams so that the external
>   look
> Of the nearby world had become confused with
>   the cobwebs inside.

Sleep here has a Whitmanian-Stevensian cast ("The Sleepers," "The Owl in the Sarcophagus") and the gorgeous solipsism so directly celebrated here has its sources in the same ultimately Emersonian tradition. Though "he," the poet or quest-hero, is distinguished from his fellows as not having yielded to such solipsism, the poem ends in a negative apotheosis:

> He shoots forward like a malignant star.
> The edges of the journey are ragged.
> Only the face of night begins to grow distinct
> As the fainter stars call to each other and are
>   lost.
>
> Day re-creates his image like a snapshot:
> The family and the guests are there,
> The talking over there, only now it will never
>   end.
> And so cities are arranged, and oceans traversed,
>
> And farms tilled with especial care.
> This year again the corn has grown ripe and tall.
> It is a perfect rebuttal of the argument. And Semele
> Moves away, puzzled at the brown light above
>   the fields.

The harvest of natural process, too ripe for enigmas, refutes quest, and confirms the natural realism of all solipsists. This poem, urging us away from the Emersonian or Central Self, concludes by yielding to that Self, and to the re-birth of Dionysus, Semele's son. Like his precursor, Stevens, Ashbery fears and evades the Native Strain of American Orphism and again like Stevens he belongs as much to that straing as Hart Crane or John Wheelwright does. In the recent prose *Three Poems,* he ruefully accepts his tradition and his inescapable place in it:

> Why, after all, were we not destroyed in the conflagration of the moment our real and imaginary lives coincided, unless it was because we never had a separate existence beyond that of those two static and highly artificial concepts whose fusion was nevertheless the cause of death and destruction not only for ourselves but in the world around us. But perhaps the explanation lies precisely here: what we were witnessing was merely the reverse side of an event of cosmic be-

atitude for all except us, who were blind to it because it took place inside us. Meanwhile the shape of life has changed definitively for the better for everyone on the outside. They are bathed in the light of this tremendous surprise as in the light of a new sun from which only healing and not corrosive rays emanate; they comment on the miraculous change as people comment on the dazzling beauty of a day in early autumn, forgetting that for the blind man in their midst it is a day like any other, so that its beauty cannot be said to have universal validity but must remain fundamentally in doubt.

> **("The Recital")**

The closest (though dialectically opposed) analogue to this passage is the great concluding rhapsody of Emerson's early apocalypse, "Nature," when the Orphic Poet returns to prophesy:

> As when the summer comes from the south the snow-banks melt and the face of the earth becomes green before it, so shall the advancing spirit create its ornaments along its path, and carry with it the beauty it visits and the song which enchants it; it shall draw beautiful faces, warm hearts, wise discourse, and heroic acts, around its way, until evil is no more seen. The kingdom of man over nature, which cometh not with observation,—a dominion such as now is beyond his dream of God,—he shall enter without more wonder than the blind man feels who is gradually restored to perfect sight.

Ashbery's apocalyptic transformation of the Self, its elevation to the Over-Soul, is manifest to everyone and everything outside the Self, but not to the blind man of the Self. The Emersonian Self will know the metamorphic redemption of others and things only by knowing first its gradual freedom from blindness as to its own glory. Ashbery's forerunners, the makers of "Song of Myself" and "Notes toward a Supreme Fiction," were primary Emersonians, involuntary as Stevens was in this identity. Ashbery is that American anomaly, an antithetical Transcendentalist, bearer of an influx of the Newness that he cannot know himself.

I leap ahead, past Frost and Pound, Eliot and Williams, past even Hart Crane, to a contemporary image-of-voice that is another strong tally, however ruefully the strength regards itself. Here is John Ashbery's **"The Other Tradition,"** the second poem in his 1977 volume, *Houseboat Days*:

> They all came, some wore sentiments
> Emblazoned on T-shirts, proclaiming the lateness
> Of the hour, and indeed the sun slanted its rays
> Through branches of Norfolk Island pine as
>   though
> Politely clearing its throat, and all ideas settled
> In a fuzz of dust under trees when it's drizzling:
> The endless games of Scrabble, the boosters,
> The celebrated omelette au Cantal, and through
>   it
> The roar of time plunging unchecked through
>   the sluices
> Of the days, dragging every sexual moment of it

Past the lenses: the end of something.
Only then did you glance up from your book,
Unable to comprehend what had been taking
    place, or
Say what you had been reading. More chairs
Were brought, and lamps were lit, but it tells
Nothing of how all this proceeded to materialize
Before you and the people waiting outside and
    in the next
Street, repeating its name over and over, until si-
    lence
Moved halfway up the darkened trunks,
And the meeting was called to order.

                I still remember
How they found you, after a dream, in your
    thimble hat,
Studious as a butterfly in a parking lot.
The road home was nicer then. Dispersing, each
    of the
Troubadours had something to say about how
    charity
Had run its race and won, leaving you the ex-
    president
Of the event, and how, though many of these
    present
Had wished something to come of it, if only a
    distant
Wisp of smoke, yet none was so deceived as to
    hanker
After that cool non-being of just a few minutes
    before,
Now that the idea of a forest had clamped itself
Over the minutiae of the scene. You found this
Charming, but turned your face fully toward
    night,
Speaking into it like a megaphone, not hearing
Or caring, although these still live and are gener-
    ous
And all ways contained, allowed to come and go
Indefinitely in and out of the stockade
They have so much trouble remembering, when
    your forgetting
Rescues them at last, as a star absorbs the night.

I am aware that this charming poem urbanely confronts, absorbs and in some sense seeks to overthrow a critical theory, almost a critical climate, that has accorded it a canonical status. Stevens's Whitman proclaims that nothing is final and that no man shall see the end. Ashbery, a Whitman somehow more studiously casual even than Whitman, regards the prophets of belatedness and cheerfully insists that his forgetting or repression will rescue us at last, even as the Whitmanian or Stevensian evening star absorbs the night. But the price paid for this metaleptic reversal of American belatedness into a fresh earliness is the yielding up of Ashbery's tally or image of voice to a deliberate grotesquerie. Sexuality is made totally subservient to time, which is indeed "the end of something," and poetic tradition becomes an ill-organized social meeting of troubadours, leaving the canonical Ashbery as "ex-president / Of the event." As for the image of voice proper, the Whitmanian confrontation of the night now declines into: "You found this / Charming, but turned your face fully toward night, / Speaking into it like a megaphone, not hearing / Or caring." Such a megaphone is an apt image for Paul de Man's deconstructionist view of po-

etic tradition, which undoes tradition by suggesting that every poem is as much a random and gratuitous event as any human death is.

Ashbery's implicit interpretation of what he wants to call "The Other Tradition" mediates between this vision of poems as being totally cut off from one another and the antithetical darkness in which poems carry over-determined relationships and progress towards a final entropy. Voice in our poetry now tallies what Ashbery in his **"Syringa,"** a major Orphic elegy in *Houseboat Days,* calls "a record of pebbles along the way." Let us grant that the American Sublime is always also an American irony, and then turn back to Emerson and hear the voice that is great within us somehow breaking through again. This is Emerson in his journal for August 1859, on the eve of being burned out, with all his true achievement well behind him; but he gives us the true tally of his soul:

> *Beatitudes of Intellect.*—Am I not, one of these days, to write consecutively of the beatitude of intellect? It is too great for feeble souls, and they are over-excited. The wineglass shakes, and the wine is spilled. What then? The joy which will not let me sit in my chair, which brings me bolt upright to my feet, and sends me striding around my room, like a tiger in his cage, and I cannot have composure and concentration enough even to set down in English words the thought which thrills me—is not that joy a certificate of the elevation? What if I never write a book or a line? for a moment, the eyes of my eyes were opened, the affirmative experience remains, and consoles through all suffering.

Of the many contemporary heirs of Whitman and of Stevens, John Ashbery seems likeliest to achieve something near to their eminence. Yet their uncertainty as to their audience is far surpassed in the shifting stances that Ashbery assumes. His mode can vary from the apparently opaque, so disjunctive as to seem beyond interpretation, to a kind of limpid clairvoyance that again brings the Emersonian contraries together. Contemplating Parmigianino's picture in his major long poem, **"Self-Portrait in a Convex Mirror,"** Ashbery achieves a vision in which art, rather than nature, becomes the imprisoner of the soul:

> The soul has to stay where it is,
> Even though restless, hearing raindrops at the
>   pane,
> The sighing of autumn leaves thrashed by the
>   wind,
> Longing to be free, outside, but it must stay
> Posing in this place. It must move as little as pos-
>   sible.
> This is what the portrait says.
> But there is in that gaze a combination
> Of tenderness, amusement and regret, so power-
>   ful
> In its restraint that one cannot look for long.
> The secret is too plain. The pity of it smarts,
> Makes hot tears spurt: that the soul is not a soul,
> Has no secret, is small, and it fits
> Its hollow perfectly: its room, our moment of at-
>   tention.

Whitman's Soul, knowing its true hour in wordlessness, is apparently reduced here and now to a moment only of attention. And yet even this tearful realization, supposedly abandoning the soul to a convex mirror, remains a privileged moment, of an Emersonian rather than Paterian kind. Precisely where he seems most wistful and knowingly bewildered by loss, Ashbery remains most dialectical, like his American ancestors.

The simple diction and vulnerable stance barely conceal the presence of the American Transcendental Self, an ontological self that increases even as the empirical self abandons every spiritual assertion. Hence the "amusement" that takes up its stance between "tenderness" and "regret," Whitmanian affections, and hence also the larger hint of a power held in reserve, "so powerful in its restraint that one cannot look for long." An American Orphic, wandering in the Emersonian legacy, can afford to surrender the soul in much the same temper as the ancient Gnostics did. The soul can be given up to the Demiurge, whether of art or nature, because a spark of *pneuma* is more vital than the *psyche,* and fits no hollow whatsoever. Where Whitman and Stevens are at once hermetic and offhand, so is Ashbery, but his throwaway gestures pay the price of an ever-increasing American sense of belatedness. (pp. 1-16)

Harold Bloom, in an introduction to John Ashbery: Modern Critical Views, *edited by Harold Bloom, Chelsea House Publishers, 1985, pp. 1-16.*

Claude Rawson   (review date 4 July 1986)

[*Rawson is an English educator and critic. In the following review of* Selected Poems, *he compares Ashbery's poetic development to that of Wallace Stevens and discusses the fractured and fragmented qualities of Ashbery's verse.*]

John Ashbery is probably the most highly regarded living poet in America. He is, in more ways than one, the heir of Wallace Stevens, and like Stevens some three decades ago is acquiring a belated minority-following in Britain (Carcanet have been publishing him for some years, and Penguin have also been in on the act, though partly through the Viking connection). The *Selected Poems,* first published by Viking in the US last year, is, like Stevens's corresponding volume, a highly personal stocktaking, which may disconcert the critics by its refreshing omission of some of the poems they most like to talk about (" 'They Dream Only of America' ", for example, or "These Lacustrine Cities").

Ashbery is nevertheless in many ways a critics' poet, like many modern and postmodern masters, the product of a culture whose reading is shaped in the seminar-room and which accepts "explication" (even defeated explication, which is a permanent invitation to more explication) as an essential part of its reading experience. This need not imply inauthenticity. It is a natural (and by no means the ugliest) product of the hegemony of university English departments over the literary consciousness of the more affluent regions of the anglophone world, and, as Alvin Ker-

nan showed some years ago, deeply rooted in the economics of (especially) American publishing, which have identified even for imaginative writers the profitability of the teacherly text.

The phenomenon of an academicized literary idiom is wider and older than the institutional hypertrophy of literary studies which it nowadays reflects, and doubtless more complex. Its roots lie partly in an earlier modernism, in the works of Joyce, Eliot and Pound, whose principal writings precede the proliferation of literature departments since the Second World War and may in some ways be thought of as late incarnations of the ancient idea of the learned poet. One variant of this is the poet whose learning shows not in his mastery of earlier poets but in his adoption of the style of professors, a narrowing of the old ideal to classroom dimensions which occurred quite early in this century and was not confined to university poets. It appears fully-formed, and in a manner Ashbery was to assimilate, in Stevens's "Notes Toward a Supreme Fiction" (1942), whose very title mimics academic discourse, while a still earlier Stevens poem is actually called "Academic Discourse at Havana", though it first appeared in 1923 as "Discourse in a Cantina at Havana" and acquired its "academic" label in 1929.

That there is derision and indeed self-derision in such scholarly gesturing does not diminish its academic character. Stevens spoke jeeringly of poets of a certain kind as "introspective exiles, lecturing" (he may have meant Eliot, in 1918), but it's a truism that academic and mock-academic often come to the same thing. This is not only because deriding the academic is the academic community's favourite tribal custom. It is also that, in the high self-conscious mix of postmodern Shandyism, the ubiquitous element of parody, instead of implying rejection, tends to cherish what it mimics along with the mimicking self.

Ashbery's best-known poem, "Self-Portrait in a Convex Mirror", takes its title from a famous painting by Parmigianino, but is as much of an "Academic Discourse" as any Stevens poem: its form is that of a lecture or treatise on that painter. Like Stevens's "Notes", it is an extended exploratory statement of aesthetic principles, and has something of the same centrality in Ashbery's *oeuvre,* and the same authority as a doctrinal key. It is difficult to be sure whether it's the intrinsic power of these poems, or our culture's sensitized receptivity to the academic, that has contributed most to this "classic" status. Certainly the volume containing and named after "Self-Portrait" is the one which first established Ashbery as a major figure, winning the three big book prizes (Pulitzer, National Book Award, National Book Critics Circle Award) for 1976.

Perhaps predictably, Ashbery's poem goes even further than Stevens's in its half-joky apparatus of professorial pretension, citing authorities ancient (Vasari) and modern (Sydney J. Freedberg, author of *Parmigianino: His Works in Painting,* Harvard, 1950), and affecting a pedantic gusto for periodizing pronouncements or the explanatory aside or afterthought: "The words are only speculation / (From the Latin *speculum,* mirror)." The donnish parenthesis functions here as a didactic counterpart to the poetic *trouvaille,* a small leap of discovery that settles, somewhat limply, into punning congruence with the poem's principal image. It's interesting that Ashbery's didactic flourishes, like Stevens's before him, often strain to transpose themselves to a nondidactic wave-length of poetic epiphany. Few poets have been more self-consciously self-repeating than Stevens. And perhaps none has so confidently claimed, or with more didactic insistence, that repetition, and the endless restatement with variations, are of the essence of the imaginative quest, a hovering that precedes the homing in:

> One of the vast repetitions final in
> Themselves and, therefore, good, the going
>   round
>
> And round and round, the merely going round,
> Until merely going round is a final good,
> The way wine comes at a table in a wood

Such "mere repetitions" in Stevens's "Notes" are a key to the structure of entire poems, to their "circular" rather than linear progression to discovery. But they operate insistently in local ways, with words repeated and repeated and each repetition a nudge towards perceptual finality. The manner easily turns to mannerism, in Ashbery as well as in Stevens. In **"Two Scenes"**, the opening poem of Ashbery's volume, the line "Destiny guides the waterpilot, and it is destiny" shows the pedagogue's emphatic manner put, rather clumsily, to tentative or exploratory purposes. The repeated word purports to be an advance on the first usage, a redefined confirmation of insight, enacting the process of discovery as well as its product. It's as though "What oft was *Thought*" were shown labouring towards the "ne'er so well *Exprest*" in a blackboard demonstration, while purporting to be surprised by joy.

Ashbery has frequented the world of art scholarship and earned his living in the college classroom, unlike Stevens, who after studying at Harvard neither had nor sought close connections with the university world. And Stevens's exercises in didactic delivery sometimes resemble a philosophy seminar hammed up in a businessmen's boardroom. It's amusing to see this feature rubbing off on Ashbery, whose experience of boardrooms must be considerably less even than Stevens's exposure to pedagogues. This comes over in poems like **"Decoy"**, whose entire form suggests parody of public speaking ("We hold these truths to be self-evident: / That ostracism, both political and moral, has / Its place in the twentieth-century scheme of things"), or **"Soonest Mended"**, where there seems at times to be self-conscious mimicry of a public man's Commencement Address ("the learning process is extended in this way, so that from this standpoint / None of us ever graduates from college").

But it also occurs in Ashbery's many poems of more straightforwardly aesthetic exploration, with their repetitious precisions and their pleasure in the prim revolving of platitude:

> The mark of things belongs to someone
> But if that somebody was wise
> Then the whole of things might be different
> From what it was thought to be in the beginning,
> before an angel bandaged the field glasses.

The idiom, the "doctrinal" content, the quaint angel image, are recognizably Stevensian, unlike the metrical spillage of the long last line, which is the kind of thing critics like to ascribe to the influence of Whitman. And it's true that America's most un-Whitmanian poets, Stevens and Ashbery no less than Pound, have often felt obliged more or less ostentatiously to make their "pact" with Whitman. But what such lines imitate is the surface garrulity, not the driving rhapsodic delight. Whitman's metrical capaciousness turns in Ashbery into a fussy exercise in extended pointmaking ("Now all is different without having changed / As though one were to pass through the same street at different times"), just as Whitman's expansive enumerations turn elsewhere in Ashbery (in the list of rivers in **"Into the Dusk-Charged Air"**, for example) into self-indulgent pieces of low-pressure variation.

Stevens is metrically more restrained, more "classical", but Ashbery's loping Whitmanian lines merely open out into a more relaxed version of Stevens's discursive prosiness. (There is nothing of the pedagogue or boardroom orator in Whitman's garrulities.) This effect is already visible, in a small incipient way, in **"Two Scenes"**:

> This is perhaps a day of general honesty
> Without example in the world's history
> Though the fumes are not of a singular authority
> And indeed are dry as poverty.

This goes back to the Stevens of *Credences of Summer*, "This is the last day of a certain year / Beyond which there is nothing left of time", whose definitional tautness is pointedly slackened in Ashbery, in a traducing which out-Stevenses Stevens's own lecturese.

[Ashbery is] in many ways a critics' poet, like many modern and postmodern masters, the product of a culture whose reading is shaped in the seminar-room and which accepts "explication" . . . as an essential part of its reading experience.

—*Claude Rawson*

Ashbery's formative involvement with professional art-criticism has of course left other marks on his poetry than this predisposition to pedagogic utterance. The strong painterly interests which he shared with his close associate, the late Frank O'Hara, "poet among painters", derived much of their stimulus from the Abstract Expressionists. That influence might be expected to tend away from the academic, and is reflected most fully perhaps in an interest in randomness, in vitality of surface and in some strong energies of colouring. Both poets are variously "painterly" (though Ashbery, as Marjorie Perloff has pointed out, affects to play down the visual aspect of his art and claims to be "much more audio-directed", with John Cage as a seminal influence). But their pictorialism tends to be sharply though often unconventionally "representational", and strongly anchored in narrative. The "story" element in Ashbery comes over in fragmented and nonsequential ways, but the fragments have a strong power of visual evocation, and a startling precision of outline even in their most surreal effects:

> Behind the steering wheel
>
> The boy took out his own forehead.
> His girlfriend's head was a green bag
> Of narcissus stems.

This is painterly, but hardly Abstract Expressionist. Its visual counterpart is Magritte.

Ashbery has always been interested in Surrealism and Dada. He once began a doctoral dissertation on Raymond Roussel, and his works reflect a fascination with Roussel, Reverdy and other writers in the Surrealist tradition. He seems to know French better than most American poets, especially than Stevens, and seems correspondingly less addicted to peppering his own poems with snippets from that language. Stevens was in his way a painterly poet too, though Surrealism may not be what first comes to mind when we think of Stevens's pictorialism. Yet even here the connections are close, and early. Ashbery's **"Illustration"** is written in an idiom of aesthete *bizarrerie* which recalls one of Stevens's most delightful early styles:

> A novice was sitting on a cornice
> High over the city. Angels
>
> Combined their prayers with those
> Of the police, begging her to come off it.
>
> One lady promised to be her friend.
> "I do not want a friend," she said.
>
> A mother offered her some nylons
> Stripped from her very legs. Others brought
>
> Little offerings of fruit and candy,
> The blind man all his flowers.

Readers of Stevens's "The Plot against the Giant" and "Cy Est Pourtraicte, Madame Ste Ursule, et les Unze Mille Vierges", will recognize the ingredients: a more or less scabrous episode sharply and elegantly sketched, the dandy-decorative "slight lyric grace" hardened by a grasp of ugly realities, the festive offerings of flowers coyly fraught with bawdy meanings, devotional proprieties lightly but uncompromisingly defiled.

One might, on the basis of this evidence, propose an analogous progress in both poets from early "dandy" lyric to the more extended and abstract meditations on imagination and reality in the later work. In fact this "later" manner is to some extent already present in the early Ashbery. A second part of **"Illustration"** moves on to reflections on what the narrative may be thought to illustrate, and reads like a pastiche of middle or late Stevens:

> Much that is beautiful must be discarded
> So that we may resemble a taller
>
> Impression of ourselves. Moths climb in the
>   flame,
> Alas, that wish only to be the flame:
>
> They do not lessen our stature.

We twinkle under the weight

> Of indiscretions.

It's perhaps the first of several minimalist variations on Stevens's theme of the "major man", and occurs earlier in Ashbery's than in Stevens's work. Ashbery's progress in one sense replicates Stevens's progress from early to late, but his own early phase also picks up where Stevens left off. It is striking to see, not only in **"Illustration"** but in **"Two Scenes"**, many features of the older poet's middle and later style.

Where Ashbery from the start differs from Stevens is in a recurrent atmosphere of menace, a violence of feeling or of natural process. This may be sensed in the surreal lyricisms of **"Glazunoviana"**, which ends, like "Sunday Morning", in the massive melancholy of a movement of birds, but a melancholy of explosive rather than elegiac suggestion:

> In the flickering evening the martins grow dens-
>   er.
> Rivers of wings surround us, and vast tribula-
>   tion.

It is also conveyed in fragmentary hints of narrative (**"Popular Songs"**, **"A Boy"**) and in a more fully-formed state in the story of the novice in Part I of **"Illustration"**, which ends in a lurid finale of sexual exposure and suicide:

> With that, the wind
> Unpinned her bulky robes, and naked
>
> As a roc's egg, she drifted softly downward
> Out of the angels' tenderness and the minds of
>   men.

It's not often that Ashbery gives us a completed narrative. In **"The Instruction Manual"** the speaker, seeking escape from humdrum labour, imagines a rose-coloured novelette set in Guadalajara, a variation on Stevens's Latino-exotic dreamlands. But **"A Long Novel"**, also from *Some Trees,* is neither long nor a novel. Nor, however, is it a Borgesian compression of a large narrative into a few paragraphs, as you might expect instead, but an elusive anecdotal surface concerned with speculative aesthetics rather than any story of human lives.

The professed anecdote is a favourite ploy in Stevensian poetics. Stevens himself has six poems entitled "Anecdote", one of which, "Earthy Anecdote", opens the *Collected Poems.* They tend to be fully-formed little fables, not fragmentary like Ashbery's, but in the best-known, "Anecdote of the Jar", both suggestions of "Anecdote" (story, informal chat) are subverted: the narrative is nugatory, and the poem's spare and resonant proposition of aesthetic principle is no more informal or chatty than "Notes Toward a Supreme Fiction" are scribbled jottings.

Ashbery's poems are not called "anecdotes", but their titles often suggest anecdotal chatter caught in mid-flow: **"And You Know"**, **"Soonest Mended"**. And the poems themselves, while not telling fully formed stories, are full of narrative intimations which erupt into the discourse with a surreal, unsettling urgency in precisely that idiom of innocent colloquial triviality: "The funniest little thing. . . . That's how it all began". A poem like **"What Is Poetry"**, whose title does announce aesthetic discourse, proceeds much more in the anecdotal mode than do Stevens's "anecdotes":

> Beautiful images? Trying to avoid
>
> Ideas, as in this poem? But we
> Go back to them as to a wife, leaving
>
> The mistress we desire?

Such analogies seem flip, but they are not foreign to formal arts of poetry. Pope's *Essay on Criticism* has several: "*Wit and Judgement* often are at strife, / Tho' meant each other's Aid, like *Man* and *Wife*", "A Muse by these is like a Mistress us'd". Ashbery's procedure, however, is not that of illustrative or conclusive analogy but of suggestive narration, incipient and open-ended, its propositions about art as open as the outcome of any speculative event: "It might give us—what?—some flowers soon?"

The snatches of gossip imply the insufficiency of formal stories. They explore instead the discontinuity of events or our perception of events, suggesting an intermittent "eavesdropping" on a "private language", the "rejected chapters" of a novel. He speaks in **"The New Spirit"** of "an open field of narrative possibilities. Not in the edifying sense of tales of the past that we are still (however) chained to, but as stories that tell only of themselves . . .". In fact, his stories aren't always free of "allegory" and their openness to "possibility" is (as in Stevens or in Borges) definable against, rather than free from, "tales of the past".

Thus, a note of mystery-story menace, or hints of an unexpounded sexual drama, chat their way across a poem, detached from their conventional novelistic context, though inevitably calling such a context to mind in its very absence: "A man in her room, you say. / I like the really wonderful way you express things . . .". The effect hovers uncertainly between the fraught and the flip. The poem from which this example comes is called **"Unctuous Platitudes"**, but that self-violating title is another blind, harshly at odds with the limpid delicacy of lyrical probing which is in fact the poem's dominant note:

> I like the really wonderful way you express
> things
> So that it might be said, that of all the ways in
> which to
>
> Emphasize a posture or a particular mental climate
> Like this gray-violet one with a thin white irregular
> line
>
> Descending the two vertical sides, these are
> those
> which
>
> Can also unsay an infinite number of pauses
>
> In the ceramic day. Every invitation
> To every stranger is met at the station.

The air of platitude in the last line is perhaps lapidary, not especially "unctuous", but lapidary, as another poem says,

with a "special, lapidary / Todayness". And since the meaning is by any standard opaque rather than obvious, the suggestion of "platitude" is itself, as the postpeople say, deconstructed. Titles in Ashbery regularly exist in a kind of adversarial tension with the rest of the poem. What the invitations to strangers met at stations really evoke are not truisms but the shadowy convergences of mystery-plots. Their strange potency comes from the fact that the general proposition is made to carry an urgency of particular events, like Gulliver's descriptions of war, but transposed from Swift's over-explicit to an inexplicit (suspenseful or "mysterious") mode. These closing lines are, in a specific sense, story-lines, but stripped of context and generalized to a kind of pregnant meaninglessness. Suggestions of "anecdote" are again, as in Stevens, subverted, but subverted by incompleteness rather than by a belying of informality.

"Rivers and Mountains" is a "mystery-poem" whose narrative surface misleads expectation in the way that some of Ashbery's titles do:

> On the secret map the assassins
> Cloistered, the Moon River was marked
> Near the eighteen peaks and the city
> Of humiliation and defeat . . .

The lines are remarkable for evoking not one but at least two narrative styles which conventionally presuppose conclusive explication: that of the suspense thriller and, more surprisingly, that of traditional allegory (add initial capitals, and "the city / Of humiliation and defeat" might have come out of Bunyan, though Auden is in this, as in other things, an intervening influence). The free-floating preoccupation with narrative style, "not events" but "rather . . . their 'way of happening' ", is nowhere more evident than here, since the idiom of allegory offers no allegory, only an atmosphere of doom, and the mystery-plot is never unravelled.

Ashbery reports that when he was asked by Kenneth Koch whether his poems had "hidden meanings", he said no, "Because somebody might find out what they were and then the poems would no longer be mysterious". The reply belongs with the statement about Parmigianino's "Self-Portrait" that its "secret" is that there is "no secret", and thus with the poetics of *surface* which, as Marjorie Perloff says, Ashbery has derived from Action Painting. It can also be read as an extreme formulation of the old modernist dogma of the irreducibility of poems to meanings, and it contains an element of Dada tease. Narrative has become a form of play, "almost / very important" in the words of Frank O'Hara. In **"Rivers and Mountains"**, a sinister atmosphere of Kafkaesque menace doesn't escape an Auden-like feeling that deadly conspiratorial doings are not far removed from schoolboy adventure, and the withholding of explanation has something of the "I shan't tell you" of children's play.

The detective or mystery-story has enjoyed a rather solemn vogue in postmodern letters. The new novelists in France, Orton and Fowles in England, Vonnegut and Pynchon in America, have exploited it as a structural frame for experiments with the well-made plot and enquiries into the play of artifice in art. Borges has been cited as an analogue to the Ashbery of **"Rivers and Mountains"**. But if Ashbery can be said to share with all these writers a feeling for violence subjected to stylish containments, he hardly ever plays with the structure of the suspense plot, only with fragments of its surface. "Story" is for him, in Perloff's words, "a point of reference, a way of alluding, a source . . . of parody", though even "parody" is misleading to the extent that it suggests stylistic reversal rather than dislocation.

In her recent book *The Dance of Intellect* Perloff speaks of "the return of story in postmodern poetry". I doubt whether "story" had receded from poems in the way she implies, and whether its present prominence is confined to the "postmodern". Ashbery's methods invite comparison for example with the "secret narrative" element in some recent British poetry, hardly postmodern, where the undisclosed or partially disclosed event also exerts an unsettling pressure of feeling. One difference is that Ashbery's narratives seem "fractured" to a point where disconnection or randomness go beyond a mere sense of information withheld, whereas in the poems of Andrew Motion or perhaps of Tom Paulin the idea of a chain of events hovers over the poem even if we can't reconstruct it. I suspect too that in these British poets the implied narrative acts in a "lyric" way, as a carrier of personal feeling in a manner similar to what Wordsworth had in mind when he said that in the narrative of "lyrical ballads" the feeling "gives importance to the action and situation" and not the other way round. Motion's narratives are, unlike Wordsworthian ballads, implied rather than overt, with the "secrecy" supplying part of the emotional charge. I suppose that Ashbery would have no truck with such "lyrical" purposes. His focus is on a bravura artifice, a depersonalized surface crackling with "possibility", a brilliant randomness in which the analogy with Action Painting asserts itself with special force, and should not be underestimated merely because the paint strokes take an auditory anecdotal form. (pp. 723-24)

Claude Rawson, "A Poet in the Postmodern Playground," in The Times Literary Supplement, *No. 4344, July 4, 1986, pp. 723-24.*

Gene Frumkin   (essay date 1986)

[*Frumkin is an American poet and critic. In the following essay, he presents a positive assessment of Ashbery's* Selected Poems, *focusing on Ashbery's evocation of the "private voice" possessed by individuals and the emphasis on process and structure in his poems.*]

A distillation of more than thirty years of work, John Ashbery's **Selected Poems** articulates the inherent contradiction dividing us as humans from the world surrounding us and even from the language that proposes standards for coherence. These poems comprise a sustained meditation on the voice that speaks to each of us but not to everyone. This is our private voice: it tries to think what we feel and feel what we think, yet it never quite finds the words to speak a cloudless meaning either to itself or another.

The clue to Ashbery's work, at one level, is not hard to uncover: he means only what you, the reader, mean when you take in the multitude of sensations that become, on the instant, your psyche with its vast memory, its process of selectivity. We are all bodies moving as objects in the world in accord with our need to communicate, but this does not coincide with how we explain ourselves to others or with their explanations to us. "Understanding" is a misused word, confined as it usually is to conceptual discernment. Implicit in this is some form of linear reasoning, yet much of what we understand is hidden, the mysteries we can only intuit or theorize about in zigzag ways.

> The half-meant, half-perceived
> Motions of fronds out of idle depths that are
> Summer. And expansion into little draughts.
> The reply wakens easily, darting from
> Untruth to willed moment, scarcely called into being
> Before it swells, the way a waterfall
> Drums at different levels. Each moment
> Of utterance is the true one; likewise none are true,
> Only is the bounding from air to air, a serpentine
> Gesture which hides the truth behind a congruent
> Message, the way air hides the sky, is, in fact,
> Tearing it limb from limb this very moment . . .
>   (**"Clepsydra"**)

This is early Ashbery, but the ruminating tone, the evocation of disjointedness at the heart of things is characteristic particularly of the middle of the *oeuvre;* **Three Poems** and **Self-Portrait in a Convex Mirror** deal more self-consciously with the act of writing than do the earlier and later poems.

What we are given to mull over in Ashbery's binaries of apprehension is precisely that which is barely mullable: the distinction between the world's thingness and the language we use to signify it. Ashbery suggests that no other course is open to us, in honesty, but to recognize the contradiction of the arrow of things/others and the arrow of speech/self pointing in opposite directions. One of Ashbery's redemptive graces is his knack of going two ways at once and still getting there, at a place of mediation: "a serpentine/Gesture which hides the truth behind a congruent/Message."

So it is perhaps fair to speak of these poems as both disease and cure; for every fact, it would seem, Ashbery can produce an anti-fact. This is so because "All things seem mention of themselves / And the names which stem from them branch out to other referents" (**"Grand Galop"**). These two lines put emphasis on the making rather than the made, on process as against whatever objects call themselves to our attention; reading through the **Selected Poems** is like going on a boat ride on an endless, exotic river. Since nothing is sure, nothing can have the final word.

An almost egoless voice runs through the book; its privacy is not lyrically personal but more in the public domain. First, second and third person pronouns are used variously and interchangeably. This provides both a screen for Ashbery, the man, and an epic-like movement—the sense that **Selected Poems** is all one poem—for the poet. The poet is a public man, discoursing about anything, from

"Daffy Duck in Hollywood" to **"The Ivory Tower."** However, since few of these poems provide us with the stability of a developed scene or event or person, they are collage-like in their grouping together of diverse elements, i.e., Ashbery's new book has no beginning and presumably will have no ending in terms of an evaluative design. It is a continuity with digressions.

> We were a seesaw. Something
> Ought to be written about how this affects
> You when you write poetry:
> The extreme austerity of an almost empty mind
> Colliding with the lush, Rousseau-like foliage of
>   its desire to
>   communicate
> Something between breaths, if only for the sake
> Of others and their desire to understand you and
>   desert you
> For other centers of communication, so that un-
>   derstanding
> May begin, and in doing so be undone.
>   **("And *Ut Pictura Poesis* Is Her Name")**

Thus understanding is the source of not understanding.

The sumptuousness of Ashbery's language and his self-consciousness as a poet writing something like a supreme fiction places him as an heir of Wallace Stevens, but the inheritance is disputable. When one takes into account the egoless subjectivity, the often abstract discursiveness, the non-lyric recording of what is going on at the time and in the act of writing, and the consequent collage-narrative effects, Ashbery seems to be at least as much a descendant of Pound and Olson—and a precursor of the Language writers—as he is a disciple of Stevens.

The fusion of these strains in Ashbery's poetry gives credence to the view that insofar as he is involved with the possibilities of dream as material his preoccupation is with structure rather than content. It would not be accurate to place him in too strict a connection with the surrealists, because for him the often evasive boundaries between "ordinary" reality and dreamworld have not resulted in an attempt to probe images of the unconscious in order to get at a deeper truth than the daylight can offer. The truth of dreams for Ashbery lies not in their meaning but in the phenomena they apprehend in mystery.

His rationale—he is quite reasonable, given his context of assumptions—is overt in this passage from **"The System,"** the only poem of ***Three Poems*** published in the present volume.

> . . . We know not what we are to become, therefore we can never completely rule out the possibility of intellectual understanding, even though it seems nothing but a snare and a delusion; we might miss out on everything by ignoring its call to order, which is in fact audible to each of us; therefore how can we decide? It is no solution either to combine . . . two approaches, to borrow from right reason or sensory data as the case seems to warrant, for an amalgam is not completeness either, and indeed is far less likely to be so through an error in dosage. So that of the three methods: reason, sense, or a knowing combination of both, the last seems the least like

> a winner, the second problematic; only the first has some slim chance of succeeding through sheer perversity, which is possibly the only way to succeed at all. Thus we may be spared at least the agonizing wading through a slew of details of theories of action at the risk of getting hopelessly bogged down in them: better the erratic approach, which wins all or at least loses nothing, than the cautious semi-failure; better Don Quixote and his windmills than all the Sancho Panzas in the world; and may it eventually turn out that to risk all is to win all, even at the expense of intimate, visceral knowledge of the truth, of its graininess and contours, even though this approach leads despite its physicality to no practical understanding of the truth, no grasp of how to use it toward ends it never dreams of ?

This passage shows Ashbery not at his most quixotic but his most theoretical; we can get a fair grasp on how well his poetry coheres to his concept of what is involved in approaching truth and also of a pragmatism not usually associated with him. Not only truth but the uses of truth.

Don Quixote's charge against the windmills is not simply a demented act. To suspect the windmills of being an opposing army is an illusion, but the attack against them is a serious act that contains an element of play. Dream content often seems to us of the same order. In structuring his "erratic approach" open-endedly, Ashbery is engaged in his own form of *bricolage*. It is questionable whether or not this suspension of meaning (taking it that truth must contain meaning), this "making do" with abeyance, can ultimately lead to anything besides a clear focus on incoherence.

Some readers have refused to accept the terms of Ashbery's play, to view his sometimes bitter, sometimes whimsical humor as more than a poetry of inconsequence, a fashionable and decadent mode pleasing to those reacting against the moral and political fervor of the 1960's. Charles Molesworth has written in reference to **"Clepsydra"** in particular and Ashbery's work generally:

> Havelock Ellis once characterized decadence as a style that subordinates the whole to the part, and we can glimpse something analogous here with the sense that each moment of the poem is true (and the further implication that *only* in its moments is the poem true, as all larger significance is illusory). And the paradox that no moment is true (because its truth must immediately be displaced by the next moment) suggests a sort of polymorphous perversity of contextuality.

It is difficult to argue with this because what Molesworth requires from the poem—presumably any poem—is closure. Each poem in order to be significant and vital must, in this view, subordinate its parts to an overall statement, a synthesis, which will allow the poem to be examined critically with hope of a neatly-packaged reward for the reader. But if such a package, such a conceptual entity, is not forthcoming because the poem refuses to define itself, insisting instead on its provisional status in a more comprehensive cultural flux, then either the reader must reject such a poem or accept the notion that closure (the whole) is not necessarily the sole "end" it might have.

What matters, finally, is the voice in its time. Charles Altieri finds in Ashbery a central figure in today's effort to rescue poetry from a dying romanticism through a fully self-conscious expression that exemplifies poetic thought purified, so to speak, of its purity. At this time in the national life and culture, Altieri writes, "impurity of language becomes a mark of authenticity, since it registers the poet's awareness of the duplicity of discourse and the complexity of intentions. In impurity is our freedom and our salvation." Perhaps this is too confining an attitude, in its amplitude, toward the regeneration of poetry from the romantic, lyric ego's swansong in high modernism, yet it does posit an Ashbery who, despite his private use of the public tongue, offers "poetry as a model of forms of consciousness that public life cannot provide . . . "

> One is forced to read
> The perfectly plausible accomplishment of a
>   purpose
> Into the smooth, perhaps even bland (but so
> Enigmatic) finish. Is there anything
> To be serious about beyond this otherness
> That gets included in the most ordinary
> Forms of daily activity, changing everything
> Slightly and profoundly, and tearing the matter
> Of creation, any creation, not just artistic cre-
>   ation
> Out of our hands, to install it on some mon-
>   strous, near
> Peak, too close to ignore, too far
> For one to intervene?
>   **("Self-Portrait in a Convex Mirror")**

This quotation, coming as it does from the poem even Ashbery's critics consider a masterpiece, may well sum up the theoretics he has established to claim his ground in the late twentieth century American vista. What one is "forced to read" spurns the notion of closure, declaring it to be a "smooth," "bland" approach to composition. "This otherness" depends upon the impurities that accumulate in daily activities, the organic flaws which permeate all human endeavors. They take "any creation . . . out of our hands" and so become impossible to ignore. The case **"Self-Portrait"** makes is strong and decisive as to process, arguing for the movement of thought as against its finished product, which is never finished anyway and has only a businessman's sort of programmatic effectuality in life.

"Self-Portrait" (1975) culminates Ashbery's most overtly theoretical writing. Four books have intervened between that work and the *Selected Poems.* In these he has returned, with greater maturity and finesse, to the freer flowing, odder language juxtapositions of the early work. This is not to say he has abandoned his critique of binary oppositions; far from it, since critique is inseparable from his content—it *is* his content. But now there is mastery. When he begins one of his latest poems, **"A Wave,"**

> To pass through pain and not know it,
> A car door slamming in the night.
> To emerge on an invisible terrain,

the sympathetic reader will not be mystified. The words

are not too private, not really impossible. Ashbery's body moves through our quotidian life, impure surely, unfinished, the body's speech carrying on, prolix at times, a stream of awareness and confusion, not ontologically different from ours but still a distinctive vision in the face of a general corruption. (pp. 258-63)

Gene Frumkin, in a review of "Selected Poems," in Conjunctions, *Vol. 9, 1986, pp. 258-63.*

Susan Stewart   (essay date September-October 1988)

[*Stewart is an American poet and literary theorist. In the following essay, she discusses the relationship of language to both perception and daily existence in Ashbery's poetry collection* April Galleons.]

John Ashbery's most recent collection of poems, **April Galleons,** explores the conditions of language at the end of the world—that is, that world we know through language. Like his earlier long poem **"The Skaters,"** the poems of **April Galleons** bear a glancing relation to [T. S. Eliot's] *The Wasteland* in speaking to issues of saying and knowing in the twentieth century. But Ashbery also reminds us that we are at the close of the millennium, at the century's other, perhaps less hopeful, perhaps less nostalgic, end. **April Galleons** is a book constructed by a principle of recursiveness, where language examines its own conditions of emergence and disappearance within a social life equally regenerative and fleeting. Through the experience of reading, we become aware of the particularity of our experience and of the ways in which that particularity is given shape and the capability of change through its relation to the movement of tradition. Thus in this work post-modernism's dual tasks are to temporalize the modernist narrative and to subject the scene of the avant-garde to a critique of novelty. In a cubist experiment very much like David Hockney's recent "Cameraworks," Ashbery's book moves the reader into an acute awareness of the time of form. **April Galleons** thereby glosses the recurrent metaphor of a wave in Ashbery's work—a wave that is the material yet invisible movement of sound through time. And, as well, the book reminds us of that other wave, constant and constantly changing in form, both agent and recipient of time and oblivion, controlled by an unseen contingency of nature, yet spoken only by the history of our seeing of it.

If **April Galleons** is a book with a typical Ashberyian sense of humor, it is also, because of its broad and timely ambition, one of the dark books. It is shadowed by pestilence and fire—the holocausts of plague and nuclear destruction. The thematic of the book becomes the temporal possibility of understanding. And the mutuality implied by the very notion of theme is both put into question and presented as the only possibility for the social as the carrying forth of tradition. In lines like "Something / In the darkness understands, tries to make up for it all. / But it's like a new disease, a resistant strain," (**"Alone in the Lumber Business"**) and "how we were all going to be lovers / When a climatic change occurred" (**"Too Happy, Happy Tree"**), in titles like **"Forgotten Sex"** and **"Savage**

Menace," in poems like **"Riddle Me,"** recalling the subjection of the body to tests determining its destiny, Ashbery presses upon us the urgency and limits of our self-consciousness as we move inevitably, and often in an untimely way, toward death. In the process of reading the book, we experience a growing perception of an ominously hopeful content, of a decision, first, *to live*—"Dreams I had, including suicide" (**"A Mood of Quiet Beauty"**) and

> Is it because we think nobody's
> Listening that one day it comes, the urge to de-
> lete yourself,
> "Take yourself out," as they say?
> > (**"Someone You Have Seen Before"**)

—and then *how to live:*

> There are two ways to be.
> You must try getting up from the table
> And sitting down relaxed in another country
> Wearing red suspenders
> Toward one's own space and time.
> > (**"Ostensibly"**)

Hence, in this work, the redemption offered by assuming the position of the other in constituting one's self—and art as the paradigm for that redemption.

Although *April Galleons* is full of the talk of contemporary everyday life, it is also almost wholly without the usual Ashbery allusions to popular culture. Instead, the book is replete with allusions to more ancient forms of discourse, particularly philosophy and folklore. The presiding spirit of the book is the weeping philosopher, Heraclitus. This is the philosopher of **"Concerning Nature,"** but it is also the philosopher of Max Jacob's "La Rue Ravignan":

> On ne se baigne pas deux fois dans le même fleuve," disait le philosophe Héraclite. Pourtant, ce sont toujours les mêmes qui remontent! Aux mêmes heures, ils passent gais ou tristes. Vous tous, passants de la rue Ravignan, je vous ai donné les noms des défunts de L'Histoire! Voici Agamemnon! Voici Mme Hanska! Ulysse est un laitier! Patrocle est au bas de la rue qu'un Pharaon est près de moi. Castor et Pollux sont les dames du cinquième. . . .

Thus Heraclitus' insight, that one cannot step twice into the same river, that Time's flow is constantly changing and changing us, is extended into an insight regarding the multiplicity of identity and the singularity of death. In *April Galleons* Heraclitus' river of flux is juxtaposed to two other rivers we can never cross twice—Lethe, the river of forgetting, and Styx, the river of speechlessness: "The underground stream that has never stood still is the surface / And the theater for all that is to come . . . " (**"Forgotten Sex"**). *April Galleons* repeatedly reminds us that a culture lives because it is practiced, spoken, uttered. Only speaking can save us from forgetting. Thus the book's lyric voice is a kind of ventriloquist's act in which others' voices (the social) are taken up and dispersed, taken up and dispersed, in a miming of the flow of language itself.

Yet it is a disservice to these poems to imply that they are simply *about* these allusions. Rather the allusions function to remind us of the various conditions we need in order to make meaning. Each poem, like a *saltimbanque*—isolated, archaic, and urbane at once—comes forth to present or enact the relation of language to understanding. This saltimbanque, for example, itself is not a random allusion. It appears often in *April Galleons* in a constellation combining Pierrot's theatrical white powder, cocaine, snow, Baudelaire, Jacob, of course, and, finally, Picasso, the most prominent, though unmentioned, resident of "La Rue Ravignan." Allusion is not simply a matter here of talking to one's own generation, of making "statements of membership." Rather, Ashbery takes on the process of emergence, opacity, misapprehension, and disappearance by which language comes into currency and fades in time. Gradually we achieve the specific historical insights into forgetting and speechlessness that the book purports are the experience of the life of language, the life in language.

In talking about the book, we become aware of all of the traps of the "overview," for it is the impossibility of this view, with its haughty claims of a kind of posthumous vatic mode, that *April Galleons* is out to subvert. "It's still too early to make concessions" claims **"Alone in the Lumber Business."** To enter into the conditions of *April Galleons* it is necessary to abandon the possibility of paranoia—to refuse to admit a point of over-reading, for this "diary," as a manifesto of speculation and resonance, returns us to the very origins of the process of reading and its relation to prophecy. In scenes of reading ranging from auguring to the overdetermined scene of Augustine in the garden, *April Galleons* finds its method. Reciprocally, we might borrow a term from writing practice and attempt a kind of "cross-hatching" of the book, a writing over it, reminding us of the prophecy of **"Railroad Bridge"**:

> The reader is reading your brain,
> That fluid but even surface. No scar
> Resolves it. From pentimenti to waste water
> All the subjects have been scanned.
> The sewers are clogged.

These fifty-three pieces echo to the weekly time of life, flowing in and out of overheard conversations, quoted snatches of talk, outbursts of feeling. They are not "poetry monuments," aloof and expert. Rather, they move through each other, summoning an ongoing consciousness built between their signs and the reader's work. The reader remembers analogous experiences: standing on the dock or in the station, is it we who move or what we are viewing? Or both, the claim of the last line of the book: the mutual vehicle of "the old eyes of love."

The opening poem of *April Galleons* takes its title, **"Vetiver,"** from the French and Tamil word for an East Indian grass whose roots yield a fragrant oil for perfume. The word means "root that is dug up," and so here the gesture of etymology (the Indo-European "root") is also the gesture of recovering the senses (the smell as the most antique of the senses). A pleasure in origins is manifested in the beauty of the opening lines—

> Ages passed slowly, like a load of hay,
> As the flowers recited their lines
> And pike stirred at the bottom of the pond.

—the litany of things and forms of life at the opening of the poem dissolves at the close of the stanza into language itself, particularly the alphabet as a set of natural figures transformed: "keeping the melancholy / Already distilled in letters of the alphabet."

From the end of summer ("The pen was cool to the touch"), the poem moves to "It would be time for winter now, its spun-sugar / Palaces and also lines of care / At the mouth, pink smudges on the forehead and cheeks." By this point the poem has arrived at its fulcrum, the moment on which the book as a whole pivots—a change in life, in weather, in seasons, in history. And this pivot is signalled at mid-poem by a catachresis or fault in the language of the poem: "The color once known as 'ashes of roses.' " We cannot hear "ashes of roses" without noting its attraction to and resistance to "attar of roses"; thus we go from color to smell in a kind of anti-synesthesia, a distillation that signals both loss and gain, substitution and fetishization—hence another gloss on the meaning of **"Vetiver."** As we attend to this fragment of life, it shatters, as a rose does: "It had all been working so well and now, / Well, it just kind of came apart in the hand."

The second stanza has moved us from a world where reference can be a matter of indexicality, where description is a matter of pointing, to a common world where *all this is language,* where a change in language signifies to us that we are not the "we" we thought we were. The passage is thereby replete with clichés:

> How many snakes and lizards shed their skins
> For time to be passing on like this,
> Sinking deeper in the sand as it wound toward
> The conclusion.
>
> . . . . .
>
> As a change is voiced, sharp
> As a fishhook in the throat, and decorative tears
>   flowed
> Past us into a basin called infinity.

Thus Ashbery, in the time of the poem, reminds us that time passes regardless of the clichés of time's passing.

In the third and final stanza we receive our instructions for reading the book:

> There was no charge for anything, the gates
> Had been left open intentionally.
> Don't follow, you can have whatever it is.

And the reader is linked to an erotic and lyrically argumentative "you" as addressee in the plaintive cry of the poem's closure:

> O keep me with you, unless the outdoors
> Embraces both of us, unites us, unless
> The birdcatchers put away their twigs,
> The fishermen haul in their sleek empty nets
> And others become part of the immense crowd
> Around this bonfire, a situation
> That has come to mean us to us. . . .

Clearly the anxious imagery of "The Wasteland" is appearing here, but just as clearly both the anxiety and the imagery means something different. In Ashbery's poem allusion will not signal fragmentation so much as an array

of possibilities set out in a hope for entry: "you can have whatever it is." And this line, which echoes the imploring phrases one might address to a burglar in an attempt to save the body, shows that it is the endurance of a tradition, an erotic, that links human time and not a hypothetical fixity of words and things. The final "unless" here, the last lines of the poem, links the Heraclitean flux of fire, the autumnal sacrifice of the leaves, the endurance of emotion, and—echoing to the book's title—the burning of the past, as modes of willed forgetting: "the crying / In the leaves is saved, the last silver drops." But just as importantly, as in "ashes of roses," our understanding, full of the self-confidence called forth by the fact that we are "at closure," must do a double-take. For "the last silver drops" can serve as an appositive for the crying in the leaves or, ominously, it can be a fall of mercury. We are deeply within the realm of the Miltonic serious pun here, for a fall of mercury can be the killing of the messenger (i.e., the poet's death implied in the "climatic change") and, in one and the same gesture, the spun sugar palaces of the beginning of the poem transformed into an image of a nuclear winter.

> It hurts, this wanting to give a dimension
> To life, when life is precisely that dimension.
> —**"Vaucanson"**

All utterance in context as hopeful, resolute, creative. All utterance in time as tragic, limited, bound by contradiction. Writing about **"Vetiver"** as I have done here is impossible, almost florid. Once one reads all of *April Galleons,* going back to individual poems is a matter of reading against, of juxtaposition, belated resonance, and decorative—because applied—sentiment. Thus the problem of understanding the present gets worked out in the texture of reading.

> Like an unruly eyebrow, something that wasn't
>   there
> Moments ago, can stop you in your tracks. I
>   mean the way
> Things have of just happening once the principle
> Of happening has been laid down for them can
>   be alarming
> Or like a rush of bubbles to the nose, depending.
> **("No I Don't")**

When one quotes, one both cuts off the quoted material from meaning and imbues it with meaning. In *April Galleons* all looking becomes a kind of quotation, a matter of negotiating the relation between the particular and the general, the specific and the applicable. Ultimately, this negotiation is just a utopian daydream—the fact is that as soon as we attend to something, we suppress something else, just as in this essay the unmentioned allusions, lines, aspects of the poems remain to haunt us like a reproach. Everyday life appears as a dream, clear and luminescent, yet a dream whose temporality nevertheless occludes a view of "the big picture." From **"Gorboduc"**:

> Tackle the infinite, basing our strategem
> On knowledge of one inch of it. But then the
>   story blows away,
> And what can you do, howling without a script?

Or from **"Someone You Have Seen Before"**:

> So much that happens happens in
> small ways
> That someone was going to get around to tabu-
> late, and then never did. . . .

Thus we proceed by processes of exclusion. In talking about the book we have a demonstration of the ways in which we talk about life. "Wanting to give a dimension to life," we simply or not so simply make more talk—that is our project and its consequences are a carrying of the language (and a shared, assumed reliance upon the language) forward at the same time as we are dropping back into death, losing resonance and meaning, doing violence to language and to context. We are always already "under different auspices," and it is Ashbery's genius here to remind us of that and to remind us relentlessly of the situated nature of our longing for some original and/or total "auspice" of being.

> Sure was pretty
> Close back there, I got scared, didn't you? The
> feeling that something
> Enormous, like a huge canvas, is happening
> without one's having the
> Least suspicion, without one single scrap of in-
> formation being vouchsafed?
> **("Dreams of Adulthood")**

What is the unit of the work of art here? Why, as poetry, does *April Galleons* resist being read as poetry? Every aspect of every poem, every poem in the book, and ultimately *April Galleons* as the culmination of Ashbery's *oeuvre*, pulls the reader into a situation where abstraction appears as a matter of resonant particulars. All reference is allusion, all allusion echoes to its conditions of meaning, and every formal feature is thereby located as a semantic feature. Voice, image, metaphor, symbol, metrical organization, traditional form—all the accouterments of poetic discourse are temporalized and hence located within a context that forces them to signify. It is all content and all content is formal and so we are able to recognize it. In other words, we are reading a scene of reading and we are in it. Ashbery often reminds us of this situation. He looks up from his book of "us": "My finger in the book," "I was reading about dinosaurs." We have only to see such gestures as counterpoints to the descriptive and musical closure of Stevens's "The House Was Quiet and the World Was Calm"; in Ashbery the pretensions of disinterestedness are put into their specific historical relations.

Thus the most dominant technique in the book is interruption. Ashbery's diarist is always "experiencing audio difficulties" (**"Fall Pageant"**), always about to be interrupted. This technique constantly reminds us of a life cut short and it also reminds us that experience comes cut this way—for the art work to present itself as a totality would be precisely the abandonment of the possibility of understanding: "From this valley they say you are leaving. / Remember to tie your shoes" (**"Fall Pageant"**). We are called to a halt; Ashbery presents us with an everyday aporia of incomprehension, yet we know enough to sense we are missing something. In **"Riddle Me,"** consider the lilting trochees of the opening lines of the first and second stanzas: "Rainy days are best" and "Even as they spoke." Yet each of these starts is stopped in its tracks by a change

in metrics, a consequent clotted syntax like an overvoice coming in to drown out the music: "There is some permanence in the angle / That things make with the ground" and "All right so it's better to have vague outlines."

Interruption is also worked by two other devices: the metrical stutter and the double-take. **"When half the time they don't know themselves . . . "** begins with a bursting set of spondees, reminding us of the above-cited bubbles at the mouth and also of the prophet's stutter, one of the prominent figural allusions in the book:

> Old cathedrals, old markets, good and firm
> things
> And old streets, one always feels intercepted
> As they walk quickly past, no nonsense, cab-
> bages
> And turnips, the way they get put into songs:

The doubletake is worked on a number of levels: first, the dissolving image as in "the last silver drops" of **"Vetiver"**; second, the notion that all speech here is double-voiced by the other, a "twice-told tale"—in **"Unreleased Movie,"** for example, the prophet/poet/law-giver explains,

> Ever since I burnt my mouth
> I talk two ways, first as reluctant explainer, then
> as someone offstage
> In a dream, hushing those who might wake you
> from this dream,
> Imperfectly got up as a lutanist.

And, thirdly, as in the following example from **"The Ice Storm,"** a voice constantly qualifying itself, incorporating and anticipating objections:

> isn't really a storm of course because unlike most storms it isn't one till it's over and people go outside and say will you look at that. And by then it's of course starting to collapse. [. . .] are you sure it's this you were waiting for while the storm—the real one—pressed it all into the earth to emphasize a point that melts away as fast as another idea enters the chain of them in the conversation about earth and sky and woods and how you should be good to your parents and not cheat at cards. The summer's almost over it seems to say. Did I say summer I meant to say winter it seems to say. [. . .] i.e., the winter, our favorite of the seasons, the one that goes by quickest although you almost never hear anyone say, I wonder where the winter has gone. But anyone engaged in the business of swapping purity for depth will understand what I mean.

Swapping purity, disinterestedness, for depth, engagement, is precisely the business of *April Galleons*; we are reminded, not coincidentally, of another phrase, impressing upon us the urgency of the book's appearance: "We interrupt this program in order to bring you an important message." Modestly, Ashbery uses interruption as a vehicle for his sense of the politics of the book; that is, the politics of this book and all books. The commitment to read moves forward despite, and in recognition of, interruption and hence represents our hopeful and cynical relation to intersubjectivity. In **"Forgotten Song,"** he writes,

the continual stirring
That we come to recognize as life merely acts
   blindly,

In pursuit of small, selfish goals, but the repercussions
Are enormous though they concern no one.

. . . . .

A force erupting so violently
We can't witness any of it.

The process of reading forces us to become aware of how
we mishear, how ignorance works, how language necessarily becomes a commodity, how we cannot see. It
doesn't tell us what to do; it tells us how we refuse to notice.

Please play this back. All the recording
In the world won't help unless you or someone
   else listens. . . .
                              —"A Snowball in Hell"

In *April Galleons* Ashbery has radically altered the conditions of lyric voice. The speaker, or diarist, is constantly
pointing to the situated quality of his discourse. And we,
as readers, are constantly aware of our status as already-
anticipated, already part of the speaker's self-picture:
"Your uniqueness isn't that unique" (**"Morning Jitters"**);
"We catch up / To ourselves, but they are the selves of
others." We are always aware that what the speaker is saying is what he has in fact already heard, and that what we
are hearing is what we are in fact already listening for, and
that somewhere in between is both the social ground of
meaning and the assumption of that social ground. Thus
all speech is already twinned or doubled in its "saidness,"
and all dialogue is already multiplied, more than two. In
"Wet Are the Boards," the "Nymph of the fashions of the
air" points out

" . . . We are all
Friends here,
And whatever it takes to get us out of the mess
   we're in
One of us has."

We are reminded that this nymph herself is "Comus" 's
"Sweet Echo, sweetest nymph, that liv'st unseen" within
her "airy shell." And hence we are also reminded of another, richly perfumed, allusion to "Comus":

I was all ear,
And took in strains that might create a soul
Under the ribs of Death.

Ashbery's allusions are therefore a gesture against forgetting and silence:

You can still find those pleasures somewhere,
In old stalls. Negative
Listener response hasn't drowned
The very simple thing of this world. . . .
                              ("Insane Decisions")

But beyond the willed intentionality of "negative listener
response," Ashbery also insists upon the necessity of misapprehension, the havoc wreaked upon language by
changes in time and context. **"Dreams of Adulthood"**'s
image of London Bridge amid Lake Havasu City is the

model for these shifts in meaning. In **"Amid Mounting Evidence,"** the speaker says,

every potential is realized if one waits
   long enough,
Only by that time the context may have faded,
   fragile
As summersweet or the light on a windowsill,
   and then,
And then, why the text will be seen as regular
Only no one wants to play anymore; games
Have their fashions much as truth does. . . .

Here Ashbery is once again using the catachrestic doubletake to jolt us into an awareness of such shifts. We
would expect this aphorism to carry its weight by making
games the vehicle and *truth* the tenor. But instead the
terms are not simply inverted, they are made "regular,"
that is, no longer distinguishable within the old hierarchy
of values.

The philosopher of language Mikhail Bakhtin wrote in his
last notebooks that every dialogue takes place as if it were
within a background made up of the understanding of an
invisibly present third party—a party bracketed and assumed by the participants. He wrote that the torture
chamber or hell is precisely that place where this background is missing—where no one hears, where there is no
such third party. And he follows this comment with a notion from Marx: "That only thought uttered in the word
becomes a real thought for another person and only in the
same way is it a thought for myself." For Bakhtin, following Marx, this prospect of the third person, the third person embodying the social in all language, is in the social
gesture of utterance itself. And it is this embodiment that
we see in Ashbery's use here of a particular account of the
utterances of the poet/prophet and the role played by such
utterance in carrying forth tradition. For Ashbery, the
poem becomes the locus of insight—the poem as the utterance of a language the poet has already received from the
life of speech, the poem returning meaning to the poet as
well as to his audience.

Thus we find in *April Galleons* a particularly Ashberyian
variant of the Galatea story. For making poems is not simply a matter of producing what he calls, in **"October at
the Window,"** the "enameled word." Rather, it is a matter
of animation, of producing something that returns, that
gives life to thought. Those selves we make in time, including our own, are our stake in making a history that will
give back context and meaning to us. We remember that
Pygmalion's Galatea gave her name to an English ship
and to the sailor suits of little boys. Here we see the importance of the tradition of animation in Ashbery's *oeuvre*,
from the moving statues of *The Meno* to Popeye, Daffy
Duck, and the halted movements of Raymond Roussel's
technique of the "tableau vivant." Yet within the context
of *April Galleons*, animation is not represented so much
as considered:

This time we take in and lavish so much affection on

It starts to like us, changeling though it be, and
   sees
Some point in the way we were made.

("Forgotten Song")

And, in **"Becalmed on Strange Waters"**:

> In the sky's sensual pout, the crazy kindness
> Of statues, the scraps of leaves still blowing
>   around
> Self-importantly after winter was well under
>   way;
>
> . . . . .
>
> Was matter enough for one or more
>   dreams. . . .

Finally, this book of arrested life, as a poetic manifesto of "untimeliness," states in **"The Mouse"** (i.e. a possible answer to the question "What are you?"):

> I like what you have given me,
> O my songs, scalloped chessmen
> Of emotions or of elaborate indifference.
> Your determining factor is a thing like the
>   weather
> That comes and goes, and stays. . . .

The Galatea story gets tied here to the book's recurring metaphor of the animated flower: the rose in **"Vetiver"**; the rose covered by a sheath of ice in **"The Ice Storm"**; the Japanese paper flower in **"Becalmed in Strange Waters,"** "still compacted in the excitement that lies ahead." But that excitement is first anticipation, and then dissolution, "the defeated memory gracious as flowers." Excitement and beauty will shatter, just as the porous youth of **"Vetiver"** does. Thus this ice-covered life is resonant with the snowball as a metaphor for experience: "Your life snowballed and hardened" and "after that there was nothing / To do except wait for colors to leach through" (**"Railroad Bridge"**). The animation of the rose, the rewinding of the movie—these are gestures that take the risk of shattering, of exposing memory to time, yet Ashbery's language of flowers is already mediated by metaphor and so rescued from the temporality of the material world. If we find here Campion's laughing "rosebuds fill'd with snow" and Mallarmé's poetic flower, absent from all bouquets, we also find a worry that language will stop, that meaning will be voided. Making the poem out of this condition, one acquires another possibility, one goes forward talking, "miming freshness tracked by pathos" (**"The Ice Storm"**), even if talking is silence:

> It was all notes for a book that has been written,
>   that nobody
> Is ever going to read. A bottle with a note in it
> Washes up on shore and no one sees it, no one
>   picks it up.
>   ("By the Flooded Canal")

If this version of Galatea is at times rather cheery, Ashbery also reminds us of the diffident side of the story: "Besides they're just statues one can take along, / If one wants" (**"Bilking the Statues"**). And **"April Galleons"** concludes, "a winged guitar would be major / If we had one." In this compression of Pound's dream of the troubadour/poet and Stevens's dream of the transcendent imagination, we are presented with a fault-line, the crack of history and historical judgment putting any poetic immanence into suspicion and, ultimately, resignation. Ashbery

is, as he says in the passage quoted above from **"Unreleased Movie,"** "imperfectly gotten up as a lutanist." In fact, the poet is not rewarded for surrendering to time and nature; he does not thus achieve a sublime music. Perhaps no other lines of poetry take the wind out of Shelley's sails so much as these:

> . . . it diminishes us
> In our getting to know it
> As trees come to know a storm
> Until it passes and light falls anew
> Unevenly, on all the muttering kinship:
> Things with things, persons with objects,
> Ideas with people or ideas.
>   ("Vaucanson")

What kind of poems are these? One would have to answer that they are lyric meditations brought dramatically up against the limitations of their moment in time. They are written in time and against time. We are aware of this aspect precisely in the ways in which the poems avoid mere novelty—i.e. novelty as an experiment which would seek to transcend, or move ahead of, time. They attempt to speak before language disappears, before an erotic disappears, before "new strains" destroy "old strains"—the latter exemplified by the endurance of "song."

In **"Offshore Breeze"** there is an account of the decay of language: "sharp / As a word held in the mouth too long. / And he spat out the pit." The poignancy of the poet's position in a culture of novelty is brought forward in these lines, as it is in the many disparaging and yet somehow incredulous references to commodities throughout the book. First the dead word in the mouth, losing its meaning, is made analogous to the coin in the mouth of the dead, Charon's fare. Thus the coinage of words is connected to the arbitrary value of other social goods. Gold and silver are, too, a kind of dross; the verses to **"London Bridge"** proclaim, "silver and gold will be stole away"—as, we know, will be the Bridge itself. Ashbery insists upon the ways in which language itself is a consumer good. Those things he "likes"—paintings, lakes and poems—are all in the business of "ruffling the surface," of exchanging "purity for depth," that is, of responding to time by posing as still surfaces whose history must be a matter of a supplement. Yet this pose is momentary and ideal; the relation of language to time becomes inevitably a matter of loss and deracination. When we are brought "an important message" it could be the urgent bottled fact of another's stranded existence or it could be an advertisement.

The hauntingly too-pretty **"A Mood of Quiet Beauty"** closes, after its discussion of burst dreams, "including suicide," with a vivid gesture of listening at the other's (i.e. the lover's) chest:

> We hear, and sometimes learn,
> Pressing so close
>
> And fetch the blood down, and things like that.

It is typical of Ashberyian sincerity to be moderated by irony, but here we find instead a sense of resignation. We are late in the century: "fetch the blood down" has lost its freshness; it is a thing "like that." But only by its constant application, and hence erosion—by its lived relation to experience—does language continue. Hence language lives at the expense of metaphor. The lines following close the poem: "Museums then became generous, they live in our breath." When the facing poem to this one, "When half the time they don't know themselves . . . ," suggests that we have had "some kind of shine" put on us "We didn't consent to, / As though we were someone's car: / Large, animated, calm," we are aware of a new addition to the repertoire of metaphor. But we are also aware, as we are throughout the book, that we must pay a price for the freshness of such a metaphor—it will "wear us" as it moves through time; we will become dated by our entry into such a point of language.

The museum that lives in our breath is the museum of oral tradition in the broadest sense. This is not a museum of static objects, but a museum of change and transformation. Ashbery has often used allusions to traditional culture in his work: his **"Fantasia on a Nut-Brown Maid,"** for example, is a master copy of the psychological situation underlying that traditional ballad's dialogue of sincerity with inauthenticity. In *April Galleons* traditional culture is the culture most recently lost, what is no longer on our breath, but what might be caught in snatches, in a kind of half-heard way, on the brink of its disappearance.

Although there is much contemporary language and phrasing here—allusions to cocaine, "Chinese restaurant tea," early retirement, "middle-echelon apparatchiks," "some arts project," "Steve" 's and "Brian" 's— everything is, as Ashbery says in **"Postures of Unease,"** both "new and worn." **"No I Don't"** plaintively explains,

> Our fathers, who had so many catego-
> ries
> For so few things, could have supplied a term
> Like a special brush for bathing, and in due
> course this
> Particularity would have faded into the sum of
> the light,
> An entity no more.

When the word disappears the thing disappears. When our way of talk disappears, we disappear. Ashbery constantly reminds us of this process in a variety of ways—the fading lines of old songs, the problem of putting together names and faces, forms of love and emotion on the brink of destruction. If Pound and Williams felt that "the language is worn out," and hence it was time to make it new, Ashbery reminds us that it is the function of time to wear out the language and that making it new is a conservative as well as an innovative convention—that is, a convention nonetheless. In **"Some Money"** we find references to the Biblical Joseph, to nineteenth-century genre painting, to "the queen" who is in her parlor eating bread and honey, to the pigsty of the prodigal son, to Moses' "blasted bush," to the lobster from Lewis Carroll, and to sentimental songs of World War I. The poem concludes, "No pen mightier than this said the object." The point is not eclecticism, but the social, contingent bond into which we enter in connecting these meanings. Such allusions, like money, only represent within a *system* of meanings and the system only works because of our shared assumption that it should do so. We are always positioned in relation to these languages; even judgments like "mispronunciation" be-

come problematic here, that is, matters of the hearer's agenda and the speaker's intention. Thus a kind of catachrestic violence is always at the heart of what seems to be the bearing of tradition.

Consider, for example, the problem of the titles. Putting together names and faces and subjects is made analogous to putting together pieces of time in order to make history. The titles here are sometimes "captions," that is, descriptions or references to what is happening in the poem and the book, as is the case with the inaugural **"Vetiver."** But at other times, the titles simply resist interpretation by their singularity. Sometimes they strike our ear as "being a little off." For example, **"When half the time they don't know themselves,"** like "ashes of roses," sounds more like what it *isn't*, i.e. "When half the time they don't know what they're talking about," than what it is. Thus this title brilliantly and economically makes Ashbery's point regarding the constitution of being in language within a demonstration of the shifting temporal grounds of linguistic certainty. Or one must go look up Ashbery's titles in the library and then try to put them together with their "faces," the poems. We come to rely upon records of reference rather than upon the living experience of speech. Something is always left out, something always fades to obscurity. And meanwhile the library is always subject to fire. "There are too many of us ever / To be remembered let alone recorded," writes Ashbery in **"Letters I Did or Did Not Get."** Hence he provides titles like **"Vetiver," "Riddle Me"** (the traditional opening to a Caribbean riddling session), the inexplicable **"Adam Snow," "Vaucanson"** (the early eighteenth century French mathematician, mechanician, and author of *Automata*), and **"Gorboduc"** (or *Ferrex and Porrex,* one of the earliest English tragedies, written by Norton and Sackville and taken from the legendary chronicles of Britain. Gorboduc is a king whose sons Ferrex and Porrex quarrel over the kingdom and civil war ensues). Each of *April Galleons*'s titles bears a skewed relation to its referent and so words and things constantly betray each other. As during revolutions, the titles get lost. The reader is forced to develop his or her own mnemonic system for remembering the lines in the poems and the poems in the book. Thus all readers are expatriates here from a utopia of reference, the imaginary childhood where, as Humpty Dumpty proclaimed, things mean exactly what we choose them to mean.

Through the book's references to giants, kings, princes, castles, magic fish, wedding-cake drawbridges, and Tom Tiddler's ground (a place where money is easily made, from the children's game in which one side chants, "We're on Tom Tiddler's ground, picking up gold and silver"), we are drawn to the diminutive past, the past that established the order of this world and then bowed out, invisible to us except through marks upon the landscape and the landscape of language. The prophets here, Isaiah, Elijah, and Moses the stutterer, and the sufferers such as Jonah, have burned their mouths or otherwise experienced a pain at the foundation of linguistic experience. In **"Disguised Zenith,"** Ashbery asks "there is no meaning but in suffering / And where is the suffering in that?" But even this declamation strikes us catachrestically, for we expect the clause to end "where is the *meaning* in that." By substituting *suf-*

fering, Ashbery once again asserts the temporal: here displacement appears as inversion, yet temporality could as easily change the terms in other ways. The next stanza continues, "Their meaning is *for* our meaning, and where / Is the meaning in that?" Only a pure repetition is precluded by time.

Ashbery is not just employing folklore, he is generating the folklore of poetry itself. As is often the case in his work, he aggressively inserts references to minor poets, reminding us of the fleeting nature of all fame, including his own. Here echoing Eliot, Thomas Lovell Beddoes is his model for a kind of "Death's Jest Book." Motifs from Henry Austin Dobson would seem to include "the Rose is beauty, the Gardener, Time," the Sermon on the Mount, "the paradox of time," and, of course, the "galleons of Spain." Or, to choose another source of galleons and outlines, we hear Kipling's "Last Chantey": "Then stooped the Lord, and He called the good sea up to Him, / And 'stablished its borders unto all eternity, / That such as have no pleasure / For to praise the Lord by measure, / They may enter into galleons and serve him on the sea." John Clare, a frequent Ashbery character, is the source of a fleeting glimpse of nature. And as he has done elsewhere, Ashbery makes use of metrical allusion. In **"Adam Snow,"** for example, we find the lines " . . . such a personal call. Sometimes it's nowhere at all / Or a faint girl will make light of it," lines which necessarily echo to the dazzling "call" rhymes of Plath's "Lady Lazarus," as well as to her suicide itself. **"The Romantic Entanglement"** accounts for "Response being, by its very nature, romantic, / The very urge to romanticism." Hence the "mussel gatherers" of this poem, as well as Adonais's frost-bound head and "winter come and gone," are important resonances, or responses, of *April Galleons* to Romanticism. **"Too Happy, Happy Tree"** takes its title from Keat's "In Drear' Nighted December." The "Ode to a Nightingale" 's happy Dryad and "Darkling I listen; and, for many a time / I have been half in love with easeful Death . . . " (see "the darkling purple air" of **"Wet Are the Boards"**), as well as its use of allusions to "Lethe," "bubbles" at the "purple-stained mouth," and fairy imagery make it a key text for *April Galleons* as a whole; the "Ode on a Grecian Urn" 's "happy, happy boughs," "unheard melodies," sacrifices and statues thread throughout in a deep allusion to Keats's strains and untimeliness. Yet **"Too Happy, Happy Tree"** also makes reference to one of Ashbery's best-known poems, **"Into the Dusk-Charged Air,"** in its allusions to the Tigris and the Monongahela:

> Generations of reciters told the tale
> From the factory of your worn roots
> And it made some difference because look how
>   multiplied
> Everything is. Your own image refracts
> Again and again greeting you at embarrassed
>   moments in the silent
> History. . . .

Sometimes even a lexical choice, such as the use of *guerdon* in **"Finnish Rhapsody,"** will strike us—here we recall the use of that term in Williams's "Asphodel" and then this erotic "flower" floods in upon us once more with a whole set of related allusions: Kora, the fiery ring around

Brunhilde, and all the shared aspects of these two long, late-life poems on love and death.

Ashbery here also relies frequently upon the dinosaur genres, the extinct forms of poetry: that is, the ballad and the epic. The ballad, as a form which is a matter of assembled snatches from its outset, is quite violently evoked in *April Galleons.* For example, **"Forgotten Song"** opens with an "insane" couplet merging "The Sands of Dee" and "Lord Randall": "O Mary, go and call the cattle home / For I'm sick in my heart and fain would lie down." And closes with a line from "The Unquiet Grave": "*The stalk is withered dry, my love, so will our hearts decay.*" If we know the latter ballad, we go on to hear the fuller context of this quote: " 'Tis down in yonder garden green / Love, where we used to walk, / The finest flower that ere was seen / Is wither'd to a stalk . . . " and "So make yourself content my love. Til God calls you away. . . . " Consequently, we also hear this ballad weaving in and out of other phrases, "June and the nippers will scarcely look our way. / And be bold then . . . " in **"Riddle Me"**; the references to the shattered flower throughout; reflections on the conditions of weather and gardening as, punningly, "natural" languages; allusions to death and Judgment Day. Or, and this is the point, all these other allusions make us remember a ballad it is impossible to remember, a ballad beyond our possibilities of hearing, necessarily subject to a mispronunciation. And the ballad is furthermore mixed with "Asphodel" and "The Wasteland." If we put our ear closely enough, we hear the frightening consequences of a slant rhyme between "nippers" in the early **"Riddle Me"** and "Lepers" in the final **"April Galleons."** How nippers become lepers becomes a record of the passage of time and nature, but also the passage of legislation. Contingency acquires nightmare-like proportions and is mimed by the reader's by-now-inevitable and finely-tuned hearing.

April Galleons's most brilliant and complex use of tradition appears in the long poem **"Finnish Rhapsody."** The title signals the poem's connection to the great compilation of Finnish epic verse, the *Kalevala,* which Ashbery had previously made reference to in his well-known poem, **"At North Farm."** But the *Kalevala* is here used beyond mere thematic allusion. We are reminded of its origins in those runes used in giving an account of the origins of sickness and in warding off evil. Even more significantly, Ashbery ingeniously employs the *technique* of the *Kalevala* to structure his poem as a double-voiced work, thus dramatically illustrating his sense of "talking two ways," the double-tongued stuttering/talking of the poet-prophet. The *Kalevala* is traditionally performed by pairs of bards who alternate lines, and thus construct the tale by an incremental and glancing form of repetition. Thus **"Finnish Rhapsody,"** as did Longfellow's "Song of Hiawatha" before it, works by lines constructed around such a process of doubling: statement/caesura/restatement, as in "He managed the shower, coped with the small spattering drops / Then rubbed himself dry with a towel, wiped the living organism," and "Day extended its long promise, light swept through his refuge. / But it was time for business, back to the old routine." The sixty-two lines of the poem all work this way, the comma signifying a change in voice that is often a change in diction and so a change in context or "climate" as well: "The sad children, the disappointed kids," "Don't fix it if it works, tinker not with that which runs apace. . . ." The "narrative" of **"Finnish Rhapsody"** is an account of time passing that ends with a stunning meditation on the nature of singularity:

> As moments, then years; minutes, afterwards
>   ages
> Suck up the common strength, absorb the every-
>   day power
> And afterwards live on, satisfied; persist, later to
>   be a source of gratification,
> But perhaps only to oneself, haply to one's sole
>   identity.

The poem only arrives at that point after the long and difficult work of doubling comprehension, of presenting at least two voices listening and speaking to each other until a point of closure that establishes identity.

Like Sade, Mallarmé, and Roussel before him, Ashbery has melded a book's practice and theory. To analyze the book is to re-trace the steps of reading, to uncover a philosophy of technique that refuses immanence. What one arrives at is the necessity to turn back as one turns forward, each time moving deeper into the situation of the language and the situation of one's temporal experience of the language. Thus in this book we see the end, in both senses, of formal experiment. For **April Galleons**'s relentless questioning of making and novelty, its thematic as the very possibility of thematic—that is, of speaking through a language always already necessarily another's—has an originality that could only evolve from such a profound immersion in the method posed by tradition. We thereby sense—that is, we experience—the urgency of this work; it is as serious a matter as matters get, this business of making that is what we are to do as we decide, in time, to live. (pp. 9-16)

Susan Stewart, "The Last Man," in The American Poetry Review, *Vol. 17, No. 5, September-October, 1988, pp. 9-16.*

I don't know what the content of my poems is or what their form is either. . . . I begin writing without knowing what I'm thinking, and stop once I feel I've finished. The form seems to be the content and vice-versa for me.

—*John Ashbery in* The American Poetry Review, *1984.*

Mark Jarman   (review date Spring 1992)

[*Jarman is a Canadian short story writer and poet. In the following scathing assessment, he faults the rambling, "evasive" style of* Flow Chart.]

C. G. Jung discovered that as much of a patient's unconscious could be revealed by having him freely associate with letters from the Cyrillic alphabet as by the more traditional psychoanalytic method of working from the patient's dreams. My own experience reading John Ashbery's new book-length poem [**Flow Chart**] proves Jung correct. Time and again I found what Ashbery himself refers to as the "appealing nonsense" of the poem a stimulus for the associations of my own mind. Or better yet, I recalled the protagonist's dilemma in Ashbery's **"The Instruction Manual,"** from his first book, **Some Trees.** He admits that he wishes he "did not have to write the instruction manual on the uses of a new metal" and finds himself, instead, dreaming of Guadalajara. I knew exactly how that dreamer felt each time I guided myself back into **Flow Chart.** The poem is more flow than chart. Its discursiveness is more a ramble from topic to topic—if topic is the right word—than a coherent argument from point to point.

The only time I thought I knew where I was was during passages of self-reference, when the poet acknowledged my presence as a reader:

> And if I told you
> this was your life, not some short story for a con-
>   test, how would you react?
> Chances are you'd tell me to buzzoff and contin-
>   ue writing . . .

Ashbery has always displayed a droll wit. Here it has given him a canny sense of what must be going through an honest reader's mind as he makes his way through what the poet calls his "wrenched narrative" as it "drips on, decays." I say honest reader, because Ashbery has many dishonest readers. They are his admirers. They include anyone who claims that a poem like **Flow Chart** is not boring, not devoid of any subject except its own composition, and not finally unrereadable. By unrereadable, I mean that, having read it once, I hope never to read it again. How can a poem do this to a reader, except by being bad? I cannot think of a single poem I have read and admired, of whatever length, that I would not willingly read again. By the time I reached page 201 of **Flow Chart,** fifteen pages from the end, and read "there is / always the possibility something may come of something, and that is our / fondest wish though it says here I'm not supposed to say so," I felt as if Ashbery and I had formed one of those bizarre intimacies kidnappers and hostages form. I had tried to cooperate and he knew it. Also on page 201, he writes:

> Excuse me while I fart. There, that's better.
>   I actually feel relieved.

This is the only declaration in the poem not shaded into evasive circumlocution. Still, it reflects the poem's existence as a running commentary on the poet at his typewriter. The poem makes a kind of musical noise, something like the easy listening jazz of the Windham Hill productions. But why is it in chapters? Why sections? Why even page numbers? They must be part of the joke. I think that, unlike his admirers, Emperor Ashbery knows he is naked. (pp. 158-59)

Mark Jarman, "The Curse of Discursiveness,"

in The Hudson Review, *Vol. XLV, No. 1, Spring, 1992, pp. 158-66.*

Lawrence Joseph   (review date 20 April 1992)

[*In the following excerpt, Joseph asserts that* Flow Chart *"portrays the essence of Ashbery's process" in its free-flowing, conversational style and possibilities for multiple interpretations.*]

John Ashbery's poetry has always been, if anything, contemporary. For Ashbery, the concept is defined by a Modernist tradition that goes back not only to [Wallace] Stevens but to Gertrude Stein, who believed that a writer's language should capture as much of a sense of the present as possible. That's what Ashbery tries to do: Everything, including what it means to write poetry, is fair imaginative game. But that isn't all. Ashbery also possesses a highly sophisticated, idiosyncratic feeling for the avant-garde. Combining configurations of present existence with indications of how meaning is discovered and formed, he imagines contemporaneity in its fullest sense. Every Ashbery book approaches the contemporary world—and what poetry is within it—differently. Yet every book aspires toward, and achieves, some idea of what we experience and know. For Ashbery, language contains multiple meanings; his poetry reflects—you might even say bears witness to—this. Subjects replace subjects; the "I" stays in a state of referential and definitional flux. Various feelings are expressed continuously through different types of voices arranged within beautifully formed yet syntactically and colloquially diverse sentences. You may disagree with how, in a given poem, Ashbery chooses to figure it all out—an autotelic imagination has a propensity for excess. But Ashbery knows his limits: Part of what the poetry does is stay ahead of what you might be thinking about it. By investigating the unfathomable connections between aesthetic and political domains, he creates an ever-new poetic space.

Flow Chart, more than any of his other books, portrays the essence of Ashbery's process. The title indicates the book-length poem's central preoccupation: Like a flow chart, it may be read according to what the reader desires. If the title's metaphorical signal is somehow missed, the poet reminds you, at the end of the first of the poem's six parts, what he's up to:

> But if it interests you
> you can browse through this catalog and, who
> knows, perhaps come up with a solution that
> will apply
> to your complicated case, just conceivably, or
> perhaps you know someone better informed
> in the higher echelons where the view is distant
> and severe,
> the ground blue as steel.

The passage is one of many that reveal the book's recurring awareness of its own pursuits. *Flow Chart* is a catalogue, which Ashbery presents as endlessly expansive and open to interpretation, encompassing within its subject matter—well, as much as the poet may imagine.

Yet although you can't quite locate what *Flow Chart* is

"about," certain subjects are insistently noticed: the nature of the city ("Still in the published city but not yet / overtaken by a new form of despair, I ask / the diagram: is it the foretaste of pain / it might easily be?" the poem begins); memory; death (of a mother in particular); religion; art, politics and work; and a revelatory preoccupation with love and love talk. The poem sounds like a diary of how we talk about ourselves and our world:

> There isn't much you can do, and it's a little
> darker. Tell it the time. And on no account lose
> your bearings
> unless you want to wash up like a piece of poly-
> ester at the gulf's
> festering edge. That tanker took on more water.
> The consensus was that there *would be* a
> symposium, if anyone could be found to host it.
> Meanwhile things are getting a little better
> on that front too, which includes romance . . .

You're supposed to take the poet at his word: Read the poem where and how you want, look or listen for language that catches your ear, eye or sensibility. Reading it is like listening to an intriguing conversation, or returning to a piece of music whose powers you're convinced of, to listen to parts of it, or the whole in relation to the parts—like focusing, for example, on the interstices between abstraction and figuration in a Modernist painting.

Written for the most part in long (flowing), conversational, almost meditative lines (a form of personal tonal talk that Ashbery's been refining for years), the poem is composed into sections that are, more accurately, verse paragraphs. The language has a formal feel to it that diffuses the vocal intimacies just enough—you never quite know how attached to the speaker or listener the person speaking is:

> I don't know where this one came in—but wait,
> it is of myself I speak, and I do know!
>   But the looks I got convinced me I was some-
> one
> else as I walked in, not at all sure of myself or
> (rightly, as it turned out) of
> the reception I would be getting. . . .

Because of the feel of the language and all it maintains, reading *Flow Chart* provides a definite pleasure—wherever you choose it. You come away when you've had enough satisfaction, go back when you want more:

> Any day now you must start to dwell in it,
> the poetry, and for this, grave preparations must
> be made, the walks of sand
> Raked, the rubble wall picked clean of dead vine
> stems, but what
> if poetry were something else entirely, not this
> purple weather
> with the eye of a god attached, that sees
> inward and outward? . . .

"Voices of autumn in full, heavy summer; / algae spangling a pool. A lot remains to be done, doesn't it? I haven't even begun to turn myself inside-out yet," the poem says near its end, after turning its radically comprehensive perceptions outside-in. (pp. 531-32)

Lawrence Joseph, "The Real Thing," in The

Nation, *New York, Vol. 254, No. 15, April 20, 1992, pp. 531-33.*

Ralph Angel   (review date May-June 1992)

[*In the following review, Angel provides a positive assessment of* Flow Chart, *praising Ashbery's depiction of the mental processes and prosaic events that comprise daily life.*]

Some things *don't* change. Thirteen books on down the road, John Ashbery remains a most generous poet. And **Flow Chart,** his new book-length journey, reads like a prolonged spell of good health. No other poet so validates the range of human experience, our vast and fragile complexity. Unlike most poetry, Ashbery's never fails to accommodate the huge, mundane drama of mental life. He attends to all the little processes, the most minute considerations, machinations, courtesies, and lapses that really aren't ordinary at all, but the stuff of life itself. This is not to say that the big picture or the central theme is any less important, for what else does mundanity lead up to, and away from, and become again? One is the life of art, the other the art of life, and they're as distinct as mind and body, and as true as their indivisibility. In fact, for Ashbery, all the little pictures, secondary themes and parenthetical digressions, though no more or less real, feel most human and in that way make possible the greatest good in this life. It's what he refers to in **Flow Chart** as "my Sonata of Experience."

> . . . Here's how it goes: the first
> theme
> is announced,
> then fooled around with for a while and goes and
> sits over there. Soon the second
> arrives, less appealing than the first or so it
> seems but after you get to know it you find
> it deeper and somehow more human, like the
> plain face of an old lady who has seen much
> but who has never been known to utter an opinion on anything that happens to her: quite
> extraordinary, in fact . . .

It's classic, friendly Ashbery. Another layer of paint cracked and peeled from the wall. It was a beautiful color, but so is the dull, curious wallpaper beneath it. And this isn't just one more instrument rising up from the symphonic flow; it's a settling down again into the whole orchestral collaboration, though who knows? The next time we're not only somebody else altogether, but just that many more layers of ourselves.

> . . . Then comes a hiatus in the
> manuscript;
> the last bits of it keep seeming to move farther
> and farther away, like houses on a beach one is
> leaving in a speeding motorboat: wait though!
> isn't that them we're approaching now? Of
> course—we had been going around in a circle
> all the time, and now we have arrived at the
> place of resolution. The stakes are high
> now, but you couldn't tell it from the glum air
> of things: bored crows, seedlings.
> And then, what passion

brought you to your knees? Suddenly your
> whole face is bathed in tears, though no one
> saw you cry. This kind of makes me review my
> whole plan of action up to now; fishing around
> for a handkerchief to hand someone does that to
> a person, I think, don't you?
> And it will mean staying up later which in turn
> will screw up
> tomorrow's well-laid plans, and then suddenly
> everything ends in a climax, or a cataract.
> I think this *is* the way it was supposed to be,
> though I can't be sure now, so much has happened;
> It will look better on a cassette, which is where
> I wanted it anyway, so I guess
> we can go home now, each to his own bed, for
> each of us has one: that's what "calling it a
> night" means.
> But I never meant to disturb anything, or harm
> a hair on your head: that would have been false
> to our beginnings, and nothing could stand up
> to that, nothing good I mean.

The stuff of human life *is* the stuff of poetry, and vice versa. We don't value or pay much attention to either. We do what we can. And those two words—life and poetry—like many other words—fishing, lady, tears, no one, cassette—are nearly interchangeable. In life it's not what happens (everything happens!) but how we react to it. In poetry it's how we hear and transcribe what happens, because some other human being might also react to it, one way or another. Each process is an act of faith.

> Any day now you must start to dwell in it,
> the poetry, and for this, grave preparations must
> be made, the walks of sand
> raked, the rubble wall picked clean of dead vine
> stems, but what
> if poetry were something else entirely, not this
> purple weather with the eye of a god attached,
> that sees
> inward and outward? What if it were only a
> small, other way of living,
> like being in the wind? or letting the various settling sounds we hear now
> rest and record the effort any creature has to put
> forth to summon its spirits for a moment and
> then
> fall   silent,   hoping   that   enough   has
> happened? . . .

We are, after all, in this boat together. *Of course* enough has happened and, like Ashbery's method and his capacity, more will happen. A person who's frightened or just flat-out sick of life might try to prevent it, and then something else happens anyway. What to do about it?—that's the question. Not that questions need answers necessarily. But fortunately, like a hand extended, **Flow Chart** makes room for both.

> Yet there are other times as in a quarry where
> no breeze stirs; nothing
> indicates it; poetry scarcely drips from vines, the
> weather is hugely oppressive, yet
> you do know something is at work in you, something else: take death away and still
> a vast alteration remains to be made. We know
> this decade doesn't fit,

that we can do nothing about it except swear, yet
it *will* do, it will have to . . .

One might say that *Flow Chart* looks like a novel, and it
does. A title, a book divided into six numbered sections,
a slew of individual (though related) paragraph-looking
stanzas, a first and last page. But it reads more like the
Tao. This pool, thank goodness, is not restricted. Swim
laps or just jump in anywhere. An act of kindness, the will
to friendship, forgives us either way. And it helps.

> . . . Were we needed then?
> Almost casually, gigantic
>   cardboard cutouts
> of mammoths and hydras appear in the wings,
> and one knows, not having done one's home-
> work,
> that the spells will materialize as dots joined to-
> gether, and the casual
> whirlwind that vaporizes moods and intensity of
> expression was an astrologer's error;
> here, it sits on a doorstep, waiting for the "back
> in five minutes" tenant to materialize
> with all the lawsuits and indecent percentages in
> its wake, but that's no matter,
> it's a river and one must keep up with it.

It's an honor to be alive during the lifetime of this kind
of human affirmation and tenderness of spirit. (pp. 54-5)

> *Ralph Angel, "In Praise of Good Stuff: Eight
> Books," in* The American Poetry Review, *Vol.
> 21, No. 3, May-June, 1992, pp. 45-55.*

Helen Vendler   (essay date 3 August 1992)

[*Regarded by many as one of America's foremost critics
of poetry, Vendler has written acclaimed book-length
studies of the poets W. B. Yeats, George Herbert, Wallace Stevens, and John Keats, as well as the award-
winning essay collection* Part of Nature, Part of Us:
Modern American Poets *(1980). Known as one of the
best close readers of poetry, she is frequently praised for
her explication of individual poems. In the following
essay, she offers a positive evaluation of* Flow Chart *and
asserts that the work is an exploration of contemporary
moral consciousness.*]

What is John Ashbery's single-poem book *Flow Chart*? A
two-hundred-and-fifteen-page lyric; a diary; a monitor
screen registering a moving EEG; a thousand and one
nights; Penelope's web unravelling; views from Argus'
hundred eyes; a book of riddles; a ham-radio station; an
old trunk full of memories; a rubbish dump; a Bartlett's
"Familiar Quotations"; a Last Folio; a vaudeville act. It
is maddening, enthralling, and funny by turns; its sentences are like chains of crystal alternating with jello. It
makes Ashbery's past work (except for those poems in *The
Tennis Court Oath,* his experiment in the surreal) seem serenely classical, well-ordered, pure, shapely, and, above
all, *short.*

Since the sixties, Ashbery has consistently been writing experimental poems that have both continued and revised
American lyric. In interviews he has professed a bland astonishment that his ruminations should seem to his readers different from their own. He is probably right in as-

suming that what Stevens called "the hum of thoughts
evaded in the mind" must be, in a given time and place,
rather alike from mind to mind. In my own case, by entering into some bizarrely tuned pitch inside myself I can find
myself on Ashbery's wavelength, where everything at the
symbolic level makes sense. The irritating (and seductive)
thing about this tuning in is that it can't be willed; I can't
make it happen when I am tired or impatient. But when
the frequencies meet, the effect on me is Ashbery's alone,
and it is a form of trance.

Ashbery is, above all, a poet of the moral life, but his
means are the means of farce: pratfalls, absurd scenarios,
preposterous coincidences, a Chaplinesque wistfulness,
and—something often absent in farce—a hatful of colored
scarves of language. He says awful things about life, but
he puts a comic spin on them, a double take of irony. He
excels especially in the fertility with which he imagines catastrophe:

> Then the fun begins
> in earnest, blows rain
> down from all over, chopping-block sounds,
> you think mechanically of Mary Stuart and
> Lady
> Jane Grey, holding on to your forelock, cap in
> hand, of course.

In Ashbery's amiably malign universe, however, no sooner is the speaker crushed by circumstance than he's up and
running again. As if in a speeded-up film, we are allowed
a brief frame of comedy—

> Yet certainly
> there are some bright spots, and when you listen
>   to the laughter
> in the middle of these it makes for more than a
> cosmetic truth

—but no sooner does cheerfulness break in than something silently menacing heaves into view: "The hangar
gets unbearably hot and very smelly."

Like the continually recycled rolling theatrical backdrop
used to simulate a landscape seen from a train, Ashbery's
recurrent farce of naïve hopes rudely demolished keeps
being run past us throughout *Flow Chart.* A mimicry of
innocence-constantly-turning-into-experience is hardly
new in literature, but Ashbery rewrites the theme in slang
and slapstick, and creates on that music-hall background
various silhouettes of love, landscape, and art. There he
is, "like a daisy on muck," as the pristine poem rises out
of the slime of life and language.

There's a brave despair in *Flow Chart*—more, I think,
than in Ashbery's earlier books. Philosophically, he has always been a skeptic, and his incorrigibly comic side precludes the satisfying comfort of gloomy skepticism of the
German variety. His pretense is always one of genial chat,
but the chat increasingly includes moments of guilt, dismay, self-reproach, sadness, and exhaustion. The superficial camaraderie eventually seems a treble ostinato against
which we hear more clearly the sighs and screams from
the torture chamber. To present torture in terms of farce
is a Beckettian ideal that Ashbery shares: "And behind /

the barn it behooves us again to take up the principle, so like the art / of tragedy and so unlike." It is not quite tragedy, because it has no ultimate sanction from God or Fate: "I see / far, in looking, out over a life, the strange, wrenching mess of it." And Ashbery is a master of the unexplained mess, here the dissolution of a former bond:

> Patiently you again show me my name in the
> register where I wrote it.
> But I'll be off now, there's no point in thanking
> me for what I haven't done, nor in
> my thanking you for all the things you did for
> me, the good things and the less good.
> In riper times of trial we stayed together. But in
> this kind of bleached-out crisis-
> feeling, the best one can do is remain polite while
> dreaming of revenge in another key.

Just when something in life has acquired "variation, texture," then "the sanitation department decreed / it was coming through," and, helpless, one sees one's possessions—friendships, loves—ground up in the hopper of Fate's garbage truck.

The despair in Ashbery is peerlessly matched by his superb dramas of the complacent self-justification we all resort to. There is very little to be said for life, for its listless or agonized days followed by an inevitable execution:

> Still, life is reasonably absorbing
> and there's a lot of nice people around. Most
> days are well fed
> and relaxing, and one can improve one's mind
> a little
> by going out to a film or having a chat with that
> special friend; and before
> you know it it's time to brush your teeth and go
> to bed.

Not that this pabulum of self-reassurance can last long. Truth breaks in:

> Why then, does that feeling
> of emptiness keep turning up like a stranger
> you've seen dozens of times, out-of-focus
> usually, standing toward the rear of the bus or
> fishing for coins at the newsstand? . . .
> Unfortunately we must die, and after that no one
> is sure what happens. Accounts vary.

Yet ostrichlike defenses against the truth recur, as a heaven is supposed after death:

> But we
> most of us feel we'll be made comfortable for
> much of the time after that, and get credit
> for the (admittedly) few nice things we did, and
> no one is going to make too much
> of a fuss over those we'd rather draw the curtain
> over, and besides, we can't see
> much that was wrong in them, there are two
> sides to every question.

If a *frisson* of emptiness follows our perception of oncoming death, then the excuses of self-regard immediately obscure the *frisson*. In this way Ashbery traces the flirtings of the mind with moral awareness, and exposes its quick scurrying to its preferred and pathetic holes of security.

Perhaps no other recent lyric poet has so swallowed the entire range of the spoken and written language of his time and then, like a mother bird, regurgitated it (delicately rearranged) as food for readers. Eliot, Pound, and Moore all incorporated "low" language that fin-de-siècle lyric had tried to do without, but Ashbery has taken the modernist experiment to its end point: to boilerplate, advertising, doggerel, obscenity, technology, media talk—the subliterary of all kinds. At the same time, he adds piquancy to his offered dish with the condiments of the past: archaisms, the dated language of flappers and lounge lizards, quotations from the canon, ancient children's books, nursery rhymes. This happens not only at the level of words but at the levels of grammar and syntax. Rarely has an exquisite writer deliberately written so banally.

At the level of genre, Ashbery is a joyous parodist. There is scarcely a received genre that doesn't emerge here doing a comic turn as a parody of itself. Most of these passages in *Flow Chart* are too long to quote: a nice one can be found on pages 106-107 parodying parataxis—a syntax in which sentences are joined by connectives like "and" or "then" or "but." This is the interminable linear syntax in which most of us tell our dreams or the plots of movies. Yet a nobler paratactic style descends to us from the grand simplicities of Genesis, the Gospels, and fairy stories, and interference from these transmissions keeps breaking into Ashbery's modern broadcast:

> And Joan she said
> too it was like being dead only she didn't care,
> she might as well be anyway, for all
> she cared, and then someone came back with
> beef. And said here
> put a rose on this, you're not afraid, you do it,
> and someone said, O if the law
> decree it he must do it. . . .
> And then in the shade
> they put their heads
> together, and one comes back, the others being
> a little way off, and says, who
> do you think taught you to disobey in the first
> place? And he says, my father.
> And at that they were all struck dumb . . . and
> it was all over for that day.

Ashbery's absurdly long lines seem to say that the nutrition in this contemporary paratactic language is so thinned out that we need a lot of words to get anywhere at all. The miraculous concision of "real poetry" is thereby laid bare as the highest "artificiality" (in the best sense).

The necessity of recording everything, of being "one of those on whom nothing is lost" (Henry James, in one of Ashbery's raisin-quotations elaborating the pudding), is a theme to which Ashbery often returns. "Did it ever occur" to preachers, he says, that we human beings "aren't / as they imagine us, or even as we imagine ourselves, but more like bales / of hay, already harvested but still sitting around, waiting for someone to put them / in the barn before rain and rodents have their way with them?" The labor of the Keatsian harvester—to shelter, in the "rich garners" of poems, himself, his readers, and their culture before the rains and rats get them—is never-ending. If Ashbery is convinced of anything under his affable skepticism, it is that tomorrow won't be like today; his poetry is a continual approximation of Zeno's paradox: No matter how you hasten toward your goal, you will always be unable to reach it.

> [In *Flow Chart*] **Ashbery is rendering an account, at once strict and voluminous, of a naked contemporary moral consciousness that most of us still shrink from, and doing so in a language more ample than most of us can wield as our own.**
>
> —*Helen Vendler*

As Ashbery waits for "my / boulder that rushes to me yet hangs suspended / like mistletoe," he harvests his bales, his gathered stacks of paper. The daily burden of living in constant awareness is now (Ashbery is over sixty) harder and harder labor:

> The page
> that was waiting to be turned had grown heavy
> as a barren mountain range, and armies
> of civil engineers equipped with the latest in pulleys, winches, sprockets, and windlasses
> were just at that moment attempting to negotiate
> its sheer sides, with little success.

One feels reading these lines a pulse of buoyant recognition that someone has here recorded the sullen effort of shifting, in late middle age, into a new phase. At the same time, one recognizes that Ashbery (whose lexical range is enormous, and who rarely repeats a word) is absolutely delighted to have found a use in lyric for the unlikely words "civil engineers," "pulleys," "winches," "sprockets," and "windlasses." The old metaphor of the soul's multiple powers (intellect, will, imagination, reason, etc.) pulling together has been Napoleonically updated to the technology of empire, retaining just enough old-fashionedness to be charming, and given just enough metallic modernity to quell all that nonsense (so Ashbery implies) of medieval psychology.

Flow Chart, though it is divided into six sections, and though it masquerades as a narrative, is really a lyric poem, in that it imitates the structure of narrative while not having a narrative theme. There is no real end to the flow of the flow chart, and no one ever progresses in it except in circles. It is true that the beginning of each section of the poem acts like a beginning, and the end like an ending, but there are any number of mini-beginnings and crypto-endings scattered through the whole book. At times, Ashbery even seems to be telling us that this is his last work, that henceforth we are on our own:

> I have no further bread and cheese for you; these
> days I count little
> but the linens folded in my scented cedar closets,
> folded up against time, in case

> I ever have a use for them; and you, you others,
> have only to break away
> like chunks of ice from the much larger iceberg
> to accomplish your destiny, that day in court
> the monkeys and jesters seemed to promise
> you—or was it a bad dream?

The infrastructure of all this—folded sheets of poems in closets ("presses," in the old sense), the Melville/ Bishop iceberg, the vaguely Shakespearean monkeys and jesters, the ambiguous Keatsian "or was it a bad dream?"—is constructed from the flotsam and jetsam of culture. While Arnold and Eliot tended to quote their poetic touchstones directly, Ashbery, though perfectly willing to insert the odd line of "The Castaway," prefers to embed his allusions in weird and funny ways. The Bible, Homer, Virgil, Dante, Shakespeare, Marvell, Cowper, Blake, Keats, Arnold, Hopkins, Whitman, Lewis Carroll, Edward Lear, Henry James, Stevens, Eliot make cameo appearances here but chimerically altered: Hamlet's "slings and arrows of outrageous fortune" turns up, for instance, as "the snakes and ladders / of outrageous fortune." Both the stately "Game of Chess" and "What the Thunder Said," from "The Waste Land," appear in parodic form:

> Even in my late forties I patiently awaited
> this. After dinner she played Kjerulf. We sipped
> tea, looking at each other. . . .
> Another day we read the thunder its own prepared statement.

Datta. Dayadhvam. Damyata. The sheer effrontery of Eliot's incorporating a "prepared statement" for thunder amuses Ashbery, and his wit at Eliot's expense marks a deep debt to and love for Eliot. But a scavenger hunt for manhandled quotations is not what Ashbery's reader is in the game for. Rather, the reader receives a highly idiosyncratic introduction to the contents of what Stevens called "a trash can at the end of the world," where all culture comes eventually to rest as pieces of itself.

In the past, the symbolic code that all poets resort to has usually been a fairly self-consistent one, no matter how heterodox. Scholars have felt that they could figure out Blake's or Yeats' "system," and make reasonable deductions about the author's symbolic intent. Ashbery of course has to write partly in the inherited code—the autumn of life, harvest as one's final ingathering, palaces as elaborate constructions, earthquakes and storms as catastrophe, etc.—but he also departs from old poetic codes for a freakish one of his own. In his code, "the sanitation department" stands temporarily for whatever mysterious extinction-machine vacuums up relationships; the next time the force of destruction shows up, however, it will be called "rain and rodents," or a dam that overflows, or the fate that makes you "wash up like a piece of polyester at the gulf's festering edge." Metaphors in Ashbery succeed each other vertiginously. One reads on the qui vive, riding the crests of ever-new imagery while, on some subliminal level, doing the decoding and relishing the sport.

The code is not always breakable. Ashbery feels free to use private information inaccessible to his reader (if only so that his autobiography in verse can be an intimate one, and the reticence that means so much to him will remain unviolated). We know that he will not reveal personal particulars; when he speaks, in one of his characteristic mixed metaphors, of "the skein of secret misery lobbed from generation to generation," we will not be told what went wrong among the Ashberys. But we are grateful to have the secret misery named as the shameful burden it is, and to see noted the parental insouciance with which it is passed down: "Here, it's *your* serve; *you* knit something with it." And when the code works it becomes a wonderful shorthand.

Here, in shorthand, is something about (so I gather) growing up among adults, and growing up gay, and changing by night (in one's own mind and perhaps in that of others) into a monster, and (another source of adolescent embarrassment) shooting up to over six feet. A recollection of adult advice opens the passage:

> Retreat, retreat! was all they ever said,
> and seemed sometimes not to know what they
> meant. Thus night
> appears to have existed always, and to one's sur-
> prise one finds oneself
> adapting to it as though one had never known
> anything else, and growing fangs and howling
> at the moon and avoiding questions from loved
> ones and overreacting.
> Now it was time to be tall too, a further compli-
> cation.

This sort of disguised autobiography runs all through Part IV of *Flow Chart.*

It is discouraging to be Ashbery, because the very culture of which he is the linguistic recorder cannot read him, so densely woven is the web of his text. His very effect—that one is gazing down through a stream of transparent words into pure consciousness—depends on the reader's noting, at least subconsciously, the whole orchestral potential of the English language, high and low, sufficiently to register the oboes here, the triangle there, the snare drums somewhere else. *Flow Chart* is like one huge party line, with everyone in the English-speaking world, past and present, from Chaucer to Ann Landers, interrupting each other in incessant fragments. This apparently aleatory music is conducted only by an invisible master at the synthesizer. The whole is too big to be subordinated to criticism: no critical essay could hope to control, except in very general terms, the sheer volume of linguistic and psychological data presented by the poem.

A couple of years ago, I came across (in *Poetry New York 3,* published by the CUNY Graduate Center) a poem written by a philosopher named Frank White; it is called "On First Looking Into Ashbery." It recognizes how uninhibited Ashbery is, and how stuffy he makes his academic readers feel:

> When you read the real thing,
> A living poet speaking your language,
> Colloquial, but in the poet's own give-away
>   tones,
> Picking over your common existence
> Like a practiced hand at a rummage sale,
> You almost choke on your own discourse,
> Wonder how you can ever wear it in public
>   again—

> So out of date, so over-worn, so ill-suited to the
>   occasion
> It somehow suddenly seems.

And yet the philosopher-speaker bounces back, realizing that Ashbery's unfettered voice has the exhilarating effect of altering his own constricted one:

> But only for a moment. The panic passes.
> Soon you are having your say again,
> Scared but talking back,
> Accent barely detectably affected,
> Having added one more high-fidelity speaker
> To your sound equipment.

All poets are "high-fidelity speakers," transmitting what Hopkins called "the current language heightened"; but Ashbery, like such narrative or dramatic writers as Chaucer and Shakespeare, and unlike most lyric poets, has made this linguistic fidelity to the entire current language a notable area of experiment. His total "Sonata of Experience" has by now had such a sing-along effect that the literary magazines are full of his imitators, trailing inconsequence, slang, and jokes. But the imitators don't have Ashbery's inexhaustible vocabulary, and they don't have his Proustian syntax, not to mention his rueful self-mockery and his lavish decorativeness. *Flow Chart* contains, for example, a double sestina; its end words, according to Ashbery, are borrowed from a double sestina by Swinburne. (And with the mention of Swinburne another Ashbery affiliation is revealed. Both poets are makers of a liquid cascade of words: "Come speak with me," says Ashbery, "behind the screen of the waterfall's Holophane.")

For all his appearance of decadence and camp, Ashbery is rendering an account, at once strict and voluminous, of a naked contemporary moral consciousness that most of us still shrink from, and doing so in a language more ample than most of us can wield as our own. Poetry, says Ashbery, usually appears as "this purple weather / with the eye of a god attached, that sees / inward and outward." That definition speaks of poetry's psychological acuteness and also of its claim to render the objective world.

But there is another poetry, written in what Keats called "a finer tone," which passes beyond both psychology and description, and leaps into a savage and thrilling authority of language. No more than any other poet would Ashbery assert that such poetry is in his voluntary power, but, in the single most transfixing passage in *Flow Chart,* he imagines it:

> And then everything you were going to say
>   and
> everything they were going to say to you in reply
> would erupt
> in lightning, a steely glitter chasing shadows like
> a pack
> of hounds, once they tasted the flavor of blood,
> and then this light would gradually
> form prickly engraved letters on a page—*but
> who would read that!*

Lightning-letters—let him read them who dares. But also engraved, formal; the letters of an invitation. And prickly—they draw blood. Who would not want to read that? (pp. 73-6)

Helen Vendler, "A Steely Glitter Chasing Shadows," in The New Yorker, *Vol. LXVIII, No. 24, August 3, 1992, pp. 73-6.*

Susan Salter Reynolds   (review date 30 August 1992)

[*In the following review, Reynolds describes the style and tone of* Hotel Lautreamont.]

The title of this new collection [**Hotel Lautreamont**] . . . from a great master refers to the pseudonymous Count de Lautréamont, a 19th-Century poet about whom little is known save that he spent his brief adult life in various hotels in Paris, and died in 1870 at the age of 24. As a jumping off point, the image of this young poet's transient life, frozen in history, permeates the book. The language is ever so slightly disjointed and cinematic, and Ashbery refers often to loose connections and broken lines of communications:

> As it is I frequently get off before the stop that is mine / not out of modesty but a failure to keep the lines of communication / open within myself. And then, unexpectedly, I am shown a dog and asked to summarize its position in a few short, angular adverbs / and tell them this is what they do, why we can't count / on anything unexpected.

It's as though Ashbery were pondering the order of things, questioning the perspective of history with the tone of some vague ruler sweeping her hand across the landscape. Images and ideas crash together

> like a / twenty-one-vehicle pileup on a fog-enclosed highway. / This is what it means to be off and running, off / one's nut as well. But in a few more years, / with time off for good behavior . . .

Reading the poems straight through is a little like having many conversations at a party, some of them important.

Susan Salter Reynolds, in a review of "Hotel Lautreamont," in Los Angeles Times Book Review, *August 30, 1992, p. 6.*

Travis Looper   (essay date Fall 1992)

[*In the following essay, Looper focuses on "Self-Portrait in a Convex Mirror" as an example of Ashbery's characteristic exploration of perception and reality and of art as means of describing experience.*]

Barbara Johnson may well have had in mind Ashbery's **"Self-Portrait in a Convex Mirror"** in speaking of the deconstructivist willingness to focus on what she calls the "warring forces of signification within the text itself" [quoted in Steven Lynn's "A Passage into Critical Theory" in *Conversations: Contemporary Critical Theory and the Teaching of English Literature,* edited by Charles Moran and Elizabeth F. Penfield, 1990]. Nothing is more commonplace among critics of Ashbery's work than remarks upon the difficulty of determining the significance

behind the text that comprises that work. Alfred Corn frankly admits [in "A Magma of Interiors," *Parnassus,* Vol. 4, 1975], "I don't understand every line in **'Self-Portrait . . .'**." Regardless of the difficulty, we can see the signs doing battle one with another, vitiating against traditional meaning and unity. This textual war of sign against sense is evident in **"Self-Portrait"** as the author uses words against themselves.

The poet persona, in the first strophe of the poem, discovers that no signs are adequate for conveying what he perceives about the soul of the person depicted in Parmigiano's painting ["Self-Portrait in a Convex Mirror"]. That soul, says Ashbery, has no objective existence apart from what he calls "our moment of attention." Consequently, the soul (about as immaterial a thing as one can imagine) exists only in the viewer's perceptions and resultant verbalizings. Although the sense of the painting, at this early stage of the poem, seems clear enough to the poet, he begins to reflect upon his inability to articulate that understanding. He can, to use his own analogy, hum the melody; but, he says, "there are no words," no signs adequate to objectify the nonobjective, or the material for that matter. The poet indicates that any words spoken of the soul (itself a second-hand inference) "are only speculation," *speculation* being a word derived from the Latin for *mirror.* And since he is speaking of a painting of mirrored materiality, he suggests that the words of the poem are not synonymous with or tantamount to that spoken of—any more than the painting is equivalent to that which it depicts. Words are themselves speculative mirrors, inadequate reflections of that toward which the poet and we momentarily aim our attention. In short, neither paint nor words (even those of the poem) can hope to capture the essence of that portrayed, anymore than Fra Pandolf could hope to reproduce "the faint / Half-flush . . . along the throat" of Browning's duchess. That inability is the war mentioned earlier: the war between Ashbery's attempts to describe an experience or object (in this case not even an object but a mere soul) and the inevitable inability to do so.

He who is the subject of the painting, Parmigiano himself, is trapped within the dimensions of the spherical canvas spoken of by the poet as "life englobed." The subject of the painting is confined within the medium, or "dimension," wherein he is depicted, perhaps longing to escape its restraints. But when the poet speaks of "one" who "would like to stick one's hand / Out of the globe," he is not talking just about Parmigiano. That word "one" speaks of all of us—the painter, the poet, and you and me. Each of us is restrained, the poet indicates, by a personal, culture-specific medium—even as our understanding of the painting is delimited by the words of the poet, who uses those signs in an attempt to escape from the signs themselves.

Although the painter's hand, as depicted, seems near to the viewer, even "big enough to wreck the sphere" of the microcosmic world of the painting, the man in the picture cannot break out. For there *exists* nothing but the one-dimensional portrayal on canvas. Ashbery says, of the pictured painter, "your eyes proclaim / That everything is surface. The surface is what's there / And nothing can exist except what's there." In other words, all that anyone can perceive of anything, whether of a picture or of some surrounding milieu, is superficial externals. And the battle that rages within us and within the poet consists of the effort to penetrate below those surfaces to some elusive reality. But Ashbery sees this effort, which is largely manifested in our signs, our words, as futile. He says, "there are no words for the surface, that is / No words to say what is really is, that it is not / Superficial but a visible core." There are no words to "describe" even the object's surface as "it really is," and certainly nothing to indicate that which is not just surface but "core" turned "visible." Ironically, what seems like superficial surface to us is really "it," says Ashbery. That "it" is by itself all of the inner core we can ever hope to find. Such a surface-core rests "on a pedestal of vacuum," Ashbery suggests, a vacuum of nothing-else.

And it is precisely here that the poet's words do battle with what he senses. For he knows, even as he writes the words of the poem, that the signs are themselves paltry substitutes for the object-realities he would describe. While using the signs, he knows they are inadequate, near-useless mouthings of that which, like the ancient name for Jehovah, can never be spoken. But he does not stop using the signs, thereby undermining the poem even as he writes it. Rather, in human fashion, he persists in that which is ultimately hopeless. I too must admit that my present attempt, to speak of that which Ashbery has already indicated is unspeakable, is in itself merely one more step removed from that initial surface-bound experience of Parmigiano, one more stage in our linguistic game of smoke and mirrors.

Any art, suggests Ashbery, whether painting or writing, is an effort to get beyond the limitations of signs and the objects they describe. David Shapiro, in speaking of **"Self-Portrait"** [in his *John Ashbery: An Introduction to the Poetry*], calls it an effort to "escape the text, get out of it as into a realm of existence beyond language. . . ." It is this "existence beyond language" that concerns both Ashbery and the reader in the platonic imagery of strophe three. Ashbery quotes Sydney Freeberg's study of Parmigiano as saying of the picture "that the painting, itself a symbol of the poem, has indeed lost, in the very act by which it was created, a measure of that ideal which it was intended to describe." On another level, Ashbery seems to indicate here that the old transcendental forms, that once served so well, are slightly tarnished, having lost as much a measure of their ideality as had the Renaissance classicism that preceded Parmigiano's mannerism.

Obviously one sees that this painting, says Ashbery, "No longer produces an objective truth, but a *bizzaria.* . . ." That is, the mannerist painter went beyond reality, twisting it to conform to some outlandish creation of the imagination. It may even be, suggests art historian H. W. Janson, that Parmigiano wanted ". . . to demonstrate that there is no single 'correct' reality." At any rate, the old transcendental forms are just a human creation, a mental construct. Although, the poet readily admits, "The forms retain / A strong measure of ideal beauty," they

have, by implication, also lost a strong measure of that beauty. "Fed by our dreams," he says, the very forms themselves have become inadequate for the painter or the wordsmith, becoming so "inconsequential" that they leave a "hole" in our imaginings. For nothing can replace that which was never there. Consequently, there is no longer any ideal form sufficient to our modern needs. There is no transcendent to which words or paint can hope to conform. There are only the signs here and the objects there.

This very absence of old transcendental idealities is nourished by the love of the artist, whether painter or poet, for distortion. Indeed, supposes Janson, for Parmigiano "distortion is as natural as the normal appearance of things." And Ashbery says clearly that the forms "forage in secret on our idea of distortion," which cannot itself survive without the transcendent—any more than the hypocrite can exist without some better to emulate, albeit in twisted fashion. Without some ideal touchstone beyond mere materiality, Parmigiano could never have depicted his rather bizarre world. For without that which is distorted there is simply nothing, nothing to be distorted. Lest we think, however, that the existence of the distortion implies the existence of a transcendental other to be distorted, Ashbery claims that the ideals have existence only when "Fed by our dreams," dreams with less than vapor for subject.

From this we would think that Shapiro is accurate in seeing the poem as a rejection of structuralist "reification" and as "a criticism of mimesis." Ashbery here certainly appears opposite that older criticism typified by F. R. Leavis. For Leavis, as Terry Eagleton says [in *Literary Theory: An Introduction*], "This whole notion of language rested upon a naive mimeticism: the thoery was that words are somehow healthiest when they approach the condition of things, and thus cease to be words at all." It would seem obvious, as it does for the first half of the poem, that Ashbery was scorning just such an identification of object and sign when he said, "There are no words / The words are only speculation." As Shapiro says, "The sign . . . is imminently cut off from the world."

After all this, we must stop for a moment to remind ourselves that a writer may say one thing and mean another. Or as Jonathan Culler puts it, discourse often ". . . undermines the philosophy it asserts" [quoted in Steven Lynn's essay]. Indeed, in the poem's final strophe, Ashbery appears to whittle away at the concepts explored earlier in the poem. He speaks, for instance, of

> a vague
> Sense of something that can never be known
> Even though it seems likely that each of us
> Knows what it is and is capable of
> Communicating it to the other.

An inner struggle occurs as the poet contemplates in greater depth Parmigiano's painting. Where he seemed so certain that signs are merely the subject's speculative referents in regard to objects, he now seems hesitant, speaking, in strophe five, of "the word that can't be understood / But can be felt." The poet is, for a while, caught between his own post-structuralist Scylla and Charybdis. On the one hand, he has suggested that signs are inadequate to their task—in that they are incapable of adequately naming either that which they describe or that to which the object refers—and on the other hand, he now hints of something beyond real comprehension but not beyond some kind of knowledge. Comparing that which can be understood with that which can be felt, Ashbery toys with a new disturbing idea: It just may be that something exists beyond rational understanding but neither beyond personal experience nor beyond communication.

At war within himself, the poet cannot say what this something is, if it is. But he does know this: "The sample / One sees is not to be taken as merely that." That which we experience is not mere "gesture" but, he says, "all, in the refined, assimilable state." What we have is not some amorphous, other-worldly dream of an ideal, but what he terms in the final strophe "*This* thing, the mute, undivided present." And such a state is not, he says,

> . . . a bad thing
> Or wouldn't be, if the way of telling
> Didn't somehow intrude, twisting the end result
> Into a caricature of itself.

The problem is not, finding ourselves without the solace of the extra-temporal and extra-spatial, that we are limited thereby. Ashbery's concern is for the adequacy of the signs that we employ to describe experiences and objects. The "way of telling" is the problem, for it comes between ourselves and the object, and between the object and those hearing it described. The result is mere "caricature," he says, verbal finger painting that hinders perception. Ashbery's poem is in itself just such a linguistic travesty, for he decries the adequacy of the very signs he uses. The problem "always happens," he asserts, as is manifest in the childish game of "gossip," whereby "A whispered phrase passed around the room / Ends up as something completely different." The artist, similarly, whether that artist is Ashbery or Parmigiano, creates an "otherness," declares the poet. That artist, we are told, begins with one conception and ends with something totally different. As pleasing as the results may be, the artist often finds that more likely than not, in Ashbery's words, "He has omitted the thing he started out to say / In the first place." Ashbery claims to be speaking of "art" and the "artist," but he does not say, as he could have done so easily, that the artist omits to "paint" what was intended. Instead—and here we see his true, reflexive position—he affirms that words, such as those he is using, turn out differently than first anticipated. All we can see, all that Parmigiano could see, the poet says, is "this / Not-being-us [which] is all there is to look at / In the mirror."

This "Not-being-us," which the poet also terms "otherness," is as close as the artist, whether painter or writer, comes to a traditional ideal. Having considered and reconsidered the possibility of such, Ashbery, in the very act of making this poem, devises his own transcendent. For him, at least within the confines of this poem, the only possibility for rising above human limitations is, he says, "what is outside." For the artist, "what is outside" consists of the object resulting from the act of creation. Ashbery, like Parmigiano with his painting, has created in **"Self-Portrait"** that which is separate from himself, at once

greater than, and incomprehensible to, himself. (pp. 451-56)

Travis Looper, "Ashbery's 'Self-Portrait'," in Papers on Language & Literature, *Vol. 28, No. 4, Fall, 1992, pp. 451-56.*

Michael Dirda   (review date 3 January 1993)

[*In the following excerpt, Dirda praises Ashbery's sense of humor in* Hotel Lautreamont.]

[No] poet is more surreal, more disjunctive and musical, more subtly allusive (note the nod to Stevens in **"It Must be Sophisticated"**) than John Ashbery. In *Hotel Lautreamont* he is also tremendously funny. You don't have to understand these poems to love them; you need only that suspension of disbelief that constitutes an audience's pleasure before the magician's flourishes and wonders. "A yak is a prehistoric cabbage: of that, at least, we may be sure." "The boss made it official. / Then a cherub came out and sassed us. / 'Why do you listen to all this *chamber music?* / Why don't you ever listen to church music?' " One could quote such campy non sequiturs all day for their humor, their cadences, for the undercutting of the orotund by the vernacular: They sound like Wallace Stevens writing Frank O'Hara's "Lunch Poems" after a couple of martinis. (p. 10)

Michael Dirda, "Classics and Contemporaries," in Book World—The Washington Post, *January 3, 1993, pp. 9-10.*

FURTHER READING

Criticism

Altieri, Charles. "John Ashbery and the Challenge of Postmodernism in the Visual Arts." *Critical Inquiry* 14, No. 4 (Summer 1988): 805-30.

> Argues that critics should view Ashbery as an innovative modern artist rather than as a poet working solely within literary tradition.

Evans, Cynthia. "John Ashbery: 'A Movement Out of the Dream.' " *The American Poetry Review* 8, No. 4 (July-August 1979): 33-36.

> Examines the development of Ashbery's career as it relates to the reflexive nature of his works and his concern with capturing his experience of the present in his poetry.

Holden, Jonathan. "Syntax and the Poetry of John Ashbery." *The American Poetry Review* 8, No. 4 (July-August 1979): 37-40.

> Discusses style and content in Ashbery's poetry and finds that Ashbery's verse is the poetic equivalent of "abstract expressionist" painting.

Jackson, Richard. "Writing as Transgression: Ashbery's Archeology of the Moment—a Review Essay." *Southern Humanities Review* XII, No. 3 (Summer 1978): 279-84.

> Considers such themes as time, motion, language, and the writing process in *Houseboat Days* and finds that *Houseboat Days* advances a deconstructionist philosophy.

——. "The Elegies of Style." *The Georgia Review* XLII, No. 4 (Winter 1988): 856-69.

> Discusses Ashbery's writing style in *April Galleons.*

Lehman, David, ed. *Beyond Amazement: New Essays on John Ashbery.* Ithaca, N.Y.: Cornell University Press, 1980, 294 p.

> Contains selected essays that address common questions and misunderstandings regarding Ashbery's works.

Macoubrie, John. "A Survey of Five." *North Stone Review* 8 (Fall-Winter 1978-79): 111-18.

> Includes a brief positive review of *Self-Portrait in a Convex Mirror.*

Mohanty, S. P., and Monroe, Jonathan. "John Ashbery and the Articulation of the Social." *Diacritics* 17, No. 2 (Summer 1987): 37-63.

> Focuses on the "individualist idealism" of Ashbery's poetry and describes this idealism in relation to his long poem *A Wave.*

Nathanson, Tenney. "Private Language: Ashbery and Wittgenstein." *Raritan* 2, No. 3 (Winter 1983): 91-108.

> Discusses the roles of language and speech in Ashbery's poetry with regard to the theories of linguistic philosopher Ludwig Wittgenstein.

Stead, C. K. "O Harashbery!" *London Review of Books* 14, No. 8 (23 April 1992): 20, 22.

> Disputes assessments of Ashbery's works by John Bayley, Helen Vendler, and Harold Bloom, and finds Ashbery's poetry unconvincing.

Interview

Poulin, A., Jr. "The Experience of Experience: A Conversation with John Ashbery." *Michigan Quarterly Review* XX, No. 3 (Summer 1981): 242-55.

> Ashbery comments on such issues as his aims and influences as a poet as well as the obscurity and difficulty of his works.

Additional coverage of Ashbery's life and career is contained in the following sources published by Gale Research: *Contemporary Authors,* **Vols. 5-8, rev. ed.;** *Contemporary Authors New Revision Series,* **Vols. 9, 37;** *Contemporary Literary Criticism,* **Vols. 2, 3, 4, 6, 9, 13, 15, 25, 41;** *Dictionary of Literary Biography,* **Vol. 5;** *Dictionary of Literary Biography Yearbook: 1981;* **and** *Major 20th-Century Writers.*

Alan Bennett

1934-

English dramatist, scriptwriter, and nonfiction writer.

The following entry focuses on Bennett's career through 1993. For further information on his life and works, see *CLC*, Volume 45.

INTRODUCTION

Bennett first gained recognition, along with Jonathan Miller, Peter Cook, and Dudley Moore, as a member of the English comedy revue *Beyond the Fringe*. Since his success in the early 1960s, Bennett has completed more than thirty works for stage, screen, and television, many of which have been highly praised by critics. Much of Bennett's work retains the wit of *Beyond the Fringe* but focuses on what he perceives to be the decline of British culture since World War II. Richard Christiansen has commented: "Alan Bennett is not as celebrated or prolific a playwright as his contemporaries Tom Stoppard and Simon Gray, but he ranks right up there with them as a witty and humane observer of England in particular and of mankind in general."

Bennett was born in Leeds, England, into a working-class family. He received his bachelor's degree and graduated with honors from Exeter College at Oxford in 1957. Bennett became a lecturer in medieval history at Oxford University, then left to collaborate with Miller, Cook, and Moore in *Beyond the Fringe*, which was noted for its revolutionary approach to traditional music-hall shows and featured extended humorous sketches inspired by the work of such socially conscious American comedians as Lenny Bruce and Mort Sahl. *Beyond the Fringe* enjoyed tremendous success in both England and the United States, garnering praise for its irreverent English outlook on such topics as nuclear holocaust, the cold war, and religion. Bennett's first play, *Forty Years On,* introduces what he perceives as Britain's disillusionment with social change, a theme common to many of his plays. Set in a boys' school that serves as an allegorical representation of contemporary England, *Forty Years On* revolves around the school's departing headmaster and his younger, more progressive replacement. In *Getting On* Bennett depicts an ill-tempered member of Parliament who expresses his disenchantment with post-World War II British culture through his scathing comments on contemporary society and his adherence to traditional virtues. The plot of *The Old Country* centers on a British diplomat and his wife who, after being accused of treason, have defected to the Soviet Union but nevertheless retain their British mannerisms and values. When visitors arrive from Cambridge, they try to convince the couple to return to a drastically changed England, one that will ostensibly overlook their offense and eventually raise them to celebrity status.

Bennett's more recent dramas incorporate political satire and concern historical events and figures. In *Kafka's Dick,* a controversial play produced in 1986, Bennett satirizes literary biographers, whom he portrays as more interested in biographical trivia than in their subjects' writings. *Kafka's Dick* concerns novelist and short story writer Franz Kafka, who, with his father and his literary executor, materializes in the home of a contemporary insurance agent. Anxious to establish his reputation as a literary critic, the opportunistic agent plots to discover and reveal the true size of Kafka's penis. Two of Bennett's one-act plays, *An Englishman Abroad* and *A Question of Attribution,* were produced together in 1988 as *Single Spies.* The first of the two plays, *An Englishman Abroad,* is based on the true story of the 1958 meeting between Coral Brown, an Australian actress, and Guy Burgess, an exiled English spy, in Moscow. *A Question of Attribution* is set in the late 1960s and concerns Scotland Yard's interrogation of the English spy Anthony Blunt, who masqueraded as director of the Queen's personal art collection on behalf of the Russian government. Richard Hornby remarked that *A Question of Attribution* explores "the nature of art and reality, and how we perceive them. [It] is the perfect play for its time, in a country struggling to redefine the nature of government and of art, and the relationship between them." In *The Madness of George III* Bennett discusses both medicine and politics, satirizing the medical theories and debates concerning the cause of King George III's madness. Although Donald Lyons claimed Bennett's talent for representing the minute details of society was wasted in his epic treatment of the royal family, Robert Brustein applauded *The Madness of George III*, commenting: "Nothing in Bennett's career as a wit and social satirist could have prepared us for the authority and maturity he displays in *The Madness of George III*. The play signals the arrival of an important epic playwright."

Bennett's teleplays have been characterized by John Russell Taylor as dealing with "boredom and emptiness and the aimless filling up of time . . . without being in themselves boring and aimless." One of the more popular pieces, *Me, I'm Afraid of Virginia Woolf,* is about a bored, dissatisfied literature professor who falls in love with one of his young male students. The teleplay *One Fine Day* deals with "male menopause" and depicts a middle-aged real estate agent's struggle to escape the monotony of his everyday life by listening to operas by Puccini and camping out on the roof of his office building. The character eventually overcomes his escapist tendencies and decides to actively engage in improving his situation. *Talking Heads,* a 1987 British television series, consisted of half-hour monologues spoken by such characters as an alcoholic vicar's wife who seeks happiness in sexual relations with an Asian grocer in his storeroom. Bennett's stage adaptation of *Talking Heads,* which he describes as "stripped-down versions of short-stories," was produced in 1992.

Bennett has yet to achieve the kind of international celebrity status enjoyed by the other members of *Beyond the Fringe.* To date, his audience consists mostly of critics, British television viewers, and a small circle of theater-goers. Addressing Bennett's lack of notoriety, Jack Kroll commented: "Bennett, the least famous of the four [original members of *Beyond the Fringe*], is arguably the most gifted as actor, comic, director and prolific author of [plays, TV drama, and movies]." In a discussion of his status as an author and dramatist, Bennett himself remarked: "I've been very lucky in that the films I've written, at any rate for television, have all actually ended up on the screen and in a form not too distantly related to what I imagined when I wrote them. Adding though that, being television, those films have about as much permanence as a fart in the wind."

PRINCIPAL WORKS

Beyond the Fringe [with Peter Cook, Jonathan Miller, and Dudley Moore] (comedy revue) 1960
On the Margin (television series) 1966
Forty Years On (drama) 1968
Sing a Rude Song [with Caryl Brahms and Ned Sherrin] (drama) 1969

Getting On (drama) 1971
*A Day Out (teleplay) 1972
Habeas Corpus (drama) 1973
Sunset across the Bay (teleplay) 1975
The Old Country (drama) 1977
†Doris and Doreen (teleplay) 1978
A Little Outing (teleplay) 1978
‡Me, I'm Afraid of Virginia Woolf (teleplay) 1978
†A Visit From Miss Prothero (teleplay) 1978
‡Afternoon Off (teleplay) 1979
‡All Day on the Sands (teleplay) 1979
The Hedgehog (teleplay) 1979
‡The Old Crowd (teleplay) 1979
‡One Fine Day (teleplay) 1979
Enjoy (drama) 1980
*An Englishman Abroad (teleplay) 1982
*Intensive Care (teleplay) 1982
§Marks (teleplay) 1982
§Our Winnie (teleplay) 1982
§Rolling Home (teleplay) 1982
§Say Something Happened (teleplay) 1982
§A Woman of No Importance (teleplay) 1982
A Private Function (screenplay) 1984
║*The Insurance Man* (teleplay) 1986
║*Kafka's Dick* (drama) 1986
Uncle Clarence (radio play) 1986
#Talking Heads (teleplay) 1987
Prick Up Your Ears [adaptor, from the biography by John Lahr] (screenplay) 1988
**Single Spies (drama) 1988
The Wind in the Willows [adaptor, from the children's book by Kenneth Grahame] (drama) 1990
The Madness of George III (drama) 1991

*These works were collected in *Objects of Affection, and Other Plays for Television* (1982).

†These works were adapted and produced for the stage as *Office Suite* (1987).

‡These works were collected in *The Writer in Disguise* (1985).

§These works were collected and produced for television as *Objects of Affection* (1982).

║These works were published as *Two Kafka Plays: Kafka's Dick* [*and*] *The Insurance Man* (1987).

#This work was adapted and produced for the stage as *Talking Heads* (1992).

**This work includes two one-act plays: an adaptation of the teleplay *An Englishman Abroad* (1982) and *A Question of Attribution.*

CRITICISM

Anthony Curtis (review date Winter 1977-78)

[*Curtis is an English critic, editor, and educator. In the following excerpt, he offers a positive assessment of* The

Old Country, *noting that the work is most effective when discussing the English aristocracy.*]

> . . . People who were in charge of intelligence work against the Soviet Union were political illiterates who did not have the slightest idea what communism was about. They chose to believe that only simple moral depravity could cause a man to betray his country, and it seems that their defenders still choose to believe this, although it is quite unnecessary to approve of Philby's actions to see that he was activated by idealism quite as much as any of us who remain on the narrow path of nationalist rectitude.

Thus wrote Bruce Page, David Leitch and Philip Knightley, three *Sunday Times* journalists, in the 1969 preface to their *Philby: The Spy Who Betrayed A Generation* the appearance of which . . . coincides opportunely with Alan Bennett's **The Old Country** at the Queen's Theatre. I don't think I am giving away any secrets when I say that Mr. Bennett's play is inspired by the career of Philby. . . . It is about three-quarters way through the first half before we realise that [Hilary, a] paunchy, stocky, middle-aged intellectual with his open-necked shirt, his supercilious drawl, his slightly tipsy gait, is indeed based on Philby. Mr. Bennett cleverly teases us for about half-an-hour as to the location of his play, the identities of the couple we see who are clearly enjoying a great deal of enforced leisure as they potter about their ranch-style summer home surrounded by shrubs and pine-trees. This setting could be any place where you might see a perspective of tall conifers through the huge picture-window of the wooden-slatted sitting-room which is knee-deep in magazines and clutter. As the husband and wife, for so they seem, bat the aphorisms to and fro, tracing the graceful parabolas of a softly knocked shuttlecock, we tick off in our minds where we are not: Hampstead—no; Bournemouth—no; Wester Ross—no, not quite; Norway—yes, perhaps. Finally the long twist of blue touch-paper reaches the cordite, as Hilary's wife, Bron . . . spits at him: 'Except that you are all traitors'. At that point the whole thing comes into focus. We are in a dacha a few hours' drive from Moscow and the house and garden in front of us is little better than an open prison in which Hilary has been languishing since his defection.

His brooding has a nostalgic tinge as he thinks back upon the lost world of Cambridge, E. M. Forster, Gaitskell, Elgar. His whole outlook seems more aesthetic than political, more true perhaps of Isherwood in California than the real Philby in Moscow. His head is full of literary allusions and he lives mainly for music. He compares himself to those other exiles, Beerbohm, Berenson, Maugham. Where indeed is the idealism of which Philby's real-life biographers speak? It has become here submerged by a quiescent acceptance of the fact that he has ceased to matter to his masters and that he might as well enjoy what solace of the flesh and the spirit is still available to him. (p. 45)

Monotony is a dangerous mood for a playwright to sustain but it is essential to Mr. Bennett's strategy in this play and there is nothing that [the director] can do—indeed dare do—to relieve it for most of the first act. In a sense we have all been here before in plays by Chekhov or Turgenev where the setting is an isolated country estate in which a group of impoverished aristocrats and their dependents sit around playing games waiting for something to happen. There is a loaded pistol in a drawer somewhere and in the final scene someone will temporarily dissipate the boredom by firing it at his temples.

> **Where [Bennett has] his sights fixed unerringly [in *The Old Country*] is that influential section of our society which has in theory repudiated paternalism but which has not yet found an efficient substitute for it and is hoping vainly to get along on irony and charm.**
>
> **—Anthony Curtis**

Here the aristocrats have all turned into spies and the faithful retainers into security-guards whose proximity can be felt as Hilary raises his hand in a clenched-fist salute to a figure off-stage; and then he looks at his fingers distastefully as if they had been soiled with ordure. But without his fully realising it the situation is changing; beneath the heavy surface boredom a trap is being sprung. We are not just passing time waiting for Godot; we are waiting for Hilary's sister Veronica and her husband Duff, whose hand like Mr. Wilcox's is on all the ropes. At length this couple enter the dacha, bearing gifts from England for the exiles, two pots of gentleman's relish and an LP of the choir of King's College, Cambridge, extra fuel for Hilary's nostalgia. The malicious accuracy with which Mr. Bennett manages to hit off in Duff all the chief characteristics of the contemporary establishment frontman reminds one that many years ago he was one of the authors of *Beyond The Fringe*. . . . (pp. 46-7)

After a number of entertaining comparisons between England then and now, Mr. Bennett, well into the second half, at last gets down to business. Hilary's 'case' is examined. E. M. Forster's credo, 'If I had to choose between betraying my friend and my country, I hope I should have the guts to betray my country' is torn to shreds before our eyes. Why, his sister asks Hilary in brutally direct language, did he do it? He has no answer at all, only an evasive scepticism, an infinitely beguiling turn of phrase.

But he does recount the circumstances of his eleventh-hour escape from England. Someone had tipped him off by scribbling a cryptic allusion to *Great Expectations,* the words 'Wemmick's warning' on his pad when he returned from lunch, and he knew the game was up. I discussed this episode with that acute critic, Mr. T. J. Binyon of Oxford, who suggested that as the brother-in-law is shown as being a confirmed Dickens-lover one may assume that it was in fact he who wrote the warning. Mr. Binyon may well be right; it would certainly fit in with the picture of the incredible incestuousness of English life which is one of the things the play exposes, but I must confess it had not occurred to me. At any rate the brother-in-law's genius for non-sequitur is stretched to the full when the other traitor, a younger man who worked as a clerk in naval intelligence, reminds him of a homosexual encounter they had had some years before. Mr. Phillips looks down upon him from a great height and does not blink an eyelid; yet his game is up too.

If Hilary is evasive about his motive in betraying the old country he is absolutely clear about one thing: he does not wish to return to be rehabilitated. When his brother-in-law finally shows his hand he hints at an official offer on behalf of Her Majesty's Government; only when it is rejected by Hilary (but not by his wife) does it emerge that it is not an offer so much as an order. Hilary has become a pawn in a diplomatic game and the Russians are using him as part of an exchange deal. He is being banished from the dream-world of exile. Like that other hubristic figure of English childhood mythology Mr. Toad his days of exile, his imprisonment by the wild-wooders, are over thanks to the old-boy network.

There remains the alternative of the pistol-shot to the temples. In the last moments of the play [Hilary] toys momentarily with this option; his fingers reach instinctively for the drawer containing the revolver but then in one of those many tiny eloquent gestures of which this great performance consists he rejects it. He is not Prince Hamlet, nor was meant to be. He exits to the waiting car taking refuge once more in cosy English irony mouthing Mr. Toad's celebrated 'Poop-poop, poop-poop.'

What we have seen is a work of uncommon distinction, directed and played with understanding of all the nuances and grace-notes in which it abounds. It is not ultimately a satisfactory portrait of a traitor and Mr. Bennett certainly does not begin to fathom the mechanics of betrayal with the thoroughness of a Le Carré. Where he does have his sights fixed unerringly is that influential section of our society which has in theory repudiated paternalism but which has not yet found an efficient substitute for it and is hoping vainly to get along on irony and charm. (pp. 47-8)

> *Anthony Curtis, in a review of "The Old Country," in* Drama, *London, No. 127, Winter, 1977-78, pp. 45-8.*

Peter Shaw   (review date April 1978)

[*Shaw is an American historian, editor, and critic. In the following excerpt, he asserts that in* The Old Country *Bennett addresses the English people's fear that "something similar to Russian totalitarianism awaits England in its socialist future."*]

[The hero of Alan Bennett's ***The Old Country,*** Hilary], has been a radical, indeed the ultimate radical—a spy for the Russians who has defected from England and gone to live in the USSR. When the play opens, the hero's sister and brother-in-law are visiting him at his *dacha* in an effort to persuade him to return to England, where token punishment and a pardon await him. The brother-in-law's position as a representative of the Establishment is further

enhanced by his having recently been knighted, a circumstance which makes him the initial target of the play's humor.

As the argument proceeds, however, the upper-class brother-in-law and his wife, who have come to praise England, almost succeed in burying it. The most the new knight can say in England's defense is that it is now possible to get a decent meal in London, since there are finally a few good (foreign) restaurants there. The wife, in turn, tells of having witnessed a man urinating in Jermyn Street, from which event she adduces the end of Western civilization. And she has a few racist quips to offer as well: the zoos are frequented by people who come from the same countries as the animals, etc.

It remains for [Hilary] to serve as sentimental champion of the old English verities. He works for the Soviet state, yet he spends his time listening to Elgar on the phonograph and apprehensively searching the London *Times* for signs of change in his homeland. He objects (in an ironical-serious mode) to liberalizations in the Anglican service, carries on over the imminent closing of the Lyons teahouse chain, and nostalgically describes how he fell in love with the tacky houses and shops of the London suburbs while in the course of handing over government secrets on his espionage assignments in those precincts.

The play treats Soviet society rather mildly (though the characters are shown to be under constant surveillance), yet the author is clearly suggesting that something similar to Russian totalitarianism awaits England in its socialist future. The [hero] spends his weekends in a people's forest, a vacation area set aside by the state, where the trees have been planted in perfectly parallel rows with every trunk equidistant from every other. A day's walk is not long enough to bring one to the end of this man-made forest, itself an illustration of the sort of society for which, presumably out of idealism, the spy-hero has betrayed England and which, presumably, England will one day resemble also. (p. 89)

> *Peter Shaw, "Staging England's Decline," in* Commentary, *Vol. 65, No. 4, April, 1978, pp. 88-90.*

Nicholas Wapshott   (essay date 27 November 1978)

[*Wapshott is an English journalist, editor, political commentator, and critic. In the following essay, Bennett discusses his work for the stage and screen, his use of language, and his aims as an English writer.*]

There is a clear line between the work Bennett does for the stage and that which he writes for television. His stage plays are highly structured and artificial, indulging his obvious delight in verbal trickery. "When a society has to resort to the lavatory for its humour, the writing is on the wall", says the headmaster in ***Forty Years On,*** while Hilary, the exile in ***The Old Country,*** muses: "If one was a drunkard and one's name was Johnny Walker, one could form a society called Alcoholics Eponymous. Or if there, were two of you called Johnny Walker, Alcoholics Synonymous". In contrast, his television plays are naturalistic, rambling studies of everyday characters from the north of England and NW1.

All his plays share the precision and perfection in writing which the others in *Beyond the Fringe* often found tiresome.

He likes to write lines as they could be said and, in this respect, all his plays are collections of detailed conversations which together make a play. His lines are directly inspired by reality and he is a compulsive recorder of overheard sayings. He keeps a little black book for the purpose and scampers off to jot down the raw material for a future character. It is an art he inherited from his father, a Yorkshire butcher, who used to imitate his wife's sisters, to the great amusement of the young Bennett.

> The only reason I write down lines or remarks I overhear is that I would forget them if I didn't. My memory is so bad that I could apply for the geriatric ward now, if there were an early entry scheme. I find the lines I've written down useful when I come to try and shape a character for a play. The character can be built up from actual remarks, rather than from an abstract idea. Olga, the Stalinist in *The Old Country,* is a failure as a character because I have have never met such a person or eavesdropped on her conversation.

But isn't this clever aping of others' innocent remarks patronizing? Bennett thinks not.

> You don't patronize or make fun of someone when you laugh at them. Very often you are celebrating them. In *Me, I'm Afraid of Virginia Woolf,* Thora Hird plays a northern woman, mother of a 35-year-old bachelor. She's funny and puzzled; but because she's recognizable she's not diminished or, as you say, patronized. Half the battle is getting accurately the way such women talk. Northern English is often written and played simply as a roughened up version of standard English. It isn't. It's structurally different, the wit in it lying not in what is said but in the way it's put.

> [My plays] wander, they joke and they don't reach many conclusions. Certainly they don't suggest how society can be improved or reconstructed. Mind you, the playwrights who write these kind of direct plays often seem to me to have more in their heads than they have in their hearts. Which is not to say they have a great deal in their heads.
>
> —*Alan Bennett*

In addition to this savouring of moments, Bennett celebrates the peculiarities of the English character, the paradoxical nature of England and the English which is more clearly articulated in the north. For this he depends upon his keen powers of social observation, his love of the north and its people and his knowledge of himself. He is a model Englishman, at once bluntly straightforward and reserved; enthusiastic yet difficult to impress; a private person who loves to perform; holding strong views on everything but with no logical framework; a hard working professional who likes to make out that he is merely a lucky amateur. In *The Old Country,* Hilary says: "In England we never entirely mean what we say, do we? Do I mean that? Not entirely. And logically it follows that when we say we don't mean what we say, only then are we entirely serious." However, to be English and to want to write about England is not fashionable.

> It's funny how one can be *accused,* of being English. It's somehow a failing. Of course I'd quite like to be more European and indeed a little more timeless (if only for financial reasons) but how do you start? Cut the jokes, I suppose. The films I've made with Stephen Frears are all very English because he's of a similar cast of mind; they're diverse, and, I hope, humane. I think this is why I've never been able to accumulate any lasting credit at the BBC. (The BBC was offered my LWT plays but turned them down.) At the moment the BBC seems to favour plays that make very direct statements. Mine don't. They wander, they joke and they don't reach many conclusions. Certainly they don't suggest how society can be improved or reconstructed. Mind you, the playwrights who write these kind of direct plays often seem to me to have more in their heads than they have in their hearts. Which is not to say they have a great deal in their heads.

> I feel less English than I used to do. I lived in New York during the Broadway run of *Beyond the Fringe.* I couldn't wait to get back to England. These days I rejoice in New York, feel a different person there. Private medicine or no private medicine, the Americans are a graver, fairer and more honest people then we are. They lack irony but we have an overdose of it. It's got into our bones. We kid ourselves we are a kind and considerate people and maybe we still are in our private lives and outside our large cities. But London life these days seems to me churlish, avaricious and grudging. Whereas New York is vigorous, generous and witty. People talk to each other in the street. They lead a public life and they make up their language as they go along, something we have long since ceased to do.

His mind is turning increasingly towards New York and, between working on a screenplay based on John Lahr's biography of Joe Orton, *Prick Up Your Ears,* he is thinking of using the city as the subject of his next play. He is plainly not entirely happy living in London. *The Old Country* was about exile and the prospect of returning home to a changed and fast changing Britain. The characters indulge themselves in fashionable reaction, bemoaning the demise of Pathé News, the lending library at the Army and Navy and the traditional Holy Communion, the rise of universal jean wearing, antique shops in Walton Street, muggers in

Malmesbury and the desecration of English cities like Bath, Worcester and Brighton.

It is, perhaps, no accident that Bennett once adapted Evelyn Waugh's overstatement about the end of great country houses, *Brideshead Revisited,* for John Schlesinger. (It was never made.)

If anything keeps him in Britain it will be his dependence upon a small, close knit group of friends, mainly stemming from his university days and now mostly working in broadcasting or journalism. (He also keeps up with the *Beyond the Fringe* team.) He meets few people outside of this circle and uses this distance from the world—he reads *The Times,* watches a small television but rarely goes to the cinema or the theatre—too, as he says, "pump himself up" for inspiration. Apart from occasional bouts of northern gloom, he is a happy person.

> I have a small group of friends and we do laugh a great deal. Giggling is a great divider, I find. Any set up where giggles are out repels me. Covent Garden I put in this category. I like opera on record but hate it in live performance because of the reverential atmosphere that surrounds it. No giggles there. I once went to a dress rehearsal of *Eugene Onegin* at Covent Garden some years ago now. Solti was conducting and the audience was full of Isaiah Berlin and other social and intellectual grandees. Some unfortunate person coughed, maybe they even breathed. Solti stopped and glared and the whole atmosphere was so reverent it made you want to fart (though anonymously). I've no time for any of that. We make too much of art. When a society sets too much store by art there is something wrong. I only wish I was clever enough to know what.

He is extremely sensitive to social embarrassment and this also affects the way he views his own work. He is his own sternest critic.

> My stage plays vaguely embarrass me. Once they're staged and running I don't like going along to see them. I do go into the theatre. I'll sit backstage and gossip with the actors or wait in a dressing room with the tannoy turned down. This reluctance isn't so much modesty as shame. In a story about a writer, Borges remarks "All the books he had ever published filled him with a complex feeling of repentance". And that's it exactly. It's a pity as it takes away a lot of joy in the job. I suppose it's a way of saying I like writing, but don't like what I've written. Television doesn't affect me in quite the same way, though I don't like watching one of my television plays in company. The technology distances them more. They're less immediate, not so much to do with me. I still wince a lot, though. I suppose that's what I'm saying: I quite often make me wince.

> *Nicholas Wapshott, "Alan Bennett: Quite Often Managing to Make Himself Wince," in* The Times, *London, November 27, 1978, p. 7.*

John Russell Taylor   (review date Spring 1979)

[*An English editor, journalist, and critic, Taylor's works include* The Second Wave: British Drama for the Seventies *(1971). In the following excerpt, he provides a thematic analysis of six teleplays Bennett produced for London Weekend Television.*]

It is no longer the fashion to ask what plays are about. Except, possibly, at the BBC, where, Alan Bennett says, they seem at the moment to favour plays that make very direct statements and come to conclusions. Which may be why, as the story goes, the BBC turned down the six plays which have recently been done instead as a sequence by London Weekend Television. (The story, as usual, is simplistic: the BBC actually offered to do three of them, one a year, starting maybe this year; at the time they were sitting on a fourth which they had bought a while before.) But then television is, as they keep saying, a writer's medium rather than a director's, and the question may still be of use in pin-pointing just what is satisfactory or unsatisfactory in a play. Certainly, if it suggests itself as relevant it should not be brushed aside. With this sequence, or some of them at least, it suggests itself rather strongly. What is the play about? Is it about enough? Is it, finally, about what the playwright wants it to be about and thinks it is about? Then, but not before, one may be able to ask also whether all this matters.

For a start, though, a few more practical details about what the sequence is, and how the plays fit together. Certainly the six of them were never conceived as a sequence. Three, perhaps: whichever three were initially offered to the BBC. But the idea of six together seems to have been the brainchild of Michael Grade, mainly because six would be easier to sell than three or four. Nevertheless, Tony Wharmby, the executive producer, considers that they hold together as a series, and even that the precise order in which they are shown is significant, setting up as it does resonances, repetitions, meaningful references forward and back. To be unkind, one might say that this is to an extent making a virtue of necessity. Bennett does have his little jokes, his favourite little lines of dialogue, and it is difficult to tell whether the lady whose stomach is on a knife-edge constitutes a meaningful cross-reference between the first play, *Me! I'm Afraid of Virginia Woolf,* and the second, *Doris and Doreen,* or whether Bennett is just repeating himself.

Certainly, however it came about, there is a network of verbal reminiscences and cross-references among the plays, which are otherwise fairly miscellaneous. Three of them, *Me! I'm Afraid of Virginia Woolf, Afternoon Off* (number 4) and *All Day On the Sands* (number 6), are meticulously notated pictures of life in the North, the first set very specifically in Sheffield and the other two in Morecambe. The first is largely, and the other two entirely, shot on film. Number 5, *One Fine Day,* is also shot on film, but takes place equally specifically in London and is, unlike the rest, hardly comic at any level. Numbers 2 and 3, *Doris and Doreen* and *The Old Crowd,* are both shot entirely on videotape, in the studio, and are very different again in style and content, both from each other and from the rest of the six. *Doris and Doreen* is an approach to

Theatre of the Absurd, a day in the life of cogs in some unspecified bureaucratic machine, in some unspecified office location. *The Old Crowd* is even more abstract—a sort of surrealistic farcical tragedy set among the crumbling relics of the upper classes in a still unfurnished house about two hours from Horsham.

What, then, do the plays have in common? They are all, one way and another, about *temps mort,* between whiles, when nothing is happening. It has been said that they are all about crisis points, when people's lives take a decisive change of direction. But if so, this usually happens off-screen, or right at the end of the play, almost imperceptibly prepared for. The only real exception to this is *One Fine Day,* which is also in certain respects the most ambitious, and certainly the most cinematic, of the six. It is perhaps not entirely accidental that the title has echoes of Olmi, whose *Un Certo Giorno* was called the same in English. And the piece is not unlike an Olmi's-eye view of *8½*—the Italian references being reinforced by the constant quotations from Puccini on the soundtrack.

It concerns—or seems to concern—our old friend of a few years back, the male menopause. George Phillips, head of the commercial property section of a large estate agents, is at the outset crumpled, listless, neurotically inactive. He hardly connects with other people at the office, gets nowhere with disposing of the company's white elephant office-block, contracts out of home life with his wife, who keeps herself busy with pointless evening classes, or his teenage son, who glumly brings home an equally uncommunicative girl for the night. Instead he withdraws to his Puccini, listened to on an earphone set. Later he withdraws still further, camping out on the unfinished top floor of his office block. Then, suddenly, he pulls himself together, gets busy selling the block, outwits the bright young man around the office and gets him sacked, and returns home to order his son's new girl-friend out of the house. The dangerous corner, it appears, is past.

At least, that is how I understand the script. The studio synopsis, without actually misdescribing what happens, makes it sound far different, as though everything follows crisply and surely from what went before and it is a simple social comedy. Maybe this is what Alan Bennett intended, though from his way with mere plot elsewhere I would rather doubt it. His hero seems as lost in his familiar world as the Chinese hero of *Afternoon Off* is marooned in wintry Morecambe with a smattering of English. Nothing seems quite to make sense to him except his (understandable) desire not to be bothered with the people around him. Whether his return to 'normality' at the end, by dint of reversing all the vaguely reasonable things he has done and disposing of the one possibly progressive, practical person in his company, should be regarded as a positive, let alone a happy, ending is a moot point. Perhaps he has just decided that he loves Big Brother. But neither Bennett nor Stephen Frears, who directed this one (and three of the others, as well as producing all six), seems to be hinting at such a cynical or despairing conclusion. Olmi has always got into trouble with the left for apparently endorsing, or at least accepting, the company ethos; Bennett and

Frears, on this evidence, could join him in the liberal dog-house.

Where the piece does not finally work very well is not in its overall conception (if we do not ever feel we know for sure what the play is about, there is no reason why, in that sense, we should), but in its lack of specificity. Bennett's talent seems essentially (1) comic and (2) realistic. *One Fine Day* is almost entirely lacking in the little memorable details of dialogue and the tiny, quirky observations of how people really live and behave (especially in the North) which enliven the best of Bennett's work, and the best of these six plays in particular. It is as though, in elaborating his grand design for this, the most 'serious' and the longest of the series, he has deliberately denied himself the miniaturist detailing which usually serves him best. As he says of his own plays, 'They wander, they joke and they don't reach many conclusions.' This one wanders too little, jokes too little, and reaches a conclusion which implies conclusions.

All this reflects back on the play most unlike *One Fine Day* in the set, *The Old Crowd.* While it is difficult to know quite what one should label *One Fine Day,* which is written and directed entirely like what we would normally call a film, *The Old Crowd* is definitely, even defiantly, a play. It is written in artificially measured tones; it is played like high comedy, or at least high farce. Anyway, I suppose that is how it is played; what that means in practice is that it is played with the sort of tranced slowness English actors assume when they have little idea what they are talking about but are sure it is very sophisticated and probably fraught with deep significance. Admittedly, with London Weekend's publicity machine going into top gear, it might have been difficult at the time of the show's screening to approach it without preconceptions of some sort. (I hasten to add that I saw a preview, knowing nothing of the fuss which was to follow.) We were told that it had cost a quarter of a million pounds, which is apparently unprecedented for a taped studio production of just over an hour; that it was very experimental; and that Lindsay Anderson, who directed . . . , called it 'anti-television', 'destroying the myth of the television play', and presumed it was going to prove somewhat beyond television audiences. In the circumstances, it was hardly avoidable that critics and public might get their backs up a bit, and demand a masterpiece or nothing.

So, the worst that anyone could possibly say was perhaps what I heard said at the preview: after a long pause, on the way out, 'Well, it's a *nice* little play . . . Bit long . . . ' In Bennett's work it is probably nearest to *Habeas Corpus,* which he describes as 'a very mannered kind of farce'; in Anderson's, it comes closest to his production of Joe Orton's *What the Butler Saw.* In general, it comes closest—too close for comfort, indeed—to a poor man's *Discreet Charm of the Bourgeoisie.* Much the same image of a present or slightly future society is offered, with creeping chaos within the walls of the empty house (the furniture has vanished on the way and the ceilings crack ominously, while the servants start to rehearse the uprising down in the kitchen), and outside the strange virus which kills in hours, holes opening in the streets and rabies in Burgess Hill.

And the people, as in Buñuel, try to go on behaving naturally, as though nothing untoward is happening. If it were played at a reasonable speed it might work better, but the emphases are so theatrical—in the worst sense of the term, and in a way, strangely, that Anderson's theatre work hardly ever is—and there is so much posing around, big entrances and exits accompanied by peculiarly obtrusive snippets of Mickey-Mousing music, that the life of the thing oozes out through the cracks. There are, it is true, extraordinary moments, like the whole episode in which Frank Grimes, one of the out-of-work actors doubling as servants for the evening, makes kinky advances to Jill Bennett's foot under the table, then meets her upstairs for some hanky-panky under the unconcerned gaze of Cathleen Nesbitt, who is far more interested in her television set. Rachel Roberts howling with desire for her young adopted nephew is also a curious effect, somewhat muffed in the execution. But most of the play is arid and sterile. Very well, it is mirroring arid and sterile lives, but it is desirable in such circumstances that the medium should not be too infected by the message.

It is perhaps in some attempt to remedy this that Lindsay Anderson has introduced a few showy effects in the direction: occasions—maybe half a dozen of them—where the camera follows characters round four sides of a three-walled set to reveal the technicians off-set, or catches the crew reflected in a mirror or, at the climactic death scene, cranes up and away to show the whole extent of the set and the monitors flickering above. There is also one period of about thirty seconds when the action for no apparent reason goes into black-and-white, then returns to colour. The latter effect I cannot explain except as a little 'in' reference to *If*. . . and other Anderson films, but the former I suppose is meant to produce a sort of Brechtian distancing and underline the artificiality of the whole dying society depicted (rather as Ken Russell explained that people kept losing their trousers in his television version of *The Diary of a Nobody* to symbolise the shaky basis of Victorian bourgeois society).

Whether these devices work is clearly a matter of taste; to me they seemed too stilted and self-conscious to carry any sort of effect at all. I suspect that if Anderson had simply filmed the whole thing, or gone to the other extreme and treated it like a stage play which would then be recorded in the usual rather arbitrary way by four cameras in continuous performance, it would have worked far better. But such a weight of thought about television and its myth could hardly at the best of times be supported by Bennett's polished but fragile text.

The other scripts in the series come to varying degrees into the same medium-vs.-message bind. They all concern boredom and emptiness and the aimless filling up of time, and have to do it, naturally, without being in themselves boring and aimless. *Doris and Doreen,* the other one done entirely on tape, is able to overcome this, to a large extent, by being very thoroughly, unashamedly theatrical: it is in effect a two-character play built much along the lines of early Ionesco and Adamov plays, with the two clerks end-

lessly arguing about administrative grades, shuffling pink and green forms from tray to tray; and then, with the fascinated horror of a rabbit hypnotised by a snake, watching the inexorable approach of their fate, computerised redundancy. This is very much actors' television . . . and Alan Bennett and Stephen Frears provide merely the slight framework, making the very lack of action into an advantage by deliberately using it, Theatre of the Absurd-style, to play on our nerves.

The other three scripts are naturalistic film comedies shot on location (bar a few noticeably taped scenes in *Me! I'm Afraid of Virginia Woolf*). The two Morecambe plays are like a matched pair. *Afternoon Off* is a winter play, about the hopeless quest of a Chinese hotel worker for a girl called Iris, who is alleged to like sallow skins and may therefore gratify his interest in bed without too many preliminaries beyond the box of Milk Tray he clutches in his hand. It is frankly episodic, with the uncomprehending Lee as the still centre and occasional catalyst in a succession of scenes from provincial life, drawn with sharp observation and sometimes mordant humour. The only thing wrong with it is that it does go on a bit, though very prettily shot (by Stephen Frears again) and immaculately acted.

Much the same verdict would apply to the summer Morecambe play, *All Day on the Sands,* directed by Giles Foster. It is a simple story of a day in the life of a small private hotel with pretensions (beautifully captured in the Portofino Room with its hanging chianti bottles and the owner's constant commentary to guests on his little loudspeaker system), and particularly of one family trying with painful refinement to hide the fact that the husband is unemployed. Bennett is particularly good at the minor tortures of keeping up a front, not being 'let down' in public by one's children, and clinging to the terminological niceties in which everyday jobs have to be clothed for one's own self-respect. And while winter Morecambe looks temptingly bizarre, summer Morecambe looks all too formica-clad and unappealing—an oddity of which, one feels, Bennett entirely approves.

Which leaves the first and in every way the most successful of the pieces, *Me! I'm Afraid of Virginia Woolf.* It could be regarded as a film, and would probably look pretty good on a smallish large screen—again, a comparison in tone and manner with Olmi and the Czech Forman films comes irresistibly to mind. But at the same time, with its technical mixture of film and tape, and its narrating voice (Alan Bennett's own) commenting intimately on the action, it does seem to belong with perfect conviction on television more than anywhere else: it achieves the theoretically desirable goal of being 'pure television' mainly by clearly working according to no theory and not worrying itself at all about what it is. (If *The Old Crowd* worried less it would work far better.) It is a comedy-drama—again, categories do not matter—about a lost and lonely 35-year-old literature teacher in a Polytechnic who realises he is becoming a compulsive liar and chronic hypochondriac from sheer self-disgust and inability to connect with anyone around him. As the commenting voice says at one point, in the midst of a wonderfully awful scene of dutiful love-making ('Other people got foreplay; he got

Bruckner') with the troll who teaches yoga, what Hopkins really wanted was someone who didn't want him, since his opinion of himself was so low he could have no respect for anyone who did not share it.

Into this drab and depressing life comes Skinner. Skinner is the only bright, irreverent, alive member of Hopkins' literature class where, the week in question, he is teaching E. M. Forster and Virginia Woolf. Skinner's presence is a mystery: the only explanation he offers is that it is better than sitting at home watching colour telly with the wife and kid. Skinner frightens Hopkins—partly because, as the narrating voice tells us round the half-way mark, he does not yet realise that he loves him. And since this is a play with a happy ending, Hopkins ends up by, in some fashion, getting his man. Though common sense may tell us that the chances of a plain, middle-aged teacher being propositioned by the most evidently glamorous young member of his class (of whichever sex) are remote, still, the prospective coupling, overtly homosexual or not, of these two emotional and intellectual outsiders does make enough human sense to carry us over; and the vulgar gesture of the end, in which a freeze of the two faces is accompanied by a lusty rendition on the soundtrack of 'I'm In Love with a Wonderful Guy', does actually work like a dream.

In other words *Me! I'm Afraid of Virginia Woolf* pulls off what all six plays—indeed, all drama, I suppose—try to do: to take us by surprise and yet make us feel that everything is inevitable. It is, throughout, a beautifully crafted play, and one cannot help noticing that the jokey lines that recur elsewhere work best in this context because here they are furthest away from the spectre of the revue sketch, most closely integrated into a serious, though never solemn, observation of complex and thoroughly understood characters.

The series as a whole, by accident or by design, gives us a very fair conspectus of the range of effects and stylistic approaches available to television drama, and neatly forbids us to make any over-tidy generalisation. This is a film, and it works on television. This is theatre, and it works on television. This is neither (or both) and it works. This is neither (or both) and it doesn't. Possibly the slow development of *Afternoon Off* would look better if it were shown on a cinema screen, with the particular kind of concentrated attention that enforces. Equally, its extremely episodic structure might work against it more there than on a small screen. Film or tape or half-and-half (or for that matter live), it is all grist to television's mill. Perhaps the only myth of television drama is that there is no myth of television drama. And the sum total of the Bennett plays is two hits, two half-hits, two misses. Any more theory than that, and you are really in trouble. (pp. 117-18)

John Russell Taylor, "The Bennett Plays," in
Sight and Sound, *Vol. 48, No. 2, Spring, 1979,*
pp. 116-18.

Alan Bennett (essay date Spring 1984)

[*In the following excerpt, Bennett discusses the differences between film and his television dramas.*]

In 1982 I took part in a symposium at the NFT during the London Film Festival. Most of the discussion that afternoon was about what was wrong with the production of films in Britain, whether for distribution in the cinema, for television or both. It struck me afterwards (and I was as much to blame as anyone else) that the six of us on the panel had sat there having a jolly good whine. Many of the audience were students, who were probably only too anxious to make films whatever the conditions. We, who in our various capacities were in the happy position of being able to do so, should have taken account of that. We didn't. So I'd preface my remarks here by saying that I've been very lucky in that the films I've written, at any rate for television, have all actually ended up on the screen and in a form not too distantly related to what I imagined when I wrote them. Adding though that, being television, those films have about as much permanence as a fart in the wind.

Maybe it's because I've never directed a film, but I don't share that passionate attachment to film that many of my (slightly younger) contemporaries have. To me it's just another way of telling a story and if the story can be told better on tape and in the studio, well and good. I don't enjoy the taping process as much, but that's because filming generally comes with bacon sandwiches.

On my own subjective scale writing for the theatre comes first, feature films second and television (whether film or tape) last. This is partly because at the moment I find television easiest to write, theatre well nigh impossible and feature films (or grown-up films as I tend to think of them) somewhere in between. But the scale has more to do with the permanence of the various forms. A theatre play, once put on, will normally get into print and so can be read and reproduced. A feature film, once shown in the cinema, starts out on its career and has a history, a life. A BBC television film has no history. It is an incident, with luck an occasion, the bait for the writer a nationwide audience and his work a topic of general discussion the next day. If cable catches on it will put paid to that. In New York for instance one seldom hears TV discussed, because with umpteen channels the audience is by now too fractured. If similar fragmentation happens here the lure of writing films for television, the chance of in some small way addressing the nation, disappears. But long before that, I suspect, the television companies will have ceased to finance films and the single play or TV film will be as rare on television here as it is in America.

I've written about a dozen TV films, eleven of which have been produced. I've written four feature films and to date none of them has been produced. My first film script was a farcical comedy, *The Vicar's Wife* (1966) for Ned Sherrin, then at Columbia. In 1973 I adapted Evelyn Waugh's *Handful of Dust* for John Schlesinger. I was quite pleased with this script, but it proved too expensive to make. In 1981 I adapted John Lahr's life of Joe Orton, *Prick Up Your Ears,* for Stephen Frears and Chrysalis Records. The boss of Chrysalis thought he was getting another *Cage aux Folles,* so it's not surprising that didn't get made. I also did an adaptation of *The Old Crowd,* my TV play that Lindsay Anderson directed, as a film for Lindsay and the

Swedish Film Institute, but there was a boardroom revolution in Stockholm and our script went out of the window.

At the moment I have a film I've written with Malcolm Mowbray that seems to be going ahead, but I'll believe it on the first day of principal photography. Unless one counts a short sketch in *The Secret Policeman's Other Ball,* nothing I have ever written has ended up on the cinema screen. And actually (because it was too dirty) they cut the sketch. So my answer to any question about the difference between films for TV and films for the cinema is that in my experience one gets made and the other doesn't.

My scripts, where the infantry is recruited from aunties and wheelchairs make up the armoured division, are not ready-made movie material. But the European directors I admire, like Truffaut or Olmi, don't eat their hearts out because they're not big in Arkansas.

—Alan Bennett

In terms of writing I don't think one can talk of feature films and TV films in the same breath, and it's not simply a question of scale or scope. It seems to me to have something to do with the space between an audience and the screen. On television one does not have to raise one's voice. The relationship with the audience is intimate, the tone conversational. A cinema audience is physically further away from the screen, so that one's tone, and the tone of the writing, has to be different, projected more. Somehow (I can't explain this) the space between the audience and the cinema screen must be matched by a corresponding sense of space in the film. Perhaps air is a better word. There has to be more air in a film. This may be utter nonsense, but there are definite practical differences. I watched *An Englishman Abroad* with an audience at BAFTA. Several crucial lines got lost because the laughter from previous lines overlapped. Watching it at home this didn't happen. If it had been written for the cinema the dialogue should have been less dense, the possibility of laughter catered for. This is partly what I mean by air.

I was slightly taken aback by the success of *An Englishman Abroad.* None of my previous TV films has received anything like the attention devoted to this one. Some of this was undoubtedly due to it being shown first at the London Film Festival and reviewed by a better class of critic. And then the upper classes and espionage are always dear to English hearts, more so certainly than the touching stories of sudden incontinence north of the Trent in which I generally specialise. *An Englishman Abroad* is bolder and more polished than my earlier films thanks entirely to John Schlesinger, but I did feel that if some of my earlier stuff, particularly the films directed by Stephen Frears for London Weekend, had been put in a similar film festival showcase they would have fared almost as

well. As it is they now languish in the archives (sic) of LWT, with no prospect of ever being seen again.

The frustration of such situations confirms my old-fashioned faith in print and I try whenever possible to get my television scripts published. But writing TV films would seem a more purposeful and worthwhile activity if the BBC and the independent companies developed a sensible and accessible archive system, where one's work was in a library and could be made available with the minimum of fuss. I know Channel 4 was supposed to cure everything from the decline of the film industry to unwanted hair, but its contribution in the matter of repeats has been more modish than helpful (i.e. I haven't figured in it). If only out of respect to Lindsay Anderson, I feel Channel 4 owes him a showing of *The Old Crowd,* his only TV play. It was screened once opposite 'Match of the Day' as part of LWT's 'New Look to Saturday Night'. As a result it was seen by about six people (Richard Ingrams considers it the worst play he has ever seen: there can be no higher praise). I could go on, but this is the kind of whining I referred to at the start.

Behind a lot of the questions that are raised lurks an unspoken one: how do we make it big in America? Risking being hauled before Colin Welland in the Barnes Magistrates Court, charged with insulting behaviour, I'd like to ask why do we want to? The answer is: because we don't just want to make films, we want to Make Movies. Or some of us do. The essential difference it seems to me is not between films for the cinema and films for television but between films and movies. There is a lot of playing soldiers about it. Forget film, there are many directors who would be just as happy conducting a small war. To which movie-making is the next best thing: getting the troops off Omaha Beach appeals to them as much as getting the dialogue on to the screen. By talent and temperament I am not in this game. My scripts, where the infantry is recruited from aunties and wheelchairs make up the armoured division, are not ready-made movie material. But the European directors I admire, like Truffaut or Olmi, don't eat their hearts out because they're not big in Arkansas. Why should we? Mrs Thatcher has the answer, but does she know anything about films? (pp. 121-22)

Alan Bennett, in an excerpt from Sight and Sound, *Vol. 53, No. 2, Spring, 1984, pp. 121-22.*

Andrew Hislop (essay date 6 September 1986)

[*In the following excerpt, Hislop examines the controversy surrounding* Kafka's Dick.]

Some writers just read great novels, others such as Jean Rhys or Peter Ackroyd rewrite them. Playwrights, however, encouraged by the wish of television to send all literature down the cathode tube, are keener than novelists to adapt the work of their favourite authors. They also like to have them strutting on their stage.

Alan Bennett, satirist, dialogist supreme, and founder member of the SDP, is about to put one of his literary heroes on the Royal Court's stage in a new play, *Kafka's Dick*. . . .

Bennett has made theatrical use of famous writers before—but at a distance in the comical pastiches of the school play within his play about a school, *Forty Years On.* However, the authors he has made most use of in his work, particularly in his many delicately cadenced television plays, are anonymous, commonplace, full of the pathetic absurdities of everyday mutterings—men and women on the Clapham omnibus, even if it is the Clapham in Yorkshire where he has a cottage.

Many a throw-away line destined for quick extinction in a faulty hearing-aid has been rescued by Bennett, stored in his notebook, then mouthed exquisitely into life again. . . .

Bennett's interest in Kafka was in part prompted by other writers who have "rewritten" his life. Among them is Philip Roth who, in a celebrated piece of fantasy, made the troubled genius become a poor, unknown Hebrew teacher in America.

Bennett's first use of Kafka was in his award-winning television play, *The Insurance Man,* which portrayed in all but name the great writer in a Kafkaesque world as though to suggest that his writing was not so much disturbed, metaphysical fantasy as an accurate reflection of his surroundings. Now comes the contentiously-titled *Kafka's Dick.*

Bennett had been "in two minds" about the title which, with its echoes of *Prick Up Your Ears,* John Lahr's biography of Joe Orton . . . filmed with a Bennett screenplay, does suggest a singular approach to literary figures.

His doubts have been recently revived by the arrival of a telegram from that celebrated theatrical rewriter of Kafka. Steven Berkoff: "I find your stupid title abusing Kafka grossly offensive . . . So easy for hacks like you to mock the dead." "I sent back a nice postcard", chuckled Bennett. "I said perhaps he should wait to see the play."

Bennett insists that it is not a work of sacrilege, even if some people might think so. Indeed, he sees Kafka, who himself reacted so strongly to his authoritarian father, as a sort of father figure to all modern writers, almost religiously sacrificing everything to his writing: "I feel very much in awe," says Bennett.

Kafka's Dick, in which . . . an insurance man turned obsessional biographer of Kafka, is intended as an examination of the relationship of a biographer to his subject and a writer to his reputation. It is also about Bennett's own reaction: "In a sense, *Kafka's Dick* is about writing *The Insurance Man.*"

"I don't have 'literary interests'. Literature is what I'm made of," wrote Kafka in his diary. Bennett too writes a diary which, unlike Kafka, he intends to publish, but he is much more modest about his place in literature, joking about his fear of being "rumbled", even providing ammunition for would-be rumblers by admitting he has never read *The Castle.*

Despite critical acclaim of his television work and the far-

cical element in his most popular stage plays, he does, however, still believe that theatre is nearer to serious literature than television. Though he greatly enjoys writing television dialogue, there is a yearning to get away from the naturalism he tends towards in his work for the small screen.

Significantly, his television play which most called into question this naturalism, *The Old Crowd,* . . . received widespread, misplaced critical disapproval. However, *Kafka's Dick* is his first work for the theatre since *Enjoy* (1980), which was even more subversive of its superficially realist setting and was the least acclaimed of his full length stage plays.

Both *The Old Crowd* and *Enjoy* are faintly reminiscent of Kafka's story *The Married Couple* in their use of a socially embarrassing corpse. But Bennett sees no influence of Kafka in his work before he started writing about him. He does think, however, that he would have liked Kafka—though not Joe Orton.

It is difficult not to like Bennett himself. Still impishly spry in his early fifties, looking suspiciously as young as his self-portrait as a boy which hangs on his wall, he has made the change from satirist to writer of substance without losing a healthy talent for mockery and self-mockery.

When I met him he had just been standing, sneakered but unsporty, holding the telephone to his television set so that a friend in New York could hear the European Games 1500 metres final. He still acts, however, as a vehicle for lines of those less famous than Orton, Kafka or David Coleman. Recently he heard a would-be member of a group of local winos thus rejected, "No, no, go away, stop trying to get on our bandwagon."

I'm not sure what Kafka himself would have made of *Kafka's Dick.* Though Kafka once charmingly said of a barmaid lover that a whole cavalry regiment had ridden over her body, he had an abhorrence of dirty jokes. Whether the joke turns out to be on Kafka or Bennett himself, I feel that other writers already on the Kafka bandwagon should listen to what their hero says for himself at the Court.

> *Andrew Hislop, "About to Raise the Roof Again," in* The Times, *London, September 6, 1986, p. 10.*

Robert Gore Langton   (review date November 1986)

[*In the following excerpt, Langton outlines the action of* Kafka's Dick *and lauds Bennett's "unfailing ear for middle-class domestic banality and that famous, honed sense of the ridiculous."*]

After *The Insurance Man* Bennett continues on the Kafka trail with [*Kafka's Dick*], this dazzling entertainment about the Prague novelist, his penis, and literary fame. . . . Literary fame is defined, by the way, as being known even by people who haven't read your books. This is foremost a comedy, of course, with the author exploiting his unfailing ear for middle-class domestic banality and that famous, honed sense of the ridiculous. It must be said that Steven Berkoff's nasty insult to Bennett (he chastised him for taking the name of Kafka in vain) appears doubly foolish since his play lobs question marks at the nature of biography and literary criticism without ever intending or doing violence towards Kafka's stature as an author.

The play opens with a dreaming Kafka in conversation with Max Brod, friend, fellow novelist and his biographer—the man who ignored Kafka's wish to have all his manuscripts burnt. Brod reminds him that when the Nazis come to power they will burn the books anyway, assuring him immortality; in fact he's surprised the publishers hadn't thought of book burning first. Brod has a nice line in Jewish humour. In a momentary transformation. . . . we are time-warped into the black and white suburban sitting room of an insurance man, Sydney, and his wife Linda. Sydney is writing an article on Kafka for the journal of insurance, *Small Print.* The door bell rings and Max Brod himself appears. Dumbfounded, Sydney becomes positively ecstatic when the tortoise in the kitchen metamorphoses into Kafka himself. A life-long hero in his own lounge. Kafka is unaware that he is a leading literary figure of the century, so Brod implores Sydney to conceal his detailed knowledge of the author. A farcical attempt to hide all the Kafka publications in the house fails and Kafka realises his posthumous fame.

Here the myth of Kafka is that he was forced to expend his energies in an insurance office while also having to put up with the opprobrium of his despicable, brutish father. We view art not as a gift but as a transaction, says Bennett. We prefer art to be produced at a price: be it a life of squalor, ill-health or unrecognition. So here the father of the cringing, tubercular Kafka returns to set things aright. Why should he go down as the villain of the piece? Hasn't the injured party exaggerated? He blackmails his son by threatening to reveal the tiny dimension (the sort biographers love) of the object referred to in the play's title. Kafka complies and gingerly confirms that he and his father did in fact get along famously. [Kafka's father, Herman], is a swaggering northerner, gross, uncouth and superbly comic. . . . The sight of him abusing and dominating [the] gaunt Kafka remains an abiding image: 'I read one of your books once—flat as piss on a plate', he jibes. But even he comes to realise that the only way he is to survive in literary history is by being the bullying father. To be a nice parent is to be forgotten in the land of biography.

Wedged into this crowded meeting of ideas and figures from opposite ends of the century is the story of Sydney and Linda's relationship. . . . [Linda is portrayed as an] unliterary wife whose ignorance is nurtured by her fact-obsessed husband. She comes in the end to condemn in a roundly feminist critique' the basis of her marriage, and the disappearance of women in literary history. Her flirting with Kafka is a release and gives Bennett the opportunity to indulge in literary pastiche: he has Kafka describe in the detailed minutiae of existentialist observation her actions in seductively offering him a chocolate. [Brod is garrulous and horny, while] Kafka deports himself like a chrysalis that will never burst open: his suited, phthistic frame is accompanied by an aura of personal misery,

though Bennett makes it clear that he enjoyed being miserable.

The author's trial, with old grandad's walking frame as a makeshift dock (let's not forget Charles Lamb's truly Kafkaesque attempts to prove himself sane to characters that he thinks all along are health inspectors) ironically confirms the need for biography to make the most of the insignificant detail. And in a final scene in heaven where Kafka's father is God, a whole celebrity-clogged cocktail party nightmare gives Kafka, on waking, pause to reflect that Heaven is hell.

There is so much buzzing in this almost over-dense battery of interleaved scenes and literary gamesmanship that it is all [the director] can do to orchestrate the events coherently on stage. The result is one of surfeit; but at least it is a case of too much of a good thing. . . . Certainly after seeing this it will be hard to pick up a Kafka novel without a chuckle first. (pp. 18-19)

Robert Gore Langton, "Kafka's Duck," in Plays & Players, No. 398, November, 1986, pp. 18-19.

Patrick Skene Catling   (essay date 2 April 1988)

[*Catling is an English-born American journalist, nonfiction writer, and critic. In the following excerpt, he offers a positive assessment of* Talking Heads, *which he finds representative of Bennett's other works.*]

'I don't know why it should be only Catholics who are thought never to escape their religious upbringing,' Alan Bennett writes in the jocularly confessional introduction to *Talking Heads,* 'I have never managed to outgrow mine. When I was 16 and not long confirmed I was devoutly religious, a regular communicant who knew the service off by heart. It might be thought this would rejoice a vicar's heart and maybe it did, but actually I think the parish clergy found my fervour faintly embarrassing. A fervent Anglican is a bit of a contradiction in terms anyway. . . . ' (p. 27)

[The six elegantly underwritten, emotionally allusive monologues for television that comprise *Talking Heads*] offer a decent, mild catharsis which may leave many viewers feeling as if they have had a not too strenuous visit to the lav. Mr Bennett evidently cares, not at all indelicately, about the lav. He writes comedy about all sorts of human activities with tolerant smiles rather than laughs and tragedy with sympathetic frowns rather than tears. Repressed fervour is a mode of northern reticence of which he, among playwrights, is the supreme master.

He was born in Leeds, a butcher's son, 54 years ago. He has lived slightly more than half his life up to now in the south. After the army and Oxford, he achieved his first public success in *Beyond the Fringe* in 1961. His most memorable contribution to that epochal review was a sermon in the painfully sincere, authentically Anglican manner yet utterly devoid of meaning. He gave Canon C. H. E. Smyth of Cambridge a copy of the text, at his request, apparently to help teach apprentice ministers how not to preach. Mr Bennett still lives in London, in a house opposite Jonathan Miller's and beside Colin Haycraft's, but sets most of his plays in the north.

In the introduction to **Objects of Affection,** a 1982 collection of his television plays, which the BBC have just republished, he writes:

> I don't have any illusions about the north being more 'real', or think that it is, like the muesli cake in **Intensive Care,** wholesome but gritty. I was brought up in the north, but, like the hero of the same play, in such humdrum circumstances that I was deprived only in that I suffered no deprivation. The language and rhythms of northern speech come naturally to me. Its characteristic habit of saving the subject until the very end of a sentence gives northern dialogue a tension lacking in standard English. It also helps the jokes.

He is a dramatist of the humdrum without humbug. The plebeian ordinariness of many of his characters and the banality of their speech invest his plays with the extraordinary excitement of universal revelation. Prosaic experiences are made to seem significantly poetic.

More candidly than some other writers, he acknowledges the autobiographical origins of even some of his weakest protagonists. He called a collection of plays produced for London Weekend Television in 1978-9 **The Writer in Disguise.**

> Hopkins, the polytechnic lecturer, Lee, the Chinese waiter, and Phillips, the estate agent, share the same character, indeed *are* the same character. Passive, dejected, at odds with themselves, they are that old friend, the Writer in Disguise. A doleful presence, whatever his get-up, he slips apologetically in and out of scenes being heartfelt, while the rest of the cast, who are invariably more fun (and more fun to write, too), get on with the business of living. . . . Lee, the Chinese waiter, who scarcely speaks but only smiles, is the ineffectual hero taken to a logical conclusion and the natural condition of all three is what Lee ends up doing—namely, lying in his underpants staring at the ceiling.

Mr Bennett obviously takes great care to select the *mot juste* to achieve his casually realistic effects. In a diary he kept while making **All Day on the Sands,** he wrote:

> What nobody ever says about writing is that one can spend a whole morning, like this one, just trying to think of a name . . . the name of a character, the name of a place, or, as in this case, the name of a boarding house. The boarding house has been jazzed up, made into a 'private hotel', rooms given the names of Mediterranean resorts: the Portofino Room, the Marbella Lounge. What should the establishment as a whole be called?

> Somerset Maugham set himself to write 2,000 words a day.

> Did you ever have this problem, Somerset?

> I eventually settle on the Miramar.

His new monologues, which were written and filmed last

year, are his most strictly disciplined, ostensibly simplest, and, perhaps, but only for him, his most difficult plays of all.

The viewer is required to exert his imagination more than usual when watching television, but the slight effort is an enjoyable one of participation. As the playwright points out, 'to watch a monologue on the screen is closer to reading a short story than watching a play.' As the narrators are 'artless,' giving only their subjective accounts of events, the viewer must construct his own interpretation of what the unseen characters off-screen really must be like. Suggesting a well-rounded story through the narrow viewpoint of a prejudiced narrator requires skill, of which Mr Bennett fortunately has an abundance.

He says he is disturbed by noting how much he writes about the same sorts of people. 'There are droves of voluntary workers, umpteen officials from the social services, and should there be a knock on the door it's most likely to be a bearded vicar.' Twenty-seven years after **Beyond the Fringe,** he certainly retains an interest in the Church. Vicars 'turn up in all but one of these pieces, earnest, visitant and resolutely contemporary.'

He resists contemporaneity, especially as represented by parsons in pastel dress, nuns who have 'lost their old billowing, wimpled innocence and now look like prison wardresses on the loose,' grey hearses and 'the dismantling of the Book of Common Prayer.'

> **[Bennett] is a dramatist of the humdrum without humbug. The plebeian ordinariness of many of his characters and the banality of their speech invest his plays with the extraordinary excitement of universal revelation. Prosaic experiences are made to seem significantly poetic.**
>
> *—Patrick Skene Catling*

The values he respects are the orthodox morality and social rules that his mother taught him. His disparagements of red paint, yellow gloves and two-tone cardigans date back to home and childhood, where they were items in a catalogue of disapproval that ranged through (fake) leopardskin coats, dyed (blonde) hair to slacks, cocktail cabinets and statuettes of ladies with alsatian dogs on leash. 'In our house and in my mother's scheme of things they were all common. Common is not an easy term to define without seeming to brand the user as snobbish or socially pretentious, which my mother wasn't.'

He remains loyal to her code and applies it to the present state of affairs. 'Common persists. It's not a distinction I'd want to be detected making,' he says, 'but to myself I make it still.' Thus he classifies as common such minor modern phenomena as lace or nylon curtains gathered in the middle, which 'look to me like a woman who's been to the lav and got her underskirt caught up behind her,' mock Geor-gian doorways and Kentucky fried chicken.

He has a keen eye for vulgar fripperies and a keen ear for clichés and the fun he makes of them seems to be based on serious disdain, possibly softened by pity, but not much.

Five of the six narrators are women. . . . Alan Bennett himself plays the other part, that of a middle-aged bache-lor who possessively loves his senile mother. . . .

> 'I always think Graham would have made a good parson,' Mother said . . . , 'only he doesn't believe in God.' 'That's no handicap these days,' Mr Turnbull said.

Well, there the reverent and irreverent Mr Bennett goes again, in heavy disguise. (pp. 27-8)

> Patrick Skene Catling, "O Uncommon Alan Bennett," in The Spectator, Vol. 260, No. 8334, April 2, 1988, pp. 27-8.

Terry Coleman   (essay date 17 February 1989)

[An English journalist, editor, critic, poet, novelist, and nonfiction writer, Coleman's works include a collection of interviews entitled Movers and Shakers: Conversa-tions with Uncommon Men (1987). In the following essay, based on an interview with Bennett, he chronicles Bennett's discussion of his life, career, and his double bill, Single Spies.]

Alan Bennett—playwright and "actor on the side", which is his own description—had just come offstage at the Na-tional after a matinee of his own double bill, **Single Spies,** the one in which the Queen is portrayed and given all the good lines. That is the scene between HMQ and Anthony Blunt, art historian, keeper of the Queen's collection, and spy.

"Fusillade of coughs today," he said, "They seemed able to cough on exactly the right word to kill the lines." Given that Mr Bennett himself plays Blunt in that most subtle of scenes, he didn't seem at all put out by the coughs.

We settled down in the room off the foyer where the Na-tional gives drinks to underserving journalists and other guests, he stretching his legs straight out in front of him, sticking his hands deep in his pockets, and explaining that he was the sort of man of whom Nabokov had said that he might be able to write, but spoke like a child. "I just flounder all over the place," he said.

All I can say is that an interviewer ought to be quite happy to flounder round with him, back, for instance, to his ma-ternal grandmother's family who were Peels from Halifax and always said they were descended from Sir Robert Peel, the prime minister: but that, he thought, was social-climbing fantasy. On the other side, his family were Lin-colnshire labourers. His father was a butcher but should not have been.

He played the violin, but had had a stepmother straight out of a fairy story, who starved him, made him practise his violin in the dark, and put him to butchery. "He had

perfect pitch. He never had a bad word for anyone except her, but he said that the day of her funeral everybody was happy."

Alan Bennett went to Leeds Modern school, was con-firmed at 14, and was for three or four years after that very religious, fond of the Church of England, its hymns, and the old prayer book. By the time he got to Oxford the idea of taking holy orders was fading. Those were the days of **Beyond the Fringe,** which made his first reputation. One of the sketches takes the form of a sermon, with the parson preaching on the text, "My brother Esau is an hairy man." He says that at first this was thought offensive, but it was done out of affection. "And the same applies really to the Queen in this. It's done out of affection. And if it isn't, it doesn't work."

Before Oxford he did his National Service in the Intelli-gence Corps doing a Russian course at Cambridge and Bedmin. During the course they were officer cadets, but at the end they went to Mona officer training school, and he failed.

> 'And almost, looking back, I think of that as being . . . I think that if I'd become an officer I would have been much more a fully fledged member of the establishment than I ever be-came. Because it's slightly "the iron entered the soul." We had to go back to the Intelligence Corps camp, and I went back as a private. Other people like Michael Frayn—he was a close friend—he was an officer. And the last few weeks were much worse than basic training. I re-member a sergeant made me scrub out a urinal with my bare hands.

How well had he learned Russian? Well enough to become a spy? (Prolonged laughter from Mr Bennett.) "If we were to become spies they'd have an enormous number of us. Some people did monitor radio broadcasts, but it was never spelled out."

He did get to speak Russian almost unthinkingly, and could read Dostoevsky, who was very difficult, but nowa-days reads nothing. "When it was over, that was the end of it."

At Oxford he read history and then for two years taught it, researching the topic of Richard II's retainers, 1388-99, discovering what they had been paid and so on, reading medieval Latin rolls in the Public Record Office, and thinking it a very broad subject.

And afterwards, had he ever written a historical play or anything? "No." So that had gone the way of the Russian? (Laughter) "Yes, that's right. Wasted."

Though when he was in New York for the Broadway run of **Beyond the Fringe,** from August 1962 to April 1964, microfilmed medieval documents were sent over to him, and he read them in the Fifth Avenue public library. And it was only last year that he threw his old notebooks away.

New York then seemed a sort of penance, another Nation-al Service, whereas now he would think it wonderful. Now the city was different; the food was better, the people were nicer. The days of **Beyond the Fringe** now seemed another life, but they had given him a bit of financial slack which he had managed to maintain ever since. He found it hard to work to commission, and thought you worked less if you did only what you wanted.

In the British Museum catalogue he is entered as "Bennett, Alan (satirical actor)", presumably to distinguish from the Bennett, Alan who is a member of the Bow Group and the Bennett, Alan who writes on gastroenteritical mobility. He is amused by this, saying that there is also an Alan Bennett who is a Savile Row tailor, and that anyway he doesn't convice himself as an actor.

How many actors did? "I think they do. It's partly that I generally play things I've written myself. The sense of immersing yourself in the text, which actors do; I don't do that. You can't really immerse yourself in your own text because you know how shallow it is. I think with real actors it's different. I'm an actor on the side."

Last year he did the television series of **Talking Heads,** half hour programmes, all monologues—the nervous, beautiful, alcoholic wife of a trendy vicar; the brisk Home Counties widow putting on a brave face; the young actress who thinks she's getting her big chance, when, as it emerges, all she has is a bit part in a porn film. The monologue is a form Mr Bennett likes and has used before, going as far back as **Beyond the Fringe.** He says it can be a risk, just having one character talking, and yet it also limits the risk. With a monologue, you have more control, because there is only one actor to worry about. If you wrote the same story as a play, with several characters, then your control was dissipated.

The monologue I found most moving was [the one concerning] Susan the vicar's wife, who is made love to by an Asian grocer in his storeroom, "there among the lentils on the second Sunday after Trinity." And then at the end, I said, when Mr Ramesh went back to India to fetch his young wife, and Susan finds a boy writing Under New Management on the window. . . . [Bennett notes:]

> She doesn't cry but she's on the edge of it. I think that's wonderful . . . But it seems to me a bit that I get credit for things which—well, if you get the dialogue right, if your ear is accurate enough, you often get credit for sympathies and for insight which you don't necessarily have; just because you've reproduced the dialogue properly, people assume that you've got it. I do have a bit, but I don't think I have the kind of insight that I get credited for. To some extent it comes with the ear, I think.

Well, since he was a Yorkshireman that might be so if the monologue he was reproducing was northern, but what about his splendid Home Counties women? "You do hear that, in art galleries. You hear them here, quintessentially here. The National is like that."

Surely the National was SDP territory?

> Well, yes. A bit Torier than that. It's that kind of robust confrontation of life. I once went to an exhibition of Tantra art at the Hayward. And there's this sculpture of this Indian couple doing absolutely everything to each other, through

every possible orifice. And there were two ladies like the one in the monologue, who stood looking at this, and one said, "My, what a busy lady." I just like that spirit of resolute unshockability. That's why I like class in a way, the difference between the classes. I suppose it's a contrast with me, who's so easily embarrassed, admiring people who aren't.

Mr Bennett is a great man for nuance and detail. I recalled a published fragment from his diary for 1968 in which he had written down his mother's descriptions of her clothes:

> My other shoes
> My warm boots
> That fuzzy blue coat I have
> My coat with round buttons

He said:

> I used to read medieval wills, where they do list possessions like that. My Dad was the same. He always wore a suit. He used to have what he called "my suit" and "my other suit." The other suit was the best suit. I like lists, somehow bodying something forth from a bare recital of facts, but I never managed to do it as a historian.

In Mr Bennett's double bill [**Single Spies**], is the second play, **A Question of Attribution,** in which Blunt and the Queen appear, having met by accident one afternoon in a corridor of the palace while he is taking down a picture. The first play, **An Englishman Abroad,** has already been seen on television. It is the one in which Coral Browne, playing in *Hamlet* in Moscow, meets Guy Burgess in exile, who commissions her to get some suits and shoes made for him in London. One of the scenes is in a bootmakers.

> All those lasts. It's just a wonderful set. It was Lobbs where we were filming this. And the people watching, a peculiar mixture of the upper classes and cobblers, and then a customer came in who was black, very well dressed, and he just sat and took no notice of the filming, which was quite difficult because it disrupted the shop. He took no notice. And one of the cobblers edged up to a makeup girl and said. "You want to be careful of him. He'll eat you." She was scandalised at this racist remark. But who it was was Boukassa; he did keep bits of babies in his fridge. He'd come in for some shoes.

Between us, on a low table, lay a programme of **Single Spies,** open at a quotation of Graham Greene's which said, "Who among us has not committed treason to something or someone more important than a country?" What about that?

Mr Bennett said that some papers recently released under the 30-year rule had shown that the Macmillan government had covered up a disaster at Windscale, and asked why the guilt for those deaths was not greater than that for the deaths caused by Blunt.

Because, I said, Windscale was an accident.

> Yes, but the people who covered it up were saving their own skins, pretending it hadn't happened. And something might have been able to be done about it. I mean, I've no sympathy with

communist philosophy at all, but you could say, well, he did this because he actually believed in it. Over Windscale, they were doing it for no better reason than that their careers were on the line. I find it very hard to think of the guilt of traitors as greater than. . . .

Than personal guilt for betraying other people, which, God help us, we did all the time? "Yes. The Graham Greene thing is quite true."

And as for Blunt on the stage, he hadn't meant to portray him in a sympathetic light, thinking him edgy and disdainful, and quite smarmy with the Queen, but now he was told Blunt appeared sympathetic.

Well, Blunt did appear as an entertaining man, didn't he? "I suppose if it makes people laugh. But then he *did* make people laugh."

In that scene HMQ had all the good lines, hadn't she? At one point she says, "If I am doing nothing. I like to be doing nothing to some purpose. That is what leisure means." Which sounded a bit like Lady Bracknell? "It is a bit Wilde-ian. Somebody told me about the royal family, that they are very much at a loss unless they have a programme, even if they're staying with people. They do actually what it laid out."

Wasn't it strange that the *New York Times* had been more astonished than any English paper that the Queen should appear on stage. "I was surprised there wasn't a row. We kept it very very quiet. What I was bothered about was that the story would be garbled and that they would think we were going to take the piss out of the Queen. I was pleased there wasn't a row. If there's a row, the play's about the row."

There have been letters from a former palace policeman, saying the Queen rang bells, and from a former lady in waiting saying the portayal was plausible. Mr Bennett had seen the Queen only twice in his life, the last time in 1966, but really the resemblance is very close.

"That's Pru (Prunella Scales). It seems to me they behaved very well."

Who, the royal family? "The palace, whatever. Not made a fuss. It couldn't have happened 20 years ago, and it's right. Because in fact the impression you get from the audience is just a wave of affection. In a way it's a fruitless scene for me to play. Of course they're laughing with her, and I felt like saying, 'Look, I wrote these lines.' "

Of course, a lot of people said he looked like a don anyway? (Laughter.)

> And I capitalise on it? When I was going to be a clergyman I thought it was probably because I looked like a clergyman. Then when I started wearing glasses I began to think that I was going to be a don, on the same basis. But that's what people do—look in a mirror and do what the mirror tells them they're suited for, and it's not good advice.

No? Well, he said, when he was doing his own play **Forty Years On,** in 1968, the cast wanted him to go out riding.

He said he couldn't, that he was hopeless, because he never had. He'd never looked as if he was good at sports. But they made him have a go, and he thought it was wonderful, and kept it. Mind you, at about the same time he tried to learn to ski, and that was a disaster.

Hadn't he been a founder member of the late SDP? He said he had been, and couldn't stand it when they started fighting. He was now totally disillusioned. "I can't see Mrs Thatcher going. And you see people converted to her way of thinking, and they're slightly contemptuous of you, as if they're realists and you're not. Which I suppose is true."

He really did deplore her? "I just don't like that attitude of mind that says the government knows best."

But surely she would say she was a libertarian and wanted as little government as possible?

> Well, it's just not true. There's more and more Government. Oh, I just flounder about. But she does not basically know there are people who cannot help themselves, and they have to be helped. I do feel passionate about the health service. It is wrong what's happening. If she had to wait in an out-patients, and see it. Labour politicians too.
>
> You see, in Yorkshire the health service works very well, because it's small, and there's a local medical centre and they know the doctors at the hospital. My Dad died after a heart attack in 1974, and it was a bank holiday. He had this heart attack at six in the morning. The local doctor came out and she rang for the ambulance. Two police cars with the ambulance, one in front and one behind, because of the holiday traffic. They got him to hospital but he died.
>
> But, you know, he was someone whose social usefulness was nil. He was at the end of his life, and yet everything was geared to him, and it seems to me that's what a health service is about—bringing everything to bear. It doesn't matter what people's social position is. And I don't think that means anything to the Government.

We had met between a matinee and the evening performance. Mr Bennett had to go. On the way out of room where the National does its entertaining Mr Bennett glanced at the empty bookshelf by the door.

"There used to be one book there," he said. "Peter Hall's diaries. I think the new regime removed it." (Laughter.)

> *Terry Coleman, "Private Bennett," in* The Guardian, *February 17, 1989, p. 26.*

Noel Annan (review date 13 April 1989)

[*Annan is an English educator, critic, and author of* The Curious Strength of Positivism in English Political Thought *(1959). In the following excerpt he examines how Bennett's views on patriotism and treason are represented in* Single Spies.]

The British obsession with spies and spycatchers continues to seethe. Books thud from the press and you cannot get a seat at the National Theatre for Alan Bennett's *Single Spies,* an evening consisting of two short plays, one about Guy Burgess, the other about Anthony Blunt. Bennett belongs to that remarkable generation of John Osborne, Harold Pinter, and Michael Frayn, and is as gifted as any of them. He has a marvelous ear and is as merciless to the pompous as he is understanding of the failures in life. A series of monologues he wrote for television (each an hour-long talking head, the TV producer's nightmare) was so admired that it has just been repeated; and one of them, *Mrs. Silly,* was recently shown on American television.

Bennett's piece on Blunt is, perhaps, more of a charade than a play. [*A Question of Attribution*] begins with the art historian lecturing on *pentimenti* and displaying on the screen an X-ray photograph of a work by Titian. This reveals that this painting of two men contained a third man that was painted out; and on the verso is the head of a fourth man. The scene moves to Buckingham Palace, where, as surveyor of the royal pictures, Blunt (played by Bennett) is removing a painting from the wall. In his view it has been wrongly attributed. By chance the Queen walks that way. Does the Queen know what Blunt really is? Their ambiguous dialogue is a delight. No, she wouldn't much care to sit for a portrait by Francis Bacon. "I might come out as a screaming queen." . . .

Bennett's play about Burgess [*An Englishman Abroad*] began as a television drama based on a real encounter. In 1958 Michael Redgrave and Coral Browne found themselves in Moscow playing *Hamlet.* In the TV version Guy Burgess, in exile in Moscow, lurches into her dressing room, is sick in the basin, and subsequently makes off with her soap and cigarettes. But he leaves a note inviting her to lunch. Coral Browne did in fact go to see him. She is an Australian and renowned in the theater for her unbridled language. She endures hours of Burgess asking after Cyril Connolly, Harold Nicolson, Auden, and others whom she has never met, and has to listen three or four times to his record of Jack Buchanan singing "Who Stole My Heart Away?" As she leaves she lets fly and tells him that she, at any rate, among the people he has charmed, is not conned. "You pissed in our soup and we drank it." Still, she agrees to do what he asks because she is sorry for him and his ghastly loneliness.

What he asks her to do when she gets back to London is to order him a suit, shoes, pajamas, and an Old Etonian tie. Burgess's Savile Row tailor is courtesy itself. Mum's the word she says to him: "Mum is always the word here, madam, Moscow or Maidenhead." But when she goes to the store for pajamas, Bennett puts the other side of the case. She is met by an affronted refusal and she says,

> You were quite happy to serve this client when he was one of the most notorious buggers in London. Only then he was in the Foreign Office. "Red piping on the sleeve, Mr. Burgess, but of course. A discreet monogram on the pocket, Mr. Burgess. Certainly. And perhaps you would be gracious enough to lower your trousers Mr. Burgess: and we could plunge our tongue between the cheeks of your arse." . . . I tell you, it's

pricks like you that make us understand why he went. Thank Christ I'm not English.

Alan Bennett shares her irritation. In the program note he says he finds it hard to drum up patriotic indignation against any of the spies. What harm did they really do?—except perhaps Philby, who sent a few agents to their deaths. Anyway, even he was quite a congenial figure: clubbable, a good drinker, and popular with journalists. Bennett puts into Burgess's mouth the words: "I can say I love London, I can say I love England, I can't say I love my country because I don't know what it means." He thinks that is a fair statement of what many people feel—and that the Falklands war made them think that way. He's probably right in believing that to be so. The Falklands war, more than any other issue, enraged the intelligentsia, who considered that Margaret Thatcher sent men to their death to avenge the government's blunders and to save her own face. (The "country"—government and opposition in Parliament and the majority of ordinary people—of course, thought otherwise.) (p. 24)

With all the distaste of the artist for those who are in politics or are concerned with affairs of state, Alan Bennett is skeptical about the damage Blunt, Philby, and the rest did to their country. He should not be skeptical about the damage they did to their friends. And not only their friends. Those who shared the same enthusiasms in their student days were to be exposed by the spies to suspicion, interrogation, rumor, and loss of respect and trust.

But for Bennett, as for other writers, D. H. Lawrence's famous dictum remains true. "Never trust the artist. Trust the tale. The proper function of the critic is to save the tale from the artist who created it." Whatever the generous sympathies of the artist toward Burgess in his loneliness in Moscow and toward the bold *tricheur* Blunt, Bennett's plays tell a different tale. "I'm sorry you think my poor painting a fake," says the Queen to Blunt. "Oh no! Not a fake, ma'am: merely a wrong attribution." "What is a fake?" A brief pause. "An enigma," replies Blunt. "That is the sophisticated view," says the Queen. The unsophisticated will continue to think the spies scoundrels. (p. 29)

> *Noel Annan, "The Upper Class and the Underworld," in* The New York Review of Books, *Vol. XXXVI, No. 6, April 13, 1989, pp. 24-9.*

Richard Hornby   (review date Winter 1990)

[*An American educator, actor, and critic, Hornby has written such works as* Script Into Performance: A Structuralist View of Play Production (1977). *In the following excerpt, he offers praise for* Single Spies *and characterizes the one-act play* A Question of Attribution *as "the perfect play for its time, in a country struggling to redefine the nature of government and of art, and the relationship between them."*]

[Alan Bennett's *Single Spies*] is actually two plays, the first of which, *An Englishman Abroad,* was shown on U.S. television a few years ago. It is the true story of actress Coral Browne's meeting with the spy Guy Burgess in Moscow in 1958; it plays well, but is little more than a character study. The second play, *A Question of Attribu-*

tion, goes deeper. Set in the late 1960s, it concerns another spy, Anthony Blunt (superbly played by Bennett himself), when he was Director of the Courtauld Institute and actually in charge of the Queen's own art collection. He has secretly confessed, and is being interrogated by Scotland Yard about his contacts; there is also a scene with the Queen . . . which gave the play a bit of notoriety and no doubt added to its commercial success. Bennett makes the Queen marvelously ambiguous; one never knows whether she is being naively comic or making shrewd double-entendres. "Portraits are supposed to be frightfully self-revealing," she says, chatting with Blunt. "Show what one's really like. The secret self. Either that, or the eyes are supposed to follow you round the room. I don't know that one has a secret self. Though it's generally assumed that one has." We of course know that Blunt does have a secret self, but whether this is just blather or sly probing is a mystery. The play is full of such intricacies, which explore the nature of art and reality, and how we perceive them. *A Question of Attribution* is the perfect play for its time, in a country struggling to redefine the nature of government and of art, and the relationship between them. (p. 636)

> *Richard Hornby, in a review of "Single Spies,"*
> *in* The Hudson Review, *Vol. XLII, No. 4,*
> *Winter, 1990, pp. 629-36.*

J. B. Miller   (essay date 30 September 1990)

[*In the following essay, Miller provides an overview of Bennett's career since* Beyond the Fringe.]

In April, 1961, the fourth man of a comedy revue seemed quiet and less anarchic than his fellow performers. He and his cohorts—Jonathan Miller, Peter Cook and Dudley Moore—had created a new satirical revue called *Beyond the Fringe,* and they were doing a run-through of the show in a theater bar in London for a prospective producer. Afterward, the impresario sighed and said he wasn't at all sure it would work. In any case, "The fair-haired one will have to go."

The fair-haired one was Alan Bennett, and he stayed. *Beyond the Fringe* ran for over a year in the West End with the original cast, and then over a year on Broadway, playing to a vast audience that included the likes of President Kennedy, Bette Davis, Charles Boyer and Noël Coward. It played until 1965 in New York, and a substitute cast kept it going in London until 1966. No one had ever seen anything like it. Where the BBC radio "Goon Show" with Spike Milligan, Peter Sellers and Harry Secombe defined comedy in the 50's, *Beyond the Fringe* set the standard for the 60's. Its influence ranged from the playful antics of the Beatles in *A Hard Day's Night* and *Help!* to such groups as Monty Python and influenced almost every BBC situation comedy of the last two decades.

Now, with his successful London play *Single Spies* published in America (a Broadway transfer is in the planning stages) and the recent PBS broadcast of his series of monologues, *Talking Heads,* Alan Bennett is again a voice in America, displaying his singular talents that have until now largely eluded our attention. Besides *Beyond the Fringe,* he is probably best known here for his screenplays of *A Private Function,* starring Maggie Smith and Michael Palin, and *Prick Up Your Ears,* based on John Lahr's biography of the playwright Joe Orton.

But if Bennett's theatrical confections are increasingly produced and celebrated (*Single Spies* won the 1989 Olivier Award for best comedy), his post-*Fringe* career began with great uncertainty, especially compared with the successes of his famous teammates.

Consider the alumni notes of the *Beyond the Fringe* graduating class: Jonathan Miller, M.D., went on to become one of Britain's leading directors of stage and opera, lately stewarding the Old Vic Theater back to its former glory, and Peter Cook became involved with the controversial British satirical magazine *Private Eye* (now an institution, deplored by the Government, but read by everyone) and formed a comedic partnership with Dudley Moore, who later escaped to Hollywood and became big box office.

But Alan Bennett seemed to drop from view. "I was a bit beat then," he says in his distinctive Northern accent, a musical, reedy dialect that sounds a bit like a punctured bagpipe. He is slumped into a chair in his drawing room, the afternoon light, dim as it is, struggling to filter through the slats of the wooden Venetian blinds.

Though just a little over six feet, Bennett nevertheless gives an impression of enormous size as he sits with his legs sprawled out before him and speaks in methodical slow motion. Throughout our conversations, although he obviously enjoys discussing his work, he seems a little ashamed to be talking about himself. Musing on his years with Miller and the others, he says: "We'd all been so interdependent that I wasn't sure that I'd be able to do anything on my own. I didn't know what I could do. I'd only written sketches; I'd never written anything else."

It must be said that he had a peculiar image right from the start: in publicity photos of the *Fringe* clan, Bennett is the unamused one who looks like he doesn't want to be there. He could have been a chartered accountant who happened to be passing by, kidnapped by the comedy trio and forced to pose in the picture. He looks like he doesn't get the joke.

But in many ways, that *was* the joke. Bennett was the one who didn't have to don a priest's garb to resemble a vicar; he could deliver a sermon and look and sound so close to the real thing that it was both hilarious and slightly surreal. If not quite the "straight man" of the group, he was certainly the most serious. During the last six months of the Broadway run, he insisted on doing a monologue on "death and its supposed comic aspects in the North of England." This was delivered, as he has conceded, in a broad Yorkshire accent that may have alienated the few audience members who cared to listen to such a subject. It was an unlikely skit for a comedy revue, but it signaled a later preoccupation with infirmity and old age (his work includes such titles as *Getting On, The Old Crowd, A Woman of No Importance, Say Something Happened*).

"I think I was an old man before I was out of my teens," says Bennett a little mournfully. "It was partly from seeing my dad. He wanted to retire, he wanted to have a garden. After *Beyond the Fringe* in New York, I made me enough money so I could buy him a cottage in the country and he could retire early. And I always think that was a good thing. That was on my mind really before I even started writing plays."

Born in Leeds, North England, in 1934, Bennett grew up in a largely bookless household. Both his parents had left school at 13.

> My dad had this butcher's shop, and a local customer by the name of Fletcher had this daughter who went to London to secretarial college. Then she became a secretary at a publisher's, and she did very well and became assistant to one of the directors, whom she married. Well, the firm was Faber & Faber, and the director was T. S. Eliot. And for years I thought that the only connection to literature I'd have was that I used to deliver meat to T. S. Eliot's mother-in-law.

Enough of those years were spent in the local library to win Bennett a place at Exeter College, Oxford, where he received a B.A. degree in history in 1957; he briefly served as a junior history lecturer at Magdalen College and seemed headed for a university career.

Could he see himself now in academia? "I suppose," he says skeptically. "Though I wouldn't have been very good at it. They started having efficiency checks, and I think I would have been weeded out." As his friend and London neighbor Jonathan Miller says: "I think both he and I have a rather flinching and evasive attitude to being in the theater at all. He's always been rather shy and retiring and had some slight suspicion that being on the stage encouraged showing off, vanity and competitiveness."

He did, however, engage in enough "showing off" in an Oxford cabaret to be noticed by John Bassett, a young producer and trumpeter who played in a jazz band with a pianist named Dudley Moore. It was Bassett's alchemy that brought Bennett and Moore together with two bright lights from a Cambridge revue, Miller and Cook, at a small Italian restaurant in London in 1960. The ensuing comedy cocktail scored its first hit at that year's Edinburgh International Festival and went on to sidetrack the four members' various careers.

Despite admitting to having a "streak of pure tinsel," Bennett had always been infatuated with British literary history, a large portion of which he put into a blender to produce his first stage play, *40 Years On,* in 1968. This collection of literary and historical skits presented under the guise of a prep-school pageant could be described as *Beyond the Fringe, Part II,* and it enjoyed a West End run with Sir John Gielgud and Bennett himself heading up the large cast. The playwright has admitted that "one way of looking at *40 Years On* is as an elaborate life-support system for the presentation of bad jokes." ("Sandy will accompany you, disguised as a waiter. That should at least secure you the entree.") It was filling enough seats for a Broadway transfer to be bruited about, but a last-minute bad notice from Clive Barnes in *The New York Times* may have soured the plans. Bennett is still bitter about it.

Although the play was very amusing, it was not distinctive

drama, and it was a few years before Bennett found his voice, writing plays for television that centered on the lives of working-class people in seaside resorts, hospitals and nursing homes. "If I have a favorite, imaginary landscape, it seems to be an empty corridor," he says.

There are, in fact, two Alan Bennetts: the celebrated West End playwright who lives in a big London house and writes about spies and government ministers, actors and authors, and the Yorkshire Bennett who still resides spiritually in the North of England, chronicling the lives of quiet desperation so common to working-class families. As he has written: "I still have the voice I was born with and the one I acquired." The effect his uprooting has had on him is difficult to underestimate; it's said that in 1961 he even considered removing himself from the projected *Beyond the Fringe* on the grounds that he would be the only Northerner in the cast.

Still boyish-looking at 56, Bennett lives alone in a smart section of Camden Town, a chic area in North London popular with film people and writers. When he bought his large Georgian house in 1967, it was already in a literary enclave of sorts: V. S. Pritchett and Angus Wilson resided nearby, and new writers were moving in. "It's been gentrified," says Jonathan Miller, who lives across the street. "This part of London has always retained a sort of Dickensian, Bohemian shabbiness about it, which I think is what both Alan and I like about it."

Bennett's house is more literary than theatrical; missing are the framed production posters, the authographed actor photographs and theater mementos. It's more Bloomsbury than Shaftesbury Avenue, with shelves stuffed with volumes by E. M. Forster, W. H. Auden and Virginia Woolf; the bare, green-mottled walls are hung with late-18th century glass paintings and the work of the British Impressionists.

There are several desks, on both the ground floor and in the basement, testimony to the literary and business clutter that the author is apt to collect. When he is working, he likes to move from desk to desk. One of these bears two uncapped fountain pens and a couple of dip-ink pens. A manual typewriter lies ostracized at the edge of the desk, beside a collection of baroque correspondence to the London Electricity Board. ("We both send off irritable letters to people," says Miller. "I think we're going to descend into a sort of strange, cantankerous old age.")

With his comfort, Bennett has acquired enough middle-class guilt (or healthy sense of social responsibility, depending on how you look at it) to endure some odd physical hardships. Consider the story of "The Lady in the Van."

For 15 years, the writer allowed an eccentric, often abusive bag lady (or what might more accurately be described as a "vehicular lady") to live in a dilapidated van parked in his front garden. Visitors had to squeeze by the van to get to Bennett's front door and were often heckled along the way. The playwright supplied his indigent guest with electricity and heat, listened to her constant political grumblings (usually several steps to the right of Bennett) and even did her shopping for her when she was sick. He admits she was exasperating and thankless and generally a pain. So why did he do it?

> It wasn't a big decision, it just crept up on me. The thing was, she was right opposite my window, on the other side of the street. And I spend a lot of my time looking out that window, so I'd see everything that went on, you know, and people did bang on the van and persecute her, and I used to see it and it used to upset me in a way that just made me angry. And in a sense I thought, maybe less angry if she were inside instead of outside.

Says Stephen Frears, who directed *Prick Up Your Ears* and many of Bennett's television plays: "Going to his house was a sort of nightmare. She was a rather frightening figure. And there used to be these wires taking electricity in from the house. She always looked rather fierce. Extremely disagreeable."

Bennett contends that if he'd known she'd be there for 15 years, he wouldn't have let her move onto his grounds in the first place. "But once she moved in, then I forgot about it really," he says. "It didn't bother me." (She died in 1989.)

Being a habitual diarist, Bennett—whose interest in the woman is described by Miller as "an interesting compound of philanthropy and curiosity"—recorded the ongoing Van Lady saga in a series of journals, part of a larger project he is in the process of collating for possible publication. A portion recently appeared in *The London Review of Books:*

> June 1984 Miss S. has been looking in Exchange and Mart again and has answered an advert for a white Morris Minor. "It's the kind of car I'm used to—or I used to be used to. I feel the need to be mobile." I raise the matter of a license and insurance, which she always treats as tiresome formalities. "What you don't understand is that I am insured. I am insured in heaven." She claims that since she has been insured in heaven there has not been a scratch on the van. I point out that this is less to do with the celestial insurance than with the fact the van is parked the whole time in my garden. . . .

Bennett's most recent play, *Single Spies,* which enjoyed a good run in London in 1989, is an elegant double bill about one of Britain's greatest obsessions: espionage. The British have an odd preoccupation with spies and double agents, ranging from the colorful comic-book heroes of the James Bond variety to the mangy also-rans of the foreign service. The interest appears to be especially piqued when the spy hails from the upper reaches of British society, as was the case of the notorious "Cambridge spies": Guy Burgess, Donald Maclean and Kim Philby.

These were not disgruntled office workers selling secrets to the highest bidder, but well-educated upper-middle-class gentlemen who had been recruited from Cambridge in the 1930's. It's been said that their alliance with Russia was probably due more to dissatisfaction with England than to love of Soviet Communism. As Bennett has his character Burgess say: "So little, England. Little music. Little art. Timid, tasteful, nice. But one loves it. Loves it.

You see, I can say I love London. I can say I love England. I can't say I love my country, because I don't know what that means." The playwright has let it be known that the statement could just as well apply to himself.

Bennett's own twist on the espionage genre began with a play called *The Old Country,* in which Hilary, a retired British diplomat, waxes nostalgic on the pleasures of old England while sitting on the porch of what appears to be a house somewhere in the British countryside. In fact, in what must be one of the more memorable *coups de théâtre,* the house turns out to be a dacha outside Moscow, and the diplomat an exiled traitor.

Hilary was taken by many people to be a thinly disguised portrait of Philby, but the author has said he was thinking more of another kind of self-imposed exile, like W. H. Auden, who misses some version of England and tries to recreate it in often inhospitable surroundings.

In the original production, the part of Hilary was played by Sir Alec Guinness, and many of the eminent visitors backstage enjoyed telling their own spy stories. One of these was the actress Coral Browne, whose encounter with Guy Burgess was slightly altered by Bennett for the stage. In 1958, Browne was touring with the Shakespeare Memorial Theater in Moscow, performing *Hamlet* for senior party officials and the British foreign service. During intermission one night, in Bennett's version, a drunken Englishman burst into her dressing room and proceeded to be sick in her sink. On his way out, he stole Browne's British bar of soap (a prized item in shabby Moscow). The next day, the actress received a note at her hotel from the mysterious visitor, apologizing for his inelegant behavior the evening before and inviting her to his flat for lunch. It was signed "Guy Burgess."

Receiving a note—or a visit—from Guy Burgess in 1958 was about as likely as winning an audience with Howard Hughes or J. D. Salinger. Although it was known that Burgess had defected to Russia, no one knew exactly where he was, and every tabloid in England was braying for his story. Browne visited the spy in his dreary Moscow flat, spending a very odd afternoon with him, measuring him, at his request, for a new English suit.

Bennett was so taken by this story that he wrote it as a television play, *An Englishman Abroad,* which was filmed by John Schlesinger with Alan Bates as Burgess and Coral Browne as herself. Rewritten slightly to fit the stage, it makes up the first half of *Single Spies,* and it looks a bit like a Noel Coward play as revised by Tom Stoppard—a bittersweet tale of a man who has lost everything except his conscience and his natural British charm.

If Guy Burgess was a tabloid sensation from the time of his exile, Sir Anthony Blunt was the subject of quiet rumors for years. Long suspected of being the "fourth man" in the Cambridge spy ring, Blunt still served in Buckingham Palace as surveyor of the Queen's pictures, a highly prestigious post that won him entree to the highest circles. There was more than a passing frisson when his true identity was finally revealed.

The second half of the bill, *A Question of Attribution,*

takes place around the time of Blunt's secret confession to British authorities in 1964, but before the story broke on Fleet Street. It is by turns highly polemical and extremely funny, with a now-famous scene between Blunt (played in London by Bennett himself) and Queen Elizabeth. Caught in the act of removing one of the royal paintings for study, Blunt has an unexpected conversation with the Queen (home early from a royal visit) that on the surface appears to be about art, but has an uncomfortable subtext about politics and betrayal. The Queen, discussing a painting that is not by whom it is claimed, calls the work a "fake." Blunt prefers the designation "enigma." It is a fascinating intellectual tug of war between two people who are accustomed to speaking in riddles, and it was the most talked-about scene in the London West End.

The playwright has given Her Majesty a curiously Bennettian sense of humor. At one point, Blunt and "HMQ" are discussing portrait painters. Says HMQ, "One Minister of the Arts wanted to loose Francis Bacon on me. . . . He did Screaming Pope, didn't he? I suppose I would have been Screaming Queen." And illustrating the inappropriateness of avant-garde painters doing the royal portrait:

> One doesn't want two noses. Mind you, that would make one no more unrecognizable than some of their efforts. No resemblance at all. Sometimes I think it would be simpler to send round to Scotland Yard for an Identikit. Still, I can understand when they get me wrong, but some of them get the horse wrong, too. That's unforgivable.

This is the London Bennett writing, knowingly, of art and royalty. The Yorkshire Bennett's specialty, by contrast, is the Northern woman. "The language and rhythms of Northern speech come naturally to me," he says.

> Its characteristic habit of saving the subject until the very end of the sentence gives Northern dialect a tension lacking in standard English. It also helps the joke. Social distinctions are subtle and minute. There are advantages to be drawn from status, however lowly. It's social climbing, albeit very much on the lower slopes. I was once on top of a tram in Leeds with my auntie. We were passing Wellington Road gasworks. She laid a hand on my arm. "That's the biggest gasworks in England," she said. "And I know the manager."

Bennett's recent television work, *Talking Heads,* was a series of six monologues that display his impressive empathy toward lonely, older women. Susan, the unhappy vicar's wife in **"Bed Among the Lentils,"** (played by Maggie Smith) can't see why she is expected to attend church every Sunday: "A barrister's wife doesn't have to go to court, an actor's wife isn't at every performance, so why have I always got to be on parade? Not to mention the larger question of whether one believes in God in the first place. It's assumed that being the vicar's wife one does but the question has never actually come up, not with Geoffrey anyway." She finally finds a comfort of sorts in Alcoholics Anonymous.

Talking Heads has certainly been his best-selling script, with over 80,000 copies of the British edition in print—an impressive number for any book, but especially for a work of drama. (It was published here this year by Summit Books in a paperback edition with *Single Spies.*) In England, the sales have been helped by drama students who like to use the monologues as audition pieces. "I pity the boards of drama schools because they must get fed up of hearing them," says Bennett.

His next theatrical venture is an adaptation of Kenneth Grahame's children's classic *The Wind in the Willows,* which is being produced at the National Theater at Christmas.

So, is he rich? "No-o-o," he protests, a bit exasperatedly, as if sincerely puzzled by what must be an oversight. "I'm not like Ayckbourn or Michael Frayn, or any of those people who do make a vast amount, 'cause they're the stuff of rep, and mine aren't, really."

Still, Bennett's canvas encompasses broader (some would say more mundane) experiences than other playwrights like Simon Gray, who tend to chronicle the small, intellectual circuit that delineates their lives. His typical television characters are weary survivors, apt to let loose the kind of careless racial remark ("And don't smile that inscrutable Oriental smile, Genghis") that can slip out among the working class. They are not generally racist, but they are not likely to be seen joining a solidarity march.

But if Bennett records the carelessness of the working class, he also records the alienation of those at the edge of society. If many of his characters have anything in common, it is that they are exiles of some sort—the spy Guy Burgess stranded in Russia, the ostracized chiropodist of *A Private Function* or a bag lady who spends 15 years living on a playwright's front lawn in the north of London. These are the heroes and heroines of Alan Bennett, all celebrated by the playwright and all sharing the eloquent self-consciousness of the tall, gangling Northerner living well in Camden Town. "It always seems the edge of things is more interesting," he says. "The edge of class, the edge of sexuality. . . . " His voice trails off, as if he's said something regrettable.

Calling him a few weeks later, I reach him just returning from a brief visit to his mother in Yorkshire. When I ask what he's been working on lately, he cagily admits to having just completed principal photography on a new project, *102 Boulevard Haussman,* a television film about Proust. "There's a motor-racing driver called Alain Prost, and I'm sure that's what the BBC thought it was," he jokes. "I don't think they'd ever heard of Proust." The film is about a period in the reclusive author's life when he was confined mostly to bed, sleeping during the day and working on his vast opus, *A la Recherche du Temps Perdu,* at night. "He had this quartet come and play for him some of the music he was using in the book," Bennett says. "His chauffeur went out and fetched them in the middle of the night." Alan Bates plays Proust ("He's a bit hefty for Proust."), and the film is scheduled to be screened at the London Film festival in November. It will be broadcast on British television next year. When I point out that Bennett has never mentioned the Proust script before, he sighs apologetically. "I tend to lose confidence in things," he says, explaining that the screenplay had been lying in a drawer for 18 months before the financing finally came together to film it.

Will there ever be a **Beyond the Fringe** reunion? "People are always trying to get the four of us together to photograph us," he says, but confesses that the prospect of their performing together again is about as likely as a Beatles reunion. Recently, however, three of the original four **Fringe** members had dinner in London. "It was the first time we'd been together in a long, long time," Bennett says. "If Dudley had been in England, he would have been there as well, and it would have been historic." What did they talk about? "Oh, we talked about the disasters of our various lives," Bennett says with a crisp laugh. "We talked about Dudley's marriage breaking up and his having to pay a million dollars. We've all of us shipwrecked in different ways. Peter is very, very fat now, which is extraordinary to think—he's not a naturally fat person. And Jonathan is always depressed, and I am too."

I think of the last time I saw Bennett in London; he was standing on the sidewalk by Gloucester Crescent, grumbling about the roadwork. Construction men were ripping up the street, and he had to walk around the mounds of rubble to get to the main street. "It's for cable television, which no one wants," he moaned. It's just another item on the long list of Things That Are Wrong With England. Alan Bennett is an Englishman abroad in England, tiptoeing outside the class system and gleefully applying pins, as he has done for 30 years, to all facets of the society. Even he would have to admit, it's a wonderful arrangement. (pp. 36, 82, 90-1)

> *J. B. Miller, "Far Beyond the Fringe," in* The New York Times Magazine, *September 30, 1990, pp. 36, 82, 90-1.*

Jack Kroll   (review date 21 January 1991)

[*In the following excerpt, Kroll praises Bennett's stage adaptation of* The Wind in the Willows *and asserts that if* "Wind in the Willows *comes to the United States . . . Bennett will get the international fame that has so far eluded him."*]

English children are notoriously well behaved, so the kids who call out advice to the actors in **The Wind in the Willows** do so not raucously but with grave concern. At the National Theatre, Alan Bennett's stage version of Kenneth Grahame's 1908 classic is just about the hottest ticket in London. The Olivier, largest of the National's three houses, has practically become a theme park, a thinking tot's Disneyland for the adventures of Mole, Rat, Badger and Toad. Throats of all ages emit sounds of delight as the vast stage, turntable wheeling, elevator rising and falling, becomes a road, a railway, a river, Mole's underground condo, Rat's shipshape galley, Badger's clubby study, Toad's stately home.

There's also a barge, a van, a locomotive and a sporty red roadster. Toad, one of literature's first motormaniacs, can't resist joyriding in somebody else's car and he winds up in jail. This leads to the political dimension of the story

as his estate, Toad Hall, is taken over by a rabble of weasels, stoats and ferrets. For kids these squatters are just mean slobs, but for Grahame they embodied his fear of the forces of anarchy and revolution. Alan Bennett gives these furry Bolsheviks a nice contemporary twist: his weasels plan to turn Toad Hall into a leisure center.

Bennett handles such touches with a lightness that adds to the fun for wised-up adults and doesn't spoil it for kids. A self-styled "old-fashioned liberal," Bennett nonetheless has great affection for the conservative Grahame's utopian fantasy that embraces the old, pastoral England and rejects the smoke and stress of the modern world. . . .

Richard Eyre, director of the National Theatre, at first wanted Bennett to write a play that would weave together Grahame's life and his masterpiece. "But I couldn't do it," says Bennett. "His life was a terrible story. His mother died when he was 5. His dad was an alcoholic. He had a troubled marriage and his son, Alastair, was born blind in one eye and committed suicide at 20 by lying across a railway track."

Bennett, a butcher's son, never read *Wind in the Willows* as a child. Books like that or *Alice in Wonderland* looked too "forbidding" in their leather bindings at the local library. "I'd say, 'That looks like a classic, so I'm not going to read it'." Instead he read comics. But he grew up to go to Oxford and became one of the four university wits—the others were Jonathan Miller, Dudley Moore and Peter Cook—whose satirical revue **Beyond the Fringe** in the early '60s changed the shape of comedy on both sides of the Atlantic.

Bennett, the least famous of the four, is arguably the most gifted as actor, comic, director and prolific author of plays (**Single Spies**), TV drama (**Talking Heads**) and movies (**Prick Up Your Ears**). Once, at a dinner with Prime Minister Harold Wilson, Bennett identified himself as one of the **Fringe** men. The P.M. looked at him sternly and said: "I don't remember you. You weren't one of the original four." Bennett felt, he said, "like Trotsky when he was cut out of the history of the revolution." If **Wind in the Willows** comes to the United States . . . , Bennett will get the international fame that has so far eluded him.

> *Jack Kroll, "The Toast of London Town," in* Newsweek, *Vol. CXVIII, No. 3, January 21, 1991, p. 60.*

David Nokes   (review date 16 December 1991)

[*In the following excerpt, Nokes offers praise for* The Madness of George III *and observes that* "Bennett has largely abandoned domestic detail for the broader, cruder strokes of historical and political satire."]

Alan Bennett's beguiling modesty has all but deflected recognition that he is probably our greatest living dramatist. His characteristic style is unpretentious, small-scale and domestic. His genius lies in an unerring ear for the idioms of lower-middle-class life, the verbal doilies of self-respect and self-repression. Less mannered than Beckett, he works on the same precise and intimate scale, conjuring a lifetime of submerged panic from the fussy, tragi-comic monologues of his suburban *Talking Heads,* miniaturizing paradise lost to a digestive biscuit irretrievably dropped beneath a sofa.

Recently he has attempted grander themes, raising his gaze beyond the privet hedges and net curtains to peer at royalty. Yet the success of *A Question of Attribution* was largely due to regal monologues which domesticated monarchy, turning the Queen into a house-proud matron. *The Madness of George III* has little of this affectionate intimacy. Although the hapless monarch and his wife address each other at bedtime in nursery terms as "Mr and Mrs King", Bennett has largely abandoned domestic detail for the broader, cruder strokes of historical and political satire.

> **[Alan Bennett] is probably our greatest living dramatist. . . . His genius lies in an unerring ear for the idioms of lower-middle-class life, the verbal doilies of self-respect and self-repression.**
>
> **—David Nokes**

This play is deliberately two-dimensional, an animated Rowlandson cartoon. Its cast of historical names are walk-on caricatures, spouting one-liners which might be set in speech-bubbles above their heads. Burke is the stage Irishman, a repetitive ranting buffoon; Sheridan is a human calculator, a cynic who "thinks like a moneylender" both as dramatist and politician. Pitt (or Piss) the Younger is thin and priggish, while Fox is fat and raucous. Fattest of all, naturally, is the Prince of Wales, played in a camp, over-ripe style that out-Gillrays Gillray as a flabby, flouncing fop. "It takes character to withstand the rigours of indolence", sighs the effete heir to the throne, one of several lines in which Bennett contrives to sound less like himself than Oscar Wilde.

In one typical transition, characteristic of the play's didactic format, we move from the foppish prince being laced into a corset to the mad king being manacled and tortured back to sanity. . . . [George III descending] from the magnificence of rude health to the nightmare of a remedial torture chamber and back again (the play's structure has an almost classical symmetry) is a theatrical *tour de force.* But the emphasis is very much on theatricality rather than interior drama. We admire a bravura performance but are offered little insight into the workings of a troubled mind. This is a play written not in terms of character but to expound a thesis about the politics of medicine. Insistent parallels are drawn between a rogue's gallery of eighteenth-century comic quacks, each with his own darling theory (the pulse-man, the stool-man, the blisterer and the moral tyrant), and the self-serving politicians propounding rival catchpenny panaceas in the bedlam of parliament. And, in case we miss the point, Bennett inserts his own theatrical footnote, bringing on stage a modern

white-coated medical expert to assure us George was never mad at all, merely off-colour with porphyria.

Unlike most of Bennett's best work, this is a play which appeals not to the ear but to the eye. [The director] fills the Lyttelton stage with striking visual tableaux of parliament, the court, the asylum, in which historical rhythms of speech are drowned by pompous bursts of Handel and the crackle of stage epigrams which gain most laughter when scoring obvious modern hits. Bennett takes his greatest risk when, in the process of regaining lucidity, he has George read from *King Lear.* Despite being given a deliberately farcical intonation, the haunting sublimity of Lear's lines to Cordelia, "but I am bound upon a wheel of fire, that mine own tears do scald like molten lead", is sufficient to remind us that the politics of royal madness need not be treated in cartoon-strip fashion. The humanity of Shakespeare's lines, and the sudden charge of real dramatic power which they evoke, are almost like a deliberate act of sabotage. It is as if Bennett is reminding himself, and us, of his own talent for poignant and profound human drama when not playing the showman's part as a crowd-pleasing latter-day Sheridan.

> David Nokes, "The Body Politic," in The Times Literary Supplement, *No. 4627, December 16, 1991, p. 18.*

Robert Brustein   (review date 17 February 1992)

[*An American drama critic, artistic director of the American Repertory Theatre Company, and former dean of Yale University's School of Drama, Brustein is well-known and highly respected for his devotion to excellence in all aspects of theater production and his beliefs in theater's "higher purpose." His works include* The Theatre of Revolt *(1964),* The Culture Watch *(1975), and* Critical Moments: Reflections on Theatre and Society, 1973-1979 *(1980). In the following excerpt, Brustein applauds* The Madness of George III *as Bennett's most mature and authoritative satirical drama to date.*]

Nothing in Bennett's career as a wit and social satirist could have prepared us for the authority and maturity he displays in *The Madness of George III.* The play signals the arrival of an important epic playwright. On the surface, the work is an effort to redeem, mostly on the basis of recent medical evidence, a much-maligned historical figure from his traditional characterization as a tyrant, buffoon, and madman. George, it seems, was not mad, as he alone believed, but suffering from porphyria, a disease characterized by symptoms of madness (and also by purple urine, hence its name). To settle for another clinical explanation of George's condition, however, is to fall into the same snare that Bennett satirizes so brilliantly throughout the play, namely the belief that curing the malady is less important than naming it properly. One of George's doctors ascribes the king's disease to "flying gout" or "rheumatism in the head"; another to his stool; another to his arrogant spirit—and each prescribes another ghastly method of treatment, whether purges, bleeding, blistering, straitjackets, or "a good spew and a good sweat." I doubt if the new nomenclature will result in any better treatment, much less a cure.

Bennett's satire on benighted medical practices reminds me of *The Doctor's Dilemma* (and of Shaw's Dr. Walpole, whose universal cure is to "stimulate the phagocytes"). But the uniqueness of his play lies in the way it manages to evoke an entire historical epoch. The action begins with four red-coated equerries walking backward down a set of golden stairs . . . , followed by magnificently dressed courtiers entering upon the stage to Handel's brilliant *Royal Fireworks* music.

Before long we are deep in the intrigues of Georgian politics, represented by the opposition of two Whig parties: those serving the king (led by the younger William Pitt), and those seeking to displace them (led by Charles Fox). The Fox party hopes to replace George with his son, the Prince of Wales, a fat ignoramus with a weakness for furniture. . . . In this seedy atmosphere of power politics, George's growing dementia becomes a sacrifice to human ambition as the various politicians propose their own doctors and remedies in an effort to ensure that the king will never recover.

George himself . . . is depicted as a simple, uxorious man with a passion for farming who disintegrates before our eyes from a robust and wily Hanoverian (who adds "What, what?" to every declaration) into a tormented, slovenly, Lear-like figure afflicted with colic, sweats, running sores, and pains in the legs ("my blood is full of cramps—lobsters cramp my bones—my limbs are laced with fire"). Eventually, a physician suggested by Lady Pembroke seems to alleviate his agony through a torture of his own devising; his primitive mental therapy consists of breaking down the king's spirit. But it is more likely that the disease just runs its course. At any rate, the king is eventually, if temporarily, restored to sanity, with the capacity to name his own children, though not to name the lost colonies (he still splutters over the word "America"). Told that he now seems more like himself, he replies, "I have always been myself—I have just learned how to *seem*. What, what?" The "what, what?"—and the appearance of yellow urine—signal the restoration of sanity, and, only mildly shaken by reports of "minor disturbances in Paris," he returns to the task of ruling his kingdom.

Actually, George's affliction returned to plague him for the last twenty years of his life, removing him from the throne and giving the corpulent Regent a long-deferred opportunity to indulge his infatuation with (regency) furniture. But the final ascent of the court up those golden stairs to Handel's shimmering trumpets describes a circle of English history as well as anything to be found in modern theater. (pp. 29-30)

> Robert Brustein, "Melting the Concrete," in The New Republic, *Vol. 206, No. 7, February 17, 1992, pp. 28-30.*

Bennett's gift, of course, is for that absurd dialogue, meaningless in itself, but conjuring up class, period and attitude with quite undemonstrative exactness.

—*David Roper, in* Plays and Players, *June, 1984.*

Donald Lyons   (review date September 1992)

[*In the following excerpt, Lyons faults Bennett for ambiguity in* The Madness of George III, *characterizing his "talent [as] that of a miniaturist—epyllion rather than epic."*]

Alan Bennett has always had a merry way with royals and nobles. He started out in the theater, as did Jonathan Miller, Peter Cook, and Dudley Moore, as one of the creators and stars of **Beyond the Fringe,** which after some thirty years remains the cream of satirical revues. The ceremonially pompous RADA style of doing Shakespeare, then dominant, was never the same (or should never have been the same) after their foppish prancing: "Sussex, get thee to Essex. Essex, get thee to Sussex" . . . "O saucy Worcester." Mr. Bennett is now a playwright of some note, specializing in monologues about lonely, mad souls on the one hand and, on the perhaps not illogical other hand, in plays about royals. In 1988 the RNT staged his short *A Question of Attribution,* which features Queen Elizabeth II enigmatically chatting about fraud with Anthony Blunt, Keeper of her pictures, scholar, and traitor. The talk is, nominally, about art fakes—how to detect them and whether or not they do any real harm—but a chill undercurrent possibly runs beneath the smooth surface of the royal commonplaces. It is a gem of ambiguity.

George III, beside losing the colonies (they became his King Charles's head), was, as the present Prince of Wales has been eager to establish, an accomplished and attractive man. In 1788 his royal eccentricities began to turn to outright madness, and it is then the play opens. Its successful scenes involve the Royal Family: chatterbox King; plumply domestic and devoted Queen (they cuddle in bed, calling each other "Mr. King" and "Mrs. Queen"); and the grotesque and dandified Prince of Wales, toward whom the usual Hanoverian antipathy of father to son reaches homicidal intensity (the King tries to strangle him). The preposterous Prinny, Prince of Wales, has the best lines: when a madwoman's knife merely cuts the King's waistcoat, he declares that mishap to be almost as "vexing" as assassination. Prinny is a dim descendant of Algernon Moncrieff.

Surrounding the mad King and the ambitious Prince are interested politicians: the ins (Prime Minister Pitt and his party) want to hush up the madness; the outs (Fox and his party) want the King declared mad and a Regency installed. Each side employs corrupt doctors, who are, in time-honored theatrical tradition, nothing but sycophantic and venal ignoramuses ("With any patient I undertake a physical examination only as a last resort; it is an intolerable intrusion on a gentleman's privacy. With His Majesty it is unthinkable").

Bennett writes these pols and docs on one note; once put on stage, they wrangle all too predictably. He has no Shavian knack for dramatizing ideas, or, better to describe what Shaw does, to play and toy articulately with ideas. (pp. 60-1)

As the doctors quibble about the exact name to affix to the royal mania (is it "flying gout" or "rheumatism in the head"?), the King declines into incoherence and incontinence. At this point appears one of Bennett's two medici ex machina—a dour, black-clad clergyman called Francis Willis who runs in remote Lincolnshire an enlightened madhouse where he treats his patients with reason, fresh air, and kindness. He is, in fact, a representative of the best of eighteenth-century civilization, the civilization of Samuel Johnson, who himself respected George III. But Willis . . . has a darker, tougher side to his therapy as well: as George howls scatologically, Willis orders him strapped to a "restraining chair," a contraption resembling an electric chair. Handel's *Coronation Hymn* swells as George screams: "I am the King of England." "No, sir," answers Willis with icy and undeferential calm, "you are the patient." It makes an effective first-act curtain.

In the next act Willis battles the snobbery of the metropolitan medical establishment and "cures" the patient by a regime of systematic humiliation and punishment/reward (as theater it owed something to the taming of Helen Keller by Annie Sullivan in *The Miracle Worker*). At last, the King is made to kneel before a page he has struck and to beg forgiveness; the moving moment is re-enforced when the recovered King reads from *King Lear* at home in Windsor and recognizes himself in the sad, mad monarch. . . . Bennett does not quite earn the injection of Lear here (not to mention the snippets of *Richard II* and *Henry IV* injected elsewhere); they are borrowed feathers. There remains a final necessity for the King to swallow his last distaste and publicly embrace his wastrel and frivolous son. He brings himself to do it on the grounds that "we must be a model family to the nation" (this got a huge laugh in the summer of 1992, an uneasy time for some of George III's descendents). Bennett gets a few final laughs at the expense of Pitt, who assures the King that the recent disturbances at the Bastille will come to nothing. And then there is the last banana peel: a modern doctor steps forward in white to explain that the King was suffering not from a psychological disturbance at all, but from a chemical imbalance called porphyria. A clue was at hand all the time in the King's purple urine, but it was illegible to eighteenth-century science. The physicians scoffed at its importance, while it fascinated the servants, who delighted in puns about "piss the younger" and "piss the elder." The

modern doctor thinks all Willis's efforts as much a waste of time as the stool-gazing of the fashionable physicians, and we are left in some uncertainty as to what extent this is Bennett's voice, too. In one sense, it cannot be, for the play's two heroic portraits—the poor King and the stern doctor—survive the final cynicism, but it seems rather Bennett than history that cannot make up its mind. Bennett's talent is that of a miniaturist—epyllion rather than epic—and the epic scale of this RNT production has not served that talent well. (pp. 61-2)

Donald Lyons, "On the Superiority of European Methods," in The New Criterion, *Vol. XI, No. 1, September, 1992, pp. 59-63.*

FURTHER READING

Caless, Bryn. Review of *A Private Function,* by Alan Bennett. *British Book News* (March 1985): 182.
Praises Bennett's "ear for natural [dialogue]" and his ability to create three-dimensional characters in *A Private Function.*

De Jongh, Nicholas. "Prime Time at Last." *Illustrated London News* (25 December 1988): 40, 42.
Feature article in which Bennett surveys his life and works.

Hobson, Harold. "Plays in Performance: Hobson's Choice." *Drama,* No. 127 (Winter 1977-78): 39-44.
Positive assessment of *The Old Country,* which Hobson describes as "one of the best plays of the year," noting that it is "constructed as meticulously as *Oedipus Rex, Phèdre,* or *Ghosts:* and which, though being so, has the atmosphere of inexplicable things which Pinter and Duras bring with them."

———. "Hobson's Choice." *Drama,* No. 139 (1981): 27-30.
Commends Bennett's "strange and valuable talent for combining the affectionate with the uncomfortable" in *Enjoy.*

Segedin, Benjamin. Review of *Prick Up Your Ears,* by Alan Bennett. *Booklist* 84, No. 13 (1 March 1988): 1087.
Characterizes *Prick Up Your Ears* as "witty, irreverent, and occasionally brilliant."

Tynan, Kenneth. "The Antic Arts: A Quartet with a Touch of Brass." *Holiday* 32, No. 5 (November 1962): 127-32.
Surveys the lives and careers of the cast members of *Beyond the Fringe.*

Wolf, Matt. "Master of Eavesdropping and Empathy." *The Times* (London) (20 January 1992): 10.
     Feature article examining Bennett's affinity for interior monologue and his experience as an actor in *A Chip in the Sugar*.

Additional coverage of Bennett's life and career is contained in the following sources published by Gale Research: *Contemporary Authors,* **Vol. 103;** *Contemporary Authors New Revision Series,* **Vol. 35;** *Contemporary Literary Criticism,* **Vol. 45; and** *Major 20th-Century Writers.*

Angela Davis

1944-

(Full name Angela Yvonne Davis) American autobiographer, nonfiction writer, and essayist.

The following entry provides an overview of Davis's career through 1993.

INTRODUCTION

Davis is best known as a political activist who champions the rights of African-Americans, women, and victims of political and economic oppression. Delineating the problems of segregation, discrimination, and inequality, her writings are frequently perceived as espousing a Marxist viewpoint that advocates radical social reform and redistribution of wealth and power.

Born into a middle-class family in Birmingham, Alabama, Davis was raised in "Dynamite Hill," an integrated neighborhood where the Ku Klux Klan actively harassed and attacked blacks. She attended the prestigious Elizabeth Irwin High School in New York and then Brandeis University. In 1968 she became a devoted Marxist and joined the Communist Party. After completing graduate work at the University of Frankfurt in Germany and the University of California, San Diego, Davis began teaching at U.C.L.A., where she gained national attention in 1969 when the school's board of regents fired her for her political views at the insistence of then California governor Ronald Reagan. A trial ensued, and Davis, who remained socially and politically active, won the case and was reinstated. In 1970 she protested on behalf of three convicted black felons who were accused of murdering a white prison guard. The correspondence and friendship that developed between Davis and one of the defendants, George Jackson, led to charges that Davis was connected with an escape attempt led by Jackson's younger brother at a California courthouse in August 1970. Some of the guns Jackson used were registered in Davis's name, and she was charged with kidnapping and murder; she fled the state and was placed on the FBI's Most Wanted List. Arrested in New York and imprisoned, Davis became the focus of an international controversy and was found not guilty in 1972. Davis remains active in numerous political organizations, including the National Alliance Against Racist and Political Repression, the National Black Women's Health Project, and the Black Panthers, and was the Communist Party's vice-presidential candidate in the 1980 and 1984 presidential campaigns.

Angela Davis, her autobiography and best-known work, relates Davis's upbringing, academic career, and public life as an activist through age thirty. Many critics contend that the work lacks a confessional attitude and insight into Davis's private and emotional life. Davis, however, avers

that her intent was to demonstrate the injustices of racism, with which, she maintains, all African-Americans are familiar: "When I decided to write the book after all, it was because I had come to envision it as a *political* autobiography that emphasized the people, the events and forces in my life that propelled me to my present commitment."

If They Come in Morning: Voices of Resistance was written while Davis was awaiting trial and includes essays and letters by other contributors, including George Jackson. In this work, which addresses the disproportionality of poor blacks in American penal institutions, Davis charges that American prisons are used as instruments of political oppression as well as racial and economic domination, claiming that many poor and minority inmates are actually political prisoners, incarcerated not for their crimes but to protect the social status quo. She explains: "The offense of the political prisoner is his political boldness, his persistent challenging—legally or extra-legally—of fundamental social wrongs fostered and reinforced by the state. He has opposed unjust laws and exploitative, racist social conditions in general, with the ultimate aim of transforming these laws and this society into an order harmonious with the material and spiritual needs and interests of the vast majority of its members."

Davis's other nonfiction works address chiefly black feminist concerns. The essay collection *Women, Race, & Class* examines the restrictions placed on black women by race, socioeconomic status, and gender within the historical context of the women's liberation movement. In addition to detailing the extent to which white suffragists ignored and distanced themselves from black women, Davis discusses the issues of rape, birth control, and child care. *Women, Culture, & Politics* explores such diverse topics as the myth of the black rapist and the role of Western and third-world women in the home and society. Many critics have faulted these collections for presenting commonplace beliefs and assumptions from a solely Marxist perspective, which, they argue, robs Davis's writing of the emotional honesty and personal voice that is necessary for political and social reform; others contend that Davis fails to provide any solution, Marxist or otherwise, to the problems of inequality. Nevertheless, Toks Williams asserts: "Angela Davis's single-minded dedication and hard-headed idealism provide more than enough positive encouragement for those who may think there is little left to fight for in the civil rights movement."

PRINCIPAL WORKS

If They Come in the Morning: Voices of Resistance [with Ruchell Magee and others] (essays) 1971
Angela Davis (autobiography) 1974
Women, Race, & Class (nonfiction) 1981
Women, Culture, & Politics (nonfiction) 1989

CRITICISM

Emile Capouya (review date 30 October 1971)

[*Capouya is an American essayist, editor, translator, and educator. In the following review of* If They Come in the Morning *he assesses the strengths and weaknesses of Davis's argument that most inmates are victims of political oppression.*]

The central argument of [*If They Come in the Morning: Voices of Resistance*] is that the greatest number of the persons confined in the jails, lock-ups, reformatories, houses of detention, and penitentiaries in our country are, properly speaking, political prisoners, the victims of political oppression. The principal author, Miss Angela Davis, pushed the argument to its furthest point in an essay that appeared, after the book was in the press, in *The New York Times* of October 8, under the title, **"Lessons: From Attica**

to Soledad." Referring to the uprising in Attica prison, and its bloody aftermath, Miss Davis's article offers these observations:

> The damage has been done. Scores of men are dead; and unknown numbers are wounded. By now, it would seem, more people should realize that such explosive acts of repression are not minor aberrations in a society not terribly disturbing in other respects. We have witnessed Birmingham, Orangeburg, Jackson State, Kent State, Mylai, San Quentin, Aug. 21, 1970—the list is unending. None emerged *ex nihilo;* rather all crystallized and attested to profound and extensive social infirmity.

Perhaps, though, the events of Attica finally awakened greater numbers of people from their socially inflicted slumber. If this be true, they must recognize that their duty is twofold: to subject governments and prison bureaucracies to unqualified criticism and to acknowledge the rational and human kernel of the struggles unfolding behind prison walls through forthright supportive action.

Despite the confusing syntax of the last clause, Miss Davis's point is perfectly clear. She would like to persuade us that there is a genuine connection between the conduct of American troops at Mylai, of the Guardsmen at Kent State, of the State Police at Attica, and the occurrence of prison revolts—that these are, indeed, a response to officially sanctioned brutality, the end-product of systematic social injustice. Since Miss Davis is herself a prisoner, charged with murder, kidnapping, and criminal conspiracy, since this book is designed to arouse sympathy for her and for her cause, the argument can fairly be regarded as a case of special pleading.

But is it therefore to be rejected? For it is one thing to recognize that Miss Davis might never have arrived at so radical a formulation of her thesis had she herself not been in peril of the law; it is quite another to dismiss that thesis as unfounded. It is one thing to recognize that Miss Davis stands to gain by arousing public sympathy for her plight as the victim of a generalized social inequity; but that does not dispose of a larger question: whether we might not all be the gainers—prisoners, police, soldiers, students, citizens—whether the nation as a whole might not be the better for taking her contention seriously.

Put briefly and crudely, the case stands like this. The population of our prisons is drawn—with exceptions so few as to be statistically negligible, and negligible in terms of any attempt at formulating social policy intelligently—from a single class, the poor. A disproportionate number of the poor are black or brown, and they contribute disproportionately to the prison rolls. In regions of the country where black and brown people are few, the prison populations are poor-white. The recurring feature is poverty. That being the case, we have, philosophically and politically, two choices. We may conclude that our human stock is so tainted that a sizable number of us will always be shiftless and immoral, hence poor and potentially criminal. That is in practice the conclusion on which much of our social policy is founded—though the notion was expressly and specifically rejected by the Founding Fathers of this republic. Or we may conclude that the plant, man, grows best under certain conditions, that those conditions can be ascertained, that deliberate social policy can promote them, that it is the historic mission of America to attend to that enterprise before any other.

This latter principle, so much more congruent with our idea of who we are—the spiritual descendants of the American Revolution and the Rights of Man—runs nevertheless into one great practical difficulty. It is so far from being the doctrine of our present leaders and the inspiration for our most important public actions that only a handful of professed radicals appear to be on speaking terms with it. Discussing that principle in a fitting manner—that is, openly and passionately—has earned for one radical, Miss Angela Davis, a most doubtful criminal prosecution. And as the charges against her are in the highest degree suspect, giving off the gamey odor of political persecution, so the hugger-mugger of her imprisonment in New York and subsequent extradition (fully detailed in this book) looks nothing at all like "equal protection under the laws." I think that is perhaps the most immediate reason for attending carefully to Miss Davis's thesis. What is at stake is American freedom. That is what gives point to the concluding sentence of James Baldwin's eloquent "Open Letter to Angela Davis," which first appeared in *The New York Review of Books* and is reprinted here by way of introduction: "If they take you in the morning, they will be coming for us that night."

Emile Capouya, in a review of "If They Come in the Morning: Voices of Resistance," in The Saturday Review, *New York, Vol. LIV, No. 44, October 30, 1971, p. 44.*

The Times Literary Supplement   (review date 12 November 1971)

[*In the following excerpt, the critic enthusiastically endorses the political and sociological ideas addressed in* If They Come in the Morning.]

One can only review **If They Come in the Morning,** the manifesto of letters and statements from prison, by saluting Miss Davis in her threefold capacity as Black woman, communist and intellectual. She is a young Black philosophy professor, who first lived in Birmingham, Alabama and whose young friends were bombed mercilessly to death while they sat at Sunday school. She saw Malcolm X, Martin Luther King and many others die as she pursued her studies of the kind of society which killed the best of the "brothers and sisters" about her. Who can blame her for concluding that the murders of Black leaders and the packed death rows of the prisons were sure signs of a capitalist society willing to pull out all the stops to terrify her own people and to undermine the working-class movement as a whole? And who can blame her for responding to and developing the theories of her master, Herbert Marcuse, whose doctrines about a society which binds down its people with silken chains were only wrong in so far as the chains for the Black prisoners were the same old chains as in the days of slavery?

Miss Davis's book is, if you like, a book on American pris-

ons; but it is that only because it is in the prisons today that the politically conscious Negro is fighting for his life and where the un-politically conscious, the framed as well as the properly convicted, are learning the meaning of true political struggle. Parts four, five and six of this deeply passionate book record some of the names of the "brothers and sisters" who are allowed to lie rotting in the jails.

In terms of the sociology of minorities Angela Davis's story is of the next stage beyond the ghetto; not yet, it is true, the stage of the systematic extermination-camp, but somewhere reasonably far along that road, where the Black Panthers and any other group which thinks that the lesson of Watts and all the other smouldering ghettoes is to take up arms and defend itself can be systematically eliminated. So, the Soledad brothers and so Attica, and so also Angela Davis, who does not deny that she bought a gun but who now stands trial for a murder and kidnapping for which no evidence which implicates her has yet been produced. If she is convicted, or if she is shot dead during one of those daily scuffles with the warders, she will not be the first of Black America's revolutionary martyrs; and unless and until the Californian courts show that she has done something that denies the purposes of a truly free society, her Black friends, her radical friends and her intellectual friends will want the whole world to know that it is not one Black revolutionary but the entire American political and legal system which will stand trial.

"Ghettoes and Beyond," in The Times Literary Supplement, *No. 3637, November 12, 1971, p. 1407.*

Brian Neal Odell   (review date 8 January 1972)

[*In the following review, Odell acknowledges the validity of Davis's argument that American jails are filled with victims of racism, economic exploitation, and a discriminatory judicial system, but faults* If They Come in the Morning *as "self-serving" and its language as trite and hyperbolic.*]

According to Angela Davis and the other authors of **If They Come in the Morning,** America's jails and penitentiaries are populated by the victims of racism, economic exploitation and a discriminatory judicial-penal system. Says Miss Davis: "While cloaking itself with the bourgeois aura of universality . . . the prison has actually operated as an instrument of class domination, a means of prohibiting the have-nots from encroaching upon the haves."

Although Miss Davis' rhetoric is trite and her stance self-serving, her thesis remains valid: Prison and the punishment for crime are class-related phenomena. The inmates of our prisons are the poor. They may be the white poor, the black poor or the brown poor, but they are almost always the poor.

Criminologists explain this phenomenon in terms of "life chances." The poor, the criminologists point out, are usually the unskilled, uneducated, under-socialized members of society. Cut off from the traditional avenues to success, the poor are forced to achieve their goals of wealth or power through "alternate" means—means which are illegal and frequently lead to imprisonment. Thus, the poor who populate our prisons are not viewed as rebels or deviants; rather, they are seen as incompletely socialized individuals who have used illegitimate means in an attempt to get their "piece of the action."

Angela Davis, Bettina Aptheker and the other authors of *If They Come in the Morning* reject this explanation of criminality. (p. 25)

The problem with such politically motivated hyperbole is that it could sabotage the efforts of concerned penologists attempting to overhaul our barbaric penal system. To be sure, Miss Davis and the other authors of *If They Come in the Morning* are correct when they argue that our judicial-penal system oppresses the poor. But they are wrong when they attribute this oppression to a conscious plot and political design. Our legal system oppresses segments of society not because we are fascists who have succeeded, but because we are well-intentioned men who have failed. (pp. 25-6)

> *Brian Neal Odell, in a review of "If They Come in the Morning: Voices of Resistance," in* America, *Vol. 126, No. 1, January 8, 1972, pp. 25-6.*

Steven V. Roberts   (review date 24 March 1972)

[*Roberts is an American editor and journalist. In the essay below, he acknowledges the truthful but sometimes formulaic nature of Davis's political rhetoric in* If They Come in the Morning *and assesses some of the volume's contradictions.*]

James Baldwin, in an open letter to "my sister, Angela Davis," writes: "what has happened, it seems to me, and to put it far too simply, is that a whole new generation of people have assessed and absorbed their history, and in that tremendous action, have freed themselves of it and will never be victims again. . . . The secret is out: we are men!"

In that passage Baldwin identifies what this hodge-podge of a book really is: a chronicle of a new consciousness among American blacks, of their cries for pride and humanity, of their fearsome determination never to be victims again. (pp. 68-9)

The best parts of *If They Come in the Morning* are several essays by Miss Davis, the former philosophy teacher now accused of providing the guns for a bloody and abortive escape attempt at the Marin County, Calif. courthouse in 1970. Most of the remaining pages are padded with statements and letters from George Jackson, Ruchell Magee, Bobby Seale and other "political prisoners," an imprecise term which ostensibly means someone prosecuted for political beliefs, not criminal acts. Lately the title has been conferred on almost any inmate who can make a fist and shout "power to the people." And at times, this book degenerates into stupefying radical rhetoric, with all the originality of a child's writing "I won't pull Susie's hair" one hundred times on the blackboard.

In spite of the rhetoric, however, and sometimes because

of it, this is an infuriating book, and rousing that sort of emotion is no small achievement. For instance, Miss Davis describes how a glaring double standard is often applied to violence by militants and police. J. Edgar Hoover has labelled the Black Panthers the gravest threat to domestic tranquility, and the mere sight of one on television starts locks clicking shut across America. But it was the Chicago police who murdered Panther leaders Fred Hampton and Mark Clark in their beds, the National Guard who killed four students at Kent State, and the state troopers who shot most of the inmates and hostages at Attica.

Moreover, Miss Davis argues, the courts are often used as "instruments of oppression" against blacks—and whites—bold enough to challenge the existing order. Look at some of the cases. Twenty-one New York Panthers were accused of conspiring to blow up public buildings, and many of them, who could not raise the bail, served more than a year in jail before they were acquitted. Seven black inmates of California's Soledad prison were charged with murdering a guard and placed in isolation. At the trial, the prosecutor asked for a dismissal when his chief witness admitted that he had been bribed into testifying. Lee Otis Johnson, a civil rights worker in Houston, is serving a 30-year jail sentence on charges of possession and sale of one marijuana cigarette, Miss Davis herself has spent more than a year in jail without being convicted of anything because her repeated appeals for bail had been denied.

Even allowing for exaggeration, these accounts leave one outraged; "equal protection of the laws" rings hollow. But the book is maddening in another way. Its whole tone implies that the only acceptable response is an enthusiastic "right on," without any questions or doubts. The fact remains, however, that the book bristles with contradictions.

The authors repeatedly assert their independence and self-determination, yet they say that virtually all criminals are "victims" of socio-economic forces and are not responsible for their actions. They want the protection of the courts, but do not admit the right of a free society to protect itself. They talk about forging a "united front," but even the Panthers are rent by petty squabbling. They praise the "working class" in the abstract, but have nothing but contempt for the police, who belong to the working class if anybody does. They denounce racism, but they canonize the three black prisoners who died at the Marin County courthouse, while ignoring the fourth victim, a white judge.

In essence, then, this is a book written by revolutionaries, true believers, who can justify anything in the name of their cause. And I have to give a wishy-washy, liberal response: "Right on, but . . ." (p. 69)

> *Steven V. Roberts, in a review of "If They Come in the Morning: Voices of Resistance," in* Commonweal, *Vol. XCVI, No. 3, March 24, 1972, pp. 68-9.*

Elinor Langer (review date 27 October 1974)

[Langer is an American journalist and author of the biography Josephine Herbst: The Story She Never Could Tell *(1984). In the following essay, she praises* Angela Davis *as a narrative of "political communication."]*

When Angela Davis finally obtained access to the library in the Women's House of Detention during the long incarceration that preceded her trial, she found among the cockroaches and the literary trash a handful of books that had some meaning for her—the autobiography of W. E. B. DuBois, a book on China by Edgar Snow, a work on communism. These, she eventually realized, were the remnants of the imprisonment of Elizabeth Gurley Flynn and Claudia Jones, Communists like herself, imprisoned in the same jail under the Smith Act and also made to leave behind the books they received as inmates. Her own book is destined for the same shelves. It is meant to strengthen the next generation of prisoners, as the books left by her predecessors strengthened her.

Angela Davis: An Autobiography is not so much revealing as "exemplary." Writing it was not an act of self-discovery; it was an act of political communication. Yet it is no prose poster. It takes its structure from her arrest, imprisonment, trial and acquittal and, for that reason and because the prison movement is her political work, it is sometimes the voice of Every Prisoner, a little familiar. But it is also a strong, idiosyncratic account of her childhood, youth and growth, and her choice of the Communist party as the agency through which to act. To the personal narrative she brings such precision and individuality that she reminds us out of what universal, bitter, private experiences the black movement coalesced in the first place. Her account of her involvement with the party is so plausible and fresh it turns back the burden of explanation to those who feel the C. P. is so irrelevant, drenched with the blood of history, or populated by Government agents, that anyone who would willingly join it is stupid, unserious, an agent him/her self, or fond of losing.

Davis, born in 1944, grew up in a violent Birmingham, Ala., neighborhood her parents were the first to integrate. She spent summers in New York. Caught between the conflicting racial styles of South and North, her experience was confusing. In New York, her favorite bus seat was behind the driver; at home, on her first ride, a worldlier older cousin tricked her into the back. In Birmingham, the only movie theater with first-run shows and a glitter that compared with the thrilling showcases of New York was reserved for whites; the black children had run-down auditoriums and re-runs of Tarzan. A good passage—there is a lot of nice writing in the book—recreates those baffled childhood comparisons. " 'If only we lived in New York. . . .' I constantly thought. . . . In New York we could buy a hot dog anywhere."

If she became a good sociologist and philosopher, it is not surprising. She had a lot to figure out. She bore her enforced piano and ballet lessons bravely, but her love of reading was real. When the black library was built it became her hangout. Frustrated by high school, and not yet caught up in the civil-rights movement, she plotted her escape from the provincial, restrictive South. She had a

choice between an early-admissions program at Fisk University, which she thought would facilitate her dream to become a pediatrician, and a program sponsored by the American Friends Service Committee through which black students from the South attended integrated schools in the North. There were pros and cons and family discussions; too many beatniks in New York (Mother), but too much socializing at Fisk (Father) for Angela's private nature. New York won, and she went off to live in Brooklyn with the family of a white, Episcopal minister who had lost his church during the McCarthy period, and attend Elizabeth Irwin High School.

And there in some ways is the heart of it, for it was at Elizabeth Irwin, one of the cultural nurseries of the New York Left, that Davis discovered Communism. "When I learned about socialism in my history classes, a whole new world opened up before my eyes." The *Communist Manifesto* bound up her childhood experiences like epoxy.

> I read it avidly, finding in it answers to many of the seemingly unanswerable dilemmas which had plagued me. . . . Like an expert surgeon, this document cut away cataracts from my eyes. The eyes heavy with hatred on Dynamite Hill, the roar of explosives, the fear, the hidden guns, the weeping Black woman at our door, the children without lunches, the schoolyard bloodshed, the social games of the Black middle class, Shack I/Shack II [her segregated school], the back of the bus, police searches—it all fell into place. What had seemed a personal hatred of me, an inexplicable refusal of Southern whites to confront their own emotions, and a stubborn willingness of blacks to acquiesce became the inevitable consequences of a ruthless system which kept itself alive and well by encouraging spite, competition, and oppression of one group by another. Profit was the word: the cold and constant motive for the behavior, the contempt and the despair I had seen.

That cohering, that understanding: an intellectual's version of being saved. But it was not yet a professional, political commitment. She went to Brandeis, took a year abroad, studied French literature, worked privately with Herbert Marcuse, and spent two years in advanced study of Kant, Hegel and Marx at the Institut für Sozialforschung in Frankfurt, where Theodor Adorno was directing her doctoral dissertation. Then, in 1967, drawn by action in the black community she could no longer ignore, she returned to the United States to find her own combination of theory and practice. Her experience with sophisticated European Marxists left her with a bias against traditional Communist parties it took her some time to overcome. She solidified her affiliation gradually, after the repeated discovery in black political meetings and on the streets of Los Angeles that only the Communists seemed to have the analysis and skills necessary to channel the undifferentiated, emotional, anti-white feelings stimulated by the Black Power Movement into lasting political gain.

The Communist party seemed the most durable organization. It had the most developed ideas. It was least susceptible to the deadly flattery that tied so many black organizations to the reputations of their leaders, then conveniently destroyed the organizations by murdering the leaders. Davis is not self-effacing, but she was not seeking stardom. She wanted to be smaller than something. In July, 1968, while she was teaching at U. C. L. A., she turned over her first dues (50 cents) to the chairman of the Che-Lumumba Club, the Black C. P. unit in Los Angeles, thereby unleashing the California headhunters in search of another black trophy and casting herself in precisely the heroic role she had hoped to avoid by her choice.

Davis's book, particularly her description of the events and discussions that were the foundation of her choice of the C. P. is a useful new look at black and radical politics of the 1960's. But her need to present her evolution as fully "objective" bothers me. Along with her need to represent herself as "unexceptional," I think it leads to distortions. She was not a typical Southern black child: Her mother worked on the Scottsboro case in the 1930's; her family always had Communist friends; she joined Advance, the Communist youth group, when she went to Elizabeth Irwin. This made for attractions, comfortableness, predilections—invisible standards by which later situations are evaluated—even if they do not crudely dictate choices.

Both the anticapitalist theory she studied and the interracial Communist community to which she was accustomed must have affected her negative analysis of the American black political scene. Private factors do not invalidate the public ones, and her conclusions ought to be considered in political argument, not in ad feminem speculation. But I wish she had chosen to present herself in a slightly more rounded way. Psychologizing can undercut the political argument, true, but political autobiography can be propaganda. She would say that is an honest function, and indeed the one she chose. I think she is too large to be confined in stereotypes, even heroic ones. (pp. 5, 55)

> *Elinor Langer, in a review of "Angela Davis: An Autobiography," in* The New York Times Book Review, *October 27, 1974, pp. 5, 55.*

What people have to start doing is to build that collective spirit. To overcome that notion of bourgeois individuality which separates one person from the next and which defines the individual as someone who can assert himself at the expense of his neighbor, at the expense of his brother by destroying his brother.

—Angela Davis, in an interview excerpted in Life, *11 September 1970.*

Walter Clemons   (review date 28 October 1974)

[Clemons is an American short story writer and critic. In the following excerpt, he criticizes the lack of personal revelation in Davis's autobiography.]

At the start of her autobiography, Angela Davis rebukes curiosity about "a 'real' person separate and apart from the political person" and warns that her book, written with reluctance, will demonstrate only that

> the forces that have made my life what it is are the very same forces that have shaped and mis-shaped the lives of millions of my people . . . The one extraordinary event of my life had nothing to do with me as an individual—with a little twist of history, another sister or brother could have easily become the political prisoner whom millions of people from throughout the world rescued from persecution and death.

Very well, but how did *you* feel about all this? One can respect Angela Davis's austerity and self-effacement, but it's hard not to find her book a little dry. Of her childhood in Birmingham, Ala., as the daughter of educated middle-class blacks, she remembers only incidents that pointed a future political course. She went to New York for her last two years of high school, then took a magna cum laude in French literature at Brandeis, with a junior year at the Sorbonne. If she fell in love, if she ever enjoyed a frivolous moment, it's none of our business. Herbert Marcuse considered her one of his best students at Brandeis and encouraged her to seek a graduate degree in philosophy at Frankfurt under Theodor Adorno. This was "a very intensive learning experience"; she gives us little more than reading lists.

Her most revealing passages are those in which Davis's feelings of guilt as a privileged intellectual come to the fore. In high school in New York she regretted her absence from Birmingham when the first Freedom Riders arrived there; when she sailed for Germany, she notes, Watts was burning. Ambitious to learn, she felt herself "hidden away in West Germany [while] the black liberation movement was undergoing decisive metamorphoses . . . The more the struggles at home accelerated, the more frustrated I felt at being forced to experience it all vicariously." Her subsequent activism was a struggle to break out of the bookworm's cocoon.

When she first met her co-defendant Ruchell Magee at their pre-trial hearing, Angela Davis was shamed to learn that his prison life had begun at 16, at which age she was entering Brandeis on a scholarship, and that while she pursued her education in Europe and worked toward her Ph.D., Magee had been studying law books in his cell: "One small twist of fate and I might have drowned in the muck of poverty and disease and illiteracy. That is why I never felt I had the right to look upon myself as being any different from my sisters and brothers who did *all* the suffering, for *all* of us." In this light, her disappointing memoir can be read as an act of abnegation. Instead of revealing herself, she has made an attempt to divest herself of individuality, and in that sacrificial effort she has pretty thoroughly succeeded. (pp. 97, 100)

> *Walter Clemons, "While Watts Burned," in* Newsweek, *Vol. LXXXIV, No. 18, October 28, 1974, pp. 97, 100.*

Ivan Webster   (review date 16 November 1974)

[*In the following review, Webster faults* Angela Davis *for its trite prose style and lack of introspection and analysis.*]

I note on the jacket of [**Angela Davis**] that Angela Davis was born 10 days after I was. By an embarrassingly slim margin, that makes me her elder. I felt something like a proud, anxious elder brother as I read her autobiography. Her look backward takes in her childhood in Birmingham's black lower middle class, where the seeds of radicalization were planted as she saw neighbors' homes bombed, black children's education scandalously neglected, and bitter social spite swallowed like daily bread.

In Davis' narrative we are swept along with her to high school in New York (where at age 15 she discovered Marxist thought and knew almost at once that it was for her), to student days at Brandeis, to graduate study in Frankfurt, Germany, doctoral work in California under Herbert Marcuse, her appointment in philosophy at UCLA, to dismissal by the university board of regents, to flight from the FBI as one of its 10 most wanted fugitives, her arrest and imprisonment in New York, 16-month confinement awaiting trial in California on conspiracy, kidnapping and murder charges, acquittal. All of this before reaching 30. My temptation is to take a deep breath and then review Angela's life rather than her book. What do I have to show for my 10-day head start?

It turns out that this is less an autobiography than a preliminary probe of her own fiber, her humble realization that she is made of stern stuff. Davis elaborates on this discovery in the context of her prison experience, and concludes that her only possible response to our system of criminal justice is to dismantle it: she is eloquent, tough and stubborn in her moral integrity. Both her New York confinement and her 16-month California ordeal are painful, unanswerable testimony to her inner strength and her power to inspire political resistance in others.

Soon after her arrival in jail other inmates, knowing Angela was among them, were emboldened by her presence into organizing, protesting and talking back to their keepers. The horrors of the penal system, the racist treatment it embodies, the wild screams, despair and rotting lives that are *really* locked up in those cells so the rest of us won't have to ask why—all this provides Davis with a proper target for her rage. The story needs telling, and she tells it powerfully and well.

I'm deeply respectful of the descriptive problems she faced, because some of the events she narrates I saw first hand. I was a student at UCLA while she waged her battle to continue teaching there, and before she arrived had earned some black activist scars of my own. Her presence on campus was electrifying. I'll never forget cutting class to sneak into her packed lectures on "Recurring Philosophical Themes in Black Literature" and being enthralled at the rigor and range of her mind.

It's when she moves away from hard, stark issues that the book falters. I also heard (and heard tell of) Angela when she took to the political rostrum. While she was a gener-

ous political battler—always stressing the plight of others more than her own—as an on-the-lines rouser she was often less than stirring. The rhetoric sounded hackneyed, the terms were not fresh, and one didn't feel the riveting quality of mind that could be heard in her lectures and in her political speeches.

A similar failing, on the intellectual and analytical plane, pervades her book. She has taken a rather narrow approach, propping up this account of her life with tract-like doctrine, reprising speeches, listing political debts and settling old movement scores. She is conscious of class conflict at seven and cannily unmasking the evils of the profit motive at 15, which doesn't sound like reminiscence. Why did these things happen to *this* woman, we keep asking, and get only partial answers.

There isn't a sharp enough sense of history in these pages, either the immediate history she is surviving and trying to change, or a place in the continuum at the end of a long line of forebears. She tells us, for instance, that just before making her final decision to join the Communist party, she reread Lenin, and also took a look at the writing of W. E. B. Du Bois around the time he made the same decision. She joined, but she fails to tell us what Du Bois said. What were his reasons and how did they clarify her own? (He was past 90 when he finally took that step; she was in her mid-20s.) She writes as if she were in a vacuum; there is no sustained discussion of how she thinks an onslaught on capitalist power ought to proceed.

She speaks as a black intellectual, but reading this book you'd never know that other black intellectuals in America have made similar decisions to ally themselves with the party and then, for reasons they've amply documented, eventually came to have serious reservations about their choice. She neglects the experiences of men like Richard Wright and Ralph Ellison. How is her case like or unlike theirs? One would relish hearing her response to the critique of the role of blacks in the party by Harold Cruse in *The Crisis of the Negro Intellectual.* The book isn't mentioned; indeed she has very little to say about her reading in any case, or how she fared under Marcuse's tutelage. Instead of an exploration of the development of her political thought, she contents herself with romantic posturing—in effect, with challenging the capitalist monolith to put up its dukes, avowing that her Marxist dad can lick anybody on the ideological block.

One would have thought that if anyone possessed the theoretical equipment to provide an in-depth situation-based discussion of what the black left accomplished in the '60s and where the movement ought to go from here, it would be Davis. But her discussions, such as they are, of Carmichael, Cleaver, Newton and cultural nationalist Ron Karenga rarely grapple with these men's theory or practice. Purely, and scantily, descriptive, she offers little analysis and thus has botched a splendid opportunity.

It may be more correct to say, bypassed. I can only speculate, but I think the book is ill timed. It doesn't crackle with the convictions of a woman with a world to win. Perhaps she shouldn't have undertaken her life story at 30, though one can understand why she wanted to try. But no one should make the mistake of writing her off at 30. Like many of us of her age, she may still be something of a mystery to herself; major pieces of her puzzle still may not have fallen into place. From my 10 days' vantage point, that's the only explanation for this book's limitations I can come up with. (pp. 30-1)

Ivan Webster, "Political Fury," in The New Republic, *Vol. 171, No. 20, November 16, 1974, pp. 30-1.*

Julius Lester (review date February 1975)

[*Lester is an American poet, historian, critic, editor, and author of children's books. In the following essay, he questions Davis's emphasis on the political rather than the personal in her autobiography, but commends her evocation of the American black experience.*]

The cover photograph of Angela Davis shows an unsmiling woman, an African mask in Ektachrome. The eyes are large, but all expression has been so carefully removed from them that one is deprived of an opening through which to glimpse even the shadow of her soul. We are presented with an almost archetypal representation of the black woman, an image to be engraved on a stamp, or currency—after the revolution.

The photograph accurately reflects [*Angela Davis: An Autobiography*], for this is one which can be judged by its cover. ". . . to write about my life," Angela Davis warns in the preface, ". . . would require . . . an assumption that I was unlike other . . . black women." Her denial of unique individuality is typical of the politically committed, for whom there is no self separate from "the community of struggle against poverty and racism." Whether or not this is true, it is the premise on which Davis bases the narrative of her life, and it is within this context that any judgment of that life, as she presents it, must be made.

To be born black is to know one's self as politically defined, and negatively so, before there is the opportunity to experience one's self as a person. Davis is eloquent as she communicates her childhood bewilderment at being an object of hate, and the book is most personal when she recounts her attempts to resist through anger, ridicule of whites, confrontations with them, and fantasies.

> I constructed a fantasy in which I would slip on a white face and go unceremoniously into the theater or amusement park. . . . After thoroughly enjoying the activity, I would make a dramatic, grandstand appearance before the white racists and with a sweeping gesture, rip off the white face, laugh wildly, and call them all fools.

Between the ages of six and ten, however, she spent the summers in New York with friends of her parents. (Among her childhood friends was Margaret Burnham, who would be one of her chief defense attorneys.) This exposure to another world was significant, for although New York was not a heaven for blacks, the range of opportunities for human experience were greater there. Increasingly stifled by life in Birmingham, Angela Davis left when she was fourteen to attend school in New York through a program sponsored by the American Friends Service Committee.

> [One] must respect and admire Angela Davis's basic and unshakable instinct toward caring. Whatever else her autobiography does, it communicates the risks and sacrifices she has endured in her efforts to right inhuman wrongs. Amid a variety of responses to her, one must be a re-examination of how one is living his or her own life.
>
> —*Julius Lester*

She attended Elizabeth Irwin High School, a private institution, and there discovered Marxism-Leninism, which clarified political reality for her. "What had seemed a personal hatred of me . . . became the inevitable consequence of a ruthless system which kept itself alive and well by encouraging spite, competition, and the oppression of one group by another." She attended meetings of a Marxist-Leninist youth group, where she became acquainted with Bettina Aptheker, as well as the children of other Communist Party leaders.

Her interest in Marxism led to the study of philosophy, particularly Hegel, during her undergraduate years at Brandeis and her graduate study at the University of Frankfurt. Her commitment to the intellectual life was slowly eroded by the events of the late 1960s and her own increasing feelings of isolation from them.

She returned to America, hoping to combine the intellectual life with that of the political activist. That was not to be. She did nothing which thousands of her contemporaries were not doing, but the state of California attacked her because of who she was—a black, female Communist. Without forewarning, she was shoved onto the stage of history; she reluctantly left her doctoral dissertation unfinished.

One is left with the impression of a woman who lives as she thinks it necessary to live and not as she would like to, if she allowed herself to have desires. She seems to be a woman of enormous self-discipline and control, who willed herself to a total political identity. Her will is so strong that, at times, it is frightening. On the death of George Jackson, she writes that "the deeply personal pain I felt would have strangled me had I not turned it into a proper and properly placed rage. . . . It would refine my hatred of jailers, position my contempt for the penal system and cement my bonds with other prisoners."

Davis has used her politics to eradicate everything in her which would interfere with her commitment to revolutionary change. If there is an Angela Davis separate from the Communist woman, Davis does not know her and has little desire to do so. If one shares Davis's view of reality as wholly political, this is admirable. I do not find it so. Human existence is not summarized by Marxism-Leninism, and one must wonder if Davis is using Marxism-Leninism to try and save the world or herself. No matter. A political ideology is unsuited for either task.

However, when one considers that the choice of most Americans is an intense indifference to injustice and the suffering of others, one must respect and admire Angela Davis's basic and unshakable instinct toward caring. Whatever else her autobiography does, it communicates the risks and sacrifices she has endured in her efforts to right inhuman wrongs. Amid a variety of responses to her, one must be a re-examination of how one is living his or her own life. (pp. 54-5)

Julius Lester, "Young, Female, Black, and Revolutionary," in The Progressive, *Vol. 39, No. 2, February, 1975, pp. 54-5.*

Janet Burroway   (review date 2 May 1975)

[*Burroway is an American novelist, short story writer, author of children's books, poet, and educator. Here, she describes* Angela Davis *as a book of poor literary quality about a life of uncompromising courage.*]

Out of one of the luminous lives of our time Angela Davis has produced [an autobiography] like a damp firecracker. In part, this is deliberate. She professes reluctance to tell her story at all, lest it should require 'a posture of difference, an assumption that I was unlike other women—other Black women', and in the wilful assumption that she is like other women, she has left out her identity. No *auto*, in fact; no particularising sense of her ambitions, her talents, her personal griefs and personal beauty. Worse, her determination to concentrate on the struggle against global exploitation, guilt-motivated legal systems, the spectre of fascism, etc., has led to a total exclusion of internal struggle, without which no autobiography rings true.

Her childhood in Birmingham, Alabama, passed, according to her account, in such unruffled familial accord that it might be the envy of us all, and it is striking that it is more recognisable as an American and a middle-class childhood than a Black one. There are ballet and tap lessons, organdy dresses, piano recitals in the Methodist Church, college-educated parents (her father found owning a service station more lucrative than teaching school), vacations in New York and California, profound parental ambitions for her betterment, intellectual enlightenment, scholarships Back East and graduate school abroad. The shape of the story (including the catapult to fame) is perfectly consistent with a national myth in which Henry Ford outranks Robin Hood for heroism. The virtues involved are those of the American work ethic: self-discipline, self-reliance, familial piety and dogged optimism; and the vices are its vices: false modesty, intolerance and a political stance that is, however communist, near-Nixonian in its lack of scope. Through all this, of course, run the horrors of Black childhood in the Deep South, but unfortunately these are reported in a tone of distanced self-righteousness. Since we are not allowed to

share in the personal emotions, including the less heroic ones, of the narrator, we shall not be moved.

Ms Davis is forever refusing to feel sorry for herself. Bombs go off, friends are beaten, humiliated, falsely arrested, murdered. She is never frightened or discouraged but that she musters her discipline to transform fear into 'proper and properly placed rage'. The propriety of such rage requires, alas, an obfuscating racist rhetoric. Blacks are 'vibrant' and 'serene and strong'; they have 'the energy of stallions and the confidence of eagles', and 'tremendous arms' like 'sculptures of an ancient strength'. All whites except those who help the cause (and who rarely merit adjectives) are 'mean-faced', 'decadent' and 'voracious'; they 'waddle'; their voices 'quiver' and are 'fury-laden'. Each of their institutions is 'filthy' and 'musty with the odor of San Diego Justice'; or 'the sparkling marble walls and antiseptically clean floor almost seemed designed to hide the dirty fascist business being conducted there'.

What are we to do with this, essentially literary, failure?—literary because what Ms Davis has done is to take the oratorical skill of a political activist and employ it in a form for which it is embarrassingly ill-suited. She can write otherwise. When she permits herself to quote from two of her letters to George Jackson in Soledad Prison (one of them was used as evidence against her and so public anyway), we are suddenly treated to felt flights of metaphor. But for the most part whatever is personal, passionate or sexual is skirted with a visible Victorian *moue* (of Jackson she confesses that 'my feelings for him had grown deeper than a political commitment to struggle for his freedom', and when a mad landlord tries to run her down and then presents her with a sheaf of poems, she mincingly records that she was 'in his eyes at least, somewhat physically attractive'). And whenever personal suffering can be wrenched into rhetoric, it is duly wrenched, to the frustration of our natural sympathies. She describes the battle of the NY Detention Centre women against mice as

> symbolic of a larger struggle . . . barricades being erected against the larger enemy . . . hundreds of women, all over the jail, politically conscious, politically committed . . . acting in revolutionary unison.

One may be permitted to say that this is overwritten without condoning mice in jails.

And through the skrim of cant, the facts are eloquent enough. The facts are that Angela Davis was fired from her job in the UCLA Philosophy Department on blatantly political grounds, that her involvement in the movement to free the Soledad Brothers began as one of a dozen such involvements, and that the attempt to convict her of 'murder, kidnapping and conspiracy' on the basis of her love letters to George Jackson represented a palpable absence of a case for the prosecution. The fact is that Jackson was shot in the back, and that Ms Davis spent more time in jail awaiting trial on charges of which she was acquitted than any convicted Watergate criminal has spent or is likely to spend. One can easily believe (but we already did) that she would nevertheless have been convicted had the California authorities not been convinced that too many people knew about it. And in spite of, rather than because of, Ms Davis's over-insistence, one can continue to believe in the provocative vengefulness and stupidity of the Los Angeles police.

Well, it is not a good book. But neither does it undo the uncompromising courage of the life. No doubt the price of the 'uncompromising' is the mental and emotional over-simplification. People who rip up paving stones must believe that by doing so they will utterly alter human nature and the course of human events. They are in error, but if they did not do so from time to time it is likely that the rest of us would not have the leisure to point it out. (pp. 593-94)

> *Janet Burroway, "All American," in* New Statesman, *Vol. 89, No. 2302, May 2, 1975, pp. 593-94.*

George E. Kent   (review date March 1976)

[*In the excerpt below, Kent praises* Angela Davis *as an educational tract.*]

[**Angela Davis: An Autobiography**] is conceived to be a political autobiography, one which stresses "my overwhelming sense of belonging to a community of humans—a community of struggle against poverty and racism." Hopefully, the book would make people understand why a large number of persons feel that they have no alternative but to offer their total lives to the battle against oppression and inspire more to join the struggle. . . .

Davis places herself in the historic context of the black struggle. Part 1 registers the personal emotions but pushes an analysis of situations based upon institutional corruption and the vagaries of the capitalistic system. In this way, she guards herself from being overwhelmed by her situation as a purely individual predicament and keeps her vision clear for understanding how individuals are crushed in an oppressive system. (p. 101)

[Other] chapters are educational with respect to the resistance and elaborately thought-out strategies necessary to overcome prejudicial circumstances and unexpected events. Davis's resources in prison dramatize and underline the kinds of suffering and injustice the penal system affords for the anonymous prisoner, and the portraits of both prisoners and officials outline a discouraging picture.

Despite its single-minded emphasis upon proper ideological response, the passion with which this political autobi-

---

Angela Davis's single-minded dedication and hard-headed idealism provide more than enough positive encouragement for those who may think there is little left to fight for in the civil rights movement.

—Toks Williams, in "Still Fighting," in New Statesman and Society, *16 March 1990.*

---

ography is written enhances its educational objective. (p. 103)

> *George E. Kent, "The 1975 Black Literary Scene: Significant Developments," in* PHY-LON: The Atlanta University Review of Race and Culture, *Vol. 37, No. 1, March, 1976, pp. 100-15.*

Angela Davis with Sid Cassese   (interview date August 1981)

[*In the following excerpt, Davis comments on the black condition in contemporary American society.*]

[*Cassese*]: *Are Black students as interested in the struggle today as they were ten or 15 years ago, when they were part of the Civil Rights and antiwar movements that led to college takeovers and the calling for Black studies programs on college campuses?*

[Davis]: There may be an even greater interest today than during that period. I don't mean greater involvement because, in terms of the organized struggle, we don't have as vast a movement as we had then. But I suspect that over the next several years, particularly with Ronald Reagan in the White House, that involvement will equal if not surpass the movement of the late sixties and early seventies.

One reason there isn't as great a visible face of the movement as there was then is that the organizing skills have not yet been rebuilt. Organizing is very important, even though most people underestimate its value. But if one does not know how to call a meeting, mimeograph literature and do all of that, then, regardless of what the sentiment might be, it never achieves expression. That's one of the real problems on campus—the lack of understanding about organizing. You may have a tremendous desire to see things change, a really profound sense of the need to resist, but it doesn't always achieve the best kind of expression without organization.

Is anything different today for Black people? There seems to have been no substantive betterment of conditions for the majority of Black people over the past decade even though a growing number of Black men and some women have gained access to the supposed goodies of middle-classness.

You're not talking about the majority but a very minute minority, really. The [U. S.] Labor Department statistics indicated that more Black people were falling into poverty, but because Black people who are "middle class" are much more visible today than they were ten or 20 years ago, the illusion is that Blacks have achieved their goals in life, have achieved liberation, and that, in fact, the masses of Black people must be doing much better.

When you say that Black people are more visible, are you talking in terms of just seeing them in the media or in politics?

No. I was watching the return of the space shuttle on television, and a Black man was the master of ceremonies for the festivities that were being held. You see individual Black people in all kinds of positions that we did not see them in before.

Is that bad?

I'm not saying that it's bad but that it creates the illusion that Black people have achieved their liberation; and that is used as an argument against affirmative action when we need it now more than ever. Proportionally, we have fewer Black students on college campuses, a widening wage differential between Black workers and white workers and problems intensifying in education, health and other areas.

Given the state of today's economy, are President Reagan's actions toward the poor and minorities any worse than would have been the case under Carter or Kennedy?

Fundamentally, there really is no great difference between Carter and Reagan. The deterioration of Black people's situation occurred during the Carter administration, and Carter proposed no solutions that could lead us in a progressive direction. But at the same time, I think that there is a whole new tone that's associated with the Reagan administration—an overtly blatant racist tone, as well as a tone of belligerence in U. S. foreign policy, particularly concerning Namibia and South Africa. That racist tone was obvious even on the campaign trail, when Reagan was in Mississippi talking about states' rights.

Is there any possibility of our correcting that under this political system unless we do something drastic?

We've got to organize. And, yes, I think something drastic has to happen. But it's not going to happen unless we organize the kind of movement that brought about the change that resulted from the civil rights struggle.

How? Can we, for instance, use the same tactics of street demonstrations, boycotts and riots that were effective ten or 15 years ago?

I think we can. We ought to use all the tactics that are still applicable. We've always had to have mass demonstrations. Some people say that those are out now. But if you're talking about people without power, then essentially the only power you have is your combined energy, your combined visibility.

But how can we possibly change the system when even the most abject of us appear to want to join it?

Well, we should definitely be able to partake of the wealth. But this society has demonstrated that there is no way in the world that we are going to be allowed to move forward, because this system is based on monopoly capitalism, and monopoly capitalism is based on profit, not on the needs of people.

But isn't the growing divisiveness that exists between Blacks who've gained economically and those who live in poverty, particularly in urban areas, a manifestation of our trying to join this system?

Yes. And those middle-class Black folk who don't identify with the masses of Black people are doing what the man wants. I really hate to put it that way, but that's the truth.

*But many middle-class Blacks would argue that they have houses to maintain and rising taxes, and live in communi-*ties *that poor Black people are now moving into, which leads to deterioration of the neighborhoods.*

What they ought to be thinking about is using whatever skills and knowledge that they have acquired to lift the entire race. The Black women's club movement used to have a slogan that I think is apt. We're talking about Black educated women who basically associated with the middle class, and their slogan was "Lifting As We Climb." And if Black middle-class people don't attempt to do that today, not only are they going to be contributing to the oppression of the sisters and brothers on whose backs they have climbed up the ladder, but they will eventually be hurting themselves. Because certainly as the condition of the masses of Black people has worsened, the condition of middle-class people has also worsened. Now, who can buy a house in California today, when the average cost of one is $100,000?

Let me make another point. I had some very interesting, very instructive experiences when I was the Communist party's vice-presidential candidate last year. What we were calling for—and we still are—is the creation of a new political party. It's not the Democratic party and certainly not the Republican party. It's a coalition party that would be antimonopoly in nature and would involve progressive Democrats. I see members of the [Congressional] Black Caucus, for example, as being leading forces in that kind of party, but the party would also include labor unions and Black liberation organizations. It would be a party that would be able to pull away from the influence of the big corporations.

You mentioned labor unions as part of the coalitions, but aren't they under the influence of the big corporations?

Well, the masses of the workers aren't. I'm not talking about the top collaborationist leadership. Some very exciting things are happening in the labor movement. There have been more strikes in this country over the last couple of years than since the thirties. Workers have refused to unload ships coming from South Africa. All kinds of things are happening within the labor movement, and we need to draw on that progressive energy. As a matter of fact, that's what it's going to take, since the masses of people are workers and the masses of Black people are workers. Now, what's instructive about this is that people in the strangest of circles agree with me.

During my campaign I addressed a Black political association in California that involved a range of Black politicians, and I got the most overwhelming response. Lionel Wilson, the Black mayor of Oakland, even agreed that we really did need a new party—that the Democratic party was not responsive to the interests of Black people.

Doesn't the National Black Political Party that was created in Philadelphia [in November of 1980] respond to that?

That's an important step. But I think we've learned that although as Black people we have our own struggle for liberation to conduct, we can't achieve any really significant victories if we are not involved in coalitions.

Why? Because of numbers or ideas?

Well, OK, because of numbers. But that's not the important thing. Whenever Black people have moved forward in this country, there has been an overall forward movement. White people have benefited from it. Certainly other people of color have benefited. The struggle for Black liberation has always served as an index to what is happening in the entire society—what's happening to women, what's happening to other people of color, what's happening to workers in general. In a sense I think that, as Black people, we have a responsibility to oppressed people in the country and all around the world.

But isn't the total society either more repressive or willing to be more repressive now than during the sixties?

The only way you can counteract that is by building a movement against that repression. I think that's an important point. My political work is concentrated on that area. Since 1973 I have been co-chairperson of the National Alliance Against Racism and Political Repression. And we see our job as challenging the whole structure of the repression and protecting people's right to organize. Ben Chavis [the leader of the "Wilmington 10"—a group who were convicted of a firebombing in North Carolina] is the other co-chairperson. And we consider the victory of the "Wilmington 10" really important, a key victory. We started working on that case in 1973, and it took seven years of active organizing to free them. But it was done.

We have Alliance chapters in about three different cities across the country. We're working on a whole number of cases on a national level. Individual chapters work on cases that emerge in their communities. And we've won a lot of victories over the last years. We're having our sixth national conference in Birmingham. My mother is the coordinator of the Alliance in Birmingham, incidentally.

I know that your mother has long been involved in the struggle, but did her involvement in more direct action come about as a result of your imprisonment?

Well, my mother was involved in the struggle to free the Scottsboro Boys back in the thirties. She's always been active.

Where are these traditional Black organizations such as the NAACP, the Urban League, PUSH [People United to Save Humanity] and the SCLC today? Are these organizations still benefiting Black people?

There are some ways, of course, in which the NAACP and the Urban League are very conservative. But I know that there are differences from chapter to chapter across the country too. I was once asked to be the keynote speaker of an NAACP chapter in Florida, and the national organization got very upset about that, and I didn't go. But the woman who was president of the chapter there resigned as a result of it. So I know there are some really good, dedicated Black people working within the NAACP.

We should attempt to involve the NAACP in progressive coalitions all over. I know that whenever we put something together, we always approach the NAACP. If we're going to hold a rally against, say, the murders in Atlanta, the NAACP will of course be approached and asked to be involved in the organizing and the sponsorship.

So in effect you think that the NAACP and the Urban League have a place in the Black struggle for freedom?

Definitely. You see, the involvement of all kinds of forces within the Black community is needed. We need to get everyone we can. That's the only way we're going to achieve our liberation. Members of the Alliance, for instance, range from the Communist party to some social clubs. We have large numbers of ministers and churches in the Alliance. At the other end of the spectrum, we have radical, revolutionary groups and the Communist party. (pp. 61, 98, 100, 103)

You mentioned earlier and correctly that fewer of our young people are in the college and university system. Shouldn't we also be considering how to deal with the fact that more of them, especially young men, are dropping out of school and are going to jail and are being murdered by the police and each other? It seems that is an ever growing danger to us. Now, we understand about coalitions, but it seems that unless we change something for our youngsters, we're going to be a very small part of any coalition. What can we do, for instance, to prevent the murder of Black youth by the police?

The only thing that I think we can do is to intensify a mass movement. The Alliance has, for example, worked on model legislation for a police-control commission. We recently held a conference in Los Angeles that was actually a national inquiry into police crimes. We had victims of police crimes testify. We had judges and lawyers and others testify. We had a series of workshops out of which emerged this model legislation for the creation of police-control boards across the country. And out of that emerged a strategy to struggle for the implementation of that kind of legislation in a number of other areas.

Have you been able to push through the police-control legislation anywhere in the country?

Work is being done toward it in L.A., and there is a great deal of activity on it in New York, but if you want more information on that you should get in touch with the [National Alliance against Racism and Political Repression].

Are Black women today becoming involved in progressive movements to the extent that you would like?

Yes. I think so. I'm really excited about the reemergence of Black women in leadership positions. We have a tradition of leadership and involvement, going all the way back to slavery. You know, it's really exciting to travel around to the different college campuses and see young women giving leadership to the Black student organizations. On this campus a Black woman is the president of the student government, a Black woman is the treasurer. And in the Alliance we have a whole number of Black women. The executive secretary of the Alliance is Charlene Mitchell, who has been involved in the struggle since she was 16. She's 50 now. I think that she's probably the best organizer in the country. We have Margaret Burnham, a young Black woman who is a judge in Boston and is vice-chairperson. Oh, I could spend hours talking about that. I'm excited, too, about the young Black men who I think are becoming more aware of the efforts that were made to recruit them to the ranks of the male-supremacist. On this campus one of the major Black organizations put together a program on Black women, and the young brothers were really excellent in terms of the comments that they made about the need to defend the right of Black women to participate on an equal level.

What does your course on Black women's music deal with?

It's basically a course in aesthetics. I emphasize the relationship of music to the struggle for Black liberation, specifically focusing on the contributions that Black women have made—from the classic blues singers to the present.

We start with Ma Rainey, Bessie Smith, Ida Cox, and do the whole classic blues tradition. We also spend a great deal of time talking about Billie Holiday, trying to correct some of the misconceptions resulting from the propaganda that tends to emphasize her personal problems at the expense of recognizing the indispensable cultural legacy that she left, and that left virtually no musician uninfluenced by her. And we talk about the significance of her decision to include "Strange Fruit" [a song about Black lynchings in the South] in her repertoire wherever she was. This was at a time when the organized struggle against lynching was becoming stronger. And she definitely established a relationship to the Black liberation struggle, particularly through that song.

Billie's predecessor more or less was Bessie Smith, who sang a very political song called "Poor Man's Blues," which she composed herself. "Poor Man's Blues" bears the same relationship to the struggle that "Strange Fruit" does.

I also teach a course on the history of Afro-American women. It's a huge course. We talk about Black women from Africa to America. We focus in the early part of the course on the situation of Black women during slavery. We try to emphasize the special contributions that Black women have made to the fight for the liberation of their people. And we focus on a number of individuals, such as Sojourner Truth and Ida B. Wells.

Angela, have you changed in the last five or ten years, or are you just stronger in your convictions?

Let me put it this way. The same kinds of problems exist today as they did ten years ago. As a matter of fact, they have worsened in a lot of respects. And basically, I still attempt to participate in seeking solutions to those problems. Hopefully, I have matured. Hopefully, I have learned. Hopefully, I can apply some of the lessons that emerged from the struggles of the sixties and seventies to make a more substantial contribution today. But I still consider myself a revolutionary. I'm still doing whatever I can to reach out to Black people, people of color, oppressed people in general, and to heighten the development of a radical liberation struggle. (pp. 104, 108)

Sid Cassese and Angela Davis, "Angela Davis," in Essence, *Vol. 12, No. 4, August, 1981, pp. 60-1, 98, 100, 103-04, 108.*

Ann Jones (review date 10 January 1982)

[*In the following essay, Jones praises Davis for discussing issues vital to women in* Women, Race, & Class, *but argues that the collection lacks emotional honesty and a personal voice.*]

The notion that poor black women are triply oppressed—by class, race and sex—is by now a truism; but the ragged course of those biases in the past and the points at which they converge today are not easily sorted out or even spotted. It is like Angela Davis, who has never shied from impossible tasks, to try. In **Women, Race and Class** she untangles some strands of that triple knot.

Her approach, through most of this ambitious volume, is historical. She begins with a powerful account of slavery, reminding us that virtually all black women were, from the beginning, workers—and not "Mammies" but field hands. Those female slaves worked side by side with men, sabotaged slavery at every turn, Miss Davis says, sometimes even killed their own children to spare them servitude, and, "passed on to their nominally free female descendants a legacy of hard work, perseverance and self-reliance, a legacy of tenacity, resistance and insistence on sexual equality—in short, a legacy spelling out standards for a new womanhood."

In carrying that new womanhood down through history, black women at first were aided by white women in the antislavery movement—and particularly by Sarah and Angelina Grimke, the South Carolina sisters who wrote and lectured on behalf of both abolition and feminism and whom Miss Davis rightfully admires because they had "such a profound consciousness of the inseparability of the fight for Black Liberation and the fight for Women's Liberation [that] they were never caught in the ideological snare of insisting that one struggle was absolutely more important than the other."

According to Miss Davis's succinct account, that early promise of unity was pathetically short-lived. In 1848 Elizabeth Cady Stanton and Lucretia Mott, distressed by "male supremacy" in the antislavery movement, called a convention at Seneca Falls to consider "the wrongs of society in general and of women in particular." The declaration the convention issued, demanding equity in marriage, property laws, education and "profitable employments," had little to do, as Miss Davis sees it, with "the circumstances of women outside the social class of the document's framers"; working women were not mentioned and black women were not even present. Three years later former slave Sojourner Truth rose at another women's rights convention in Akron, Ohio, to answer the male argument that "delicate" women need protection rather than rights; her thundering question "Ain't I a woman?" was probably aimed not only at men in the gathering but at those white "ladies" who tried to prevent her speaking. By 1866, when the Fourteenth Amendment on apportionment of representation inserted the word "male" for the first time into the Constitution, excluding women (black and white), a betrayed and outraged Mrs. Stanton protested:

"The representative women of the nation have done their uttermost for the last thirty years to secure freedom for the negro; . . . but now, as the celestial gate to civil rights is slowly moving on its hinges, it becomes a serious question whether we had better stand aside and see "Sambo" walk into the kingdom first. . . . Are we so sure that he, once entrenched in all his inalienable rights, may not be an added power to hold us at bay?"

The dream of a unified black and women's liberation was dead. (Mrs. Stanton's racism is undeniable, even though her fears have been borne out. Only a few years ago a black male legislative caucus in Illinois, flexing political muscle to avenge a slight by party leaders, voted down the Equal Rights Amendment.)

During Reconstruction many black and white female teachers worked together to erase black illiteracy, but for the most part, in Angela Davis's account, black women were on their own, forming their own clubs and unions to campaign for black rights and, though spurned by the white suffragists, for women's enfranchisement. And black women drudged on in virtual "slavery." In 1940, 60 percent of black women in the labor force were household workers; in 1960, one-third were still in domestic service—and their employers were white women.

Against this intricate background of the separate and unequal histories of black and white women, Miss Davis sets in perspective some contemporary women's issues: rape, reproductive freedom, housework and child care. And it is here, in the resonances between past and present, between received history and observed life, that one hears some false notes. In her discussion of rape, for example, Miss Davis, who is a member of the Communist Party, offers one more time the familiar frayed old party line of Scottsboro days. One of the reasons black women have avoided the anti-rape movement, she says, is because they know that if "the notion is accepted that Black men harbor irresistible and animal-like sexual urges, the entire race is invested with bestiality," and black women become targets (as they have been throughout history) for rape by white men. In addition, the argument runs, black women know that they must protect black men from white women's false cries of rape. "The anti-rape movement," Angela Davis concludes, "must be situated in a strategic context which envisages the ultimate defeat of monopoly capitalism." Maybe so, but Miss Davis simply underestimates the number of black women in the anti-rape movement, just as she overestimates the number of women, black and white, who will still "protect" rapists. (Crime studies show that most black rapists rape black women; but that fact, of great concern to many black women, is not broached here.) Juggling race, class and sex through history is a difficult feat, so it is understandable that Angela Davis should sometimes pocket one issue while treating the other two as though she still had the full complement aloft. The factor that drops out, invariably, is sex. In [an essay] called **"Communist Women,"** Miss Davis offers adulatory thumbnail sketches of half a dozen black and white women, from Lucy Parsons to Elizabeth Gurley Flynn. But the tenacious and self-reliant women she admires fight for the interests of their race or class—or in the case of well-born white women like Anita Whitney, for

somebody else's race and class—never primarily for themselves as women. Even for Miss Davis, it seems hard to revive that dream of a truly united black and women's liberation without suggesting that one struggle is, after all, "absolutely more important than the other."

It is the historian's job to "inform" the present, to give back to us a version of our past that makes plain the life we observe around us and makes the future thinkable. In a poem about "Heroines" Adrienne Rich asks of the early suffragists: "How can I fail to love / your clarity and fury / how can I give you / all your due / take courage from your courage / honor your exact / legacy as it is / recognizing / as well / that it is not enough?" Angela Davis faces precisely the same question, and I wish that she had spoken to us here, as she has so movingly in the past, in a voice less tuned at times to the Communist Party, more insistently her own. But she is herself a woman of undeniable courage. She should be heard. (pp. 8, 14)

> Ann Jones, "Black Women: On Their Own," in The New York Times Book Review, January 10, 1982, pp. 8, 14.

Anne Laurent   (review date 31 January 1982)

[*In the excerpt below, Laurent argues that Davis neglects to offer solutions to the problems of sexual and racial inequality outlined in* Women, Race, & Class.]

The moral majority is on the offensive. Ronald Reagan is celebrating his first year in the White House. The Left is still picking up the pieces and learning the lessons of its near dissolution in the '70s. And the women's movement is torn by dissent over a range of troubling issues from equal rights to welfare rights to the rights of lesbian mothers.

It's an opportune moment for Reagan's old nemesis Angela Davis to remind us that to break the contemporary impasse we must mine history for insights and guidance. **Women, Race & Class** is a collection of 13 essays by Davis on the most problematic of the historic divisions rending the women's movement. In it she places in context the often acrimonious debate over the whiteness and elitism of feminism.

Davis traces a disgraceful history of racism and betrayal of black women by the predominantly white women's movement of the 19th and early 20th centuries. She notes the absence of black women at the first women's rights convention at Seneca Falls in 1848. She details the rapid growth of racism in the movement after the Civil War when the Republican party moved to enfranchise black men to ensure Northern control of the South. Davis quotes abolitionist and leader of the women's rights and suffrage movements, Elizabeth Cady Stanton, on black male suffrage: "It becomes a serious question whether we had better stand aside and let 'Sambo' walk into the kingdom first."

Stanton's compatriot Susan B. Anthony said of the Fifteenth Amendment, "I will cut off this right arm of mine before I will ever work for or demand the ballot for the Negro and not the woman."

Davis follows this strain of racism as it wends its way through the history of women's struggles. In 1909 Gertrude Stein characterized one of her female characters as possessed of "the simple promiscuous unmorality of black people." Birth control pioneer Margaret Sanger fell prey to the white race salvationist theories of eugenics and in 1919 advocated, "more children from the fit, less from the unfit."

Women, Race & Class also treats the exclusion of white and black working women's concerns from the agenda set by the doctors' and preachers' wives who ran the women's rights movement. Davis describes conditions in the early textile mills whose workers were for the most part black and immigrant women: "Incredibly long hours—twelve, fourteen or even sixteen hours daily; atrocious working conditions; inhumanly crowded living quarters." The primary interest of these women in working conditions and wages was largely ignored by suffragettes like Stanton and Anthony who encouraged women to cross the picket lines of striking workers to gain entry into new trades.

Black women suffering under the double oppression of racism and sexism saw early that they needed far more than just the vote. Davis grimly reminds us that, "after the long-awaited victory of woman suffrage, Black women in the South were violently prevented from exercising their newly acquired right."

Never one to shy from struggle, Angela Davis conjures up the images of black women fighting to educate their children, surreptitiously under slavery and openly under segregation. She devotes a too brief chapter to the Black Women's Club movement organized in 1892 in the aftermath of a speaking tour by Ida B. Wells. Wells, a remarkable black newspaper publisher and reporter, spent her life building an international campaign against lynching. In . . . "Communist Women," Davis celebrates the lives of five other activist women, among them Wobblies Lucy Parsons and Elizabeth Gurley Flynn.

While Davis' treatment of the early years of women's rights offers little new information, it is a well-documented compilation of information vital to the discussion of the movement's current problems. Her comments on recent history, however, seem curiously dated, almost as though she's been out of the country since the late '70s.

Davis repeats the now familiar charge of racism against Susan Brownmiller for her 1975 book, *Against Our Will: Men, Women and Rape.* She also justly excoriates Jean MacKellar for her claim in *Rape: The Bait and the Trap* that over 90 percent of all rapes are committed by black men.

About the "myth of the black rapist," Davis observes that it has been used to imprison and execute black men since slavery began. From 1930 to 1967, 405 of the 455 men executed for rape convictions were black. Black women have not joined the anti-rape groups because their white members are insensitive to the danger of the myth, according to Davis.

On reproductive rights, Davis reveals the ugly cooperation of birth control advocates with the Eugenics Society. She explains the absence of black and Puerto Rican women from the ranks of the pro-choice movement. These women were suspicious of an abortion rights movement which failed to address their serious concern with sterilization abuse. Davis quotes a 1970 Princeton University study which showed that 20 percent of all married black American women had been sterilized. Thirty-five per cent of all Puerto Rican women of childbearing age had been sterilized by the 1970s according to Linda Gordon's *Woman's Body, Woman's Right,* quoted by Davis.

Despite its factual abundance, *Women, Race & Class* is ultimately disappointing because it is incomplete. By failing to focus on ways to mend and reinvigorate the movement, the book becomes merely a gathering of disparate essays. While Davis calls repeatedly for the overthrow of monopoly capitalism and its replacement with socialism, she hardly suggests how racism and sexism are to be overcome in the progress toward a new society. Perhaps a longtime affiliation with the Communist Party has limited her view, for she also fails to present a vision of an authentic American socialism. . . .

No doubt Angela Davis will soon update and complete her analysis of race, class and the women's movement. Her experience and scholarship will then give her recommendations great resonance. Meanwhile, the point is not just to understand the historic failings of the women's movement, but to remedy them.

> *Anne Laurent, "Race against History," in* Book World—The Washington Post, *January 31, 1982, p. 10.*

One of the most important things that has to be done in the process of carrying out a revolutionary struggle is to merge those two different levels, to merge the personal with the political where they're no longer separate.

—Angela Davis, in an interview excerpted in Life, *11 September 1970.*

Jacqueline Jones (review date 20 February 1982)

[*Jones is an American historian and educator who has written extensively on history, race relations, and cultural and ethnic issues. In the following essay, she examines the strengths and weaknesses of* Women, Race, & Class.]

"The uplift of women is, next to the problem of the color line and the peace movement, our greatest modern cause. When, now, two of these movements—woman and color—combine in one, the combination has deep meaning." So wrote the great scholar-activist W. E. B. Du Bois in his 1921 essay "The Damnation of Women." Du Bois realized that three vital strands of American history—

race, gender and class—were entwined within the experiences of black women and that a better understanding of those experiences would reveal the underpinnings of American society.

Yet despite the burgeoning literature on Afro-American history, women's history, labor history and family history, black women remain a neglected group. Feminist scholars have explored the connection between work and the family, but for the most part they have concentrated on white women. Historians of Afro-American culture tend to focus on men in their discussions of slaves, freed people or blacks in general.

Contrary to the implicit assumptions of social historians, black women are not an anomalous group in either black or women's history. Rather, their story reveals a good deal about the oppression of all blacks (regardless of gender), the roles of all women (regardless of race) and the status of all workers (regardless of race or gender).

In her new book, *Women, Race and Class,* Angela Davis seeks to redress this historical imbalance and at the same time to indict the system of "monopoly capitalism," which, she charges, is responsible for the exploitation of black women in their dual roles as wage earners and homemakers. In thirteen essays covering the period from slavery to the present, she explores the sporadic alliance between the black liberation and the women's rights movements. Specifically, she shows how the women's rights campaign of the nineteenth and early twentieth centuries was confined by a white middle-class bias that deprived it of any potential for effecting revolutionary change. Too often, white women—even "liberals" on the race issue like Elizabeth Cady Stanton—believed their own interests to be in conflict with and more important than those of blacks.

This book represents Davis's second major contribution to the field of black women's history. In her insightful article **"Reflections on the Black Woman's Role in the Community of Slaves"** (*The Black Scholar,* December 1971), she suggests that slave women, in carrying out their community and family responsibilities, built a "house of resistance" in the midst of degradation and violence. (Davis's argument about the historical and political significance of slave family life in some respects presaged Herbert G. Gutman's monumental work, *The Black Family in Slavery and Freedom, 1750-1925.*) The article, completed while she was being held in the Marin County, California, jail, demonstrates that she (a philosopher by training) perceived the study of Afro-American history to be a political act in itself.

At the beginning of *Women, Race and Class,* Davis concedes that she approaches her subject as a lay historian. Still, her work must be judged as a piece of historical scholarship. In it she seeks to advance the cause of socialism by exposing the mistakes and the narrow-mindedness of past reformers. To this end she has compiled much useful information not easily obtained elsewhere. She has included chapters on the link between abolitionism and women's rights; the domination of the women's suffrage movement by white women, most of whom launched rac-

ist attacks on enfranchised black men in order to further their own cause; the racist beliefs of early twentieth-century proponents of birth control and abortion. She also describes the pioneering efforts of white and black women and men (Ida B. Wells, Frederick Douglass, the Grimké sisters) to emancipate women as well as people of color. She has sections on the black women's club movement, on Communist women and on the ways in which the "myth of the black rapist" was used to justify the physical abuse of both black men and women.

Davis's work deserves a wide readership, for her ideas about the racist edge of various forms of the American women's movement are sound. Nevertheless, she has not always been careful in her research and writing. In view of her polemical ends, several of her mistakes are especially ironic. For example, Davis lauds the Wobblies for their egalitarian approach to union organizing, yet she consistently refers to the group as the International (instead of Industrial) Workers of the World. In another instance she hails the "unity and solidarity" of "Black and white women [who] together led the post-Civil War battle against illiteracy in the South." Yet she fails to realize that the white women involved in this crusade—the Northern teachers of the freed people—tried to impose their own bourgeois notions of individualism, self-control and time discipline on a folk who had a cooperative and anti-materialistic culture. There is precious little evidence of compassionate understanding or honest friendship between members of the two races, although they shared a commitment to black "education."

The book's title suggests that it will deal with the trilogy of forces that have shaped American society, but Davis is principally concerned with the issue of race. White working-class women, and the oppression they share with black women, are barely mentioned. In her eagerness to castigate middle-class reformist organizations for their racism, Davis glosses over the racist policies and rhetoric of workers' and radical groups. When she does find evidence of racial antagonism among workers, she assumes that it "was consciously planned by the representatives of the economically ascendant class." This superficial analysis of American working-class history masks the complex tensions between groups which were united by their experience of economic exploitation, yet divided by ethnic, religious, racial and gender prejudices.

At this late date we hardly need another book that documents the racism of white reformers, even those with impeccable liberal credentials. The more daring and demanding task before Davis was actually to examine the issues indicated by her title. How, in fact, do "racism and sexism frequently converage," and why is "the condition of white women workers . . . often tied to the oppressive predicament of women of color"? How do we explain the male supremacist ethic within black (as well as white) family life and political movements? Curiously, Davis fails to deal with the black power movement of the 1960s and with Stokely Carmichael's infamous description of the desired position of women within it ("prone"). She describes the rape issue as a racist ploy designed to terrorize black men, without acknowledging that black rapists attack women of their own race. But even had she addressed the themes announced in her title, the absence of a coherent theoretical framework in **Women, Race and Class** would doubtless have made her discussion of these issues unsatisfactory.

Perhaps the most challenging issue not raised in the book involves the relations between black male and female family members. Historically, American capitalism has stressed personal ambition and material success for white men while systematically denying both to black men. (The strength and endurance of nineteenth-century black family life has been well established by Gutman and others; it is a waste of Davis's time and energy to browbeat Harriet Beecher Stowe and Daniel Patrick Moynihan.) Ultimately, the role of the black family under American capitalism presents a thorny problem for feminists, black activists and socialists alike. For if, as Davis showed in **"Reflections on the Black Woman's Role in the Community of Slaves,"** the black family has served as a bulwark against racism, then it cannot be dismissed (as she dismisses domesticity in general) as an example of counterrevolutionary privatism.

Over the years, millions of black women—domestics, factory workers and field hands—have yearned, in the course of their long and ill-paid work days, to stay at home with their children. It is unlikely that they would have agreed with Davis that "the assembly line is doubtlessly the most powerful incentive for women to press for the elimination of their age-old domestic slavery." To care for one's own family without interference from slaveholders, welfare bureaucrats or "workfare"-minded politicians is the freedom that black women have struggled for throughout their history in America. They have perceived the nurturing of their children as an "oppressive predicament" only insofar as they have been denied the time and the financial resources to do it to their satisfaction. Nevertheless, Davis asserts that the shifting of housework and child-care from "[women's] shoulders to the society" constitutes one of the "radical secrets of women's liberation." Her contention that housework is rapidly becoming "obsolescent" indicates that, among American Communists, hope continues to spring eternal.

In **Women, Race and Class,** Angela Davis makes clear her belief that black liberation is a more crucial matter than women's rights (the latter issue she identifies almost exclusively with middle-class white women). But in these days of federally subsidized racism, persistent opposition to the Equal Rights Amendment and calls for workers to renounce hard-won benefits and wage increases, we should avoid placing the rights of one group over those of another. Hierarchical power systems based on race, class and gender are mutually reinforcing and equally oppressive. (pp. 213-14)

> *Jacqueline Jones, "Three Strands of History," in The Nation, New York, Vol. 234, No. 7, February 20, 1982, pp. 213-14.*

Gloria I. Joseph   (review date Autumn 1983)

[*In the essay below, Joseph praises* Women, Race, &

Class *as a well-documented historical account of women's struggles, but faults Davis for overlooking the contributions of twentieth-century feminist and lesbian critics.*]

Angela Davis's **Women, Race and Class** could readily be subtitled, "Twentieth-Century Feminists Marching to the Beat of Nineteenth-Century Feminism and Getting Nowhere Fast." Davis, a superb historical scholar, discusses the history of Black and white women's struggles to remove the economic, social, and sexual shackles that have traditionally restricted their freedom. Her well-documented, perspicacious account demonstrates parallels between the debilitating, internecine effects of racism and classism within the nineteenth-century and contemporary women's movements.

Davis justly acclaims the accomplishments of early feminist leaders Elizabeth Cady Stanton, Susan B. Anthony, Lucy Stone, and Margaret Sanger. At the same time she reveals "how defenseless they remained—even after years of involvement in progressive causes—to the pernicious ideological influence of racism." Davis insightfully shows how twentieth-century feminists have failed to move beyond the racism and classism of their predecessors. She validly criticizes the works of Susan Brownmiller, Jean MacKellar, Diana Russell, and Shulamith Firestone for their contributions to racist myths.

The author's description of the Black club women of the 1800s, along with outstanding figures like Ida B. Wells, Mary Church Terrell, Josephine St. Pierre Ruffin, Sojourner Truth, Lucy Parsons, and Mary Talbert, attests to the fact that Black women were working for the benefit of their race as well as for all women. Unfortunately, modern Black feminists and Black lesbian feminists are not mentioned. The inclusion of their contributions would have been an important and noteworthy complement to the attention Davis gives to Black women's historical struggle for equal rights.

Another omission concerns the [essays] detailing the impact of the experiences of Black women, white women, working-class and middle-class women on the women's movement. These sections contain frequent references to Black male scholars such as W. E. B. DuBois and Frederick Douglass. From a Black feminist perspective it would have been refreshing to hear more about the accomplishments of Black women, particularly Sojourner Truth, a visionary concerned with removing the barriers to freedom for all.

Davis employs a Marxist analysis throughout the book. While there may be little doubt that a Marxist analysis can be more productive, progressive, and capable of bringing about some modicum of equality for the working classes, Davis's argument is weakened by her tendency to use materials selectively to substantiate her claims while ignoring information that points to other possible conclusions. For example, in her final [essay], **"The Approaching Obsolescence of Housework: A Working Class Perspective,"** Davis argues forcefully but unconvincingly for the socialization of housework and child care on the grounds that it can help end the separation of domestic life from economic production that prevails under capitalism. Her condemnation of capitalistic greed and her assessment of housework as unstimulating, uncreative, and nonproductive drudgery form the basis of her argument. As proof of the deadly effects of housework she cites the destruction of the main character in Ousmane Sembene's film, *Black Girl*, who "is so overwhelmed by her despair that she chooses suicide over an indefinite destiny of cooking, sweeping, dusting and scrubbing." More accurately, the dehumanization of the young African woman is brought about by her white employers' total disregard for her African traditions and religious beliefs, combined with psychological depression resulting from her employers' conceptualization of her as an object to be capriciously manipulated.

Contrary to the evidence Davis presents, housework in and of itself need not be drudgery. Only its devaluation and its repetitiveness make it undesirable. Household maintenance once or twice a week can offer a welcome balance to routine office, factory, or classroom work. Similarly, rewards can be gained from having and raising children. From someone as analytically astute as Davis, the attempt to force facts into a specific political framework is disconcerting.

These minor criticisms in no way detract from the value of the book as a scholarly contribution to the academic disciplines of history, sociology, economics, Black studies, and women's studies. . . . **"Rape, Racism and the Myth of the Black Rapist"** should be required reading for all students in women's studies programs. By tracing historical changes in the treatment of the subject, Davis offers an outstanding explanation for the complexity of the social context of rape today.

Far too few white feminists realize the extent to which they have internalized racist ideologies or the degree to which their white solipsism operates. Pretentious and incomplete analyses concerning rape and sexism from authors such as Susan Brownmiller perpetuate the dogmatic, unsubstantiated claim that rape is the worst crime perpetrated against women and sexism the ultimate oppression.

Davis's book is extremely important for twentieth-century feminists concerned with building coalitions between Black and white women. Mainstream white feminists must realize that feminist theory, feminist organizing, women's conferences, and women's studies courses generally lack an ideological philosophy capable of systematically encompassing the histories, experiences, and material needs of Black and working-class women. As Black and working-class women become increasingly aware of this neglect, many have come to feel that coalitions are not in the cards. Those clubs and spades keep getting pushed around and shuffled to the bottom of the deck, while the dealers keep dealing from the top. Davis conveys this message well. (pp. 134-36)

> *Gloria I. Joseph, in a review of "Women, Race and Class," in* Signs, *Vol. 9, No. 1, Autumn, 1983, pp. 134-36.*

In terms of the sociology of minorities Angela Davis's story is of the next stage beyond the ghetto; not yet, it is true, the stage of the systematic extermination-camp, but somewhere reasonably far along that road, where the Black Panthers and any other group which thinks that the lesson of Watts and all the other smouldering ghettoes is to take up arms and defend itself can be systematically eliminated.

> **—*Ernest Krausz, in his "Ghettoes and Beyond," in* The Times Literary Supplement, *12 November 1971.***

Angela Davis (lecture date March 1987)

[*In the essay below, which Davis originally presented in March 1987 at a Harvard University conference entitled "Poetry and Politics: Afro-American Poetry Today," Davis examines the relationship between art, aesthetics, and politics in the African-American community.*]

I was asked to reflect upon some of my experiences during the sixties and to suggest on the basis of those experiences what I see as some of the major political and aesthetic challenges of the eighties. But I want to go back to the forties for a moment to talk about an experience I had as a very young child. I think I must have been about three years old when my mother took me to a reading by Langston Hughes. My mother tells me that I was absolutely enthralled by his poetry, and that afterwards, when she took me up to meet him, I audaciously informed him that I could also recite poetry. "Mary had a little lamb" was the evidence I hastened to present to him. And to this day, forty years later, I cannot reflect upon that episode in my life without feeling utterly embarrassed.

My embarrassment emanates from the fact that I had nothing more substantive to offer this great poet of Afro-American liberation than "Mary had a little lamb." It emanates from the fact that at that young age—as continues to be the case with many people who have grown to maturity—I thought that poetry was only about form and technique, not about substance. Thus, in my eyes, I could offer him "Mary had a little lamb" in exchange for "The Negro Speaks of Rivers" or "The Negro Mother," as if there were some fundamental kinship between them by virtue of the poetic form. Why didn't I think to recite or sing, for example, one of the many spirituals I had learned in Sunday school and church? Years later when I read Langston Hughes' manifesto, "The Negro Artist and the Racial Mountain," I was once again reminded of my own personal encounter with him, and upon reading the first paragraph of that essay, I began to more clearly understand the source of my embarrassment.

"One of the most promising of the young Negro poets," Langston Hughes said,

> said to me once, "I want to be a poet, not a Negro poet," meaning, I believe, "I want to write like a white poet," meaning subconsciously, "I would like to *be* a white poet," meaning behind that, "I would like to be white." And I was sorry the young man said that, for no great poet has ever been afraid of being himself. And I doubted then that, with his desire to run away spiritually from his race, this boy would ever be a great poet. But this is the mountain standing in the way of any true Negro art in America— this urge within the race toward whiteness, the desire to pour racial individuality into the mold of American standardization, and to be as little Negro and as much American as possible.

This message announced the beginning of a Renaissance in the literary and visual arts of the twenties. And one of its clearest implications was that the great Black poet would never seek to ignore or evade politics because that would mean that the poet was seeking to dismiss the significance of the historical experience of her or his people. And of course Afro-American artists have been repeatedly criticized because the content of their work has involved the politics of Black liberation. They have been called provincial, meaning that their work, in focusing on the specifics of the Afro-American experience, fails to achieve the universality required by great art.

But then, of course, in a larger sense politics has been considered anathema to art in the United States, and especially since the experience of the thirties. Robert Bly once asked the question, why have so few American poems penetrated to any reality in our political life? "I think," he said, "one reason is that political concerns and inward concerns have always been regarded in our tradition as opposites, even incompatibles." For Black artists, however, the politics of racism have always conditioned inward concerns even for those who have denied the racial or national character of their work.

Looking back on the history of Black people in America, it is hard to deny that periods characterized by mass political movement have also been periods of aesthetic renewal and resurgence. The civil rights era reawakened the music which had initially arisen among our enslaved ancestors. The political militance of the late sixties served as a catalyst for the literary and visual arts.

In 1965, when the Watts rebellion occurred, marking a new phase in the movement for Black equality, I was doing graduate studies in Europe. As a philosophy student, much of the work I was doing focused on aesthetics. When news of the Black movement motivated me to interrupt my studies there and to return to this country to directly participate in Black community organizing, I drew no connection at all between my philosophical interests in art and my desire to become a political activist. But like so many of the activists of that era, I instinctively understood that our movement would have been seriously lacking without our poets, without our musicians, our Sonia Sanchezes, Amiri Barakas, June Jordans. Nina Simone's "Mississippi God Damn" and Max Roach's and Abbie Lincoln's "Freedom Suite" were as indispensable to our work as our rallies and demonstrations.

Yet I think we tended to take the artists of our movement for granted, perhaps in the same way that Black people take the music and poetry which has always permeated our lives for granted. It was simply there as it had always been there. It may have been that we recognized the extent to which the new collective political courage of our community gave birth to a more politically courageous art. But I don't think that most of us grasped the extent to which this poetry and this music had rendered our psyches receptive to the difficult requirements of the political struggle during those days. In order to persevere through the veritable war which was being waged against the Black community, we very clearly needed our cultural and aesthetic nourishment. We needed our painters and our poets and our songsters.

As I look back on that period of the late sixties, I realize how much I suffered from our collective failure to contend with the deleterious influence of sexism within our movement. I never doubted my own unshakeable commitment to stand together with my brothers as a soldier in the war against the deadly racism of that period. But I was also passionately opposed to the attitudes many of them expressed about their inherent masculine right to relegate their sisters to an inferior place in the struggle. Some went so far as to say that as women we were supposed to be content with the role of inspiring our men and bearing and educating their children.

I remember how utterly confused and frustrated I felt when I received a message, when I was a graduate student down in San Diego, from some male leaders of a prominent Black organization. The message warned that if I continued to play such a visible role as a Black community organizer I might find myself dead in some back alley. Women were not supposed to be so aggressive, and they were certainly not supposed to be political spokespersons.

What was at issue then was a campaign to protect a young brother who had circulated a petition in the navy accusing the Johnson administration of racism. At that time, he was facing a very serious court-martial. Ironically, I emerged as the spokesperson for that campaign because no one else was willing to do the work. I hardly considered myself a leader and I would have been more than willing to follow the leadership of any Black man at that time who took on the responsibility of organizing the campaign. Yet I found myself the target of an assassination threat because my heart had gone out to this young brother and I wanted to do everything I could to generate support for him within the Black community. For the first time in my life I purchased and carried a gun because I feared that I might be attacked by those Black men who felt threatened by the fact that a woman was emerging as a political leader in the Black movement.

At that time I had not yet conducted any serious scholarly research on the age-old tradition of female leadership in the struggles of the Black community. I did not really know about the pivotal role Ida B. Wells had played in the anti-lynching campaigns of the turn of the century, nor did I know the work of Mary Church Terrell. I did know the names of Sojourner Truth and Harriet Tubman, and I knew that during the early sixties there had been Fannie Lou Hamer and Ruby Doris Robinson and Rosa Parks and Ella Baker. I knew that what I was doing was far from extraordinary, but that I was simply following in the footsteps of my foremothers. And I felt affirmed in what I was doing by a Black woman poet named Mari Evans when she wrote "I / am a black woman / tall as a cypress / strong beyond all definitions still / defining place / and time / and circumstance / assailed / impervious / indestructible / Look / on me and be / renewed."

As a political activist of the 1980s, I can hardly believe that twenty years have already gone by. And I am deeply concerned about the immediate problems we face as we encounter this rising tide of racism directly associated with the forces of the Reagan administration. I know that we must continue to engage in and encourage the kind of grass-roots political organizing which brought so many people into the arena of struggle during the sixties. And along with many other veteran activists, I continue to organize against racist violence, police crimes, prison repression; for jobs; for women's equality; for peace; for international solidarity with our sisters and brothers in South Africa, Central America, the Middle East.

But I also want to talk about some of the cultural forces which have shaped and continue to affect us as a people. And I am specifically, at this time, interested in the historical role music has played as a powerful social and political force in our lives and in our struggles. My own interest in the political dimension of Afro-American music has evolved in a very direct fashion from my groping efforts during the late sixties and early seventies to assist in the resuscitation of some awareness of women's roles in Black peoples' struggles for liberation. My research led me directly from Ida B. Wells to Gertrude "Ma" Rainey, from Mary Church Terrell to Bessie Smith, from Claudia Jones to Billie Holiday. And I began to realize that if we truly wished to understand the political legacy forged by Black women, we not only needed to assess the contributions of our sisters who were political leaders, but we also needed to become cognizant of the politics of Black women's music.

Over the last few years I have been attempting to seriously study the role of Black women in forging the blues tradition for the purpose of uncovering the social implications of their music. The work that I am doing now has naturally evolved both out of my political activism and out of the scholarly studies I have undertaken. As a matter of fact, many people find it difficult to believe that I'm interested in music today. "What," I have been asked, "does music have to do with politics?" And I think I understand the confusion because if someone had told me in 1967 that I would be studying music in 1987, I probably would have had the same reaction.

When I was a young soldier for freedom, an activist of the sixties, in my twenties, I was convinced that the revolution was going to arrive tomorrow. No one could have convinced me that our marches, our rallies, our demonstrations were not going to immediately usher in a new revolutionary social order. We had our poets, our songsters. But at that time, it seems to me, we demanded that they be judged by the very same criteria as we judged ourselves, by the immediate requirements of our political creations. Their aesthetic vision had to conform to the immediacy of our political goals. And indeed, in order to be a political artist, we demanded that the poetic or musical content be political in an immediately and literally discernible fashion.

Of course, we do need the poems and the murals and the songs and the novels that educate us in a literal way about our contemporary political realities. But at the same time we cannot dismiss as apolitical those works whose social and political implications may not be so immediately visible. And I want to take just one example from the work that I am doing now, an example taken from some studies on Billie Holiday. Most people understand the pivotal political function of a song like "Strange Fruit" which was recorded in 1939, with respect to creating a broad awareness, a broader awareness of the inhumanity of racist violence. But I would argue that we could also discover wrathful politics in her love songs. The aesthetic rescue by Billie Holiday of so many of the current popular tunes, which would have otherwise drowned in the commercial mediocrity of the capitalist market, made her a powerful advocate for human freedom. And many who were so profoundly moved by her singing—and this continues to be the case today—no doubt instinctively grasped what she was about. While she may not herself have been aware of this, her aesthetic transformations directly parallel the creations of her enslaved ancestors who generations ago had offered the gift of Negro spirituals to the world.

One of the very earliest songs Lady Day recorded in 1935 with Teddy Wilson and his orchestra is called "What a Little Moonlight Can Do." This was an utterly unnoteworthy tune from a British musical, whose words are as follows:

> ooh what a little moonlight can do
> ooh what a little moonlight can do to you
> you're in love, your heart's a-fluttering
> all day long you only stutter
> cause your poor tongue just will not utter
> the words "I love you."
> ooh what a little moonlight can do
> wait awhile, for a little moonbeam comes
> peeping through
> you'll get bold
> you can't resist him
> and all you'll say
> when you have kissed him
> is, "ooh what a little moonlight can do."

Now if you recall the way in which Billie Holiday sings this song, as a result of the aesthetic form she confers on this rather trite song about love under the cliché spells of the moon, and as a result of the emotional impact it acquires under the profound spell of her music, it becomes an authentic commentary on human love. And in her statement on love, Billie Holiday sings into "What a Little Moonlight Can Do" such complex layers of emotional meaning that her message reaches far beyond the limits of individual romantic heterosexual love. Indeed, she seems to follow her music toward a realm where the nature of human relations in general is fundamentally conditioned by love. It is as if the theme of the lyrics, the transformative power of moonlight, is explored by her music in such a powerful symbolic way that the lyrics lose their significance. The music itself becomes a process of negation which annuls the literalness of the lyrics, thus purging the song of its content. In this way the song's form is set free to receive a new, more complex and more profoundly human content, the content forged by the magical musical instrument which is Lady Day's voice.

Pursuing the social implications of this process, it can be said that the negation of the lyrics contains another hidden negation, a call to overthrow the social order which is mirrored in the superficiality of the song's words. I would even venture to suggest that there is a hint of revolutionary meaning in that higher, more human love announced by the music. For as love is to provide the connecting force of human relations in general, then the old society with its attendant relations of domination and oppression must certainly be overthrown and replaced with the new harmonious social order. In "What a Little Moonlight Can Do," Billie Holiday extends an invitation to us to ascend on the notes of her music to a place where we can catch a brief glimpse of human love and light.

That she was not herself conscious of this process and probably never reflected on her music in these social terms, does not in any way invalidate the interpretation. Indeed, it is her absolute brilliance as an artist which draws her to offer us social insight which she herself could never understand or reveal to herself. As an artist, she gives us music, her music as the context for an aesthetic experience. It allows us to glimpse a new and different order founded on freedom and love. To be sure, what we see is an aesthetic illusion, but perhaps it can inspire us to work toward the social realization of this revolutionary social order.

Someone once said that poets are never liberals or conservatives. They are always radicals or revolutionaries. And this is especially true of Afro-American artists. For the Black aesthetic, in its overt as well as camouflaged forms, has always been an aesthetic of resistance. Now is the time to invite all of our poets to return to the fold. Historically, our poets have been *griots*, spokespersons, advocates for the community. At a time when racist violence is erupting around the country, when the Reagan administration encourages systematic attacks on all of the victories against racism won by the struggles of the last three decades, we need to call upon our artists to nourish our hearts, to refine our consciousness, and to arouse us to collective action. We need to become activists against racism, activists against sexism, activists against economic injustice. We need to challenge homophobia, ageism, prejudice against the disabled. We must act against US aid to counterrevolution in Nicaragua, and against US support for apartheid in South Africa. We must act in support of Palestinian liberation. We must all become activists who resolutely oppose the policies of the Reagan administration which daily thrust humanity closer to the brink of nuclear armicide.

Our poets should heed the words of their sister June Jordan, who once said,

> I am for the continuance of all life, and hence, I oppose nuclear weaponry, genocide and every form of domination. I believe that life demands an always vigilant dedication to justice. And that justice depends upon the absolute support of self-determination everywhere in the world. As a poet, I express what I believe and I fight against whatever I oppose in poetry.

> (pp. 1, 21)

Angela Davis, "Strong beyond All Definitions . . . ," in The Women's Review of Books, *Vol. IV, Nos. 10-11, July-August, 1987, pp. 1, 21.*

Davis on reading Marx's *Communist Manifesto*:

I read it avidly, finding in it answers to many of the seemingly unanswerable dilemmas which had plagued me. . . . Like an expert surgeon, this document cut away cataracts from my eyes. The eyes heavy with hatred on Dynamite Hill, the roar of explosives, the fear, the hidden guns, the weeping Black woman at our door, the children without lunches, the schoolyard bloodshed, the social games of the Black middle class, Shack I/Shack II [her segregated school], the back of the bus, police searches—it all fell into place. What had seemed a personal hatred of me, an inexplicable refusal of Southern whites to confront their own emotions, and a stubborn willingness of blacks to acquiesce became the inevitable consequences of a ruthless system which kept itself alive and well by encouraging spite, competition, and oppression of one group by another. Profit was the word: the cold and constant motive for the behavior, the contempt and the despair I had seen.

Angela Davis, in her autobiography Angela Davis, *Random House, 1974.*

Jackie Stevens (review date 27 February 1989)

[*In the following excerpt, Stevens argues that* Women, Culture, & Politics *is an ineffective attack on capitalism because of Davis's failure to offer solutions to the problems of racism or speak of her own experiences.*]

Political leaders often need to use the broad stroke, to master the art of making complicated things appear straightforward. Sometimes the goal is to evoke the visceral truths in twenty-second sound bites; at other times, the objective is to reassure the converted at rallies. In books, however, that technique calls attention to itself, as readers notice how the broad strokes avoid complexity, minimize contrasts, perhaps even bore them. There are few surprises for any audience in [*Women, Culture, and Politics*] this collection of speeches and essays written between 1983 and 1988—neither new truths nor affirmations of old sensibilities in new ways. And there is no sign that Davis herself has come to any special understandings since *Women, Race and Class* was published in 1981 (to which *Women,*

Culture and Politics is less a sequel than a re-edited version, with a couple of new scenes thrown in at the end).

Both books contain the same argument: Since the abolitionist movement there has been a coincidence of strategy and ideology between labor and African-American organizations, but feminists inevitably sabotage the alliance. According to Davis, capitalism is the root of all contemporary evil, and feminism has nourished that root. Thus, class analysis alone can lead us through the quagmire of oppressions comprising racism, elitism, sexism and homophobia, and socialism will be waiting for us at the other end.

For instance, in **"Slaying the Dream: The Black Family and the Crisis of Capitalism"** Angela Davis with Fania Davis, her sister, confront Daniel Moynihan's "blame the victim" rhetoric. They write that the high rate of pregnancy among African-American teen-agers

> is a symptom of a deeply rooted structural crisis in the U.S. monopoly-capitalist economy. . . . There is a direct correlation between the unprecedented rates of unemployment among Black teenagers and the rise in the birthrate among Black women under twenty. Yet the Reagan administration's policy shapers consistently formulated the problem of teenage pregnancies in terms that implicitly held Black girls partially responsible for the depressed state of the Black community.

The final sentence of that essay (similar to Angela Davis's conclusion in other pieces) states:

> If we as Black people in the United States want to guarantee that the dream for a better life is realized through our children, we must recognize the importance of setting our sights on a socialist future.

Although there is much to applaud in Angela Davis's focus on the role of monopoly capitalism in the perpetuation of racism and classism, the book leaves important questions unaddressed, to say nothing of unanswered.

Davis's structuralism is like an unassembled Tinkertoy set. All the pieces are there (the defense industry, homophobia, consumerism, sexism, denial, racism), but Davis never puts them together in a coherent model. In the passage on African-American teen-age pregnancy—as in the sections where she observes that sexism, homophobia, racism and classism are cut from the same cloth, and that these patterns can only be destroyed after the socialist revolution—Davis is miserly with the details of causality. Why the correlation between unemployment and teen-age pregnancy? Do people without jobs have sex more often? Do they make different decisions about abortions? Are they dependent on Aid to Families with Dependent Children, which gives them an incentive to procreate (Moynihan's argument)? The same problem arises with respect to other issues. I have my own ideas about the relation between homophobia and racism; why do I have no understanding of the link that, according to Davis, binds them together?

Davis's thesis that capitalist relations harm people is non-

controversial compared with the second of the book's not-so-leit motifs. She states that the women's movement as such has an essentially middle-class (and that means white) agenda, and so has done little to challenge capitalism or racism. In an address to a conference on women and racism, sponsored by the Minnesota Coalition for Battered Women, Davis says of white feminist leaders,

> Their theories and practice have frequently implied that the purest and most direct challenge to sexism is one exorcised of elements related to racial and economic oppression—as if there were such a phenomenon as abstract womanhood abstractly suffering sexism and fighting back in an abstract historical context. In the final analysis, that state of abstractions turns out to be a very specific set of conditions: white middle-class women suffering and responding to the sexist attitudes and conduct of white middle-class men. This approach leaves the existing socioeconomic system with its fundamental reliance on racism and class bias unchallenged.

Even worse, white feminists have been prone to unabashed racist attitudes themselves: "It would not be inappropriate to raise questions concerning the underlying racism of some of Geraldine Ferraro's supporters."

In **Women, Race and Class** Davis offers some especially nasty examples of racist feminists, which clearly inform her assertions in **Women, Culture and Politics.** For instance, Elizabeth Cady Stanton, who was a major actor in the women's suffrage movement, wrote in an 1865 letter to the editor of the *New York Standard*: "If the 2 millions of Southern black women are not to be secured the rights of person, property, wages and children, their emancipation is but another form of slavery. In fact, it is better to be the slave of an educated white man, than of a degraded, ignorant black one."

And yet, if Davis truly believes that feminism per se is irrelevant to socialist revolution, and if the struggle between the sexes is only a distraction, lecturing middle-class feminists on their misconceived priorities is like blaming the pine tree for not bearing acorns. If so-called bourgeois feminist interests are intrinsically opposed to those of proletariat men and women (her jargon, not mine), it is hard to see why she even speaks to these women's organizations. Surely Davis had better speak to the proletariat if she intends to foment a working-class revolution, but there is not a single address to a labor audience in this collection. Seventeen of the eighteen speeches and articles are directed toward white feminists or the African-American middle class. In her earlier work Davis was far less concerned with white feminist racism than with black male sexism. In *An Autobiography,* published in 1974 and just reissued, she criticized black nationalists LeRoi Jones (Amiri Baraka) and Ron Karenga, in part because of what they said and in part because of her experience in working with their political organizations. Indeed, a major topic of letters between Davis and George Jackson, who wrote *Soledad Brother* and was murdered by a San Quentin prison guard, was his previous sexism; Davis expressed more than a little pride in her role in changing his belief that African-American women needed to be subservient to African-American men. The absence in *Women, Culture and Politics* of a single reference to the misogyny of black nationalists such as Eldridge Cleaver, Baraka and Ishmael Reed is confusing and troubling.

Davis's actions speak more complexly than her words. At some level she must recognize that there are indeed progressive forces within feminism that she wishes to encourage. That is not the same as issuing a general appeal to the humanistic impulses in all of us: She makes no speeches to the Rotary Club, for instance. Why is Davis reluctant to elaborate on her tacit commitment to feminism? She seems to assume that her audience is incapable of understanding anything complicated.

Perhaps that is why Davis's voice in this book is not especially compelling. Bent on convincing feminists and others of their evils, Davis can manage only a recitation of statistics and anecdotes. Whether despite or because of the strong polemics, her observations sound thin.

An excerpt Davis quotes from June Jordan's "Poem of My Rights" displays a different way of making an argument. Jordan writes that she feels out of place and fears going out alone. In France, she explains, if the guy doesn't ejaculate it isn't a rape; she compares herself to Namibia, and asks how one knows what it looks like when Pretoria ejaculates. Jordan's writing is effective, and not only because of the power of poetry to show connections. Her political points resonate because they seem to come from an honest construction of her own experience. Davis displays that quality in but a single essay.

That essay is **"Women in Egypt: A Personal View,"** which was Davis's contribution to *Women: A World Report* [1985]. The article is politically informative and provocative not only because of Davis's perceptions but also because of the verbatim quotations from her meetings with Egyptian feminists. Egyptian women were outraged that Davis accepted an assignment to write on women and sex with respect to Egyptian women. Many of the feminists Davis met rejected the Western obsession with the sexual practices of the Third World as racism; but some pointed out that women who are sexually oppressed are stifled in other ways as well. Davis discusses the implications of each position with feeling and intelligence. It is unfortunate that the conundrum of women, culture and politics in the United States does not receive such treatment. (pp. 279-81)

Jackie Stevens, "Talking about a Revolution," in The Nation, *New York, Vol. 248, No. 8, February 27, 1989, pp. 279-81.*

Eleanor J. Bader   (review date Summer 1989)

[*Bader, an American critic and essayist, is the news editor of* New Directions for Women. *In the following essay, she contends that Davis's examination of racism, classism, and sexism in* Women, Culture, & Politics *neglects adequate evaluation of solutions.*]

A truism in community organizing is that both personal and political empowerment are essential for social change. For long-time activist Angela Davis, empowerment has

particular resonance, harkening back to the turn of the century, when the National Association of Colored Women's Clubs created the motto "lifting as we climb" to indicate the responsibility of group members toward others.

Now, as then, there are many to lift. As our sisterhood joins hands with people around the globe who are challenging racism, sexism, homophobia, and imperialism, we are linked one to another, learning as well as teaching, lifting as well as being lifted. And that, says Davis, is the only way for barriers to be broken and communication enhanced.

Davis is partisan. An unabashed communist, she sides with the disenfranchised, the "wretched refuse" struggling to survive in a hostile world. Whether on behalf of the functionally illiterate, the homeless, or the jobless, Davis's commitment is passionate and vigorous; her anger at misguided political priorities is palpable as she rails at a Pentagon budget that she says wastes $41 million an hour, or $700,000 a minute.

In the eighteen essays that make up *Women, Culture and Politics,* Davis argues for a new social order—a socialist one. But she also addresses the difficult issues of racism and classism that have kept North American social movements from being as inclusive as they could be. She hammers away at the elitism that has strained relationships with women in and from the Third World and raises important questions about the unintentional exclusion of women in low-income communities from much of our local work. Her analysis is concrete and pointed.

One particularly instructive chapter describes a trip to Egypt that she made prior to the United Nations Decade for Women Conference in Nairobi. The focus of feminists from the United States on the practice of clitoridectomy as evidence of abysmal conditions of Arab women has, Davis says, inadvertently caused rifts between the two groups and contributed to racist stereotyping.

> Even if it were possible to envision the success of an isolated campaign targeting female bodily mutilation, the fact that Egyptian women represent barely 10 percent of the labor force would remain unchanged. That 71 percent of the female population suffers from illiteracy would be unaltered. The personal status of women with respect to polygamy, divorce and guardianship would remain one of socially enforced powerlessness.

Which is not to say that we need be silent on genital mutilation. Instead, Davis and the Egyptian women she met argue for evaluation of the whole of women's oppression before jumping to conclusions about something that seems odious to those schooled in Western mores.

As right as she is, however, something is missing from *Women, Culture and Politics.* And it is troubling. Although most of Davis's arguments are supported with irrefutable information and figures, her conclusions are often glib and somewhat weak. While racism and classism are thoroughly examined, neither socialism nor communism comes in for the same kind of scrutiny. As a result, many of the essays seem to conclude with a facile, formulaic, "socialism is the answer" simplicity.

Now changes in the Soviet Union are rocking the world progressive movement, and discussion is under way among progressives of all stripes on everything from the Soviet economy to Third World socialism, domestic relationships, abortion, and birth control in the republics of the USSR. The fact that none of these issues is even mentioned is, at the very least, disappointing. Davis indicts capitalism successfully, using the power of numbers to convince us of the casualties resulting from the actions of a callous, reactionary government. Yet the book does not convince us that socialism is, in fact, better suited to meeting human needs.

I believe, as she does, that it is imperative that the United States thoroughly rearrange the economy and eliminate the forces of market manipulation that now reign. But it is not because of Davis that I believe this. And that is too bad; for in the end, convincing us is the responsibility of a political theorist and writer, part of the process of lifting as she climbs.

Eleanor J. Bader, "Mountain Climbing," in Belles Lettres: A Review of Books by Women, *Vol. 4, No. 4, Summer, 1989, p. 20.*

FURTHER READING

Biography

Aptheker, Bettina. *The Morning Breaks: The Trial of Angela Davis.* New York: International Publishers, 1975, 284 p.
    Discusses the events surrounding the Marin County courthouse trial. Aptheker argues that the book represents "a personal account of my experiences in the movement to free Angela Davis" and draws on her notes, trial transcripts, and the files of the National United Committee to Free Angela Davis.

Major, Reginald. *Justice in the Round: The Trial of Angela Davis.* New York: Third Press, 1973, 314 p.
    Examines people and events related to Davis's trial.

Criticism

Anderson, Karen. Review of *Women, Race, & Class,* by Angela Davis. *The Journal of American History* 69, No. 3 (December 1982): 717-18.
    Offers a mixed assessment of *Women, Race, & Class,* noting that the book lacks "new information or theoretical breakthroughs on the issues of race, class, and gender," but provides useful "information on the status, circumstances, and activities of black women, including material on the civil rights activities of club women and other activist black women."

Bardsley, Barney. "Black & Female." *New Statesman* 104, No. 2692 (22 October 1982): 31.
    Review of *Women, Race, & Class* in which Bardsley as-

serts that while Davis's "research is thorough, the conclusions are uninspiring."

Cunliffe, Marcus. "Angela Doesn't Feel Free." *The Guardian* 112, No. 23 (7 June 1975): 14.
    Faults *Angela Davis* for lacking the emotional tone that is characteristic of autobiographical works.

Dennis, Peggy. "Our Political 'Criminals'." *The Nation* 221, No. 4 (16 August 1975): 118-19.
    Includes reviews of *Angela Davis* and Bettina Aptheker's *The Morning Breaks: The Trial of Angela Davis.*

Durbin, Karen. "First Person Impersonal." *Ms.* CXI, No. 8 (February 1975): 38, 40, 42.
    Examines the different personas Davis employs in her autobiography and the volume's lack of insight into her emotional life.

Erickson, Carolly. "Davis Works Over the Founding Mothers." *The Los Angeles Times Book Review* (4 April 1982): 4.
    Laudatory review of *Women, Race, & Class.* Erickson argues: "If the women's movement is to regenerate itself . . . , the roots of that regeneration may lie in the analytical clarity Davis brings to these and more intractable issues."

Giddings, Paula. Review of *Angela Davis,* by Angela Davis. *Black World* XXVI, No. 5 (March 1975): 93-7.
    Discusses the strengths and weaknesses of *Angela Davis.*

"The Path of Angela Davis." *Life* 69, No. 11 (11 September 1970): 21-7.
    Includes a biographical study of Davis's life and reprints quotes from an interview Davis gave in June 1970. This was published at the time Davis was a fugitive charged with murder and kidnapping.

MacPike, Loralee. Review of *Women, Race, & Class,* by Angela Davis. *West Coast Review of Books* 8, No. 2 (April 1982): 56-7.
    Positive review of *Women, Race, & Class* in which MacPike praises Davis's analysis of contemporary feminist issues.

Painter, Nell Irvin. Review of *Women, Race, & Class,* by Angela Davis. *Ms.* X, No. 10 (April 1982): 99.
    Praises *Women, Race, & Class,* calling it an important addition to the neglected field of black women's history.

Wenzel, Lynn. Review of *Women, Culture, & Politics,* by Angela Davis. *The New York Times Book Review* XCIV, No. 13 (26 March 1989): 17.

>   Questions the polemic intent of *Women, Culture, & Politics,* but lauds Davis for her insightful analysis of women in modern societies.

Additional coverage of Davis's life and career is contained in the following sources published by Gale Research: *Black Writers; Contemporary Authors,* Vols. 57-60; and *Contemporary Authors New Revision Series,* Vol. 10.

Ariel Dorfman

1942-

Argentinean-born Chilean novelist, nonfiction writer, essayist, short story writer, poet, playwright, journalist, and critic.

The following entry focuses on Dorfman's works published between 1988 and 1992. For further information on his life and career, see *CLC,* Volume 48.

INTRODUCTION

Dorfman is best known for works in which he examines such topics as exile, life under authoritarian rule, the influence of popular culture on social and political values, and the interaction of power, language, and ideology. Pat Aufderheide has commented: "Like many Third World writers, Dorfman denies the neat division between art and politics; more impressive, he also refuses to collapse the two categories into one."

Born in Buenos Aires, Dorfman was two years old when his family was forced to flee to the United States because of his father's opposition to the Argentine government. Dorfman spent the next ten years in New York City, where his father worked for the United Nations, before the family settled in Chile in 1954. After completing his education at the University of Chile, Dorfman became a naturalized Chilean citizen in 1967. A year later, while working as an activist, journalist, and writer, he published his first book, *El absurdo entre cuarto paredes: El teatro de Harold Pinter,* a critical analysis of English playwright Harold Pinter. Following the overthrow of Chilean president Salvador Allende by Augusto Pinochet in 1973, Dorfman was forced into exile, intermittently living in Argentina, France, the Netherlands, and eventually the United States. As a contributor to English and Spanish journals and a frequent guest on television news programs, Dorfman has remained an active participant in Chile's political and social affairs. He returned to Chile in 1990 after Pinochet relinquished his position to popularly-elected successor Patricio Aylwin.

The interaction of culture and politics is a recurrent theme in Dorfman's nonfiction. In *Para leer al Pato Donald (How to Read Donald Duck: Imperialist Ideology in the Disney Comic)* and *Reader's nuestro que estás en la tierra: Encayos sobre el imperialismo cultural (The Empire's Old Clothes: What the Lone Ranger, Babar, and Other Innocent Heros Do to Our Minds),* Dorfman argues that such forms of popular literature as cartoons, comic books, picture novels, children's stories, and the magazine *Reader's Digest* subliminally promote capitalism and encourage passivity. In his most recent work of nonfiction, *Some Write to the Future: Essays on Contemporary Latin American Fiction,* Dorfman focuses on the themes of repression and violence

in the work of several Latin American novelists. Critics have been particularly impressed with his interpretation of Gabriel García Márquez's magic realism, which Dorfman defined as a cultural experience rather than a literary technique.

Dorfman often focuses on Chilean political life in his fiction and plays. Published the same year as Pinochet's overthrow of Allende, the novel *Moros en la costa (Hard Rain)* questions the value of writing in the midst of mass murder, exploitation, and poverty. *Viudas (Widows)* centers on the struggle between an autocratic government and thirty-six women who suspect that their missing husbands were abducted and killed by the authorities. Although Dorfman set the novel in occupied Greece during the 1940s to avoid censorship, he changed the setting to Chile when he adapted it for the stage. The stories in *Cría ojos (My House Is on Fire)* examine how people retain a sense of hope despite living under a repressive military regime, while *Death and the Maiden,* a play about a woman who believes she has found the man who tortured her years earlier, addresses morality and justice in post-Pinochet Chile.

Although commentators have criticized his short stories as simplistic and unimaginative and his poetry as a mere recording of the horrors of prison and torture, most critics consider Dorfman's narrative techniques in his novels highly original. For instance, *La última canción de Manuel Sendero* (*The Last Song of Manuel Sendero*) combines narratives from several different perspectives: unborn fetuses who refuse to enter a world filled with violence and fear, two exiled Chilean cartoonists and characters within the cartoonists' comic strip, and a scholar who teaches a course thousands of years in the future. Dorfman uses similar techniques in *Mascara,* in which he incorporates the monologues of a voyeuristic photographer, an amnesiac woman with multiple personalities, and a plastic surgeon whose operations eliminate the past and give politicians the faces that the public expects. Concerned with human identity and the paranoia created by authoritarian regimes, *Mascara* has been hailed by critics as an innovative political allegory and has been compared to the work of novelists Franz Kafka and Günter Grass. As Robert Atwan has commented: "[One of] Dorfman's main achievements in fiction has surely been his ability to create methods of storytelling that enact, not merely record, a political vision, [and] that fuse both the political and the literary imaginations."

PRINCIPAL WORKS

El absurdo entre cuatro paredes: El teatro de Harold Pinter
   (criticism) 1968
Imaginación y violencia en América (essays) 1970
Para leer al Pato Donald [with Armand Mattelart]
   (nonfiction) 1972
   [*How to Read Donald Duck: Imperialist Ideology in the Disney Comic,* 1975]
Moros en la costa (novel) 1973
   [*Hard Rain,* 1990]
Ensayos quemados en Chile: Inocencia y neocolonialismo
   (essays) 1974
Superman y sus amigos del alma [with Manuel Jofré]
   (essays) 1974
Culture et resistance au Chile (essays) 1978
Cría ojos (short stories) 1979
   [*My House Is on Fire,* 1990]
Pruebas al canto (poetry) 1980
Reader's nuestro que estás en la tierra: Ensayos sobre el imperialismo cultural (essays) 1980
   [*The Empire's Old Clothes: What the Lone Ranger, Babar, and Other Innocent Heroes Do to Our Minds,* 1983]
Viudas (novel) 1981
   [*Widows,* 1983]
Missing (poetry) 1982
La última canción de Manuel Sendero (novel) 1983
   [*The Last Song of Manuel Sendero,* 1987]
Hacia liberación del lector latinoamericano (essays)
   1984
Dorando la píldora (short stories) 1985

Patos, elefantes y héroes: La infancia como subdesarrollo
   (essays) 1985
Pastel de choclo (poetry) 1986
   [*Last Waltz in Santiago, and Other Poems of Exile and Disappearance,* 1988]
Mascara (novel) 1988
*Widows (drama) 1988
Some Write to the Future: Essays on Contemporary Latin American Fiction (criticism) 1991
Death and the Maiden (drama) 1992

*This drama is an adaptation of the novel *Widows.*

CRITICISM

Marjorie Agosin (review date 2 June 1988)

[*An American poet, educator, and critic, Agosin is the author of* Scraps of Life, the Chilean Arpilleras: Chilean Women and the Pinochet Dictatorship *(1987). In the following excerpt, she maintains that the poems in* Last Waltz in Santiago *lack imagination.*]

Ariel Dorfman is one of Chile's better-known writers living abroad. Like so many others of his generation, he writes fiction and political essays that deal with contemporary Chile and the dictatorship of Gen. Augusto Pinochet. Dorfman's most recent novel, **The Last Song of Manuel Sendero,** describes a generation of fetuses refusing to be born until the political climate of an imaginary country—undoubtedly Chile—changes.

The Last Waltz in Santiago represents Dorfman's attempt to explore through poetry the daily lives of people living under a dictatorship. Intense and colloquial, these verses speak of a world of endless disappearances and torture, as well as the lives of relatives left behind to search for those who have disappeared. It's a symphony of distinct voices: a mother telling her daughter that the missing father is neither dead nor alive; a father hoping his son still lives because someone heard his scream from the torture chambers.

It is difficult to write about the missing, about the howls of those condemned to death, and Dorfman, in this straightforward collection, does not succeed completely. His lyrical voice is not convincing. I am not saying it lacks authenticity, but that these poems seem to have been written to advance a cause or an urgent need to wake up readers concerning the reality and atrocities of a dictatorship. The metaphors don't add up to a vision; the poems are factual accounts of horrors and sorrows of a besieged people.

   Marjorie Agosin, "Latin America Seen through the Eyes of Contemporary Writers," in The Christian Science Monitor, *June 2, 1988, p. 20.*

Cecile Pineda (review date 30 October 1988)

[*Pineda is an American novelist, playwright, short story*

writer, poet, and essayist. In the following review, which first appeared in the Los Angeles Book Review, *she praises Dorfman's novel* Mascara *for its distinctive narrative structure and suggests that the novel is a metaphor for American politics and culture.*]

Ariel Dorfman, the Chilean-born novelist and man of letters, has already established a distinguished career investigating the relationship of words to politics. Two of his works, *How to Read Donald Duck* and *The Empire's Old Clothes* explore the way children's literature and cartoon heroes mold public consciousness. Though within the tradition of political fiction, Dorfman's works have courageously burst the bonds of conventional realistic narrative with its benchmarks of straightforward narrative, character delineation, and historical fidelity. His ability to elaborate ingenious narrative strategies which speak to political realities while at the same time engaging the life of the imagination, and his commitment to creating literature-as-event (in contrast to narration) have lent his work a very unique and welcome kind of distinction.

"So we're finally going to meet, Doctor. Face to face, so to speak." With these opening words, *Mascara,* Dorfman's first novel written in English, establishes its major premises. The work will deliver on its promise of a sinister confrontation (with astonishing results); and the immediacy of its tone will differentiate it throughout as a literary play of event (as opposed to a more conventional narration). What is less readily apparent is that its opening pun hints from the start at a literary strategy which, despite its indirection, will raise what in less consummate hands might remain merely a fantastic thriller, to the level of a political and metaphysical metaphor. As such, *Mascara* places Dorfman in the exalted cultural Parnassus inhabited by [Franz] Kafka and [Kobo] Abé.

Mascara consists of three sections closely resembling monoplays. The personae are a faceless photographer, a plastic surgeon named Marivelli, and the woman, identified only as Oriana, a victim of multiple personality disorder. The first monologue, which occupies very nearly half the book's length, consists primarily of an obsessive harangue directed at Doctor Marivelli. In it, the protagonist describes himself as a voyeur, a clandestine photographer, and an informer whose bureaucratic position in the Department of Traffic Accidents permits him to infiltrate a spreading network of victims-become-accomplices. All his successes, however, are attributable to his self-admitted "invisibility." "Nobody remembered me. . . . The world acted as if I had not been born." His viscerally pornographic, racist, and self-pitying digressions are mercifully interrupted by the arrival of a woman named Oriana who remembers neither her real name nor her past. His diatribe is nearly matched in length by the Doctor's own response.

No run-of-the-mill face cranker, Dr. Marivelli is by his own admission

> a plastic surgeon who had sculpted and sewn up the most pre-eminent faces in the country, the public faces with which the powerful governed . . . the elder ones, that they may continue to reign under the newer faces. And the

youngest, that they may aspire someday to infiltrate the proudest faces of ancient power.

But Dr. Marivelli has a further ability: "My operations have such an incredible degree of success because along with the old skin, they eliminate old habits, the past."

Sandwiched between the voices of what must be two of contemporary literature's more revolting personae, Oriana shows the disturbing signs of multiple personality. Entombed in the mummy case of her walking-talking doll persona, one who is completely forgetful of her past, is the memory of the recording angel who "like(s) the dead, the people who are about to die, (who) hear(s), in the miserable cities where people are not the owners of their own hands, thousands of men, thousands of women who await (her)." The hands she describes are the hands of slaves; the mysterious secret police ("Don't you remember them? A pair of men always in a hurry, blunt, . . . with their knives (and) their photos") are

> the real owners of all the hands in the universe . . . (And) because I remembered them, they would come to take my very own hands, even before I had passed away. . . . I (would have) to witness and watch . . . what those men would do to my hands, . . . stuffing (them) into boiling water, extracting them pale as sheets, without a wrinkle, without a line that could remind anyone of what they had once caressed.

With the persona of Oriana, bordering on the archetype where the exterminating and recording angels meet, Mr. Dorfman bursts the bonds of political allegory as a genre to include the ultimately inviolable territory that exists between death and life, the regenerative Bardo of the universe. In this section above all others he reveals the extraordinary power of his imagination.

Is Oriana's double personality intended to reflect on the one hand the innocent notion we hold of American democracy, undisturbed by covert memories, and, on the other, what happens when, as a result of political repression, the notion of liberty survives only as a memory? Does Mr. Dorfman mean to imply that the manipulators of power and their supporting infrastructure of secret police are ultimately interchangeable? Or that Dr. Marivelli's chameleon name changes are there deliberately to suggest that his number is legion? Has Mr. Dorfman temporarily switched from the Spanish of his native Chile, with its on-going legacy of political terror, in order to address us directly in English? And can it be that in Dr. Marivelli's words *Mascara* encodes some disturbing reminders of our own pre-election masquerade?

Mascara proves to be a marvelously inventive story of suspense. Not only is the fate of the world at stake, but the outcome of a first-class thriller as well. One suspects, however, that what the author admits is a "sort of" epilogue may have been editorially generated to make the book-as-plot more accessible to the hypothetical "average reader." It is to Mr. Dorfman's great credit that he manages to bring off this rather obvious tying of loose ends with such magisterial skill. Because, politically speaking, the story has no end. Secret governments and political repression continue to proliferate. No one is immune. In a clear reiteration of his larger meanings, Dorfman chooses to break off his epilogue abruptly:

TO BE CONTINUED

Cecile Pineda, "The Fiction of Sinister Confrontations," in San Francisco Review of Books, *Spring, 1989, p. 38.*

Robert Atwan   (review date 6 November 1988)

[*In the following review, Atwan maintains that although* Mascara *can be read on several different levels, the novel is ultimately an examination of the paranoia and deception that can arise under authoritarian governments.*]

With the publication of Ariel Dorfman's taut, eerie novel, contemporary American literature welcomes one of Latin America's most versatile writers. Though all his previous books have been published here in translation, *Mascara* is the first he has written in English. A novel of deceit and desire, it is also an excursion into a world where human identity, as in a skillful composite photograph, no longer refers to verifiable identification.

In his previous novels and essays, Mr. Dorfman (a Chilean citizen who teaches literature and Latin American studies at Duke University, and who lives in the United States) has explored the connections between language and politics. Like George Orwell, he has written wonderfully on mass culture and popular literature; his *How to Read Donald Duck* and *The Empire's Old Clothes* are insightful accounts of the way cartoon heroes and children's books shape public consciousness. But Orwell's fictional investigations into language and politics stayed pretty much within the boundaries of conventional realistic narrative. In Mr. Dorfman's work, we encounter a new type of political novel, one that takes enormous risks. He tackles political themes in ways that may seem disorienting to readers accustomed to political novels that depend exclusively upon straightforward narrative, true-to-life characters and historical realism. One of Mr. Dorfman's main achievements in fiction has surely been his ability to create methods of storytelling that enact, not merely record, a political vision, that fuse both the political and literary imaginations. In *The Last Song of Manuel Sendero,* published in the United States [in 1987], Mr. Dorfman pushed the premise of Günter Grass's *Tin Drum* into deeper literary territory. Where Mr. Grass created a 3-year-old protagonist whose protest takes the form of refusing to grow up, Mr. Dorfman weaves into a complex narrative the voices of revolutionary fetuses who refuse to be born.

Mascara, Mr. Dorfman's third novel, is not on its surface a political book. Ostensibly, it is the story of an unnamed character who is born without a recognizable face; no one, not even his parents, even remembers who he is. Practically invisible ("I lived as if I were missing") and a perfect voyeur, he has been obsessed since childhood with photography and lives solely to capture the faces of others. He finds a Kafkaesque job as an assistant to the "archivist of photography files at the Department of Traffic Accidents," where his convenient invisibility coupled with his uncanny memory for faces allows him to compile a personal collection of photographs, "an authentic gallery of human privacy—thousands of faces at their worst, their most intolerable."

This anonymous character, who has systematically destroyed all records of his identity, including fingerprints, has led a miserable life despising the false, recognizable faces of others. Like a 19th-century physiognomist, he believes he can see through the mask of any face into the true character. Featureless himself, he has fashioned an analytical philosophy of the human face. All faces are false from the start. They are scripted from infancy, continually rehearsing the features we invisibly learn from the adult world. Our faces are not so much biological as historical, authorized by society, truly made up: "Human beings are trapped inside the dead faces of their remote ancestors, repeated from generation to generation."

> *Mascara* itself is an intricately layered book. It can be read as an ominous fairy tale, a literary horror story, a post-modern version of Jekyll and Hyde. But the book is also a parable of human identity and paranoia engendered by authoritarian politics.
>
> —*Robert Atwan*

Through his photography, Mr. Dorfman's invisible man can capture moments that disclose the deep hidden faces of others. He "captures" the expression literally, for the photograph becomes an act of possession, usually of erotic possession. His photographs have given him power over people whom he has photographed in compromising situations. But his secret empire begins to dissolve when he falls in love with the woman of his Edenic dreams and is forced to seek help from his physiognomic rival, Dr. Mavirelli.

The photographer needs Dr. Mavirelli's skills as a plastic surgeon to keep the enigmatic woman he loves from becoming "the ordinary everyday person she once was." Oriana—no one is ever sure of her real name—is blessed with what her lover believes is a supreme virtue: her memory has been arrested at the age of 5. He desires an intimacy without the burdens of false identities. It would be the perfect match: "I with no face and she with no past, the two mirrors reflecting nothing more than each the other and the other again." The photographer knows Mavirelli has the skills to perform what he wants, but when he takes a bandaged Oriana to be operated on and meets the doctor face to face he discovers—in a grotesque surprise twist—even deeper layers of self-deception and sinister dominance.

Mascara itself is an intricately layered book. It can be read as an ominous fairy tale, a literary horror story, a post-modern version of Jekyll and Hyde. But the book is also a parable of human identity and paranoia engendered by authoritarian politics. Oriana is hounded by two unidentified investigators; Dr. Mavirelli has been reconstructing prominent public figures, giving them the faces that opinion polls show people expect; and throughout the book there is the recurrence of controlled memories and missing people. Ariel Dorfman has handled these themes directly in his other works. In **Mascara** he takes a more oblique approach to capture the true face of political power.

> Robert Atwan, "He with No Face, She with No Past," in The New York Times Book Review, November 6, 1988, p. 14.

Ariel Dorfman with Peggy Boyers and Juan Carlos Lertora   (interview date Spring-Summer 1989)

[*In the following interview, which took place in December 1986, Dorfman explains how being in exile has affected his writing and discusses the relationship between ideology and art.*]

[*Lertora*]: *As a highly political writer living in exile, do you find there are contradictions between the way you live and the political ideas you espouse? What do you think appropriate political action would constitute for an intellectual in exile?*

[Dorfman]: I prefer not to recommend to other intellectuals what they should do, but I would like to say, in general, that too many intellectuals seem incapable of understanding how difficult it is to radically change things. Perhaps they believe that you can change the world just as you write—not that writing is easy, but it is something that you have real control over, that you can do over and over until it is right. It may be that Vargas Llosa's constant criticism of how things are done is a result of his never having done those things; he has never participated in trying concretely to organize a form of liberation for his own people.

You mean, in Peru?

In Peru or anywhere else. Once he becomes involved in Peruvian politics, as he has recently indicated he intends to do, he will have a sharper sense of the real problems. But to get back to the original question, I am no model for anyone, because I do not live anywhere near the way I would like to live, according to my ideas. This may be the product of years of defeat, you know, having to put as a first priority the fight against the dictatorship in Chile. One has just so much energy, and once a lot of it is spent trying to get rid of Pinochet, there is not much left to change one's own life. Or this may be mere wisdom, that comes with age, the ability to accept ourselves the way we are, not to self-destruct. A long time ago, when I was very young, and perhaps not as radical as I am now, but as impatient, I toyed with the idea that I should go and live in the shanty-towns. But I was not so blind that I could not see that whenever one of my friends did this, dropping out of a more comfortable existence, he would come back with typhoid and have to be nursed to health. Now I have learned that one should not go out of one's way to look for suffering that will make one whole—suffering will come to you, unfortunately, without your looking for it.

But at any rate, early on, I discovered that I was not a saint—there were more sacrifices I was not prepared to make for what I believed in. That does not mean, however, that I or others of my generation can act as if there were not an enormous mass of people in my country and in most of Latin America who are left outside the land, the work, the body of politics and the body of words. There are fundamental conditions that intellectuals cannot fail at least to acknowledge. If intellectuals can use certain forms of their knowledge, of their words, as part of the ongoing social struggle, I am all for it. This participation can assume many forms—it does not automatically mean a contingent subordination to that struggle.

As you understand your own work as an intellectual, as a writer, is all of your work inscribed within this political perspective?

My work is political, to begin with, because my life is very political—and one writes about one's life, right? But there is another way to put it: I am fascinated with power, the way power is distributed and exercised. This is not only a problem of turning one class out and putting another class in. Power is found on many levels and I am particularly interested in the power of the word, the dominant word and the liberating word, the word which has been imposed upon people. I'm interested in the power of Machismo or the power that defines children and makes them act in certain pre-established ways. Power and language are, above all, what draw me as a writer.

> **I do think that there is ideology in everything, but not everything can be reduced to ideology or be explained by it in every aspect.**
>
> **—Ariel Dorfman**

At the beginning of your career as a writer and sociologist, you published an analysis of comic strips, **How to Read Donald Duck.** *Recently in* Contraviento *Vargas Llosa caricatured what he calls the "chic intellectual," in Vargas Llosa's terms somebody who finds ideology in comic strips, in the visit of the Boston Symphony Orchestra to Lima, in films, only then to apply for a Guggenheim fellowship and take up a position in the United States. What do you think about this condition? Does it sound familiar?*

Well, I don't know whether Mario was thinking of me, because he's never said this to me to my face and he's a straightforward person. It's certainly, in any case, a valid question. First, let's talk about the first part of what you asked, about finding ideology everywhere.

Yes, I do think that there is ideology in everything, but not everything can be reduced to ideology or be explained by it in every aspect. When we find ideological patterns in Donald Duck comics, what we are doing is revealing the underlying political message of an apparently innocent piece of entertainment. It's not a coincidence that Donald and his nephews are incessantly rushing off to Third World countries and siphoning off their treasures and suggesting to the savages there how to become successful in the modern world. There is a hidden thesis in Disney's works and in many other mass media expressions—I've studied *Babar the Elephant, The Reader's Digest,* the superheroes, *E.T.*—about development, growth, values. And by pointing that out, you are making a subversive reading of a dominant, official language. But this look underneath, this exploration of what we are being massively fed, does not exhaust the meaning of Donald Duck. He can mean many different things. You can even find forms of social criticism in some comics of Donald. It is, therefore, a caricature of my position to suppose that all I am doing is reducing everything to mere ideology.

But there is a second aspect I'd like to confront in what you said. There is, undoubtedly, a good deal of ideology in art as well. But I don't think that what is good in art is precisely ideology. What makes art so harrowing and liberating is that it is such an anti-ideological form, a form which breaks up ideology. To reduce everything an artist does to his or her ideology is to incarcerate that artist, to exclude him or her—and to prepare the way for doctrines and, who knows, commissars. The best way of answering art that you disagree with is with your own art.

The second part of the question is whether there is a conflict between criticising an empire and living off that empire. You know the argument: why is it that these exiled intellectuals seldom if ever choose to live in the countries they defend, namely Cuba, or the USSR?

In my case, there are a number of quite concrete reasons which may, or may not, be the same for others. For many years, paradoxically, I resisted coming to live in the States—my politics had little to do with my decisions. You see, I had been brought up as a kid in the U.S. and was incredibly involved in American culture. But I said to myself, after the coup, if I go somewhere where I feel that much at home, maybe someday I won't want to go back to Chile—and I needed to tell myself that I would return as soon as possible. I think I subconsciously kept myself—which certainly was not fair to my wife, Angelica, who has accompanied me so faithfully in all our wanderings these years—from settling down. We went to Paris first, and then to Amsterdam and when we finally came here, it was to spend a year in Washington on a Wilson Center Fellowship, where Vargas Llosa, incidentally, was finishing *The War at the End of the World.* I intended to go on to Mexico—where we could bring up our kids in Spanish and where we would be nearer to the struggles of Latin America, but the Mexican government denied me a visa and so we got stranded in the States. But beyond the anecdotal aspect of this decision, it is worth asking what it means to apply for one of these fellowships. I think what matters is that you should not change what you write or what you stand for in order to receive this sort of help. If you ask for one of those fellowships, being who you are, and they give it to you, I see no problem. You just have to be sure enough in what you believe and not sell yourself.

I didn't hide what I was going to write when I applied to work on *The Last Song of Manuel Sendero*—a book narrated by revolutionary fetuses, about exiles who discuss how to deal with defeat after having tried to change Chile under Allende. I didn't cover up the comic book sequences where a country is turned into a laboratory experiment for the multinationals. I wrote what I promised to write in my project. And if I wrote it with money from the country that is considerably responsible for my exile because it intervened with its secret services in my country and destroyed our democracy, well, then maybe there's something fair in that.

But there are other aspects of this supposedly sacreligious journey to the North which should be confronted. People should be free to travel where they want—and the U.S., which is the dominant power in our lives, constitutes an enormous attraction. The influence you can have here in relation to our continent exceeds any influence you can have elsewhere. Not to mention what you can learn! And then, of course, you are not only coming to the country which destabilized your own democratic government. Am I coming to the land which created the Underground Railroad in the last century or the Sanctuary Movement recently? Or am I coming to the land that supports the contras?

[Boyers]: I'd like to come back to the issue we discussed earlier, namely, the connection between ideology and art. Camus once wrote of feeling "more than a writer." Do you feel yourself to be more than a writer? Do you ever fear that your political involvements and activities distract you from your "real work," making you less rather than more than a writer? And is it possible to be only *a writer, now, not just for you, but for other Latin American writers?*

All my life I have been trying to work out a fertile relationship between literature and politics. There have been times when I have felt very comfortable with the relationship I have established and other times when I have lived in real anguish. At this moment, you're catching me in the midst of what I might call a soul-searching crisis. I've been reading Dante a lot: "in the middle of life, I lost my way . . ." I've been wondering about where I go next in my literature and my life. And, as Pepe Donoso is here in our audience, I'd like to bring him into this. Just this year I was having dinner with him in Chile and he asked me what I was busy with and I told him I was writing a long piece for the *New York Times Magazine* and he looked at me and asked—it was a wonderful question: "What for?" And of course I gave him a series of reasons: this was the way of explaining Chile to an enormous audience, this was how I explored the country that had been denied to me for so many years of exile. And all that was true—that article did, in fact, have considerable importance politically in helping to further knowledge about the iniquities of Pinochet and the dilemmas of the opposition, but later I asked myself that very question: "What for? Ariel, why are you writing this?" Because I spent six months on that, perhaps as a pretext not to do other things—it may have been a way of keeping busy while I settled down to what was supposed to be my definitive return to Chile. Up until then I had felt I could do my best immediate political work, my work as a citizen, let's say, as a journalist (or a spokesperson) and that, right next to that, I could explore the deeper relationship between power, language and imagination in my fiction, my poetry and some essays. But I had begun to feel that the immediate tasks of finishing with Pinochet were strangling my possibilities of expressing myself in other dimensions. Not only because the politics is so time-consuming, but because it focuses you excessively on the immediate task and not on the more profound sort of meditation that is needed. What would happen if I wanted to begin to write as if Pinochet did not exist? On the other hand, can I write without taking into account that my country is held hostage? I have coined a phrase for the sort of literature I want to do: socialist irrealism. It sounds better in Spanish, *irrealismo socialista.* Maybe I now have to dip into the real meaning of that phrase.

Do you mean by "socialist irrealism" an attitude that informs your writing with an "unrealistic" hope founded on a utopian ideal rather than on an acknowledgement of what is possible or even likely?

I think the main word there is "hope." Writing itself is an act of extraordinary hope and faith. There is no rational reason why I should have any hope, or why my characters should, or why anybody in this world should. I look at the situation in Chile and I have to agree with Donoso that it's *"la desesperanza."* But at the same time, I do not forget that there was a period in the history of Chile, full of mistakes, full of problems, the Allende years, when the people in my country who had been told all their lives they were nothing and less than nothing, lazy and no good, when those people who had been told that the only way to get out of that situation was for them to compete, when those people decided to take their destiny into their own hands and became the protagonists of History. That is one certainty in a very confusing world: I don't want to betray what I learned from those people. Because if they can do it, those peasants, those workers, the excluded women, then I don't know why I should not be able to do it. History is full of silent people who in fact have created a very vibrant, strong culture of their own. And I have kept, in a corner inside me, the burning sense that that memory, those people, are still alive, that we will one day come to the surface again, step forth from the shadows. This has kept me alive—or should we say perpetually resurrected—during these years.

I see exile as a terrible loss, the pain of being distanced from everything that gives you a meaning.

—*Ariel Dorfman*

And this has to do with exile. I see exile as a terrible loss, the pain of being distanced from everything that gives you a meaning. There are two basic myths that come out of humanity's experience of that loss. One is the foundational myth. You break the past, you rupture the umbilical cord of the past to found a new society. You create something new—no matter what problems that new vision or society or life cause you. And the other myth of exile, the other form of redemption that exile offers, is the opportunity to go back, to return and with what you have learned outside, to renew your original society. One myth speaks of birth, the other of rebirth. I can't believe that our species would have kept those myths of Eden and Utopia alive all these millenia if they had not been the product of profound needs—although later these needs and these myths have been manipulated and sugared and packaged and sold. People have the need for their community, the old one renewed or the new one to be created, a place where they can find some sort of redemption. I would not like someone to come away from reading one of my books and feel that there is no hope for human beings. But I will tell you, when I began *The Last Song of Manuel Sendero,* I started out with a sense of extraordinary despair, trying to find the threads of hope in the midst of that despair. There is no rosy optimism in my stories, in the poems of missing people, in *Widows.* If we are going to overcome, as the song suggests, it's going to be difficult. Nobody guarantees that we can find our way out of these tunnels. You don't know if you can come out of the labyrinth once you've gone into it. And the same goes for the labyrinth of language, which you also explore to find something with which to light your way and that of others. I would not want the horrors of life that I have witnessed or uncovered to contradict the hope I feel about life. Many exiled writers, such as Kundera or Naipaul, find only a desolate barrenness. And if that is how they feel, that is the truth they must tell. But I don't see why people should dismiss my politics because they cannot find, in their lives, the basis for hope. Nor is that hope the rosy and false hope of Donald Duck or the superheroes or the *Reader's Digest* or the ducky optimism of a President Reagan.

There is a passage in Borges about the ideal library in which the books of one's dreams would affirm everything, deny everything, confuse everything. Would you be pleased if readers of **The Last Song of Manuel Sendero,** *for example, came away with that sort of experience of it?*

That novel and much of my work is "open," in the Umberto Eco sense of the term, and that leaves a lot of the interpreting up to the reader. But even though there is a constant mixing of different languages and dimensions of reality, the fairy-tale, the "realistic," the scholarly footnotes, the mass media expressions, this should not be understood as a post-modernist gliding over surfaces all of which have identical value. I think that in the midst of all the confusion, there are certain ethical certainties which guide us or should guide us. I don't impose these on the text, or at least I hope I don't. You know, something similar happens in my second play, **Reader**—which is based on the story you are publishing in *Salmagundi.* The play develops at length, as the story did not, the way in which the person—who is reading and suppressing a book in which he is secretly the central character—confuses fiction and reality, is forced to live the anguish of not being able to distinguish between his fears and his everyday life. In the story I am implying, and in the play I am more than implying, that if you lose your values you will not be able to tell the difference between your inner and your outer life, between the fictions that others weave around you and your own consciousness. It begins by being about a man who is an accomplice in a Latin American dictatorship and ends up by being about a man who lives in a society where the boundaries of reality have evaporated—not that different from what you find in ordinary people in the United States, in fact, where there is not a dictatorship. But in **Reader,** and **The Last Song,** and in **Mascara,** my latest novel, it is the reader who must discover this need for anchoring his reality in certain human values—this is not something I have decided for the reader. There is a difference, at any rate, between telling the reader what to think and how to act, and creating a world and a language complex enough so that he must draw—or be unable to draw, perhaps—his own conclusions.

[Lertora]: *Sometimes, not necessarily in your case, exile favors the writer's career. In what way has exile affected you? Do you think your writing would have been different had you not had to go into exile?*

It would certainly have been different. If I hadn't gone into exile, in fact, my writing would have been so different that it would have been non-existent, because I would have been killed. Later, in fact I did die—my body was found in Chile in 1986 according to newspapers—while of course I was still alive. Perhaps those who read the story I told about this in *The Nation* or *El Pais* will remember the episode. At any rate, to be dead would have affected my writing considerably. But to answer the question about how exile affected me, first let me quickly sketch out my life, because that is related directly to language. I was born in Argentina in 1942; at two and a half, my family went to the States where I spoke only English until I was twelve, when we went to Chile, for many years. I felt an irrepressible nostalgia for the States. It was as if I was exiled from the States, looking back at it, from Chile. But when I finally settled down in Chile, began living deeply in that country, it seduced me—and one woman in particular, who was to be my wife, Angelica, and who is Chilean, enchanted me. I fell in love with a country. And that is the place where I feel the most hope for the future. Even the vices of Chile I feel as if they were my own. In a sense, you could say that I feel at home there. So when I had to leave the country, I left with an extraordinary sense of guilt. Others were dying there, my brothers and sisters in arms (or without arms, in fact, because we were confronting the Junta in a peaceful resistance). And it was also my adopted land, a land I had originally not even wanted to come to. My first writings in exile—after a first period of two, almost three years of shocked silence—were all as if I were still there. My poems (collected in English in **Last Waltz in Santiago**) and the stories (**My House Is On Fire,** forthcoming in English) are written from the perspective of somebody who has not left the country. These writings circulated clandestinely in Santiago, and people would say to me, when they came out, "you're writing as if you were still in the country. How can you know what we're living here?" So my first writing is based upon a refusal to consider myself an exile, to make believe I was back home.

Widows is the first step towards the acceptance of exile.

I wanted a piece of fiction on the disappeared to circulate in Chile and the whole Southern Cone—so I wrote it under a pseudonym, attributing the book to a Danish resistance fighter during the Second World War and set the action in Greece. That double distancing—of mediation through an author who was not me and a country which was not my own—allowed me to write an allegory which is simultaneously realistic, a literary solution to the problem of how to write about overwhelming horror and sorrow. But exile is already structuring the book, its form, its language: the fact that in order to write about a home which was already far in time and space, I had to use indirection and obliqueness.

[Boyers]: *And that is now transformed into a play. What differences are there between the novel and the play?*

Generic differences, to begin—and I spent many years simply trying to work these out. It wasn't until I had effectively destroyed the novel in my head that I could really write the play. I only wrote one version of the novel—with revisions, you know, as I went along, but the version people read is from beginning to end the one I sent to the publisher. On the other hand I must have written some twenty or so finished versions of the play. What to do with the inner life of the characters, their monologues, how to create a chorus, what to do with the magic that in the novel is in the lyrical vision of the characters, but that in the play must function as action and conflict? But there were other, perhaps more interesting problems. For the play to work I decided to set it in Latin America, and therefore to destroy the basic distancing premise that had given a form to the novel. That made it more immediately political—in the most politically ignorant society in the world, the United States. And at the same time I wanted to keep the universality, the fact that this is happening right now, that it happened a thousand years ago, that unfortunately it may well happen tomorrow. For that I had to descend into myth more than I think I did in the novel. And of course there is also the fact that to work on a play, and to write it in English, is in a way to accept that you have a community outside your country, that you are speaking primarily to an audience which is not necessarily the one back home. This can only happen if you have somehow become—perhaps this is not the right word, but here it goes—reconciled to exile, have found out that exile can also fertilize you, be a form of growth.

[Lertora]: **The Last Song of Manuel Sendero** *is openly about exile.*

Yes. I started to write the voice of the fetus, of the son of Manuel Sendero, and around the fourth chapter, another voice, that of Eduardo, the baby's rival, began to attack the fetus, his fairy-tale style, demanding that the real story be told, with people we can identify with, that we can compare to those who lived that period. So a pair of exiles, David and Felipe, were born—in a Mexican traffic jam, which is a terrible place to be born and have to live out your existence forever. I look the dilemmas and sorrows of exile directly in the face there. It was as if I were accepting what had been done to us, what we had done to ourselves, what we had allowed to be done to us in defeat and before defeat by blinding ourselves to reality. But to make sure that readers understood this was, in itself, a construction, and that the mythic world of Manuel Sendero was as real as the supposedly recognizable and immediate world of David and Felipe, I invented a series of footnotes, a sort of academic spoof, which commented on the exiles' dialogue as if it were an extant manuscript discovered by archaeologists thousands of years in the future. That also is related to the way in which time and language are constructed in the novel.

[*Boyers*]: *At least one reviewer of* **The Last Song** *compared it to* The Tin Drum. *I wondered if you had* [*Günter*] *Grass in mind when you wrote your book.*

I admire Grass enormously and his book may have influenced mine significantly. But there was not a conscious attempt to take his basic premise of a child who refuses to grow up one step further by creating a revolution by babies who will not be born until adults show themselves to be responsible. Originally, when I was planning the novel, I had a singer, Manuel Sendero, who had lost his voice in a concentration camp and comes out and finds his wife has fallen asleep. Then I decided it would be more dramatic if she were pregnant and ever so slowly I came to realize that it was the baby that would be telling the story and when the baby began to speak—and I mean this literally, the characters simply take over, to my enjoyment and often to my dismay—he decided that enough was enough, that we mature people had made a total mess of things and it was time for the unborn—who are, after all, at least potentially, the majority—to have a say. And did he have a mouthful!

You've consistently availed yourself of a whole variety of cinematic narrative techniques. Is film as important a medium to you as it has been to Puig and other Latin American writers?

Our whole generation was brought up in a mass media world and film therefore is one of the major influences on our work. But film is not only a technique, a way of organizing perceptions and messages, but also one of the many popular forms of culture which younger intellectuals in the continent share with large audiences. We may often be critical of those forms, but are at the same time immersed in them. There is a bridge there to our public which older generations did not have, not even as a challenge. (pp. 148-60)

In [*the United States*], *and in England, you have been as well known for your journalism as for your fiction. But lately I've not seen you in* The Nation *or* Granta *and I wonder if it's because you've decided to take a break from that kind of writing for a while?*

I've always felt attracted to journalism. In the last few years, I have basically concentrated on Chile as the source of that journalism—because there was an urgent need for information about my country and the struggle for democracy there. Most of this has been a series of endless op eds in *The New York Times, The Washington Post, The Los Angeles Times* and *El Pais* and some more ambitious reporting in the *Village Voice*—which I also reproduced elsewhere, in *Der Spiegel, Le Nouvel Observateur,* etc . . . Once we get rid of Pinochet, I believe—but this may be

a mere daydream—, then I will withdraw from this sort of journalism and perhaps go back to the more reflective work I used to do a couple of years ago. My wife says I will never cease to find causes, that I need to go back to the urgency of journalism and that I'll always be like that. I have, at any rate, a non-fiction book for Pantheon that should be out shortly in which I embark on two parallel voyages, one through contemporary North American media culture and the other through what we could call the counter culture of poverty in Latin America. As that book advances, you'll see excerpts appearing here and there. But I have concentrated a lot on my fiction and my plays in these last years—perhaps as a counterbalance for the need to be extremely immediate and up to date with the writing that deals with the ups and downs of the fight against the Chilean dictatorship. I do think, however, that this journalistic streak will eventually find its way into a novel I have planned after **Mascara**—where the whole problem of the genre of *testimonio* will come up and one of whose protagonists might well be a journalist returning from exile to Chile.

[*Lertora*]: *Most of your journalistic writing has been in English. Does speaking and writing English in this country, where you reside most of the time, affect your Spanish, especially your written Spanish?*

Because I am so thoroughly bilingual that question has been haunting me for some time now. During the early part of my life I wrote in English and never in Spanish; then I reversed myself and said I would write only in Spanish. Exile has forced me—and I mean this literally, because when we got stranded in the States I had to write in English in order to survive economically (we lived on the brink for several years)—to write again in English. I thought, then, that my journalism and many of my essays on mass culture would be in English; and my fiction primarily in Spanish. But from the beginning this was not so. I wrote a lot of journalism for Spanish newspapers and Latin American magazines which I then worked into English; and vice versa. And of course they ended up being quite different versions. The language speaks you, as Alistair Reid once told me. An example: when I wrote that piece on my death for *The Nation,* I began with Mark Twain's famous words about reports of his death being greatly exaggerated. I tried to start the *El Pais* article with that and it didn't work, because that phrase was not part of our Spanish American culture. So I began it with an evocation of imagining one's own death in childhood, something much nearer to the idea of what has been called "magical realism" and as I kept on writing, Don Quixote imperceptibly crept into the narrative.

For a time, this really worried me, that I had these two languages. When you're in exile, you constantly examine your own actions for signs of betrayal, of forgetting where you come from. I was afraid that I would lose Chile, as I already explained. But as time went by, and particularly as of late, I started just enjoying the dialogue between the languages. English certainly influences my Spanish and working with English language editors, such as Tom Englehardt at Pantheon or Nan Graham at Viking, has made me look closely at my Spanish—to the point that I have rewritten Spanish texts (*Widows* and *The Last Song,* for instance), after editing them in English. *Mascara* is the first novel I am doing in both languages. Maybe it is an attempt to find some sort of unity in a fragmented life. But instead of lamenting the fragments, I am delighting in their confluence and conflict. I have a novel somewhere in the future—it is a long, epic novel, perhaps in several volumes—where this problem of language is central. One of its protagonists is simultaneous translator in . . . well, in California in the middle of the nineteenth century, when the Hispanic and the Anglo fought out a cultural battle (and a political and economic one as well) which is still not resolved to this day, even if North America won and has been winning ever since. How long will I be able to live switching one language on and the other off? I really don't know, but I don't intend to spoil my creativity, for the moment, by putting more obstacles in my path than I now have. Let's see if I can also find a way of bringing together my very disparate audiences. And there is of course the question: what will happen to my work, and this particular dimension of it, when we return to Chile? (pp. 161-63)

Ariel Dorfman, Peggy Boyers, and Juan Carlos Lertora, in an interview in Salmagundi, *Nos. 82 & 83, Spring/Summer, 1989, pp. 142-63.*

Bharati Mukherjee   (review date 31 December 1989)

[*An Indian-born American novelist, short story writer, nonfiction writer, and journalist, Mukherjee often writes about Third World emigrants to North America. In the following review, she states that while the political situations depicted in* My House Is on Fire *are shocking, the narratives are simplistic and the characters predictable.*]

The finest political fiction of our time goes beyond the indictment of specific political monstrosities. Gabriel Garcia Márquez, Günter Grass, Salman Rushdie, Nadine Gordimer and Thomas Pynchon all convert the literal into hallucinated visions of absolute tyranny. For the duration of the text, they capture our souls as well as our minds. In his novels *Widows* and *Mascara,* the Chilean writer Ariel Dorfman, who now lives in the United States, came close to transforming political protest into universal nightmare. His first collection of short stories is, however, a lesser work.

All 11 stories in *My House Is on Fire* are grounded in the politics of a regime reminiscent of that of Gen. Augusto Pinochet. In these stories, an unnamed dictator lays siege to democracy with the efficient apparatus of repression: death squads, interrogation chambers, prison beatings, surreptitious executions, censorship and disinformation. In such a country, innocence is forbidden. Even children must take sides. Men and women of conscience must become guerrillas or exiles.

Mr. Dorfman's aim is to exorcise the demagogue who has, until very recently, dominated and brutalized his beloved nation. But the intoxicating nobility of that aim turns out to be the collection's main problem. For where his novels triumphed because they were dense, inventive meditations on power and paranoia, his stories disappoint because they are merely stories about politics rather than complex, compelling narratives invigorated by a politicized imagination.

What shocks in most of these tales is the situation. In story after story, the shadowy dictator infiltrates the lives of ordinary citizens, forcing them to choose between courage and cowardice, between torture and ignorance. In the title story, this infiltration is at its most frightening. At the story's start, a young brother and sister play at keeping house in a "home" they have erected out of blankets and chairs in their father's library. When the children hear a car noisily pulling up on the street outside, they assume at once that "the enemy"—a squad of state-sponsored thugs—has arrived to trap them into letting slip what little they know about their parents' links with resistance movements. The oppressor roots himself in every mind, grows there and bloats. In such a situation, families discover that to try to protect one another, even to love one another, is to risk betraying and being betrayed. The little girl in the story, seeing that the car contains only a single man, makes what may be a fatal error, assuming this visitor is a mysterious friend of her father's, whom she addresses as Uncle Leandro.

In **"Family Circle,"** a son comes home on leave from the army and tells his parents that he will soon be sent as a guard to the prison where his uncle is being held. "So, what are you going to do?" his father demands. The old man was himself once jailed and tortured for trying to unionize millworkers. "What kind of damned question was that?" despairs the son. "Go, of course, you hard-headed old man! When an order was given, you had to go; you had to obey. . . . What else could I do?"

Mr. Dorfman makes clear what his characters *should* do when faced with a repressive regime's narrow choices. These people fall into unsubtle categories: docile or fearless, demonic or saintly. I longed to be surprised by them.

The weaker stories—**"Putamadre," "Lonely Hearts Column"** or **"Godfather,"** for instance—are awkwardly plotted exercises in political irony. **"Reader,"** a story about a low-level civil servant in the Ministry of Censorship, strains for Kafkaesque effects. The language in these stories, rendered from the Spanish by George Shivers with the assistance of Mr. Dorfman, too often calls attention to itself as a translation. Insensitive prose ("The old man's words fell on me like a ton of bricks, a slap in the face, crushing me like some miserable bug") alternates with unfortunate Americanisms ("potatoes cooked to a T").

This is all the more disappointing because the stronger stories, particularly **"Backlands"** and **"Titan,"** are fueled by an extraordinary lyricism. Consider, for example, the thoughts of Theo, the young hero of **"Titan,"** who has been detained and tortured for small acts of civil disobedience, then set up by the authorities to be killed as he breaks out of prison. Somehow, Theo finds within himself an enormous strength and is able to survive the warden's stratagems:

> I listen to those cutting, definitive, glorious words that the Colonel spits at Mama, trying to bite them before they are born into the universe, proving that nobody is dreaming me, that no-

body has the right to tell my story but me, the words the Colonel did not release to the press, those words that I am forcing him to state, as if I were kicking them out of his mouth, those words which to Mama will mean that I may be wounded, but that I am whole, and that someday we have a chance of winning, we have a chance of telling this story our way.

The collection's final entry, **"Backlands,"** offers a powerful, unsettling glimpse of apocalypse. A man and a woman, survivors of a civil war and the last defenders of democratic decencies, huddle within the ramparts of a bombed-out castle while the city behind them burns. Torturers have left the woman with a hideously scarred body, a melted face and mutilated breasts. "Look at me, coward," the woman begs. "Do you really think there's any hope?" The man's answer is unequivocal: "I say yes, that in spite of everything, yes, I believe there is hope."

My House Is on Fire is a slim, uneven collection, but there are moments, as in this story, when it can be both challenging and disturbing. Its value lies in forcing even the most self-absorbed reader to experience the blank horror of political depravity.

Bharati Mukherjee, "A Land Where Innocence Is Forbidden," in The New York Times Book Review, *December 31, 1989, p. 8.*

Jim Shepard (review date 21 January 1990)

[*Shepard is an American novelist. In the following review, he faults* My House Is on Fire *for its uneven characterization, flat language, and thematic simplicity, but praises the work as a potent examination of social suffering.*]

Hans and Sophie Scholl, in the second leaflet produced by the White Rose, the heroic and short-lived undergraduate resistance group centered in Munich University in 1943, articulated in advance its would-be readers' resistance to the hard and horrible truth in this way: "Why tell you these things, since you are fully aware of them—or if not of these, then of other equally grave crimes?"

Their answer is Ariel Dorfman's: because you are *not* truly aware; because something can, must, be done. Since leaving Chile in 1973, Dorfman has chronicled, obliquely and directly, the devastation of his country under Pinochet and Pinochet's legacy of repression. In his earlier fictions (*Widows, The Last Song of Manuel Sendero* and *Mascara*), he writes of exiles, living in a land that is not theirs and dreaming of redemption in the opportunity to return and help renew one's homeland. In his new collection of stories, *My House Is on Fire,* all set in Chile under Pinochet, he's still writing about exiles: all those living in a world they helped construct; but cannot enjoy; all those not allowed to become the protagonists of their own stories, not allowed the voices that will make them narrators of their own lives.

Over and over the fictions in this new collection are concerned with brothers and sons, fathers, mothers and daughters: the ways in which the political will always kick in the door of the familial, the impossibility of private life.

And more than that: the stubbornness with which the need to connect survives.

"Crossings," one of the longer stories, concerns a man whose job it is to signal illicit incoming couriers, whom he does not know, that all is well or not well when they arrive at the Santiago airport. The narrative alternates between his quietly excruciating wait and his speculation on what the courier, a woman he has seen only once and imagines with great tenderness, also must be enduring. The crosscutting echoed in the title effectively evokes the grinding anxiety of his particular and everyday situation, and evokes as well the importance, and the tenuousness, of these oddly intimate human connections in such circumstances—such connections seem precious and illuminated when they involve a man whose job it is to tell by his very presence the woman he's been imagining and has never known, and hundreds like her, that things are, for now, fine, that they are, for now, safe.

Some of these stories are not particularly lyrical and not of an overwhelming thematic complexity, but what powers them is the intensity of the political commitment behind them: the intensity of the understanding and the intensity of the caring. There is throughout the collection a desire to face and to understand enormous suffering, enormous sadness, and that need is compelling.

When could such an intensity of political commitment possibly be an aesthetic drawback? When it prevents the sorts of connections to those other characters that Dorfman needs to tell all the stories that this collection seeks to tell: It's not that stories such as **"Family Circle,"** narrated by a soldier soon to accept a post as guard at a political prison, or **"Putamadre,"** about three right-wing cadets on shore leave in San Francisco, seem too openly to indict their narrators (why shouldn't such narrators be openly indicted?), as that one feels that the attempt to get inside those men was incomplete and that those voices, simply too repugnant to the author, never fully came alive.

Yet in the best stories—**"Reader,"** with its Borgesian premise of a government censor discovering himself as the protagonist of a novel he is examining, or **"Lonely Hearts Column,"** with its sinister Chilean Dear Abby counseling a "Distraught Patriot" who fears her husband may be fooling around sexually and politically ("I suggest that you watch your husband closely for the next several days, *without his realizing it . . .* When you have more substantial evidence, come to my office at the newspaper, so we can talk the matter over, woman to woman . . . Hold onto your faith, and don't be surprised if the solution to your dilemma is just around the corner."), or the surreal power of **"Consultation,"** in which the torturer asks the blindfolded doctor to prescribe a moderate diet for him—the voices are assured, heartbreaking and are bearing witness to an all-encompassing social suffering, seemingly taking in all aspects of a society divided against itself. Finally it is the generosity and the sadness of *My House Is on Fire* that stays with the reader, that accepting of what has been done to us, of what we have done to ourselves.

Jim Shepard, "In the Shadow of Chile's Dictator," in Book World—The Washington Post, *January 21, 1990, p. 8.*

Christine Schwartz (review date 30 January 1990)

[*In the following review, Schwartz unfavorably assesses* My House Is on Fire, *describing the stories as unimaginative and simplistic.*]

My House Is on Fire is like a romantic paean to political opposition. Ariel Dorfman's well-meaning message—faith in the human heart, courage, and political change through individual action—is conveyed by prosaic story concepts, simplistic psychology, and unadorned, often drab prose. The brevity and explicitness of these stories contrast sharply with the geographical transfigurations and other complexities of his previous works. *The Last Song of Manuel Sendero,* for example, was a wonderful, delirious web, its subplots combining and recombining into an allegorical rebellion of fetuses. Most of the stories in *My House Is on Fire* are simply unadorned allegories.

Presumably Dorfman has his reasons for replacing passionate sophistication with raw simplicity. Perhaps the changing political situation in his native Chile, notably the decline of Pinochet, necessitates directness. The stories in this collection were written after Chile's government allowed him to return home following 10 years in exile. Dorfman's work has always urged the reader not to forget that Chile exists and its situation is tragic. *My House Is on Fire* continues this valuable lesson. The problem is that it feels so much like a lesson.

In **"Reader,"** for instance, an "infallible" censor in a publishing house—none of the books he's approved over a 20-year career have ever been condemned by the government—gets a new book for review. Because of "the soft spell of the prose," and the fictional protagonists' resemblances to his son and himself, the censor awakes to a higher, bolder political reality, that of the opposition. In **"Consultation,"** a doctor saves his own life by persuading his overweight, dwarfed torturer that he can overcome his handicaps and prevent the deaths of his victims.

Dorfman's treatment of women in *My House Is on Fire* is also irritatingly simplistic. Though the women protagonists of **"Lonely Hearts Column"** and **"Godfather"** stand on different sides of the fence—the first is close to "the Junta" and suffers from her political and emotional betrayal by her husband; the second, mourning her left-wing husband's death, faces the Registry Office's refusal to let her name his last child after him—both are subdued characters who resort to soapy expedients or stubborn inertia to achieve their ends. Male protagonists, on the other hand, always appear smart and resourceful.

A few jewels just save this disappointing collection. In **"Family Circle,"** Dorfman shows what a glowing writer he can be. Long, rhythmic, sometimes breathless sentences and graphic metaphors brilliantly communicate the flood of memories, emotions, and sensuality overwhelming Lusho as he comes home from military service. In **"Backlands,"** Dorfman's message finds a strong voice in a man left alone to defend the remnants of his city—a ruined castle and his brother's disfigured wife—after its devastation by "the enemy." The story is patient and terse, conveying a slow triumph of compassion and a raging appetite for life over solitude, blindness, and desolation.

"Backlands" finds its eloquence precisely by *not* being explicit.

These two stories never rush to meaning; their virtuosity and psychological finesse belie the hammering rectitude of the others. If only the entire collection were this good. *My House Is on Fire* could have been so much more than another stodgy, politically correct volume by another Latin American intellectual.

> *Christine Schwartz, "False Alarm," in* The Village Voice, *Vol. XXXV, No. 5, January 30, 1990, p. 63.*

Michael Ugarte (review date 19 February 1990)

[*Ugarte is an American educator and critic. In the following review, he compares* My House Is on Fire *to Dorfman's earlier works and identifies the collection's principal themes.*]

Consider a passage from Mother Goose that appears as an epigraph for the title story of Ariel Dorfman's new collection of short narratives in English translation, *My House Is on Fire:* "Lady bug, lady bug, / Fly away home. / Your house is on fire. / Your children will burn." From the perspective of the child, what does this gentle ladybug represent—that is, of course, if she is gentle? Is she a mirror image of the child, or a mother figure? What is the significance for the child of the ladybug's house? What thoughts kindle the speaker's sense of urgency and fear that the house is on fire? And how does the child read that curious semantic contradiction, "Fly away home"? Questions such as these on the nature of fairy tales and children's rhymes are difficult, and although there have been many attempts by psychiatrists, psychologists, anthropologists and literary critics to offer responses, the meanings remain mysterious.

As a Chilean, a writer of fiction, a professor, an activist who worked to elect Salvador Allende and later participated in his government, and as an exile, Dorfman may not provide answers, but he continues to ask pressing questions about the children of dictatorship and their families. He has always been concerned with images and myths that serve political ends, and what better foci to study these cultural artifacts than those embedded in the minds of children and adolescents: Donald Duck and the entire gamut of Disney characters; Superman; the Lone Ranger; and even *Reader's Digest,* which, as Dorfman explained in his *The Empire's Old Clothes,* infantalizes its readers in offensive and oppressive ways. These were the objects of Dorfman's scrutiny in his early essays, and in his fiction he has continued to approach political problems through the perspective and study of the young mind (as in his most ambitious novel, *The Last Song of Manuel Sendero,* in which would-be children rebel by refusing to be born until adults buckle down and solve the world's problems).

My House Is on Fire is yet another example. Although its treatment of children is by no means its only concern, youngsters of all varieties populate this *House:* sons and daughters of dictatorship's *persona non grata,* young soldiers, adolescents caught in a web of oppression and thought control, and children of a not-too-remote past now struggling as adults to deal with a tragic political reality. The collection is typical of Dorfman (a true *mensch* of a writer) in its humane yet critical treatment not only of children but of those who encircle them: parents, other relatives, even authorities.

In **"Crossings,"** a haunting tale of espionage and fear, the reader must play the role of a child listening to a bedtime story to decipher the plot. The identity of the characters and their motivations are not readily available, never made explicit. Through an imagined dialogue between a man in an airport and an unknown woman on a plane whose arrival he awaits impatiently, we learn of other characters: a poor woman dressed in black accompanied by her children; lovers in a passionate embrace; and two men furtively observing certain people as if they were prey. Yet there is a story within the story. The speaker also imagines a man on the plane telling his son a tale of a muleteer who risked his life crossing the Andes more than a century ago to give messages to the troops fighting the Spanish for Chilean independence. Through this children's story the identities of the other characters begin to take shape, and the woman on the plane becomes a modern version of the muleteer, a messenger in service of the resistance against Pinochet.

Fear is clearly the watchword in **"Crossings,"** as it is in several other stories. In **"My House Is on Fire"** two children hide under a blanket as the authorities come to their house looking for their parents. The brother reassures his younger sister that they are playing a game, so that she won't be frightened, but the reader is never sure if in fact the children *are* playing a game, if they are rehearsing for a time when the police will come or if the person who finally weeds them out is a friend or an enemy. This childlike uncertainty lies at the root of a horrific situation; as Dorfman shows us, to be a child is to be riddled with fears of all types, and in a police state the terror increases tenfold.

These youthful fears manifest themselves in a variety of ways, including in the acts of young males who collaborate with the dictatorship. Dorfman deals earnestly with the mentality and the contradictions that lead to compliance, treating these characters with sympathy and critical understanding. In the story that opens the collection, **"Family Circle,"** a young man is terrified at how his progressive, salt-of-the-earth father will react to his having become a soldier, and worse still, to his having been assigned as a guard in a prison for political transgressors. Near the story's end, at home, the son clutches the handle of a pot of boiling stew and announces that if anyone tries to escape while he is on duty, he will shoot "full-blast." Dorfman skillfully leads to that pathetic declaration with the image of fire, a constant motif in the collection. The father helps his son carry the pot to the table, but neither of them will let go. The son observes his father's movements: "His hands moved implacably over the metal, they must be burning by now; it must be singeing his skin, sinking to the bone; his blood had to be boiling." Dorfman has pene-

trated a father's disgrace and a son's shame in the midst of a regime that turns innocent people into killers.

The object of Dorfman's political search is a language that is open but never arbitrary or without motive, dialogical but never vacuously pluralistic.

—*Michael Ugarte*

Dorfman's stories are by no means single-minded or preachy, even though his writing exposes its own ideology, unlike that of other Chilean dissidents, such as Antonio Skármeta and Jorge Edwards, who have not been as committed as Dorfman to imagining progressive alternatives to capitalist and neocolonialist culture. The object of Dorfman's political search is a language that is open but never arbitrary or without motive, dialogical but never vacuously pluralistic. Dorfman is interested in relations. Although the women are not given the same depth as the men, all his characters are developed in conjunction, in collusion or in conflict with others: sons with their fathers, brothers with their sisters, children with their families, rebels with their enemies, exiles with those who stay to continue the battle, adolescent soldiers looking for a good time with North American prostitutes—who refuse to give it to them because they are boycotting all Pinochet's merchandise. This last situation occurs in **"Putamadre"** ("whore-mother"), a story titled after the nickname of its male protagonist. Although there is something of the myth of the Happy Hooker in the tale, Dorfman underscores the clash between men who think of women as whores and real prostitutes who are wiser and more politically sophisticated than their johns.

The burning question of ***My House Is on Fire,*** of course, is the future, especially for Chile, with its new political and social possibilities as it cautiously (perhaps too cautiously) returns to democracy. Is Dorfman's sense of urgency dated in the wake of the recent Chilean elections? Is his house no longer on fire—is it merely smoldering in Pinochet's ashes? The answers, or the suggestions of answers, might be found in the final story of the collection, **"Backlands,"** in which the protagonist insists on protecting a dreamlike castle as everything around him burns. He refuses to gaze at the flames of "the city," concentrating instead on the castle and imagining possibilities for it in spite of the advice of those few left around him to let it burn:

> The city's savage breath beats at my back, like an oven lit by a man gone insane. It was then I decided not to turn around. The fire would die out, finally there would be nothing left to burn. The flames would lap at my walls, like bound, like tamed ocean waves. Let the enemy squeeze the city till it was only a rind. Could not a new fruit be dreamed from the peelings?

And sure enough, the dream seems closer to reality than we readers would have thought. Almost as a prediction of the return of Chilean exiles, the protagonist imagines his departed brother back from wherever he has been speaking "a different language," imagines him unable to recognize his family. As he passes by, the protagonist calls his son to witness the event: "And then, taking my son by the hand, I will let my brother disappear into the distance. And then, yes, at that moment, I will turn around to look our city in the face." These culminating words of the collection could be read as a synthesis of the present political and social reality of Chile.

In **"Backlands,"** an allegorical yet open-ended story, Dorfman, like the protagonist, is unwilling to let his house burn in spite of the damage done by the flames of the police state. The appearance of the son, the last of Dorfman's children, is an affirmation that if the ladybug and the brother do as the rhyme admonishes, if they "fly away home," face the house, the children will not burn. (pp. 245-47)

> Michael Ugarte, "The Children and the Flame," in The Nation, *New York, Vol. 250, No. 7, February 19, 1990, pp. 245-47.*

Helen Birch   (review date 18 November 1990)

[*In the following excerpt, Birch comments on Dorfman's concept of realism as expressed in* Hard Rain.]

[For] Ariel Dorfman, writing about the events in Chile involves a process of disruption, even of the narrative structure itself. **Hard Rain,** first published in Spanish in 1973, was written in the twilight hours of Allende's government. In a preface to this first English edition, Dorfman suggests that the battle for power raging in Chile during those final months of 1972 was also a struggle to determine 'who would get the chance to tell [the] story, to write history'. **Hard Rain** is a kind of dossier of his country's literature, compiled through reviews, essays, encyclopaedia entries, snatches of fiction, letters and dialogues, which together form an incessant debate about how history might be told.

Beginning with a convoluted detective story set in different torture chambers across the world, the novel goes on to discuss the work of a Marxist nun, a literary/artistic exhibition of toilet paper called SHIT, a book called *The First Forty Measures,* written by well-known writers who support Allende.

It ends with a fictional interview with Dorfman, in which he says his intention in writing this fragmentary novel was to kill the author, 'but not after having tortured him and the reader for hours, I at least wanted a relative to be able to identify the body'.

In the final passages he takes this idea further. Realism, he seems to suggest, attempts to convey everything, to order it, monopolise it. But to give each facet of a culture a voice, and by implication, to allow each person an active citizenship, you have to take sense apart and give birth to meaning through 'the senseless piling up of data'.

> Helen Birch, "Patriots Peel Back the Skin of the Body Politic," in The Observer, *November 18, 1990, p. 62.*

Richard Burgin   (review date 16 December 1990)

[*Burgin is an American educator and critic. In the following review, he offers a mixed assessment of* Hard Rain.]

Jorge Luis Borges became justly famous for creating stories purporting to be articles about real books that actually only existed in Borges's imagination. In Ariel Dorfman's first novel, **Hard Rain,** the Chilean writer radically extends this Borgesian conceit to a vertiginous degree.

Originally published in Spanish in 1973 (as **Moros en la Costa**) and now deftly translated into English by the author and George Shivers, **Hard Rain** is a collage of fictitious book reviews, editorial reports, encyclopedia entries, prologues to anthologies, student term papers, sales pitches to film companies, letters and newspaper articles, interspersed with fragments from the imaginary books themselves.

Mr. Dorfman's ambitions transcend formal literary experimentation; indeed, most of the book's pieces grapple directly with the political reality of Chile in the last months of Salvador Allende's Socialist Government and, specifically, with the way writers reacted to the reforms that provoked a military coup. Throughout, Mr. Dorfman ponders, paradoxically, the value of writing itself in a time of crisis.

"Does it make any sense," asks one of Mr. Dorfman's fictitious essayists, "to use the resources of a Borges, the labyrinths, the double personalities . . . to work a metaphor, to correct and balance a verb, if mass murder, the invisible wall of exploitation and death are still going on?"

Mr. Dorfman never answers that question without some ambivalence, but he clearly opposes both political and esthetic dictatorships, as well as exercises of literary technique that are devoid of genuine human empathy. Sometimes his positions are dramatized metaphorically, as in a long essay about an imaginary mystery novel called *Concentrations,* which deals with a series of identical murders of prisoners in death camps in, among other places, Nazi Germany, Rhodesia and several countries in South America.

In each case, the detective's investigations are hampered by too much or too little compassion for the victims. Finally, Agatha Christie's famous detective, Hercule Poirot, arrives. (This isn't entirely surprising, since Mr. Dorfman is as fascinated by pop culture as Borges was by ancient texts.)

His powers of ratiocination unclouded by any emotional consideration, Poirot is about to reveal the dazzling solution to all the murders when the scene shifts to a hacienda in Chile, where a new murder has been committed. This time the policeman knows the identity of the killer but arbitrarily refuses to reveal it. *Concentrations* ends with the willfully passive policeman focusing his attention on daily reports of poverty, alcoholism and death by starvation. Mr. Dorfman's essayist concludes that "the moral seems clear: the world itself is a concentration camp, and those really responsible, the true criminals, are not the ones we insist on searching out and denouncing."

Other parts of *Hard Rain* are much more lighthearted. There is a review, for example, of something called a "novel-object" in which "the story being told is basically the story of the roll of [toilet] paper on which it is written," and an article on a novel called *Story of a Potato*, which describes the people and experiences a potato encounters from the moment it germinates until it vanishes into the mouths of the family it nourishes.

Hard Rain is intellectually fascinating, but it lacks narrative tension and a fully satisfying shape. Nonetheless, it is eloquent in dramatizing both the inability of art to capture reality and the unthinkableness of life without art.

> Richard Burgin, "With Poirot in Chile," in The New York Times Book Review, December 16, 1990, p. 22.

Ariel Dorfman with John Incledon (interview date May 1991)

[*In the following interview, Dorfman discusses politics, the influence of other writers on his work, and the relationship between reader and writer.*]

[*Incledon*]: *Let's [discuss] your literary works. Looking back, which book are you most satisfied with?*

[Dorfman]: I think *The Last Song.* It's the one I feel most comfortable with. I can remember when I finished it, I told my wife Angélica, "Now I can die." In other words, I felt that I had done something which would touch people very deeply if they opened themselves to this book.

It's your most difficult book.

It's a difficult book. That's the kind of book I wanted to write. The satisfaction I feel from *Windows,* for instance, when people come up to me and say, "Oh, thank you so much for writing this," is quite different. Or when someone comes up to me and recites one of my poems to me from memory. I occasionally get letters which say things like, "I picked up your book in a bookstore and began crying as I read it." Wonderful things—wonderful because you know that you've touched your readers. I think what I have done in *The Last Song* is a combination. It's as if the politics and the literature are exactly the way I want them to be, as if I've pushed everything as far as I can in a certain direction. It doesn't mean that the books that come afterwards aren't satisfying. I'm working on some very ambitious projects now, and I'm pleased with their progress. In fact, the ambition of *The Last Song of Manuel Sendero* might even be its downfall. I know the book has certain problems. But I would rather have written it with those problems than not to have pushed the boundaries as far as I possibly could. I mean, I think I pushed in many different directions. I took all the risks in that book. I could have written a very safe yet engaging novel of exile. I could have taken a set of characters and written an interesting, straightforward story of exile. But I decided not to do that. I could have written the typical—I hate the word—"magical realist" novel. But I didn't. *Manuel Sendero* is a very self-conscious, self-reflexive book. It's a novel which takes one risk after another. When you think you've come to the point where you can say, "Oh, now I

understand," I try to push things even farther. I demand a lot from my reader. You can't get involved with that book and not be moved by it. Or hate it. There are those who don't like it at all.

It's not your most readable book. It's not as readable as **Widows.** *The Last Song seems like a more personal book. For example, I can imagine the sequences with David and Felipe as something rather close to your own experience.*

They're close, but I am neither one of them. A lot of the things that happen to them I either saw or happened to me in an oblique way.

What about literary references in **The Last Song?** *I thought I heard echoes of Julio Cortázar's* A Manual for Manuel *in the conversations between David and Felipe, in the comic book project, etc.*

Actually, not at all. Cortázar is a major influence in my literature and a major influence in my life as well. He was one of my dear friends, a truly extraordinary human being. I love most of Cortázar's work except for *A Manual for Manuel,* which I find a frustrated work. I like a lot of the sequences. What I don't like is the revolutionary part. Julio knew nothing about the revolution. I mean, he knew everything about "the revolution," but he knew nothing about revolutionaries. I think Cortázar incorporated politics into that novel all wrong. He was so obsessed by what was happening in Argentina and so hurt by it. I think his writing wasn't prepared for that leap. Whereas I do think that several of his stories afterwards are wonderful political stories. So, *A Manual for Manuel* is hardly an influence. There are, however, echoes of a lot of contemporary fiction in *The Last Song of Manuel Sendero*—Günter Grass and Cortázar, but more the Cortázar of *Hopscotch.* That's where the basic lesson of Cortázar's work is to be found, in the idea that you've got to push yourself up against the wall, and you've got to push your reader up against the wall—and then you've got to push the wall itself. I mean, what you ask of yourself you can ask of your reader as well. I think that's a major point.

The idea of the "reader-accomplice."

Yes, the "reader-accomplice." Bringing the reader into the work. Writing as if your life depended on it. I think that's very important. But in terms of my own work I would say that García Márquez is very important for me as well. The names I'm mentioning—Carpentier, Asturias, Roa Bastos and Borges, in other words, the writers of the "Boom" in the Latin American novel—all of them, of course, are in some sense shaped by the Latin American novel which came before them. But they also tend to look to the United States and Europe for their models. The difference with my generation of writers is that we can now can look to these Latin American writers for our models. They opened up an enormous literary terrain for the rest of us. We're harvesting their crop right now.

Who are your favorite writers? Or the ones who have most influenced you?

I think Cortázar . . .

You mentioned some of the later stories that Cortázar wrote as being political works. Of course, those are not the works on which Cortázar's reputation is based.

No, not at all.

What about the fact that the most significant work by Cortázar, Borges and a whole generation of writers of "fantastic literature" has nothing to do with social issues? Does that bother you?

First of all, I think it's political enough to say that we have the right to the whole world. In other words, just because I am obsessed with social issues and political issues, doesn't mean that I don't have the right to dream, to have fantasies, and to enjoy myself in a series of other ways. I don't think we should allow ourselves to be compartmentalized. For example, just because I'm writing about General Pinochet, does this mean that I must write a realistic novel with torture scenes described in complete detail? I won't be forced into doing that! That's the first thing. The second is, I think there's a difference between Borges and Cortázar. I think Cortázar is enormously political from his very first stories. He is dealing with the liberating force of the imagination all the time. He writes about people who are shut up inside incredibly narrow worlds. And the world that erupts in the middle of all this is basically that of the Latin American bárbaro, the imagination that will not let this person build a European existence. What could be more political? One of my great heroes in Latin American literature is Arguedas, who is very different from Cortázar. But I think that both of them, one from the point of view of the city and the other from the point of view of the backlands, confront the fact that Latin America is a hybrid, a contradictory continent made up of enormously interesting tensions. I think that the best writers are the ones who feel those tensions and try to form some kind of unity out of them. Some writers, like García Márquez, are fortunate and talented enough to find a style which brings together the surrealistic European quality and the mythic indigenous quality of Latin America. This synthesis creates a unified and original style. My style isn't at all unified. I'm full of fragments and contradictions. I haven't been able to find that unity in my work, in my vision. My life has been very fragmented and my vision is as well. Of course Cortázar was constantly struggling with repressive forces. *The Winners* is just that. And Oliveira in *Hopscotch* is unable to find a sense of community. I've had discussions about this with a number of people on the Latin American left. There are those who attack Cortázar because he's an escapist. I don't believe that any great writer creates escapist literature.

Well, how is Borges different? You seem to distinguish Borges and Cortázar.

I think that Borges is much more afraid of the bárbaro. His work has nothing to do with anything I believe in politically. But he does give us a sense of being very careful about the way in which we use language, about how language can be used to deceive, and so on. Borges is the first person who gives the art of the parasite a central position in literature. He is an author who writes at the margins. As Fernández Retamar says, only a writer from a "marginal" society would know everything about world litera-

ture. You learn and you take from everybody. I've learned from Quevedo. A great influence in my writing has been Cervantes, for instance. Anybody who reads **The Last Song of Manuel Sendero** in Spanish will realize that. It's very Cervantine.

Tell me more about that.

I just think that Cervantes, once again, is a writer who pushed the limits. He used the genres of his day and split them wide open. There's an important lesson to be learned from him. I wonder whether I've learned it quite yet. What his work suggests, if you listen to him hundreds of years later, is that the important genres of our day are the mass media. The popular literary forms of his day were the pastoral novel, the chivalric romances—which he hated and loved—and the picaresque novel. He took all of them and put them into Part One of the *Quixote*. And then he exploded them in Part Two. I can understand how one might be able to write in the vein of Part One of the *Quixote,* but I have no idea how anybody could possibly write the way Cervantes wrote in Part Two. Maybe *One Hundred Years of Solitude* is that, and that's why it's so extraordinary. It is a literature of foundation. Nobody can write like García Márquez. When someone tries to imitate him, it's a disaster. You can't do that. You also have to kill the fathers. I mean, you have to kill your literary antecedents every time you start to write. That's very important.

> I've always felt that the struggle against the dictatorship of the author upon the reader is one of the central questions in my work. Of course, this means that my books are complex, ambiguous, open-ended, provocative, and very often difficult.
>
> —*Ariel Dorfman*

Why is the relationship of the author to his reader so important? What kind of reader are you hoping for? Or hoping to create?

I'm really not sure, but I do know why it's so important. We seem to control very little of our existence, in that we are determined by so many forces—biological, social and political. And in troubled times like these, very often your life is taken away from you just like that. I think that art and the relationship that you establish in art is like a love relationship, in the sense that you create something that has a center, a foundation. It is something that you can control up to a point. I feel that many writers have a tendency to dominate the reader, in that their text does not allow for multiple interpretations, does not provoke and challenge the reader. The more this is true, the less human the reader can become, the more of a soliloquy the work turns out to be. So I've always felt that the struggle against the dictatorship of the author upon the reader is one of the central questions in my work. Of course, this means that my books are complex, ambiguous, open-ended, provocative, and very often difficult. And at the same time, thinking in political terms, there is the desire in the back of my mind to reach as many people as possible. My real wish is to be read by the happy few, as Stendhal would say, but at the same time to be read by everybody. I was recently on a television program in Holland with Umberto Eco, and the interviewer asked him why *Foucault's Pendulum* is such a difficult book. "My wish," he said, "is to be bought by everybody but to be read by the happy few." I would like those happy few to be everyone. But it's probably not going to happen.

So liberation is not just a theme of your work, but a process which takes place in the reader, too?

It's a process and it's part of the formal creation in the sense that there may be a moment in which I say to myself, "I'm letting the reader off the hook. I'm making this too easy. I'm not really forcing the reader to be creative." I've got to do this. I've got to make the reader work. Of course, this is not the way to become a popular writer. And let's face it, my books are not bestsellers. I would love for that to happen, but I'm not going to compromise my writing. Right now I'm revising the stage version of *Widows.* In a play you can do some of those things. You can reach the masses, but it's very difficult. I'm always wary of being too soft. You know, I'm a very gentle person. Yet in my fiction, I think I'm very hard on the reader. If you look at the essays I've written, in which I analyze fiction for popular consumption, including children's literature, my major criticism is that these books tend to "infantilize" the reader. They're not even geared toward real readers, toward imaginative, wonderful, extraordinary children. They don't even see children as they really are. Popular fiction closes the universe, projects a distorted image of its readers. (pp. 97-100)

Why did you set **Widows** *in Greece? The old woman is an Antigone figure, isn't she?*

Yes, I would say a cross between the protagonists of *Antigone* and *The Trojan Women,* in the sense that she's also a captive. There's another story of mine called **"Family Circle,"** in which I use epigraphs from *Iphigenia* and *Orestes.* The story deals with a very poor Chilean family who display enormous dignity in the midst of terrible struggle and strife. They have all the dignity of a Greek tragedy, which comes to the surface when they rebel. The narrative strategy in **Widows,** as I've said in the prologue, was to publish it under a pseudonym.

In Chile?

In Chile, or somewhere else in the Southern Cone. I'm not at liberty to reveal the name of the editor who then turned the book down, in spite of the idea of using a pseudonym. But when I reread the novel, and a couple of friends who are editors said to me, "Why don't you set it in El Salvador, in a Latin American country," I found that I liked the distance that the Greek setting gave me. In other words, what started out as a pretext, a political strategy to get the book published, turned out to be a literary strategy which allowed me to talk about the missing and about

the situation in Chile without having to be realistic about that material. Because, once again, I probably could not have written a realistic novel about this. I could not have written *The Official Story.* I just couldn't have done that.

So, what started as a strategy to get the book published worked out fortuitously for you as a novelist.

Yes, although perhaps not so fortuitously. Perhaps it was not such a coincidence. I'm not so sure that the novel was not written by that Danish author. I'm not so sure he wasn't there dictating to me. Because it was written very quickly, feverishly. **The Last Song** took many years to write. **Widows** took perhaps a month and ten days. I wrote it very quickly, as if I were possessed, though I generally write as if I were possessed. Writing is a painful experience for me. So I would not call it fortuitous because I may have been searching for some strategy which would allow me to speak about this situation. I was obsessed with the plight of the young people in my country. I asked myself, "How can I get to them? How can I reach them?" It's strange, because as soon as I finished **Widows,** I began writing a column every month or so under my own name in the only major opposition magazine, *Hoy,* which was timidly beginning to appear. I began to realize that there were ways in which I could write about this. But, in point of fact, there is no village in Chile or anywhere in the world where all the men have disappeared and only women remain, along with an occupying military force. So if I had set the novel in Chile, the old "reality principle" would have come into play. I would have said to myself, "Come on, Ariel. You know very well . . . " It's something which I've always had to fight, because I think it's part of the tradition in political fiction—the sense that your subject has to be real. In the case of **Widows,** that was the solution. Now in the stage version, I've set it in a Latin American country. I had to do that.

It sounds like you've used the play as an opportunity to rewrite the novel.

I've done twenty-seven versions of the play thus far. I mean twenty-seven finished versions. Versions where I've said, "OK. It's done." It's gone on and on and on. And now I'm coming down to the last one. It probably won't be completely ready until it's had its major production in Los Angeles. Then I won't touch it again.

Is this version of the play what the novel might have been if you had not had any restrictions at all as far as having it published?

I don't think so.

So much time has passed?

So much time has passed and the making of a play is the result of a collective process, which is something I had never done before. Like most writers, I'm rather solitary. So this has been a complicated experience because I've had to work with directors, with actors, I've had feedback and things like that. It's different. Actually, Angélica's my main collaborator. She reads everything. There are things she likes and things she backs away from. For instance, she likes parts of **The Last Song,** but there are other parts she likes less. I had to leave them in, in spite of her. But she's always my first reader, my first audience. My first "reader-accomplice."

That's right. So you know how your work affects that "reader-accomplice."

Yes, except that she is a very special reader. Because she is not the typical literary reader. I mean there are a whole lot of things in **The Last Song** that I like and which she is not very fond of—the game-playing, the different time frames and things like that. She prefers my writing to be a bit more simple and straight-forward. I can remember when I told her about the section set in the future, I told her "Angélica, I've got this incredible idea!" "Oh, no," she said. "Not again!" But the process of writing the play has been very complicated, because there's the generic difference between a novel and a play. I have never realized it before as fully as I do now. I mean you can never really understand the difference until you try to move from one form to the other.

The novel itself [**Widows**] *is very dramatic. It's almost visual.*

Absolutely. Yet the actors ask me for motivation. They say, "How do I move from here to here." Then the next problem is political. How do you write a political piece of theater for a relatively apolitical audience, even if those who go to the theater in the States tend to be more savvy than most of their compatriots? And do it in such a way that the audience understands what's going on.

How did you deal with that problem?

It's hard. You set limits as to how much you're prepared to compromise. In the latest version, for instance, I try to make the forces in conflict absolutely crystal clear. What does the Captain represent? What do the women represent? What does the priest represent? What does the lieutenant represent? And so on. I'm laboring to make this play work so that people will understand it. There are a lot of things that aren't clear in the novel, that don't have to be clear. But in the play they have to be clear.

For example?

For example, the relationship with the earth is presented through lyrical monologues in the novel. You can't do that in the play, even though I do have a series of monologues. You need the women to be very clear about what they are doing, how they are doing it, where they're going, that there is a dramatic need propelling the characters, and so on. You have to create a universe on stage. And there are other dilemmas as well. For example, the problem of presenting the mythic. Presenting the mythic dimension in a novel—I'm not saying it's easy, but it's part of what fiction is. Fiction tends to be mythic. In your mind, you create this universe. Using myth on stage is very complicated. Especially in an age that doesn't believe in myths.

Mascara *was a turn in your career.*

I haven't got a career! (we laugh) . . . in my evolution.

OK. Well, you've talked about the specter of Pinochet in this novel, his presence . . .

And his absence.

Yes. To what degree would you say that **Mascara** *is a political novel?*

I think it's a departure in that it is not an overtly political novel. It doesn't deal with events in Chile or Latin America. There are no human rights violations. So, in that sense, it's a radical departure. In another sense, a lot of my political obsessions are present in **Mascara.** For instance, alienation; the use of deception in relation to the public and the private world; memory, the need for memory; the erasure of memory as a form of control; and the idea of a hidden structure that acts like a vampire in our lives. All these questions are very much related to my previous essays and fiction. I mean, I've been interested in these problems before. And my experience in shaping these characters comes out of my experience with the horror of these past years. Of course, it is easy from this point in time to suggest that the novel has an underlying political foundation. But the truth of the matter is that none of this was conscious in the novel to begin with.

How did you start writing **Mascara?**

A voice came to me. That's what's so scary.

A voice of one of the characters?

The voice of the man without a face. In fact, at that point the voice didn't even have a face. I didn't know anything about it. All I knew was that this person was somehow a voyeur. A man who was looking at a woman—probably a woman—as if she were taking off her clothes. She was ringing the doorbell. And I knew that it had something to do with faces. At the beginning it might have been that the man couldn't remember a face. But more than that I knew that this guy had such an arrogance in his tone. And yet there was something in the way the words were written which indicated to me that the man, arrogant as he was, was somehow incredibly hurt, terribly damaged and twisted. Underground, not there. It was very strange, how that man could have so much power in his voice, but not be there. Then it came out. I put the plastic surgeon in, answering him. The first voice wasn't really directed toward the plastic surgeon in the beginning. I mean, it was just a man who was there. And then slowly I began realizing how important the presence of the plastic surgeon was. It was very slow. It was as if it were there in reality. I'm telling you, it was scary. I did that rather quickly. This novel took seven months to write. And I would say that I finished the main body of the novel in three months. Then I spent perhaps four months trying to figure out the section on Oriana, the girl with whom the faceless man falls in love. I knew there was something missing in the middle, between the two men talking past each other, but I couldn't figure out what it was. It came out very painfully. Only when that was done, when I had heard the three voices, was I able to realize what the epilogue should be. In fact, there's a second book which will come out of this, which uses two of the characters. It's a detective story set in Chile, a very different book.

Are the two characters in **Mascara,** *the man without a face* *and the doctor, somehow two sides of the same coin? Their obsession with power?*

I'm very puzzled by this novel. It's very difficult for me to try to understand it. But there seem to be several levels at which you can read it. One of them suggests these might be the three parts of a personality of only one human being, mingling together. Or, who knows, you may have Adam and Eve and God. A strange triangle. It can work itself out in many ways. You may have realized that the theme of father and son is something which repeats itself over and over again.

*I read **Mascara** and thought I was doing quite well with it until I got to the Epilogue. Can you help me out a little bit?*

What do you think about it? I mean, I can't help you too much because . . . the "reader-accomplice," you know. I'm not supposed to help you too much. (we laugh)

Touché!

No, no, no. That's all right. It's organized as a puzzle, no? Stylistically it's as different as you can find. It's supposed to tell you what happened.

The Epilogue?

Every epilogue is supposed to tell you what happened afterwards. And I think it does. I mean, I think it refuses to close the novel.

"To be continued . . . " it says, no?

To be continued. But to be continued in many senses. I think you need to read the ending again. With great care. It's a book which must be read very carefully. Probably you're going to read it the second time and understand it immediately. I mean, basically it's clear. There are two men who are interrogating the Nurse or Secretary of Dr. whatever his name is . . .

Mavirelli, Marivelli . . .

Exactly. And you have to discover who these two men are. You have an idea who they are. And then you've got to piece together what happened in that studio. That can be done. Except there are two alternatives, and it's not certain which one happened. There are clues. There are hints.

*Tell me about **Missing Continents**.*

Missing Continents is a book which will come out in 1991. It's a very strange book. I say this about all my books.

Is it novel or essay?

It's an essay. It's really two trips through the Americas. One of the trips is from the perspective that is prevalent in the United States about the Third World and particularly about Latin America in the 80's. It's a trip that you can take without moving away from your television set. Just by observing the world through the newspapers. It has to do with the culture and, to put it in a nutshell, about how the United States makes the people of Latin America and the Third World disappear from sight, from consciousness. The introductory chapter is basically, with modifications, what I will be reading at Albright, talking about the challenge of the missing. From there I go on to

talk about the problem of the missing as portrayed in American films. Then I talk about missing people right here in America—MIAs, missing children. And finally I get into a series of rather outlandish subjects from E. T. to Indiana Jones to contemporary American pulp fiction. Having completed that journey, I then set out on a second journey through a series of counterculture initiatives by grass roots organizations in Latin America—people who are trying to make themselves appear in our consciousness, who are seeking empowerment. And in the conclusion I ask myself what chance there is of these two worlds ever coming together, of making the necessary adjustments. It's very strange. They are two opposite worlds, but in some ways they are interconnected. Because the world that America tries to keep out of sight is always challenging America, and that's why it's constantly made to disappear. And the world that is trying to appear is constantly being molded by the United States success story, its development model and a series of other things which I've looked at in other books, such as *The Empire's Old Clothes.* I took a whole year off to write *Missing Continents* because I felt that it was time for me to go back to my essays. I hadn't written an essay since *The Empire's Old Clothes.* I don't know what people are going to think about this book.

It's finished?

I've finished a first draft. There are two stages to my writing. One is getting everything in place and finishing a first draft. That's the most painful part. The second part is playful, wonderful in the sense that I can play around with the book. I already know what the foundation is, I know what I'm building. It's like painting a house after you've built it. The basics are there. The first stage is complicated because, until I put in the last brick, I never know if the whole structure isn't going to come crumbling down. In fact, I'm never even sure if I'm not building the wrong house, if I haven't used the wrong materials, and so on. I mean it. It's very anguishing. Now I may have a couple more months of work, but it's a question of bringing things in and making things a bit clearer and reordering, rearranging ideas. But the basic structure is there. I'm pleased with it. I don't think it's going to make me many friends. I'm very harsh with the United States during the Reagan years. It's as if the Reagan years had made me scream *¡Basta!* I mean, never before have I seen a whole people cheat themselves out of reality. It was a very painful thing to watch, day after day. One of the main discussions in this book is what happened with Vietnam, I mean how the Vietnamese were made to disappear. Really they were! Literally. The Vietnamese were the quintessential thirdworlders. They filled the television screens for months on end. And when the Americans left Saigon, the Vietnamese disappeared from sight. As if they were never there. They're hardly there now. It's amazing! This is one of the central metaphors of the book. It's a book which zeros in on my basic experience of living here [in the U.S.], including the outrage and indignation I have felt regarding these matters. Because I think that America should do better than that. It has such wonderful people. It's such an extraordinary continent. It has such a wonderful tradition of insurgency and insurgent thought. Yet it's growing into a nation of comfortable, self-indulgent people who are scared. Really, they're much more afraid than Chileans are.

How so? And why?

I think they're afraid of losing their comforts and looking at the pain of the world. And of taking on moral responsibility. Of growing up. So there's an urgency, a somewhat strident tone to this book which *The Empire's Old Clothes,* for example, did not have.

Actually, I'm glad to hear that. When I read in the opening of **The Empire's Old Clothes** *that you were toning things down a bit for your American audience, I thought to myself, "That's a pity."*

I toned them down in part because when you're living with people I think that it's difficult to write that way. I mean, **Missing Continents** isn't finished yet, OK? But, I open, for example, with the image of 1984. Because I started the book in 1984. I've been working on it for a long time. This last year I sat down and wrote it, but I had been writing notes and outlining it since 1984. In 1984, you had the United States obsessed with the East-West conflict, right? That's all the politicians spoke about. One saying the Soviet Union was like this, and the other one saying the United States was like that. Nobody was looking at the fact that if indeed the Orwellian prophecy was coming true, it was coming true in the Third World. We're imagining a world in which the great majority of humanity is being left out. The minority in power is going to destroy the resources of the world not only for themselves but for the rest of humanity as well. That's in the book. I'm worried about this. It's a very hopeful book, by the way. But that brings us back to my politics. I do believe that ideas can help people to change the world and understand it better. And you don't have to hit people over the head with ideas in your fiction. By presenting your readers with these fictional worlds, you give them the opportunity to address these issues within themselves, and to ask themselves how they are involved with that destiny. Now I'm not saying that everyone has to do this. But I can't help but ask myself why it should be that those of us who are doing that are labelled as second-rate writers, just because we're interested in the survival of the world. It seems that being interested in the survival of the world means being relegated to an inferior status, being likened to an editorial columnist. And that's unfair. I have fits of frustration over this, though I should be used to it by now.

I see a great deal of continuity between your essays and your novels. You try to get people to look at things in a new and different ways and you use a Marxist perspective to do this. For you as a writer and as a perspective for the 1990's, how relevant is Marxism today?

This is obviously not something that can be answered briefly, particularly given the fact that I am answering in a society that has demonized Marxism, that has effectively marginalized it. For me Marxism has been extremely important in two ways which I'll separate merely for the purposes of answering the question. To begin with, Marxism is related to the struggle of people everywhere, those who

> The tremendous problems that socialism has accumulated does not necessarily mean that people should no longer exercise control over their collective destiny and, in particular, control over the economy. I'm for returning to the democratic, subversive, liberating, participatory aspects of Marxism—and ending all dogma, revising everything about it.
>
> —*Ariel Dorfman*

have nothing but their bodies, who have worked all their lives yet remain powerless and impoverished. In that sense, it has been a foundation for my community and my culture. It has given us a set of tools with which to question and challenge an unjust world. Over the last one hundred and forty years it has provided the means by which a vast contingent of people, intellectuals as well those who are dispossessed, has voiced a call to change reality. In Chile, Marxism has served as a vehicle for communion. It has provided a common language, an everyday heritage for a great many people, including those who attempted a revolution through democratic means. The Chilean road to socialism attempted to solve problems of poverty and inequality and brutality which capitalism, after hundreds of years, had not solved. Problems which, in fact, capitalism has produced. But Marxism was also born out of the intellectual tradition of the West, and is an attempt to deal with a whole series of economic, social, and philosophic problems which arose during the Age of Reason and the Industrial Revolution. Many of those questions are still around. Regardless of what neoconservatives boastfully claim, I certainly don't think that capitalism has provided a very humane answer or a very satisfactory one to those dilemmas. In that sense, the way in which Marx and many of those who followed after him tried to make sense of the world is still—perhaps valid is not the right word—it is still extremely valuable as an instrument for understanding the structure of the contemporary world. As Fred Jameson [a Marxist literary critic at Duke University] has suggested, in the age of late capital where the Western model has penetrated virtually every surface and depth of the planet, where it has become an overwhelming world system, some (though not all) of Marx's ideas seem more pertinent today than ever. Having said this, we must also realize that Marxism today, as an intellectual tradition and as a social system based upon that tradition, is in crisis. Actually, it's a healthy crisis with a double dimension which roughly corresponds to the two dimensions I mentioned before. One is a crisis at the intellectual level. There are contemporary challenges in the world today to the way in which Marxists—and there are many types, of course—have looked at the world and tried to know and change it. The question of women's rights, the problem of ecology, establishing limits to industrial growth—all these issues make demands on Marxism and are in fact changing it quite drastically. Then there is the other aspect of this crisis, which has to do with Marxism as an instrument for social change in specific political surroundings and the future of socialism as an alternative for humanity. We are at an extremely promising moment, when those societies that have tried to develop under socialism find themselves in great difficulty. Having lived through a process where we Chileans tried to create a socialist system through democratic means, and having suffered the intervention of the United States and the boycott and sabotage of the wealthier sectors of my country, I know how hard it is to build something new in the midst of the old structures, when you are being invaded, blocked, cornered, and provoked. But at the same time I have been critical of the authoritarian solutions imposed upon so many people in the name of socialism, the result of which is that socialism, for many people, has become a discredited term. For example, we have a government in China today which on the one hand is trying to incorporate capitalism and the resultant injustice into its economy, and on the other hand is suppressing the freedom of its people with guns. All in the name of socialism! The question then becomes, how can these societies find political freedom, more participation, no censorship, and at the same time not reinstate the degrading aspects of capitalism? It is a daunting task. When people in Poland say—and I've been a strong Solidarity supporter from the beginning—when they say that they want capitalist solutions in Poland, I think they're crazy. Surely Polish workers don't want a corporation run by a few executives to decide whether or not to close a factory. Surely they don't want five per cent of the population to have its wealth increased many times over, as was the case during the Reagan years. They want consumer goods, but surely they don't want only the well-to-do to have health care or child care. They can't want millions of homeless people, or increased pollution, or growth through the exploitation of Third World countries. At least I hope that they don't want that. The tremendous problems that socialism has accumulated does not necessarily mean that people should no longer exercise control over their collective destiny and, in particular, control over the economy. I'm for returning to the democratic, subversive, liberating, participatory aspects of Marxism—and ending all dogma, revising everything about it. We're at the point where we should question everything.

Tell me where your work is now. What other projects are you working on that you can tell me about?

Well, this year will be dedicated to finishing the stage version of **Widows** and to **Reader,** another play. I will also be revising **Missing Continents.** You're finding me at a moment when I'm simplifying my life by finishing several projects. Beyond that, I've got several novels ahead of me. One is the continuation of **Mascara.** It's a detective story. I think the problem of memory, how you investigate memory and how different social groups try to appropriate memory for their own ends will be very central. There will be a detective who is looking for some answers in his own life and for society in general. And there probably will be a parallel sequence where someone goes back to Chile trying to dig up information. It's a novel which I've already started working on. Then I have a second project, an his-

torical novel on an epic scale. The more I research it and the more I work on specific parts, the more complicated it gets. At the same time I would like this to be a simple novel if at all possible. But it doesn't seem like that will happen.

Dealing with what event or events?

It spans the history of Latin America from the end of the eighteenth century to the present. The axis of the novel is California in the 1840's. From there it moves backward into the past and forward into the future.

The California of the goldrush.

Let's call it the California of the goldrush. Lots of Chileans went there to mine gold.

I didn't know that.

Oh yes. A large number of them. I've been working on this for many years, nibbling here and there. I've got the main characters in my head—I have a notion of who they are and where they're going. My basic stumbling block has to do with the problematic nature of the historical events. I can't believe that what I'm writing really happened. In the end, I'm going to have to come to terms with the problem of history and allegory. I'm not sure whether it will turn out to be several novels or one immense novel—like **The Last Song** or maybe even larger—or perhaps several versions, a popular version and a more difficult, more hermetic version. I'm working on all these possibilities. I don't want to decide just yet. I've discovered that you work on something when it's ready. When I was younger I didn't understand when a novelist would say, "It took me ten years to write this." Now I do. I also have ideas for several plays, one of which I already mentioned, which deals with this idea of how you live side by side with those who have wronged you. Does it bring out the worst in you? Does it bring out the best in you? I'm not sure whether it's a play or a novel. It's there as a possibility. And then there are several other things. I have a book on exile that I'd like to complete. I've got enough work for a good ten years. So I have to figure out how these projects will fit in with our plans for returning to Chile. The return may be so traumatic that I may not be able to do these things. Or I may become interested in doing other things. I'm not sure. You know, there was a time that I thought I could write everything I ever wanted to write. And now . . . I'm forty-seven. I'm beginning to feel that time is running out. I never had that sensation until I finished **Mascara.** I started to feel that I should be careful with my priorities, with my time. (pp. 101-07)

Ariel Dorfman and John Incledon, in an interview in Chasqui, *Vol. XX, No. 1, May, 1991, pp. 95-107.*

James Polk (review date 2 June 1991)

[*In the following excerpt, Polk favorably reviews* Some Write to the Future, *noting particularly Dorfman's analysis of magic realism.*]

It is the business of the literary critic (as opposed to the mere book reviewer) to provide context for a work, site it somewhere in the cultural firmament and relate it to neighboring stars and galaxies. In *Some Write to the Future,* Ariel Dorfman, the Chilean poet, novelist, critic and playwright, turns criticism into a personal quest as well—for his own context, both as writer and citizen of Latin America.

He comes to the job with ample qualifications. A critic who has explored popular culture (*How to Read Donald Duck,* etc.), and a novelist who has examined the particularly Latin American thesis of fiction as political act (*The Last Song of Manuel Sendero,* etc.), Dorfman was also a defender of the Allende government and later a highly vocal exile. From these last, he brings to his criticism a sense of engagement and participation in the world around him.

As both political and literary being, he belongs to the Latin American traditions of the committed writer. An elite corps—numbering Neruda, Garcia Marquez, Fuentes, Carpentier, Vargas Llosa and Paz among its members—has made personal involvement in affairs of state and society into something of a creative act, an involvement that simultaneously exists apart from and is enmeshed with their art.

That commitment to an external, to a reality outside the particular work of fiction, is what this intelligent and thoughtful book is all about. It is not an easy thesis to explore. On one hand, Dorfman holds out his "fierce belief that our literature has an important role, indeed an essential one, to play in the liberation of the people of Latin America." But against this article of faith, he admits that the native readership of that literature is extremely limited. So how can an elite talking only to another elite liberate anyone? His answer to this question, which at first glance sounds unpersuasive and looks unclear, is to mythologize, to explore the super-reality that seems to so dominate daily life in Latin America.

What the author apparently means is suggested in the eclectic range of titles he examines. Not included are the social realist novels that predominated in post-revolutionary Mexico, or the Brazilian "novel of the northeast," or the "literature of the disappeared" produced by Argentine writers (mostly from exile) during that country's "dirty war."

Instead, except for a single long and provocative essay on the "testimonies" of Chilean survivors of the dark night of Pinochet, Dorfman focuses on "literary" works. Myth and fantasy are the staples here, and immediate political references are clouded in metaphor.

None of the works he discusses—by Miguel Angel Asturias, Jorge Luis Borges, Jose Maria Arguedas, Alejo Carpentier, Augusto Roa Bastos and Gabriel Garcia Marquez—is much concerned with the historical present. Instead, these authors offer a reading of the human condition (and of the Latin American condition) through abstraction and mystery. Whatever answers might be glimpsed here, in other words, are not to specific questions but rather to a kind of generalized uncertainty about life.

That glimpse calls for what Dorfman, in his essay on Gar-

cia Marquez, calls "a need to communicate in a new way" the special reality of the continent. As practiced by these writers, that way requires the evolution of a structure of magic and myth to explain the world. It also requires recognition of "the presence of the marvelous" as "a cultural experience that comes from the way people in Latin America cope with their existence."

The marvelous is Dorfman's synonym for that old chestnut, magical realism, a term he objects to because it implies mere literary technique rather than the strategy ordinary people employ to get them through the day. It is what Garcia Marquez in his Nobel Prize lecture called "this outsized reality," and is what unites writers as seemingly incompatible as Borges and Asturias.

It is also what Dorfman's "writing to the future" is all about. When Asturias in *Men of Maize,* for example, writes of the land and the people taking collective revenge against their ravagers, or when Carpentier's tyrant in *Reasons of State* searches for ways to "escape history," we are not in a world of the everyday. Instead, these authors operate in territory of enlarged metaphor and abstraction. They write about a Latin America where the mundane and the marvelous coexist. At present, the two don't always get along, but those who write to the future, as Dorfman shows us, provide a context in which they might.

> *James Polk, "Where the Mundane Meets the Marvelous," in* Book World—The Washington Post, *June 2, 1991, p. 11.*

Richard Hornby   (review date Winter 1992)

[*Hornby is an American educator and critic. In the following excerpt, he favorably compares the play* Widows *to a Greek tragedy, but criticizes the work as too episodic.*]

In [1992], the Mark Taper Forum presented Ariel Dorfman's *Widows,* an earnest piece dealing with Chile under the recent, brutal regime of General Augusto Pinochet. One of the worst evils of that government was the practice, common to many totalitarian countries, of "disappearing" people—arresting and murdering them, all the while disavowing the arrests or any knowledge of the individuals. The relatives are denied even their loved ones' bodies.

In the foreground of the play is a struggle between two army officers sent to develop a rural valley after a recent civil war. Both are tough individuals who have employed ruthless tactics in the past, but in this instance the Captain, of middle-class, professional background, prefers the carrot of a new fertilizer factory to pacify the region, while his cynical lieutenant, an aristocrat with important political connections, insists on using the stick of more terror.

In the background to the officers' personal struggle are the women of the valley, who are like a chorus in a Greek tragedy. All of their men have disappeared, apparently without a trace. One day, however, a body is washed up from the river, so battered and decayed that it is impossible to identify. The Lieutenant, acting against orders, simply burns the body, and intimidates the woman who insists it is that of her dead father. When another body is washed up, the Captain adopts a more clever tactic; when a woman comes to claim it, he sets up a rival claimant, who maintains that it is that of her husband, who died in a drunken accident.

The fact that the bodies are all but unrecognizable and can be claimed by almost anybody leads the women to a clever ploy of their own: 36 widows all claim to recognize the corpse, and demand it for burial. They demonstrate with bonfires until finally the Captain, under increasing political pressure, orders them slaughtered.

Despite the simple, austere plot outline, with its echoes of *Antigone* and *The Trojan Women*, *Widows* has an episodic sprawl. Adapted from Dorfman's novel by the author and Tony Kushner, the play remains too novelistic in structure, with many slow, loosely connected incidents, including an odd scene in a wealthy villa that is completely different in tone from the rest of the play. It occurs too late to be an effective counterpoint, and spoils the previously developed feeling of a ruthless power structure operating invisibly. The Captain is a well-developed, complex character, and his relationship with the Lieutenant is interesting because his supposed underling is actually more powerful than he, but the Lieutenant himself is a villainous stereotype, the man you love to hate, as are the aristocrats in the villa scene. The women are stolid, peasant folk; since they lack an articulate spokeswoman like Antigone in Sophocles' play or Hecuba in *Trojan Women*, their only force is one of sheer inertia. No one could deny the sincerity of the play, or the importance of its message, but it needs fewer scenes, with more development and complication within them, and more sharply developed conflicts. (pp. 632-33)

Richard Hornby, "Theatre in Southern California," in The Hudson Review, *Vol. XLIV, No. 4, Winter, 1992, pp. 631-38.*

John Butt (review date 28 February 1992)

[*In the following review of* Death and the Maiden, *Butt praises Dorfman for confronting audiences with the difficulties involved in establishing a democracy in a formerly totalitarian state.*]

The setting of Ariel Dorfman's harrowing play [*Death and the Maiden*] is timely: a new democracy, precariously established after a long period of brutal dictatorship; the country is recognizably Chile, although it could be any post-communist state. And its theme is intensely relevant: one of the dictatorship's victims, a woman devastated by rape and torture, suddenly and unexpectedly confronts the man who she is convinced brutalized her years before. She overpowers him and tries to force a confession from him under the threat of death.

Whereupon the audience is caught in a neat moral trap and is made to confront choices that most would presumably rather leave to the inhabitants of remote and less favoured countries; the image of the play itself as a mirror set before the comfortable liberal conscience is central to the work. The pressures on the spectators are cleverly managed. Juliet Stevenson's fine portrayal of the victim, Paul-

ine, spares us no discomfort as she oscillates between screeching vindictiveness and an unnerving coolness and flippancy. Our instinctive liberal distaste for her extremism is fortified by the possibility, which she herself admits, that she may have picked the wrong man, and by the fact that her mediocre but well-meaning husband eloquently presents the usual case for the normal processes of justice. We support her demand for summary justice, but her instability undermines her case, and we protest against the way she abuses the overwhelming moral authority that her dreadful experiences have conferred on her. We long, with her husband, for her to put down her gun and forget the whole damned business.

But our retreat from her extremism is blocked precisely by the character of her husband Escobar, whose decent and humane blandness is deeply suspect, as Bill Paterson makes brilliantly clear in his exposure of a lenient and adult reasonableness that is really motivated to an indeterminate extent by political ambition. Escobar's longstanding professional goal has just been reached: he has been nominated to the presidential commission of enquiry into the old regime's crimes, and the commission will name no names and bring no one to book. His wife's demand for revolutionary justice genuinely offends his humanitarianism, but he also fears its potential for embarrassing his career. Nor can we step sideways out of the impasse by endorsing the convincing argument that, whatever the facts of the case, the cycle of revenge will bring back fascism. This solution is advanced by the alleged torturer, and the play invites us to conclude, admittedly on slender evidence, that he really is guilty.

> [*Death and the Maiden*] offers no easy answers to the question of how the new democracies should deal with the criminals in their midst without either sinking back into violence or sweeping hideous crimes under the carpet.
>
> —*John Butt*

More than one critic has commented on this production's formal perfection, the way it unwinds with a remorseless inevitability that recalls the finest classical tragedy. Such praise hardly seems exaggerated. This version, directed by Lindsay Posner, has an economy, clarity and moral complexity that make it in some ways a definitive liberal tragic statement about the intractable dilemmas posed by the reestablishment of liberal democracy after a period of sadistic oppression.

But it is in the nature of essentially liberal statements like this play that they get their dramatic effect from presenting vast dilemmas and at the same time almost flaunting their inability to suggest solutions to them. The play offers no easy answers to the question of how the new democracies should deal with the criminals in their midst without either sinking back into violence or sweeping hideous crimes under the carpet. For this reason, it will incense everyone who thinks that it is reactionary obfuscation to suggest that some problems can't be cleared up by simple choices, in this case either by forgiving or by pulling the trigger. In fact, the play's depressing message is that none of the three characters can offer a solution because all are still re-living the past. It says that the worst injuries inflicted by those obscene regimes can't be healed merely by a quick change either of regime or of outlook on the part of the victims. Such tyrannies spawn misery that infects generations, not only destroying the minds and bodies of people who actually fell foul of the torturers, but returning years later to undermine the happiness and relationships of everyone, even those who, like Escobar, think that anything is better than the interminable perpetuation of violence.

> *John Butt, "Guilty Conscience?" in* The Times Literary Supplement, *No. 4639, February 28, 1992, p. 22.*

John Simon   (review date 30 March 1992)

[*An American writer and critic, Simon has served as a drama critic for* New York *magazine as well as a film critic for* Esquire *and* New Leader. *In the following excerpt, he criticizes Dorfman for trivializing torture and suffering in* Death and the Maiden.]

Ariel Dorfman, the Chilean writer, brings us his **Death and the Maiden,** a drama set in a country that, the program coyly tells us, "is probably Chile." A long era of dictatorship has yielded to a new democracy, and Gerardo Escobar, a lawyer, has been appointed to the presidential commission investigating political crimes. Driving back to his beach house, he blows a tire and, having neither a spare nor a jack (much is made of these two unconvincing circumstances), gets a stranger, Dr. Miranda, to give him a lift home. By an even less persuasive device, Miranda drops in after midnight, and Gerardo's wife, Paulina, recognizes him (or so she thinks) as the man who, fifteen years ago, participated in torturing her and repeatedly raped her. But she keeps mum.

Miranda accepts Gerardo's invitation to spend the night (more stretching of credibility), and while he sleeps, Paulina knocks him out, drags him into the living room, ties him to a chair, and gags him. In the morning, she is seated beside him with a gun. She tells her flabbergasted husband that they will hold a trial; Gerardo is to be the defense, Paulina the witness, prosecutor, and judge. Miranda, when he does get a chance to speak, flatly denies being *that* doctor. Paulina, we gather, has been mentally unbalanced since those terrible events: Is she capable of determining what's what? And how will she deal with Miranda if he is found guilty?

But we do not get enough of the Escobars' home life to infer just how crazy Paulina is. Or enough about this society to deduce whether Miranda's loving Schubert's famous quartet and quoting (or misquoting) Nietzsche constitute enough grounds for identifying a person. We don't even know what to make of the fact that former evildoers

are to be ferreted out but granted amnesty. Yet these are small matters compared to the basic insufficiency of reducing a national and individual tragedy to a mere whodunit. For despite the little grace (or disgrace) notes of humorous squabbles and troubled personal relationships, the play is really all is-he-or-isn't-he, did-he-or-didn't-he: too trivial for the amount of suffering on which it is predicated. Can you imagine *Hamlet* if its only real concern were whether Claudius did or did not poison his brother?

Yet even as a whodunit, **Death and the Maiden** fails because it avoids coming satisfactorily to grips with the one question it raises. Would Agatha Christie leave a murder unresolved and then pride herself on her ambiguity? And it isn't as if the wit, pathos, or language here were good enough to carry the play or even a half-pound paperweight. (pp. 87-8)

> *John Simon, "The Guary Apes," in* New York Magazine, *Vol. 25, No. 13, March 30, 1992, pp. 87-8.*

Kay Raymond   (review date October 1992 & February 1993)

[*In the following excerpt, Raymond provides an overview of* Some Write to the Future.]

In his latest work of criticism [**Some Write to the Future: Essays on Contemporary Latin American Fiction**], Ariel Dorfman, the Chilean professor, novelist, poet, and dramatist includes six essays translated from Spanish as well as one on Gabriel García Márquez written in English for this volume. Each essay deals with the work of a contemporary author (or in the case of the essay on Chilean testimonial literature, seven authors) from a different Latin American country, from Cuba to Guatemala, Columbia, Peru, Paraguay, and Argentina. Despite this wide geographical range, the essays all deal with narrative prose, generally with novels, and are unified by Dorfman's constant interest in the relationship between culture and politics.

For Dorfman, literature can never be separated from the goal of the social and economic liberation of Latin America. In the Introduction to **Some Write to the Future,** he states that the principal link between these essays is the fact that "all of these meditations stem from the same fierce belief that our literature has an important role, indeed an essential one, to play in the liberation of the people of Latin America." He admits that this affirmation of the revolutionary function of literature may appear more naive than it did twenty years ago, that in the world of the 90s it is harder to envision "significant change," but still maintains that "only an exploration of the ways in which our contemporary fiction subverts prevalent power, or submits to it, can reveal that fiction's true character."

Two of the essays were written more than twenty years ago. **"Men of Maize**: Myth as Time and Language,"** on Miguel Angel Asturias' novel, and **"Borges and American Violence"** were published in Dorfman's first collection of essays (*Imaginación y violencia en América*). They are published as they originally appeared with only a few changes to reflect current concerns. The author adds a parenthetical remark not in the Spanish version that there are hardly any women in Borges' works, and omits a short but rather gratuitous attack on another critic who has devoted too little attention to *Men of Maize* in an article. These essays, however, both fit into the general theme of repression and violence. Dorfman's attempt to "humanize" and make Borges' work central to the Latin American experience must be seen as an important contribution to the criticism of the outstanding Argentinean writer.

In the longest essay in the volume, **"Fathers and Bridges Over Hell: *Deep Rivers*,"** Dorfman concentrates on the social novel of José María Arguedas, defining its social message as one of final hope. **"Sandwiched Between Proust and the Mummy: Seven Notes and an Epilogue on Carpentier's *Reasons of State*"** is a 1980 essay about one of the Cuban writer's lesser-known works. **"The Rivers of Roa Bastos,"** a study of *Son of Man,* was written as an introduction to an English translation of the work.

Dorfman's 1982 piece, **"Political Code and Literary Code: The Testimonial Genre in Chile Today"** studies the testimonial literature of seven of the Pinochet regime's political prisoners. According to the author, not only does this literature witness the power of the written word and hope that fights against tyranny, but it is obviously one that affects him personally. This regime forced him to go into exile in 1973 (from which he did not return to his native country until 1990) to avoid being taken prisoner. He has chosen all male authors: Alejandro Witker, Rodrigo Rojas, Rolando Carrasco, Carlos Lira, Anibal Quijada Cerda, Manuel Cabieses, and Jorge Montealegre. His analysis includes excellent generalizations about the function and style of these works. Furthermore, despite his own commitment to leftist politics, he is capable of seeing the stylistic weakness of many of these:

> The reason, however, why I mention this first great defect of these accounts is that I believe that their carelessness with language, the fact that they consider it a mere vehicle for a truth that is already preestablished, that is, as an instrument that is almost extraneous to what is really important, is one of the most pronounced weaknesses of the left in Chile and, beyond them, of those who want to change the world in a revolutionary way.

Although Dorfman the critic has previously defended the validity of language used for propaganda, as a writer he sees that writing well, integrating form and substance, will produce a stronger, more vital, and more powerful literature.

Dorfman's writing varies in quality. At times his style is extremely difficult. This difficulty stems often from the complexity of his thought. However, the sentence and paragraph structure become convoluted, as when he discusses Ernesto's dreams in the essay on *Deep Rivers:* "There are, therefore, allies in this world, but they are not messianic saviors; and there are renewing spaces, but not to withdraw to, separating oneself from the day-to-day crossroads of life." The translations are done well, but perhaps with too much attention to accuracy of thought and

too little homage to English style. On the other hand, there are moments when the author uses a felicitous turn of phrase, as when he is describing the desire for fame in the essay on Carpentier's *Reasons of State:*

> The Head of State is, therefore, essentially colonized: his deepest desires are to leave behind his original earth and interfuse with the values of those who are "superior," to be a conspicuous member of the select group of humanity who happen to own the cannons, the factories, and the phonemes and who can guarantee him a place in their dictionaries.

We have, obviously, left the best for last. **"Someone Writes to the Future: Meditations on Hope and Violence in García Márquez"** must be read by anyone preparing to teach or discuss *One Hundred Years of Solitude.* Dorfman's analysis serves as a catalyst for thought, and as a corrective for the overuse, indeed the abuse of the term "magic realism" or "magical realism" (at one point Isabel Allende was called "The Queen of Magical Realism" in a television sketch about her!). Too frequently today any Latin American literature automatically falls under the denomination of "magical realism." Dorfman points out the two traditions in Latin American culture, that of the literature of the educated minority, found principally in cities, and that of the majority, the popular/oral or folk tradition, found mainly in the countryside. He situates García Márquez's style at the confluence of these two traditions, and explains that the presence of the marvelous proves that "that term ['magical realism'] attempts to explain what happens in novels such as these as merely literary strategy rather than a cultural experience that comes from the way people in Latin America cope with their existence." His formulation certainly expands the horizons and goes beyond any simplistic formulae in explaining the artistic achievements of Gabriel García Márquez.

Some Write to the Future is definitely worth reading, if only for the essay on García Márquez. But Dorfman's extensive review of the literature on each of the writers he includes is also invaluable for the professional who is looking for a deeper analysis of these works; the notes are extensive and show a wide knowledge of the bibliography. Central ideas from works found in the bibliography in Spanish are provided in summary form to the reader of English. Dorfman's ideas are provocative and challenging, and the book should prove invaluable to the study of many areas of contemporary literature. (pp. 256-58)

Kay Raymond, in a review of "Some Write to the Future: Essays on Contemporary Latin American Fiction," in College Literature, *Vol. 19, No. 3 & Vol. 20, No. 1, October, 1992 & February, 1993, pp. 256-58.*

FURTHER READING

Doughty, Louise. "Under the Oppressor." *The Times Literary Supplement,* No. 4656 (26 June 1992): 22.
    Review of *My House Is on Fire* in which Doughty praises Dorfman's humanistic depiction of political oppression and his ability to locate hope in the midst of tragedy.

Graham-Yooll, Andrew. "Dorfman: A Case of Conscience." *Index on Censorship* 20, No. 6 (June 1991): 3-4.
    Interview in which Dorfman discusses Chile's transition from dictatorship to democracy and his plays *Death and the Maiden* and *Reader.*

Kramer, Mimi. "Magical Opportunism." *The New Yorker* LXVIII, No. 6 (30 March 1992): 69.
    Review of the 1992 New York production of *Death and the Maiden* in which Kramer faults Dorfman's simplistic treatment of violence and Latin American politics.

Lyon, Ted. "Review of *Hard Rain.*" *Books Abroad* 49, No. 1 (Winter 1975): 84-5.
    Argues that although the tone in *Hard Rain* is often pedantic and sarcastic, the novel is a valuable cultural account of Chile during the early 1970s.

Nieto, Margarita. "In Chile: The Lingering Stench of Fear." *Los Angeles Times Book Review* (28 January 1990): 3, 10.
    Criticizes Dorfman's lack of character development in *My House Is on Fire,* but praises his poetic language and talent as a storyteller.

Smith, Wendy. "Ariel Dorfman." *Publishers Weekly* 234, No. 17 (21 October 1988): 39-40.
    Interview in which Dorfman comments on his novel *Mascara.*

Additional coverage of Dorfman's life and career is contained in the following sources published by Gale Research: *Contemporary Authors,* Vols. 124, 130; *Contemporary Literary Criticism,* Vol. 48; and *Hispanic Writers.*

Bob Dylan

1941-

(Born Robert Allen Zimmerman) American songwriter, poet, singer, and screenwriter.

The following entry presents criticism on Dylan's career as a performer and songwriter. For further information on Dylan's life and career, see *CLC,* Volumes 3, 4, 6, and 12.

INTRODUCTION

Among the most dynamic and popular songwriters of his day, Dylan is praised for the spontaneity and sometimes caustic honesty of his lyrics. Reflecting the rebellious attitudes of his generation toward authority, politics, and institutionally prescribed norms, the diverse songs of Dylan's career consistently challenge the preconceptions and expectations of his audience. Critics generally agree that Dylan has accurately reflected the alienation, anger, anxiety, desperation, and philosophy of the generation of young adults who came to maturity in the 1960s. Biographer Anthony Scaduto noted: "For millions of the young, Dylan has been a poet of the streets, crying out in pain against society's indifference and stupidity; his voice, his words, his visions gave substance to their radicalization."

The son of a furniture and business salesman, Dylan spent his childhood and youth in Hibbing, Minnesota. During his teens, he taught himself guitar, piano, and harmonica, and gained an appreciation for country music, particularly that of Hank Williams, as well as the music of Little Richard and other black performers who combined elements of gospel, rhythm and blues, and rock and roll. While at the University of Minnesota, Dylan became interested in the folk revival that was then sweeping the country and began playing folk music at The Ten O'Clock Scholar, a local coffeehouse. He soon dropped out of school and moved to New York City, where he began playing in Greenwich Village in the early 1960s.

At the age of twenty, Dylan released his first album, *Bob Dylan.* A collection of blues and folk songs by such artists as Jesse Fuller and Blind Lemon Jefferson, the album contained only two original songs, "Talkin' New York" and "Song to Woody," and achieved only limited success. Within a year Dylan had completed *The Freewheelin' Bob Dylan,* a collection of primarily original songs united by related themes of protest and apocalypse. By the time Dylan released *The Times They Are A-Changin'* in 1964, he had been designated as a prominent media spokesperson for the counterculture protest movement. Uncomfortable with the role, and growing increasingly pessimistic about the ability of the counterculture to affect change, Dylan remarked: "What Joan Baez is doing, and all those people demonstrating, they're not gonna save the world. It's not true they can change men's hearts. . . . Nobody's gonna learn by somebody else showing them or teaching them. People have to learn by themselves." In his ensuing albums Dylan created music that continually confounded his followers' expectations. *Another Side of Bob Dylan,* a collection of highly personal folk ballads and introspective love songs, was followed by *Bringing It All Back Home,* in which Dylan returned to his roots in rock and gospel. Although as critical of society as before, he made no direct references to racism, war, or political activism in his songs of the mid-1960s. During this period, Dylan enraged audiences accustomed to his image as an acoustic folksinger by appearing at public performances with an electric guitar. While he lost many fans who considered such an act a capitulation to commercialism and a betrayal of his folk image, Dylan greatly broadened his audience with *Highway 61 Revisited* and *Blonde on Blonde,* which most critics consider among his best works due to their successful fusion of folk and rock influences and use of mystical, apocalyptic lyrics dense with images and allusions.

In July 1966, at the height of his popularity, Dylan broke his neck in a near-fatal motorcycle accident that led to public speculation as to whether he was alive or dead. While recuperating in Woodstock, New York, he reexamined his Judaic roots and began writing and recording demo versions of new songs with his backup group, The Band. Several of these recordings were released in 1975 as *The Basement Tapes.* Ignoring popular trends as before, Dylan's first release following the accident was a slow-paced, predominantly acoustical album, *John Wesley Harding.* This was followed by two unusually optimistic volumes, *Nashville Skyline,* a collection of pure country music, and *New Morning.* Both of these works reflected Dylan's happiness in his personal life at the time yet seemed to some a denial of his protest and civil rights responsibilities at the height of the Vietnam War.

Dylan's musical output diminished somewhat during the early 1970s. In 1971 he published *Tarantula,* a loose collection of prose, poems, letters and other pieces written between 1965 and 1966 that had been informally circulating amongst Dylan collectors for several years. Widely dismissed as uncohesive, the book was described by Michael Rogers as "the hallucination of a methed-up poker player, rapidly dealing the cards, all of which reveal only parts of himself in a cosmically tricked deck." Following the release of *Planet Waves* in 1974, Dylan garnered major media attention as he undertook a comeback tour in which audience demand greatly exceeded available seating for his concerts. In 1975 Dylan released *Blood on the Tracks,* an album most critics celebrated as Dylan's best since the 1960s. Using ideas more related to visual art than music, Dylan employed unusual imagery and blurred distinctions between reality and illusion to challenge common notions of the everyday world. This work, as well as his next album, *Desire,* achieved widespread success in both the United States and Europe, and marked a second high point in his career.

In 1977 Dylan became involved in a divorce with his wife Sara and a bitter custody struggle for his children that biographers assert drained him emotionally and stifled his artistic output for two years. In 1978, while touring to support his album *Street Legal,* Dylan experienced a religious vision ("a bornagain experience, if you want to call it that") that he later asserted made him question his moral values and saved him from self-destructive behavior. Professing a belief in fundamentalist Christianity, Dylan began to incorporate into his music a concern with religious salvation and impending apocalypse. While many fans expressed dissatisfaction with Dylan's overt proselytizing on such albums as *Slow Train Coming* and *Saved,* others detected in his lyrics a continuation of his earlier concerns with change and social prophecy. Although *Slow Train Coming* was a surprise commercial success, the ensuing albums, *Saved* and *Shot of Love,* were generally considered commercial and critical failures.

By 1983, with the release of *Infidels,* Dylan was forced to contend with the transition the music industry was making toward video on MTV. During this period, critics asserted that Dylan allowed others to take over video productions of his songs, which failed to incite commercial or critical interest. However, Dylan remained a prominent public figure during the mid-1980s due to performances in both the 1985 single "We Are the World" and the Live Aid benefit concert which were designed to secure funds for famine relief in Ethiopia. The same year Dylan released *Biograph,* a highly popular five album set of previously released recordings and "bootlegs" (unreleased recordings in circulation amongst Dylan collectors) on which he also provided brief commentaries. Beginning in 1988, Dylan collaborated with veteran music stars George Harrison, Jeff Lynne, Roy Orbison, and Tom Petty on two albums, *Traveling Wilburys* and *Traveling Wilbury Volume 3.* Dylan's releases of the late 1980s included *Knocked Out Loaded, Oh Mercy,* and *Under the Red Sky.* His 1992 album *Good as I Been to You,* an acoustic collection of blues and folk standards, is reminiscent of his first album *Bob Dylan,* released thirty years earlier.

The various shifts in Dylan's career are apparent in the many notable songs that he has written. *The Freewheelin' Bob Dylan* contains some of Dylan's best known protest lyrics, including "Blowin' in the Wind" and "A Hard Rain's A-Gonna Fall." "Blowin' in the Wind," which became a civil rights anthem during the 1960s, suggests the tortuous problems of Dylan's generation through powerful imagery and shifts in the narrator's perspective, yet offers no easy solution for his audience, for whom "the answer is blowin' in the wind." In "Hard Rain" Dylan similarly protests injustices that threaten to destroy the world, but uses a prophetic tone and apocalyptic imagery that suggests a kind of cumulative catalog on the order of Biblical lists or Allen Ginsberg's poem "Howl." Dylan's rejection of his early role as a politically committed folksinger and his shift to electric music is exemplified on *Bringing It All Back Home* in songs such as "Subterranean Homesick Blues." In this insistent and angry lyric Dylan implies that the uniquely creative individual is forced into outsider status by society, which shuns individuality and imagination and seeks to instill arbitrary cultural norms.

On *Highway 61 Revisited* Dylan continues in the vein of indirect social criticism by returning to the themes of alienation and loss of identity in such songs as "Like a Rolling Stone" and "Ballad of a Thin Man." Dylan's 1975 album *Blood on the Tracks* features songs reflecting the sorrow, passion, and bitterness of his personal life at the time. For example, "Tangled Up in Blue" ("a song it took me ten years to live and ten years to write") relates a quest for an idealized woman, and "If You See Her, Say Hello" directly refers to the breakup of his marriage. Among Dylan's most popular songs from the time of his conversion to Christianity is "Gotta Serve Somebody" from *Slow Train Coming,* which became a top-selling single and won Dylan a Grammy Award for Best Male Vocal Performance despite its message—atypical for a rock song—about the need for humanity to commit either to the Devil or to God in the search for truth.

Dylan's work has elicited a wide variety of critical responses, including journalistic, literary, and biographical commentaries. One group of critics, asserting that Dylan's lyrics are inseparable from the metrical structures of his music, have examined his vocal delivery and alteration of meaning in live performance. Others have scrutinized Dylan's lyrics as poetry. Admired by such Beat poets as Lawrence Ferlinghetti, Kenneth Rexroth, and Allen Ginsberg, to whom he is sometimes compared for his vocal delivery—which often makes use of an angry, derisive syntax, more chanted than sung—Dylan has also drawn comparisons to such diverse American and European poets as Walt Whitman, William Blake, and Arthur Rimbaud for his emphasis on individuality, personal fulfillment, pure subjectivism, and rebellion. Ginsberg credited Dylan with having "altered the course of poetics in America. . . . Dylan has almost single-handedly brought language back to its original poetic form which is minstrelsy."

PRINCIPAL WORKS

Bob Dylan (songs) 1962
The Freewheelin' Bob Dylan (songs) 1963
Another Side of Bob Dylan (songs) 1964
The Times They Are A-Changin' (songs) 1964
Bringing It All Back Home (songs) 1965
Highway 61 Revisited (songs) 1965
Blonde on Blonde (songs) 1966
Bob Dylan's Greatest Hits I (songs) 1967
John Wesley Harding (songs) 1968
Nashville Skyline (songs) 1969
New Morning (songs) 1970
Self Portrait (songs) 1970
Tarantula (prose writings) 1970
Bob Dylan's Greatest Hits II (songs) 1971
Dylan (songs) 1973
Pat Garrett and Billy the Kid (film soundtrack) 1973
Words (poem) 1973
Writings and Drawings (songs, poems, drawings, and writings) 1973; expanded as *Lyrics: 1962-1985*, 1985
Before the Flood [with The Band] (songs) 1974
Blood on the Tracks (songs) 1974
Planet Waves (songs) 1974
The Basement Tapes [with The Band] (songs) 1975
Desire (songs) 1976
Hard Rain (songs) 1976
Bob Dylan at Budokan (songs) 1978
Bob Dylan: Masterpieces (songs) 1978
Renaldo and Clara (screenplay) 1978
Street Legal (songs) 1978
Slow Train Coming (songs) 1979
Saved (songs) 1980
Shot of Love (songs) 1981
Infidels (songs) 1983
Real Live (songs) 1984
Biograph. 3 vols. (songs) 1985
Empire Burlesque (songs) 1985
Knocked Out Loaded (songs) 1986
Hearts of Fire (film soundtrack) 1987
Down in the Groove (songs) 1988
Traveling Wilburys [with George Harrison, Jeff Lynn, Roy Orbison, Tom Petty] (songs) 1988
Dylan and the Dead [with The Grateful Dead] (songs) 1989
Oh Mercy (songs) 1989
†*Traveling Wilburys Volume 3* (songs) 1990
Under the Red Sky (songs) 1990

Bootleg Series I-III (songs) 1991

*The songs on *The Basement Tapes* were recorded in 1967.

†No second volume by the Traveling Wilburys was released.

CRITICISM

Frank Kermode (essay date May 1972)

[*Kermode is an English critic who combines expert traditional scholarship with modern critical approaches from such fields as structuralism and phenomenology. In the following excerpt, Kermode examines Dylan's intentional use of obscurity in his lyrics of the 1960s and early 1970s.*]

According to Dylan himself, anything he can sing is a song and anything he can't sing is a poem. It's a useful distinction, but here it will have to be flouted, since the subject is precisely the poems Dylan sings. Everybody knows that the words, or for that matter the notes, on the page give a very poor idea of what a Dylan song really sounds like—he is a virtuoso executant, and since he writes the words with virtuoso performance in mind, they can't, on the page, be more than the musical notes are: reminders, hints, or shadows. All the same, there's quite a lot of good poetry which started life in a similar way—Greek tragedy, medieval ballad—and has survived the loss of music and performance. How do Dylan's poems stand up?

In his own kind it goes without saying that he has no close rival; The Beatles' "Eleanor Rigby" is a more accomplished lyric, probably, than any of Dylan's, but it isn't of the same kind. Some of Dylan's work is avowedly based on traditional models, but he always reinvents them; a poem that starts **"As I Went Out One Morning"** soon loses its resemblance to its predecessors, and even in straight imitations of ballads about folk heroes he tends to shed the regularities of rhyme and meter which, in the old days, were an unconscious tribute by the poet to high-class culture.

> Jesse went to rest with his hands on his breast;
> He died with a smile on his face.
> He was born one day in the county of Clay,
> And came from a solitary race.

That's closer to Wordsworth than Dylan will ever want to be.

Some folk song acquires obscurities simply by long transmission, or because special meanings are lost. (Who can be sure that *the foggy dew* is a euphemism for virginity?) Sea chanteys are obscure and distorted because they are work songs, and the scribes probably had trouble sorting out words from grunts. Art songs can be transformed into poetic obscurity within a few years of their adoption by folk singers. This kind of obscurity interests Dylan; it has what he called in an interview "mystery"—"its meaninglessness is holy," he said, and he likes to put that kind of mystery into his own lyrics from the start. He has achieved this in a variety of ways. A recent song, **"If Dogs Run Free,"** uses the delicious wordless vocal scribble of a black scat-singer to render mysterious a rather empty lyric, and this seems just as much in character as those unfocused color photographs on his record sleeves. Certainly his long-established preference for mystery in the verbal texture has been an important factor in his development.

Dylan's career of a decade or so is already conventionally divided into three periods. The first is Protest. The second is marked not only by the use of electric guitar and so forth, but by a change of tone more easily recognized than described: protest offered too simple a kind of authenticity, and the songs of 1964-65 have to do with a more complex notion of the truth, with what he called in **"Tombstone Blues"** "the geometry of innocence." There is now no alternative society, no easy way to drop out of the general guilt, no absolute freedom: "Are birds free / From the chains of the skyway?" The recommendation, insofar as there is one, is against "lifelessness," the sort of self-betrayal against which he warns Ramona, and for some kind of recognition that after you've escaped from the meaninglessness of appearance into unglamorous reality—down the manhole, or into Desolation Row—innocence and authenticity lie only in responding truly to the casual challenges of precisely the kind of mystery represented by the incoherence and irrationality of Dylan's own texts. The third period is what we now have: musical experiment and pastiche or re-exploration of old styles—country, blues, rock and roll, etc., including reminiscences of his own earlier manners.

Shakespeare and Beethoven are traditionally allowed four periods, so how is Dylan using his up so fast? There are two interrelated reasons, one personal and the other public. Dylan is a great rejecter—he rejects his own role-playing ("I'm really not the right person to tramp around the country saving souls"), his own audience (he says he's not a "performer" and the songs would exist without an audience), and his own songs. He dislikes anything programmatic, mistrusts the wrong kind of relevance or specificity ("there's nothing, absolutely nothing, to be specific *about*"). If you look at the song that had the greatest political effect—**"Blowin' in the Wind"**—you'll see that even there the questions are not all about pacifism or liberty or equality, and those that are lack specificity, are very abstractly presented, and answered only by the mysterious ballad refrain. **"With God on Our Side,"** though undoubtedly more pointed and ironical, is more complex, notably in the Jesus and Judas reference, than its simple occasion requires. Dylan often speaks of his distrust for "messages," and even in the relatively straightforward **"Who Killed Davey Moore?"** the message is partly concealed behind an ancient and practically universal folk motif.

This preference for mystery, opacity, a sort of emptiness in his texts, a passivity about meaning, is no doubt a deep temperamental trait. Some of the best of the early poems are talking blues, and even then he was a master of the obliquely subversive dropout lines at the ends of the stanzas, as in **"Talkin' World War III Blues"** ("And I drove down 42nd street / In my Cadillac / Good car to drive after a war"), or in the celebrated closing lines. The movie *Don't Look Back* has some casual remarks that illustrate a refusal to accept the responsibility of being explicit or suasive. "I just go out there and sing 'em . . . I got nothing to say about these things I write." The gushing High Sheriff's Lady of Nottingham is presented with a mouth organ, which constitutes a parable about mystery in personality and in song: Hamlet gave the tiresome and unmusical Guildenstern a recorder for the same reason. "Why, look you now," says Hamlet, "how unworthy a thing you make of me! You would play upon me, you would seem to know my stops, you would pluck out the heart of my mystery . . . 'Sblood, do you think I am easier to be play'd on than a pipe?" The second and third periods, different as they are, have in common bigger and more various musical sound and the rougher, more random verbal texture that ensures the protection of mystery. The listener provides the response, brings his own meanings; he is offered no message, only mystery. Dylan says that audience reaction "doesn't matter," but also that he welcomes "with open arms" people who analyze his songs.

This necessary public participation is a factor in his rapid changes of style. For earlier poets change was a slower process, issuing from an active dialogue with an audience that was always ready for a manageable extension of the poet's language. Of course the whole process speeded up when it became an ambition on the part of poets to shock by dropping out of public syntax and crossing commonplace semantic limits—say, after Rimbaud. Now, however, there is a new factor: instant response from a public which is not interested in old styles of verbal precision, doesn't care much if the words are inaudible or obscure, seeks the gut before the mental response. In this situation there is no interpretive feedback, no check on sense; liberated from linguistic responsibility the poet cultivates his own mystery, does his own thing only.

Dylan can rely on the crispness, accuracy and immediacy of the musical performance to cover semantic blur. Thus the brilliant second-period **"Subterranean Homesick Blues"**—modern skeltonics delivered with great pace and verve—has as a very general theme the hostility between dropout drug users and the police, with observations on obscenity of the whole social and education system; but it is full of allusions to which every man brings his own key. The most ambitious example of these procedures is **"Desolation Row."** This strange narrative begins: "They're selling postcards of the hanging / They're painting the passports brown." We're in a surrealist town with a circus, a beauty parlor for sailors, a restless riot squad. Behind all this stands the unattractive but apparently stable Desolation Row. From it may be seen a procession of figures, all behaving uncharacteristically: Cinderella, Romeo, the Good Samaritan, Ophelia, "Einstein disguised as Robin Hood" and, having abandoned the electric violin, on the bum; a Doctor Filth, the Phantom of the Opera in disguise, Casanova; finally T. S. Eliot and Ezra Pound in a seascape with mermaids. All this is a deliberate cultural jumble—history seen flat, without depth, culture heroes of all kinds known only by their names, their attributes lost by intergenerational erosion—all of them so much unreality against the background of Desolation Row, the flat and dusty truth, the myth before the myth began. That this is the plot Dylan makes clear in a last verse which rejects a correspondent for trying out culture figures on him: "I had to rearrange their faces / And give them all another name." Send me no more such letters, he adds; send no more letters at all, "Not unless you mail them from / Desolation Row." Here the general deviance, the lack of stereoscopy in the cultural references, gives the poem its whole force.

The later work continues to be unpredictable, offering no interpretive handholds. There is even an alteration or extension of the quality of Dylan's own voice. How different from the characteristically rebarbative whine is the baritone assurance of **"Lay, Lady, Lay."** This song also has a very accomplished lyric: no explanations, but enough suggestiveness (in "His clothes are dirty but his, his hands are clean," for example) to keep it clear of the banality of pop love song. **"New Morning"** is a simple sketch which the dependable buffs have filled with enormous symbolisms of rebirth; what's characteristic here is the line "Automobile comin' into style," which doesn't belong to the pictures in any obvious way, and might push the date of the action back a century. This is tough on the allegorists, but good for Dylan, who needs organized ambiguity rather than automatic writing to preserve himself best as a poet.

And Dylan remains a poet, as he has remained a virtuoso of the voice—snarling, pushing words and tunes askew, endlessly inventive. His peculiar relationship with his audience—they must teach themselves to do the work of performance and interpretation—has its dangers, which is why he often tells them that it is not his business to solve their problems but simply to get on with his own work. They can be co-creators if they want to, or drop out. So far, despite the occasional outburst of dismay, they have stayed with him, and he has himself probably seen that he can be too inward, too solipsistic. What he offers is mystery, not just opacity, a geometry of innocence which they can flesh out. His poems have to be open, empty, inviting collusion. To write thus is to practice a very modern art, though, as Dylan is well aware, it is an art with a complicated past. (pp. 110-18, 188)

Frank Kermode, "Bob Dylan: The Metaphor at the End of the Funnel," in Esquire, Vol. LXXVII, No. 5, May, 1972, pp. 109-18, 188.

Michael Gray (essay date 1972)

[*Gray's* Song and Dance Man: The Art of Bob Dylan *is a seminal study that definitively established Dylan as a viable subject for serious critical study. In the following excerpt from his introduction to* Song and Dance Man, *Gray insists that in his songs Dylan offers "the artistic recreation of the individual's struggle in our times—a vision of life within chaos—a very contemporary, and yet universal, vision for the English-speaking world."*]

Dylan uses much more than language in his art: his words are presented not as poems but as parts of songs. This is not to suggest that Dylan is no poet—but simply to re-

I remember going in and talking to [Dylan] and playing him some of the *Sgt. Pepper* album. He said, Oh I get it, you don't want to be cute any more! That summed it up. That was sort of what it was. The cute period had ended. It started to be art, that was what happened. Dylan brought poetry into lyrics so you found John doing his Dylan impression on "You've Got To Hide Your Love Away". We were highly influenced by him . . .

—*Paul McCartney, in an interview with* The Telegraph *reprinted in* Wanted Man: In Search of Bob Dylan, *Black Spring Press, 1990.*

member that he is certainly a composer, and a singer too, at the same time. Where some attempt is made to isolate the words—to study verses like stanzas of poetry proper—it ought to be kept in mind that the selection and organisation of Dylan's language is governed by the artistic disciplines of a medium not solely linguistic or literary. It cannot be emphasised too strongly that Dylan's finished works of art are his recordings—that like his vocal performances and his music, his words are just ingredients.

To lift off the lyrics (using that word in the song-writing sense) is to disrupt the intimacy of connexion between words and music. Structurally, the words of a song differ necessarily from those of a poem. They are not the sole arbiters of their own intended effects, rhythmically or in less technical ways.

In print, the rhythmic pattern of the following lines, for instance, might be as indicated here:

Eīnstĕin dĭsguīsed ăs Rōbĭn Hōod
Wĭth hĭs mēmŏrĭes ĭn ă trŭnk . . .

whereas in context—the context of the song as recorded (it is **'Desolation Row'**, from the 1965 album *Highway 61 Revisited*)—the rhythmic pattern is this:

Eīnsteīn dĭsguīsed ăs Rōbĭn Hŏod
Wĭth hīs mēmŏrĭes īn ā trūnk . . .

I am suggesting the kind of thing that must be borne in mind if we approach analysis, and not that no analysis should be tried. Too many of those who stand by Dylan's art as they see it contend, apparently as proof of its rare quality, that it cannot or should not be analysed. Add to this the mass uneasiness which talk of 'literary criticism' produces at the present time and one has enough to explain, in the rush of 'enthusiasm', the lamentable absence of critical concern which has greeted Dylan's work.

To analyse is first to find a context, which involves asking definite questions. Who are today's artists? What, of real consequence, has appeared since the work of D. H. Lawrence? This book tries to explain why my answer has to be that Bob Dylan is the artist who has vitally enhanced our perceptive abilities in the last ten years. A great artist.

It seems obvious to me, in consequence, that by the beginning of the twenty-first century, and for a long time after that, those who want to understand the generation which has been growing up in the West in the 1960s and 1970s to alter the rest of our times, will find it vital to study Bob Dylan's art very closely.

It is, of course, hard to make firm contemporary judgements—yet for precisely the reasons which have enforced my sense of the difficulties involved, it is necessary to state a case for Dylan *now*. I have cited Lawrence deliberately—conscious that he provides, unhappily, an example of an artist who went uncredited for far too long by the generations he was addressing so urgently. Dylan gives no such impression of being a sage in haste, and in many ways has hardly gone uncredited: but it would be a comparable disaster were a knowledge of Dylan's work to remain confined to those who explore it at the moment. I have tried, therefore, in what follows, to assess the great value of Bob Dylan's art—and so to get it more widely listened to and discussed.

Eight years ago, rock music was largely despised by the mass of those American and British students who follow it so devotedly today. Though they have since been put right on this—largely at Dylan's instigation—the older intelligentsia has not caught on. It has in the end recognised that films can be works of art, but rock music—no, surely not, not that!

So ignorance widens the generation breach. A student of today who can move calmly from, say, a consideration of Edmund Spenser to one of the Rolling Stones gets told that such facility is, deplorably, symptomatic of what T. S. Eliot called 'the dissociation of sensibility'. This simply exposes a similar limitation to that under which the Victorian critic struggled. Think of poor, brilliant Matthew Arnold, breathing in the sexual panic of his times and so deciding that Chaucer's work, because it showed no such panic, was 'lacking in high seriousness'.

It is time it was more generally recognised that to use rock music, as Dylan has done, is not to be, *ipso facto,* lacking in such high seriousness; and the corollary of this is to analyse, not shudder at, what Dylan has achieved.

There is a sense in which, more fully than F. Scott Fitzgerald did, Dylan has created a generation. For those of us within that generation, the possibilities of our inner lives have been intrinsically enhanced by the impingement of Dylan's art—by the impact of his consciousness on ours. The point that needs equal emphasis is that this impact, this impingement, need not be, as direct experience, exclusive to one generation, any more than the effects of Dylan's achievement, as indirect experience, can be discounted as a vital part of contemporary, changing, everyday life.

Whenever an artist of such real power emerges, there is a fatalistic desire, on the part of those who appreciate it, not to analyse but to submit. People can hardly be expect-

ed to question critically the quality of the artist's achievement when they are so much more concerned with the style of their own surrender to it. The critical questioning is necessary, though, if, unlike politicians, we are concerned about the direction in which our civilisation moves as well as with its methods of getting along. There is a collaborative process involved in art's impingement: the artist's work must be receptively approached before it can function fully.

I am not arguing that Dylan's work has been ignored on every level, but it is the case that though the Underground, obviously, has picked up on it, the real impact of Dylan's art has passed unnoticed by both the literati and the mass-media, while that other impact—the impact of the show-biz phenomenon—has been far from ignored. Dylan has been interviewed, his concerts written up, his records reviewed, with relish and persistence; but reviews and interviews are rarely designed for analysis so much as for a kind of flippant prying. The review is as far removed from real criticism as is the interview from real dialogue.

In Dylan's case there has been plenty of this superficial Message-Hunting. It provokes, in the artist, an appropriate defensiveness:

> DYLAN: . . . I do know what my songs are about.
>
> PLAYBOY: And what's that?
>
> DYLAN: Oh, some are about four minutes, some are about five minutes, and some, believe it or not, are about eleven or twelve.

The kind of insensitivity which lends itself readily to the interview is, of course, an occupational malaise. The journalist cannot afford the time or the perceptions needed for telling the truth—or even recognising it. He is trained to extract stories from life, to produce inaccurate outdated timetables of miserably external events, and to deny, in the process of extraction, the centrality of individual experience. And then again, editors must 'give the public what it wants'. The artist is the inevitable enemy of the journalist because he stands absolutely on the other side from any such obligation.

Dylan, of course, is hardly the only man to speak out honestly against what adds up to the contemporary dehumanising process—a process of discrediting imagination, of removing, in schools and via the media, any assertion of real individuality, and of obliterating our resources for a valid human dignity.

One must, though, distinguish between intention and effect in such a 'speaking out'. The phrase has qualitative implications. I don't know what Nietzsche had in mind when he wrote that people should not know more than they can creatively digest, but I take it as recognising that, for example, while the polemicist offers 'Freedom!' as a slogan and can communicate no more than the hysteria of the *word* to his audience, the creative artist can offer in his vision the living experience of freedom as a real force. Like the man said, all art is propaganda, but not all propaganda is art.

It is this power of the artist's which lends his ability to

'speak out' its quality. Great art is highly effective art; and Dylan's comes into this category. He seems to me better equipped creatively to 'speak out' for life and growth than any of his contemporaries.

What Dylan does not do—and consequently, whatever the mode of approach, the journalist's Message Hunt must fail—is consciously to offer a sustained, cohesive philosophy of life, intellectually considered and checked for contradictions. What I think he does offer is the artistic re-creation of the individual's struggle in our times—a vision of life within chaos—a very contemporary, and yet universal, vision for the English-speaking world. His work is truly educative, and thereby truly entertaining. Its virtue lies not in the immediacy, or pace, but in the perceptiveness of what it offers. It is too much like faint praise to say that Dylan adds a fresh voice to the cluster of modern writers' attempts to deal with the problem of loss of identity and individuality. At its best, Dylan's work possesses much more than freshness: it has that clear individually-disciplined integrity which is capable of 'representing the age' and competent, therefore, to go beyond and outside it—to clarify by focusing, with a vital intelligence, on its confusions.

From the most elementary consideration of Dylan's art it is plain how different is its capacity from a facility for collating a few common denominators of sentiment to which everyone feels susceptible, as (say) the Beatles did. The process whereby *their* work functioned engaged no individual consciousness: it was 'dealing in the known and the cheap' and sustained its pretence at a connexion with the individual focus only by the careful preservation and inclusion (to a formula) of an ostensibly *playful* eccentricity. Lennon and McCartney were self-stylised 'amateur' parallels of Walt Disney. They used their own persona as Hollywood used Bambi, with Ringo—forgive the pun—as a cute Liverpudlian Thumper.

It follows that the *rapport* which *this* level of evocation produced applauds, in effect, a fundamental and wilful ignorance. The Beatles offered glossy sketches of a world that we must fool ourselves into seeing: a world that could be 'if only'—or 'once upon a time'. What they ignored, and what Dylan always deals with, is the human world as it really is.

At one time Dylan wrote songs explicitly 'about' war, exploitation and suffering. That he no longer does so is not a mark of any lack of concern—of any retreat from responsibility. As Jon Landau has pointed out, Dylan could not have written (Lennon-McCartney's) 'Fool On The Hill' contemporaneously with the Vietnam war. The imagination, however wistfully or humorously engaged, must connect with the real spirit of the age; 'Fool on the Hill', 'Lucy in the Sky with Diamonds' and the rest connect only with a self-indulgent falsity.

In contrast, an early Dylan song like **'A Hard Rain's A-Gonna Fall',** with its clear didactic glimpses:

> I met one man who was wounded in love
> I met another man who was wounded in hatred

—evinces the same kind of exploratory awareness which has matured, not disappeared, in Dylan's later work.

On a political level, in any case, Dylan's work has become more important as it has moved beyond the early explicit rhetoric. Compare **'The Times They Are A-Changin'** with **'Desolation Row'.** As Nigel Fountain has expressed it, whatever happened to all the senators and congressmen who were supposed to heed the call? Dr Filth is still around. With his later work, in fact, Dylan is politically *ahead,* almost a kind of pied piper of dissent. It can be said of the ('non-political, non-progressive') album **Self Portrait,** 1970, that once again, Dylan had anticipated the direction in which the New Left in America must move. While the Weathermen were increasingly an isolated, alienated, psychotic group bereft of any public support, Dylan was directing the hip/aware/active crowd towards the American white working-class masses, via their music—and doing so at a time when the New Left needed to move precisely in the direction of those workers.

There is, then, a fundamental sense in which Dylan cannot be placed alongside most heroes of the mass-media: he is incapable of that falsity of consciousness, that bland superficiality on which they depend, and which they purvey to the ulcerated tribesmen of [Marshall] McLuhan's global village.

In this achievement, Dylan proves how right a part of McLuhan's thesis is. It *is* true that Dylan's vast young audience has been attracted by the medium as well as the message, indeed that the two are bound up. It is true that the kind of thinking, the kind of perceiving, spawned by the old print technology seems increasingly foreign to those whose real attention is caught by the audio-visual media; that because the TV set and the record-player are more vocal and articulate parts of people's homes than their parents are or were, so now the home is open-ended and 'all the world's a stage'. It is true too that the traditional education sysem is at last being seen as a pathetically outdated, imaginatively bankrupt, mind-shrinking affair. And while schools, along with much else that is crumbling, stand for categorisation, detachment and what Mailer calls 'the logic of the next step', so electric technology 'fosters and encourages unification and involvement'. And the medium Dylan works in is the most powerfully attractive form of electric technology yet available—since, that is, films still involve having to sit in cinemas, and TV is in the hands of those Dylan once called 'men and women who look like cigars—the anti-happiness committee'.

At least one wheel has come full circle. Folk-music married to poetry has been reasserted; in Dylan . . . the subcultures have surfaced.

This is not hard to explain. Dylan's generation has packed together its discoveries of innumerable 'sub-cultures' and re-formed them into chaotic, kaleidoscopic but living experience. The contemporary student of, say, literature, gets far more from a life only peripherally concerned with the cultural mainstream than does his professor, who never stops swimming in it. The student has, with a free intelligence, derived a dynamic vision from rock music, cinematic experiment, comic books, communal living, philosophy, existential politics, trips (upon the tambourine man's magic, swirling ship), and an early tacit recognition that the cultural mainstream has done little, in our times, to combat the moral and imaginative imbecility of the Great Society and its Establishment intelligentsia. As Mailer has said of this generation:

> Their radicalism was in their hatred for the authority—the authority was the manifest of evil to this generation. It was the authority who had covered the land with those suburbs where they stifled as children while watching the adventures of the West in the movies, while looking at the guardians of dull genial celebrity on television; they had had their minds jabbed and poked and twitched and probed and finally galvanised into surrealistic modes of response by commercials cutting into dramatic narratives, and parents flipping from network to network—they were forced willy-nilly to build their idea of the space-time continuum (and therefore their nervous systems) on the jumps and cracks and leaps and breaks which every phenomenon from the media seemed to contain within it.

Under these conditions, the very term 'sub-cultures' becomes meaningless. Everything connects and makes redundant the sorts of distinction implied by the term. It is to this re-processing that Dylan's work so eloquently testifies, and I think it true to say that it is in this context that an understanding of his art can best be attained. (pp. 3-10)

> *Michael Gray, in his* Song & Dance Man: The Art of Bob Dylan, *Hart-Davis, MacGibbon, 1972, 337 p.*

It's funny but people still attach a lot of mystery to Bob. I mean, Dylan's just a guy like anybody else, except he's a guy who has something to say. And he has a personality that makes it his own. There's not many people that can walk into a room of 20,000, stare at them and get their attention. That's not an easy trick.

—Tom Petty, in a 1986 interview with The Telegraph *reprinted in* Wanted Man: In Search of Bob Dylan, *Black Spring Press, 1990.*

R. Serge Denisoff and David Fandray   (essay date 1977)

[*In the essay below, Denisoff and Fandray assert that Dylan has been unjustly characterized as a propagandist and revolutionary by left- and right-wing American political forces.*]

Bob Dylan appears as the most enigmatic and controversial artist of the turbulant 1960s. Dylan was all things to many people, at least at one point in that decade. His fans and the media enjoyed a love-hate relationship with the singer that has rarely been witnessed. He was labeled a voice of a generation, yet turned his back on the role. His importance was immense long before **"Like a Rolling Stone"** finally reached the pop charts. Very few people aware of Dylan are neutral about him. His aesthetic changes have been roundly criticized.

The stormiest side to Dylan is in the sphere of politics. Originally heralded as the heir apparent to Woody Guthrie, Dylan was roundly condemned as an "opportunist" and a "sell-out" by the same people who championed his career. Counter culturists who bootlegged records chose Dylan as their first and main target. A. J. Weberman, a self-proclaimed revolutionary, even started a Dylan Liberation Front. The underground Weathermen chose their name from **"Subterranean Homesick Blues."** Nowhere but in the radical press has Dylan been so violently attacked and yet so loudly praised. Several biographers and critics have attempted to explain this Janus-like relationship. Craig McGregor, perhaps, summed it up best writing "Dylan is a master of masks. If any proof were needed, his manipulation of the mass media and his deliberate choosing among images to present to the public are sufficient" [see *CLC*, Vol. 4]. Certainly there is a manipulative aspect to Dylan's career as Toby Thompson and Tony Scaduto have aptly illustrated in their biographies [*Positively Main Street: An Unorthodox View of Bob Dylan* and *Bob Dylan: An Intimate Biography*]. However, Dylan's relationship with the Left, Right, and indeed, political Middle are not merely a symptom of the man's personality.

Dylan is a child of the folk music revival which exploded upon the consciousness of American youth in the waning years of the 1950s. Triggered by "Tom Dooley," the revival found literally hundreds of guitar carrying youths wandering into the world of Greenwich Village. The Village was more than just a string of "basket houses" such as Gerde's where guitar pickers could exhibit their wares for a few dollars and an occasional free beer. The Village had an entire zeitgeist. The Village was the home of Bohemianism and progressive politics going back to the days of John Reed, John Dos Passos, and the literary Masses. It was here that the Almanac Singers—Woody Guthrie, Pete Seeger, Lee Hays, and numerous others—held the first hootnannies to pay their rent and help various political causes. The short-lived Weavers paid their dues at the Vanguard. Folk music as well as jazz dominated the MacDougal Street music scene. During the 1950s, folk music was mere replication of Child and Lomax ballads. Only Pete Seeger and a handful of ex-People's Songsters [contributed] to topical song traditions of the post-war years. Some of the early Village artists looked with some degree of crypticness at topical song-writing. In 1959 Dave Van Ronk and Dick Ellington put out a satirical songbook titled *The Bosses Songbook: Songs to Stifle Flames of Discontent.* This is an obvious parody of the Industrial Workers of the World (IWW) *Little Red Songbook.* In the lyrics, Van Ronk and Ellington mocked the agit-prop material of previous years. One verse commented tersely:

> Their material is corny
> But their motives are the purest

And their spirit will never be broke,
As they go right on with their great noble cru-
    sade
Of teaching folk songs to the folk.

While generally discarding the political ideology of the preceeding decade, singers did find the works of Woody Guthrie and other artists to be of considerable value. Guthrie was somewhat of a saint in the dingy folk clubs. There were few village performers that did not toss in at least one "hard travelin'" number from the Dust Bowl days. (pp. 31-2)

In the early 1960s the underground heritage of the American Folk Music movement began to surface. Its uneasy alliance with the Left of the 1930s and 1940s suggested musical directions at a time when many collegiates were finally awakening from the deep sleep of the 1950s. Labor songs and the topical material of Guthrie, Seeger, and Leadbelly appeared contemporary in light of Selma and the Bay of Pigs. Still, only Seeger seemed to be carrying the political torch.

There is a good deal of controversy as to who was the first topical songwriter in the New York milieu. Phil Ochs claims he was the first, and their is little reason to dispute that assertion. But it was Bob Dylan that drove the vehicle to stardom.

Dylan's original involvement with topical material seems to have been motivated more by his roommate than by any deeply felt political convictions. Tony Scaduto suggests:

> Suze was working for CORE [Congress of Racial Equality] as a secretary and envelope stuffer. She spent many hours telling Bob about the realities of the black man's life as she saw it from her desk at CORE, where the phones rang day and night as field men called in to describe the latest segregationist brutalities. And so one of Dylan's first protest songs, **"The Ballad of Emmett Till,"** was written for CORE.

"The Death of Emmett Till" was a narrative depicting the murder of a young black youth in Mississippi. The true story was somewhat of a cause celebre in civil rights circles as Till's killers went free. While not as well written as some of his later material, the song did create a pattern. The motif was a social injustice and lack of public reaction, or better yet indignation to it. Songs like **"The Lonesome Death of Hattie Carroll," "Percy's Song," "Only a Hobo," "Oxford Town"** and **"Hollis Brown"** were all in this vein. Dylan's concluding verse included "Your eyes are filled with dead man's dirt" and **"Hattie Carroll"** concluded with "Now is the time for your tears." His second protest song, **"The Ballad of Donald White,"** an executed black, ended with "When are some people gonna wake up . . ." This type of material greatly appealed to those involved in movement politics. A basic premise of any social movement is that if the false conscience of the public could only be eradicated, then social change would take place.

Dylan's writing of topical and protest material revived in the Village an aura of the 1940s where the Almanac Singers sang for various causes, followed after the war by Peo-

ple's Songs, Inc. The role of the folksinger then was fairly well defined by liberal and "progressive" politics. The balladeer was the social conscience of the people. Phil Ochs labeled this orientation "the Guthrie-Seeger tradition." Needless to say, many veterans of the earlier years were only too happy to proclaim Dylan "the great white hope" of the 1960s. Dylan was to be the "new Guthrie," a role which he did not originally totally reject. In fact, his first album as well as official record company biography stressed his heritage of the Dustbowl Balladeer. **Bob Dylan** included **"Song to Woody"** as well as the following liner notes: "Although they are separated by thirty years and two generations, they were united by a love of music, a kindred sense of humor, and a common view toward the world."

Dylan's actual connection to Guthrie is [difficult] to establish. In fact, the famous hospital visit has been denied by Dylan himself on several occasions. Some observers claim that even if Dylan did go to the Greystone Hospital in New Jersey, Woody was incapable of communicating with his visitor. In a 1966 interview, Phil Ochs indicated that Dylan was in fact using the politics of the Village to further his own career. Ochs' charge may be a bit strong; however, there is little historical evidence to refute the argument that Dylan's career was substantially aided by veterans of the Old Left as well as a new generation of politically conscious youths.

Sing Out! magazine, the dominant folk music publication, first sang Dylan's praises to their audience in 1962. Gil Turner wrote an article introducing him as a dedicated and committed singer of topical and political songs who refused to have his material watered down [see *CLC*, Vol. 12]. Gordon Friesen wrote a similar essay in *Mainstream*. When *Broadside* magazine first appeared in 1961, Dylan's **"Talking John Birch Paranoid Blues"** was included. *Broadside* was the brainchild of ex-People Songsters Pete Seeger and Malvina Reynolds who felt that *Sing Out!* was not publishing enough political material. Agnes "Sis" Cunningham and her husband Gordon Friesen started the mimeographed publication in 1961 with the help of Gil Turner who solicited material from his contemporaries at Gerde's folk club. The orientation of *Broadside* was openly movement directed. Early issues stressed disarmament, civil rights, and anti-Radical Right songs. Dylan fit the mold with **"Talking John Birch Paranoid Blues," "Let Me Die in My Footsteps,"** and in the sixth issue **"Blowin' in the Wind"** which became an anthem for the desegregation movement.

Because of his songs, Dylan by 1963—the year of the March on Washington—was firmly established as the leading "new" topical song writer in the folk music revival. Few people doubted Dylan's commitment to the cause. Pete Seeger introduced his songs at concerts, the *New York Times* reported a "Bob Dillon" at a rally in Greenwood, Mississippi; and Dylan was at the historic March on Washington as well as at the finale of the 1963 Newport Folk Festival. For the folk music revival and the protest song vogue, the 1963 Newport convention was the highpoint. It ended appropriately with Joan Baez, Peter, Paul, and Mary, the Freedom Singers, Pete Seeger, and Bob

Dylan, arms linked, leading the crowd with "We Shall Overcome" and **"Blowin' in the Wind."**

Dylan's dedication to the civil rights movement and the New Left was questionable. Unlike his forebearers Seeger, Hays, and sometimes Guthrie—Dylan was not the voice of any given movement. His songs may have reinforced the belief systems of those involved in changing the social conditions of the 1960s, but he was not physically one of them. First and foremost Dylan was a performer very aware of audience preferences. In the folk world tying up with the Guthrie-Seeger tradition was a definite plus. However, Dylan could never accept the demands of politics upon him.

The Guthrie-Seeger balloon was finally popped at a dinner staged by the Emergency Civil Liberties Committee where he was given the Tom Paine Award. At the dinner Dylan denounced the participants. The reasons are not clear, but later he explained to a friend "All they can see is a cause, and using people for their cause. They're trying to use me for something, want me to carry a picket sign and have my picture taken and be a good little nigger and not mess up their little game. They're all hung up on games. But games don't work any more". Dylan obviously was turned off to much of the civil rights movement. In an interview with Nat Hentoff [see *CLC*, Vol. 12], Dylan admitted some affinity for the Student Non-violent Coordinating Committee (SNCC), but later added "I agree with everything that's happening . . . but I'm not part of no Movement. If I was I wouldn't be able to do anything else but be in 'the Movement.' I just can't have people sit around and make rules for me. I do a lot of things no Movement would allow." Musically Dylan made similar statements beginning with *Another Side of Bob Dylan* and his farewell song to protest and perhaps even folk music with **"My Back Pages."** Dylan's reasons for the change are not totally clear. Several writers have indicated that Dylan desired to reach the youth market of popular music rather than just the folkies who could not give him a gold record. While many called Dylan's artistic retreat "opportunism" it should be remembered that the economics of folk music revival benefited very few artists. Pop acts like Peter, Paul, and Mary, The New Christy Minstrels, and several others did enjoy the bounties of the college concert circuit. However, most folksingers were almost totally dependent upon a handful of urban night clubs and a host of coffee houses where the pay was marginal. Few acts had recording contracts with major labels. There Dylan was fortunate as most of his Village contemporaries did not have the promotional and distribution power of Columbia Records. Most artists found themselves with Prestige, Elektra, Vanguard, or Verve, companies with limited budgets who in many instances did nothing for the artists except press their records.

Many advocates of the Guthrie-Seeger tradition disdained the commercial aspect of folk music. The Kingston Trio, Limelighters, and the New Christy Minstrels were frequently denounced for their "commercialism." Not surprisingly Dylan's behavior at the Paine Awards, the Hentoff interview, and **"My Back Pages"** sparked a bitter debate in Greenwich Village and in the pages of *Sing Out!*

and *Broadside*. Most of Dylan's original critics were old-time guardians of the Guthrie-Seeger tradition. Irwin Silber attacked Dylan in [the Vol. 14, 1964 issue of] *Sing Out!* for "selling out." Silber, a veteran left-wing polemicist, wrote "The American Success Machinery chews up geniuses at a rate of one a day and still hungers for more . . . through noteriety, fast money, and status, it makes it almost impossible for the artist to function and grow. It is a process that must be constantly guarded against and fought." Paul Wolfe in [the Vol. 53, 1964 issue of] *Broadside* labeled Dylan's "defection" as being "innocuous" showing utter "disregard of the tastes of the audience" and a symptom of "self-conscious egotism." The Silber-Wolfe articles sparked a considerable controversy. Dylan had his defenders. Phil Ochs, already being heralded as the "new" master of the Guthrie-Seeger tradition, wrote [in *Broadside* 54, 1964]: "As for Bob's writing, I believe it is as brilliant as ever and is clearly improving all the time. On his last record **'Ballad in Plain D'** and **'It Ain't Me Babe'** are masterpieces of personal statement that have as great a significance as any of his protest material." In the same issue a reader commented "I found Paul Wolfe's article 'The New Dylan' sad and depressing. It brought me back to the old sectarian days of *Sing Out*— when a song was 'male chauvinist' or 'racist' if it didn't hew to the left wing line." While much of the attack on Dylan was ideologically motivated there were also a number of underlining causes. Dylan was a symbol of what was happening to the folk music scene. Its old mentors at *Sing Out!* and in the Village who had long labored in the folk music vineyard were losing control of it. Record sales and recording contracts were rapidly displacing topicality as a major criterion of success. The star system so long condemned was entering into the scene. Dylan's ever-present entourage offended many. The reaction was generated both by fear and some jealousy, but perhaps an even more significant cause was a general dislike of Dylan as a person. Dylan's ascendency to stardom was not filled with grace. He had used and bumped many people. Singers at Gerde's told many stories of having Dylan walk in and take over the stage. Stories abounded in the Village about his mistreatment of Suz-Rotolo. Rumors about Dylan's penchant for money were plentiful. *Esquire* may have labeled Dylan the voice of a generation, but many of his contemporaries disliked and envied him intensely.

The final break between Dylan and the folk music scene occured at the Newport Folk Festival in 1965. Dylan appeared with a dreaded symbol from rock and roll: a Fender electric guitar. Prior to that time rock music was a source of scorn for those in the folk music. Rock was trivia for adolescents and another symptom of American commercialism. Few people in the folk music movement saw it as having any merit. Joan Baez, Peter, Paul, and Mary in fact did parodies of rock songs at their concerts. The Animals' "House of the Rising Sun" was considered almost sacreligious. Dylan's roots, however, were in rock. In 1965 after hearing the Byrd's version of "Mr. Tambourine Man" he decided to follow suit. The best description of what occurred at Newport was provided in Dylan's first biography [*The Bob Dylan Story* by Sy and Barbara Ribakove]:

The sight of the instrument infuriated the crowd. It was to them the hated emblem of rock 'n roll, the tool of performers whose only air was to take big money from dumb kids. In the hands of the man who had been their god, it was the symbol of the sell-out.

Jeering and heckling finally drove Dylan from the stage momentarily to return the Fender to its case. He emerged with his Martin and sang **"It's All Over Now, Baby Blue."** It was.

Once again the pages of *Sing Out!* and *Broadside* served as a forum for another Dylan debate. Tom Paxton labeled Dylan's new sound "folk rot." Izzy Young wrote "He is forced to a brilliant obscurity in his writing so that people will continue to buy his records." Irwin Silber added "I do not believe that Dylan's vision of the world is really where it's at." One reader of *Sing Out!* wrote a poem:

McCartney sings, backed up by a celli
And no one gets a pain in the belly.
Why do folkies, then, get cramps
On hearing Dylan play with amps?

A more direct statement was "[The] fact is, he has caught the general ear while you have yet to be heard above a whisper." Dylan's record sales supported his defenders. ***Bringing It All Back Home*** would in time be his first gold album. There is little question that Bob's artistic sense of timing was correct. The charge that he was one of the main factors for the dissolution of the folk revival has some merit as his success did point other performers in similar directions.

Dylan's relationship to the progressive parts of the folk music scene is a complex one. It is too simple merely to dismiss him as an "opportunist" unless one accepts the notion that a performer must be a "cry for justice." Dylan did go where the audience was when he started writing topical songs. How calculated a move this was is impossible to establish. All artists play what people want to hear. However, there is a point where individual creativity interjects itself. There is little question that this—at least partially—was the case in the evolution of Bob Dylan.

Dylan's protest songs also offended another segment of the American polity: The Radical Right. Since the early days of the Martin Dies Committee, spokesmen for the Right have taken an interest in topical songs especially those in the folk idiom. Woody Guthrie and Pete Seeger became favorite targets of those testifying before the infamous House Un-American Activities Committee and those writing Right-wing literature. A number of folk performers—at least those not willing to "cooperate" with HUAC—were blacklisted during the McCarthy period. Pete Seeger had to wait seventeen years to make a network television appearance. Early in his career Bob Dylan encountered the wrath of those with a Rightist perspective. Dylan wrote and recorded **"Talking John Birch Paranoid Blues"** in 1962. The song was destined for the *Free Wheelin'* album. The talking blues attacked the paranoia of the Right. "Found out there were red stripes in the American flag . . . Oh Boy!" CBS Records released the album with the anti-Right number only to quickly remove it from circulation. The original copies are now valuable collec-

tors' items. Dylan encountered a similar problem with the CBS network censors who refused to allow the song's performance [on] the Ed Sullivan show. Dylan walked off the program screaming "Bullshit! I sing that or I sing nothing." At that point in his career the act was fairly daring as Bob could have used the national exposure provided by the Sunday night program.

In 1964 Dylan became the target of numerous right wing articles. *American Opinion,* the John Birch Society magazine, began the attack [in its Vol. 7, 1964 issue] with:

Dylan, whose personal characteristics include his scorn for baths and disdain for haircuts and razors, has been called the 'most important writer of folk songs in the last 20 years.' *The New York Times* has praised him as a moralist, a pamphleteer, an angry young man with a guitar, a social protest poet . . . perhaps an American Yevtushenko. Dylan, who usually travels with two bearded bodyguards, is a student of old-time Communist Woody Guthrie.

Having linked Dylan with the Soviet poet and Guthrie—who was never a member of the Communist Party—*American Opinion* went on to describe Dylan's songs as "filled with the bitter polemic which characterized the Communist folk song." David Noebel of the Christian Crusade, who became the Right's authority on subversive music, devoted a chapter [of his *Rhythm, Riots and Revolution*] to Dylan calling him the "prince of rock and folk." Noebel's portrayal of the singer was that of a dirty, long haired subversive who was a threat to American morality and security. [In *Christian Crusade,* March, 1967] he would write: "Dylan might not be fit to marry the household pet, but Columbia Records feels he's fit to influence the psyche of millions of our teenagers." Ironically, this description of Dylan appeared several years after the famous Newport incident. In 1969 *American Opinion* repeated its charges of Dylan's Communist connections. At the same time portions of the New left and the Con III movement were bitterly attacking Dylan for having sold out their values. A. J. Weverman was launching his ludicrous Dylan Liberation Front while bootleggers were releasing Dylan tapes as a "public service." Once again the Radical Right missed the boat as Dylan was never an overt Leftist or even an ideologue.

Bob Dylan's conversion to rock and roll seemed to substantiate all of the fears of both the Left and the Right. Most notably through the successes of such singles as **"Like a Rolling Stone"** and **"Rainy Day Women,"** Dylan began to reach the mass of young rock fans who heretofore had only the Beatles and Rolling Stones to claim as major objects of adulation. Dylan quickly assumed a position of importance in the growing youth culture of the mid-60s. He was playing the electric music that young people wanted to hear; he had a reputation for being critical of "the establishment"; and the songs of his ***Highway 61 Revisited*** and ***Blonde On Blonde*** period, while not carrying overtly political messages, reflected the general sense of alienation that was growing in young people throughout America. Thus, Dylan quickly was elevated to a status equal to that enjoyed by The Beatles and The Stones among members of this group of young people. In fact, he may even have superceded these two bands in significance, as his appeal was not only musical, but intellectual because of the stress placed on the lyrical side of his songs.

As a result, Dylan became the spiritual, if not actual, leader of yet another group of people. This man who has repeatedly denied that he is anything more than a musician and entertainer now had not only the Left and Right interpreting his every move and note played, but he had this vast and unorganized mass of young people in the middle looking to him as the symbol of America's counter culture. He could no longer function as a mere entertainer without the critical analysis of every young person who looked upon him as the American prophet of the 60s.

Dylan, however, did not spend much time in the eye of his newly-found public. The summer of 1966 brought with it Dylan's near-fatal motorcycle accident. Rumors of death, dismemberment, and brain damage immediately spread across the country. Rumors continued to wax and wane throughout the year that Dylan spent in convalescence in upstate New York. The injured prophet did little to stop the rumors and speculation about the effects of the accident on his career. He remained quiet, maintaining little or no contact with his public.

While he was recuperating, Dylan underwent a drastic change in his orientation to his music. It was a change that was taking him far away from the course popular music was taking as it moved into the summer of 1967. While *Sergeant Pepper* and San Francisco psychedelicism were sweeping this country's young people and musicians into an era of musical complexity and experimentation, Bob Dylan was jamming with The Band, creating music that was raw and stark in its simplicity.

By the October of 1967, Dylan was ready to record again. He went to Nashville, and recorded ***John Wesley Harding,*** an album so subdued in its country flavor that it made even Dylan's work that summer seem like raucous rock and roll. The Band, at least, knew how to rock, but the session man used in Nashville played with such restraint as to make their presence on the album almost unnoticeable.

When the album was released in January, 1968, many Dylan fans were shocked by the musical style. The lyrics were unmistakably Dylan, but what did this have to do with the music he was making on ***Blonde On Blonde***? This shock was nothing, however, compared to reaction voiced the following year when Dylan released ***Nashville Skyline.*** This album appeared in the spring of 1969, and many of those who had begun to look on Dylan as a leader and symbol a few years earlier were nothing less than scandalized. Like its predecessor, ***Skyline*** was recorded in Nashville and featured a distinctly country sound. Unlike ***John Wesley Harding,*** though, it not only featured Dylan singing duets with the likes of Johnny Cash, but its lyrics touched upon little except the usual country themes of love and simplicity. For those dedicated to opposing the entire way of life idealized in country music, ***Nashville Skyline*** was worse than disappointing; it was betrayal. Dylan, either of his own volition or due to his failure to

stand up to corporate pressures, was seen as selling out the movement he had been chosen to lead.

Dylan, of course, was only following his own artistic impulses. Many in the counter culture, however, saw Dylan only in his role as symbolic leader of a generation. This made him public property; and as public property he had no right to release as little as one album every year or so, and have this precious album go against the things he was supposed to symbolize in both the artistic and ideological senses.

While some merely criticized, others who would save Dylan from himself acted. Thus, several Dylan enthusiasts took a step that was calculated (at least in their official statements on the matter) to bring some of Dylan's best music to the people, regardless of what Dylan and Columbia Records wanted to release. In doing so, they introduced the "bootleg" record to the rock music industry.

The practice of bootlegging is an old, and almost venerable institution. In general practice, bootleggers take records or tapes of what they consider to be significant performances that are no longer, or never have been available through commercial recording companies. Using these sources, they transfer performances to a master tape; which is, in turn, taken to a commercial pressing plant, where the performances are put on record. These records are then distributed to anyone interested in having a copy of the performance.

Bootlegging has been common among fans of jazz, blues, and classical music. Through the practice, historical performances that would never have been available may be obtained and preserved. (A good example of this is the bootlegging Maria Callas' performance of Verdi's *Macbeth*—a performance that has never been available commercially). In blues, jazz, and the classics, the practice has largely been condoned by record companies because it can be seen as a preservation of history, and the bootleggers have rarely tried to compete with the companies by issuing recordings of commercially available performances.

Bootlegging was introduced to rock and roll in the fall of 1969. At this time, a plainly packaged album that became known as the *Great White Wonder* appeared on the shelves of record stores on the West Coast. Although it has been traced to a tape librarian at Columbia Records the exact producer of the original *Great White Wonder* remains unknown. Whatever the album's origin, however, it quickly became a fast-selling item. What made it important was the fact that it was Dylan. The double-album set consisted of some tracks recorded in 1961 in a hotel room in Minneapolis, most of the songs recorded by Dylan and The Band in the summer of 1967 (the legendary "basement tapes" which included such notable selections as "This Wheel's On Fire," "I Shall Be Released," and "Tears Of Rage"), and one song recorded from Dylan's appearance on Johnny Cash's television show.

The recording quality was poor, and the performances were unpolished, but the set captured Dylan before he has eaten "country pie." In the face of ***Nashville Skyline,*** this album was extremely important to those who saw Dylan's music as something sacred to a generation. In addition, by

1969, anything recorded by The Beatles, The Stones, or Dylan was considered important due to the growing infrequency of their releases.

By December of 1969, the album was available in major cities across the country. On the West Coast, its price ranged from seven to twelve dollars. Its cost rose as it became available in the east, reaching a price of $20 a copy at one store in New York City. Despite the high price, it was estimated that between 60,000 and 100,000 copies had been sold. In addition, two more Dylan bootlegs had become available. *Troubled Troubadour* was a single-record set that contained some material from the first bootleg, plus a few new songs. *Stealin',* another single-disc set, was a collection of alternate takes from Dylan's ***Bringing It All Back Home*** and ***Highway 61 Revisited*** sessions. The recording quality of this latter record was so good compared to the other two that Columbia believed the tapes had been stolen from its own vaults.

As the sales figures indicate, the bootlegs were warmly-received by the public. Music fans were merely glad to obtain new music by Dylan. Those who saw Dylan as a cultural symbol welcomed the bootlegs because they were seen as a public reclamation of Dylan's music, and an attack on the corporate system of which he and Columbia Records were a part. It was considered a political act; and once again Dylan was pulled into the middle of an ideological confrontation.

The bootleggers' primary line of justification drew on both political and artistic elements. As one told the *Los Angeles Free Press:*

> Some of the songs are better than the shit Columbia has released. They just keep sitting on them, so you might say in a sense, we're just liberating the records and bringing them to all the people; not just the chosen few.

Grail Marcus, who gave some modicum of legitimacy to the bootlegs by reviewing them in the *Rolling Stone,* did not give the records unrestrained approval. However, he did note:

> In a way, the bootleg phenomena may well force artists to respond to what the public wants—or lose a lot of bread. One obvious way to squelch the *Great White Wonder* album, without arousing any bad feelings, would have been to issue the basement tape. . . . the bootleggers might well force more albums out of The Stones and Dylan, in particular.

It must be noted, however, that for all of the claims of benevolence made by the bootleggers, they were making money. Since they paid no royalties or recording costs, they had few expenses other than the cost of delivering the records and the costs of manufacturing them, which was probably little more than $.35 an album.

The response to bootlegging by the recording company and the artist was immediate and unfriendly, however. Columbia's initial reaction to the first bootleg was:

> We consider the release of this record an abuse of the integrity of a great artist. By releasing material without the knowledge or approval of Bob

Dylan or Columbia Records, the sellers of this record are crassly depriving a great artist of the opportunity to perfect his performances to the point where he believes in their integrity and validity. They are at one time defaming the artist and defrauding his admirers. For these reasons, Columbia Records, in cooperation with Bob Dylan's attorneys, intends to take all legal steps to stop the sale and distribution of this album.

The label then sent a group of private investigators out to find the producers of the album. The original producers had fled to Canada with the proceeds from 8,000 albums, but two record store owners, Norton Beckman and Ben Goldman, had begun making their own pirated recording of the bootleg. The detectives ultimately located Beckman and Goldman, and Columbia filed in federal court for a restraining order and asked for injury to plaintiff Dylan. Beckman and Goldman ceased production of the record. Record stores that carried it began to remove *Great White Wonder* from their shelves, either in response to the court ruling or as a result of pressure from Columbia's field representatives.

Dylan's exact role in the suppression of *Great White Wonder* and the other bootlegs is somewhat ambiguous. At first glance, it would appear that the action was primarily carried out in the interests of his record company. However, spokesmen for the label said that the bootlegging did not hurt the company. Since the albums did not duplicate any albums released by Columbia, the company did not stand to lose money. These spokesmen maintained that the appearance of these albums merely injured the artist who lost royalites for his performances and songwriting, and the right to determine what he wanted to release to the public.

Thus, it would appear that the fight against the albums was carried out on Dylan's behalf. This view is supported by Columbia's statement that it was working with Bob Dylan's attorneys, and the assertion in the restraining order that the bootlegs were causing injury to Dylan.

Dylan's tacit approval of the campaign against his bootleg albums could be viewed as further evidence that he was betraying the generation that had come to look on him as a leader. Here was an example of the people demanding his music. In effect, they were saying that they wanted to hear anything he had to offer, no matter what the quality. Yet, he both refused to make the material available legitimately and sanctioned the efforts to keep it from reaching the people through other means.

This only fanned the flames of anger against the performer. Was he so greedy that he wanted to stop the loss of performing and composing royalties? Did he feel that he was above being responsive to the desires of his public? Dylan's reasons for not releasing the basement tapes in the 60s, and for at least allowing his attorneys to seek the restraining order against *Great White Wonder* may never be entirely known—especially in light of the fact that he allowed the release of the tapes officially in the summer of 1975. It seems, however, that the real key to his behavior in this situation can be traced to his insistence that he is a musical artist rather than a public servant.

As noted by Greil Marcus in his review of *Great White Wonder* [in *Rolling Stone,* 29 November 1969], "Like any artist, Dylan chooses what to reveal and what to keep for his own. That such choice has, in this case, been taken out of his hands is something about which most must feel ambivalent." This view was further substantiated by Columbia's insistence that the record "defamed" Dylan because he simply did not want that material released.

His reasons for not wanting the tapes released can be understood. As he told *Rolling Stone,* the songs on the basement tapes were recorded merely to be circulated to other artists as part of his publishing company's portfolio. "They weren't demos for myself. They were demos of the songs. I was being pushed again . . . into coming up with some songs." He maintains additionally that they were merely "a kick to do," not performances meant for public consumption.

That these were Dylan's primary thoughts in dealing with the bootlegs is the view maintained by biographer Anthony Scaduto. In his book, Scaduto states, "Dylan conceives an album the way a writer conceives a book of poetry, or a novel." Because of this lack of artistic control, Dylan, then, was understandably upset by the bootlegs. As proof of this, Scaduto recalls an incident that occured while he was finishing his book:

> During one of his visits to my apartment I was playing one of the bootlegs . . . When he walked in the door and heard the album, he said: "Oh, the basement tapes. You should hear the originals. They're fantastic. The crap they're putting out doesn't even sound like me. And they're sure not in the order I'd put them on an album."

It hardly seems surprising that an artist would object to a product bearing his or her name without having had any amount of control over its complete synthesis.

This, of course, has always been Dylan's major problem in relating to the label-makers and demagogues. As any artist, he was absorbed into the important events and feelings in his environment, and brought them together in potent form in his art. Whether he has done this in a calculated effort to gain popularity, or simply in a natural step in the perfection of his art may be debated. What cannot be debated, however, is Dylan's reluctance to do anything not in the interests of his music and-or career. While those who viewed him as the leader of a generation of young Americans decried his musical progression, and the bootleggers boasted their benevolence, calling themselves modern day Robin Hoods, Dylan merely concerned himself with his music. As a result of this overriding preoccupation, he was drawn into yet another ideological skirmish. As before, the battle raged and died while Dylan moved calmly into a new decade.

During the turbulant 1960s Bob Dylan began as a prophet who quickly was transformed into a false one. He was never the pamphleteer or the revolutionary that the Left and indeed Right demanded. He was condemned by both, but for different reasons. What political radicals failed to realize was that Dylan was just Bob Dylan not the Savior or Devil of the 1960s. (pp. 32-40)

R. Serge Denisoff and David Fandray, " 'Hey, Hey Woody Guthrie I Wrote You a Song': The Political Side of Bob Dylan," in Popular Music & Society, *Vol. V, No. 5, 1977, pp. 31-42.*

Dylan on poetry:

I can't define that word poetry. I wouldn't even attempt it. At one time I thought that Robert Frost was poetry, other times I thought Allen Ginsberg was poetry, sometimes I thought Francois Villon was poetry—but poetry isn't really confined to the printed page. Hey, then again I don't believe in saying, "Look at that girl walking. Isn't that poetry?" I'm not going to get insane about it. The lyrics to the songs . . . just so happens that it might be a little stranger than in most songs. I find it easy to write songs. I been writing songs for a long time and the words to the songs aren't written out for just the paper, they're written as you can read it, you dig? If you take whatever there is to the song away—the beat, the melody—I could still recite it. I see nothing wrong with songs you can't do that with either—songs that, if you took the beat and melody away, they wouldn't stand up. Because they're not supposed to do that, you know. Songs are songs . . . I don't believe in expecting too much out of any one thing.

Bob Dylan, in a September 1965 interview reprinted in Bob Dylan in His Own Words, *Quick Fox, 1978.*

John Herdman (essay date 1982)

[*In the essay excerpted below, Herdman examines the "intensity of feeling" in Dylan's songs.*]

'Like a Rolling Stone' has been described [by Steven Goldberg in *Bob Dylan: A Retrospective*] as "Dylan's quintessential work", and with good reason. The first line of its refrain, "How does it feel? How does it feel?", rendered by Dylan in many different versions of the song with varying emphasis and interpretation but always with rock-bottom intensity of feeling, gives us the very kernel of his art. It is the element of feeling which, in interviews, he has consistently stressed as the essence of his work, and in one [*Rolling Stone,* 16 November 1978] he gives us a picture of himself "trying to figure out whether it was this way or that way, just what *is* it, what's the simplest way I can tell the story and make this feeling real." In this process lies the key to his almost limitless emotional range, which has led many a Dylan enthusiast to remark that whatever one is feeling in any situation, Dylan has always written a song which says it all. He tells us what he feels himself, he projects himself with eerie immediacy into the feelings of others, and in so doing he shows us what *we* feel too.

This is the underlying activity of all his writing and his music-making, but nowhere is it more apparent than in that large body of songs which deal with personal relationships: not simply those which are addressed to lovers or former lovers, though there are many of those, but all which find their subject in the infinite varieties of human confrontation, which give us human beings acting upon and reacting to each other. Such songs stand at the centre of Dylan's achievement.

When Dylan talks of making a "feeling real" he does not of course mean necessarily a single, simple, indivisible feeling which can be isolated from a wider range of experience. More often the songs deal with a nucleus or complex of feelings from which may radiate tentacles which reach out towards areas connected to the centre only by the links of resonance and association. There *are* however songs, particularly some early ones, which seek no more than to communicate as faithfully as possible one emotional truth, and in some of these we can see at work, at a local level, the kind of effects which Dylan also deploys as part of a larger undertaking in more complex works. As an example of the most straightforward of these we can take **'Girl of the North Country'**, which is simply a tender rememberance of a past love and works by means of evocation, drawing upon the universal experience of the way in which our memories of people are indelibly associated with the scenes in which we have known them. But by using the device of asking another to "Remember me to one who lives there", and to see to her well-being on his behalf, Dylan unobtrusively heightens the poignancy of the emotion by indicating at once his desire to communicate his feeling to the girl, and the impossibility of doing so in a direct way. It is a device which he was to use again years later, as we shall see.

In **'Tomorrow is a Long Time'** (once recorded by Elvis Presley) the emotion to be expressed is again as simple as possible: grief at being parted from his true love. Here he indicates a subjective state of mind by means of figurative imagery, and in this very early song it is already characteristic Dylan:

> I can't see my reflection in the waters,
> I can't speak the sounds that show no pain,
> I can't hear the echo of my footsteps,
> Or can't remember the sounds of my own name.

The authenticity of the feeling is indicated in the second line by the singer's inability to achieve the conventional putting-on of a brave face. It is also worthy of note how, on the early concert version of the song released on ***Greatest Hits Volume Two,*** Dylan obviates the danger of mawkishness in the lines from the last verse, "But none of these and nothing else can touch the beauty / That I remember in my true love's eyes", by a sudden, unexpected hardness in his delivery of the last phrase, which takes us by surprise just as we are about to give way to a mood of sweetness. Such vocal contributions to the sense of the words are inseparable from their total "meaning", and serve as a constant reminder that Dylan's lyrics cannot be discussed without our continually maintaining in the forefront of consciousness the memory of the way—often, indeed, the alternative ways—in which Dylan delivers them.

In **'One Too Many Mornings'** these approaches are combined and expanded in the communication of a feeling which is a little more complex, a little more ambiguous. The situation behind the song is not clearly defined: we know only that the lovers have parted, perhaps in acrimony, each maintaining his or her point of view. This, indeed,

we learn only from the last verse: the first two are devoted to establishing that "restless hungry feeling", and we are half-way through the song before the basis of the regret is suggested by the lines "As I turn my head back to the room / Where my love and I have laid." The evocation of atmosphere is subtle:

> Down the street the dogs are barkin'
> And the day is a-gettin' dark.
> As the night comes in a-fallin',
> The dogs'll lose their bark . . .

Having made use of the barking dog image in the first line, a lesser writer would probably have sought for something new to enhance the effect in the third; instead of which Dylan returns to it and extracts from it a subtler potential. The dogs don't just cease to bark but *lose* their bark. The line not only makes a recognisable feature of evening come alive in our mind's ear, but in passing says something sympathetic, strangely poignant and quite unparaphrasable about the nature of doggishness. Equally effective is the image of the silent night shattering "from the sounds inside my mind", which serves as a first specific link between the atmosphere evoked and the human drama associated with it. "The crossroads of my doorstep" at the beginning of the second verse hints at a crossroads in the relationship which is just about to be mentioned for the first time, and as the singer gazes back "to the street, / The sidewalk and the sign," we know that he does so not just from his stance at the crossroads reached at that moment summoned back from the past, but also from the longer perspective from which the song itself is sung. It is from that perspective that the last verse reaches back:

> It's a restless hungry feeling
> That don't mean no one no good,
> When ev'rything I'm a-sayin'
> You can say it just as good.
> You're right from your side,
> I'm right from mine.
> We're both just one too many mornings
> An' a thousand miles behind.

This is one of those songs in which Dylan looks back on a relationship from an attitude of "calm of mind" (though not necessarily of "all passion spent"), and with a creative effort of fairness and impartiality towards things as they are or have been. Yet it is seldom quite as simple as that. The balance of that last verse, as sung, is slightly illusory. "You're right from your side, / I'm right from mine": the two halves of that proposition look equal and congruent on the page, but in the original version of the song Dylan places slight, unobtrusive but definite emphases on the words "I'm" and "mine". This is a typical gesture of artistic honesty, recognising as it does the truth that whatever one's objective impartiality, the view from within one's own skin always finally carries the most weight.

It is interesting to compare **'One Too Many Mornings'** with a very much later song of the same type, **'If You See Her, Say Hello'** from the ***Blood on the Tracks*** album. It too has a simple feeling to put over—in spite of everything that has passed between them he wishes her well, and he wants her to know it; and as with the songs we have been considering much of its effect comes from the beauty of its melodic line. Its method however is utterly different. Evocative imagery is almost absent, reduced to a single line in the last verse which merely gestures towards that associative resonance which was so important an element in **'One Too Many Mornings'**: "Sundown, yellow moon / I replay the past". Instead of building up an atmosphere and understating the story, leaving it largely to be inferred from slender hints, this song gives us a great deal of information. We learn that the girl has departed, probably for Tangier, in early spring; that the singer hasn't forgotten her in spite of their separation; that they fell out and that she made the move to end the relationship; that he desires her happiness in spite of the resultant bitterness which still "lingers on"; that he can't get her out of his head and, finally, that he would like to see her again. The device employed for telling the story is that already used in **'Girl from the North Country',** the addressing of the song to a third party who is given certain simple instructions, in this case to say hello to the girl, deliver a kiss, and "Tell her she can look me up / If she's got the time." All this is achieved with the utmost economy, in five verses of eight very short lines each, and the way it is done is to make each piece of information given at once an essential link in the story, and as emotionally telling as possible without self-indulgence. Dylan is thus enabled to convey a much greater sense of complexity, of emotional subtlety in the presentment of a relationship, than in the earlier song, while at the same time giving expression to a basically uncomplicated and spontaneous *feeling*. He is expressing, again, a fully assimilated experience, so that the statements made are a thousand miles from the raw sentiments which made failures of such songs as **'I Don't Believe You'** and **'Ballad in Plain D',** in which Dylan first attempted to analyse the dynamics of human relationships, as opposed to giving form to an emotional deposit as in the early successes.

Part of the success of **'If You See Her'** is, once more, closely bound up with the way he sings it. Cliché is the lifeblood of love songs, but if it is to be effectively used it must be cleansed of its vulgarity without in the process being stripped of its sincerity. Dylan deals with cliché in this song—and the cliché lies as much in the situation as in the words used to describe it—either by handling it in a "knowing" way, by saying "yes I know this sounds corny but I'm telling it the way it really was"; or by confronting it head-on, driving through the sentiment of the words to the base of passion which underlies them. To list the various phrases which he copes with in these ways would be valueless: the achievement is a triumph of intelligent instinct which can only be appreciated as it is heard.

It is worth noting here that all the songs we have been looking at have been what might be called after-love songs. It will be found in fact that the great majority of Dylan's love (and hate) songs come into this category. Those that deal with a happy and continuing relationship are comparatively few, nor, with one or two exceptions, are these among the most striking. This may have as much to do with the nature of love songs—and perhaps of love—as it has to do with Dylan. The habit of singing about past relationships is at any rate so inveterate that even a song like **'You're Gonna Make Me Lonesome When You Go'**—a witty and light-hearted number which celebrates an on-going and possibly none too serious affair—takes its direction, as the title implies, by paradoxically looking ahead (I had better not say forward) to the time when the lover addressed will be gone.

Many of the songs which have been described as "put-downs" are really aiming at a mood of emotional realism. Jon Landau, after condemning **'Don't Think Twice, It's All Right'** as an unsympathetic, unsubtle and one-dimensional put-down [in an essay reprinted in *Bob Dylan: A Retrospective*], is forced to concede that "the beauty of Dylan's vocal-guitar-harmonica performance doesn't really say what the words do and, in fact, really transforms the verbal meaning of the song into something much deeper and much less coarse". The point must be repeated that the "meaning" of a Dylan song is *not* necessarily just what the words say (though they may make the predominant contribution), and indeed may depend for its realisation precisely on tensions between the words and the other elements involved; but that apart, it does not seem to me that the words of **'Don't Think Twice'** have the unsympathetic qualities which Landau attributes to them. The feeling that is being aimed at is a balanced reconciliation between a sense of hurt and a realistic understanding, and the rather flip tone serves as a defence against the hurt suffered, which is more than hinted at in lines like "Still I wish there was something you would do or say / To try and make me change my mind and stay"; and "It ain't no use in callin' out my name, gal / Like you never did before"; and "I ain't sayin' you treated me unkind / You could have done better but I don't mind". The attitude of defence is itself, of course, part of the feeling which Dylan is trying to "make real". The effort to sympathise with the girl's point of view is not easy, and in the lines in which he tries hardest to do so—recognising that this woman is emotionally a child—he switches, in order to make objectivity easier, from addressing her as "you" to referring to her in the third person:

> I'm a-thinkin' and a-wonderin' all the way down
>   the road
> I once loved a woman, a child I'm told
> I give her my heart but she wanted my soul
> But don't think twice, it's all right.

The return to the direct address in the refrain is in that context a return to outgoing human sympathy, even though a doubt remains as to whether it really is as "all right" as he claims. (That doubt is underlined in the *Budokan* version, in which at the end of the song Dylan repeats the phrase again and again in a variety of conflicting intonations, ending with a particularly flat, drawn-out kind of howl.)

There are a number of songs of the period up to *Blonde on Blonde* which present, with varying degrees of irony and from differing vantage points, such a "sane man's view" of finished, dying or unpromising relationships. Several are valedictory, like **'It Ain't Me, Babe'** and **'It's All Over Now, Baby Blue',** offering probably unwelcome but certainly sound advice as a parting gift. **'It Ain't Me, Babe'** is a warning-off song, aimed at discouraging a starry-eyed admirer, while **"Baby Blue"** advises a dismissed lover to put the past behind her (or, as we are confidently informed by a number of commentators, him) and "start anew". There is certainly an element of hardness in these songs which can look like cruelty:

> Go melt back into the night, babe,
> Everything inside is made of stone.
> There's nothing in here moving
> An' anyway I'm not alone.

In **"Baby Blue"** Dylan gets into the skin of the person whose world is breaking up with vertiginous images like "the sky, too, is folding under you", and "The carpet, too, is moving under you". This implacable quality should however be seen as part of the effort towards emotional realism. In neither song is Dylan putting someone down; rather he is advising them to "think positively", in a way which implies a genuine concern:

> Leave your stepping stones behind, something
>   calls for you.
> Forget the dead you've left, they will not follow
>   you.
> The vagabond who's knocking at your door
> Is standing in the clothes that you once wore.
> Strike another match, go start anew
> And it's all over now, Baby Blue.

'One of Us Must Know (Sooner or Later)' is a postmortem song in which Dylan admits a sense of his own fault in ways which are subtler than might at first appear:

> I didn't mean to treat you so bad
> You shouldn't take it so personal
> I didn't mean to make you so sad
> You just happened to be there, that's all.

The apparent naïveté of the approach is undercut by the singing: clearly he understands very well that it was entirely natural that she should "take it so personal", while the fourth line implicitly confesses to the unthinking egotism with which he has treated her. Against this is balanced the evident sincerity with which he sings each time the last line of the refrain: "That I really *did* try to get close to you."

But there *are* of course songs which deal with people in a very much harsher idiom. A group in particular springs to mind from the time of *Highway 61 Revisited*—**'Like a Rolling Stone', 'Queen Jane Approximately', 'Ballad of a Thin Man'** and **'Positively 4th Street'**. A remark which Dylan made to Anthony Scaduto [published in Scaduto's *Bob Dylan*] may be mentioned here. "I discovered that when I used words like 'he' or 'it' or 'they' and talking about other people, I was really talking about nobody but me," he said. ". . . You see, I hadn't really known before, that I was writing about myself in all those songs." This interesting comment has been taken in an absurdly literal way by several writers on Dylan, leading Craig McGregor, for instance, to conjecture [in his introduction to *Bob Dylan: A Retrospective* (see *CLC*, Vol. 4)] that Queen Jane may be "Dylan himself". Actually, of course, it is quite impossible to write a song "about" oneself, in a literal sense, and remain unaware of it. What Dylan was talking about was surely what Keats called "negative capability", the capacity of certain kinds of sensibility to imagine the experience of others *as if* it were their own, to enter, for

the time being, another personality, and to project one's own experience into one's understanding of another's. It relates, too, to the words of Dylan's master Rimbaud, *'Je est un autre.'* Dylan possesses to an exceptional degree the quality of imaginative empathy, and it is just this which in a strange way humanises his most bitter and corrosive attacks. By entering the skin of his "victims" he ensures that he does not treat them as mere objects, he acknowledges their common humanity. So when, with terrifying exultation, he intones "How does it fee-eel? How does it fee-ee-eel?" we know that he understands, himself, just how it must feel.

Such an understanding always implies a degree of sympathy. This is borne out by a marvellous line in **'Queen Jane Approximately'**. Throughout most of this song Dylan appears to be revelling in the discomfiture which he envisages Queen Jane as experiencing in the future, and it sounds as if, when he sings "Won't you come see me, Queen Jane?", he is looking forward to crowing over her plight. Then, in the last verse, comes the line "And you want someone you don't have to speak to", and we see that he has another motive in making his plea—he sees himself as offering that unvocal sympathy which, perhaps, "negative capability" alone can provide. In fact, both motives are probably present: he does want to crow too, but in the last analysis the more generous impulse takes pride of place. There is always, too, with Dylan the feeling that all positions are potentially reversible. This sense is expressed in the ending of **'To Ramona'**:

> And someday maybe,
> Who knows, baby,
> I'll come and be cryin' to you.

The further import of Dylan's remark to Scaduto relates to his fundamental purpose in writing all his songs—to get to the truth of a feeling. The feelings in question are generally his own, and in that sense the songs may be said to be about himself. But those feelings are nonetheless usually concerned with other people. Often the emotions expressed are quite primitive: they can be far removed from the balanced, objective summings-up to which some of the songs we discussed earlier were devoted. To complain that a song like **'Positively 4th Street'** is "bitter" is to present Dylan with no case to answer. To give expression to the feeling of undiluted, remorseless bitterness—something which a good many people must have experienced at times—is precisely its purpose. By its success in conveying that feeling it adds to the repertoire of the emotions which have been realised and sublimated in art. (And to see how little this repertoire is increased by an attempt which fails we need look no further than **'Ballad in Plain D.'**)

'Like a Rolling Stone' seems to be one of a pair with **'Queen Jane Approximately'**—Dylan goes in for matching or contrasting pairs of songs on several of his albums. What is envisaged in **'Queen Jane'** seems, in **'Like a Rolling Stone'**, to have happened, and Dylan is now crowing. The "jugglers and the clowns" who frown when they do "tricks for you" could indeed be the same clowns that Queen Jane "commissioned." From the first lines he seems to be rubbing her face in it:

> Once upon a time you dressed so fine

You threw the bums a dime in your prime,
    didn't you?

That taunt gives the tone of the song: he wants her to admit that she is down and out. He piles up images that suggest a person successful, extraverted and full of confidence (if somewhat unaware), only to reveal her feet of clay. Yet if ever there was a case of the total sense of a Dylan song springing from much more than the words, and of the other elements modifying the verbal meaning, it must be this. The song has had a lot of attention and I don't want to comment on it at length; but its greatness lies in its capacity to expand and take on new resonances and emotional tones, and this it owes largely to its magnificent, celebratory, affirmative melody. After the hard confidence of the original treatment, and the Dionysiac exultation of the version on *Before the Flood,* it becomes, on the *Budokan* album, a profoundly sad, wise and sympathetic piece, closer in mood to what is expressed in the last lines of that wonderfully tender and evocative song, **'It Takes a Lot to Laugh, It Takes a Train to Cry':**

> Well, I wanna be your lover, baby,
> I don't wanna be your boss.
> Don't say I never warned you
> When your train gets lost.

'Like a Rolling Stone' is a work which grows and matures in as moving and unexpected ways as does the man who wrote it. (And shrinks, also, with his temporary retreats: it is rather poignant to hear that pulsing rhythm held in unnatural restraint so as to accommodate the stubbornly tame interpretation which Dylan gives us on the Isle of Wight track included in *Self Portrait*—so tame and so reductive of the song's real mood that in the words "How does it feel?" he even puts almost as strong an emphasis on "does" as on "feel".)

'Positively 4th Street' has no such potential breadth of sympathy but it does have its own prickly integrity. It is an extremely tightly constructed song with an unending, circular musical pattern, each verse formally corresponding to one musical unit but the variable rhyme scheme being based on two, which allows for some neat effects making use of matching verses. The jaunty, carefree tune—we can picture Dylan strolling whistling down 4th Street, hands in pockets—ironically offsets the pitiless, clinical exposure of hypocrisy which is the song's unrelenting business. It is probably addressed to some friend who has let Dylan down; but in the one verse where 'he' is referred to in the printed text, "it" is substituted in the song as sung:

> Do you take me for such a fool
> To think I'd make contact
> With the one who tries to hide
> What it don't know to begin with

The purpose of this could be to leave the person's sex indeterminate, but more likely it is to reduce his status to that of an object. This does not, I think, contradict my earlier contention that Dylan humanises his attacks on his victims by putting himself in their position; for he is calling the person "it" here for a conscious purpose of invective and not out of a failure of imaginative sympathy. Indeed his innate tendency to put himself in the other person's shoes is here made literal, again with a polemical object in view, in what must be the ultimate in gestures of rejection:

> I wish that for just one time
> You could stand inside my shoes
> And just for that one moment
> I could be you
>
> Yes, I wish that for just one time
> You could stand inside my shoes
> You'd know what a drag it is
> To see you

The refined cruelty of this is remarkable. The repetition of the proposition keeps the listener in suspense, perhaps hoping for a more sympathetic line than the song has so far displayed; for the wish that the other "could stand inside my shoes" might be expected to mean "understand my point of view" rather than what it does mean, "see you as I do"; and in the light of that expectation "And just for that one moment / I could be you" could even seem to express an outgoing impulse instead of the sneer which it later proves to be. The "feeling" behind the whole song is perfectly embodied in those last lines and the way Dylan sings them; and to have allowed any element of charity to creep in would have been to be untrue to the feeling which grows out of the first verse:

> You got a lotta nerve
> To say you are my friend
> When I was down
> You just stood there grinning

'Ballad of a Thin Man' is a song which has been subjected to a profusion of interpretations. I have seen Mr Jones confidently identified as variously a newspaper reporter, a "representative of the unhip world", "the respectable man in the street and probably you and I", "the pop equivalent of Mr Charlie", and Bob Dylan. Dylan has said that he is "a fella that came into a truck-stop once." It is also suggested (by Craig McGregor, Michael Gray and others) that the situation in which Mr Jones is lost involves a homosexual propositioning. None of this really matters: what matters is that he is someone—anyone—who finds himself vulnerable, exposed and alone in a situation which he does not understand and cannot control:

> You raise up your head
> And you ask, "Is this where it is?"
> And somebody points to you and says
> "It's his"
> And you say "What's mine?"
> And somebody else says "Where what is?"
> And you say, "Oh my God
> Am I here all alone?"

The helplessness, the confusion, the feeling that you are being laughed at and that whatever you say next will be wrong—everyone must at some time or another have felt something like this and said to himself "Oh my God / Am I here all alone?" Mr Jones is observed from the outside but we are obliged to feel with him because we know no more about what is "happening here" than he does; the story is told from an implied position of omniscience which we are not permitted to share—Dylan understands what it's all about, we feel, but we don't, any more than

Mr Jones does (which is why we feel obliged to attempt an interpretation). He is being mocked, but we are not able to go comfortably along with the mockery because the victim is too close to ourselves. That Dylan is able to bring off such an effect is, of course, dependent on his own act of empathy.

There is a passage in the section of *Tarantula* called "Sand in the Mouth of the Movie Star" which seems closely related to **'Ballad of a Thin Man'** (both belong to roughly the same period). It is worth looking at as an illustration of how Dylan seems to need the disciplines of song writing to define and direct his insights. The prose passage is unfocused, diffuse and lacking in impact, and would probably go unremarked without a knowledge of the song, which provides a clue to what the writer is driving at. It would be interesting to know which came first; most likely the prose contains the germ of the song.

We have been looking at songs which appear to be mainly negative in attitude. But the point is really—and this is something that will crop up again and again—that Dylan is one of those artists who most often define their *values* negatively—in terms of what they are against rather than of what they are for. This can be clearly seen in a song which has a very positive outlook and tone—**'All I Really Want to Do.'** This is one of the wittiest and most high-spirited of the early songs, very sharp psychologically, full of nimble internal rhyming, and delivered in a chuckling, irreverent, half-mocking but very engaging tone of voice. The whole song is devoted to a catalogue of the things Dylan *doesn't* want to do to the girl, set only against the recurrent protestation: "All I really want to do / Is, baby, be friends with you." This disclaimer is, of course, tinged with irony, for whatever he may *not* want to do it is certain that he is interested in being more than just "friends" with her. But the phrase points effectively to a straight-forward and uncomplicated attitude which stands in contrast to the kind of intense, soul-searching approach to sexual relationships which is what he is satirising—what D. H. Lawrence used to call "sex-in-the-head":

> I ain't lookin' to block you up,
> Shock or knock or lock you up,
> Analyse you, categorize you,
> Finalize you or advertise you.

The picture that is built up of the woman he is addressing is of one who likes to accuse her lover of such objectives precisely because she herself is stuck firmly in her head. Against this claustrophobic cerebral closeness Dylan asserts his own self-sufficient singleness:

> I ain't lookin' for you to feel like me,
> See like me or be like me.

This is a perennial Dylan theme. We find it again in **'Maggie's Farm'**:

> Well, I try my best
> To be just like I am,
> But everybody wants you
> To be just like them.

It crops up once more as late as the *Slow Train Coming* album, in **'I Believe in You',** where his friends show him the door " 'cause I don't be like they'd like me to".

What Dylan is saying in **'All I Really Want to Do'** is entirely positive in spirit, but it is highly characteristic of him that it is presented in a negative form. The lover who receives perhaps his highest and most finely-wrought praise—the woman of **'Love Minus Zero / No Limit'**—has attributes which are formulated either negatively or by means of such suggestive paradoxes as are used to describe spiritual things in the language used by Eastern religion. Thus "she speaks like silence, / Without ideals or violence", "she laughs like the flowers"; her insights and attitudes belong to the spirit of Zen:

> She knows there's no success like failure
> And that failure's no success at all.
>
> . . . . .
>
> My love winks, she does not bother,
> She knows too much to argue or to judge.

The values represented by this lover are defined in contrast to the ways of the world—the insincere gestures, the lost and futile talk, the insubstantiality of material things, the confused spiritual strivings—all suggested in marvellously rich and concrete language. The positive values find their place within a harsh, elemental world:

> The wind howls like a hammer
> The wind blows cold and rainy,
> My love she's like some raven
> At my window with a broken wing.

The "broken wing" is one of those flashes of imaginative insight which only a great artist can make livingly concrete. It comes as a surprise, for all the previous imagery has suggested someone secure, confident, untouched, almost remote, standing above the common exigencies of living by virtue of spiritual strangths; but when the image comes it impels our assent, for with its suggestion of vulnerability-within-strength it establishes her humanity: this is no goddess and no abstraction, but a woman who lives out her values in the world. (pp. 14-26)

'She Belongs To Me' has sometimes been taken for a similar hymn of praise, but it does not appear so to me. It does seem to make a pair with **'Love Minus Zero'**, but such pairings among Dylan's songs generally imply some degree of contrast. The irony surely begins with the title, for it could much more aptly be called "I Belong To Her", and the song is almost as much about what it feels like to belong to her as it is about the woman herself. Her dominance is complete: she is self-centred, imperious, probably capricious, certainly predatory. The singer's thraldom is such that his lover colours the very texture of his days and nights:

> She can take the dark out of the nighttime
> And paint the daytime black.

This woman too has a certain spiritual power, or power of personality, but unlike the other she uses it to dominate and to feed her ego:

> You will start out standing
> Proud to steal her anything she sees.
> But you will end up peeking through her keyhole
> Down upon your knees.

(Dylan admits this as his own experience implicitly,

through the title.) Again, unlike the other, she appears invulnerable, untouchable in a way which seems only doubtfully a compliment:

> She never stumbles,
> She's got no place to fall.
> She's nobody's child,
> The law can't touch her at all.

The basis of the relationship is succinctly summed up in the lines "She's a hypnotist collector, / You are a walking antique"; and when Dylan suggests buying her a trumpet for Halloween, we are left wondering whether this is so that she can blow her own. The mood of the song is of a kind of despairing admiration for the enormity of it all. But of course it is not an objective summing-up of an actual woman: it is a putting-out-there of a specific feeling. It is even possible that the women of the two songs are actually one, seen from the vantage-point of different feelings, of different motions of the will. James Joyce attributes to Shem the Penman in *Finnegans Wake* the two complementary functions of the artist: "He points the deathbone and the quick are still . . . He lifts the lifewand and the dumb speak." If in **'Love Minus Zero'** Dylan lifts the lifewand, **'She Belongs To Me'** is one of the songs in which he points the deathbone. (pp. 26-7)

> *John Herdman, in his* Voice Without Restraint: A Study of Bob Dylan's Lyrics and Their Background, *Delilah Books, 1982, 164 p.*

To me, Dylan always represented rock'n'roll—I never thought of him as a folk singer or poet or nothing. I just thought he was the sexiest person since Elvis Presley—sex in the brain, y'know? Sex at its most ultimate is being totally illuminated, and he was that, he was the King. And he still has it. I don't think his true power has been unleashed. I haven't stopped believing in him.

—*Patti Smith, in an interview with* The Telegraph *conducted on March 18, 1977, and published in* Wanted Man: In Search of Bob Dylan, *Black Spring Press, 1990.*

Richard Tillinghast (essay date 1987)

[*Tillinghast is an American poet, critic, and educator. In the following essay, he examines Dylan's evocation in his songs of the idealized female muse, a figure he compares with American poet Robert Graves' "White Goddess."*]

In 1960 Bob Dylan "burst on the scene already a legend, / The unwashed phenomenon, the original vagabond," as Joan Baez later described him in her song "Diamonds and Rust." He seemed cut according to the Woody Guthrie

template, a workshirt-wearin', guitar-pickin' person with a lot to say about migrant workers and sharecroppers. The Baez song, however, talks more about eros than about social consciousness:

> You strayed into my arms
> And there you stayed, temporarily lost at sea.
> The madonna was yours for free, yes the girl on
> 　the half-shell
> Could keep you unharmed.

Dylan's interest in the protest song would fade faster than a pair of Levi's, but he would continue to court the idealized lady whom poets from the Greeks to the troubadours of medieval Provence to Dante to many of our contemporaries have looked to for inspiration. Robert Graves, of course, called her the White Goddess. Jung wrote of the *anima:* the hidden, feminine side of a man's psyche, which he sought out in women, and when encountered, made him feel he had at last discovered his true self or twin. The search for this other self, twin, muse, madonna, has turned out to be a strikingly insistent lifelong quest for Dylan. Though sardonic and a master of the put-on, this is one subject he has not tended to joke about. And over the long haul this lady has not proved to be his "for free."

Dylan's early songs addressed to women are, like his early songs addressed to everyone else, confrontational, biting, and derisive. **"Just Like a Woman,"** for example, takes for its title a traditionally derogative male comment. The emotions run deep here, but they are bittersweet:

> It was raining from the first, and I was dying of
> 　thirst,
> So I came in here.
> Your longtime curse hurts, but what's worse
> Is this pain in here. I can't stay in here,
> Ain't it clear?
> That I just can't fit.
> Yes I believe it's time for us to quit.
> And when we meet again, introduced as friends,
> Please don't let on that you knew me when
> I was hungry and it was your world.

Standing out among the hard-edged, overexcited songs on the 1966 album *Blonde on Blonde,* where **"Just Like a Woman"** also appears, **"Sad-Eyed Lady of the Lowlands"** takes one whole side of a record and is a hymnlike wedding song to his wife Sara, whom he married in 1965. At that stage in Dylan's career it was a bit of a shock to see him this mellow. These are song lyrics, meant to be heard, so listen to the record if you have it. The printed words don't convey their full effect, but the band Dylan assembled in the Columbia studios in Nashville, with Kenny Buttrey's measured drumming and Al Kooper's lush organ, backed up a Dylan who for once sounded fulfilled and at peace:

> With your Mercury mouth in the Missionary
> 　Times,
> And your eyes like smoke and your prayers like
> 　rhymes,
> And your silver cross and your voice like
> 　chimes,
> Oh who did they think could come bury you?

He is clearly laying his gifts in the traditional manner at

this lady's feet: "My warehouse eyes, my Arabian drums: / Should I leave them by your gate, / Or sad-eyed lady, should I wait?"

Like many writers who present an autobiographical surface, Dylan, it turns out, works with the illusion of an actual life—autobiography as a poetic convenience, a resource, a vehicle for communication with an audience. A realization that emerges from acquaintance with apparently autobiographical narratives by writers one knows, is that "I" really *is* "another," and that particularly for persons who create lyrics and tell stories, the self shifts, is not a fixed commodity.

One key to the magnetism of Dylan's songs is his ability to lose himself in his material, to exercise negative capability—though when seen as a psychological trait and not just an artistic mode, negative capability has, as Aristotle would say, the defects of his qualities. Dylan has often been lost. His song, **"Too Much of Nothing,"** makes that clear. Significantly the album *Self Portrait* (1970) primarily highlights songs written by other people, including pop standards like "Let It Be Me" and "Blue Moon."

Perhaps the absence of a fixed, clearly defined self makes his search for the spiritualized, feminine ideal standing behind many real women all the more crucial. His best songs of intensely romantic, star-crossed love appear on *Blood on the Tracks* (1975) and *Desire* (1976), coinciding with the breakup of his marriage to the woman for whom he wrote **"Sad-Eyed Lady of the Lowlands."** The lady in one of my favorite Dylan songs, **"Tangled Up in Blue,"** is not the usual dark-eyed, dark-haired beauty, but a redhead:

> Early one morning the sun was shining,
> I was laying in bed,
> Wondering if she'd changed at all,
> If her hair was still red.
> Her folks they said our lives together
> Sure was gonna be rough.
> They never did like Mama's homemade dress,
> Papa's bankbook wasn't big enough.

The song recounts the adventures, split-ups, and reunions of this couple, separated by circumstance and reunited by fate. But after you listen a few times, you sense that all these stories couldn't all have involved the same woman, that this romance must be a composite. And Dylan hints at the poet-muse connection when the woman, whom he has at this point rediscovered working in a topless place— "I must admit I felt a little uneasy / When she bent down to tie the lace of my shoe"—in New Orleans, takes him to her apartment, "lit a burner on the stove / And offered me a pipe," then hands him a book of poems by "an Italian poet / From the fifteenth century." The century is wrong, but who else could it be but Dante? The poetry brings an instant shock of recognition:

> And every one of those words rang true
> And glowed like burning coals,
> Pouring off of every page
> Like it was written in my soul,
> Brought me to you,
> Tangled up in blue.

Blue is the blue of her eyes, a blue mood, blue of the sky—

and then there's Dylan's earlier song, **"It's All Over Now, Baby Blue."**

"Simple Twist of Fate," the next track after **"Tangled Up in Blue,"** tells of an encounter, seemingly casual, on the waterfront somewhere—a one-night stand that leaves him with "an emptiness inside." So he goes looking for this woman, walking by the docks, "where the sailors all come in. / Maybe she'll pick him out again. / How long must he wait / One more time for a simple twist of fate?" The song fudges beautifully on point of view, sliding meaningfully out of the third person to show that he was the "he" in the song: "They walked along by the old canal / A little confused, I remember well." In the last stanza of this haunting song, Dylan drops all pretense that it's a story about someone else:

> People tell me it's a sin
> To know and feel too much within.
> I still believe she was my twin,
> But I lost the ring. . . .

These songs mingle rapture and regret, and there is an air of poignant sadness to them. The series is topped off by **"Sara,"** from the album *Desire,* an elegiac song that marks the end of his twelve-year marriage, a gesture as final and as painful as the $10-million-dollar divorce settlement.

Dylan is one of our truest poets, and only our discomfort with an aural medium prevents us from seeing this. It's fascinating though not surprising to see that over the course of his career social themes easily lost out to eros and the encounter with the muse. How consistent this is with Robert Graves's classic account of the poet's encounter with the White Goddess in his poem "To Juan at the Winter Solstice":

> Dwell on her graciousness, dwell on her smiling,
> Do not forget what flowers
> The great boar trampled down in ivy time.
> Her brow was creamy as the crested wave,
> Her sea-blue eyes were wild
> But nothing promised that is not performed.

(pp. 172-76)

Richard Tillinghast, "Bob Dylan and the White Goddess," in The Missouri Review, *Vol. X, No. 3, 1987, pp. 172-76.*

Aidan Day   (essay date 1988)

[*A British critic and educator, Day often focuses on English and American poetry. In* Contemporary Authors *(Vol. 132), a Gale companion series to CLC, Day remarked that his study* Jokerman: Reading the Lyrics of Bob Dylan, *from which the following essay is taken, "was written to suggest a few of the ways in which Bob Dylan's lyrics sustain literary, critical, close reading." Below, Day examines Dylan's treatment of identity in "Ballad of a Thin Man" and other songs.*]

> light of feelin'
> as I listen t'one of my own tongues
> take the reins
> guide the path
> an' drop me off . . .
> **'11 Outlined Epitaphs'** (1964)

[To] this day, where great rock music is being made, there is the shadow of Bob Dylan over and over and over, and Bob's own modern work has gone unjustly underappreciated for having to stand in that shadow. If there was a young guy out there writing "Sweetheart Like You", writing the *Empire Burlesque* album, writing "Every Grain Of Sand", they'd be calling him the new Bob Dylan.

—*Bruce Springsteen, in a speech delivered on the occasion of Dylan's induction to the Rock 'n' Roll Hall of Fame on January 20, 1988, and reprinted in* Wanted Man: In Search of Bob Dylan, *Black Spring Press, 1990.*

'I cannot say the word eye any more' wrote Dylan in the 1965 album notes to **Highway 61 Revisited.** The observation forms part of a prose passage which, punning on the homophone I/eye, playfully hints at a scepticism regarding the attribution of a fixed meaning to the term 'I'. It is a scepticism elaborated in the passage as Dylan explores a self that is divided—observing itself as it might observe another—by virtue of its very self-consciousness. In place of the single reality conventionally identified by the first-person pronoun the passage substitutes an image of 'mouths' of the self. Such a plurality of mouths, tongues or voices, calls into question the monolithic authority of the conscious 'I' that is associated with the upper reaches (the 'rooftop') of the mind:

> I cannot say the word eye any more. . . . when
> I speak this word eye, it is as if I am speaking
> of somebody's eye that I faintly remember. . . .
> there is no I—there is only a series of mouths—
> long live the mouths—your rooftop—if you
> don't already know—has been demolished. . . .

The preoccupation with questions of identity, and the punning, carry over into the lyrics of **Highway 61 Revisited.** 'Like a Rolling Stone', for example, inquires into the disquiet of living unprotected by the learned values of established culture. 'You've gone to the finest school alright, Miss Lonely', but 'nobody has ever taught you how to live on the street':

> How does it feel
> To be without a home . . . ?

And how does it feel to be without the reassurance of accepted ways of thinking about the self? Living on the street is in this lyric expressly a matter of living without a rooftop. The rhyme pattern in the second stanza recalls the sleeve-note pun on I/eye:

> You said you'd never compromise
> With the mystery tramp, but now you realize
> He's not selling any alibis
> As you stare into the vacuum of his eyes

It is within an interior cityscape that the denizen of the streets, the 'mystery tramp', is encountered. Looking forward to the figure of the joker in Dylan's 1983 **'Jokerman'** (*Infidels*), the 'mystery tramp' images possibilities of the psyche not contained solely within the field of the conscious or rational self. Guaranteeing no alibis, these possibilities expose the hollowness of the notion that the self can be posited in any one, verifiable position: 'the vacuum of his eyes'. Perhaps ultimately unmanageable, the 'mystery tramp' reflects identity as unsettled, evading fixture and formulation. Always on the move, he has a number of family relations in another lyric from **Highway 61 Revisited,** 'Ballad of a Thin Man'.

'Ballad of a Thin Man' consists simply of a voice scornfully addressing a certain 'Mister Jones': 'something is happening here / But you don't know what it is / Do you, Mister Jones?'. Throughout the lyric Mister Jones is envisaged as one who enters upon a scene—a scene that is never precisely delineated—in which he is out of place and of which he has no knowledge. It is upon questions of knowledge that the speaker's censure of Mister Jones turns. In the first place there is hostility to the gathering of mere information. At the very opening of the lyric: 'You walk into the room / With your pencil in your hand.' The note-taking implied by that pencil is deemed by the speaker incapable of coping with the phenomena Mister Jones now faces:

> You try so hard
> But you don't understand
> Just what you'll say
> When you get home

Though this is not to say that the documentary approach will not turn even more reductively empirical when its inadequacies are pointed out, as the speaker is very well aware:

> You have many contacts
> Among the lumberjacks
> To get you facts
> When someone attacks your imagination

The mind that is sustained by data alone may also be one that proceeds only by cold abstraction. 'You've been with the professors', the speaker tells the unfortunate yet resilient Mister Jones in stanza five:

> And they've all liked your looks
> With great lawyers you have
> Discussed lepers and crooks
> You've been through all of
> F. Scott Fitzgerald's books
> You're very well read
> It's well known

Not that F. Scott Fitzgerald is not a proper object of knowledge. The objection in this lyric is to a way of knowing that defines knowledge purely in terms of that which is available to the discursive intellect: 'With great lawyers you have / Discussed lepers and crooks.' With insiders, in other words, you have debated outsiders. But the satiric insinuation is of the absence in such discussions of an imaginative comprehension of conditions of alienation.

From one point of view **'Ballad of a Thin Man'** constitutes an attack on an ideology of rationalism, in much the same vein as the speaker of **'Tombstone Blues'**, also from *Highway 61 Revisited,* declares:

> Now I wish I could write you a melody so plain
> That could hold you dear lady from going insane
> That could ease you and cool you and cease the
>   pain
> Of your useless and pointless knowledge

In **'Tombstone Blues'** the sensuality of the young—relatively free of inscribed knowledge—may temporarily unsettle authorized orders and abstractions: 'The geometry of innocence flesh on the bone / Causes Galileo's math book to get thrown'. But the 'king of the Philistines . . . / Puts the pied pipers in prison' and in this lyric it remains an open question whether freedom from a cultural dead hand will not always be betrayed into servitude:

> The geometry of innocence flesh on the bone
> Causes Galileo's math book to get thrown
> At Delilah who sits worthlessly alone
> But the tears on her cheeks are from laughter

In **'Ballad of a Thin Man'** an ideology of rationalism is apprehended, in the first place, in external terms. It dramatizes, with an acid wit, a scene where the representative of a dominant, rationalistic culture encounters another kind of culture (or, perhaps, subculture). But such encounters, recognizable in their outward features, do not happen only at the surface of things. Nor are the players in the drama necessarily just different kinds of people. The tension between opposing forces in **'Ballad of a Thin Man'** may be played out within the individual mind and, at the same time as the lyric visualizes an external confrontation, it enacts that confrontation as an interior drama, as a matter of the rational self's repression of deeper impulses of personality. The limitations of such a repression are not merely asserted in the lyric. They are demonstrated at those points where Mister Jones is brought up against things that cannot simply be rationalized. Most striking are his encounters with a series of figures drawn from the tradition of circus or carnival. In the third stanza, 'You hand in your ticket / And you go watch the geek'; in the sixth, 'the sword swallower, he comes up to you'; and in the seventh, 'Now you see this one-eyed midget.' These figures invoke the freely creative, if anarchic, potencies of the imagination. Confronting them, Mister Jones is put in the position of negotiating 'something' that is 'happening' deeper than the reach of merely the rational self. No doubt the antitypes of his conversations with professors and lawyers, his encounters with them comprise darkly funny exercises in confronting the absurd:

> you go watch the geek
> Who immediately walks up to you
> When he hears you speak
> And says, 'How does it feel
> To be such a freak?'
> And you say, 'Impossible'
> As he hands you a bone
>
> the sword swallower, he comes up to you
> And then he kneels
> He crosses himself
> And then he clicks his high heels
> And without further notice

> He asks you how it feels
> And he says, 'Here is your throat back
> Thanks for the loan'

Language marks the divide that is dramatized in **'Ballad of a Thin Man'** between the conscious self and unconscious potentiality. A series of present-tense verbs thinly disguises the fact that these episodes involving Mister Jones and the carnival figures are deficient in normal causal connections. As the 'geek', 'sword swallower', and 'one-eyed midget' present a challenge to reason and the rational self so they challenge the logical sequences of syntax. There is in each episode a disturbance of predictable lexical arrangement. And, as words are displaced from their usual contexts, the straightforward meaning, the assumed transparency, of the most ordinary words and speech patterns is called into question. It is an independence which would render them opaque to the eye attempting to read them according to customary usage. Dylan's passages achieve a surrealist effect in which the rebellion of words becomes a measure of the rebellion of the imagination against rational censorship. A notable moment of collision with syntactic control comes in the seventh stanza as the 'one-eyed midget', abrogating the accepted continuities of dialogue, seeks to cut the connection so desperately insisted upon by Mister Jones between reason, meaning and language:

> Now you see this one-eyed midget
> Shouting the word 'NOW'
> And you say, 'For what reason?'
> And he says, 'How?'
> And you say, 'What does this mean?'
> And he screams back, 'You're a cow
> Give me some milk
> Or else go home'

At once vital and grave ('you say, "Impossible" / As he hands you a bone'), Dylan's comic-grotesque figures are instinct with that carnival laughter which, in the words of Mikhail Bakhtin [in his *Rabelais and His World*], is 'gay, triumphant, and at the same time mocking and deriding', which 'asserts and denies. . . . buries and revives'. They are informed by the carnival spirit that, in its hostility to all that is 'completed', exposes the 'gay relativity of prevailing truths and authorities'. But only to some degree. Dylan's exotic carnival figures are shown finally to be in no position to celebrate an unconditional emancipation from established orders. And the domestic Mister Jones, while disconcerted at glimpsing what it is to be without a home, remains unrepentant. It is with complacent indignation that he reacts to the momentary disruption in stanza two of a usual pattern of interrogative exchange:

> You raise up your head
> And you ask, 'Is this where it is?'
> And somebody points to you and says
> 'It's his'
> And you say, 'What's mine?'
> And somebody else says, 'Where what is?'
> And you say, 'Oh my God
> Am I here all alone?'

Mister Jones is here led to put inadvertently what could be construed as a radical question about identity, about what may be said to belong to the self. But Mister Jones would be blind to such a construction. The attempted disorientation of his terms of reference throughout the lyric never succeeds in reconstituting him within a discourse by which he might reread the entire question, 'What's mine?' Endorsing reason and meaning even to the end Mister Jones remains closed to the imaginative possibilities erupting before him. Equally, however, this very resilience denies unqualified potentiality to the forces that refuse to conform to the rules of his rationality.

What is crucial in the lyric is that the relationship between those forces and those rules is not a matter of mutual indifference. Each side behaves as if under compulsion to confront the other. And it is more than a matter of simple opposition. While the figures of carnival and Mister Jones appear caught in stark contrast at the surface level of the lyric the narrative itself contains elements which collapse any absolute distinction between them. Mister Jones never gives up hope of being able to frame order out of chaos. The 'one-eyed midget' assumes the possibility of exploiting—even drawing some kind of sustenance from—Mister Jones: ' "Give me some milk." ' Mister Jones may also have something that the 'sword swallower' needs, however disparagingly the sword swallower may phrase his gratitude for the satisfaction of that need: ' "Here is your throat back / Thanks for the loan." ' Conversely, the sword swallower's asking Mister Jones how 'it feels' and his thanking Mister Jones for the use of his 'throat' add up to a picture of Mister Jones as a swallower of swords. Mister Jones and the sword swallower may be at odds with each other but only in the special sense that different dimensions of one psyche may be at odds with each other. There is a comparable effect when the 'geek', inverting the obvious terms, asks Mister Jones how it feels to be a 'freak'. But the different personae of the lyric discover their interconnections most tellingly in the speaker's own final perception of Mister Jones. In the closing stanza of the lyric Mister Jones is no longer envisioned simply as the narrow man defined by a world of 'facts' and 'books' and a society of 'professors' and 'lawyers'. Instead he appears to the speaker in the guise of the absurd itself:

> Well, you walk into the room
> Like a camel and then you frown
> You put your eyes in your pocket
> And your nose on the ground

While **'Ballad of a Thin Man'** speaks, from one point of view, as a one-sided assault, its deepest sensitivity is to the interdependence of the rational and the irrational, the interinvolvement of meaning and the absurd. That the lyric speaks at all presumes the necessity of that interdependence. Julia Kristeva has said [in her *Revolution in Poetic Language*] that literature of the avant-garde, a modernist literature characterized by teasing perversions of logical construction, is a kind of writing in which the energies of the unconscious graphically break through the strict, constraining orders of reason: 'Magic, shamanism, esoterism, the carnival, and "incomprehensible" poetry all underscore the limits of socially useful discourse and attest to what it represses.' But repressor and repressed cannot simply be divorced. The energies of imagination that are felt within a literary text may be 'indifferent to language, enigmatic'. They may constitute a 'space underlying the writ-

ten' that is 'rhythmic, unfettered . . . musical, anterior to judgement', but it is a space that is 'restrained by a single guarantee: syntax'. It is a space necessarily restrained, if not contained, because such restraint is the condition of intelligibility. Speaking of the interrelations between the irrational and the rational in poetry Kristeva invokes Mallarmé's view of the ' "mysterious" functioning of literature as a rhythm made intelligible by syntax'. In **'Ballad of a Thin Man'**, however much they may rail against an arid rationalism, and however much they espouse the cause of a surrealist subversion, the lyric and its speaker never entirely divest themselves of the rational syntax of language. **'Ballad of a Thin Man'** refuses, ultimately, to allow that imagination or the unconscious are able to speak in a way that is not complicit in the language that defines Mister Jones. In the last resort no hard separation is allowed between reason and imagination. Speaker and lyric, for they are one and the same, are implied simultaneously in the beings of Mister Jones and the carnival figures.

Yet the dialectic in **'Ballad of a Thin Man'** is never finally resolvable. The work comes to a conclusion by an arbitrary act of establishing an ending. But as a drama of the relation between reason and free creative desire, between language and the unconscious, the lyric's text is endless. Syntax will continue to attempt to rein in the asyntactic, which will in turn continue to slip complete harnessing. The sword swallower's gratitude for the loan of Mister Jones's throat, the instrument and mechanism of utterance, also conceals a recognition that imagination's articulation is coincident with Mister Jones's language. The mutual suspicion involved in this transaction images a negotiation between interests that are inextricably linked but not conformable to each other. The relationship between Mister Jones and the forces of carnival is one of tense interaction that never achieves a synthesis. It is a relationship that, as a paradigm of the connections between language and the unconscious, becomes a paradigm of the lyric itself. (pp. 8-17)

> *Aidan Day, in his* Jokerman: Reading the Lyrics of Bob Dylan, *Basil Blackwell, 1988, 189 p.*

Stephen Scobie   (essay date 1991)

[*Scobie is a Scottish poet, critic, and educator. In the essay excerpted below, Scobie offers a favorable assessment of Dylan's 1990 album* Under the Red Sky.]

The first thing that struck me when listening to **Under the Red Sky** [1990] was how different it was from **Oh Mercy.** And that was good news—it took me back to the days when no two consecutive Bob Dylan albums were the same, when you could never tell from one album to the next which direction he would be heading. So if you approach **Under the Red Sky** expecting to hear **Oh Mercy,** you're going to be disappointed. But if you approach **Under the Red Sky** on its own terms, then you may find that it is a very strange, mysterious, and wonderful work. If I had to invoke any previous recording by Dylan to compare it with, I would say that to find a collection of songs like *Under the Red Sky* you have to go all the way back to *The Basement Tapes.*

Of course, there are similarities and continuities from *Oh Mercy,* perhaps slyly signaled by the appearance of the word 'mercy' itself, which sneaks into *Under the Red Sky* in the last line of the last song, like a signature signing off: 'may the Lord have mercy on us all.' But the differences are more immediately obvious. We move from the precisely controlled production values of Daniel Lanois to Dylan's more accustomed ragbag approach, with its stray assortment of superstar guests dropping in on individual tracks. *Under the Red Sky* never sounds as well crafted as *Oh Mercy,* but on the other hand it's much more fun. The difference in tone is obvious in the opening songs: after the solemn socio-religious statement of 'We live in a political world' comes the cheerful informality of **'Wiggle Wiggle.'** Who would have thought a 'serious artist' like Bob Dylan would write a song with such a title? He's not just letting down his hair, he's letting down his pants.

The casual appearance may be deceptive though. Even **'Wiggle Wiggle,'** which seems like a throwaway opening number, almost a joke song, is the product of extensive revision. If you listen to the versions of the song performed by Dylan on tour (for instance, at Toad's Place in January, 1990), you will note that apart from the title phrase not one line is the same as the track released less than nine months later.

Nevertheless, there is something very scattered and incomplete about the album. In contrast to the tight, well-made songs of *Oh Mercy,* these new songs wander all over the place. I tend to remember individual lines and images rather than whole songs, and often these lines stick out from their surroundings in quite incongruous ways. Take, for instance, the very striking little narrative

> Once there was a man who had no eyes,
> Every lady in the land told him lies,
> He stood beneath the silver skies
> And his heart began to bleed

The theme of blindness is important to the album, but what are these lines doing in the middle of **'Unbelievable'**? How do they relate to the rest of the song? A blinded man suddenly shows up for four lines, and then disappears again; no connections are made. This use of the 'bridge' passage to effect a sudden shift of perspective is not new in Dylan's work: think back to **'Señor (Tales of Yankee Power)'** or **'Going Going Gone.'** Often the power and mystery of such songs arise not so much from the individual line as from the juxtapositions of apparently unrelated images.

Similarly, though I love almost every line of **'Handy Dandy'** taken by itself, I can't combine them into any coherent picture of the song's protagonist. At times he seems like Dylan ('controversy surrounds him'); at times he seems like Christ, living in that heavenly mansion where 'no thieves can break in'; at times he seems like a cheap gangster; at times he seems like an excuse for some easy rhymes on 'candy' and 'brandy.' The only thing that ties this song together is the exuberance of its music and Dylan's bravura delivery of its long, rolling lines.

By describing these songs as incoherent I am not necessarily finding fault with them but rather trying to describe the kind of writing that's going on. Coherence is only one kind of virtue. In the language of literary criticism, *Oh Mercy* displays a modernist urge toward the perfect lyric while *Under the Red Sky* reaches for postmodernist indeterminacy and open-endedness. There is a sense of risk-taking in *Under the Red Sky.* Every line takes a deep breath and plunges recklessly in an unexpected direction:

> Hey! Who could your lover be?
> Hey! Who could your lover be?
> Let me eat off his head so you can really see!

It is this craziness, as well as the down-home barnyard apocalypse of a song like **'Cat's in the Well,'** that reminds me of *The Basement Tapes.* Describing that album [in his liner notes to the LP], Greil Marcus wrote of 'strange adventures and poker-faced insanities' in songs that 'seem to leap out of a kaleidoscope of American music no less immediate for its venerability.' A line like 'Back alley Sally is doing the American jump' seems to come straight out of the ethos of *The Basement Tapes.* From folk songs to the blues, from nursery rhymes to traditional counting songs, *Under the Red Sky* is filled with echoes. Even the apparent casualness of its craft, after the highly polished professionalism of *Oh Mercy,* suggests a deliberate courting of the naïf. This is Bob Dylan's Grandma Moses album.

Pop music itself is part of this eclectic range of sources. The title *Under the Red Sky* recalls an album by U2, *Under a Blood Red Sky,* while the cover image, a black and white photograph in a desert setting, further evokes U2's *The Joshua Tree.* Other echoes and borrowings abound. The main riff in **'Unbelievable'** is similar to Robert Palmer's hit a few years ago, 'Simply Irresistible,' which ended up as a Pepsi commercial. The music of **'Handy Dandy'** echoes everything from Dylan's **'Like a Rolling Stone'** (in Al Kooper's organ) to 'Hang On Sloopy.' When **'Wiggle Wiggle'** appeared at a few concerts in 1990, Dylan scholars were unsure whether it was an original composition or another obscure 1950s B-side dredged up from the memories of late night radio in Hibbing.

The blues are also evident, in the format of **'10,000 Men'** and **'Cat's in the Well.'** (Perhaps **'Handy Dandy'** is, after all, W. C. Handy.) And the blues' fondness for repeated lines shows up to stunning effect in the title song, **'Under the Red Sky,'** a rhythmic *tour de force* in which the same lines are repeated at double speed. The effect of this repetition is one of simultaneous progression and stasis: a story is told, but the situation remains the same. It has both the linearity of narrative and the timelessness of myth.

The title song, **'Under the Red Sky,'** also invokes the feeling of nursery rhymes, though in a totally perverse manner, in which all the conventions of the form are viewed through a veil of desperate black humour:

> Let the wind blow low, let the wind blow high,
> One day the little boy and the little girl were
>   both baked in a pie.

The saccharine melody enables Dylan to sing these lines

with a straight face, so that at first you don't quite believe what you're hearing. By substituting 'the little boy and the little girl' for, let us say, 'four and twenty black-birds,' Dylan simultaneously uses and parodies the original form of the nursery rhyme. The parody works by exaggeration or by *literalizing* the image. There is something uncomfortably specific about these lines, something that invites us actually to see and experience the cruelty which is often present in nursery rhymes but is usually glossed over. The same thing happens in a later song, when the nursery rhyme 'Ding dong dell, pussy's down the well' becomes 'Cat's in the well, the wolf is looking down. . . . '

Nursery rhymes provide a major intertextual matrix for the text of *Under the Red Sky.* [In a pamphlet published by *Rolling Tomes,* P.O. Box 1943, Grand Junction, Colorado 81502], Simon McAslan has pointed out a series of echoes and direct quotations from *The Real Mother Goose,* including such key phrases as 'Every lady in this land,' 'feed the swine,' and 'The bull's in the barn.' The 'ten thousand men' may recall the Grand Old Duke of York while a nursery rhyme entitled 'Boy and Girl' opens with

> There was a little boy and a little girl
> Lived in an alley,
> Says the little boy to the little girl,
> 'Shall I, oh, shall I?'

Compare Dylan's lines 'There was a little boy and there was a little girl / Lived in an alley under the red sky.' The nursery rhyme references are not, however, *simple* quotation. The black-comedy context of **'Under the Red Sky'** parodies the supposed innocence of nursery rhymes by insisting on an uncomfortably literal reading of what might otherwise be passed over as a conventional image. This technique of literalization is also used in two other areas of popular culture present in **Under the Red Sky:** numbers and clichés.

In a few key songs, a stress on numbering is strongly characteristic of folk culture. **'2 x 2'** is the most obvious example: it takes the form of a traditional counting song, but again the form is pushed toward the edge of exaggeration and parody. If one takes the numbers literally, the pictures they produce become absurd and surrealistic: 'Ten thousand women all sweepin' my room.' Biblically, ten may be the number of perfection (ten Commandments, ten tribes of Israel), but equally it may be the number of retribution (ten plagues sent on Egypt). 'Thousand' is an intensifier, a higher degree of whatever the number signifies; seven is another number of perfection. But together (ten thousand men, each of them with seven wives) they go just too far. Seventy thousand wives? The arithmetic is too precise for this numerology to be taken seriously.

The same thing happens with cliché. Dylan continually takes words or phrases gone dead in conventional usage and sets them in new contexts that twist their meaning and force them back into life. Some reviewers have complained that the language of **Under the Red Sky** is banal, but the point is precisely the banality and what is done with it. The reviewer in *Rolling Stone,* for instance, quoted with great disdain the couplet, 'They said it was the land of milk and honey / Now they say it's the land of money.' Taken by themselves, these two lines are banal, but the

next line must be included too: 'Who ever thought they could ever make that stick?' Now the change in social values is something imposed, a con job, and 'make that stick' suddenly and ironically evokes the literal image of 'honey.' The promised land has become a sticky mess.

Sometimes Dylan deconstructs cliché by simple inversion: 'Beat that horse and saddle up that drum.' This is an old Dylan trick, as in 'he just smoked my eyelids / An' punched my cigarette,' but it puts both halves of the phrase in a new context and invites us to see them freshly. We get, for instance, an uncomfortably literal picture of someone beating a horse, which in turn echoes 'beating on a dead horse' in *Oh Mercy;* at the same time 'saddle up that drum' eerily foreshadows those 'ten thousand men' who are 'Drummin' in the morning, in the evening they'll be coming for you.'

Most obviously, the song **'God Knows'** takes a phrase that all of us, God knows, use without thinking and, by sheer repetition, restores it to literal meaning, so that the song moves from the casual 'God knows you ain't pretty' to the entirely serious assertion of divine omniscience: 'God knows everything.' As another example, 'Truer words have not been spoken' is simple cliché; but when the rhyme adds 'or broken,' the entire phrase twists back on itself. 'Word' changes from its declarative sense, as a unit of meaning, to its performative sense, as a promise; and the truth, not only of this word but of all words, is questioned. 'Truer words have not been broken' is a tortuously difficult sentence to untangle, even syntactically: how many negatives and double negatives are in there? The same is true of 'None of them doing nothin' that your mama wouldn't disapprove.' Does she approve or doesn't she?

And what are we to make of that extraordinary line 'Cat's in the well, and the barn is full of the bull'? It seems almost a nonsense line, produced by internal alliteration and rhyme (barn/bull/full); at the same time it suggests the colloquial use of 'bull' as bullshit, another kind of nonsense. The farm does seem neglected—perhaps the barn is literally full of shit. The words also might suggest a very large bull, an unnaturally large and threatening animal. The song is full of such strange inversions of the natural order, and this oversize bull takes its place, with the wolf and the dogs, as an image of menace.

The verbal texture of **Under the Red Sky,** though appearing casual at first glance, is rich and rewarding. And, of course, no Dylan album is without the occasional startling, vivid, or beautiful image: 'Ten thousand men dressed in Oxford blue,' or 'Back alley Sally is doing the American jump,' or 'You're blowing down the shaky street.' I wouldn't trade the complete works of Bruce Springsteen for that single adjective 'shaky.'

But what do all these scattered effects actually *say?* Here I feel less certain: the album's apparently casual and scattered nature is part of its theme, and to propose a coherent thematic interpretation is to work against the directions suggested by the text. But two areas of investigation are possible for a thematic analysis of **Under the Red Sky.** One is very general—the continuing Dylan theme of apocalypse—and the other is more specific—the strange treatment of vision and blindness.

We live in a political world, and this is no less true of *Under the Red Sky* than of *Oh Mercy*. 'Unbelievable' speaks of social disintegration while 'T.V. Talkin' Song' burlesques the degeneracy of the media. Signs of impending catastrophe are everywhere: '2 x 2' is about Noah's flood while the 'fire next time' in 'God Knows' evokes both the Negro Spiritual ('God gave Noah the rainbow sign, / No more water, the fire next time'), and also James Baldwin's impassioned account of black experience in America. The only previous appearance in Dylan's work of 'ten thousand men' is the 'ten thousand talkers whose tongues were all broken,' in the apocalyptic 'A Hard Rain's A-Gonna Fall.'

In 'Under the Red Sky,' the impending catastrophe is imagined in ecological terms: the sky turning red, the rivers running dry. This 'red sky' has many possible sources and implications. Its field of play includes the album's cover photograph, which is in black and white. (Inside, the lettering of the lyrics, white on black, reverses the normal order.) Dylan squats on his heels in a desert landscape, one in which indeed the rivers have run dry, and the only things red (and read) in the sky are the letters of his own name. But the pose in the photograph is highly reminiscent of the inner sleeve photograph in *Infidels*, where Dylan also squats on stony ground and where the sky is red. In the background of the *Infidels* photograph, under the red sky, is the holy city of Jerusalem, the city of the end of time.

According to weather lore, 'Red sky at night, shepherd's delight; red sky in the morning, shepherd's warning.' This proverb is quoted by no less an authority than Jesus, who uses it to give his own 'warning,' in Matthew 16:1-4:

> The Pharisees also . . . came, and tempting desired him that he would shew them a sign from heaven.
>
> He answered and said unto them, When it is evening, ye say, It will be fair weather: for the sky is red.
>
> And in the morning, It will be foul weather to day: for the sky is red and lowring. O ye hypocrites, ye can discern the face of the sky; but can ye not discern the signs of the times?
>
> A wicked and adulterous generation seeketh after a sign; and there shall be no sign given unto it, but the sign of the prophet Jonas. And he left them, and departed.

Christ's warning speaks to a 'wicked and adulterous' generation, and this brings us back perhaps to 'Wiggle Wiggle.' The song appears to be a straightforward call for its audience to get out there and wiggle. But there are some uneasy lines: 'Wiggle till you vomit fire' doesn't sound like much fun. A line from the earlier version, 'Wiggle on the 4th of July,' suggests that it could even be a State of the Union message on America's wicked and adulterous generation. The 'big fat snake' in the last line is suitably ambiguous: the snake is a standard phallic symbol and a symbol of mystical wisdom, but he is also, of course, Satan.

He is the animal *not* named in 'Man Gave Names To All the Animals.' On the album's cover photograph, what is Bob Dylan doing wearing snakeskin boots?

Satan also appears in 'Under the Red Sky' as the 'man in the moon.' Dylan has a thing about the moon; there's a 'blue moon' in 'Wiggle Wiggle' and a 'sanctified' moon in 'Unbelievable.' In 'License to Kill' he claimed that 'man has invented his doom, / First step was touching the moon.' Now this man, who not only touches the moon but is in it, causes the sky to turn red and the river to run dry. In 'God Knows'

> God knows there's a river,
> God knows how to make it flow,
> God knows you ain't gonna be taking
> Nothing with you when you go.

Again there is the association of water, either as flood or as drought, with death. For Dylan the 'political' world is always near its end. Consistently throughout his work he has been drawn to the eschatological vision of the final days; this is always what gives his songs their urgency, morally, socially, and theologically.

'Cat's in the Well' is the fullest statement of this apocalyptic vision, though typically, it is conveyed in terms of a barnyard fable. (It is pertinent to note that some 1990 Dylan concerts opened with an instrumental version of 'Old MacDonald Had a Farm'! The repeated title phrase, besides echoing the nursery rhyme, suggests both the cat's helplessness and the potential pollution of the source of life. From the cat menaced by the world through increasing levels of generalization, 'The world's being slaughtered.' The 'natural' order of the barnyard has collapsed. Besides the comic yet menacing bull, the 'dogs are going to war' (another example of a literalized cliché): the animals are taking over. The human forces of order and salvation, whether matriarchal or patriarchal, are helpless. The 'gentle lady is asleep,' and this sleep is not just passive indifference but a condition of being under attack: 'the silence is a-stickin' her deep.' The father is equally ineffective, 'reading the news' while 'His hair's falling out and all of his daughters need shoes.' By the end of the song, disaster gathers: autumn closes in, and all that is left is a desperate prayer for mercy to an absent God.

The theme of vision and blindness may be approached through one of the lighter, more comic pieces, the 'T.V. Talkin' Song.' This is a cunningly balanced song: what it says about the dire effects of the media is carefully distanced through two levels of characterization. Much of it sounds like a rant, but the overstatement is acknowledged by the fact that the rant is placed in the mouth of a Hyde Park preacher, an admitted crank. It is further filtered through the divided consciousness of the narrator, who admits that 'My thoughts began to wander' yet still remembers enough of what he heard to narrate it to us. The preacher's attack on T.V. is covered and repeated on T.V. The medium co-opts its own criticism and appropriates it as entertainment. What in the end does the narrator really remember: what he saw or what he saw on T.V.? What is at stake here is a problematic of *sight*. The preacher warns against letting your mind be soiled by 'something you can't see.' This is an odd warning against television, the primary visual medium of our time, but it presumably means that you don't *really* see things on T.V. True sight, clear moral vision, must be direct.

Yet curiously, heaven is also something you can't see:

> God know there's a heaven,
> God knows it's out of sight.

Heaven as 'out of sight' is another play on cliché: in colloquial speech 'out of sight' means both wonderful and unbelievable, but heaven is also literally out of sight. It can't be seen, even on T.V. It has to be (seen to be) believed.

Not being able to see heaven, we are in effect blind: 'Two by two, they step into the ark, / Two by two, they step in the dark.' This numbered procession, attempting to escape the catastrophe of the flood, approaches heaven. 'Seven by seven, they headed for heaven, / Eight by eight, they got to the gate.' But here they stop, drink wine, and then drink it again, before the song retraces its steps to begin the numbering again. They have not passed through the gate of heaven; they are back down in the flood, in the dark.

Physical blindness, then, is a metaphor for spiritual blindness; yet, in another of the paradoxes in which this album abounds, it is often also a sign of prophetic insight. In the song **'Unbelievable,'** 'there was a man who had no eyes. . . . ' This man could simply be the victim of the 'unbelievable' political world that surrounds him. But he may also be a blind prophet or poet, someone who is not believed: Homer, Tiresias, or Oedipus. Blind Oedipus was guided by his daughter, Antigone, but this man is betrayed even by his daughters: 'Every lady in the land told him lies.' This use of 'lady' looks forward to the sleeping 'gentle lady' of **'Cat's in the Well.'**

Other connections multiply between these songs. In **'Cat's in the Well,'** the father who reads the news is unable to provide his daughters with shoes, but in **'Under the Red Sky,'** the 'little girl' is promised that 'Someday . . . you'll have a diamond as big as your shoe.' But who makes this promise? Is it the singer, or is it the sinister 'man in the moon'? And how does it relate to the mysterious second bridge of the song?

> This is the key to the kingdom and this is the
>   town
> This is the blind horse that leads you around

The 'key to the kingdom' should unlock heaven's 'gate' at which 'eight by eight' arrive. But if heaven is out of sight, does the 'blind horse' lead you toward it or away from it? Is agreeing to be lead around by a blind horse a sign of humility or a sign of the reversal of the natural order? And how does this horse relate to the horse being beaten, the dead horse of *Oh Mercy,* the pale horse of the Apocalypse?

Strangest of all is the line from **'10,000 Men'**: 'Let me eat off his head so you can really see.' The singer appears to argue that the woman being addressed will only 'see' truly and clearly when she can look through her own eyes: at the moment she sees only through her lover's eyes, which the singer generously offers to remove. Perhaps the exact meaning is less important than the bizarre shock effect of

the line, but it does imply an interchangeability of identity, eye and I.

Throughout this book I have argued that the metaphor of sight is central to Dylan's songs and that the double sense of eye and I is continuously at play. The references to sight and blindness in *Under the Red Sky* are not in themselves conclusive, but they indicate the persistence of these motifs in his work. Look one last time at the cover photograph: one eye open, one eye almost closed; the gaze that returns the camera's gaze is wary, suspicious, defensive. Retreating from a relationship in **'Born in Time,'** the singer, who has always preferred the disguise of an alias, complains that it was 'too revealing.' What is revealed in *Under the Red Sky* is like heaven—it's out of sight.

As always, Bob Dylan leaves us with more questions than answers. In 1991, at fifty years of age, he remains as much an enigma as when he first assumed the alias 'Bob Dylan' more than thirty years ago. *Under the Red Sky* is, in my view, a triumphant reassertion of his creative power—but it is a very open-ended album, offering no firm conclusions except the always-present possibility of Apocalypse. (pp. 171-80)

> *Stephen Scobie, in his* Alias Bob Dylan, *Red Deer College Press, 1991, 192 p.*

Paul Williams   (essay date 1992)

[*The founder of* Crawdaddy!, *the first American rock music magazine, Williams is a prominent scholar and critic of Dylan whom* Library Journal *called "one of the architects of serious rock criticism." In the following excerpt from the second volume of his* Performing Artist: The Music of Bob Dylan, *Williams critiques Dylan's live performances during the period of his conversion to Christianity in the late 1970s.*]

The importance of identifying Bob Dylan as a performing artist, as distinct from the popular perception that he's a songwriter and recording artist, is immediately clear when one has a chance to hear his fall 1979 concerts. **"What Can I Do for You?," "Solid Rock," "Saving Grace," "Covenant Woman"** and **"In the Garden"** as performed at these shows are some of the finest works in Dylan's oeuvre, but you'd never know that from listening to *Saved,* the 1980 studio album that features these compositions. The *Saved* performances are technically adequate, but they fail to put across the essential character of any of these songs, which I suppose tells us that that essence is not automatically present in the words and music of a song; it is possible (and in this case it happened) that these elements can be in place and yet whatever it is that makes the song meaningful can still be missing.

Which is to say, your awareness and appreciation of Dylan's greatness is incomplete until you hear these songs (and **"When He Returns"**) as performed live in the fall of 1979, in San Francisco (fourteen shows November 1-16) and in southern California, Arizona, and New Mexico (twelve shows between November 18 and December 9).

The first thing that distinguishes these early "gospel" or "born again" shows is that Dylan performed only songs he had written in the last twelve months, that is to say the songs from the *Slow Train Coming* album plus eight newer songs (one of these, **"Blessed Is the Name of the Lord Forever,"** is identified by Clinton Heylin as a traditional gospel song). "All old things are passed away," Dylan told the audience at one of the San Francisco shows, in response to requests for **"Lay Lady Lay"** and **"Like a Rolling Stone."** Even in 1965-66 fans got half a concert of acoustic Dylan before being confronted with his new persona of rock and roller. But in 1979 Dylan is uncompromising: new songs (i.e., Christian songs) only. No exceptions.

The second immediately striking aspect of these shows is the size of the theaters. In 1978 Dylan was playing in sports arenas, with 14,000 or 15,000 seats, and selling out most of his concerts. A year later he's playing 2000- or 3000-seat theaters. Embracing Jesus and refusing to play greatest hits has required some sacrifice on his part (more than expected—originally the Warfield shows were meant as a warm-up for a tour of larger venues, which had to be scaled down; even in the smaller theaters, some shows were canceled because ticket sales were poor). But artistically, in terms of the sound quality of the performance and the level of interaction between performer and audience, the small theaters are a tremendous leap forward. Clearly the Dylan we hear on the fall 1979 tapes is delighted to be a performing musician again after almost a year's break, and clearly he's very excited about his new music and the good news he wants to share. But it seems fair to assume that another factor in his evident joy is the opportunity to perform with a hot band in a human-size setting. The intimacy in his new music and the intimacy of the environments he finds himself working in reinforce each other very nicely.

The third thing we notice right away is that this is not the same person who recorded *Slow Train Coming*. Bob Dylan has transformed himself again. He's still singing about God (still singing the same songs, in fact), but every note he sings tells us that his God of vengeful righteousness has also turned out to be a God of restoration and love.

The first show, November 1, 1979, proved to be an exact model for the concerts that followed (the sequence and choice of songs were almost unchanged from night to night). The lights went down and a black woman walked on stage. "Regina McCrary [Havis] played with me for a while," Dylan recalls in the *Biograph* notes. "She's the daughter of Preacher Sam McCrary from Nashville who used to have the old gospel group the Fairfield Four. She would open these shows with a monologue about a woman on a train, she was so incredibly moving. I wanted to expose people to that sort of thing because I loved it and it's the real roots of all modern music . . . " Regina's performance is indeed riveting and sets a tone of intimacy and (as she transitions into the first song) excitement and spirited joyousness that is sustained throughout the evening. She and Mona Lisa Young and Helena Springs, with Terry Young backing them on piano, sing six glorious gospel numbers, "Let Me Ride," "The Rainbow Sign," "Do Lord, Remember Me," "Look Up and Live by Faith,"

"Oh Freedom," and "This Train." I attended eight of the San Francisco shows and this opening set was more of a delight each time I heard it; on that great day when a recording of one of these concerts is made available to the public (I recommend November 6, 8, or 16, but almost all of them are very good), the women's gospel set should definitely be included.

Lights down again at the end of "This Train"; when they came up a moment later the full band and Dylan had taken the stage and started right into **"Gotta Serve Somebody,"** Dylan in a black leather jacket over a white t-shirt, the three women remaining on stage to sing back-up harmonies on almost every song. He followed with **"I Believe in You," "When You Gonna Wake Up," "When He Returns"** (no band, just Dylan on electric guitar and Spooner Oldham on grand piano), **"Man Gave Names to All the Animals," "Precious Angel," "Slow Train,"** and then the first new song of the evening, **"Covenant Woman."**

Dylan introduced Regina Havis, who sang "Put Your Hand in the Hand" backed by the band, while Dylan took a cigarette break (other nights it would be Mona Lisa Young singing "Ordinary People" or Helena Springs singing "What Are You Doing with Your Heart?"). Without an intermission, Dylan returned to sing the two remaining *Slow Train Coming* songs, **"Gonna Change My Way of Thinking"** and **"Do Right to Me Baby,"** and then launched into a string of new songs: **"Solid Rock," "Saving Grace"** (Dylan played lead electric guitar between verses of this one, drawing cheers from the crowd), **"What Can I Do for You?"** (featuring extended harmonica solos), **"Saved,"** and, climax of the set, **"In the Garden."** He and the band came back and played **"Blessed Is the Name of the Lord Forever"** as an encore (he introduced the musicians before the song), and then, after much applause (very few people jeered or walked out, despite the reports in the newspapers), a second encore, **"Pressing On,"** Dylan playing piano on the first verse, then walking to the front of the stage and clapping his hands, singing the second verse and chorus into a microphone with no guitar between him and the audience.

The show lasted two hours. The same script was followed for the next 25 concerts, except for a couple of nights in Arizona when one or both encores were omitted, a night in San Francisco when **"Precious Angel"** was omitted, and the last night in San Francisco when Dylan sang an extra song after **"Covenant Woman"**—**"Ain't No Man Righteous, No Not One,"** originally recorded at the *Slow Train Coming* sessions but not included on the album.

Of the seventeen songs Dylan sings, there isn't one that isn't a rewarding performance (on a good night, and most of the nights at these November and December shows were good nights). Minor songs like **"Do Right to Me Baby"** and **"Man Gave Names to All the Animals"** become genuinely endearing (the latter is also a lot of fun, notably on November 16, when Dylan clowns around with the lyrics—"wasn't too big, think I'll call it a . . . giraffe!"—and evidently clowns around on stage, maybe doing a little dance, judging from the audience's delighted response). Songs like **"When You Gonna Wake Up"** and **"Change My Way of Thinking"** that sound great musically on the album but make me uncomfortable with their lyrical belligerence, are transformed by Dylan's apparent shift in attitude (whether this is a function of the months that have gone by or, just as likely, the way it feels to be performing to a live audience instead of a dimly imagined one) into songs that, for this listener anyway, are much more available. I can identify with them now (the words haven't changed, but the emphasis certainly has), I find myself moved by them without misgivings, I like the spirit that's coming through. **"When You Gonna Wake Up"** can be a low-key rocker, earnest and friendly; it can also be, particularly in shows from the second week onward, keen and demanding and fiery. Both readings (and they have more in common than my description suggests) are splendid; in concert the song has an integrity and warmth that assures me that it is about what I want it to be about, which is the need for awakening. "Strengthen the things that remain"—yes, the real values. And let go of everything else.

"I Believe in You" is sincere and effective. **"Precious Angel"** and **"Slow Train"** make a fine crescendo, it sounds so good to hear them, they lend themselves to live performance, this is a mini-climax each night, and each night it turns out to be a set-up for the real climax of the first set, the new song, **"Covenant Woman."** There's a particularly sweet **"Precious Angel"** November 6, an especially invigorating **"Slow Train"** November 16 (with a fine rap preceding it—but I also like the quick phrase he throws in as introduction November 6: "from a hard rain to a slow train . . . ").

But the most memorable performance from among the *Slow Train Coming* songs is, almost every night, **"When He Returns."** The performance on the album, vocal and instrumental, can't be recreated, so Dylan doesn't try—instead he and the piano player go off in another direction, gentler, more restrained, but equally electrifying. What a mood this song sets! And how much it has to say to its listener, once listener and pianist and singer are sharing the same mood. The live version manages to go beyond the gloriously dramatic, self-conscious vulnerability of the album track into a shared vulnerability, a welcoming (with no softening of the song's fiercely honest language), a fellowship. What results is a performance worthy of a great singer and a master creator—Dylan at his most naked and his most inspired, quite a combination. Just to hear him sing "wilderness" (long drawn-out vowel in the last syllable) makes the whole evening worthwhile, and speaks volumes about his view of the contemporary world and how it feels to live here.

And there's a lot more to come. **"Covenant Woman"** is extraordinarily affecting. Dylan's greatness as a songwriter is often associated in people's minds with tour de force extravaganzas like **"Mr. Tambourine Man"** and **"Hard Rain"** and **"Desolation Row,"** with the result that he has become a sort of symbol of the modern poet as a person with a gift for fancy (and penetrating, timely, accurate) language. That's fine, but Dylan himself would be the first to say that what distinguishes most great songwriters is their gift for simplicity (he says this when he chooses the songs other than his own that he likes to sing).

True simplicity is awesome. Consider the lyrics of **"Knockin' on Heaven's Door"** or **"Lay Lady Lay"** or **"Oh Sister,"** and the easy, graceful way these lyrics work with their respective melodies, song structures, vocal and instrumental settings. **"Covenant Woman"** has a lot in common with **"Oh Sister,"** except that in **"Covenant Woman"** Dylan sings as though he's already found the lady he seems to be looking for in the earlier song: a woman who will make him feel at home in this great mysterious world, a woman who will make him feel at times that she is the friend he's dreamed of being with since childhood, and at other times that he and she are together in that Friend's presence.

The love in the song is overwhelming (I'm listening to the November 6 performance from San Francisco). Dylan this time has no difficulty communicating love for a woman and love for God in the same song, perhaps because this time he *is* singing directly to the woman, giving her his full attention; even when he takes a verse to tell the past, present and future of his relationship with life and the Lord, she's the one who's brought forth this confession, and he rewards her patient attention by ending the verse with a marvelous (and simple) (and very sweet) uniting of his two themes: "He must have loved me oh so much to send me someone as fine as you."

The song is in fact full of great lines, some of them clichés given dignity and emotional power by their musical settings and the way Dylan delivers them ("you know that we are strangers in a land we're passing through") and others startlingly fresh ("who sees the invisible things of Him that are hidden from the world"). "I've been broken, shattered like an empty cup" is striking in the power of its imagery, in the effectiveness of its meter and the wonderful phrasing that that meter and the rising melody lend themselves to, and in its placement within the song, opening a new verse amidst the emotional reverberations of the vocal and musical climaxes the last chorus just built to. The interplay between organ, piano, voice, and rhythm section during this eight-word phrase is extraordinary, as it is throughout the performance.

I don't know how simple a piece of music is that relies on two interwoven keyboard parts (with a vital additional percussion role for the drums-and-bass), but I know it *sounds* simple, as though the music were picked out on the piano by a student whose hands have just found a delightful and playable progression, something he can pour his half-formed rhythmic and melodic longings into. Dylan's success at getting this very basic sound from the back of his mind out to where we can hear it sitting in the audience, is again the result of his gift for music, gift for words, gift for song-creating, gift for performance. Awesome simplicity. He opens his mouth, the band plays, and suddenly our hearts are feeling what's in his heart.

Great singing at these shows.

"Solid Rock," more precisely "Hanging On to a Solid Rock Made before the Foundation of the World" as Dylan introduced it at these concerts, is a tremendous crowd-pleaser—so much so that in 1979, fresh from being part of that crowd, I wrote that the song "is sure to become one of his all-time classics." This didn't happen, partly because of what Dylan in the *Biograph* notes calls "religious backlash" (the old fans didn't want to hear this message, and the anticipated new fans never really got on board), but also I think because Dylan failed to capture the song on record. Even in live performance the song deteriorated subtly as the weeks went by, eventually losing its core of incredible power and becoming just an up-tempo noisemaker.

This points to an aspect of performing art that I find rather mysterious: the fragility of some great songs, the ease with which their seemingly indestructible power can be lost forever if they're not captured (i.e. recorded) at the right moment. **"Subterranean Homesick Blues"** as recorded in 1965 for *Bringing It All Back Home* is recognizably brilliant and its power seems likely to endure for many more years to come. But if we knew the song only through its later live performances (1988, 1989) I doubt that we'd pay it much attention. It sounds good, has a nice beat and some clever lyrics. On a good night, Dylan performs it quite well. But it's nothing special, which is to say, in my opinion, the greatness of the song is not apparent and, arguably, not even present. Where did it go?

To be able to answer this question, we'd have to know where it came from in the first place. It comes, I think, from a feeling, or from a gestalt of feelings; it comes (greatness comes) from having something to say, something you need to say, something that feels like it won't be communicated unless you do it right. It comes from inspiration. "Hanging On to a Solid Rock Made before the Foundation of the World" is an inspired song and, on November 6, 1979, for instance, it communicates something very real and palpable, "you can feel it, you can hear it." But you can only feel and hear it when the performer feels and hears it. Greatness goes, disappears, when that intensity of need is not present, for whatever reason. You can't fake it. Thus, performance is the most demanding of art forms, or, put differently, is at the center of all creative experiences. The performer makes a bridge. He passes on his inspiration, recreates it, lives it or relives it so we can live it. He needs something. His performance is an expression of that need.

"Solid Rock" is a remarkable achievement, both lyrically and musically (not that the two are separated for Dylan; but it's unusual for a songwriter to be so original and so fluid in both realms at once). Lyrically, Dylan's achievement is not unrelated to what distinguished him earlier in his career: his ability to absorb a language-of-consciousness quickly and deeply intuitively, and then to speak things that that language had been wanting to say but hadn't found words for yet. He gave voice to a movement, in the 1960s, that only fully recognized itself once it heard him speak. This did not occur in relation to his embrace of born-again Christianity, for reasons that don't need to concern us here (basically, the movement already had plenty of voices, many of them rather jealous of their territory). What is significant is to realize that Dylan, in the new fall 1979 songs, began a process of, in effect, adding to and extending and modernizing the language of the Christian faith and of the primary work of Western lit-

erature, the Bible—not intellectually but from the heart and in the spirit, inspired, filled with *enthousiasmos*.

I do not know the Bible well enough to assert that the image and actual language of Dylan's chorus, "I'm hanging on / to a solid rock / made / before / the foundation / of / of the world" (the separations indicate the actual form in which this phrase is vocalized, with a full stop and musical embellishment after each segment), does not come whole cloth from some part of the King James or Revised Standard editions. However, Bert Cartwright (a Protestant minister whose theological degrees are from Yale) describes the phrase as "combining the imagery of the love the Father had for Jesus 'before the foundation of the world' (John 17:24) with Paul's writing about the Rock that was Christ (1 Corinthians 10:3)." Cartwright, in his booklet *The Bible in the Lyrics of Bob Dylan* [see Further Reading list], says that in this phrase and in his line from another song, "the saving grace that's over me," Dylan "although seeking to stick close to the biblical teachings he is learning . . . allows his poetic mind to roam across pages of the Bible and freely express thoughts [from] his own depths." Helena Springs, recalling to Chris Cooper in 1985 the Dylan she knew when he was "exploring Christianity" in 1978 and 1979, describes him as "a very inquisitive person" trying "to learn everything he could . . . You know, he's a sponge, he absorbs so much."

A sponge. We've heard this word before, but I think we perhaps forget how central it is to the riddle of "who is Bob Dylan?" In any case, what I want to point to here is the vital power of this image Dylan has come up with (he is undoubtedly drawing on his pre-conversion experience of the song "Rock of Ages" as well as on more immediate sources). This title phrase, and the rest of the chorus ("Won't let go and I can't let go / Won't let go and I can't let go / Won't let go and I can't let go no more"), and the hard rockin' gloriously melodic rhythmic netting in which words and singer and audience are suspended, articulate with phenomenal clarity and accuracy an image and a felt spiritual awareness of Jesus as fundament (and what that means and how it feels in one real person's life) that I suspect is not grasped (or hung onto) much of the time by most born-again Christians. The song serves both to introduce the singer's faith and attract others to it, and to articulate and reawaken the faith that may already be present in the listener. It is absolutely brilliant (referring always to the early San Francisco performances, not to the frustrating close-but-no-cigar reading on *Saved* that somehow sabotages the song's revelatory power even as it attempts to preserve it for posterity). The verses, with lines like "It's the ways of the flesh / To war against the spirit" and "Nations are angry / Cursed are some" and the extraordinary rhythmic energy of the music they contain and are contained by, are almost as effective as the choruses. Every breath, every pause, every emphasis in the song is inspired, even though there is no single night (that I've heard) when Fred Tackett totally gives himself to the lead guitar break and lets it take on its full fierceness, or when Dylan is so committed to the song that he doesn't swallow one or more vital phrases in the course of his delivery. It's a difficult piece, Dylan is trying to invent heavy metal gospel and he and his band aren't quite adequate (technically and, in Tackett's case, emotionally) to the full realization of the song's potential. But they come close enough to leave you absolutely awestruck (crawling back the next night to hear it again). This is not a song about an idea. It is an expression of the singer's experience of a more substantial reality than this everyday world. Its words are not from the Bible so much as they are a carrying on of a conversation initiated by the Bible. This is living literature, living art, contemporary Logos (or perhaps Logos and Eros combined).

I'm not done raving. The next song, **"Saving Grace,"** is a good enough song to move this listener any time Dylan performs it, but it becomes a transcendent experience on those rare nights when Dylan feels the inspiration and the courage to really sing it directly to the One he loves. On November 6 in San Francisco his vocal is so sensitive and vibrant that every word of the song is infused with life and meaning and intimacy; in such a state the performer can do no wrong, so that for example when he hurries the first line of the second verse (singing the words a half-beat or more ahead of the accompanying music) the mood of the song is not broken but actually strengthened, the melody responding to his leadership and reshaping itself, improving itself, on the spot.

Dylan is writing his own spirituals. As **"Solid Rock"** reaches back to "Rock of Ages," **"Saving Grace"** is (lyrically) a cousin to "Amazing Grace." The singer describes the joy of living in a state of trust and vulnerability, living by God's will, as opposed to the hell of living in a state of cynicism where one follows nothing except the voice of one's own ego (he identifies the "search for love" as vanity, narcissism; in this sense the philosophy expressed here is opposite to—and arises naturally from—the state of mind that expressed itself on *Street-Legal*). **"Trouble in Mind"** from the *Slow Train Coming* sessions described the problem; **"Saving Grace,"** which touches on many of the same issues, describes the solution, not theoretically or as taught but as experienced. Dylan is bearing witness. The song's delicacy and sweetness derive in part at least from the fact that the despair, fear of death, and sense of hopelessness he speaks of are not in the past but still here in his present; God's love has not rescued the singer from this pit but rather allows him to live in the midst of it. "Thy rod and thy staff they comfort me." In **"Saving Grace"** Dylan gives this comfort a name and a location, and allows us to feel (ah those rippling guitar lines) how sweet its presence can be.

"What Can I Do for You?" is the supreme achievement of this astonishing song cycle. Another elegantly simple composition, its essence is summed up in its opening lines: "You have / Given everything to me / What can I do for you?" This is what the singer wants to say; the rest of the song is simply an expansion of this phrase. Each of the three verse-chorus stanzas (with the chorus coming first) begins with the same words, "You have—," and ends with "What can I do for you?" In between Dylan orchestrates a glorious crescendo (lyrical and musical) of tension, release, tension, release, each phrase building on the one before, each bit of musical and vocal phrasing seemingly more powerful and startling and satisfying than the last.

The song is so well-constructed, so pretty, and so wonderful to sing, it literally takes on new meanings every time he performs it. This is odd, because its essential message of humility, devotion, gratitude, and eagerness to serve never changes. The song is a story, the everchanging story of the situation and feelings and hopes and fears of the person delivering its never-changing message. Or you could say, what Dylan has to say to God here never changes, but how he feels about God, and about his audience (he's a performer, he knows they're out there), and about himself, and about his relationship with God, and about his role as prophet or artist or preacher or public truth-teller, these feelings change constantly, and in so many subtle ways you could never describe or list them. But you can hear them. This is the complexity within the simplicity. The song is a question without an answer. Surely it answers itself—surely there is no greater gift a singer could give God than to sing and play his harmonica for Him—and yet for the singer to be satisfied with this answer invites the sin of pride and the renewed blindness and self-absorption that comes with it. To stay true to Spirit, one must keep asking, without presuming as one asks that one already knows the answer. Thy will, not mine. Return always to the question.

"What can I do for you?" The second and third verses each build into what I want to call harmonica solos but they're not, they're ensemble performances, fantastic journeys, led by the harmonica but also featuring bass, drums, keyboards, and a chorus of female voices ("oooohhh, oooohhh") harmonizing with and counterpointing against Dylan's structured but unpredictable harmonica eruptions. Here, by conscious prearrangement, the performer's heart is split open and he shares as much as he's able to share.

The song scares Dylan a little, understandably, and he tends to stumble over the opening. November 6 is perhaps the most perfect performance (although November 16 is also indispensable), but the first line is all wrong—he accidentally sings "you have done" instead of "you have given," which robs the song of its cornerstone image and instead gives the impression that he thinks of God and himself as equals. The only solution is for the listener to mentally insert the proper words and let the performance go on from there, which it does, exquisitely. Indeed, there are a number of places in the song where Dylan has had trouble making the words mean what he wants them to say. ("You opened a door that couldn't be shut.") He sings them anyway, and so powerfully that the listener feels the intended meaning, and (usually unconsciously) scrambles the words to make them fit the felt truth.

The biggest problem is in the next-to-last line of the song. At early shows Dylan sings, "I don't deserve what I have come through," or "I don't deserve it, but I have come through." I'm fairly sure what he wants to say is that he has come through an amazing experience, a gift of the Lord which he feels he doesn't deserve but which he gratefully accepts. But his inability to get the words to actually say this and at the same time to have the necessary punch required of this line (the verbal climax of the final verse) causes him fairly early (by the second week of performances) to let the line alter itself to "I don't deserve it, but I sure did make it through," with vocal emphasis on "sure did," which unfortunately is a boast, at exactly the point in the verse where a well-intended boasting of how willing he is to serve is supposed to give way to heart-opening expression of humility. His heart does open, every time, in the great harmonica foray that follows, but these new words and (often) the way they're sung are false to the spirit of the song. This leaves it up to the listener to mentally alter or disregard the words that don't fit, or else perhaps be put off or distracted, consciously or unconsciously, by the prideful language that's slipped back into this song of humble supplication.

What I'm saying is the song and performance are great, are great even in their imperfection; this imperfection or awkwardness is a perfect expression of the authentic struggle going on within the artist, and it emerges here because this is not a set piece. Dylan is renewing his vows of spiritual poverty every time he sings it. It isn't easy for him. What is most astonishing and most moving about the song is that he almost always succeeds. This is a song of letting go, a song of love, a song of giving oneself away.

The harmonica makes the difference.

Almost every show Dylan performed during his overtly religious period, from November 1979 to November 1981, started (his entrance) with **"Gotta Serve Somebody"** and ended (end of the regular set, before the encores) with **"In the Garden."** Where other songs talk about the singer's relationship with Jesus, this last song is a passion play, a formal work, Dylan's way of bringing the Gospel—that is, the story of Jesus—directly into his concert, in the most honored place. It's a fascinating song, different from anything else he's written (in the *Biograph* notes he says, " 'In the Garden' is actually a classical piece; I don't know how in the world I wrote it but I was playing at the piano, closed my eyes and the chords just came to me"), majestic in performance at these autumn 1979 shows, full of colors and shapes not normally encountered in whatever sort of music it is that Bob Dylan usually makes. Very deeply affecting.

And it is characteristic of Dylan that he manages to tell the story as a series of questions, questions that are more than rhetorical, questions that somehow escape our natural tendency to think we know exactly what the asker intends the answer to be. "When they came for Him in the garden, did they know? Did they know he was the son of God—?" The primary question in each stanza is repeated four times, twice at the beginning and twice at the end, with two lines that are sometimes statements, sometimes questions, but always additional information, sandwiched in the middle. I don't know of any other narrative, poetic or otherwise, structured this way. It's hypnotic. It's impassioned.

It's Dylan attempting to yield his stage to a more worthy subject for our attention. He does it very gracefully (ironically, after beating us over the head with the cheerful—but, for the nonbeliever, very confrontive—"I've Been Saved by the Blood of the Lamb"). I don't know how you measure the success of evangelism (that is, of this sort of

supportive evangelism, which doesn't actually invite people to step forth and accept Jesus right now), but in artistic terms **"In the Garden"** is a stunning accomplishment. It is intended to invoke wonder—like a medieval chapel—and it does. The singer is using his Voice.

And **"Pressing On,"** the second encore, is a simple but very special gift from Dylan to his live audience. He plays the piano (a moment of conscious intimacy, like the harmonica solos but even rarer); he sings out in a stirring, full-hearted voice; and finally he stands before us and (rare moment indeed) acknowledges and accepts our love, communicating by his presence how much he does in fact appreciate it.

And then he disappears into the night. (pp. 151-63)

The *Saved* recording sessions close out this period. Dylan hasn't often recorded with his touring band; he tried it with *Blonde on Blonde* and was dissatisfied, ultimately keeping only one track that he cut with the Band (they had not yet been touring with him when *Planet Waves* was recorded, so that doesn't count). He tried it on *Street-Legal.* In the case of *Saved* he broke his own rule in a grander fashion: where he usually comes into the studio with new songs and sits down to record them live, with musicians who often haven't met him before and who've heard the songs once if at all, this time he came in with his travelling band and recorded songs they'd been performing together for three and a half months.

It didn't work. Not only is the spark missing, that energy of hot pursuit (of the creative will o' the wisp) that seems to get Dylan through his studio shyness, but the error is compounded when Dylan either came up with or allowed someone else to suggest a batch of uninspired new arrangements for several of the best songs. On **"Covenant Woman,"** for example, the drum part is dreadful, and the lovely keyboard-and-percussion riff on which the live performance was based is lost, which in turn leaves the vocal with nothing special to play against. **"What Can I Do for You?"** is given a generic intro, and the slowness and depth of the original arrangement are replaced by a hurried blandness. **"Pressing On"** starts off powerfully and then degenerates into an overbaked crash-and-thud I find almost unlistenable.

The only song from the fall 1979 shows that can be said to be well-performed on the album is the title track, **"Saved,"** which is tight and full of life and actually sounds better to me on the record than it did at most of the concerts. The closing track of the album, **"Are You Ready?",** is also an uplifting performance; Dylan and band grab hold of a strong riff and ride it for all it's worth. The song's lyrical content is predictable, but to the point: Dylan sees himself as being in the business of saving souls, and he wants to leave you thinking about what condition yours is in.

And there's a little miracle here as well. The opening track, a country standard called "Satisfied Mind," is absolutely magnificent. This is spontaneous Dylan, inspired Dylan, the performing artist at work; you can hear the man's genius not only in his voice but in the astonishing performance of the back-up singers and in Tim Drummond's delightful bass playing. Dylan, when the spirit moves him, breathes out great music as easily as another person laughs.

Dave Kelly says, "I think Bob himself was unhappy with that album [*Saved*]. He certainly tried to stop its release." Be that as it may, the album did come out, in June 1980. Like *Slow Train Coming* it had a painting on the cover, but where that album's art had been subtle and intriguing and attractive, the cover of *Saved,* and the very title of the record, seem carefully chosen to give the finger to any and all of Dylan's "so-called fans" who haven't already seen the light. Songs that had the potential to open some well-defended ears to a new message end up doubly buried, limp performances wrapped in repellent packaging. The desire to reach out to the world that Dylan demonstrated in the care he took with *Slow Train Coming* and in the love he poured into the Warfield shows seems to have slipped away somehow with the new year, new decade. (pp. 168-69)

> *Paul Williams, in his* Bob Dylan Performing Artist: The Middle Years, 1974-1986, *Underwood-Miller, 1992, 334 p.*

FURTHER READING

Bibliography

Wissolik, Richard David, et al. *Bob Dylan—American Poet and Singer: An Annotated Bibliography and Study Guide of Sources and Background Materials, 1961-1991*. Greensburg, Penn.: Eadmer Press, 1991, 97 p.

Annotated bibliography containing five short introductory essays, a list of primary and secondary materials, and a catalog of "Selected Background Studies to the Folk Revival of the Sixties."

Biography

Heylin, Clinton. *Bob Dylan behind the Shades: A Biography*. New York: Summit Books, 1991, 498 p.

This biography covers Dylan's career through his involvement with the Traveling Wilburys. Includes a list identifying personages alluded to in the text, a selected bibliography, and a "Bob Dylan Sessionography."

Scaduto, Anthony. *Bob Dylan*. New York: Grosset & Dunlap, 1971, 280 p.

Possibly the most frequently cited biography of Dylan, this work draws on Dylan's statements as well as those of fellow musicians and close friends.

Shelton, Robert. *No Direction Home: The Life and Music of Bob Dylan*. New York: Beech Tree Books, William Morrow and Company, Inc., 1986, 573 p.

Combines criticism and biography.

Spitz, Bob. *Dylan: A Biography*. New York: McGraw-Hill Publishing Company, 1989, 639 p.

A largely speculative portrait that draws on interviews with Dylan's friends, family, and fellow musicians.

Thompson, Toby. *Positively Main Street: An Unorthodox View of Bob Dylan*. New York: Coward-McCann, Inc., 1971, 187 p.

Prefaced with a 1969 quote from Dylan, "That boy . . . this fellow, Toby . . . has got some lessons to learn," this unauthorized work investigates Dylan's youth through interviews with teachers and other early acquaintances.

Criticism

Bauldie, John, ed. *Wanted Man: In Search of Bob Dylan*. London: Black Spring Press, 1990, 224 p.

Combines short essays by such Dylan specialists as Clinton Heylin and Paul Williams with reminiscences of Dylan, drawn from the British fanzine *The Telegraph*, by such prominent music personalities as Johnny Cash, Eric Clapton, and Roy Orbison.

Bloom, Fred A. "Seeing Dylan Seeing." *The Yale Review* 71, No. 2 (January 1982): 304-20.

Affirming the need for "art which lives in the present day," the critic attempts a "psychobiographical" portrait of Dylan by commenting on "the history we share in common: in the common world we found growing up in the fifties."

Booth, Mark W. "The Art of Words in Songs." *The Quarterly Journal of Speech* 62, No. 3 (October 1976): 242-49.

Briefly compares Alfred Hayes' song "Joe Hill" with Dylan's "I Dreamed I Saw St. Augustine" in an examination of the distinctions between lyrics in songs and poetry.

Bowden, Betsy. *Performed Literature: Words and Music by Bob Dylan*. Bloomington: Indiana University Press, 1982, 239 p.

Concentrates on the flexibility and malleability of Dylan's lyrics in performance, particularly "how his vocal inflections interact with words and music to create aural meaning."

Brown, Richard. " 'I Want You': Enigma and Kerygma in the Love Lyrics of Bob Dylan." In *American Declarations of Love*, edited by Ann Massa, pp. 174-94. New York: St. Martin's Press, 1990.

Asserts that throughout Dylan's writing "there has been a kind of consistency in producing lyrics on the subject of love which may be thought of as a central theme of his songs."

Cott, Jonathan. *Dylan*. Garden City, N.Y.: Doubleday & Company, Inc., Rolling Stone Press, 1984, 246 p.

Oversize volume containing "Bob Dylan: The Joker and the Thief"—a biographical commentary by Kott—and many beautiful photographs from Dylan's career.

Dowley, Tim, and Dunnage, Barry. *Bob Dylan: From a Hard Rain to a Slow Train*. London: Omnibus Press, 1983, 176 p.

Scrutinizes major shifts in Dylan's career and philosophy; includes a detailed discography.

Dunaway, David K. "No Credit Given: The Underground Literature of Bob Dylan." *Virginia Quarterly Review* 69, No. 1 (Winter 1993): 149-55.

Discusses "fugitive" materials on Dylan, including xeroxed copies of his 1970 novel *Tarantula*, songs written by Dylan for other musicians but not credited to him, and various "bootlegs" (recordings never officially released but in circulation among Dylan collectors).

Earl, James W. "Beyond Desire: The Conversion of Bob Dylan." *University of Hartford Studies in Literature* 20, No. 2 (1988): 46-63.
Demonstrates how Dylan's conversion to Christianity is consistent with other phases of his career.

Gonzalez, Alberto. "Rhetorical Ascription and the Gospel According to Dylan." *The Quarterly Journal of Speech* 69, No. 1 (February 1983): 1-14.
Asserting that the "palatability of Dylan's gospel songs (for his secular audience) is significantly predicated upon a listener's ability to associate their lyrical and musical features with Dylan's pre-conversion songs," this study examines the associative rhetorical features evident in Dylan's earliest gospel songs performed on stage.

Gremore, Robert B. "The Social Roots of Imagination: Language and Structure in Bob Dylan's 'Baby Blue'." *American Studies* XXI, No. 2 (1980): pp. 95-107.
Formalistic critique in which the critic discerns "in the underlying musicolinguistic structures of 'Baby Blue' a symbolic re-enactment of behavioral patterns that were important to members of the disaffected subculture."

Hattenhauer, Darryl. "Bob Dylan as Hero: Rhetoric, History, Structuralism, and Psychoanalysis in Folklore as a Communicative Process." *Southern Folklore Quarterly* 45 (1981): 69-88.
Addressing the role of formalism in folklore studies, the critic uses Dylan's role as cultural hero to test Joseph Campbell's theory of the monomyth, in which the "hero quest" is "divided into three stages: the departure, the initiation and the return."

Humphries, Patrick, and Bauldie, John. *Absolutely Dylan: An Illustrated Biography*. New York: Viking Studio Books, 240 p.
Oversize volume combining over 200 photographs of Dylan, a chronology, discography, and bibliography, and a biographical and critical overview by Humphries as well as notes by Bauldie.

Kramer, Daniel. *Bob Dylan: A Portrait of the Artist's Early Years*. New York: Citadel Press, 1991, 160 p.
Collection of photographs from Dylan's early career, first published in 1967. Contains a reminiscence of Dylan by Kramer.

McGregor, Craig, ed. *Bob Dylan: A Retrospective*. New York: William Morrow & Company, Inc., 1972, 407 p.
Compendium of valuable early essays, record and performance reviews, and interviews with Dylan by such commentators as Robert Shelton, Nat Hentoff, and Robert Christgau.

Mellers, Wilfrid. "God, Modality and Meaning in Some Recent Songs of Bob Dylan." *Popular Music I* I (1981): 143-57.
Examines Dylan's ambiguous treatment of existential themes in his songs of the late 1970s and early 1980s.

———. *A Darker Shade of Pale: A Backdrop to Bob Dylan*. New York: Oxford University Press, 1984, 255 p.
Examines Dylan's public image and relationship to American folk, country, and pop music.

Pickering, Stephen. *Bob Dylan Approximately: A Portrait of*

the Jewish Poet in Search of God—A Midrash. New York: David McKay Company, Inc., 204 p.
Asserts "that Dylan is operating out of the Hassidic tradition in which hope is garnered and nourished out of the perception of certain paradoxes." Contains many photographs and illustrations from the Kabbalah and other religious texts.

Rodnitzky, Jerome. "Also Born in the USA: Bob Dylan's Outlaw Heroes and the Real Bob Dylan." *Popular Music and Society* 12, No. 2 (Summer 1988): 37-43.
In response to ambivalent critical attitudes toward Dylan and his work, as well as Dylan's often contradictory statements concerning his personal beliefs, the critic suggests that "Dylan is best understood by analyzing the heroes of his songs."

Roos, Michael, and O'Meara, Don. "Is Your Love in Vain?—Dialectical Dilemmas in Bob Dylan's Recent Love Songs." *Popular Music* 7, No. 1 (January 1988): 35-50.
Asserts that Dylan's music of the 1980s may be considered generally inferior to his earlier material due to "a complex combination of factors all pertaining to [his] attempt to balance the dialectical forces pulling at him from both the public and private areas of his life."

Rotundo, E. Anthony. "Jews and Rock and Roll: A Study in Cultural Contrast." *American Jewish History* LXXII, No. 1 (September 1982): 82-107.
Scrutinizes the careers of Dylan, Phil Spector, and Paul Simon to determine "why rock and roll, among all the popular art forms, has especially repelled creative young Jews."

Spender, Stephen. "Bob Dylan: The Metaphor at the End of the Funnel: But Is It Art? . . . No, If You Think Mass Art Should be Confined to the Masses." *Esquire* LXXVII, No. 5 (May 1972): 109-110, 118, 188.
Explores the folk roots of Dylan's music.

Sumner, Carolyn. "The Ballad of Dylan and Bob." *Southwest Review* 65, No. 1 (Winter 1981): 41-54.
Demonstrates how Dylan's art reflects a conflict "between security and freedom, and the search for a saving balance in which these do not become mutually exclusive."

Tierce, Mike, and Crafton, John Michael. "Connie's Tambourine Man: A New Reading of Arnold Friend." *Studies in Fiction* 22, No. 2 (Spring 1985): 219-24.
Asserts that American writer Joyce Carol Oates consciously associated Dylan with the symbolically "demoniac character" of Arnold Friend in her short story "Where Are You Going, Where Have You Been?"

Williams, Paul. *Dylan: What Happened?* South Bend, Ind.: And Books/Entwhistle Books, 1979, 128 p.
Accounts for Dylan's conversion to Christianity through critical analysis of his live performances and song lyrics of the late 1970s.

———. *Performing Artist: The Music of Bob Dylan: Volume One, 1960-1973*. Novato, Calif.: 1990, 310 p.
Perceptive critique of the various changes in Dylan's music and style as a live performer up to 1973; includes a discography, filmography, and bibliography.

Williams, Richard. *Dylan: A Man Called Alias*. New York: Henry Holt and Company, 1992, 192 p.

Combines color and black-and-white photography with
biographical commentary by Williams, a journalist who
has followed Dylan's career closely since 1966.

Other

Dundas, Glen. *Tangled Up in Tapes Revisited: A Collector's
Guide to the Recordings of Bob Dylan.* Thunder Bay, Ont.,
Canada: SMA Services, 1990, 278 p.
　　Detailed discography, session, and concert guide.

Shepard, Sam. *Rolling Thunder Logbook.* New York: The Viking Press, 1977, 184 p.
　　A renowned American dramatist and personal friend of
　　Dylan recounts the Rolling Thunder Revue tour of
　　1975.

Sloman, Larry. *On the Road with Bob Dylan: Rolling with the
Thunder.* New York: Bantam, 1978, 412 p.
　　Journalistic account of Dylan's Rolling Thunder Revue
　　tour with such musicians as Joan Baez, Joni Mitchell,
　　and Jack Elliot.

**Additional coverage of Dylan's life and career is contained in the following sources
published by Gale Research: Contemporary Authors, Vols. 41-44, rev. ed.; Contemporary
Literary Criticism, Vols. 3, 4, 6, 12; and Dictionary of Literary Biography, Vol. 16.**

E. M. Forster
A Passage to India

(Full name Edward Morgan Forster) Born in 1879 and deceased in 1970, Forster was an English novelist, short story writer, essayist, and critic.

The following entry presents criticism on Forster's novel *A Passage to India* (1924). For further discussion of Forster's life and works, see *CLC*, Volumes 1, 2, 3, 4, 9, 10, 13, 15, 22, and 45.

INTRODUCTION

Considered Forster's masterpiece, *A Passage to India* is esteemed by critics for its complex depiction of the social and political realities of colonial India. Set several decades before the end of British rule, the novel portrays the English and Indian communities as well-intentioned but fundamentally uncommunicative and incompatible. Suggesting that the self-proclaimed "civilizing mission" of the British empire was morally bankrupt, Forster's novel is credited with anticipating the waning of British Imperial power.

Forster visited India twice before completing *A Passage to India*. After his first visit in 1912-13, he returned to England and began working on the novel, but he reached an impasse and put the book aside for nearly ten years. In 1921 he returned to India and worked as the private secretary to the Maharajah of the Hindu Princely State of Dewas; he wrote about this experience in *The Hill of Devi: Being Letters from Dewas State Senior*. During both of these visits Forster observed the deleterious effects of colonialism on Indian society and the governing Anglo-Indians. While Forster was writing *A Passage to India,* he became dissatisfied with the clichéd and self-assured descriptions of India which appeared in contemporary English novels. As he writes in a letter to an Indian friend in 1922: "When I began the book I thought of it as a little bridge of sympathy between East and West, but this conception has had to go, my sense of truth forbids anything so comfortable."

A Passage to India begins with Adela Quested, a sincere young Englishwoman, arriving in Chandrapore to meet Ronny Heaslop, a colonial official with whom she is considering marriage. She has been accompanied to India by Ronny's mother, who shares Adela's disdain for the arrogance of British colonial society and her desire to discover the "real" India. They meet Dr. Aziz, a doctor who is the embodiment of the well-intentioned, Western-educated Indian straddling the cultural divide which separates the colonial society. With Dr. Aziz they visit a local tourist attraction, the Marabar caves. While in the caves, Adela comes to believe that she has been sexually assaulted by Dr. Aziz, though the reader is uncertain whether or not

she hallucinated the incident. During the ensuing trial Adela recants her accusation against Dr. Aziz, but the rage and terror which are revealed beneath the surface of the orderly relations between the British and Indians suggest that sincerity and goodwill alone are ultimately insufficient to overcome the inequities of colonial society.

In critical commentary devoted to *A Passage to India* two principal readings emerge. The first views Forster's work as a realistic novel that is vitally concerned with depicting the social and historical milieu of colonial India. While some critics have claimed that Forster insufficiently represented the nascent Indian nationalist movement or is too concerned with native Anglophiles, most agree that *A Passage to India* is a penetrating criticism of Anglo-Indian colonial society, one which is pessimistic about the ability of the British and Indians to reconcile their differences. A recent trend in this line of criticism sees *A Passage to India* as part of a group of imaginative and scholarly texts which implicitly justify imperialism by creating Eurocentric knowledge about India; others have demonstrated ways in which the novel subverts this enterprise. In contrast to these socio-historical perspectives, a second reading exists which analyzes *A Passage to India* on a symbolic level.

Such a reading tends to universalize the novel as a broad commentary on the human condition and to suggest a theme of reconciliation between conflicting forces. Critics have shown, for example, that the influence of Hinduism on the novel allows a redemptive embrace of opposites and that the positive religious symbolism of the temple in the final section of the book counterbalances the negative implications of the rape trial of Dr. Aziz. Forster himself suggests that a broad interpretation of the book was his intention: "the book is not really about politics. . . . It's about something wider than politics, about the search of the human race for a more lasting home, about the universe as embodied in the Indian earth and the Indian sky. . . . It is—or rather desires to be—philosophic and poetic. . . . "

PRINCIPAL WORKS

Where Angels Fear to Tread (novel) 1905
The Longest Journey (novel) 1907
A Room with a View (novel) 1908
Howards End (novel) 1910
The Celestial Omnibus, and Other Stories (short stories) 1911
Alexandria: A History and a Guide (nonfiction) 1920
The Story of the Siren (short stories) 1920
Pharos and Pharillon (nonfiction) 1923
A Passage to India (novel) 1924
Aspects of the Novel (criticism) 1927
Abinger Harvest (essays) 1936
Two Cheers for Democracy (essays) 1951
The Hill of Devi: Being Letters from Dewas State Senior (nonfiction) 1953
Maurice (novel) 1971

CRITICISM

Rose Macaulay (review date 4 June 1924)

[*In the following review, originally printed in the* Daily News, *Macaulay cautiously praises* A Passage to India.]

Mr. E. M. Forster is, to many people, the most attractive and the most exquisite of contemporary novelists (for a contemporary novelist he has, fortunately, now once more become). Further, he is probably the most truthful, both superficially and fundamentally. His delicate character presentation—too organic to be called drawing—his gentle and pervading humour, his sense and conveyal of the beauty, the ridiculousness, and the nightmare strangeness, of all life, his accurate recording of social, intellectual and spiritual shades and reactions, his fine-spun honesty of thought, his poetry and ironic wit—these qualities have

made him from the first one of the rather few novelists who can be read with delight.

No one now writing understands so well as he the queer interaction of fantasy and ordinary life, the ghosts that halo common persons and things, the odd, mystic power of moments. Neither does anyone, I think, understand quite so well, or convey with such precision and charm, what ordinary people are really like, the way they actually do think and talk. His people are solid, three-dimensioned, and he sees them both from without and within.

A Passage to India is his fifth novel, and his first for fourteen years. Those who fear that his peculiar gifts may be wasted in a novel about India can be reassured; they have full scope. He can make even these brown men live; they are as alive as his Cambridge undergraduates, his London ladies, his young Italians, his seaside aunts; they are drawn with an equal and a more amazing insight and vision. And in the Anglo-Indians, male and female, he has material the most suitable ready to his hand.

Never was a more convincing, a more pathetic, or a more amusing picture drawn of the Ruling Race in India. A sympathetic picture, too, for Mr. Forster is sympathetic to almost everyone. Here, for instance, is the Club, after a supposed insult offered by an Indian to an Englishwoman:

> They had started speaking of 'women and children'—that phrase that exempts the male from sanity when it has been repeated a few times. Each felt that all he loved best in the world was at stake, demanded revenge, and was filled with a not unpleasing glow. . . . 'But it's the women and children,' they repeated, and the Collector knew he ought to stop them intoxicating themselves, but had not the heart.

Somewhere between the two camps, the Anglo-Indians and the Indians, are the newcomers to India—an old lady and a girl, not yet hardened and harrowed into the Anglo-Indian outlook, but full of honest, interested curiosity. These two women are alive with all the imaginative actuality with which Mr. Forster invests his old and his young females. He is almost alone in this, that he enters into the minds of old ladies, and attributes to them those sensitive reactions to life, those philosophic, muddled speculations as to the universe and personal relationships, which most novelists only find younger persons worthy to contain or to emit. The old lady in this book is the most clear-sighted, sensitive, civilised and intellectually truthful person in her circle. She speculates like a male or female undergraduate. 'She felt increasingly (vision or nightmare?) that, though people are important, the relations between them are not, and that in particular too much fuss has been made over marriage. Centuries of carnal embracement, yet man is no nearer to understanding man. And to-day she felt this with such force that it seemed itself a relationship, itself a person who was trying to take hold of her hand.' What other novelist would attribute such thoughts to a lady of sixty-five who has just been told of the engagement of her son?

It is such patient, imaginative realism as this that distinguishes Mr. Forster from most writers. His young woman, too, is an achievement—a queer, unattractive, civilised, logical, intellectually honest girl, who wanted to understand India and the Indians, and came up against the wall of Anglo-India between herself and them. *A Passage to India* is really a story about this Anglo-Indian wall, and the futile occasional attempts, from either side, to surmount it. I suppose it is a sad story, as most truthful stories of collective human relationships must be; it is an ironic tragedy, but also a brilliant comedy of manners, and a delightful entertainment. Its passages of humour or beauty might, quoted, fill several columns. But they cannot profitably be isolated; Mr. Forster is not, in the main, a detachable epigrammist; his wit and his poetry are both organically contextual. This novel has a wider and a deeper range than any of his others.

He has quite lost the touch of preciousness, of exaggerated care for nature and the relationships of human beings, that may faintly irritate some readers of his earlier books. He used once to write at times too much as a graduate (even occasionally as an undergraduate) of King's College, Cambridge (perhaps the most civilised place in the world), who has had an amour with Italy and another with the god Pan. In *A Passage to India* (as, indeed, in *Howards End*), Pan is only implicit, the mysticism is more diffused, the imagination at once richer, less fantastic, and more restrained. It is a novel that, from most novelists, would be an amazing piece of work. Coming from Mr. Forster, it is not amazing, but it is, I think, the best and most interesting book he has written.

But I should like very much to know what Anglo-Indians will think of it. (pp. 196-98)

Rose Macaulay, "Women in the East," in E. M. Forster: The Critical Heritage, *edited by Philip Gardner, Routledge & Kegan Paul, 1973, pp. 196-98.*

E. A. Horne   (essay date 16 August 1924)

[*In this letter to the editor, which appeared in the* New Statesman, *Horne, a member of the Indian Education Service, gives an Anglo-Indian perspective on* A Passage to India.]

Sir,—The publication of a new novel by Mr. Forster, after twelve years' silence, is a great event—perhaps, *the* literary event of the year. This, in itself, is sufficient excuse for a good deal of ink being spilt about it; but, apart from its character as a literary event, the book is one which I think will be much discussed. Mr. Ralph Wright has already reviewed it in *The New Statesman;* and what I now feel impelled to write is not another review, but something which will convey to English readers how the book strikes an Anglo-Indian—a task for which I claim to possess qualifications, having spent the last fourteen years of my life in Chandrapore itself. And with all respect to English literary critics, a knowledge of Cambridge and the suburbs of London, while it may equip them to appraise Mr. Forster's earlier novels, is scarcely sufficient for the appraisement (apart from the purely literary merits of the work, to which they have done full justice) of this latest one. For, after all, this is not a case of mere local colour, as in novels

one might mention, the scene of which is laid in Egypt or Morocco, but of Mr. Forster's own 'passage to India.' The centre of his universe is shifted, for the time being, from Surbiton to Chandrapore. It is this rare faculty to identify himself with the little world he is describing, to live its life from the inside, which gives to all Mr. Forster's novels their special quality; and, incidentally, as I shall try to show later, it is to this peculiar faculty of his that his latest novel owes not only what is so strangely beautiful and true, but elements which are unreal and strangely distorted.

A Passage to India is a novel, not about India (though the Indian background is wonderfully worked in), nor about Indian 'problems' (though these are plentifully implied), but about Indians—and more particularly, Indian Muhammadans. Fielding, who is the author's mouthpiece, when asked how one is to see the real India, replies: 'Try seeing Indians.' This is the way in which Mr. Forster himself has seen India; and it makes his book different from all other books about India. Mr. Forster has created some wonderful characters. The dear old Nawab Bahadur (whose favourite remark was: 'Give, do not lend; after death who will thank you?'); the polished and charming Hamidullah; Mohammed Latif ('a distant cousin of the house, who lived on Hamidullah's bounty and who occupied the position neither of a servant nor of an equal . . . a gentle, happy and dishonest old man'); Hassan (Aziz's servant)—Aziz himself. And some wonderful scenes! How perfect is Aziz's first appearance in the book; and how it strikes a key-note! 'Abandoning his bicycle, which fell before a servant could catch it, the young man sprang up on the verandah. He was all animation.' The first meeting of Aziz and Fielding, and the incident of the collar-stud. The chapters—among the most beautiful in the book, and to me the most moving—when Fielding calls on Aziz. ('Aziz thought of his bungalow with horror. It was a detestable shanty near a low bazaar.') Aziz is in bed, with slight fever. The room is full of people, many of them sitting on his bed. Of some he is acutely ashamed—'third-rate people.' His spiritual restlessness and discomfort—until he gets rid of the others, and has Fielding to himself, and shows him the photograph of his wife. The gorgeous episode at the railway station in the early morning, when Fielding and Godbole miss the train to the Marabar hills—the elephant, the caves and the picnic—all sustained on the full-spread wings of comedy until the crash into sordid tragedy. Such portraits, such scenes, by the hand of a Westerner, are something never before achieved, and are worthy of the cunning of Mr. Forster's hand at its deftest. And how lovingly are these characters studied—with the affectionate understanding which, while it glosses over none of their faults (some of them very odious), just because it understands, forgives. There is one thing, for me, unsatisfactory about Aziz. We are told too little, we are told practically nothing, about his social and spiritual antecedents. ('Touched by Western feeling' is the most that we are told on the subject.) Hamidullah we can 'place'; but Aziz we cannot, and are left groping.

Many readers will be dissatisfied with the central incident in the book—the thing, unpleasant but nameless (since no one can say what really happened), that befell Adela in the cave on the Marabar hills. Here is rich material for the psychoanalyst. My private theory is as follows. The 'hallucination' was not Adela's, but Aziz's. His the sexual vanity, the physical obsessions (on which Mr. Forster lays somewhat painful stress throughout the book); not Adela's, with her college-bred questionings about love. When she 'innocently asked Aziz what marriage was like,' it was the man who was thrown off his balance; 'and she supposed that her question had roused evil in him.' That it did, we may conclude from the gross image which Aziz conceived of the girl's attitude afterwards, putting these words into her mouth: 'Dear Dr. Aziz, I wish you had come into the cave; I am an old hag, and it is my last chance.' The hallucination was Aziz's; but it communicated itself to Adela, just as old Mrs. Moore's obsession by 'evil spirits' communicated itself to the girl's impressionable mind.

To some readers, the epilogue or pendant to the book (Part III., Temple), of which the scene is laid in a Native State on the other side of India, will savour of an impertinence. But a virtuoso passage of the finest is the description of the Hindu festival, the Gokul Ashtami (the birth of Krishna).

It is when one turns from the Indians, who are the real theme of the book, to the Anglo-Indians, who are its harsh but inevitable accompaniment, that one is confronted by the strangest sense of unreality. The 'English' people are real enough. Fielding, the author's mouthpiece; Adela, with her frank, questioning, but ever baffled nature; old Mrs. Moore, with her rather shiftless, rather tiresome, mysticism, but her authentic beauty of soul. Indeed, they are types with which the reader of Mr. Forster's earlier novels will feel instantly at home. But the Anglo-Indians? Where have they come from? What planet do they inhabit? One rubs one's eyes. They are not even good caricatures, for an artist must see his original clearly before he can successfully caricature it. They are puppets, simulacra. The only two of them that come alive at all are Ronny, the young and rapidly becoming starched civilian, and the light-hearted Miss Derek.

Many of Mr. Forster's generalisations about Anglo-Indian society are both witty and penetrating. This, for example: 'The orchestra played the National Anthem. Conversation and billiards stopped, faces stiffened. It was the Anthem of the Army of Occupation. It reminded every member of the club that he or she was British and in exile. It produced a little sentiment and a useful accession of will-power.' Or, again: 'Their ignorance of the Arts was notable, and they lost no opportunity of proclaiming it to one another; it was the Public School attitude, flourishing more vigorously than it can yet hope to do in England. The Arts were bad form.' The incident of Aziz's tonga, commandeered without a word of explanation or apology by two ladies wanting to get to the club, rings true. The self-complacency too, of a young man like Ronny, when faced with the apparent impossibility of mixing with Indians on terms of social equality. 'One touch of regret would have made him a different man, and the British Empire a different institution.'

Even about the general background, however, there is a slight air of unreality. This is partly because the picture is out of date. The period is obviously before the War. Not that this matters, provided it is clearly understood. It is not only that Lieutenant-Governors and dogcarts are out of date. All the fuss about the 'bridge' party will strike the Anglo-Indian reader as hopelessly out of date, it being nowadays very much the fashion—not in Delhi and Simla only, but in the humble mofussil station also—to entertain and cultivate Indians of good social standing.

But it is of Mr. Forster's Anglo-Indian men and women that I wish to speak. Of Turton, the Collector, who is addressed individually and in chorus, and at every turn—as by children in school—as 'Burra Sahib'; and about whom all the other Europeans scrape and cringe. Turton, who is for ever hectoring Fielding, a man not much his junior in years and occupying a sufficiently important official position, telling him (speaking 'officially,' whatever that may mean) to stand up, or 'to leave this room at once,' or to be at the club at six, always addressing him as 'Mr.' Fielding. 'Pray, Mr. Fielding, what induced you to speak to me in such a tone?' This man is not an Indian civilian; he is a college don, and ridiculous enough as that. Of Callendar (of the Indian Medical Service), that incredible cad and bully. Of McBryde, the Superintendent of Police, who, though he does use phrases (speaking of the Collector) like 'Sort of all-white thing the Burra Sahib would do,' is represented as being, morally and intellectually, by far the best of the bunch. And yet we are asked to believe that McBryde commits adultery with Miss Derek while she is staying in his own house, and his wife in the next room! And what is one to make of the women? But I think they are scarcely worth discussing, so inhuman are they without exception. And if these people are preposterous, equally preposterous are the scenes which they enact. The scene at the club, when an 'informal meeting' is held to discuss the situation created by the alleged assault on Adela; the scene in the courtroom at the trial, which ends with Callendar ('on a word from Turton') standing up and bawling: 'I stop these proceedings on medical grounds.'

And why is this? Why are these people and these incidents so wildly improbable and unreal? The explanation is a singular but a simple one. Mr. Forster went out to India to see, and to study, and to make friends of Indians. He did not go out to India to see Anglo-Indians; and most of what he knows about them, their ways and their catchwords, and has put into his book, he has picked up from the stale gossip of Indians, just as the average Englishman who goes out to India picks up most of what he knows about Indians from other Englishmen. It is a curious revenge that the Indian enjoys in the pages of Mr. Forster's novel which profess to deal with Anglo-Indian life and manners; and some would say a just one. All the same, it is a thousand pities that Mr. Forster did not see the real Anglo-India, for he would have written an incomparably better and truer book; and we venture to suggest to him, next time he goes to India: 'Try seeing Anglo-Indians.'

But there is yet another reason why Mr. Forster's picture of Anglo-Indian society is distorted; and this may be told by means of a parable. Even when Aziz blasphemes hideously against their friendship, accusing Fielding of having made Adela his mistress (immediately after the trial); even under this provocation, Fielding understands and forgives his friend. But for the offending members of the European club, he has in his heart no understanding, no forgiveness. To Aziz 'he made a clean breast about the club—said he had only gone under compulsion, and should never attend again unless the order was renewed.' I have said that Fielding is Mr. Forster's mouthpiece; and nobody can describe people as they really are unless he has some affection for them. (pp. 246-51)

> E. A. Horne, in a letter to the editor on August 16, 1924, in E. M. Forster: The Critical Heritage, *edited by Philip Gardner, Routledge & Kegan Paul, 1973, pp. 246-51.*

St. Nihal Singh (review date September 1924)

[*Singh, an Indian nonfiction writer and journalist, speculates on the political significance of* A Passage to India. *This review originally appeared in* Modern Review.]

A Passage to India is of an entirely different character. Not that it refrains from showing up the weak traits in the Indian character. On the contrary, it gives the impression that there is no such thing as an Indian, for the Muslim disdains the Hindu and is in turn hated by the Hindu and Hindus and Muslims alike are slack, prevaricating, not quite honest, unreliable, sexually loose—in a word, inefficient from every point of view. The author is, however, not content with such an expose but mercilessly tears away the gaudy vestments and gewgaws which Anglo-Indians, or 'Europeans' as they prefer to call themselves, have draped about themselves and displays a sight which will revolt some persons, shame others and enrage still others.

The scene is laid in a small civil station probably in Behar and Orissa, where the universe revolves round the Collector. His assistant, who is also the City Magistrate, the District Superintendent of Police, and the Civil Surgeon, a Major in the Indian Medical Service, constitute his satellites. The only Briton who does not kow-tow to him, or care to associate much with the others, is the Principal of the Government College.

Into this 'little England' enter the City Magistrate's mother and the girl who has come out from 'Home' to look him over and decide whether or not she wishes to marry him. They insist upon knowing the 'real India', and since the people among whom their lot is cast loathe and despise India and Indians, they have to seek the good offices of the teacher-man, who is the only 'European' who associates with the 'natives.'

The one Indian—the Assistant-Surgeon (Dr. Aziz)—with whom these two ladies become really acquainted, is a little later accused by the younger woman of attempted assault. He is promptly locked up by the Collector; the District Superintendent of Police works up a case against him, and denies the Principal of the College, who believes in his innocence, the opportunity to see him; the elder Englishwoman, who also believes him innocent, is packed off lest she may complicate matters for the prosecution. The City Magistrate's fiancee however realises in the middle of the

trial, that hysteria had led her to make the charge and withdraws it.

Dr. Aziz has become so embittered by the treatment which he has received at the hands of the British Colony that he resigns his position and takes service under a Hindu Raja. The Englishman in the Educational Service, who had stuck to him during his days of trial even at the expense of ostracism from the Anglo-Indians, pays a visit to that State, accompanied by his wife (who happens to be a step-sister of the City Magistrate) and her brother. Aziz avoids him because he is an Englishman, and he has had enough of them.

Chance brings them together, however, and an attempt at reconciliation is made but proves useless, because the iron has sunk too deep into the Muslim doctor's soul, while the Englishman, now an Inspector, has himself become an Anglo-Indian.

The plot, though quite thin, has enabled the author to accomplish two purposes. It has first of all given him the opportunity to show how the British in India despise and ostracise Indians, while on their part the Indians mistrust and misjudge the British and how the gulf between the two is widening and becoming unbridgeable. It has further given him a chance to demonstrate the utter hopelessness of expecting any improvement from the efforts of Englishmen of superior education who arrive in India at a mature age, because they can resist the bacillus of Anglo-Indianitis only for a time, and even then not completely, and in the end fall victim to it.

The author's pictures are faithful and vivid. That is particularly the case in regard to the Anglo-Indian characters he has created.

In making that remark, I do not mean to suggest that the Hindus and Muslims depicted by Mr. Forster are not faithfully sketched. On the contrary, there are unquestionably young Muslims in India like Dr. Aziz who, despite the advantages of education they have enjoyed, look down upon Hindus and belittle their culture, and fall below even a reasonable standard of truthfulness and efficiency. There also are Hindus like Professor Godbole and Dr. Panna Lal, who return the compliment to men like Aziz and are not his superior either in respect of truthfulness or efficiency.

There are, however, Indians who are neither full of religious prejudices nor the footling muddlers that Mr. Forster has painted. Perhaps his limited opportunities did not permit him to come in contact with them, or possibly the plan of his book did not permit him to introduce them into it. Unfortunately, however, the British reader, as a rule, is so ignorant of India of our day that he is likely to take Aziz and the others as typical of all modern Indians, and, therefore, become confirmed in his prejudices. Such as the notion that India is a congeries of clashing races and creeds, that the Indian standard of morality is low, that Indians cannot dispense with the British crutches, and the like.

Any harm, which the book may do to the Indian cause by laying such emphasis upon our shortcomings will, however, be more than counterbalanced by the good that may result through the exposé of Anglo-India by an Englishman who has evidently taken the trouble to study it and who possesses the moral courage to tear from it all the sham trappings which a spirit of self-adulation had wrapped round a hideous skeleton.

The head of the district is described as a man who 'knew something to the discredit of nearly every one of his (Indian) guests at the bridge party' (not the game 'but a party to bridge the gulf between the East and the West'), and was consequently perfunctory. 'When they had not cheated, it was *bhang,* women, or worse, and even the desirables wanted to get something out of him'. He had had twenty-five years' experience in India and had 'never known anything but disaster result when English people and Indians attempt to be intimate socially. Intercourse, yes. Courtesy, by all means. Intimacy—never, never.' The whole weight of his authority was against it. 'When he saw the coolie asleep in the ditches or the shopkeepers rising to salute him on their little platforms, he said to himself, "You shall pay for this, you shall squeal" '. 'He longed for the good old days when an Englishman could satisfy his own honour and no questions asked afterwards.' As it is, not only the Indians, but 'the Government of India itself also watches—and behind it is that caucus of cranks and cravens, the British Parliament.' In India 'the Turtons (the Collector and his wife) were little gods; soon they would retire to some suburban villa and die exiled from glory.'

The City Magistrate is made out to be a man who lives up to the principle that the British are not in India for the purpose of behaving pleasantly. They are there 'to do justice and keep the peace.' 'Here we are, and we're going to stop, and the country's got to put up with us,' he declared. He was out in India 'to work, mind, to hold this wretched country by force.' He was 'not a missionary or a Labour Member or a vague sentimental sympathetic literary man. . . . Just a servant of the Government.' The British, he said, were 'not pleasant in India' and do not 'intend to be pleasant.' His task was a difficult one. 'Every day he worked hard in the court trying to decide which of two secretive accounts was the less untrue, trying to dispense justice fearlessly, to protect the weak against the less weak, the incoherent against the plausible, surrounded by lies and flattery. That morning he had convicted a railway clerk of over-charging pilgrims for their tickets, and a Pathan of attempted rape. He expected no gratitude, no recognition for this, and both the clerk and Pathan might appeal, bribe their witnesses more effectually in the interval, and get their sentences reversed.' When the day's work was over, he wanted to play tennis with his own kind or rest his legs upon a long chair. He frankly did not like the 'natives'. Soon after he came out, he had asked one of the Pleaders to have a cigarette with him. He found afterwards that he had sent touts all over the bazaar to announce the fact—had told all the litigants that Vakil Mahmoud Ali was 'in with the City Magistrate'. And he believed that 'whether the native swaggers or cringes, there's always something behind every remark he makes—if nothing else, he's trying to . . . score.' He did not consider it worth while to conciliate the educated Indians. They

would be no good to the British in case of a row, and so did not matter.

The District Superintendent of Police was the most reflective and best educated of the officials in the place. Himself born at Karachi, his theory was that 'all natives are criminals at heart, for the simple reason that they live south of latitude 30,' and that 'when an Indian goes bad, he not only goes very bad, but very queer.' His attitude was, 'Everyone knows the man's guilty, and I am obliged to say so in public before he goes to the Andamans.' And in the end he, a married man, was caught in a lady's bedroom and divorced by his wife—and probably 'blamed it to the Indian climate.' According to him, there was nothing in India but the weather—it was the Alpha and Omega of everything.

The Civil Surgeon, a Major in the Indian Medical Service, was full of the 'details of operations which he poured into the shrinking ears of his friends. The boredom of regime and hygiene repelled him.' He was not well disposed towards his Indian Assistant, considering that he had 'no grit, no guts,' and was not any better disposed towards him when by operating he saved an English lady's life. It never occurred to him that 'the educated Indians visited one another occasionally. He only knew that no one ever told him the truth, although he had been in the country for twenty years.' He 'put the fear of God into them at the hospital.' As he described to his fellow 'Europeans' at the club the appearance of the grandson of the leading Indian loyalist:

> His beauty's gone, five upper teeth, two lower and a nostril. . . . Old Panna Lal brought him the looking glass yesterday and he blubbered. I laughed; I laughed, I tell you, and so would you; that used to be one of these niggers, I thought, now he's all septic; damn him, blast his soul—er—I believe he was unspeakably immoral—er—. He subsided, nudged in the ribs, but added, 'I wish I'd had the cutting up of my late assistant too; Nothing's too bad for these people.'

The womenfolk of these persons, as described by Mr. Forster, are a vulgar lot. They were amazed when the heroine and the lady who expected to be her mother-in-law expressed a desire to see Indians. 'Wanting to see Indians!' they exclaimed, 'Natives! why fancy!' and they explained that 'Natives don't respect one any the more after meeting one.' The kindest thing one could do to a native was to let him die.

When the Collector gave a 'bridge party,' his wife refused to 'shake hands with any of the men unless it has to be the Nawab Bahadur.' She reminded the strangers that they 'were superior to every one in India except one or two of the Ranis, and they're on an equality.' She 'had learnt the lingo, but only to speak to her servants, so she knew none of the politer forms and of the verbs only the imperative mood.' She was more distant with Indian ladies who had travelled in Europe and 'might apply her own standards to her.' She told the men that they were 'weak, weak, weak.' The Indians ought to be made 'to crawl from here to the caves on their hands and knees whenever an Englishwoman's in sight, they ought not be spoken to, they ought to be spat at, they ought to be ground into the dust, we've been far too kind with our Bridge Parties and the rest.' No wonder her husband thought that 'After all, it's our women who make everything more difficult out here.'

Then there was the wife of the District Superintendent of Police, who, at her husband's bidding, gave purdah parties until she struck; and the lady who was visiting her, who was companion to a Maharani in a remote Native State, who had taken leave 'because she felt she deserved it, not because the Maharani said she might go.' She burgled the Maharaja's motor car at the junction, as it came back in the train from a Chiefs' Conference at Delhi. 'Her Maharaja would be awfully sick, but she didn't mind, he could sack her if he liked.' 'I don't believe in these people letting you down,' she said. 'If I didn't snatch like the Devil, I should be nowhere. He doesn't want the car, silly fool! Surely it is to the credit of his State I should be seen about in it at Chandrapore during my leave. He ought to look at it that way. Anyhow he's got to look at it that way. My Maharani's different . . . my Maharani's a dear. That's her fox-terrier, poor little devil. . . . Imagine taking dogs to a Chief's Conference! As sensible as taking Chiefs, perhaps, she shrieked with laughter.' She it was in whose bedroom the District Superintendent of Police was later caught.

The Anglo-Indians are not used to being talked about in this manner. They will hate Mr. Forster for giving them away.

I wonder if the book will open the eyes of the British people. I see that it is being widely reviewed in the London and the provincial press, and the critics are writing of it in glowing terms. I have not seen it pointed out anywhere, however, that the author has come to realise that the Anglo-Indians are acting in the manner in which he has described them as acting because they are determined to hang on to India and because they feel that that is the only way they can hang on. The problem, in other words, is not social, but political, and therefore, no end of homilies can have any effect upon improving the manners of the British in India. The political elevation of Indians is the only remedy which can cure them of their habit of looking down upon us—of belittling our past and our capacity—of desiring to keep us at a distance. (pp. 264-69)

St. Nihal Singh, in an excerpt from E. M. Forster: The Critical Heritage, edited by Philip Gardner, Routledge & Kegan Paul, 1973, pp. 264-69.

Edwin Muir (review date 8 October 1924)

[*Muir was a distinguished Scottish novelist, poet, critic, and translator. With his wife Willa, he translated works by various German authors unfamiliar to the English-speaking world, including Gerhart Hauptmann, Hermann Broch, and most notably, Franz Kafka. Here, Muir praises* A Passage to India *in an early review which appeared in* The Nation.]

A Passage to India is a very accomplished novel. It is the kind of novel which could be written only by a very cultivated man, but it shows Mr. Forster's cultivation more clearly than it does his intuition. He does not convince one that he understands his characters; he convinces one only that he understands their misunderstandings, that he knows where they are wrong. His theme is the antagonism, founded largely upon misapprehension, between a colony of Anglo-Indians in a little Indian town and the natives; but although he never shirks the subject he never gets to close grips with it. His picture of mutual misunderstanding is consummate. He presents English people and Indians speaking together, the Indians at a word flying off at an incomprehensible tangent, the English blankly amazed. Nothing could be better than his account of the party at Fielding's, where some English people and two Indians, chatting amiably, find themselves, without knowing why, moving poles asunder. There is the most exquisite artifice in this economically managed scene. The trial, too, is beautifully rendered, and the riot after it is wonderfully neat, a little too neat. Mr. Forster always says the right word, selects the significant detail; yet his art is essentially a kind of impressionism. Miss Quested, the open-minded young Englishwoman who comes to India resolved to know it and refusing to be put off with "a frieze of Indians," gets little more than that in the end, nor do we; for Mr. Forster's Indians have the coldness of a procession, and, if more delicately exact than Mr. Kipling's, they have less personality. The author gives us glimpses of their psychology, but he does not understand that psychology, and cannot explain it to us. It is here that a reader who wants to pursue one path until he comes to the end will rebel against Mr. Forster's intelligent resolve to go only half the way. There is no end, Mr. Forster would no doubt reply. Here is a picture of the muddle: if you try to probe it farther it will only become more baffling. At any rate, his picture is wonderfully drawn. He holds the balance evenly between the Anglo-Indians and the natives, without a hint of prejudice, idealistic or imperialist, and with no fear of the opinions of the English public. He is above the quarrel, and without much hope for its issue. It required courage of a rare kind to write the book.

The story is simple. Mrs. Moore and Miss Quested, the prospective fiancée of Mrs. Moore's son, come to India, and are at first repelled by the English official attitude to the Indians. When they suggest a more sympathetic attitude they are always told from the height of a ten or twenty years' experience, "That is not the point"; and baffled

Forster on writing *A Passage to India*:

The genesis of the book is worth mentioning. I began the book after my 1912 visit, wrote half a dozen chapters of it and stuck. I was clear about the chief characters and the racial tension, had visualized the scenes, and had foreseen that something crucial would happen in the Marabar Caves. But I hadn't seen far enough.

E. M. Forster, "Three Countries," in the Forster Typescripts, King's College Library, Cambridge, as cited in Robin Jared Lewis, E. M. Forster's Passages to India, 1979.

by the English, they turn to the Indians. But by these they are baffled in a different way: they find good-will, even gratitude, but they are misunderstood at every turn. Their sympathy eventually involves them in an adventure in which the younger woman is sexually assaulted, or thinks she is (the point is not clear), in a cave to which a young Moslem doctor has conducted her. The doctor, who is innocent, is arrested and tried; there is a prodigious racial fuss raised by the English, and hysterical indignation among the natives. In the end the doctor is acquitted by the testimony of the woman who accused him, who comes to the conclusion that she was suffering from hallucination. For letting them down she is forthwith ostracized by the Anglo-Indians. A tumult follows the legal decision, and the English fear violence, but the riot passes into a farce. The novel, one feels, should have ended here; but Mr. Forster adds a final section portraying, with an unconvincing irony, an aspect of Indian religious life. It is the only feeble part of the novel, and, seeing that it is the end, the part which could least suffer to be feeble. But, apart from it, the book is executed with rare scrupulousness. The writing, when it does not slip into fine writing, as it does once or twice, is a continuous delight. The novel is a triumph of the humanistic spirit over material difficult to humanize. It is this first of all; it is also a work of art exquisite rather than profound. Last of all, it is a peculiarly valuable picture of the state of India seen through a very unembarrassed and courageous intelligence. (pp. 379-80)

> *Edwin Muir, "Mr. Forster Looks at India," in* The Nation, *New York, Vol. LXIX, No. 3092, October 8, 1924, pp. 379-80.*

Nirad C. Chaudhuri   (essay date June 1954)

[*In the following essay, originally published in* Encounter, *Chaudhuri argues that Forster is misguided in his representation of the failure of British colonialism in India.*]

Reading *A Passage to India* some time ago, I was led to think not only of the final collective passage of the British from India but also of Mr. Forster's contribution to that finale. Such an association of ideas between a novel and an event of political history may be objected to, but in this case I think the association is legitimate. For *A Passage to India* has possibly been an even greater influence in British imperial politics than in English literature.

From the first, the more active reaction to it followed the existing lines of political cleavage, its admirers being liberal, radical, or leftist sheep and its detractors conservative, imperialist, and diehard goats. The feud between English liberalism and the British empire in India was as old as the empire itself. Except for a short period of quiescence when Liberal-Imperialism was in vogue, it raged till 1947. Mr. Forster's novel became a powerful weapon in the hands of the anti-imperialists, and was made to contribute its share to the disappearance of British rule in India.

On those, also, who did not follow clear party cues in respect of India, its influence was destructive. It alienated their sympathy from the Indian empire. As it was, the British people taken in the mass were never deeply in-

volved in this empire, emotionally or intellectually. To them it was rather a marginal fact of British history than what it really was—a major phenomenon in the history of world civilisation. Mr. Forster's book not only strengthened the indifference, it also created a positive aversion to the empire by its unattractive picture of India and Anglo-Indian life and its depiction of Indo-British relations as being of a kind that were bound to outrage the English sense of decency and fair play. Thus, the novel helped the growth of that mood which enabled the British people to leave India with an almost Pilate-like gesture of washing their hands of a disagreeable affair.

Even intrinsically, the novel had a political drift. There is of course no necessary connection between a writer's own intentions and the manner in which he is accepted or exploited by his public. It has even been said that it is only when they are debased or deformed that philosophical ideas play a part in history. But in regard to *A Passage to India,* it can be said that the author's purpose and the public response more or less coincided. The novel was quite openly a satire on the British official in India. Perhaps in a veiled form it was also a satire on the Indians who were, or aspired to be, the *clientes* of the foreign patriciate. As such it was, at one remove, a verdict on British rule in India. At the risk of depriving it of its nuances, but perhaps not misrepresenting its general purport, I might sum it up as follows. This rule is the cause of such painful maladjustment in simple human relations that even without going deeply into the rights and wrongs of the case it is desirable to put an end to it. The intention seems to have been to bring even English readers to agree with the last outburst of the hero of the novel, Aziz: "We shall drive every blasted Englishman into the sea, and then you and I shall be friends."

Accordingly, one is almost forced to appraise the novel as a political essay on Indo-British relations, and as soon as it is considered as such, a striking gap in Mr. Forster's presentation of these relations fixes attention. It is seen that the novel wholly ignores the largest area of Indo-British relations and is taken up with a relatively small sector. The ignored area is the one I watched at first hand from the age of seven to the age of fifty. The other sector, in contrast, was known to me only by hearsay, because I feared its contact almost as much as a Pharisee feared the contact of publicans and sinners.

The Indo-British relations I was familiar with were contained, for the most part, within the conflict between Indian nationalists and the British administration. Here I saw great suffering and distress, but also exultation, a brave acceptance of ill-treatment and conquest of weak tears. The longer the men had been in jail, the more they had been persecuted, the more "sporting" they seemed to be. In the other sector, the conflict was between associates, the British officials and their Indian subordinates or hangers-on, and had all the meanness of a family quarrel. It sizzled without providing any ennobling or even chastening release for passion, only distilling rancour. It contributed much to the pathology of Indo-British relations but virtually nothing to the final parting of ways. If we can at all speak of having driven the "blasted Englishman into the sea," as Aziz puts it, it was not men of his type who accomplished the feat. Those who fought British rule in India did not do so with the object of eventually gaining the Englishman's personal friendship. Just as personal humiliation did not bring them into the conflict, personal friendship did not also lure them as a goal.

But of course there was good reason for Mr. Forster's choice. The reason is not however that the political conflict was impersonal and could not be treated in a novel. It could be, though the result would have been a tragedy of mutual repulsion and not a tragi-comedy of mutual attraction. Mr. Forster chose the sector of which he had personal knowledge. As an Englishman paying a short visit to India, he naturally saw far less of Indians in general than of his own countrymen and of the Indians with whom the latter had official business or perfunctory social relations. Being an Englishman, of humane sensibilities, he was also shocked by the state of these relations, as among others Wilfrid Blunt was before him. On the other hand, he could not observe the larger and the more important area without going considerably out of his way and making a special effort.

There is also another and not less fundamental reason for Mr. Forster's choice. That is the character of his political consciousness. I should really call it humanitarian consciousness. For his is an appeal in a political case to the court of humane feelings to what he himself calls "common humanity" in a later essay. Now, the relationship between common humanity and politics is even more complex than that which exists between morality and politics. I firmly believe that ultimately, politics and morals are inseparable; even so, the most obvious moral judgement on a political situation is not necessarily a right judgement, and for humane feelings to go for a straight tilt at politics is even more quixotic than tilting at windmills.

The consequences of pitting humane feelings against a political phenomenon are well illustrated in *A Passage to India.* One consequence is that it leads to pure negation. In the sphere of Indo-British relations the novel has no solution to offer except a dissolution of the relationship, which is not a solution of the problem but only its elimination. The good feeling that such a dissolution can generate, and has in actual fact generated between Indians and the British after 1947, is the sort of kindly feeling one has for strangers or casual acquaintances. It is of no use whatever for a sane ordering of political relations which one is struggling to raise from an amoral or even immoral level to a moral one.

Another consequence is that the humanitarian prepossession leads Mr. Forster to waste his politico-ethical emotion on persons who do not deserve it. Both the groups of characters in *A Passage to India* are insignificant and despicable. I have, however, my doubts about Mr. Forster's delineation of his countrymen. I am no authority on the life of White officials in India, for I never cultivated them. Still, observing them in their public capacity, and at times laying incredible stupidities at their door, I did not consider them quite so absurd a class as Mr. Forster shows them to be.

Of one implied charge I will definitely acquit them. Mr. Forster makes the British officials of Chandrapore nervous about the excitement of the Muharram to the extent of making the women and children take shelter in the club, and after the trial of Aziz he makes them reach home along by-ways for fear of being manhandled by a town rabble. Of this kind of cowardice no British official in India was to my mind ever guilty, even in their worst time since the Mutiny, in the years 1930 to 1932, when the Auxiliary Force armoury at Chittagong in Bengal was raided by a band of young revolutionaries, British officials were shot dead in Calcutta and the districts, and attempts were made on the life of the Governor of Bengal and the Police Commissioner of Calcutta. As a class, the British officials kept their head. The courage shown by the District Magistrate of Chittagong on the night of the raid, when an insurrection of unknown magnitude and danger faced him, was admirable. The shortcoming of the British official was not in courage, but in intelligence.

On the other hand, Mr. Forster is too charitable with the Indians. Aziz would not have been allowed to cross my threshold, not to speak of being taken as an equal. Men of his type are a pest even in free India. Some have acquired a crude idea of gracious living or have merely been caught by the lure of snobbism, and are always trying to gain importance by sneaking into the company of those to whom this way of living is natural. Another group of men are more hardboiled. They are always out to put personal friendship to worldly profit, perhaps the most widespread canker in Indian social life even now. Indian ministers and high officials feel this even more strongly than Ronny in Mr. Forster's novel. These attempts at exploitation are making them more outrageously rude than any British official, and all the more so because in India there is no tradition of kindliness among people in power. In British days this bickering gave rise to a corrosive race conflict, now it is fomenting an equally corrosive class conflict. But it is futile to grow censorious over this, no sane or satisfactory human relations can be built up with such material.

Mr. Forster appears to have felt this himself. He is too intelligent to be able to overlook the weak points in the Indian character, and too honest to suppress them in his book. Indeed, he shows himself so acute in seizing them that it is impossible to imagine that he was representing Aziz and his associates as fine fellows who deserved to be treated as equals by the British, and was not conscious of their utter worthlessness. I detect a personal admission in the comment he puts in the mouth of Ronny about the Nawab Bahadur, the "show Indian": "Incredible, aren't they, even the best of them?" So I am not surprised to find a streak of satire even in his presentation of Indians. But such satire not being his aim, he is driven into a corner, from where he can plead for satisfactory Indo-British relations on the only basis which could be proof against disillusionment, the basis of the least respect and the largest charity. Inevitably he has also to make a moralist's impossible demand on human nature.

But even if Mr. Forster's Indians had been good as individuals as they are malodorous, he would not have had a very much stronger case. For he had not chosen his Indian types happily. In regard to the Hindu characters, he relied mostly on the types found in the Princely States. Certainly they were more traditional than those in British India, but they were so traditional that they did not represent modern India at all. For instance, to those of us who are familiar with the teachings of the Hindu reformers of the 19th century, Godbole is not an exponent of Hinduism, he is a clown. Even for us, friendly personal relations with these men became possible only if we assumed we were in an anthropological reserve. Although the States have now been incorporated in India, the unevenness persists, and it presents a serious problem of *Gleichschaltung* for the future.

But Mr. Forster's more serious mistake was in taking Muslims as the principal characters in a novel dealing with Indo-British relations. They should never have been the second party to the relationship in the novel, because ever since the nationalist movement got into its stride the Muslims were playing a curiously equivocal role, realistic and effective politically, but unsatisfying in every other respect. The Muslims hated the British with a hatred even more vitriolic than the Hindu's, because it was they who had been deprived of an empire by the British. Yet they found themselves wooed by the latter as a counterpoise to the Hindu nationalists, and they did not reject these overtures.

They were shrewd in their calculations. They knew that their own battle was being fought by the Hindus and that in an eventual victory their share of the spoils was guaranteed. In the meanwhile, it was profitable to exploit the British, make the best of both worlds. This game, played with boldness and hardheaded realism, succeeded beyond expectation and created an independent state for the Muslims of India.

But a colossal Machiavellian game of politics like this could be played without moral risks only by men of very great strength of character, as indeed all the Muslim leaders, from Sir Sayyid Ahmad Khan to M. A. Jinnah, were. On the rank and file of the Muslims, so far as this policy influenced them, it had a deplorable effect. It left one section unweaned from its barren and rancorous hatred and made another pine for British patronage. Aziz and his friends belong to the servile section and are all inverted toadies. With such material, a searching history of the Muslim destiny in India could have been written, but not a novel on Indo-British relations, for which it was essential to have a Hindu protagonist.

But I think I know why Mr. Forster would not have a Hindu. He shares the liking the British in India had for the Muslim, and the corresponding dislike for the Hindu. This was a curious psychological paradox and in every way unnatural, if not perverse. On the one hand, the Islamic order was the natural enemy of the Christian-European, and the British empire in India was in one sense the product of the secular conflict between the Christian West and the Islamic Middle East, which is still running its course. More than one British Foreign Secretary found the pitch of British policy queered by the incurable phil-Islamic attitude of the British Indian Government, and once Sir Edward Grey expressed frank annoyance at it.

On the other hand, there was between European civilisation and the Hindu in its stricter form a common Indo-European element, which was discovered and described by British Orientalists in the first century or so of British rule, but which came to be forgotten and ignored by Englishmen in later times. Modern Hindu thinkers did not, however, lose sight of the affinity. Swami Vivekananda, speaking at the end of the last century, said that two branches of the same people placed in different surroundings in Greece and India had worked out the problems of life, each in its own particular way, but that through the agency of the British people the ancient Greek was meeting the ancient Hindu on Indian soil, and thus "slowly and silently the leaven has come, the broadening out, the life-giving revivalist movement that we see all around us." The British in India never gave this fruitful idea any encouragement. They were taken in by the deceptive simplicity of the Muslim and repelled by the apparent bizarrerie of Hinduism and its rococo excrescences. I wonder if it was the Hebraic element in the British ethos which was responsible for this.

This leads me straight to my objections to the politics of *A Passage to India* and my one positive comment on its central theme. My most serious criticisms are the following. It shows a great imperial system at its worst, not as diabolically evil but as drab and asinine; the rulers and the ruled alike are depicted at their smallest, the snobbery and pettiness of the one matching the imbecility and rancour of the other. Our suffering under British rule, on which a book as noble as Alfred de Vigny's *Servitude et Grandeur militaires* could have been written, is deprived of all dignity. Our mental life as depicted in the book is painfully childish and querulous. Lastly, attention is diverted away from those Indians who stood aloof from the world the book describes and were aristocratic in their way, although possessing no outward attribute of aristocracy. When I consider all this I feel Mr. Forster's literary ability, which has given the book its political importance, as a grievance.

At the root of all this lies the book's tacit but confident assumption that Indo-British relations presented a problem of personal behaviour and could be tackled on the personal plane. They did not and could not. The great Indians who brought about the Westernisation of their country and created its modern culture had none of the characteristic Indian foibles for which Mr. Forster invokes British compassion. They were men of the stature of an Erasmus, Comenius, or Holberg, who could hold their own with the best in Europe. Yet some of them were assaulted, some insulted, and others slighted by the local British. None of them had any intimate personal relations with any member of the British ruling community. There were also thousands of Indians who had adopted Western ideals and were following them to the best of their ability, who were not only not cultivated but shunned with blatant ostentation by the British in India. "What you have got to stamp on is these educated classes," they all said, like the subaltern in the novel. This was due, not to any personal snobbery, but to that massive national snobbery which refused to share British and Western civilisation with Indians.

Those who remember the powerful championship of Westernisation by Macaulay usually forget that his best supporters were Indians and his most determined opponents his own countrymen. In spite of the formal adoption of this policy, the British ruling class in India never felt happy about it and carried it out half-heartedly. Towards the result, the attitude of the thoughtful Englishman was one of regret, while the average Englishman grew maliciously quizzical.

To give only one example, there was hardly one Englishman who had a good word to say about our employment of the English language. I still remember the pleasure I felt when for the first time in my experience, I read praise of our English in Sir Michael Sadler's report on Calcutta University. Normally the better our English the more angry did the Englishman become, and the worse it was the greater was the entertainment of the Memsahib and *ergo* the larger the favours of the Sahib. Even so great a personage as Lady Minto was not above the weakness, and in his kindly manner even Mr. Forster has felt amused by our English.

Of course, I cannot deny that much of our English as indeed much of our Westernisation was quaint. But ours were the shortcomings of self-taught and unguided men everywhere. If, in their days of power, the British had not looked askance at our employment of English, today the battle for English in India would not have been already lost, and we should not have needed the forlorn crusade of the British Council, too late for love, too late for joy, too late, too late!

Once the premise of cultural apartheid was admitted, there could be no advance on the personal plane, for men do not treat as equals those who are not of their psychological species. The British in India clinging to the obsolete idea of zoological speciation for mankind, could only cry as the District Collector does in *A Passage to India*: "I have never known anything but disaster result when English people and Indians attempt to be intimate socially. Intercourse, yes. Courtesy by all means. Intimacy—never, never."

A real Englishman, greater than Mr. Forster's Turton, had come to the same conclusion. Sir Edwin Lutyens, the builder of New Delhi, tried friendship with Indians and wrote in disenchantment: "The natives do not improve on acquaintance. Their very low intellects spoil much and I do not think it is possible for the Indians and Whites to mix freely and naturally. They are very different, and even my ultrawide sympathy with them cannot admit them on the same plane as myself. They may be on a higher plane or a lower one than a White, but the ethics of their planes are different to ours, and for one or the other to leave his plane is unclean and unforgivable."

On the other hand, putting the cultural impact in the foreground, Indians propounded a strikingly contrasted thesis. At that level our personal humiliations ceased to matter and even our great *injuria temporum,* political subjection, presented a second face. Rammohun Roy was grossly insulted by a British baronet and official. He protested against it to the Governor-General but did not allow it to

influence his views on Westernisation or even those about British rule in India. He surprised a young French scientist, Victor Jacquemont, who saw him in Calcutta, by an expression of opinion which the Frenchman set down verbatim in his journal: "*La conquête est bien rarement un mal, quand le peuple conquérant est plus civilisé que le peuple conquis, parce qu'elle apporte à celui-ci les biens de la civilisation. Il faut à l'Inde bien des années de domination anglaise pour qu'elle puisse ne pas perdre beaucoup en ressaisissant son indépendance politique.*"

Bankim Chandra Chatterji, the creator of Hindu nationalism, was actually assaulted by a British official though a magistrate himself, but he too, when it came to assessing the larger consequences of British rule in India, argued persuasively that it was in many ways providential. Personal grievance, even when well-founded, did not influence men of this type.

The contrast between the generosity of such Indians and the British narrowness furnishes the key to the real failure of the British in India. It was the failure to see that a nation which was not willing to propagate its civilisation and extend its spiritual citizenship was also incapable of perpetuating, not only an empire, but even friendly political relations with other nations not belonging to its own culture complex. The challenge before the British was to create an open society in the order of the mind. Their opportunity was to make India an extension of the Western world. But they failed as completely in using their opportunity as they did in meeting the challenge. Compared with this failure, which was a betrayal of the West in India, their bad manners were mere peccadillos.

This political evaluation of *A Passage to India* has not been attempted for its historical interest, great as that interest is. I believe that the questions which British rule raised in India have only been put aside and not answered by what happened in 1947. I also believe that the British failure to understand the true nature of the Indo-British relationship has a moral, whose application is likely to widen as time passes, for a new set of international relations taking shape today over an area very much larger than India. It is this moral that I have to draw now.

But as a preliminary I should define my position. I represent no school of thought in India, past or present, and there is nothing characteristically Indian in my views except the fact that they are those of an Indian by birth and are based on Indian experience. I differ fundamentally from the nationalistic majority of my countrymen who speak of 19th century imperialism but forget that the century also had its nationalism. I differ no less fundamentally from the influential minority in India who believe in world government, who pin their faith to a world government of the contractual type, carried on by means of a world assembly in which the national representatives will be wise, reasonable, and just. I cannot say, like a Christian, that this conception is bound to be wrecked on the innate sinfulness of man, but I would say that it would hurtle against man's inherent urge to power.

It seems to me that the West is now showing the same incomprehension which destroyed British power in India.

The economic and the political impact of the West is being felt. What is absent is that proselytising cultural impact which alone can counteract the mental resistance to the extension of Western culture into the non-Western parts of the world. Instead, there is the same uncritical faith in the promotion of economic prosperity and the converting power of *Pecunia Americana* as there was in the maintenance of law and order and the indispensability of *Pax Britannica*. The West ought to, and in my opinion can, think in terms of something higher than effective diplomacy, higher even than world government, for converting the single zoological species called man into one psychological species. Of course, that might not be possible. But one can never speak of impossibility before an effort has been made. (pp. 115-20)

> *Nirad C. Chaudhuri, "Passage to and from India," in* Perspectives on E. M. Forster's "A Passage to India:" A Collection of Critical Essays, *edited by V. A. Shahane, Barnes & Noble, Inc., 1968, pp. 115-20.*

Forster on "the Indian mind":

The Indian who attempts to interpret his country to the Westerner is apt to become part of the mystery he offers to solve. He is too often full of vague platitudes, of illustrations that explain nothing, of arguments that lead nowhere, and such interpretation as he gives is unconscious. He leaves us with the sense of a mind infinitely remote from ours—a mind patriotic and sensitive—and it may be powerful, but with little idea of logic or facts; we retire baffled, and, indeed, exasperated.

> *E. M. Forster, "The Indian Mind" in his* Albergo Empedocle and Other Writings, *1971.*

Glen O. Allen (essay date December 1955)

[*In the following essay, originally published in* PMLA, *Allen discusses the structure of* A Passage to India.]

For the thirty years since its publication, E. M. Forster's *A Passage to India* has enjoyed the somewhat paradoxical status of being valued without being understood. It is generally recognized as one of the finest literary productions of this century; it is also commonly thought to be one of the most puzzling. No doubt, part of the reason for our difficulty in interpreting it is that the literary problems it raises are continuous with its philosophical problems, or, to put it another way, that the obscurities of the novel duplicate or disappear into the obscurities of life itself. We cannot, of course, expect to explain the latter mystery before attempting to explain the former, nor need it be necessary; yet, if we are to succeed in interpretation, we must guard against that most common critical error of assuming that our own philosophical predilections must apply universally. As Earl R. Wasserman recently observed, "Our failure to grasp as total and integrated experiences such works as . . . E. M. Forster's *A Passage to India* results from our not having succeeded as yet in bringing to

these works the proper controlling cosmos, for each cosmos is the creation of the author." Discovering the nature of this "cosmos" and relating it to structure, symbol, and theme of the novel will be the concern of the following pages.

Among the general critical treatments of Forster's novels those of Lionel Trilling, Austin Warren, and Morton D. Zabel deserve special mention for their sensitivity and discernment. All of them, however, suffer the limitation of having comparatively little to say about *A Passage to India.* More recently, three attempts have been made to probe more directly into the meaning of this novel. E. K. Brown has applied one of Forster's own concepts, *rhythm,* in an analysis of his narrative technique, but without any very fruitful results in the interpretation of the book's meaning. Paul Fussell, Jr. has suggested the possibility of the identity of Mrs. Moore and Madame Blavatsky, apparently unaware of Forster's aversion to "psychical research, that dustbin of the spirit." Finally, Gertrude M. White has attempted to embrace the three parts of the novel in an Hegelian triad. Her recognition that beneath the details of the story runs a philosophical under-current of the broadest dimensions is a valuable contribution; yet I believe her interpretation does violence not only to the meaning of the novel, but to Forster's own philosophical views. The alleged synthesis and the optimism of Hegelian doctrine are quite at odds with Forster's quietism.

One would think that the publication of Forster's Indian correspondence of 1911 and 1921 would throw light upon the significance of the novel. The letters do, in fact, contain a number of descriptions of incidents and scenes which appear in the text almost without change. Reported to his mother, or one of his other correspondents, were: an incident in which a wild animal leaped out of a ravine and charged an automobile; an instance in which a small dead tree is mistaken for a snake; a description of an Indian song approximating the strange chant of Professor Godbole; and finally nearly all the details connected with the ceremony of the birth of Shri Krishna. Considering the degree to which Forster has called upon the unembellished incidents of his own experience in the construction of his novel, one is tempted at first to believe that much of the text of the novel might go under the name of "local color" and thus account for the difficulty of synthesizing its many diverse details.

Nothing, however, could be farther from the truth. Few novelists discipline themselves to the omission of extraneous detail more severely than Forster. The following passage from his Clark lectures, delivered three years after the publication of *A Passage to India* and later published as *Aspects of the Novel* (New York, 1927) assures us that a Forster novel should be approached not as a muddle but as a mystery inviting discerning analysis.

> The plot-maker expects us to remember, we expect him to leave no loose ends. Every action or word ought to count; it ought to be economical and spare, even when complicated it should be organic and free from dead matter. It may be difficult or easy, it may and should contain mysteries, but it ought not to mislead. And over it, as it unfolds, will hover the memory of the reader

(that dull glow of the mind of which intelligence is the bright advancing edge) and will rearrange and reconsider, seeing new clues, new chains of cause and effect, and the final sense (if the plot has been a fine one) will not be of clues or chains, but of something aesthetically compact, something which might have been shown by the novelist straight away, only if he had shown it straight away it would never have become beautiful.

The structure of *A Passage to India* is built around its threefold division into "Mosque," "Caves," and "Temple." Forster, in his notes to the Everyman edition, tells us that the three parts stand for the three seasons of the Indian year. The action of "Mosque" takes place during the cool spring, that of "Caves" during the hot summer, and of "Temple" during the wet monsoon season of the autumn. But he is not limiting the significance of this division to the times of the year or to the characteristic weather of these seasons, though, to be sure, the weather constitutes an important part of the symbolic structure. In the text itself, the author hints at another meaning of the threefold division. "Ronny's religion was of the sterilized Public School brand, which never goes bad, even in the tropics. Wherever he entered, *mosque, cave,* or *temple,* he retained the spiritual outlook of the Fifth Form, and condemned as 'weakening' any attempt to understand them." Caves, then, like mosques and temples, represent some kind of religion. But by religion Forster means something more than that which attracts the western peoples into church on Sundays and Easter, as one may assume from his indifference to the minutiae of creed and practice. Speaking of the mosque through Aziz, he says, "Here was Islam, his own country, more than a Faith, more than a battle-cry, more, much more . . . Islam, an attitude towards life both exquisite and durable, where his body and his thoughts found their home." Similarly with caves and temples, Forster is endeavoring to represent what is much more than a faith or a battle-cry, much more than orthodox Christianity or the worship of Shri Krishna. These creeds are specifically mentioned, but they are not the basic categories in which Forster conceives "attitudes toward life."

It is easier to understand Forster's treatment of mosque, caves, and temple if we accept as his basic categories the emotional nature, the intellect, and the capacity for love. He has accordingly selected religions to represent his views, each of which offers exercise predominantly to one of these faculties. In Islam, he sees a mode of expression for the emotional nature, an attitude towards life where Aziz's "body and his thoughts found their home." Islam, however, provides no sanctuary for the intellect. " 'There is no God but God,' doesn't carry us far through the complexities of matter and spirit; it is only a game with words, really a religious pun, not a religious truth." Nor, indeed, does the worship of Shri Krishna, in which the exercise of the faculty of love predominates, offer satisfaction to intellect or will. Its quietism in the face of the unjust accusation of Aziz is a source of great exasperation to Fielding, while its religious practices are described as a muddle, "a frustration of reason and form." Godbole, the Brahman, charming as he is, remains utterly inscrutable to both Aziz

and Fielding, who at the very end of the novel show in one instance continuing indifference and in the other continuing puzzlement over his strange faith. The mysticism underlying devotion to Shri Krishna amounts to an utter renunciation of the intellect, the disintegration of the categories which make distinction—and, therefore, thought—possible. Hence the futility of Fielding's attempt to grasp its meaning.

At the third corner of this triangle of religious attitudes are Fielding and Adela, exemplars of peculiarly western traits. Neither emotional nor strongly endowed with mystical insight, they approach the deeper problems of life and human relationships through the mind and whatever is not reducible to intellectual categories is therefore beyond their grasp. It is this devotion to reason, form, and the sense of purpose as the *sine qua non* of right behavior and attitude that Forster represents as the religion of caves. As Aziz is the principal character in "Mosque" and Godbole in "Temple," so Fielding and Adela dominate the action of "Caves."

Mrs. Moore, the other major character of the western group, bears a strong though subtle resemblance to Fielding and Adela. Though endowed with some of the emotional spontaneity of an Aziz and the mystical sensitivity of a Godbole, her strongest moorings are of ultimate intellectual origin. Though not doctrinaire in her beliefs, she is nevertheless a practising Christian, and so deeply embedded are the roots of Christianity in the traditions of western thought that Mrs. Moore, without being intellectually disposed, is intellectually committed; without having the capacity for thought, she is nevertheless a victim of her intellectual heritage. Because of her widely diverging traits, Mrs. Moore appropriately exercises an influence in all three parts of the novel: in "Mosque," as an active character spanning the gulf between Fielding and Adela and the volatile Aziz; in "Caves," as the pettish old woman disappointed by her vision of the mystical realm beyond the limits of the intellectual categories; and, in "Temple," both as a spiritual residue and as the progenitor of the mystically inclined Ralph and Stella.

It is not surprising that India, which, according to Forster, "mirrors the universe" and likewise has no unity itself, should in the history of its religious philosophy have embraced an approximation of each one of these "attitudes towards life" as a way of salvation. The historians of Hindu philosophy provide ample documentation for this trichotymous division; however, for its succinctness of expression, I have chosen the statement of E. W. F. Tomlin.

> Indian philosophical tradition has fully recognized the different degrees in wisdom to which the three great elements of Hindu scripture approximate. In the first place there is the so-called Path of Activity, or *Karmamarga.* To this path belong the Vedas, songs to be chanted in public as a stimulus to effort: the anthems of a people engaged in a communal exploit needing for its accomplishment a burning faith in its mission. In the second place there is the so-called Path of Knowledge, or *Inanamarga.* To this path belong the *Upanishads,* explorations by the mind in se-

cret conclave of that which is permanently knowable behind the world of appearances and illusion. In the third place there is the so-called Path of Devotion, or *Bhaktimarga*. To this path belongs the *Bhagavad-Gita*.

The principal function of the threefold division of the novel, then, is to represent these three "attitudes toward life" both as they partake of regularized religious views and as they are expressions of varying types of culture and of individual character.

Within this embracing architectural structure, Forster has spun a web of marvelously rich and complex detail. Characteristic of his technique is the repetition of detail in different contexts and with slight variations, and to this method Forster has applied the term, "rhythm." The effect of this rhythm is not only to knit together aesthetically the detail of the novel; it also contributes very considerably to the meaning of it.

The wasp, for instance, is mentioned in three different contexts—first, when Mrs. Moore finds it on a coat-peg; second, when the missionaries consider the possibility of admitting wasps to heaven; and third, when Godbole is described as impelling the wasp to completeness of union in God. In all of these instances the wasp retains its identity as a pretty creature but somewhat undesirable because of its sting, as "good-and-evil," to use a term of Forster's coinage, but it functions differently according to each context in which it appears. It is not, that is to say, a full-fledged symbol, but rather an instance of repetition for the sake of its unifying effect. Our first acquaintance with the wasp comes directly after Ronny has demonstrated to his mother the "official" way of penetrating the subterfuges of the Indian character, and his mother cannot deny that his accusation of Aziz "sounds very sensible," though she thinks to herself, "how false a summary of the man." Similarly, there are two ways of looking at a wasp, as a creature possessing a stinger and capable of inflicting great pain, or, as Mrs. Moore did: " 'Pretty dear,' said Mrs. Moore to the wasp."

When the wasp next appears in the remarks of the missionaries, its function is quite subservient to the function of the whole parable. It remains a pretty but dangerous creature which even the advanced Mr. Sorley can not readily find room for in the house of many mansions. The whole parable exists to comment on the inclusions and exclusions involved in the invitations to the bridge party at the club, a British-style heaven. But the ultimate significance of the parable reaches out to one of the basic ideas of the novel, the necessity of exclusion to make inclusion meaningful, or, in the most general terms, the necessity of distinction to intellectual processes and hence the basic repugnance of the western mind to mysticism.

The last mention of the wasp illustrates the consequences of the complete indifference to distinction which results in "the frustration of reason and form." Had he been a Christian missionary, Godbole might have concentrated on Mrs. Moore and then, as a second choice, perhaps Fielding. But no, for the Hindu no such distinctions exist. God is equally immanent, though perhaps not equally evident, in man, wasp, and stone, and no one is to be preferred

above another. "Thus, Godbole, though she was not important to him, remembered an old woman he had met in Chandrapore days. Chance brought her into his mind while it was in this heated state, he did not select her, she happened to occur among the throng of soliciting images, a tiny splinter, and he impelled her by his spiritual force to that place where completeness can be found. Completeness, not reconstruction. His senses grew thinner, he remembered a wasp seen he forgot where, perhaps on a stone. He loved the wasp equally, he impelled it likewise, he was imitating God."

The effect of rhythm is achieved in the case of the wasp by virtue of the material similarity of wasp in one instance with wasp in another. In passing I noted also the parable of the missionaries, another example of rhythm, but in this case repetition occurs not in the material but in the formal similarities existing between invitations to the club and admission to heaven. A more complex and significant instance of this sort of rhythm lies in the similarities between the accident involving "the savage pig" and Adela's entrance into the cave. The essential features of the accident are the approach to the scene during which Adela is concerned with the problem of marriage, the collision with the animal, the confused attempt at identifying the animal, and the return in Miss Derek's car. These features are reproduced in the incident of the cave. "As she toiled over a rock that resembled an inverted saucer, she thought, 'What about love?' The rock was nicked by a double row of footholds, and somehow the question was suggested by them. Where had she seen footholds before? Oh yes, they were the pattern traced in the dust by the wheels of the Nawab Bahadur's car. She and Ronny—no, they did not love each other." Thereafter, Adela asks Aziz her offensive question, enters the cave, believes herself attacked, and descends wildly from the summit of Kawa Dol to return to Chandrapore in Miss Derek's automobile. The incidents are basically similar in form, and the reference to the earlier accident is an invitation to us to infer further similarities. The obvious inference to make is that just as the accident is not to be unilaterally explained by appeal to a naturalistic cause, so too the incident of the cave is not to be accounted for by blaming Aziz or the guide. In both cases Adela's wish for explanation at all cost is the source of her error.

I have avoided using the word symbol in referring to those repeated items composing the rhythm of the novel in order to preserve its significance for reference to the major symbolic structure of the book—the Marabar Hills, the caves, the sun, echoes, serpents, snakes, and worms. A distinction between the two can be made on this basis: the former, to which I have referred as instances of rhythm, take their meaning from their context; they have no stable meaning but grow and wane in significance according to the way in which they are used. The wasp, the circumstances of the accident and the affairs of the cave, the speculations of the missionaries, Godbole's song, the Tank of the Dagger, and a host of others fall under the head of rhythm because their meaning is not stable but varies according to context.

The Marabar Hills and related symbols, on the other

hand, while they are certainly not unconnected with the other details of the novel, derive their essential meaning from sources outside the novel itself. This no doubt accounts for the silence in some critical quarters and the puzzlement in others when the inevitable question of the caves arises. Mostly, the practice has been to look the other way; however, Austin Warren sees the caves as something "bare, dark, echoing," echoing "eternity, infinity, the Absolute." Gertrude White declares that they are "the very voice of that union which is the opposite of divine; the voice of evil and negation." Virginia Woolf suggests hesitantly that "the Marabar Caves should appear to us not real caves but, it may be, the soul of India," while Lionel Trilling, after observing the radical alterations undergone in their depths by Mrs. Moore and Adela, offers to call them "wombs."

Of the Marabar Hills and Caves, the most important characteristics are that they are "flesh of the sun's flesh"; that "nothing, nothing attaches to them," that is, that they are without attributes; that they reflect, either as a mirror or as an echo, all the light and sound which touches their surface; and that that echo is spoken of sometimes in the image of a serpent, sometimes as a snake, and sometimes as an "undying worm."

"Nothing, nothing attaches to them." We remember that Godbole attempted to describe the caves at Fielding's tea-party but discovered that he could predicate no attributes of them. "Neti, neti," the Hindus say of their conception of deity, "I know not, I know not," for to predicate attributes of deity is to limit him and the Hindu deity extends universally comprehending all that exists. "All that exists" is embraced in the terms of Indian philosophy by Atman and Brahman, the Self and the Not-Self. But Atman and Brahman are not truly distinct; rather they are parted by Maya, the veil of illusion, and when the mystical release comes, whether from the discipline of sacrifice or knowledge or love, Maya is dissipated and Atman and Brahman, the Self and the Not-Self, are seen to be one. With the release, all distinction, all individuation ceases to exist. Thus Mrs. Moore, dejected by her experience in the cave, could reflect: "Pathos, piety, courage—they exist, but are identical, and so is filth. Everything exists, nothing has value."

The *Upanishads,* which are the sacred philosophical scriptures of Hinduism, contain the basic revelations of this doctrine. In them we find fairly frequent reference to Brahman and Atman as "in the cave." In the *Katha-Upanishad,* for instance, Yama, the teacher, says to his pupil, Nakiketas: "The wise who, by means of meditation on his Self, recognizes the Ancient, who is difficult to be seen, who has entered into the dark, who is hidden in the cave, who dwells in the abyss, as God, he indeed leaves joy and sorrow far behind." Again, in the same Upanishad, the teacher says: "There are the two, drinking their reward in the world of their own works, entered into the cave . . . dwelling on the highest summit. Those who know Brahman call them shade and light." Atman and Brahman, the Self and the Not-Self, which are truly identical, dwell in the cave on the highest summit.

The relation between Atman and Brahman is ultimately a mystical one, not truly to be understood except intuitively on the occasion of release. However, one of the imaged relationships specified in the *Vedanta-Sutras* which approximates that relationship is that of the snake to its coils. As it is explained by Shankara in his commentary: "We therefore look on the relation of the highest Self and the soul as analogous to that of the snake and its coils. Viewed as a whole the snake is one, non-different, while an element of difference appears if we view it with regard to its coils, hood, erect posture, and so on." The import of the snake symbol, then, is the equivalent of the cave symbol itself—the ultimate identity of Brahman and Atman.

The echo which assaulted the ears of Adela and Mrs. Moore also has its counterpart in Hindu scriptures and religious practice. Forster writes the echo as "Boum" or "ou-boum," but there is little phonetic difference between it and the mystic syllable, *Om.* The pronunciation of and meditation upon this syllable is a very important part of the discipline of those seeking Brahman. In the *Prasna-Upanishad,* we find this discipline prescribed for meditation upon the syllable *Om:* "The syllable Om (AUM) is the highest and also the other Brahman; therefore he who knows it arrives by the same means at one of the two. . . . He who meditates with this syllable AUM of three Matras, on the Highest Person, he comes to light and to the sun. And as a snake is freed from its skin, so is he freed from evil. . . . He learns to see the all-pervading, the Highest Person."

These few passages from Hindu scriptures will suggest what Forster has in mind in the symbols of cave, echo, and snake. What of light, the match struck within the cave?

> The visitor arrives for his five minutes and strikes a match. Immediately another flame rises in the depths of the rock and moves towards the surface like an imprisoned spirit: the walls of the circular chamber have been most marvelously polished. The two flames approach and strive to unite, but cannot, because one of them breathes air, the other stone. A mirror inlaid with lovely colours divides the lovers, delicate stars of pink and grey interpose, exquisite nebulae, shadings fainter than the tail of a comet or the midday moon, all the evanescent life of the granite, only here visible. . . . The radiance increases, the flames touch one another, kiss, expire. The cave is dark again, like all other caves.

Surely this is one of the most exquisite images ever put into words. It is even more remarkable for the abstruse thought it expresses. The light and sun imagery in Hindu philosophy is associated with intelligence even as it is in the West. Forster here is pointing to the inadequacy of intelligence or reason in its effort to discover within the limits of its categories the ultimate nature of the universe. The concept of time implies the irrational idea of eternity; the concept of space implies the irrational idea of infinity of space; the concept of causality implies an infinite regress in the concatenation of causes and their effects. The flames touch, kiss, expire, and light is followed by darkness. Elsewhere, Forster uses again the image of the match to illustrate a philosophical subtlety. "Even the striking of a match starts a little worm coiling, which is too small to complete a circle but is eternally watchful." His purpose here is similar to that which I have explained above: Even the smallest glimmer of intelligence implies a total conception of the universe. The coil of the serpent implies the whole serpent; the concept of time implies the irrational concept of eternity. It is these limitations of reason which support the monistic idealism characteristic of Hindu philosophy and which lead its interpreters to the point of view that all philosophy is ultimately a critique of mind.

In addition to Hindu scriptures, Forster's symbolism has still another source of significance in the work of the western philosopher, Schopenhauer. Though greatly separated in time and in cultural background, the system of Schopenhauer has a great deal in common with the philosophic teachings of the *Upanishads*. Thus, though these sources may at first seem widely disparate, they are in fact almost of one piece and one moves readily from one source to the other in interpretation. The principal difference between the metaphysics of Schopenhauer and Shankara, the great Hindu enlightener, is that the ultimate monism of the former lies in that single substance, the blindly striving will, while that of the latter is a monism in which no qualities can be attributed to ultimate being. On the other hand, Schopenhauer specifically states that an equation exists between his *principium individuationis* and the Hindu Veil of Maya such that the categories of space, time, cause and the like occupy the same position in his thought as in the thought of Shankara.

A Passage to India contains one direct allusion to Schopenhauer in the mention of "the world of dreams—that world in which a third of each man's life is spent, and *which is thought by some pessimists to be a premonition of eternity.*" Indirect allusions are frequent: Schopenhauer's work provides the explanatory context for Mrs. Moore's game of Patience; for the mirror-like quality of the interior of the caves and such phrases as "the mirror of the scenery was shattered"; and the frequently echoed phrase, "Before time, it was before space also," which may be regarded as referring to the will as a thing-in-itself logically prior to the *principium individuationis*. The phrase, "undying worm," though taken from the New Testament, nonetheless alludes indirectly to Schopenhauer's blindly striving will.

More important, however, than these occasional allusions is the light that Schopenhauer's work throws on the meaning of the major symbols—the Marabar Hills, the caves, and the sun. On at least three occasions Forster speaks of the "fists and fingers" of the Marabar Hills. According to Schopenhauer, "The parts of the body . . . completely correspond to the principal desires through which the will manifests itself; they must be the visible expression of these desires. Teeth, throat, and bowels are objectified hunger; the organs of generation are objectified sexual desire; the grasping hand, the hurrying feet, correspond to the more indirect desires of the will which they express." There is perhaps an intended phallus in the Marabar symbol, but surely Forster, in speaking of the "fists and fingers" of the Marabar Hills, is representing the intellect as under the service of the will—knowledge as power and

power expressed as the desire to possess. The symbol of the sun bears out this contention. It is represented to us in two aspects—as the source of light and as the source of heat. In the former aspect, it has its usual identification with intelligence; in the latter, it is represented as will and power. "Strength comes from the sun," we learn at the opening of the book, and "Caves," which is concerned principally with the western attitude, the way of knowledge, shows us a malignant sun, "with power but without beauty . . . through excess of light" failing to triumph, a "treacherous sun," "insanely ugly." According to Schopenhauer, "As man is at once impetuous and blind striving of will (whose pole or focus lies in the genital organs), and eternal, free, serene subject of pure knowing (whose pole is the brain); so, corresponding to this antithesis, the sun is both a source of *light,* the condition of the most perfect kind of knowledge, and therefore of the most delightful of things—and the source of *warmth,* the first condition of life, i.e., of all phenomena of will in its higher grades. Therefore, what warmth is for the will, light is for knowledge."

Like Schopenhauer, Forster, too, is forever reminding us of the insignificance of human endeavor. His reminders take the form of an observation on the vastness of the universe which stretches arch beyond arch into the blue infinity of space; or he observes how tenuously held is the human empire against the burgeoning nature which surrounds it. Again, he sees his characters from a gigantic perspective as "dwarfs shaking hands," or he shows their trivial bickerings in contrast to the supreme indifference of the beautiful punkah wallah who has not been touched by moral or intellectual enlightenment. But what if man, by some desperate contortion of mind, should reduce the universe to the scale of his own thoughts? The world might indeed be his idea, but the consequence of this effort would remain the same; the Marabar "robbed infinity and eternity of their vastness, the only quality that accommodates them to mankind." The universe, so reduced, would no longer eclipse the human being; but the human being, in turn, for being everything, would, as a result, be nothing. This is "the twilight of the double vision," a "state where the horror of the universe and its smallness are both visible at the same time."

With this introduction to the significance of the Marabar Hills and related symbols, we are prepared to study the events which took place there and discover their meaning. Mrs. Moore and Adela both wished to "see India"; their efforts to do so had their first promise of success at Fielding's tea party, but the intimation that it would be strange and unpleasant came at the same time in Professor Godbole's song. Both Adela and Mrs. Moore traced their uneasiness to this beginning. Godbole had called upon Krishna to come to him, but in spite of the ardor of his prayer, he "neglects to come." Mrs. Moore suggested hopefully that he "comes in some other song," but is assured that he does not. This song and its token, "come, come, come," runs like a thread through the entire novel; it is connected, on the one hand, with the formlessness, the muddle of India, the India which is "not a promise, only an appeal," and, on the other, with the natural repugnance of western intellectuality toward what is formless, what is not infused with order and purpose.

Although Adela and Mrs. Moore are very different in temperament, they are both expressions of western intellectuality in that they both demand that orderly and purposeful conception of the universe. Mrs. Moore, a Christian, demands a universe supported and justified by a divine being who is the promise of righteousness and of ultimate reward for good works. It is in this respect that Mrs. Moore shares with the others of the western group a commitment to the way of knowledge. Adela, like the liberal, Fielding, is skeptical, agnostic in her religious views, but, though she does not affirm or deny deity, she nevertheless refuses to believe that the categories in which she conceives of the spatio-temporal world are not sufficient to her needs. Every problem for Adela is "something more to think out." Whether the western attitude is shown through the temperament of a Mrs. Moore or an Adela, it is in either case distinctly at odds with that of the Orient which accepts from the beginning the inadequacy of the intellect, under what Schopenhauer would call the principles of sufficient reason, to approach a conception of deity. The mind, in order to perform its functions, must necessarily identify, individuate, and force into a causal pattern all the events which come before it, but the mystical conception of deity occurs only with the disintegration of these categories. The experience of the caves thrusts upon these western women the inadequacy of the Christian and the intellectual points of view.

What did in fact happen in the caves? In treating this question we must recognize that there are two answers—one natural, and one supernatural—just as there are two answers to the question of what caused the strange automobile accident. It is characteristic of Forster to portray incidents from two points of view and it is this double perspective (or, as he refers to this trait in Mrs. Moore, "double vision") which has been the source of a great deal of confusion in the interpretation of his novel. When we ask the question, "What did in fact happen in the caves?" we are asking for a naturalistic explanation, because we are puzzled that a nice girl like Adela could so malign a decent fellow like Aziz. Forster does give us such a naturalistic explanation, though he deliberately subordinates it in two dependent clauses. Mrs. Moore and Adela, prior to the visit to the caves, have had somewhat similar experiences and have reacted similarly. They both wished to see India, though they have gone about it in their different ways. They both attended Fielding's party, and both were subtly affected by Godbole's song. At the Marabar, both were strangely stricken by their experiences in caves. Even as Adela is approaching the cave in which the assault is alleged to have occurred, Mrs. Moore is at the base of the summit meditating peevishly on her experience. "She tried to go on with her letter, reminding herself that she was only an elderly woman who had got up too early in the morning and journeyed too far, that the despair creeping over her was only her despair, her personal weakness, and that *even if she got a sunstroke and went mad,* the rest of the world would go on." In the next paragraph, we pick up Adela and Aziz ascending the summit of Kawa Dol and are reminded that "the sun was getting high. The air

felt like a warm bath into which hotter water is trickling constantly, the temperature rose and rose, the boulders said, 'I am alive,' and small stones answered, 'I am almost alive.' Between the chinks lay the ashes of little plants." And in the following paragraph we learn that Adela's mind was "blurred by the heat." Surely, if we demand a naturalistic explanation, we may accept this invitation to infer that Adela, upon entering the close confines of that last cave, "got a sunstroke and went mad," and that her impression that someone had attacked her was hallucinatory. Later on we find a confirmation of this hypothesis coming from the disinterested Professor Godbole. "Suffering," he points out to Fielding with meticulous care, "is merely a matter for the individual. *If a young lady has sunstroke, that is a matter of no significance to the universe.*"

On the other hand is the supernatural explanation of the incident partaking of the symbolical significance of the caves. Adela enters her cave with the problem of love and marriage on her mind. Love is for her "something to think out" and the declaration of having discovered an answer is marriage. What assails her in the cave, however, is beyond thinking out, and her false charge against Aziz is witness to the inadequacy of her means to do so. She had a terrifying experience, hallucinatory to be sure, but nevertheless terrifying. Her only recourse, within the limitations of her mode of behavior, was to eliminate the terror by trying to understand. The intellect took over; the causal pattern was imposed; and Aziz was arrested and brought to trial. Adela was some time recovering. There was the sunstroke, the shock, the cactus needles she had picked up in her precipitous descent of Kawa Dol: "She lay passive beneath their fingers, which developed the shock that had begun in the cave. Hitherto she had not much minded whether she was touched or not: her senses were abnormally inert and *the only contact she anticipated was that of mind.* . . . 'In space things touch, in time things part,' she repeated to herself while the thorns were being extracted—her brain was so weak that she could not decide whether the phrase was a philosophy or a pun." Adela was awakening from her experience of contact with an immaterial world and convincing herself of the consequences of living in a world of space and time.

Although she manages the physical recovery, Adela retains ringing in her ears the echo of the caves, and she will not be rid of it until she has withdrawn her charge against Aziz. We see this foreshadowed in Professor Godbole's parable of the Tank of the Dagger. Just as the rajah cannot rid himself of the dagger with which he had murdered his nephew until he has offered water to the cow, so Adela cannot rid herself of the echo until she recognizes the common being of humanity by defaulting on her accusation. However, her own reason and the evidence of the prosecution have justified the false accusation, and thus, in order to make her default honest, she must transcend the sphere of reason. She does so in a vision in which she is released from the limitations of the self, the principle of individuation: "She didn't think what had happened or even remember in the ordinary way of memory, but she returned to the Marabar Hills, and spoke from them across a sort of darkness to Mr. McBride. The fatal day recurred in every detail, but now she was of it and not of it at the same time, and this double relation gave it indescribable splendour." That evening Adela could report to Fielding, "My echo has gone." But neither she nor Fielding was ever able to understand what had really happened at the Marabar. Such things transcend rational explanation, and rational explanation was all that she and Fielding could accept.

Although Adela's experience in the cave carries the story, that of Mrs. Moore is more complex and more important. Her heightened sensitivity allowed her to grasp what was denied to Adela, and though her vision was not a total one, she captured the essential meaning of the caves. She was not able to explain that meaning to Adela any more than Professor Godbole could describe the caves for Aziz, for the meaning of such an experience transcends the principle of individuation and hence defies all attempts to conceptualize it. Moreover, Mrs. Moore was not the kind to fret over explanations; the experience did not touch her intellect, but her soul, her sense of values. "Suddenly at the edge of her mind, Religion appeared, poor little talkative Christianity, and she knew that all its divine words from 'Let there be light' to 'It is finished' only amounted to 'boum'. Then she was terrified over an area larger than usual; the universe, never comprehensible to her intellect, offered no repose to her soul, the mood of the last two months took definite form at last."

Mrs. Moore, on her arrival, had been immediately attracted to India "with its cool nights and acceptable hints of infinity." "To be one with the universe. So dignified and simple." She had not calculated the costs of this union. For her India was a mystery, inscrutable perhaps, but certainly not confused, disorderly, purposeless. And Mrs. Moore liked mysteries; in this she differed from the clear-headed Fielding and Adela. "I do so hate mysteries," said Adela, and Mrs. Moore replied, "I like mysteries, but I rather dislike muddles." "A mystery is only a high-sounding term for a muddle," Fielding declared. "India's a muddle." And Mrs. Moore, unsettled by Fielding's statement, expressed her uneasiness: "India's—Oh, what an alarming idea!" Fielding's statement was shortly thereafter borne in upon her by Godbole's song. To her plaintive question, Godbole replied assuredly that Krishna never does come, and to Mrs. Moore this meant that that state of perfection called Heaven which Christianity shrouds in mystery and promises as a reward for good works is always becoming, never being. In this sense, India is an appeal, not a promise. At once, the justification of moral purpose was undermined. Mrs. Moore grew peevish; her duties became onerous. She had hoped for a glorious union of mankind through love, and her contribution to that endeavor, she felt, lay in assisting the marriage of her children. But Godbole had suggested to her what she was to find confirmed in her experience in the caves— that the costs of being "one with the universe" are the loss of a transcendent sanction for values, the loss of absolute distinctions between good and evil, the loss of that ultimate reward for good works which made her accept duties as bearable, and, finally, the loss of that sublime emotion which comes from contemplating God in the infinitudes.

Such costs were too great. In the cave, the echo spoke out to her of the oneness of all things; it revealed itself to her

as a serpent, the universal will, composed (under the principle of individuation) of a manifold of wills, writhing independently, struggling against each other. From that moment forward, she lost all desire for ultimate union; she lost interest in her "duties" to her children; she conceived of life as a game of Patience, always another card to turn, another duty to be done, with no final consummation. The individual will had reasserted itself in her. "What had spoken to her in that scoured-out cavity of the granite? What dwelt in the first of the caves? Something very old and small. Before time, it was before space also. Something snub-nosed, incapable of generosity—the undying worm itself."

But Mrs. Moore's vision, Forster suggests, was not a complete one. As she left Central India on the way to Bombay, there passed before her eyes the fortress at Asirgarh which ten minutes later reappeared seeming to say, "I do not vanish." Here is a kind of permanence not touched by the vision of the caves. And when she set sail "thousands of coconut palms appeared all round the anchorage and climbed the hills to wave her farewell. 'So you thought an echo was India; you took the Marabar caves as final?' they laughed. 'What have we in common with them, or they with Asirgarh? Good-bye!' "

Forster's handling of Mrs. Moore is characteristic. As with Adela, with Fielding, with Aziz and Godbole, there is something in her nature which he affirms; but in none of these instances does he affirm without qualification. Thus, if *A Passage to India* may be said to have a theme, may be said to express symbolically some predication about the way life is or ought to be, we cannot expect to find that expression in the person of any of his characters. Nor may we expect to find it by generalizing the outcome of action in the story, for nothing is so apparent as the absence of complete resolution of dramatic conflict. We must, in fact, look beyond the single character and beyond the story itself for the theme, for neither Forster's conception of the form of the novel nor his view of the human predicament allows him to permit a single character or a single element of the novel to pronounce the whole of his theme. Life and the novel are more complex than that, and the novel as a representation of life must speak through all its parts. "Expansion," Forster says of the form of the novel, "that is the idea the novelist must cling to. Not completion. Not rounding off but opening out." Nor is the complete resolution of the conflicts which comprise the plot consistent with his view of life. "The business man who assumes that this life is everything, and the mystic who asserts that it is nothing, fail, on this side and on that, to hit the truth. . . . Truth being alive [is] not halfway between anything. It [is] only to be found by continuous excursions into either realm, and though proportion is the final secret, to espouse it at the outset is to insure sterility."

Critics writing on *A Passage to India* have unconsciously deferred to Forster's philosophy of the novel by failing to show anything like unanimity of opinion on its theme. Gertrude M. White would seem to imply that the novel is an espousal of the Hindu religion. Peter Burra declares that "the real theme of the book" is the "friendship of Fielding and Aziz." Rose Macaulay finds the "moral" of the book in the criticism of "the legions of ought and ought not." Some critics find a multiplicity of themes. E. B. C. Jones discovers three, while Lionel Trilling mentions at least half a dozen, perhaps eight. Strangely, in spite of the lack of agreement, none of these conclusions is wholly insupportable. They fail for not being sufficiently comprehensive. It is owing to its comprehensiveness that the statement of Morton D. Zabel, though it was made of Forster's novels in general, seems the most applicable of them all to *A Passage to India.* Forster, he says, "made his object the search for the wholeness of truth; the synthesis of matter and essence, of civilization with its inhibitions and nature with its blind energy, of the fragments and denials on which life is commonly founded and the total vision of reality that man's sloth or cowardice forbids him to unveil." But we must particularize this statement somewhat before it will become significant with respect to *A Passage to India.*

In "Temple" as in "Caves" the dominant symbolism is drawn from the landscape. On the hill overlooking the tank at Mau stands a fortress from which centuries earlier a Mohammedan saint had released prisoners, but, in doing so, had lost his own head. As Forster reports the legend, his head had been severed at the top of the hill, but, disregarding its absence, he had fought his way back to the bottom to report his feat to his mother. This heroic fight had necessitated the erection of two shrines—the Shrine of the Head and the Shrine of the Body. This divided shrine and consequent divided allegiance, Forster implies, is the awkward dichotomy with which the varying plans of salvation by religion have left us—the mutual exclusion of mind and body, spirit and flesh. In effect this description of the physical scene is a restatement of the conflict which has evolved in "Mosque" and "Caves." The Way of Works which we have identified with "Mosque" and its principal character, Aziz, is associated with the Shrine of the Body which stands in Aziz's garden. The Way of Knowledge, which we have identified with "Caves" and the western protagonists, is associated with the Shrine of the Head and its infestation of bees which attack Fielding and Ralph. At the foot of the hill lies the third element of symbolism—the tank at Mau where the ceremony connected with the birth of Krishna is to take place. Needless to say, we have here represented the Hindu factor and the Way of Love, associated throughout the novel with Godbole and, by implication, with his western counterpart, Mrs. Moore.

Over this scene hang the heavy clouds of the monsoon, intermittently wetting the earth, but through them, occasionally, "the friendly sun of the monsoons shone forth and flooded the world with color." These are the symbols of life and fertility, and it is under their influence that the reunion of Aziz and Fielding will take place. The principal event of the long ceremony, the event to which all of the characters will be drawn, is the drowning of the village of Gokul, birthplace of Shri Krishna. Here in the midst of wind and rain, the confusion of crowds, the trumpeting of elephants, the sounding of artillery, thunder and lightning, the boats containing Aziz and Ralph, Fielding and Stella, will collide, upset, dumping them ignominiously into the tank. "That was the Climax," Forster observes, "as far as India admits of one." The fusion of the three

ways of life—mosque, caves, and temple—comes to pass in the tank at Mau. Fielding and Aziz, British and Indian, are brought together (though not completely united) under the influence of the Hindu Way of Love.

As Forster moves from mosque to cave and from cave to temple, from the Way of Works to the Way of Knowledge and the Way of Love, his acquiescence is always tentative. We hear the judgment—made quietly and more in the comic spirit than with compassion—"yes, but. . . ." Each of these ways of salvation has something to offer to the whole life, but each also contains the defects of its qualities. Aziz, whom we have taken as representative of the Way of Works, is made charming by his volatile affections, but he is also victimized by the very emotional traits which we find most winning. We see also, and even more distinctly, the limitations of the purely intellectual attitude, the Way of Knowledge, as it is represented, for instance, in Fielding. For all of his well-meaning liberalism, there is something lacking in his nature, something the intelligence cannot supply. "After forty years' experience, he had learnt to manage his life and make the most of it on advanced European lines, had developed his personality, explored his limitations, controlled his passions—and he had done it all without becoming either pedantic or worldly. A creditable achievement, but as the moment passed, he felt he ought to have been working at something else the whole time—he didn't know at what, never would know, never could know, and that was why he felt sad." The moment referred to was the advance of the Marabar Hills moving "graciously towards him like a queen" in the evening sky. This was Fielding's opportunity for mystic vision, missed on this occasion and again thereafter when "he lost his usual sane view of human intercourse, and felt that we exist not in ourselves, but in terms of each others' minds—a notion for which logic offers no support and which had attacked him only once before, the evening after the catastrophe, when from the verandah of the club he saw the fists and fingers of the Marabar swell until they included the whole night sky." "Clarity," we are told, "prevented him from experiencing something else."

Unlike Fielding and Adela, who were blinded by their own clarity of thought, Mrs. Moore achieved full recognition of her failure. "I think everyone fails," she said early in the novel, "but there are so many kinds of failure." And having undergone her experience in the caves, she concluded, "There are different ways of evil and I prefer mine to yours." In short, the Way of Knowledge, whether it be of the sort belonging to Fielding and Adela or that belonging to Mrs. Moore, is not enough: "Though the intellect is our best friend," Forster wrote in his biography of G. Lowes Dickinson, "there are regions whither it cannot guide us."

In the Way of Love, represented in Hindu ceremonies attending the birth of Shri Krishna, Forster again finds inadequacies. Here is no beauty, no taste, no sense of the appropriate; the entire ceremony is a muddle, a frustration of reason and form. Love is a good, Forster seems to say, but not in its extreme nor to the exclusion of all other goods. The final friendship of the protagonists, like "the God to be thrown," is but an emblem of passage, "*a pas-*

sage not easy, not now, not here, not to be apprehended except when it is unattainable." Passage is the mystical return which can occur only with complete renunciation of
the will and utter loss of individuality in union with the
whole. Such renunciation and loss is the equivalent of
death. Forster does not propose this unhappy extreme:
"There was death in the air, but not sadness; a compromise had been made between destiny and desire, and even
the heart of man acquiesced." Intimations of passage had
occurred to Adela, to Mrs. Moore, to Aziz, and to Fielding himself, but in each instance the experience was momentary, and, to all, ultimately uncongenial. Like the Way
of Works and the Way of Knowledge, the Way of Love
has its repugnant extreme. And thus, as the novel ends,
Fielding and Aziz, whose friendship had been reborn in
the tank at Mau, are preserved from consummate union
as the hundred voices of the earth speak out and say, "No,
not yet" (not in time), and the sky says, "No, not here"
(not in space).

Does the novel contain a statement of theme? With all its
negations, does it yet affirm some unequivocal truth about
the way life is or ought to be? Indeed it does. "Proportion
is the final secret," Forster had observed in *Howards End.*
Works, knowledge, love—these are the ingredients of the
good life, but no one of them is to be affirmed to the exclusion of the others. Nor can that proportion be realized except as the product of vital activity. "Truth being alive [is]
not half way between anything." Thus it is only when Fielding is passing through "that exquisite lake" between the
extremes of India and England that we learn that "the
Mediterranean is the human norm," for here is exemplified "the harmony between the works of man and the
earth that upholds them, the civilization that has escaped
muddle, the spirit in reasonable form, with flesh and blood
subsisting." (pp. 121-41)

> Glen O. Allen, "Structure, Symbol, and
> Theme in E. M. Forster's 'A Passage to
> India'," in Perspectives on E. M. Forster's "A
> Passage to India:" A Collection of Critical Es-
> says, edited by V. A. Shahane, Barnes &
> Noble, Inc., 1968, pp. 121-41.

Michael Spencer   (essay date February 1968)

[In the following essay, Spencer claims that the double
vision between the "transient and transcendent" that
other critics have noted in A Passage to India is the result of Forster's borrowings from Hinduism.]

Hinduism permeates *A Passage To India.* While recognizing this fact, none of the critics have so far displayed an
understanding of Hinduism which is adequate for the
analysis of this novel. The type of Hinduism which has
been popularized in the West, that of Vedantic philosophy, has been stressed in their studies. Further pursuit of
this critical task will show unmistakably that Hinduism of
an entirely different kind pervades the novel.

Before dealing with this matter it is necessary to consider
the following three related questions: Was Forster's
knowledge of this religion more than superficial? Is the religion very important in the purpose of the novel or is it
more a part of the cultural pattern which forms the background of the lives of the characters? Is Mohammedanism
actually more important to the novel than Hinduism, in
view of the fact that Aziz is more central in the story than
any Hindu?

Concerning the quality of Forster's knowledge of the religion, any illusion on this matter should be dispelled by
reading *The Hill of Devi,* a book of collected letters which
are packed with the novelist's perceptions of the Indian
scene, He had shown in an early short story, **"Mr. An-
drews,"** an interest in Hindu belief. In *The Hill of Devi*
we watch his interest and knowledge grow during his two
visits to India. We see him speaking enthusiastically about
the literature of Hinduism, learn of his discussions with
the Maharajah about religion, and hear of his participation in the Festival of Krishna's birth, perhaps something
no European had done in Dewas before him.

This study will attempt to answer the second question.
Hinduism, it will be clear, is fused into the development
of the plot and it determines the character of at least one
important figure in the novel. It can be seen to be involved
in his purposes and his use of symbols in the book. Certainly, the very skies of India call out for some sort of resolution to the religious problems that have plagued man
through the ages. "Outside the arch there seemed always
an arch, beyond the remotest echo a silence." The reason
for Forster's increasing concern with such questions since
his preceding novel, published fourteen years before, is
partly accounted for by comments made in the novel that
it is difficult to resist the supernatural as one grows older.

The third question asks whether or not the place of Aziz
in the novel gives Hinduism more of a central place in its
scheme than to the other religion. Forster's comment in
The Hill of Devi that he admired the superiority of the
form of Mohammedanism to Hinduism has often been
cited in order to suggest this. However, to turn to the
novel itself—the best method of dealing with such an
issue—we can see Mohammedanism dismissed with the
comment that it, like Christianity, does not penetrate very
far into the mysteries of reality. At one place in the book
we are shown Fielding thinking about the echo in the
Marabar Caves and then we are told that "it belonged to
the universe that he had missed or rejected. And the
mosque missed it too. . . . 'There is no God but God'
doesn't carry us far through the complexities of matter
and spirit; it is only a game with words, really, a religious
pun, not a religious truth." Apparently, Mohammedanism has a purely cultural importance in the novel.

Why does the echo in the caves have the influence it has
on Mrs. Moore? What does it represent? Obviously, the
meaning of the caves incident is very complex and rich;
no attempt will be made here to propose a complete solution to these questions. However, while the implications
in their meaning are complex, it does seem clear that the
response they evoke can be linked to the perspective of a
particular type of religious world-view.

Imagery foreshadowing the events which occur in the
caves helps define the nature of the experience. As the expedition Aziz has organized approaches the Marabar

Hills, for some mysterious reason everything around it seems to begin to lose its solidity. "Everything seemed cut off at its root, and therefore infected with illusion." Imagery of light and darkness is used in a very suggestive way. These antithetical qualities are fused into a borderland state: the train approaches the caves in "timeless twilight," the sun hangs somewhere about the horizon, seeming to rise in a false dawn, Mrs. Moore has a "twilight" vision. In the caves the darkness overwhelms the two Englishwomen and they panic. These colors, most clearly the darkness of the caves, suggest the antithetical qualities of good and evil. However, Forster resolves their duality—he fuses the two into a single condition until the darkness triumphs and then evil spreads like a disease beyond control through the lives of both native and Anglo-Indian communities in Chandrapore. As will be seen at a later point in this paper, this blending of dualities into a single condition and the symbolic equilibrium of good and evil expresses conceptions which have an important place in Hindu belief.

As Godbole had said, there is something about the caves which is very strange. The caves seem to swallow up all of Mrs. Moore's efforts to think. What does she feel after she hears the echo? " 'Boum' is the sound as far as the human alphabet can express it, or 'bou-oum,' or 'ou-boum.' . . . the striking of a match starts a little . . . worm coiling, which is too small to complete a circle, but is eternally watchful." The sound "had managed to murmur . . . 'Pathos, piety, courage—they exist, but are identical, and so is filth. Everything exists, nothing has value' . . . no one could romanticize the Marabar because it robbed infinity and eternity of their vastness, the only quality that accommodates them to mankind. Suddenly, at the edge of her mind, Religion appeared, poor little talkative Christianity, and she knew that all its divine words from 'Let there be Light' to 'It is finished' only amounted to 'boum.' " And then later, when the impact of the caves has sunk further in: "She had come to that state where the horror of the universe and its smallness are both visible at the same time—the twilight of the double vision in which so many elderly people are involved. If this world is not to our taste, well, at all events, there is Heaven, Hell, Annihilation. In the twilight of the double vision, a spiritual muddledom is set up for which no high-sounding words can be found; we can neither ignore nor respect Infinity." The thought of Adela's having been assaulted there enters her mind and "The unspeakable attempt presented itself to her as love: in a cave, in a church—Boum, it amounts to the same."

The double vision is the vision of both the transcendent and the more limited reality of our environment. Perhaps Forster here remembers a deceptively simple line of Blake's: "May God us keep / From single vision and Newton's sleep," which he later quotes in "Prophecy," in the section of *Aspects of the Novel* which also warns us against having a limited vision. This vision of the transcendent gives an insight into a realm of the infinite beyond human imagining: not into eternity, not into any other conception which bears the suggestion of the limitations of space and time (as he points out when he tells us that the caves rob infinity and eternity of their vastness), but

rather into infinity. The reality of a totally transcendent state of being which spurns the limitations of the world in which we live and act is here suggested.

Embodied in this experience are attitudes important to certain of the Eastern religions. Action, no matter how virtuous, can lead us only to another reincarnation in the illusory world of time and space in which we presently exist. Good action will lead us to a higher reincarnation, evil action to a lower one, neither to freedom from time and space. To be liberated from the inevitability of an infinite series of lives, in which we will be doomed to live and die endlessly, over and over, we must escape in one way or another from action altogether. In the novel, the categories of time fade away into meaninglessness, the idea of the beginnings and the endings of things, "Let there be Light" and "It is finished" is seen with horrified contempt. All distinctions are eliminated—filth and beauty are identical. Heaven, Hell, and Annihilation, conceptions which have been used to expand the belief in the importance of human action to a cosmic scope, are reduced to triviality. Heaven and Hell themselves are the fruits of action, whether good or evil, and along with our lives are unimportant. If this is the experience, it is not surprising that Mrs. Moore, like Adela, is driven into a panic, into wild confusion. Life becomes so insignificant in her eyes that she renounces all action altogether. The impact of the experience is all the greater on Mrs. Moore, we are told, because she was getting old. But perhaps also the fault lies in the fact that she is a Westerner. Certainly, the Anglo-Indians are all marked by their concern for the more practical issues of life, in contrast with the Indians who are more concerned with a realm beyond matter. The novelist further suggests with his use of the terms "Let there be light" and "It is finished" that Western religions have magnified this fault.

In Forster's earlier fiction he glories in the Pans and the Stephen Wonhams of this world, in creatures in the most fundamental connection with the earth. Had Forster changed drastically before he wrote this novel? Evidently, he had not. The caves are the source, not of some inspiring insight, but of great evil. They are the central event in the second portion of the novel, the Hot Season. The terrific heat of the sun destroys and kills. Mrs. Moore dies from it. It is the heat, it might be said, not of purgation, but of hell. Forster indicated that the caves had perverted the double vision. They express his ideal vision "with its back turned." Mrs. Moore had been life affirming, the image of an ideal woman. Suddenly she saw the other half of the double vision with shattering forcefulness. She is caught, bewildered, between life and the infinite and then entirely and disastrously by the second.

The monistic strain of oriental belief teaches that everything is a part of a Supreme existence, that the world of our environment is entirely illusion or delusion. And so Mrs. Moore speaks of people as being only a part of a dream. She cares little for what happens to others—it is of no concern to her if her son's fiancée was attacked in the caves or not. She does not try to save Aziz by speaking to Adela although she knows he is innocent. In Hinduism, the monistic approach to reality is represented primarily by Vedantic philosophy, where everything is a part of Brahman, an impersonal God without any qualifying attributes capable of making Him conceivable to the mind. But when the caves are named in the trial scene, it is not Hinduism which is associated with them. "In which cave is the offense alleged, the Buddhist or the Jain?" . . . "All the Marabar Caves are Jain." Buddhism is less optimistic about the value of our lives than Hinduism. Jainism is far more pessimistic yet. To the Jain ascetic the greatest and most noble of acts is the renunciation of life by committing suicide. The Jain feels that only by continual self-renunciation can one escape from the bonds of a life whose unpleasantness is only partly explained by the fact that one is alive. The sound "om" which Forster has the echo play with means a variety of things to the Hindus, but to Buddhist and Jain it means Brahman.

Does Forster actually favor the belief in such a monistic God? The sound in the cave suggests this. Obviously, Mrs. Moore thought little and undoubtedly she knew less about the religions of India and she could not be expected to know about such sacred sounds. It could not be simply a hallucination. However, the main religious stream which flows through the novel is alien to this belief and it is this the novel glorifies. The only certainty is that here Forster indicates a belief in a transcendent realm which in some way should be harmonized with the world which encompasses us.

Forster is a symbolist: a fact quite significant in particular for understanding many of his short stories and his last two novels. In his lecture on "Prophecy" which was made a part of *Aspects of the Novel*, Forster speaks of that which is derived from religion or felt so strongly that it is raised to the level of religious faith. This is that level of the double vision which infused power and meaning, he implies, into the pages of great novels. Prophecy expresses a meaning which cannot be spoken, but only sung. Similarly, the echo itself is unnameable: "Mrs. Moore, what is the echo?" "Don't you know? . . . If you don't know, you don't know; I can't tell you." Symbolism provides a meaning of rich and suggestive beauty. With such artists as Virginia Woolf or James Joyce the meaning of the superior reality is suggested with little attempt made to describe it. Forster does this also. The images used in symbolist literature are meant to open out on a transcendent, spiritual reality where there is unity. These tendencies greatly influence Forster's handling of religion in *A Passage To India* and are important not just in interpreting the caves incident, but his picture of the festival as well, the antithesis of the caves incident.

The festival is an uncomplicated ceremony, a re-enactment of the birth of Krishna, his life and his death. Krishna is the most popularly celebrated of the ten incarnations of Vishnu. To his sect, one of the two great ones in India, Vishnu is the Supreme God. In each of his ten incarnations Vishnu is born into the world in order to drive back the forces of evil, represented usually by demonic powers which threaten to overwhelm or to rule the earth. The festival reenacts certain popularly celebrated events in the life of Krishna. Regional differences prevent the festival from being similar everywhere in India, but

clearly we see this one celebrating his birth, the failure of King Kansa to take his life because of his escape into the cowherd tribe, Krishna's life as a child among the cow-herds when he was full of playful pranks such as his thefts of butter from the cowherd wives, and his sexual prowess with the cowherd women, who were overpowered by his irresistible charm. Then we see the joyous procession through the streets of the city after the god is carried out of the temple. The festival culminates when clay models of Krishna and other characters involved in the myth, placed on a model of the village where the god was born, are all carried out into the pond at Mau where they dissolve into the water. The ceremony continues many hours and is marked by an orgiastic confusion, filled with cries, music, dancing, gun-fire and chanting to Radha, shown here as Krishna's favorite wife, and to Tukaram, the greatest of the Maratha poet saints. The festival blends together the ludicrous (in celebration of Krishna's boyhood tricks we see a man placing butter on his forehead and waiting for it to slide down into his mouth), the trivial (as seen by the attention Godbole pays to a wasp), the joyful (the freeing of a prisoner), with the noble (the birth of the god), and much more into one ecstatic complexity of impressions of sight, sound and color, bodying out of the swirl of images.

The festival is the antithesis of the experience of the caves. It is the fruit of bhakti Hinduism. Bhakti means devotion. In Vedantic philosophy, for example, the goal is to fuse ourselves with an impersonal God. Bhakti is a theistic belief which calls for loving devotion to a personal God. In the caves, as a result of her vision of the infinite, Mrs. Moore ends believing that life is unimportant. The festival reflects the dualistic tendencies of the bhakti movement. In the tradition of which it is a part, the world is not maya, illusion. Our lives are important, action is meaningful. Krishna is incarnated into the world in order to drive back the forces of evil. In contrast with the type of life suggested by the caves, which causes Mrs. Moore to renounce action in the manner of Eastern asceticism, bhakti blends flesh and spirit. The festival itself celebrates the god's sexual feats as a cowherd youth. Tukaram, whose name is chanted in the ceremony, denounced asceticism in words which indicate the rigors of many of its adherents. "Some people tense their body uselessly for the sake of spiritual realization. They wear brown clothes; but a dog is also brown. They bear matted hair; but a dog also has got matted hair. They live in caves; but even rats live in caves." The festival, like the echo, encompasses the infinite, but the result on the participants is reversed. Instead of a rejection of the concerns of human action, the bhakti festival gives it purpose. Forster said at one time that the festival represents the same thing as the caves, but reversed. It is "turned inside out." Godbole is uninterested in the trip to the cave. One of the author's jokes in the novel is to have him delayed by his prayers until he misses the train. Because of its great inclusiveness, no part of life, even evil, as will be seen, fails to find its due place in the festival. The caves call out for renunciation rather than incorporation. In a passage which has become a favorite among the critics, Forster laughs at the inability of a Christian missionary of "advanced" attitudes to include a wasp adequately in his scheme of values. Godbole, dancing on the carpet before the statue of the god, exults in his love for the wasp. The Hindus see exclusion as a kind of sin, an overthrow of a condition we are obligated to sustain. Since to state them would be exclusive, because it would be to use definitions, the Hindus make a kind of poetry out of their beliefs. They can sing of God that "He is, was not, is not, was" without any concern whatsoever for the contradictions involved in the statement. Forster laughs at Aziz for falling asleep dreaming of the ninety-nine names of God neatly inscribed on the walls of the mosque. This desire to suggest rather than to state, which causes the Hindus to dislike the Western religions, one would think, would appeal forcibly to the symbolist tendencies in Forster's thinking.

A further and notable aspect of bhakti devotion is to be seen in its unconcern for the caste system, a social pattern which is the creature of orthodox Hinduism in India. The novel itself fails to deal in any detail with this aspect of Indian civilization. One would think that this was a factor which allowed Forster to deal with the bhakti movement as favorably as he did. The rajah himself refuses to sit in the temple enthroned, since it would be a blasphemy. In India the festival represents a complete overturning of the caste system, since everyone is mingled together in the act of worship, a condition which would never occur in the daily routine of the average Indian village.

The ceremony embodies the double vision. Even the aimless, as the playful, becomes an integral part of the ceremony. "By sacrificing good taste, this worship achieved what Christianity has shirked: the inclusion of merriment." This incredible mixture of all aspects of human existence mingles everything in wild confusion. In *Howard's End* Forster speaks of two groups of people, those who see life clearly and those who see it whole. The Anglo-Indians see things clearly. The Indians see them whole. The myth is suggestive rather than clearly defined in its meaning, the feature that makes myth so attractive to the Indian mind. Emotionally, the festival is as diffuse as a cloud. Men are blended together without regard for caste. Radha is metamorphosized from Krishna's mistress into his wife. God becomes an idol and participates in the ceremony. Godbole dances on the carpet, unconscious of his own existence, as the fragments of his experience merge together in his mind. Personality itself is extinguished. Distinctions dissolve away as the rain approaches and then pours down in a terrific storm. Two boats and a servitor with God on a tray collide in the water. English, Moslem and Hindu join and mingle amidst the confusion of the festival. Fielding's letters to Aziz, tokens of their estrangement, float away on the water.

The India of the novel is a place of great confusion and muddle. The festival itself is only a partly ordered chaos of events. Things do not fall into a pattern, one thing is mistaken for another, the truth cannot be guessed. Does a ghost strike a car? Is a snake actually only the projection of a log? Aziz mistakenly thinks Fielding has married Adela Quested. In the very center of the plot there is confusion. Adela believes she has been attacked by Aziz when she has not. We are never told what actually had happened. The novel is filled with ambiguities and suggestions. Disorder itself is intensified until it receives a cosmic universality. Perceiving this, we are meant to ask where meaning is to be found.

The English rank men and categorize everything according to a pre-determined pattern. They expect order to encompass everything. The Anglo-Indians, never the Indians, complain repeatedly about the muddle which encloses their lives in the novel. The Hindus have a more satisfactory perspective on experience: by their conception of an ideal unity of things, involving a transcendent realm which allows things to achieve union, they are able to find all of life meaningful. The Hindus see life wholly rather than partially and so chaos does not upset them. This fact is strikingly apparent in Godbole's case, as will be seen. The transitoriness of life, the uncontrollable and unpredictable flux of things to the Hindus of the novel is not unsettling. In his essay **"Art for Arts Sake,"** Forster states that there are two valid ways of ordering experience into a meaningful whole, through religion and through art. Forster, like his character Godbole, does not seek to unravel the meaning of a completely ordered world, nor does he suggest that there is any method of readily creating a pattern of existence for mankind in which confusion, suffering and error will be eliminated. In his essay he emphasizes his belief that order is an interior condition, a vital harmony evolved from within. Hinduism, obviously, provides one method of ordering human perceptions into a meaningful totality.

How does he look at the festival's central myth? Certainly, the festival is dealt with favorably. The myth is a belief handled with more sympathy than he has given to any other organized belief in his fiction. Religious myth has been used by many other contemporary European authors without an allegiance being given them as full as the Hindus in the novel give to theirs. However, such authors usually use mythology in an ironic criticism of contemporary civilization and its members. Forster uses it to show how the myth sustains the values of living men. Nevertheless, as might be anticipated, Forster is not concerned about the truth of the myth, about whether or not it reproduces in any way actual events, and the novel makes it clear that if the Hindus in the festival had gained some clear insight into ultimate reality, the experience quickly would become meaningless. " . . . The human spirit had tried by a desperate contortion to ravish the unknown. . . . Did it succeed? . . . How can it be expressed in anything but itself? Not only from the unbeliever are mysteries hid, but the adept himself cannot retain them. He may think, if he chooses, that he has been with God, but as soon as he thinks it, it becomes history, and falls under the rules of time." The novelist's attitude towards the myth, as well as towards the ceremony itself, is suggested by the fact that although Mrs. Moore's daughter, a woman in whom is to be rediscovered that great insight into life her mother had once shown, finds in the festival something very meaningful and helpful, she does not care about the religion's forms. Apparently, Forster could better describe what is not contained in the transcendent reality which subtly reveals its existence through the novel, than he could say what it is. Before he had written this novel he had rejected the claims of Christianity and its mysteries, and we have seen that the novel gently ridicules Mohammedanism and unsparingly assails oriental monism and asceticism. Now we see that Forster felt that even the Hindus were much too definite as to what that final reality actually was. Forster, it seems, takes a psychological approach to mythology. Its great inclusiveness, he indicates, its wisdom and innocence, before our eyes makes the lives of the Hindus who participate in its celebration seem very full. Myth can be very beautiful, it can give us confidence in the ultimate value of human experience. It can sustain us imaginatively and fulfill us emotionally. It can be a very rich and powerful influence, as it is to even the least educated of the Hindus in the ceremony.

In an incident recorded in *The Hill of Devi,* Forster was struck by the Maharajah's answer to the problem of evil. ". . . When I asked why we had any of us ever been severed from God he explained it by God becoming unconscious that we were parts of Him, owing to His energy at some time being concentrated elsewhere. 'So,' he said, 'A man who is thinking of something else may become unconscious of the existence of his own hand for a time' . . . Salvation, then is the thrill which we feel when God again becomes conscious of us . . . " Here the Western religious conception of providence is lacking, the belief that evil will be turned inevitably into good by the due course of events. Evil, the Hindus feel, is an integral part of existence and it is irredeemable. It can be overcome, but not transformed into good. In *Howard's End,* Forster describes the goblins, the embodiments of evil, being driven away, only to return again and again with unceasing vigor. Lionel Trilling has written of the novelist's conception of good-and-evil, in which one seems necessarily and inevitably associated with the other. Godbole, as a milkmaiden calling to Krishna, cries to the God who does not come. "Good and evil are different, as their names imply," Godbole tells Fielding later in the novel. But God "is present in the one, absent in the other. . . . Absence implies presence, absence is not non-existence, and we are therefore entitled to repeat, 'Come, come, come, come.' " This picture of good and evil is more than the belief of one of the characters, it plays an intimate role in the unfolding of the story. In the myth Krishna comes into the world, inflicts disaster on his demonic foe and finally dies. The goblins will return again, but Vishnu will be reborn in another incarnation and drive them back again. Never does Krishna overcome evil. He is incarnated for the sole purpose of restoring the balance of good and evil in the world. The image of Krishna dissolves away in the pond, carried there in the hands of a servitor whose job is "to close the gates of salvation." The pattern of events recorded in the mythology of Vishnu is repeated in the novel. Although it covers only the period of a little more than two years we can clearly trace a movement from good to evil to good, from hope for new and fruitful relationships between the Anglo-Indians and their subjects, to spreading evil, and then finally on to the regeneration of good. Such is the general development of the three sections of the novel, each section, perhaps deliberately, following this suggested pattern, possessing contrasting elements, the first marked by the prejudices of the Anglo-Indians, the second marked by Fielding's striking courage and love of justice, the third by the estrangement of Fielding and Aziz. We are taken through one cycle of good-and-evil and evil-and-good, and then on into half of the next. Aziz makes friends with Ralph Moore and recalls his earlier friendship with the boy's mother and he sees that another cycle is beginning. Significantly, the cycle of good and evil follows the pattern of the seasons. Another rainy season is inevitable, the rains again symbolically generating goodness and life, but there inevitably will be another hot season of spreading evil. As if to suggest the final section is not the last word, the novel ends with Aziz's furious cries against the presence of Fielding's people in India and his statement that they cannot be friends before the English are driven out.

Forster was attracted to the Hindu conceptions of good and evil, to its union of flesh and spirit, to its inclusiveness. These elements receive their greatest concentration in the myth of Krishna, and this contains the meaning of the festival in small, in which is contained much of the nature of the novel in small, in which the purposes and condition of life itself are thought by the novelist to be found.

Religion also enters into the way in which the characters in the novel are fashioned. In order to see that the English lack insight into some elemental aspect of life, it is unnecessary to understand Hinduism. Even the best that Fielding, the best of the Anglo-Indians of the novel, can do lacks some essential quality. His life is missing something, but what this is he will never be able to say. Sometimes with his wife, Mrs. Moore's daughter, he feels half dead and half blind. Both he and Adela, after she has renounced her charges and lost her place in the Anglo-Indian community through her assertion of integrity, are said to lack the apparatus for judging if the universe is one or if it is not. Like the rest of the Anglo-Indian community, Fielding has no more than one half of the double vision, that of their environment. Fielding is capable of the best reason can do, but this is not enough. He is troubled by his knowledge that he lacks something basic in life; he cannot understand his wife any more that Mr. Wilcox in *Howard's End* could understand his first or his second wives. Adela and the entire Anglo-Indian community drop completely out of the novel before the end and finally the scene shifts to a point two years later in time, to the native state of Mau. It is as if Forster were tired of them and their limited outlook on life and he had decided to permit only the presence of Fielding and his relatives in the story. The force of character Mrs. Moore had possessed and her secret, mysterious understanding are recreated in her son and daughter, who now appear in the novel for the first time, and perhaps a third is to be born. They replace the Anglo-Indians who are contemptuously dismissed, Forster having shown adequately how their lives are circumscribed around rigid patterns of actions, memories and attitudes, being capable of seeing others only in terms of their externals, particularly in the perspective of the group of which they are members. They are unable to rise above their experience and trace a larger pattern in life than the one they had learned.

Hinduism plays the key role in the nature of the character of Godbole, a man whose greatest role is in the third section of the novel. To fully appreciate this fact, it is necessary to understand the Hindu attitude towards personality and towards attachment. First of all, Hinduism demands an escape from personality, that is, from all of that which makes us unique as individuals and so distinct from everyone else. In Hinduism the tendency is to see all that which forms the personality, which includes will, thought and self-consciousness, as being only a part of material nature. This factor helps make Godbole seem as colorless as he is. Inclusiveness, unity is the goal for him. In the festival the participants lose their individuality and seem to merge into one another when they see the idol of the god. " . . . A most beautiful and radiant expression came into their faces, a beauty in which there was nothing personal, for it caused them all to resemble one another during the moment of its indwelling, and only when it was withdrawn did they revert to individual clods." While the claims of our environment on our concern are recognized in bhakti, nonetheless, the final goal is the liberation from the world of matter. And so also we must escape from the limitations of our personality. The bhakta, like any Hindu, must renounce the world of action. However, one method of doing this is by renouncing the desires which lead to action rather than action itself, to act only out of a disinterested sense of duty. Godbole seems remarkably unconcerned about the events the novel portrays. In **"What I Believe"** Forster expresses his belief that a decline in allegiance to the concept of personality will destroy interest in personal relationships. Furthermore, he shows that he believes that Hindu disassociation from the world of action through the renunciation of desire, while it allows room for the bhakti's wholehearted commitment to a theistic God, can produce a total unconcern for others. One passage emphasizes this element in Godbole's character. " 'I hope the expedition was a successful one,' " Godbole asks Fielding. "The news has not yet reached you yet, I can see.' 'Oh yes.' 'No; there has been a terrible catastrophe about Aziz.' 'Oh yes. That is all round the College.' 'Well, the expedition where that occurs can scarcely be called a successful one,' said Fielding with an amazed stare. 'I cannot say. I was not present.' " In the first two sections of the novel this mysterious figure wanders in and out of the story, never becoming involved, vanishing before all the climatic scenes. When he was expected to travel on the crucial trip to the Marabar Caves he missed the train. "He always did possess the knack of slipping off." He takes a central role in the festival, but the festival itself is not accounted for by the plot; nothing which has previously occurred in the novel causes it. It has been removed from the time scheme of the novel, whose central aspect is this cause and effect development by which it moves forward by the force of the inevitable march of events from the past into the future. The festival seeks to create unity between the transcendent and the concrete, and with this effort, disassociates itself from the aimless flux and movement of the pattern of human existence beyond its bounds. The ceremony has only an unintentional and indirect effect on Fielding, Aziz and Mrs. Moore's two children. It participates in the novel in the same way as Godbole. The festival is a self-enclosed universe. In *The Hill of Devi* Forster created a far more vivid picture of a Hindu. But the Maharajah of that book remained enigmatic to Forster until the end, and the Englishman never even felt he knew what the Indian thought of him. In this case Forster had personally experienced the characteristic of disinterested-

ness, although *The Hill of Devi* shows that he knew it did not always go to Godbole's extreme.

Is this renunciation of personal feelings "vision or nightmare?" Forster often has stressed his belief in human relationships as a fruitful source of human fulfillment. If one is to say that Forster believed in something quite definite, this is it. Characters who by their affection and concern nourish the lives of others as well as their own recur constantly in his stories and essays. Mrs. Moore had been such a person, as the Indians knew. Perhaps Forster wrote this novel when he had begun to despair about the value of personal relationships. The Anglo-Indians with their terrible and cruel self-righteous enmity towards the Indians and to Fielding are Forster's bleakest fictional portrayal of humanity. Personal relationships of any real value would be a rarer experience than he had once thought if men are capable of such terrible evil. Many Europeans had been embittered by the experience of World War One. Men had become more pessimistic about human nature than they had been a few years before. The effect of the War is, perhaps, present in this last novel of his. Possibly, Forster felt that now the primary issue was how modern man was to revitalize his existence since personal relationships seemed in such a dismal state, as Adela feels at one point in the novel. But ironically, while Forster admired much that he saw in Hindu belief, Godbole as a human being left him cold. The novelist warms when he writes of Aziz. The Moslem is a flightly character, unable to solve his personal problems, a man who by the end of the novel has built his life upon a mistake. He has, perhaps, too much personality. Yet it is he that Forster loves. In spite of the fact that Hinduism pervades the novel, the central Indian character is a Moslem. Forster has not been able to fit personality into the unity the Hindus strive to achieve since they do not respect it, and so, while Godbole might in his way be an admirable character, he is not loved.

Mrs. Moore is similar in certain ways to Godbole. The novelist has been more interested generally in depicting an ideal state than an action with his heroines, in being rather than becoming. Mrs. Moore is loved but her influence on others has its limitations; she is more ineffectual than many of Forster's earlier heroines. While her very name is enough to cause Aziz to renounce his intention to sue Adela Quested for damages, she was unable to help direct the troubled personal affairs of her son and Adela, although she had come to India for this purpose. At first, she does not seem to be a very dynamic character because she is almost completely incapable of having an immediate influence on others. After her experience in the caves she becomes totally uninterested in what happens to everyone else. If she had told Adela forcefully that she knew Aziz was innocent, the girl might well have renounced her charges because of it. But the older woman doesn't care. The echo had seemed to make life meaningless and had caused her to develop complete contempt for the individual and all his concerns. "The human race would have become a single person centuries ago," she says at this time, "if marriage was any use. And all this rubbish about love, love in a church, love in a cave, as if there is the least difference, and I held up from my business over such trifles."

But soon before she dies, Mrs. Moore's shattered personality begins to reform when she sees that while the world is filled with the flux and flow of changing things, it actually has an importance and reality of its own. The turning point comes on the train to Bombay when she sees the fortress of Asirgarh appear, flicker out of view and reappear. It seems to say "I do not vanish." And then as the boat bound for England puts to sea the palm trees on the harbor's shores wave to her: "So you thought an echo was India; you took the Marabar caves as final?" they laughed. "What have we in common with them, or they with Asirgarh?" Such a perspective on the material world is like that of the bhakti movement and represents a recovery.

Mrs. Moore dies on the ocean soon after she leaves India, but this does not mark the end of her presence in the world of the novel. Until she had left Chandrapore for good, her passage to India had been a passage to muddledom. But then, it seems, it becomes a passage to a transcendent realm. An Indian had become terrified by his belief that a ghost struck the car in which Adela and others had been touring. Without being given the idea by anyone else, Mrs. Moore is frightened by the possibility of it having happened. The incident remains mysterious and ambiguous. This event foreshadows Mrs. Moore's own influence later in the novel, as if suggesting, as it certainly does, some mysterious realm beyond death. During the trial scene the Indians chant the name of Mrs. Moore in the street; by then they have deified her into a goddess. Almost immediately after this Adela recants her confession. In an interview Forster has said "I was interested in the imaginative effect of someone alive but in a different way from other characters—living in other lives." Then he was asked a further question: if this expresses the concept of vicarious immortality, practiced by Samuel Butler, another novelist who otherwise influenced him. Forster said it doesn't. Whatever the case, she is dead and passed beyond personality, she is now pure character, a complex of traits whose presence others somehow seem to feel with beneficial results. We are never told in the novel precisely what did happen. However, the novelist did speak of it as an "imaginative effect." Probably, her influence is no more meant to be taken seriously than the myth is. Forster has said that Mrs. Moore's influence continues on even into the third section of the novel. Certainly, the son and daughter of Mrs. Moore are like her, but this does not seem to be what the novelist meant. Perhaps in some vague way Forster links her with the revitalization of goodness in the last portion of the book, personality already having become character, now character becoming a shadowy creative force.

So far the influence of Hinduism has been associated with Forster's purposes, plot and characterization. Finally, it can be seen that Forster was influenced by Hindu symbolism. A variety of images, such as sun, bird, snake, echo, arch, and wasp, run through the novel. As one could expect in a symbolist author, they suggest much of the book's meaning. Certain of these images receive a special content from their association with Hindu practices and their use in story and myth. One of these is very important, a few others have a lesser place in the novel. Two minor images are to be seen in the presence of the Marabar

Hills and Caves in the story. In Hindu mythology Siva, the chief god of the Hindu ascetics, makes his abode in the Himalaya Mountains, where he performs rigorous penances in a comforting isolation. If one reads how the hills are described during the expedition to them from the city it will not seem inappropriate to associate them with this symbolism, a symbolism resulting from the difficulty of attaining the summit. And again, caves have long been associated with ascetic austerities and are still used in India for this purpose. Certainly, the meaning of the Marabar Caves and Hills is very complex and rich. However, it seems that these particular associations have been used to increase their total meaning.

One major image which has not been properly appreciated as yet is water. Water is, of course, a universal symbol of dissolution, regeneration and eternity. It is not necessary to read far in Hindu mythology to see the peculiar role of water symbolism. As in Christianity, water is frequently used as an emblem of regeneration and as a means of producing purification. A myth which helps explain the significance of the River Ganges to the Hindu embodies this factor. In order to destroy a demon which had taken refuge in the water, the ascetic Agastya swallowed all the oceans. Only after a thousand years of terrible penances was King Bhagiratha able to persuade the god Shiva to help by sending down the River Ganges to the Earth. In this way the oceans were replenished. Like the Ganges, the torrential seasonal rains are linked to a time of reinvigoration in the novel. But water has a much greater importance, one which it lacks in the West. The Hindus have a cyclic view of history. One cycle of history will occur and then the universe will dissolve away. After a time the Supreme God, the only remaining being, will refashion the universe and a new cycle will begin. This occurs over and over again, an infinite number of times. Each time the universe dissolves away into water, the womb of the next creation. For water is the primal state of being, in which everything is blended into a formless mass, where all dualities are reconciled. In one scene, after being told of how the crocodiles eat corpses which float down on the river, Mrs. Moore stands watching the Ganges. In this short scene the Hindu symbolism is apparent. " 'What a terrible river! What a wonderful river!' and sighed. The radiance [of the river] was already altering whether through shifting of the moon or of the sand; soon the bright sheaf would be gone, and a circlet, itself to alter, be burnished upon the streaming void." She perceives antithetic qualities in the river. We are told the water will dissolve and refashion. Apparently Mrs. Moore's death, on the ocean significantly enough, and her later presence in the novel is suggested. Water symbolism is supremely significant in the third section of the novel and its presence is most pervasive in the climactic scene in which the servitor bearing the village of clay and the boats collide together in the pond as gusts of rain issue without warning from the skies in confusion. Death has already been mingled with life when Aziz sees the haunting image of the dead rajah across the water and thinks it a living man. Here in this last scene the village of Gokul dissolves into the water as if into its primordial elements, the token of death and the dissolution of the past and of all existing things at the end of the world. At the same time the old friends, Aziz and Fielding, collide at the moment when the clay figures on the tray have dissolved completely. Here also, life and death, extinction and regeneration are intimately fused into a totality.

The symbolic India contains the total spiritual condition: English, Moslem, Anglo-Indian, Hindu and Jain. Ideally it embodies the double vision, which Forster associates in this novel with the bhakti movement. Running through Forster's fiction is the portrayal of a sharp cleavage between the worlds of matter and spirit, of money and culture, of pragmatism and idealism, of the transient and transcendent. Clearly, Hinduism presented Forster with new methods of reconciling the two realms. Nevertheless, Hinduism did not present a totally satisfactory solution to the problems in contemporary life and civilization created by this split, since one-half of it was too mysterious and transcendent for an ideal union with the rest, it treats personality with contempt, and in short, it embodies "a passage not easy, nor now, not here, not to be apprehended except when it is unattainable." (pp. 281-95)

> *Michael Spencer, "Hinduism in E. M. Forster's 'A Passage to India',"* in The Journal of Asian Studies, *Vol. XXVIII, No. 2, February, 1968, pp. 281-95.*

Malcolm Bradbury (essay date 1969)

[*An English man of letters, Bradbury is best known as the author of such satiric novels as* Eating People Is Wrong *(1959) and* Stepping Westward *(1965). He has also written extensively on English and American literature, especially the works of E. M. Forster. In the following essay which has also appeared in his* Possibilities: Essays on the State of the Novel *(1973), Bradbury claims that the complexity of* A Passage to India *is the product of Forster's reconciliation of two distinct modes of thought, Victorian liberalism and the emerging modernism of the twentieth century.*]

There are major writers whose work seems to us important as a contribution to the distinctive powers and dimensions of art; there are others whose work represents almost a personal appeal to value, and who therefore live—for certain of their readers, at least—with a singular force. There have not been many English novelists of our own time who have established with us the second function, but E. M. Forster is certainly one of them. He has served as an embodiment of the virtues he writes about; he has shown us their function and their destiny; he has left, for other writers and other men, a workable inheritance. Partly this is because he has always regarded art as a matter of intelligence as well as passion, honesty as well as imagination. In making such alliances he has given us a contemporary version of a once-familiar belief—that art can be a species of active virtue as well as a form of magic—and has thus sharply appealed to our sense of what man can be. Literary humanist qualities of this sort are not always easy to express today within the impersonal context of modern literary criticism—which tends, more and more, to ascribe virtue to structural performance within the text and to neglect what lies beyond. In fact, they are crucial virtues, and we fortunately have enough personal testimony—particularly from writers like Christopher Isherwood

and Angus Wilson—to see the kind of inheritance he has left. At the same time, what Tony Tanner has called the "trace of totemism" with which Forster has been and is still regarded—and I must assert here my own sense of indebtedness, intellectual, moral, and literary—has its dangers, and to his role and his influence may be ascribed certain slightly odd and uneasy features of Forster's present reputation. That he is a major writer I have no doubt, yet criticism has repeatedly expressed an unsureness about him, has wondered, time and time again, whether he really stands with the other great writers of the century we feel sure of—with Joyce or Conrad or Lawrence.

Why is this? One reason is surely that Forster stands much exposed to our modern predilection for historicist thinking—our inclination to substitute, in Karl Popper's phrase, "historical prophecy for conscience". Forster once told us that he belongs to "the fag-end of Victorian liberalism", and the phrase is often taken with complete literalness and applied against him. As a result his intellectual and his literary destiny has been too readily linked with that strange death of liberal England which historians have dated around 1914, when the equation of economic individualism with social progress lost political force. Since it is easy to explain the exhaustion of political liberalism as a historical necessity, as the inevitable failure of a synthesis proven unworkable by the new social conditions of the second-stage Industrial Revolution, then it is also possible to see Forster's ideas and faith as historically superannuated, too. This view, indeed, has taken root—even though Forster recognises the ironies of the situation and works with them, even though he raises all the crucial questions about elevating social determinism above value; and we often overlook the fact that the liberalism he speaks for so obliquely has had a longer history as a moral conviction than as a political force, that it has as much to do with our idea of man and culture as with our political solutions, that it speaks for a recurrent need for the criticism of institutions and collectivities from the standpoint of the claims of human wholeness. But coupled with this there has been another distrust: distrust of the entire idea of art and culture as Forster suggests or expresses it.

In this century critics have increasingly accepted modernist norms for the judgement of literature, even though, of course, many of our writers have not been modernists in the strict sense. Forster is a paradox here; he is, and he is not. There is in his work the appeal to art as transcendence, art as the one orderly product, a view that makes for modernism; and there is the view of art as a responsible power, a force for belief, a means of judgement, an impulse to spiritual control as well as spiritual curiosity. The point perhaps is that Forster is not, in the conventional sense, a modernist, but rather a central figure of the transition into modernism; and that is surely his interest, the force of his claim. He is, indeed, to a remarkable degree, the representative of two kinds of mind, two versions of literary possibility, and of the tensions of consciousness that exist between them. He stands at the beginning of the age of the new, speaking through it and against it. In this way his five novels—and particularly his last two—can be taken as reflecting the advantages and disadvantages of the humanist literary mind in an environment half hostile to it; they clearly and often painfully carry the strain of a direct encounter with new experience. Forster has been, by training and temperament, sufficiently the historian to see the irony: that culture itself is in history, that a humanist view of the arts as a way of sanely perceiving and evaluating is itself conditioned, for it has its own social environment and limits. So Forster is at once the spokesman for the transcendent symbol, the luminous wholeness of the work of art, out of time and in infinity, and for its obverse—the view that a proper part of art's responsibility is to know and live in the contingent world of history.

If Forster is indeed a Victorian liberal, as some of his critics charge, he is also deeply marked by the encounters that the moralised romantic inheritance must make with those environments which challenge it in matters of belief, technique, and aesthetics. Of course, Forster's confession that he belongs to the fag-end of Victorian liberalism does express a real inheritance; but that end is also the beginning of new forms of belief and of new literary postures and procedures. My point is that he emerges not as a conventionally modernist writer, but rather as a writer who has experienced the full impact of what modernism means—a hope for transcendence, a sense of apocalypse, and *avant-garde* posture, a sense of detachment, a feeling that a new phase of history has emerged—while retaining (with tentative balance that turns often to the ironic mode) much that modernism would affront.

Forster's traditional literary inheritance, which reaches back through the Victorian period to roots in English romanticism, is something which he himself has sketched clearly and well in books like *Marianne Thornton.* He has shown us the formative influence of the world of the Victorian upper-middle-class intelligentsia in its liberal radical mode—that world of "philanthropists, bishops, clergy, members of parliament, Miss Hannah More" which reached into evangelical Christianity and into agnostic enlightenment, that world which he draws upon and values, and against which he also reacts. To the cultural historian, its interest lies in its unconditioned spirit, its sense of disinterestedness, its capacity to act beyond both self and class interest and to transcend its economic roots without losing its social standing. Its view of the critical intelligence working in society is therefore accompanied by no strong sense of disjunction, and it takes many of its terms from the moralised line of English romantic thought. What Forster inherits from it is apparent—something of the flavour of that engaging marriage made by the most influential English romantics, Wordsworth and Coleridge in particular, between the claims on the one hand of the imagination and the poet's transcendent vision, and on the other of right reason and moral duty; something of its power, therefore, to make a vision of Wholeness which embraces the social world in all its contingency. So the personal connection between inner and outer worlds—a connection forged through the powers of passion and imagination—has its social equivalent, in the notion of an obligation on society that it, too, be whole; that it grant, as Mill stresses, "the absolute and essential importance of human development in its richest diversity", that it sees, in Arnold's terms, that perfection can be both an *inward* condition of mind and spirit and a *general* expansion of

the human family. Forster draws on the full equation for his fiction, taking as his proper field the social realm of action as well as the life of individuals in their personal relations, and criticising his characters and their society now from the standpoint of right reason and culture, now from that of the heart, the passions, the power of visionary imagination that can testify, however inadequately, to the claims of the infinite. Thus there come under fire "the vast armies of the benighted, who follow neither the heart nor the brain"; and the connective impulses embrace not only man and man, and man and infinity, but the social order, too.

But if Forster is undoubtedly an inheritor of that world of value, he inherits with a due sense of difficulty. In *Howards End* he touches in with deep force those powers and forces in history which are process, and can't be gainsaid; the pastoral and vividly felt landscape of England is turned by the demanding processes of urbanisation and industrialism into a civilisation of luggage; while the very economics of the intelligentsia he belongs to become a matter for ironic exposure. In *A Passage to India* the final nullity of romanticism is exposed in the cave, where the worlds within us and without echo together the sound of *boum;* this is the extreme beyond Coleridgean dejection, for the visionary hope is lost in the face of an unspeaking and utterly alien nature, a nature only self-reflecting. The will to vision and the liberal thrust to right reason, the desire to connect both with infinity and all mankind, are placed against unyielding forces in nature and history—obstructing the movement of Forster's visionary themes and producing, particularly in these two last novels, a countervailing, ironic reaction. This countervailing sense, this sense of historical apocalypse coupled with spiritual abyss, is surely recognisably modernist. And what in the early novels appears as a species of social comedy—a comedy exercising the claims of moral realism against the liberal wish to draw clear lines between good and bad action—emerges in these latter novels as an essential irony of structure: indeed, as a direct challenge to the values Forster is so often supposed to represent. If, to cite Lionel Trilling (who writes so well of this ironic aspect of Forster), there is an ironic counterpart in the early work whereby while "the plot speaks of clear certainties, the manner resolutely insists that nothing can be quite so simple", these complexities increase in the later work into the mental and aesthetic possession of two colliding views of the world.

Forster's way of assimilating two modes of thought—one an inheritance, the other an urgent group of ideas about contemporary necessity—is matched by the curious aesthetic implications of his techniques in fiction. He is often considered as a writer technically a coeval of his Victorian predecessors (Walter Allen calls him "a throwback"), and in asserting his own debts has particularly named three writers: Jane Austen, Samuel Butler, and Marcel Proust. The indebtedness to the first two of his species of moralised social irony hardly needs elaborating; it is the third name which suggests that the "traditionalist" account of his technique is misleading. Of course, in his novels the omniscient author mediates, with the voice of the guidebook or essay or sermon, the proffered material—though as much to sustain fiction's place in the field of intelligence and thought as to establish the authenticity of fact. But at the same time he offers his work as the symbolist or autotelic artefact; a work of art is "the only material object in the universe which may possess internal harmony". What is so fascinating about his most extended aesthetic statement, **Aspects of the Novel,** is its attempt to place the modes of symbolism and post-impressionism in the context of what might be considered the more "traditional" story-telling function; the novel *tells* (rather than *is*) a story, and it lives in the conditioned world of stuff, of event, of history. (So, finally, Forster puts Tolstoy above Proust.) Yet it has transcendent purposes; art, "the one orderly product which our muddling race has produced", (*ibid.*) has Platonic powers to touch infinity, reach to the unity behind all things, prophesy (in the Shelleyan sense).

In this respect Forster is as post-impressionist or post-Paterian as anyone else in Bloomsbury, and the ultimate field of action for the arts is that of the "unseen". Procedurally this symbolist power seems to lie in the analogue with music, and is gained from aspects of the novel outside and beyond story, in thematic recurrences, leitmotifs, pattern and rhythm, prophetic song. The problem of whether art can redeem life by transcending it is crucial to modernism; the encounter between the formally transcendent—the epiphany, the unitary symbol—and the world of history recurs throughout its works. And Forster's view is, like that of most modernism, dualistic: art may reach beyond the world of men and things—the world of "story"—but it can never leave that world behind, and must seek meanings and connections in it. What distinguishes Forster is the faint hope which he entertains on behalf of history: the hope that by understanding and right relationship men may win for it a limited redemption.

I have suggested that Forster is deeply involved in some of the largest intellectual, cultural, and aesthetic collisions that occur in the transition into this century; and it is his sharp sense of the contingent, of the powers that rule the world of men, that makes him so. The result is a complex version of modern literary disquiet. An intermediary between those two literary traditions of "moderns" and "contemporaries" that Stephen Spender sees as the two main lines of modern English writing, he bears these burdens so as to expose the crucial choices that a writer of this transitional period might make. Divided as he is between infinite and contingent, he is none the less more available to the offered pressures than most of the more confirmed modernists. This is because his sense of the "crisis" of infinity is so much bound up with his sense of the divisive and changing forces of the world of time. For he is increasingly concerned with the problems of the infinite view within the cultural movements of the modernising world; and in his growing sense of the need to synthesise an ever more eclectic experience he testifies to the new multiverse, the chaotic welter of values, which has confounded the modern mind. Hence his visions, though they may suggest an order or unity in the universe, are defined, increasingly from novel to novel, in terms of an anarchy that they must always comprehend. Thus they are never fully redemptive, since the world of time persistently enlarges our feelings of intellectual, moral, social, and spiritual relativism,

creating a world in which no one philosophy or cosmology accounts for the world order—where it is possible to believe with Mrs. Moore that "Everything exists; nothing has value." This, with its suggestion that in seeing life whole one may see nothing except multiplicity, is the obverse of the unitary vision; and in *A Passage to India,* his fullest and most eclectic book, Forster gives us in full that possibility—and its sources in social relations, personal relations, and the realm of spirit.

Forster may have an ideal of unity, a will to a whole solution, but we mistake him if we see only that in him. For he is characteristically not a novelist of solutions, but rather of reservations, of the contingencies and powers which inhibit spirit. The power of sympathy, understanding, and community with all things is for him an overriding power; but its claim to wholeness is always conditioned, and mystery, to which we must yield, co-exists with muddle, which we must try to redeem, or even accept in its nullity. Indeed, it is because Forster is so attentive to the forces in our culture and world-order which induce the vision of anarchy—and threaten through its very real powers not only the will to but the very insights of the whole vision—that he seems so central a writer; a novelist whom we in our turn have not always seen whole.

Forster is a difficult and ambiguous writer, a writer who has often made his critics uneasy and caused them to feel how strangely elusive his work is. His observation of his materials, and his way of making his structures, usually involves two tones that come into perplexing relationship. There is the instinct towards "poetry", which goes with the view of art as a symbolist unity; and there is the comedy and the irony, the belittling aspect of his tone, which brings in the problems and difficulties of the contingent world. Because of this it is often possible simultaneously to interpret his work positively and negatively, depending on the kind of critical attentiveness one gives.

Thus for some critics, like Wilfred Stone, *A Passage to India* is Forster's most affirmative and optimistic novel, the one which most suggests, as Stone puts it, that "unity and harmony are the ultimate promises of life." "The theme which this book hammers home," says Stone, "is that, for all our differences, we are in fact *one*. . . . Physically of one environment, we are also psychically one, and it is reason's denial of our commonality, the repression of that *participation mystique,* which has caused man to rule his Indias and himself with such futility and blindness." But other critics like James McConkey and Alan Wilde have come to precisely the opposite view, seeing the work as a novel of the final dissociation between the chaotic life of man and an intractable eternal reality. In part the decision depends upon whether one insists, like Trilling, on a relatively realistic reading of the book, or whether, as E. K. Brown does, one reads it as a "symbolist" novel. If the world of men and manners, of politics and human behaviour, which it depicts suggests divisiveness, the world of the work itself as single "orderly product" suggests profound correspondences within it, a power to resolve its meanings which lies beyond any given character. Of this aspect of the book, Frank Kermode has remarked that it depends upon faking—faking a universe of promised wholeness, of rhetorical and structural unity, of a testing of the world of men from the standpoint of total coherence: "All that civilisation excepts or disconnects has to be got in for meaning to subsist." What this means is that the world of men and the world of order must exist in paradoxical relationship, and this is what Lionel Trilling seems to imply, too, when he remarks that the novel has an unusual imbalance between plot and story: "The characters are of sufficient size for the plot; they are not large enough for the story—and that indeed is the point of the story." But it is typically in such contrasts of time and transcendence that Forster deals, and to clarify the relationship between them one needs to look very closely at the overall working of the novel.

To a considerable extent, the book deals in themes and matters we have learned to associate with Forster from his previous novels. Here again are those rival claims upon men and nature which dichotomise the universe—the claims of the seen and the unseen, the public and the private, the powers of human activities and institutions and of the ultimate mysteries for which the right institutions and activities have yet to be found. And here again Forster's own sympathies are relatively apparent. The book is focused upon the testing-field of human relationships, with their various possibilities and disasters; on the "good will plus culture and intelligence" which are the necessary conditions of honest intercourse; on the clashes of interest and custom which divide men but which the liberal mind must hope, as Fielding hopes, to transcend. Its modes of presentation are familiarly complex—moving between a "poetic" evocation of the world of mystery and a "comic" evocation of the world of muddle, which is in a sense its obverse and refers to the normal state of men.

But what is unmistakable, I think, is that in this book Forster reveals new powers and resources—of a kind not previously achieved in his fiction—and that this extension of resource is linked with an extension of his sensibility, and above all with a new sense of complexity. For instance, *A Passage to India* is not simply an international novel—in the Jamesian sense of attempting to resolve contrasting value-systems by means of a cosmopolitan scale of value—but a global novel. The contrast of England and India is not the end of the issue, since India is schismatic within itself; India's challenge is the challenge of the multiverse, a new version of the challenge that Henry Adams faced on looking at the dynamo. What the city is as metaphor in *Howards End,* India is in *Passage;* it is a metaphor of contingency. Forster is not simply interested in raising the social-comic irony of confronting one social world with the standards of another; he stretches through the social and political implications to religious and mystical ones, and finally to the most basic question of all—how, in the face of such contingency, one structures meaning.

The geographical scale of the novel is, in short, supported by a vast scale of standpoint. Forster attempts a structure inclusive of the range of India, and the judgements of the book are reinforced by the festivals and rituals of three religions, by the heterodoxy—racial, political, cultural, religious, and mystical—of this multiple nation, and by the physical landscape of a country which both invites mean-

ing ("Come, come") and denies any. "Nothing embraces the whole of India, nothing, nothing," says Aziz; the landscape and the spirit of the earth divide men ("Trouble after trouble encountered him [Aziz], because he had challenged the spirit of the Indian earth, which tries to keep men in compartments"); and even the sects are divided within themselves just as the earth is:

> The fissures in the Indian soil are infinite: Hinduism, so solid from a distance, is riven into sects and clans, which radiate and join, and change their names according to the aspect from which they are approached.

Forster's social comedy works to provoke, among a variety of different and sympathetically viewed groups, those ironic international and intra-national encounters that come when one value system meets another and confusion and muddle ensue. But his other aim is to call up, by a poetic irradiation, the ironies lying within the forces of mystery and muddle in the constituted universe of nature itself. For here, too, are deceptions, above all in the absence of Beauty, which is traditionally a form for infinity, so that the very discourse of Romanticism becomes negative under the hot sun—who is "not the unattainable friend, either of men or birds or other suns, [who] was not the eternal promise, the never-withdrawn suggestion that haunts our consciousness; he was merely a creature, like the rest, and so debarred from glory." There is much in India that invites a cosmic meaning, but it places both man and infinity:

> Trees of a poor quality bordered the road, indeed the whole scene was inferior, and suggested that the countryside was too vast to admit of excellence. In vain did each item in it call out, "Come, come." There was not enough god to go round. The two young people conversed feebly and felt unimportant.

All this stretches the Whitmanesque enterprise called up by the title to a vast level of inclusiveness. It also involves Forster in a placing of the social and human world of his novel in a way he has never approached before. One way of putting the situation is to say that the human plot of the novel is set into singular relation to the verbal plot, with its radiating expansiveness of language. The human plot of the novel is essentially a story hinging on Adela Quested, who comes to India to marry, has doubts about her marriage when she sees what India has made of her fiancé, and tries herself to create a more reasonable relationship between British and Indians. She takes part in an expedition, arranged by an Indian, to the Marabar caves, in one of which she believes she is attacked by him. She accuses him of attempted rape, and, although at the trial she retracts her accusation, the incident has sown dissent and discord, and has exposed the political and institutional tensions of the country.

The plot moves us from the world of personal relationships to the social world (which in this case involves political relationships), and is set largely in and around the city of Chandrapore, at a time not stated but evidently intended to be in the 1920s. The dense social world that Forster delinates so skilfully consists primarily of racial or religious groups with their own customs and patterns. The English, whom we see largely through the eyes of Adela Quested and Mrs. Moore, visiting India together, are identified with their institutional functions. Mostly professional middle-class people, they have gone through a process of adaptation to their duties, which are, as Ronnie says, "to do justice and keep the peace." They have learned the importance of solidarity, conventions, rank, and standoffishness; and their judgements and their social order are those of a particular class in a particular situation. Their ethics are dutiful and serious; they have a deep sense of rational justice; they are distrustful of mysticism and lethargy; their deep Englishness has been reinforced by their situation. They operate at the level of political and social duty, and their relationships—the ties that bind the characters together and enable Forster to thread the way from one to another—are those of the political and social roles they play.

The other group, which we see first largely through the eyes of Aziz, consists of Indians, though these are themselves divided by religions and castes. Here again what we see are primarily the professional classes, linked to the British by their duties and to their own people by their familial and friendly relationships. The two main groupings that emerge here are, of course, the Hindus and the Moslems, and Forster differentiates carefully between them, and their respective versions of India. Where they differ radically from the English is in their long and adaptive response to the confusions of their country, a response which obscures the firm lines of value that the British in their isolation can protect, and permits lethargy, emotionalism, and mysticism. Forster explores Indian custom and faith in great detail, noting its own patterns of classification, its own way of making and not making social and moral distinctions, above all recognising that Indians have adapted to a different physical environment by being comprehensive or passive rather than orderly or rationalistic.

These worlds—Anglo-Indian (to use the phrase of the day), Hindu, Moslem—are given us in full as they connect and draw apart, and Forster enters imaginatively into each of them. And to a large extent what interests him is not the relations between people, the normal matter for the novelist, but their separation. In the novel's social scenes we are always conscious of those who are absent, and much of the discussion in the early part of the novel is devoted to those not present—the whites are talked of by the Indians, the Indians by the whites. And this suggests the vast social inclusiveness of the novel, which spreads beyond the communities established for the sake of the action into a cast of thousands: nameless marginal characters who appear for a moment and are gone, like the punkah wallah or the voice out of the darkness at the club, and the inhabitants of Chandrapore who seem made "of mud moving."

Out of this complex social world derives a complex moral world, in which the values of no one group are given total virtue. The English may have thrown the net of rationalism and "civilisation" over the country, but India's resistance to this—"The triumphant machine of civilisation may suddenly hitch and be immobilised into a car of

stone"—puts them in ironic relation to Indian reality; they scratch only the surface of its life, and theirs is a feeble invasion. On the other hand, the passive comprehensiveness of India is seen as itself a kind of social decay, debased as well as spiritual, leading to a potential neglect of man. The traditional repositories of Forsterian virtue—goodwill plus culture and intelligence—function only incompletely in this universe; and Forster's own liberal passion for social connection motivates a large section of the action, but does not contain its chief interest. In the deceptively guide-bookish opening chapter Forster establishes an appeal beyond the social world, to the overarching sky; it looks, at first, like a figure for the potential unity of man, the redemption that might come through breaking out of the social institutions and classifications that segregate them into their closed groupings, but the gesture has an ambiguous quality. The civil station "shares nothing with the city except the overarching sky", but the sky itself is an infinite mystery, and reaching away into its "farther distance, . . . beyond colour, last freed itself from blue." Certainly, beyond the world of social organisation is that world of "the secret understanding of the heart" to which Aziz appeals; this is the world that is damaged when Ronnie and Mrs. Moore discuss Aziz and she finds: "Yes, it was all true, but how false as a summary of the man; the essential life of him had been slain."

Forster is, as usual, superb at creating that "essential life" and showing what threatens it, and much of the book deals with its virtues and its triumphs. So at one level the social world *is* redeemed by those who resist its classifications—by Adela and Mrs. Moore, Fielding, Aziz, Godbole. Forster does not belittle their victories directly except in so far as he sees their comedy. But he does place beyond them a world of infinitude which is not, here, to be won through the personal. For this is not the entire realm of moral victory in the novel; indeed, these acts of resistance, which provide the book's lineal structure, are usually marked by failure. Adela's is a conventional disaster; she makes the moral mistake of exposing the personal to the social. Fielding's is more complicated; he is an agent of liberal contact through goodwill plus culture and intelligence, but he, like Mrs. Moore, meets an echo:

> "In the old eighteenth century, when cruelty and injustice raged, an invisible power repaired their ravages. Everything echoes now; there's no stopping the echo. The original sound may be harmless, but the echo is always evil." This reflection about an echo lay at the verge of Fielding's mind. He could never develop it. It belonged to the universe that he had missed or rejected. And the mosque missed it too. Like himself, those shallow arcades provided but a limited asylum.

As for Mrs. Moore, who does touch it, she encounters another force still—the moral nihilism that comes when the boundary walls are down. Her disaster dominates the novel, for it places even moral and mystical virtue within the sphere of contingency; it, too, is subject to spiritual anarchy. Beyond the world of the plot, the lineal world of consequences and relationships, there lies a second universe of fictional structure, which links spiritual events, and then a third, which in turn places these in history and appeals to the infinite recession of the universe beyond any human structure that seeks to comprehend it.

This we may see by noting that in this novel, as compared with the earlier ones, the world of men is clearly granted reduced powers. The universe of time and contingency is made smaller, by the nature that surrounds man, by the scale of the continent on which man's presence is a feeble invasion, by the sky which overarches him and his works. It is a world of dwarfs and of dwarfed relationships, in which the familiar forces of romantic redemption in Forster's work—personal relationships as mirrors to infinity, a willingness to confront the unseen—undertake their movements toward connection without the full support of the universe. The theme recurs, but Mrs. Moore expresses it most strongly in Chapter XIV, when she reflects on her situation and grows towards her state of spiritual nullity in the cave:

> She felt increasingly (vision or nightmare?) that, though people are important, the relations between them are not, and that in particular too much fuss has been made over marriage; centuries of carnal embracement, yet man is no nearer to understanding man. And today she felt this with such force that it seemed itself a relationship, itself a person who was trying to take hold of her hand.

The negative withdrawal is, of course, an aspect of that "twilight of the double vision in which so many elderly people are involved," and it is not the only meaning in the book. But it is the dominant one. It is by seeking its obverse that Adela compounds her basic moral error:

> It was Adela's faith that the whole stream of events is important and interesting, and if she grew bored she blamed herself severely and compelled her lips to utter enthusiasms. This was the only insincerity in a character otherwise sincere, and it was indeed the intellectual protest of her youth. She was particularly vexed now because she was both in India and engaged to be married, which double event should have made every instant sublime.

Human relationships are dwarfed not only by the scale of the historical and social world, which is potentially redeemable, but by the natural world, which is not.

Of course, intimations of transcendence are present throughout the novel. Structurally they run through the seasonal cycle, from divisive hot sun to the benedictive healing water at the end, and from Mosque to Caves to Temple. By taking that as his order, Forster is able poetically to sustain the hope of a spiritual possibility, a prefiguring of the world beyond in the world below. The climax of this theme is Godbole's attempt at "completeness, not reconstruction." But what happens here is that divine revelation is shifted to the level of the comic sublime; Forster's rhetoric now puts what has been spiritually perplexing—the webs, nets, and prisons that divide spirit as well as society—back into the comic universe of muddle. The Mau festival is the celebration of the formlessness of the Indian multiverse, seen for a moment inclusively. The poetic realm of the novel, in which above all Mrs. Moore and Godbole have participated, and which has dominated the book's primary art, is reconciled with the muddle of the world of men, in an emotional cataract that momentarily repairs the divisions of the spiritual world (through Godbole's revelation) and the social world (through the festival itself). It satisfies much of the passion for inclusiveness that has been one thread in the novel, the desire that heaven should include all because India *is* all. Earlier the two Christian missionaries have disagreed: Mr. Sorley, the more advanced,

> admitted that the mercy of God, being infinite, may well embrace all mammals. And the wasps? He became uneasy during the descent to wasps, and was apt to change the conversation. And oranges, cactuses, crystals and mud? and the bacteria inside Mr. Sorley? No, no, this is going too far. We must exclude someone from our gathering, or we shall be left with nothing.

Godbole's universe of spirit is much more inclusive:

> Godbole consulted the music-book, said a word to the drummer, who broke rhythm, made a thick little blur of sound, and produced a new rhythm. This was more exciting, the inner images it evoked more definite, and the singers' expressions became fatuous and languid. They loved all men, the whole universe, and scraps of their past, tiny splinters of detail, emerged for a moment to melt into the universal warmth. Thus Godbole, though she was not important to him, remembered an old woman he had met in Chandrapore days. Chance brought her into his mind while it was in this heated state, he did not select her, she happened to occur among the throng of soliciting images, a tiny splinter, and he impelled her by his spiritual force to that place where completeness can be found. Completeness, not reconstruction. His senses grew thinner, he remembered a wasp seen he forgot where, perhaps on a stone. He loved the wasp equally, he impelled it likewise, he was imitating God. And the stone where the wasp clung—could he . . . no, he could not, he had been wrong to attempt the stone, logic and conscious effort had seduced, he came back to the strip of red carpet and discovered that he was dancing upon it.

His doctrine—"completeness, not reconstruction"—is, of course, a species of transcendence, a momentary vision of the whole, the invocation of a universe invested with spirit. It links up with the symbolist plot of the novel, its power as a radiant image, rather than with plot in the linear sense, with its world of "and then . . . and then . . . " Threading its way through the novel, to an old woman and a wasp, it takes these "soliciting images" and puts them in new association—not with all things, but with each other and with what else comes almost unbidden into the world of spirit. But the stone is left, and equally spirit may or may not invest the universe in any of its day-to-day affairs: "Perhaps all these things! Perhaps none!" Things, in freeing themselves from their traditional associations, social and historical, form a new order, beyond dialogue, beyond human plot, in the realm where poetic figures function on their own order of consciousness. Yet here, too, irony is at work: mystery is sometimes muddle, completeness is sometimes the universe where "everything exists, nothing has value." If history ultimately obstructs, and does not give us a final, rounded structure in terms of human events, if the horses, the earth, the clutter of human institutions say, "No, not yet," then like obstructions dwell in the realm of spirit and symbol, too: the sky says, "No, not there."

The linear, social plot, then, has stretched a long way in search of a structure of its own that will provide coherence in the world, but if it finds one it is in the form of an oblique, doubtful and ironic promise; personal relations only go so far to solve the muddle of history. As for the symbolist plot, it transcends but it does not redeem; it is there but "neglects to come." The power of the novel lies, of course, in the Whitmanesque ambition to include multitudes, to find eternity in some order in the given world. But is this ambition realised? Intimations of eternity may have their symbols in the world of men (in love and relationship) and in the world of nature (in the force of mystery that resides in things); the social and the natural worlds have in them touches that promise wholeness. But they do not of themselves have unity; they are themselves afflicted by the double vision which is all that man can bring to them, grounded as he is in history and hope at once. The world stretches infinitely about us, and there is infinity beyond us. But questions bring us only to the unyielding hostility of the soil and the unyielding ambiguity of the sky.

The universe, then, is less intimation than cipher; a mask rather than a revelation in the romantic sense. Does love meet with love? Do we receive but what we give? The answer is surely a paradox, the paradox that there are Platonic universals beyond, but that the glass is too dark to see them. Is there a light beyond the glass, or is it a mirror only to the self? The Platonic cave is even darker than Plato made it, for it introduces the echo, and so leaves us back in the world of men, which does not carry total meaning, is just a story of events. The Platonic romantic gesture of the match in the cave is the dominating ambiguity of the book. Does it see *itself* in the polished wall of stone, or is the glimmer of radiance a promise?

> There is little to see, and no eye to see it, until the visitor arrives for his five minutes, and strikes a match. Immediately another flame rises in the depths of the rock and moves towards the surface like an imprisoned spirit: the walls of the circular chamber have been most marvellously polished. The two flames approach and strive to unite, but cannot, because one of them breathes air, the other stone. A mirror inlaid with lovely colours divides the lovers, delicate stars of pink and grey interpose, exquisite nebulae, shadings fainter than the tail of a comet or the midday moon, all the evanescent life of the granite, only here visible. Fists and fingers thrust above the advancing soil—here at last is their skin, finer than any covering acquired by the animals, smoother than windless water, more voluptuous than love. The radiance increases, the flames touch one another, kiss, expire. The cave is dark again, like all the caves.

Isn't it less the transcendence of a Whitman, uniting all things through the self and the ongoing lines of history,

than the ambiguous and narcissistic transcendence of Melville, where the universe is a diabolical cipher, where the desire to penetrate meaning ends only in our being swallowed up in the meaning we have conferred? Isn't the novel not Forster's "Passage to India", but rather, in the end, Forster's *Moby Dick*? (pp. 123-42)

> *Malcolm Bradbury, "Two Passages to India: Forster as Victorian and Modern," in* Aspects of E. M. Forster, *edited by Oliver Stallybrass, Edward Arnold, 1969, pp. 123-42.*

D. H. Lawrence on *A Passage To India*:

To Martin Secker.

Dear Secker,—

Am reading *Passage to India*. It's good, but makes one wish a bomb would fall and end everything. Life is more interesting in its undercurrents than in its obvious; and E. M. does see people, people and nothing but people: *ad nauseam.* . . .

Yrs.,

D. H. Lawrence.

> *D. H. Lawrence, in* The Letters of D. H. Lawrence, *1924.*

John Beer (essay date 1970)

[*In the following essay, Beer examines the symbolism of* A Passage to India.]

Forster visited India twice, in 1912-13 and 1921. He has recalled some of his impressions, and included letters written at the time, in *The Hill of Devi.* But the seeds of *A Passage to India* lie scattered still further back. They were growing when [in *The Longest Journey*] Herbert Pembroke, addressing his house at Sawston School, pointed to portraits of empire-builders on the wall and quoted imperial poets.

There is an inevitability in the choice of theme for this culminating novel. In the earlier ones, Sawston never quite found an antagonist worthy of its powers. In England, it was faced on one side by an aristocracy which patronized and used it, on the other by a working class with which it had long ago compromised. It existed only with the connivance of other classes of society which in their turn kept some check on it. Even when it set itself against the more spontaneous life of Italy, it was facing a society which in its treatment of women and relatives was even more rigid than itself.

But in India, Sawston could flourish with greater freedom. As a class it was single and distinct, not subject to checks from above or below: and the opposition to it came from a separate civilization which although more comprehensive, more venerable and more alive to the human condition than itself, was seen by its blinkered vision as naïve and primitive. The characteristics of Sawston were bound to become exaggerated in a situation where it lived both complacently assured of its own rightness and consciously embattled against forces which could easily, through some error or miscalculation, overwhelm it. A novel with such a setting is necessarily alive with dramatic tensions.

Into this precarious situation, as localized in the small station of Chandrapore, step Mrs Moore and Adela Quested, two visitors from England. Adela has come because a marriage is being arranged between her and Ronny Heaslop, the district magistrate; Mrs Moore in order to accompany her. Adela expresses a desire to see the 'real' India, and in order that she may do so Dr Aziz, a young doctor, arranges a trip to the famous Marabar caves. But during the expedition Adela enters a cave and on emerging has the impression that Aziz followed her in and assaulted her. Her accusations are made publicly, an explosive situation is created in the small town, and a trial is arranged at which she is to be called as a witness. Then, when the tension is at its height during the trial, Adela suddenly declares that no one followed her into the cave. The trial collapses; there is a temporary crisis during which there are fears for the breakdown of public order, and then life resumes its normal tenor. Adela, who has incurred universal dislike for her action, returns to England without marrying Ronny. The novel concludes with a long section devoted to an Indian festival which is attended by Mrs Moore's son and daughter. Mrs Moore herself, who stood throughout the novel as a reconciling power between English and Indians, has died on the voyage home after an illness which began, like Adela's crisis, with her experiences in a Marabar cave.

The dramatic situation of the novel, involving as it does an explosive human situation which can be ignited by the failure of a single individual, is finely conceived. If one regards plot as a means for manipulating the reader's expectations and responses, on the other hand, the novel is less successful. It is a major disappointment to readers who have been brought up on detective stories to find that there is no spectacular dénouement, no final revelation concerning the events in the cave, only Adela's denial that Dr Aziz followed her. And if this negation is all that is to be offered, the key events of the trial ought to come at the end of the novel. Why is there a long sequence dealing with irrelevancies such as the festival?

Forster has explained his introduction of the Hindu festival in his *Writers at Work* interview. *Interviewers.* 'What was the exact function of the long description of the Hindu festival in *A Passage to India*?' *Forster.* 'It was architecturally necessary. I needed a lump, or a Hindu temple if you like—a mountain standing up. It is well placed; and it gathers up some strings. But there ought to be more after it. The lump sticks out a little too much.' But this answers one question only to raise another. Why, when the climax of the book has been passed, should such a lump be 'architecturally necessary'? The answer can only be that it is there for some purpose other than the dramatic demands of the plot. In other words, we have to cope with the possibility that the structure of the novel does not consist simply of an arrangement of events. Behind that structure there is another, an arrangement of the novel's meaning.

A reader who is looking for further meaning in the novel may well be attracted to the idea that it is intended as a piece of anti-imperialist propaganda, polemic against British rule in India. As a picture of that rule, however, it contains some major distortions. Some of the characters could be typical only of the sort of Princely State in which Forster spent most of his time, not of modern India. And as both Nirad Chaudhuri and George Orwell have pointed out, little attention is paid to the sheer vastness of the political and economic forces at work there. But the novel ought never to have been read as an essay in *realpolitik*. It is at once too local and too universal. As a contribution to a 'practical' solution of the Indian problem as it existed at that time its value was limited, and the last chapter acknowledges the fact.

Beyond these immediate questions, the pettinesses of officials in a small Government station do have their relevance: for racial and economic questions are, ultimately, questions of human relations and it can never be out of place to say so. And Forster's satire is not directed only against the British: as so often in his work, we are being presented not with propaganda, but with a dialectic, of which the British and the Indians furnish respective limbs. The British may act badly in Forster's India, but so do the Indians. There is never any doubt that they need the justice and fair administration that the British give them. It is the hostility and lack of communication between the two sides that marks the failure—the old failure to 'connect'.

The gap between the two sides is, roughly speaking, the gap between head and heart. In his **'Notes on the English Character'**, Forster says that it is the 'undeveloped heart that is largely responsible for the difficulties of Englishmen abroad'. Forster's Indians, on the other hand, make up for any failure in cold judicial reasoning by their highly developed hearts. Between the two groups there is a failure. But if the British are to be blamed for the failure, that is only because they were the group from which any initiative must necessarily have come.

Throughout his novel, Forster is at pains to stress the quality of achievement of the British and in particular their desire that justice be done. His central points both for and against the régime are made in his account of the work of Ronny as City Magistrate at Chandrapore:

> Every day he worked hard in the court trying to decide which of two untrue accounts was the less untrue, trying to dispense justice fearlessly, to protect the weak against the less weak, the incoherent against the plausible, surrounded by lies and flattery.

Adela listening to his defence of his behaviour, is not satisfied however:

> His words without his voice might have impressed her, but when she heard the self-satisfied lilt of them, when she saw the mouth moving so complacently and competently beneath the little red nose, she felt, quite illogically, that this was

not the last word on India. One touch of regret—not the canny substitute but the true regret from the heart—would have made him a
different man, and the British Empire a different
institution.

Throughout the novel, this failure of connection between
British and Indians is a running theme. There is no need
to illustrate in detail what every reader can see for himself.
Towards the end of the novel it is symbolized perhaps in
the temple at Mau which has two shrines—the Shrine of
the Head on the hill, the Shrine of the Body below. At all
events, the separation is strongly emphasized in the last
chapter, when the two characters who have tried hardest
to come together, Fielding and Aziz, are out riding. The
final passage, in which the whole landscape confirms
Aziz's words about the impossibility of friendship between
British and Indians, finely epitomizes this element in the
novel:

> But the horses didn't want it—they swerved
> apart; the earth didn't want it, sending up rocks
> through which riders must pass single file; the
> temples, the tank, the jail, the palace, the birds,
> the carrion, the Guest House, that came into
> view as they issued from the gap and saw Mau
> beneath: they didn't want it, they said in their
> hundred voices, 'No, not yet,' and the sky said,
> 'No, not there.'

For Fielding, a moderate man who is content with friendliness and sweet reasonableness in his dealings with other
men, there can be no solution in India. He finds what he
is looking for only when he visits Italy on his way home
to England and rediscovers the beauty of its cities. 'He had
forgotten the beauty of form among idol temples and
lumpy hills.' The account of his visit concludes:

> The Mediterranean is the human norm. When
> men leave that exquisite lake, whether through
> the Bosphorus or the Pillars of Hercules, they
> approach the monstrous and extraordinary; and
> the southern exit leads to the strangest experi-
> ence of all.

This observation is sometimes taken to be Forster's final
message in the novel: and it is true that in so far as it is
a study of the conflict between two civilizations, at extreme poles from each other and separated by the Mediterranean, the passage offers the only hint of a solution. But
it also has to be read in conjunction with another statement of Forster's: 'though proportion is the final secret,
to espouse it at the outset is to insure sterility'.

The point of the novel lies not in an assertion of normality,
but in an exploration of extremes. And this exploration is
not simply social and political. Further issues are involved, which reflect Forster's basic preoccupations as a
thinker, and his own experiences in India.

The relationship between Forster's experiences and the
final shape of his novel is a good deal more subtle than one
might at first imagine. If one turns to *The Hill of Devi*,
the later factual record of his visits, some points of contact
with the novel stand out immediately. . . . And longer incidents sometimes find their way into the novel, when

some important purpose is to be served. There was, for example, his adventure during a walk:

> There we had an exciting and typical adventure.
> Our train of villagers stopped and pointed to the
> opposite bank with cries of a snake. At last I saw
> it—a black thing reared up to the height of three
> feet and motionless. I said, 'It looks like a small
> dead tree', and was told 'Oh no', and exact spe-
> cies and habits of snake were indicated—not a
> cobra, but very fierce and revengeful, and if we
> shot it would pursue us several days later all the
> way to Dewas. We then took stones and threw
> them across the Sipra . . . in order to make
> snake crawl away. Still he didn't move and when
> a stone hit his base still didn't move. He *was* a
> small dead tree. All the villagers shrieked with
> laughter.

During the ascent to the caves in *A Passage to India,* there
is a corresponding incident:

> Again, there was a confusion about a snake
> which was never cleared up. Miss Quested saw
> a thin, dark object reared on end at the farther
> side of a watercourse, and said, 'A snake!' The
> villagers agreed, and Aziz explained: yes, a black
> cobra, very venomous, who had reared himself
> up to watch the passing of the elephant. But
> when she looked through Ronny's field-glasses,
> she found it wasn't a snake, but the withered and
> twisted stump of a toddy-palm. So she said, 'It
> isn't a snake.' The villagers contradicted her.
> She had put the word into their minds, and they
> refused to abandon it. Aziz admitted that it
> looked like a tree through the glasses, but insist-
> ed that it was a black cobra really, and impro-
> vised some rubbish about protective mimicry.
> Nothing was explained, and yet there was no ro-
> mance.

In *The Hill of Devi* there is also an account of an incident
which puzzled Forster a good deal, and led him to wonder
whether his Maharajah might possess super-normal faculties. A couple described how they had been motoring from
Dewas to Indore, and how their car had been hit by some
animal just as they crossed the Sipra so that it swerved and
nearly hit the parapet of the bridge:

> His Highness sat up keenly interested. 'The ani-
> mal came from the left?' he asked.
>
> 'Yes.'
>
> 'It was a large animal? Larger than a pig but not
> as big as a buffalo?'
>
> 'Yes, but how did you know?'
>
> 'You couldn't be sure what animal it was?'
>
> 'No we couldn't.'
>
> He leant back again and said, 'It is most unfortu-
> nate. Years ago I ran over a man there. I was not
> at all to blame—he was drunk and ran on to the
> road and I was cleared at the enquiry, and I gave
> money to his family. But ever since then he has
> been trying to kill me in the form you describe.'

Forster relates that he was left with the sense of 'an unexplained residuum'. In *A Passage to India* there is a similar incident, which takes place when Adela and Ronny are out driving. An estrangement between them is just being resolved by their consciousness of physical attraction when the car is brought to a standstill by the impact of something against it. They get out and decide that a hyena has hit them. Shortly afterwards, Adela tells Ronny that she has no intention of breaking with him after all. When the incident is recounted to Mrs Moore, she shivers and says, 'A ghost!' No one can explain why she says this, least of all herself: but we later learn that the Nawab had hit a drunken man there some years before, just as Forster's Maharajah had done in real life.

An examination of the use of these incidents shows that Forster is not simply putting in useful local colour. A more subtle purpose is being served. Both help to suggest Adela's state of mind during the expedition to the Marabar caves, as we shall see later.

A good deal of Forster's experience must have been used in producing the details which give the novel its deceptively causal appearance—its air that 'this is how things usually happen, one after another'. But the fact that some of the most important incidents appear, not at random but in order to subserve a particular effect, harmonizes with a statement by Forster in *The Hill of Devi,* in which he tries to explain the relationship between his Indian experiences and his Indian novel:

> I began this novel before my 1921 visit, and took out the opening chapters with me, with the intention of continuing them. But as soon as they were confronted with the country they purported to describe, they seemed to wilt and go dead and I could do nothing with them. I used to look at them of an evening in my room at Dewas, and felt only distaste and despair. The gap between India remembered and India experienced was too wide. When I got back to England the gap narrowed, and I was able to resume. But I still thought the book bad, and probably should not have completed it without the encouragement of Leonard Woolf.

Only away from India could the patterns which were being woven to interpret his Indian experiences flourish without being swamped by the sheer mass of meaningless experience in everyday life there.

In the early part of the novel the 'pattern' consists mainly of a suggestive atmosphere. There is a constant emphasis upon the existence, side by side, of attractiveness and hostility in the Indian scene. The two interweave constantly. They are represented with particular strength in the tension between sky and earth—the sky benevolent, the earth hostile. The most important statement of this tension comes at the end of the first chapter:

> The sky settles everything—not only climates and seasons but when the earth shall be beautiful. By herself she can do little—only feeble outbursts of flowers. But when the sky chooses, glory can rain into the Chandrapore bazaars or a benediction pass from horizon to horizon. The sky can do this because it is so strong and so enormous. Strength comes from the sun, infused

in it daily, size from the prostrate earth. No mountains infringe on the curve. League after league the earth lies flat, heaves a little, is flat again. Only in the south, where a group of fists and fingers are thrust up through the soil, is the endless expanse interrupted. These fists and fingers are the Marabar Hills, containing the extraordinary caves.

The juxtaposition of beauty and hostility continues. When Aziz is on his way to the beautiful mosque where he first meets Mrs Moore, Forster comments on the difficulty of walking in India. 'There is something hostile in that soil. It either yields, and the foot sinks into a depression, or else it is unexpectedly rigid and sharp, pressing stones or crystals against the tread.' Mrs Moore notices the sky continually and feels a kinship with it. 'In England the moon had seemed dead and alien; here she was caught in the shawl of night together with earth and all the other stars.' But at the end of the chapter, when she murmurs a vague endearment to a wasp which she finds sleeping on a clothes peg, it is against a sinister background. '. . . jackals in the plain bayed their desires and mingled with the percussion of drums.' Her voice floats out, 'to swell the night's uneasiness'. The double theme persists throughout the novel. At the climax, in the Hindu festival, there is a momentary reconciliation, symbolized when Aziz looks down on the tank from the road above. 'Reflecting the evening clouds, it filled the netherworld with an equal splendour, so that earth and sky leant toward one another, about to clash in ecstasy'. But this is the nearest approach to fusion. In the last episode of the novel, earth and sky alike are made to agree in the impossibility of reconciliation between English and Indians here and now.

The discussion so far might suggest that the sky is only associated with benevolence, the earth only with hostility. This is not so, however. Forster's symbolism has to be referred back to his purposes in *Howards End.* Here, as there, Forster is concerned with the finite and the infinite. The earth represents the finite, the sky the infinite. But both are morally ambivalent. When the moonlight shines on the mosque, it offers 'acceptable hints of infinity'. But when the sun beats down on a parched landscape, infinity becomes unbearable. In the same way, the finite earth can either harden to the hostility of rock, or relax to the benevolence of a fertile plain.

This moral ambivalence provides the warp and woof of the novel. But at its extreme points, the utmost of hostility is found in the finite intractability of rock, the utmost of benevolence in the infinite sun—not the unbearable sun which beats down on noonday India, but the gentler, more glorious sun which is seen for a moment at sunrise and which symbolizes the splendour of true love.

The two poles of the novel are narrowed and focused into more precise symbols. The hostility of rock is particularized in the Marabar caves. As Professor Frank Kermode has pointed out, Forster achieves a good deal of his effect here by an insistent use of the word 'extraordinary'. The first sentence of the whole book reads, 'Except for the Marabar Caves—and they are twenty miles off—the city of Chandrapore presents nothing extraordinary.' The last sentence of the first chapter ends with a mention of 'the

Marabar Hills, containing the extraordinary caves'. The innocent word recurs in a later dialogue, when Aziz tries to make Godbole explain why the Marabar caves are famous—but at each move in the conversation the listeners are further from discovering 'what, if anything, was extraordinary about the Marabar Caves.' Even when the visitors are on their way, no one will tell them exactly why they are going or what they are going to see. In the meantime, however, there has intervened a description of the caves. Nothing, says Forster, distinguishes one cave from another: 'It is as if the surrounding plain or the passing birds have taken upon themselves to exclaim "extraordinary", and the word has taken root in the air, and been inhaled by mankind.'

This peculiar atmosphere, where all is ordinary to the point of being extraordinary, where nullity hardens into hostility, where lack of value turns dully malignant, is crystallized in another image. Elsewhere Forster has described the sinister atmosphere of the Grand Canyon, where the Colorado River 'rages like an infuriated maggot between precipices of granite, gnawing at them and cutting the Canyon deeper.' In **'The Machine Stops'**, there is a horrifying scene where the hero, trying to escape, finds himself seized by hideous long white worms which overcome his struggles and suck him back from the surface of the earth into the Machine beneath. This image-pattern is used by Forster to describe Mrs Moore's experience of the Marabar caves. The echoes in the cave are little worms coiling, ascending and descending. What speaks to her there is 'something snubnosed, incapable of generosity—the undying worm itself'. In this negative vision, the serpent of eternity is 'made of maggots'.

Against the nightmarish nullity of the caves there is to be set another voice which rings insistently in the novel. Professor Godbole represents the old Hindu tradition of love. At one point he sings a song expressing the earth's yearning for the heavens—the song of the milkmaid calling to Krishna, who refuses to come. In answer to a question from Mrs Moore, he explains that the god never comes in any of his songs. ' "I say to Him, Come, come, come, come, come, come. He neglects to come". '

When Ronny and Adela pass through the countryside in the car, their estrangement unresolved, the landscape is described as too vast to admit of excellence. 'In vain did each item in it call out, "Come, come." There was not enough god to go round.' The outward scene here expresses their own inward landscape, from which the visionary sun-god of love is absent. Again, when the train is steaming towards the Marabar caves, there is a long passage on India, culminating in the statement, 'She knows of the whole world's trouble, to its uttermost depth. She calls "Come" through her hundred mouths, through objects ridiculous and august. But come to what? She has never defined. She is not a promise, only an appeal.'

Godbole's song may express the yearning of India, but the spirit of love which he also represents cannot cope with the intractability of the caves. As we have seen, he insistently refrains from specifying exactly what is 'extraordinary' about the caves: in particular, he does not mention the echo. Similarly, after the disastrous expedition, his

lack of concern about it disconcerts Fielding. He explains that his unconcern is due to the fact that good and evil are 'both aspects of my Lord':

> 'He is present in the one, absent in the other, and the difference between presence and absence is great, as great as my feeble mind can grasp. Yet absence implies presence, absence is not nonexistence, and we are therefore entitled to repeat, "Come, come, come, come." '

A similar limitation is apparent in his dance-ecstasy at the festival. As he dances his love, he brings more and more things into his vision, but when at last he imagines a stone, he finds that he cannot include it. Certain things always resist the harmonizing vision, which can only ignore them.

Yet, if the caves represent one extreme of India, its 'reality' in one sense, Godbole's spirit of love, rising to ecstasy, expresses its other extreme, its other 'reality'. And if the two extremes cannot quite meet, that does not mean that mankind ought to turn away from both and seek a compromise halfway between them. One is reminded again of that vehement assertion in *Howards End*:

> No; truth, being alive, was not halfway between anything. It was only to be found by continuous excursions into either realm, and though proportion is the final secret, to espouse it at the outset is to insure sterility.

By this time, it will be observed, symbolic implications have transformed the pattern of the novel. What seemed at first sight to be only a conflict between British and Indians has broadened into a conflict between earth and sky—which in its turn veils the conflict between spirit and matter, between love and the intractable.

The title of the novel might have suggested these depths to us. Walt Whitman's poem, 'Passage to India', from which it is taken, begins as a poem about human voyaging. But as it proceeds, it turns into a poem about the voyage of the soul to God.

> O thou transcendant!
> Nameless—the fibre and the breath!
> Light of the light—shedding forth universes—
>   thou centre of them!
> Thou mightier centre of the true, the good, the
>   loving!
> Thou moral, spiritual fountain! affection's
>   source!
> thou reservoir!

The poem continues with the reiterated cry, 'Passage to more than India!' Forster's use of Whitman's title has a distinctly ironical flavour, however, for if his two visitors are to find in India 'more than India', it will also be something very far removed from the transcendent or the Ideal: Mrs Moore will find herself confronted by the very negation of her values. The main events of Forster's novel are dominated not by the 'Light of light' but by an oppressive and hostile sun. Yet Whitman's ideal is not irrelevant. The symbolic events of Forster's first section, at least, are lit by a gentle moon, and throughout the novel there is suggestion of a greater power, a sun-like spirit of love which never quite manages to become incarnate. And Godbole's point becomes relevant: 'absence implies presence, absence is not nonexistence. . . .'

Moreover, if Forster has not Whitman's full optimism, his central point is the same. Mrs Moore and Adela Quested, who think that they are making an ordinary tourist's trip to India, and that they know what they mean when they ask to see the 'real' India, are to find that they are making a spiritual passage, and that they will be brought face to face with 'reality' in a very different form. This confrontation reverberates throughout the novel, shedding light on and affecting everything else that happens in it.

It is here that the boldness of the novel becomes apparent. At the level of events, the plot which promises so much fizzles out in a negation. To find positiveness we have to move behind the simple action—first to the moral significance of the events and then, quite naturally, to a pattern of symbolism which rises behind the plot just as the Marabar caves rise silently against the sky behind the busy little station of Chandrapore.

We have already touched upon some of the symbolic themes. Their point of interaction with the plot, however, lies chiefly in the experiences of Mrs Moore and Adela Quested, and we cannot do justice to the subtlety of the interweaving without examining those experiences more closely.

There is one important respect in which an appreciation of what is going on at the symbolic and psychological level helps to unravel the plot itself. A point which troubles many readers is whether Aziz actually assaulted Adela or not. At first she declares that she was assaulted; then at the trial she says with equal conviction that Aziz did not follow her into the cave. Either or both statements as they stand might be the result of hysterical delusion. Which are we to believe? Even as close a friend as Goldsworthy Lowes Dickinson asked Forster, 'What did happen in the caves?'

Confusion on this point has to do with a confusion concerning the place of 'reality' in this novel. Here, as in *The Longest Journey,* 'reality' is on the anvil. We are back with Forster's idea that its importance consists not only in its objective nature, but also in its psychological function. Whatever philosophical position they take up, men will normally agree that reality is one and unchanging. But a sense of reality can fluctuate: and according to Forster all men lose their sense of reality to a greater or lesser extent when they fail to connect head and heart.

This was what happened to Lucy Honeychurch when she entered the 'armies of the benighted', and to Rickie when he married Agnes and taught in Sawston School: it is also what happens to Adela Quested in this novel. She has arrived with the double intention of seeing the 'real' India and settling the question of her proposed marriage to Ronny Heaslop. Early in the novel, having observed the effect of India on Ronny, she has decided that she will not marry him after all. But the incidents just afterwards when they go out for a drive and are thrust together first by the jolting of the car then by the impact of collision with an animal, restore the relationship for the time being by reminding them of their physical attraction towards each other.

So the relationship stands until the day when Adela is climbing up towards the Marabar caves. Two incidents affect her state of mind on this occasion: first the confusion over the snake, then, as she is thinking about her marriage, a reminder of the animal impact:

> But as she toiled over a rock that resembled an inverted saucer, she thought, 'What about love?' The rock was nicked by a double row of footholds, and somehow the question was suggested by them. Where had she seen footholds before? Oh yes, they were the pattern traced in the dust by the wheels of the Nawab Bahadur's car. She and Ronny—no, they did not love each other.

She considers the position, pausing thoughtfully:

> Vexed rather than appalled, she stood still, her eyes on the sparkling rock. There was esteem and animal contact at dusk, but the emotion that links them was absent.

Like Rickie at a corresponding moment, however, she fails to respond to the symbolic moment and decides to go through with the marriage. To break it off would cause too much trouble, and she is not at all sure that love is necessary to a successful union. She dismisses the thought and enters on a discussion of marriage with Aziz. Like Lucy Honeychurch, she is in the process of muddling herself: and it is in this state of muddle that she enters the cave.

The clue to her subsequent behaviour lies not in any outward event but in this muddled state of her mind at the crucial moment. It is still the vital clue when, after a long period of illness, she arrives at the trial to give her testimony. In the intervening period one important event has taken place. She has visited Mrs Moore, talking to her first about the persistent echo in her head, then about love and marriage. Afterwards, although in fact nothing has been said about the subject directly, she emerges with a conviction that Aziz is innocent and that Mrs Moore has said so. Questioned later, Mrs Moore denies having mentioned Aziz—but also says irritably, 'Of course he's innocent.'

The remark does not deter Adela from going forward, but it has disturbed her. It has cracked, without breaking, the state of unreality in which she has been living since the day of the expedition. The state was created because she muddled herself about her relationship with Ronny, and Mrs Moore's ramblings have probed the muddle without exposing it. The exposure does not come until she is standing in the courtroom: and then, significantly, she thinks immediately of Mrs Moore:

> The Court was crowded and of course very hot, and the first person Adela noticed in it was the humblest of all who were present, a person who had no bearing officially upon the trial: the man who pulled the punkah. Almost naked, and splendidly formed, he sat on a raised platform near the back, in the middle of the central gangway, and he caught her attention as she came in, and he seemed to control the proceedings. He had the strength and beauty that sometimes come to flower in Indians of low birth. When

that strange race nears the dust and is condemned as untouchable, then nature remembers the physical perfection that she accomplished elsewhere, and throws out a god—not many, but one here and there, to prove to society how little its categories impress her. This man would have been notable anywhere: among the thin-hammed, flat-chested mediocrities of Chandrapore he stood out as divine, yet he was of the city, its garbage had nourished him, he would end on its rubbish heaps. Pulling the rope towards him, relaxing it rhythmically, sending swirls of air over others, receiving none himself, he seemed apart from human destinies, a male fate, a winnower of souls. Opposite him, also on a platform, sat the little assistant magistrate, cultivated, self-conscious, and conscientious. The punkah wallah was none of these things: he scarcely knew that he existed and did not understand why the Court was fuller than usual, indeed he did not know that it was fuller than usual, didn't even know he worked a fan, though he thought he pulled a rope. Something in his aloofness impressed the girl from middle-class England, and rebuked the narrowness of her sufferings. In virtue of what had she collected this roomful of people together? Her particular brand of opinions, and the suburban Jehovah who sanctified them—by what right did they claim so much importance in the world, and assume the title of civilization? Mrs Moore—she looked round, but Mrs Moore was far away on the sea; it was the kind of question they might have discussed on the voyage out before the old lady had turned disagreeable and queer.

While thinking of Mrs Moore she heard sounds, which gradually grew more distinct. The epoch-making trial had started. . . .

At this, the crisis of the novel, there has been an irruption from an old world, the world of Forster's mythologies. The figure who catches Adela's attention is an incarnate god, an Indian Apollo. He is as real as the garbage-heaps of the city, yet he is also a visionary figure. His glory outshines the muddle which has made her confuse a mixture of desire and esteem with love, and releases a power which reminds her again and again of Mrs Moore, dissolving the cloud of unreality which has shrouded her since the day of her muddle, and restoring her sense of reality.

Looking at Aziz in the courtroom, she is once again wondering whether she has made a mistake, when the memory of Mrs Moore is unexpectedly reinforced. Her name is mentioned in court, and the defence suggests that she has been deliberately hidden in order that her witness may not clear Aziz. The grievance spreads to the crowd outside, who begin chanting

Esmiss Esmoor
Esmiss Esmoor
Esmiss Esmoor

in the way that at a festival they would chant 'Radakrishna Radakrishna'.

Just afterwards, Adela rises to give her evidence. She has always been shy of this moment, because in spite of her desire to tell the truth, she remembers that her entry into the cave was associated with thoughts about marriage, and thinks that her question to Aziz on the subject might have roused evil in him. Yet she would find it hard to recount a matter so intimate in open court. By the time that she rises, however, the 'naked god' and Mrs Moore have done their work.

> But as soon as she rose to reply, and heard the sound of her own voice, she feared not even that. A new and unknown sensation protected her, like magnificent armour. She didn't think what had happened, or even remember in the ordinary way of memory, but she returned to the Marabar hills, and spoke from them across a sort of darkness to Mr McBryde. The fatal day recurred, in every detail, but now she was of it and not of it at the same time, and this double relation gave it indescribable splendour. Why had she thought the expedition 'dull'? Now the sun rose again, the elephant waited, the pale masses of the rock flowed round her and presented the first cave. . . .

Because her head has once again made contact with her heart (the 'Mrs Moore' in her) her sense of reality has been restored, and the memory of what happened is not only clear but magnificent. Imagination and perceptions have been reunited to make that state which is commonly acknowledged to be the true 'reality', where the universe of the heart and the universe presented to the senses form a single pattern. She is no longer separate from the scene—instead, the masses of the rock 'flow round her' in a symphony of experience.

The reality so presented to her governs her testimony, which brings the trial to its abrupt close. And at the close of the trial, the chief symbol in it is left in full possession of the scene.

> . . . before long no one remained on the scene of the fantasy but the beautiful naked god. Unaware that anything unusual had occurred, he continued to pull the cord of his punkah, to gaze at the empty dais and the overturned special chairs, and rhythmically to agitate the clouds of descending dust.

Once one has observed the symbolism of this figure, coupled with the train of mental development that has elapsed, it becomes clear that Adela's new state of mind is not and cannot be another hysterical state: it is a recovery from hysteria. The important thing is not what happened in the cave but what has been happening to Adela.

In the eyes of British India she is now finished. She has committed the unforgivable sin of betraying her fellow-countrymen and bringing about the possibility of rebellion. Certainly there can now be no question of her marrying Ronny Heaslop, even if she wanted to. She can only return to England, lucky that Dr Aziz does not press for heavy damages.

For her as an individual, however, the events have a decisive and formative effect. As Fielding talks to her later, he is impressed by her new attitude. 'Although her hard school-mistressy manner remained, she was no longer examining life, but being examined by it; she had become a real person.' Nevertheless, the progress has been made within strict limitations. She remains a creature dominated by her head, and so her behaviour cannot impress the Indians:

> For her behaviour rested on cold justice and honesty; she had felt, while she recanted, no passion of love for those whom she had wronged. Truth is not truth in that exacting land unless there go with it kindness and more kindness and kindness again, unless the Word that was with God also is God. And the girl's sacrifice—so creditable according to Western notions—was rightly rejected, because, though it came from her heart, it did not include her heart. . . .
>
> (pp. 186-204)

The limitations of Adela's experience in the courtroom have now been exposed—her heart came into play in the service of truth but did not become engaged. The vision of the 'naked god' was a temporary stimulus, not a lasting revelation. The crisis of the novel over, Adela, now realized as a person but still a creature of the head, emerges in contrast to Mrs Moore, whose heart is developed, but who cannot face the nakedness of truth.

This gives us the cue for an examination of Mrs Moore's experiences in India. In the early part of the novel, when the atmosphere is not oppressive and the two women are merely two travellers who are seeing the sights of the state, Mrs Moore figures in an incident which sets the tone of her character for the rest of the novel. Venturing into a mosque one evening she encounters Aziz, who is still smouldering under recent insults from the British. He speaks to her sharply, but she replies with friendliness, establishing a bond with him which is never afterwards broken. It is a peaceful, moonlit night as she returns to the club, but she is soon given to understand that she has behaved in an un-English way by speaking to Aziz. After an argument with her son Ronny she emerges from the club to find a small wasp on the peg where her cloak is hanging. ' "Pretty dear," said Mrs Moore to the wasp. He did not wake, but her voice floated out, to swell the night's uneasiness.'

Mrs Moore's kindness to Aziz, and her treatment of the wasp, introduce one of the novel's main themes. Where is love to end? Mrs Moore has a developed heart and is kind to those whom she meets, but what is she in the face of India's teeming millions and manifold sufferings? Love in India: is it not like a snow-flake dropping into the ocean? It is not even simply a question of people, for India is shown to be a country which human beings have not quite dominated. In mentioning the wasp, Forster comments on the fact that no Indian animal has any sense of an interior. The animal and vegetable kingdoms have a prominence which they have lost in Western Europe and behind them stretches something still more intractable—the hardness of rock itself.

At the moment, however, we are still at the more manageable level of animals and insects, and this theme is reinforced in the next chapter, where there is an account of Mr Graysford and Mr Sorley, the two missionaries of Chandrapore. Mr Sorley, who is more advanced than his older companion, considers that God's hospitality may extend to the animal kingdom, to monkeys for example. Even jackals might be included. But he is less sure about wasps.

> He became uneasy during the descent to wasps, and was apt to change the conversation. And oranges, cactuses, crystals and mud? and the bacteria inside Mr Sorley? No, no, this is going too far. We must exclude someone from our gathering, or we shall be left with nothing.

The uneasiness about extending love to wasps foreshadows the more sinister atmosphere of the next section, which is dominated by the Marabar caves. The description of the caves at the beginning of the section is no mere chunk of local colour, but a statement of significance which 'places' the caves before they begin to act in the narrative. Their rockiness is not merely beyond the reach of civilization: there is a sense that they extend behind the time process itself, untouched by any human quality.

> They are older than anything in the world. No water has ever covered them, and the sun who has watched them for countless æons may still discern in their outlines forms that were his before our globe was torn from his bosom. If flesh of the sun's flesh is to be touched anywhere, it is here, among the incredible antiquity of these hills.

Hostility is a keynote of the whole section. The main scene of the first section took place in moonlight, a moonlight which helped to establish the atmosphere of human kindness. But even in that section the Marabar hills were always 'fists and fingers'. In this section, where they come into their own, the sun is the dominating presence, always hostile. This part of India is 'flesh of the sun's flesh.' On the morning of the ill-fated expedition to the Marabar caves, the sunrise which the visitors are looking forward to fails them.

> They awaited the miracle. But at the supreme moment, when night should have died and day lived, nothing occurred. It was as if virtue had failed in the celestial fount. . . . Why, when the chamber was prepared, did the bridegroom not enter with trumpets and shawms, as humanity expects? The sun rose without splendour.

Symbolic interpretations press hard here. Like Blake and Coleridge, Forster sees the moment of sunrise as the nearest approach in the universe at large to the splendid birth of love in human experience. For one moment an almost transcendent glory is revealed. But on this occasion, an unglamorous sunrise only serves to stress the hostility of a sun in which heat predominates. During the day the presence of the sun is mentioned again and again, always as a hostile presence. The experiences undergone by both Mrs Moore and Adela are ascribed partly to sunstroke and correspond to recorded case-histories of it.

The sun beats down on them as they toil up towards the caves and banks the oppressiveness that pervades the scene. It bars escape from the experiences that await them. Mrs Moore, entering a cave, finds the interior unpleasant and even horrifying. The cave is immediately filled by their retinue and begins to smell. Some 'vile naked thing' (which later turns out to have been a baby, astride its mother's hip) strikes her face and settles on her mouth. For an instant she goes mad, hitting and gasping like a fanatic, alarmed not merely by the crush and stench, but by the unexpected and terrifying echo.

The echo is the culminating horror of the novel. It reminds one directly of the echo that oppressed Margaret Schlegel in St Paul's and indirectly of the 'goblin footfalls', also in *Howards End.* It has the same nullity, the same ability to deny value: it is 'entirely devoid of distinction'.

> Whatever is said, the same monotonous noise replies, and quivers up and down the walls until it is absorbed into the roof. 'Boum' is the sound as far as the human alphabet can express it, or 'bou-oum', or 'ou-boum'—utterly dull. Hope, politeness, the blowing of a nose, the squeak of a boot, all produce 'boum'. Even the striking of a match starts a little worm coiling, which is too small to complete a circle but is eternally watchful. And if several people talk at once, an overlapping howling noise begins, echoes generate echoes, and the cave is stuffed with a snake composed of small snakes, which writhe independently.

The echoes turn swiftly into worms and serpents, which reinforce the hint that their significance is reaching out beyond the cave. The worm and serpent have associations with an evil which is characterized more closely later, when Mrs Moore comes to reflect upon her experience:

> She minded it much more now than at the time. The crush and smells she could forget, but the echo began in some indescribable way to undermine her hold on life. Coming at a moment when she chanced to be fatigued, it had managed to murmur, 'Pathos, piety, courage—they exist, but are identical, and so is filth. Everything exists, nothing has value.' If one had spoken vileness in that place, or quoted lofty poetry, the comment would have been the same—'ou-boum'. If one had spoken with the tongues of angels and pleaded for all the unhappiness and misunderstanding in the world, past, present, and to come, for all the misery men must undergo whatever their opinion and position, and however much they dodge or bluff—it would amount to the same, the serpent would descend and return to the ceiling. Devils are of the North, and poems can be written about them, but no one could romanticize the Marabar because it robbed infinity and eternity of their vastness, the only quality that accommodates them to mankind.

> She tried to go on with her letter, reminding herself that she was only an elderly woman who had got up too early in the morning and journeyed too far, that the despair creeping over her was merely her despair, her personal weakness, and that even if she got a sunstroke and went mad the rest of the world would go on. But suddenly, at the edge of her mind, Religion appeared, poor little talkative Christianity, and she knew that all its divine words from 'Let there be Light' to 'It is finished' only amounted to 'boum'.

The moment is a crucial one in Forster's writings, and Mrs Moore becomes here an allegorical figure. She possesses within herself all the virtues of the heart, only to find at this moment that her values are nullified by an echo.

There have been many visionary moments in the novel, but this is a moment of anti-vision—a vision of the horror of the universe which contrasts completely with Adela's moment of vision in the court-house. Mrs Moore passes into what Forster describes as 'that state where the horror of the universe and its smallness are both visible at the same time—the twilight of the double vision in which so many elderly people are involved'. And he goes on to work out the significance of the echo:

> What had spoken to her in that scoured-out cavity of the granite? what dwelt in the first of the caves? Something very old and very small. Before time, it was before space also. Something snub-nosed, incapable of generosity—the undying worm itself. Since hearing its voice, she had not entertained one large thought, she was actually envious of Adela. All this fuss over a frightened girl! Nothing had happened, 'and if it had', she found herself thinking with the cynicism of a withered priestess, 'if it had, there are worse evils than love'. The unspeakable attempt presented itself to her as love: in a cave, in a church—Boum, it amounts to the same. Visions are supposed to entail profundity, but—Wait till you get one, dear reader! The abyss may also be petty, the serpent of eternity made of maggots. . . .

It would be easy to see this moment of nightmare vision as the core of the novel. For many readers, it leaves a deeper impression than anything else, and it is not therefore surprising that they should invest it with central significance. Such centrality, however, is not assigned by Forster, who has called it 'a moment of negation . . . the vision with its back turned'. Nor is it assigned in the novel itself, for as Mrs Moore leaves India, other voices speak to her. The train passes a place called Asirgarh, which consists of bastions and a mosque. Ten minutes later, Asirgarh reappears, the mosque now on the other side of the bastions. The train has described a complete semicircle round it. She has nothing with which to connect it: 'But it had looked at her twice and seemed to say: "I do not vanish."' It evidently reminds her of the moonlit mosque of the first section, which had offered a more agreeable India, a less hostile infinity. Similarly, the hostility of the caves is contrasted with the scene where her boat moves out of the harbour and thousands of coconut palms wave her farewell. ' "So you thought an echo was India; you took the Marabar caves as final?" they laughed. "What have we in common with them, or they with Asirgarh? Good-bye!" '

The echo, after all, does not undermine Adela, who also experiences it. It enters her only for a time, echoing and re-echoing in her head during her illness, but disappears during her conversation with Mrs Moore. Mrs Moore's failure, on the other hand, is the physical enforcement of a physical lack. She is old, and after a lifetime of developing her heart rather than her head, she cannot stand against a re-orientation of reality. When this basis is gone, the cave becomes the universe, her values are destroyed and she dies. Nevertheless, even then her spirit is not extinguished. It can still, even when she is rambling, suggest to Adela that Aziz is innocent. And it survives in the memories of those who have known her. As with Rickie and Mrs Wilcox, her vicarious survival is a form of redemptive immortality. She is resurrected in the mind of Adela during the trial and the crowd outside chant her name. She is resurrected again towards the end of the novel, when Professor Godbole is dancing himself into an ecstasy of love at the Hindu festival. The image of Mrs Moore then comes into his mind:

> Chance brought her into his mind while it was in this heated state, he did not select her, she happened to occur among the throng of soliciting images, a tiny splinter, and he impelled her by his spiritual force to that place where completeness can be found. Completeness, not reconstruction. His senses grew thinner, he remembered a wasp seen he forgot where, perhaps on a stone. He loved the wasp equally, he impelled it likewise, he was imitating God. And the stone where the wasp clung—could he . . . no, he could not, he had been wrong to attempt the stone, logic and conscious effort had seduced, he came back to the strip of red carpet and discovered that he was dancing upon it.

Later, the ecstasy over, he steps out of the temple into the grey of a pouring wet morning, thinking, 'One old Englishwoman and one little, little wasp. It does not seem much, still it is more than I am myself.'

The images that occurred in his ecstasy reiterate themes of the novel. Unlike the two missionaries, but like Mrs Moore, Godbole can extend his love to include the wasp. His failure to include the stone is equally significant. There is always something that resists and denies love, and the stone is reminiscent of the intractable Marabar caves.

Forster's inclusion of this intractable element even in Godbole's ecstatic dance is another indication of its importance in the novel as a whole. Once again, he insists on having a Caliban on his island. But the Marabar caves, which make no pretentions at all to humanity, are better than Caliban or Leonard Bast for his purpose. As symbols, their excellence can be measured by the number of significances which critics have found in them. They have been respectively described as 'bare, dark, echoing', echoing 'eternity, infinity, the Absolute'; 'the very voice of that union which is the opposite of divine; the voice of evil and negation'; 'wombs'; and 'it may be, the soul of India.'

Forster's own account of them in his *Writers at Work* interview helps to point their significance:

> When I began **A Passage to India** I knew that something important happened in the Marabar Caves, and that it would have a central place in the novel—but I didn't know what it would be.
>
> . . . The Marabar Caves represented an area in which concentration can take place. A cavity. They were something to focus everything up: they were to engender an event like an egg.

Everything in the novel has to be confronted by the caves.

The head of Adela and the heart of Mrs Moore are equally challenged by the negation of a cave which can only reflect sights and sounds. For them it is a confrontation with 'reality' in the worst sense of the word: matter without mind, substance devoid of imaginative appeal. But this is not full reality even if it is an element without which reality cannot exist. The attempt to love a stone breaks into Professor Godbole's ecstasy and brings him back to the strip of red carpet where he is dancing, but it does not stop him dancing. Similarly the existence of the Marabar caves in India does not prevent thousands of palm-trees from waving farewell to Mrs Moore, nor does the hostility of the sun invalidate the hints of a more benevolent infinity offered in the first section of the novel.

The Marabar caves are not a revelation of reality, but a touchstone by which reality is tested. They are a 'vortex', in the sense in which Blake used the word. The forces of the novel are attracted towards the experience which they offer, and in passing through it are transformed. They are drawn in and englobed, to emerge with form and new life. Adela becomes a person. Mrs Moore is destroyed in the body but, as we have seen, her spirit lives on in the lives and spirits of others: and in the last section of the novel it is actually reincarnate in physical form, when her children Ralph and Stella visit India.

At this point, moreover, the spirit of Mrs Moore is absorbed into the total spirit of Love which is shadowed, however uncertainly, by the Hindu festival of the same section. We have already mentioned Forster's reference to this as 'architecturally necessary', meeting the need for 'a lump, or a Hindu temple if you like—a mountain standing up'. The image which he is here using may well derive from a wartime experience which he described in a broadcast talk and later in a book review. Writing of an exhibition of Indian temples which Stella Kramrisch (together with Dr Saxl) devised in London in 1940, he says:

> Briefly she showed me the temple as the World Mountain on whose exterior is displayed life in all its forms, life human and superhuman and subhuman and animal, life tragic and cheerful, cruel and kind, seemly and obscene, all crowned at the mountain's summit by the sun. And in the interior of the mountain she revealed a tiny cavity, a central cell, where, in the heart of the world complexity, the individual could be alone with his god. Hinduism, unlike Buddhism, Islam and Christianity—is not a congregational religion: it by-passes the community and despite its entanglement with caste it by-passes class. Its main concern is the individual and his relation to reality, and however much it wanders over the surface of the world mountain it returns at last to the mountain's heart. This happens to appeal to me.

In retrospect, the Hindu festival evidently seems to him to possess some of the same qualities. It is a final image of all-inclusive reality, through which some of the chief characters must pass before his novel can be concluded.

Together with Fielding, to whom Stella is now married, Mrs Moore's children come to take part in the festival. They take a boat on the water when the festival is at its height and are joined grudgingly by Aziz, who has been moved by Ralph's resemblance to his mother to set aside, at least for an evening, the hatred for English people which has possessed him since his trial.

Unfortunately, a slight gale is running on the tank, heralding a storm: and the result is that they lose control of the boat, which, having collided with another boat, drifts towards the servitor with his tray and strikes it. Stella, by shrinking first towards her husband, then flinging herself against Aziz, capsizes the boat and plunges them all into the warm shallow water. Meanwhile there is a crescendo of noise from artillery, drums and elephants, culminating in an immense peal of thunder. The climax, 'as far as India admits of one', has been reached, and rain sets in steadily to wet everything and everybody.

Symbolic meaning surges again at this point. It is significant that the capsizing is caused by Stella throwing herself at both Fielding and Aziz in quick succession; it is significant that afterwards letters from Ronny and Adela float on the water. This mêlée at the feast of Krishna, prince of love, is the nearest approach to a birth of brotherly love in the novel—it at least marks the release of Aziz from the hatred which has confined him since his trial. It is equally typical of Forster's firm realism in this novel that the approach should only be made in the middle of the upsetting of a boat, and that the accompanying climax of the festival should immediately dissolve in rainy confusion. If there is a mystery of love in India, it subsists only at the heart of a huge muddle.

Unlike the civilization of Sawston, which has gradually selected a manageable segment of human experience to be its world, India represents the whole of human experience. It contains at one extreme the ecstasy of human and divine love, at the other the sort of basic stony 'reality' which baffles an undeveloped head and challenges an undeveloped heart. When someone remarked earlier in the novel that India was a muddle, Mrs Moore recoiled. Her 'undeveloped head' could not deal with muddles:

> 'I like mysteries but I rather dislike muddles,' said Mrs Moore.
>
> 'A mystery is a muddle.'
>
> 'Oh, do you think so, Mr Fielding?'
>
> 'A mystery is only a high-sounding term for a muddle. No advantage in stirring it up, in either case. Aziz and I know well that India's a muddle.'
>
> 'India's—Oh, what an alarming idea!'

Fielding represents the British attitude which has done so much for India in clearing away administrative inefficiencies and giving her improved communications, but which is dead to other perceptions. Yet he, too, can still recognize other possibilities. When he is saying good-bye to Adela later, they sense a certain similarity in their outlooks and gain satisfaction from it.

> Perhaps life is a mystery, not a muddle; they could not tell. Perhaps the hundred Indias which fuss and squabble so tiresomely are one,

and the universe they mirror is one. They had not the apparatus for judging.

After that it is fitting that when they part, 'A friendliness, as of dwarfs shaking hands, was in the air.' They seem for a moment to see their own gestures from a great height—there is a wistfulness, the shadow of a shadow of a dream.

Adela and Fielding for their part have missed something great: and so, for her part, has Mrs Moore. The familiar broken dialectic between head and heart is still operative. The final events of the novel confirm the impression that Fielding has failed by his disregard of mystery, Mrs Moore by her dislike of muddles. In this way, they have each shown that they are still half in touch with the Sawston which tries to evade both muddles and mysteries at one and the same time. India, on the other hand, because it contains the extremes of human experience, is both a vast muddle and a concealed mystery.

In his culminating view of India, Forster thus achieves his greatest fusion of vision and realism, for each quality has its objective correlative in this great panorama. India's muddle needs all the efficiency which British administrators brought to it: at the same time its mystery asks for the reverence of a fully developed heart. In presenting the situation, moreover, Forster is able to present the 'muddle' with a completeness which Virginia Woolf, like most readers, finds highly attractive:

> We notice things, about the country especially, spontaneously, accidentally almost, as if we were actually there; and now it was the sparrows flying about the pictures that caught our eyes, now the elephant with the painted forehead, now the enormous but badly designed ranges of hills. The people too, particularly the Indians, have something of the same casual, inevitable quality. (Virginia Woolf, *The Death of the Moth and Other Essays* (1942))

D. A. Traversi has commented on the fact that this casualness becomes an essential part of the novel's meaning: Godbole declares that Krishna '*neglects* to come'; the echo comes upon Mrs Moore when she '*chanced* to be fatigued'; '*chance*' brings Mrs Moore into Godbole's mind while he is dancing, and so on. The casualness is an essential part of the Indian mind, as compared with the English. And so the 'reality' which is so broad and casual and attractive can also be refined to the point where echoes and reflections in a cave mirror the terrifying, casual, incomprehensibility of the entire universe: the 'Pan' of Forster's early short stories, the 'earth' of *The Longest Journey,* which is best avoided unless it can be met with a fully developed head and heart. In the same way, 'vision' can be presented broadly in the spirit that informs the actions of Fielding and Mrs Moore, but it can also be intensified to the ecstatic love which is still to be found in the old Hindu traditions of Forster's India.

Vision and reality are not at one, even in India, and Forster is at pains to emphasize the fact. But his last words on the festival are a way of suggesting that somehow, somewhere, India, at least, manages to preserve a connection between them:

Looking back at the great blur of the last twenty-four hours, no man could say where was the emotional centre of it, any more than he could locate the heart of a cloud. (pp. 204-15)

> *John Beer, "The Undying Worm," in* E. M. Forster A Passage to India: A Casebook, *edited by Malcolm Bradbury, Macmillan and Co. Ltd., 1970, pp. 186-215.*

Jeffrey Meyers   (essay date March 1971)

[*In the following essay, Meyers examines the historical and political references of* A Passage to India *which, he suggests, have been neglected by previous critics.*]

Although *A Passage to India* has been thoroughly and perceptively analyzed, critics have been mistaken about three political aspects of the novel. They are wrong about the chronological point of view; they are unaware of the important political events that occurred in India between the end of the Great War and the publication of the novel in 1924; and they are unjustified in their criticism of Forster for ignoring these events in the novel. I believe, on the contrary, that Forster carefully controls the chronological point of view; is fully aware of the postwar political events that he wrote about during 1921-22 while living in India; and that he alludes to these events in his novel and uses them to enforce his political theme.

When asked about the composition of *A Passage to India,* which he wrote over a period of twelve years, Forster said, "I had a great deal of difficulty with the novel, and thought I would never finish it. I began it in 1912, and then came the war. I took it with me when I returned to India in 1921, but found what I had written wasn't India at all. It was like sticking a photograph on a picture. However, I couldn't write it while I was in India. When I got away, I could get on with it." Rose Macaulay is therefore inaccurate when she writes that the novel "deals with the India of one period [1912], is written largely from material collected and from a point of view *derived from that* [1912] *period,* and was published twelve years later." Actually, Forster writes about India from a 1924 viewpoint not a 1912. He depicts the reactionary pre-War colonial ideas and attitude of 1912 (when the book takes place) as if they still existed in 1922-24 (the dates of composition and publication). He therefore intends the people in the novel to seem totally unaware of the vast changes that had occurred in India and the rest of the world since 1912. The dramatic tension between the pre-War point of view of the characters and the postwar point of view of the author, intensifies the political significance of the novel and heightens its persuasive power and irony.

The important postwar political events have been ignored by critics like K. W. Gransden, who mistakenly writes, "the wartime gap would *not* have had much significance, for the World War had *little* effect on India, where the social and political pattern imposed by the British continued largely *unchanged* until almost the time of the final withdrawal." Even Lionel Trilling states, "its data were gathered in 1912 and 1922 *before* the full spate of Indian nationalism." On the contrary, the 1912-22 period was of the

greatest significance for India and had a profound effect on the country, and it is precisely during this period that the forces of Indian nationalism first began to operate with potent effect.

One small example will suggest the difference between the two periods. As the "Bridge Party" commences, Mrs. Turton haughtily instructs Mrs. Moore and Adela, "You're superior to everyone in India except one or two of the Ranis, and they're on an equality." In **"Reflections on India"** (1922), Forster writes, "the lady who said to me eight years ago, 'Never forget that you're superior to every native in India except the Rajas, and they're on an equality,' is now a silent, if not extinct species. But she has lived her life, and she has done her work."

Martin Green claims that Forster's novel ignores the recent nationalist movements: "*A Passage to India* is 'out of time'—does it take place before or after the Great War?—surely no other intelligent book published in 1924, and so concerned with the modern mind, so completely ignores what just happened to the world." Andrew Shonfield agrees that "one gets the impression that Forster had little understanding and no sympathy for the complicated and courageous politics of the Indian independence movement." And even Natwar-Singh, an Indian diplomat and fervent admirer of Forster, states that the novel "depicts a pre-1914 India and by the time it was published in 1924 events had overtaken it. It appears to be an almost antinationalist book, since it makes no mention of the political ferment that was going on in India in the early 'twenties . . . It seems odd that a person of Forster's awareness could have been so totally oblivious of what was going on in India in 1921."

I believe that Forster's understanding of the overwhelmingly important events that occurred in India and in the entire world between 1917 and 1922 gives *A Passage to India* its political significance, and that in the novel Forster emphasizes the political implications of race relations, fear of riots, English justice and government, Hindu-Moslem unity, Indian Native States, nationalism and the independence movement. As Forster says, "You cannot understand the modern Indians unless you realise that politics occupy them passionately and constantly."

Between Forster's first and second visits to India in 1912 and 1921, the world experienced the Great War, Wilson's Fourteen Points (1918) and the League of Nations (1919), the Russian Revolution, and the revolutionary Sein Fein movement (1918-21) that led to the creation of the Irish Free State. The First World War, like the other events, provided a violent stimulus for Indian nationalism, for "agitation against the British . . . did not reach formidable proportions until the twentieth century, and particularly after World War I." The fifth of Wilson's Fourteen points demanded "a free, open-minded and absolutely impartial adjustment of all colonial claims," and seriously weakened the imperialist position. In Asia the idea of the self-determination of peoples was acclaimed as a doctrine of liberation. In 1917 Lenin published the inflammatory *Imperialism: The Highest State of Capitalism,* and imperialism meant something totally different after Lenin's insistence on the liberation of subject peoples. In 1921, for example, Grigory Zinoviev, Chairman of the Comintern and Politburo member, told the predominantly Moslem Congress of the Peoples of the East in Baku, Georgia: "The Communist International turns today to the people of the East and says to them, 'Brothers, we summon you to a Holy War [the Moslem *jihad* against the infidel], first of all against British imperialism.' "

Immediately after the War, India experienced Gandhi's rise to prominence, the Montagu Declaration (1917) and the First Government of India Act (1919), the Amritsar Massacre (1919), the Moplah Rebellion (1921), and the Khalifat Movements (1921-22). Gandhi returned from his career as a lawyer and political agitator in South Africa in 1914. In 1919 he launched his first campaign of passive resistance against the Rowlatt Acts that permitted judges to try political cases without juries and extended the power of internment without trial to provincial governments. Gandhi initiated civil disobedience in 1920, and was arrested and sentenced to prison in 1922. The first important concession to Indian nationalism was made in the Montagu Declaration which provided for the gradual development of self-governing institutions that would eventually lead to Dominion status. This proposal was embodied in the First Government of India Act which opened the road to parliamentary government, and was the first serious challenge to British rule since the 1857 Mutiny.

The most notorious and violent post-war event was the Amritsar Massacre. Without warning, the English General Dyer broke up a prohibited meeting of ten thousand people by firing 1650 rounds, killing over three hundred people and wounding over a thousand more. He stopped only when his ammunition was exhausted. Louis Snyder writes:

> Among the orders passed by General Dyer at Amritsar was an order that has been styled 'Crawling Order'. . . . The order was to the effect that no Indians should be allowed to pass through the street, but if they wanted to pass they must go on all fours, and pickets were placed at certain points in the street to enforce obedience to this order . . .
>
> within a few minutes after he had passed the order and put the pickets, twelve persons had to be arrested for being insolent and he ordered them to be taken into custody, and the police took them through the street and the picket enforced the crawling order on them.

There is an oblique but unmistakable reference to this infamous crawling order in *A Passage to India.* At the height of the ugly British hatred, hysteria and fear, when the innocent Aziz is freed and the mob is rioting, just after Major Callendar boasts of his medical cruelties to the "buck nigger" Nureddin and says "there's not such a thing as cruelty after a thing like this," Mrs. Turton virulently responds " 'Exactly, and remember it afterwards, you men. You're weak, weak, weak. Why, they ought to *crawl* from here to the caves on their hands and knees whenever an Englishwoman's in sight, they oughtn't to be spoken to, they ought to be spat at, they ought to be ground into the dust' ".

The bitter epilogue is that though General Dyer was retired after the Massacre, the readers of the London *Morning Post* rallied to his support and subscribed a testimonial of £26,000.

The Moplah Rebellion took place on the *Malabar* Coast in August 1921, two years after Amritsar. Several thousand fanatical Moslems were killed by troops and violent crowds after they had skinned alive and slaughtered thousands of Hindus. The Marabar caves would remind every one who knew India of the recent horrors on the Malabar Coast.

The Khalifat was the only mass movement in the recent political history of India in which the Hindus and Moslems collaborated fully. The Indians demanded that the Sultan of Turkey and caliph of all Islam, who had recently been defeated in the Great War, should not be deposed or deprived of his power in the Arabian peninsula. (T. E. Lawrence had successfully led the Arab Revolt against the Sultan and had promised his followers independence.) In 1922, while in India, Forster wrote a sympathetic article on the Khalifat movement in which he said that the Indian Moslem "believes that under God's will the guardianship of Holy Places has passed to the Turks, and that Constantinople itself has become half-holy . . . [this belief] is decent, it is human, and even if it cannot be furthered it should not be wantonly insulted."

Finally, Forster enlarged his own experience and ideas about colonialism by working with the International Red Cross in Alexandria from November 1915 until January 1919. In 1921 he was commissioned by the Labour Party Research Department to write on British colonial policy in Egypt. In his pamphlet, *The Government of Egypt,* he describes England's broken pledges and mistreatment of Egypt, and recommends independence. He criticizes the British High Commissioner, Lord Cromer, for his profound distrust of Orientals, and asserts that Cromer's sympathy with Nationalism was purely academic. Forster's social and political attitudes in this work anticipate *A Passage to India,* for he writes that "I have walked alone, both in the native quarters of the towns and in the country, and have always met courtesy and kindness," and that Cromer's colonial administrators and "still more their women-folk, introduce a racial arrogance from which the regular Anglo-Egyptian officials are free."

The political themes of *A Passage to India* are crucial to the meaning of the novel, and are closely related to the social and philosophical ideas. Forster says that "the political side of it was an aspect I wanted to express," and his political purpose was to ameliorate the world by helping Indian aspirations. The novel was a set book for the Indian Civil Service, and Forster claims "It had some political influence—it caused people to think of the link between India and Britain and to doubt if that link was altogether of a healthy nature." As the Indian writer Nirad Chaudhuri states, it "became a powerful weapon in the hands of the anti-imperialists, and was made to contribute its share to the disappearance of British rule in India."

Forster's political reasoning is inductive; he begins with individuals and then moves to nations. The enormous difficulties that Aziz encounters when he prepares the expedition to the caves, suggests in miniature the difficulties of social life in all of India, and the multifarious differences that separate races and religions. Forster believes that colonial problems are primarily the result of personal misunderstanding and mutual incomprehension. He believes the personal relationship is most important to the Oriental, and that in the East, the individual must succeed as an individual or he has failed.

The opening description of Chandrapore emphasizes the physical opposition of the Indians in the squalid city near the river and the English in the civil station on the hill. In the next chapter, Aziz and his friends immediately introduce the social-political theme with which the novel is largely concerned: whether friendship with an Englishman is possible, and the contrapuntal chapters of the "Mosque" section reflect upon this question. The pleasant meeting in the mosque is followed by the frigidity of the Club; the Indians discuss the "Bridge Party" invitation, and the party fails. This disastrous party, Ronny's boorish and rude interruption of Fielding's tea party, the failure of the Bhattacharyas to fulfill their invitation, and the Nawab Bahadur's car accident, all indicate that friendship between a dominant and a subservient people is rarely possible. The final answer to the question of friendship is emphatically negative: English and Indians cannot be friends until Indians are politically independent. Aziz's vow to Fielding, "India shall be a nation! . . . We may hate one another, but we hate you most . . . we shall drive every blasted Englishman into the sea, and then . . . you and I shall be friends," echoes the belief of the Hindu nationalist Bankim Chatterjee: "So long as the conqueror-conquered relationship will last between English and Indians, and so long as even in our present degraded condition we shall remember our former national glory, there cannot be any hope of lessening the racial hatred." *A Passage to India* embodies the truth that Orientals hate their European oppressors.

Forster's answer to such political hatred, which he again presents on the individual level, is an ideal of personal behavior and personal relations that is perhaps the major theme of the book, for it is echoed by three sympathetic characters, English and Indian, and embodied in the actions and fundamental good will of the hero, Fielding. Mrs. Moore expresses the beliefs of Aziz and Hamidullah when she appeals to her uncharitable son with a plea for "Good will and more good will and more good will," and begins to quote I Corinthians xiii.1, " 'Though I speak with the tongues of . . . ' men and of angels, and have not charity, I am become as sounding brass, or a tinkling cymbal." Forster also emphasizes the need for kindness in **"Reflections on India"** and writes that

> The decent Anglo-Indian of today realizes that the great blunder of the past is neither political nor economic nor educational, but social. . . . The mischief has been done, and though friendship between individuals will continue and courtesies between high officials increase, there is little hope now of spontaneous intercourse between two races. . . . Never in history did ill-breeding contribute so much towards the dissolution of an Empire.

The potent justification of the truth of Forster's social and political beliefs, which are fundamentally religious (though he is opposed to institutionalized and sectarian Christianity), comes from the Indians themselves. Forster's insistence on the need for kindness, charity and good will and his emphasis on the disastrous political effects of ill-breeding, are at the core of the charge made against the British by Gandhi: that they "were 'incompetent' to deal with the problems of India—which were not primarily administrative at all, but *social and religious.*" And Vinoba Bhave, a contemporary Indian saint and Gandhi's adopted son, criticizes the West in purely Forsterian terms: "You have developed the head; the heart did not keep pace. With us it was the opposite—it was with the development of the heart that we have been concerned in India." Adela's sacrifice was rightly rejected by the Indians because it did not include her heart.

In *A Passage to India* Forster also attacks the traditional (and mythical) justification of imperialism, that the natives are better off under English domination. Sir Alan Burns, former Governor-General of the Gold Coast, presents this argument as late as 1957: "the subject peoples of the British Empire have greater liberty and better conditions of living than many of the inhabitants of independent countries." Fielding deliberately rejects this view, and in a political discussion with Indians is too honest to give the conventional answer that England holds India for her good, which Ronny gives earlier in the novel. Aziz's assertion that there can be no self-respect without independence expresses Forster's understanding that Indians yearn for political freedom and do not care about economic, that they prefer to be ruled badly by themselves than well by others, and that no amount of progress can compensate for lack of liberty and personal dignity, a lack that degrades every aspect of personal, cultural, social and moral life. This belief has always been held by Indian nationalists. Deshbandu Das, in his presidential address to the Indian National Congress in the 1920s, said, "Morally, we are becoming a nation of slaves. . . . Intellectually we have become willing victims to the imposition of a foreign culture upon us . . . there is inherent in subjection something which injures national life and hampers its growth and fulfillment."

The trial of Aziz is a political allegory on this theme. Adela's accusation of Aziz is also Britain's accusation of India—that she is poor, backward, dirty, disorganized, uncivilized, promiscuous, uncontrollable, violent—in short, that she needs imperialism. His innocence is equivalent to India's right to freedom, which is symbolized by Aziz's transformation from subservient and passive before the trial to independent and nationalistic after it. Before his arrest he is not interested in kicking the British out of India; after his release he is more formidable and proudly announces that he has become anti-British.

Adela's echo also has political implications, for it functions as a sonant conscience, sounding doubts about her charge against Aziz and expressing the guilt and fear of the English imperialists. When Mrs. Moore remains secluded, and Ronny supports Adela's charges, "the echo flourished, raging up and down like a nerve in the faculty of her hearing, and the noise in the cave, so unimportant intellectually, was prolonged over the surface of her life." It resounds and haunts her periodically when she considers her accusation, diminishes when she thinks of retracting the false charges, and disappears only when she tears the veil of illusion and releases Aziz. After the trial when she tells Fielding she no longer has any secrets, the evil echo leaves her and discharges itself into the Indian atmosphere of hatred, hostility, recrimination and animosity.

Finally, Forster's political ideas are prophetic. Aziz predicts not only the Hindu-Moslem unity against the British, but also that independence will be achieved in the next European war. He even prophesies a conference of Oriental statesmen such as that which took place thirty years later (1955) in Bandung, Indonesia. He deplores the policy of racial discrimination and declares colonialism an evil that should be eradicated.

Thus, political events and political ideas are closely related to Forster's moral ideas, which find their most profound expression in *A Passage to India.* (pp. 329-38)

> *Jeffrey Meyers, "The Politics of 'A Passage to India'," in* Journal of Modern Literature, Vol. 1, No. 3, March, 1971, pp. 329-38.

Bikram K. Das   (essay date 1975)

[*In the following essay, Das shows how miscommunication between the Indians and British in* A Passage to India *results from different socio-cultural uses of English.*]

Stylistics has not yet been defined precisely by its practitioners; very loosely, we may call it the application of descriptive linguistics to literary texts. In the past, descriptive linguisticians were preoccupied with the spoken forms of language but more recently they have begun to feel that the language of literature also is amenable to the techniques of descriptive analysis since it may be said to comprise a special language-variety or dialect.

Linguisticians who have interested themselves in literature claim that the linguistic sciences can aid close textual analysis, by making precise and explicit the critic's intuitive response to language. However, most literary critics are not certain if the linguistician can tell them anything about what makes literary text *valuable:* at best, they feel, stylistic analysis can be a useful pre-critical activity.

The linguistician is concerned with linguistic form—with the structures of language and their distribution in a given corpus of language (spoken or written). He is totally unconcerned with matters outside the text. Several schools of modern criticism—for instance, the New Critics—seem to share, to a large extent, this unconcern with extratextual elements; to them, the 'printed word' is everything. But in the most influential critics, concern with language is interpenetrated by other kinds of concern, such as the moral and the sociological; in F. R. Leavis's criticism, for example, the value of language-organization appears to be almost therapeutic. It is felt, therefore, that if the linguisti-

cian aspires to the status of a literary critic, he must be prepared to go beyond the level of form. Formal organization and structure must be linked with extra-linguistic elements, such as theme.

One school of linguistics now current in Britain—the neo-Firthian School—makes use of the concept of *context,* to identify those elements in language which relate demonstrably to elements in the extra-linguistic situation. Since language is a social phenomenon, a complete description of language will include a description not only of formal patterns but also of the social context of situation in which language is used, i.e. of the users of language, the use to which language is being put, the relationship that exists between the users, etc. The branch of linguistics which studies these aspects of language is termed sociolinguistics and the linguistic concept of style belongs to this particular branch of the study.

'Style' is the relation existing between elements of language form and elements in the extra-linguistic situation. More simply, style is what distinguishes between one utterance and another, which are equally possible or permissible as grammatical alternatives and convey approximately the same information: for example, "I can see you" and "I am able to perceive you". The choice between this pair will be determined by such considerations as: who is speaking to whom; what is the relation between speaker and hearer; what is the topic or subject of discourse, i.e. whether the utterance is taken from a simple real-life situation or a philosophical discourse, etc. Stylistic analysis attempts to relate each set of formal features (e.g. syntax, morphology, lexis) to some features of context and to classify the relationships so obtained.

In any given context of situation, a certain style is regarded as the norm; for instance, when two friends are speaking to each other in an informal situation, "I can see you" is the norm, while "I am able to perceive you", is a deviation from the norm; the converse is true if we imagine two philosophers formally discussing the nature of sensory perception. This concept of stylistic norms and deviation from norms is exploited in stylistic analysis.

But when a critic is examining a literary work, it is not enough to be able to say what the stylistic norm is and to point out instances of deviation; one must also be able to analyse why a deviation from the norm is significant in the total organization of the work.

To decide on the issue of significance, another concept is used, that of *foregrounding.* The author of a literary text, it is argued, wishes to highlight those features of his use of language which carry a 'functional load' or, in other words, are particularly relevant to his thematic or structural organisation. If we find a significant deviation from the stylistic norm or norms, we can assume that this deviation is functional, and is related to important extralinguistic concerns.

With this brief and totally inadequate enumeration of the theoretical notions involved, let us now attempt an analysis of a particular literary text—E. M. Forster's *A Passage to India* in order to trace how far the formal and contextual deviations are functional and appropriate to Forster's theme; how far the language in this text carries the burden that artistic structure and organization impose upon it, and which elements of language form are foregrounded by the author as appropriate to the theme.

First, let us attempt to identify Forster's theme in order to see how far the use of language is relevant to it. Forster's *A Passage to India* has been interpreted, inter alia, as a portrayal of the human predicament in a mysterious and hostile universe, bordering on tragedy; it has been read, also, as an ironic picture of human institutions, verging on social comedy. Some critics have seen it as a liberal manifesto, with important political overtones; still others have regarded it, not as a generalized and symbolic representation of human existence, but as a sketch of a particular society at a particular point of time.

The interpretation which appears to be most relevant to our purpose is one which has been noted by most critics but taken by some to be at the most superficial level of organization. This is the theme of social interaction between two cultures: the Indian and the British. Elsewhere in Forster's writings we have evidence of his interest in interpersonal, inter-group and inter-cultural relationships: the theme appears again and again in his fiction, for example in *Where Angels Fear to Tread* and *A Room With a View,* as well as in his occasional writings, e.g. on Egypt and India. The confrontation between different or alien cultures is also present in a number of instances. A part, at least, of the significance of Forster's theme is the failure of human beings on communicating across group or cultural barriers; the words which Forster uses as an epigraph in *Howards End*—'*Only Connect* . . .'—could serve as the leitmotif for his fiction.

In *A Passage to India,* Forster found an appropriate frame for his theme: the confrontation between two cultures is heightened and dramatized by the fact that one group of persons stands to the other group in relation of the rulers to the ruled. The presence of the British in India is resented by the Indians, while most of the British feel it a waste of time to attempt to communicate with the Indians. The gap cannot be bridged, in spite of the fact that a certain amount of goodwill exists; individuals do attempt the passage but fail.

The breakdown of communication between two cultural groups may be regarded, then, as the central element in the theme, and one may set out to investigate how far this is foregrounded through the use of language. As has been stated above, the theme is particularly suited for stylistic representation. Language being the main channel of communication between the different groups, the breakdown in communication is *signalled* through language; moreover, communication, or the loss of it, is determined by the social and cultural—hence stylistic—restraints placed on language. The situation is made more piquant by the fact that the two interacting groups constitute two different language-communities, in the Bloomfieldian sense, the members of each sharing the same responses to identical linguistic stimuli; but the two groups must communicate with each other in a language which is foreign to one, so that language serves to divide, rather than to connect, the two communities. Obviously, those elements of language

will be foregrounded in Forster's use which serve to signal the breakdown in communication. Within each language community, it will be noticed, communication is total; it is only when communication is attempted across linguistic communities that it fails.

Like other authors writing in English about India and Indians, Forster had to grapple with the two-fold stylistic problem of:

(a) trying to represent, in English, how Indians converse among themselves in languages other than English: and

(b) trying to represent how Indians use English.

The first of these problems has been of special interest to Indians writing in English about India (the term 'Indo-Anglian' is in use currently to describe this body of literature). Most writers belonging to this group try to interpret India to the English-speaking world; they highlight those aspects of Indian life and culture which might be of special interest to the English-speaking world, and these include Indian speech. Also, many of them are trying to forge a new idiom which seems to them appropriate to the Indian sensibility. The result is the creation of a dialect, or series of idiolects, which nowhere exist except in works of imagination; nor is it the intention of such writers to suggest that this pseudo-dialect actually exists. It seems somewhat strange that Kachru, in his two important papers on 'Indian English," has drawn most of his illustrations from this pseudo-dialect. A few citations will suffice: 'Spoiler of my salt'; 'sister-sleeper'; 'May the vessel of your life never float on the sea of existence'; 'turmeric-ceremony', etc. These are purely literary coinages, having no actual currency in any situation in India in which English is used; they are *not* examples of Indian English, which is a very real socio-linguistic phenomenon.

Of Englishmen writing about India, few have had the necessary knowledge of Indian languages to attempt to represent Indian speech in English. Kipling attempts it, but his representation mostly takes the form of a courtly, archaic, almost biblical style, interlarded with Indian conversation-initiators and lexical items. Here is an example from *Kim:*

'Thus do we beg who know the way of it. Eat now and I will eat with thee. *Ohe, bhissti!* ' he called to the water-carrier, 'give water here. We men are thirsty.'

There is no resemblance here to the actual syntax and lexical range of Indian speech, though the syntax of the first sentence, with the defining relative clause separated from the antecedent by the lexical verb, is strange enough to sound exotic. (pp. 78-82)

Forster seems uninterested in representing in English the nuances of Indian speech; partly, this may have been because of his inadequate knowledge of Indian languages. More important is the reason that Forster did not feel that this was central to his theme; he was concerned with showing that when individuals in a homogeneous linguistic group converse in a language which is native to all of them, communication is natural, spontaneous and unhindered; when, on the other hand, communication is through a language not native to all the participants, it is likely to break down. The language-signals are missed, or misinterpreted; wrong stylistic choices are made, and social confusion results. The language forms which Forster selects to illustrate the two phenomena are completely determined by the extra-textual context: the field, mode and tenor of discourse, relationships between participants (who is speaking to whom), etc. There is no manipulation of forms for the sake of effect, or what is traditionally (not in linguistic meta-language) termed style.

Forster was intrigued by the fact that Indians frequently used English for internal communication in preference to any native language. Here is an extract from his essay **"India Again"**, published in *Two Cheers For Democracy;* it is quoted at some length because it is highly relevant for this paper:

> The Indians I met mostly talked English. Some of them spoke very well, and one or two write in our language with great distinction. But English, though more widely spoken than on my last visit, is worse spoken, more mistakes are made in it, and the pronunciation is deteriorating—'perpendicule' for 'perpendicular'. 'Pip' into my office for 'pop'. Here are two tiny slips which I noted in a few minutes, and both of them made by well-educated men. The explanation, I think, is that Indians at the schools and universities are now learning their English from other Indians, instead of from English teachers as in the past. Furthermore, they have little occasion to meet our people socially and so brush it up; intercourse is official and at a minimum, and even when there are mixed clubs the two communities in them keep apart. So it is not surprising that their English is poor. They have learnt it from Indians and practise it on Indians.

> Why talk English at all? This question was hotly debated at the P.E.N. Conference of All-India writers . . . Meanwhile, in this uneasy interregnum, English does get talked and gets interlarded in the oddest way with the Indian vernacular . . . And my reason for wanting English to be the common language for India is a purely selfish reason: I like these chance encounters, I value far more the relationships of years, and if Indians had not spoken English my own life would have been infinitely poorer.

To illustrate my thesis that communication within a language community is facilitated by socio-cultural conventions which determine context, I quote an instance from *A Passage to India* illustrating a piece of coversation in which all the participants are Indians:

> 'Hamidullah, Hamidullah, am I late?' he cried. 'Do not apologise', said his host. 'You are always late—.'

> 'Kindly answer my question. Am I late? Has Mahmoud Ali eaten all the food? If so, I go elsewhere. Mr. Mahmoud Ali, how are you?'

> 'Thank you, Dr Aziz, I am dying.'

> 'Dying before your dinner? Oh, poor Mahmoud Ali.'

> 'Hamidullah here is actually dead. He passed away just as you rode up on your bike.'

> 'Yes, that is so,' said the other. 'Imagine us both as addressing you from another and happier world.'

> 'Does there happen to be such a thing as a hookah in that happier world of yours?'

> 'Aziz, don't chatter. We are having a very sad talk.'

Stylistically, this could not have been a conversation between a group of L-1 speakers of English. All the speakers are intimate friends, but their register betrays a kind of formality which might be 'un-English'.

'Do not apologise', 'Kindly answer my question', etc. belong to what Martin Joos might have called the 'frozen' style. The humour in this piece of conversation is laboured, even slightly awkward; death is not generally a topic for humour, except in a grimly ironic style. There is an element of the grotesque about the conversation, which is un-English again, if one remembers that Forster's English dialogue is 1924 vintage. But the banter is perfectly effective because all the participants share the same linguistic and stylistic conventions; if one of the speakers had been an Englishman, the humour would have misfired—in fact, this happens repeatedly in exchanges between the English and the Indians in *A Passage to India.*

A stylistic problem faced by Forster was the representation of the English used by Indians, both among themselves and in conversing with native speakers of English. The extract from **"India Again"** shows Forster's awareness of 'Indian English', which has interested many British writers on India. Traditionally, the Indian speaker of English has been a figure of fun—almost a character from music hall comedy, caricatured and burlesqued from Kipling to Peter Sellers. 'Babu English' has been described at length, though not with precision. One may note, among its other characteristics, confusion of the phonology of Standard English; its tendency to confuse registers, juxtaposing highly ornate and formal features with informal, even 'slangy' patterns; its use of archaic and obsolete forms, resulting from 'book learning'; unusual syntax and lexis, resulting from L-1 interference.

All deviations from Standard English in *Kim* are of the grossest kind, conforming fairly closely to the stereotypes of 'Indian English'. The inappropriateness of the English used by Kipling's Indian characters is fundamental—grammatical rather than stylistic; they used 'bad English', but this does not matter at all because Kipling's Englishmen (who are thoroughly at home in India) expect Indians to use bad English and make every allowance for it. There is no confusion, no breakdown in communication.

Forster, on the other hand, is not fundamentally interested in caricatures of Indian English; as an observer of the social scene, he could not have helped noticing this phenomenon (vide his remarks in **"India Again"**), and he does, in a very few instances, attempt to depict—in rather an impressionistic way—far less accurate than Kipling's—how Indians typically use English. But his main concern is with the loss of communication resulting from utterances inappropriate to certain situations, since this alone contributes to his theme. Violations of grammar are less relevant than stylistic deviation; wrong or 'bad' grammar is less likely to create confusion in sophisticated communication than wrong context. In the former case, one is liable to reject an utterance as being unacceptable; one either understands or fails (refuses) to understand, but there is less likelihood of one's *misinterpreting* an utterance. Contextual ambiguity is more complex than grammatical, and for an artist like Forster, who is trying to manipulate social situations to reveal group-interaction, stylistic choices are more challenging technically than more gross deviations of grammar. Consequently, Forster passes very lightly over the grammatical deviations in the speech of his Indian characters and concentrates on contextual deviance.

Most of Forster's Indian characters speak fairly 'good' English, consistent with their education, intelligence and refinement; they are highly articulate in English and have a 'feel' for the language. Forster himself had a relatively short stay in India—during 1912-13, 1921-22 and 1945. His most fruitful contacts with Indians were in Britain; among his close friends were people like Syed Ross Masood (who is said to be Forster's model for Dr. Aziz). Forster seems to have been impressed with the command of English which these Indians displayed. In *A Passage to India,* Fielding—who might resemble Forster himself—has occasion to reflect on this:

> He was often struck with the liveliness with which the younger generation handled a foreign tongue. They altered the idiom, but they could say whatever they wanted to say quickly; there were none of the babuisms ascribed to them at the club.

We may, in passing, note a few instances of the more obvious deviations in grammer, lexis and phonology in the speech of the Indian characters. Some of these occur in the speech of Aziz:

> 'Then we are in the same box,' he said cryptically. 'Then is the City Magistrate the entire of your family now?'

> 'Sir, excuse me, I did. I mounted my bike and it burst in front of the Cow Hospital.'

> 'Goodbye, Miss Quested' . . 'You'll jolly jolly well not forget those caves, won't you?'

> 'Well, here's luck! chin-chin!'

> 'Here's luck, but chin-chin I do refuse,' laughed Fielding.

Some of the other Indian characters also use noticeably deviant English:

> 'You will make yourself chip,' suddenly said a little black man.

> 'The shorter lady, she is my wife, she is Mrs Bhattacharya. The taller lady, she is Mrs Das.' (This is an instance of two subjects in apposition in a single clause—a common feature of Indian syntax.)

> 'Half one league onwards!' The Nawab Bahadur fell asleep.

> 'Even when the lady is so uglier than the gentleman?'

These deviations, interesting though they are as representations of Indian English, are not functional in Forster's scheme. They do not signal the breakdown in communication which results from stylistic confusion. Forster's depiction of this other kind of linguistic deviation is highly subtle—it takes into account the various contextual parameters such as addressee-relationships, forms of address, tenor of discourse, etc.

The personal tragedy of Aziz is largely stylistic. He is warm, eager to respond to friendship, generous and highly emotional. His intimate friends understand and respect him, but with others—particularly those who do not share his language—he is likely to be misunderstood and to misunderstand, to look for signs of intimacy or equally for slights where none are intended, to become patronizing or garrulous in the wrong situations, and also to become 'frozen' or appear to be frozen on the wrong occasions. Ultimately, he is unable to communicate, even when the ground has been prepared for communication.

The first meeting between Aziz and Mrs. Moore, which is also the first instance of the two cultures meeting, illustrates this. Aziz has entered the mosque in order to be alone with his thoughts, when he sees Mrs. Moore:

> . . Suddenly he was furiously angry and shouted: 'Madam! 'Madam! Madam!'

> 'Oh! Oh!' the woman gasped.

> 'Madam, this is a mosque, you have no right here at all; you should have taken off your shoes: this is a holy place for 'Muslims'.

> 'I have taken them off.'

> 'You have?'

> 'I have left them at the entrance.'

> 'Then I ask your pardon.'

The ferociousness of his address and the inadequacy of his apology reveal ignorance of the socio-cultural constraints on the use of language in English-speaking societies, particularly in addressing women. But he makes matters worse:

> 'Madam!'

> 'Please let me go!'

> 'Oh, can I do you any service now or at any time?'

> 'No, thank you, really none—goodnight.'

> 'May I know your name?'

Without intending it, Aziz is being boorish; he is totally mishandling his language. A little later he appears to patronize her, again without intention:

> ' . . I shall tell my community—our friends—about you. That God is here—very good, very

fine indeed. I think you are newly arrived in India?'

'Yes—how did you know?'

'By the way you address me.'

Within seconds, Aziz begins to assume an air of intimacy and to address Mrs. Moore informally; fortunately for him, she is not offended, as another English lady might justifiably have been.

'And why ever do you come to Chandrapore?'

'To visit my son. He is the city magistrate here'.

'Oh, no, excuse me, that is quite impossible' . . .

The implication in the last remark might have been that Mrs Moore was lying in order to impress Aziz: the ambiguity is contextual.

Mrs Moore, at this first encounter, is being extraordinarily polite to Aziz, but he mistakes conventional politeness for friendship, misreading the linguistic signals. Mrs Moore makes a very guarded comment about Mrs. Callendar—the Civil Surgeon's wife—and Aziz immediately responds with a flood of confidences that takes her by surprise.

> He was excited partly by his wrongs, but more by the knowledge that somebody sympathized with him. It was this that led him to repeat, exaggerate, contradict. She had proved her sympathy by criticizing her fellow-countrywoman to him but even earlier he had known. The flame that not even beauty can nourish was springing up, and though his words were querulous, his heart began to glow secretly. Presently it burst into speech.
>
> 'You understand me, you know what others feel. Oh, if others resemble you!'
>
> Rather surprised, she replied, 'I don't think I understand people very well.'

Aziz has gone 'hay-wire 'stylistically; there is no real communication, and he makes the mistake of assuming too much. He is impulsive, undoubtedly, but the linguistic context is plainly too much for him.

In a complete study of Forster's style, the speeches of Aziz and Godbole must claim thorough analysis. The present paper has aimed at indicating the nature of stylistic deviation from accepted norms and its relevance to artistic organization. (pp. 82-8)

> *Bikram K. Das, "A Stylistic Analysis of the Speech of the Indian Characters in Forster's 'A Passage to India',"* in Focus on Forster's "A Passage to India:" Indian Essays in Criticism, *edited by V. A. Shahane, Orient Longman, 1975, pp. 78-88.*

Chaman L. Sahni (essay date 1975)

[*In the following essay, Sahni analyzes the symbolism of the Marabar caves in* A Passage to India *with respect to Indian philosophical and literary thought.*]

The latent mythology evident in [cosmic-egg motif and]

Forster on English-Indian relations in 1921:

I have been with pro-Government and pro-English Indians all the time, so cannot realise the feeling of the other party: and am only sure of this—that we were paying for the insolence of Englishmen and Englishwomen out here in the past. I don't mean that good manners can avert a political upheaval. But they can minimise it, and come nearer to averting it in the East than elsewhere. English manners out here have improved wonderfully in the last eight years. Some people are frightened, others seem really to have undergone a change of heart.

But it's too late. Indians don't long for social intercourse with Englishmen any longer. They have made a life of their own.

E. M. Forster, in his The Hill of Devi, *1953.*

the unconditioned potential of the Marabar Caves has been brought out by various critics of [*A Passage to India*]. The present essay will complement their discussion by expounding the significance of the cave symbology from the Indian standpoint. It will first seek to establish that the Marabar Caves represent the complex variety of Indian thought, and then demonstrate the religious, mythological, and conceptual concentration that takes place in these caves. Further, an attempt will be made to illuminate the nature of Mrs Moore's experience in the cave in the light of Indian thought.

The history of Indian architecture reveals that the Marabar Hills, near Gaya, in Bihar, contain the most ancient rock-cut cave-temples of India.

From inscriptions of later date we also learn that the caves were for centuries occupied by Brahmanical ascetics. On the highest peak of Barabar, there is still a Siva temple with a lingam sacred to Siddheswar.

The history of the Barabar caves clearly indicates that although they were originally associated with the three non-Vedic monastic schools of thought—Buddhism, Jainism, and the Ajivika doctrine—they are now known by names connected with Brahmanism and later Hinduism. It seems to me that Forster uses the symbol of the caves in the plural to suggest the various off-shoots of Indian thought, echoing the Impersonal Absolute. The Marabar Hills, containing these "extraordinary caves", symbolize the ancient mythical past and the mystical heritage of India, which has always been a great attraction for the foreigner but at the same time a source of great bafflement also.

"The incredible antiquity of these hills" is testified by geology. Geologically, they are part of the Deccan plateau which is certainly older than the Himalayas and much more so than the Indo-Gangetic plain from which it is separated by the Vindhya and the Satpura mountains. In the novel Forster uses the phrase "the high places of Dravidia," for what he calls "the Vindhya and Satpura hills, the plateau of Deccan" in the manuscript. In Hindu mythology, "the Vindhya Mountains, at one time, in an excess of pride, so enlarged themselves that they fairly eclipsed the sun and even blocked its path. Their pride was humbled by a mighty ascetic, Agastya, the patron saint of South India, who is also associated with the myth of the Descent of the Ganges. Since Forster starts the "Caves" section with the myth of the Descent of the Ganges, probably he might have read about the myth of saint Agastya who is said to have swallowed the entire ocean, depriving the earth of its life-sustaining waters, and thus making it imperative for another ascetic Bhagiratha to exercise his yogic powers to release the celestial Ganges from heaven and bring it down to earth. It seems to me that Forster is recounting the myth of Agastya and the Vindhya Mountains in his remark. "If the flesh of the sun's flesh is to be touched anywhere, it is here, among the incredible antiquity of these hills." Again, in Hindu legend the Vindhya Mountains, which separate the North Indian plain from the highlands of the Deccan, form the summit over which the sun rises to begin its daily transit of the firmament. Thus in his initial concept of the caves, Forster is recapitulating not only the physical configuration of India but also the great Aryo-Dravidian synthesis that had taken place as a result of this configuration.

These hills have, then, seen not only "the upheaval of the Himalayas from a sea" but also the rise of all formal religion and mythology, for they existed even before "the gods took their seats on them." They are "older than all spirit" because they represent matter, the primordial matrix of *Prakriti*. The expedition to these hills is symbolically a journey into the timeless past, an effort to fathom the mystery of the Primal Cause, a quest for Ultimate Reality, for a Timeless Absolute in relation to which our time-bound existence acquires meaning and significance.

Mrs Moore connects the Marabar caves with infinity, eternity, and vastness. "The Infinite," as Betty Heimann puts it "is boundless, but is still conceived under a vague notion of space." The caves symbolize pure space cut out of solid rocks. Hence they suggest the Infinite. In all religio-philosophical systems of India, the Infinite is visualized under the symbol of *Sunya*, the Void, which, as Heimann says, mean "not a thing, but a no-single thing." This concept of emptiness, the void, vacuity, as Zimmer says, has been employed as "a convenient and effective pedagogical instrument to bring the mind beyond the sense of duality which infects all systems in which the absolute and the world of relativity are described in contrasting, or antagonistic terms."

Since the Absolute is beyond any fixed notions of empirical knowledge and valuation, it can be expressed only in negative terms, *Na-iti, Na-iti* (not-this, not-this). The Absolute is also beyond the ethical concepts of good and evil, beyond any definition given by human reason. Forster is, therefore, right in saying that "if mankind grew curious and excavated, nothing, nothing would be added to the sum of good or evil."

Again, in the Indian concept of the Infinite, "matter and spirit, combined, form the transcendental and superempirical fullness. Spirit alone is considered not wide enough a concept to suffice to represent the Whole, the *purnatva*." Jainism, the daughter religion of Hinduism, has emphatically stated that there is a living soul in stones also, as in the higher organized beings. No wonder if during the ascent to the Marabar caves, "the boulders said, 'I am alive', the small stones answered, 'I am almost alive.'" According to the Sankhya system, all unconscious matter (*prakriti*) is in a state of pure potentiality, and its evolution can take place only through the presence of the consicous spirit (*purusha*). Since in his comments on Fielding's reflections about the Marabar echo Forster implies that "a religious truth" must encompass "the complexities of matter and spirit", the Marabar caves enshrine "a religious truth" by incorporating both matter and spirit as suggested by the exquisite image of the flame in the cave.

The passage referred to suggests the mystery inherent in the development of life-monads (*purushas*) from unconscious matter (*prakriti*). The reflection of the match flame in the stone suggests that all matter is potentially infused with spirit but lacks consciousness. Hence the flame in the stone appears only when the flame in the air is lit.

From the Vedantic point of view, the match flame is the symbol of *Atman* (the *Katha Upanishad* compares *Atman* to a flame); the pure space of the cave represents Brahman (the *Chandogya Upanishad* makes frequent references to space as Brahman); the walls of granite suggest the phenomenal world; and the flame mirrored in the wall symbolizes the world of appearances created by Maya which displays universal consciousness as duality by separating the self from the true reality. So long as this illusion remains, there can be no merging of *Atman* and Brahman, for *Moksha* (liberation) comes by extinction, through enlightenment, of individual consciousness. Hence the world of appearances must be re-integrated into the Vast Immensity, that is, Brahman. According to Indian thought, there is no greater good than the joy of merging with Brahman, the eternal substratum of existence.

The cave's association with eternity is suggested by the recurrent image of the serpent and its coils. The Hindu and other ancient scriptures picture eternity under the old symbol of a snake swallowing its own tail. The circle thus formed represents eternity, without beginning and without end, in itself infinite, but enclosing a portion of finite space. The cycle of time continually revolves like the "eternally watchful" worm in the cave. The desending and ascending of the serpent has a special meaning in Jainism. According to the Jains, Zimmer tells us, "the present 'descending' (*avasarpini*) period was preceded and will be followed by an 'ascending' (*utasarpini*). *Sarpini* suggests the creeping movement of a 'serpent' (*sarpin*); *ava-* means 'down' and *ut-* means 'up'. The serpent-cycle of time . . will go on revolving through these alternating 'ascending' and descending' periods forever." In Hinduism, the circular coils of the snake also represent the wheel of *Samsara* (the endless round of transmigration of soul) from which the Indian mystic seeks release (*Moksha*), meditating on the divine symbol *OM*. As Lord Krishna says in the *Bhagavad-Gita*, "Aum is the one indestructible (sound), the Immensity. He who, his mind intent upon me, abandons his body and leaves the world uttering this syllable attains the supreme purpose of his destiny."

It seems to me that Forster uses the composite image of

the caves to suggest the various facets of the all-embracing Whole (*purnatva*), represented by the various non-Vedic and Vedic schools of Indian thought. The caves may then simultaneously represent the "impersonal cosmic principle" of the Ajivika sect, the total renunciation and isolationism of Jainism, the Nirvana or the Void of Buddhism, the irresoluble dichotomy of *purusha* (life-monad, always represented in the Sankhya system as an "imprisoned spirit") and *prakriti* (matter) represented by Sankhya and Yoga, and the undifferentiated oneness that lies at the root of the concept of Brahman in Advaita-Vedanta.

In one of the caves, Mrs Moore undergoes a tremendous spiritual experience which annihilates her inherited sense of Christian values and makes her ponder over the inadequacy of "poor little talkative Christianity." From the Indian standpoint, she has a vision of the Vast Immensity, the Hindu view of the Timeless Absolute, but from the Western standpoint her vision embodies a confrontation with Nothingness. She hears a "terrifying echo" which proves to be nerve-shattering for her. Her reflections on the nature and significance of the echo suggest that it represents a particular aspect of Indian thought, and that it cannot be accounted for in Western religions and philosophies of life.

The echo in a Marabar cave is "entirely devoid of distinction," and "as far as the human alphabet can express it," its sound is "Boum" or "bou-oum", or "ou-boum." It is difficult to say, for certain, what Forster meant by this sound, but as Glen O. Allen and James McConkey have pointed out, it does have close phonetic resemblance with the Indian mystic symbol *"AUM"* or *"OM"*, which stands for the inexpressible Absolute. Both these critics, however, associate the echo with evil, whereas *OM* is the most auspicious and spiritual symbol of the supreme One in Indian thought. It is, therefore, beyond good and evil. Only those who cannot understand the real meaning and significance of this mystic sound would associate it with evil. Mrs Moore certainly thinks, "Nothing evil had been in the cave, but she had not enjoyed herself."

The significance of the echo has been discussed in many *Upanishads.* We are told that the sacred syllable *OM* consists of three and a half morae. The three morae are *A, U, M,* and the half mora is represented by the echo (*nada*). It is this half mora which bears the deepest meaning and leads to the supreme goal. *Dhayanabindu Upanishad* says:

> Higher than the original syllable
> Is the point, the echo higher than this;
> The syllable vanishes with the sound,
> The highest state is silent.

The highest state is that of *turiya,* supreme silence, corresponding to *samadhi,* representing Spirit in its undifferentiated unity. The supreme goal of every individual, according to Indian thought, is total reintegration—that is, return to fundamental unity underlying this cosmos.

The undifferentiated oneness suggested by the echo to Mrs Moore lies at the root of Advaita-Vedanta, and signifies the ultimate perception of the Hindu mystic. For Mrs Moore, however, such a concept is puzzling, for it cuts at the root of all her Western values. The echo points out to

her that all is one: "Everything exists, nothing has value." Even the categories of time are meaningless, for the idea of the beginning and the end of things suggested by "Let there be light" and "It is finished" does not hold good in view of eternity. The echo eliminates all distinctions. The concepts of Heaven, Hell, and Annihilation, which have sprung from the ethical importance attached to human actions, are all reduced to triviality, for action itself loses its significance because it prepetuates existence. Although soon after her arrival in India Mrs Moore had become aware of the inefficacy of her concept of God, as is evident from her spiritual awareness that "outside the arch there seemed always an arch, beyond the remotest echo a silence," her vision in the cave terrifies her. She feels mystified and at the same time spiritually isolated. In her isolation even the elephant becomes "a nobody" for her. It is the isolation of spirit in spirit, abiding in one's own essence. It is soul's isolation from its own eterna and timeless essence, as Hinduism holds. She is later restless to know: "What had spoken to her in that scoured-out cavity of the granite? What dwelt in the first of the caves? Something very old and very small. Before time, it was before space also. Something snubnosed, incapable of generosity—the undying worm itself. Since hearing its voice, she had not entertained one large thought . . ."

The *Katha Upanishad* says: "The wise who, by means of meditation on his Self, recognises the Ancient, who is difficult to be seen, who has entered into the dark, who is hidden in the cave, who dwells in the abyss, as God, he indeed leaves joy and sorrow far behind." But Mrs Moore's concept of God is monotheistic and she cannot comprehend the metaphysical subtleties of the Advaita-Vedanta. Nevertheless, under the spell of her vision in the cave, she shrinks away from the forces of life and contemplates retiring into "a cave of (her) own." She loses interest in everything, in her children, in social responsibilities, in religion, even in God. She even mortifies her will-to-live by refusing to leave her bungalow when an attack was expected on the last night of Mohurrum. She not only renounces all action but develops an attitude of apathy and inertia. She is no longer willing to continue her assigned role on the stage of life.

Judged by purely rational standards, she deteriorates into a state of psychic paralysis; but, from the Indian point of view, she is spiritually heading toward a state of supreme "isolation" (*Kaivalya*). Since the Absolute is beyond the confines of time and space, since it is before creation, it cannot be approached without turning one's back upon the phenomenal world. As a result of her experience in the cave, therefore, Mrs Moore not only turns inward, but also she lapses into a state of invincible noncooperation and detachment . . . But that part of her which she has imbibed from personalized Christianity cannot easily be reconciled with her soul's newfound vision, for she is still imprisoned in her Ego.

Forster's description of her state as "the twilight of the double vision" in which "a spiritual muddledom is set up" remains deliberately ambiguous. In such a state, he says: "we can neither act nor refrain from action, we can neither ignore nor respect Infinity." In this state Mrs Moore lies suspended between the noumenal and the phenomenal world. Her experience in the cave has taught her that this world is empty and meaningless, and that all rational conceptions are inadequate to comprehend the mystery of the Infinite; but whether she attains that enlightened vision in which the soul is enwrapped in its own effulgence remains doubtful, for Forster gives no indication of her having come out of the state of "spiritual muddledom". Perhaps, as Ernest Beaumont has said, "the author's sincerity does not allow him to portray unambiguously an experience which was itself puzzling and unsatisfactory, an experience which cannot be clearly expressed, because it never was clear to the person undergoing it." Or, perhaps she was destined to see only the "twilight" and not the irradiant light, of the mystic vision.

Forster later called her experience a vision "with its back turned." The woman who had been life-affirming, who had a staunch faith in the world of personal relationships, and who wanted to be one with the universe is caught between life and infinity and is utterly bewildered by the latter. The vision of the Vast Immensity—the Indian view of the Timeless Absolute—has strained all her nerves and tapped her spiritual resources. Now she seeks peace in quiet contemplation and longs for extinction in a state of purely negative isolation, as advocated by Jainism and Sankhya-Yoga. The Hindu *Upanishads* also recommend complete renunciation of the world as the only sensible way to attain the world of Pure Being.

Such a world-view may appear to be utterly pessimistic, unnatural, and incomprehensible to a Westerner because it seems to contradict the instinctive force within man, what Schweitzer calls, the "will-to-live" but all the religiophilosophical systems of India, whether Vedic or non-Vedic, are agreed in regarding the attainment of final emancipation from *Samsara* (existence-influx) as the true status of the individual. To attain that status, they postulate that all the ties that ever fettered the life-monad must dissolve away and the soul be purified of all *karmic* matter. This demands not only renunciation and isolation, but also, as Schweitzer says, "the concentration of the spirit on the Suprasensuous . . The repetition of the sacred sound 'OM' plays a great part in such exercises of self-submergence." Hence it is not without significance that for Mrs Moore "the echo began in some indescribable way to undermine her hold on life." Finally, she quit the stage of life as quietly as possible and met her death on the Indian Ocean. As she was departing from India, the thousands of coconut palms seemed to laugh: "So you thought an echo was India; you took the Marabar caves as final?"

Of course, to treat the Marabar caves as "final" is to pinpoint a particular facet of Indian thought to be "India". The Marabar caves represent only that aspect of Indian religious and philosophical thought which concentrates on the Impersonal Absolute and stresses the importance of complete renunciation, detachment, and isolation to achieve the trinity of transcendent reality (*sat*), awareness (*cit*), and freedom (*ananda*). As the "Caves" section comes to a close, Fielding remarks: "There is something in religion that may not be true, but has not yet been sung. . . . Something that the Hindus have perhaps

found." This remark directly leads to the third section, "Temple", which, as Forster told Alan Wilde, "represents the same thing as the scene in the cave, "turned inside out". After her death on the Indian Ocean, Mrs Moore is spiritually reborn in the supreme moment of cosmic unity, symbolized by the Krishna Janamashtmi festival. Her vital presence in the mind of Professor Godbole at the Birth of Lord Krishna hints at the fulfilment of her supreme destiny, her absorption in the Absolute. In the *Bhagavad-Gita* Krishna is represented as the highest Godhead, the physical embodiment of the metaphysical Absolute, and, at the same time, the symbol of Cosmic Love and Unity. The Caves embodied *nirguna* (super-personal, without attributes) Brahman; the Temple represents *saguna* (personal, with attributes) Brahman—both being aspects of the same Lord. (pp. 105-13)

> *Chaman L. Sahni, "The Marabar Caves in the Light of Indian Thought," in* Focus on Forster's "A Passage to India:" Indian Essays in Criticism, *edited by V. A. Shahane, Orient Longman, 1975, pp. 105-14.*

Benita Parry   (essay date 1979)

[*In the following revised version of an essay originally published in* E. M. Forster: A Human Exploration (*1979*), *Parry discusses the representation of India in* A Passage to India *with respect to Edward Said's theory of orientalism which suggests that the West constructs images of Asia which implicitly justify imperialism.*]

> Perhaps the most important task of all would be to undertake studies in contemporary alternatives to Orientalism, to ask how one can study other cultures and peoples from a libertarian, or a non-repressive and non-manipulative perspective. But then one would have to rethink the whole complex problem of knowledge and power.
>
> —Edward Said, *Orientalism* (1978)

> This pose of 'seeing India' . . . was only a form of ruling India.
>
> —*A Passage to India*

The discussion on *A Passage to India* as a political fiction has for long been dominated by the followers of a mimetic theory of literature, whose quest for empiricism tied to didacticism is achieved when they find the narrative content to be an authentic portrayal of India and a humanist critique of British–Indian relations during the last decades of the Empire. Since the accession of critical methods concerned with representation as an ideological construct, and not a truthful, morally inspired account of reality, however, the politics of the novel have demanded another mode of analysis, where the articulations of the fiction are related to the system of textual practices by which the metropolitan culture exercised its domination over the subordinate periphery; within this theoretical context, *A Passage to India* can be seen as at once inheriting and interrogating the discourses of the Raj. In common with other writings in the genre, this novel enunciates a strange meeting from a position of political privilege, and it is not difficult to find rhetorical instances where the other is designated within a set of essential and fixed characteristics: 'Like most Orientals, Aziz overrated hospitality, mistaking it for intimacy'; 'Suspicion in the Oriental is a sort of malignant tumour'; and so on. It is equally possible to demonstrate that while the idiom of Anglo-India is cruelly parodied, the overt criticism of colonialism is phrased in the feeblest of terms: 'One touch of regret—not the canny substitute but the true regret from the heart—would have made him a different man, and the British Empire a different institution.'

Yet to interpret the fiction as an act of recolonisation which reproduces the dominant colonial discourse would be to ignore—egregiously—the text's heterogeneous modes and its complex dialogic structure. Even the most superficial consideration of the 'India' construed by Western texts, an India which was virtually conterminous with the European consciousness of it, will show that this canon of historical, analytical, propagandist and fictional writings (official minutes, political treatises, scholarly studies, geographical surveys, missionary tracts, journalists' copy, memoirs of civil servants and army officers, educational manuals, school text books, adventure stories, children's books, Anglo-Indian romances, the works of Kipling) devised a way of dividing the world which made British rule in India appear a political imperative and a moral duty. The strategy of discrimination and exclusion can be deduced from the series of meanings produced by the word 'exotic': dissimilar, unrelated, extraneous, unconformable, untypical, incongruent, eccentric, anomalous, foreign, alien, abnormal, aberrant, deviant, outcaste, monstrous, fantastic, barbarous, grotesque, bizarre, strange, mysterious, unimaginable, wondrous, outlandish. Only by wilfully suppressing its initiation of an oppositional discourse is it possible to insert *A Passage to India* into the hegemonic tradition of British–Indian literature.

Written from within the liberal-humanist ideology, and in its realist aspect using the style of ironic commentary and measured ethical judgement, the fiction does act to legitimate the authorised cultural categories of the English bourgeois world. Indeed, so far as it imitates 'the beauty of form . . . the harmony between the works of man and the earth that upholds them, the civilization that has escaped muddle, the spirit in a reasonable form,' the narrative organisation underwrites the value of Western cultural norms. Other rhetorical modes converge, however, to subvert the certainties of the fiction's own explanatory system as these are put into confrontation with foreign codes. It has been repeatedly alleged in the critical literature that Forster's India is an amorphous state of mind, a figure of inchoate formlessness, a destroyer of meaning. This is to substitute the firm stance on epistemology discernible in traditional fiction for the ontological puzzlement of a modernist text, where India's difference is represented not as a Manichean opposition threatening Western precepts and practices, but as an original system of knowledge and an alternative world view. Without embracing or consolidating the cosmic perspectives and aspirations institutionalised in some of India's major cultural traditions, the novel does, in its triadic structure of Mosque, Caves and Temple, undermine the politically constructed concept of India (as well as refusing the scented East of legend, and

the India to be seen as pageant or frieze from the seat of a dogcart) to produce instead a set of radical alternatives to the meanings valorised by an imperialist civilisation.

Thus, within the novel's colloquy, the gestures of performance and force are countered by icons of restfulness and spiritual silence; the rhetoric of positivism, moral assurance and aggression is transgressed by the language of deferred hope, imponderables and quietism. Against the grain of a discourse where 'knowing' India was a way of ruling India, Forster's India is a geographical space abundantly occupied by histories and cultures distinct from the Western narrative of the world and the meanings this endorses. But if *A Passage to India* can be seen to act as an ideological catalyst, it can also be seen as constrained by its conditions of production. What is absent is a consciousness of imperialism as capitalism's expansionist, conquering moment, and the enunciated critique of the Raj is consequently toned down. Imperialism's triumphalist rhetoric is present, but modulated and made safe by irony. Lampooned in the conversations of the Anglo-Indians, it is without the danger such declamations arouse in Conrad's writings, where a language extolling might, force, domination and supremacy, conflating a mystical zeal for conquest with a utilitarian preoccupation with exploitation, engenders a ruthless criticism of imperialism's beliefs, practices and styles. All the same, given the evasions in the novel's articulations of imperialist ideology, *A Passage to India* is the limit text of the Raj discourse, existing on its edges, sharing aspects of its idiom while disputing the language of colonial authority. Forster's reputation as the archetypal practitioner of the domestic, liberal-humanist, realist English novel, has inhibited contemporary readers from engaging with *A Passage to India* as a text which disrupts its own conventional forms and dissects its own informing ideology. Where criticism has not applauded the novel's humanist political perceptions, it has scorned its equivocations and limitations; it should now address itself to the counter-discourse generated by the text, which in its global perspective refuses the received representation of the relationship between the metropolitan culture and its peripheries, and interrogates the premises, purposes and goals of a civilisation dedicated to world hegemony.

The symmetrical design and integrative symbolism of *A Passage to India* confirm Forster's wish to make a coherent statement about human realities through art—for him the one internally harmonious, material entity in the universe, creating order from the chaos of a permanently disarranged planet—while the deeper structure to the novel holds open-ended, paradoxical and multivalent meanings, discharging ideas and images which cannot be contained within the confines of the formal pattern. In a text consisting of a political fiction, an allegory, a philosophical novel, a social tragedy and a metaphysical drama, both centrifugal and centripetal forces are at work: the themes diverge from the axis and realign, the literary forms radiate and join, the ostensibly poised whole emitting ambiguity, dissonance and contradiction which are formally repossessed and transfigured in an affirmative if allusive coda. The novel's mythopoeic mode strains after models of universal and ahistorical order, composing an archetypal symbolism intimating that there exists a metaphysical wholeness of all the antinomies in physical reality, social formations and the psyche. Countermanding this cosmic vision of vistas beyond the time-space world is a pessimism which perceives a universe apparently random and inhospitable to habitation, a disjunctive historical situation and the human mind divided against itself. The one orientation points towards an escape from the dislocations in the material world to the timeless womb of myth, the other confronts the present disarray in all its specificity and contingency. But finally, in the 'not now, not here,' 'not yet, not there,' another direction is indicated, one which forecasts that the visionary and the secular will be reconciled. This anticipation of a future still to emerge, a tomorrow radically different from what exists, is rooted in the belief that institutions are not inviolable nor is consciousness fixed; with this hope, the novel's metaphoric and realist modes merge, establishing that the flight into emblematic resolutions has been abandoned, and history reaffirmed.

Forster's nonconformity was evident in his distance from both the orthodoxies and heresies of British society. Though he shared the ideology of the middle-class milieu to which he was born, he was at crucial points disengaged from it, was a part of Bloomsbury yet apart, a socialist without doctrine, a reverent humanist reassured by the sanity of rationalism and the sanctity of individual relationships, who came to speculate on the satisfactions of sacred bewilderment and the dissolution of self in a transcendent other. With the accelerated disintegration of the old order after 1914, Forster's refuge in liberal-humanism, never wholly proof against the elements, was drastically damaged. Confronted by the breakdown in established values, the ravages of European competition, intensified class conflict within British society and growing disaffection amongst the colonial peoples, he looked outside England for a focus on this multiple disorder and, in choosing a route which passed from fiction centred on the condition of England to the global context created by imperialism, initiated a meeting with a defining condition of his times.

Forster has written of his visits to India in 1912 and 1921 as transforming experiences. For a small but significant number of English writers, brought through circumstance or choice into contact with the colonised world, the encounter exposed their consciousness to rival conceptions of civilisation, culture and community, to cosmologies postulating variant orderings to the universe, other definitions of the human condition and alternative versions of personality structure. In negotiating the contrary modes of awareness, the divergent precepts and goals devised by the West and by India, Forster produced a novel which neither fully accepts nor entirely repudiates the standards and usages of either. The text reveals the crisis of liberal-humanist ideology—its impotence as a code in an embattled social situation where moderation and compromise are not possible, its inadequacy as an explanation of a universe more extensive than the environment made by human intervention, and the insufficiency of its insights into the potentialities of mind whose experiential range exceeds ratiocination and sensory cognition. Nevertheless, although the work ventures no affirmation of its creed, it

is the product of an intelligence and sensibility nurtured within the cultural and intellectual context of liberal-humanism. It is because the novel is mediated through this world view and returns there for repose that the advance into new and profoundly astonishing perceptions is accompanied by retreats to the confines of known sterilities. The narrative voice oscillates between faith and disbelief in the validity of humanist mores, observing that, within an India divided into cultural groups not always sympathetic towards each other and ruled over by aliens hostile to all, community is both a refuge and a laager; that, if immersion in mysticism wastes secular proficiency, adherence to rationalism atrophies other possible facets of personality; that, whereas empiricism can provide a rigorous arrangement of appearances, it misses essences, and, if exclusion and definition lead to functional and aesthetic excellence, only the suspension of discrimination and the abolition of barriers will facilitate the making of a total explanatory system.

To these polarities no resolution is suggested, yet, because *A Passage to India* calls on resources outside the norms and priorities of Western societies, summoning other social configurations, ethical codes and philosophical systems, evaluations which have been made of Forster's 'medium mind' and his imprisonment within a superannuated system of ideas and values should be rephrased, for this novel both articulates in ontological and moral terms a radical dissent from the conventions and aspirations of the late bourgeois world, and omits to make the critical connection between these and the social and political structures they accompanied and sustained. Because of this, there is a vacuum at the core of the political fiction. Forster, always a cultural relativist, was amused at the rhetoric of a 'high imperial vision' and came to applaud the colonial people kicking against imperialist hegemony, but just as liberalism was unable to produce a fundamental critique of Western colonialism, so is a consciousness of imperialism's historical dimensions absent from *A Passage to India.* Imperialism inflicted a catastrophic dislocation on the worlds it conquered and colonised, generated new forms of tension within the metropolitan countries and brought the West into a condition of permanent antagonism with other civilisations; yet about this very epitome of contemporary conflict the novel is evasive.

But if such elisions tend to disembody the criticism, suggesting an evaluation of a superstructure uprooted from its base, the British-Indian connection is nevertheless represented as the paradigmatic power relationship, and the encounters possible within the imperialist situation are perceived as grotesque parodies of social meetings. The chilly British circulate like an ice stream through a land they feel to be poisonous and intending evil against them; British domination rests on force, fear and racism, generating enmity in articulate Indians sustained by memories of past opposition to conquest and mobilised by prospects of the independence to be regained. It is the politically innocent Mrs Moore who challenges her son's brutal pragmatism with an appeal for love and kindness, a gesture towards humanising an inhuman situation, which is repudiated in the novel's recognition that hostilities will increase as Indian resistance grows (a process to which passing references are made) and British determination to retain power hardens. Aziz, the Moslem descended from Mogul warriors, and the Brahmin Godbole, whose ancestors were the militant Mahrattas, may have conflicting recollections of an independent Deccan resisting British conquest, but they are united by their distinctively expressed disinclination to participate in their own subjugation, a shared refusal which culminates in a Hindu-Moslem entente. On the other side, the British make up their differences and close ranks, with even Fielding throwing in his lot with Anglo-India and so betraying his ideals.

The effeteness of liberal codes in the colonial situation is established in the novel by the catastrophic failure of British and Indian to sustain personal relations. The friendship between Fielding and Aziz, disturbed throughout by differences in standards and tastes, is finally ruptured when each withdraws, as he inevitably must, within the boundaries of the embattled communities, and it is Forster's consciousness that social connections will fail which sends him in pursuit of spiritual communion between Mrs Moore and both Aziz and Godbole. But perhaps the most eloquent demonstration of liberalism's impotence is its inability to offer any opposition to the enemies of its values. The obtuse, coarse, arrogant and bellicose deportment of Anglo-Indians, as realised in the novel, is the very negation of those decencies defined through Fielding: 'The world, he believed, is a globe of men who are trying to reach one another and can best do so by the help of good will plus culture and intelligence.' When Fielding, after his courageous stand against his countrymen and women, aligns himself with the rulers of India, he is submitting to the fact of imperialism, deferring to a mode of behaviour and feeling made and needed by an aggressive political system and conceding that his liberal principles and hopes of doing good in India exist only by favour of a Ronny Heaslop. Forster's tone can be mild, but the integrity and toughness of his pessimistic acknowledgement that here there is no middle way to compromise and reconciliation marks a break with his previous, though increasingly hesitant, appeals to rapprochement between contending social forces.

In an essentially speculative novel, intimating a universe which is not human-centred and departing from the romantic humanism of his earlier works, Forster—without relinquishing trust in reason—reflects on the numinous as he perceives its presence in India's religious traditions. The liberation to ecstasy and terror of the psychic energies subdued by modern industrialised societies, as represented in *A Passage to India,* is significantly different from Forster's former domesticated exhortations to connect the outer and inner life, the prose with the poetry, for the sublime now contemplated has heights and depths never discerned in 'dearest Grasmere' or artistic Hampstead, and recognition of this augurs existential possibilities still to be assimilated by the West. 'Inside its cocoon of work or social obligation, the human spirit slumbers for the most part, registering the distinction between pleasure and pain, but not nearly as alert as we pretend.' The awakenings of two Englishwomen dislocated by an India that confutes their expectations take cataclysmic form and result in derangement and delusion, the one mimicking in her feelings

and behaviour the ascetic stance of isolation from the world but misunderstanding its meanings as meaninglessness, the other assailed by knowledge of sexuality and misinterpreting this as a sexual assault. Both are negative responses to their perceptions of India's 'otherness': Mrs Moore shrinks the august ambition of quietism to the confines of personal accidie, while Adela Quested experiences cultural differences as a violation of her person. When the urbane Fielding has intuitions of a universe he has missed or rejected, of that 'something else' he is unable to know; when he and Adela Quested, both devoted to commonsense and clarity, speculate on the possibility of worlds beyond those available to their consciousness—then they are not yielding to concepts of heaven or hell, but (stirred by an India that is difficult, intricate and equivocal) recognising the possibility of other states of awareness.

What the novel produces in its transmutations of the numinous are dimensions to experience which are authenticated by their psychological truthfulness alone—expressing a hunger for perfection, a discontent with the limitations of the present and an aspiration to possess the future. The need for the unattainable Friend 'who never comes yet is not entirely disproved,' the yearning after the 'infinite goal beyond the stars,' the longing for 'the eternal promise, the never withdrawn suggestion that haunts our consciousness,' these are signs of that permanent hope which will persist 'despite fulfilment,' just as the images, substitutions, imitations, scapegoats and husks used in religious ritual are figures of 'a passage not easy, not now, not here, not to be apprehended except when it is unattainable.'

Signicantly *A Passage to India* is a novel from which God, though addressed in multiple ways, is always absent—necessarily excluded from the caves of the atheist Jains, and failing to come when invoked in the form of the Hindu Krishna or the Moslem's Friend—the Persian expression for God. As represented in the novel, the numinous is not divinely inspired nor does it emanate from arcane sources; it needs no religion and meets with no God. Forster's disbelief in the power of the human spirit to 'ravish the unknown' informs his transfigurations of the mystical aspiration:

> Did it succeed? Books written afterwards say 'Yes'. But how, if there is such an event, can it be remembered afterwards? How can it be expressed in anything but itself? Not only from the unbeliever are mysteries hid, but the adept himself cannot retain them. He may think, if he chooses, that he has been with God, but as soon as he thinks it, it becomes history, and falls under the rules of time.

What Forster does acknowledge is that faith confers grace on the believer during 'the moment of its indwelling,' and he affirms the gravity of religion's concerns, the fruitful discontent it speaks and the longings it makes known: 'There is something in religion that may not be true, but has not yet been sung. . . . Something that the Hindus have perhaps found." This paradox signifies the meanings which Forster assigns the institutionalised routes to an understanding and changing of human existence devised by India's religious traditions.

Theme and symbol in the novel's component modes converge on India. It is interesting that Forster's perceptions are in the tradition of Walt Whitman and Edward Carpenter, the one a passionate believer in popular democracy, the other a romantic socialist, both mystics and homosexuals disassociated by temperament and conviction from the conventions of their respective societies. Instead of the bizarre, exotic and perverse world made out of India by Western writers in the late nineteenth and early twentieth centuries, a compilation serving to confirm the normality and excellence of their own systems, Whitman and in his wake Carpenter found in that distant and antique civilisation expressions of transcendent aspects to experience and access to gnosis, predicting that, when connected with the secular, these would open up new vistas to democratic emancipation, international fellowship and progress. But if Forster's India does have affinities with these poetic evocations, the perspectives in *A Passage to India* are informed by inquiry into, rather than new-found belief in, alternative ways of seeing, and the altogether more complex configuration centres on its difference and originality as a challenge to the authorised categories of Western culture.

It is as if the defining concepts of the major Indian cosmologies are objectified in the landscape made by the novel, and this presents to the alien a new awareness that humanity's place is within a chain of being linking it with monkeys, jackals, squirrels, vultures, wasps and flies, and on a continuum of existence extending to oranges, cactuses, crystals, bacteria, mud and stones. Drawing on Indian traditions, the text constructs an ontological scale situating the species in a universe indifferent to human purpose and intent, contiguous to an unconcerned inarticulate world, planted on a neutral earth and beneath an impartial sky. It is a position which seems to reduce existence to a respite between two epochs of dust, inducing a view of people as moving mud and contesting the centrality of human aspiration and endeavour. The Marabars, as a figure of eternity, and the distance behind the stars, as the sign to infinity, create mythological time-space, challenging the myopia of empirical observation and measurement. In the environs of the Marabars, where hills move, fields jump, stones and boulders declare themselves alive and plants exercise choice, hylozoistic notions formulated by archaic philosophies, and still extant in some Indian religious traditions, are confirmed. To the rationalist this failure to delineate and define, this obliteration of distinctions, spells disorientation and chaos; to the metaphysician it speaks of a continuous series accommodating disparate modes of being within one coherent structure.

It is this theoretical organisation of reality that is produced through the multiplex metaphor of India: an India which with its various cultures, religions, sects and classes, is difficult, arbitrary, intricate and equivocal, a microcosm of the 'echoing, contradictory world,' and an India which is the emblem of an organic entity, an all-including unity accommodating paradox, anomaly and antinomy. For if 'no one is India' and 'Nothing embraces the whole of India,' it may all the same be the case that 'the hundred Indias which fuss and squabble so tiresomely are one, and the universe they mirror is one.' This possibility is translated in the gravitation of Aziz and Godbole towards a united front. Aziz attempts consciously to identify with India—'I am an Indian at last'—and unwittingly becomes absorbed, as had his ancestors, in India; Godbole, while continuing to live obediently within the sects and castes of Hinduism, assists Aziz in moving to a Hindu Princely state and declares himself his true friend. But it is in the Hindus' ritual celebration of the entire universe of living beings, matter, objects and spirit taken into the divine embrace that the conception of a dynamic blending of opposites is symbolically enacted, that enigmas and contradictions are ceremonially resolved and fusion is abstractly attained.

Although he was not a scholar of Indian metaphysics, Forster was familiar with the myths, epics and iconography of India's varied cultures and found their innately dialectical style congenial. On rereading the *Bhagavad-Gita* in 1912 before his first visit to India, he noted that he now thought he had got hold of it: 'Its division of states into Harmony Motion Inertia (Purity Passion Darkness).' These three qualities, constituting in the classical Indian view the very substance of the universe, are permuted in *A Passage to India* as Mosque, Caves and Temple, a sequence with multiple meanings—one of which is the ontological and psychological significance pertaining to three major Indian philosophical-religious systems: they are figures, respectively, of consciousness and the present, the unconscious and the past, and the emergent metaconsciousness and the future. The novel offers this triad as the form of differences contained within a whole: incorporated in the enclosing frame is the gracious culture of Islam in India, a society where personal relations amongst Moslems do flourish; the unpeopled Jain caves, place of the ascetic renunciation of the world; and the buoyant religious community of the Hindus, internally divided and internally cohesive. The approach to the component meanings of these systems is, however, profoundly ambiguous, moving between responsiveness and rejection, making the myth and subverting it.

Mystical Sufi tendencies are represented in the unmistakably Indian incarnation of Islam, a monotheistic and historically recent religion, dually committed to the mundane and the sacred. But, having confronted the more ambitious theories of older India, Forster now relegates Islam's consummation of the prose-poetry connection as too symmetrical, shallow and easy. With 'Caves', the novel passes back to the world-rejecting atheist tradition of the Jains, a post-Vedic heterodoxy of the fifth century BC but, like Buddhism—with which it has historical and theoretical affinities—rooted in the ancient, aboriginal metaphysics of primal, Dravidian India. Here the novel produces a version of this uncompromisingly pessimistic outlook, one which disparages bondage to the phenomenal universe as the source of pain and suffering, and pursues liberation from all involvement with matter. The contemplation of negatives and Nothing within the text culminates in the transfiguration of the ascetic world view, and, if 'Everything exists, nothing has value' is a statement of nihilism, it has an alternative meaning, one which acknowledges the material world as verifiable but assigns significance only to Nothing, to complete detachment:

'Nothing is inside them, they were sealed up before the creation of pestilence or treasure; if mankind grew curious and excavated, nothing, nothing would be added to the sum of good and evil.'

There is a striking ambivalence to the imagery of the Caves; their 'internal perfection' is evoked through crystalline figures of pure emptiness. But competing with and countermanding the delicate transparency of their interiors is the opaque menace of their external form:

> There is something unspeakable in these outposts. They are like nothing else in the world and a glimpse of them makes the breath catch. They rise abruptly, insanely, without the proportion that is kept by the wildest hills elsewhere, they bear no relation to anything dreamt or seen. To call them 'uncanny' suggests ghosts, and they are older than all spirit.

This speaks of the formless, primordial abyss before time and space, threatening to overwhelm consciousness, an enunciation which undermines the representation of Nothing as an authentic negative aspiration.

Moving forward to the Hinduism of India's Aryan invaders, the novel represents that tradition's ecstatic affirmation of the entire world, the ceremonial celebration of all matter and spirit as originating from and sharing in the Lord of the Universe. But if the text participates in the ambition of Hinduism—itself compounded over aeons through the assimilation and reworking of many other existing beliefs—to tie, weld, fuse and join all the disparate elements of being and existence in a complete union, it withdraws from the incalculable and unassimilable enormity of the enterprise. While *A Passage to India* applauds the refusal of the present as it is, the wish to supersede all obstacles in the way of wholeness, it rejects emblematic resolutions. The impulse to the ceremonies is shown as magnificent:

> Infinite Love took upon itself the form of SHRI KRISHNA, and saved the world. All sorrow was annihilated, not only for Indians, but for foreigners, birds, caves, railways, and the stars; all became joy, all laughter; there had never been disease nor doubt, misunderstanding, cruelty, fear.

But when the celebrations end, the divisions and confusions of daily life return. Just as consciousness of political conflict and social divergence transgresses against the will to union, so is there here a humanist's repudiation of symbolic concord. The allegory is over before the novel ends, the aesthetic wholeness dismembered by the fissures and tensions of the disjoint, prosaic world that the novel represents; the permanent is dissolved in the acid of contingency. In the last pages emblems of reconciliation and synthesis compete with their opposites: 'the scenery, though it smiled, fell like a gravestone on any human hope.' The illimitable aspiration is not consummated: 'a compromise had been made between destiny and desire, and even the heart of man acquiesced.'

In retrospect it is apparent that the authority of the allegory is throughout undermined by other modes within the text; as each positing of universal abstractions is counter-

manded by perceptions of the specifics in the historical situation, so the cosmic is cut down to size by the comic—the squeals of a squirrel, though 'in tune with the infinite, no doubt,' are not attractive except to other squirrels; trees of poor quality in an inferior landscape call in vain on the absolute, for there is not enough God to go round; there are gods so universal in their attributes that they 'owned numerous cows, and all the betel-leaf industry, besides having shares in the Asirgarh motor-omnibus,' and a god whose love of the world had impelled him to take monkey flesh upon himself. From the infinite the novel returns to the ordinary; from eternity there is a bridge back to the mundane. The worth of human effort, ingenuity and creativity is restored in the view Mrs Moore has on her last journey across India, where the symbolic landscape is pervaded by history and culture:

> She watched the indestructible life of man and his changing faces, and the houses he had built for himself and God. . . . She would never visit Asirgarh or the other untouched places; neither Delhi nor Agra nor the Rajputana cities nor Kashmir, nor the obscurer marvels that had sometimes shone through men's speech: the bilingual rock of Girnar, the statue of Shri Belgola, the ruins of Mandu and Hampi, temples of Khajuraho, gardens of Shalimar.

The balance is redressed, and in the retreat to the Mediterranean it is overturned in favour of the secular and the 'normal'. The relief and pleasure known by both Adela Quested and Fielding on their return voyages from India is confirmed by that narrative voice which has throughout posited and endorsed Western norms and values; and the paean to Venice is eloquent of an ambivalence within the text's discourse towards the alternatives it poses:

> the harmony between the works of man and the earth that upholds them, the civilisation that has escaped muddle, the spirit in a reasonable form. . . . The Mediterranean is the human norm. When men leave that exquisite lake, whether through the Bosphorus or the Pillars of Hercules, they approach the monstrous and extraordinary; and the southern exit leads to the strangest experience of all.

But neither this tenuous repose nor the symbolic solutions, neither the inevitability of compromise nor the permanence of conflict is the final word, for these are superseded by the generation of hope in a future when the obstacles the novel has confronted will have been overcome in history. On their last ride together, Aziz and Fielding, after misunderstanding, bitterness and separation, are friends again 'yet aware that they could meet no more,' that 'socially they had no meeting place.' But Aziz, anticipating the time of freedom from imperialist rule, promises, 'and then . . . you and I shall be friends' (p. 316); and when Fielding asks why this cannot be now, earth, creatures and artefacts intercede to reject the possibility: 'they didn't want it, they said in their hundred voices, "No, not yet", and the sky said, "No, not there." '

A Passage to India is Forster's epitaph to liberal-humanism. In search of other systems he had contemplated traditions to which ironically he had access because of the global space created and divided by imperialism, and if he withdrew from the sheer magnitude of the ambition to liberation nurtured within Indian philosophical modes, he had acquired a perspective on a transfigured tomorrow that made the social hope of his earlier fictions seem parochial. But as fascism, persecution, war and the repression of the colonial struggle brought force and violence near and made the 'not yet' seem ever more distant, Forster retired to essays, criticism, biography and broadcasts, media in which it was still possible to reiterate an adherence to liberal values, an option unavailable in self-interrogating fictional texts. In 1935 Forster attended the International Association of Writers for the Defence of Culture in Paris, a meeting organised by the Popular Front to unite communists, socialists and liberals in defence of 'the cultural heritage'. It is possible in retrospect to be cynical about the political humanism which the congress opportunistically advocated and to observe that Forster would have been quite at home in such a gathering. At the time it was surely an act of integrity by an untheoretical socialist determined to demonstrate his opposition to fascism. In his address Forster used the vocabulary of liberalism—justice, culture, liberty, freedom—and conceded that the times demanded another language which he could not speak:

> I know very well how limited, and how open to criticism, English freedom is. It is race-bound and it's class-bound . . . you may have guessed that I am not a Communist, though perhaps I might be one if I was a younger and a braver man, for in Communism I can see hope. It does many things which I think evil, but I know that it intends good. I am actually what my age and my upbringing have made me—a bourgeois who adheres to the British constitution, adheres to it rather than supports it. . . .

Forster needed no critics to tell him of the ambiguities, contradictions and limitations in his intellectual stance; brought to *A Passage to India,* such categories reveal the constraints on the text's system of representation—an analysis which should not hinder the perception that this novel is a rare instance of a libertarian perspective on another and subordinated culture produced from within an imperialist metropolis. (pp. 27-43)

> *Benita Parry, "The Politics of Representation in 'A Passage to India',"* in A Passage to India: Essays in Interpretation, *edited by John Beer, The Macmillan Press Ltd., 1985, pp. 27-43.*

Jenny Sharpe (essay date Spring 1991)

[*In the following excerpt, Sharpe analyzes the treatment of rape in* A Passage to India *and in subsequent feminist criticism on the novel with respect to contemporary theories of patriarchy and imperialism.*]

E. M. Forster's *A Passage to India* reenacts in the drama surrounding a rape the fears and fantasies of an imperial nation over the intermingling of two races, the colonizer and the colonized. Adela Quested, who is English, accuses the educated Muslim, Dr. Aziz, of sexually assaulting her in one of the Marabar Caves. By reading Aziz's "crime"

Forster on writing *A Passage to India*:

When I returned in 1921 to stay with the Maharajah I took the chapters with me and expected that the congenial surroundings would inspire me to go on. Exactly the reverse happened. Between the India I had tried to create and the India I was experiencing there was an impassable gulf. I had to get back to England and see my material in perspective before I could proceed. Perhaps the long wait was to the good and the religious atmosphere of Dewas certainly helped to establish the spiritual sequence I was seeking, particularly in the last section of the book.

E. M. Forster, "Three Countries," in the Forster Typescripts, King's College Library, Cambridge, as cited in Robin Jared Lewis, E. M. Forster's Passages to India, *1979.*

---

as "the unspeakable limit of cynicism, untouched since 1857," the English residents of Chandrapore place the alleged rape within the racial memory of the Mutiny, also known as the Sepoy Rebellion. Eighteen fifty-seven has entered the colonial records as nothing less than the barbaric attack of mutinous Sepoys on innocent women and children. Yet, as one of the largest anti-British uprisings, 1857 is also known to Indian nationalists as the First War of Independence. During the 1920s when Forster was finishing his novel, Vinayak Savarkar's *Indian War of Independence of 1857*—a highly polemical book written to rouse Indians into armed struggle against the British—was widely circulated despite its proscription. The memory of 1857 was thus a site of historical contention during those volatile years of early decolonization. I take from Forster's presentation of Adela's attack within the frame of 1857 the license to read his novel as a narrative that reveals the limits of an official discourse on native insurgency. It is a discourse that racializes colonial relations by implicating rebellion in the violence of rape.

A Passage to India holds up for public scrutiny the racialization of imperial discourse by generating its narrative desire through the indeterminate status of the rape. Since the reader is not privy to what happened in the caves, she or he is faced with the contradictory evidence of Adela's accusation and Aziz's denial. The accuracy of Adela's judgment is undermined during the trial when, upon interrogation, she suddenly withdraws the charge. Forster's staging of the court scene around the reversal of a rape charge disrupts the taken-for-grantedness of the racially motivated assumption that "the darker races are physically attracted by the fairer, but not *vice versa*." The roles of assailant and victim are now dramatically reversed as the novel reveals the "real crime" of imperialism to be an abuse of power that can only lead to its demise. Yet we are never told whether the attempted rape was real or imagined, and the question of what happened in the Marabar Caves continues to intrigue readers of the novel. Whereas early inquiries investigated the mystery for what it revealed about Forster's narrative technique or Indian metaphysics, recent criticism has shifted the terms of the debate toward issues of race and gender.

I situate my own reading of the rape in *A Passage to India* within the current effort of feminist theory to account for the heterogeneous text of women's history. As we attempt to pry apart the singularity of a female tradition, we often presume "race" to be a unified and homogeneous field of otherness. By treating race as a transhistorical category, we thus fail to dislodge the dominant discourses that wrench racial (and sexual) constructions out of history and present them as essentializing categories of difference. The demand on contemporary feminism, then, is to disrupt the taken-for-grantedness of such categories through an excavation of the histories that produce racial and sexual difference. In response to this demand, I trace the signification of rape in Forster's novel to the historical production of a colonial discourse on the native assault of English women in India. Upon making this move, however, I do not wish to suggest that literature and history are repetitions of each other. While the historical records produce a racial memory that is silently constitutive of Anglo-Indian fiction, the familiar plots of such fictions render India "imaginable" for historical narration. In this regard, my interest in *A Passage to India* lies in the particularly strategic role it has played in establishing the terrain for recent revisions of the Raj.

A replaying of the last days of the Raj in the ongoing drama of movies like *Gandhi*, *The Jewel in the Crown*, and *A Passage to India* exhibits a nostalgia for Empire even as it masquerades as self-criticism. Forster's critical look at imperialism presents a problem that is particularly vexing for feminists. Upon questioning whether the real crime is Adela's accusation or Aziz's assault, *A Passage to India* sets up an opposition between "the English woman" and "the Indian man." If one decides, in keeping with the novel's anti-imperialist theme, that the crime lies in a system capable of reducing an Indian man to his pathological lust for white women, then even the slightest hint of an actual rape cannot be entertained. Conversely, a defense of Adela's fear of assault brings with it a condemnation of the Indian patriarchy and Aziz's objectification of women as sex objects. The ambiguities surrounding the alleged rape thus force the critic to defend either the native man or the white woman against his or her opponent. It is this either/or decision (but never both) that has divided an anticolonial criticism of *A Passage to India* along gender lines.

Critical opinion tends to favor Adela's hallucination as the most likely explanation for what happened in the caves. Offering her sexual repression as evidence, such accounts discredit Adela's charge against Aziz as not only mistaken but also misguided. Even those readings that critically engage the problems of colonial representation treat Adela's cry of rape as an expression of her desire. Although *A Passage to India* does suggest the imaginary nature of the attack, it does not provide sufficient evidence for presupposing that Adela's musings on Aziz's handsome appearance should translate into a sexual fantasy of rape. In his screen adaptation of the novel, David Lean legitimates this common reading by adding a scene which eliminates any doubt that, on at least one other occasion, the unattractive Adela suffered a bout of sexual hysteria. The scene shows Adela leaving the safety of the European compound to

venture out on bicycle alone. She chances upon an ancient Hindu temple, whose sexually explicit carvings arouse her curiosity and interest. The threatening aspect of her sexual arousal is figuratively represented in the aggressive monkeys that swarm over the statues and scare her away. Adela returns to Chandrapore breathless, pale, and sweating. Having just broken off her engagement to Ronny Heaslop, she now says she will marry him. His query—"What happened?"—and her response—"Nothing"—are emblematic of the film's message regarding the cave scene. In a flashback of Adela staring fixedly at Aziz's silhouetted shape looming in the cave's entrance, Lean repeats the image of her pale and frightened face after her encounter with the monkeys. The conclusion to be drawn is so obvious that the film does not find it necessary to provide further elaboration.

A masculinist reading of the mystery in the cave (such as Lean's) is based on the "common knowledge" that frigid women suffer from sexual hysteria and that unattractive women desire to be raped. This interpretation works backward from the imaginary rape, positing the effect of an effect as its cause. The argument consequently produces its own tautology: Adela hallucinated the rape because she was sexually repressed, the proof of which lies in her hallucination. Feminist criticism of *A Passage to India* has dismantled this tautology by revealing the "making into meaning" of its assumptions. Rather than discounting the imaginary nature of the attack, feminists respond to the critical verdict against Adela by retracing her hallucination to a "first cause" of patriarchal authority rather than sexual hysteria. Elaine Showalter, for instance, reads the hallucination in terms of Adela's apprehensions about committing herself to a loveless marriage that is nothing short of "legalized rape." In "Periphrasis, Power, and Rape in *A Passage to India*," Brenda Silver also links the imaginary rape to the gender roles suggested by marriage. Since Adela enters the cave disturbed about her forthcoming marriage to Ronny Heaslop, argues Silver, she is forced to acknowledge her social status as a sex object and thus to confront "the material and psychological reality of what it means to be rapable."

Although they are correct to situate the alleged rape within the larger frame of women's oppression, Showalter and Silver fail to address the historical production of the category of rape within a system of *colonial* relations. Feminist criticism has thus replaced the masculinist tautology with another one. The feminist tautology goes something like this: Adela experiences the conditions of rape because she is objectified as a woman, the proof of which lies in her experience of rape. What does it mean for an English woman's experience of her oppression to be staged as a scenario in which she is the potential object of a native attack? In other words, how does the feminist critic negotiate the either/or opposition between the colonial female and the colonized male that the novel sets up? I would begin by insisting that Adela's confrontation of "what it means to be rapable" is framed by racial tensions that cannot be understood as simply another form of patriarchal violence.

What is immediately noticeable about the representation

of gender roles in *A Passage to India* is the fracture between Adela's social positioning and that of Anglo-Indian women. From the early pages of the novel there are suggestions that colonial women are protectively cloistered behind an anachronistic code of chivalry and honor. "Windows were barred lest the servants should see their mem-sahibs acting," the narrator informs us, "and the heat was consequently immense." Fielding's refusal to behave chivalrously toward English women "would have passed without comment in feminist England," we are told, but not in Anglo-India. Unfamiliar with their customs, Adela is surprised that club members have chosen to perform *Cousin Kate,* a play Showalter reminds us is "a mildly anti-feminist comedy." Thus establishing an opposition between the emancipated women of England and the stalled liberation of the *memsahibs, A Passage to India* plots Adela's movement from one side of the East-West divide to the other.

It is not just that Adela enters the cave contemplating a marriage that will subsume her identity into that of her husband. More importantly, she recognizes the danger of assuming the Anglo-Indians' racist assumptions about India and its inhabitants. "Well, by marrying Mr. Heaslop, I shall become what is known as an Anglo-Indian," she says to Aziz as they make their way toward the caves:

> He held up his hand in protest. "Impossible. Take back such a terrible remark." "But I shall! it's inevitable. I can't avoid the label. What I do hope to avoid is the mentality. Women like—" She stopped, not quite liking to mention names; she would boldly have said "Mrs. Turton and Mrs. Callendar" a fortnight ago.

Adela's inability to identify Mrs. Turton and Mrs. Callendar as the insensitive imperialists that they are demonstrates her new-found loyalty to Anglo-Indian women. Her transformation into a *memsahib* was already under way the moment she agreed to marry Heaslop. "She was labeled now," she thought to herself at the time. If the label is inevitable, the mentality is inescapable. A disregard for Indians to the degree of rendering them invisible is an offense that Anglo-Indian women repeatedly commit. By the time Adela enters the cave, her self-consciousness about what it means to be an Anglo-Indian is forgotten. After presuming that Aziz has more than one wife by virtue of being a Muslim, Adela is oblivious to having offended him and, being so wrapped up in her own thoughts, she is not even aware of his presence. "Quite unconscious that she had said the wrong thing, and not seeing him, she also went into the cave, thinking with half her mind 'sight-seeing bores me,' and wondering with the other half about marriage." Only half of Adela's mind is on thoughts of marriage; the other expresses a boredom with Aziz's elaborate efforts to show her "the real India." Her divided mind reveals a tension between the Anglo-Indian woman's double positioning in colonial discourse—as the inferior sex but superior race. It is a contradiction that must be addressed in any discussion of the sexual assault.

When Adela emerges from the cave accusing Aziz of rape, she consolidates the identity she would rather deny. That is to say, she reconfirms the colonizer's racist assumption that, given the slightest opportunity, the native will revert to his barbaric ways. In her haste to escape she flees through cacti, lodging thousands of minuscule spines into her flesh. Her mutilated condition confirms the violence of the attack, but it also reduces her sensibility to her tortured body. "Everything now was transferred to the surface of her body, which began to avenge itself, and feed unhealthily." Her fellow expatriates react to the news of the assault from within their code of honor and chivalry: they treat Adela as a mere cipher for a battle between men. "Miss Quested was only a victim, but young Heaslop was a martyr; he was the recipient of all the evil intended against them by the country they had tried to serve; he was bearing the sahib's cross." The age-old equation of female chastity with male honor is reinscribed within the language of the colonial civilizing mission. By virtue of that mission, the white man reenacts a Christian allegory of self-sacrifice so that the weaker races might be raised into humanity. The objectification of Adela into a passive victim denies her an entry into the grand narrative of the white man's burden even as that victimage reaffirms the self-sacrifice of the men who serve the colonial mission. *She* cannot save the natives from their depravity, but neither can she save herself. Adela, the *memsahib,* the Anglo-Indian woman, has strayed far from the borders of "feminist England." She may have entered the caves with some semblance of her former identity, but she emerges as a violated body bearing the visible signs of the native's ingratitude.

A Passage to India consciously invokes, in its animation of a sexual assault that transforms Adela into a sign for the victimage of imperialism, a nineteenth-century colonial discourse of counter-insurgency. During the 1857 uprisings, a crisis in colonial authority was managed through the circulation of "the English Lady" as a sign for the moral influence of colonialism. A colonial discourse on rebellious Sepoys raping, torturing, and mutilating English women inscribed the native's savagery onto the objectified body of English women, even as it screened the colonizer's brutal suppression of the uprisings. When the Anglo-Indians of Chandrapore read "rape" as "the unspeakable limit of cynicism, untouched since 1857," they are not only associating the attack in the cave with the racial memory of those earlier "unspeakable" acts, but also reproducing its effects.

Feminist explications of *A Passage to India,* however, tend to ignore the racial memory that forms the historical frame to its theme of interracial rape. Silver, for instance, does not allude to a colonial past but, rather, a history that demystifies the myth of the black rapist in the American South. Her discussion of "the Negro" in the place of "the Indian" suggests a continuity between the divergent histories of slavery and imperialism. To read racial stereotypes in terms of the discontinuous histories of colonial conquest, slavery, and imperialism is to see that the selection of certain attributes for exaggeration has to do with the ideological sanction they provide. In her careful documentation of lynching, Ida B. Wells reveals that the fearful stereotype of "the Negro rapist" sanctioned the upsurge in violence against black men, women, and children that was aimed at reversing their political and economic gains. Her evidence is reinforced in Eugene Genovese's observation that "the violence-provoking theory of the superpotency of that black superpenis, while whispered about for several centuries, did not become an obsession in the South until after emancipation, when it served the purposes of racial segregationists." The myth of the black rapist presupposes even as it reproduces the Negro's lustful bestiality. The Oriental male, by contrast, is constructed as licentious, not lustful, duplicitous rather than bestial.

In the absence of its colonial constructions, Silver discusses racial codes on a level of generality that reduces out geopolitical differences. It is an absence that permits her to write the condition of both the black rapist and the colonized under the name of "woman." By understanding rape to be a discourse of power that objectifies colonial women and colonized men alike, she suggests that Aziz is figuratively raped by the accusation of rape. "When spoken of as Indian within the discourse of English and Indian, sahib and native," she writes, "he himself [Aziz] is objectified; he enters the 'category' of woman and becomes rapable." Although Silver expresses that she is "aware of 'feeling privileged *as a woman*' to speak to and for third-world women (and in this case third-world men as well)," it is her problematical reading of third-world men as occupying the space of first-world women that permits the latter to serve as a model for all oppressed peoples. Since she *is* attentive to the dangers of substituting gender for race, I do not dismiss her essay as misinformed. Rather, I regard her informed reading as symptomatic of the persistent difficulty Anglo-American feminism has with dislodging the (white) woman as a privileged signifier for "otherness." It is a privilege that can be unlearned, but only through an attention to the historical production of our categories for class, race, and gender relations. If feminism has anything to teach us, it is that an official history has produced a category of "woman" that keeps women, to invoke Sheila Rowbotham, hidden from history. By deploying "rape" as a master trope for the objectification of English women and natives alike, Silver produces a category of "Other" that keeps the colonized hidden from history. (pp. 25-30)

A Passage to India recreates in the drama surrounding Aziz's arrest the precariousness of the imperialist mission under threat of insurrection. It is a vulnerability that necessitates the positing of a native desire for white women as the "chief cause" for interracial conflict. In all those scenes that allude to Dyer's command at Amritsar and the racial memory of the Mutiny, the novel also shows the fear of a native assault on English women to be a screen for imperialist strategies of counterinsurgency. In other words, it draws attention to a discourse of rape deployed in the management of anticolonial rebellion. Such stagings, however, do not disrupt the dominant Mutiny narrative but simply question its premises. What does reveal the fictionality of colonial truth-claims is the element of doubt Adela introduces into the certainty of a crime confirming the native's depravity.

During the trial, Adela delivers a verdict that throws the place of imperial law into chaos. "Dr. Aziz never followed me into the cave," she declares, "I withdraw everything."

When situated within the racial memory of the Mutiny, her extension and withdrawal of her charge drives a wedge of doubt between a colonial discourse of rape and its object. In other words, Adela's declaration of Aziz's innocence undermines the racist assumptions underpinning an official discourse that represents anticolonial insurgency as the savage attack of barbarians on innocent women and children. Yet, Forster does not replace the certainty of an attack with its negation but rather with a narrative suspension that opens up the space for a mystery. After the trial, Fielding explores with Adela four possible explanations for what happened: either Aziz did molest her, she claimed he did out of malice, she hallucinated the attack, or someone else followed her into the cave (the guide and a Pathan are offered as two likely assailants). Although Fielding rules out the first two possibilities, Adela gives no indication to him (or the reader, for that matter) whether she reacted to a real or imaginary assault. She finally admits that the only one who knows for sure is Mrs. Moore, whom she claims to have acquired her knowledge through a telepathic communication. As he keeps forcing Adela to return to the question of what happened in the caves, Fielding soon realizes that the very multiplicity of explanations offer no easy resolution to the mystery: "Telepathy? What an explanation! Better withdraw it, and Adela did so . . . Were there worlds beyond which they could never touch, or did all that is possible enter their consciousness? They could not tell . . . Perhaps life is a mystery, not a muddle; they could not tell." As readers, we are perhaps less satisfied than Fielding with the "life is a mystery" response, for critics have, and still do, search their imaginations for an explanation. Forster himself imagined at least one possibility in a scene that does not appear in the published version of his novel.

The deleted scene contains such a detailed description of the assault in the cave that it would be practically impossible to read what transpired there as Adela's hallucination. Here we have no helpless woman seeking the protection of others, but one who calculates the right moment to make her move and manages to fight off her attacker:

> At first she thought that <she was being robbed,> he was <holding> /taking/ her hand /as before/ to help <out>, then she realised, and shrieked at the top of her voice. "Boum" <went> /shrieked[?]/ the echo. She struck out and he got hold of her other hand and forced her against the wall, he got both her hands in one of his, and then felt at her <dress> /breasts/. "Mrs. Moore" she yelled. "Ronny—don't let him, save me." The strap of her Field Glasses, tugged suddenly, was drawn across her throat. She understood—it was to be passed once around her neck, <it was to> she was to be throttled as far as necessary and then . . . [Forster's suspension points] Silent, though the echo still raged up and down, she waited and when the breath was on her wrenched a hand free, got hold of the glasses and pushed them at /into/ her assailant's mouth. She could not push hard, but it was enough to <free her> hurt him. He let go, and then with both hands /on her weapon/ she smashed <him to pieces> /at him again/. She was strong and

had horrible joy in revenge. "Not this time," she cried, and he answered—or < perhaps it was > the cave /did/. [Oliver Stallybrass, *The Manuscripts of A Passage To India*]

Like the Anglo-Indian women who survived the 1857 attacks, Adela's act of self-defense is at odds with a dominant discourse that constructs the "English Lady" as a passive victim. As a consequence, one cannot help but notice a resemblance between the absent text of her struggle and an official discourse which erases colonial women's agency. In fact, feminist critics have submitted Forster's deletion of this scene as the sign of a more pervasive silencing of women or the repression of a misogyny that returns in subtler forms throughout the novel. What these readings cannot account for, however, is that the "passive victim" is recorded in the deleted script as "feminist England," but only at the risk of confirming the attempted rape. A clearing up of the mystery in favor of Adela's guilt or innocence consequently adheres to the terms of a discourse that displaces racial signification away from colonial relations onto narratives of sexual violence. We see that a restoration of the silenced stories of English women alone cannot disrupt a colonial plotting on interracial rape.

The racial and sexual significance of rape in *A Passage to India* does not issue from Adela's experience in the cave; the answer is not to be found there. To clear up the mystery of what happened in the caves by searching our imagination for the missing details involves reading Forster's novel according to the narrative demands of the Mutiny reports. To read the mystery itself as an effect of that colonial history, however, is to see in its indeterminacies the imprint of a racial memory and "to trace the path which leads from the haunted work to that which haunts it" [Pierre Macherey, *The Theory of Literary Production*]. In the place of "what happened in the caves," I offer a different kind of question, one suggested by Adela's cry in the deleted assault scene. Managing to free herself from the grip of her attacker, Adela screams—"Not this time." What are the other times, the other assaults to which her triumphant cry alludes? I think that I have already answered that question.

If we are to study literature for its disruption of an ideological production that prevents social change, we can no longer afford to restrict our readings to the limits of the literary text. Rather, we should regard the literature as working within, and sometimes against, the historical limits of representation. *A Passage to India* contends with a discourse of power capable of reducing anticolonial struggle to the pathological lust of dark-skinned men for white women. Adela serves the narrative function of undermining such racial assumptions but then, having served her purpose, she is no longer of interest to the concerns of the novel. The "girl's sacrifice" remains just that, a sacrifice for advancing a plot centered on the impossibility of a friendship between men across the colonial divide. As feminists, we should not reverse the terms of the "sacrifice" but, rather, negotiate between the sexual and racial constructions of the colonial female and native male without reducing one to the other. Like Fielding and Adela who confront the mystery in the multiplicity of explana-

tions, we should recognize that there are no easy resolutions. (pp. 40-2)

> *Jenny Sharpe, "The Unspeakable Limits of Rape: Colonial Violence and Counter-Insurgency," in* Genders, *No. 10, Spring, 1991, pp. 25-46.*

FURTHER READING

Appasamy, S. P. "Forster's Attempt to Connect Britain and India." *Indo-British Review* 111, No. 3 (January-March 1971): 19-24.

> Asserts that *A Passage to India* "has become a modern classic, not because it is a piece of anti-imperialistic propaganda, or a polemic against British rule in India, but because [Forster] tries to isolate the reasons for the failure of the great civilising mission of Britain."

Armstrong, Paul B. "Reading India: E. M. Forster and the Politics of Interpretation." *Twentieth Century Literature* 38, No. 4 (Winter 1992): 365-85.

> Argues that Forster has been treated unjustly by critics who consider him an upholder of discredited political views and a practitioner of outmoded literary techniques.

Babu, M. Sathya. "Godbole in 'The Temple'. " *The Literary Criterion* IX, No. 2 (Summer 1970): 70-8.

> Disputes previous critical interpretations of the character of Professor Godbole in *A Passage to India*, claiming he is a much more important and complex character than is usually assumed.

Beer, John, ed. *A Passage to India: Essays in Interpretation.* London: Macmillan Press, 1985, 172 p.

> Includes essays by Benita Parry, G. K. Das, and John Drew.

Beyer, Kathleen Collins. "Intertextuality in E. M. Forster." *The Literary Half-Yearly* XXXIII, No. 2 (July 1992): 23-30.

> Claims that *A Passage to India* and Forster's nonfiction account of his experiences in India, *The Hill of Devi*, both develop the same themes: "the hunger for friendship; the human attempt to harmonize."

Bodenheimer, Rosemarie. "The Romantic Impasse in *A Passage to India*." *Criticism* XXII, No. 1 (Winter 1980): 40-56.

> Contends that *A Passage to India* "must be seen as a narrative deeply and frankly divided against itself, split between Forster's aesthetic and moral belief in the formal beauty of romantic vision, and his serious distrust of the fictions created by language and memory."

Bradbury, Malcolm, ed. *E. M. Forster: "A Passage to India."* London: Macmillan, 1970, 252 p.

> Representative collection of essays divided into sections covering the composition of the novel, its early reception, and recent studies of the book. This volume contains many of the most important essays on *A Passage to India*, including those by Lionel Trilling, Frederick Crews, John Beer, Gertrude White, and Frank Ker-

mode, as well as reactions from Virginia Wolf and D. H. Lawrence.

Clubb, Roger L. "*A Passage to India:* The Meaning of the Marabar Caves." *CLA Journal* VI, No. 3 (March 1963): 184-93.

Examines the significance of the Marabar caves in *A Passage to India,* claiming that their mystery is the key to a spiritual interpretation of the book.

Gardner, Phillip, ed. *E. M. Forster: The Critical Heritage.* London: Routledge & Kegan Paul, 1973, 498 p.
Compilation of early reviews.

Goonetilleke, D. C. R. A. "Colonial Neuroses: Kipling and Forster." *Ariel* 5, No. 4 (October 1974): 56-60.

Examines *A Passage to India* and Kipling's stories set in India as works that reflect the racial and cultural fear experienced by the British living among their colonial subjects.

Gowda, H. H. Anniah. "To the Caves." In *A Garland For E. M. Forster,* edited by H. H. Anniah Gowda, pp. 23-39. Mysore, India: The Literary Half-Yearly, 1969.

Analyzes the characters in *A Passage to India* as well as the symbolic significance of the Marabar caves.

Hale, Nancy. "A Passage to Relationship." *The Antioch Review* XX, No. 1 (Spring 1960): 19-30.

Discusses the treatment of human relationships in *A Passage to India.*

JanMohamed, Abdul R. "The Economy of Manichean Allegory: The Function of Racial Difference in Colonialist Literature." *Critical Inquiry* 12, No. 1 (Autumn 1985): 59-87.

Claims that *A Passage to India* operates within the ideological framework of "Orientalism," the discourse that creates knowledge about the East to justify European hegemony.

Kipnis, Laura. " 'The Phantom Twitchings of an Amputated Limb': Sexual Spectacle in the Post-Colonial Epic." *Wide Angle* 11, No. 4 (October 1989): 42-51.

Application of feminist cultural theory to the recent film adaptions of *A Passage to India* and *Out of Africa,* suggesting that they comprise specific "readings" of the texts. In particular, Kipnis claims that the ideological project of these films is "to disavow the moral culpability for a tainted history and to sanitize that history by reenacting colonialism as a female disease."

Lebowitz, Naomi. "*A Passage to India:* History as Humanist Humor." In her *Humanism and the Absurd in the Modern Novel,* pp. 67-83. Evanston, Ill.: Northwestern University Press, 1971.

Discusses *A Passage to India* and Forster's humanism with respect to theories about the writing of history.

Levine, June Perry. "Passage to the Odeon: Too Lean." *Literature Film Quarterly* 14, No. 3: 139-150.

Discusses David Lean's film adaptation of *A Passage to India,* claiming that it demonstrates "a Western preoccupation with Western issues, even in a film set in India based on a novel about India, and a lack of curiosity about other peoples . . . that can most kindly be termed parochial."

Lewis, R. J. "The Literature of the Raj." In *Asia in Western Fiction,* edited by R. W. Winks and R. R. Rush, pp. 53-70. Manchester: Manchester University Press, 1990.

Contrasts *A Passage to India* with other British colonial literature set in Asian countries.

Noble, R. W. "A Passage to India." *Encounter* LIV, No. 2 (February 1980): 51-2, 54-61.

Explores the origins of *A Passage to India* in Forster's experience in India.

Pathak, Z., Sengupta, S., and Purkayastha, S. "The Prison-house of Orientalism." *Textual Practice* 5, No. 3 (Summer 1991): 195-218.

Comments on the teaching of *A Passage to India* in an Indian university in light of Edward Said's theory of Orientalism.

Phillips, K. J. "Hindu Avatars, Moslem Martyrs, and Primitive Dying Gods in E. M. Forster's *A Passage to India.*" *Journal of Modern Literature* 15, No. 1 (Summer 1988): 121-40.

Suggests that the concept of a "dying God," a god "who knows that the taking of form is both necessary and necessarily limited," appealed to Forster as an image of the tentative nature of human understanding and art."

Shahane, V. A., ed. *A Focus On Forster's "A Passage to India": Indian Essays in Criticism.* Bombay: Orient Longman, 1975, 137 p.

Collection of essays from Indian critics, including Chaman Sahni, Bikram Das, Anniah Gowda, and M. K. Naik.

Silver, Brenda. "Periphrasis, Power, and Rape in *A Passage to India.*" *Novel* 22, No. 1 (Fall 1988): 86-105.

Discusses the avoidance of direct descriptions and the naming of rape in *A Passage to India,* suggesting that the novel operates within a system of control by men/colonizing subjects over women/colonial objects.

Singh, Frances B. "*A Passage to India,* the National Movement, and Independence." *Twentieth Century Literature* 31, No. 2 (Summer-Fall 1985): 265-78.

Places the novel in the historical context of the Indian nationalist movement between 1912 and 1924.

Stallybrass, Oliver, ed. *Aspects of E. M. Forster.* London: Edward Arnold, 1969, 195 p.

Collection of essays commemorating Forster's ninetieth birthday that includes Malcolm Bradbury's "Two Passages to India" and Stallybrass's "Forster's 'wobblings,' " which examine the manuscripts of *A Passage to India.* Elizabeth Bowen and K. Natwar-Singh, two other noted critics, are also included.

Thomson, George H. "Thematic Symbol in *A Passage to India.*" *Twentieth Century Literature* 7, No. 2 (July 1961): 51-63.

 Analyzes the symbolism of the mosque, caves, and temple sections of *A Passage to India* as representing three different stages of spiritual development.

Additional coverage of Forster's life and career is contained in the following sources published by Gale Research: *Authors and Artists for Young Adults,* Vol. 2; *Concise Dictionary of British Literary Biography,* 1914-1945; *Contemporary Authors,* Vols. 13-14, 25-28 (rev. ed.); *Contemporary Authors Permanent Series,* Vol. 1; *Contemporary Literary Criticism,* Vols. 1, 2, 3, 4, 9, 10, 13, 15, 22, 45; *Dictionary of Literary Biography,* Vols. 34, 98; *Major 20th-Century Writers; Something about the Author,* Vol. 57; and *World Literature Criticism.*

Julien Green

1900-

(Full name Julien Hartridge Green; also known in English translation as Julian Green; also wrote under the pseudonyms Théophile Delaporte and David Irland) Simultaneously an American citizen and a lifelong resident of France, Green is a novelist, playwright, diarist, autobiographer, biographer, essayist, and translator.

The following entry provides an overview of Green's career through 1993. For further information on his life and works, see *CLC*, Volumes 3 and 11.

INTRODUCTION

Green is considered one of the most prolific and highly esteemed French-language authors of the twentieth century. While much of his fiction is noted for its psychological symbolism and pessimistic world view, his autobiographies and journals explore such matters as spirituality and sexuality. Praised for his graceful and sensuous use of the French language, Green was the first American citizen to be elected to the prestigious Académie Française.

Green was born in Paris, France, the youngest of seven children. His parents, originally from the southern United States, relocated to France for business purposes, and Green learned to speak English at home while he was formally educated in French schools. Influenced by his mother, a strict Episcopalian, Green became interested in religion during his youth; in 1916 he converted from Protestantism to Roman Catholicism. Green travelled to the United States in 1919 to attend the University of Virginia, where he developed an interest in the American South and an awareness of his homosexuality. Green returned to France in 1922 without completing his degree, and two years later he published his first work, "Pamphlet contre les catholiques de France," which criticized the Roman Catholic establishment for its pervasive apathy and insincerity. During the 1930s Green began questioning his faith and left the Catholic church, a decision, critics contend, that accounts for the pessimism and alienation found in his early novels. Green returned to Catholicism in 1939 and was often viewed strictly as a Catholic writer due to the more structured moral context of his works published at this time. During the 1950s Green's works acquired an increasingly autobiographical tone and often directly addressed his homosexuality, establishing him as a confessional and a mystical writer. With the exception of his college education at the University of Virginia, Green has resided in France throughout his life while retaining his American citizenship.

Green's early fiction often incorporates psychological symbolism. These works are largely pessimistic, often depicting characters who suffer from isolation, despair, and

insanity and who represent, critics argue, Green's emotions and conflicts. The winner of the Harper Prize for literature in 1929-30, *Léviathan* (*The Dark Journey*) portrays a man whose jealousy leads him to assault and permanently disfigure a woman who betrayed him and then to murder another man whom he fears will reveal his crime. *Adrienne Mesurat* (*The Closed Garden*) concerns a sheltered and friendless young woman who, overwhelmed by her obsession for a man whom she only knows from a distance, ultimately kills her domineering father and descends into insanity when her love is rejected. Dreams, hallucinations, and fantasies are also prominent motifs in Green's early novels. For instance, *Le visionnaire* (*The Dreamer*) focuses on an unattractive and lonely youth who seeks refuge in a vivid romantic fantasy, while *Si j'étais vous* (*If I Were You*) describes the adventures of a young man who escapes the confines of his own identity by willfully assuming others' personalities.

In his journals Green attempts to reconcile the spiritual and sensual aspects of his personality, focusing particularly on the moral dilemmas posed by carnal desire. His later works, including the autobiographical series *Partir avant le jour* (*To Leave Before Dawn*), *Mille chemins ouverts*,

Terre lointaine, Jeunesse, and *Fin de jeunesse,* also juxtapose eroticism and spirituality. *To Leave before Dawn,* for instance, presents a detailed account of traumatic events of Green's early childhood, his sexual experiences during adolescence, and his concern with the concept of sin. In *Jeunesse* Green explores the disparity between his worship of physical beauty and the feelings of revulsion he associated with casual sexual encounters experienced during his youth. Green examines similar themes in such fictional works as *Le mauvais lieu* and the critically acclaimed *Le malfaiteur (The Transgressor),* which emphasize the emotional devastation associated with romantic love, the nature of evil, and the conflict between physicality and transcendent experience.

Critics frequently emphasize Green's French and American heritage as a formative influence on his career. While Green is regarded as a renowned stylist in the French language, much of his writing reveals a distinctly southern American sensibility: Green's *Sud (South), Les pays lointains (The Distant Lands),* and *Les étoiles du sud* focus on life in the American South and are often associated with his experiences at the University of Virginia and the influence of his mother, who was a lifelong supporter of the Confederate States of America. In *The Distant Lands,* for example, Green presents a picturesque version of nineteenth-century Southern life that many reviewers deemed reminiscent of Margaret Mitchell's *Gone with the Wind* (1936). The novel focuses on an English girl who becomes acquainted with the lifestyle of the Southern aristocracy when she comes to live with wealthy relatives in Georgia. While immensely popular in Europe, the work has received mixed comments in the United States, where it has been praised for its vivid atmosphere and eerie sense of mystery, but criticized for its superficial treatment of the antebellum South. Jeffery Paine asserted: "In *The Distant Lands* Julian Green returns to that time before all the honors and laurels, before his 60 published books, before his friendship with Cocteau and Gide, to write a novel that embodies the half-remembered, half-indescribable terrors and charms that encapsulated his boyhood. The mesmerizing peculiarity of the novel derives, however, from the fact that Mr. Green is fashioning a world he both did and did not know."

The winner of numerous awards, including the Grand Prix National des Lettres and the Grand Prix Arts, Sciences et Lettres de Paris, Green has garnered critical acclaim in both Europe and the United States with numerous scholars citing the universal appeal of his works. Glenn S. Burne asserts: "Green is the total artist. Insofar as it is possible to say this, he *lives,* he *is* his work. . . . We may not always like what we find [in his works]; we may not accept all his problems as ours or agree with all his values; but of one thing we are certain: Green's novels are admirable blendings of art and life and, once experienced, are unforgettable. They are powerful documentations of the sense of alienation and loss that haunts modern man and of the devastating consequences when man can no longer harmonize his physical life with the invisible spiritual world that lies beyond."

PRINCIPAL WORKS

"Pamphlet contre les catholiques de France" [as Théophile Delaporte] (nonfiction) 1924; published in journal *La revue des pamphlétaires*

Mont-Cinère (novel) 1926; also published as *Mont-Cinère* [enlarged edition], 1928
  [*Avarice House,* 1927; also published as *Monte-Cinère,* 1937]

Adrienne Mesurat (novel) 1927; also published as *Adrienne Mesurat* [revised edition], 1991
  [*The Closed Garden,* 1928]

Suite anglaise (essays) 1927

Un puritain homme de lettres: Nathaniel Hawthorne (nonfiction) 1928

Léviathan (novel) 1929
  [*The Dark Journey,* 1929]

L'autre sommeil (novel) 1930; published in journal *La nouvelle revue française*

Le voyageur sur la terre—Les clefs de la mort—Christine—Léviathan (short stories) 1930
  [*Christine, and Other Stories,* 1930]

Epaves (novel) 1932
  [*The Strange River,* 1932]

Le visionnaire (novel) 1934
  [*The Dreamer,* 1934]

Minuit (novel) 1936
  [*Midnight,* 1936]

*Les années faciles, 1928-34 (diaries) 1938; also published as *Les années faciles, 1926-34* [revised edition], 1970

*Derniers beaux jours, 1935-39 (diaries) 1939

Varouna (novel) 1940
  [*Then Shall the Dust Return,* 1941]

Memories of Happy Days (memoir) 1942

*Devant la porte sombre, 1940-43 (diaries) 1946

Si j'étais vous (novel) 1947; also published as *Si j'étais vous* [revised edition], 1970
  [*If I Were You,* 1949]

*L'oeil de l'ouragan, 1943-46 (diaries) 1949

Moïra (novel) 1950
  [*Moira,* 1951]

*Le revenant, 1946-50 (diaries) 1951

Sud (drama) 1953
  [*South,* 1955]

L'ennemi (drama) 1954

Le malfaiteur (novel) 1955
  [*The Transgressor,* 1957]

*Le miroir intérieur, 1950-54 (diaries) 1955

L'ombre (drama) 1956

*Le bel aujourd'hui, 1955-58 (diaries) 1958

Chaque homme dans sa nuit (novel) 1960
  [*Each in His Darkness,* 1961]

**Journal: 1928-1958 (collected diaries) 1961
  [*Diary, 1928-57* (abridged edition), 1964]

†Partir avant le jour (autobiography) 1963
  [*To Leave before Dawn,* 1967]

†Mille chemins ouverts (autobiography) 1964

†Terre lointaine (autobiography) 1966

*Vers l'invisible, 1959-66 (diaries) 1967

**Journal, 1928-66 (collected diaries) 1969

L'autre (novel) 1971

[*The Other One,* 1973]
Ce qui reste de jour, 1966-72 (diaries) 1972
†*Jeunesse* (autobiography) 1974
Liberté cherie (essay) 1974
**La bouteille à la mer, 1972-76* (diaries) 1976
Memories of Evil Days (memoir) 1976
Le mauvais lieu (novel) 1977
**La terre est si belle, 1976-78* (diaries) 1982
**La lumière du monde, 1978-81* (diaries) 1982
Frère François (biography) 1983
   [*God's Fool: The Life and Times of Francis of Assisi,*
   1985]
Paris (essay) 1983
†*Fin de jeunesse* (autobiography) 1984
Histories de vertige (short stories) 1984
L'automate (drama) 1985
Demain n'existe pas (drama) 1985
Le langage et son double/The Language and Its Double
   (essays) 1986
Les pays lointains (novel) 1987
   [*The Distant Lands,* 1991]
**L'arc-en-ciel, 1981-84* (diaries) 1988
Les étoiles du sud (novel) 1989
**L'expatrie, 1984-90* (diaries) 1990
Journal du voyageur (travel journal) 1990

*These fourteen volumes of Green's diaries are collectively known
  as his *Journal.*

**These works respectively contain the seventh and eighth volumes
  of Green's *Journal.*

†These works are collectively known as *Jeune années.*

CRITICISM

Dayton Kohler   (essay date April 1932)

[*In the following essay, Kohler views Green as a unique
voice in contemporary literature and discusses Gothic
and fatalistic elements in Green's works.*]

Terror and despair brood over the pages of Julian Green
like shadows of approaching doom. Life holds no escape
for his characters, and the sharp shock of tragedy, when
it falls, is never blunted by irony or pity. His books reflect
the mood of their creator, cold, impersonal, aloof. His art
burns only with a darkly luminous flame; there is little
heat behind the somber brilliance of his prose. Men and
women are driven to crimes of violence and insanity, but
fate remains as remote and serenely implacable as the
stars.

No one can read *The Closed Garden* or *The Dark Journey*
without recognizing in their author an individual talent
and a vast power of concentration. In an age of experiment, when his contemporaries are seeking new material
for fiction and new forms of expression, he adheres closely
to the classic tradition of the novel. He is not a modern

writer in the sense that James Joyce and Ernest Hemingway, for example, are modern. *Ulysses,* that lode-star of
younger novelists, has failed to influence a single page of
his work. Contrary to the prevailing fashion of young
writers, his books are not records of adolescent autobiography or futile gestures toward the moon, but full-bodied
novels which deal with authentic and universal human experiences. Style, or the purely decorative side of art, does
not interest him, although the compactness and proportion of Flaubert were never more exquisite in restraint and
fine economy of detail than the method which Green has
made indubitably his own. He belongs to no contemporary
school of writing, he is neither a realist nor a romanticist
in the accepted meaning of those terms, and he is content
to tell a simple story with compelling force. "All I aim at
is correctness; the subject must stand by itself." That is his
most direct comment on his own purpose and achievement. Clearly, the case of Julian Green presents many
points of departure from the standards of his literary generation here and abroad.

Much has been made of the fact that he should choose
French as a medium for literary expression, but the reasons for his choice are not so strange as they appear on the
surface. His nationality can be regarded only as an inci-
dental factor in the process of his development toward creative writing. Born in Paris of American parents, but
French in temperament by education and association, he
is no literary expatriate in flight from the American scene
and an industrial civilization. The explanation which
would account for the voluntary exile of T. S. Eliot or
Ezra Pound must, in the case of Julian Green, be ruled
out. Those few years at the University of Virginia served
only to define his perspective of two different racial backgrounds and cultures. It is no more remarkable that he
should write in French than it would be for any European,
born in the United States and educated in our schools, to
write in English. It would be a fallacy of criticism to regard him as an American novelist. Parisian critics are justified when they claim him as one of the most distinguished talents among younger French writers.

To understand the unique position Julian Green holds in
the literature of our time, it is necessary to recognize his
literary kinship with older novelists, for he has succeeded
to the heritage of Emily Brontë, Hawthorne, and Flaubert.
It is significant, perhaps, that among his critical papers not
yet available in translation there should be sympathetic
studies of the Brontë sisters on Haworth moors and the
dark genius of Nathaniel Hawthorne, for these were the
great writers who worked in solitude, finding within their
limited social experience a depth and richness rather than
a variety of life.

His imagination, like that of his predecessors, seeks out
the unexplored, fantastic regions of the human soul, creating against a background of physical reality an atmosphere haunting and inscrutable with the harsh passion of
life. With the art-magic of a Poe, a Dostoievsky, a Baudelaire, he achieves a macabre intensity of narration which
aims at a shuddering portrayal of demoniacal, elemental
forces in the lives of his characters. His subjects are like

those of a Balzac or a Dostoievsky: the eternal conflict of the human spirit with an ultimate destiny.

In the world of Julian Green men and women are fore-doomed to certain failure. Their tragedies are the tragedies of frustrated lives, their struggles are against internal and external forces which they dimly perceive but never wholly understand. In the end they lose the world and their own souls as well, for the tragic essence of his work is the disintegration of the human soul into chaos. Thus, the final tragedy is an inner defeat of spiritual undoing. Life becomes a stark and despairing revelation of fear, weakness, bitterness, cruelty, and consuming love that is its own agent of destruction.

These minor themes of tragedy, however, eventually revolve themselves about the more impressive spectacle of man's insignificance against his doom. But fatality, as we see it here reflected, is altogether impersonal; humanity is not a race of irresponsible toys in the hands of sardonic, sportive gods. There is not the same "catharsis by pity and terror" of which Aristotle wrote, and we miss the divine irony of Sophocles and Thomas Hardy. Julian Green portrays life upon a different level of tragic elevation. His point of view sees men and women broken by powerful, incomprehensible forces within and without themselves, forced by heredity or environment into set ways of conduct which serve partly as chemical reaction upon their own personalities. They fail not through turn and play of circumstance but because they lack strength to struggle and endure in their attempts to rise above that circumstance.

For this reason, the writer's sense of tragedy is less Greek than Gothic. Ethical and philosophical concepts of life have been dismissed from his consideration; the dramatic values alone provide those timeless and universal qualities of his art. And the spirit of his work is Gothic in a rare and curious manner. He builds no Castle of Otranto or gloomy House of Usher in which to stage his effects of tragic terror; he creates no Lygeias or Frankensteins to portray the weird and abnormal in human character. That driving intensity of violence and despair he finds in the commonplace ranks of life. Or perhaps because he portrays the outward aspect of human existence as a uniform flat surface, the hidden life holds so much drama and significance. His backgrounds are the college towns and lonely farm districts of rural Virginia and the small villages of French provincial life, where time passes with a monotonous succession of days, nights, and years. His characters are men and women who seem at first view as ordinary and quiet as their surroundings. They remain commonplace and dull until the writer breaks through the surface of their daily lives to show the seething life within.

His books are revelations of an inward drama which is strange and appalling, yet powerful and beautiful because of its affirmation of the passionate demands of living. His characters are caught in the dungeons of their inner lives as inexorably as Fortunato was trapped in the terrible crypt of the Montresors. If the living force within these uncomprehending and unrational beings is to find expression, they must assert their humanity by violence and agony of the spirit. But the escape is often as disruptive

and baffling as the slow doom of confinement. Minds dwarfed and twisted by long habits of restraint breed unearthly ghost shapes from which they cannot free themselves, and the greater tragedy results. All of Green's books end upon this note of final catastrophe. Daniel O'Donovan commits suicide. Emily Fletcher dies in the conflagration she has kindled. Adrienne Mesurat goes insane. The characters of *The Dark Journey* are moved to brutal assault and betrayal. Such conclusions show the writer's constant brooding over the enigma of the eternal skull.

Melodrama, the motivating action of the old Gothic romance, is inseparable from his method. Since his art is directed toward a complete intensification of human experience, action which will convey the full implication of intensity must be pushed beyond the limits of common social experience. While the spirit of his narrative may be exaggerated or strained beyond the conventional limits of art, Julian Green preserves the convincing illusion of reality through his heightening of the laws of circumstance against a commonplace background. Theme and setting are thus held in adequate balance and the intense cries of his situations are subdued to the tone of realistic simplicity. Even the Gothic element of horror has been transmuted into the explainable strangeness of human emotions. It is the method and spirit of the modern Gothic, a fantastic realism achieved through the physiological melodrama of terror, violence and despair in the consciousness of ordinary people.

The use of recurring motives of melodrama in all of his novels shows the peculiar pattern to which the world has shaped itself in his imagination. For Julian Green does not describe; he creates. He has asserted that he must write of persons and events as far removed as possible from the boundaries of his own personal experience. Only in the mood of complete detachment can he construct characters and situations and combine these elements in an inevitable conclusion. Here again we see the working of the Gothic temperament, shown also in the strange and terrible beauty of a Poe or a Doré.

It seems to me that everything Julian Green has written fulfills the promise of a short story, his one venture into English prose, published in the student literary magazine while he was enrolled at the University of Virginia, in 1920. At that institution Green is remembered as a quiet, bilingual youth who worked a great deal and read widely and with even greater diligence than he worked. Certainly he was not identified with that flamboyant and self-conscious group of juvenile literati from which Lawrence Lee and Charles Wertenbaker have since emerged. His story was called, curiously enough, **"The Apprentice Psychiatrist"**, and the omnipresent themes of madness and murder indicate plainly the subjects which in the days of his early attempts at writing appealed most to his creative fancy.

Casimir Jovite is the apprentice psychiatrist of the story. He has a true scholar's interest in neurology, which he regards as the merging of psychology and natural science. When his father refuses to send additional funds for his course of study at the Ecole de Médecine, he is forced to find employment as a tutor to Pierre-Marie de Fronsac. Both tutor and pupil are characters that have appeared under different guises and in different situations in his later novels. The serious-minded and studious Jovite, with his "somewhat melancholy nature and very fine, eager, inquisitive eyes that looked at everything with a sort of impassioned interest", becomes, transformed, the harassed tutor of *The Dark Journey* and the sinister Jalon in the long story, **"The Keys of Death"**. And Pierre-Marie, with his dreamy, tragic vision that to the tutor's imagination "seemed to look clean through him, beyond him, beyond the world of matter, down into abysses of thought and phantasy", is the masculine prototype of those uncanny, perceptive girls who appear in other novels and short stories. It is this psychic quality in the nature of his pupil that fascinates and puzzles Jovite until he realizes that the boy is slowly going mad.

Here at his hand is a laboratory case by which he may test the knowledge acquired through years of study. Curiosity grows more powerful than any regard for the boy in his care while he fills page after page with notes and observations that chart the slow progress of disease. Jovite's enthusiasm for research combines something of the fanatic and the zeal of the scientist. Realizing that events are rapidly approaching a crisis, and Pierre-Marie is on the verge of complete insanity, he resorts to subtle methods of torture in order to bring the case to a close. The ending comes with an irony of tragic surprise. After the tutor has gone to his pupil's room, the household is startled by the explosion of a pistol, followed by a burst of hysterical laughter . . . "When the policemen entered the room, half an hour later, they found, lying on his stomach, Pierre-Marie de Fronsac, shot through the temple, and, playing in the corner with a pistol, a raving maniac."

> **[Green's] books are revelations of an inward drama which is strange and appalling, yet powerful and beautiful because of its affirmation of the passionate demands of living.**
>
> **—Dayton Kohler**

This story, told with all the cumulative passion and tragic finality of Julian Green's method, has never been included in any of his bibliographies. Yet it would appear that **"The Apprentice Psychiatrist"** contains in adequate measure within its limited space those distinctive elements which he was later to develop upon a wider canvas with greater intensity of characterization and theme. Green himself dates his literary career from his return to France in 1922, where, after six months at an academy of art, he began to write, producing first a critical article on William Blake. This was followed in 1924 by his short novel, *The Pilgrim on the Earth.*

Antedating *Avarice House* by almost a year in time of composition, *The Pilgrim on the Earth* contains certain crudities of structure and a lack of artistic control which are not apparent in later novels. The story is told by means of a young boy's diary and a series of letters written after his death by those interested in the facts of his strange suicide. These letters, while they explain much that the hero of the story cannot understand or relate, divert the attention of the reader from the psychological study revealed in the diary itself. Daniel O'Donovan is the victim of a strange psychic disease, partly the result of heredity and partly of environment. What psychoanalysis would term a persecution complex becomes an obsession in his adolescent mind. He believes that he is entirely under the control and evil influence of an uncle with whom he lives; consequently he spends most of his time in loneliness and gloomy introspection. Entrance to an American university offers a means of escape from his imaginary tyranny. Disaster overtakes him in this new freedom, for the dual parts of his personality now separate and he entrusts himself to the guidance of this unreal being whom he knows only as Paul. The spiritual crisis which arises from this conflict of a double personality marks the turning point of the story . . . "Now the world would come to an end and life depart from me. All visible things existed only for my temptation and by an impulse of the soul which broke my last resistance, I renounced in an instant the possession of all these things, all affection for the world, all hope of earthly happiness." The finding of Daniel's body points to a suicide as inscrutable as his life.

Avarice House, published in this country in 1927, contains less of the mystic and supernatural. It is a grim study of overmastering passions and a conflict of wills, in which one is reminded at times of Emily Brontë and that dark, brawling household at Wuthering Heights. Emily Fletcher, the chief character about whom the movement of the story centers, lives on a small Virginia estate with her mother and grandmother. Old Mrs. Elliott and her granddaughter dislike one another, but they are united in a common sense against the miserliness of Mrs. Fletcher. We see these three women, hating and fearing one another, reacting to the daily incidents of their intimate life with sadistic intensity. When Emily views her mother satisfying a grasping nature by selling those things which the daughter should someday inherit, she is driven to revolt against her mother's avarice. She had hoped for a protector against the older woman when she married a young man from a neighboring farm, but she discovers too late his brutality and greed. In desperation, she hits upon the idea of destruction as the only means of thwarting all schemes for possession, and, setting fire to the house, she sacrifices herself in the flames. Few novels of our time have portrayed with such somber reality the annihilating power of human desires.

The Closed Garden presents a similar morbidity of subject matter and theme. In this novel the writer turns from the American backgrounds of his earlier works to the setting of a dull provincial town near Paris. As in *Avarice House,* there is a constant clashing of motives and wills among members of a single household. Adrienne Mesurat is a young girl who has never known associations beyond those with a tyrannical father and a consumptive older sister, Germaine. Unable to know her father or sister, she withdraws more and more to herself until a casual encounter with the town physician becomes an adventure to arouse her temporarily from moods of introspection and despair. Believing herself in love with the doctor, she walks out in the evenings to watch the house in which he lives, but after the secret is discovered she is forced once more into the old monotonous round of service to the semi-invalid sister and obedience to her father. When Germaine finally runs away, Adrienne is left to bear the force of her father's cruelty and anger. There is a scene in which M. Mesurat strikes his daughter while they stand quarreling at the top of a flight of stairs. On a sudden impulse she hurls herself against him, and he is killed by his fall. In spite of the fact that the accidental appearance of his death deceives the authorities, Adrienne is unable to free herself from the established order of her existence, in which every venture of escape becomes a futile, despairing gesture. She is terrorized by a solitude which has grown almost unbearable. Eventually she confesses her secret to the doctor, who is unable to aid her. Nothing remains but a black shadow of madness growing longer and longer across her narrow world.

The Dark Journey, the Harper prize novel of 1929, indicates a broadening scope of Julian Green's powers as a novelist. His theme, however, is still that of inevitable tragedy. Against a background of French provincial life he presents a small group of characters whom he portrays with the depth and sureness of an insight that is conscious art. Paul Guéret, the central figure of the novel, is a tutor curiously reminiscent of Casimir Jovite. He is a man grown prematurely into middle age, embittered by memories of his youth, unhappy in the futility of his marriage and career. Three women have a part in his life: Angèle, the young girl who awakens in him the force of pent-up emotions and a vague dissatisfaction with the bleakness of his existence; Mme. Londe, proprietress of a café, whose days are given over to constant spying on the affairs of others and the acquisition of knowledge by which she can hold the community in moral bondage, and Mme. Grosgeorge, mother of Guéret's pupil, in whom the starved passions of her girlhood have turned to a tortured kind of love that finds its outlet in treachery.

Guéret, driven to desperation by the knowledge that Angèle, at Mme. Londe's direction, has shared her favors among other clients of the restaurant, first breaks into the girl's empty bedroom and later, in a fit of brutal fury, assaults her, disfiguring her for life. In his flight he murders an old man whom he fears because of a suspected knowledge of his crime. Finally he is betrayed by Mme. Grosgeorge, who shoots herself at the realization of her action. Mme. Londe is left in her corroding pride to view the ruins of her life when she can no longer, through Angèle, pander to her customers and know the secrets of the community. Humanity reduced to its elemental passion has broken through the surface of these repressed lives and its manifestations of assault, murder and treachery have been raised to the serene levels of tragedy because they affirm the fundamental principle that the vitality of the human spirit cannot be restrained or ignored. Julian Green gives a universal significance to his work through an objective

fatalism and his keen interpretation of human values when all barriers of restraint have been broken down.

The short stories in *Christine* reflect in miniature the spirit and purpose of his novels. The title story is a brief episode of eccentric characterization which contains a suggestion of unexplained lunacy. In **"Leviathan,"** its scenes laid on shipboard, the writer presents the monotony of life at sea. Here, as in all of Green's works, there is the hint of a mysterious crime and an equally mysterious death. **"The Keys of Death"** suggests the earlier story of Daniel O'Donovan in that two related manuscripts are employed to tell the story of a boy's obsession for murder and a girl's supernatural, clairvoyant powers. Jalon, who exercises a strange and disturbing influence over the household in which he lives, is a figure of diabolical characterization.

The stories of Julian Green are built always upon a single theme: the terror and frustration of solitude. Within the limits of his art he is an acknowledged master, but in these limitations we find his greatest weakness and his greatest strength. His is a tragic world that has been stripped of all but the bare essentials in order to show the full intensity of those forces toward which his art is directed. We miss the diversity of interests which the older novelists could command when we consider how narrow and limited is the imaginative experience he offers us. We miss also the relieving grace of humor to provide dramatic contrast for the materials of tragedy. There is not even the mordant humor of an ironic conception of the universe, only a grim terror and futility tempered by madness. In the portrayal of meager and monotonous lives that mask the tortuous emotional forces within lies the full depth and power of his art. Although he pays scant attention to the sensuous imagery of his situations, he is a master of dominant impression. How sharply etched in its vivid concentration of detail the flight of Adrienne Mesurat to a neighboring town: the unforgettable dreariness of the rain, the haunted solitude of the dingy hotel, the young workman she encounters in the street! Equally beautiful in its stark impressionism is Guéret's flight after his attack on Angèle, when the mood of his consuming passion reaches its climax in the murder of an innocent old man.

At the age of thirty-one, with his most important books unwritten, Julian Green has won an international reputation that few writers ever gain until the close of their careers. He is one of the most significant talents in the whole field of contemporary literature, and for those who can follow him across the borderline of tragedy his books hold the dark, unearthly beauty of man's madness and despair. (pp. 139-48)

> *Dayton Kohler, "Julian Green: Modern Gothic," in* The Sewanee Review, *Vol. XL, No. 2, April, 1932, pp. 139-48.*

Milton H. Stansbury   (essay date 1935)

[*In the following essay from his* French Novelists of Today, *Stansbury considers the macabre and pessimistic aspects of Green's novels through* Le visionnaire.]

America follows with special interest the career of her

brilliant expatriate, Julien Green. Not that there remains overmuch of the American in a man who was born in France and who, except for three years of study at the University of Virginia, has always lived abroad. However, neither his choice of a foreign home nor the adoption of French as his literary medium can alter the fact that he is an American. With admiration mingled with pride we have marveled at his precocity and rejoiced in his rapid rise to fame. This came when he was a young man in his twenties, for with *Adrienne Mesurat,* his second novel, he was pronounced a master. The recipient of various literary awards, included in every list of the best contemporary French novelists, he was more generously praised in France than many a talented French writer. If, ironically enough, he was known to most of his countrymen only through translation, at least they hastened to read him. Nor was his American vogue solely dependent on his availability in English, for even the average Anglo-Saxon linguist could read this simple, unassuming French with comparative ease. The fact that it does present so little difficulty suggests that Green's is not a distinctively Gallic medium, even if the Americanisms in his early works were not additional evidence. Indeed, it would be interesting to know whether some of his early work was not written first in English. At present, with five novels to his credit, he has acquired a much more fluent style, although even now, Green prudently limits his aspiration to what he calls "invisible prose," where thought, not phrase, is given precedence.

He was particularly suited to the American mind from another point of view. Retaining, as it were, one last vestige of his Anglo-Saxon descent, he is one of the most reticent of authors when his subject is sex. Where writers such as Henri de Régnier would have alienated American readers by their lewdness, Julien Green covertly implies but never frankly confronts the physical aspect of love, and so escapes unscathed. He is more communicative on other and no less unlovely themes, but since he stresses the passions and never passion, the most puritanical can plunge with confident relish into this world of thwarted lives, blind injustice, and ferocious hate.

For Green has a somber imagination, and believes that happy people have no story, that the ugly offers greater interest than the beautiful. At first this attitude might have been attributed to his youth, for many a young author, fresh from Baudelaire and the Realists, adopts a morbid point of view. But since Green is now thirty-four and still sees black, it must be assumed that his point of view is adult and natural to him. If it were only a question of settings, his are neutral enough. Unfortunately, he must people these backgrounds, and he too frequently peoples them with monsters. Placing his characters in the most commonplace surroundings, he excels in endowing them with an abnormality of feeling and a violence of passion all the more dramatic because of their everyday background.

From the first, abnormal psychology had a fascination for him, and his youthful stories, **"Le Voyageur sur la terre,"** **"Les Clefs de la mort,"** **"Christine"** and others, depicted morbid, sensitive young people afflicted with hallucinations and leading isolated, misdirected lives. This interest in the so-called "idiot fringe" was soon to manifest itself on a larger scale in his novels. In the earliest of these, *Mont-Cinère* (1926), named after the estate in Virginia where his characters live, Green introduces us to his first really full-fledged monsters. A widow, whose economical habits have grown with inexorable intensity into an all-absorbing mania, Mrs. Kate Fletcher subjects her daughter, a neurotic girl of fifteen, to such cruel and pointless privations—for in possessing Mont-Cinère this family is far from poor—that the child becomes deranged. Mrs. Fletcher renders equally miserable the old age of her mother, who is ill and forced to share her roof. With such a deplorable family life as a background, this dismal tale recounts the daughter's unnatural proposal of marriage to their ex-gardener, a young widower with a child, by means of whom she plans to usurp her mother's place; and her incendiary burning of Mont-Cinère upon discovering that the gardener husband means to assert his mastery.

Since the infinitely more mature *Adrienne Mesurat* was to appear just one year later, the crudity of this earlier novel is all the more outstanding. Far from developing convincing characters in *Mont-Cinère,* Green has done little more than supply *leitmotifs* which, in spite of their insistent repetition, are not sufficient to create the impression of reality or even of remote plausibility. It is not enough to remind the reader at every page that Mrs. Fletcher is a sort of female Harpagon and that the daughter has an equal lust for possession. By concentrating on a single facet of their personality to the point of ignoring all other traits, he has created unbalanced characters for whom there is neither law nor reason.

As a foreshadowing of his future work, however, this early story presents several points of interest, for the author is already experimenting with certain themes which in his later novels he develops with greater subtlety and skill. At first it may be surprising to discover that husband and wife, mother and daughter, in not only one but several generations, should so completely detest one another. With each succeeding book, we learn to expect this family-hate *motif,* which eventually becomes inseparably linked with the name of Julien Green. In the three hundred pages of *Mont-Cinère,* there is not a civil word exchanged. On the rare occasions when these people do converse, their speech is abrupt and churlish, suggestive of a lower stratum of society than that with which this book is dealing and which, for lack of a better name, must be called the "gentry." The adverbs selected to qualify their conversation are reduced to "briefly," "dryly," "curtly," superfluous reminders in view of the words they utter. It is possible to believe in the acidity prevailing between members of Green's family groups, but where the outside world is involved such bad manners and disregard for social amenities become increasingly shocking and improbable.

With *Adrienne Mesurat,* Green revealed the full measure of his talent. Turning to France, and the small provincial town where the Mesurat family lives, Green is perfectly at home. Although the heroine herself is not a monster, she is surrounded by them. Persecuted by a tyrannical father and a dour, malignant older sister, the embittered Adrienne has lived until her eighteenth year in a coma of unrelieved and apathetic boredom. Into the dreary vacuum of this existence comes the chance encounter with the new doctor who lives across the street. This first momentary glimpse—for no words have been exchanged—is sufficient to inspire the lonely girl with an irrational and tenacious passion. From this point on, everything and everyone conspire against her—but chiefly Julien Green. It required no little ingenuity to make things go so incredibly wrong. In a fit of hysteria she pushes her father down a flight of stairs, and causes his instant death; she is blackmailed by an adventuress, a neighbor who has divined her guilt; and her love is rejected by the doctor. Her last hope shattered, there snaps what little remains of her already tottering reason. If the author's success is to be gauged by the measure of suffering he has created, this book is a grim fulfilment of his fondest hopes. We may question why he wished to place his heroine on this rack of pain, but his genius as a torturer is beyond dispute.

To offer still further proof, he wrote *Léviathan* (1929), a novel of greater variety and range, though inferior to *Adrienne Mesurat* as a work of art. This reference in the title to the biblical monster Leviathan does not belie the nature of the story. Some avenging spirit pursues the hero Guéret, who, as a result of his unrequited passion for a village girl, leaves murder, rape, suicide, and insanity in his trail. A curse was also placed on the pathetic little Angèle, the laundress whom he mutilates, though why, as a public prostitute, she steadfastly refused his love, is never satisfactorily explained. No less unfortunate is the frustrated and vindictive Mme Grosgeorge, the familiar Green monster, who "having detested her child from the moment she felt it struggling within her entrails, darkened its earliest years with uncalled-for punishments," a woman so inhuman, the author informs us, that "her nature produced nothing in which poison was not in some way mingled, warping her simplest feelings and corrupting every affection at its source." Of the plot, always Green's special bugbear, suffice it to say that in spite of its skilful presentation, the level hardly rises above that of a harrowing melodrama.

Conscious of only malice and cruelty, [Green] places a cancerous soul in every character he paints.

—*Milton H. Stansbury*

After the publication of *Léviathan,* Green announced that with these first three novels he had completed his observation of a certain phase of life and would henceforth write in a different vein. However, in his next novel, *Epaves* (1932), which is the least effective of all his books, aside from the shifting of the scene from the provinces to Paris, and the application of less violent colors, there is little indication of a change of heart. The inevitable obsession is still present—cowardice this time—and the familiar family dissension. The story itself is very simple: a young mar-

ried couple have never loved each other since their wedding night; the woman who really loves this faint-hearted and fatuous man is his wife's older unmarried sister, who shares their apartment, and who, though only thirty-one, is described as "a shriveled old maid with wrinkles"; the wife meanwhile is meeting secretly another man whose sole and rather incredible attraction is his squalor. Where *Adrienne Mesurat* and *Léviathan* stimulated interest through the steady progression of horror built up around a central theme, in *Epaves,* where little happens and where there is no crescendo to a tragic culmination, all that remains are three eccentric and rather silly people arbitrarily housed within a single apartment. The most significant comment is that except for certain naïve and improbable episodes, the story quickly fades from memory.

In Julien Green's latest novel, *Le Visionnaire* (1934), a much more successful work, he reverts once more to his favorite setting of the province, and chooses for his hero a forlorn young man who finds himself thwarted and unhappy. Ugly, timid, servile, and dying of tuberculosis, he seeks relief from reality by immersing himself in a world of dreams. But his sufferings have so permeated his subconscious being that the visions he evokes are no less horrible than the life he is striving to forget. The realities of his existence are the shrewish aunt with whom he lives; his bestial and miserly employer; and his cousin whom he loves, but who, being only a schoolgirl in short dresses, is unresponsive to his passion. For his imaginary world he chooses a nearby château which he has never entered but which has always haunted his dreams. Supposing himself to be employed there as a servant, he pictures its weird inhabitants as a cruel and haughty young viscountess; her aged father dying of cancer; her half-demented brother, likewise tormented by the fear of death; and Death itself, vaguely incarnated in a ghoulish housekeeper. The feverish dreamer writes these visions in his journal, until its abrupt termination at the point where the viscountess, unexpectedly entering the young man's bedroom, suddenly locks the door behind her, and blows out the light—the moment in every amorous scene where Green always drops the curtain. The narrative is resumed at a later period by the young girl whom he loves and who relates her cousin's sudden collapse and death during a walk with her in the neighborhood of the real château. The people who actually figure in this unfortunate young man's life are quite as fantastic as the fictitious creations of his dreams. The aunt, who, though cruel to everyone else, makes a fetish of all sick people and would have loved her dead husband more had he been unhealthy, who despises her daughter because she enjoys good health, is as improbable as the imaginary viscountess with her brusque and unaccountable fits of silent laughter, her aimless barefoot wanderings through the night, and her brooding curiosity as she spies upon her dying father's agony. In other words, a nightmare atmosphere is maintained throughout. If, in this agonizing fifth in a series of lugubrious novels, Green has again proved himself a master, the reader's surprise proceeds not so much from the choice of subject matter in any single book, as from the fact that any writer should be content to reign in such an exclusively morbid domain.

The contemplation of so much suffering would be a greater emotional experience were it not apparent that for most of it Julien Green and not life itself is responsible. The failure of these ill-starred destinies to move us more deeply is due to our realization that though fate may be cruel, it is not so immutably perverse. Green has no desire to arouse sympathy for his characters; his ambition is rather to make us say: "How true, how real that is!" but he has a far greater chance of capturing our pity than gaining our credulity. His weakness as a psychologist lies in not having masked his own sinsiter intentions in the cataclysms he lets loose. It is his own ruthless hand which adds the touch of salt to every wound; which shoves these luckless people over their tragic precipice. Like Zola before him, he resembles a scientist injecting a helpless specimen with malignant bacteria in order to study the disease thus artificially induced. The poison once in circulation, Green gives a magnificent demonstration of its deadly course; but the fact remains that all this had to be concocted in a laboratory, and no amount of skilful chemistry can make of it the stuff of life. More applicable to Green is Pierre Lièvre's criticism of André Gide: "The author has only observed his characters' extravagant, anomalous side, without taking into consideration that only by supplying the rest of their personality would this extravagance or this anomaly be rendered human. What we seem to have, therefore, is the portrayal of a disease made independently of the victim."

And yet, so great is Green's talent, that we forget at times the test tubes. The landscape seems so trustworthy, small wonder if we are thrown off our guard. For in the creation of his pictorial background he has adhered with the strictest fidelity to truth. Able to vivify his stories with descriptive minutiæ of almost uncanny accuracy, he has obviously documented himself from actual localities. Indeed, no one since Balzac has so successfully conveyed the immured and stifling atmosphere of the provinces, that colorless existence where it would be revolutionary to pick the geraniums on Friday when one always picked them Saturday; to go for a walk at ten in the morning, when five in the afternoon was the usual hour. How doubt the reality of characters in this almost photographic setting? When we can hear the opening of every shutter around them, the creak of every chair? Nothing but the severest shock will waken our suspicions as to the unsubstantiality of this world. Unfortunately, it is Green himself who administers these shocks.

The greatest tax on the imagination is that any people, even in the most remote provincial town, could lead such isolated, antisocial lives. His characters are represented as without friends or social contacts, and although at times they bemoan their solitude, they apparently cannot alter this state of affairs. Their restricted life simplifies the author's task considerably, and in Adrienne's case—arbitrarily cut off as she is from all the friendships usually allotted to a young and beautiful girl—permits the apparition of a total stranger to produce such a catastrophic effect. Green allows her to meet only one man, and automatically he becomes the one she never should have met. Naturally, people so removed from their fellow-men will be ignorant of the world and of themselves; naturally, in their seclusion they will become the prey to dangerous obses-

sions and develop abnormal natures. Least of all are they permitted to love or be loved within the four walls of their homes, for Green may be called the destroyer of the legend of family love. Even his characters pause at times to marvel at their misery, and interrupt the narrative with frequent, if rather self-conscious, lamentations such as: "Never before have I felt so sad," or "To suffer more than I have today would be impossible," or like Adrienne, who, passing the night in a strange hotel, scribbles on a piece of paper: "Here at Montfort, the 11th of June, 1908, I have been more unhappy than has ever been the lot of anyone before."

The spirit behind Green's writing is strikingly akin to that of the painter Goya, who, having a marked preference for horrible scenes, used to decorate his walls with the more gruesome of his pictures: men buried alive, and monsters gorged with human flesh. Green too is attracted by the sight of human misery, and writes: "People always feel more at home in places where they have greatly suffered." Conscious of only malice and cruelty, he places a cancerous soul in every character he paints. When he presents a restaurant proprietress seated peacefully among her clients, he distorts her otherwise placid features by tracing in her eyes a gleam of demoniac curiosity. When it is a woman watching over her sick nephew's bed, he stresses the atrocious satisfaction she experiences at the young man's plight. Who but Goya could so dramatically evoke a murderer in a coalyard and flood the scene with moonlight? And just as in the case of the Spanish painter, the works of Green, with the possible exception of *Epaves,* are stamped forever on the mind.

If with *Adrienne Mesurat* Green had been content with one success in macabre vein, if he had not decided to assume permanently the rôle of bugaboo, perhaps the world would never have suspected that he was himself the bugabooed and that his own social adjustment was at fault. Undoubtedly one of the most sincere of men, he is at the same time the most diffident, and this clash of honesty and timidity may account for much of the implausibility of his writings. Shrinking from every social contact, trembling with terror when confronted by his fellow-man, he reduces to the barest minimum his first-hand knowledge of the world, an initial handicap for which no amount of talent and imagination—and Green has both—can entirely compensate. However, it would be unjust to accuse him of wilfully distorting fact. Just as dreamers never doubt the reality of their nightmares, Green in his panicky flight from his fellow-creatures would be the last to suspect that he was falsifying them in his books. Whether or not his creations are true to life, they are true to what he thinks of life. Since it is evident that he accomplishes, and beautifully, what he sets out to do, we are at a loss whether to censure him for his curtailed vision, or to praise him for his skill as a maleficent conjurer. (pp. 147-56)

Milton H. Stansbury, "Julien Green," in his French Novelists of Today, *University of Pennsylvania Press, 1935, pp. 147-56.*

Helmut Hatzfeld (essay date 1957)

[*A German-born American author and educator, Hatzfeld wrote extensively on the literature of many countries and was a noted scholar of stylistics. In the following excerpt from his* Trends & Styles in Twentieth Century French Literature, *Hatzfeld considers Green's treatment of madness, dreams, and reality in his fiction.*]

Green knows so well the psychology of the lust-stricken and libidinous that he pictures the power of sensual temptation as a fiendish urge. In *Le Visionnaire* (1934), Manuel, the ugly, sick young man, yearns to be loved in spite of his ugliness. But he rejects the idolatrous, seemingly maternal love of his fifty-year-old aunt. When in his plight he tries to embrace his fifteen-year-old cousin Marie-Thérèse and her girl companions, he only arouses scandal in the house and the town. So he invents a hallucinatory romance, imagining that the viscountess of the neighboring castle loves him, and after the death of her father comes in the night to his room to love him so tremendously that she dies in his embrace. This dream event was the last jotted down in his diary by Manuel who then dies himself from this traumatic shock. Marie-Thérèse, who found the diary after his death, has no difficulty in surmising the connection of the events. The imaginary viscountess was supposed by Manuel to have often had hallucinations of death, such as visions of horsemen with embroidered white cotton uniforms, speaking a strange language, riding through vast prairies; or a carriage with dangerous horses running down a hill and endangering her life. Marie-Thérèse with regard to Manuel's notebook asks herself,

> si le visionnaire, après tout, ne jette pas sur cette terre un regard plus aigu que le nôtre, et si, en un monde, qui baigne dans l'invisible, les prestiges du désir et de la mort n'ont pas autant de sens que nos réalités illusoires.

These are exactly the questions of Jung and Adler.

The personal visionary power of Julien Green himself was made known by the publication of his lengthy and explicit *Journal.* Therefore we look with particular interest at his novel *Minuit* (1934). Here we are confronted with people living in Fontfroide, a kind of mental sanitarium, but we are confronted at the same time with symbolized human passions. The only sound person among the mental patients seems to be the girl Elisabeth. After the death of her mother she was confided to her aunts. Antagonized by their eccentricity, Elisabeth gives herself up to the doorman Serge whose brutal sexual instinct seems to her the only acceptable passion since it makes no attempt at a false or biased justification. The other inhabitants of Fontfroide are all under the insane spell of M. Edme who thinks he can only breathe at night, and in order to have company for his whim sells to the other patients as the highest wisdom, the secret of moon-adorers of old, that night is superior to day and a link to the invisible. His credit is enhanced by the propaganda of his mother and of Mlle Eva who has fallen in love with him. Edme's hypocritical rhetoric makes him a prophet in the eyes of M. Agnel, who for his part cannot live without a leader, without an idol. Mme Angeli tries to break the thraldom of M. Edme's nightwatchers. In order not to lose her sleep, she invents a story about having to make the one o'clock train to meet her husband somewhere. This novel of the world of the insane sheds much light on the other novels and also on the tormented soul of Julien Green. A fervent convert in his youth, after a lost vocation and a critical attitude towards Catholicism, he returned seriously as a mature man to his Catholic convictions.

Green's over-all pattern, the fusion of hallucination and crime, also characterizes Miss Fletcher in *Mont Cinère* (1926). Mistreated by her greedy mother, after maddening privations, she marries her mother's gardener to get her freedom. But no less dominated by her proletarian husband, she becomes so unbalanced that she burns down the Virginia house with all the family inside. There is still *Adrienne Mesurat* (1927) running wild after having been rejected by the doctor for whose sake she practically killed her tyrannical father, pushing him down the stairs when nobody else was around. Madness is lurking everywhere; when Green, similar on this point to the painter Vincent van Gogh, "presents a restaurant proprietress seated peacefully among her clients, he distorts her otherwise placid features by tracing in her eyes a gleam of demoniac curiosity. When it is a woman watching over her sick nephew's bed, he stresses the atrocious satisfaction she experiences at the young man's plight," says M. H. Stansbury [in *French Novelists of Today*], hinting at *Léviathan* and *Le Visionnaire.*

Green, who came close to an evident visionarism in certain moments of his life, declared:

> Certaines réalités ne me semblent vraies que si le fantastique les grandit. . . . Ce don de voir ainsi m'est accordé, puis retiré, puis rendu sans que je sache pourquoi. Parfois des années passent sans que l'exercice m'en soit possible; enfin il vient un jour où, l'heure et l'endroit étant propices, je retrouve cette faculté se représenter faiblement par l'esprit. (*L'Autre sommeil,* 1931)

The stylistic principle of Julien Green is not only an uncanny fusion of thought and action, but of the real world and the dream world which normally are unbridgeable in reality. These two worlds, however, coalesce in the sensibility of highly nervous personalities. The esthetic advantage of using this fusion lies in the element of suspense because the action, contrary to the method of Proust, branches out from a sharply delineated view into a haze of hallucinations where the fringes of the actual and the dream-reality can no longer be distinguished. This upsets the logical calculations of the reader; Bernanos does much the same thing. Green, giving to all of his novels the same structure, fails nonetheless to reach a truly interesting presentation. This is so because the moral elements involved in any human action are necessarily minimized when the individual who performs it is neurotic and cannot be made responsible for it. (pp. 88-91)

Helmut Hatzfeld, "Introspection, New Aspects of Love, 'Acte Gratuit',' " in his Trends & Styles in Twentieth Century French Literature, *The Catholic University of America Press, 1957, pp. 66-113.*

Nicholas Kostis on Green's preoccupation with death:

The force which defines reality in Green's world is death. The only certainty, it constitutes the foundation of being and reality. It makes his world a disquieting one of unresolved tensions, conflicts, and contradictions. A precarious metaphysical truce rarely endures. The ultimate source of every antithesis is the life-death antithesis. Instead of *cogito ergo sum* Green implies *morior ergo sum*.

Nicholas Kostis, in his The Exorcism of Sex and Death in Julien Green's Novels, *1973.*

Martin Turnell   (review date 22 October 1964)

[*Turnell was an English literary critic and scholar who wrote several notable studies of French literature, including* The Art of French Fiction *(1959) and* The Rise of the French Novel *(1978); he has also translated works by Jean-Paul Sartre, Blaise Pascal, and Jean-François Revel into English. In the following review of Green's* Diary, 1928-1957, *Turnell discusses Green's treatment of religious and moral themes.*]

Although the diary as a literary form is by no means a French monopoly, it has become something of a French speciality. We are naturally inclined to assume that any French diary will be filled with scandalous revelations and savage comments on the writer's contemporaries, that the rake will regale us with detailed and vain glorious accounts of his sexual conquests. We are not invariably disappointed. Stendhal's diary contains some useful tips on rape; Amiel records the sensations of a middle-aged professor of aesthetics on the belated loss of his virginity; the Goncourts tell us that the Empress Eugénie suffered from corns in an unlikely part of her anatomy. More recently Montherlant has warmly advocated what he elegantly calls "affectionate copulation" as a substitute for love and Gide has given us scarifying descriptions of the problems of the married pederast.

Gide himself once complained that Mr. Green's diary was too "reticent." This was simply blaming Julian Green for not being André Gide. The two men could scarcely have been more different. Mr. Green is happily free from Gide's overweening vanity. His [*Diary, 1928-1957*] is not sensational or scabrous or malicious, and unlike Gide's it is never boring. The personality that emerges from it is engaging: modest, serious, responsible, deeply religious. His aim like Stendhal's is a practical one: the diary is an instrument of self-knowledge and perhaps of personal salvation.

Julian Green was born in France of American parents sixty-four years ago. At the age of sixteen he followed his Presbyterian father into the Catholic Church and at one moment thought of becoming a monk. He went to America for the first time when he was nineteen and took a university course. He tells us in the diary that his outlook is essentially French and that the French language is his natural means of expression. It is evident, however, that his American ancestry and background played a vital part in

his formation and development as a writer. They not only provided him with the setting of two of his finest novels—*Moira* and the still untranslated *Chaque homme dans sa nuit*—they enabled him to project the conflict between the puritan and the hedonist which is the core of the man and his work.

A number of themes recur constantly in the diary and do much to illuminate the novels. They are nightmares, the novelist's vision of reality, the writer's sense of being born out of due time, above all the clash between the religious and the sexual impulses:

> Last night, a familiar nightmare roused me from sleep, the nightmare of being pursued. How well I recognized all those steep slopes, those almost vertical paths winding around gigantic stones! I leapt from rock to rock to drop, finally, shrieking at my enemy's feet. As I woke, it occurred to me that this enemy was my own self and that what my adversary pursued and wished to subdue was my body.

> For the last few years, the problem of the window that won't open has counted for more and more in my life. It is, generally speaking, the problem of every life. To escape . . .

> Disturbed by the problem that I am in the habit of calling the problem of the two realities: the carnal reality and the metaphysical reality. Am I to be their battle-ground to the end of my life?

"For the novelist," he said in another entry, "there is a conventional reality and a reality that might be called the reality of vision." There is one pronounced difference between the novels written before and after the war. No one would dream of accusing Mr. Green of describing "conventional reality" in any of his novels, but "vision" is not to be had for the asking. The difference might be expressed by saying that the earlier novels deal with *hallucination* and the later with *vision*. The characters in *The Closed Garden, The Dark Journey,* and *Midnight*—the English titles of the first two books are much more expressive than the French—are prisoners: the prisoners of their own abnormal states of mind. They are prey to nightmares, to nameless fears, and to a claustrophobic urge to escape from themselves. The novels are powerful and exciting to read, but in the last analysis there is no vision, no pattern, no ultimate meaning. The diary tells us the reason. "No one suspects," Mr. Green said in 1946, "that during the years when I was writing those inexplicably gloomy books, I was so happy that such bliss sometimes kept me from sleeping and I wept for joy." We may feel that "inexplicably" is not altogether the right word. The books are surely a record of the novelist's successful attempts to escape from his own inner pressures by transferring his problems to the creatures of his imagination.

The earlier novels belong to a period when the writer's adherence to the Church was tenuous and he had apparently abandoned the practice of his religion. He returned to the Church in 1939. The effect on his writing was considerable. The later novels are not exactly cheerful reading. The violence and the nightmares are still there, but there is something else besides. The novelist's strong religious feeling and the insight that goes with it bring characters and events into focus, provide the framework that was lacking. The protagonists of **Moira** and **Chaque homme** are fanatics, but they are not monsters like those of the earlier novels. Mr. Green tells us that there is something of himself in all his characters, but there is a great deal of himself in Joseph Day, the Bible Protestant, and Wilfred Ingram the Catholic. They are both profoundly religious and at the same time men who are, as their creator remarks of himself, "subject to ungovernable fleshly appetites." Joseph Day is seduced by a flighty girl and murders her in revenge. Wilfred Ingram could say with the novelist: "The idea that God might not exist has never so much as grazed me," but it does not prevent him from pursuing women with a frenzied promiscuity seven nights a week until he meets his death, shot down by another fanatic who is torn between religion and perverse inclinations. Wilfred Ingram suffers from the particular anguish described in an entry in the diary for 1934:

> I was suddenly seized with anguish. As I walked down the Rue Garancière, it occurred to me to go to Saint-Sulpice and there, in this church, I went and hid in the darkest spot, in front of the Lady chapel. I thought as I knelt: "I have not come to make promises that I could not keep. There are things that I cannot give up. I simply want to receive *strength* . . . "

What we find in the later novels is something that belongs to a great tradition, but today is slightly out of fashion: the conflict between duty and inclination, between spirit and flesh, restated in contemporary terms. The novels are studies in violence, but there is none of the sensationalism, none of the complicity, that we meet in the work of a Francois Mauriac or a Graham Greene. The novelist is no longer looking for alibis or ways of escape; the issues are faced squarely and unflinchingly; the conflict is genuine and the outcome tragic.

It would be wrong to give the impression that the diary is nothing but nightmares, anguish, and sin. There are astute comments on life and literature. The writer expresses his dislike of political parties and adds endearingly:

> I am the kind of man who is stood up against a wall and shot in all revolutions.

His observations on his fellow men are not only free from malice, they are informed by a charity which is rare among men of letters. His account of Gide's efforts to undermine his religious convictions, indeed, goes beyond the demands of charity:

> It would be understanding him very badly to say he played the part of Satan. Quite the contrary, his purpose was to *save* me. He wanted to win me over to his unbelief and exerted all the zeal of a missionary trying to convince an infidel.

But his judgment on Gide as a writer is admirable in its penetration:

> He writes beautifully and every page is crammed to overflowing with a wealth of ideas, yet, while he gives all he has to give, he chills the heart, and the more you read, the less you believe, the less

you hope, and—I say this regretfully—the less you live.

His judgments on English writers are often acute. He fails, as other Frenchmen have done, to appreciate *Macbeth* in spite of its religious implications, but shows a remarkable understanding of poets as difficult as Donne and Hopkins. In a couple of sentences he goes straight to the heart of Auden's weakness:

> Read Auden, at first with admiration, then with a certain weariness. His extraordinary felicity of phrase reminds one of a man who always wins in a lottery.

Julian Green's diary was originally published in seven volumes between 1935 and 1958. A selection from the first two volumes was translated into English in 1940. An omnibus edition, from which ephemeral material had been omitted but which still ran to 1200 pages, appeared in French in 1961. It is from that edition that the present selection, consisting of roughly a quarter of the French text, was made by Kurt Wolff. One could have done with a more generous portion, but the essentials seem to be there. The translation by the novelist's sister is competent, but her continual use of the historic present, which is ill-suited to the English idiom, is an irritation to the reader. (pp. 16-17)

> *Martin Turnell, "Puritan Hedonist," in* The New York Review of Books, *Vol. III, No. 3, October 22, 1964, pp. 16-17.*

James Lord   (review date 1 October 1967)

[*In the following review of* To Leave before Dawn, *Lord focuses on Green's depiction of several childhood experiences that influenced his emotional and artistic development.*]

Julian Green was born in 1900 in Paris, where his American parents had come to live, for business reasons, the year before. He grew up there, deeply influenced both by the Puritan Anglo-Saxon heritage of his forebears and the Catholic Latin animus of his surroundings. The emotional stress of this formative duality had a decisive effect upon the young author. It is starkly reflected in his novels, all written in French, of which the most notable are **Avarice House, The Dark Journey, Then Shall the Dust Return** and **Each Man in His Darkness.** These works are obsessed by sin, brooding with a sense of cruelty and violence, and engrossed in the eventuality of derangement and death. Such characteristics are also present in Green's plays, **South, The Enemy** and **Shadow,** presented since the war, and they inevitably figure as well in the author's autobiographical works.

To Leave Before Dawn is the third volume of autobiography that Julian Green has published. But it describes the very beginning of his life, those decisive, formative years in Paris, years of indecision and turmoil not only for the young boy but also for France and for the world. Accordingly we may look into it with the expectation of learning why this man has written as he has.

We have not far to look. A boy of 5 lies in bed, uncovered,

exposed, naked. He has been found playing with parts of himself which are "forbidden." His mother stands over him, brandishing a saw-toothed bread knife and shrieking, "I'll cut it off!"

The shadow of that knife extends with sinister and shocking effect across every page of this book, and beyond it, enormously, across the life of its author—for he was that child. But the act of the mother was no more perverse than the reaction of the son. He adored her: "Her sole outbursts of tenderness were reserved for me." Indeed! And some years later, observing the boy in his bath, which she supervised till he was 12, the mother exclaimed, "Oh, how ugly that is!" One is stricken anew, as if it had never been revealed before, by the insidious, arbitrary and amoral nature of human love. It will have its way.

And it is shown to us with brilliant, sober immediacy in *To Leave Before Dawn.* Julian Green wrote these pages in his early sixties, endeavoring not so much to re-create the sensuous world of his youth, though he does this vividly, as "to see more clearly into that part of conscience that so often remains obscure as we move away from our childhood." That was his purpose, and in his own way he has fulfilled it with noble candor and subtlety.

Without ever forgetting or denying that he has become the son of that child, the author describes how he gradually grew to understand that nature and human nature were to demand more of him than those ecstatic moments of blind participation in the universe which all children experience and which all children naturally imagine to be unique. The prose which Green has devised for this use is supple and unpretentious, calling no attention to its delicate virtuosity, and has been translated in like spirit by his sister Anne, who herself is portrayed here with affection.

Mr. and Mrs. Green, their several daughters and their last child Julian all live persuasively and with the dimensional variety of truth in this narrative. Their servants Jeanne and Sidonie live. Their households live; their very furniture lives by force of the author's creative vitality. But what animates his work at its core is the conflict that raged within him between the requirements of his faith in a divinity of infinite understanding and goodness on one hand, and on the other the imperious demands of his own human nature to be granted the fulfillment of its instincts and desires. It is this conflict which obtains the fascinated participation of the reader as well as of the author, and which induces in both considerations of implacable universality. It is this conflict which is central to all of Green's literary work and which has decisively affected his private life as well.

Julian Green is a deeply religious individual, a disposition which was logically and inexorably established by his mother. His personal, intellectual and moral adherence to the tenets of Roman Catholicism appears to be complete. The omniscient participation of a deity in man's life is explicitly pronounced as individual and universal truth. There is no argument with mysticism. However, one may look upon its works and wonder: Julian Green has invited us to do so. His candor has been great; it deserves like response.

Not one word, not one intimation, not one aura in this entire book suggests that the author is aware of the events so momentous for all of humankind which already for some years before his birth had been taking place in an obscure, overstuffed consulting room on the Berggasse in Vienna. Sigmund Freud nevertheless is more compellingly present in the pages of *To Leave Before Dawn* by his decisive absence from them than if Green had at least attempted to relate in terms of psychogenic reality the tormenting problems of his youth. Both as a boy and as a man, however, he chose the other way. His conscience allowed him, or compelled him (the awful shadow of the knife!) to seek a conviction of infallible assurance, which is the access to reality always sought by those who crave the comfort of a stable self.

Significantly, the first memory of which the infant author still retains a vivid impression is one of physical pain. Next he remembers lying naked on his mother's lap, filled with vague happiness. Soon he becomes aware of his body. From the first it is considered with aversion, and the eventuality of sexual pleasure is at once and repeatedly described as *the enemy.* The boy felt ill at ease when undressed. "The impure should be hidden," he writes. But he adds, "What was wrong in all this? That is what I cannot make out, even at present." Young Julian questioned his parents about the sexuality which appears in the Bible. He was told, "You don't need to know about it." At the age of 12 he saw a boy at school open his trousers in front of the class. The author declares, "I wonder if I have ever seen evil more perfectly incarnated in a human being?"

He was appalled by the impulses of the flesh: "Flesh meant anarchy, meant the horror that darkened every face. Even now, how I loathe that inexorable force that reduces men to slavery by its all-powerful whims!" Not surprisingly, Green had never masturbated till he was 14, and it seems significant that by then his mother was dead. But masturbation was to him, of course, no pleasure: "It meant that a world ended, and ended shabbily." He felt that, "Any priest could have shown me the danger toward which I ran." Convinced that his life would have been different if he had been warned of that danger, he explains that in the past his mother's' presence had guarded him "in a way that neither she nor I could suspect."

The presence of his father, who remains throughout this narrative a neutral figure, seems neither to have protected nor to have attracted the boy. Later Green repeatedly participated in sexual play with one of his schoolmates, but each time he felt compelled afterward—and in order, he says, to insure his complete enjoyment—to run to the confessional for absolution.

And yet, the innocence with which the adult author demonstrates by his own observations both the deviousness of his youthful self and the morbid ingenuity of his mature rationalizations forbids us to enjoy any indignation or levity at his expense. Our very respect, however, compels us to consider the terrible effects of psychological naiveté and moral equivocation.

Green was, and is, obsessed by sin. But the sin that obsesses him is of the sort which he believes to occur when young boys meet in darkened rooms and to be absolved by whisperings through the green curtain of a confessional. For the torment caused by such an intimacy with sin one may feel sympathy, even compassion, but the fact remains that in the urgent rationale of human circumstances, sin has long since been displaced by evil.

And the contemporary personification of evil, *the enemy* whose dominion every man must oppose, is not a sniggering Priapus who undoes his trousers in public. He is a mild-mannered gentleman who likes Renoir, speaks well of things as they are and with polite competence presides over the workings of gas chambers or the uses of napalm. From the efficiency of his doings there is no guaranteed verity on the other side of a confessional curtain to absolve any one of us.

It is not surprising that Julian Green's first memory of his infant self should be one of pain, for he is an inveterate masochist. The pleasure which he found as a child in reading accounts of torture and executions and which he has prolonged as an adult in writing about violence and sadism is but a superficial expression of this proclivity. Its full effect is demonstrated by the author's congenital inability to accept on their own terms the realities of human nature. (That this may have provided the decisive motor impulse for his talent as a writer is beside the point.)

To explain the somber incident of the bread knife the author instructs us to believe that this mother's hysterical attitude toward the male sexual organs was caused by the trauma she sustained when her brother died from the effects of syphilis. Such an explanation, of course, was acceptable to both mother and son. It enabled them without compunction to pursue the ambivalent fantasies and oedipal compulsions of their relationship, enlivened still further by the exaltations and dilemmas of religion. The author is certain that his mother loved him with all her heart. In that spirit he tells us that she once said to him, "Now, listen. If you were ever to do something wrong, I would rather see you dead. Dead at my feet." The particular nature of wrongdoing was all too memorable and explicit. The boy was then 6 years old. Where is the kingdom of God?

In the end Julian Green answers the sin, the doubt and the anguish of his youth by saying that he did not know what he was doing. That is every man's excuse, of course, and Green reminds us that on the cross Christ invoked it in favor of mankind. Ultimately, then, he entrusts to God's grace the responsibility for human freedom. But, alas, ignorance of the truth does not render truth less desirable or ignorance less deplorable. And the responsibility for human freedom rests solely upon those human beings who because they have had the courage and the vision to acknowledge both physical and historical reality for what they are can then freely act to establish a reality of their own.

The ways of art are no less mysterious than those attributed to heaven. What Julian Green intended that we should see in *To Leave Before Dawn* may not prove to be what we do, in fact, see. No matter; life is there. (pp. 5, 46)

James Lord, "In the Shadow of a Knife," in

The New York Times Book Review, *October 1, 1967, pp. 5, 46.*

Green on the creative process:

There exists for the novelist, both a conventional reality and a reality which one may call a reality of vision. Anyone whose profession it is to tell stories will understand what I am trying to express. There are times when words assemble as it were themselves, and create pictures in the mind which may have a verisimilitude, a certain appearance of truth about them, by which a bad writer and a careless reader may easily be taken in. Accuracy of vision calls for a sterner effort, a kind of self-sacrifice. For example, it is not enough to write, "She shrank before his gaze." The writer must realize, in his inmost self, what these words imply. If he fails to do so, the sentence which follows it will be a little less accurate (that is to say, it will not have the ring of that truth which comes from within, which is the only genuine truth), and so the next sentence will be still less accurate, and so on, until the author pulls himself together.

Julien Green, 21 October 1931, quoted in R. L. Mégreoz's
Thirty-One Bedside Essays, *1951.*

Robert Speaight   (review date 7 February 1975)

[*Speaight was an English actor, theater scholar, nonfiction writer, critic, and lecturer. In the following review, he asserts that* Jeunesse *reveals Green's characteristic examination of the opposition between the human body and spirit.*]

The latest volume of Julien Green's autobiography [*Jeunesse*] reminds one of François Mauriac's observation about André Gide that he was "determined nothing about him should remain hidden". Green recalls his first meeting with Gide; the idiosyncrasies of his speech and his air of effortless authority. There were to be many more such meetings, of which one can read in the fascinating volumes of Green's *Journal* to which this book is a kind of preface. It prepares us for the diarist and the novelist that he was to become, ending with the writing—though not, as yet, the publication—of his first novel, *Mont-Cinère.* Gide is not among the leading dramatis personae of Green's *Jeunesse,* but he affords an interesting point of comparison and contrast. Both men were avowed and practising homosexuals, but where in the case of Gide this was a cause of complacency, in the case of Green it was a cause of conflict. Both have recorded their sexual lives with perfect candour, and neither regarded as in any way unnatural what came quite naturally to themselves.

The narrative covers only three years—from 1922, when Green returned to Paris with his father and three sisters, up to his debut in the world of letters. He had only lately finished his studies at the University of Virginia, and had left his heart there. But in 1923 he took to "prowling", and the effect of these casual encounters was a nightmare of horror and disgust. He combined a worship of physical—or more exactly facial—beauty with a revulsion against the sexual act; and when love entered into the relationship he took care that it was not killed by pleasure. This was the classical conflict between "the marriage of true minds" and "the expense of spirit in a waste of shame". Mauriac, though his temptations were different, was a victim of the same tensions, and arrived at similar conclusions. In each case the precept of chastity, as the Church understood it, interposed its prohibition.

Green, a convert to Catholicism, had once felt a call to the religious life, and had not forgotten it. The nostalgia for a state of grace was strong in him. He might dally with vice but, unlike Gide, he never justified it. In later years Gide was to see in Julien Green, not a sensualist with the same tendencies as himself, but yet another victim of the faith which had captured so many of his friends—Copeau and Rivière, Mauriac and Charles Du Bos—and threatened his own cherished *disponibilité*.

When Green told Mauriac that the Devil had been looking over his shoulder, Mauriac replied that he was privileged in having been given this proof of what they both believed in. It would be naive to expect the average reader to share this belief, but the atmosphere of evil which both writers had the power to generate is more easily understood in the light of it.

Jeunesse is not, however, an exclusively sombre book. Green has a sense of humour, not least about himself. His first efforts to earn a living included the unsuccessful purveying of pots of orange marmalade, and the abortive attempt to tutor a boy who locked himself in the lavatory and refused to come out. Painting attracted him before he decided to become a writer; it was something to illustrate, even if one could not realize, one's fantasies. [One of his works] was entitled *Le Voyageur sur la terre;* and that is very much how Green himself appears in all his personal writings. He seems to be walking alone in a strange land with the unexpected always round the corner.

It is a world which he only half believes in—an "unreal city"—and it was to the audacity and innocence of William Blake, and the haunted vicarage of Howarth, that his imagination most readily responded. Supernatural terror stalks the pages of his own fiction and drama, and the more effectively when its footsteps are scarcely audible, as in masterpieces like *Moïra* or *Adrienne Mesurat*.

The Puritan tradition of his American forebears and the Jansenist inheritance of Port-Royal combined in opposition to an ardent sensuality. What he wrote of his first publication—a pamphlet **"Contre les Catholiques de France"**—might have been written of pretty well everything he has written since: "Behind every sentence of my little book one can divine the horror and the attraction of lust. Lust led to atheism, and it was the road to Hell." The advice of Barrès to the young Mauriac—"surtout il faut être bien élevé"—is scrupulously followed in these pages, where the most candid avowals are purged, so to speak, by the purity of style. The *gravitas* is never inflated, and the moralist is not tempted into the pulpit. Julien Green is a perfect illustration of Graham Greene's definition of a great writer as "a man obsessed".

Robert Speaight, "Alone in a Strange Land,"

in The Times Literary Supplement, *No. 3805, February 7, 1975, p. 146.*

John M. Dunaway   (essay date May 1977)

[*An American educator and critic specializing in French literature, Dunaway is the author of* The Metamorphoses of the Self: The Mystic, the Sensualist, and the Artist in the Works of Julien Green *(1978). In the following essay, he discusses the progression of Green's artistic development and suggests that his writings reveal a process of self-discovery.*]

The works of Julien Green bear witness to a perpetual duality that is fundamental to his psychological makeup. Green says in his *Journal* that he can understand only two types of human personalities: the mystic and the sensualist. These are precisely the two selves that are at odds in Green's inner struggle, a kind of "Spleen et Idéal" conflict that recalls the manichaeism of Baudelaire's statement that within all men there are two simultaneous forces, one leading toward God and the other toward Satan. In all of his writing, Green is constantly addressing himself to what he calls the problem of the two realities—the carnal reality versus the metaphysical reality—and seeking his own place in the tension between the two forces. With the mystical and erotic selves constantly struggling for ascendency, Green's first reaction was a desire for escape and a refusal to accept reality on such difficult terms—a reaction reflected in the "magic realism" which characterizes his early fiction. But the eventual result of the inner tension is the affirmation of a third self that resolves the first two at a deeper level of meaning.

There have been various labels attached to Green in an effort to characterize cogently for the public the nature of his writing. The most persistent epithet has been that of the Catholic writer. The aspect of Green's writing that is most neglected in the Catholic interpretation is the strong erotic element that conflicts so violently with the spiritual aspirations of his protagonists. The struggle of these two forces is the basic opposition of the first two Greenian selves, the mystic and the sensualist. The former identity arose from the context of Julien Green's diary, which was published in installments over the years of his long career; the latter, from the long-repressed confession of the autobiography, whose publication began in the 1960s.

The fact that the erotic dimension of Green's writing is often homosexual intensifies the violence of the inner struggle, given his puritanical background. The level on which Green's fiction treats homosexuality preserves the solemn dignity of the subject in the same sense that Racine preserved the solemn dignity of incestuous passion in *Phèdre*. Nevertheless, it must be remembered that sexuality in all its manifestations was regarded as impure by the young Julien Green. And because of his puritanical background, sexual inversion has always carried a moral stigma for him.

It is only natural for misleading images of this writer to have arisen. One of the peculiar aspects of his writing is the process of *dédoublement* that so many of his characters experience. Daniel O'Donovan in *Le Voyageur sur la terre* (1926), for example, has a companion and guide whom we eventually discover to be an imaginary projection of a particular aspect of his own personality. Indeed, the very act of writing for Julien Green is an attempt to resolve a profoundly divided self and to reach new depths of self-discovery. Especially in the world of Green's fiction, the amorphous, bewildering metamorphoses of the self are intimately involved in the drama of each protagonist. Ultimately, they lead to a personal myth of a heroic visionary artist.

In the *Journal,* Green states repeatedly that his novels constitute his true diary. A major trend in modern literary criticism has been to reaffirm Mallarmé's contention that the artist's true identity may be appreciated only from his imaginative creations—"Tel qu'en Lui-même enfin l'éternité le change." Indeed, the subject of much of the art and literature of the last one hundred years has been the apotheosis of the artist himself. The Socratic quest for identity that is instrumental in both Green's *Journal* and his autobiography is equally important in his fiction, where the self is liberated and passes through new transformations that lead to a personal myth of the artist.

Julien Green was destined to arrive at his own myth of the artist because of his method of writing. He has never believed in making a preliminary outline of a book because he never knows in advance what will happen in it. He writes only what he sees his characters in the process of acting out. Therefore, he does not invent: he recounts what he witnesses. For this reason, writing fiction for Green is as much a process of discovery as one of creation. His characters lead him to a fuller understanding of his true self. The fictional self, then, has a spark of authenticity that is not equalled in the confessional context because of its spontaneous origins. It has what Green calls "une réalité de vision" which contrasts with the "réalité conventionnelle" in that it is the product of a self-giving on the part of the novelist. It is not enough for the Greenian novelist to describe a character's actions. He must see *from within* what the words describe.

Green's fictional reality imposes itself on him in the form of an intense vision in which he must participate. The complicity that is established between the novelist and his characters is such that their sins, in a sense, become his own. In identifying with his characters, he is captured by the "envoûtement de cette chose monstrueuse qui sort de son cerveau." The novelist must become what he is writing. Indeed, Green himself had no alternative. Perhaps the strongest motive in all of his writing is to find a kind of rebirth, to change, to become another. The desire to become *autre,* which obviously figures in the identity quest, partly explains the attraction that metempsychosis had for him. The hero of *Si j'étais vous* (1947), Fabien Especel, has the power to reincarnate himself as different persons, and other Greenian protagonists project certain of their own personality traits as doubles. The possibilities that fiction provided Green for becoming transformed were the only means by which he was able to discover a self that he could live with.

Writing fiction is a compulsive activity for most serious novelists but the case of Julien Green is an extreme one.

He says in the diary that without that vocation, he might well have gone insane. Because of the turmoil that has always raged within him, because of a life style of self-imposed solitude, Green has always been obliged to write his novels in order to maintain his psychological equilibrium. It is the most efficacious means at his disposal for exorcising the demons of his divided self.

Green's method of writing has had great therapeutic value for him, but by the same token it has intensified a dramatic debate within him which he has discussed in the *Journal.* Is the act of writing a novel compatible with the state of grace? Can the artist err otherwise but in sin? The answer: The very source of fiction, according to Green, is essentially involved in the realm of the impure, and if the artist tries to purify the source there is no more fiction.

> **Green has said that the common ground of the mystic and the sensualist is that each is in search of the absolute. The seemingly conflicting forces of eroticism and mysticism in Green's works are ultimately geared toward the same goal and must be understood as such.**
>
> **—*John M. Dunaway***

Thus, the vocations of novelist and of Christian appear incompatible, and the problem of art and morality is a very disturbing one for Julien Green. His close friend Jacques Maritain, who had an important influence on his spiritual development, wrote about the problem of the two vocations in *Art et Scolastique.* He, like Green, stated that art is pagan in origin and inevitably involved in sin. Even though it is very difficult, it is not impossible to combine the two vocations of novelist and Christian. The essential difficulty is that one must reconcile two absolutes.

For art is, according to Maritain, an absolute. It is a fully autonomous domain that can never be subjected to morality. Its sole end is the creation of beauty, whereas the end of morality is reconciliation with God. Maritain goes to great lengths to establish the unquestionable purity of art. "L'Artiste est soumis, dans le ligne de son art, à une sorte d'ascétisme, qui peut exiger des sacrifices héroïques."

In the character of Daniel O'Donovan, protagonist of *Le Voyageur sur la terre,* Julien Green discovered intuitively this heroic destiny. Daniel has a recurring dream in which he sees himself led from his bed to a roaring chasm filled with the precipitous churning of a river. The angelic guide who has led him there calls it "la source des eaux-vives." In the dream, Daniel's double swoons, only to find, upon awakening, his other self broken and transfigured on the bed. The dream is a prophetic revelation of Daniel's destiny, for he commits suicide at a river bluff that resembles the one in the dream. For Green, it is the first partial revelation of his deepest identity, that of visionary artist. In beginning the vocation of writer (*Le Voyageur* was his first work of fiction), Green was bringing himself to the great chasm of his subconscious, which contained the fearful desires of an erotic nature. The descent into the raging waters of his obsessions and anxieties was a perilous one. But Green knew, if only subconsciously, that those raging waters also represented the living water of regeneration that the author finds in the vocation of writer-hero.

Daniel O'Donovan, then, revealed to Green the identity that would eventually prove to be his most authentic self. The heroic role of the visionary artist developed in Green's mind to the point of representing a personal myth in his later fiction. In *L'Autre sommeil* (1930), he became increasingly aware of the gift of seeing by means of *la seconde vue* of the visionary artist. In *Le Visionnaire* (1934), the figure of Manuel recounting his vision was one version of the third self incarnated.

Le Voyageur sur la terre and *L'Autre sommeil,* however, were not typical of Green's early fiction because of their highly autobiographical content. Most of what he wrote before 1950 was apparently very unlike him. His own *vérité* was clothed in mystery in these early works, which were full of female protagonists and fantastic plots that bore little resemblance to his own life. Even his unobtrusive style was designed to hide the personality of the author. Because of his fictional disguise Julien Green was not recognized in his early works. *L'Autre sommeil,* for example, was never really understood as a kind of confession until the last part of Green's career. The theme of sexual inversion in it was long ignored, as it was in *Moïra* (1950) and even *Sud* (1953). Indeed, the latter work was first taken to be a historical play about the problems of the South in 1861. Not until the great confession of *Partir avant le jour* (1963) did the public appreciate the true importance of the erotic in Julien Green's works.

The evolution of Greenian criticism has followed a pattern quite similar to that of Green's fiction itself. Before 1939 his novels were involved in a seemingly unautobiographical world of hallucination and were interpreted as examples of magic realism. In the 1940s his novels were less popular, and the importance of religion in his diary led critics to regard him as essentially a Catholic writer. With the increasingly autobiographical accent of *Moïra,* the trilogy of plays published in the 1950s, *Chaque homme dans sa nuit* (1960), and, of course, the autobiography itself, critics began slowly to accept the erotic aspect of Green's fiction and to appreciate the violence of the conflict in which it was born. Green himself became more aware of having found a vocation in expressing his deepest *vérité.*

The image that recurs most frequently in Green's works is the staircase. The author himself was the first to discover the obsessive recurrence of the staircase in his writing. In the April 4, 1933, entry of his diary he listed examples of stairways in moments of fear or other intense emotions in nearly all the novels and short stories he had written at that point in his career. Since that time, there have been numerous interpretations of the staircase image ranging from the obvious Freudian connotations to the equally obvious notion of the mystic's progress toward heaven.

In *Le Voyageur sur la terre,* the old captain's nightly climbing of the stairs throws Daniel O'Donovan into fits of superstitious fear. Denis, in *L'Autre sommeil,* is seated on a stairway when his erotic fantasy ends in a swoon. Once in *Minuit* (1936) and twice in *Moïra* the creaking of the stair as the protagonist mounts toward his room reminds him of the crack of a whip. Green tells us in *Terre lointaine* (1966) that he often wrote stories as a boy in which he was being chased on a staircase and had to take refuge in a basement. In these stories he imagined himself killing many people.

In *Memories of Happy Days* (1942) he recounts the nightly drama of having to go to bed before the older members of the family during the summers at Andrésy. Much too frightened to go all the way upstairs to his dark room, he would sit on the stairway and read. The painful ordeal of the *drame du coucher* was a poignantly oedipal one in the same sense that it was for Marcel as he reluctantly climbed the familiar stairway in Proust's *Du Côté de chez Swann.* It was this experience, suggests Green, that was the origin of the prominence of the staircase image in his fiction.

There was, however, another important experience in Green's life that helped crystallize the staircase image in his mind. The moment that determined his fate, he says in the diary, came one afternoon in April of 1919 as he was leaving the crypt of the chapel at the rue Cortambert. Stopping on the stairway, he suddenly felt an intense sadness at the thought of what he would have to give up in order to follow the monastic vocation. "Tout à coup je sentis se formuler en moi 'le grand refus' qui devait prêter à ma vie un aspect si particulier." Indeed, the great refusal of monasticism was a fateful decision in his life, and it was to result in the nostalgia for sainthood that never could be satisfied. In that moment, it seemed that all the world was being offered him: " . . . sortant d'une espèce de Moyen Age, j'abordais en pleine Renaissance." After leaving the chapel, he was sure that his life had just reached an important turning point. He was moving away from the realm of the spirit and beginning to explore the strange world of the flesh that was beckoning to him.

Green has said that the common ground of the mystic and the sensualist is that each is in search of the absolute. The seemingly conflicting forces of eroticism and mysticism in Green's works are ultimately geared toward the same goal and must be understood as such. For this reason, the staircase image is significant as a *liaison* between the first two selves of Julien Green and points toward the visionary third self.

Julien Green's fiction is the meeting place of various levels of being. The third self is the consciousness that recounts in a visionary manner the communication between cosmic zones for the reader. The staircase illustrates the phenomenon of analogous realities that is presented in Green's fiction. Another image that is closely related to this visionary quality is that of the threshold. In *Mille chemins ouverts* (1964), we see the adolescent Green immobile on the threshold of a friend's room as he contemplates his captivating beauty. When Ian first sees his *bourreau* in *Sud,* Erik is standing immobile at the threshold of the plantation house. Similarly, Denis of *L'Autre sommeil* says that the nude statues he contemplates in hallucinatory fashion exist on the threshold of an unexplored world, and in the diary, Green tells us that *Le Visionnaire,* a book that obviously explores communication between levels of reality, was originally to be entitled *Au Seuil de la nuit.* In *Partir avant le jour,* Green speaks of the ineffable secrets of God that only children hear and that are forgotten as we leave the world of childhood. He says that in seeking to regain the intuitive revelations of childhood, he knows that he must remain silent because they are hidden beneath the threshold of language.

The images of the staircase and the threshold reveal the ultimate drama of Green's fiction. They occur at moments when the protagonist is on the verge of discovering a new reality. Often it is the shattering revelation of sexuality, the impure realm that is so fearful to the product of puritanical heritage. Sometimes it is a fleeting glimpse of the mystical reality to which the first Greenian self aspires.

The threshold experience is much more than an intermediate position between divine and earthly realities. It is a moment of passage in which self-annihilation and rebirth are involved in the hero's progress toward the universal source. It partakes of the artist's mythic role of visionary hero. Like Daniel O'Donovan, Julien Green's vocation entails a perilous interior descent through the metamorphoses of the self that culminates in "the source of living waters."

The puritanical heritage of Julien Green made it impossible for his first self, the mystic, to transcend his second identity of sensualist. The horror of sexual inversion for the Puritan mystic rendered him incapable of resolving his identity crisis in religious terms. The third self of the visionary artist was the only identity that Green could assume in order to integrate the various aspects of his own personality. In the most recent works of Julien Green we find the basic duality of spirit and eros in its most finished form. The current stage of his fiction began in 1950 with *Moïra.* His three plays, especially *L'Ennemi* (1954), explored the struggle in increasing depth. *Chaque homme dans sa nuit* represented an even more radical polarization of forces in the character of Wilfred Ingram, the *coureur* who is also the chosen vessel of divine grace. Finally, in *L'Autre* (1971) the polarity is expressed in still another metaphysical *dédoublement.* There are two main characters, each of whom has his own narrative, as in *Le Visionnaire.* And, as in *L'Ennemi,* there is a dual movement of spiritual and erotic forces represented by the two main characters. Significantly, a great deal of this long novel is devoted not to narrative but to dialogue between Karin and Roger, constant debates between spirit and flesh.

The evolution in Green's career that we have just outlined comes more clearly into focus in the light of one of Jacques Petit's most significant theories, articulated in *Julien Green, l'homme qui venait d'ailleurs* (1971). According to Petit, one of the most essential sources of Green's writings was an experience that is described in *Terre lointaine* and later in *Jeunesse* (1974). Mark, the student at the University of Virginia whom Green had loved silently for two years, was visiting his friend in Paris in 1923. As they strolled together by the Seine, Green resolved at last to tell

Mark of his passion, but was unable to confess the nature of his feelings. Petit observes that there are repeated variations of this scene of "l'aveu impossible" throughout Green's novels up until 1960. Denis and Claude in *L'Autre sommeil,* Simon and Joseph in *Moïra,* and Ian and Erik in *Sud* are examples of the male's impossible avowal of homosexual passion, and the examples of heterosexual and female versions of the scene are numerous. In *Chaque homme dans sa nuit,* however, Angus actually does confess his love for Wilfred by means of a letter. This scene, says Petit, marks the resolution of an all-important theme in Green's fiction which he calls "le poids d'un silence." Significantly, *Chaque homme dans sa nuit* is the last book written by Julien Green before his autobiography, which is a uniquely frank and explicit confession of his personal erotic drama that had been only partly revealed by any of his preceding works.

The movement of self-discovery and of confession throughout Green's career may thus be understood as culminating in the autobiography. In the early stages of his writing, he was unable to face his most disquieting problems and deal with them directly. The motive of escape, then, is naturally the most prevalent one in the early fiction. With *Moïra,* Green seemed to have found a new determination to explore more thoroughly the meaning of his own erotic drama. The increasingly autobiographical aspect of the fiction beginning with *Moïra* is a reflection of this determination. Indeed, the end of *Moïra* suggests a turning point not only in Joseph Day's life but also in the life of his spiritual cousin Julien Green.

After Joseph has submitted to the loss of his virginity and committed the murder, Bruce Praileau offers him a means of escape. The fact that Joseph accepts Praileau's proposal and begins his flight is characteristic of the abortive escapes in the conclusions of Green's earlier novels. While he is fleeing through the woods, he takes satisfaction in the deepening snow that has fallen since he buried Moïra, knowing it will abet his escape attempt. Joseph, at this point, is fleeing the dreaded sexual instinct that Moïra represents and vainly seeking to recapture the inhuman purity (represented by the snow) that characterized him before he met Moïra. But the cathartic experience of tragic suffering he has undergone is effectual. Finally, he does decide to return, to give himself up, to face his realities, and to confess his crime.

Julien Green, in writing *Moïra,* was embarking on a new stage of writing characterized by more direct self-discovery and confession. The tragic conclusions of *Moïra, Sud, L'Ennemi, Chaque homme dans sa nuit,* and *L'Autre* all suggest the possibility, at the same time, of the action of grace. The avowal of homosexual passion was impossible for Green's heroes until the definitive confession of the autobiography. The resulting "poids d'un silence" was important in lending a special tension and mystery to the pre-autobiography novels. Now that Green has finally exorcised the demons of his divided self in the autobiography, the question is whether those demons, whether that weight of silence were essential to the fertility of his artistic creation.

L'Autre has, indeed, much less of the authenticity of the

Greenian fiction of the fifties. It is somewhat longer and tends to belabor the duality of spirit and flesh, which all somehow seems to have been said before. The duality in *L'Autre* is too neatly delineated in a rather self-conscious fashion. Likewise, the fourth volume of the autobiography (*Jeunesse,* 1974) is still more explicit than the previous ones and none the better for it. *Jeunesse,* when compared to *Terre lointaine,* lacks much of the tension of the shadowy erotic identity, struggling to express itself. It leads one to ask whether Green's autobiography has drained the mystery from the richest source of his inspiration. It appears that any future works inevitably will be either less ingenuous than *Moïra* and *Chaque homme dans sa nuit* or will mark a radically new stage in his writing. One can only hope that Green's long career—*né avec le siècle*—will once again renew itself in a different vein, as Hugo's so often did in spanning the century before him.

It was a mysterious process by which the myth of the visionary artist imposed itself on Julien Green. While it was still an unconscious myth it expressed itself in starkly primitive form. When he was drawing pictures as a child, he felt the first effects of the mysterious identity within that insisted on expressing itself. A fearful hallucinatory process seemed to take possession of his imagination. "Ce que j'imaginais, je le voyais comme un visionnaire voit une vision."

In this sense, the mysterious identity of *l'autre* in Green's most recent novel may be considered the third self of the artist. The evolution of Green's writing has been a movement from mystery to self-discovery, during which the transformations of the self led him to the most profound revelation of his *vérité*. Although the mechanisms of the third self are obscure, its presence is unmistakable, as Green indicates in the following passage from his *Journal:*

> A propos du roman que j'écris, je voudrais dire ceci, qui est vrai de tous mes livres: il arrive un moment où de grandes brèches se forment par où passe quelque chose qui ne vient pas de moi, mais d'un autre dont parfois j'ai peur comme d'un moi plus impérieux, plus autoritaire et plus sûr de lui que le moi que je connais. Quel écrivain n'a éprouvé cela? Et d'où cela vient-il?

Thus, there is evidence that Julien Green himself embraces the belief in the existence of a unique identity in the works of great writers. In his introduction to an English translation of Péguy, he included parenthetically this amplification on the idea that Péguy's own poetry had a providential influence in leading him to his conversion. "What lies deepest in us is very often beyond our ken until we go through the struggle to express it, and then it begins to react on us." Green's writing has led him to the revelation of a hidden identity, a self that witnesses with the eyes of *la seconde vue* a fictional reality with a unique visionary quality. (pp. 85-93)

> John M. Dunaway, *"The Motive of Self-Discovery in Julien Green," in* South Atlantic Bulletin, *Vol. XLII, No. 2, May, 1977, pp. 85-93.*

Kathryn E. Wildgen   (essay date Fall 1987)

[*In the following essay, Wildgen examines the nature of evil and sexual desire in* Le mauvais lieu *and relates the novel's themes to Green's life.*]

[In his article "A Study of Julien Green" published in *The Journal of Abnormal and Social Psychology,* Vol. 41 (1946)] Milton C. Albrecht stated: "Is [Julian Green] not likely to remain in a whirlpool and to be classed finally among the decadents of our time? . . . one wonders what his ultimate development will be considering the nature of his personality." *Le Mauvais Lieu,* Green's latest novel, may help to answer these questions since it is a sort of *summa* involving most of Green's archetypal characters, images, and, especially, ideas, particularly those concerning evil. Green stated in 1924 in the **"Pamphlet contre les catholiques de France"** that the world was diabolical. He has evidently not changed his mind, his statement in *La Lumière du monde* notwithstanding.

Le Mauvais Lieu is, to be sure, an outrageous book in many ways and can seem to be an atrocious novel until one realizes that it is not really a novel at all, but, as Jacques de Ricaumont points out [in "Julien Green à travers ses derniers livres," *Revue des deux mondes* (August 1978)], a "symbolic narrative—in fact, one could almost call the work an apologue." It is also a kind of grotesque fairy tale, "Sleeping Beauty" gone awry. The principal message of the book is twofold: every place on earth is an evil place; and, as Perrotte, one of the more wretched characters in the story puts it, 'It is dreadful to love someone.'

The story involved Louise, a blonde, blue-eyed, beautiful child on the threshold of adolescence. She is surrounded by a bevy of actual and would-be child molesters, male and female, yet she manages to avoid physical or moral contamination of any sort. She is finally sent to Chanteleu, a gorgeously situated finishing school that is nothing but a harem for the totally Lesbian staff, and from this horror one day she disappears forever into the snow.

Several years before the creation of *Le Mauvais Lieu,* Nicholas Kostis stated [in *The Exorcism of Sex and Death in Julien Green's Novels* (1973)] that Green's is an "extremely private, perhaps hermetic work of art, which, while it has the conventional form and characteristics of a novel, is nonetheless a system of signs which represent forces and states of mind that one feels are directly affecting, even torturing the author." That statement appears to be truer of *Le Mauvais Lieu* than of any other of Green's works. This study is an attempt to elucidate some of the signs of this most enigmatic novel.

First, it is necessary to consider the title. The loci of the novel are, almost without exception, both beautiful and strongly tinged with evil. The story opens in a children's park, full of joy, sunshine and the cries of youngsters having fun. In this lovely setting, Louise's aunt Gertrude muses on her unhappy marriage and on the indecent proposition she thinks a worker has just made to her. At the end of the novel, in a similar park, perhaps the same one, Gertrude's brother Gustave cuts his own throat as children's cries again fill the air. The grotesque corruptness of the characters and their actions is in sharpest possible con-

trast with the gorgeousness and opulence of their surroundings. Gertrude's house, the setting for the major
portion of the story, is full of flowers and pastel colors and
delicious pastries. (Her *patissier* is named Gloppe—who
ever said Green doesn't have a sense of humor?) Her house
is divided into three areas, each with its own particular
sinister aspect. The salon, the scene of Gertrude's popular
receptions, is also one of the domains of Félix, a procurer
for dirty old men who wish to dupe themselves into believing that they are making love to *fillettes* when, in fact,
quite the contrary is true. It is here that Félix comes to terrorize Monsieur Brochard, one of Gertrude's regulars.
And it is here that Gustave announces to his sister that he
plans to extort Louise's tutelage from her. The bedroom
area, the floor above the salon, is the scene of Gertrude's
violent, morbid nightmares. It is in Louise's room that
Gustave announces to her that she must leave her aunt's
house for a boarding school. The third area, the attic, is
Louise's refuge, the place to which she is irresistibly
drawn, a place where she nevertheless feels both fear and
sadness. She is frightened by the clothes that move in
drafts and seem animated. She is fascinated by the *porte-
fenêtre*, a variation of the theme of the *gouffre* which can
be a temptation to suicide. Lina, the maid, dies on the floor
of the attic as a result of a near fall out of the *porte-fenêtre*.
She had been attempting to wave to the departing Louise,
and in a real sense, the child's departure killed her.

The filthy squalor of the *nid d' amour*, a place of assigna-
tion used by Félix's clients, and the pathetic tawdriness of
Brochard's house are more appropriate to them than the
Victorian splendor of the ironically-named boarding
school, Chanteleu, where Louise is sent by her uncle
Gustave. Chanteleu is, as I mentioned, populated entirely
by Lesbians. It, like Gertrude's house, is all flowers and
pastels and physical appeal masking turpitude. The pupils
are the staff's harem. At Gertrude's house, Louise's bedroom had been joined to her aunt's by a connecting door.
A similar arrangement exists at Chanteleu where Louise's
room is joined to staff member Marthe Réau's by a connecting sitting room, suggesting that Louise has simply
traded one *mauvais lieu* for another.

On a more symbolic level, the title of this novel refers to
the world in which man is forced to work out his salvation
while surrounded by temptation. This is a *lieu commun* in
Green's thought. The body is also an evil place in which
the soul is imprisoned. In fact, Green considered the Incarnation to be a principal suffering of Christ:

> "Réfléchi à la grande douleur que l'Incarnation
> a dû être pour le Christ. Qui de nous . . . n'a
> souffert de se sentir emprisonné dans un corps?
> Prison que nous portons avec nous, avec les lim-
> ites continuelles qu'elle impose à l'âme." (*Oeu-
> vres complètes*)

> ("Thought about the intense suffering that the
> Incarnation must have been for Christ. Who
> among us . . . hasn't suffered from feeling im-
> prisoned in a body? A prison that we carry
> around with us, with the continuous limits it im-
> poses on the soul?")

Green's protagonist Louise is almost pure symbol. Inno-

cence incarnate, she moves from one evil place to another
and remains utterly uncorrupted by the vice-ridden who
surround her. She is a pivotal character in the truest sense
in that all characters love her, desire her in some way, and
are wretched because of her. This curiously mute child
holds her world in thrall. Louise's attitude towards Gertrude and Gertrude's reaction to her, reported early in the
novel, are typical of Louise's relations with everyone:

> Louise . . . leva les yeux sans mot dire vers sa
> tante . . . Dans l'ovale de ce visage . . . les pru-
> nelles bleues frappaient par leur immobilité
> attentive . . . Comme d'habitude, Gertrude
> demeura . . . interdite devant cette beauté qui
> lui éetait pourtant familière, puis elle retrouva sa
> voix, mais devenue rauque d'émotion.

> (Louise looked at her aunt without saying a
> word. Gertrude was struck by the fixed stare of
> concentration in her blue eyes, framed by her
> oval face. As usual, she was speechless in the
> presence of such beauty, which by now was quite
> familiar to her. Finally she spoke in a voice
> hoarse with emotion.)

Green conveys here several facts that will be reiterated
throughout the story: Louise is silent; Louise is passive in
the presence of certain persons; Louise's beauty causes
pain to those who look upon her. The Greenian theme of
the *aveu manqué* is carried to its paroxysm in this novel
in which Louise's purity makes it completely impossible
for the people around her to express their feelings of passion to her. Marthe Réau and Mademoiselle Perrotte manage to convey only the spiritual part of their love. Uncle
Gustave and Monsieur Brochard leer and make veiled,
equivocal comments. But no one dares to express the plen-
itude of his feelings to this child.

Louise is arguably Green's most perfect creature and the
only successful person portrayed in his works. She alone
escapes the "disintegration of the human soul into chaos"
which Dayton Kohler properly identifies as the lot of all
of Green's characters. She is unique in that she vanishes
before she becomes entrapped by habit and insanity like
Adrienne Mesurat, or set in her ways and destructive like
Emily Fletcher, enslaved and mutilated like Angèle, or a
suicide like Elisabeth of *Minuit.* She disappears from all
evil places while yet uncorrupt. To be sure, all of this is
a result of her youth—she has not had a chance to be ruined. We find her just at the threshold of awakening sexuality just like the fairy-tale characters Sleeping Beauty and
Little Red Riding-Hood mentioned several times in the
story. She looks at the young, attractive worker in the
street. She looks at her naked body in the mirror. But all
she does is look. She makes no contact whatsoever. Gertrude's insinuation that Louise may be tempted by "the
act performed by those who don't respect their bodies"
leaves Louise utterly stupefied.

Perhaps the most important aspect of Louise's persona is
that she not only realizes that "la vraie vie est ailleurs,"
she lives that realization. She not only believes that Paradise exists, she claims to have been there. She *knows* what
the others, Perrotte and Marthe for instance, only believe.
Green himself feels that Louise's insistence on the existence of Paradise is the center of the novel (*La Terre*).

Louise lives both the "real" life and the imaginary life of Green's characters as described by Janine Carrel [in her *L'Expérience du seuil dans l'oeuvre de Julien Green* (1967)]:

> Le mystére du personnage greenien est en effet de vivre en même temps dans sa vie ordinaire, qui est souvent une prison, et dans une vie imaginaire qui, sans s'intégrer dans la vie quotidienne, s'y intercale, de sorte que le personnage, vivant au seuil de deux réalités, se meut tantôt dans l'une, tantôt dans l'autre. . . .

> (The mystery of the character in a Green novel is that he is quite able to function in his ordinary life which is often a prison, and, at the same time, in an imaginary life which, without becoming part of daily life, inserts itself into it, so that the character, living on the threshold of two realities, moves now in one, now in the other.)

This is what Green meant when he called Louise a "mystic wandering about in hell, a hell which is the world" (*La Terre*). She is able to penetrate what Brian Fitch calls the "dimension of the supernatural, that 'elsewhere' referred to by M. Edme in *Minuit,* a 'beyond' just beneath the surface at every moment, not only at the moment of death."

Le Mauvais Lieu is probably the novel in which one finds the highest number of nominally practicing Catholics: Louise, Gertrude, Marthe, Perrotte. Gertrude is the quintessential Catholic of Green's 1924 **"Pamphlet"**:

> Les catholiques de ce pays sont tombés dans l'habitude de leur religion, au point qu'ils ne s'inquiètent plus de savoir si elle est vraie ou fausse, s'ils y croient ou non; et cette espèce de foi machinale les accompagne jusqu 'à la mort. (*Oeuvres complètes*)

> (The Catholics of this country have fallen into a religion of habit, to such an extent that they don't even care if it is true or false, or whether they believe in it or not; and this type of mechanical faith stays with them till death.)

Gertrude's shallowness and foolishness are frequently placed in juxtaposition with the Crucifixion. Her most

Green in 1935.

characteristic gesture is a careless sign of the cross, a carelessness specifically castigated in the sixth paragraph of the **"Pamphlet."** And she is forever placing all her trivial woes "au pied de la croix." She wears a gold cross and has a crucifix on the wall of her bedroom. Green's description of the latter suggests that this practice is close to blasphemy: "This Christ with outstretched arms seemed to her to be both an art object and a good luck charm. The idea that it depicted a dying man never even crossed her mind." Her emotions are as shallow as her faith. She was out shopping while her husband Alfred was on his deathbed. At a moment when Louise was missing and Lina was out frantically searching for her, Gertrude went to bed and fell asleep. And, finally, she relinquished Louise to Gustave in exchange for money. Gustave gets to the heart of the matter when he points out to Gertrude the vicious circularity of her feelings towards the child: 'You despise her because she frightens you, and she frightens you because you are in love. And you don't want to be in love.' In a certain sense, that statement is true of all the characters who revolve around Louise. Their love for her tortures them. It is also noteworthy that Gustave uses the adjective *amoureuse,* with its sexual connotations, rather than the more sexually neutral verb *aimer.*

Gertrude's selfish love for Louise and her decorative ivory crucifix find their counterpoint in the latter part of the novel in Marthe Réau's tender affection for the child and in her "little cross of black wood." Marthe, like Julien Green, has homosexual tendencies which she suppresses in order to practice her faith. She is irresistibly drawn by Louise's purity but is also repelled by it because it is an important obstacle to the union she desperately desires. Like Green, she loves what is inaccessible precisely because of that which makes it inaccessible. She could say, with Green: "Innocence remained for me an insurmountable obstacle" (*Oeuvres complètes*). Marthe's love for Louise saves the child, but in the most ironic manner possible. A heartbroken Louise leaves Chanteleu because of Marthe's words which she completely misunderstands, a situation typical of this novel of *amour inutile, amour refusé.* The girl sees Marthe at prayer, knows there is something terribly wrong, and wonders from what "mysterious evil" the woman is suffering:

> Tout à coup, dans le silence troublé seulement par une plainte assourdie, [Louise] distingua des paroles qui la glacèrent:—Cela me fait trop de mal de la voir . . . Elle ne sait pas et je suis trop faible. Ayez pitié d'elle et de moi . . . Louise porta la main à sa bouche pour étouffer un cri et s'en alla. Dans sa chambre, elle s'assit sur son lit et pensa: "Elle ne m'aime plus."

> (Suddenly, in the silence broken only by a muffled groan, Louise heard words which froze her to the spot: It hurts me too much to see her . . . She doesn't know and I'm too weak. Take pity on her and on me . . . Louise stifled a cry with her hand and hurried to her room. She sat on her bed and thought: "She doesn't love me anymore.")

Green's frequently expressed notion that words exist to

disguise thought and distort meaning and intention is poignantly illustrated here.

Le Mauvais Lieu is full of other ideas and themes typical of Julien Green's work. Louise, like many other Greenian characters, makes several moves but finds refuge nowhere. Like Adrienne Mesurat and Elisabeth of **Minuit,** she is strongly attracted to young workers and, like Adrienne, she spends a lot of time looking out of windows, daydreaming. There are the usual references to *taches lumineuses* on the floor made by sunlight streaming in through the windows. The seemingly-animated clothes in the attic closet come straight from Green's own childhood memory of his mother's closet. But the theme most typical of Green, one with which this novel is deeply imbued, is that of the devastation wrought by love. In his early twenties, while at the University of Virginia, Green made the following discovery:

> Tout à coup, la liberté m'était enlevée. A cause de quelqu'un que je n'avais vu que trois ou quatre secondes, je devenais un esclave . . . L'amour, je le voyais bien, était un malheur. (*Oeuvres complètes*)

> (Suddenly, I was no longer free. Because of someone I had seen for only three or four seconds, I became a slave. It was obvious to me that love was a bad thing.)

It does not take long for a beautiful face to cause irreparable damage to the human heart, both Green's and his characters'. This idea is both illustrated and expressed on several occasions in this work. Its most poignant expression is made to Louise by Perrotte, desperate at the thought of separation from the child: 'It is terrible to love someone.' Gustave has a similar notion: 'Love is hell. . . . ' The directress of Chanteleu, Léonie Dange, is described as being "in the twilight of a long existence in which love had played its devastating role." And love is, of course, the *mal mystérieux* with which Marthe Réau is afflicted.

But one may legitimately wonder if Julien Green wrote *Le Mauvais Lieu* simply to reiterate themes that are, by now, thoroughly familiar to his readers. Was he simply stating or showing yet again that love is hell, that the world is constantly on the attack against innocence, that too many Catholics lead lives of unthinking, superstitious habit? Or is it possible that the evil places and particularly Louise are symbols having nothing to do with morality? To suggest an answer to these questions, it is necessary to bear in mind two attributes of Louise that are of paramount importance: her muteness and her successful escape. It is also vital to realize that the real subject of most of Green's pondering, in his fiction, in his journal, and in his autobiography, is the profound mystery of literary creation. Milton Albrecht noted as early as 1948 [in "Psychological Motives in the Fiction of Julien Green," *Journal of Personality,* Vol. 16] that "Green's adult life is characterized . . . by devotion to the past, to art, literature, and his own creative efforts." Green is more tormented by human inability to communicate than by any other demon that plagues mankind. Even his obsession with splotches of light on

walls and floors is connected in his psyche with this problem. On 13 October 1945 he wrote:

> [J]'ai admiré la manière dont les maisons d'un côté de la rue . . . dessinaient leurs ombres inégales sur les façades du côté opposé. Il y avait là quelque chose qui échappait au langage humain, quelque chose que les mots ne pouvaient dire. Bien des fois . . . j'ai eu cette impression de l'inexprimable, mais rarement d'une façon aussi vive . . . je suis resté immobile devant ces maisons . . . qui parlaient aujourd'hui un langage nouveau. Et tout à coup j'ai été envahi d'une tristesse sans nom. Il n'y avait là, pourtant, rien de triste; rien que du soleil dorant de vieilles pierres sous un ciel gris. Mais cette tristesse venait d'ailleurs. (*Oeuvres complètes*)

> (I admired the way in which houses on one side of the street cast shadows of varying dimensions on the facades of the opposite side. There was something there that escaped human language, something that words could not express. Many times I have had that sensation of the ineffable, but rarely in such a vivid fashion. I remained motionless in front of those houses which that day were speaking a new language. And suddenly I was overwhelmed by a nameless sadness. However, there was nothing sad there, nothing but the sun gilding old stones under a gray sky. But that sadness came from somewhere else.)

It is farily clear that Green was forever frustrated by the fact that thought cannot be communicated as the purely spiritual thing it is, but must be clothed in the flesh of words. This idea is expressed in the **"Pamphlet"** in which Green states that thought is of divine essence; it is that which establishes the resemblance between the Creator and man. Thought intuits important things and struggles to free itself from the world: "All of its ties are out of this world, it knows this and struggles to free itself from the world" (*Oeuvres complètes*). Thought also struggles to free itself from the *word*. Green states in *Jeunesse* that the writing of the **"Pamphlet"** was a sexual act:

> On eût dit que le fait d'écrire devenait un acte sexuel . . . et que la chair se mêlait irrésistiblement à l'esprit dans ces moments qui semblaient exclure le désir. (*Oeuvres complètes*)

> (One would have thought that the act of writing was becoming a sexual act, that the flesh was becoming irresistibly mingled with the spirit in these moments that seemed to exclude sexual desire.)

In light of these statements, the following hypothesis becomes plausible: Louise, in her silence, in her purity, in her familiarity with Paradise, represents all of Green's deepest thoughts and feelings, thoughts that are incommunicable in their pure state; those around her represent his frustrated attempts at expressing these thoughts. They are the flesh that insists on imposing itself on these ideas. This perhaps would explain why every person in this strange novel feels sexual desire for Louise. In other words, sexual desire in this story represents a desire to communicate the ineffable. And the *mauvais lieu* is the body insofar as it is incapable of expressing the pure thought of the soul. It is not morally evil, but simply impotent. For Nicholas Kostis, the body as an obstacle to the salvation of the soul is a principal "theme around which the symbols of [Green's] novels are organized." I suggest that the obstacle is to the true, clear expression of thought. Louise's escape at the end of the novel signifies the perpetual elusiveness of successful communication. In other words, her success signifies Green's failure. This, I believe, is the central message of *Le Mauvais Lieu,* a message which does much to illuminate the anguish that permeates the entire body of Julien Green's work. (pp. 43-51)

Kathryn E. Wildgen, "Evil in Julien Green's 'Le Mauvais Lieu'," in Renascence, *Vol. XL, No. 1, Fall, 1987, pp. 43-52.*

Alfred Cismaru   (essay date 1989)

[*A French-born American, Cismaru is a professor of French, Italian, and Spanish who has published several studies on notable French writers. In the following essay, he discusses Green's views on such matters as women, sexuality, politics, and religion.*]

It is always sad to read a celebrated person's memoirs. Such an activity brings inescapably to mind the fact that a life is near its end; and that near the end there is no looking straight forward anymore, nor to the future, but only backwards. One realizes, too, that the writer's inspiration has probably run its course and finds nothing new to express, except, perhaps, some additional or different comments on what has taken place already, in the past. Action is reduced to looking at action, as contemplation, the forerunner of passivity, preceeds the angel of death.

All this is better than silence, of course, and there is a long tradition in French letters that a famous author does not stop writing until the very last moment. For example, Jean-Paul Sartre, in his seventies, dictated when he could no longer see well enough to put pen to paper; Simone de Beauvoir, in her late seventies, wrote even when hospitalized for weeks at a time and continued to publish assiduously, keeping editors and readers interested from her bed; Samuel Beckett, in his eighties, composes play after novel after play, although no longer at the rate of about one title per year as he used to when he was merely in his seventies; Eugéne Ionesco, a septuagenarian now himself, writes, directs and even acts on several of the world's stages. And these are only contemporary examples. One could go back to Victor Hugo and Chateaubriand, to Voltaire and Rousseau, and even earlier, to many other French writers of repute who proved not merely that senescence is only a state of mind, but that the exercise of memory and introspection can keep the mind alive even after inspiration has been tamed by time.

Not long ago Julien Green published his monumental historical novel, *Frère François* (1985). It was an astonishingly popular work both with reviewers and readers, even though it was the product of an eighty-five-year-old person, who has a reputation of being very Catholic, often obscure, and always a writer who directs his efforts towards the upper level of the intelligentsia. Only three years later, at the even more advanced age of 89, he showed that he

is still capable of surprising his *aficionados* by yet another title, *L'Arc-en-ciel, Journal 1981-1984* which appeared in the bookstores in May 1988. At the time of this writing there is no English translation of it, but by August 1988, in France and in French-speaking countries the book has already sold more copies than any of Green's previous titles, and more than any text by an American expatriate in France to date.

It will be recalled that a few years ago, when Julien Green became a candidate for membership in the French Academy, he refused to give up his American passport and thus fulfill the requirement that all members must be French citizens. The French people, then, considering that extreme merit surpasses the importance of rigorous and long-standing laws, supported enthusiastically a bill introduced in Parliament which made an exception in the case of the American writer and allowed him to join the forty Immortals. These events are mentioned in this context because they reveal his popularity abroad, one not always enjoyed with the American public which is ever so reluctant to bestow an aura of glory upon the head of a writer of genius (an examination of the reasons for such reluctance is best left to another essay).

The word *Journal* in Green's title does not mean autobiography. George Bernard Shaw, who did not mince words, said often that such a presumptuous enterprise can only contain lies: not inescapable ones, but rather willed and deliberate because, as he put it, "No writer ever takes off his pants in order to reveal a minuscule genital construction." To be sure, an author will sometimes tell his faults, even the great ones, but he will always do so in order to show his superiority over those who go astray and never confess; or else, he will dwarf his great sins by listing his still greater virtues. In addition, such a confessor is always cognizant of the fact that an error aired tends to be forgiven by those who find the confession of others personally cathartic. Julien Green, however, is not the Romantic writer à la Rousseau or Chateaubriand, who told in order to praise themselves and to rise about their readers who did not dare do likewise. Although he does not like Ernest Renan for political and religious reasons, he quotes the author of *The Origin of Language* and reveals the why and the how of his first-person narration: "Childhood, youth, and adulthood have powerful but confused intuitions; only the clear light of old age can analyse them."

From the vantage point of distance, then, the author ponders over his narcissism, over the simplifications of the psychoanalysts who had attempted an exegesis, and on the reasons of writing, above all, for he considers it the most solitary, the most painful, and yet the most exorcising of all human activities. The introspection of a *journal,* however, is replete with barred windows through which it is impossible to escape or to see clearly. At best, the blurred vision afforded the writer by the poor light is revelatory of only vague landscapes filled with fog and low, floating clouds. It is difficult to peer through these clouds, and when you catch a glimpse of something the vision is fleeting, the memory of it uncertain. For example, does narcissism precede homsexuality, or is it the cause of it? Is homosexuality the best way to avoid, albeit in part, the curse of *others,* those who breathe your oxygen, who poison you with their carbon dioxide and who commit the highest atrocity of all, that of judging? Or is homosexuality simply a first step towards masturbatory, therefore ultimate self-sufficiency? And, finally, is the latter what others call freedom, without realizing that theirs, because it is not masturbatory, is dependent on laws and on the good will of their fellow men whom, in their weakness, they cannot help but need?

Some of the *others,* women for example, Julien Green considers as utter abominations. They are the ones who become glued to you and who do not let go. They can be appreciated as nurses, he opines, or as mothers of very young children, but in all other endeavors they are all liars. In a novel which was published a year before the *Journal,* but on which Julien Green had been working for many years, *Les Pays lointains,* woman's duplicity is related in caustic, even brutal terms. In the more than nine hundred pages of the text he tells the story of a young girl in the state of Georgia during the Civil War. She falls in love with an immigrant from Austria who returns to his native country in order to marry another woman. On the rebound, she marries another man whom she does not love, then appears to forget her first infatuations and to fall in love deeply with her husband—only to continue corresponding with her former boyfriend to whom she sends passionate letters. Can a woman love more than one man at a time? Of course, the author thinks, and not just two, but any number within reach because "she has been cursed with the uncontrollable need of sexual satisfaction at any cost."

Even holy women are prey to this need. In fact, the more holy they are, the more they are apt to cause the perdition of even the holiest men. In *Frère François,* for example, he told how much Saint Francis had suffered at the hands of Sainte Claire. He was twelve years older than she when they had met, but she drew his attention through self-effacement and through apparent mortification of her flesh. Only the flesh, in a female, Julien Green strongly believes, is always stronger than the soul:

> To be sure, as a child she lived a quasi-angelic existence. One of her most characteristic traits was her desire not to be seen by anyone. Moreover, under the silky, elegant clothes in which she was dressed by her rich parents, next to her skin she would wear another article of clothing made of rough, Cilician goat hair. In secret, she always found a way of putting aside and then giving to the poor some of the elaborate dishes served at her table. In secret, too, she would spend hours praying, much as a mature and devoted nun.

But, Julien Green went on to comment, in a woman, basic, animal carnality always fights back and always wins. That is why she later lured Saint Francis into secret meetings, even though he was scared of her and even though he had interdicted the monks of his own order to speak to women or to practice any other intercourse with those "luring creatures, so dangerous and so bound to lead even the strongest to utter perdition."

Boldly, in *Frère François* Julien Green had discussed fac-

ets of the life of Saint Francis which are usually left out by other biographers. He had probed his hero's *fall* and had tried to rationalize it. Sure, it was prudent to avoid women; facing them, however, and then resisting their bewitchment, must have appeared to him to be the braver course of action. Yet, the trap extended by Claire was unavoidable. Since they had met often in the woods, the biographer concluded to the possibility of real love between the two, even of sexual intercourse. After all, on 18 March 1212 did not Claire furtively leave her parents' home and take refuge in the Saint Mary of the Angels Church where Francis was waiting for her? And did he not, after all, go through the unprecedented gestures (because a much lesser prelate was usually in charge of such chores) of shaving her head, of taking custody of her clothes, and of seeing to it that she was clad in Franciscan garb? The author's insistence on such events in long, orphic passages explains, perhaps, his later conclusion in the *Journal* that "women love men just as the Germans love France: they must invade it."

Of course, there is a great deal more in the *Journal* than the writer's misogyny. Throughout there is the antithesis of Catholicism emerging from Protestantism; of an American in love with the language of Montaigne; of an introvert who has very precise opinions about things and people and who, when facing only the blank paper in front of him, is not at all shy about expressing his thoughts with astonishing vigor. When discussing his colleagues, for example, his comments are often without charity. André Gide is castigated not only for not knowing English, but also for ignoring Anglo-Saxon literature. André Malraux is seen as a petty Communist in his youth, while his later conversion to the extreme right is considered dubious and of little importance. Jean-Paul Satre is also guilty of leftist political views and of atheism, although he is somewhat redeemed by his generosity vis-à-vis the poor and the disadvantaged.

The author is equally intolerant when mentioning his Catholic *confrères:* Gabriel Marcel caused merely a few waves in his lifetime, while being properly ignored by contemporary generations; and Paul Claudel, of devout reputation, nevertheless wrote often about God as if the two had been in the habit of sharing a bottle of wine together in some neighborhood bar. Only François Mauriac is held in high esteem for he alone, Green points out, mastered the art of appearing to sympathize with the plight of women's submissiveness to husbands, while all the time he showed how the Thérèses of this world poison men spiritually and physically.

There is less vigor in the writer's comments about the political events which he noted between 1981 and 1984. It is as if he considers a certain amount of aloofness superior to Sartrean-like commitment. He estimates that few historical happenings are actually meritorious of an artist's attention. The latter might indeed be affected by some, such as world wars, or economic catastrophies, but the smaller events that he witnesses hardly deserve his scrutiny. To be sure, in the period covered certain tropisms draw the attention of those who have little better to do, or those who find their own passivity tolerable by facing the activity of of others. The lazy might be drawn by the Romantic revolt in Poland which, in fact, does not profit the Polish people at all. They might draw catharsis from the epic voyage of the British fleet to reconquer the Malouine Islands, a reconquest devoid of even the most minimal significance. Those who fight Communism from the comfort of their living room, armchair strategically placed in front of the television set, might be properly shocked by the blind fury of Brejnev, and properly gladdened by his death, but a tyrant is only replaced by another, he thinks, and little, if anything, ever changes.

Actually, Julien Green has little hope for the world, which, he opines, is bent on self-destruction because it is so disgusted with itself. How else can one explain, he asks, drugs, cults, mass suicides, and false prophets forecasting dooms and amassing millions? Governments do not want to deal with these problems because politicians know they have no power except that of lulling the governed to sleep and opening Swiss bank accounts while the somnolent let them rule. And as for the Vatican itself, the only authority having a God-given chance and responsibility to save humanity, little can be expected from it because it too is infiltrated with politicians concerned only with the preservation of their own riches and power. The author even goes so far as to lend credence to a long-standing suspicion in Europe that "the best Pope of our time, Jean-Paul I" was assassinated with the full consent of many cardinals who had objected to the Pontiff's habit of giving Church money to the poor.

In fact, Julien Green questions the necessity of vast treasures being in the hands of the Vatican, and even wonders why there is no privatization of Vatican-owned businesses and sale of works of art which now adorn churches and museums controlled by the Holy See. How many thousands of people, he asks, would eat well and for weeks with the proceeds from one single painting? Yet, not far from such questions are descriptions of his travels to Italy, Germany, and Spain during the period covered, where he revisits museums and looks again at this or that favorite canvas. He does not question the lay governments' control of the latter, nor does he suggest that they be sold for abatement of social problems.

To be sure, there are many passages in the *Journal* which reveal the writer's contradictions, stemming from the powerful struggle, within him, of opposing forces, some on the winning side at one time, some victorious at another. It is not clear that hindsight manages to throw more light on these contradictions, or on earlier ideas and activities. More often than not, persons age without changing, and it is difficult to note, as time passes, any remarkable reverses in Green's personality. Memory recalls past events, and the rest of the mind explains or defends them. As the writer proceeds, however, defense winds up being a great deal more important than explanation. After all, it is eminently difficult to admit that one could have thought or could have done differently. To admit it, would be, partly, to negate one's past; and since, when writing memoirs there is very little time left, the loss would be unacceptable.

On the other hand, Green's efforts are sincere for he does

wish and does set out to dissect, as objectively as possible, the earlier development of his ideas and of his career. If his explanations are not always satisfying, or if they fall short of the highest expectations, it may be that, as alluded to above, the vehicle selected is not the most propitious. It may also be that the already mentioned antithetical background of the autobiographer precludes a totally conclusive exegesis. Other writer's memoirs, those in whose personal history there is only one religion and only one country, must surely have an easier task. On the contrary, Green, the Protestant-turned-Catholic and the American-become-almost-French, has to deal with complexities which often remain cryptic in spite of one's best efforts. Nevertheless, the *L' Arc-en-ciel, Journal 1981-1984* adds considerably to our knowledge of one of the most profound and durable novelists of our time. (pp. 136-41)

Alfred Cismaru, "Julien Green's 'Journal': A Contemporary Look Backwards," in Mid-American Review, *Vol. IX, No. 2, 1989, pp. 136-42.*

Patrick Lindsay Bowles (review date 17 May 1991)

[*In the following review, Bowles assesses Green's* Oeuvres complètes, Tome 6; Journal du voyageur; *and* The Distant Lands.]

In 1979, Julien Green (b 1900) received a letter from a well-wisher, beginning, "As you are soon to depart into the realm of the invisible . . .". Notwithstanding that diapasonal *bon voyage*, M Green, having already produced an *oeuvre* that many 120-year-olds might well envy, is marking the start of his ninth decade with the publication of over 3,000 pages of work, including a 900-page novel, *The Distant Lands,* completed in his mid-eighties; [*Oeuvres complètes, Tome 6,*] the sixth volume of his complete works in the Pléiade (putting him, somewhat absurdly, one volume ahead of Proust); and a travel album, *Journal du voyageur*—both texts and photographs by the author—spanning over half a century, Green having travelled widely (and always with his Bible) since his youth, frequently, as he says with rather disarming ingenuousness, "for sexual reasons".

The *éminence rose* of world letters, Green has a special place, next to Bloy, Péguy, Bernanos, Claudel and Mauriac, on the shelves of every thinking Christian. If he has consciously avoided what he calls the "frivolity" of turning religion, or for that matter sex, into a "mere literary subject", both of these themes rumble beneath the surface of his work like a thorough-bass. They are rather more on the surface than usual in the latest Pléiade volume, which, although it contains no fiction or theatre, quaintly juxtaposes an excellent biography of St Francis, a credo (*Ce qu'il faut d'amour à l'homme*) and scattered references to Pusey and Pevsner and papal encyclicals and Kierkegaard on the one hand, with, on the other, a couple of rather funny anti-hetero jokes, some wan day-dreaming on a bull ("what a colossal hullabaloo of meat that must be in action") and the description of a journal which Green started keeping in his early twenties, when one could have set a clock by his nocturnal forays as surely as by Kant's constitutionals: ("Every night at eight-thirty, I had an appointment with the Devil"). For many years he stowed what were, by his own account, throbbingly monotonous and maniacally precise descriptions of each and every one of his encounters in a notebook, now, alas, lost.

The indispensable autobiographical writings, interviews and prefaces (by diverse hands) also included [in the *Oeuvres complètes*] provide an outline of the principal erotic and religious stages on life's way: Green's first sexual experience cut, almost literally, short when, at five years old, having fondled himself, his knife-wielding mother emerged into the candlelight and threatened unanaesthetized amputation (this did not affect his lifelong devotion to the memory of his mother, who died in 1914, but it certainly elucidates his famous, matter-of-fact assertion that the normal outcome of eroticism is murder); his conversion to Catholicism at sixteen (he was christened in the American Cathedral in Paris, an Anglican church); his awakening, a few years later, to his homosexuality at, appropriately enough, the University of Virginia, and his initiation thereunto at twenty-three in, appropriately enough, Paris. This blend of the prurient and the pious, while unusual, is not, of course, unique. From the thrawn theologies of Huysmans and Rozanov to John Updike's Rabbit-breeding Redeemer, modern fiction and nonfiction alike are full of cloven-hooved angels and mystic roués, some of whom (Rasputin, for example) are standard figures of pop mythology. Yet the image that glows forth from this volume, of the young Green leaving his parents' flat in the rue de Passy every night, walking down to Trocadéro and along the banks of the Seine, sometimes as far as Notre-Dame, cruising for wild boys with a rosary or the Book of Job in his pocket, not only prophesies the grandiose dereliction of Genet, it embodies more pathetically and precisely than perhaps any other human image in modern letters the mystery of the *sacer.*

The other, more famous, journal—here covering the period from 1972 to 1981—is breathtaking in scope: sixty years of "whatever pops into my head": notes on luncheons with kings, doctors' appointments, landlord problems, lexicographical debates at the French Academy, literature, travel and current events (a nice passage on the death of Elvis). If by the sky-high standard of Gide's journal, some of this does sound a bit like Pierian spring-cleaning ("How to shorten my novel?" he wonders at one point without revealing a solution) and some of the entries are taken up with head-scratching over what to enter, Green remains a modern Pepys, with a jeweller's eye for the droll or macabre anecdote: the mayor of Milan replying to Napoleon, who had just said that all Italians were thieves, "Non tutti ma una buonaparte"; the Oxford dons elevating a cat to the status of dog *honoris causa* to avoid its removal from their college; a girl brutally murdered in Central Park whose final observation in the diary she was carrying read "Nothing ever happens to me"; or the saintly Jacques Maritain leaving his heart to America in his will, only to be told that it had first to be disinfected.

A dust-jacket describes the author as "Julien Green, Julien Green, American citizen, French writer, French Academician, English writer". Although Green has written

quite infrequently in what is, strictly speaking, his mother's tongue (but not his mother tongue), we do have a good sampling of it here in *The Language and its Shadow,* some exercises in self-translation, with English and French texts on facing pages. In a preface to these writings, called, mysteriously, "experiments", Giovanni Lucera makes some wildly extravagant claims for Green's bilingualism, although Lucera, who says "last not least", speaks, in a footnote, of "Mounbatten" and evokes the "deplorable" (why not terrifying?) accent of New Yorkers, may not be the best judge of English currently alive. There would seem to be some confusion too in Green's own mind about his adopted idiom. When Jane Birkin interviewed him last October for *Femme* magazine, she was surprised to hear him speak with an Irish accent. "My mother was from Kent", he explained. Prim at best, and peg-legged at worst, the English on display in the Pléiade selections is so over-cautious and so lacks the lilt and spin of authentic English that, where one might want to give the benefit of the doubt between a misprint and ignorance to a Nabokov or a Kosinski, one regretfully hesitates to do so for Green.

Completing the Pléiade volume are some occasional pieces and a chronology for the years 1972-85, comically—no writer has ever been more efficiently embalmed before his death—complete: (November 12, 1980: Green undergoes knee operation by Dr Judet. December 22, 1980: Dr Judet dies. January 23, 1981: Julian Green is back on his feet. "I am walking normally now, without a cane." March 1982: At Oxford, Green working in the Bodleian).

The image of the cultured French writer among the sexually hospitable savages of exotic lands is a grand iconological tradition: Rimbaud in Abyssinia, Gide in the Congo, Green at Oxford. And in the *Journal du voyageur* we have, far more than in *The Language and its Shadow,* an excellent example of how truly, uniquely cosmopolitan Green is, as he captures the disturbing beauty of local youth and some of the architectural niceties of Christendom with pleasantly conventional snapshots and fine descriptions of fifty dream destinations (Oxford, Siena, Venice, *et al*). Even the one or two mortally boring destinations here included, such as Hammerfest in Norway, are so beautifully described as to make one want to set off at once. It is a collection of ideal postcards from an ideal friend, the perfect thing for a summer-house. Plans to include a series of Green's photographic studies of Greek statues were cancelled. Judging from the single example of these included here, a marmoreal bottom taken in 1937, that is a pity.

Finally, *The Distant Lands,* a black Catholic antebellum romance begun in the 1930s as an *hommage* to the author's mother, "herself a Southern belle", abandoned *en route* when *Gone with the Wind* was published, and taken up again in 1984. Set in Georgia and Virginia from 1850 to 1853, it is the story of sixteen-year-old Elizabeth, a blonde aristocrat from Devonshire who arrives with her mad, ruined mother to live with cousins at Dimwood, the family plantation. It contains every delicious cliché of the genre, from the moonlight and magnolias on page one to the obliquely Oedipal ending. Elizabeth falls in love with one man, marries another, duels are fought, Negro spirituals are sung, fried chicken is eaten, babies are born, a dog barks. In addition to Elizabeth, who goes from wilting English solipsist "with a tendency to see in the visible world a kind of hallucinatory phenomenon" to Americanized can-do widow-with-a-whip, there are a prophesying, odoriferous Welsh witch, a half-breed *fidei defensor,* the bland Aunt Laura, vehicle of the implicit and wayward Catholic apologia. Add a family tree at the end to tidy up the sometimes complicated relationships, and you have this saga of doodah *Angst* and crinolined schizophrenia.

There are two major problems with **The Distant Lands.** One of these is the translation. Even if we overlook the dozens (upon dozens) of mistranslations, notably of *faux amis* like *susceptible* and *sauvage;* and the fact that the Southern characters, who are said to speak with a drawl, sound uniformly and teddibly British (indeed, some sound positively Woosterish: " 'My word,' said Uncle Douglas, 'it's dreadfully like a wedding cake.' " Uncle Charlie says "jolly good!" and "poor old chap"), there is still the insurmountable problem, in every paragraph, of translatorese: "That very formal, respectable behaviour that had survived the languor of the waltz gave way now to that familiarity that passes for dangerous." "War emerged from words proffered millions of times, it sufficed for there to be sufficient of them." "He about whom you must no longer think is looking for you in the gardens." This is, to be fair, less the fault of the translator than of the publisher, who has seen the book into print without having seen the book.

The second problem exists in the French original (**Les Pays lointains,** first published in 1987). Even if the translator calls *argent massif* "massive silver", it is not she but Green who, rather than, for example, letting us catch quite offhandedly a glimpse of the *poinçon* on a single fork, trundles out the sterling on every possible occasion and says, each time, that it is sterling. It is not the translator but Green whose shameless repetitiveness, whose posh vulgarity and whose outrageous padding finally, here as in far too much of his work, obscure his true gifts as a master of chiaroscuro and a peerless story-teller. Gide, as usual, got it exactly right when he wrote in 1929: "It's almost as if he didn't really care. The main thing for Green is to plough ahead until he can finally get to the parts where his true power shines through, where that special dark genius of his, once it does shine through, puts him with the very best."

Patrick Lindsay Bowles, "When He Was Good . . . ," in The Times Literary Supplement, *No. 4598, May 17, 1991, p. 6.*

Joan Aiken   (review date 29 September 1991)

[*Aiken is an English novelist, short story writer, dramatist, poet, and author of children's literature. In the following review, she characterizes* The Distant Lands *as an entertaining but somewhat superficial depiction of Southern life.*]

I always enjoy the kind of novel that opens with the poor orphan girl's arrival at the house of wealthy relatives, where she has to be kitted out in someone else's cast-off clothes; but it must be said at once that Elizabeth Escridge is a most exasperating heroine, continually stamping her foot and asserting that she is a brave English girl. It is fortunate that she is so stunningly beautiful and golden-haired, or how could her cousins endure her disagreeable ways and her total self-absorption?

The year is 1850, the place Savannah, Ga., and Elizabeth and her mother have just come, stony-broke, from England. The pace of [**The Distant Lands**] is so wonderfully leisurely that we do not in fact learn until page 621 precisely what happened in England to send the ladies overseas; and it is not until page 807 that Elizabeth loses her virginity; but never mind, there they are, settling into the great plantation house, Dimwood, all Spanish moss and live-oaks. There's also a sinister grove, the Wood of the Damned, haunted by ghosts of Seminole and Creek Indians, massacred in earlier centuries, an equally alligator-infested river, and a mysterious little circular, windowless room with a skylight made from alabaster, which no one ever remains in for more than a few minutes.

People at Dimwood are frequently given to saying things like, "Never ask me that, child!" or "Certain things are not mentioned in this house." Indeed, the whole place creaks with mystery. What happened to Cousin Laura? Who is the mysterious lady, swathed in white, who appears from time to time, riding round the property, escorted by wicked Jonathan Armstrong, rightful owner of Dimwood, whose father Harold frittered away a fortune and was obliged to sell out to the Hargroves? Why does Uncle William Hargrove go into a tremor every time he lays eyes on Elizabeth, "his little English violet"? Why is Elizabeth's mother called Mrs. Escridge when she was married to Sir Cyril, so presumably ought to be Lady Escridge? Why do people keep taking other people away to their bedrooms in a meaningful and confidential way, and then not divulging anything in particular, but merely issuing vague warnings, such as "You will be careful, won't you? *Do you understand me?*" To which the answer is invariably, "Yes . . . no." Or: "Shall I tell you who made me so unhappy?" To which the answer is simply, "No."

People suddenly embark on long explanations of family feuds: Aunt Maisie had a terrible row with Aunt Amelia, over the household accounts, and the two sisters have not entered each other's houses from that day to this; one is, from time to time, irresistibly reminded of Jane Austen's "long and minute detail of past adventures and sufferings in which the worthlessness of lords and attornies might be set forth; and conversations which had passed twenty years before be minutely repeated."

We are told that American-born Julian Green, who is a writer immensely respected both in England and in France (where he lives, and has been elected a member of the Académie Française) began this monumental antebellum novel back in the '30s. Then he apparently learned that Margaret Mitchell was undertaking something of the same kind, so abandoned his manuscript for 50 years. One can't help wondering whether also, possibly, he came across a copy of Stella Gibbon's classic *Cold Comfort Farm* (1932) and wondered if its satire on the gothic cut just a little too close to what he was producing. One would dearly like to know whether he had completed the entire 902-page oeuvre when he put it away, or whether he broke off in the middle, but left an outline of how he intended the story to continue.

At any rate, no visible join can be detected; the story proceeds smoothly on its apparently meandering, inconsequential (but highly readable) course. Immense meals are eaten, always off snowy-white cloths laden with shining silver; mint juleps are drunk; much of the family conversation is taken up with the possibility of war (still 10 years ahead however); and the English poor relations are often warned always to be civil to the slaves, for we don't want a revolt.

Exasperating Elizabeth falls in love with wicked Jonathan, after one glimpse of him through a magnolia-screened verandah. And other people fall in love with her. Fred does. Billy does. Daniel does. Uncle Will lusts after her. Ted does. Ned does. As Aunt Charlotte remarks, in a pensive tone: "Life . . . It's a good job there is laudanum to help us put up with it." Lots of ladies take laudanum in *The Distant Lands,* and Miss Charlotte distils her own, in the washroom, from the very best ingredients.

People are always warning Elizabeth. Old Souligou, the West Indian seamstress, has premonitions, and tells her fortune on Tarot cards, concealing the Hanged Man. Miss Llewellyn, the sinister Welsh housekeeper, shows her how to perform a magic rite with a scroll of paper and a lock of hair, which will bring her heart's desire but death in its wake.

It is impossible not to make fun of this book, and impossible not to admire it also. What an opus! Imagine launching out on those nine hundred and two pages. (*Gone With the Wind* has 1,037, but then *Gone With the Wind* included the Civil War, while *The Distant Lands* stops 10 years short of it.)

What this novel can marvelously evoke for the reader is the excruciating, intolerable boredom and misery of adolescence. Elizabeth Escridge may not be a likeable heroine, but by golly she will strike a chord in the heart of all as she scribbles letters alternately to both her loves (most of which will not get posted, but some, unfortunately, will) and snaps at poor old black Betty and is rude to Uncle Charlie. She is a young cousin of Emma Bovary. Perhaps it was this endemic boredom, this chronic languor in the South (also most marvelously and nostalgically called up) that finally catapulted the region into the War between the States? Because no one could endure the monotony another day, and war was preferable to endless inertia with a mint julep and a palm leaf fan?

Julian Green conveys all this at the start with a gluey relish. "Suddenly the indescribable was everywhere, consuming the air . . . Finding oneself on the edge of a precipice would not have been as hard as this. An eternity of damnation was setting itself where time had flowed freely an instant earlier."

I have a feeling that, in the earlier version, the writer had stopped short of the conclusion, and that when he did finish the book, it was in a different, and considerably more

ironic frame of mind. There is a wonderfully funny conversation between Ned and his father, in which Papa advises Ned not to let his wife experience sexual pleasure.

> "It's preferable for it to be that way with women," Charlie Jones continued gravely. "Otherwise there is a danger of them turning into . . . mmm . . . nymphomaniacs . . . "
>
> "But that's monstrous, Papa. What do these wretches do?"
>
> *"They write novels."* (My italics)

This strikes me as a different, and more tongue-in-cheek voice, than that at the start of the book. And the conclusion, when it comes, is quite startlingly sudden, with a duel in the Wood of the Damned (we are now back in Georgia), two deaths, and Elizabeth left alone to mourn in her Savannah mansion, and to bring up little Charles-Edward who bears an unfortunate likeness to the wrong one of the two duellists.

And we never do discover precisely what happened to poor Aunt Laura's quadroon daughter. But at least she will inherit Dimwood and its malign housekeeper.

This is the sort of novel that, in the happy old days, would have been gloriously serialized in women's weekly magazines in 119 parts. Maybe it still will. Anyway I am sure it will give a great deal of pleasure to anybody prepared to undertake it.

The novel was written in French and translated by Barbara Beamount, who does a good job, but sometimes falls into present-day idiom such as "Uncle Douglas was keeping his cool."

> Joan Aiken, "Mysteries and Magnolias," in Book World—The Washington Post, *September 29, 1991, p. 5.*

Henri Peyre on Green:

The originality of Julien Green lies in his total disregard of literary trends and fashions and in his aloofness from all groups, theories, and schools. He is one of the most cultured of contemporary novelists, at home in the world of painting and of music, in love with English and French poetry, a student of religion. His *Journal* may well some day rank above that of Gide for its psychological penetration, for its spiritual profundity, and for the incisiveness of literary opinions modestly offered on writers of the past and, more discreetly and never in a spirit of slander or cant, on contemporary writers.

> Henri Peyre, in his French Novelists of Today, *1955, reprinted in 1967.*

John Weightman   (essay date 5 December 1991)

[*In the following essay, Weightman assesses the significance of* South, The Distant Lands, Paris, *and* Adrienne Mesurat *in Green's oeuvre.*]

Julian, or Julien, Green, an American born and brought up in Paris, is one of the most unusual figures in contemporary French literature. He is probably—after the eighteenth-century *philosophe* Fontenelle, who lived to be a hundred—the longest surviving French-language author known to history. He was ninety-one on the sixth of September; he made his mark in 1926 with his first novel, ***Mont-Cinère,*** and he is still writing. Indeed, he is probably the most prolific French author of the century, since he has produced not only novels, plays, polemical writings, critical essays, and biographies, but also, in addition to a lengthy autobiography, many volumes of an ongoing diary, the published part of which is apparently only a fragment of the full text, much of which is being held in reserve during his lifetime. And, more significantly, he is at once Catholic and homosexual; his Catholicism is fervent, and his homosexuality has been open since the early 1950s.

A relatively small portion of his vast output has been published in English, and then only sporadically over the years. It follows that, although Green's name is known in the English-speaking world, he has not hitherto enjoyed the general fame accorded to François Mauriac, the Catholic novelist to whom he is perhaps nearest in religious sensibility, or the notoriety of André Gide, who preceded him in the prewar years as a declared homosexual. In France, he has always had his faithful readers, who ensured him a solid *succès d'estime;* he has won many literary prizes and, in 1972, he was elected to the Académie Française, in succession precisely to Mauriac. Recently, however, there has been a change in his status. In extreme old age, and as the sole survivor of the prewar literary generation, he has entered upon a sort of Indian Summer of celebrity in his Parisian setting. He has made some successful television appearances and, according to his publishers, the first two volumes (***Pays Lointains*** and ***Les Etoiles du Sud***) of the trilogy on which he is now working have become best sellers in France and on the European continent.

This no doubt explains why two American publishers, thinking that the time is ripe for a more general recognition of Green's talent, have simultaneously decided to represent him to the English-language audience. Marion Boyars has chosen the first volume of the trilogy now in progress, together with ***Paris,*** a collection of essays written at intervals since 1945, and ***South,*** a play first published in 1953. Holmes and Meier have reissued a revised version of the original English version of the novel ***Adrienne Mesurat,*** which dates back to 1927. We are dealing, then, with four texts, written at long intervals over more than half a century, and it is logical to ask how coherent a picture they present of Green, and whether they show him in his most characteristic and interesting light.

I confess that my reaction is rather negative. To begin with, the four books are so different from one another in tone and theme that they cannot be easily comprehensible to readers unfamiliar with the complex strands of Green's Franco-American, Protestant-cum-Catholic, Catholic-cum-homosexual makeup. In fact, they might seem, at first sight, to be from the hands of two, or perhaps three, different writers.

Paris is a collection of nostalgic prose poems, devoted to various topographical aspects of the French capital, where Green was born, and where he has lived most of his life. It is illustrated with a score of photographs taken by the author himself. The tone is mainly elegiac, contrasting the charm of the old Paris of his childhood with the brashness of the new, and the style is exquisitely literary in a traditional French manner. The book is good of its kind; it will please lovers of "fine writing," but it is more of a pious tribute to the evanescent *genius loci* than a vital part of Green's output. The author sounds so completely French that he might have no connection with America at all, witness the highly rhetorical hymn to the river Seine, of which I quote a few sentences:

> "I am the road running through Paris," says the Seine. "I have carried off many images since you were a child and reflected many clouds. I am changeable, but as people are: I have my moments of happiness in the June dawn and my sinister times some December evenings. Above all, I am inquisitive—you call it being in flood. We have something in common, you everlasting passers-by and I, the fleeing water, which is that we never go back: your time is my space.

> "The lights my surface has reflected! My memory is a great kaleidoscope in which you will find all that has gone to make up the history of your century. . . ."

The Distant Lands exploits a totally different local color. It is set in the American South on the eve of the Civil War, and it could be described as a romantic blockbuster in the style of *Gone with the Wind.* The heroine is a spirited, aristocratic English girl who, after being impoverished by her father's death, is taken to live with her rich American relations. The theme is her education in southern ways, and her gradual awakening to love. There is an abundance of white-colonnaded houses, tree-lined avenues, Spanish moss, magnolias, full moons, picturesque slaves, southern beauties, and dashing young men.

Green says he began the book in the Thirties, but put it aside after the appearance of Margaret Mitchell's best seller, to which it was too close in subject matter. However, I think we can assume that, had he completed it then, it would have been very different from the book it now is. He must have written the bulk of the present text in his eighties. The typical novels of his early and middle periods are all extremely somber psychological dramas, set in grim claustrophobic households either in France or America, and full of dark passions, murders, suicides, and madness. ***The Distant Lands*** is, by comparison, quite sunny, as if, in old age, Green had sloughed off most of his previous pessimism and had entered a more indulgent, and perhaps self-indulgent, phase.

True, the tragedy of the Civil War is about to happen; two of the young men kill each other in a duel; there are unhappy love affairs and various frustrations, but the tone is overwhelmingly romantic in the more facile, sentimental sense, with ghosts, premonitions, fortunetellers, coincidences, and so on. The book is pleasant enough to read, but I cannot see it as part of Green's serious contribution to literature; it is rather an entertainment with which he has filled his later years and, if it is already a best seller on the European continent, this may well be because it appeals to a middlebrow audience, for whom he never wrote in his somber prime. However, I may mention that it did not make much of an impression when it appeared in England a year ago.

Of the four works under review, only two are fully characteristic of what I take to be the essential Green—the novel *Adrienne Mesurat* (1927) and the play *South* (1953)—but they too may seem very remote from each other. The first is set in an unnamed French provincial town in the days of horse-drawn carriages, that is, presumably before the First World War, and tells the bleak story of a frustrated girl who kills her father and goes mad. *South,* on the other hand, is almost a companion piece to *The Distant Lands,* in the sense that it too is set in the American South on the eve of the Civil War, but it is as remorselessly grim as *The Distant Lands* is romantically superficial. It may also seem puzzling, because the motivation of the characters cannot be entirely clear to uninstructed readers.

To understand what the play is really about, one has to be familiar with the central sexual-cum-religious obsession in Green's life, and its connections with his Franco-American background. These complexities also have a bearing on the unadulterated pessimism of *Adrienne Mesurat.* In fact, I don't think any of Green's readers could have guessed what his fundamental concern was until he began publishing his confessional writings in middle life. Since it has to be explained, I will try to summarize the issue as briefly as possible, drawing not only on the diary, but also on the three-volume autobiography (*Partir avant le jour,* 1963; *Mille chemins ouverts,* 1964; *Terre Lointaine,* 1966), only the first volume of which appears to have been translated.

Green has a dramatically divided personality, but he is probably more French than American. Although English was spoken in the Green household in Paris, all Julian's schooling was in French up to the pre-university stage, so that French is his dominant language, and the only literary medium in which he feels completely at home. It will be generally agreed, I think, that he is a considerable stylist in the traditional French classical manner. He has, incidentally, made some very interesting comments, in the diary and elsewhere, on the problem of double identity, which may afflict individuals brought up simultaneously in two languages.

However, in his case, the linguistic dichotomy is only one of several. On the American side, while he admits to having been enormously influenced by Nathaniel Hawthorne, an author who might seem far removed from the atmosphere of the American South, Green is first and foremost a southerner with an old-fashioned, antebellum sensibility. This is a result of his family connections and, more especially, of the influence of his adored mother, who instilled southern patriotism into him in childhood. His parents came of rich southern stock, but after his father lost his fortune through misguided speculation, a wealthy uncle

volunteered to finance Julian's studies at the University of Virginia from 1919 to 1922. These three years were tremendously important for his career, and we might say that he has lived on them ever since. He absorbed the southern local color, which he has used several times, usually showing it through the eyes of an ambiguous insider/outsider like himself. But above all, in the company of his fellow students at the University of Virginia, he suffered the homosexual temptations and the pangs of unrequited love on which he was to ring the changes—at first in a disguised form, then later more or less openly—in so many structurally similar plots.

Like the tension between his French and American loyalties, the tug-of-war between religion and sex also began in childhood, but with much more serious consequences. His strong-minded and anxiously puritanical mother brought him up as a pious Anglican, with daily Bible readings in English and prayers at her knee. She had remained faithful to the religion of her English ancestors, but there was also perhaps some Evangelical influence present, since she kept assuring him from an early age that he was "saved." He grew up with an intense respect for the Bible as a guide in all circumstances, and an unshakeable belief in a personal God and a personal Devil.

However, his mother also took him to museums and, as he explains, from the age of six he was obsessed by the nude male figures everywhere on show, and in particular by the prostrate, naked, and callipygous corpse in the foreground of *The Bearers of Bad Tidings,* a historical picture by the academic painter, Lecomte de Nouy, which he saw in the Musée du Luxembourg. Soon he had fixations on beautiful boys at school, without understanding the nature of his feelings. His mother died when he was fourteen, so that her loss coincided traumatically with the onset of puberty. After that, for a while, he was inveigled into masturbation by a school friend, but soon experienced a complete revulsion against sex in general. This may have been a factor in his conversion to Catholicism at the age of sixteen, since it enabled him to reinforce his original puritanism with the Catholic ideal of celibacy. At any rate, from then on until his return from America in 1922, it was his declared intention to enter a monastery.

By 1923 he had changed his mind again, and decided that he was not suited to be a monk. And in 1924 he underwent an extraordinary crisis, which seems almost to have amounted to an attack of schizophrenia. On the one hand, his Catholic fervor led him to publish a **"Pamphlet contre les catholiques de France,"** a violent attack on the tepid faith of average French believers, in which he goes so far as to maintain that the Spanish Inquisition, in its severity, had been a necessary and virtuous organ of the Church. On the other hand, it was now that he had his first, fully realized homosexual encounter—with a stranger, as it happened, and on the banks of the Seine. This initiated an apparently long period of homosexual cruising, at first mainly after dark, hence perhaps the exceptional predominance of nighttime wanderings on the part of the anguished heroes and heroines of his novels. During these years, he seems to have stopped being a regular churchgoer, while still retaining his faith in God.

It is perhaps useful, at this point, to emphasize the difference between his and André Gide's view of homosexuality. Gide, to his own rather dubious satisfaction, argued himself into a state of pagan innocence or amorality with regard to his seduction of boys. Green could not "come out" in this way about his relations with young men, because he saw his irresistible need to "sin" as recurrent submission to the Devil, who, for him, is as personal a being as God. His sexuality was something for which he might eventually burn in Hell since—regrettably—there was no modern Inquisition to send him to the stake for it immediately.

He himself recognizes that the creative pressure which drove him to produce his main series of novels probably arose from this conflict between his fierce piety and his uncontrollable sex drive. He repeatedly explains that, during this long period of turmoil, he wrote his fictions under an obscure compulsion, as if he were transcribing a waking dream, without knowing where the characters and the plots were taking him. This no doubt means that they were a form, if not of autotherapy (in Green's system of thought, there can be no cure for the Devil), at least a kind of defense mechanism, warding off a general breakdown through a symbolic displacement of tensions. It is significant that neither the homosexual obsession nor its counterweight, religious faith, is overt in any of the works published before 1950. Instead, there is an overwhelming sense of doom: the main character, male or female, is in the grip of an unappeasable monomania—it may be the all-consuming desire to get possession of a house, as in *Mont-Cinère,* or the impossible love of a woman for a man she hardly knows, as in *Adrienne Mesurat,* or of a man for a woman he hardly knows, as in *Léviathan*—and the outcome is suicide by an act of arson, or a murder followed by madness, or two murders leading to arrest. It is also notable that the *idée fixe* of the protagonist, i.e., the transposition of the author's dilemma as an unjustified sinner, is intensified by the machinations of secondary figures (usually—for some reason one can only guess at—Machiavellian females), who have almost the status of agents of the Devil.

All these novels, with their inspissated gloom, have in parts a hallucinatory power which suggests that some hysterical sense of damnation is finding an oblique outlet. They can almost be defined as superior horror stories, and it is understandable that they should have their admirers, especially among those readers who can appreciate the author's poetic effects in the original French. The plots may be rather uncertain and repetitive, as in *Adrienne Mesurat,* but there are many brilliantly realized scenes in the imaginative-realist style.

I repeat that the central sexual-religious tension in Green's life is not directly expressed in these characteristic novels; the sexuality is always presented as heterosexual and usually cerebral, and the author's Catholicism is not prominent. Indeed, in *Le Visionnaire,* there is a satirical description of life in a Catholic school which might have been written by a non-believer, as if Green had moments of revolt when he saw Catholicism more from the Devil's point of view than God's. Certainly, to appreciate the literary quality of these novels, one does not need to share, or even sympathize with, the sexual/religious dilemma which fueled them.

With the approach of old age, and perhaps also because of the general change in the cultural atmosphere during the last twenty-five years, this central tension in Green's life seems to have slackened a great deal. Now that the Devil has ceased to torment him so acutely, he may feel more secure in the house of God. Here again, however, there is something of a contradiction. Green has long lived openly with a younger man, now his adopted son, and some recent diary entries imply discreet reservations about the sexual conservatism of the Pope. But at the same time, in the later novels, where the homosexual theme becomes explicit, there is no example of happy, or even tolerated, homosexuality. In *Moïra* (1950), the hero's passion is still disguised as heterosexuality, and it leads him to murder the desired but hated object of his lust. In *Le Malfaiteur* (1956) and *Chaque homme dans sa nuit* (1960), the overtly homosexual men are all doomed; one compounds the curse with the additional sin of suicide, and another commits a murder.

Incidentally, what helps to make *The Distant Lands* so untypically bland is the almost complete absence of any reference, indirect or direct, to homosexuality; I have noticed only one tiny episode in which a rather hysterical young man makes a pass at a friend, and is immediately repulsed with contempt. We must suppose, then, that although Green appears serenely content with his lot when he appears on television, he maintains his fundamental disapproval of deviance. Perhaps the fourth volume of his autobiography, which has apparently been completed but remains unpublished, will shed some light on this puzzle.

But if the reader will bear with me, there is a still further complexity to be mentioned if the meaning of the play *South* is to be made clear. Within Green's homosexuality, as he describes it in the autobiography, there is also a split. On the one hand, he falls deeply in love with beautiful young men—"Greek gods," as he calls them, fusing pagan imagery with his Christian sensibility—for whom his feelings remain platonic, or at least cannot easily be transposed onto the crude physical level, because of a paralyzing inhibition. On the other hand, he can have sex with any number of people who, far from being Greek gods, may even be, like his very first partner, "powerfully ugly," as befits incarnations of the Devil. In other words, with a strangely naive simplicity, he seems to see male beauty as a bewitching yet forbidding sign of angelic innocence, whereas sexual seductiveness, unaccompanied by formal beauty, is essentially diabolical. In either case, the emotions aroused may be so intense that, in the fictions at least, the lover usually kills the beautiful or alluring object of his love to rid himself of his intolerable obsession. Or, reversing the process, he kills himself, directly or indirectly, to escape from his guilty longing. This pattern repeats itself, sometimes in quite remotely transposed forms in the earlier writings, but more clearly and indiscreetly in the later.

To go back now at last to *South*—in that play, the violent, sinful, but liberating act takes the form of an indirect suicide. The hero, Jan Wicziewski, a Yankee officer of aristocratic Polish origin, is on leave in a well-to-do southern household on the eve of the Civil War. He is a handsome, enigmatically brooding figure, admired by all. He is present as a friend of the family, because his grandfather once did a great service to Edward Broderick, the head of the household. Also present is Regina, an orphaned niece of Broderick, secretly in love with Wicziewski, who knows her feelings and plays a sadistic cat-and-mouse game with her. Broderick has a sixteen-year-old daughter, Angelina, who is in love with a young neighbor, Eric MacClure, and he with her; he is only talked about in the first act, and appears in the second. Meanwhile, Wicziewski, on a sudden impulse, asks for Angelina's hand, but is gently turned down by Broderick *père,* who, being himself ambiguously attracted to Wicziewski, has guessed his secret and hints that marriage would not be a solution. Then, suddenly, MacClure appears, and Wicziewski is thunderstruck by his beauty. The dénouement follows rapidly. Hopelessly drawn to MacClure, whom he has known only for a few hours, Wicziewski deliberately provokes the young man to a duel with sabers and, in the unseen combat offstage, allows himself to be killed. The play ends with Regina weeping over Wicziewski's body, center stage, just as the Civil War begins.

South apparently enjoyed some success when it was first put on in France and England. I have not seen it performed, but I wonder if it would stand restaging now, after an interval of some forty years. As I read it, it is little more than a melodrama exploiting Green's usual theme of homosexual doom in a transparently mechanical way, and without any of the literary virtues to be found in the better parts of the novels. Wicziewski, not the fate of the South, is the center of interest throughout, and so the title is inappropriate; the coming Civil War and the misunderstandings between North and South are not organically related to his plight, but simply used to provide him with an ominous background; that is, the broader social issue is emotionally subordinated to the individual sexual problem, and this creates an unpleasant imbalance. Also, in a superfluous and embarrassing scene, Uncle John, a pious blind old Negro with the gift of prophecy, is brought in to forecast death and disaster.

Then there are two *invraisemblances.* Is it conceivable that the first glimpse of an unknown young man, however beautiful, would precipitate such an immediate and violent crisis? And is there not a technical difficulty with the duel? It is presumably easy to commit suicide in a pistol fight, simply by refraining from aiming at one's opponent, but how can this be managed in a duel with sabers? But, on second thought, it occurs to me that Green's unconscious may have so arranged matters that Wicziewski's death is not a pure suicide, but a suicide which, through a slip of the foot or a wrong stroke, might have turned into a murder, thus holding in suspense both of the author's usual solutions to sexual desire—self-obliteration or obliteration of the Other. In either case, I find the episode strangely repugnant and not at all conducive to those feelings of pity and terror that are supposed to be aroused by tragedy.

I have to admit that this feeling of repugnance comes partly from the fact that I cannot sympathize with the way Green turns sex into a cosmic issue. He sees the essential drama in life as the tension between a longing for individual salvation in the bosom of a personal God in competition with the contrary, seductive wiles of a personal Devil, operating mainly through sexual desire. As an agnostic humanist, I cannot myself conceive of God as a Person, even with a capital letter, because, in that case, He or She would be limited to a certain temperament as human beings are (or like the jealous God of the Old Testament) and to limit the limitless is a logical contradiction. Then the idea that the universal, creative Something might prefer to "save" one particular soul and "damn" another, on the basis of an instinct It Itself has implanted, is surely only a distorted effect of human self-importance. Moreover, if God is all-powerful, the Devil can only be that part of Himself that He allows to misbehave so as to give variety to the universe; such a supposition is, to say the least, disrespectful.

To my mind, Green has—with muddled consequences—hitched his sexuality to a relatively simple version of the Christian metaphysical structure, a version which he absorbed in childhood and has never consciously questioned, whatever emotional difficulties he may have had from time to time with the Church. The tension within his makeup produced what I have called the "horror stories" and, to that extent, it can be said to have had a positive literary result within a fairly narrow range. But he is not one of those existentialist Christians, such as Pascal or Simone Weil (or even, in his lesser way, François Mauriac), who see the problem of evil as being coextensive with the whole of creation and who, being aware of the agnostic position, make a deliberate leap into faith in order to transcend it. Green's is a more archaic, less sophisticated, religion, perhaps as much Old Testament as New Testament in flavor, and with the supposed sinfulness of sex as its main concern, as is transparently obvious in *South.*

In short, he does not seem to have "come to terms" in any sense with his homosexuality. Instead, he can be said to have oscillated between God and the Devil, with the Devil winning symbolically in most of the fictions, through murder, suicide, and other acts of violence, and through the almost total absence of any concept of human love unrelated to sexual desire. Wicziewski's ambiguous death in *South,* whether a successful suicide or a halfhearted murder attempt, is a facile, imaginative canceling out of a problem which remains unsolved—or if a solution is too much to ask for—intellectually unbroached, on the plane of ordinary human reality. All this having been said, it also seems odd to a non-Christian that a Christian author should dispatch his admired hero to the Judgment Seat, burdened with the extra sin of having gratuitously challenged an innocent man to a duel. The Devil wins twice over, as it were.

But, as I have already implied, Green should not be judged on this play, which is a creaking theatrical vehicle. His real quality lies in certain unique and haunting passages of the typical novels, and also, and perhaps mainly, in his curiously honest autobiography, in which he expounds the interlocking contradictions of his "case" in minute detail, yet without, I think, ever seeing them fully in perspective. If the fourth, as yet unpublished, volume is of the same standard as the first three, I should expect the complete text to be his major achievement and to survive as a singular classic of confessional literature. (pp. 53-6)

John Weightman, "Sex and the Devil," in The New York Review of Books, *Vol. XXXVIII, No. 20, December 5, 1991, pp. 53-6.*

Jeffery Paine   (review date 22 December 1991)

[*In the following review, Paine characterizes* The Distant Lands *as a long-winded but stylistically effective novel.*]

"We need another good book like *Gone With the Wind*." The speaker is the good-humored, not-so-bright mother in Flannery O'Connor's story "The Enduring Chill," but she expresses the devout wish of many readers. And, curiously, long before Alexandra Ripley's *Scarlett,* there was another *Gone With the Wind* of sorts in the works, and its fate is as peculiar a story as exists in the history of publishing.

First, it seems peculiar that the author of that other Southern epic, **The Distant Lands,** should be a lifelong Parisian and a member of the French Academy. Or is the real peculiarity that a member of the Académie Française is an American? "I find it marvelous," wrote the philosopher Jacques Maritain of Julian Green, "that an American should be the greatest French writer of our time." Certainly no other living writer, French or American, can boast a career studded with the names and honors that have surrounded Mr. Green: his friends included Gertrude Stein, André Gide and Jean Cocteau; his works were translated by T. S. Eliot and praised by Hermann Hesse, Carl Jung and George Orwell. And yet Julian Green, that last survivor of this literary firmament, is all but unknown in America.

He was born with the century, in 1900, in Paris—to which his parents had immigrated from Georgia and their beloved South, in ruin after the Civil War. He himself spent little time in America—only his college years and later the World War II period—so that in the early 1930's, when he began this Southern novel, he perhaps believed he was venturing into virgin territory. If so, he was soon to be cruelly set straight. After witnessing the publication of *Gone With the Wind* and the resultant ballyhoo, he quietly put away his own unfinished manuscript in a safe place, where more than a half-century later he rediscovered it, resumed writing and produced a book that became a best seller in France.

And here it all is, once again—*the South:* the plantations and the perfumed magnolias; the belles and the balls and the gallant boys; the "South's timeless forms of politeness" and generous hospitality; the devoted black servants, with "more love, and, above all, more goodness . . . in those great pupils as black as night"; and, above everything, the shadow of encroaching war that will soon darken everything and everything destroy.

The heroine of the novel is Elizabeth Escridge, a "little English violet" with the requisite "mass of golden hair," "full of the freshness of adolescence that heralded beauty to come." Poverty drives her and her recently widowed mother in the year 1850 to accept the kindness of strangers—of their rich cousins in Georgia. Elizabeth's luck is better than Scarlett O'Hara's, for she gets both Ashley and Rhett: that is, she both marries the kind, bland Ned and enjoys a *liaison dangereuse* with the rogue Jonathan. But Jonathan and Ned kill each other in a duel, and poor Elizabeth must console herself with her baby as the novel thumps to its melodramatic ending. Over her little Ned's crib, she whispers, "You haven't forgotten our secret? . . . Sleep well then, my Jonathan, good night, my Jonathan."

The plot of this 900-page novel, thus stated, seems barely sufficient to animate a 9-page story. And, in truth, little else in the way of action happens. An outing from the plantation to Savannah to buy a dress is the labor of a hundred pages; chapter after chapter is taken up preparing for a ball, in dizzying anticipation of which the characters ingest laudanum to sleep at night. The heroine is so inefficient she requires 800 pages to lose her virginity. Meanwhile, every room passed through is detailed lovingly, sumptuously; every meal is sampled with a gourmand's lust, course by delicious course. But in those chambers and at those suppers little but talk transpires.

Were 650,000 Frenchmen wrong, or rather, disappointed when they snapped up **Distant Lands**? Perhaps not. If considered as an American pre-Civil War epic, Mr. Green's novel, serviceably translated by Barbara Beaumont, is melodrama minus the drama; but as a French novel, it can be read another way. Julian Green worked in the French tradition of authors like Villiers de l'Isle-Adam, who wrote, "We who have thought so much would not deign to act," and then added the line that so thrilled Yeats, "As for living, the servants will do that for us." Mr. Green's contemporary, Julien Gracq, employed in his novel *The Chateau d'Argol* a Gothic castle but then filled it not with frightful happenings but with a philosophical *ménage à trois* and psychological innuendo. Frequently, in French literature, action is simply not where the action is.

And if one has a taste—and the time—for Mr. Green's lack of action, something quite hypnotic eventually happens. A reader will be initiated almost bodily, inducted experientially, into the slower pulse rate of an earlier era. Yielding to this spell, you will discover no additional action in the narrative, but the very absence of action lets the luxurious ambiance—the exquisite interior decoration—reverberate with the force of an event. There is a forgotten ease and dallying here, quite unlike the dramatic urgency of *Gone With the Wind,* where there lurks in the shade of each magnolia and is heard rustling in every crinoline the South's impending doom.

Mr. Green's novel, for all its period-piece décor, has little to do with the actual antebellum South. The South in 1850 was filled with more raucousness, high jinks, cruelty, racial antagonism, class tensions, heated debate and labors (even for the wealthy) than this suave, genteel novel could possibly convey. Instead, we get a highly elegant fuss about refinement, the characters' polite talk that avoids saying anything substantial, their need to fill time, to avoid boredom, all of which belong to a later period—to Edith Wharton's *Age of Innocence,* say, and, not incidentally, to Julian Green's own childhood.

Indeed, the spell of hypnagogic languor that *The Distant Lands* casts comes from Mr. Green's recreating something like those eternal afternoons of childhood that were filled with adults' talk one couldn't quite follow and with over-sized objects that dwarfed one's small presence. If the novel's terrors remain always hinted at and never made explicit, it is because, as Mr. Green said, "Childhood terrors have an indescribable quality."

In *The Distant Lands* Julian Green returns to that time before all the honors and laurels, before his 60 published books, before his friendship with Cocteau and Gide, to write a novel that embodies the half-remembered, half-indescribable terrors and charms that encapsulated his boyhood. The mesmerizing peculiarity of the novel derives, however, from the fact that Mr. Green is fashioning a world he both did and did not know. In that Paris apartment the young Julian would look at "the graveyard," as he called the wall with the portraits of his American relatives, staring blankly at them in stupefied boredom. But it was a different matter, a romance, when his mother would describe, over and over, the Old South, always with tears in her eyes.

Later, Mr. Green would be furious when Freud's colleague, the psychoanalyst Wilhelm Stekel, used a novel of his to illustrate the unconscious Oedipus complex. But here it seems touching, a full circle come round, to see Julian Green, a very old man, dedicating—and writing—his novel, his homage, to that woman who sighed for distant lands and another time. "To the memory of my mother, daughter of the South."

Jeffery Paine, "Whistling 'Dixie' in French," in The New York Times Book Review, *December 22, 1991, p. 10.*

Alan Riding   (essay date 22 December 1991)

[*In the following essay, based on an interview with Green, Riding and Green discuss the writing process for Green's last two novels as well as his literary influences which include his American heritage.*]

"Welcome to the South," Julian Green said, receiving a visitor to his apartment in the heart of Paris. A Confederate flag hung at the end of a narrow corridor. First-person accounts and other Civil War documents filled bookcases. Furniture from Georgia brought here by his father at the turn of the century has pride of place in the dimly lighted sitting room. "This is the American South in France," he added, with a smile that acknowledged his poetic license.

Born in Paris 91 years ago, Mr. Green is recognized today as one of France's foremost writers. He has lived here most of his life; in 1972 he became the first American to be elected to the 40-member Académie Française, and he is one of the few living writers to see his works collected in Gallimard's prestigious Pléiade library. All but two of

his 18 novels, 5 plays, 14 volumes of diaries, 4 books of autobiography, 6 collections of essays and 2 history books were written in French. "I am not prolific," he likes to say. "I am just very old."

Yet it seems right that Mr. Green should be returning to the South at this stage of his life. It always served as a nostalgic backdrop for him. And with the American publication of his romantic antebellum novel, *The Distant Lands,* he now hopes to be rediscovered in the United States as a Southern writer. But the writing of this book and its sequel, *The Stars of the South,* also transported him back to his Parisian childhood, when each day he would leave school, cross the road and enter the dream world of his Southern belle mother.

His father had been sent to Europe in 1895 by the Southern Cotton Oil Company. Given a choice of living in France or Germany, his mother insisted on France because, she said, "The French had been defeated in 1870 and would understand the Southerners." Julian was the youngest of her eight children, and he listened to her stories of the South with wonder. "She told us all about the splendid victories we had," he recalled, "but she was always bursting into tears. She didn't tell us until very late in the day that we lost the war."

She died in 1914, and in 1919 Mr. Green went to the United States to attend the University of Virginia, where for the first time he saw the South for himself. Although he returned to live in Paris in 1922, he subsequently spent long periods in the United States. During one visit in 1933, he began what more than 50 years later would become *The Distant Lands.* But he heard that Margaret Mitchell's *Gone With the Wind* was about to come out. With just two chapters written, he abandoned his project for fear of being accused of plagiarism.

By that time, Mr. Green had already enjoyed some success in the United States. "But after the war, I didn't go back to America and they called me an expatriate," he explained in soft, clipped English. *L'Expatrié,* that's the title of one of my diaries. They said it as a form of rejection, you know, he has gone, he has left us." In France, though, his fame began to grow, as much for his diaries as for his novels. He was known for his elegant and sensuous use of the French language, but also for his pessimistic view of life, marked by the perennial tension between his Roman Catholicism and his homosexuality.

He converted from Protestantism at the age of 16 after he found a book on Catholicism "that had all the answers." Years later he learned Hebrew so that he could read the Old Testament, and to this day he attends Mass weekly, studies the Bible daily and picks religious books over contemporary literature to keep by his bedside. He insists, though, that he is not a Catholic writer. "Several of my characters are Catholics, but most are Protestants and atheists," he noted. "I have never written a book with the idea of writing a Catholic novel. I am a writer and I am Catholic."

By his own admission, his homosexuality frequently tested his faith. "You've heard of the flesh and the spirit," he explained in an almost conspiratorial tone. "Well, the flesh played an enormous part when I was young."

He has recounted how he finally won the battle between the "intensely carnal and profoundly religious" sides of his character when he renounced sex 30 years ago. "Sexuality is an obstacle that stands between God and man," he told one French interviewer.

Today, with such trials behind him and his longtime French friend, Eric, whom he has adopted as his son, caring for him, Mr. Green seems very much at peace with himself, continually peppering his conversation with ironic asides—a habit, he insists, that is proof of his English blood. He still travels in Europe and enjoys a big following in Germany, but he rarely bothers to attend sessions of the French Academy a few blocks from his home. "It's a little tiresome," he said apologetically. "You see, they're grammarians and experts in the origins of words, and they go on and on arguing."

Yet he chose France not only because he was born and brought up here, but also because he was drawn by the challenge of the language. "French is actually a very poor language," he went on. "There are very few words. In the 16th century there were 50,000 words. Today the French only use about 4,000 words. But it means there is only one word to describe a certain thing, not two. You have to find 'le mot juste,' whereas in English there are many words."

Today he still works for three or four hours a day, writing in longhand, correcting as he goes along and never rereading the completed manuscript. "I begin with a very clear idea of what the characters are like," he explained. "It probably makes me sound like a lunatic, but my ideal is to begin with a sort of hallucination. In Europe it's called 'automatic writing.' It's like someone dictating something, and I have to be very careful to write down exactly what I hear. It's surrealist. When I write page 1, I don't know what page 2 is going to be like. I write the book to know what's inside."

At the same time, he keeps up the diary he began in 1919. "When it came out in 1938, it was the first diary of its kind to be published in France," he recalled. "André Gide kept a diary from the 1890's, but he only published excerpts in literary magazines. Gide was interesting to me. He was a strange man in many ways. He knew I kept a diary and he knew that I wrote about him. We had an agreement because he wrote about me in his diary and we exchanged our diaries so we could see what we had to say about each other."

This year has seen the publication of three additional works by Mr. Green in the United States: the novel *Adrienne Mesurat,* first issued here in 1928; the play *South,* which had its debut on the London stage in 1955; and *Paris,* a collection of essays written over the course of the past four decades.

Until 1984, *Gone With the Wind* seemed to stand in the way of his unfinished antebellum novel. "I remember going to see the movie version in 1939, but I left after the opening scene," he said. "I thought, if this isn't sufficiently Southern, I'm not going to sleep, so I'd rather not see it.

I finally read the book when I had almost finished *The Distant Lands.*" And your reaction? "Great admiration for certain things," he replied cautiously. "There is something artificial about the characters, but the setting and the writing of the story are very good."

After the success in France of *The Distant Lands,* which is set between 1850 and 1854, he continued the epic in *The Stars of the South,* carrying the story to 1861. And now he hopes to complete the trilogy, to be called *Dixie,* with a final volume on the Civil War itself. But he is hesitating. "I want to write a third one," he said. "The doctors say I'll have another five years, perhaps another ten years." He then whispered mischievously. "The trouble is that it will have to end with another Southern victory."

> *Alan Riding, "A Nonagenarian in Paris: A Conversation with Julian Green," in* The New York Times Book Review, *December 22, 1991, p. 11.*

FURTHER READING

Biography

Burne, Glenn S. *Julian Green.* New York: Twayne, 1972, 159 p.
>   Biographical and critical survey of Green's life and career.

Criticism

Alter, Jean. "Julien Green: Structure of the Catholic Imagination." In *The Vision Obscured: Perceptions of Some Twentieth-Century Catholic Novelists,* edited by Melvin J. Friedman, pp. 151-85. New York: Fordham University Press, 1970.
>   Examines *Epaves* in the context of Green's assertion that "all my books, however removed they may seem from the usual and generally accepted notion of religiosity, are nonetheless religious by nature."

Biddle, Francis. "Frenchman from Savannah." *The New Republic* 157, No. 20 (11 November 1967): 26-30.
>   Discusses several autobiographical events and themes presented in *To Leave before Dawn.*

Billington, Rachel. "A Saint in His Own Days." *The New York Times Book Review* (29 September 1985): 14.
>   Presents a balanced review of *God's Fool: The Life and Times of Francis of Assisi,* describing the work as "as a labor of love, a quest to discover the nature of a man who inspired the novelist so deeply in his youth."

Courtines, Pierre. Review of *To Leave before Dawn,* by Julien Green. *America* 117, No. 18 (28 October 1967): 484.
>   Examines *To Leave before Dawn,* concluding that the autobiographical work "serves to explain Green's private daemons, so admirably exorcised by him in his internationally famous novels."

Davidson, Donald. "Painful Literature." In his *The Spyglass: Views and Reviews, 1924-1930,* edited by John Tyree Fain, pp. 93-5. Nashville: Vanderbilt University Press, 1963.

Laudatory review of *The Dark Journey* dated 8 December 1929. Davidson focuses on Green's depiction of evil and pain in *The Dark Journey*, which he asserts is "perfection itself."

Davis, Clive. "Return to the South." *New Statesman & Society* 3, No. 120 (28 September 1990): 36-7.
Questions the literary merit of *The Distant Lands.*

Doering, Bernard. "Jacques Maritain, George Bernanos and Julien Green on the Mystery of Suffering and Evil." *Religion & Literature* 17, No. 3 (Autumn 1985): 37-55.
Discusses the significance of the philosophical problem of suffering and evil in the works of three major French writers.

Englund, Steven. Review of *God's Fool: The Life and Times of Francis of Assisi*, by Julien Green. *The Los Angeles Times Book Review* (22 December 1985): 1, 8.
Asserts that Green fails to present an objective and thorough exploration of his subject in *God's Fool.*

Field, Trevor. "The Literary Significance of Dreams in the Novels of Julien Green." *The Modern Language Review* 75, Part 2 (April 1980): 291-300.
Discusses the relationship between dreams, reality, and literature suggested in Green's novels.

Fowlie, Wallace. "Man as He Is and as He Would Be." *The New York Times Book Review* (27 September 1964): 7.
Reviews Green's *Diary, 1928-1957*, highlighting Green's artistic concerns and the progression of his religious beliefs.

Gascoyne, David. "Good Places and Bad." *The Times Literary Supplement*, No. 4148 (1 October 1982): 1072.
Presents a positive assessment of the eleventh volume of Green's autobiography, *La terre est si belle, 1976-1978*, focusing on Green's travels and his use of language.

Glassman, Deborah. "An American in Paris: Deborah Glassman Chats with Julian Green." *The San Francisco Review of Books* 18, No. 1 (January-February 1993): 14.
Briefly discusses the major achievements and influences of Green's career, emphasizing his bilingualism and the duality of his cultural heritage.

Joiner, Lawrence D. Review of *Memories of Evil Days*, by Julien Green. *The Modern Language Journal* LXII, No. 3 (March 1978): 145-6.
Presents a brief review of Green's lecture collection *Memories of Evil Days.*

Keating, L. Clark. "Julien Green and Nathaniel Hawthorne." *The French Review* XXVIII, No. 6 (May 1955): 485-92.
Presents a comparative study of Green and Nathaniel Hawthorne.

Lewis, Naomi. "The Lost Country." *The Listener* 81, No. 2097 (5 June 1969): 797.
Brief positive review of *To Leave before Dawn.*

Review of *The Other One*, by Julien Green. *The New Yorker* XLIX, No. 15 (2 June 1973): 122-23.
Presents a brief negative assessment of *The Other One.*

In addition to faulting the translator's work as "lumpish," the critic laments the book's predictability and "incredibly drawn-out arguments and explications of the antagonism between the body and the spirit."

Orwell, George. Review of *Personal Record 1928-1939*, by Julien Green. In his *The Collected Essays, Journalism and Letters of George Orwell: My Country Right or Left, 1940-1943*, Volume II, edited by Sonia Orwell and Ian Angus, pp. 19-21. London: Secker & Warburg, 1968.
Reprint of article originally appearing in *Time and Tide* in April 1940. Orwell praises Green's impressions of the politically turbulent era preceding World War II.

Robinson, Christopher. "Christian Convictions." In his *French Literature in the Twentieth Century*, pp. 178-200. London: David & Charles, 1980.
Includes a discussion of the religious aspects of Green's novels.

Sturrock, John. "Dying Fall." *The Times Literary Supplement*, No. 3961 (24 February 1978): 236.
Brief assessment of *Le mauvais lieu* that focuses on the novel's pessimistic tone.

"Eros on the Cross." *The Times Literary Supplement*, No. 3360 (21 July 1966): 638.
Discusses Green's focus on love and sexuality in his *Terre lointaine.*

"A Fortunate Accessory." *The Times Literary Supplement*, No. 3610 (7 May 1971): 522.
Assesses the strengths and weaknesses of *L'autre.*

Ziegler, Robert. "Burning *Mont-Cinère.*" *Rocky Mountain Review* 43, Nos. 1-2 (1989): 35-45.
Asserts that Green explores the futility of possessiveness and greed on three different levels in *Mont-Cinère.*

————."In the Eyes of the Father: Narcissism and Identification in Julien Green's *Chaque homme dans sa nuit.*" *University of Dayton Review* 20, No. 1 (Summer 1989): 99-107.
Explores psychological aspects of *Chaque homme dans sa nuit.*

————. "Autobiographical Discourse in Julien Green's *L'Autre Sommeil.*" *Essays in Literature* XVII, No. 1 (Spring 1990): 131-41.
Examines the significance of the confessional nature of *L'autre sommeil.*

————. "(L)imitations of Silence: The Implications of Reader Exclusion in Julien Green's 'Leviathan: La traversée inutile'." *Studies in Short Fiction* 27, No. 3 (Summer 1990): 339-45.
Analyzes the role of the reader in Green's short story "Léviathan: La traversée inutile."

———. "Castles in the Air: Vision and Narrativity in Julien Green's *Minuit.*" *Studies in 20th Century Literature* 16, No. 2 (Summer 1992): 233-45.

    Examines Green's "interest in the function of storytelling, the explicitness of narrative, and the importance of what it does and does not disclose" as related in *Minuit.*

Additional coverage of Green's life and career is contained in the following sources published by Gale Research: *Contemporary Authors,* Vols. 21-24, rev. ed; *Contemporary Authors New Revision Series,* Vol. 33; *Contemporary Literary Criticism,* Vols. 3, 11; *Dictionary of Literary Biography,* Vols. 4, 72; and *Major 20th-Century Writers.*

Julia Kristeva

1941-

Bulgarian-born French linguist, psychoanalyst, literary theorist, and novelist.

The following entry provides an overview of Kristeva's career through 1992.

INTRODUCTION

One of the foremost thinkers to emerge from the political and social unrest of France in the 1960s, Kristeva is best known for her intellectually rigorous critiques of structuralism and semiotics and for her psychoanalytic studies of horror, love, and melancholy. Although her thought and intellectual development have been closely associated with the work of other theorists—notably Roland Barthes, Jacques Lacan, Louis Althusser, Michel Foucault, and Mikhail Bakhtin—Kristeva has formulated a unique approach to critical theory by drawing on and revising elements from such diverse systems of thought as Marxism, structuralism, and Hegelian philosophy.

Kristeva was born in Soviet-controlled Bulgaria to educated, middle-class parents. She attended Bulgarian- and French-language primary schools and, though originally intending to study astronomy and physics, earned her degree in linguistics from the Literary Institute of Sofia in western Bulgaria. She worked briefly as a journalist during the early 1960s, but in 1966, with the fall of Nikita Krushchev and an upsurge of Soviet repression, Kristeva emigrated to Paris on an academic scholarship. During her doctoral studies in Paris, Kristeva worked and studied with such thinkers as the structuralist and Marxist critic Lucien Goldman, structural anthropologist Claude Lévi-Strauss, literary theorist Tzvetan Todorov, and most importantly critic Roland Barthes, who helped get her work published and became her mentor. Within her first year in Paris, Kristeva began publishing articles in prestigious scholarly journals, including *Tel quel,* the most prominent of the radical structuralist and Maoist periodicals at the time. Kristeva later married the editor of *Tel quel,* Philippe Sollers, a noted critic and avant-garde novelist. Kristeva received her doctorate in linguistics in 1973 after publishing her first two books, *Semeiotke: Recherches pour une sémanalyse* and *La texte du roman: Approache semiologique d'une structure discursive transformationelle.* In 1974 her dissertation was published as *La révolution du langage poétique: L'avant-garde à la fin du XIXe siècle, Lautréamont et Mallarmé (Revolution in Poetic Language);* in this work she blends literary criticism and philosophical analysis in a description of the extra-linguistic, non-syntactic characteristics of French avant-garde literature at the end of the nineteenth century. Inspired by the Marxist/Leninist philosophy espoused by Communist leader Mao Tse Tung, Kristeva visited China

in 1974; her book *Des chinoises (About Chinese Women)* marked the beginning of what some commentators consider to be the overtly feminist phase of her career. Although some critics denounced the book at the time of its translation for self-indulgence and for ignoring the egregious abuses of human rights that occurred during Mao's Cultural Revolution, *About Chinese Women* was the first of Kristeva's works to be translated into English and helped establish her reputation in the United States. In the mid-1970s Kristeva started practicing as a psychoanalyst and began teaching linguistics at the University of Paris. Since that time, Kristeva has continued to teach and has maintained her psychoanalytic practice. In 1990 she published her first novel, *Les samouraïs (The Samurai),* a semi-autobiographical work that contains veiled characterizations of Barthes, Lacan, Foucault, and other famous figures of the French intelligentsia.

Kristeva's theoretical work draws on the principles of many disciplines. Commentators note that her work essentially attempts to describe the nature of poetic language and its relation to human subjectivity. Her works of the 1960s—primarily *Semeiotke* and *La texte du roman*—undertake the development of a theory describing, in John

Lechte's words, "the dynamic and unrepresentable poetic dimension of language: its rhymes, rhythms, intonations, alliterations—melody; the music of language, in short; music which is even discernible in everyday speech, but which is in no sense reducible to the language of communication." Specifically, Kristeva works from French structuralist Ferdinand de Saussure's semiotic theory of language—which holds that meaning does not inhere in words or symbols but results from their relational position within a linguistic or semiotic system—to propose that the poetic aspects of language represent intrusions upon and threats to the stability of the communicative, signifying system. For Kristeva, the dynamism specific to the "rhymes and rhythms" of poetic language—as in Edgar Allan Poe's line about "the tintinnabulation of the bells, bells, bells, bells, bells, bells, bells"—signifies an additional dimension of language which listeners and readers can understand intuitively but have no means of describing. In her work of the 1970s, primarily *Revolution in Poetic Language,* Kristeva endeavors to describe the content of this "dynamic and unrepresentable" component of language. Here Kristeva refines the psychoanalytic theory of Jacques Lacan, who had revised many of Sigmund Freud's central concepts by proposing a linguistically based theory of the unconscious. Lacan's theory asserted that the child's acquisition of language is predicated upon the alienation from an undifferentiated sensory experience of the mother, with the child consequently being thrust into the symbolic, cultural realm characterized by paternal law and castration anxiety. Challenging Lacan, Kristeva argues that the child's pre-linguistic experience is maternal in nature and not completely lost with the acquisition of language, becoming the part of the unconscious Kristeva refers to as the "semiotic chora" (*chora* meaning both receptacle and distinctive mark). For Kristeva, the semiotic chora—the repressed, maternally-oriented psychic energy—re-emerges as the "unrepresentable" aspect of language and as such poses a continual challenge to the dominance and stability of the paternally-oriented realm of signification. Kristeva's elaboration of this dialectic formed the basis of her political commitment and feminist philosophy in the first two decades of her career.

Kristeva's major studies of the 1980s refine her psychoanalytic theories by focusing on the nature of three intense emotional states: horror or abjection, in *Pouvoirs de l'horreur: Essai sur l'abjection* (*Powers of Horror: An Essay on Abjection*), which examines the role of the mother in psychoanalysis and further revises Lacan's theory of language acquisition; love, in *Histoires d'amour* (*Tales of Love*), which studies the concept of narcissism and attempts to determine how ego-ideals are formed; and depression, in *Soleil noir: Dépression et melancholie* (*Black Sun: Depression and Melancholia*), which revises Freud's concept of melancholia and argues that the depressive's sadness is "the most archaic expression of a non-symbolisable, unnameable narcissistic wound." These works make extensive use of Kristeva's experiences with her patients and are written in a more accessible style than her works of the 1960s and 1970s. *Etrangers à nous-mêmes* (*Strangers to Ourselves*) ponders the psychoanalytic and sociopolitical implications of the increasing concentration of non-native peoples in Europe and the United States.

Her description of the unconscious, psychoanalytic roots of xenophobia and her argument that each individual must recognize his or her own inner foreignness demonstrate the extent to which Kristeva has expanded her unique psychoanalytic theory to address contemporary issues. Although some critics have regarded her work of the 1980s and 1990s as an abandonment of the Marxism and the politically engaged critique of Western philosophy that marked her early work, Kristeva is nonetheless esteemed for the rigor and variety of her thought and remains one of the leading intellectuals in the West.

PRINCIPAL WORKS

Semeiotke: Recherches pour une sémanalyse (nonfiction) 1969

La texte du roman: Approache semiologique d'une structure discursive transformationelle (nonfiction) 1970

Des chinoises (nonfiction) 1974
[*About Chinese Women,* 1977]

La révolution du langage poétique: L'avant-garde à la fin du XIXe siècle, Lautréamont et Mallarmé (nonfiction) 1974
[*Revolution in Poetic Language,* 1984]

Polylogue (nonfiction) 1977

† *Desire in Language: A Semiotic Approach to Literature and Art* (nonfiction) 1980

Pouvoirs de l'horreur: Essai sur l'abjection (nonfiction) 1980
[*Powers of Horror: An Essay on Abjection,* 1982]

Le langage. Cet inconnu: Une initiation à la linguistique (nonfiction) 1981
[*Language—The Unknown: An Initiation into Linguistics,* 1989]

Histoires d'amour (nonfiction) 1983
[*Tales of Love,* 1987]

Au commencement etait l'amour: Psychanalyse et foi (nonfiction) 1985
[*In the Beginning Was Love: Psychoanalysis and Faith,* 1987]

The Kristeva Reader (selected essays, edited by Toril Moi) 1986

Soleil noir: Dépression et melancholie (nonfiction) 1987
[*Black Sun: Depression and Melancholia,* 1989]

Etrangers à nous-mêmes (nonfiction) 1988
[*Strangers to Ourselves,* 1991]

Les samouraïs (novel) 1990
[*The Samurai,* 1992]

*This work is a partial translation of *La révolution du langage poétique.*

†This work includes "The Bounded Text" and "Word, Dialogue and Novel," translated from *Semeiotke: Recherches pour une sémanalyse,* as well as translations of eight of the twenty essays in *Polylogue.*

CRITICISM

Philip E. Lewis   (essay date Fall 1974)

[*In the following excerpt, Lewis discusses Kristeva's doctoral thesis* La révolution du langage poétique, *examining the essay's main philosophical concerns and its relation to the work of Jacques Derrida, Karl Marx, and G. W. F. Hegel.*]

It is doubtless all too easy to discuss Kristeva's work in terms of her visible relationship with Sollers, *Tel Quel,* and the avant-garde, and to subject that relationship to a facile attitude, ranging from awe through self-reassuring irony to derision. Yet Kristeva, in representing her work as a conceptual extension of the textual work of the avant-garde, compels us, with great insistency in *La Révolution du langage poétique,* to question that relationship seriously (intellectually rather than journalistically), to rethink the status of the critical text in relation to the literary text. Does the interpreter produce a subordinate, supplemental, weakly mimetic postscript, or does the critical text itself become scriptural, thus originary and programmatic, subject to interpretation in the work of the artist? The history of Symbolism and Surrealism in France may suggest that literary avant-gardes inevitably raise this question, and also that the question is ordinarily articulated in the nominally theoretical texts of a practicing artist—a Mallarmé, a Breton, an Artaud, a Sollers—and thus immediately resolved in the dynamics of an individual's work. Yet Kristeva's case is special, closer to the problematics of scholars and teachers, for, however unremitting her commitment to the avant-garde, she remains an academic critic, holding a university chair, writing in a foreign language, at times as a polemicist, but not as an artist, not even as a critic like Barthes who is clearly a writer in his own right. Both the avant-garde and academic critics have considerable stakes in her work, for both are obliged to examine it as a wager which tests—i.e., testifies to and contests—the legitimacy of their own work.

La Révolution du langage poétique is an enormous (620 pages) and difficult doctoral thesis which is distinguished first and foremost by the immense scope of its problematics. At first glance, one might qualify the study as interdisciplinary because it embraces many areas of investigation: anthropology, history, linguistics, poetics, psychoanalysis, and so forth. But interdisciplinary is an inadequate epithet: first because Kristeva pursues forcefully the development of a broadly conceived ideological position; second, and more consequentially, because her theoretical reflection overpowers disciplinary categorization, encompassing the very conception of interdisciplinary study, ultimately focusing upon the most fundamental philosophical questions of intelligibility. The crucial issues, then, are "superdisciplinary"—conceptual and epistemological. While their importance and complexity preclude rapid evaluation in terms of particular problems in specific fields (readers should be wary at least of dismissing her thesis upon discovering particular analyses or readings with which they disagree), there is hardly any alternative to relatively partial, fragmented perceptions of this monumental work, if only because it so readily absorbs and outdis-

tances the overviews or contextual accounts which might be proposed. In short, it would be unduly presumptuous to venture to adopt, for evaluative purposes, a more general, more fundamental, or more incisive critical position than that of this, as it were, all-encompassing book, nominally devoted to poetic language; the full-scale assessment of *La Révolution du langage poétique* should doubtless be long-range and collective. (p. 28)

In the earlier stages of her research, represented by *Le Texte du roman* (1970) and by the collections of essays entitled *Recherches pour une sémanalyse* (1969), Kristeva sought to elaborate a revisionary, materialist semiotics in opposition to the predominant structural semiotics which was developing rapidly in the late 1960's. She followed her teacher and eventual collaborator Roland Barthes in granting initial priority to linguistics over semiotics, and in at least two important respects, she appropriated Derrida's critique of Western logocentrism: (1) resistance to the "natural" complicity with phonocentrism in Saussurrian linguistics, carried out by Kristeva via the importation of analytic models from mathematics and formal logic; (2) rejection of any tacit subordination of the signifier to the signified, insistence on treating the signified as a signifier. Both of these tactics are designed to subvert an unselfconscious semiology, to enforce an awareness of the inescapably ideological status of the new discipline, which emerges in opposition to inherited forms of scientific reflection on man. The most remarkable aspect of this hybrid semiology is its claim to formulate incessantly its own philosophical problematics, to develop simultaneously as a theory and a practice, thus to test and correct its own first principles. In Kristeva's own terms,

> At every moment of its elaboration, semiology thinks its object, its instrument, and their relation, thus thinks itself, and becomes in turning back upon itself the *theory of the science that it is.* This means that semiology is in every case a re-evaluation of its object and/or its models, a *critique* of its models (thus of the sciences from which they are borrowed) and of itself (as a system of constant truths).

As an autocritical critique constructing the theory of its own criticology, Kristevan semiology is a perpetually self-revising, reflexive, open-ended, self-validating process, pursuing the formulation of a knowledge which is always immediately relativized, confronted with alien concepts, subjected to theoretical analysis. At the open end of a semiological investigation, there is nothing to be found other than the basic ideological gesture of its own movement, which it recapitulates and denies prior to re-enacting the same critical trajectory, but with a modified object. In and through the process of taking and maintaining cognizance of its ideological import, this permanently revisionary semiology purports to break with the Hegelian vision of a science which presents itself as a circle turned back upon and into itself, incapable of radical self-interrogation, subordinated to a teleological outlook which imposes an established system upon the sciences that it subtends and which removes the validation of scientific inquiry from the conduct of the inquiry itself. [In a footnote, Levis adds: "Kristeva is bound to incur many attacks for what will be called her Hegelianism. Hegel is extraordinarily prominent in ***La Révolution du langage poétique,*** and whereas the Husserlian discourse on the subject is an object of attack, the Hegelian concept of negativity undergoes elucidation and appropriation. . . . Yet this appropriation plays a decidedly subversive role in Kristeva's thesis, which hardly acquires a thoroughgoing Hegelian cast. Her relations to both Hegel and Marx, which are exceedingly complex and never acquiescent, certainly do not allow cursory characterization"].

Here Kristeva's solidarity with the Marxist critique of scientific reflection is transparent. The aim of the attempt to subvert scientific discourse as it is practiced in the various academic disciplines is to show how science is born within ideology, within a particular, although broadly conceived, capitalist ideology characteristic of Western European civilization since the Renaissance. The initial *object* which the semiologist's subversive research seeks to apprehend is a phenomenon of resistance, an idiosyncratic or iconoclastic factor which is not subsumed by the suspect logic of Western culture, which can play against it from within it, challenging it by dislocating it, by unveiling heterogeneous forces that belie its apparent homogeneity. The framework of this reflection is the Marxist analysis of work and production, carried out from the point of view of the circulation of values and thus bound within the capitalist system which is its object. But Marx, according to Kristeva, at least adumbrates the possibility of apprehending work without reference to its value, prior to its insertion in the system of merchandise; he foresees dimly, without being able to preceive what the neo-Marxist will attempt to grasp directly, another concept of work, another scene [in Kristeva's words] "on which work no longer represents any value, does not yet intend any statement, has no meaning, a scene on which it is a question of the relationship between a body and an expenditure." The disclosure of this concept of work required a long critical meditation on the limits of the Logos as the archetypal model of the communicative system of meaning (value), a painstaking exposition of the systems of exchange which govern conventional thinking about language. (In this context, Kristeva, like Derrida, recognizes a considerable debt to the structuralism which she indicts.) The idea of a silent production—one which nonetheless leaves its mark and transforms language prior to the appearance of circulatory speech, communication, exchange or meaning, first becoming accessible through the Freudian concept of dream-work, where production is represented, not as a process of exchange or usage, but as a premutational play which models production—is crucial for it is only in the work of the avant-garde that the diacritical concepts of textual production and semiotic process come into play as discernible features of the particular semiotic practice called literature. Indeed, Kristeva tends to dismiss literature as a conventional structure, to reserve the term *écriture* for the writing of the avant-garde, for texts which make the problematics of semiotic production more visible than others, for texts whose irreducibility to the structures of normative linguistics or to the *concepts* of representation is discernible and unsettling. What makes the text or textual work a difficult concept is its strangeness, its otherness, its inaccessibility to conventional logic [as Kristeva writes]: "In effect, the text is exactly that which cannot be thought within the whole conceptual system that grounds present-day understanding, for it is precisely the text which delineates the limits of that understanding." If it is already adventuresome to envisage a literary evocation of the unthinkable which is the sustaining limit of our thought, it is doubtless still more so to make this unthinkable outside the object of a scientific investigation. Yet the validity of Kristeva's entire critical enterprise probably depends fundamentally on the success or failure of her attempt to elaborate a rigorous description and explanation of the workings of the text and the semiotic process.

In ***Le Texte du roman,*** Kristeva undertakes just such a scientific investigation, performs an analysis which is paradoxical to the extent that it develops a structural and generative account of *Le Petit Jehan de Saintré* in order to expose a conception of textual work which Antoine de la Sale was not in a position to practice because the socioeconomic conditions of the fifteenth century provided an overpowering confirmation of an expressive or representative vision. His novel manifests two conceptions of the book—as a narrative phenomenon and as a literary discourse—but not as textual or scriptural work, which turns against representation, "becomes the inscription of its own production," brings into play the dynamics of writing. Kristeva's remarkable essays on poetic language, on Saussure's anagrams, on Barthes' *Système de la mode,* on Lautréamont and Raymond Roussel, all carry on her attempt to position the text in its unspeakable otherness by discerning within it the marks of writing itself [as Kristeva writes]: "Freud opens up the problematics of *work as a particular semiotic system,* distinct from that of exchange: this work takes place within communicative speech, but differs from it in essence; it does not think, calculate or judge; it is content to transform.

According to Kristeva, the option of latter-day semiology is a choice between the conventional structuralist study of communication and the study of production—of this pre-representative production. Either we can continue to formalize semiotic systems in terms of exchange, distribution, and consumption, or we can try to open up within this initial investigation "this other scene which is production prior to meaning." Choosing the latter course, Kristeva distinguishes between two possible avenues of research: (1) Derrida's strategy, which consists in isolating a measurable aspect of a signifying system (work, production in terms of value) against the background of non-measurable concepts (the gram, the trace, differ*a*nce); (2) Kristeva's attempt to construct a new scientific problematics on the basis of the new concept of work (a concept which may seem, in its singularity, akin to Derrida's undecidables). For Kristeva, semiology thus becomes the elaboration of a new theory of production-prior-to-the-product, a search for the principle governing the play of a new, unmeasurable, barely namable object, disconnected from the representable objects of communicative exchange.

The problem appears to be straightforward: how to formulate this problematics of work which is radically different from the prevailing problematics of exchange, how to define or apprehend this work, this production prior to the product, this pre-communicative activity? Grosso modo, it seems fair to suggest that all of Kristeva's work during the past five years, including the massive doctoral thesis, derives from this question, and within her elaboration of a response, we can discern two principal, complementary movements, the first of which focusses upon the concept of *text,* the second of which articulates a more complex philosophical construct around the concept of the *semiotic process* (which we might represent initially and loosely as the generation of signifiers on a ground of psychic instincts). In each case, the writing of the avant-garde, as a dynamic and subversive process, working against the grain of spoken language, is fundamental.

"L'Engendrement de la formule," an essay of nearly 100 pages on Sollers' *Nombres,* seems to be a turning point leading to the shift in conceptual objects from the text *per se,* as the scene of *écriture,* to the semiosis process, for it works out the first version of a psychobiological model of the germination of semiosis which will be recast and expanded in the theory of the subject elaborated in ***La Révolution du langage poétique.*** This model is built upon the celebrated bifurcation of the text into *phéno-texte* and *géno-texte.* Following her usual practice of displacing and redefining key terms, Kristeva has, in effect, widened the notion of *text* so as to distinguish it from the linguistic phenomenon (pheno-text) fixed within a linear structure and bearing a given message. The concept of text is one of a process, an *engendrement:*

> an engendering inscribed in [. . .] this *pheno-text* or printed text, but which is readable only when we retrace a vertical path through its genesis: (1) of its linguistic categories, and (2) of the topology of the signifying act. The emergence of signifiers [*la signifiance*] will thus be this engendering which can be apprehended in a double guise: (1) engendering of the fabric of language; (2) engendering of this 'I' which positions itself so as to present the emergence of signifiers.

This movement back through the genesis of the pheno-text reveals the linguistic operation that generates the pheno-text, and this "signifying productivity," this fecundative process underlying the written product, is termed the geno-text. The geno-textual formula is a textual complex (neither the effect of a producing cause nor the expression of a submerged meaning), indicative of the infinite plurality of signifiers; it is "a remnant correlated with the germination of which it is neither the effect nor the cause, but the *seal* to be read as illegible, the indispensable fall which prevents germination from becoming a generation, i.e., from 'giving birth,' from having an offspring—a Meaning." This textual seal, the remnant or trace of germination deposited in the pheno-text, comes to the surface in the strangest texts of Mallarmé, Lautréamont, and Artaud: it is systematically inscribed in the texts of the contemporary *avant-garde,* and seminally—disseminally—in the numbers woven formulaically into the text of *Nombres.*

It is important to recognize that this germination process cannot be reduced to one of gestation, to a conventional structure of creation: the geno-text is not a structure, not a source or ground of linguistic structure; it is the infinite signifier, the mass of signifiers which overdetermines the particular formula displayed—or better: factored, multiplied—in the pheno-text. In ***La Révolution du langage poétique,*** dismissal of the "natural" image of creation is still more imperative, for the impersonal process of germination is inserted into a theory of the writing subject, of the producer of the textual formula, which may seem at first glance to invite the restoration of an authorial persona behind the text. The thesis lies, in fact, far beyond such an outlook: Kristeva appropriates emphatically the deconstruction of the expressive subject which is effectuated by the Lacanian critique of ego psychology and undertakes to ground the concept of a dynamized, infinitized signifying subject through an aggressive materialist critique of Husserlian phenomenology. The reconstituted poetic subject is not a stable "je" or "ego" which states meanings and thus constructs itself (its self, its identity) within the structure of language; it is a doubled subject, at once the modality of the linguistic system and of its breakdown or splitting-apart; the poetic subject is a dialectical process in which the structured language of the ego comes into contact with a violent, heterogeneous force which is its ground, with the flow of psychic instincts which Artaud represented as corporal motility and which Kristeva terms the semiotic *chora,* designating thereby a music, a rhythm, an architecture, a non-verbal articulation of the semiotic process which redistributes the linguistic and grammatical categories of a language to which the *chora* remains unassimilable.

In the initial pages of ***La Révolution du langage poétique,*** the semiotician will encounter what must be an unsettling theoretical distinction of the *semiotic* and *symbolic* modalities, a distinction which becomes the core of Kristeva's exploration of the concept (in many respects the leitmotiv of this book) of the *subject.* The displacement of the term semiotic onto unfamiliar territory resembles the conversion of the term *text* into a dynamic operative concept: in each case, the focus is downward, toward the generative process of semiosis, toward the core of corporal and psychic energy which is the ongoing heterogeneous ground out of, over, and against which all symbolic activity is articulated. The symbolic modality embraces the whole sphere of activity covered by the term semiotic in its common, loose acceptation; "it includes that which, in language, falls within the order of the sign, i.e., simultaneously nomination, syntax, signification, and denotation;" it is the broad domain of all expressive/communicative activity which emerges as a function of positionality, i.e., with the identification of a subject and its objects as the basic thetic polarity, delineating a *symbolic* space and structuring the act of enunciation. Since the primitive constitution of the thetic structure lies in the discovery of the Other (here an appropriation of the Lacanian analysis of the "mirror stage" and castration is crucial), the symbolic becomes at once the domain of *inter*subjectivity, thus of all human relations, becomes therefore the framework for an open-ended theoretical reflection on the "signifying architecture of a society," ranging from the anthropological rudiments of the social order (e.g., the analysis of sacrifice and the societal status of art) to the complex and thoroughgoing inquest into the modern political state in the final one-third of the book. For Kristeva, the interest of semiological investigation shifts from the functional, homogenic, homological account of the symbolic order to the unstable yet indissoluble relationship between the heterogeneous domains of the symbolic and the semiotic (the cleavage between these inextricably bound domains is marked by the dissection of the sign into signifier/signified). To advocate this shift of focus is not to dismiss or devalue the descriptive/analytic enterprise of conventional semiotics; it is, however, to accuse it of blindness to the internal dynamics of semiosis, to denounce its complicity with a stable, homogeneous, but *false* image of expression and communication which ignores the entrenchment of symbolization in the unstructured field of instinctual forces.

While the semiotic *chora* is normally repressed by the consolidation of the symbolic domain, the semiotic remains the inseparable condition of the symbolic and retains the capacity to irrupt—with potentially revolutionary force—on the scene of signification. In its entirety, *La Révolution du langage poétique* is a testimonial to the importance, for the revolutionary avant-garde, of recovering the semiotic *chora,* of deploying its potential for *jouissance* in the symbolic sphere, initially and most immediately by reinforcing the lingual with the release of the instinctual in its artistic activity. At stake in the recovery and reappropriation of the semiotic is the avant-garde's attempt to overcome the repressive structure of subject unity, to disrupt the status of the subject, and consequently of the individual, in the bourgeois system. The following passage from Kristeva's essay on Artaud, **"Le sujet en procès,"** i.e., the subject in process ("on trial,"—put on trial through recovery of the semiotic process), provides a kind of synopsis of the articulation (elaborated analytically and massively in *La Révolution du langage poétique*) which she envisions between the poetic work of the avant-garde and its political program:

> Through a specific practice which touches upon the very mechanism of language (in Mallarmé, Joyce, Artaud) or the mythic or religious systems of reproduction (Lautréamont, Bataille), the "literary avant-garde" confronts society— even if only on its fringes—with a subject in process, assailing all of the stases of a unitary [*unaire*] subject. The avant-garde thus assails closed ideological systems (religions), but also social structures of domination (the state), and accomplishes a revolution which, however distinct from or up to now unknown to the socialist and Communist revolution, is not its "utopian" or "anarchist" moment, but designates its blindness to the very process which sustains it. This "schizophrenic" process of avant-garde activity introduces a new historicity, a "monumental history" cutting across the myths, rites, and symbolic systems of humanity, declaring its detachment from contemporary history (like Artaud) or following this contemporary history in order to open it onto the process of negativity which propels it (like Bataille).

Given the breadth of the avant-garde's ambitions and the overt militancy of its philosophical discourse, the conception of its program obviously becomes increasingly problematic—and susceptible to misunderstanding—as it extends to the interpretation of history and the sphere of contemporary politics. Yet Kristeva's account of the avant-garde's project displays a certain critical reserve which should be kept in sight: the scene of action on which the fundamental *work* of the avant-garde takes place is, and will remain, the *specific* practice—an activity of committed intellectuals and artists—which aims at transforming the most elemental constituents of a cultural system through a combination of literary and conceptual operations that the practicioners can effectuate, here and now, but only in their own writing. The deconstruction of the unitary subject and invention of a pluralized successor imply not only the most radical of cultural revolutions, but also the strategic placement of revolutionary activity primarily in relation to its localizable object, a grounding of militant theoretical reflection in the potential repercussions of transforming that object. Kristeva notes straightforwardly the marginality—"if only on its fringes"—of the literary avant-garde vis-à-vis society, and it suffices to read *Tel Quel* with a modicum of seriousness to recognize that the Parisian avant-garde, while resolutely adhering to the necessity, both theoretical and "human," of formulating the implications of its work as a socio-political position, entertains few illusions as to the immediate efficacity of that position and perceives its fundamentally *exemplary* role as a historicizable force, as a present condition of the future possibility of a revolution which cannot be theorized within the mainstream of social evolution, which can be anticipated in its necessity only from a purposefully marginal position. (It seems inevitable that a book such as Sollers' recent *Sur le matérialisme,* still more decisively than *La Révolution du langage poétique,* will be taxed with the consequences of a marginality that is indispensable to its subversive thrust.) A major point of Kristeva's book is precisely to draw our attention to the fundamental work of the avant-garde—textual work on the subject— which, as its most difficult and challenging task, is probably also the least accessible element of its visible production. (pp. 28-32)

Philip E. Lewis, "Revolutionary Semiotics," in Diacritics, *Vol. IV, No. 3, Fall, 1974, pp. 28-32.*

Leslie W. Rabine   (essay date October 1977)

[*In the following essay, Rabine examines Kristeva's semiotic theories of language and assesses their applicability to a Marxist-Feminist study of literature.*]

Julia Kristéva is usually associated with French structuralism, or more precisely, with the post-structuralist tendency of which she is one of the foremost critics and theoreticians. In 1967 she joined the influential literary journal *Tel Quel* which, in the aftermath of May, 1968, was moving in a direction of Marxist theory as it was then understood by Parisian intellectual circles. *Tel Quel's* search for a materialist theory of language and literature led it to the thesis that bourgeois ideology is embedded in the very structure of Western language. Kristéva, in her books **Semeiotikè** and *La Révolution du langage poétique,* explores, deepens, and plays with this thesis. As a linguist she has studied Chinese, where she found ideological structures far different from our own. After her visit to China in 1974, the rise of the Women's Liberation Movement in France led her to write **Des Chinoises (About Chinese Women)**. Since the publication of **Des Chinoises,** *Tel Quel* has returned to its original status as a literary journal.

Since Kristéva aims to replace structuralism with a dialectical materialist theory of language and literature, the intent of this paper is to explicate her ideas on women in the light of their relevance to Marxist-Feminist criticism in the United States, and to clarify before evaluating them certain concepts and terms which are difficult to understand. Marxist-Feminist criticism sees a work of literature as inseparable from the historically defined socio-economic relations and ideological structures in which it is produced. In class societies a work can either perpetuate or challenge the dominant ideology oppressive to women, although most of our literature, through its internal contradictions, both perpetuates and challenges.

Therefore, the following explication of Kristéva's theory will be guided by two basic questions: 1) What tools offered by semiotics can sharpen and deepen our analysis of those literary structures which reflect a sexist ideological structure? and 2) In what way does Kristéva's theory perpetuate those structures? The difficulties of semiotic theory reside more in its rhetoric, terminology, and structural complexity than in its basic ideas and methods. An explication of the terminology will hopefully make it clear that the difficulties are related to an anti-feminist bias inherent in the theory, while the complexities of structure and terminology actually make the theoretical apparatus too cumbersome to explore adequately the even greater complexities of women's lives in society.

[*About Chinese Women*], although disappointingly incomplete and superficial as a history and sociology of women in the Chinese society and family, is an illuminating and fascinating application of the semiotic method to the study of women. Since *About Chinese Women* has . . . been reviewed by Marina Warner in *TLS* (April 22, 1977), who criticizes its observations of Chinese women from an anti-Marxist bias, and by Varina Conley in *Diacritics* (Winter, 1975), who sees it as an exciting example of post-structuralist experimentation, I shall not "review" the book here. My intention is rather to map out in *About Chinese Women,* in *Semeiotikè,* and in other essays, major principles of the Kristévan method in terms of their usefulness for feminist literary criticism.

About Chinese Women, mainly concerned with the revolution in the family and the status of women in the People's Republic, begins by looking at Western women with new eyes in order to challenge ethnocentric stereotypes of Chinese women. The introduction examines the origins of Western patriarchal ideology in the birth of Judaic monotheism:

> Towards 2000 B.C., Egyptian refugees, nomads, bandits, and insurgent peasants united, it seems without any ethnic coherence, without territory, without a state, in the desire to survive as a community, at first in their wanderings. Judaic mo-

notheism doubtless finds its roots in this will for community in face of and against every concrete, unfavorable circumstance: an abstract, symbolic, nominal community, beyond individuals and their beliefs, but also beyond their political organization.

Such a community, since its unifying principle was "nominal" (residing in the *name* of God), was spiritual, internalized, "super-egoist," and therefore stronger, more resistant and more disciplined than other communities. But on the other hand, it could not tolerate any difference, any dualism, any otherness, whether existing in other civilizations alongside it or within itself. It suppressed many neighboring agricultural societies and their mother-goddess cults, and it also suppressed the women of its own tribe:

> Monotheistic unity maintains itself by a radical separation of the two sexes: this very separation is its condition. Because without this division between the two sexes, without this localization of the polymorphous, spastic, desiring and laughing body in the *other* sex, it would have been impossible, on the *symbolic level,* to isolate the principle of a Law—One, Sublimating, Transcendent, guarantee of the ideal interest of the community.

This basic cleavage between what is considered the superior Masculine and the inferior Feminine is repeated consistently in Western ideologies—ideologies which function through hierarchized dichotomies in which the spiritual term, isolated from the material term, transcends it and governs it. Ideas are isolated from things, the soul from the body, and love from sex. In capitalistic ideology, as Kristéva interprets it, this first movement of absolute separation is followed by a second movement: the superior engulfs the inferior and makes the inferior an identical reflection of itself. Thus, in Western romantic love, the development of which coincides with the history of developing capital, the woman is not a self but the man's double, who serves to guarantee him his transcendent identity.

Kristéva sees the Chinese ideological structure as very different from that in Western Culture. Throughout Confucian patriarchal society from 1000 B.C. to 1949, elements of an earlier society have, according to *About Chinese Women,* survived. This earlier society was a highly developed matrilineal culture, differing from Western monotheism in every respect; in it feminine and masculine, matter and spirit, sexual pleasure and social constraint, yin and yang alternate in heterogenous and contradictory union within each person and within the social structure. Even in the Confucian order, where social unity was based on the name of the father, elements of this matrilineal culture survived.

Such an analysis reformulates the Freudian thesis that our Western culture is able to function because sexual repression and social constraints are deeply internalized. Kristéva's theory expands this notion in two ways. First, she explains why Western women have been identified with sexuality. As the "Other" sex, they became the receptacle for those impulses that had to be repressed in men if a cohesive, unified, and stable society were to be maintained. Then, as such receptacles, women became unworthy of inclusion in that society. From Kristéva's point of view, therefore, a study of women in literature becomes a study of the repression on which the entire social order is based. Such a theory leads to an innovative analysis of women and ideology because Kristéva sees the sexual relations, economic relations, and linguistic activities of a given society as forming a system of isomorphic structures. Sexuality, economics, and communication are all permutations of one total social structure, which is constantly reinforced by the very homogeneity of all its activities.

Kristéva defines a "structure" as any stable, cohesive, homogeneous, and unified entity such as a state, the family, a religion, a language, or a social relation. Its opposite is "process" or "impulse." A structure is established by what she calls a "cleavage," which cuts it away from process, and although process is repressed or excluded, it forms the unified structure by acting as its outside limits. In Judaic-Christian and capitalistic civilizations, the unified human subject is male, while women's exclusion from the state, from religion, from culture, from the status of subject, assures the cohesion of the society.

One quality of structure is that it be governed by what Kristéva calls the "Law of One," which decrees not only that all structures of a culture be internally homogeneous, but also that they be analogous to each other. The internal relations of each structure will therefore be models for all the others. Here, then, is the second quality of any structure: it will be modelled both on a society's form of economic practice and on its form of linguistic communication. Like the economic practices of production and exchange, each structure produces and reproduces the society and its social relations. Like linguistic communication, all structures are based on the exchange of messages which have significance for the members of a culture. All social activities, according to Kristéva, are productive practices and communicative exchange, or what she calls "signifying practice." Analyzing signifying practice, especially literary "practice," is the main focus of semiotics.

The production of meaning in bourgeois language would be analogous to the production of exchange value under capitalism. According to Marx, the capitalistic system of exchange hides and denies its exploitative process of production; it represses and excludes the producers. By the same token, according to Kristéva, our system of communication (or exchange of words) hides and denies the work of producing meaning. Semiotics attempts to study language not only in terms of its communicative structure, but also in terms of the labor process which produces it.

For Kristéva, our language of communication is based on the "sign." In Ferdinand de Saussure's *Cours général de linguistique,* a work which founded structuralism, the sign is said to be composed of a "signifier" or composite of sounds, and a "signified" or mental image. Structural linguistics divorces signs from their referents and examines them in a closed autonomous system of internal dependencies, i.e., in a structure. Each sign has meaning not in itself nor as it relates to a referent in reality, but as it is different from other signs. In other words, a sign derives its meaning from its position in the system or structure.

According to Kristéva's book *Semeiotikè,* the structure of discursive language as a system of signs makes meaning into a static, one-to-one relationship between a signifier and a signified. The two elements of the sign give each other identity and mirror each other in a unified and closed entity. Since the systems of signs is linear, it collapses the three-dimensional space of action and spectacle into a two-dimensional line. By thus excluding the space where meaning is produced, signs exclude the practice of their own production. The syntax of our language is also structured like the sign into a subject and a predicate which mirrors the subject and gives it identity. Semiotics as a critique of structuralism attempts to illuminate the practice and process repressed by the sign.

The human subject of capitalism is also structured like the sign, and, in fact, according to Kristéva, consciousness does not pre-exist language, but is actually itself formed by the acquisition of discourse. The child becomes a conscious subject of our culture when he masters syntactical speech, a moment which coincides with his final cleavage from dependence on his mother's body as he comes to awareness of himself as a separate entity. At this moment language structures the consciousness by cutting it from the unconscious, the inexpressible instinctual process which always underlies conscious language. Psychoanalysis designates this moment in the life of the child as the end of the Oedipal complex, climaxed by the castration crisis, but Kristéva sees castration as a symbol for the cleavage that initiates any structure. She says in *Des Chinoises:*

> We would prefer to situate this fundamental event [which structures every psychic act] not in castration . . . (which would be only [a] fantasmic deviation . . .), but in the apprenticeship of the symbolic function to which the human animal is subject from before the Oedipal period.

Kristéva goes on to define the symbolic function as: "signifier/signified organized in logico-syntactic structures, whose purpose is to assure social communication as exchange purified of pleasure." Social constraints, then, are so very deep because they function from within language itself. And to the cleavages "signifier/signified" and "conscious/unconscious," Kristéva adds "symbolic/semiotic." If the symbolic function comprises all communicative activity, then the semiotic designates those unconscious, instinctual, bodily impulses which precede syntactic language. The semiotic also includes the effects of pre-symbolic impulses which come into language, as "rhythms, intonations," which cannot be "captured as a sign, signifier, signified."

The child, or conscious subject, governed by the "symbolic function," enters the social structure governed by the "Law of One," a law represented by the "symbolic founding father." In Judaism, the father Abraham founded the civilization based on the law that God is One. The "paternal function" as the "support of the subject, of symbolism and of sociality," cuts the child from his maternal attachment so that he enters the family governed by the father alone. According to Kristéva, the paternal function structures both the family and social behavior by repressing the pleasurable impulsive process associated with the maternal phase. But the cleavage between masculine and feminine is broader than that. As we see in **About Chinese Women,** the woman is what man represses in order to structure his own identity, and to master the state, religion, and the economy.

In China, according to Kristéva , language, subjectivity, sexuality, and the relations between the sexes function quite differently, but are also homologous. In the Chinese language, meaning is based on tone as well as sound, and tonal distinctions are the first linguistic distinctions an infant makes. In China, says Kristéva, children acquire language at a very early age, while they are still dependent on the mother's body, so that the imprint of this psychophysical maternal attachment remains an underlying element of syntactical speech. Likewise, Chinese writing requires physical gestures, so that the memory of symbolic meaning is needed in order to write.

The Chinese language, according to Kristéva, functions in the subject without requiring a radical cleavage between unconscious process and conscious structure, between the semiotic and the symbolic, or between the material maternal and the symbolic paternal. This suggests that the Oedipal complex and the castration crisis do not determine the socialization of Chinese children, nor, therefore, sexual roles and identities. Kristéva hypothesizes that Chinese culture does not know our deeply internalized sexual repression which gives rise to our super-ego, our individualism based on guilt and sin, and our notion of transcendent identity. She suggests that sexuality and eroticism, while less repressed for both men and women in China, are more severely separated from public life in the community. The act is permitted, talking about it is not. We see, therefore, another example of instinctual process harmonizing with structured unity instead of being dominated by it or suppressed as in Western ideology.

Kristéva, along with some French feminists, argues that this alternation between masculine and feminine in society, in language, and within each individual is intolerable in Western capitalistic society where structures always function "to make an 'other' 'resemble' a 'same'." Woman is either repressed or forced to become the mirror reflecting man back to himself. Whether she accepts her role or revolts against it, either choice, according to Kristéva, will be a masquerade.

The foregoing over-brief statement of Kristéva's semiotic theory is intended only as a summary of her major concepts which are useful for literary study. Here now are two criticisms of that theory. First, given its identification of the masculine with structure, symbolism, transcendence, unity, and discourse; and of the feminine with process, semiosis, materiality, multiplicity, and silence, semiotics may perpetuate rigid roles by making socially and historically determined stereotypes into a universal feminine essence or nature which can never change. Second, semiotics, through the concept of signifying practice, may fur-

> **[Given] its identification of the masculine with structure, symbolism, transcendence, unity, and discourse; and of the feminine with process, semiosis, materiality, multiplicity, and silence, [Kristeva's] semiotics may perpetuate rigid roles by making socially and historically determined stereotypes into a universal feminine essence or nature which can never change.**
>
> **—Leslie W. Rabine**

ther reinforce the very ideological structures it aims to combat. The purpose of any dialectical materialist theory of language and literature is to re-establish the relation between practice in material social reality and the spiritual symbolic realm of ideas and literature. But such a theory should present economic, material production and the realm of ideas, ideology, or literature as *dialectically* related, i.e. as the unity of opposites, not as the homology between isomorphic structures.

Marx calls the realm of productive relations the "base," and the realm of culture, politics, art and ideology the "superstructure." In Marxist writings, including those of Marx and Mao, the base and superstructure of a society are said to contradict each other. The two realms are heterogeneous, different from each other and irreconcilable with each other, but they are also completely interdependent on each other for the survival of the total society. Semiotic theory, with its system of isomorphic structures between economic and literary production, denies not only the difference between the two realms but also their interdependence. It actually reinforces the very cleavage between matter and spirit it attempts to criticize by setting up the two realms as parallel rather than interlocking. It does not have to analyze deeply the way material socioeconomic relations influence language and literature since it claims that the signifier is itself material. By claiming that language has its own materiality, this semiotic theory also perpetuates and repeats the very process of capitalist ideology it attempts to criticize—that process by which the spiritual dominates and suppresses the material. A theory which says that the signifier is material actually excludes the material processes in all their rich complexity, while it transforms "matter" and "practice" into metaphors or symbolic entities which simply reflect language and literary creation. Conversely, language and literature become mirror reflections of economic practice rather than forces locked in contradiction with it.

In spite of these pitfalls in semiotic theory as a whole, however, it offers methods and tools which can be incorporated into a feminist approach to literature. It does show that ideology as the "Law of One" is more deeply rooted and more pervasive than a vision of the world. Even its concepts of isomorphic structures, if confined to the uncovering of homologies within the literary text, can give us the tools for examining in greater depth that ideology and the way in which literature serves and/or combats it. In analyzing a literary work we can see how the theme, the form of the text as a whole, and the language all function to reinforce the same ideology. In a series of French novels, for example, ranging at least from *Manon Lescaut* in the eighteenth century to *Le Grand Meaulnes* in the twentieth, the narrator relates the conclusion at the beginning so that the novel is structured as a closed totality in which the memory of the narrator mirrors the anticipation of the hero. Thematically, these novels portray a heroine who mirrors the hero, and who ends the tale either by dying or by retiring to a convent. It is the exclusion and silence of the woman at the end of the novel which permit the hero to close the circle of his self-identity. Her exclusion also permits him to enter the established culture as a full-fledged member of a stable social order. Finally, only the heroine's disappearance makes it possible for the hero to become the narrator of the novel, to articulate his lived experience in the realm of language, and to transform experience into literature.

There is both a danger and an advantage in using Kristéva's concepts and tools, the same danger and advantage we often have as teachers and critics of literature. It is perhaps not a coincidence that a theory which in a subtle way perpetuates traditional feminine stereotypes and key elements of capitalistic ideology also expresses itself in a language that can be understood only by a tiny intellectual elite. This danger of intellectual elitism could lead us to perpetuate the same structures we attempt to call into question. The value, however, is that if we can make some of Kristéva's ideas generally accessible, we can help to avoid a feminism which demands only that the social order allow a few women to become full members of the same kind of closed unity Kristéva and others have been criticizing. We can, instead, come to a clearer and more thorough understanding of the social order we have been inhabiting as strangers. (pp. 41-8)

> *Leslie W. Rabine, "Julia Kristéva: Semiotics and Women," in* Pacific Coast Philology, *Vol. XII, October, 1977, pp. 41-9.*

Alice Jardine   (essay date Autumn 1981)

[*In the following essay, Jardine discusses Kristeva's essay "Women's Time," analyzing how it and Kristeva's other works redefine feminism.*]

> That this rupture can be in complicity with the law or, rather, that it can constitute a point of departure for even deeper changes: that is the major problem.
>
> The Future Perfect: for an action/event which at a given time in the future will be in the past.

Julia Kristeva writes in a kind of "future perfect"—a modality that implies neither that we are helpless before some inevitable destiny nor that we can somehow, given enough time and thought, engineer an ultimately perfect future. She often uses this term herself, particularly in reference to the poetic text; a literary text is always before or after its time (because of the negativity forcing the rejection of

all theses) but also of its own time to the extent that it represents a certain linguistic and ideological configuration. In ["Women's Time"] she evokes the future perfect to characterize a new social formation now in the process of rediscovering what part of it has forgotten. I am not suggesting that Kristeva's theoretical writings are *texts* (in the strong sense that word has acquired in France) or even that they are only there to remind us of what we have "forgotten" for the present. Rather, her thought reveals such a complex stratification of predictions and echoes, progressions and regressions, that even readers most familiar with her work find themselves wondering, What will have to have happened before she can be read?

This becomes a vertiginous and difficult problem for American readers of Kristeva who are drawn through her texts into a multiplicity of temporal spaces often quite foreign to them: the time of French thought (and its massive recent present), the time of importation and exportation of French thought to the United States (about ten years), and the time of the United States, "so far ahead of France" and yet *assuming* fundamental truths that French thinkers have long since rejected.

The American feminist reader of **"Women's Time"** may experience this multiple time/space shuttle in an almost physical way: alternating, sometimes from sentence to sentence, between strong affirmation ("Yes, this is important and promising for the future") and violent rejection ("But this was said about women a hundred years ago!"). In fact, the article was published only two years ago, but in a theoretical time and space totally alien to most American feminist itineraries. At the same time, it is important for it represents a certain number of configurations which American feminists are only now having to come to terms with. [In a footnote, Jardine adds that this coming to terms "is further complicated by the fact that Kristeva writes within a conceptual vocabulary, a 'metalanguage,' which even those French feminists most familiar with the lexical paradigms find irritating—sometimes to the point of saying that it is not 'the way a woman should write.' Ironically, the strong reactions provoked by her writing often involve a form of *judgment* at the core of the very ego/identity she wants women to help explode."] In the space allotted here, I can only try to schematically situate **"Women's Time"** in its local time, its time of writing. What its American time might be remains a question for the future.

Published in 1979 (between *La Folle vérité* and *Pouvoirs de l'horreur*), **"Women's Time"** is, in some ways, Kristeva's most extensive and direct analysis of feminism as an international movement in the 1970s. It appeared in a small, modest, but excellent research journal to be read (obviously) first in Paris. This is not a negligible observation (as I have tried to suggest above) and, if nothing else, helps account for some of the more polemical points of the article.

The argument, first and foremost, revolves around a certain definition of "historical time," which may prove to be the first stumbling block outside of Paris. Indeed, this definition (slightly pejorative here, more so elsewhere, but whose force is never denied) and the ensuing extrapolations can seem out of joint to many American readers who continue to see the site of their major battles as the lack of "historical consciousness" in much American thought. We cannot even summarize here the major revolutions this word "history" has been through in France over the past twenty years. Suffice it to say that Kristeva's shorthand definition should be understood in the context of an entire "new (re)generation" of French philosophy. This (re)generation has taken place within what Vincent Descombes (rather unhistorically, but at least clearly) has termed the passage from the generation of the "Three H's" (Heidegger, Hegel, and Husserl) to the generation of the "Three Masters of Suspicion" (Marx, Nietzsche, and Freud) and, most important, beyond. It has been pointed out that the resultant "relativization" of historical modes of thought (and, essentially, of dialectical thought), has also taken place within the heritage of Russian formalism and continental structuralism. Pointing out this local history is very different from marketing it. Much of the most heterogeneous work written throughout the 1960s and 1970s "against" *both* phenomenology and structuralism (not to mention the rediscovery of Anglo-American analytic philosophy) has rapidly become a "package deal" for nonspecialists. This "false historicization" of twenty years of writing flourishes particularly well in America and England under the anachronistic paperback label of "structuralism," adding an extra twist to any foreign reading.

This overall interrogation of various systems of historical thinking and their mutual dependence on certain fundamental conceptions of language—the speaking subject and religious structures—is essential to all of Kristeva's thought. This is not to say that ["**Women's Time**"] cannot be read without this "background," only that it is once again important to evoke the place from which Kristeva is speaking: a Europe disillusioned with and closer to what seem to be the ultimate "reality principles" of traditional—and some not so traditional—approaches to history. [In a footnote, Jardine adds: "Our time machine can again seem out of kilter. E.g., French intellectuals have only recently, in a massive way, 'discovered the Gulags.' This is absurd to most American intellectuals. The ensuing emotional attacks on the Soviet Union sound astonishing—like an echo—to any American who was alive and living in the United States in the 1950s. On the surface, the utterances are the same as those fed to us then (and again now) under the banner of anticommunism. But many of these French denunciations are coming from an intelligentsia who is, was, or might have been either the established or the far Left and are, in any case, in dialogue with Marxist theory/practice in a way impossible to those who live in the United States. Traditional notions of Right and Left in France have been confused to such an extent that one has been speaking, for some time, of a total intellectual crisis. All of this is to say that an American cannot simply take an eight-hour flight to Europe and qualify 'anti-Marxist thought' as rightist, fascist or, more fashionably, anarchistic. Neither can all of those tendencies be denied as factors."]

Kristeva's definition of "historical time" as teleology and project (whether elaborated in a "Marxist" or "idealist" structure—but again, those are dangerously generic

terms) operates, however, within at least one generally accepted consensus: The West is approaching or has already traversed the *ending* of a certain strictly delimited history, that of Judeo-Christianity. To analyze this culture and society in crisis, Kristeva always keeps in sight, on her intellectual and temporal horizon, two limits: Stalinism and fascism (and thus, inevitably, anti-Semitism). This recent acceleration in the historicization of our history and its limits thus leads to a set of accelerating extrapolations (analogies elsewhere in question): History is linked to the *cogito,* to the paternal function, representation, meaning, denotation, sign, syntax, narration, and so forth. At the forefront of this rethinking is a rejection of what seem to be the strongest pillars of that history: anthropomorphism, humanism, and truth.

Here again, the American feminist reader is immersed in a strange temporality, for feminism is necessarily about *women*—a group of human beings in history whose identity is defined by that history's representation of sexuality. It is hardly necessary to point out to American feminists, faced daily with the self-conscious task of unraveling patriarchal history, that our ways of thinking about feminism are already overdetermined; that they are based—sometimes consciously, more often unconsciously—on systems of inherited thought. In most cases, they are based on empiricism or (we must not forget) on *imported* existential/concrete thinking; but in translation from one culture to another, these assumptions at least must be specified in order for there to be any dialogue at all. In any case and in whatever form, there is an insistence by feminists (myself included) on reality, on realism: a pragmatic definition of truth or, as Descombes writes in reference to Sartrean humanism, "the true is the result." This (among other things) has led to the rejection of the word "feminism" by some French women as simply the other side of humanism, or else it has culminated in an attempt to live in two times: political time (realism) and written time (elsewhere). An increasing majority, however, retains the word "feminism"; they admit there are problems with it but insist on using it now, concretely (i.e., existentially). "If humanism was about putting the word 'man' where 'God' had been used before, and if therefore feminism is nothing but another humanist gesture in that it replaces 'man' with 'woman,' so be it—for now." Some have suggested that the "End of History" and the "Death of Man" are nothing but paranoid reactions on the part of male thinkers to the concrete changes brought about by women's massive awakening. They no doubt are, as Kristeva hints in ["**Women's Time**"], but. . . .

In analyzing the logic(s) which belong to this long but presently out-of-sync history, Kristeva concentrates on its crises, on what has always threatened it, and, thus, inevitably, on "woman." [In a footnote, Jardine adds: "In Anglo-American feminist theory, 'woman' and 'women' are often used to distinguish between the abstract and the concrete, with the former relegated either to poetics ('Such is Woman!') or used to designate, negatively, the concept of 'the eternal feminine.' While the same semantic choice is valid in French, this distinction is less widely used. 'La femme' continues to be used by women theorists side by side with 'les femmes' which, in the concrete plural, is consciously put forward in countereffect."] She often situates herself as a woman-subject-theorist-foreigner-in-France— still, like women in the past, being forced to say what that history has either effaced or concealed. However, faced with the choice between (1) addressing/rediscovering what women-subjects have always said about that history from within it and (2) investigating what has functioned within that history as "the feminine," she has obviously and for multiple reasons chosen the latter. Kristeva's "feminine" is, in a sense, the glue that has held our history (or holds any system) together. She minutely analyzes the ways in which this "feminine" (and thus women?) has been sublimated, made a fetish, exalted, or liberated by *male* writers. At the same time, she emphasizes how this "feminine" is inexorably linked to both the "Mother" and mothers within the classic Western oedipal structure. Kristeva is very consciously aware of the difficulties inherent in an analysis of this "feminine." For example, in the following condensed passage she first supports the necessity for locating the position(s) of women-subjects in language; second, she adds, however, that (at the same time) the woman-subject is as much a product of language as the man-subject; third, she posits that only through this latter recognition can we short-circuit the cycle of the eternal feminine; and yet, fourth, she emphasizes that the "feminine" cannot, in turn, simply be left out of our analysis, for it is intrinsic to metaphysics:

> One could then situate the woman-subject within the complexity of these parameters [of language] without reducing her to the state of the slave-excluded-from-the-linguistic-system. Here, I am obviously maintaining the notion of *subject* for women (the metaphysical implications of this are in no way inhibiting if, at the same time, its roots in significance are recognized) and am thereby avoiding the, in effect, fetishistic reification of a 'feminine in and of itself.' [. . .] If, on the contrary, we could just understand by 'feminine' that which provides an approach to 'non-being'—to that which is impossible to say and yet is posited by metaphysics. . . .

The "woman-subject," the "feminine-in-and-of-itself," and the "feminine" as redefined by Kristeva are caught in a series of semantic networks difficult (if not impossible) to untangle fully from within the "identity" and "difference" paradigm bequeathed to us by our history . . .

This is perhaps the point where it becomes important to remember that "feminism," as a generic term, is just as semantically complex and conceptually hazardous as "woman" or the "feminine." Generally seen as a movement "from the point of view of women," it covers enormous ground and becomes particularly dangerous across the border. In the present case, involving France and the United States, any generic description of "French feminism(s)" from afar immediately homogenizes and neutralizes the specificities of struggles that, at least in Paris, are of epic (and often violent) proportions. Even the attempt to specify contexts and assumptions, as I have done above, can run into the dangers of a comparativeness rooted in nineteenth-century thought which, in turn, can lead to a bizarre, modern form of "white woman's burden." Suffice

it to say here, therefore, that when one speaks of "feminism" in France, no one is quite sure who or what is meant. [In a footnote, Jardine adds: I will risk but a few examples: The group Psychoanalysis and Politics has legally taken on the name "MLF" (Mouvement de libération des femmes: marque déposée). Thus, recently, when their group came out in support of Jian Qing during her trial, the entire Parisian journalistic machine launched into praise or blame of "feminism" in general without ever mentioning that it was only a question of this one group. This is, at the very least, ironic, given that Psychoanalysis and Politics has rejected feminism completely. Another group of women (Questions feministes) initiated the term "neofeminism" to designate, specifically, the theories of Psychoanalysis and Politics. Since then, this term has come to mean something close to what Kristeva calls here "the second generation," although many who would place themselves in that generation are diametrically opposed to Psychoanalysis and Politics. For many, feminism has no meaning outside of activism. For others, feminism is simply the "final hysterization of middle-class women." Academic feminists can be counted on one hand. And so forth. All of this is complicated by the fact that any one group tends to center itself around one or two thinkers whose work nevertheless continues to circulate in other completely different contexts.] Kristeva, while extraordinarily attuned to feminism outside of France (in the United States particularly), is necessarily in an ongoing dialogue with "feminism," local time. At the most polemical points in [**"Women's Time"**], she is often referring to a form of fetishism which, I think I can safely say, most American feminists would also be among the first to reject. But there is much more here than polemics. Kristeva quietly and consistently rejects any thought that *desexualizes* (or, as we would put it, minimizes the gender differences intrinsic to) the structures forming us and our thought. At the same time, she forcefully draws our attention to those moments when women-subjects rejoin with or valorize the same feminine whose function she so minutely analyzes in Western culture. For Kristeva, the moments when women deny culture, reject theory, exalt the body, and so forth are moments when they risk crossing over the cultural borderline into hysteria. While recognizing hysteria as potentially liberating and as one of the major forms of contestation throughout our history, she also relentlessly emphasizes its very real limits: the fantasy of the phallic, all-powerful mother through which women reconnect with the very Law they had set out to fight. . . .

[In *Pouvoirs de l'horreur,* Kristeva writes] " . . . A symbolic (social) system *corresponds* to a specific structuration of the speaking subject within the *symbolic order.*" This, then, has been and still is Kristeva's theoretical starting point. To change the system, we have to change the speaking subject, but changing its gender or its cause alone is not sufficient. The subject must be thought in entirely new ways. She takes her distance from those modern French philosophers who reject the (human) subject altogether (by replacing it with traces, modalities, forces, or numbers): "Those who refuse to think the subject-in-process/on-trial risk becoming the object of a trial." She also steps back from all those who see Western history as operating on an Exclusion Model—where "what" or "who" has been left out of history can be gathered together as a basis for a new social contract. She shows how both the Law and all that has been silenced by the Law are inseparably bound in *the* logic and history of Judeo-Christianity. Now, if that historical temporality is coming to an end (but to speak of an "end" and "beginning" is, again, already to adhere to a certain logic)—what might henceforth perform the function of religion—and "woman"—with the least religiosity?

Here is where Kristeva's major passion breaks through: the poetic text, what, since the nineteenth century, we have called "literature." She once wrote, "What has not become law is poetic." Literature as a replacement for the religion which has bound us together for hundreds of years? No, not exactly. (Kristeva's thought, whatever else it is, is never utopian.) But perhaps a place—a space—where new borders between what can and cannot be said can find the *time* to form. Kristeva ends [*Pouvoirs de l'horreur*] (where the "feminine" finds a new and frightening contemporary resonance) in this way:

> Am I only reserving for myself the calm banks of contemplation by bringing to light, from under the deceitful and policed surfaces of civilizations, the nourishing horror they are busy putting out of sight through their constant purifying, systematizing, thinking: the horror they supply themselves with in order to grow and function? I see it rather as a work of deception, frustration, emptiness . . . possibly the only counterbalance to abjection. The rest—its archeology and its exhaustion—is nothing but literature. . . .

["Women's Time"] will be judged by many as antifeminist. I cannot possibly deny that it is. But if one is willing to follow Kristeva into the labyrinth she is exploring, I think they will find a thread of that "search for the woman-non-mother, the only radical other, the sister." Kristeva is alone—almost like the artists she describes writing in the future perfect—in reminding us that any hope for a radically new ethics may be up to women. *We have certainly heard this before,* but never while standing in a place (and time) from which we might finally be able to speak: the *now* and *here* where "our species finds itself exposed to madness under an empty sky." (pp. 5-12)

Alice Jardine, "Introduction to Julia Kristeva's 'Women's Time'," in Signs, *Vol. 7, No. 1, Autumn, 1981, pp. 5-12.*

Carol Mastrangelo Bové (essay date Winter 1984)

[*In the following excerpt, Bové discusses the methodology and rhetoric Kristeva employs in her analyses of literature and literary theory.*]

Although several of her finest essays appeared in excellent translation in 1980 as *Desire in Language: A Semiotic Approach to Literature and Art,* few American critics discuss Julia Kristeva at any length and even fewer analyze the political ramifications of her theory of the literary text. Within the limits of this review essay, I attempt to describe her work more fully (especially two essays that to my

knowledge have not yet been discussed in English) and to consider the question of her radical politics.

Her methodology is formalist, but unlike that of so many persistent academic critics trained in the American New Criticism or more recently in French Structuralism, her formalism neither separates linguistic and sociological functions nor relegates the latter to a marginal position. Rather, the study of the linguistic level of the text is the necessary point of departure in explicating levels that are political as well as psychoanalytic. Her theory of linguistic form as a break with the social contract is imaginatively explored in essays ranging over an impressive variety of writers including Roman Jakobson, Mikhail Bakhtin, Samuel Beckett, Roland Barthes, and Louis-Ferdinand Céline. I have come to read these writers differently, to rethink my understanding of even classic works with which I thought I had already come to terms, and to reconsider literary history with more awareness of the social issues that are necessarily raised by linguistic forms. The difference that Kristeva's work can make in the perception of these issues will become clearer, I think, if I apply her theory of the "hermitic" Marcel Proust. Although Kristeva's book does not deal directly with Proust, her theory suggests that we re-evaluate all significant novelists like him whose political discourse has for the most part gone unheard. He supposedly withdrew from the crassness of the haute bourgeoisie by creating an elitist, symbolist text. Not so if I read him as *Desire in Language* suggests I might.

Kristeva sees the text as an unleashing of unconscious drives, a liberation of innovative, instinctual discourse from traditional, communicative language. Building on the work of Bakhtin, Freud and Lacan, Kristeva analyzes this liberation in terms of a break with the social contract and in this way uncovers a sociopolitical function in the text. This text constitutes the linguistic life of the speaking subject that exists as a sequence of different selves—narrator, but also, reader or addressee, and characters. In the act of writing, an author liberates unconscious selves and in so doing, liberates the whole tradition of rational discourse in the West which is built upon the assumption of a homogenous, logical Self. This discourse denotes more than it connotes, and fuses one proposition to the next with causal links, leading to a conclusion already implied in the opening proposition. This essentially static structure, the thought pattern of a human being who is completely rational, mirrors the Christian God and possesses a transcendent quality.

By liberating the speaking subject from rational discourse, literature frees him or her from the social structure which this discourse also reflects. In Kristeva, moving from linguistic conservatism (language as communication where denotation and logically linked propositions dominate) to political conservatism (preservation of the status quo whether class or socialist structure) is not an unjustified leap because in every literary text, the first invariably reveals the second to some extent. The text repeatedly circulates words as it does everything else as objects of exchange and supports within a logical, self-regulating economy the privileged position of a unitary Self. In this way, communicative discourse attempts to deny the subject's needs within both language and society for the negation of rational discourses and for change that will accommodate unorthodox unconscious drives.

It is by means of a formalist methodology that Kristeva dramatizes the subject's need for such negation and change. She rejects a thematic approach and instead studies the dynamic interplay between two kinds of language, symbolic or communicative and semiotic or instinctual. The distinction between these two languages sounds dangerously close to jargon when summarized, but takes on a very concrete and carefully articulated meaning within the context of Kristeva's work. She uses this distinction to explain how art becomes a privileged form of existence for the human being because it is in this form that we no longer repeat words and images into which the cogito is again fixed but rather create a new language into which the long repressed life of the instincts is projected. This new language is defined in opposition to traditional language where logically connected clauses and denotation are primary. Instinctual language highlights connotations and creates patterns that are more rhythmical than logical.

Kristeva's formalist methodology may explain the critical reticence vis-à-vis her work and even some of the hostility to it. Her painstaking analysis of subtle linguistic structures in conjunction with an elliptical style deals with the issue of social change only indirectly and in the context of complex figures like Hegel and Lacan. Her reader takes on a difficult task and is tempted in the reading process to accuse her prematurely of playing linguistic games that instead of adopting a critical stance toward society, entertain and support an elite by supplying it with cocktail party conversation during which superficial "repressions" may be lifted (sex and revolution can be bandied over a drink) so that underlying repressions may continue (governments in Eastern and Western countries for the most part appear to grow more rigid and hierarchical).

Does Kristeva's formalism constitute an approach that can legitimately be called politically radical? Among the few who discuss her work, most ignore this critical issue or treat it in a summary fashion. Philip Lewis's review essay of *La Révolution du language poétique* also treats some of the essays translated in *Desire in Language* and is probably the most intelligent introduction to Kristeva published in English but it is unfortunately only a brief overview. It does call attention to her understanding of the sociopolitical function of the avant-garde but fails to discuss this function at any length. For Lewis, the connection she makes between poetic process and political program is "problematic" and "susceptible to misunderstanding." He implies that because her politics is restricted to the sphere of writing and to a writing that is marginal and inaccessible to a large audience, it does not merit extended treatment.

Claude Bouché's remarks on the sociological aspects of Kristeva's work seem downright cavalier. In his article "Materialist Literary Theory in France, 1965-1975," he attempts to deflect the subversive thrust of her work in one short paragraph in which she is condemned along with all

of the *Tel Quel* and *Change* writers as an idealist. Bouché appears to have accepted the orthodox Marxist reading which rejects the work of *Tel Quel* and of any criticism which does not concentrate on the direct, concrete relationship between text and means of production. When confronted by a similar rejection at a conference in Milan in 1973 on psychoanalysis and politics, Kristeva underlined the necessity to move beyond orthodox Marxism (and orthodoxy in general) and the study of the direct rapport between text and economic production. She reaffirmed the political function of literature in her theory by explaining that a psychoanalytic approach demonstrates the impasse represented by forms of class society and opens up the possibility of creating new forms.

Does a careful reading of *Desire in Language* support her reaffirmation of a political function in literature? The answer is no if this function is understood as the transformation of particular social structures and historical conditions. She never discusses how literature could play that kind of role. Yet, her formalism can be considered a radical political theory to the extent that it successfully dramatizes the subject's need for upheaval of the social order. Her debt to Bakhtin, Freud, and Lacan cannot be underestimated. She derives many concepts central to her formalism from them—from Bakhtin she learns how linguistic forms mirror social ones, on the one hand, and how the first may alternately subvert the second, on the other; from Lacan she borrows the notion of literature as the text of the speaking subject who is inherently multiple. Once the derivation of key concepts has been granted, however, we can admire *Desire in Language* for the intelligence with which it, 1) combines these concepts to build an eclectic theory in which linguistic, psychoanalytic, and political functions are integrally related, and 2) puts the theory into practice in her discussions of literature and painting. Her essay, "Word, Dialogue, and Novel" is a good example. Here and throughout the other essays on literature, Kristeva formulates her theory of the text as a series of alternations between instinctual and communicative language. She dramatizes these alternations by expressing them in terms of the subject's violent movements against or through a stable barrier that is the law or a similar fundamental defense of social structure.

The subject of the essay "Word, Dialogue, and Novel" is Bakhtin's notion of the dialogic which derives from Menippean satire and carnivalesque forms. Kristeva transforms this notion into the structuring principle of all texts understood within her eclectic theory:

> In other words the dialogism of Menippean and carnivalesque discourses, translating a logic of relations and analogy rather than of substance and inference, stands against Aristotelian logic. From within the very interior of formal logic, even while skirting it, Menippean dialogism contradicts it and points it towards other forms of thought. Indeed, Menippean discourse develops in times of opposition against Aristotelianism, and writers of polyphonic novels seem to disapprove of the very structures of official thought founded on formal logic.

The poetic word, polyvalent and multidetermined, adheres to a logic [the dialogic] exceeding that of codified discourse and fully comes into being only in the margins of recognized culture. Bakhtin was the first to study this logic, and he looked for its roots in *carnival.* Carnivalesque discourse breaks through the laws of language censored by grammar and semantics and, at the same time, is a social and political protest. There is no equivalence, but rather, identity, between challenging official linguistic codes and challenging official law.

In these telling passages, Kristeva underlines literature's sociopolitical dimension—it "challenges official law" and "disapproves of the very structures of official thought." For readers unfamiliar with Bakhtin, these statements appear simply to posit this dimension. Kristeva is building upon Bakhtin and assumes his understanding of literature as a political act that, in and through linguistic forms, subverts the hierarchical tendencies of social structure (Western class societies and Stalin's rigid form of socialism). Rabelais is a transitional figure who bridges the gap between the Middle Ages and the Renaissance. He presents an image of feudal ideology in certain linguistic patterns of his work where values (and particularly the eternal) are pitted against material existence and change. These patterns are then deconstructed by others where everything of value is linked to a hardy physical entity that grows.

Whereas the source for Kristeva's conception of the political and linguistic levels of the text is Bakhtin, the source for her understanding of the psychoanalytic level, for the notion of a multiple subject who alternately constructs and dissolves structures that are at one and the same time linguistic and ideological is Lacan. Convinced of the validity of his notion of the subject, she reads Bahktin as a precursor of the imaginative interpreter of Freud, "In order to describe the dialogism inherent in the denotative or historical word, we would have to turn to the psychic aspect of writing as trace of a dialogue with oneself (with another), as a writer's distance from himself, as a splitting of the writer into subject of enunciation and subject of utterance."

This passage not only helps us to see how Kristeva meshes the psychoanalytic level of the text with the formal and sociopolitical levels but also suggests the way in which her theory is put into practice. The image of the "splitting of the writer" goes beyond its conventional use in psychoanalytic criticism. It is part of the rhetoric she employs to dramatize linguistic and social upheaval as violent action against or through a stable barrier. In this case, the barrier is the human being understood in traditional terms as a unitary Self whose resistence to such action is felt in repeated reference to this Self ("with oneself," "a writer's," "the writer," "subject of enunciation").

Other examples of this rhetoric that describes action against a barrier abound both in the rest of this essay and throughout the book. In the section where she relates Saussure's concept of the poetic paragram to Bakhtin's dialogism, she states that the latter " . . . implies a categorical *tearing from the norm* and a relationship of nonexclusive opposites." Here, as is often the case, the barrier under attack has both linguistic and social connotations—

it is described as a kind of legislative authority, "the norm". Similarly in the passage quoted above, "carnivalesque discourse *breaks through* the *laws* of a language *censored* by grammar and semantics and, at the same time, is a social and political protest." The variations of this rhetoric are endless: "opening up" of an "enclosure, "bursting" or "clashing" movement, "shattering" of a surface, "transgression." The "shattering" of a surface, for instance, is often the form taken by the subject's negating energies in Kristeva's analysis of both Bakhtin's dialogism (" . . . syntactic and semantic unity are shattered by the voices and accents of the 'others' ") and of Jakobson's innovations in linguistics and commentary on the Russian Futurists, Mayakovsky and Khlebnikov: " . . . *a code* (mores, social contract) *must be shattered* in order to give way to the free play of negativity, need, desire, pleasure, and jouissance, before being put together again, although temporarily and with full knowledge of what is involved."

Kristeva's rhetoric serves to dramatize her theory of the text as revolutionary praxis and to lend coherence and conviction to this theory. Along with the images of violent action opposing a barrier are related images that belong to Freud and that depict this barrier as, 1) a watchman at a threshold, or 2) a screen that blocks the subject's speech. Kristeva uses Freud's images in conjunction with Lacan's notion of the decentered subject in ways that appear to read Freud and Lacan into texts where a theory of the unconscious is at most only implicit, such as Bakhtin's books on Rabelais and Dostoevsky and Jakobson's essays on the Russian Futurists. Kristeva's own rhetoric, and particularly the way in which she seems to project herself as Lacanian critic onto the text she analyzes, indicates a break with traditional, wholly rational, authoritarian, critical stances. . . . [Her] rhetoric itself supports the thesis that language constitutes the linguistic and political liberation of the "speaking subject".

By projecting herself onto the text she analyzes and by making unorthodox, semiotic language her central theme, Kristeva gives this language a privileged position in her work. Revealing the charges of idealism and elitism to be misguided, she performs a political act by breaking with the social contract thematically and linguistically in her own "subjective" discourse and also (and this follows naturally from her theory) by giving individuals and groups considered marginal in the hierarchies of society and literary history a privileged role as well. Her complex analysis of a little known prose piece of the fifteenth century, La Sale's *Jehan de Saintré,* for instance, identifies this piece as central in the birth of the realistic European novel. She demonstrates how the novel breaks with the symbolic mode and the feudal world view of earlier prose and how it begins to establish a sign-oriented mode and a capitalist ideology. The analysis of La Sale is a good example of Kristeva's uncanny ability to identify and explicate subversive, transitional figures. Her early (1969) appreciation of Bakhtin as a writer at the crossroads of Russian Formalism, Marxism, and psychoanalysis is another case in point.

In addition to the "subversive intellectual" (La Sale, Bakhtin, and also Jakobson, Khlebnikov, and

Mayakovsky, particularly back in 1974 when she wrote **"The Ethics of Linguistics"**), she also gives a privileged role to others considered secondary in mainstream Western society and discourse. She has written a fascinating account of her impressions during a trip to China in 1974 that reflects on a culture still little understood in the West and especially on the status of women in both East and West (*About Chinese Women*). In *Desire in Language*, frequent reference is made to the marginal position of women.

Unlike many theorists who attempt to uncover a sociological function in art, Kristeva reveals that the dynamics of form are both complex and specific. Her analysis of Saussure's *Anagrams* and of La Sale's *Saintré*, for instance, could not be criticized for either simplifying or generalizing problems of linguistic structure (poetic logic in the first case, the birth of the realistic novel in the second). Part of the value of her formal method lies in the fact that she deals successfully with the particular elements of different works and of different disciplines, especially literature and painting. The dialectical interplay between the communicative and the instinctual that emerges in her analysis of texts emerges in different form in her essays on Medieval and Renaissance painting, **"Giotto's Joy"** and **"Motherhood According to Bellini"**. In the essay on Bellini, she projects herself with him onto the baby on the canvas whose desire for the Mother (search for *jouissance*) transforms the two-dimensional madonna into a play of color that creates a sense of volume or third dimension. Kristeva describes this projection in terms of the formal elements of the painting where traditional representation in two dimensions (madonna and child as a phallic attempt to reach the Mother) is deconstructed by the madonna's other-worldly, alienated and characterless face and the almost abstract use of blocks of color for the human figures. This dialectical movement from representation to its deconstruction functions as a political act as well as a formal procedure: representation, using "madonna and child" in the orthodox manner, reproduces the Renaissance Humanist ideology that fetishizes the Mother as a narrowly-defined figure who is child-oriented and "the seat of social conservation." By subverting that ideology and the society that is sustained by it, Bellini liberates the subject and particularly the female subject. The chapter on Bellini makes clear that Kristeva's theory is a form of materialist literary theory and of feminist literary theory as well. It is feminist not because the theme of the painting happens to be a woman, but because for Kristeva, as for Lacan, to resist the use of signs for communication (in Bellini, elements of traditional representation like the madonna and child icon) and, in general, to transgress the social contract, constitutes a rejection of the normal resolution of the Oedipal conflict. Here, the unconscious projects itself into an antisocial, antirepresentational feminine role and frees itself from authority.

Proust's work presents a clear example of the rejection of the normal resolution of the Oedipal conflict and in general an excellent model on which to test Kristeva's theory. (pp. 217-24)

Although, and maybe because, Kristeva does not offer a specific analysis of how the subject's struggles can be seen as an attempt to change a particular social structure and to have an impact on historical conditions, she does offer a broadly political perspective that enables me to see [Proust's] *Remembrance* as a liberating work that frees the subject from the narrator's symbolist aesthetic and also from repressive class society. Proust is offering a critique of this aesthetic as an attempt to transform the fluctuating movements of the psyche into a homogenous linguistic object that contains no reference to anything outside of its own coherent structure. The narrator's symbolism, his efforts to reify the ephemeral, discontinuous, sensual experiences of his apprenticeship as a writer is only one side of a double discourse. The other side negates these efforts by revealing them to be repressive—they deny instinctual drive by limiting the subject's existence to a coherent linguistic structure without discontinuity. Moments of involuntary memory lose their fundamentally disruptive character and are made to appear to testify to a transcendent Self. In the last section of the novel, the narrator often claims, for instance, that the madeleine and paving stone episodes reveal an unchanging core of being that the preceding 2800 pages of discontinuous experiences deny.

Like his attitude toward his theory of fiction, the narrator's view of salon society is double. On the one hand, it is the setting par excellence for art—he hears and discusses the fine Vinteuil sonata and meets Bergotte, the author he admires most, at the Verdurins. The salon is, on the other hand, the worst possible environment for art—objects and guests are chosen for their exchange value, i.e., their prestige within the hierarchical upper class and not for their own merits. Swann, for instance, becomes one of the Verdurin clan not for any special virtue of his own, but because he is the friend of Odette who has been selected by the authoritarian Mme Verdurin as the fashionable cocotte of the current season. Although he claims to be working on Vermeer, Swann has nothing of interest to say about the painter and actually works only occasionally on this project. For many years the narrator himself allows the beau monde to hinder his writing by devoting himself almost exclusively to the predominantly mindless repartee of the Guermantes salon. Proust delivers a critique of salon society as one that does not really encourage the artistic individual, but exploits him (Swann and the narrator, for instance) as objects of exchange in order to maintain and solidify its privileged position within a hierarchy that does not lend itself to transformation. (pp. 224-25)

Reading Proust with Kristeva leads me to reassess his position in literary history. I question the long held view that he brings the symbolist era to an elegant and elaborate culmination—it is more probably that he helps to clear the new frontiers of psychoanalysis and Marxism. At the same time, the insights that an application of her theory to the *Remembrance* yields indicate that a careful reading and assessment of Kristeva's own substantial corpus is long overdue. (p. 227)

Carol Mastrangelo Bové, "The Politics of Desire in Julia Kristeva," in boundary 2, *Vol. XII, No. 2, Winter, 1984, pp. 217-28.*

Eléanor H. Kuykendall   (essay date 1989)

[In the following essay, Kuykendall criticizes Kristeva for failing to question what she considers the male-oriented, paternalistic underpinnings of Freudian and Lacanian psychoanalysis.]

What is knowledge of language? For Ferdinand de Saussure, it is the speaker's use of signs, accepted by social consensus to constitute language, or *la langue.* For Noam Chomsky, it is the speaker's understanding grammar and word meaning, or linguistic competence. For Jacques Lacan, it is the speaker's accepting symbolic meaning, or renouncing forbidden unconscious desires and becoming a separate subject. But in **"The Ethics of Linguistics"** Julia Kristeva proposes expanding conceptions of language and its knowledge to include rhythmic and tonal—prosodic—interventions in uses of signs, syntax, and symbols. The speaker or writer alternates between syntactic and symbolic, and prosodic communication, perpetually recreating a decentered, divided subjectivity in process. Kristeva proposes that linguistics and its allied disciplines be obligated to disclose the unconscious origins of this divided subjectivity to speakers and writers.

In that which follows I want to show that Julia Kristeva's conceptions of language and its knowledge—which extend the Saussurian conception of the sign, reject the Chomskyan conception of the rational speaker, and revise the Lacanian conception of the separate speaking subject—clash with her conception of ethics itself, an ethics which leaves a Lacanian conception of subjectivity in place. First, I offer a brief account of what Kristeva takes an ethics of linguistics to be and why, for her, psychoanalysis has a positive role in it. Second, I ask whether the "speaking subject" of Kristeva's argument is masculine, gender-neutral, or possibly feminine. I do this by comparing interpretations of Freud's famous example of language acquisition—a child's game with a spool while uttering the words "fort" ("gone") and "da" (here)—by Lacan, by Kristeva herself, and by Jacques Derrida and Luce Irigaray. Third, I conclude that Kristeva's conception of ethics, which characterizes the feminine as "outlaw" or "heretical" and thus outside ethics entirely, renders a conception of "female subjectivity," at best, problematic and at worst, a contradiction in terms. Despite the apparent centrality of the feminine in her writings on maternity, Kristeva's ethics of linguistics is not, finally, feminist, in a sense of the term that Americans would accept, in that it is avowedly Freudian and leaves no place for a feminine conception of agency.

What does Kristeva take an ethics of linguistics to be? And why, for her, does psychoanalysis have a positive role in it? Kristeva both rejects Chomskyan rationality and revises a narrowly conceived Freudian and Lacanian conception of symbolic meaning. She also proposes a positive program to expand the Saussurian conception of the linguistic sign. Psychoanalysis plays a positive role in her ethics of linguistics by helping to describe interventions in symbolic meaning "admitting of upheaval, dissolution, and transformation," in which the "social constraint" perpetuated by descriptions of language as "signified structure" is also disrupted, "with the speaking subject leaving its imprint on the dialectic between the articulation and its process."

Kristeva's ethics of linguistics rejects Chomskyan rationality and revises Lacanian subjectivity. Her **"Ethics of Linguistics"** rejects Chomsky (whom she does not name in that essay though she does elsewhere), by rejecting Chomsky's conception of the primary object of inquiry—the sentence—as well as Chomsky's conception of what the speaker knows—syntax and conventional meaning which conform to the law of contradiction. For Kristeva, Chomskyan linguistics err by imposing an adult generative model of knowledge of language both on the utterances of infants, whose communication precedes conventional language use, and also on adult poetic discourse and its semiotic interventions, which evince and recreate the unconscious desires of infants before they learn conventional syntax and symbols.

Kristeva's ethics of linguistics not only rejects Chomskyan rationality, but also revises Lacanian subjectivity which repeats an error by Freud. Kristeva argues that Freud erred by attributing to the pre-speaking infant a relationship to the father and to discourse that can occur only after the child learns conventional meaning. Yet Kristeva also contends that Freud's error has not affected the structure of linguistics, which need only be expanded to include semiotics. By extension, Lacan also erred, conflating the structure of semiotic communication during the pre-Oedipal mother-infant bond, with symbolic communication, which the (male) child must learn in and by separating from the mother and identifying with the father. Lacan's reinterpretation of Freud's account of the child's resolution of the Oedipus complex by learning the symbolic discourse of the father, it follows, has not affected linguistics either.

Thus in presenting her positive proposal for an ethics of linguistics Kristeva leaves in place a Lacanian conception of the acquisition of symbols. This account does not differ structurally from Freud's account of the resolution of the Oedipus complex, in that both Freud and Lacan tie their accounts of language learning to a male child's identification with the father, acquisition of a superego or moral sense, and renunciation of forbidden erotic desires for his mother. Kristeva's proposal does, though, supplement a conception of the symbolic in which Freudian and Lacanian psychoanalysis continues to play a positive role, with her own conception of the semiotic, which she criticizes Freud and Lacan for overlooking.

Kristeva has repeatedly presented and reaffirmed a distinction between semiotic and symbolic meaning tied to Freudian and Lacanian psychoanalysis. For example, in her 1974 *Revolution in Poetic Language,* she offers the following definition of "semiotic," which is tied to Freud:

> We understand the term "semiotic" in its Greek sense: sémiotiké = distinctive mark, trace, index, precursory sign, proof, engraved or written sign, imprint, trace, figuration. . . . This modality is the one Freudian psychoanalysis points to in postulating not only the *facilitation* and the structuring *disposition* of drives, but also the so-called *primary processes* which displace

and condense both energies and their inscription. Discrete quantities of energy move through the body of the subject who is not yet constituted as such and, in the course of his development, they are arranged according to the various constraints imposed on this body—always already involved in a semiotic process—by family and social structures. In this way the drives, which are "energy" charges as well as "psychical" marks, articulate what we call a *chora:* a nonexpressive totality formed by the drives and their stases in a motility that is full of movement as it is regulated. . . .

Kristeva also offers the following definition of the symbolic, which is tied to Lacan:

> We shall distinguish the semiotic (drives and their articulations) from the realm of signification, which is always that of a proposition or judgment, in other words, a realm of *positions.* This positionality, which Husserlian phenomenology orchestrates through the concepts of *doxa, position,* and *thesis,* is structured as a break in the signifying process, establishing the *identification* of the subject and its object as preconditions of propositionality. We shall call this break, which produces the positing of signification, a *thetic* phase. All enunciation, whether of a word or of a sentence, is thetic. It requires an identification; in other words, the subject must separate from and through his image, from and through his objects. This image and objects must first be posited in a space that becomes symbolic because it connects the two separated positions, recording them or redistributing them in an open combinatorial system.

Despite many turns in Kristeva's work, a constant theme remains her distinction between the semiotic and the symbolic, a theme which she argues in **"The Ethics of Linguistics"** as well as in other works. For example, she reaffirms it explicitly in her 1985 *Au commencement était l'amour* and again in *Soleil Noir,* from 1987, where she writes: "The 'semiotic' and the 'symbolic' become the communicable marks of a present affective reality, perceptible to the reader (I like this book because it communicates sadness, anguish, or joy to me), and nevertheless dominated, separated, conquered . . . "

Kristeva's method of countering the symbolic with the semiotic, as well as her conceptions of them, also holds constant. For example, in 1970 she described her inquiry into a subjectivity in process as a "logic of dialogism," in which there appears, first, a "logic of distance and of relation between different terms of a sentence or narrative structure" and, second, a "logic of analogy and of nonexclusive opposition, in opposition to the level of causality and of identifying determination." In the second stage of this process, a Chomskyan identification of syntax with logic and rationality is turned against itself. In 1975 Kristeva wrote that the Freudian anti-logic of the first stage, with its opposition between separation and desire for merger, is perpetually recreated through the interventions of the semiotic into conventional syntax and sense. The process is continual, dynamic, diachronic—it is a historical process taking place over time, so that the writer

of the literary text, through the disintegrated perception of a subjectivity wrought by that text, is thereby transformed with the reader together as subject origins of an unconscious knowledge of language.

Consequently Kristeva's ethics of linguistics, which is a negative rejection of Chomskyan rationality and a revised and elaborated version of Lacanian subjectivity, continues to embrace Freudian and Lacanian psychoanalysis. But, critical as she is of narrower Freudian and Lacanian conceptions of symbolic meaning, Kristeva leaves untouched their conception of ethics, which is tied to their account of (symbolic) language acquisition.

Is the "speaking subject"—revealed, for Kristeva, through interventions by the semiotic into symbolic meaning—masculine, gender-neutral, feminine, or simply absent? I want to consider alternative answers to this question given by Freud (in a famous example), by Lacan, by Kristeva herself, by Jacques Derrida, and by Luce Irigaray. Freud's and Lacan's accounts, of course, are "symbolic," in Kristeva's sense of the term. Kristeva's, in which, as we have seen, she postulates a perpetually dislocated and moving subject, I shall characterize as "adverbial;" and Derrida's and Irigaray's, as "performative."

Kristeva states both that Freud was wrong in supposing that language learning begins with learning symbolic meaning, and that his error has not affected linguistics. Compounding this apparent contradiction, Kristeva repeatedly cites as authoritative Freud's conception of symbolic language acquisition, which he ties to an account of the acquisition of the superego or moral sense. And she also endorses Lacan's interpretation of Freud's conception of language acquisition.

Kristeva has reaffirmed these endorsements in her most recent writings. In *Au commencement était l'amour,* for example, she states: "The sadness of young children, their renunciation of maternal paradise and of the immediate satisfaction of their demands, which precedes the appearance of language, has frequently been observed. It is necessary to abandon the mother and to be abandoned by her in order that the father take me up and that I speak." In *Soleil Noir* she writes,

> This identification which one might call phallic or symbolic assures the entrance of the subject into the universe of signs and of creation. The father-support of this symbolic triumph is not the Oedipal father, but rather this "imaginary father," "father of individual prehistory," according to Freud, who guarantees primary identification. However, it is imperative that this father of individual prehistory be able to assure his role of Oedipal father in symbolic Law, for it is on the basis of this harmonious alliance of the two faces of paternity that the abstract and arbitrary signs of communication can to be connected to the affective sense of prehistoric identities.

According to both Freud and Lacan, the child learns conventional word meaning simultaneously with becoming a separate subject, learning to substitute words for an absent and desired object—the mother. The child in question is a boy, the identification with the symbolic is with the father, and so the Freudian or Lacanian "speaking subject" is masculine.

In Freud's example, an eighteen-month-old boy named Ernst—Freud's own grandson, a child of Freud's daughter, Jacques Derrida tells us in *La carte postale*—invents a game with a cotton-reel or spool tied to a piece of string. Throwing the spool over the edge of his curtained crib with a drawn-out "oooh," and recovering it with an elated "ah," the child, according to Freud, comes to accept his mother's absence by learning to substitute the spool for his mother and to control the spool by pulling on the string. Moreover, the child's utterance, wrote Freud, is semantically meaningful: the "oooh" and "ah" are the boy's first attempts at the German words "fort" and "da," which mean "gone" and "here." The child thus learns to control not only the spool, but also the words. Freud drew from this example the child's attempt to master a (temporary) loss of his primary object of satisfaction—the mother—as the child's mastery of language. The child perceives that his action of throwing the spool places the object out of view—destroys it—but that he can cause it to reappear or disappear again at will by manipulating the string to which it is tied. In the same way, the child learns that by uttering words he, too, can magically banish or reevoke the desired object. It was the "fort . . . da" game that led Freud to postulate the pleasure principle, the death drive, and the acquisition of language, since the child's use of words in this game is a sadistic destruction of the objects referred to, then a symbolic and omnipotent resurrection of them.

Both Freud and Lacan also argue that the child learns to reject the mother and accept, under threat of castration, the words representing the rule of the father; but Lacan's account of the "fort . . . da" example is more radical still, in that for Lacan the words themselves stand for the spool, which in turn stands for the mother symbolically and sadistically thrown away, so that the game "demonstrates in its radical features the determinacy which the human animal receives from the symbolic order." Anika Lemaire adds that the game illustrates Lacan's theory of anchoring points, in that the symbol—the spool—is substituted for the child's experience of the mother's absence, and the spool as symbol is replaced, in turn, by the linguistic symbol—the words:

> This mechanism of access to language simultaneously constitutes both the unconscious and conscious language. But it is followed by the separation of the unconscious from conscious language, as the phonemes substituted for the child's imaginary lived experience have the universal meaning of the concepts 'gone' and 'present' as well as their subjective reference. . . . To sum up: language re-produces reality.

Although critical of Freud's and Lacan's neglect of semiotic meaning, Kristeva endorses both Freudian and Lacanian interpretations of the "fort . . . da" example, adding that the Freudian fort-da is the origin of the drive to rejection, or negativity.

> This negativity—this expenditure—posits an object as separate from the body proper, and, at the

very moment of separation, fixes it in place as *absent,* as a *sign.* In this way, rejection establishes the object as real and, at the same time, as signifiable (which is to say, already taken on as an object within the signifying system and as subordinate to the subject who poses it through the sign). . . . Negativity—rejection—is thus only a *functioning* that is discernible through the *positions* that absorb and camouflage it: the real, the sign, and the predicate appear as differential moments, steps in the process of rejection.

Since Kristeva's conception of semiotic meaning turns on contradictory and shifting references and significations, the point of her own argument is that the semiotic meaning is originally not referential, but adverbial: "The well-known 'reel game' with its *fort-da,* observed around the age of eighteen months, finds, over a period of time, its linguistic realization first in demonstrative or localizing utterances and finally in personal and negative utterances." Even according to Freud's interpretation of his grandson's utterances of "oooh" and "ah," the German words "fort" and "da" or "gone" and "here" are not, of course, nouns at all, but adverbs; for they have no definite reference. Nor, according to Kristeva's reading of the example, does the speaker have a stable self-reference either. The "speaking subject" of Freud and Lacan is thus transformed into Kristeva's "subject in process." For her this subject is gender-neutral, alternating between a masculine identification with the symbolic and a feminine identification with the semiotic, in fusion with the mother. But Kristeva's adverbial account of the example does not question—indeed, it repeatedly reaffirms, as we saw at the beginning of this section—the Freud-Lacan conception of the child learning conventional word meaning in separating from his mother under threat of castration. Thus Kristeva's portrayal of the "speaking subject" as gender-neutral is problematic. But other readings of the same Freud-Lacan "fort . . . da" anecdote support an alternative to Kristeva's own expanded conception of the "speaking subject."

For example, both Jacques Derrida and Luce Irigaray have argued, with differing conclusions, that the child's game with the spool is not simply an acquisition of symbols mastering the absence of a forbidden yet still-desired mother, as in Freud and Lacan, nor even an adverbial dislocation both of the desired object and of the subject himself, as Kristeva proposes. Rather, the child's game with the spool is a performance. By uttering words suitable to the deed the child does not, of course, make the object disappear and reappear simply by uttering the words. Rather, the child utters the words repeatedly to evoke the action—making the object disappear and reappear at will.

The child's performance is not a simple matter of exercising the pleasure principle in alternation with a sadistic drive, Derrida suggests, but rather, perhaps, of Freud's own autobiography:

> We observe that something repeats itself. And (has this ever been done?) the repetitive process is to be identified not only in the content, and the material described and analyzed by Freud but already, or again, in Freud's writing, in the *dé-*

marche of his text, in what he does as much as in what he says, in his "acts" if you will, no less than in his "objects". . . .

The performance in the "fort . . . da" example, as Derrida here observes, is not only ritual but also rhythm—the rhythm of Kierkegaardian repetition, of Nietzschean external return. Perhaps it is a ritual for Freud himself, as well as a rhythm of generations and of the transmission of power from one generation to another through the intermediary of the mother. Derrida notes that Freud's daughter Sophie, mother of the little boy who played with the spool and of a second child of whom the first was extremely jealous, died when her first-born was five years old, leaving an inconsolable husband. Although Derrida acknowledges Freud's indication that he finished *Beyond the Pleasure Principle,* which includes the "fort . . . da" anecdote, before the child's mother fell sick, Freud's story can also be interpreted as the father's adjustment to the loss of his daughter, forbidden to him as the son is to his mother by the incest taboo. Thus as rhythm, the utterance of "fort . . . da" ritually invokes Freud's own contact between the generations, dispelling the separation of death.

The Freudian "fort-da" is a performance or a ritual for the mastery and control of absences other than the mother's, Derrida suggests: of truth, veiled like the child's cot or like the forbidden mother; of eros, which, as in Aristophanes's speech in Plato's *Symposium,* arises in a desire to overcome separation from the object of desire; and finally of power itself, transformed from a reflective quest for control to an ecstatic search for fusion with another. Though for Derrida this quest is mediated through an archetypal woman, he also acknowledges that the infantile castration fantasy, which Freud (followed by Lacan and Kristeva) attributes to little boys, does not exist for women. Hence Freudian and Lacanian interpretations of the origins of morality and of the power of discourse do not exist for women either, if castration does not. If the driving force toward fusion characterized by both Freud and Lacan is beyond morality, it is also beyond morality in its derivative erotic, which equates fusion with death. But the little boy's attempt to control his mother's absence, reinterpreted in a Derridean erotic, then becomes a three-stage process through which she never becomes fully visible to the beholder.

In the first stage the woman appears as truth, though veiled, much as the infant's cot was veiled so that the spool thrown over its edge disappeared from view. In the second stage the woman appears as untruth, the unlawful object of the erotic desire of a son who can enter into intimacy with her only by violating her, thus, destroying the father's morality. In the third stage, Derrida proposes, "Woman is recognized and affirmed as an affirmative power, a dissimulatress, an artist, a dionysiac. And no longer is it man who affirms her. She affirms herself, in and of herself, in man." But in presenting woman as "dissimulatress," though a specifically feminine presence, Derrida perpetuates a conception of the male child's fantasy of control, since the mother still does not act directly. Thus Derrida perpetuates the Freudian and Lacanian assumption, which Kristeva tacitly accepts, of the masculinity of the speaking subject.

The conception of an animating belief or faith in the return of what was absent ("la croyance") supporting the child's performance with the spool or the words can be regarded apart from Derrida's mythic interpretation of it. For example, according to Luce Irigaray, it is not the mother's absence merely, but the mother herself, who is the object of the male child's search for mastery and control. But for Irigaray it is rather the mother's experience of fusion with the child, preceding the child's separation from her, that provides the basis for faith in a return after separation. Then the power to speak is not a matter of a male child's control or mastery over his mother's absence but rather of a mother's exercising a power having nothing to do with the threatened intervention of a punishing father. Consequently, for Irigaray, there is no question of a further retelling of the story of the absent spool, for "In this peek-a-boo game the son plays only with himself: with himself in her, her in him, above all face-to-face between them." It is instead a question of altogether abandoning the game, with its symbolism and its conception of symbolic meaning, as imposing a nonreciprocal power on the mother.

For Irigaray, the belief that the child supposedly exercises in uttering the ritual "fort . . . da" is a belief in sexual difference, which reaffirms the mother's absence. But that belief has nothing to do with the mother's experience, or with a little girl's experience of learning language either. It is, indeed, another kind of doctrine: "Belief is not safe except in not knowing in what one communes or communicates. If one knows it, no need to believe, at least according to a certain mode of adherence. But truth, all truth, has always depended on a belief which mines and undermines it. Whether that belief announces itself or veils itself in myths, dogmas, figures, or religious rites, does that not also reveal what metaphysics holds in its crypt?" Confidence or "croyance" in a community which makes communication possible undermines both Derrida's proposal to shift the focus of speaking subjectivity to an inaccessible feminine figure, and the Freud-Lacan analysis of masculine language acquisition which Kristeva endorses.

Further, for Irigaray, both the Freud-Lacan "fort . . . da" and Derrida's revision of it tell of a banishment of the mother, and by extension of the feminine, from speaking subjectivity. This banishment creates an ethical problem for Irigaray which is no problem at all for Kristeva: Kristeva's conception of the feminine is, by definition, and in consequence of the Freudian and Lacanian conception of the "speaking subject" which she endorses, outside ethics entirely.

In several essays on the maternal Kristeva depicts an absent, hysterical, or wounded mother as a heroine. She is a two-faced being, an object of horror. She is the Virgin present at the crucifixion of Christ: the goddess-mother whom the Judeo-Christian tradition supplanted with the father-son. She is, then, a mystical being, dwelling in the semiotic, pre-Oedipal preconsciousness, beyond the reach of a punishing father who compels accession to the symbolic order of discourse and thereby to the order of phallic Law. Yet for Kristeva this mother is phallic—powerful—in the Freudian sense of the term.

Rather than reject the mystification of the mother, as Simone de Beauvoir did—too quickly, Kristeva says—and rather than respect the glorification of a subordinate mother, in accordance with conventional belief, Kristeva calls for an ethics of the "second" sex. This ethics, Kristeva says, does not exclude women, as Freud and Lacan do, or place her in a deferential position, as conventional religious belief does, but resolutely separates women from morality altogether:

> Now, if a contemporary ethics is no longer seen as being the same as morality; if ethics amounts to not avoiding the embarrassing and inevitable problematics of the law but giving it flesh, language, and jouissance—in that case its reformulation demands the contribution of women. Of women who harbor the desire to reproduction (to have stability). Of women who are available so that our speaking species, which knows it is mortal, might withstand death. Of mothers. For an heretical ethics separated from morality, an *herethics,* is perhaps no more than that which in life makes bonds, thoughts, and therefore the thought of death, bearable: herethic is undeath, love.

This conception of a "heretical" or outlaw ethics appears to give value to the feminine by resurrecting the pre-Oedipal, prerational part of the unconscious while reviving, as we have seen, the lost area of semiotic meaning evoked in poetry and *avant-garde* writing. But, by her own account, Kristeva's conception of a heretical ethics of the feminine leaves in place Freudian and Lacanian conceptions of ethics itself, which tie the acquisition of symbolic meaning to a male child's acquisition, under threat of castration, of a superego, identifying himself with the father and more generally with the Law of the Fathers. Ethics itself, for both Freud and Lacan and, as we now see, for Kristeva too, is masculine, as is consciousness, the symbolic, and the superego or what Kant called "the moral sense"—that is, rationality. Indeed, Kristeva considers that subjectivity can only be masculine; "feminine subjectivity" is, at best, problematic.

An ethics of linguistics, it follows, obligates linguists, psychoanalysts, and literary critics to disclose the hidden resources of the unconscious for the benefit of *male* writers—and it is with male writers and artists, and their portrayals of the feminine, that Kristeva is concerned. The one exception is Kristeva's discussion of the erotic works of Marguerite Duras, some of which seem to concern women primarily. But even here Kristeva concludes that Duras "recounts the psychic underground anterior to our conquest of the other sex," so that Kristeva interprets even an author's exploration of this "quasi-uterine space" in terms of a subsequent engagement with the male, or of the depression accompanying the failure of such an engagement.

And so, for Kristeva, "Belief in the mother is rooted in the fear—fascinated with a weakness—the weakness of language. If language is powerless to locate myself and state me for the other, I assume—I want to believe—that there is someone who makes up for that weakness. . . . In that sense any belief, anguished by definition, is upheld by the fascinated fear of language's impotence." Kristeva's maternal, heretical, outlaw ethics argues for the mystery or unknowability of the mother while at the same time rejecting the subordinate mother assumed by conventional morality, appearing to make the feminine primary in all experience. But the return to the mother which Kristeva celebrates in calling for a recognition of the semiotic is necessary for the creativity and even the psychic survival of the male. Of the mother's own experience—which, as Luce Irigaray pointed out and as we have seen, Freudian (and Lacanian) and Derridean tellings of the "fort . . . da" episode overlooked—Kristeva's ethics of linguistics has little to say.

Even in her most recent work, *Soleil Noir,* in which Kristeva gives numerous examples from her (primarily but not exclusively) female psychoanalytic patients, she accepts uncritically a Freudian conception of the "castration complex" and accounts for her patients' depressions by invoking a Lacanian equation between phallic power and the power to speak. Accepting a Freudian and Lacanian conception of ethics as well, Kristeva attempts to carve out a place for maternal communication within that system, and ends by placing maternal communication—indeed all communication that she identifies as feminine—outside the phallic power system entirely. Kristeva's maternal ethics of linguistics ends where rationality, cognitive knowledge, and the social order imposed by paternal law begins.

Thus, Kristeva says that the mother's body is the locus of the confrontation between nature and culture—the symbolic, the "phallic" mother who makes discourse possible—and further places the mother between the "symbolic paternal facet" and the "homosexual feminine facet" that precedes discourse. Denoting the mother's body, and more generally maternal communication, as the reference point for the male speaker's ambivalence, Kristeva adopts a patriarchal system whose structure she does not question. The mother is always there, but there is no place for her. In that Kristeva's "ethics of linguistics," here elaborated as a maternal ethics, makes no place for the mother, or, more generally, for the feminine, it is an ethics of male sexuality, male ambivalence. Subjectivity in the process of traversing and retraversing the boundary between unconscious and irrational communication and that which is cognitive and rational is primarily a male concern.

The question remaining for Kristeva's ethics of linguistics is whether its call for a recognition of the value of semiotic communication could ever be separated from the Lacanian and phallocentric conception of ethics it also espouses. If it cannot, then no conception of feminine, conscious agency is possible for it either. In **"Stabat Mater"** Kristeva writes in two parallel columns; the citations above have been taken from both. In that the one column can be taken to represent the mother's own voice, commenting on cultural mystifications of the maternal, Kristeva can be taken as offering at least one example of feminine agency. But Kristeva is not concerned with establishing a theoretical conception of feminine agency. She has written ironically of support she received from feminist women in public lectures in the United States, has mocked

American feminist publications she found ("One finds that weak, naive, and ugly"), and has otherwise distanced herself from the American women's movement. She cannot, then, be considered a feminist, as Americans understand the term. And she has distanced herself from all factions of the French women's movement as well, writing, "Are women subject to ethics? . . . The answer . . . can be considered affirmative only at the cost of considering feminism as but a *moment* in the thought of that anthropomorphic identity which currently blocks the horizon of the discursive and scientific adventure of our species." In that Kristeva remains resolutely identified with Lacan, and, above all, with Freud, even in her most recent writings, and in that, in particular, she endorses an ethics resolutely located in an irrational, pre-Oedipal preconscious, her conception of "feminine subjectivity" is, in the end, a contradiction in terms. (pp. 180-91)

> *Eléanor H. Kuykendall, "Questions for Julia Kristeva's Ethics of Linguistics," in* The Thinking Muse: Feminism and Modern French Philosophy, *edited by Jeffner Allen and Iris Marion Young, Indiana University Press, 1989, pp. 180-94.*

Adam Phillips   (essay date 24 May 1990)

[*In the following excerpt, Phillips discusses* Black Sun: Depression and Melancholia *and Kristeva's theory of the importance of loss.*]

When Freud wrote in his famous essay 'Dostoevsky and Parricide' that 'before the problem of the creative artist, analysis must, alas, lay down its arms,' he seemed to be suggesting that there was some kind of war between psychoanalysis and art. And also that the creative artist was in some sense a problem, at least for psychoanalysis. Art may not be soluble in terms of psychoanalysis—it is difficult to see now why anyone should want it to be—but it is interesting to see what kind of object it is for different psychoanalysts, both how they find themselves using it in their writing and what kind of relationship they have with it. If psychoanalysts could think of themselves as the makers of sentences rather than of truths they would feel less at odds with—feel less need to privilege and covertly disparage—what Freud called Creative Writers. The idealisation of art and artists among psychoanalysts who write is always accompanied by its shadow of envy; and it is of interest that psychoanalysis has never found a place for the idea of inspiration. But from quite early in Freud's work—both in its genesis and in its content—the connection between creativity and mourning did find a place in psychoanalytic theory, one Melanie Klein was among the first to elaborate. Freud began to believe that lives were about achieving loss, eventually one's own loss, so to speak, in death; and that art could be in some way integral to this process, a culturally sophisticated form of bereavement. A work of art was a work of mourning—and mourning itself was an art. So after Freud and Klein it becomes possible to think, as Julia Kristeva suggests in one of many striking sentences in **Black Sun,** that 'my depression points to my not knowing how to lose—I have perhaps been unable to find a valid compensation for my

loss?' Compensation only comes, in Kristeva's view, in renewing the possibilities of communication, in the commitment to language. The acquisition of language is the only way of learning how to lose. 'The Freudian way,' she writes, 'aims at planning for the advent and formulation of sexual desire . . . for named sexual desire ensures securing the subject to the other, and consequently, to meaning.' Leon Roudiez, who has produced a mostly fluent version of a difficult text, translates *arrimage* as 'secures'. The French term, which is nautical in origin, also means 'to stow'. It is through desire, in language, Kristeva is saying, that the potential for connection between people is stored and kept safe. It is this, for very good reasons of his own, that the depressed person refuses and attacks. 'The depressed person,' she writes, only apparently changing the context, 'is a radical sullen atheist.'

Black Sun opens—and it is more like a drama than a treatise—with an enquiry into depression as an absence of interest, and with the paradoxical sense that to write about depression or melancholia is to write words about a state of mind in which words can be virtually meaningless:

> For those who are racked by melancholia, writing about it would only have meaning if writing sprang out of that very melancholia. I am trying to address an abyss of sorrow, a non-communicable grief that at times, and often on a long-term basis, lays claim upon us to the extent of having us lose all interest in words, actions, and even life itself. Such despair is not a revulsion that would imply my being capable of desire and creativity, negative indeed but present. Within depression, if my existence is on the verge of collapsing, its lack of meaning is not tragic—it appears obvious to me, glaring and inescapable.

Depression is a self-cure for the terrors of aliveness, of being alive to one's losses and therefore to one's desires. From a psychoanalytic point of view, imagination—the capacity for representation—begins, or rather, is initiated by the experience of loss; and the first loss appears to be of the mother. It is only in the absence of that first essential object that the infant or child will have to give thought to the mother. He will cope with the absence, which should be temporary, by imagining her presence. It is only in the space created by the mother's absence that she can be desired and therefore imagined. Knowing people is what we do to them when they are not there. And language in Kristeva's view—and the view of the versions of psychoanalysis she uses—is the way of managing loss by making it up. 'Signs are arbitrary,' she writes, 'because language starts with a negation of loss, along with the depression occasioned by mourning.' 'Arbitrary' because they are what happen to stand in for the absent mother—as though the child is implicitly saying, 'I haven't lost her because I have the words for her'—and a negation of loss because they are a pretended substitute. If my mother and I are the same, of the same mind, so to speak, I would not need a word for her or for what I wanted; and because my desire would then be strictly commensurate with its satisfaction, there would be no desire. It is through loss that I come to want something, and to imagine, even though it is a controversial thought, that there might be an I doing the wanting. But it is only in the medium of language that such constructions become possible.

The child, it seems, depends on his mother: but his development into a separate speaking being depends upon what might be called sufficient loss. And loss is literally figured out in language. 'If I did not agree to lose mother,' Kristeva writes, bringing in the notion of choice, 'I could neither imagine nor name her.' Without language, and without the pain of acknowledged absence this entails, there is no desire. So from this point of view psychoanalysis becomes a way of understanding the obstacles to symbolisation, to the conversations that are being refused. The realm of the unspoken comes to represent, among other things, the unwillingness to mourn, or to relinquish primary involvements. 'By' analysing—that is, by dissolving—the denial mechanisms wherein depressive persons are stuck,' Kristeva writes with beguiling confidence, 'analytic cure can implement a genuine graft of symbolic potential.' In psychoanalysis you cannot, of course, force people to be interested, but you can show them that there are interesting things around, that they are making more sense than they can let themselves know. As part of this graft of symbolic potential—horticulture is always preferable to militancy in psychoanalysis—she proposes that 'vowels, consonants or syllables may be extracted from the signifying sequence' of the depressed patient's language and construed by the analyst in the service of new meanings. The analyst, in other words, can make sense of the patient's language by listening to it as though it were nonsense poetry. If the analyst looks after the sound the sense can be taken care of. And this becomes necessary because, in psychoanalytic terms, defence mechanisms, like the denial Kristeva refers to, are forms of anaesthetic, unconsciously sustained poverties of language that pre-empt a knowledge of feeling. The desolate apathy of depression is less painful than the meanings it attempts to blank off. The possibility of meaning, the release of curiosity, is what the depression works to deny. (pp. 6-7)

Mourning, Freud wrote in 'Mourning and Melancholia', is an entirely appropriate response to the loss of a loved person through death or separation, but in melancholia 'a loss . . . has occurred, but one cannot see clearly what it is that has been lost, and it is all the more reasonable to suppose that the patient cannot consciously perceive what he has lost either.' In a revealing and understated way in **Black Sun** Kristeva often obscures Freud's distinction. Not denying that there is a difference between an actual rupture between people and a prevailing mood of despondency, she keeps open the question—a question that would be meaningless to someone grief-stricken by a bereavement—of what it is that has been lost. Is the trauma, for example, constituted for the child by the excessive absence of the mother, or by a breakdown or refusal of the possibilities of representation? Is what is lost the mother (or lover) as an object, or the belief in language as a substitute for her? 'The speech of the depressed,' Kristeva writes, 'is to them like an alien skin; melancholy persons are foreigners in their maternal tongue. They have lost the meaning—the value—of their mother-tongue for want of losing the mother.' So part of the value of language is the struggle we have to believe in it. And by its commitment

to the possibilities of meaning, psychoanalysis, as Kristeva says of works of art, 'can lead us to establish relations with ourselves and others that are less destructive, more soothing'. There is no cure, but there are ways of talking. (p. 7)

Adam Phillips, "What Is There to Lose?" in London Review of Books, *Vol. 12, No. 10, May 24, 1990, pp. 6-8.*

Calvin Bedient   (essay date Summer 1990)

[*In the following excerpt, Bedient criticizes Kristeva's psychoanalytic theory of poetry, which, he argues, is reductive in that it allows for the valorization of only those poems that reflect the premises of the theory.*]

I take it that when Julia Kristeva speaks of art as a "semiotic *chora*," as "the flow of jouissance into language," she means that art utters what cannot be uttered: *instinct*. I take it that she means that poetry, in particular, subverts culture (when we thought it *was* culture), because it permits instinct to infiltrate the symbolic medium of language itself.

Judge, if you will, for yourself. First, Kristeva's notion of the *chora*:

> We borrow the term *chora* from Plato's *Timaeus* to denote an essentially mobile and extremely provisional articulation constituted by [bioenergetic] movements and their ephemeral stases. We differentiate this uncertain and indeterminate *articulation* from a *disposition* that already depends on representation, lends itself to phenomenological, spatial intuition, and gives rise to a geometry. . . . The *chora*, as rupture and articulations (rhythm), precedes evidence, verisimilitude, spatiality, and temporality.

In other words, the *chora*, as the matrix of the drives, is precultural, subsymbolic. Is it then this, this *life*, that breaks into the civilized space of representation in poetry, crashing and destroying its party (when culture is partying) or making a shambles of its solemnity (when culture is being religious)?

To Kristeva, the person writing poetry is "on trial" or, more strictly, not a "subject" so much as a bundle of nerve impulses hostile to the "edifice" of identity, indeed to all cultural molds. This is the revolution *in* poetic language. And whatever our own terminology, don't all of us assume that "in the practice of the *text*" a "subject" is "*in process / on trial* [*sujet en procès*]" and that "deep structure or at least transformational rules are [thus] disturbed and, with them, the possibility of semantic and/or grammatical categorial interpretation"? Doesn't everyone know about and respect *connotation, ambiguity, charged language*?

How radical, then, is the theory of **Revolution in Poetic Language**? Isn't the heart of Kristeva's theory in the right place? So it might seem. But such a blind, revolutionary heart! All anger at "stases" that are inevitably reactive and phony, that are mere pauses for air, clutches at straws, or lies, and condemned to demolition because not the *utter* peace of death. Question Culture—this, in effect, is what the "semiotic *chora*" cries, "because it behaves like an arrival, an end, unpacks its bags, plans to stay. Nothing must stay until there is nothing." The understanding of life couched in Kristeva's writings, and particularly in *Revolution in Poetic Language*—and no understanding of life is more modern, more radical in relation to the age-old hubris of spirituality—is thus essentially the view familiar from Freud's *Beyond the Pleasure Principle* and, further back, the substance of some of Nietzsche's reflections, such as: " 'To be released from life is once again to become *true* . . . to perfect oneself' "; or " 'Inorganic matter is the maternal breast. . . . Whoever understands this would consider the return to insensate dust as a celebration' "; or " 'The inorganic world . . . represents the greatest synthesis of forces. . . . In the inorganic, error and the limitations of perspective do not exist.' "

In this "perspective," to be free means "not to be a function." Now, the *chora*—even if it is an indeterminate Brownian motion of impulses—is a function, a factory of *drive.* Biology is error, and the aspect of drive that is "too much," its *drive,* confesses as much. It rages to undo itself. But the culturally and personally positioned "subject" is an even greater error, because it is more obviously a function. Revolutionary freedom in poetry, then, must be won at the subject's expense, at the expense of position or perspective, or, in Kristeva's term, of the *thetic,* the laid down. Insofar as poetry is propositional, it is error. Insofar as it is "instinct," it is error, too. But relatively free? A runner's anticipatory lean into the tape at the finish line—that much closer to death?

[According] to Kristeva's theory, poetry is essentially antiformal—in fact, so profoundly antiaesthetic that the proper words for describing it are not *beauty, inspiration, form, instinctive rightness, inevitability,* or *delicacy.* . . . Instead, it attracts terms drawn from politics and war: *corruption, infiltration, disruption, shatterings, negation, supplantation,* and *murder.*

—*Calvin Bedient*

We had thought that poetry was a grace beyond biology, except for the biomovements of dancers, athletes, or those we love most. We had thought it a contradictory "organic" perfection in the relatively *staying* realm of the symbolical. But, no, according to Kristeva's theory, poetry is essentially antiformal—in fact, so profoundly antiaesthetic that the proper words for describing it are not *beauty, inspiration, form, instinctive rightness, inevitability,* or *delicacy* (to leave aside unaesthetic terms such as *perception* and *truth,* which the theory also renders inappropriate). Instead, it attracts terms drawn from politics and war: *corruption, infiltration, disruption, shatterings, negation, sup-*

plantation, and *murder.* Poetry is the *chora*'s guerrilla war against culture.

According to Kristeva, poetry reverses the ritualistic theological sacrifice of the soma, a sacrifice subsequently exacted, like a sales tax, through the "thetic" element of discourse, its determinate articulations. For Kristeva, the "theologization of the thetic" is what culture is—and as such it has no fundamental right to be, since what is fundamental is the *chora* and not God. I refer here as throughout to the revolutionary Kristeva of the late sixties and early seventies, the Kristeva whose "we," as she says in **"My Memory's Hyperbole,"** was a putatively communist Parisian party for "permanent revolution." *Revolution in Poetic Language* is a monumental, late end product of this phase of Kristeva's thinking; indeed, there are signs that she had already surpassed it by the time the book was published.

Simply put, *Revolution in Poetic Language* posits that *poetry sacrifices theology,* or the thetic, to traces of nonsymbolized drive. Poetry, that is, exploits and augments the "semiotic *chora*" with which language is already charged, the prelinguistic elements at its origins (rhythm, breath impulsion, intonation). In Kristeva's use, *semiotic (le sémiotique,* not the *la sémiotique* of French semiotics) means *index* or *imprint,* after the Greek word σημειον; the semiotic *chora* is the spider of instinct at the bottom of poetry's cup. Yes, "profoundly a-theological," "art—this semiotization of the symbolic— . . . represents the flow of jouissance into language"; and *jouissance* is the bliss of the nerve ends as they undergo their destructive splitting, firing up beyond the level of the pleasure principle.

This *jouissance* is primarily anal, since the destructive anal drives are (so Freud inferred) the strongest. But what is surprising—and political—in *Revolution in Poetic Language* is the virtual benching of the so-called affirmative drives. It is as if Kristeva attends only to the aggression implicit in the word *drive* itself. A year later, in **"From One Identity to an Other,"** one of the essays subsequently collected in *Desire in Language,* Kristeva even says that poetry "utters incest" (a magnificently thrown gauntlet that is at least *seemingly* sweeter than the claim that it utters *death.* But in the last analysis *desire* parallels *drive;* desire, too, is "too much."). In **"From One Identity to an Other,"** Kristeva emphasizes *erotic orality,* leaving behind, so to speak, the anality she makes so much of in *Revolution in Poetic Language.* And even in the latter, she asks:

> Doesn't poetry lead to the establishment of an object as a substitute for the symbolic order under attack, an object that is never clearly posited but always "in perspective." The object may be either the body proper or the apparatuses erotized during vocal utterance (the glottis, the lungs), objects that are either linked to the addressee of desire or to the very material of language as the predominant object of pleasure. . . . isn't art the fetish par excellence, one that badly camouflages its archaeology? At its base, isn't there a belief, ultimately maintained, that the mother is phallic, that the ego—never

precisely identified—will never separate from her, and that no symbol [linguistic sign] is strong enough to sever this dependence? In this symbiosis with the supposedly phallic mother, what can the subject do but occupy her place, thus navigating the path from fetishism to autoeroticism?

Evidently, this is to refer poetry, not to the *chora,* or the bioenergetic "mother," but to a mental construction, "the phallic mother." If "at its base" art hungers for that belated (as against archaic) fiction rather than for the autoeroticized *elsewhere* of the inorganic, then isn't art antinature and profoundly fictional? But this contradiction is no great moment in **Revolution in Poetic Language** because the idea that poetry is fetishistic is deeply obscured by the author's running emphasis not on *eros* but on *thanatos,* or not on *orality* but on *anality.* Poetry comes off not as fetishistic but as *rejective*—that is, as a rage for more than both the imaginary and the symbolic can offer. Poetry craves not identity with a maternal power but a negative freedom from all identity: dissolution, death. It takes words—the coins in the "isolated pocket of narcissism," the subject's "symbolic" spending power—and flings them beyond the lost space of mother-protected autoeroticism into the blind nonspace of organic origins. Thus would the *chora* "practice" a retreat to the inorganic bosom, make a down payment on peace. "Art," writes Kristeva, "accepts the thetic break [from nonsymbolized drive] to the extent that it resists becoming either delirium or a fusion with nature. Nevertheless, through this break, art takes from ritual space what theology conceals: transsymbolic jouissance, the irruption of the motility threatening the unity of the social realm and the subject." "Transsymbolic jouissance"—or subsymbolic *jouissance*—is drive where it slouches from the *chora* to culture to be symbolized, drive opposed to a cultural disposition and destiny.

Again: in poetry "the repeated death drive (negativity, destruction) withdraws from the unconscious and *takes up a position as already positivized and erotized in a language* that, through drive investment, is organized into prosody or rhythmic timbres." But this positivity and erotism nonetheless betray "an explicit confrontation between jouissance and the thetic," poetry bringing "into play . . . the vehemence of drives through the positing of language." What the text manifests "through language" is "the jouissance of destruction (or, if you will, of the 'death drive'), which . . . passes through an unburying of repressed, sublimated anality." Poetry becomes "a permanent struggle to show the facilitation of drives within the linguistic order itself." Culture beware!

Whatever the checks and balances acknowledged by her formulations, the pull of "theologized" culture (symbolization, fetishization) against the push of *jouissance,* Kristeva's rhetorical sympathies lie with anal cruelty, with "revolution," not with fetishism. One could deduce that she naturally stresses the part of her theory that is new, "revolutionary." But the zeal of her analysis of rejection has, as intimated, a political level. A politics of permanent revolution posits society itself as an analogue of poetic "practice," or a continual rage for "new symbolizations," a restlessness with the element of thetic finality.

This, indeed, describes the current temperament of the humanities. But it is not good psychoanalysis to take politics as fundamental; what is fundamental is the death drive, and Kristeva gives her theoretical and rhetorical energies to it with a thoroughness that suggests, precisely, a hunger for *jouissance.*

In any case, for both politics and poetry the implications of a "rejectivity" that has no agenda *except* "rejectivity" are breathtakingly radical. Change as the blind result of the *chora*'s restiveness—and Kristeva's theory posits and allows no other mechanism of change—results, at best, in transformations that are accidental in their plans and details. "New symbolizations" exist on the blind side of "the jouissance of destruction," itself blind, just as the mounds thrown up by a mole are the pure products of its rejection of the dirt in its path.

Kristeva effectively dismisses both intelligence (in any of its forms) and a formal sense as points to consider in analyzing the "textual practice" of poetry. "Intuition" is not a part of her technical vocabulary. And "ideas" she seems to regard as hopelessly contaminated by theology and what it constitutes, the murder of the soma. She's so hostile to the element of cognition in poetry that she speaks not of poems, in which ideas could nestle like eggs in a carton in a market, but only of "textual practice," a dynamic operation that subjects everything to "the vehemence of drives." But is there never anything to fear in a poet's power of mind? No truth to absorb? Nor any value (for instance, an experience of sharing) in the absorption? Withholding recognition as she does from everything except the pulverizingly reductive concepts of *rejection* and *stasis,* and in any case implicitly identifying the thetic with theology (in still another wholesale reduction), Kristeva naturally does not suppose that poetry has anything much to say. In effect, as "thesis," it all says the same thing: "viva narcissism!" Effectively, she wipes the suggestions of perceptivity off, like mist on a windshield, but only to drive straight on into the night.

She's no less ruthless toward form, not to mention genre and even the raw subject matter. Hence she insists that "we can read a Mallarmé or a Joyce only by starting from the signifier and moving toward the instinctual, material, and social process the text covers." In other words, we cannot read them, we can only excavate them. But how can we get back to the "instinctual, material" process of poetic practice? How can we examine various authors' nerve ends in their moment-by-moment vehemence? In any case, why do so? In their ceaseless "scissions," are they not all alike? Are there qualitative differences in a Joyce's, as against a Mallarmé's, destructive drives? Is not the goal of Kristevan analysis a triumphant and *leveling* demonstration of the persistence of *jouissance,* an encounter with the zero point of the death drive?

In "poetic practice," "instinct" becomes manifest as aesthetics, but only as it pulls the latter down from its high horse, away from considerations of form and genre, and rolls about with it indistinguishably—amorously or murderously?—in the mud. Kristeva's theory is, in fact, as profoundly antiaesthetic (that is, antiformal) as it is antitheological and (but for her this is much the same thing) antithetic. The aesthetic is suffered only to the extent that it appears unpremeditated and "infiltrated" by drive that culture had as yet failed to capture.

Her approach displaces the idea of the poem as the outgrowth of a locally evolutionary "inspiration" (a protocoherent, indeterminate articulation) with a biomechanical blind process of negation. From point to point of the text, rejection (expressed through breath impulsions, rhythm, intonation, syntactic rupture) *automatically and indiscriminately* negates thesis. But (and this is Kristeva's most contradictory notion) rejection also rejects itself. The death drive fears the death drive! Rejection, finding itself in the middle of nowhere as a result of its own stubborn resistance to stases, panics and flings itself into yet another stasis (a thetic stronghold); but no sooner has this happened than, true to its "nature," it rushes out again. This is the hidden logic of poetic practice, a logic simultaneously of negation and renewal. Kristeva formulates it as follows: "rejection$_1$—stasis$_1$—rejection$_2$—stasis$_2$—(etc.)—*Thesis*—rejection$_n$—stasis$_n$."

Negation and recovery: it's as if each conception (each word? each phoneme? Kristeva's term "mark" remains obscure) were a ballasted round-bottomed toy that rocks back into position after the drives give it a whop. Again, "rejection generates the signifier and the desire adjoining it as a defense against the death that rejection brings about by carrying its logic of scission 'to the end.' " "Repeated rejection is separation, doubling, scission, and shattering" *and* "at the same time and afterward accumulation, stoppage, mark, and stasis. In its trajectory, rejection must become positive: rejection engrammatizes."

If one accepts Kristeva's conception of the ferocious strength and constancy of the death drive, then the emphasis she places on rejection as the truth of textual practice is reasonable. But this is a case of a theory in excess of the "textual" evidence. To begin with, a contrary paradigm of positive choice–positive choice, etc., would appear to suffice. And certainly it would better account—indeed, it alone would account—for the fact that a poem is more than a random "accumulation" of stases, is, in fact, more cohesive than prose, as a "heterogeneous" molecule is more dynamically cohesive than a penciled line.

That rhythm by definition rejects the "noninstinctuality" of a thesis does not mean, of course, that a thesis (a "stasis") cannot be lifted and altered by rhythm without losing its distinctiveness; perhaps access, not rejection, is feeling's aim. In poems, it's not only "subjects" but theses that put themselves "in process/on trial." Poetry makes theses (but this is not a happy word for the play of ideas in a poem) negotiate with feeling. Isn't rhythm, in any case, positive for itself, attentive to itself? Like a school of flying fish, doesn't it arch over and over the negative troughs of the "breaks," the silence? (I think of T. S. Eliot's reminder "that the music of verse is not a line-by-line matter, but a question of the whole poem.") Isn't rhythm that which is happy to be rhythm rather than an accidentally perceptible part of the nerve ends' rage?

We know from the testimony of poets that poems can seem to germinate long before they become "determinate articulations." They are not the consequence of instantaneous rejectivity. From the first bit of rhythm or whiplash of words, they are instinct not with rawness but with a new, irreducible conception- or form-in-the-making. It would seem to be *the whole mind* of the poet that heads toward some image-perspective, some structural respite, during the course of "textual practice." A final consideration: how does "practice" (as blindly thrashing rejection) know when the end has come?

Kristeva's theory doesn't so much fail to address the dynamics that make a poem something more than an "accumulation" as, rejectively, dismiss as superficial and arbitrary anything but the genuine search-and-destroy mission of the drives. The blinders on the theory are meant to fix its vision on what alone is incontestable. But is "rejectivity" really incontestable? Is it not, in any case, the poorest object of contemplation that the field of poetry affords—the same little *zero/one, negation/renewal,* limned over and over?

Kristeva associates poetry with knowledge of a single kind: knowledge of its own anarchic practice, that is, its biomaterial rejection of symbolization. Indeed, for her, poetry is rejectivity; hence what preceded the late nineteenth-century "avant-garde text" and its quieter offspring, the "modern" or "twentieth-century" text is, so she implies, more likely than not to be *rhetoric.* And she finds only one sort of text, the "modern text," which alone has psychoanalysis (standing) behind it, secure in such knowledge: "in the forefront of both its linguistic functioning and the representation that invests it, the modern *text* exhibits that which has always been the disguised mainspring of 'art' "—by which she appears to mean heterogeneity or (and) negation. Anti-"art," the modern text is art only to the degree that it knows and shows itself angry at God as meaning, meaning as God. Knowledge of textual practice as "that most intense struggle toward death, which runs alongside and is inseparable from the differentiated binding of its charge in a symbolic texture"; knowledge of the subversion of "the symbolic function" by an "anal drive that agitates the subject's body"; knowledge of "matter in the process of splitting"—such is the burden of the modern or "twentieth-century text."

In short, the only knowledge Kristeva associates with poetry coincides with her theory; it's her theory mirrored back. Which is to say that for her the only trustworthy knowledge is psychoanalytical: knowledge that escapes "religion and its dependencies," knowledge of the brute *chora*'s power and petulant persistence. "The modern *text . . .* introduces the kind of knowledge concerning the body, language, and society that sciences today might have provided." To get to the conceptual heart of the "modern text" (a term reductively singular), Kristeva has but to walk on the sinking steps of her typewriter. Poetry is here a captured specimen that confirms a theory by re-echoing it. In other words, poetry confirms the truth of psychoanalysis by becoming psychoanalytical. Where poetry coincides with psychoanalysis as "science" and "theory," just there it is truly—it is pure—poetry.

In the teeth of Kristeva's theory, perhaps some of yesterday's ideas about poetry should be brought out from the mothballs. For instance, the idea that poetry is highly arti-ficial, or at least the product of a *formal* instinct acting on the sounding qualities of words under the example and re-straints of a tradition (or a number of traditions). Second (and last, for I must be brief), the idea that the knowledge communicated by a good poem is always specific to itself. Without disappearing into a black hole of the body, this very delicate knowledge is nevertheless as much as matter of tone, rhythm, image, and nuance as it is of statement. Poetry shows the entire bundle of the individual how to feel and think—for a moment. Nor is theology usually its "position," if theology isn't too simply and hostilely equated with the repressive power of words. (pp. 807-15)

Calvin Bedient, "Kristeva and Poetry as Shat-tered Signification," in Critical Inquiry, *Vol. 16, No. 4, Summer, 1990, pp. 807-29.*

John Lechte   (essay date 1990)

[*In the following excerpt, Lechte presents an overview of Kristeva's thought and career.*]

Especially in its early phase, Julia Kristeva's work consti-tutes a particular version of semiotic studies increasingly influenced by psychoanalysis. No doubt due to the specific character of French (or Parisian) intellectual life, certain aspects of semiotic theory may seem highly elaborated, if not obscure, to an Anglo-Saxon audience. My position is that the difficulties of reading Kristeva outside France are as much due to a particular Anglo-Saxon intellectual dis-position as they are due to the intrinsic nature of her work. Kristeva herself speaks—admittedly in 1980—of 'the *dif-ference* in mental and intellectual habits that persist in spite of recently increased cultural exchanges between the United States and Europe'. . . .

To the extent that Kristeva's name is known outside France, it is usually in connection with so-called French feminism. But while Kristeva has indeed commented pub-licly, and written about issues relevant to the position of women in western society, there is a sizeable other dimen-sion to her writing which has been somewhat neglected in the literature on her work. . . . [This] includes Kristeva's theory of society and culture as inspired by Freud and avant-garde art; her consideration of writing as a practice, and elaborations of psychoanalytic theory with respect to 'horror', 'love' and 'melancholy'. It is especially these lat-ter three topics which contribute to raising fundamental questions about social life in advanced capitalist—postmodern—societies. Not to be neglected, in this re-gard, is Kristeva's postition as exile and foreigner. Her book, *Etrangers à nous-mêmes* published late in 1988, provides an important insight here. (p. xii)

Broadly considered [the three periods of Kristeva's intel-lectual trajectory] are, firstly, the writings of the 1960s and early 1970s which outline a theory of semiotics capable of describing poetic language both as the 'productivity' of the text, and as a specific form of negativity. Kristeva scruti-nizes linguistics, various logics, and some aspects of math-ematics in order to see whether they offer a rigorous way of developing a theory of the dynamic and unrepresentable poetic dimension of language: its rhymes, rhythms, into-

nations, alliterations—melody; the music of language, in short; music which is even discernible in everyday speech, but which is in no sense reducible to the language of com-munication. It is a question, for example, of creating a way of analysing the poetic aspect of Joyce's writing. This writ-ing is illustrated in *Ulysses* by Molly's monologue. Consid-er for instance the repetition of 'yes' in the final lines of the latter:

> I was a Flower of the mountain yes when I put the rose in my hair like the Andalusian girls used or shall I wear a red yes and how he kissed me under the Moorish wall and I thought well as well him as another and then I asked him with my eyes to ask again yes and then he asked me would I yes to say yes my mountain flower and first I put my arms around him yes and drew him down to me so that he could feel my breasts all perfume yes and his heart was going like mad and yes I said yes I will Yes.

Kristeva will enable us to become aware, in her writings of the late 1960s, that each 'yes' in this passage from *Ulys-ses* does not have the same meaning as it does in the lan-guage of communication. In effect, there is here a poetic 'yes' *and* the 'yes' of communication. Kristeva begins to provide a way of speaking about such a poetic 'yes'. Whereas before we relied on intuition, now it is possible to speak about what used to be unspeakable. Such then is one of the major strengths of Kristeva's work of this time.

The second discernible period of Kristeva's trajectory is the 1970s. Here, particularly with the publication of *La Révolution du langage poétique,* Kristeva takes up the issue of the theory of the subject in relation to language—and especially poetic language. This is the period of the re-finement of the concept of *'le sémiotique'* designed to help articulate the realm of the pre-symbolic, or that dimension of language which constitutes the basis of poetic language. At this time, too, Kristeva's debt to psychoanalysis begins to become more evident with the 'feminine' coming to dis-rupt the Name-of-the-Father as the embodiment of the pa-ternal function (of father/mother/child triad), and thus the Symbolic as the order of language and signification. [The] feminine element as *'chora'* (a receptacle, as well as a distinctive mark) corresponds to the 'poetic' in language. For the feminine would be located in language's unrepre-sentable materiality—its indeterminate and almost ephemeral aspect—the aspect which places in question all modes of formalization traditionally associated with 'na-tionality' (masculinity). Certain kinds of text highlight the materiality of language more than others (the poems of Mallarmé more than the novels of Balzac), and these can be analysed, as Kristeva illustrates, in relation to the socio-historical context in which they emerge. The possi-bility of poetic language becoming evident (visible) is thus linked to the nature of social relations at a particular mo-ment in history. In the highly normalized, regularized, or-dered society of *fin de siècle* France of the last century, po-etic language assumes the role of the major ethical func-tion of art. Kristeva thus begins to sketch out the political significance of the avant-garde, and at the same time offers insights into the way psychoanalytic theory can throw light on social relations. Poetry becomes, in Kristeva's analysis, a way of maintaining social bonds through what is destructive of the social, and conducive to madness. Poetry is capitalist society's carnival, a way of keeping death and madness at bay. Poetry is a refusal of a 'flight into madness'.

Finally, Kristeva's work has focused even more closely on psychoanalytic theory during the 1980s. *Powers of Horror* marks a turning point in this regard for at least two reasons. Firstly, while psychoanalysis and semiotics remain the principal instruments of explication, there is in this text a strong sense that the origin of psychoanalysis itself might be brought into the picture, via the notion of abjection. This is the effect of focusing on Freud's more 'anthropological' writings and thence on religious practices in general. Secondly, however, as several writers have noted, *Powers of Horror* introduces a marked 'lightening' of style with a more liberal use of the first person and the more frequent inclusion of personal experience as illustrative of points being made. In this respect, we find Kristeva tacitly acknowledging her debt to Roland Barthes. Moreover, whereas prior to 1980, semiotics and psychoanalysis were brought to bear on works of art (cf. poetic language), now the tendency is to invoke works of art in order to illuminate, or even explain, concepts such as abjection. Céline's work is, for instance, used in this way.

A similar stylistic approach appears in two other works of the 1980s, namely, *Tales of Love (Histoires d'amour)* and *Soleil noir.* These examine, through a psychoanalytic prism, aspects of love in western culture, and depression and melancholia, respectively. Both books are personal and theoretical odysseys which at the same time illuminate the nature of personal experience in the west in the 1980s. Art (both painting and literature), both past and present, is put in service of studies of the ego (cf. narcissism) and its vicissitudes—one outstanding example being Kristeva's analysis of Hans Holbein the Younger's 'The Corpse of Christ in the Tomb' painted in 1521. . . . (pp. 4-7)

The evolution of Kristeva's *œuvre* from the practice of a *sémanalyse* in the 1960s to reflections on art and melancholy in the latter half of the 1980s, invites us to ask about the structure of this evolution. In this regard, we note that at all stages Kristeva has never wavered from a concern to extend 'the limits of the signifiable', and to understand writing as an individuating 'experience of limits'. Poetic logic, the semiotic, and subjectivity as an open system (founded on love as a multiplicity of identifications) only seem to confirm the predominance of this Kristevan concern. Nevertheless, a change has occured in the period in question. For whereas Kristeva's writing up until, and partly including, *Pouvoirs de l'horreur* (1980), focuses on the restrictiveness of a western society which privileges a representative state apparatus and scientific logic—especially as far as aesthetic practices are concerned—her writings since 1980 embody a modified focus. Ostensibly, this consists in a more intense concentration on the subject in analysis and the importance of identification (and thus the analyst) in love and melancholy.

Looked at within a broader perspective, we see that the fight against an overly restrictive form of the Name-of-the-

Father in the bourgeois representative state, and the consequent emphasis on identification and identity to the exclusion of forms echoing the feminine, now makes way for a return of identification as both a necessary component of love and a bulwark against melancholia—if not psychosis. It is as though a too-severe dethronement of the Father—of identity—produces a need to tip the scales in the other direction. Even more. Could we not see Kristeva's work of the eighties as a transformation of her work of the seventies?

Here, it must quickly be acknowledged that Kristeva herself does not accept such a hypothesis. Rather, she suggests that this change in emphasis has resulted from her deepening personal commitment to analytic practice. Also, we need to recall, as I have suggested elsewhere [in "Art, love, and melancholy in the work of Julia Kristeva," in *Abjection, Melancholia and Love: The Work of Julia Kristeva,* edited by Andrew Benjamin and John Fletcher], that Kristeva has never argued for the privileging of either the semiotic over the symbolic, or for the dominance of the symbolic over the semiotic. On the contrary, her work urges a striving for a certain equilibrium in the social and psychic experience of individuals—between language (symbolic) as meaning, and (potentially) poetic non-meaning (semiotic): that is, for what can both erase and multiply meaning. Perhaps, then, it is not within the *œuvre* itself that a transformation has taken place, but in the relation of this *œuvre* to two different social and political contexts: the 1960s and 1970s—when the arrogance of representation was being brought into question and 'difference' was subverting the exclusiveness of 'identity'—and the 1980s, when 'postmodernism' as a celebration, perhaps of difference but certainly of variety, captures the 'colour' of the times. Depression and melancholia begin to become audible on the analyst's couch, along with a speaking that often oscillates between the lucidity and delirium of the borderline case. The mother becomes the (implicit or explicit) point of reference in the subject's sadness, in place of the father in the neurotic's painful reminiscences. Consequently, postmodern anti-Oedipus may have won the day. Of course, to win in a situation where psychic equilibrium is needed, is in fact to lose. To strive for some kind of equilibrium is not to try and impose a single meaning onto the subject's utterances, but to recognize the inevitable crisis that is constitutive of the subject. Meaning and non-meaning come to exist side by side.

When Jean-François Lyotard defined the 'postmodern' as consisting in a certain 'incredulity toward metanarratives'—by which he meant that the reduction of reality to a single meaning was no longer credible—did he, by that very act, pretend to resolve the crisis in meaning by giving us an ultimate interpretation of the times we live in at the end of the twentieth century? Similarly, is Lyotard's *interpretation* of a delirious reality where 'anything goes' a much-needed call to order before the anti-Oedipal, 'schizanalyse' of current nihilism leads to a more or less generalized terror? Or again: is Lyotard's discourse on the postmodern not a slightly belated recognition by a philosopher of the non-meaning (delirium) always contained within meaning? Is the necessity for a work of art today to become 'postmodern' before it becomes 'modern', simply another way of saying that new meaning can only arise after the dissolution of entrenched existing meaning: delirium giving rise to meaning? Needless to say, it would take more space than is available here to begin to answer these questions satisfactorily. Nevertheless, it can be said that Kristeva's work is somewhat tangential to this postmodern experience. Her focus as psychoanalyst is to confront the distress of the analysand and to mobilize interpretation—not with the aim of finding the true meaning of the subject's distress, and 'not to make an interpretative summa in the name of system of truths'; rather, the task

> is, instead, to record the *crisis* of modern interpretative systems without smoothing it over, to affirm that the crisis is inherent in the symbolic function itself and to perceive as symptoms all constructions, including totalizing interpretation, which try to deny this crisis: to dissolve, to displace indefinitely, in Kafka's words, 'temporarily and for a lifetime'.

From this statement it would seem that the psychoanalyst places the very possibility of a philosophy of postmodernism into doubt. In effect, the times we live in are postmodern because they do *not* have a name; history has been put in question; it is (simply) a time of 'laughter and forgetting' (Kundera). An older generation is dimly reminded of its past by the passion for 'retro' fashion—in the arts, as elsewhere—so that when presented with art works of, say, the 1930s, a new generation says: 'It's just like the modern art of today.' Here, 'retro' *is* modernity; for there is no memory, or knowledge, of what came before. Or rather, as Kristeva says, we can give a name to postmodernism in a spirit of equilibrium if it is in accordance with Kafka's 'temporarily and for a lifetime'. On this basis, we may begin to live our lives in crisis, but also with a degree of fulfilment. (pp. 208-10)

> *John Lechte, in his* Julia Kristeva, *Routledge, 1990, 230 p.*

Suzanne Clark and Kathleen Hulley   (interview date Fall-Winter 1990-91)

[*In the following excerpt, Clark and Hulley provide an introduction to Kristeva's thought and, in an interview conducted in 1989, solicit her opinions on such topics as foreigners and foreign-ness, psychoanalysis, the importance of history in the literature of Marguerite Duras, and her novel* Les Samouraïs.]

The Eastern Bloc was crumbling, Chinese students had recently been shot in Tiananmen Square, Europe was preparing for unification, and France was celebrating the bicentennial of its revolution. Our interview with Julia Kristeva seemed to take place in a moment of accelerating change. In the context of modernity and historical crisis we talked about her three recently published books. *Soleil noir* (translated in 1989 by Leon Roudiez as *Black Sun: Depression and Melancholia*) studies the subject of modernity, with Marguerite Duras emerging as the final exemplar of a non-cathartic historical melancholy. *Etrangers ànous-mêmes* . . . directly addresses contemporary history as a crisis in which the problems of foreign-ness and strangeness—*étrangeté*—pose political questions

that overlap with the uncanny released by psychoanalysis. Kristeva's first novel, *Les Samouraïs,* appeared on the Parisian book stands in March, 1990; we were reading it as we were writing this introduction. *Les Samouraïs* is a dialogic *roman à clef* about three women living through the intellectual and political revolution of 1968 in Paris. In each of these three books, Kristeva addresses the great crises of modernism from the perspective of the subject-in-process. Her project, as she discussed it in our interview, takes up the individual within psychoanalysis, but also within cultural history, working to provide strategies at the most concrete levels to address the global shifts which seemed to be occurring at the very moment we were speaking in her quiet office at the University of Paris VII. (pp. 149-50)

Within months of our interview with Kristeva, the Berlin Wall had fallen and Eastern Europe had thrown off the burden of Russian domination. Oddly enough, while history seemed suddenly to move to fast forward, in a very real sense, history also moved backward. It is almost as if the past eighty years had not happened; Europe seems to be confronting the same unresolved issues of nationalist, religious, and racial intolerance. It is as if, since the American and French revolutions, all the utopian questions raised by their enlightened promise of perfectibility have remained the same: how to resolve issues of individual rights with the power of social formations and the needs for community and communal responsibility; how to accommodate the formation of identity with differences; how to institute social justice. It is this crisis of private and public history, of political intolerance and the internalization of history, of boundaries and transgressions, which recur in all three of Kristeva's most recent books.

These books also mark considerable change in her work, however. *Black Sun* continues the theorizing of psychoanalysis and discourse found in *Powers of Horror* and *Tales of Love,* focusing on the relationship of melancholy, the maternal, and language, and at last taking up the question of women and language. *Etrangers à nous-mêmes* is less involved with theorizing the psychoanalytic, working instead to define cultural strangeness and to situate psychoanalytic discourse within modern political crisis. Together with *Les Samouraïs,* this work suggests that Kristeva wishes to address a broader public.

In order to focus the issues Kristeva addresses in this interview, there are three central points that we want to take up. First, how can psychoanalysis and literature play a role in political transformation and the crisis of modernity or address the differences of cultural strangeness rather than the reproduction of Western identities? Second, there is a question prompted by all her work, and appearing strongly in *Black Sun*: what is the relationship of individual subjects to language and history? Is Kristeva's insistence on a kind of individualism a resistance to the political? Third, what is the place of heterogeneous women within the structures of *étrangeté* and the unresolved contradictions of modernism?

Coming to Paris in late 1965 on the eve of the poststructuralist explosion which she helped generate, Kristeva brought a dialectical linguistics from Bulgaria and the

East, which included the Russian formalists and most importantly, Bakhtin. Not only Roland Barthes, but also Emile Benveniste were major alliances. She soon became part of the Tel Quel group that included Sollers, Derrida, Foucault—she married Sollers. Thus she became part of not only the academic world but also the avant-garde literary circles from the beginning. This intellectual community is the setting of her novel *Les Samouraïs.*

Her project has been poststructuralist from the start. Her critique of structuralism has always stressed that we cannot ignore the place of the speaking subject or the context of history—what she calls the "intertextuality" of writing and of history. Since structuralism is far from extinct—it is, in fact, becoming more dominant in French education as a mode of reading—it is important to note that Kristeva's defense of individual, particular subjectivity responds to a rationally articulated and centralized monoculture that has little to do with American ideologies of individualism. She tends, perhaps, to idealize the way community works in the United States, and to overlook how the community-building function in America is feminine. We might more usefully think of her in relationship to the Marxism shaped by the mythos of her own childhood. Like other Eastern Europeans, she thinks of Marxism as both the ideology of an oppressive social life and also as a utopian program and mode of social analysis. Like Marx, she believes that progress means working through the forms of capitalism, not simply opposing them.

American critics need to keep in mind how Kristeva locates her philosophical work on the subject within the impossibility of identity, self-knowledge, and self-possession opened up by Freud and the field of post-Lacanian psychoanalysis. The Kristevan subject-in-process emerges at the point of the unconscious which is not, she argues, structured "like" a language but rather is the materiality of language, the semiotic. The Kristevan subject is, furthermore, postmodern, located at a historical moment of crisis, at what Kristeva calls in the interview "the rupture of a structure, the rupture of an equilibrium." This rupture of identities is both internal and external, the permanent crisis of "modernity."

In the current historical situation, Kristeva characterizes state and party politics as dangerous, allied as they are with the extreme movements of nation, race, and religion appearing globally. Is there, Kristeva suggests, some second, intermediary, provisional alternative to thinking of power either in terms of isolated individuals—the fragmentation of late capitalism—or in terms of monolithic and passionate collectivities? Her investigations are related to questions about the situation of intellectuals and the avant-garde as well as the situation of women. These are not positions which represent the oppressions of class and race, yet they are both marginal and secondary in the market economy of the "first" world.

Can our experience as women-as-other be useful to our engagement with other foreigners, immigrants (and also the African-American), each a stranger who has crossed the boundaries (willingly or not) of France (but also America) in the form of the Muslim, the postcolonial subject, the

black who both is and is not us? The logic of difference can mask its specificity. Is it possible, given our position as academic first-world women, to constitute that other except as the uncanny, the "*Unheimliche,*" that which is simultaneously familiar and radically alien? our double, our other within the drive to remain the same? our differences from ourselves? If the situation of this stranger has in some sense been historically constituted, then the issue for Kristeva lies within the context of history: how can we constitute subjectivity differently in our present historical context?

We asked, then, what kind of power the subject-in-crisis might exercise in the crisis of modernity. Kristeva's response suggests that this provisional power is to be found in the mediating functions so often occupied by women—of therapist, of teacher. In *Etrangers à nous-mêmes,* Kristeva tries to address this issue by beginning with the experience of foreignness, with what she as a Bulgarian in Paris could speak about. She represents the second world—not only of Bulgaria, but also of the white intellectual woman, the occidental artistic subject. For it is at another level, between the first and third world, that the second world operates, like women, who are always caught between superpowers: mediating, acting as "relays"—"flexible."

In *Etrangers à nous-mêmes,* it becomes clear that Kristeva sees the crisis of modernity and the failure of both religion and reason as a historical moment not only of danger but of opportunity, when the open, split subject-in-process of psychoanalysis might relay the operations of power in less oppressive forms, not resisting the crisis and becoming a form then of fascism but embodying negativity in style, acknowledging the foreign as internal. The estranged, foreign, uncanny subject of historical and psychoanalytic crisis might imagine the regulation of power as a work in progress rather than the cut of identity which precipitates scapegoats and objects of desire—and woman may wrest her power from her historical construction as the prototypical stranger.

In the interview which follows, Kristeva insists on the individual as the site of subversion and ethical possibility. Because much of the feminist critique of Kristeva centers on this individual micrology, it is important to put that concept within the context of Kristeva's own highly-developed ideolect. Unlike the American subject of history, Kristeva assumes a history of colonization and takes for granted that we are always talking about discourse within the international history of power politics—the ideological politics of nations and religions which has not concluded. Unlike the self-made subject of the American frontier, Kristeva's individual can never be a self-sufficient unity. On the contrary, for Kristeva, the individual is an intersection of intertextuality, a subject-in-process, a subject in dialectical crisis. It is the refusal to acknowledge the strangeness located within that makes the individual a reactionary and dangerous subject; its circulation is blocked by any forced resolution of that crisis, or any capture of that process in a privatized self-willed notion of the individual. The Kristevan individual is already positioned in language and ideology and, therefore, in history. For

Kristeva, the dialogic which constitutes the subject is not an intersubjectivity of autonomous entities but an intertextuality. Thus the problem of isolation from history manifested by the imaginary discourses explored by Barthes (in, for example, *A Lover's Discourse*) is an illusion of aporia produced by the failure to imagine the subject as text, subject to intertextuality; "a literary text does not live in an autistic fashion, closed on the interior of itself . . ." says Kristeva in the interview. Subjectivity is always dialogic, constituted within dialogue. Thus the psychoanalytic dialogue represents the situation of the subject more accurately than the notion that the ego is an isolated individual.

Kristeva reads the notion of the individual within the context of European history, not in terms of the strength of an Emersonian mythos of free-will and uncontaminated choice which continues to dominate the American imagination.

—*Suzanne Clark and Kathleen Hulley*

Intertextuality involves differences that are not merely linguistic but historical and contextual as well. As the discussion of the term "individual" shows, in spite of the easy familiarity Americans assume with "Euro-centric" discourses (and they with ours), misunderstandings are shaped by residual foreignness. If we look at Kristeva's notion of the individual in the context of her own intellectual heritage and her theoretical work, we see that the term "individual" means something other than the self-reliant, self-willed individual of American culture. Kristeva reads the notion of the individual within the context of European history, not in terms of the strength of an Emersonian mythos of free-will and uncontaminated choice which continues to dominate the American imagination. For the American theorist, "individual" is apt to call up a unified, essentialist figure which merges with the subject of entrepreneurial capitalism. This is a problem with Kristeva: individuality is untranslatable, not so much because of linguistic differences but because of those cultural differences which connote our political relations to words. The American individual may be pluralistic, may be multicultural, but American pluralism omits the unconscious; it is not open to the *étranger* in her sense.

As her response in this interview suggests, Kristeva is reluctant to advocate a feminist subject because she is involved in a critique of the "subject" itself as a positivity. The crisis of history at the level of social institutions and the crisis of identity at the level of the individual are aspects of postmodernity which she does not view simply as suffering and wrongness. Kristeva views the situation of crisis with a certain optimism. For her, the speaking subject may be inventive and powerful, may be able to effect change precisely to the extent that a Hegelian negativity—and a Freudian uncanny—can enter discourse. We can

deal with the question of the other—of gender in familial realms and the foreign in religious and social realms—by focusing on the Freudian uncanny, the unconscious strangeness, rather than by perpetuating the sacrificial discourses of exclusion that create paranoia and scapegoating. This dialectic of the familiar and the strange is where women may enter into the question of subjectivity, in the gap opened up by the uncanny dialectic. If we acknowledge that the subject is split, we no longer worry about needing a feminine identity that would be positive and totalizing. "I am very attached to this idea of the woman as irrecuperable foreigner," Kristeva says in the interview; ". . . one can be positive by starting with this permanent marginality, which is the motor of change."

At the same time that many feminists are declaring the end of marginality for women, Kristeva is arguing that the crisis of modernity makes all of us marginal subjects. From the point of view of certain reactionary postmodernisms, Kristeva has seemed all too committed to social change, to optimism, to an ethical practice, and to discourses which are not sufficiently ironic. On the other hand, from the point of view of revolutionary feminism, Kristeva has seemed too identified with dominant male discourses of essentialism, the avant-garde, and religion. Indeed, she has frustrated feminists by her refusals—not just of practical politics, but also by her refusal to valorize women's work and by her choice to consider, primarily, not female but male avant-garde texts. More importantly, she has steadily opposed the feminist subject, even going so far as to call feminism "the last religion." For Kristeva, the production of a singular feminist identity (something in little danger of emerging, we might inject) would reproduce the logic of the sign, would reproduce, in fact, the female pseudo-center which mediates a return to the male as subject.

We need at this point to call attention to some of the differences between French psychoanalytic practices which critique the reified individual, and American psychoanalytic practices which tend either to reinstall the individual as a "normal" member of society or to liberate the individual to be her "true self." Within that model, the aim is to resolve crisis, fix boundaries. But for Kristeva such a cure would be a kind of failure precisely because for her the perverse hysteric, in perpetual crisis—in the interview she insists on the position of the hysteric as always apart from the closures of ideology—is analogous to the crisis of modernity, which can evade totality only so long as it opens itself to more and more heterogeneous foreignness (*étrangeté*).

Critics have raised questions about Kristeva's commitment to an ethical position, given her resistance to political commitments, and many accuse psychoanalysis itself of avoiding history. We therefore wanted to ask her to address these issues as they appear in ***Black Sun.*** In particular we find the chapter on Marguerite Duras important because it is the first time Kristeva has studied a woman's writing. Kristeva situates Duras both at the crossroads of an unbearable historical content and at the crossroads of personal psychoanalytic anguish. To review: Duras's explicit subject matter is the link between female desire and the unspeakable events of modern history—Auschwitz, Hiroshima, the European legacy of colonization in Vietnam and India. To subvert the disease of history, Duras suggests, one can only assume the infection and transform it, deflecting or deterritorializing it, demolishing boundaries, bringing history within. By setting most of her stories in sites of Western colonization which have been violently contested in the twentieth century, Duras prevents us from isolating the problem of female desire from the historical and rhetorical issues of colonization itself. Kristeva begins her chapter on Duras by acknowledging the intersection of history and desire in Duras's writing, but at the same time Kristeva associates Duras's ability to embody the depression of modernity with an unresolved relation to the maternal. For Kristeva, this unresolved relation makes Duras's descent into colonized desire a dangerous, non-cathartic aesthetic.

Kristeva's insight would be problematic if it suggested that although the Durassian woman is a symptom of modernity, the symptom can be removed and history cured in the private space of psychoanalysis. But Kristeva seems to associate psychoanalysis with historical events which open into the postmodern—not with a privatized space, then, but with the chance, in crisis, to work on history through literature, through discourse. Duras's language seems to deny the power of language, to reinforce the depression of modernism. When we asked Kristeva about this, she insisted on the importance of catharsis, locating psychoanalysis in a resistance to death, in a different relationship to history—and discourse—than the melancholy of modernism.

The dialogic and the uncanny emerge as governing functions in Kristeva's view of modernity, history, and the political. What can be the political force of women as heterogeneous individuals? Freud is responsible for resolving the dualism of the rational and the irrational by locating the uncanny within reason, so that not only women but all of us must learn to be foreigners to ourselves, inhabited by otherness (*étranget*). Kristeva's work on *étrangeté* develops an analogy between the state, which produces the ideology of the foreign, and the image for the ego, which in turn produces the semiotic by the cut of the symbolic.

If we resist the state ideologies producing the foreign, does that help the specific situation of foreigners? How does Kristeva's work help feminism? Can feminism make use of this permanent strangeness, this negativity, as a way to posit one mode of an effective subject position? Can feminism ally itself with a kind of anarchism? This interview reveals a Kristeva whose answers to these questions might almost be characterized as optimistic. What makes feminists in America most uneasy with poststructuralist thought may be that its negativity erases any firm position for collective action. Equally disquieting is the constant theoretical critique that such a position seems to generate. Kristeva is specifically arguing for a practice that is highly provisional, operating at the level of intertextual relationships among individuals, for which psychoanalysis is her model.

Is it the inevitable fate of even a feminine theorist to appear in our cultural imaginary as the heroic individual mounting a solitary crusade? Kristeva's valorizing of psychoanalysis and literature, her insistence on the political efficacy of the work on language which psychoanalysis and the artist might effect—do these resist any reduction to liberal humanism and the new fragmentation of late capitalism? American feminists have the virtue of being identified with contentious communal effort, but Kristeva's strange individualism provides a way to keep that contention in dialogue. *Les Samouraïs* acknowledges the position of the avant-garde intellectual as a member of a warrior class, an assemblage of superstars. But Kristeva's own position either as character or as the speaking subject cannot be fixed. Identity shifts and becomes the other, loses place. In her novel as in her theory, densely imbricated intersections of strangers circulate through the intertexts which constitute their freedom. (pp. 151-58)

. . . . .

[*Clark*]: *Your recent analysis of psychoanalysis and theology is situated within a sense of historical crisis. Can you tell us any more about this idea of crisis and how it is related to the question of modernity?*

[Kristeva]: Yes, this problem of crisis is an enormous one. We formed a "groupe de recherches," a seminar, here at Paris VII, addressing this crisis. We tried to organize an interdisciplinary reflection across history, because the crisis has multiple aspects. It does not appear in the same form every century. But, on the other hand, we can speak of a global notion of crisis nonetheless, and understand by that the rupture of a structure, the rupture of an equilibrium. Considered from this point of view, the fundamental crisis in which the contemporary world is living—and consequently the arts which interest us—began to unfold at the time of the French Revolution, and the results of this crisis are what we are living through, a crisis at once of royal sovereignty, of religion, but also of discourses in their communicative value. At the level of sovereignty, we are in the process of living new forms of democracy which are imposed by multinational states and societies, among other things. This concerns the problem of foreigners, but also the other forms of difference that a democracy is capable of harmonizing: the differences of women, of children, differences in sexual practices, and so forth. At the level of religion, this crisis poses moral questions which are very important today. In particular at the level of the reproduction of the species—genetic manipulations, the codes defining responsibilities and identities with respect to children—must we live with the former criteria? Or are the criteria in the process of changing? This is an important problem.

And at the level of discourses: as early as the eighteenth century (one cannot say this enough) a ludic discourse was developing, an erotic discourse, and a discourse of insanity. Examples can be found in Diderot as well as in Sade, or in the literature of pamphleteers, both of the right and the left, which surrounded the French Revolution. You have the royalist press, but also the populist press, which was extremely sexualized, extremely virulent, and which expressed a sort of desire for pleasure, often by procurance. "We're not the *salauds*, the others are." There was this violence of discourses which, in a certain way, was expressed by the guillotines, but in another way, was blocked and forbidden by the guillotines. We sense that the sexual liberation of the twentieth-century avantgardes—surrealism, *après-guerre,* the discourse of homosexuals, May '68, and so forth, the whole effort to find new forms of expression in language, for the libido, by changing the style—are perhaps conclusions of that crisis.

I would say, together with certain historians, that the French Revolution is now coming to an end. This can be seen clearly by taking account of the phenomena of the problems of authority, of democracy, of religion, and of language in its relationship to sexual identity. I think that the crisis has opened and there will be a succession of crises.

[*Hulley*]: *Are these crises fundamental to every culture then, or unique to our own modernist historical moment?*

I think that modernity, in particular this radical break made by the French Revolution, has rendered the crisis explicit, and minimized the moments of equilibrium. We can think of it this way: previous social forms counted on a certain calm and crisis came periodically, but now, an epoch has opened when we live in permanent crisis. What is provisional now are the moments of status-quo.

Then would you say that the subject of this crisis, the sujet en procès, *is an anarchic subject?*

Yes. Anarchy generally has a negative connotation. But for me, from this perspective of a permanent crisis, anarchy is the non-repressed state of subjectivity. So it is a permanent state of functioning. At this moment, the problem arises of two alternatives: is the crisis a suffering, is it a pathology? Or is it a creation, a renewal? And it is at this moment that recourse to a provisional and stabilizing apparatus is important.

This provisional and stabilizing apparatus—but it is important to insist on the *provisional*—is the role which a new form of power can play in society. This is the power of the therapist, the power of the educator, the power of a certain familial authority, a power which is, however, relative and flexible. We are in the process of seeking new forms of power in the city, in the state. But I think that this has nothing to do with the idea of an anarchy which is nihilism of power, nor with the idea of an absolute power.

Is it a dispersed power?

Dispersed and flexible at the same time, capable of flexibility. Relational. Taking as a starting point—I myself would imagine—the image of the analyst's power, provided we do not see the analyst as a "shrink" who reduces imaginative capacities or as a suggestive figure who exercises an indoctrination on his patients, but as an intermediary who becomes a fixed point of support and confidence and who permits the individual to find his capacities for play and for construction.

Let us find this kind of power—try to find it, again—in the therapist, the teacher, the social worker; that is, these different, flexible forms representing social authority which societies are in the process of inventing.

Can the profession of teaching play a role in this?

If the profession does not play such a role, it teaches nothing at all. Above all in the human sciences and in literature.

As for pedagogy, do you think it is possible to pay attention to differences, to individuals?

It is necessary. This will require a great deal of money, first. Because there must be many more professors. We must ask for it, not be ashamed to ask for it. But this also requires a certain personal devotion, a certain moral, pedagogical attention on the part of teachers, who are not necessarily prepared by their studies to do this. . . . (pp. 159-61)

You have extended psychoanalytic analysis into the subject of society and of the foreigner, or the stranger, in **Etrangers à nous-mêmes,** *at a moment when the problem is much discussed here in France. And in the US, though in a very different way I think. Is there a certain optimism in your view of the ethic which psychoanalysis would allow, an ethic of solidarity?*

Yes. The question which arises now is knowing on what moral basis one can regulate the problem of foreigners. Because it is evident that even if the jurists and politicians decided, for example, to let all foreigners live in France, or even to give them a right to vote—which is far from being done of course, but suppose that that happened one day—the problem arises of knowing whether morally and ethically the national populations are ready to take that step. And the answer is *no.* So, where does one start to open up this very phobic notion of national identity, to permit the mixture of races and to welcome others, in order to proceed toward what I call "puzzle" states, that is, states that are constituted from several types of citizens—immigrants, people who are part of the European community, people who come from Africa or Asia in addition to those in France—and then perhaps one day to proceed toward the disappearance of the notion of the foreigner? Montesquieu and the French revolutionaries had such an idea, but it is far from being realized.

We cannot look for the answer in religions, not even if certain religions—for example, present-day Catholicism—make steps towards the understanding of others. Why? In France, for example, we have an important Catholic assistance movement which is enormously interested in the immigrants, which gives them educational, moral, and material aid. But in spite of these current movements in religious institutions, these are discourses which welcome the other only on condition of delegitimating or annulling him. "You are accepted if you accept our moral code as Christian or Jew. The moment you do this, there is no problem. You are like us. We accept you." Still, they are moving towards more flexible forms of ecumenity, recognizing the right of the other to exist; they are not waging a religious war against heretics. This is true for Christianity, for example. But the great monotheistic religions like Islam are extremely reactionary and persecutory—look at the Rushdie affair. Orthodox Judaism also poses very grave problems—what is happening in the occupied territories demonstrates that.

> [With] the religions in crisis, we must search for other means of approaching the question [of foreigners, of "the other"]. I consider psychoanalysis as the means of approaching the other because the Freudian message, to simplify things, consists in saying that the other is in me. It is my unconscious.
>
> —*Julia Kristeva*

Therefore we lack a moral code which would permit us to think about the question of the other. And I speak of religions because the question of the other is fundamentally, I think, a religious question. But with the religions in crisis, we must search for other means of approaching the question. I consider psychoanalysis as the means of approaching the other because the Freudian message, to simplify things, consists in saying that the other is in me. It is my unconscious. And instead of searching for a scapegoat in the foreigner, I must try to tame the demons which are in me. "Hell," said Sartre, "is other people." Perhaps, but because hell is my unconscious and I do not recognize it. Therefore recognizing what is not doing well in myself—my death drives, my eroticism, my bizarrenesses, my particularity, my femininity, all these uncoded marginalities that are not recognized by consensus—I would tend less to constitute enemies from those phenomena, which I now project to the exterior, making scapegoats of others.

Beginning with such a conception of things, I think that one can proceed toward what I call in *Etrangers à nous-mêmes* a *paradoxical community,* which responds to your idea of solidarity. Because that supposes, in effect, a community. We try to help one another, all. But not a community which unifies and banalizes. We recognize each other, as foreigners, strangers. That is to say, as weak, that is to say, as potentially sick. And it is by being able to hear the other as tracked by some pathology, by some anomaly, as I myself am, that I refuse to see in the other an enemy. And this would be a basis for a form of morality.

When you said earlier that the crisis of both history and the individual may be seen as a kind of suffering, a pathology, or as an opening for creation, do you mean to emphasize the creative possibilities of crisis?

I try to see the most optimistic aspects of the crisis. Of course, when you see a bottle which is half empty you can find it half empty or half full. I tend toward the direction that it is half full. A moment of crisis is a moment when something has crumbled, something is rejected, but it is also the moment when new sources appear, and in postmodernity I myself see this aspect of renewal, which interests me.

And this possibility for renewal is the same for the individual?

Altogether—it's like the analytic process. There are many people who are afraid to undertake analysis because they are going to dissolve many defenses, and it's a crisis, and they are going to find themselves at a certain moment of analysis extremely unhappy and disarmed. But when they have touched bottom, precisely, they are going to construct other possibilities for living, and so one cannot construct without destroying the old defenses.

In Etrangers à nous-mêmes, *you make the link between psychoanalysis and what you call "solidarity" among different individuals. What adjustments in the realm of culture might follow from what you propose in this book?*

Listen, I do not know. Really, I do not know. I think at the present stage we must keep ourselves from proposing great syntheses. We must try to be the most concrete—I would even say microscopic—that we can. To work at the level of individuals. At the level of individuals, pathologies, the concrete cases of foreigners, to take care of civil society and the problems that are not being solved. But we must not try to propose global models. I think that we risk, then, making politics into a sort of religion, while it seems to me that concrete interventions are more important. For example, I consider that my work as an analyst is political work, to take it in a microscopic and individual sense. I think that the outcome of the rights of man is the veneration of the individual and of his difference. And that we should try to preserve these singularities. How can we make a politics that takes account of the singularities? Obviously, not by talking about the political, but by trying to maximize singularities. Of the political there is already too much, of political men and women. Perhaps they will finally listen to us, try to apply this. But our role, my role, as an intellectual, is to see the most exceptional things possible, what individuals have that is exceptional, what literary texts have that is exceptional. And to put the accent on irreducible things.

So literature is a way of getting to a politics of singularity, of keeping étrangeté *within discourse. Can you address the way fiction relates to the construction of gender? Nancy Armstrong, an American critic, argues that the discourses producing the idea of the middle-class woman, especially domestic fiction, are responsible for gendering difference and for creating the modern idea of the individual. How do you see women and gender in this question of individual differences?*

First, the idea of the individual as connected, as having been discovered from the feminine: I am not sure that that can be supported if one takes account of history. Because if you look, for example, at the emergence of the notion of individuality in the Renaissance, it is connected as much to the recognition of insanity in carnival as to the recognition of bizarre sexual practices. So—all forms of strangeness. It is true that the feminine, in particular in the novel of the eighteenth century, comes to crystallize marginality, psychology, discomfort, and melancholy all at once. And the feminine heroine of Richardson, Sterne, Diderot, even Sade becomes the paragon of this individuation. But I don't think we should generalize and see in the woman the only can-opener (*le seul ouvre-boîte*), so to speak, that could permit a homogeneous society to generate the notion of the individual. I think that we must take account, also, of other currents.

Why do I say this? Because in the present state of things, I am afraid that if we insist on the fact that the feminine differentiates the individual, we may arrive at a new form of homogeneity. Because, myself, I see many women—at the university as well as on the couch—and what interests me in order to think about what a woman is, is the difference between these women. In other words, I would emphasize not the notion of gender, but the notion of singularity. Of the irreducibility of individuals—whether they be men or women. Perhaps there is a woman who has the sexuality of a baby, of a child, of a little girl, of a little boy, and each can be found within the notion of "woman."

But I would like to multiply differences. I have the impression that the idea of the feminine as difference was good to begin with, but it risks fixing difference too much and making us think of only two, while there are many more. And perhaps what interests me is a democracy of the multiple, and in this perspective, it is seeing individual differences, singularities. With the singularities of women included. On that point, let me recall something that we did several years ago in a Belgian feminist journal called *Les Cahiers du GRIF* (which is still in existence). The interview was called *"Une(s) Femme(s)."* I put *"Une(s)"* and *"Femme(s)"* to show that, it is true, there are groups of women—we are communities—but that that makes no sense—these new groups of women have no meaning with respect to groups of men or of proletarians or this or that unless we take account of the singular differences of women. If not, if we put all under the same common denominator, all the women the same, it is not so interesting. That would be to replace one providential force by another providential force.

Do you see a difference between Americans and the French on the idea of the individual, the domestic, and the woman?

Surely, but it is very difficult to generalize. The French are perhaps more individualistic, and at the same time more ironic about their individualism. Americans, it seems to me—in any case, Protestant Americans—have a sense of duty and of mutual help, of the necessity of devoting oneself to another, of being able to establish a bond of community, which does not exist with the French. I first became aware of this friendly side of the American university community when I arrived in the United States with my son, when he was a baby. In twenty-four hours I had everything needed to furnish a baby's room—diapers, bottles, pots, a little bed, a swing. People were altogether warm and helpful.

As for women, there also it's an individual matter, it's unwarranted to generalize. But I think the French tradition—in spite of its misogyny and anti-feminism, which are widespread—nonetheless gives a certain valorization to feminine work, feminine spirit and wit, to a sort of social aura of woman. Through the salons of the eighteenth century, through the great writers of the eighteenth and nineteenth centuries, there is something which endures, which it seems to me is still living. I myself sense that the

women in the French university are less subjected to harassment, to surveillance, than in the United States.

There is also the question of individualism and ideology. For example, the American ideal of an autonomous individualism makes it difficult for my students to imagine a subject-in-process.

There are two aspects. There is, on the one hand, this kind of permanent exceeding of the individual, who is not an atom closed on herself, who is in fact a process—you are right to stress that. And then there is this problem which is posed more and more on the political level in French society: how to arrange it such that this aspect of singularity does not become isolation, but that there is nevertheless a kind of communication among singularities. Here we are trying to find new forms of society which are not constraining, but there are no societies which are not constraining that do not respect individuals. I think that it is one of the fantasies of feminism to think that one can make a collective without singular individuals. It's somewhat a caricature of communism into which certain feminists have fallen.

But the problem for some American feminists is that the idea of individualism is linked to a discourse which is liberal, positivist, middle class, a class controlled by patriarchal discourse, and which serves the consumerist culture only too well.

They imagine that there is an alternative which exists in the East. Because what is happening now, in Eastern countries, is that the collapse of the Marxist and socialist idea is showing something else. It shows that we can arrive at a better society not before bourgeois individualism, but after. I think that they ought to revise their ideas, seeing what is happening in the East now. Because many feminist ideas were unconsciously calculated and modeled on the image of communist and Marxist countries, as if a progressive and communitarian ideology could produce the economy of bourgeois society. Now one realizes that one cannot just make the system of a society from the model of ideology. It is necessary to transform it. But not on this side of it, but by passing to the other side.

In thinking about your new book and about the question of becoming a stranger to oneself, becoming uncanny, we wondered—given women's marginality in relation to power or to discourse, given woman's foreignness—whether women could be anything but étrangères.

I am very attached to this idea of the woman as irrecuperable foreigner. But I know that certain American feminists do not think well of such an idea, because they want a positive notion of woman. But one can be positive by starting with this permanent marginality, which is the motor of change.

So I think that for me femininity is exactly this lunar form, in the way that the moon is the inverse of the sun of our identity. From this point of view, perhaps we women have it more than the men, but the men have it also. And to try to preserve this part as unreconcilable permits us perhaps always to be what Hegel called the eternal irony of the community. That is to say, a sort of separate vigilance

[Women are] what Hegel called the eternal irony of the community. That is to say, a sort of separate vigilance which keeps groups from closing up, from becoming homogeneous and so oppressive. That is, I see the role of women as a sort of vigilance, a strangeness, as always to be on guard and contestatory.

—*Julia Kristeva*

which keeps groups from closing up, from becoming homogeneous and so oppressive. That is, I see the role of women as a sort of vigilance, a strangeness, as always to be on guard and contestatory.

In fact, it's the role of the hysteric, a little, and why not. I accept that altogether. We can play our hysterias without necessarily making a psychodrama and exposing ourselves to being the victims of the male order, but with great lucidity, knowing what we do, and with great mastery and measure. That is, perverse hysterics. Very wise.

How does this work, to take this perversity, this hysteria on oneself as a strategy?

First, it is two things. It seems to me that the possibility of perversion is less distinct and strong with women than with men, because it is more difficult for a woman to break the law, to choose different, multiple erotic objects, like a Don Juan or a Casanova, for example. This is due, probably, in part to her fusion with the maternal image, and in part to a great dependence with respect to paternal law. So, in this context feminine perversion is a rather rare phenomenon, which explains why we encounter more depression than its opposite, which is perversion in women. But in compensation, when the capacity for perversion succeeds in finding a place—notably, when a woman detaches herself from the maternal weight, or when she succeeds in arranging a lighter, freer relationship, more detached as well with respect to paternal authority—then, under those conditions, there can indeed be a perverse coloration of hysteria which permits her to play with the norm. I think that all creations go through that, and especially artistic creations, for women as well as for men. But it is very clear: when one encounters aesthetic successes in women, they are supported in individual experience on a sort of fringe that I will call *"père-perverse d'hystérie,"* the perverse father of hysteria, without putting any pejorative into this word, but simply the possibility of playing with the law.

So it is a choice that a woman can make to play this role.

It is difficult to say if it's a choice, because often they are so bound up by the maternal weight and the authority of the father that this choice is impossible. But I think that a successful analysis, for example, could lead a woman to this solution.

Speaking of a perverse hysteria as a strategy leads me to

think of another figure of the woman which you have delineated. I am very interested in this story of Io which you tell in **Etrangers à nous-mêmes.**

Oh, yes, the sacred cow.

I wondered if you had thought of proposing it as an alternative to the Oedipus narrative for women?

I haven't worked much on this, but it should be done. There are psychoanalysts who have worked on Io. Paul Claude Racamier in France has published a text on Io and the Oedipus complex in women, as it happens. But in any case what fascinated me was that the first foreigners occidental which occidental history speaks about were foreign *women,* because the initial Greek example of the foreigner is found in a fragment which remains of Aeschylus, in the play about the Danaides. Who are the Danaides? They are women who descend from the sacred cow, Io. What did she do, this sacred cow? She was a person who fell in love with Zeus, and who committed therefore an illegitimate act because she seduced the husband of Hera. One has, consequently, a sort of authoritarian couple, Hera and Zeus, a parental couple, and here is this girl—one imagines a girl—coming to commit an act of lese-maternity by making an enemy of Hera and taking the papa. And Hera, obviously, is furious. She sends a sort of insect, a horse-fly, which crazes Io, who is turned into a cow and chased from her native land. So she becomes foreign from that moment on; there are no more lands which can become her own because she is condemned to wander in the world, until the day when Zeus decides to touch her. But he cannot permit himself to do that in Greece because Hera, who is the goddess of the foyer, prevents it. Indeed, the maternal authority is so strong that even Zeus cannot transgress it. He profits by the moment when Io finds herself in Egypt, he touches her, and she becomes calm. The madness of foreignness is eliminated and Io can become the mother of children, who eventually have as descendants the fifty Egyptades and fifty Danaides. So Io is the ancestor of these Danaides who are the first foreigners.

That is, we find the Danaides at an important moment which concerns both women and the problems of foreignness. They are fifty girls who are forced to marry their fifty cousins. They do not wish to do so; they are resistant to marriage, and in certain variants of the myth, on the day of the marriage ceremony, they kill the cousins. We have the impression that this is a memory that the Greek society preserved about the passage from an endogamous society where one married in the same clan, to an exogamous society where one must leave to marry someone else who is not a cousin. And that that passage was lived in an extremely violent manner, so painful that the refusal was imagined as a murder. The women do not wish to marry their cousins, and at the extreme they would murder these cousins. So these women are viragos, against marriage. In other variants of the myth the Danaides are seen as very ambiguous characters. On the one hand, they serve the cult of Hera, who is the goddess of marriage; they carry the cask of the Danaides with which they pour the water symbolizing the domestic household. On the other hand, they participate in the cults of Demeter, which are very violent. Once a year the women gather together. They pour not water, as they do in their housekeeping tasks, but blood. As if this double myth of water and blood wished to show that marriage is an affair of extreme violence, and that if one makes water flow, one must not forget that there is the potential for making blood flow. And that this act of alliance between two persons is in fact based upon an extreme ferocity, a great aggressiveness, a great violence.

I give this example to show how violent, clear, and explicit the idea of the war of the sexes, of the difference of the sexes, was in this Greek mythical and post-mythical consciousness, and why it was necessary to follow such rites to facilitate the catharsis of that consciousness. In our societies we try, instead, to repress this idea of violence. Feminism has had the advantage of putting the accent upon it, reemphasizing the incompatibility of the sexes. This is perhaps to go too far—to declare an absolute war of the sexes seems to me an exaggeration—but such a declaration is the opposite of puritanism. I think that we can try to find an agreement: neither the discrete veil over the contradictions in order to see only harmony, nor absolute war. But that we can recognize the difficulty of an alliance between two people and try to deploy all possible tact so that these foreigners—which men and women are to one another—can find a modus vivendi, which is not easy. The developed societies, which we call decadent, have the advantage of being confronted with this truth that I would call mythical and fundamental, because it is not in Islam that we can reflect on this difficulty. It is in our society—it's in New York, or Paris, where couples are becoming impossible. It is by starting with this impossibility that one can perhaps try to live with a man, with a woman, like one lives with foreigners. . . . (pp. 163-71)

Let's now return to the question of psychoanalysis and its implications for literature. Your book **Black Sun: Depression and Melancholia** *has now appeared in translation in the United States. In it you trace the way melancholy appears in both psychoanalytic patients and literature. Here, we're especially interested in the final chapter, where you look at the work of Marguerite Duras. Can you talk about how, in Duras, history and the depressive psyche interact? How do you read Roland Barthes's* Lover's Discourse—*in particular, the idea that the lover's discourse is isolated from history—in light of the way Duras is obsessed with the way history infects both the lover's discourse and desire?*

I have already tried to answer this aporia posed by Barthes with the idea of intertextuality. Because I think on the one hand, we must maintain the autonomy of discourse with respect to the social level, because it is a level of autonomy that guarantees freedom. We can speak in a different manner than our familial and social determination. There is an undecidable part which comes perhaps out of our biology, a certain number of determinations which escape us, but in any case which are not reducible to what we know of society. And if one does not keep this autonomy of discourse, one falls very quickly into a reductionist and sociological conception where all aesthetic or personal performances are explained by the social milieu or a similar fate: from the fact that you were born red, black, white, or poor. This said, there is nevertheless an incontestable in-

teraction between discourse and society, and I myself would consider that the fact of taking society as a generalized text permits us to see how, for example, a literary text does not live in an autistic fashion, closed on the interior of itself, but borrows at all times from the discourses of the press, from oral discourses, from political discourses, and from other texts which preceded it, which provide vehicles in their turn for these cultural and political texts of history.

To take the example of Duras, I believe that one cannot understand the depression, for example, of the women she puts on the stage if one does not take the Second World War into account. That is what I try to show. She made this explicit throughout a text called *La Douleur,* and it was already present with *Hiroshima*. So it is a political context which individuals lived through, of immense physical and moral pain, of death and destruction. But it is also a metaphysical context, which is the context of a generalized doubt about values. God does not exist and nothing can replace the good and the beautiful. And, finally, the good and the beautiful do not exist. Even my own text, Duras seems to say, is neither beautiful nor good; it is nondescript; it is something unmade, a woman without makeup. It resembles a depressed woman. Thus the extremely contagious role, and the contagious effect—I say even, at moments, non-cathartic—of this text which obliges us to live through the pain without proposing a way out. Not even its own beauty. Because it does not present itself as a seduction which is going to pull us from the abyss. It shows us the importance of the abyss. But this can only be understood from the interior not only of Duras's text, which one could analyze to show how much it resonates with a problematic of depression, but also from the interior of the context of the war and of the crisis of values of which I have just spoken.

Given the interior crisis of the war which Duras explores, then how is any catharsis possible in art? She is one of the living writers who explores that crisis, the heart of that void, and shows it to us. It's true that her work is not cathartic, but once we have passed through Hiroshima and Auschwitz . . .

There are those who cannot pass through. I was surprised to see that many students, for example, said to me, "We cannot read Duras because it is so close to us that it plunges us back into the sickness." And so when one feels oneself a little fragile, there is such a force of attraction that one does not have the means to get through. This is why I say she has the force of a sorceress perhaps more than of an artist.

We wanted to know if you think that melancholy in Duras is a personal pathology or a symptom which is global, widespread. Is it private, something in her family, or history which created this melancholy?

I do not know her well enough, but I suppose in looking at her writing that she is capable of great depressive moments. This said, it would not be of much interest if she had not succeeded in making of this problem, which is perhaps personal, something general which joins a universal symptom of our generation, I think. That is why her books speak to many people. Her work is at once personal and at the same time it joins with the depression that we know. But I consider that it is not cathartic but rather, let us say, an echo, a connivance with depression. Catharsis supposes that we leave depression, while I have the sense that these books plunge us into depression and do not give us the means to get out of it.

Do you think we should try to get out of this historical depression? Because when we look at history, perhaps we ought to press the things that are unthinkable, in fact—Auschwitz, Hiroshima.

I tend to think as a therapist that it is better to come out of depression because if not, it's death.

Speaking of the same chapter from **Soleil noir,** *at the end you compare Duras and Sollers, modernity and postmodernity—melancholy and parody. Readers have interpreted this ending of the book in completely opposing ways. Some see it as a valorization of the parodic and the postmodern, and others accuse you of maintaining the melancholy of modernity, of valorizing the tragic vision.*

I think that I tried to give perhaps a more direct response through my novel, **Les Samouraïs.** The young generation has a desire to cross this after-war period, the existentialist periods, this Duras-Blanchot period when one was perhaps too close to anguish and death. They want to pass into a less burdened world, more ludic. But that is a little naive. And what I tried to do in **Les Samouraïs** was to start with the color black, but also to go toward the sun—so a sort of balance between pain and solace. I do not think that there can be a simply ludic and parodic postmodernity. I think that the postmodern crosses this black experience and in knowledge of its cause, permits itself a certain abandon. But abandon simply like that—the game for the game—that does not interest anyone.

Let us go on, then, with the question of your own writing, and your new work as a novelist. You have advocated looking at the subject of discourse as le sujet en procès. *How is this connected to the question of* style? *I should like to know how you see your own style, which in fact performs this "procès" by displacing any fixed position for the subject. How do you see your style in relation to will, to the possibility for choice and agency?*

I think that questions of style cannot be raised on the level of conscious choice. Style is one possibility of being in contact with our unconscious and, I would say, even our sensations. I am more and more interested in the importance of memory and sensation in language. And I think that the role of analysis, and also of writing, is to put the neutral surface of abstract words into contact with a whole dynamic of recollection which leads us at once to recall our traumas, the pains or the pleasures, and the most archaic sensations. And it is when we are capable of translating these sensations and perceptions and traumas or joys into the language of cognition that one obtains a style. For example: Proust.

Most of your writing, except in the parallel texts of say **"Stabat Mater,"** *has had a framework which is not literary, yet which is deeply informed by a "style." How would*

you say, even in a style which one might call "rational," that the unconscious can play a part?

We must make a distinction which is connected to my personal history and then to the nature of theoretical discourse. I think that there is a discourse of knowledge in the Occident which mobilizes or disciplines stylistic experimentation. When one wishes to appropriate this discourse of knowledge, one imposes a certain asceticism on oneself at the level of style. From this perspective, when I began to work, it seemed very important to me, as a person and as a woman, to show that I could take hold of that discourse. In the course of its development, this rational discourse has begun to interrogate its own mechanisms of asceticism, of neutrality; it has come to introduce more and more the personal side, the unconscious rapport. We have only to see philosophical discourse in France—Barthes, Derrida, Serres—which was influenced by Heidegger in a certain sense, but even more by Freud. This philosophical and theoretical discourse has become increasingly a very stylized, very fictional discourse. But I believe there is a defiance in it, a sort of critique with respect to certain restrictions on the discourse of knowledge and its pretensions to neutrality. As for myself, my pathway through psychoanalysis has perhaps reconciled me with my memory and my body, and that has had a considerable importance for the change in my style.

Does this mean that we must abandon the discourse of knowledge and what I spoke of earlier as its discipline, its ascetic side? Personally I do not think so. It is a way of clarifying certain texts or certain films or certain undeveloped societies, to take several different examples from the human sciences. Even if the understanding were schematic and neutral, it is a way of throwing light on the phenomenon. So we must not deprive ourselves of the discourse of knowledge.

Often students are pushed too quickly to write literature about literary objects, or about objects taken from human social practices. And the result is a sort of swamp of fuzzy intuitions which inhibits students' intellectual capacities and their instruction in the techniques of cognition. I think one must carefully differentiate the capacity for cognition from the capacity to exceed it, and give students the models of knowledge, of a neutral distancing. Then afterwards allow a certain softening. This for those who engage a theoretical discourse. Those who wish to do literature right away—all right, let them. But in the domain of pedagogy and knowledge we get rid of discipline, judgment, argument, and thought a little too rapidly and we often produce individuals who are incapable of reasoning.

Deconstruction was very harmful in this respect because it was misunderstood. One does not deconstruct before having constructed. Those who are not capable of a certain classicism should return to cartesian ideas, to maxims like *"Ce que l'on conçoit bien s'énonce clairement"* ("What is clearly conceived is clearly expressed")—and afterwards produce an effect of flux, of orchestration, and of polyphony. But as enrichment and not as confusion.

To finish up, many women have been hoping you would write about women writers and artists in particular; now you've done so in writing about Marguerite Duras. Do you think you will look at other women writers in your future work?

Perhaps I am becoming a "writer" myself, to do more fiction for a while, perhaps to return later to philosophy. Which does not prevent my being interested in other women writers. But it is an idea which attracts me for the moment, to try to speak about my experience in a more fictional way for a while, which is a form, perhaps, of finding the maximum of singularity and the maximum of communicability. Thus the political impact. I think that there is in fiction something which reconciles the fact of being very particular and the fact of carrying a message which is understood by the most people possible. It is a form of atomized politics, if I could say so, in the sense of the atomizer, "the spray."

So, because I think literature has importance, I have written this novel which has just come out. The title, *Les Samouraïs,* is a wink at Simone de Beauvoir and *Les Mandarins.* To tell you very briefly, it is about the intellectuals from '68 to the present, an effort to tell the life of the passions. One recognizes Foucault, Barthes, Lacan, perhaps myself. There are other characters who are prototypes and who represent our generation without being stars. On the feminine plane—I am going to stop at that—the characters are three women. One is named Olga; she is a young linguist who comes from the East—one recognizes in her, of course, myself. There is another named Carol, a woman who undergoes all the crises that we lived through around May, 1968, who is affected by depression—who I consider at once as a prototype of our generation but also as a nocturnal double of Olga. And then there is a third who is a psychoanalyst, who keeps her journal, and who sees all this French and Parisian society with distance and irony. The three can be considered aspects of the narrator. I think it will entertain you. There is also a chapter where Olga goes to the United States and has an affair with an American professor. That permits her to make a fresco of American society, which she knows a little from a distance. This gentleman who becomes her lover is named not Mrs. Dalloway, but Mr. Dalloway, a dialogue with Virginia Woolf, a sort of intertext with Woolf. I think it will make you laugh. I wanted to write a popular novel, very sensual and ironic.

Two other questions, on the subject of Bakhtin and the carnivalesque, and on the subject of the crossing of voices in your writing. We wondered if you still have the dialogic in mind.

Yes, I continue to think about that, and I tried to write *Les Samouraïs* according to this logic of polyphony, making, for example, rather short chapters which answer to one another, characters which reverberate, resonate, one in relation to the other; to fragment, to make discontinuous narrative series and make the relationship of one to another in a permanent ambivalence and dialogism. The French critics have not noticed this for the moment, because I think it is more particular to Russian or English novels. Of course in Rabelais it is evident—but the modern French novel has become thin, a little univocal—they

do not have this practice, I think, current critics. I regret it. (pp. 175-80)

Suzanne Clark and Kathleen Hulley, "An Interview with Julia Kristeva: Cultural Strangeness and the Subject in Crisis," in Discourse: A Review of the Liberal Arts, *Vol. 13, No. 1, Fall-Winter, 1990-91, pp. 149-80.*

Elizabeth Wilson   (review date 14 June 1991)

[*In the following review, Wilson offers a mixed assessment of* Strangers to Ourselves.]

The photograph of Julia Kristeva on the end flap of this book shows her with an arm round a large piece of South East Asian temple sculpture: the head of a goddess, downward looking, mysterious, its features almost erased. The authoress embraces art, and the smeared and enigmatic glance of the cultural icon contrasts with the bright elegance of the writer.

Julia Kristeva is herself something of a cultural icon, her work treated with profound reverence, especially by feminists. Yet her political path has been the familiar one from left to right. Along with the Parisian *Tel Quel* group, with which she was associated, she moved through ultra-leftism, anti-Stalinism and psychoanalysis to become a supporter of Valéry Giscard D'Estaing; an exaggeration, or even a parody of the trajectory followed by many intellectuals in the 1970s and 1980s. She rediscovered liberal individualism. Politics became the *faux pas*. More interesting than journeys to China were those to the interior of one's own subjectivity.

It is possible that Kristeva's work has continued to attract the support of feminists because—paradoxically—she has justified in her theoretical writings certain conventional or traditional feminities, or feminine preoccupations: motherhood, romantic love. In an article in *Feminist Review* in 1984, Ann Jones criticised her extraordinarily patriarchal view of womanhood, but, more often, feminist literary critics such as Toril Moi have capitulated to her intellectual power, and she has been particularly influential in the US. This is despite the fact that she always maintained a distance from feminism and became, in the 1980s, increasingly hostile to and critical of the women's movement.

Like the writers of the Frankfurt School, Kristeva has argued that the aesthetic avant-garde is the location of the truly "revolutionary", truly subversive impulses in western society. She has by implication drawn on an established tradition in western aesthetics: the idealisation of the artist, the supreme individualist, as the true social rebel. As Charles Baudelaire wrote of the figure of the dandy, this artist or bohemian stands aloof from society. He practises detachment rather than engagement. He takes a stand *against* what is, rather than committing himself to some alternative (revolutionary, socialist) world, and his perspective leads to an aristocratic critique rather than a vulgar proletarian programme for change.

The dandy, says Baudelaire, makes of himself a work of art, and the avant-garde writer or painter is different only in so far as his art is an exteriorisation of his critique of society. The *Tel Quel* group identified this stance as dissidence, and, for them, the dissident seems to be a kind of latter-day dandy, a critic who sees through both the falseness of consumer society and the hoplessness of the political project. As Kristeva said . . . in 1983, "We try not to be political." What started out, however, as good old-fashioned bohemianism mutated in their case into straightforward conservatism and adulation of the US.

The French anthropologist Georges Devereux wrote that "all theory is a kind of autobiography", and *Strangers to Ourselves* may well be rooted in Julia Kristeva's own experience of being a "foreigner". (Born in Bulgaria, she took up residence in France in the 1960s.) Yet Kristeva does not write of her own experience directly. In her opening chapter, **"Toccata and Fugue for the Foreigner"**, we move through a flood of allusive suggestions and promising insights into what it means to be a "foreigner", the nature of this particular "otherness", its alienation for the self and its symbolism for the "non-foreigner".

This is then abandoned in favour of a chronological journey through western history in order to uncover the source of contemporary attitudes towards foreigners. Chapters on the ancient Greeks, the Romans, the Jews, the early Christians, the Renaissance, the Enlightenment and 19th-century thinkers range widely yet lightly over a vast store of cultural knowledge, sometimes interspersed with psychoanalytic interpretations. At the centre of the book, a chapter on the legal status of foreigners confronts a question for our own time, to which Kristeva returns throughout. How are we to find a way of living in a global culture that is riven with nationalisms and chauvinisms of all kinds? Politics may have failed us, but there remains an ethical question.

In a fascinating chapter on the Enlightenment, Kristeva explores the paradox of modern nationalism, the seeds of which she locates in 18th-century concepts of universalism and the rights of man or of citizens. This leads to her conclusion: that the Freudian "Copernican revolution" has forced us to acknowledge our own (inner) foreignness. Consequently: "Psychoanalysis is then experienced as a journey into the strangeness of the other and of oneself, towards an ethics of respect for the irreconcilable. How could one tolerate a foreigner if one did not know one was a stranger to oneself?"

Yet the link made between this and the attempt to find a juridical solution to the status of citizens and "non citizens" alike in the new Europe, or indeed in the "new world order", is a weak one. *Strangers to Ourselves* tantalises and irritates in about equal measure, despite its elegance—or even, in part, because of it. Although the reason for the concentration on western history becomes clear, might it not still have been appropriate to explore the philosophies of some of "our" (westerners') "Others"? I should also have found it useful to learn about the attitudes of, say, Chinese and African cultures and Islam. At times it was wearisome to make the familiar journey again through Machiavelli, Montesquieu, Hegel, Freud and the rest, however lightly the author's knowledge is deployed, and in spite of the fact that I did learn much.

One easy—in fact, too easy—criticism of Kristeva might be that she is élitist. If this means that she is relentlessly and rigorously intellectual, then I see nothing wrong with that. However, in some respects this text lacks precisely the rigour the reader might have expected. Kristeva warns that the final chapter at least is "meant to be prospective, fragmentary, subjective". There is almost a kind of self-indulgence in the way she sets off a mass of ideas—free associations, almost—about the "foreigner" without subjecting these aphoristic insights to sustained scrutiny. The reader is swept on, and it requires an effort to pause and question. Her first chapter in particular displays all the shortcomings as well as the seductions of the Frankfurt School's aphoristic mode.

Kristeva's relentlessly apolitical "answer" seems but a dusty one in the face of Le Pen and his racist movement. Psychoanalysis is sometimes brought forward as a substitute for ethics, rather than a philosophy of right behaviour. *Strangers to Ourselves* had the same effect on me as Michael Ignatieff's *The Needs of Strangers,* which in a peculiar way it strikingly resembles. The similarity is in the spectacle of the elegant, yet ultimately futile, attempt of the liberal intellectual to work out a civilised ethical position, when confronted with situations, passions and ideologies that shatter liberalism from top to bottom. (pp. 34-5)

> Elizabeth Wilson, "Dandy Dissidence," in New Statesman & Society, Vol. 4, No. 155, June 14, 1991, pp. 34-5.

Wendy Steiner (essay date 15 November 1992)

[*In the following review of* The Samurai, *Steiner faults Kristeva's prose style as clichéd, arguing that the novel proves only that she possesses "a heart that thrills to the cadence of the Harlequin romance."*]

It has been a bad year for Europe's academic superheroes. On the heels of disclosures of Paul de Man's Nazi past comes news of his bigamy and messy housekeeping. We were aware that the leftist French philosopher Louis Althusser had lost his sanity and murdered his wife, but who would have believed he had not read his Marx? And now comes the revelation that Julia Kristeva, semiotician of desire and Maoist psychoanalyst, is in actuality a sentimentalist. Underneath that rugged exterior is a heart that thrills to the cadence of the Harlequin romance.

The Samurai, a transparent *roman à clef,* fluently translated by Barbara Bray, chronicles Ms. Kristeva's—and Paris's—intellectual glory days. The tale begins in 1965 with the arrival of its heroine, Olga Morena, from Bulgaria as a young student, "an active body with an active soul, in a state of weightlessness." At this point, Ms. Kristeva demonstrates a talent for cliché that never leaves her. On the slushy Boulevard du Montparnasse Olga decides that the women were worried about the spatters on their coats, but the "men (as usual) thought only of their desires." Though Olga propounds many such gender contrasts, she does like men. Or rather, she dislikes women, "probably because I think I'm better than all the rest of them."

Male academics seem to agree. Fabien Edelman (in real life, the Marxist literary scholar Lucien Goldman) invites Olga for a meal, which she photographs rather than eats. Overcome with this proof of her brilliance (and the extra portion of food), Edelman takes her on as his student. "She hadn't said anything," Olga marvels. "Was silence always golden?" Enthralled by Armand Bréhal (Roland Barthes), who invents "the real poetics of love," she overwhelms him with a seminar paper so strong that he calls her a "bulldozer." He is "delighted to have a woman by his side when he advances through Strich-Meyer [Claude Lévi-Strauss] and Lauzun's [Jacques Lacan's] minefields." In this way, miraculously, Olga finds herself accepted into the "spontaneous kinship" of these kindred spirits, like Jo in *Little Women*.

The most important of her early meetings is with Hervé Sinteuil, a thinly disguised portrait of Philippe Sollers, the aristocratic writer, theorist and editor who was to become Ms. Kristeva's husband. With his "martial view of the world," this "Pope of St.-Germain" transforms the "mermaid of the caves" into a "champion swimmer" in a rhapsody of mixed metaphors. Accepting the role of samurai, Olga's characterization of her intellectual colleagues and lovers, she vows to Hervé, "With me it'll be war." "Let it be war then!" he counters, and the samurai face off.

But Olga had an earlier samurai in Bulgaria, and on a brief visit he finds her new friends bloodless game players. She assures him that underneath they are all passion. Take, for example, Strich-Meyer, the great structural anthropologist, modeled on Claude Lévi-Strauss, who reduced "to formulas the rules that govern marriage and myth all over the world," or Scherner (Michel Foucault), the theoretician of madness, who does not realize that "since Freud there hasn't been any such thing as madness. Only *idiolects.*" The Lacan character, Maurice Lauzun, sports a Zorro-like cape and fragrant cigar, while Benserade (Émile Benveniste), a polymath linguist, teaches Olga about the etymological relation between "tree" and "trust," which she had, of course, intuited. Saïda (Jacques Derrida), a literary-theoretical guru, invents "condestruction" (deconstruction) and the three-hour seminar. If this is passion, it is the kind engendered in mirrors.

But Olga should know passion when she sees it. She was there in 1968, when the masters contemplated revolution and the women embraced feminism. Olga's friend Carole, infuriated at her lover's wife, with her "cling peach skin, destined to remain forever young," refrains from braining her with a cobblestone and throws it instead at the police. Such is the genesis of revolutions. At first, Olga is part of this feminist revolution, meeting Bernadette (Antoinette Fouque) and Aurélia (Hélène Cixous). Later she goes to China to write a book on Chinese women, but the manuscript she produces is skeptical about matriarchy, and Bernadette accuses her of being "contaminated with patriarchy." Olga, who has lived through harassment by the Komsomol, will not put up with "a feminist dictatorship." She decides that "the excited faces of Bernadette and her pals, red and white with sick ambition, were rotting peonies," and gives up feminism and political activism on the spot.

Besides, it has occurred to Olga that she might want to have a child, for she has been musing on the myth of the eternal return. But her ideas about parenthood are a bit academic. "The idea of the eternal return as child's play engendering children removes the tragic aspect of procreation and, without either degrading or glorifying it, gives it the serious insignificance of all children's games," she writes in a little lecture in which we all recognize our thoughts on motherhood.

But before engendering new life, Olga must kick up her heels. In China, her whole circle had become "Chinese" to her, unfamiliar, strange: "As she confronted a loneliness at once imposed and chosen, an amber-colored wave had frozen and clung to her, and she felt moved to reject every contact and bond she had ever had in the past or might have in the future." Hervé tells her to "follow her desire," and she departs in the amber-colored wave for a year of teaching in New York. There she promptly abandons herself—after martinis and a recitation of Céline—to a romantic American. But she realizes that it is just too much for her, "the whole unimaginable burden a little girl can amass when she acts the intellectual but still wants to remain a little girl."

The love passages that follow have no equal in modern literature, as when we learn that "their sexes kept seeking each other in the depths of a sleep that was one long embrace, watched over by spirits of song." None of my informants can identify the American lover—a sign either of Ms. Kristeva's discretion or of her creativity. But when the year is over, the American's intellectual fire is burning low and Olga returns to Hervé. The old gang is all dying, and Olga decides to enter the eternal return. Despite the fact that "she didn't want to put anything into words, and nor do other mothers," she overcomes her reluctance in fond descriptions of pregnancy, childbirth and child rearing.

Ms. Kristeva's novel may well mark the demise not only of an intellectual generation but also of an intellectual style. Inspired by Surrealism and the theatrical Lacan, the members of the French School gained power by functioning as a group, by engaging in unabashed self-promotion and by appropriating the cachet of the artistic avantgarde. The resulting image of the intellectual was unlike any in modern history. Changing theories as fast as airplanes, bridging the most divergent disciplines and subject matters, these samurai injected humanism with Surrealism, a heady infusion indeed. As Olga says, her life with Hervé was "made up of mental adventure, verbal confrontation, written murder and resurrection, and as such might have seemed idle, long-winded and abstract. But to the people living it, it was a kind of martial art." No doubt this was the case, but one finds oneself wishing them the quieter talent and deeper wisdom required to refrain from writing novels like **The Samurai.** (pp. 9, 11)

Wendy Steiner, "The Bulldozer of Desire," in The New York Times Book Review, *November 15, 1992, pp. 9, 11.*

FURTHER READING

Criticism

Baruch, Elaine Hoffman, and Meisel, Perry. "Two Interviews with Julia Kristeva." *Partisan Review* LI, No. 1 (1984): 120-32.

> Presents two interviews, the first of which primarily addresses the feminist issues raised by Kristeva's *Tales of Love;* the second interview questions Kristeva on the development of the modern French intellectual milieu.

Barzilai, Shuli. "Borders of Language: Kristeva's Critique of Lacan." *PMLA* 106, No. 2 (March 1991): 294-305.

> Compares Kristeva's critique of Jacques Lacan's linguistic theory of the unconscious with Freud's original writings on the notion of "signs."

Bové, Carol Mastrangelo. "Women and Society in Literature, or Reading Kristeva and Proust." *Dalhousie Review* 64, No. 2 (Summer 1984): 260-69.

> Examines Kristeva's revision of Lacan's theory of the unconscious, in which the critic detects a "startling parallel to Proust's attempts to break with the structures of symbolism and of salon society."

Brandt, Joan. "The Systematics of a Non-System: Julia Kristeva's Revisionary Semiotics." *The American Journal of Semiotics* 5, No. 1 (1987): 133-50.

> Examines the development of Kristeva's critical method—her means of analyzing "the relationship between language and the social system it supports"—from *Sémeiotke* and *La révolution du langage poétique* to *Powers of Horror.*

——. "The Power and Horror of Love: Kristeva on Narcissism." *The Romanic Review* 82, No. 1 (January 1991): 89-104.

> Examines Kristeva's interpretations of Freud and Lacan as presented in her work on the "unconscious, narcissistic foundations" underlying the history of discourses on love.

Ermarth, Elizabeth Deeds. "Conspicuous Construction; or, Kristeva, Nabokov, and The Anti-Realist Critique." *Novel: A Forum on Fiction* 21, Nos. 2 & 3 (Winter-Spring 1988): 330-39.

> Argues that Kristeva and Vladimir Nabokov engage in the same kind of critique of language, suggesting: "What Kristeva describes, Nabokov does."

Jardine, Alice. "Theories of the Feminine: Kristeva." *Enclitic* IV, No. 2 (Fall 1980): 5-15.

> Discusses the way in which the word and concept of "Woman" has been used in French intellectual discourse, focusing on Kristeva's notion of "the semiotic"—which Jardine describes as "the primary organization of instinctual drives by rhythm, intonation and the primary processes"—as inherently maternal in nature.

——. "Opaque Texts and Transparent Contexts: The Political Difference of Julia Kristeva." In *The Poetics of Gender,* edited by Nancy K. Miller, pp. 96-116. New York: Columbia University Press, 1986.

> Analyzes notions of ethics as they apply to such elusive concepts as modernity and feminism in Kristeva's works.

——, and Menke, Anne M., eds. *Shifting Scenes: Interviews on Women, Writing, and Politics in Post-68 France,* translated by Katherine Ann Jensen, pp. 113-24. New York: Columbia University Press, 1991.

> Interview with Kristeva which focuses on women's changing roles in modern society and "the issue of the blurring of sexual difference."

Kennedy, Lisa. "Art Ache: The Last Temptation of Julia Kristeva." *The Village Voice Literary Supplement* (November 1990): 15.

> Mixed review of *Black Sun: Depression and Melancholia.*

Kritzman, Lawrence D. "Melancholia Becomes the Subject: Kristeva's Invisible 'Thing' and the Making of Culture." *Paragraph* 14, No. 2 (July 1991): 144-50.

> Discusses *Black Sun,* analyzing in particular Kristeva's conceptualization of depression and melancholia as "linguistic maladies" which art in the postmodern age can no longer symbolically remedy.

Kurzweil, Edith. "An Interview with Julia Kristeva." *Partisan Review* LIII, No. 2 (1986): 216-29.

> Wide ranging interview that addresses such topics as the differences between French and American understandings of deconstruction, the issues of nationalism and patriotism, and contemporary politics in France and the U.S.

Lechte, John. *Julia Kristeva.* London: Routledge, 1990, 230 p.

> Critical overview of Kristeva's thought, which the critic places within the context of French intellectual history.

Reineke, Martha J. "Life Sentences: Kristeva and the Limits of Modernity." *Soundings* LXXI, No. 4 (Winter 1988): 439-61.

> Analyzes Kristeva's feminist understanding of psychoanalysis and its influence on her critical methodology.

Smith, Paul. "Julia Kristeva Et Al.; or, Take Three or More." In *Feminism and Psychoanalysis,* edited by Richard Feldstein and Judith Roof, pp. 84-104. Ithaca: Cornell University Press, 1989.

> Examines the development of Kristeva's psychoanalytically based theories of subjectivity and language, finding that her "turn in the direction of anti-feminism and anti-Marxism (concomitant with her full embrace of the practice of psychoanalysis)" has resulted in "an absolutely idealist version of subjectivity and a nonmaterialist account of language."

Van Wert, William F., and Mignolo, Walter. "Julia Kristeva/Cinematographic Semiotic Practice." *Sub-Stance,* No. 9 (1974): 97-114.

> Suggests ways in which Kristeva's theories of semiotics and combination of Marxism and psychoanalysis might be applied to film studies.

Waller, Margaret. "An Interview with Julia Kristeva." In *Intertextuality and Contemporary American Fiction,* edited by Patrick O'Donnell and Robert Con Davis, translated by Richard Macksey, pp. 280-94. Baltimore: Johns Hopkins University Press, 1989.

> 1985 interview in which Kristeva discusses primarily the term "intertextuality," which she argues originates in the literary theory of Mikhail Bakhtin.

Zepp, Evelyn H. "The Criticism of Julia Kristeva: A New Mode of Critical Thought." *The Romanic Review* LXXIII, No. 1 (January 1982): 80-97.

    Examines Kristeva's "critique of structuralism and the emergence and redefinition of semiotics in her thought."

Arthur Kroker

1945-

Canadian nonfiction writer and editor.

The following entry provides an overview of Kroker's major works.

INTRODUCTION

Kroker is known for critical works that define postmodern theory and culture. He is coeditor with his wife Marilouise Kroker of the *Canadian Journal of Political and Social Theory* and has edited a series of monographs profiling Canadian theorists and books examining such social, political, and cultural issues as postmodernism and technology. Although his works are criticized for their often difficult theoretical terminology, they are recognized as comprehensive, thoughtful introductions to current critical theories and concerns.

Kroker, a professor of political theory at Concordia University in Montreal, was born in Red Rock, Ontario. Since their marriage in 1976, Arthur and Marilouise Kroker have collaborated on nearly all of their writings and editorial projects. Kroker's first major work, *Technology and the Canadian Mind: Innis/McLuhan/Grant,* focuses on the works of Harold Innis, Marshall McLuhan, and George Grant, three Canadian thinkers who examined the impact of technology on the human condition. Kroker classifies Grant as a "traditionalist" who views technology as a source of evil and McLuhan as a "technological humanist" who sees technology as a means of solving humanity's problems. According to Kroker, Innis is a "technological realist" whose thought combines elements of both Grant's and McLuhan's stances. Kroker argues that these three writers' works evince a tension between technology and tradition which pervades all of Canadian thought and shapes a distinctive Canadian outlook on the modern world. Many reviewers commend Kroker's insight into the issues that Innis, McLuhan, and Grant confront and believe that he accurately portrays Canadian self-perception as that of a country struggling to balance the technology-centered culture of the United States with tradition-based European cultures. However, commentators criticize Kroker for overlooking such details as the differences in each writer's definition of technology and for lapsing into obscure philosophical language. Others fault Kroker for presenting a distorted conception of these writers' philosophies because he treats the works exclusively as social criticism concerned with technology and disregards other issues they encompass. Some also believe he oversimplifies the connections between Innis's, McLuhan's, and Grant's writings to conform to a clichéd image of Canadian culture and thought.

The Postmodern Scene: Excremental Culture and Hyper-

Aesthetics, written with David Cook, studies current postmodernist cultural theory and analyzes specific examples of postmodern culture, especially those drawn from television and the visual arts. *Panic Encyclopedia: The Definitive Guide to the Postmodern Scene,* written and edited with Marilouise Kroker and David Cook, incorporates contributions from twenty-four artists and writers. The authors declare that "Panic is the key psychological mood of postmodern culture," and the essays, artworks, and interviews which follow this statement examine such postmodernist icons as Panic Elvis, Panic Hamburgers, and Panic (Shopping) Malls. In both *The Postmodern Scene* and *Panic Encyclopedia,* the authors assert that Western culture is exhausted, arguing that such actualities as money and communication have been transformed by technology into a "floating reality" of computer-generated electrical pulses, and the technology that allows, for example, instant communications and the electronic management of finance has served to alienate the individual and undermine previous standards of identity and conduct. In the resulting culture of boredom and cynicism, the authors maintain, media and industry exploit the individual's need for a sense of purpose, identity, and power by marketing an ever-changing world of trends. Some critics believe that these assertions are only restatements of the commonplaces of postmodernist critical theory and that the works fail to further develop a postmodernist view of politics and society. Others find fault with the works' apocalyptic, rhetorical, and esoteric language, arguing that their pessimism and critical terminology amount to little more than a flashy surface for insubstantial scholarship. However, critics have praised the editors for their astute analysis of postmodernism's effects on contemporary art and popular culture, explaining that the examples which the authors investigate offer a comprehensive introduction to the concerns and outlook of postmodernist critics studying Western culture.

PRINCIPAL WORKS

Technology and the Canadian Mind: Innis/McLuhan/Grant (nonfiction) 1984

The Postmodern Scene: Excremental Culture and Hyper-Aesthetics [with David Cook] (nonfiction) 1987

Panic Encyclopedia: The Definitive Guide to the Postmodern Scene [with Marilouise Kroker, David Cook, and others] (nonfiction) 1989

CRITICISM

Mark Freiman   (review date Summer 1985)

[*In the following review, Freiman identifies weaknesses in Kroker's* Technology and the Canadian Mind.]

[*Technology and the Canadian Mind*] is the first in a projected series of monographs on North American thinkers and theorists published by New World Perspectives, an offshoot of the *Canadian Journal of Political and Social Theory,* a lively New Leftist periodical that has achieved something of a reputation as a gadfly in the areas of social and intellectual theory. Written by the founding editor, it will unfortunately do nothing to advance an understanding of its subject among either lay or specialist readers.

The problem begins with the title. The book is ostensibly directed at clarifying the relationship between 'technology' and the 'Canadian mind' as this latter entity is represented by the thought of Innis, McLuhan, and Grant. Surprisingly, Kroker never pauses to define 'technology,' an oversight which prevents him from confronting the fact that his authors use the term in three quite different ways and are consequently concerned with relatively dissimilar aspects of the effects of 'technology' on the individual and on society. The 'technology' that interests Grant is a sort of civil religion of human mastery over nature associated with the relativistic liberal materialism that has brought about what he sees as the spiritual bankruptcy of current

North American society. McLuhan's interest in technology, by contrast, is in the media of communications, which he conceptualizes as artificial extensions of human sensory capacities that alter the shape and significance of 'reality' as it is apprehended through human perception. For Innis, 'technology' is the 'howness' of man's interaction with his environment, the physical characteristics of his tools and modes of communication, and consequently their possibilities, limitations, and 'biases.' Kroker seems able to unify these disparate perspectives under the rubric of 'technology' by making that term roughly synonymous with what used to be called 'the system' in the 1960s—a concept so vague and all-encompassing as to drain it of any of the analytic power that, at least in the works of Innis and McLuhan, results from each thinker's detailed examination of the characteristics and consequences of the specific 'technology' under study. Instead of hard analysis or any detailed consideration of specifics, Kroker offers up flaccid clichés about the 'vortex of technology' and of man's fate to be 'trapped within the technological simulacrum.'

The second term in the title, 'the Canadian mind,' proves to be as problematic as the first. Kroker believes that Grant, McLuhan, and Innis are 'emblematic figures' whose viewpoints 'represent the major positions which might be adopted today on the question of technology.' This emphasis leads him to treat them almost exclusively as social critics, and leaves him relatively uninterested in any aspects of their work that do not bear on his chosen theme. This has important stylistic, methodological, and substantive consequences for Kroker's analysis. Stylistically, it leads him to eschew any attempt at a logical or sequential elaboration of their works; thus he largely takes their writing for granted, searching instead for citations and examples that bear on the paradigm he intends to illustrate. This mode of proceeding, combined with his rather turgid style, makes the book very tough going and is likely to defeat most general readers coming to it for an introduction to the works of Innis, McLuhan, and Grant.

Readers familiar with the subject matter are likely to be taken aback by the methodological consequences of Kroker's approach. He does not find it necessary to make use of, or even to refer to, any of the existing biographical or critical scholarship. Instead, he chooses to contextualize their work within the 'Canadian mind' by interdisciplinary references to cultural and artistic 'analogues.' The discussion of McLuhan with reference to Seurat's *A Sunday Afternoon on the Island of La Grande Jatte* works rather well (mainly because McLuhan himself made Seurat the focus of his analysis in *Through the Vanishing Point*), and Kroker's citations from that work bring home some of the force of McLuhan's crazy-brilliance. Kroker's own attempts at a similar analysis, using Colville's *To Prince Edward Island* and Don Proch's *Manitoba Mining Mask* to explicate the thought of Grant and Innis respectively, are ham-handed and unconvincing.

Finally, there are the actual paradigms with which he identifies the thought of Grant, McLuhan, and Innis—respectively 'technological dependency,' 'technological humanism,' and 'technological realism.' Like 'technology' itself, these categories remain undefined. They have little if any intrinsic explanatory power, and as applied by Kroker result more in caricature than in analysis. Nor, for that matter, is it plausible, at least with regard to Innis and McLuhan, to perceive these thinkers exclusively as social critics. In McLuhan's case, although there are some useful observations about the relationship of his Catholicism to his theory, Kroker's emphasis leads him to stress 'sub-texts' at the expense of overt themes, highlighting references to technology as 'buzz saw,' and all but ignoring the 'global village' or the theories of 'right brain' and 'left brain.' Similarly with Innis, emphasis on some of his later nationalistic pronouncements without adequately grounding them in Innis's empirical historical and economic analysis transforms this most austere and subtle of dialecticians into precisely the sort of 'political sandwichman' he so fervently decried.

If Grant seems least distorted by Kroker's approach, part of the reason is probably that Grant *is* primarily a social critic, and his outlook is perhaps not unfairly summarized by Kroker as a meditation on losing in a world in which the deck is stacked against one. Another reason—though Kroker would undoubtedly reject the suggestion out of hand—is perhaps that Grant's sensibilities are most closely in tune with his own. Certainly by the conclusion, a Jeremiad in which Boy George, rock videos, the 'digital manipulations of the silicon chip,' and 'the Bomb' are lumped together as the 'technology' threatening human freedom, one feels oneself in the presence of a temperamental pessimism as chilling as anything that blows through the work of the dour Nova Scotian.

Given the respective achievements of Grant, McLuhan, and Innis, one suspects that a temperamental and intellectual affinity with either of the last two thinkers would have produced a more satisfactory result. (pp. 448-51)

> *Mark Freiman, in a review of "Technology and the Canadian Mind: Innis/McLuhan/Grant," in* University of Toronto Quarterly, *Vol. LIV, No. 4, Summer, 1985, pp. 448-51.*

Abraham Rotstein   (review date August-September 1985)

[*Rotstein is a Canadian economist, educator, and editor. In the following review of* Technology and the Canadian Mind, *Rotstein commends Kroker's appraisal of Canadian thought.*]

Arthur Kroker is one of this country's intellectual powerhouses. He is the founder and editor of the *Canadian Journal of Political and Social Theory,* and has single-handedly redeemed the social sciences from their often pedestrian and sterile preoccupations. The present volume [*Technology and the Canadian Mind*] launches a new series of paperbacks "intended to be both a celebration of the uniqueness of New World thought and a critical appraisal of its most dynamic tendencies." Kroker seldom disappoints us and his first volume sets a very high standard for the rest of the series.

In this diffident and envious country of ours, the binding

thread is no longer the CPR. It is instead a spiritual hankering for the universal aided and abetted by the electronic age to which we seem to have a special kinship. While others have taken the lead in creating the hardware, Kroker establishes our credentials as creators of the philosophical software.

We got off to a false start in the postwar period. Pearsonian liberalism encouraged us to turn our backs on Canada in the name of the higher and loftier purposes of global this and that and the international free flows of everything. Our economists, political scientists and some of our writers needed little urging to abandon ship and race for the global visions that were a fast one-way ticket out of here. Only a few recalcitrants realized that the genuine route to the propositions of universal significance started at a profound celebration of our indigenous experience.

To launch into philosophical outer space, we need our own Cape Canaveral. Kroker has assembled one from the generation of V-2 scientists that were bred here: Harold Innis, Marshall McLuhan and George Grant. Many people have appropriated Innis, McLuhan and Grant to shore up and extend existing perspectives and personal hobby horses, but Kroker is the first to have fitted the three thinkers into a common framework (although not in historical order of appearance). He has fallen back on the grammar of discourse of both Hegelian Marxists and Christians and given us a Canadian trinity: Grant, the spiritual Father, has the widest and most uncompromising view of technology (thesis); McLuhan, the Son, offers a more humanistic chiaroscuro (antithesis); Innis, the Holy Ghost, is grounded in a political realism that is remarkably prescient in its judgment of the American empire (synthesis).

This unexpected yoking of the Nietzschean Grant with the Moog synthesizer of the media, McLuhan, may make us fidget, but when we calm down we realize that Kroker is right. Running at the technological society from these very different directions does in fact produce a new topography—a topography of the Canadian mind, at least, but one that should stake its claim to universal interest as well. For Canadian intellectuals in spiritual diaspora, there is something well worth coming home to.

In the space of 30 pages, Kroker recapitulates the classical themes of George Grant as effectively as anyone in this country has ever done. According to this retelling, we are trapped in the self-generating momentum of scientific and technological endeavour and deprived of the ancient language of justice that would allow us to articulate our despair at this blind and dynamic nihilism. In Krokers's philosophical shorthand, citing Grant:

> The limits of human dependency have been achieved when we can say "technique is ourselves"; the calculus of "reasoning and willing" . . . (is) the nucleus of the "dynamic spirit" of the New World . . . and "the pure will to technique" is the essence of human freedom.

Although Kroker refers to Grant's epiphany as "the 'lament' of the Protestant mind," the Protestantism of—or more strikingly its absence from—Grant's discourse is never dealt with seriously. Grant falls back on the ancient Greeks and does not avail himself of the ultimate spiritual disengagement from the toils of the real world that was Luther's and later Hegel's legacy to modernity (*On the Freedom of a Christian*). Grant never counterpoises Christian freedom against "the pure will to technique" and its accompanying liberal freedom. Perhaps Grant may be right, but "technique" wins by default.

Grant's Protestant lament is hardly more than a foil for McLuhan's Catholic humanism—the basis for McLuhan's "new universal community" founded on the culture of technology. This thesis is suggestive but its development is elliptic. One thinks in this context of Teilhard de Chardin as well, but McLuhan is only slightly less reticent than Grant on this issue. The full religious connection in both cases has yet to be made.

Innis is used as a mediator between the two minds although he was the precursor of both and his vocabulary stems from an earlier period. There is an art deco touch to terms like "the monopoly of knowledge," "space versus time," and the quest for a "stable society." But Innis is thoroughly grounded in the muscle and sinew of Canadian society and in Canada's ambiguous fate in the American empire. His discussion of the communications media of antiquity has a compelling and authentic ring to it, perhaps because Innis is the ancient mariner of the St. Lawrence.

Kroker's account is occasionally larger than life and some may suspect that this version of "The Canadian Mind" has been lobotomized. The liberal strand is hardly dealt with except through Grant's eyes. It often seems that Canadians have little time for these darker preoccupations; they are too busy pursuing the updated version of their original credo, "Thou shalt have condominium from sea to sea."

There is no doubt, however, that this book is an intellectual *tour de force,* written with enormous power and insight. Kroker has seized on what is unique and vital and has rendered the Canadian mind to itself on a world stage. (pp. 34-5)

> *Abraham Rotstein, "Rest for the Philosophically Weary," in* The Canadian Forum, *Vol. LXV, No. 751, August-September, 1985, pp. 34-5.*

Thomas Carmichael   (review date Fall 1987)

[*In the following review, Carmichael praises Kroker and David Cook's grasp of postmodernist cultural theory in* The Postmodern Scene, *but faults the work for its lack of new insight into the postmodern condition.*]

When the term 'postmodern' entered critical discourse over a quarter-century ago, it was used to describe the lamentable epigone of the great project of modernity. This view has remained remarkably persistent, despite the efforts of later champions of a distinctly postmodern culture; however, notions of the provenance and the limits of postmodernism have not proved so unshakeable. Most recently, postmodernism has become identified as the cul-

tural arm of the poststructuralist program, and it is this cultural configuration to which Arthur Kroker and David Cook address themselves in *The Postmodern Scene.*

The aim of this book is twofold: on the one hand, the authors attempt to uncover the 'theoretical site' of the postmodern condition; at the same time, they present an examination of the artifacts of postmodern culture, particularly the visual arts and television. Kroker initiates his theoretical interrogation of the postmodern condition (the author of each section, except the first and the last, is identified by his initials) with a discussion of Charles Norris Cochrane's work on Augustine. Reading against Cochrane, Kroker presents the 'historical thesis' that the Augustinian 'closing of the eye of the flesh' betrays an awareness of 'the nihilism at the heart of Western consciousness,' which is only reawakened with the insights of Nietzsche and Foucault. At this point, Kroker returns to the main lines of the current postmodern debate, and his subsequent discussion of Nietzsche, Bataille, and Jean Baudrillard is a more incisive contribution to this book.

Armed with Baudrillard's notion of the *simulacrum* and his revisions to Foucault's meditations on power, Kroker effectively demonstrates the role of a purely relational 'dead power' in motivating a vapid but 'hyper' contemporary culture. The postmodern scene is thus the site of a 'cycle of disintegration, exhaustion, and "viciousness for fun," ' where the real disappears into a 'vast and seductive simulation.' This analysis is applied powerfully by each author, whether in an exposure of the cynical gender reversal in a Calvin Klein ad, in an examination of Eric Fischl's art, or in David Cook's eloquent account of the career of Roland Barthes.

The Postmodern Scene is a somewhat limited book, however, in that despite the theoretical prowess of its authors and their ability to read specific works of art, the text conveys little new insight into the postmodern condition. The book is up to date: the Eurythmics, Madonna, and Carol Pope and Rough Trade all make appearances. But the notions of a 'postmodern detritus,' of 'the deadness of the spirit,' and of 'a culture of forgetting, of forgetting of origins and destinations, . . . from trend to trend, from ad to ad' are ones which have already been established among literary critics in their discussions of the contours of modernism and postmodernism. This does not, of course, undermine the veracity of the authors' claims; it is simply to suggest that in equipping themselves with 'the radical insights of poststructuralist art . . . and poststructuralist theory,' Kroker and Cook appear to promise a more potent critique of postmodern culture than *The Postmodern Scene* actually delivers.

Kroker and Cook are most successful finally in their description of the intellectual culture that informs the postmodern condition. In demonstrating how contemporary life conforms to their theoretical model, however, they can at times give the reader occasion to ponder the useful limits of cultural analysis: what is to be gained, for instance, from employing critical theory to designate AIDS, Anorexia, and Herpes as poststructuralist diseases? (pp. 144-45)

> *Thomas Carmichael, in a review of "The Post-*

modern Scene: Excremental Culture and Hyper-Aesthetics," in University of Toronto Quarterly, *Vol. LVII, No. 1, Fall, 1987, pp. 144-45.*

W. Terrence Gordon   (review date Spring 1989)

[*In the following review, Gordon describes some of the strengths and weaknesses of* Panic Encyclopedia.]

"This is the way the world ends, not with a bang but a whimper," wrote T. S. Eliot in 1925. Now we have a book describing the way the century ends, not with a frenzied scene but in the inverted panic of inertia.

Describing itself as "the dark, reverse and imploding side of all the modernist encyclopedias," the book makes only one concession to convention by alphabetically arranging its entries. These do not deal with facts but post-facts, the former having disappeared, along with 90% of contemporary society, when modernism ended at 3:32 p.m., 15 July 1972.

Entries of one to seven pages in length range over sociology, physics, technology, politics, and economics, pulling them by cultured levitation into the bright and dense vortex of panoptic knowledge. The technique of reinforcing ideas through visual art which marked the senior author's earlier book, *Technology and the Canadian Mind,* is used even more extensively. Photos of works by Alex Colville, Salvador Dali, Eric Fischl, André Masson and others are interspersed with ads for Calvin Klein and Garbage Pail Kids.

Many wonders are revealed in this book: how money imitates art, why Gorbachev may be viewed as the last and best of all the Americans, why power, money, sex and the unconscious may now be abandoned, the missing w-particles of postmodern physics as a new metaphor for the electronic media, and a deficient orthological analysis of "substance abuse."

The authors have some difficulty situating themselves at the rupture-point between frenzy and reflection without appearing dogmatic. All but the most patient of readers will grow weary of their bald assertions: camp is postmodern spirituality, shopping malls are liquid television, the computer virus is yesterday's disease, David Letterman is a media predator, there is no deconstruction.

This unremitting barrage is lightened now and then by humor, though it is not always easy to tell when it is intentional. What is one to think on reading that "the fusion of the lawn specialist and the beautician creates the 'unconsciousness' of post-hoc suburban life; the aestheticization of all the post-lawns is the ruling metaphysic of the new middle class?"

Although the influence of Marshall McLuhan is clear in the panorama of society with twenty-first century engineering and nineteenth-century perceptions, the book's predominantly bleak mood-line moves it away from McLuhan's technological humanism toward George Grant's technological determinism.

Only rarely do the authors pass judgment on the postmod-

ern scene, as when they condemn the magazine *Vanity Fair* for its insidious project of simultaneously tantalizing and appeasing consumers. Readers will be less inclined to suspend judgment on *Panic Encyclopedia* and its project of simultaneously tantalizing and unsettling consumers—and refusing to let the world end with a whimper. (pp. 147-48)

W. Terrence Gordon, in a review of "Panic Encyclopedia," in The Dalhousie Review, *Vol. 69, No. 1, Spring, 1989, pp. 147-48.*

An excerpt from *Panic Encyclopedia: The Definitive Guide to the Postmodern Scene*

Shopping malls are liquid TVs for the end of the twentieth century. A whole micro-circuitry of desire, ideology, and expenditure for processed bodies drifting through the cyberspace of ultracapitalism. Not shopping malls any longer under the old sociological formula of consumption sites, but future shops where what is truly fascinating is expenditure, loss, and exhaustion.

Shopping malls act like electro-magnets, attracting into their force field all the surrounding community activities. They involve a double movement of recuperation and dispersion. Recuperation in the sense that malls provide a temporary unity for an otherwise chaotic, random, and undetermined field of activity. And dispersion in the sense that, when the energy is shut off (life outside the mall), the force field, vectored around desire, ideology, and expenditure, immediately dissolves into its constituent particles.

Shopping malls call forth the same psychological position as TV watching: voyeurism. Except this time, they do it one better. Rather than flicking the dial, you take a walk from channel to channel as the neon stores flick by. And not just watching either, but shopping malls have this big advantage over TV, they play every sense: smelling, tasting, touching, looking, desiring, fantasizing. A whole image-repertoire which, when successful, splays the body into a multiplicity of organs, all demanding to be filled. But, of course, the shopping mall, just like all the promises of ecstasy and catastrophe before it, fulfills what it promises only virtually; and the shopping body, caught for one instant in the force field of the commodity as image-repertoire, sags back into the routine of life outside the field.

Arthur Kroker, Marilouise Kroker, and David Cook, in their Panic Encyclopedia: The Definitive Guide to the Postmodern Scene, New World Perspectives, 1989.

Dmitry Khanin   (essay date October 1990)

[*In the following essay, Khanin evaluates postmodernism as defined by Kroker and David Cook in* The Postmodern Scene.]

Postmodernists—The Sectarians of our day—proclaim that the old kingdom of historical narrative and historical subject has perished, and is now being replaced by a new one of ahistorical discourses and ahistorical characters. According to these prophets, "history" is anyway just changes in ways of talking about history. Anyone who does not agree with the ahistoricity of the postmodern world outlook may be accused—and tried on the spot—of defending the cause of the totalitarian Reason against the most liberating movement of today.

This postmodernist abuse of history is paradoxical, since the very notion of history coming to its end and giving way to the ahistorical kingdom of freedom and merry debauchery is itself a very old idea, even a mythological one. The description of history as marching toward its own demise relies on a whole tradition which portrays history as a drama. Aristotle's conception of tragedy as a sequence of actions culminating in a dénouement has no doubt shaped this view of historical process. Christian and other religious millenarians have announced the end of history already many times. Yet another notorious instance of such eschatological daydreaming is the futurology of Karl Marx, who envisaged the kingdom of communism as occupying this same ahistorical space. A rather obsolete idea, perhaps, but it seems still to attract postmodernists, though they give it a characteristic twist, since they sincerely believe theory, discourse, écriture (i.e., theoretico-symbolical activity) are much more important than any actual historical content—processes and events.

One of the most notable spokesmen for this approach is Arthur Danto, who insists that world history evolved in a good Hegelian manner until the theorists came to understand that history depends on their texts much more than theorists themselves depend on historical processes and events [Danto, *The Philosophical Disenfranchisement of Art*]. Many theoreticians working in an otherwise Marxist tradition similarly are glad to assert with Fredric Jameson that we must say farewell to Marx's positivistic illusion that history is driven by laws disguised as economic forces [Jameson, "Postmodernism in Consumer Society," in *The Anti-Aesthetic: Essays on Postmodern Culture,* edited by Hal Foster]. In the epoch of "late capitalism," says Jameson, consumption gains the upper hand over production and becomes the mainspring of history. Of course, in light of recent doings in Europe I am tempted to ask if we owe it to postmodernists—and their ahistorical, inconsistent, and generally confounding claims about history lying in ruins—that the Berlin Wall *actually is in ruins* and Václav Havel is president of Czechoslovakia.

Even more daring theorists may now declare an era of *"very late* capitalism." Here it will not be merely the mass media that act transformatively on society (as McLuhan claimed), but rather consumer goods themselves, like state-of-the-art washing machines or French perfumes, which create a new aura of intellectual discourse. *The Postmodern Scene: Excremental Culture and Hyper-Aesthetics,* a book by two Canadian authors, Arthur Kroker and David Cook, promotes such a sea change in the theoretical landscape and along the way presents a joyous recapitulation of the latest fads in postmodern thinking. The new apostolic generation of postmodern critics seems to enjoy the beautiful new things that can be bought for bucks, worrying at the same time that bucks may be losing some of their purchasing power. Like Hari-Krishnas dancing in the street they luckily possess a sort

of happy consciousness which also recalls their puritanical great grandfathers who regarded profligacy as the greatest sin and much preferred saving to spending. In what follows I want to draw a portrait of this new postmodern posture.

A few main assumptions underlie Kroker's and Cook's wake for postmodernism, which, in its peculiar genre of philosophic obituary, epitomizes and thus prepares for future oblivion views which were exceedingly popular in the preceding decade. First of all, the authors adopt Baudrillard's equation of Marx and Nietzsche: "Marx and Nietzsche shared a deep and common affinity in meditating upon historical (Christian) and materialistic (capitalist) expressions of the will of power." From Baudrillard's perspective Marx appears as a pathetic romantic who tried to defend the "referential illusion" by renaturalizing concrete labor even though its entirely abstract character was brilliantly revealed in *Das Kapital.* Baudrillard himself, in Kroker's and Cook's opinion, is a prophet of a new stage of civilization, advanced capitalism. It is an epoch when "the real does not exist anymore, or more precisely . . . the real appears to us only as a vast and seductive simulation." All that is left for us then is to hyper-theorize, trampling history into ruins in order to get an intellectual rush from experiencing the postmodern. If the sign and omen of the epoch is "its panic boredom" let us enjoy this to the full. The motto of Andy Warhol—"bored but hyper"—thus becomes a catchword for a new philosophical mood. Theorists who want to be integral in their own epoch surely must put on a postmodern mien—which means panicking to escape being bored.

There are, in fact, three principal aspects of the new postmodern outlook as proposed by Kroker and Cook. Firstly, it takes a quite definite moral stand assessing the contemporary epoch under the sign of jovial pessimism. Advanced capitalism rapidly is falling into "radical decline." What is taking place in our culture is a very pleasant degradation. Nietzsche was right (as Marx was not) in his immediate prognosis. Generally speaking this mood has nothing to do with postmodernism as such (though it is being substantiated with the help of poststructuralism). This is just a banal condemnation of a developing civilization and its vices. Such a pronouncement may be traced back to almost any social theorist beginning with the dawn of the stone age (the first decadent epoch when the "real" values of apish prehistory with its mimetic illusions were subversively undermined by new stone contraptions).

Another postulate is somewhat more specific. It claims that the mass media have already usurped power over the world and are unflinchingly remaking it in their own image. With McLuhan and Baudrillard, Kroker and Cook insist that new technologies that have transformed the mass media not only influence the contemporary ways of life and modes of perception, but have in fact replaced them and become substitutes for other practices of reality. "The TV audience may be, today, the most pervasive type of social community, but if this is so then it is a very special type of community: an anti-community or a social anti-matter. . . ."

The third argument might be termed economico-aesthetic.

The authors have no doubts about the altogether aesthetic character of the contemporary stage of capitalist society. This line of reasoning is linked on the one hand with Nietzschean pessimism in estimating the future and on the other hand with a frantic McLuhanesque belief that the new technologies of mass media are the very lever that can overturn the world. The crucial argument thus is that capital now "becomes that which it always was: an empty and nihilistic sign-system of pure mediation and pure exchange which, having no energy of its own, adopts a scorched earth policy toward the missing social matter of society."

Where Kroker and Cook succeed in being most original, transgressing the boundaries of their usually epitomizing discourse, is in their practical analysis of the postmodern mood as it is represented in art. Their chosen specimen of a postmodern artist is Eric Fischl, who portrays something "perhaps much worse than fascism . . . a whole society of dead souls who confuse leisure with freedom." The deep-rooted crises of contemporary culture, both nihilistic and cynical, are illustrated, according to Kroker and Cook, by *Daddy's Girl,* a painting in which a middle-aged man, sunbathing naked, is caressing his little daughter who has seemingly just run up to kiss her father "good morning."

There are two grave accusations that are leveled at the resting man by the authors. First, "Daddy is a potential sexual transgressor" (the drink by his side is suggested to be an oblique proof of his sensual instability); secondly, no female is to be seen anywhere which means, of course, that "Mommy has disappeared, and who cares." Mommy's disappearance from the context of postmodern painting is perhaps an even more insidious symbol of the imminent decline of our culture than the outrageous absence of the historical subject. Probably, if Mommy were sitting (also naked, sunbathing) in another chair and there were two glasses of booze served symmetrically instead of a single menacing drink at Daddy's side the painting would be just a nude and not a postmodern one. As it is, the girl's fate is "a throw of the dice between incest and fatherly love."

When someone confesses to being scared (an emotion many try not to betray), sympathy requires another either to disperse the person's fears, provided they are unreasonable, or to share them if they are justified. The panicked consciousness of these two Canadian authors suggests that they are terrified by something as menacing as an injured bear, otherwise they would not fancy terrorizing the readers of their book, people who doubtless have enough "real" trouble of their own, to which they don't need to add merely metaphysical problems. But the more I try to understand what so bothers these fellows, the more confused and bewildered I become.

Kroker and Cook assure the reader that the ascendant middle class, this historical subject of the society devoid of social matter, is actually torn between "dread over the transmission of bodily secretion and fear about the imminent breakdown of the technical system." The anxious stupor of middle-class man, the prevailing social being in our era, who was gradually stripped by the signifying systems of many of his natural abilities, receiving something

very fragile and insecure in exchange, is quite understandable. Must this uncertainty and metaphysical instability entail a panicky vacillation from one pole to another? Is this schizoid pattern so characteristic of our time as opposed to all other historical periods? This is very dubious.

Kroker and Cook ascertain that there are three principal sins (or are they gifts?) of television which cannot be redeemed by any new savior. These are seriality, postmodern technology, and entertainment as the dominant ideology. It is specifically seriality that characterizes, in the authors' minds, the type of contact between the audience and the media elite who are united in a strange kind of relationship where (following Baudrillard) only one partner is allowed to speak—though he or she has virtually nothing to say—while the other one is doomed to a perpetual silence. From Sartre they borrow the idea that the passive recipient of the serial production experiences "practico-inert" emotional states of implosive triumph. When, for example, one feels oneself to be smarter than a television personality, one experiences "impotent indignation" and the thrill of subjugation of the other. One realizes too that the communication in mass media is not a dialogue but a one-way street.

One may question the applicability of Sartre's 1940s characterization of radio broadcasting to postmodern television. More generally I would call into doubt the universality of Sartre's self-analysis as a viewer, or rather a listener. His experience has every mark of an intellectual who would rather be putting on a show inside the box than watching one outside it. It is this kind of ego, self-conscious and even envious of the other's popularity, which enjoys triumphant bliss when outsmarting a television personality, feels indignant when outsmarted, and is downright humiliated if the flickering images succeed in gaining its complete attention.

Is this, however, a universal model of television's impact on the audience? Such a projection of Sartre on Baudrillard's silent majorities looks strange to me. Specifically so with the advent of new techniques of viewer participation, on the other hand, and the much more delightful experience of TV blips directed by a less exalted person than an existentialist philosopher, on the other hand. It may well be that the silent majorities enjoy just happily watching television (without reservations and intellectual tantrums) and, yes, happily believe that this is a genuine life, and to hell with the real world, which is (let's confess) often very boring. Yet the question persists of whether such a welcome detachment from the burden of the everyday is an aspect of the human condition as such, or whether as Kroker and Cook would have it, this aloofness is peculiarly characteristic of our contemporary culture.

The antihistorical bias of the current trends in art, philosophy, and culture is evident. Can we take it for granted, though, that history itself has actually come to a standstill? Wouldn't it be a better idea to search for the actual historical reasons of this ahistorical turn? The most prominent feature of the postmodern psychological stance which can help us to grasp its true identity is, in my opinion, its antagonism towards modernism. There is something troublesome about a cultural phenomenon that seeks to naturalize within its boundaries all other historical challenges, but at the same time heavily rests on the modernist experiment, even as it rejects modernist ideology. The trait of the latter that upsets postmodernists more than anything else is the modernist belief in the constant advance of history, the ability of modernists to keep pace with this progress, and indeed the necessity of doing so.

This kind of worldview is, to be sure, consistent with the ideology of the hard sciences which sets no absolute limit to knowledge and lustfully seeks to go deeper and deeper into its subject matter at a permanently increasing speed. Modernism in art, and, perhaps, also in politics, merely parallels this indomitable forward motion in science and technology, intentionally trying to demonstrate that what is true of the overall phenomenon of progress is no less true for art and politics—that art and politics too can transform themselves at the same rate into ever new and unpredictable shapes. Postmodernism most typically attempts to arrest this incessant and hastening flow of events in order to take a long breath. Its principal means of achieving this is to make fun of the very notion of history and historical progress as mere wishful thinking, asserting that historical change actually not something real but rather a sort of transformed discourse.

Postmodernism versus modernism: this was the battle that was waged from the very beginning and it is still the crux of the whole discussion. A question naturally arises, however, as to the genetic relationship between modernism and postmodernism. To the best of my knowledge, two main answers have been given. The first, more obvious one, postulates that the word "post" should be understood quite literally; the second hypothesizes to the contrary that the "post" could well have preceded the modern, however pre-posterous it may seem. This debate of course recalls a much more ancient quarrel about the priority of hen or egg. The hen-pecked always believed, it would seem, that modernism was before, as this name was current even when no one had heard of or cared about "post"; the egg-headed stubbornly rejoined that their adversaries simply cannot understand the real importance of eggs in history.

The stylistic features of postmodernism—its playfulness, pluralism, love of disguise, and its antisynthetic fusion of different modes of human experience, or as Kroker and Cook would want us to believe, its "hypercoldness of cynical culture American style . . . where even sex is parasited just for the fun of it"—are in fact not indicative by themselves of something dashingly new. But all of these features might also be viewed as stylistic features of some other epochs, such as the baroque or romantic, or of aestheticism. However, none of these is in this regard equal to postmodernism.

Postmodernism, to be sure, is not merely a style, even though it certainly has some stylistic idiosyncrasies. It is rather a mood (here I agree with Kroker and Cook) and hence an ideology, no matter how opposed to other forms of ideologism or ideologism it may appear. Being preeminently a mood, or psychological state (both of which have ideological aspects), postmodernism, in my opinion, should be scrutinized in the light of its principal differentia

specifica: a dislike of the idea of history as an evergrowing and accumulating energy process, and a distaste for modernism as the herald of history's advance.

The thrust of the protest against the totalizing impact of great narratives, especially characteristic of philosophical postmodernism, clearly bears the stamp of our epoch, sometimes aptly named: the age of lost innocence. Somewhat similar to the Enlightenment's scorn for the medieval mentality as an assortment of prejudices, postmodernism is ready to abandon historicism insofar as it has tainted itself with totalitarianism. After a whole century of political violence and rape, a strategy commonly recommended to victims (please, relax and try to enjoy it) is being advertised as a bright, new world outlook.

Evidently, this makes a lot of sense from an economic point of view. Instead of persuading oneself that what one got, one surely wanted, a more universal approach suggests that we should not even think of the event in such emotionally charged terms as "rape." Victims, of course, might protest, as this new turn of thought robs them of the pleasure that they strained to procure from their own victimization. However, a consolation suggested by such an uncompromising solution to the problem of violence in history is quite manifest.

Disappointment with history (and what is postmodernism after all but a sneering pessimism?) was, perhaps, never so deep or ingrained as now. It is a subjective mood, highly symptomatic of our age and its mentality. One could risk saying that such a mood—a sort of gloomy restlessness and anxiety to the point of evaporation of merely natural feelings—ought to be more characteristic of the countries that put their shoulders to the heavy wheel of the societal experiments of the present century in the first place. Actually the opposite holds true. Naturally, the world is one and historical experience is indivisible, being a collective and common rather than an individual or local legacy. But nevertheless, the more developed countries are privileged to experience the living process of history in more intimate and authentic forms, as they stand closer to its epicenter, even though the less developed ones are doomed to suffer its most disastrous implications.

Modernism can be formulated as simply as this: it is a conviction that what is new is better than what is old just because it is a product of a later stage of development. What underlies this view is a particular conception of history as an evolving process whose further phases necessarily supersede the previous ones in every possible respect, using them as a platform for new breakthroughs. The debate of the ancients and the moderns in seventeenth-century France, as is often noted, might be taken as a watershed between the medieval type of consciousness which rested on the maxim, the older the better (the older being closer to the sacred truths of revelation) and the modern one, assured of the superiority of the present as more sophisticated and refined than what came before.

The Enlightenment's notorious intolerance of the Dark Ages was the first sign of modernity's impatience with all that is outdated and old-fashioned. In the nineteenth and even more specifically twentieth centuries, such contempt for former ways of living and modes of thinking reached its apogee in the technocratic positivism which rapidly spread like an oil spill in the ocean. It was adopted as the ruling ideology of a mass society, scornful of anything that does not belong to its terrain, though happily ignorant (as Ortega y Gasset emphatically put it) as to what ensured all this well-being. The technocrat's snobbery found its counterpart in the sneer of the man in the street, disdainful of everything that is not brand new. Quixote once again found his Sancho Panza.

What is at stake after all in the current controversy over postmodernism if not the idea of progress? When Arthur Danto asserts in *The Philosophical Disenfranchisement of Art* that Hegel perhaps was not wrong to maintain that history is but the story of the self-understanding of an Absolute, he is actually claiming that progress is finite rather than limitless. This is also typical of postmodern horror at the wild horizons of history and postmodern exhaustion with trying to keep up with something that exceeds the natural boundaries of the human domain. Better just to look after ourselves than try to serve as a measure for everything else in the world.

A new ultramodernist phase of postmodernism is trying now to combine the technological optimism of the 1960s with the pessimistic cynicism borrowed from the turn of the last century. A corrected model of historical being is hence put forth. Instead of the former utopia of limitless progress, ultramodernists stick to new technology with the same zest but no longer believe in the subsequent change of human nature. The image of modern observer—pathfinder and conqueror—is replaced in postmodernism by that of the voyeur. But perhaps this is just a postmodern posture. If history is gone forever we are simply left on the playground with the warped, old toys—like retarded children with no prospect of maturing. Do you fancy this new horizon for humanity? I prefer the chance to live inside history rather than to drop out of it. (pp. 239-47)

> *Dmitry Khanin, "The Postmodern Posture," in* Philosophy and Literature, *Vol. 14, No. 2, October, 1990, pp. 239-47.*

FURTHER READING

Biography

Yanofsky, Joel. "All Shook Up." *Books in Canada* XX, No. 8 (November 1991): 24-7.

> Overview of Arthur and Marilouise Kroker's careers and joint publishing ventures.

Criticism

Armour, Leslie. "A Map of Chasms." *Canadian Literature,* No. 110 (Fall 1986): 163-64.

> Notes that Kroker fails to distinguish between Innis's, McLuhan's, and Grant's differing definitions of technology in his *Technology and the Canadian Mind.*

Arnowitz, Stanley. "Technology and Culture." *Canadian Journal of Political and Social Theory* IX, No. 3 (Fall 1985): 126-33.

> Examines Kroker's portrayal of the philosophies discussed in *Technology and the Canadian Mind.*

Campbell, Robert Malcolm. "Technology, Democracy and the Politics of Economic Regeneration." *Journal of Canadian Studies* 20, No. 3 (Winter 1985-86): 158-72.

> Reviews five works, including Kroker's *Technology and the Canadian Mind: Innis/McLuhan/Grant,* that examine the role of technology in shaping Canada's political and economic future.

Keefer, Michael H. "Postmodernism." *Canadian Literature,* No. 120 (Spring 1989): 225-27.

> Review of three studies, including Kroker and Cook's *The Postmodern Scene: Excremental Culture and Hyper-Aesthetics,* which offer differing perspectives on postmodernism.

Tonkin, Boyd. "Alphabet Soup." *New Statesman and Society* 2, No. 57 (7 July 1987): 43.

> Unfavorable review of *Panic Encyclopedia: The Definitive Guide to the Postmodern Scene* in which Tonkin criticizes the unoriginal and jargon-laden prose style of postmodern theorists.

James Alan McPherson

1943-

American short story writer.

The following entry provides an overview of McPherson's career through 1993. For further information on McPherson's life and works, see *CLC,* Volume 19.

INTRODUCTION

McPherson is best known for *Elbow Room,* a short story collection for which he won the Pulitzer Prize in 1978. In this volume, as in his earlier work, *Hue and Cry,* McPherson challenges restrictive views of race, culture, and religion. McPherson also examines the emotional and psychological effects of such social problems as poverty, violence, and discrimination on working-class individuals. While McPherson often delineates the experiences of African-Americans, critics note that his stories are accessible to all readers because of their emphasis on humanistic values and social change. Throughout his career McPherson has been praised for his technical skill, the universality of his themes, and the believability and richness of his characters. Irving Howe has observed: "[McPherson] possesses an ability some writers take decades to acquire, the ability to keep the right distance from the creatures of his imagination, not to get murkily involved and blot out his figures with vanity and fuss."

McPherson was born and raised in a lower-class black community in Savannah, Georgia, a historic city comprised of several ethnic groups, including French, Spanish, Indian, English, and African. Although McPherson attended segregated public schools as a child, he grew into adolescence during the height of the civil rights movement; he has stated that living in the multicultural atmosphere of Savannah in such a politically-charged era contributed to his ability to transcend racial and social barriers. In addition to witnessing integration, McPherson was influenced by the optimism and belief in progress that pervaded the black community at this time: "[The] 1960s were a crazy time. Opportunities seemed to materialize out of thin air; and if you were lucky, if you were in the right place at the right time, certain contractual benefits just naturally accrued." As a youth McPherson worked as a grocery boy, a waiter on a train, a janitor, and a newspaper boy. These experiences would later provide McPherson with the basis for many of his stories. McPherson earned a bachelor's of arts degree from Morris Brown College in 1965, a law degree from Harvard University in 1968, and a master's degree in creative writing from the University of Iowa in 1969. He began to seriously pursue writing while attending law school, and his story "Gold Coast" won first prize in a contest sponsored by the *Atlantic Monthly.* This journal would later figure prominently in McPherson's career: the Atlantic Monthly Press co-

published his first short story collection, *Hue and Cry,* in 1969 and later that year McPherson was named a contributing editor of the magazine. During this time McPherson also met black writer Ralph Ellison, who would later become his mentor. McPherson has stated: "[Ellison affirmed] ideals that no one else, including whites, seemed to believe in—that something called America *did* exist; that it had a culture; that black Americans were, by our unique history and special contributions and the quality of our struggle, heroic; that self-imposed segregation, especially of the imagination, was a mistake. By taking this stand, he affirmed himself, but it placed him in an impossible situation, intellectually and personally. Still, I admired him for standing his ground. 'Never segregate yourself,' he advised me. At the time I needed a mentor to give me permission." In addition to his ongoing contributions to the *Atlantic Monthly,* McPherson has also worked as a professor of English at the University of Iowa Writers Workshop since 1981.

In *Hue and Cry* McPherson addresses the themes of injustice, loneliness, and self-identity. Facing such obstacles as racism, economic exploitation, and age discrimination, the characters in this collection are unable to alleviate the pain and frustration in their lives and frequently suffer in silence. "Gold Coast," for example, focuses on an elderly white couple who are shunned by their neighbors because they are unable to keep themselves or their apartment clean. "A Matter of Vocabulary" centers on Thomas, a thirteen-year-old grocery boy who realizes that because he is black he is expected to quit school if he wants to keep his job. Since his work gives him a sense of pride and responsibility, he acquiesces to the expectations of his white employer. McPherson parallels Thomas's inner turmoil and misery with the plight of a homeless woman who, having descended into madness, releases her frustration by screaming endlessly into the night.

McPherson's *Elbow Room* is generally considered more optimistic than *Hue and Cry* because of its emphasis on social improvement, personal development, and racial harmony. The characters in this collection range from college professors to ex-convicts and are willing and able to struggle for survival. While some of the stories in this work focus specifically on African-Americans trying to gain respectability and status in contemporary American society, the collection as a whole addresses the concerns of all individuals who are limited by social injustices. McPherson also emphasizes the importance of communication, critical thought, and the ability to understand others as complex and unique human beings rather than stereotypes. In "Just Enough for the City," for example, the narrator questions conventional views of religion, love, language, and race as he seeks to identify and appreciate the humanity in all people. As he is sitting in a diner at the end of the story, the narrator observes: "[When Doris, humming, brings the people at the counter] plates of sizzling hamburgers, limber lettuce, grease-drenched fries, I see them look into their meals as I would look at a beautiful woman. I see them bend their heads and close their eyes, almost in unison, over red and yellow condiment holders, plastic glasses of Coke, the steaming plates. It is such a private, natural gesture in its smoothness of reflex that I, like they, forget we are in a very public place. Something breathes quickly against the cobwebs inside me. But because I fear what I feel is love, I turn my face away." In "Elbow Room," an unidentified narrator wrestles with the moral, aesthetic, and social issues related to interracial relationships. Like the other stories in this volume, "Elbow Room" demonstrates McPherson's belief that one cannot succumb to simplistic racial stereotypes. Robert Phillips has observed that the stories in *Elbow Room* are "not so much about the black condition as the human condition."

Critical reaction to McPherson's work has been overwhelmingly positive. Throughout his career he has been the recipient of numerous honors, including a National Institute of Art and Letters grant, a Rockefeller grant, a Guggenheim Fellowship, and a MacArthur Foundation Award. Ralph Ellison reflected the opinion of most critics when he asserted: "[McPherson is] a writer of insight, sympathy, and humour and one of the most gifted young Americans I've had the privilege to read." Believing that people from all social groups have contributed to the development of American culture, McPherson emphasizes that literature must transcend racial and ethnic prejudices

if it is to have positive effects on society. McPherson has stated: "It seems to me that much of [black] writing has been, and continues to be, sociological because black writers have been concerned with protesting black humanity and racial injustice to the larger society in those terms most easily understood by nonblack people. It also seems to me that we can correct this limitation either by defining and affirming the values and cultural institutions of our people for their education or by employing our own sense of reality and our own conception of what human life should be to explore, and perhaps help define, the cultural realities of contemporary American life."

PRINCIPAL WORKS

Hue and Cry (short stories) 1969
Elbow Room (short stories) 1977

CRITICISM

Granville Hicks   (review date 21 May 1969)

[*Hicks was an American literary critic whose famous study* The Great Tradition: An Interpretation of American Literature since the Civil War *(1933) established him as the foremost advocate of Marxist critical thought in Depression-era America. After 1939, however, Hicks sharply denounced Marxist criticism, which he called a "hopelessly narrow way of judging literature," and in his later years adopted a less ideological posture in literary matters. In the following excerpt, he offers a laudatory review of* Hue and Cry.]

Hue and Cry is a collection of stories by James Alan McPherson. . . . (p. 47)

I like the title, which is also the title of one of the stories, because, taken literally, it is quite inappropriate. As epigraph McPherson has chosen a passage from Pollock and Maitland's *History of English Law:* "When a felony is committed, the hue and cry *(hutesium et clamor)* should be raised. If, for example, a man comes upon a dead body and omits to raise the hue, he commits an amerceable offense, besides laying himself open to ugly suspicion. Possibly the proper cry is 'Out! Out!'" Unlike certain other black writers, McPherson does not find it necessary to go into spasms of indignation every time he describes an act of discrimination. He is acutely aware of the misery and injustice in the world, and he sympathizes deeply with the victims whether they are black or white.

"It is my hope," he says,

> that this collection of stories can be read as a book about people, all kinds of people: old, young, lonely, homosexual, confused, used, dis-

carded, wronged. As a matter of fact, certain of the people happen to be black, and certain of them happen to be white; but I have tried to keep the color part of most of them far in the background . . . I have tried to say in these stories what I have seen of humanity: the good, the bad, the predictable things and some things not so easily understandable or predictable.

It is a book about the mass of men, who, Thoreau said, lead lives of quiet desperation; and so they do whether they are black or white. One of the fine stories tells about an old Pullman waiter who, in the great days of railroading, had a peculiar eminence because he could do his job better than anyone else; but at last, like any other champion, he is beaten by time and circumstance. Another, written from the point of view of the "apprentice janitor," describes the people in an old apartment house near Harvard Square, once part of the formidable Gold Coast, "a very fine haven for the rich," and now the abode of men and women on the way out. As McPherson understands and repeatedly shows, the problem of identity does not exist for intellectuals alone.

McPherson's book reminds me in a way of Ernest Gaines's *Bloodline* because, despite differences in their experience, both authors are Negroes who have devoted themselves to learning their craft. It also reminds me, even more strongly, of Jonathan Strong's *Tike* because both men are so gifted and so young.

I want to end by quoting from the jacket a statement made by Ralph Ellison. Not only because it justly praises McPherson's book but also because it addresses words of wisdom to all Negro writers:

> With this collection of stories, McPherson promises to move right past those talented but misguided writers of Negro American cultural background who take being black as a privilege for being obscenely second-rate and who regard their social predicament as Negroes as exempting them from the necessity of mastering the craft and forms of fiction. Indeed, as he makes his "hue and cry" over the dead-ends, the confusions of value and failures of sympathy and insight of those who inhabit his fictional world, McPherson's stories are themselves a hue and cry against the dead, publicity-sustained writing which has come increasingly to stand for what is called "black writing." McPherson will never, as a writer, be an embarrassment to such people of excellence as Willie Mays, Duke Ellington, Leontyne Price—or, for that matter, Stephen Crane or F. Scott Fitzgerald.

No one in the world is better qualified to speak such words than Ralph Ellison, and I can only add Amen. (pp. 47-8)

> *Granville Hicks, in a review of "Hue and Cry," in* The Saturday Review, *New York, Vol. LII, No. 21, May 21, 1969, pp. 47-8.*

Irving Howe   (review date December 1969)

[*A longtime editor of the leftist magazine* Dissent *and a regular contributor to the* New Republic, *Howe is one*

of America's most highly respected literary critics and social historians. In the following review, he praises Hue and Cry *and calls McPherson "a born writer."*]

At twenty-six James Alan McPherson has written a book of short stories, ***Hue and Cry,*** that one can read with pleasure and respect, caring only for the calm assurance with which he penetrates the lives of Negro train waiters, black students, white janitors. Though sometimes lacking in a culminating tension—his stories begin more strongly than they end—Mr. McPherson's writing is beautifully poised. He possesses an ability some writers take decades to acquire, the ability to keep the right distance from the creatures of his imagination, not to get murkily involved and blot out his figures with vanity and fuss. He doesn't reach as deeply into the entanglements of black life as Hal Bennett occasionally can, nor is he as familiar with the psychic lesions of plebeian blacks; but he is a more controlled writer, able to turn out a finished piece of work.

His hue and cry is over life's incompleteness, the small betrayals we all enact. James McPherson has a strong sense of injustice, almost a boy's sense, and he knows how disproportionately large a share of that injustice black men must bear; yet he manages to take human beings one at a time, honoring their portion of uniqueness. Some writers have the psychology of inquisitors, and some of victims; Mr. McPherson has none of the former and not too much of the latter, which for a black writer these days seems exactly right. In **"Gold Coast"** he writes with a shudder of sympathy about the feebleness and loneliness of an old white janitor in Harvard Square; in **"A Solo Song: For Doc"** he speaks a low-keyed paean of affection for an aging black waiter expert at "the service" on railroad dining cars. (James McPherson isn't so foolish as to suppose that all older Negroes must have been shuffling Toms, and he even knows that those who were probably had no choice and deserve their mite of respect too.) The title story is a touching portrait of a bright and sensitive black girl who has an affair with a bright and sensitive white boy; slowly the affair disintegrates ("I don't know," says Margot to Eric, "if I'm a person to you or an idea. Right now, back there, I felt like a damn cause"). The girl starts losing her nerve, she can no longer summon that shrug of independence which had set her above all the cults and causes of campus life.

James McPherson's stories need a sharper articulation, and his language could with advantage be given a freer idiomatic lilt. But he is a born writer—which means a writer who works hard on every sentence, thinks lucidly about his effects, and knows that in art meaning, even salvation, depends finally on craft. (pp. 137, 141)

> *Irving Howe, "New Black Writers," in* Harper's Magazine, *Vol. 239, No. 1435, December, 1969, pp. 130-46.*

Rosemary M. Laughlin   (essay date Autumn 1973)

[*In the essay below, Laughlin praises McPherson's depiction of dining car waiter Doc Craft in "A Solo Song: For Doc," and claims that Doc Craft is an example of the American folk hero.*]

In the spring of 1969 James Alan McPherson's first book was published—a collection of short stories entitled **Hue and Cry.** Several of the stories had appeared previously in *The Atlantic* and one of them, **"Gold Coast,"** had won that magazine's fiction prize for 1968. The critical reaction was a writer's dream for a first book—almost unanimously approving and enthusiastic. Understandably, the publishers chose to quote Ralph Ellison's evaluation on the jacket of the paperback edition which followed in 1970:

> With this collection of stories, McPherson promises to move right past those talented but misguided writers of Negro American cultural background who take being black as a privilege for being obscenely second-rate and who regard their social predicament as Negroes as exempting them from the necessity of mastering the craft and forms of fiction. . . . McPherson . . . is a writer of insight, sympathy, and humor, and one of the most gifted young Americans I've had the privilege to read.

Several of the reviewers noted that their favorite in the collection was **"A Solo Song: For Doc,"** brilliant, as one observed, for its "fusion of reportage, thematic drama and manly lyricism that seems to be unforgettable." This evaluation is certainly merited, but the story is most remarkable in that it brings to light an American folkloric hero whose time for recognition has come at last.

Doc Craft qualifies as hero both in the general tradition of folklore and in specifically American fashion. Present in his story are the elements of legend and reality, of characters that are both comic and tragic, of situations and scenes that are typically and often uniquely American, and of narrative that records an oral telling that justifies, with its rhythmic patterns of words and phrases the "song" in the title.

The fable itself does not focus on a hero of the epic or warrior type nor on one who achieves notoriety by a single deed. He belongs rather with the occupational heroes, the work giants of American folklore: John Henry the Steel-Driving Man, Casey Jones the Brave Engineer, Paul Bunyan the Giant Lumberjack, and Joe Magarac the Steel Maker, to mention a few of the better known. Indeed, like John Henry and Casey Jones, Doc Craft works for the railroad. He is a black dining car waiter and his great drive is to distinguish himself by doing a superlative job of what he must do: "the service." And this he does, with the flair, expertise, and genius that make him an idol and hero to his fellow workers even in his own time.

As the narrator, one of those fellow waiters, recounts Doc's story to a young waiter (several years after Doc's death at the age of 73 in 1965), he makes us aware that this time is also the death hour of railway passenger service. The railroad management "don't *want* to haul people anymore. The planes do that. The big roads want freight now," he tells his young listener. So it is that the railroad officers decided to regain complete control of their unionized waiters. "Look," explains the narrator, "how they hired youngbloods just for the busy seasons just so they won't get any seniority in the winter. Look how all the Old School waiters are dropping out." This is what we see as

the story of Doc is recounted, and how it is the stuff of tragedy and legend.

In the 1930's Doc joined the crew of waiters on one of the crack passenger trains (probably on the Northern Pacific or Great Northern, though the railroad is never named in the story) and quickly became the "Waiter's Waiter." He had come hungry one day into the Chicago yards from the nowhere of the ghetto and was taken into the kitchen by a sympathetic Swedish cook. In six years he had worked himself up to chef, but rather than give him that position the management transferred him to the dining section as a waiter with fellow blacks. At first he was hazed by the others who resented a new man with whom tips would have to be shared, but Doc quickly won their respect by topping their own tricks in return and by the way he handled himself in the service. "When Danny Jackson saw how cool and neat he was in his moves . . . he began to call him 'the Doctor'." And, "Mister Doctor Craft . . . Youngblood Doctor Craft . . . that's who you are," says another. From then on there was nothing but admiration:

> He was a Waiter's Waiter. He danced down these aisles with us and swung his tray with the roll of the train, never spilling in all his trips a single cup of coffee. He could carry his tray on two fingers, or on one and a half if he wanted, and he knew all the tricks about hustling tips there are to know. He could work anybody.

The Commissary even patterned the book of rules after him, but Doc was no "Uncle Tom." The brilliance with which he hustled his tips and handled himself with pride and grace scotched any such notion. In contrast McPherson portrays another of the waiters, "Uncle T. Boone," as the Tom stereotype who constantly preaches the necessity of Negro humility, fawns over the customers, and wears the detested skullcaps long after the Union won the agreement for their removal.

The longer Doc worked the more the railroad dining service became a part of his blood. "He fell in love with the feel of the wheels under his feet clicking against the track and he got the rhythm of the wheels in him and learned, like all of us, how to roll with them and move with them. After that first trip Doc was never at home on the ground." "He loved going out and he hated coming in," explains the narrator, and recalls Doc's own words: " 'Going out is my whole life, I wait for that tenth morning. I ain't never missed a trip and I don't mean to.' "

The reason for this "railroad blood" is not merely physiological conditioning. McPherson makes it clear that Doc's deepest inclinations are for freedom, the freedom to wander, to be on the move, to light out on railroad territory, to be independent and in control. In Doc's own words, "I guess I care about moving and being somewhere else when I want to be. I guess I care about going out, and coming in to wait for the time to go out again." More specifically, in the narrator's terms:

> What can I tell you? . . . He liked what I liked: the money, owning the car, running it, telling the soldiers what to do, hustling a bigger tip from some old maid by looking under her dress and laughing at her, having all the girls at the

Haverville Hotel waiting for us to come in for stop-over. . . . *He liked running free* and not being married to some bitch who would spend his money. . . . He liked getting drunk with the boys . . . setting up the house and then passing out from drinking too much, knowing that the boys would get him home (italics mine).

In short, in his own mode determined by race and circumstance Doc epitomizes the American Dream fashioned by Puritans, Transcendentalists, and the vast frontier. He possesses the vaunted independence, self-reliance, ingenuity, pragmatism and wanderlust all operating together—albeit without the restraints of Puritan morality—to make him successful and happy. He is significantly like the earliest figures of American folklore—the Yankee peddler, the Backwoodsman, and the Negro vagabond minstrel whose similarity and appeal were primarily in their characteristic need to wander over the land, to dissever themselves from established societies. More, McPherson gives to Doc, too, the appealing mystery of social anonymity. "He had no wife, no relatives, not even a hobby," says the narrator. He shares yet another trait with many an American folkloric figure in his ability to attract women, to enjoy them, and yet to remain detached from them.

Certain qualities of the tall tale that so often cloak American folkloric heroes are present in Doc's story. They are not, however, in the highly hyperbolic style of the Paul Bunyan tales (hauling snow from China over a frozen Pacific Ocean) or Pecos Bill yarns (riding a twister over three states to wear it out), but in the manner of the songs about the two great railroad heroes John Henry and Casey Jones. They are the phrases, rhythms, and details that make a "natural man" larger than life, yet still realistic.

McPherson's choice of names for the waiters is a good example. The name "Doctor Craft" bestowed on Doc by his fellow-workers is a double superlative; not only does it suggest that the man is the embodiment of his craft, but that cunning cleverness is involved as well. The honorific "Doctor" indicates the respect and admiration of the others. His real name—"Leroy Johnson, I think," says the narrator, suggests both the anonymity from which he comes and his future status as the "Waiter's Waiter", "Leroy" is French for "The King." Sheik Beasley is the waiter who shuts himself up in the dining car closet to smoke marijuana; "Sheik" connotes the colorful exoticism of the illusory world he conjures up by so doing. The "T." of "Uncle T. Boone" stands for "Tom," and Uncle T.'s character is not only the foil for Doc and the others but he is a folkloric type himself, as is Reverend Hendricks who works as a Baptist preacher in South Chicago when off the road. The narrator never gives his proper name but describes himself as a "Waiter's Waiter," all he needs to say to qualify himself as the teller of this tale. Though Danny Jackson's name is scarcely colorful, he himself is a prodigy, a brilliant literary man "who was black and knew Shakespeare before the world said he could work with it." When he speaks his remarks often have the touch of a Shakespearean line that enlarges the importance of what he says. As Doc faces his greatest test Danny says, "Now let's sit on the ground and talk about how *kings* are gonna get fucked."

Other words and phrases the narrator uses effect the feeling of legend through images and rhythms. "There was a time when six of us, big men, *danced* at the same time in that little Pantry without touching," recalls the narrator (italics mine). It is a remarkable picture of grace and in its own context as amazing as any gouging contest on a small raft floating down Mike Fink's Mississippi. So is the portrait of Doc:

> Anybody can serve, but not everybody can become part of the service. When Doc poured that pot of hot tea into that glass of crushed ice, it was like he was pouring it through his own fingers; it was like he and the tray and the pot and the glass and all of it was the same body. It was a beautiful move. It was fine service.

The balanced antithesis of the first sentence, the repeated constructions beginning with "it was" and the series of "and" phrases create a smooth rhythmic regularity that simulates the flow of tea from pot to glass as poured by Doc. McPherson's sensitivity to rhythm is evident, too, in his frequent repetition throughout the story of the word "youngblood." The narrator uses it to address his listener and to describe the young Doc. Along with phrases like "the story goes" and "from what they tell me" and "I think," this repetition creates oral formulaic patterns essential to the folkloric art.

Finally, the showdown or contest in the line of duty that tries the occupational hero for either tragic or comic glory is present in Doc's story. John Henry opposed the steam drill with his own strength, Casey Jones pitted his skill and the power of Engine 382 against time, but Doc had the entire railroad management against him. It had chosen to break the unionized Old School through him, its best representative. When the Commisary could not persuade Doc to retire for reasons of health, the General Superintendant tried to bribe him with a large pension, a party, and a lifetime pass. But that didn't move Doc. So, against this single 70-year-old black man the company moved its best lawyers. The picture of their intrigue, despite its grim occasion, is a comic one that enhances Doc's reputation of invulnerability:

> Those fat company lawyers took the contract apart and went through all their books. They took the seniority clause apart word by word, trying to figure a way to get at Doc. But they had written it airtight back in the days when the company *needed* waiters, and there was nothing in it about compulsory retirement. Not a word. . . . *Nothing* in the whole contract could help them get rid of Doc Craft. . . . There was nothing the company lawyers could do but turn the pages of their big books and sweat and promise Tesdale [the Superintendant] that they would find some way if he gave them more time. The word went out from the Commissary: "Get Doc." The stewards got it from the assistant superintendants: "Get Doc." Since they could not get him to retire, they were determined to catch him giving bad service.

And so the Commissary began arbitrarily changing its dining service rules, especially the little rules "like how the initials on the doily should always face the customer, and how the silver should be taken off the tables between meals." They sent out spotters to catch Doc giving bad service but they could never catch him doing a thing wrong. Finally, they sent Jerry Ewald after Doc. With parallel phrases and repeated ominous words the narrator creates an incantatory rhythm as he conjures up the portrait of Doc's ultimate adversary:

> Look out the window; this is North Dakota, this is Jerry's territory. Jerry, the Unexpected Inspector. Shouldn't you polish the shakers or clean out the Pantry or squeeze oranges or maybe change the linen on the tables? Jerry Ewald is sly. The train may stop in the middle of this wheatfield and Jerry may get on. He lives by that book. He knows where to look for dirt and mistakes. Jerry Ewald, the Unexpected Inspector. He knows where to look; he knows how to get you. He got Doc.

The dining car was filled with an air of tension and doom as Jerry got on that afternoon in Doc's forty-ninth year of service and seated himself at Doc's table:

> Then Jerry looked directly at Doc and said: "Headwaiter Doctor Craft, bring me a menu." Doc said nothing and he did not smile. He brought the menu. Danny Jackson and I moved back into the hall to watch. There was nothing we could do to help Doc and we knew it. He was the Waiter's Waiter, out there by himself, hustling the biggest tip he would ever get in his life. Or losing it.

The match began and Doc performed brilliantly. He scored perfectly on taking the order, presenting faultlessly polished silver, placing plates and intialed doilies, according the allotted number of crackers, ladling the soup and arranging ash tray and prayer card. The other waiters began to hope for the best. "He swung down the aisle of the car between the two rows of white tables and you could not help but be proud of the way he moved with the roll of the train and the way that tray was like a part of his arm. It was good service." The match continued with Doc giving the appropriate service for cold roast beef with mustard. But it was the lemon wedge with the iced tea that was Doc's undoing:

> "Very good service, Doc," he said, "But you served the lemon wrong. . . ."
>
> "How's that?" said Doc.
>
> "The service was wrong," Jerry said. He was not smiling now.
>
> "How could it be? I been giving that same service for years, right down to the crushed ice for the lemon wedge."
>
> "That's just it, Doc," Jerry said. "The lemon wedge. You served it wrong."
>
> "Yeah?" said Doc.
>
> "Yes," said Jerry, his jaws tight. "Haven't you seen the new rule? . . . 'As of 7-9-65. . . . Fresh lemon wedge will be served on bread and butter plate, no doily, with tines of oyster fork

stuck into *meat* of lemon.'" [Doc had placed them in the skin.] Jerry paused.

> "Now you know, Headwaiter," he said.
>
> "Yeah," said Doc.

Thus it was that Doc was written up and forced to retire. His legend ends a tragic one because, as the narrator puts it, "He was beaten and he knew it; not by the service, but by a book. . . . That's not a good way for a man to go. He should die in the service. He should die doing the things he likes. But not by a book." But the narrator would have to agree that in the most important sense Doc did die then; the five months that he continued to exist physically were scarcely more than a technicality. As much as John Henry or Casey Jones, Doc Craft died in the service.

In concluding, I would hope that this discussion has revealed in McPherson's story a character who shares characteristics with traditional American folkloric figures from our earliest times, and an occupation whose folkloric worth and color have not yet been discovered by the mainstream culture. As one reviewer remarked, "I always knew that some day the right author would catch the romance of the dining car waiter . . . because they [the waiters] were acting men's parts in the dark toilsome romance of this republic. Here it is." By mining this rich vein and displaying its treasure in the patterns of legend, James McPherson has not only added to the wealth of American folklore but has proved his own mastery of craft as a "Writer's Writer." He has made a happy irony of the narrator's closing prediction: "You have a good story. But you will never remember it. Because all this time you have had pussy in your mind, and your mind, and your fingers in the pages of that black bible." (pp. 220-26)

> *Rosemary M. Laughlin, "Attention, American Folklore: Doc Craft Comes Marching In," in* Studies in American Fiction, *Vol. 1, No. 2, Autumn, 1973, pp. 220-27.*

James Alan McPherson   (essay date December 1978)

[*In the following essay, which was adapted from a speech he delivered earlier in 1978, McPherson relates events that shaped him as a black American writer.*]

In 1974, during the last months of the Nixon Administration, I lived in San Francisco, California. My public reason for leaving the East and going there was that my wife had been admitted to the San Francisco Medical Center School of Nursing, but my private reason for going was that San Francisco would be a very good place for working and for walking. Actually, during that time San Francisco was not that pleasant a place. We lived in a section of the city called the Sunset District, but it rained almost every day. During the late spring Patricia Hearst helped to rob a bank a few blocks from our apartment, a psychopath called "the Zebra Killer" was terrorizing the city, and the mayor seemed about to declare martial law. Periodically the FBI would come to my apartment with pictures of the suspected bank robbers. Agents came several times, until it began to dawn on me that they had become slightly interested in why, of all the people in a working-class neighborhood, I alone sat at home every day. They never asked any questions on this point, and I never volunteered that I was trying to keep my sanity by working very hard on a book dealing with the relationship between folklore and technology in nineteenth-century America.

In the late fall of the same year a friend came out from the East to give a talk in Sacramento. I drove there to meet him, and then drove him back to San Francisco. This was an older black man, one whom I respect a great deal, but during our drive an argument developed between us. His major worry was the recession, but eventually his focus shifted to people in my age group and our failures. There were a great many of these, and he listed them point by point. He said, while we drove through a gloomy evening rain, "When the smoke clears and you start counting, I'll bet you won't find that many more black doctors, lawyers, accountants, engineers, dentists. . . ." The list went on. He remonstrated a bit more, and said, "White people are very generous. When they start a thing they usually finish it. But after all this chaos, imagine how mad and tired they must be. Back in the fifties, when this thing started, they must have known anything could happen. They must have said, 'Well, we'd better settle in and hold on tight. Here come the niggers.' " During the eighteen months I spent in San Francisco, this was the only personal encounter that really made me mad.

In recent years I have realized that my friend, whom I now respect even more, was speaking from the perspective of a tactician. He viewed the situation in strict bread-and-butter terms: a commitment had been made to redefine the meaning of democracy in this country, certain opportunities had been provided, and people like him were watching to see what would be made of those opportunities and the freedom they provided. From his point of view, it was simply a matter of fulfilling a contractual obligation: taking full advantage of the educational opportunities that had been offered to achieve middle-class status in one of the professions. But from my point of view, one that I never shared with him, it was not that simple. Perhaps it was because of the differences in our generations and experiences. Or perhaps it was because each new generation, of black people at least, has to redefine itself even while it attempts to grasp the new opportunities, explore the new freedom. I can speak for no one but myself, yet maybe in trying to preserve the uniqueness of my experience, as I tried to do in *Elbow Room,* I can begin to set the record straight for my friend, for myself, and for the sake of the record itself.

In 1954, when *Brown v. Board of Education* was decided, I was eleven years old. I lived in a lower-class black community in Savannah, Georgia, attended segregated public schools, and knew no white people socially. I can't remember thinking of this last fact as a disadvantage, but I do know that early on I was being conditioned to believe that I was not *supposed* to know any white people on social terms. In our town the children of the black middle class were expected to aspire to certain traditional occupations; the children of the poor were expected not to cause too much trouble.

There was in those days a very subtle, but real, social distinction based on gradations of color, and I can remember the additional strain under which darker-skinned poor people lived. But there was also a great deal of optimism, shared by all levels of the black community. Besides a certain reverence for the benign intentions of the federal government, there was a belief in the idea of progress, nourished, I think now, by the determination of older people not to pass on to the next generation too many stories about racial conflict, their own frustrations and failures. They censored a great deal. It was as if they had made basic and binding agreements with themselves, or with their ancestors, that for the consideration represented by their silence on certain points they expected to receive, from either Providence or a munificent federal government, some future service or remuneration, the form of which would be left to the beneficiaries of their silence. Lawyers would call this a contract with a condition precedent. And maybe because they did tell us less than they knew, many of us were less informed than we might have been. On the other hand, because of this same silence many of us remained free enough of the influence of negative stories to take chances, be ridiculous, perhaps even try to form our own positive stories out of whatever our own experiences provided. Though ours was a limited world, it was one rich in possibilities for the future.

If I had to account for my life from segregated Savannah to this place and point in time, I would probably have to say that the contract would be no bad metaphor. I am reminded of Sir Henry Maine's observation that the progress of society is from status to contract. Although he was writing about the development of English common law, the reverse of his generalization is most applicable to my situation: I am the beneficiary of a number of contracts, most of them between the federal government and the institutions of society, intended to provide people like me with a certain status.

I recall that in 1960, for example, something called the National Defense Student Loan Program went into effect, and I found out that by my agreeing to repay a loan plus some little interest, the federal government would back my enrollment in a small Negro college in Georgia. When I was a freshman at that college, disagreement over a seniority clause between the Hotel & Restaurant Employees and Bartenders Union and the Great Northern Railway Company, in St. Paul, Minnesota, caused management to begin recruiting temporary summer help. Before I was nineteen I was encouraged to move from a segregated Negro college in the South and through that very beautiful part of the country that lies between Chicago and the Pacific Northwest. That year—1962—the World's Fair was in Seattle, and it was a magnificently diverse panorama for a young man to see. Almost every nation on earth was represented in some way, and at the center of the fair was the Space Needle. The theme of the United States exhibit, as I recall, was drawn from Whitman's *Leaves of Grass:* "Conquering, holding, daring, venturing as we go the unknown ways."

When I returned to the South, in the midst of all the civil rights activity, I saw a poster advertising a creative-writing contest sponsored by *Reader's Digest* and the United Negro College Fund. To enter the contest I had to learn to write and type. The first story I wrote was lost (and very badly typed); but the second, written in 1965, although also badly typed, was awarded first prize by Edward Weeks and his staff at *The Atlantic Monthly.* That same year I was offered the opportunity to enter Harvard Law School. During my second year at law school, a third-year man named Dave Marston (who was in a contest with Attorney General Griffin Bell earlier this year) offered me, through a very conservative white fellow student from Texas, the opportunity to take over his old job as a janitor in one of the apartment buildings in Cambridge. There I had the solitude, and the encouragement, to begin writing seriously. Offering my services in that building was probably the best contract I ever made.

I have not recalled all the above to sing my own praises or to evoke the black American version of the Horatio Alger myth. I have recited these facts as a way of indicating the haphazard nature of events during that ten-year period. I am the product of a contractual process. To put it simply, the 1960s were a crazy time. Opportunities seemed to materialize out of thin air; and if you were lucky, if you were in the right place at the right time, certain contractual benefits just naturally accrued. You were assured of a certain status; you could become a doctor, a lawyer, a dentist, an accountant, an engineer. Achieving these things was easy, if you applied yourself.

But a very hard price was extracted. It seems to me now, from the perspective provided by age and distance, that certain institutional forces, acting impersonally, threw together black peasants and white aristocrats, people who operated on the plane of the intellect and people who valued the perspective of the folk. There were people who were frightened, threatened, and felt inferior; there were light-skinned people who called themselves "black" and darker-skinned people who could remember when this term had been used negatively; there were idealists and opportunists, people who seemed to want to be exploited and people who delighted in exploiting them. Old identities were thrown off, of necessity, but there were not many new ones of a positive nature to be assumed. People from backgrounds like my own, those from the South, while content with the new opportunities, found themselves trying to make sense of the growing diversity of friendships, of their increasing familiarity with the various political areas of the country, of the obvious differences between their values and those of their parents. We *were* becoming doctors, lawyers, dentists, engineers; but at the same time our experiences forced us to begin thinking of ourselves in new and different ways. We never wanted to be "white," but we never wanted to be "black" either. And back during that period there was the feeling that we could be whatever we wanted. But, we discovered, unless we joined a group, subscribed to some ideology, accepted some provisional identity, there was no contractual process for defining and stabilizing what it was we wanted to be. We also found that this was an individual problem, and in order to confront it one had to go inside one's self.

Now I want to return to my personal experience, to one

of the contracts that took me from segregated Savannah to the Seattle World's Fair. There were many things about my earliest experiences that I liked and wanted to preserve, despite the fact that these things took place in a context of segregation; and there were a great many things I liked about the vision of all those nations interacting at the World's Fair. But the two seemed to belong to separate realities, to represent two different world views. Similarly, there were some things I liked about many of the dining-car waiters with whom I worked, and some things I liked about people like Dave Marston whom I met in law school. Some of these people and their values were called "black" and some were called "white," and I learned very quickly that all of us tend to wall ourselves off from experiences different from our own by assigning to these terms greater significance than they should have. Moreover, I found that trying to maintain friendships with, say, a politically conservative white Texan, a liberal-to-radical classmate of Scottish-Italian background, my oldest black friends, and even members of my own family introduced psychological contradictions that became tense and painful as the political climate shifted. There were no contracts covering such friendships and such feelings, and in order to keep the friends and maintain the feelings I had to force myself to find a basis other than race on which such contradictory urgings could be synthesized. I discovered that I had to find, first of all, an identity as a writer, and then I had to express what I knew or felt in such a way that I could make something whole out of a necessarily fragmented experience.

While in San Francisco, I saw in the image of the nineteenth-century American locomotive a possible cultural symbol that could represent my folk origins and their values, as well as the values of all the people I had seen at the World's Fair. During that same time, unconsciously, I was also beginning to see that the American language, in its flexibility and variety of idioms, could at least approximate some of the contradictory feelings that had resulted from my experience. Once again, I could not find any contractual guarantee that this would be the most appropriate and rewarding way to hold myself, and my experience, together. I think now there are no such contracts.

I quoted earlier a generalization by Sir Henry Maine to the effect that human society is a matter of movement from status to contract. Actually, I have never read Sir Henry Maine. I lifted his statement from a book by a man named Henry Allen Moe—a great book called *The Power of Freedom.* In that book, in an essay entitled "The Future of Liberal Arts Education," Moe goes on to say that a next step, one that goes beyond contract, is now necessary, but that no one seems to know what that next step should be. Certain trends suggest that it may well be a reversion to status. But if this happens it will be a tragedy of major proportions, because most of the people in the world are waiting for some nation, some people, to provide the model for the next step. And somehow I felt, while writing the last stories in **Elbow Room,** that the condition precedent the old folks in my hometown wanted in exchange for their censoring was not just status of a conventional kind. I want to think that after having waited so long, after having seen so much, they must have at least expected some new stories that would no longer have to be censored to come out of our experience. I felt that if anything, the long experience of segregation could be looked on as a period of preparation for a next step. Those of us who are black and who have had to defend our humanity should be obliged to continue defending it, on higher and higher levels—not of power, which is a kind of tragic trap, but on higher levels of consciousness.

All of this is being said in retrospect, and I am quite aware that I am rationalizing many complex and contradictory feelings. Nevertheless, I do know that early on, during my second year of law school, I became conscious of a model of identity that might help me transcend, at least in my thinking, a provisional or racial identity. In a class in American constitutional law taught by Paul Freund, I began to play with the idea that the Fourteenth Amendment was not just a legislative instrument devised to give former slaves legal equality with other Americans. Looking at the slow but steady way in which the basic guarantees of the Bill of Rights had, through judicial interpretation, been incorporated into the clauses of that amendment, I began to see the outlines of a new identity.

You will recall that the first line of Section 1 of the Fourteenth Amendment makes an all-inclusive definition of citizenship: "All persons born or naturalized in the United States and subject to the jurisdiction thereof, are citizens of the United States. . . ." The rights guaranteed to such a citizen had themselves traveled from the provinces to the World's Fair: from the trial and error of early Anglo-Saxon folk rituals to the rights of freemen established by the Magna Carta, to their slow incorporation into early American colonial charters, and from these charters (especially George Mason's Virginia Declaration of Rights) into the U.S. Constitution as its first ten amendments. Indeed, these same rights had served as the basis for the Charter of the United Nations. I saw that through the protean uses made of the Fourteenth Amendment, in the gradual elaboration of basic rights to be protected by federal authority, an outline of something much more complex than "black" and "white" had been begun.

It was many years before I was to go to the Library of Congress and read the brief of the lawyer-novelist Albion W. Tourgée in the famous case *Plessy v. Ferguson.* Argued in 1896 before the United States Supreme Court, Tourgée's brief was the first meaningful attempt to breathe life into the amendment. I will quote here part of his brief, which is a very beautiful piece of literature:

> This provision of Section 1 of the Fourteenth Amendment *creates a new* citizenship of the United States embracing *new* rights, privileges and immunities, derivable in a *new* manner, controlled by *new* authority, having a *new* scope and extent, depending on national authority for its existence and looking to national power for its preservation.

Although Tourgée lost the argument before the Supreme Court, his model of citizenship—and it is not a racial one—is still the most radical idea to come out of American constitutional law. He provided the outline, the clothing, if you will, for a new level of status. What he was proposing in 1896, I think, was that each United States citizen would attempt to approximate the ideals of the nation, be on at least conversant terms with all its diversity, carry the mainstream of the culture inside himself. As an American, by trying to wear these clothes he would be a synthesis of high and low, black and white, city and country, provincial and universal. If he could live with these contradictions, he would be simply a representative American.

This was the model I was aiming for in my book of stories. It can be achieved with or without intermarriage, but it will cost a great many mistakes and a lot of pain. It is, finally, a product of culture and not of race. And achieving it will require that one be conscious of America's culture and the complexity of all its people. As I tried to point out, such a perspective would provide a minefield of delicious ironies. Why, for example, should black Americans raised in Southern culture *not* find that some of their responses are geared to country music? How else, except in terms of cultural diversity, am I to account for the white friend in Boston who taught me much of what I know about black American music? Or the white friend in Virginia who, besides developing a homegrown aesthetic he calls "crackertude," knows more about black American folklore than most black people? Or the possibility that many black people in Los Angeles have been just as much influenced by Hollywood's "star system" of the forties and fifties as they have been by society's response to the color of their skins? I wrote about people like these in *Elbow Room* because they interested me, and because they help support my belief that most of us are products of much more complex cultural influences than we suppose.

What I have said above will make little sense until certain contradictions in the nation's background are faced up to, until personal identities are allowed to partake of the complexity of the country's history as well as of its culture. Last year, a very imaginative black comedian named Richard Pryor appeared briefly on national television in his own show. He offended a great many people, and his show was canceled after only a few weeks. But I remember one episode that may emphasize my own group's confusion about its historical experience. This was a satiric take-off on the popular television movie *Roots,* and Pryor played an African tribal historian who was selling trinkets and impromptu history to black American tourists. One tourist, a middle-class man, approached the tribal historian and said, "I want you to tell me who my great-great-granddaddy was." The African handed him a picture. The black American looked at it and said, "But that's a *white* man!" The tribal historian said, "That's right." Then the tourist said, "Well, I want you to tell me where I'm from." The historian looked hard at him and said, "You're from Cleveland, nigger." I think I was trying very hard in my book to say the same thing, but not just to black people.

Today I am not the lawyer my friend in San Francisco thought I should be, but this is the record I wanted to present to him that rainy evening back in 1974. It may illustrate why the terms of my acceptance of society's offer had to be modified. I am now a writer, a person who has to learn to live with contradictions, frustrations, and doubts. Still, I have another quote that sustains me, this one from a book called *The Tragic Sense of Life,* by a Spanish philosopher named Miguel de Unamuno. In a chapter called "Don Quixote Today," Unamuno asks, "How is it that among the words the English have borrowed from our language there is to be found this word *desperado?*" And he answers himself: "It is despair, and despair alone, that begets heroic hope, absurd hope, mad hope."

I believe that the United States is complex enough to induce that sort of despair that begets heroic hope. I believe that if one can experience its diversity, touch a variety of its people, laugh at its craziness, distill wisdom from its tragedies, and attempt to synthesize all this inside oneself without going crazy, one will have earned the right to call oneself "citizen of the United States," even though one is not quite a lawyer, doctor, engineer, or accountant. If nothing else, one will have learned a few new stories and, most important, one will have begun on that necessary movement from contract to the next step, from province to the World's Fair, from a hopeless person to a desperado. I wrote about my first uncertain steps in this direction in **Elbow Room** because I have benefited from all the contracts, I have exhausted all the contracts, and at present it is the only new direction I know. (pp. 53-7)

James Alan McPherson, "On Becoming an American Writer," in The Atlantic Monthly, *Vol. 242, No. 6, December, 1978, pp. 53-7.*

McPherson on *Hue and Cry:*

It is my hope that this collection of stories can be read as a book about people, all kinds of people: old, young, lonely, homosexual, confused, used, discarded, wronged. As a matter of fact, certain of these people happen to be black, and certain of them happen to be white; but I have tried to keep the color part of most of them far in the background, where these things should rightly be kept.

James Alan McPherson, in a 1969 advertisement for Hue and Cry, *later published in* Dictionary of Literary Biography, *Vol. 38, 1985.*

Edith Blicksilver (essay date June 1979)

[*In the following essay, Blicksilver examines the female characters in several of McPherson's short stories, stating that McPherson "is at his artistic best when he depicts weak and dispossessed women who still are sympathetic creatures. We may not like them, but we understand what complex terrors motivate them."*]

James Alan McPherson, who was awarded the Pulitzer Prize for fiction in 1978, is a writer and a black, but his narrative approach is not that of a black writer, since he has refused to permit his fiction to be categorized by color or by ethnic labels. As McPherson commented, "certain of the people happen to be black and certain happen to be white; but I have tried to keep the color part of most of them far in the background, where these things should rightly be kept."

But, on the other hand, not to remember that McPherson is a black writer would do him a disservice because he retains in his works the "morality of fiction," which Ralph Ellison said means that a writer "starts with anger, then. . . . he immediately translates it through his craft into . . . understanding, into insight, perception." Ellison, who called McPherson "a writer of insight, sympathy and humor and one of the most gifted young Americans I've had the privilege to read," goes on to say that you see "a situation which outrages you, but as you write about the characters who embody that which outrages you, your sense of craft and the moral role of your craft demands that you depict those characters in the breadth of their humanity." And herein lie the appeal and ultimate success of McPherson's stories. He does start with anger, the tragic repercussions of racial exploitation, for example, in **"A Matter of Vocabulary,"** but he is concerned with "the density of the human" and most important of all, the "moral role" of his craft.

McPherson, in this story and in others, illuminates a situation of paramount importance by directing attention to a significant social issue involving a young man's sudden self-awareness and loss of innocence. In this work and also in **"Gold Coast,"** which, incidentally, first appeared in the *Atlantic* in November, 1968, and won the *Atlantic Monthly* prize, the narrator, a black, bright teenager tries to ignore or overcome racial barriers with limited success.

McPherson's stories actually tend to reflect the dilemma confronting the black intellectual in America: on the one hand attracted by much that the white society has to offer, such as quality education, on the other hand embittered by that same society's racist record. His approach avoids the fiery bitterness of Eldridge Cleaver or James Baldwin, but McPherson is sensitive to the bigotry and injustice which permeate American life and which nullify the attempts of those seeking, like the narrators in both **"A Matter of Vocabulary"** and **"Gold Coast,"** to try to overcome racial discrimination.

But even if McPherson is not as revolutionary as Cleaver or Baldwin, he is sensitive to injustice and his concerns are about people rather than with slogans. And so this paper will focus upon selected female characters in several of his short stories. These women are white and black, strong and weak, well-favored and dispossessed.

McPherson's other female characters will be developed in another study since in order to probe the complexity of personality exhibited by Margot Payne, for example, in **Hue and Cry** and by Virginia Valentine in **Elbow Room** requires in-depth analysis.

This perceptive author, whether dealing with major or minor female characters, is at his artistic best when he depicts weak and dispossessed women who still are sympathetic creatures. We may not like them, but we understand what complex terrors motivate them.

Thus, in **"Gold Coast,"** ever fanatic, obsessively clean Miss O'Hara, whose energies are directed toward disrupting the pitiful lives of the bigoted old Irish janitor, James Sullivan, and his endlessly screaming, mad wife, Meg, are sketched with sympathy and even with some measure of respect for all the sufferings that old age and lonely despair can bring.

Although many of McPherson's stories reflect their author's sense of cultural tension, such a concern appears more as an undertone than as a dominant theme. His interests range from the neurosis attached to religious fanaticism in **"Just Enough for the City,"** or the Black Power cause in **"Cabbages and Kings"** to love in its many guises: **"Hue and Cry," "A New Place," "Elbow Room," "Widows and Orphans,"** and **"All the Lonely People."** Several of these stories are concerned with the emotional impact of what it is like to be a woman, and especially a black woman, in a white male, power-dominated world. His range of subjects represents much of the vitality of current writing. Most of his stories are moving in their separate ways as he explores the complex, demanding, sometimes unsatisfactory arrangements that women make with men.

Usually his older black women are treated with respect although sometimes they are never fully developed. They transmit wise sayings from one generation to another, being in a unique position to look forward and backward, to decide how much of the past is worth salvaging, such as the jaded woman with the scar who remembered that her friend, Red Bones, had advised her to avoid putting on airs by quoting grandmama: "It don't make no difference how well you fox-trot if everybody else is dancing the two-step."

The venturing-outward thirteen-year-old narrator in **"A Matter of Vocabulary"** was very obedient to his mother, afraid to disobey her or his teacher nuns and skip church services. Although he had never thought of these nuns as real people because they were completely different in dress and color from the people he knew, his mother exerts a powerful influence in his life, teaching him both morals and manners. He must "speak to people in the streets because Southern blacks do not know how to live without neighbors." But when strangers do not respond to his greetings, he wonders if he has been rejected by whites because he is black. He therefore begins to question his mother's wisdom.

However, when she claims that she knows exactly who will be damned and who will be saved on the day of judgment, he is fearful of disobeying her.

> "The hour's gonna come when the Horn will blow," his mother told him while he cowered in the corner behind her stove, feeling the heat from it on his face. "The Horn's gonna blow all through the world on that Great Morning and all them in the graves will hear it and be raised up," she continued.
>
> "Even Daddy?"
>
> His mother paused, and let the spoon stand still in the pot on the stove. "Everybody," she said, "both the Quick and the Dead and everybody that's alive. Then the stars are gonna fall and all the sinners will be cryin' and tryin' to hide in the corners and under houses. But it won't do no good to hide. You can't hide from God. Then they gonna call Roll with everybody's name on it and the sheeps are gonna be divided from the

goats, the Good on the Right and the Bad on the Left. And then the ground's gonna open up and all them on the Left are gonna fall right into a pool of fire and brimstone and they're gonna be cryin' and screamin' for mercy but there won't be none because it will be too late. Especially for those who don't repent and go to church."

> Then his mother stood over him, her eyes almost red with emotion, her face wet from the stove, and shining black, and very close to tears.

After all, she had been raised as a Southern Baptist, going to the same minister all her life.

When young Thomas is caught, after seeing several deacons keep some of the children's collection money, he secretly stops going to church in spite of fearing both damnation and his mother's wrath.

He became a model student in school, afraid of violence, because he had learned that in complete silence lay his safety when angry nuns slapped students with a wooden ruler.

So his mother and the nuns represented the fear-filled authority symbols of home, school, and church, but the sensitive non-communicative narrator finds it difficult to reach out to adult females for understanding or for companionship as he seeks his place in this same adult society.

Another older black woman, Ella, in **"The Faithful,"** symbolizes, instead of conservative traditionalism, the need for community change when she reprimands her barber-minister husband because he refuses to give Afro haircuts, unable to recognize outside of his shop that the world is changing. She reminds him that he is "too possessive about the past and determined not to allow the present to slip into focus."

Another woman, Marie Gilmore, the wife of a church leader who threatens to transfer to a more liberal congregation, is understanding and compassionate, admonishing her husband not to cause trouble because the elderly barber "ain't got much longer to go." Finally, even Marie became exasperated with the man's uncompromising rigidity and she came to church, no longer to hear the sermon. Instead she sat in at the back of the room wearing a purple dress instead of her traditional white one. When the minister-barber calls his parishioners "stiff-necked people" who will be judged for their actions, Marie replies with fiery determination, "Who's to say what's to be judged and what ain't? Who's left to say for certain he knows the rules or can show us where they written down?"

In another story, in which McPherson described the actions of an exploitive street gang that is seeking acceptance through violence as they test their manhood, matronly Bertha Ray, sweating in the kitchen of a bar, admonishes the boys, and she tells them to go home. "You oughta be shame of yourselfs," she says, but one youthful offender comments with worldly wisdom, "A fat mouth make a soft ass." Finally, when the extortion attempt fails, Bertha's chastizingly stern voice is the only one they hear as they face derision and shamefully flee: "Your momma outhta give you a good whippin!" Here perhaps the female is a castration symbol, robbing these young men of their macho victory.

Another castrating symbol was ruthless Red Bone, who "had broke every man she ever had and had never seen a man with no hand-holes on him."

Murphy, the celibate Irishman in **"Gold Coast,"** was used by Miss O'Hara, who had always dominated him. When he had first come to the apartment building "fresh from Montgomery's Campaign, he must have had a will of his own," but Miss O'Hara, who called him "Frank Dear," had drained it all away, so that now he would "do anything just to be agreeable," even sign a complaint about mad Meg's pitiful dog, although he did not "really mind the dog: he did not really mind anything."

So the older women in McPherson's stories are not cut out of one pattern although his black characters tend to be strong-willed, religious matriarchs frequently representing the conservative elements of the Establishment— Southern good manners, the laws of an ordered society, traditional morality. They are forceful without being abrasive within the safe confines of the black community. They do not threaten the precariously dignified position of their elderly black husbands when these men venture out into the more powerful, less safe white society.

Younger black women are not treated with as much dignity in many of McPherson's stories. They are exploited by selfish pleasure-seeking men as the women in **"All the Lonely People"** and in **"Of Cabbages and Kings."** Some women mistake exploitation for love. The scarred woman claimed that her jealous lover disfigured her because he loved her so much that he chose violence rather than accept rejection and betrayal. Some women are bored and restless with good men, as was this same scarred woman with Billy Crawford. She looked instead for "a sweet-talkin' young dude."

Sometimes McPherson's narrators seem snobbishly class-conscious, impressed with the power that wealth can buy. There is, for example, in **"A Matter of Vocabulary"** The Rich Old Lady in the supermarket, who pushed her cart slowly, with dignity, always bought parsley and when thirteen-year-old Thomas passed her and smelled her perfume which was light and "did not linger in the air like most other perfumes. . . . it seemed to him that she must have made it just for her and that it was so expensive that it stayed with her body and would never linger behind her when she had passed a place."

The young boy feels superior to Miss Hester, the produce manager, who, although she has the power to fire him, is jealous of both his youthful dexterity and his superior intellectual ability. But his intellectual pride is challenged when a younger brother, Eddie, also working in the supermarket, is reprimanded for putting an order in the wrong car.

Responding that "evidently someone took my cart by mistake," Eddie has demonstrated his language competence all too well, and Miss Sarah Feinberg, the market owner, retorts: "Evidently! Evidently! Miss Hester, you should please listen to *that!* Evidently. You let them go to school

and they think they know everything." Eddie, almost in tears, quits the job and, with youthful pride, denies that his folks need the money; later he tells his brother in anger: "I'm gonna learn all the big words in the world . . . [and when] I go back in there I'm gonna be talking so big that fat old Miss Sarah won't even be able to understand me." McPherson has given some good insights into why a sensitive young black man becomes bitter toward certain members of the white economic power structure, intent upon exploiting and keeping him in his place.

The girl, Lynn, in **"Private Domain,"** is used to show Rodney's internal torments. Because he lives in an urban culture of educated people, he takes pride in being racially liberal, but he is, in actuality, ashamed of his black cultural roots. He is also insecure and fearful of offending his white acquaintances who sincerely admire black jazz musicians. He tries to fit into an acceptable social mode instead of viewing himself as an individual. He feels responsible for the ideas and the image of those around him, so he reprimands Lynn for sitting on the floor while girls sit on chairs. Rodney, "trying desperately to make up for a lifetime of not knowing anything about Baroque," was ashamed of Lynn, showing her panties and "her bay-bee and the loose ways she had, Rodney assumed, picked up from living among whites too long. Sometimes she made him feel really uncomfortable and scared." He resents his sexual need for her and only wants to make love at night, in the dark, feeling uneasy if he made sounds while making love, "although he felt uneasy if the girl did not make any." So he isn't too secure about either his masculinity or his black identity.

Girls are used as sex objects in several of McPherson's stories. In **"Of Cabbages and Kings,"** Claude, the slightly mad adherent of the Black Power mystique, uses blonde white women to reinforce his own faltering sense of self-worth. He was not comfortable with any of the girls and was never in control.

> He used his virility as a tool and forged, for however long it lasted, a little area of superiority which could never, it seemed, extend itself beyond the certain confines of his room, no matter how late into the night the records played. I [his roommate] could see him fighting to extend the area, as if an increase in the number of girls he saw could compensate for what he had lost in duration. He saw many girls: curious students, unexpected bus-stop pickups, and assorted other one-nighters. And his rationalizations allowed him to believe that each one was an actual conquest, a physical affirmation of a psychological victory over all he hated and loved and hated in the little world of his room.

> But then he seemed to have no happiness, even in this. Even here I sensed some intimations of defeat. After each girl, Claude would almost immediately come out of his room, as if there was no need for aftertalk; as if, after it was over, he felt a brooding, silent emptiness that quickly intensified into nervousness and instantaneous shyness and embarrassment so that the cold which sets in after that kind of emotional drain

came in very sharp against his skin, and he could not bear to have her there any longer.

McPherson's purpose in using women as sex objects is obvious, and he shows that objectivity coupled with close observation and technical skill can evoke strong emotions. In spite of just using women as sex objects, the author in **"Of Cabbages and Kings"** focuses upon a superbly moving and haunting description of the exploitation resulting in tension among black men, between brotherhood and separateness, actually between the irrational and the rational in men of all colors.

McPherson's narrators occasionally mouth philosophic theories about human nature, such as the disfigured woman in **"The Story of a Scar,"** who comments with world-weary knowledge to an attractive stranger: "The best mens don't git married. They do they fishin' in goldfish bowls," and his own sophisticated conclusions about why she wore a honey-blond wig and a purple pantsuit because she represented women who had "a natural leaning toward the abstract expression of themselves. Their styles have private meanings, advertise secret distillations of their souls." He concluded that "this woman was the true sister of the man who knows how to look while driving a purple Cadillac."

Sometimes, stereotyped observations about other ethnic groups appear. One ambitious postal employee, concerned about being replaced by a computer, noted that the Jews and the Puerto Rican postal employees were not "settin' up their beds under these tables" where mail was hand sorted but instead were "trying to improve themselves."

Occasionally, references to other ethnic groups were not only stereotyping labels but also less flattering. Meg Sullivan's berserk rages and snobbish, neurotically clean Miss O'Hara's fanatic attempts to get rid of the aged Sullivan's dog, mask the lonely attempts of both women to seek the attention of Robert, the young college boy and temporary apprentice janitor. Miss O'Hara, who had "a great deal of Irish Pride" and who "loved animals much more than people," hated the Sullivans because "they were a couple of lushes who haven't been sober a day in twenty-five years."

They also symbolized the dirty metaphysical smell of sick old age and drunk despair. Miss O'Hara found a purpose in life by hating the Sullivans and their dirt. She hoped to outlive James Sullivan and attend his wake "with a knitting ball and needles" devoured by vengeance—like Dickens' Mme Defarge. But she seems to have repressed maternal instincts, and while Robert was mopping the second floor she offered him root beer, apples or cupcakes while trying to pump evidence from him about that "filthy old man Sullivan."

She was also a sexually repressed old maid who heard everything that went on in the building. Robert had the feeling that he should "never dare to make love with gusto for fear that she would overhear and write down all my happy-time phrases, to be maliciously recounted to me if she were ever provoked."

Sullivan, on the other hand, labeled Miss O'Hara an "old bitch," the kind that "sat around singing hymns and watching them burn saints in this state." It was "her kind," shrewd Sullivan concluded, that cannot be trusted even though she "smiles in your face because it was her kind that laughed when they burned Joan of Arc. . . ."

The best of McPherson's stories cannot be categorized; they explore with depth and with richness the complexities of isolation and of involvement. The hauntingly anguished cries of the West Indian, slightly mad Barefoot Lady, who laments her love for mortician James, is the least developed female character in his short story **"A Matter of Vocabulary."** Actually, because we know almost nothing about the source of her sorrow, she is one of the most fascinating. She is linked in misery with thirteen-year-old Thomas, who has become aware of a prejudiced white world that seems intent upon stifling his ambitious dreams. More important, both have been linked with all suffering humanity.

McPherson's stories tell us about the interaction of women with carry-out boys, janitors, railroad dining car waiters, barber/preachers, social climbers, intellectuals, jazz musicians, Black Power leaders, religious zealots, cynical salesmen, Professional Blacks, middle-class college girls and slums swarming with petty criminals, riffraff, back-alley, prostitutes, men in drag or on drugs, hippy daughters of old families, the soiled, the failed, the crawling, faceless losers—both black and white.

Yet even Philomena Brown in **"An Act of Prostitution"** is an understandable human being, one of those pitiful people "more sinned against than sinning," and we simultaneously despise her and understand why she will be victimized by men all her life.

We have more sympathy with her because she sells her body with no deception involved; we have less respect for her cheap lawyer, who trades his integrity for a hollow victory.

McPherson shows a wide range of women, many of whom still retain a trace of humanity. Most are complicated, quietly desperate and driven only into themselves. He doesn't push his people through the standard manipulations of a standard plot.

Even when he deals with the segregation problem on a pullman train, he writes with emotional objectivity in an unhurried way that manages to link a reporter's eye for detail with a touch of unforgettable lyricism. His style is both bold and controlled and he has Hemingway's ear for dialogue. In spite of using some harsh realistic terms, he is never offensive.

Narrated with simplicity and directness, **"On Trains"** presents an assorted mixture of white and black characters, both male and female. Through the contrasting values and attitudes toward segregation of these vividly drawn characters—the grinning black waiters, the harassed conductor, the prissy, sexually inhibited Southern lady who won't sleep in the same railroad car with the dignified, elderly pullman attendant, the morally promiscuous "painted" white woman who will sleep with anyone, including the gregarious black bartender—McPherson objectively presents a microcosm of modern society, leaving the reader to make his own moral judgments regarding the dehumanizing effects of racial fanaticism.

This Pulitzer Prize winner offers no simple solutions in any of his stories and although the racial theme is present in many of them, it receives a background rather than a foreground emphasis. McPherson's images of women are seldom merely stereotyped mothers, or lovers or wives or black or white.

He views the black predicament, as he views the predicament of women, as too challenging and too complex to be dissected with false simplistic labels. Instead both are part of the larger predicaments faced by human beings of all races, all colors and both sexes in today's complex, impersonal society. Fortunately, he has not lost his humanity; his hue and cry is over life's injustices, the small betrayals we all have experienced. McPherson has a strong sense of justice and he knows how disproportionally large a share of that injustice black men and especially black woman have borne; yet he manages to project human beings one at a time, honoring their special kind of uniqueness. He is neither inquisitor nor judge. He manages to keep the right distance from his imaginative creations; he does not get murkily involved and blur his figures with emotion-clad traps. He is, instead, a controlled writer, beautifully poised and, therefore, he is able to turn out a finished, finely honed piece of work. (pp. 390-401)

> *Edith Blicksilver, "The Image of Women in Selected Short Stories by James Alan McPherson," in* CLA Journal, *Vol. XXII, No. 4, June, 1979, pp. 390-401.*

Ralph Ellison on *Elbow Room*:

Elbow Room is the most rewarding collection of short stories to come my way in quite some time. In them James Alan McPherson reveals a maturing ability to convert the ironies, the contradictions of American experience into sophisticated works of literature. To my mind McPherson ranks with the most talented and original of our younger writers. The title story alone reveals more about the spiritual condition of Americans during the 1960s than is to be found in most novels.

Ralph Ellison, on the dust jacket of Elbow Room, *1977.*

Mary A. Gervin   (essay date December 1982)

[*In the essay below, Gervin provides a psychological analysis of the characters in the short story "Elbow Room."*]

"Elbow Room" is the title story of James Alan McPherson's 1978 Pulitzer Prize winning collection of short fiction by the same name. The main story line is a tale of miscegeny: a white man from Kansas marries a black woman from outside Warren, Tennessee, despite the misgivings of their parents and in spite of the caste restrictions of society.

The author himself sublimates plot to the development of character. As a result, the narrative becomes a psychological study in character relationships. As the main characters engage in a search of a positive "sense of self," a realization of their own self-worth, they also reflect the concept of androgyny—a merging of the masculine and feminine attributes. The principals—Paul Frost and Virginia Valentine—complement each other's personality traits. Even though the two are opposites in many respects, one partner assimilates the characteristics of the other as the stronger characteristics of one mate gradually offset the weaker traits of the other.

Paul Frost is trying to "find himself"; he is trying to realize self-actualization. In an effort to understand who he is and to identify his role in life, he moves from one job to another, from place to place, and from one situation into another. Feeling out-of-touch with his own culture, Paul attempts to adapt to another by marrying Virginia Valentine, a bold, assertive black woman. Virginia is the ideal "soulmate" for Paul; she balances his weakness of character. She knows what she wants and is aware of her place within the system. She is already a self-assured person, with a "cosmopolitan" outlook. Indeed, Virginia is a woman of the world. As a Peace Corps volunteer, she has traveled to Africa and the Far East. In her travels she finds "different ways of looking at the world." In contrast, Paul's experiences are less worldly; he does hospital detail in Chicago and on the West Coast instead of serving a tour of duty in the armed forces.

Paul and Virginia are drawn to each other because they are both disillusioned with and embittered by the "caste curtains" society has drawn about them. The young woman is far from the feminine ideal:

> The girl was not at all pretty. . . . She was a little plump, had small breasts and habitually wore Levi's and a flat broad-brimmed type of cap. . . .

Certainly Virginia is not physically attractive, but she has finesse. She is compassionate and sensitive and has a unique talent for "locating quickly the human core in people." Thus she readily perceives in Paul a sense of longing. In turn, Paul senses Virginia's strength of character. Indeed, he has "keen eyes for value" and aligns himself with Virginia in part to redeem himself and partly to draw from her source of strength; for despite her assertiveness, Virginia is an embodiment of a soft, passionate, sensitive entity. But to all outward appearances she affects a swagger, feigns a raucous laugh, and contrives a booming voice. This outward display of strength attracts Paul Frost. Conversely, Paul Frost is a quiet, intense, unimposing innocent. He needs nurturing in order to become a completely fulfilled person. Of their relationship the narrator, an acquaintance of theirs, remarks:

> And after I had come to understand them better, I began to see deeper into their bond. She was an eagle with broken wings spread, somewhat awkwardly, over the aristocratic soul of a simple farm boy. Having his soul intact made him a vulnerable human being. But having flown so high herself, and having been severely damaged, she

still maintained too much grace, and too complete a sense of treachery in the world, to allow any roughness to touch the innocent. Virginia Valentine was protecting him to heal herself.

These two characters identify in each other prevailing characteristics which will make their own lives more content. In effect, whatever void is missing from their own lives, they hope a mate will fulfill. Ideally, once a man and woman enter into the commitment of marriage, they lend their strengths to creating something new. The same is true for Paul Frost and Virginia Valentine.

Virginia marries outside her race, seemingly, to shock others, to make others take notice of her. But she does not want to be identified with the white culture; she wants to be accepted as a woman, without regard to race or color. And Paul, a bewildered, introverted male, weds outside his race because he is lost and out-of-step with his own kind. He is displaced, yet he feels secure with Virginia, even though he is "ostracized" by his own parents. About Paul's conduct Virginia reflects:

> But I'm worried about that nigger of mine. I told you he had heart. In his mind he's still working through all that s—. Underneath that soft front he's strong as a mule, and he's stubborn. Right now both his eyes are a little open, but if he ever got his jaws tight he might close one eye and become blacker than I ever thought about being.

Under Virginia's tutelage, Paul develops into a wholesome, discerning fellow, at peace with himself and content with his world.

Virginia Valentine is at once aggressive, suspicious, callous, and abrasive as a result of her myriad experiences. With her union to Paul, Virginia becomes vulnerable and less ferocious:

> And yet at times, watching Virginia's eyes soften as they moved over his face, I could read in them the recognition of extraordinary spiritual forces, quietly commanded, but so self-assured as to be unafraid of advertising themselves. I am sure he was unaware of his innocence. And perhaps this is why Virginia's eyes pleaded, when he openly approached a soul-crushed stranger, DON'T HURT MY BABY! DON'T HURT MY BABY!, even while her voice laughed, teased, or growled.

Initially, Paul Frost is a confused, gullible, and naive individual. But as he associates himself with his betrothed, he becomes wizened and more self-assured:

> Because the thing that illuminated him, that provided the core of his mystery, might have been simple guilt, or outright lust, or a passion to dominate, or a need to submit to some fearful-seeming object. All such motives enter into the convention of love.

The two never really diminish themselves or stoop to dominate the other. Their alignment enables them to grow and develop a solid relationship together.

In the merger the two not only develop "different ways of looking at the world," but they also regenerate themselves and find new directions for their lives. As the narrator re-

flects: "The peasants [had become] aristocratic without any of the telling affections [whereas] the aristocrats by birth had developed an easy, common touch. They considered themselves a new tribe." In this case Paul (the peasant) and Virginia (the aristocrat) have become one. The couple forms a new breed, an androgynous strain, a hybrid of the dominant qualities of both mates. The assimilation of interests developed between the couple enables them to see beyond the confines of their own self-interests and molds them into two perceptive, wholesome beings:

> Beside him, I saw Paul lift his own head and turn fierce eyes on the old gentleman's face. In his voice was a familiar arrogance from a source he had just begun to consciously tap. . . . "This is MY WIFE. If you don't like what she's wearing, THAT'S TOUGH!" . . . I closed my own eyes and tried to lose myself in the music. But I was made humble and hopeful by that other thing, and I thought to myself, THIS ONE'S A MAN.

Paul's image of himself is considerably stronger than the pining, confused young man who earlier married Virginia. His personality has more dimension. His demeanor is more imposing; his ego more confident.

During the marriage the couple cement their bond through assimilation. As the relationship is nurtured, Virginia and Paul become parents. Virginia wants the child to develop into a classic kind of person. She muses, "Wouldn't it of been something to be a nigger that could relate to white and black and everything else in the world out of a self as big as the world is?" And Virginia and Paul set out to make the vision a reality. Paul philosophizes, "People DO grow. You may not think much of ME, but my children will be great!" Paul and Virginia do grow; they see in each other a mainstay, a source of strength and bearing. In turn they produce a strong, vital boy. In the end the child is responsible for the parents' reconciling their differences with the child's grandparents and the grandparents' resigning themselves to the union of Paul and Virginia. Their offspring is not only remarkable but also lucky; he will receive the best of both possible worlds:

> The mother is, after all, a country raconteur with cosmopolitan experience. The father sees clearly with both eyes. And when I called Kansas they had already left for the backwoods of Tennessee, where the baby has an odd assortment of relatives. I will wait. The mother is a bold woman. The father has a sense of how things should be. But while waiting, I will wager my reputation on the ambition, if not the strength of the boy's story.

The youngster, born of mixed blood, is also a by-product of two cultures. The affinity of the parents, their equivalent convictions, and the assimilation of ideals, will nurture the child as the parents have nurtured each other. They not only have matured; they have thrived. Because of their fusion of interests, feelings, and personalities, their child will develop into a paragon, beyond race consciousness.

Certainly the characters in **"Elbow Room"** grow in stature as the story unfolds. They become truly compatible, having been drawn closer by their androgynous spirit. It creates a bond, unifying their principles and attitudes so that both can adjust to each other's differences. Such a relationship is reciprocal; neither partner overwhelms the other. Accordingly, Paul Frost and Virginia Valentine are not clones of each other; they merely augment each other's tendencies and thereby contribute to the success of their marriage. Therefore the couple, as a result of their association, evolve into paradigms of androgyny, having greater bearing and more dynamic presence as they etch out some elbow room for themselves in a predominantly self-centered society. (pp. 251-55)

Mary A. Gervin, "Developing a Sense of Self: The Androgynous Ideal in McPherson's 'Elbow Room'," in CLA Journal, *Vol. XXVI, No. 2, December, 1982, pp. 251-55.*

William Domnarski   (essay date Spring 1986)

[*Domnarski is an American lawyer. In the following essay, he praises McPherson's depiction of "the black experience" in his fiction.*]

James Alan McPherson's two collections of short stories, **Hue and Cry** and **Elbow Room,** have established him as an important writer interested in illustrating the effects of racial prejudice on blacks. The two collections are integrally related, with the second expanding and defining more precisely McPherson's bleak vision of blacks seeking respectability and self-identity. A sense of misery, which sometimes develops into rage, controls McPherson's work. Through explosive moments of insight into the black experience, he enables us to know and feel the frustration and despair of his characters.

Critics have praised the diversity of McPherson's stories and noted a conscious attempt to repress the blackness of the characters, suggesting the two characteristics are complementary. This is ironically misleading, however, because the wide range of stories reflects McPherson's broad focus on the very issue critics have tended to lead us away from: the blackness of the characters. At first the handful of stories about blacks working at various jobs does not seem to have much in common with other stories about the law or the search for self-identity, yet a careful working out of the themes of McPherson's fiction reveals his attempt to analyze comprehensively the difficulties blacks face at every turn.

To outline the plight of blacks trying to establish themselves within the mainstream of American society, McPherson examines the underlying premise of the American dream—that individuals can rise socially by working hard—and shows how this premise often does not apply to blacks. McPherson's characters, instead of demonstrating through their hard work that they are no different from anyone else, find that no matter how well they do their jobs, they cannot escape those holding racial prejudices.

Thomas, the shy, insecure boy in **"A Matter of Vocabulary,"** discovers, for example, that the work he does in the local supermarket creates a dilemma he will always have to endure. His work brings praise from the owners and

gives him a sense of responsibility, pride, and even superiority, but the job's impact cuts both ways for him, as the benefits are balanced against the stereotypical role he must assume to please the owners, who expect Thomas, like all the other blacks in the neighborhood, to drop out of school.

The supermarket owners will not accept Thomas if he fails to conform to his role. To show this, McPherson has Thomas's brother Eddie, who also works in the supermarket, show his intelligence and antagonize the owners by using a precisely appropriate word in an argument. The lesson Thomas learns is clear. If he does not act in the expected manner, he threatens his job and the sense of pride and identity that goes with it. As a result, Thomas must give up part of himself to keep part of himself.

In a brilliant stroke, McPherson gives Thomas's internal misery an external equivalent by linking Thomas with the beggar woman crying desperately in the night. Her scream is "a painful sound, lonely, desperate, threatening, impatient, angry, hungry." Thomas comes to realize they share the experience of being in misery and not being able to do anything about it, yet we recognize that Thomas's agony is greater because he cannot release his frustrations by wailing at night. He must keep his anguish within him and continue with the work that paradoxically creates the anguish.

Thomas suffers quietly, as does the railroad porter in **"On Trains."** By connecting the two, McPherson expands his theme and gives us a sense of what lies ahead for Thomas. We see the porter as a man who takes great pride in his work, who wants the respect that accompanies a job well done, but instead he gets passengers who see only his color, which makes prejudice, not competence, the controlling issue. The result is that the job both builds up and tears down the porter. We are compelled to think of young Thomas when we read of the porter's broken spirit after an argument between the conductor and a woman who objects to the porter because he is black.

> The porter, who stood all the while like a child waiting for punishment, seemed to droop and wither and grow smaller; and his eyes, which had only minutes before flashed brightly from the face of the conductor to the enraged face of the lady, now seemed to dull and turn inward as only those who have learned to suffer silently can turn their eyes inward. He was a very old man and he grew older, even older than his occupation or the oldest and most obsequious Pullman Porter.

McPherson wants us to associate the painful cry of the beggar woman in **"A Matter of Vocabulary"** with the old porter. When we then reexamine the description of her cry we recognize that it contains inchoate elements of rage, some of which can be seen in **"A Solo Song: For Doc,"** the third story in **Hue and Cry** focusing on work. Here McPherson varies his theme to show a black unwilling to act obsequiously. The black railroad waiter eventually loses his battle with a vengeful, threatened management, but only after a tense, heroic struggle. In two subsequent stories in **Elbow Room,** McPherson takes his developing

theme further to detail the disappearance of obsequious-
ness and the emergence of violence.

"A Sense of Story" and **"The Story of a Scar"** are important to McPherson's vision partly because each story depicts job related frustrations leading to explosions of violence. Equally important, the stories widen McPherson's
focus yet further to show additional forces working on the
characters. In **"A Sense of Story,"** McPherson includes
a comment on a legal system that cannot find sympathy
for a mechanic who kills his boss because he is convinced
the boss has not given his invention the consideration it
deserves. The judge handling the case has little difficulty
convincing himself that the mechanic is guilty—it was
cold-blooded murder. But as readers we have ambivalent
feelings. We realize that the mechanic is guilty, yet we demand more for him. We want the court at least to recognize the frustration the mechanic endured knowing he was
deprived of something due him. The stories about work in
Hue and Cry have prepared us to understand not just the
mechanic's frustration but also the dimensions of the
problem. We leave the story feeling there have been two
injustices. The first is the white boss's successful repression of the black mechanic's talents and ambitions. The
second is the judge's reaction to the case: the facts are interesting, but nothing more. His summary conviction thus
symbolizes a general dismissal of this problem of a blight-
ed version of the American dream for blacks.

Billy's slashing of his girlfriend's face in **"The Story of a
Scar"** comes to symbolize a reaction to yet another aspect
of the problems associated with work and social mobility
for blacks: peer pressure and the difficulty of being ambitious within the black community. McPherson uses the
contrast between Billy and Teddy, both postal workers, to
illustrate the differences between those planning for the future and those living for the present. **"The Story of a
Scar"** suggests the extent of the friction between the two
groups, with those living for the present avoiding and re-
senting their opposites, attributing to them a sense of
aloofness and superiority.

"The Story of a Scar" shows that the apparently sincere
interest Billy's girlfriend has in him, an interest grounded
in her respect for his ambition, is not strong enough to
withstand the dreaded feeling of isolation she will experience at work in the post office if she continues making
Billy and what he represents her choice. Her ultimate rejection of Billy for Teddy and his view of life comes to
mean much more than a failed romance. When Billy vi-
ciously attacks his girlfriend in a moment of rage, he is
symbolically attacking an attitude within his own cultural
niche that represses and frustrates him.

The recognition that elements within the black community can paradoxically retard blacks seeking social mobility
enables us to understand **"Of Cabbages and Kings,"** one
of McPherson's most disturbing stories. It involves The
Brotherhood, a black power organization that harms rather than helps those adhering to its principles by espousing
a kind of reality-distorting mysticism and by failing to deal
effectively with the problem of self-identity for blacks.

"Of Cabbages and Kings" depicts two pathetic figures.

Claude is torn apart by paranoia, prompting him to sleep
with an endless number of white women in an attempt to
ease his anxiety. The result, however, is continued self-
hatred. He responds to the real world around him by believing in flying saucers and his own supernatural powers.
McPherson's point that The Brotherhood contributes to
Claude's evolving destruction is clear. Equally clear is the
mood of despair McPherson evokes by having Howard,
the story's narrator, succumb to his fascination with
Claude and willingly accept his teachings. The path the
once rational Howard follows thereby highlights McPherson's comment on black splinter groups that ultimately divert blacks from the real problems facing them.

By illustrating the deleterious effects ostensibly positive
forces can have on blacks, **"Of Cabbages and Kings"**
heightens our awareness to the problem blacks may face
of aligning themselves with social forces in an age in which
forces and attitudes change quickly. The Afro haircut represents one of these forces, and John Butler's refusal in
"The Faithful" to offer it in his barbershop suggests the
broader issue of blacks being forced to make decisions
about themselves and their place in the community. The
decisions are difficult to make, illustrating McPherson's
point that blacks may be forced to turn their backs on
their cultural pasts to embrace the forces of the future.

Butler sees the schoolboy, the old style haircut, as important to black pride and identity. Those around him, however, argue that blacks must now avoid the schoolboy because the very values Butler ascribes to it have come to
characterize Uncle Toms. The Afro, they point out, gives
a new sense of identity to the black seeking to assert himself in a new age. Butler's decision to oppose the Afro
shows the depth of the conflict within him, as his shop will
be unable to survive without the trade brought in by the
Afro. In this conflict of forces, Butler does not trust the
future enough to give up the past.

McPherson inverts the problem of blacks choosing between old and new values in **"The Silver Bullet."** Instead
of an older man desperately clinging to the values of his
generation, we see a young man trying to make his mark
in the world by enlisting the aid of a community organization he feels is the force of the future. His is a foolish
choice, however, because the community organization is
actually a toothless extortion operation disguised by rhetoric featuring the latest sociological jargon. McPherson
has pulled our sympathies both ways in these two stories,
giving us both young and old failing to recognize what is
best for them. By doing this, McPherson gives us a sense
of the dilemma that blacks might face in trying to sort out
the forces operating on them.

When we distance ourselves from individual stories and
see McPherson's two collections of short stories as general
statements, we see the pervasive bleakness of his vision.
The stories about a callous legal system, such as **"A Sense
of Story"** and **"An Act of Prostitution,"** complement the
group of stories focusing on work and its paradoxical effect on blacks to show layers of entrenched forces affecting
blacks. McPherson then goes further to expose elements
within the black community itself that complicate the existing institutional forces.

Important to McPherson's short stories is the mood of despair, a mood illustrated well in **"A Loaf of Bread."** The story, which at first makes us feel anger and indignation toward the white grocery store owner for charging more at his store in a black neighborhood than at his suburban store, concludes with the recognition, both by us and the story's principal black character, that the higher overhead costs created by the crime in the black neighborhood justify the higher prices. The story details an economic system adversely affecting blacks and then, almost without comment, acknowledges the logic supporting the system.

Despair strikes at the characters and destroys them from the inside. In the end, the social and economic conditions that McPherson's characters collide with rob them of their self-respect and identity. Indeed, the theme of self-identity runs through many of the stories in both *Hue and Cry* and *Elbow Room.* We see it, for example, in **"The Faithful," "A Solo Song: For Doc," "Of Cabbages and Kings," "The Story of a Scar,"** and **"Private Domain."**

But of course not all of McPherson's stories fit within the scope of themes I have outlined. There are some stories about the search for self-identity in which homosexuality, not race, plays a dominant role, while other stories present blacks who are successful at their jobs. The diversity of McPherson's work has the ironic effect of buffering the sound of the angry, tormented, and despairing voices in his fiction. My contention is that once we recognize these voices in stories such as **"A Matter of Vocabulary"** and **"The Story of a Scar,"** we begin to hear them in an increasing number of stories, leading us to conclude that they are the true voices of McPherson's work.

An analysis of **"Why I Like Country Music,"** McPherson's often-anthologized tale of first love, bears this out. If we come to the story with the understanding of McPherson's work I have suggested, we see that the black narrator's silent suffering, and not the delightful account of his youthful love, controls the story. The narrator's lengthy digression to explain why he likes country music serves on one level as a means of discrediting stereotypical beliefs, such as the idea that blacks cannot like a type of music traditionally associated with rednecks or that blacks have a natural sense of rhythm. More important, though, the story points to the narrator's wife as the unlikely source of the stereotypical thinking he must contend with.

The narrator's memory of country music, Gweneth, and his love for her is important to him. Yet he finds that his wife's staunch belief that blacks should not like country music comes between him and his fond memory of Gweneth. As a result, the narrator feels that his wife is telling him to bury that part of himself. This is the crux of the issue, as the conflict between the forces attacks the narrator's sense of self. A public-self/private-self dichotomy develops, with the narrator keeping his fondness for country music to himself. He, like Thomas in **"A Matter of Vocabulary"** and the old porter in **"On Trains,"** has learned to suffer silently, a connection made clear by the emphasis in all three stories on the words "silently" or "quietly."

The connections between **"Why I Like Country Music"**

An excerpt from the title story in *Elbow Room*

[Virginia] was not at all pretty, and at first I could not see how [Paul] could love her. She was a little plump, had small breasts, and habitually wore Levi's and that flat, broad-brimmed type of cap popularized by movie gangsters in the forties. But the more I looked into her costume, the more I recognized it as the disguise of a person trying to deflect attention away from a secret self. . . . She employed a complicated kind of defensive irony. When her voice boomed, "Don't play with me now, nigger!" it said on the underside of the very same rhythm, *Don't come too close, I hurt easily.* Or when the voice said, "Come on in here and meet my fiancé, and if you don't like it you can go to hell!", the quick, dark eyes, watching closely for reactions, said in their silent language, *Don't hurt my baby! Don't hurt my baby!* She spiced her stories with this same delicious irony. Virginia Valentine was a country raconteur with a stock of stories flavored by international experience. Telling them, she spoke with her whole presence in very complicated ways. She was unique. She was a classic kind of narrator. Virginia Valentine was a magic woman.

Paul Frost seemed attracted to her by this outward display of strength. I am convinced he was by this time too mature to view her as just exotic. He was the second generation of a Kansas family successful in business matters, and he must have had keen eyes for value. But because of this, and perhaps for reasons still unclear to him, his family and the prairies were now in his past. I think he felt the need to redeem the family through works of great art, to release it from the hauntings of those lonely prairie towns. I know that when I looked I saw dead Indians living in his eyes. But I also saw a wholesome glow in their directness. They seemed in earnest need of answers to honest questions always on the verge of being asked. This aura of intense interest hung close to his face, like a bright cloud, or like a glistening second coat of skin not yet thick enough to be attached to him. It seemed to inquire of whomever his eyes addressed, "Who am I?" But this was only an outward essence. Whatever else he was eluded my inspection of his face. And as I grew aware of myself in pursuit of its definition, I began to feel embarrassed, and a little perverse. Because the thing that illuminated him, that provided the core of his mystery, might have been simple guilt, or outright lust, or a passion to dominate, or a need to submit to a fearful-seeming object. All such motives enter into the convention of love.

And yet at times, watching Virginia's eyes soften as they moved over his face, I could read in them the recognition of extraordinary spiritual forces, quietly commanded, but so self-assured as to be unafraid of advertising themselves. I am sure he was unaware of his innocence. And perhaps this is why Virginia's eyes pleaded, when he openly approached a soul-crushed stranger, *Don't hurt my baby! Don't hurt my baby!,* even while her voice laughed, teased, or growled. She employed her country wits with the finesse and style of a magic woman. And after I had come to understand them better, I began to see deeper into their bond. She was an eagle with broken wings spread, somewhat awkwardly, over the aristocratic soul of a simple farm boy. Having his soul intact made him a vulnerable human being. But having flown so high herself, and having been severely damaged, she still maintained too much grace, and too complete a sense of the treachery in the world, to allow any roughnesses to touch the naked thing. Paul Frost was a very lucky innocent. Virginia Valentine was protecting him to heal herself.

James Alan McPherson, in his Elbow Room, *Little, Brown and Company, 1977.*

and McPherson's other stories depend more on an under-standing of just what troubles the narrator. Like Billy in **"The Story of a Scar,"** the narrator in **"Why I Like Country Music"** finds that the woman closest to him cannot give him what he needs most, an acceptance of him as he is. Thus, the narrator's frustration shares a common theme with Billy's frustration and with the frustration of the other characters encountering layers of resistance in their attempts to achieve fulfillment, whether it be economic or personal. Fulfillment, they all learn, is harder to come by because they are black. (pp. 37-44)

> William Domnarski, "The Voices of Misery and Despair in the Fiction of James Alan McPherson," in Arizona Quarterly, *Vol. 42, No. 1, Spring, 1986, pp. 37-44.*

Herman Beavers (essay date Fall 1986)

[*In the essay below, Beavers discusses the relationship between theme and narrative strategy in "The Story of a Dead Man."*]

In the short fiction of James Alan McPherson we can find a very strong relationship between the narrators' visibility and authorial intention. In stories like **"The Story of a Scar"** and **"A Solo Song: For Doc"** McPherson presents us with narrators who achieve visibility through their skill as storytellers. Certainly, one route towards visibility for these narrators lies in their being characters within their own narratives, tellers who relate experiences responsible for their present state of awareness. In this regard, **"The Story of a Dead Man"** takes a different tack. Though similar to the aforementioned narratives in that it has a narrator who is both teller and character, its main difference lies in the mode of visibility the narrator achieves. Unlike McPherson's other narrators, who distinguish themselves through a heightened sensibility that legitimizes them as storytellers, the narrator in **"Dead Man"** is distinctive because of his innocence and naiveté.

To substantiate this notion, my critical approach toward the narrator begins and ends apart from the narrative he renders. The notion of visibility, as I intend the term in this instance, is concerned with how the narrator combines technique and strategy to complete a transaction with his listener. This involves an attempt to transform the listener, bringing him or her to a new level of awareness, concerned with providing the listener with a clearer image of the narrator. What I am suggesting is that we can see the narrator in **"The Story of a Scar"** as listener, storyteller, patient, and healer. Likewise, in **"A Solo Song: For Doc"** the narrator comes to us as teacher, historian, musician, author, and in a limited sense, as priest. None of these roles is explicitly rendered in McPherson's prose, and we should not assume that discovery of any evidence to this effect is in itself of lasting value. But a sensibility

towards McPherson's narrators, mindful of the different roles they play, is helpful in illuminating his stories. As his titles suggest, McPherson's artistic intent is often discernable only insofar as one perceives his feelings toward the narrative strategy employed by the narrator. As we will see in **"The Story of a Dead Man,"** the narrator's gift is his ability to obscure himself through a rhetorical approach to storytelling.

The two main facets of visibility are authorial control and literacy, which the aforementioned stories posit as narrative goals. In **"Scar"** we see the scarred woman exert authorial control over her tale in order for the narrator to achieve a better understanding of women, which he then exhibits as a storyteller, having learned the art of listening. The narrator's task in **"Doc"** is to wrest authorial control from an illegitimate text (a book of rules), tell the story (or stories) it obscures, and bring his listener to an awareness of atextual literacy; a reliance on insight gained through experience, rather than the ability to read. In both instances, the narrators' attempts to exert authorial control reside in the use of experience and action as authenticating devices aimed at "texts" in need of revision. These storytellers are concerned with life as a living text, not as it is validated by the written word. The stories they tell represent equipment for living, and thus they are a prerequisite to action.

Essentially, **"The Story of a Dead Man"** is no different from the above stories in this regard. What is at issue here is perspective, and by this I mean that McPherson's approach towards authorial control and literacy is realized in a different fashion. Whereas **"Scar"** and **"Doc"** present two experienced storytellers, **"Dead Man"** utilizes a narrator who is neither adept as a storyteller nor concerned, in the manner of an experienced storyteller, with the creation of a viable form of kinship. McPherson's purpose in rendering the story from his point of view is to show what can happen to a story (and by implication, kinship) when placed in the hands of an inept teller. Moreover, **"Scar"** and **"Doc"** are narratives concerned with the creation of kinship linkages between two individuals not related by blood but by circumstance. **"Dead Man"** presents two men, cousins with the same first name, and chronicles the weakening, if not dissolution, of a blood tie. And, indeed, at the heart of the story is the issue of family history, for the oral narratives exchanged by kin require authenticity in order to solidify blood ties in time and space, making them legitimate in the eyes of outsiders.

"The Story of a Dead Man" is concerned with a family crisis. It is here that the question of who this story "belongs" to becomes relevant. Rather than simply describing the adventures of Billy Renfro as he undertakes "his careless search for an exciting death," the story is in the grasp of the narrator who attempts to fashion a family narrative flattering to his own perspectives on life and living. The result is a story of not one "dead" man but two. The narrator himself goes so far as to suggest this when he observes that he and Billy Renfro, his cousin (indeed, his first cousin), *"are one* with the same ancestors," concluding that "whatever fires rage in him [he] must look to find smolderings of within (him)self." The narrative tension is strikingly dramatized here; William and Billy are parts of a whole, positive and negative poles which simultaneously attract and repel one another. With this type of tension present, the question arises as to what extent we can "trust" McPherson's narrator and how honorable his intentions are when he asserts:

> Recognizing this obligation, I here attempt to deflate mean rumors circulated by his enemies, cut through the fat of Billy's own lies, and lay bare the muscles of his life.

The obligation, of course, is one of blood, but one is curious as to what benefits the narrator derives from such an act, particularly since he looks at Billy, as the two of them sit in a bar, and sees a "gangster," someone he characterizes as "not the kind of man I wanted to meet my family." At issue for the narrator is a good name, for both he and Billy have been named after Willie Joe Warner, their paternal grandfather and a jackleg Baptist preacher, which suggests an air of infidelity surrounding their names. **"The Story of a Dead Man"** is concerned with the struggle between Billy and the narrator to "live up" to their names. Their lives converge at points, diverge at others, making the task of the narrator an attempt to "break" his kinship tie with Billy as he attempts to live out an upwardly mobile, middle-class life befitting the more formal name of William, shorn of the images that a name like Billy conjures in the minds of his peers.

I want to suggest, then, that it may not be wise to accept the narrator's stated intention at face value when we consider him as a storyteller. William says of his desire to tell Billy's story, "I bother to refute these rumors because the man is my cousin, and I am honor-bound to love him as he really is." What this sentence omits is the narrator's desire to refute the rumors spread by Billy's "enemies" for the sake of Billy's honor; nor does William wish to *present* Billy as he really is. The narrator has obscured his real intention, which is to distance himself from the type of individual that he believes Billy Renfro represents. To this end, William relates several of Billy's adventures, all of which end in Billy's death. In the narrator's hands, however, these adventures achieve a level of comedy. By making Billy a comic figure, one driven by the stereotypical behavior associated with "street types," he turns his life into a caricature. This obscures the heroic qualities implicit in the tales, replacing them with the value-laden "readings" the narrator imposes upon them. William's narrative intrusion into Billy's tales transforms them into "representative anecdotes" intended to show just how "low" Billy really is. They are designed to sustain authorial control over his own "narrative," a fact he attempts to veil rhetorically as he struggles for control over his own name.

Thus, when William relates Billy's experiences in Houston as he tries to reclaim a defaulted automobile, he immediately interferes with the tale's shape. He begins:

> It is not true that Billy Renfro was killed during that trouble in Houston. The man is an accomplished liar and likes to keep his enemies nervous. It was he who spread this madness.

This invalidates the end of the tale, which, we must assume, consists of Billy's death in Houston. The narrator attributes this ending to Billy himself, then says, "The truth of what happened, he told me in Chicago, was this." This suggests to us that William has heard what actually happened directly from Billy. However, what he relates is laden with his own value-judgments. He locates Billy at the room of the defaulted car owner; then, rather than relating events as Billy would recount them, he begins to toy with particulars as he observes that Billy's "common sense was overwhelmed by the romantic aspects of the adventure. That was why he kicked open the door, charged boldly into the room, and shouted, 'Monroe Ellis, give up Mr. Floyd's cadillac that you done miss nine payments on.' " Instead of telling what happened, William intrudes upon the tale, offering reasons for Billy's actions where none, we can assume, have been offered. The rhetorical overload exhibited by a phrase such as "romantic aspects of the adventure" obscures Billy's rendering of the tale so that the listener does not hear the facts as they happened but as William sees them. Thus, when William quotes Billy, we see a fool, not a hero. Though William notes that Billy was shot in the side with a .38, he dismisses any possibility that Billy may in fact have died by saying that the "wound did not slow Billy's retreat from the room, the rooming house, or the city of Houston." Again, the rhetorical strategy here is to present Billy as both a fool and a coward, for the word "retreat" bears this silent inference.

The stilted rhetoric employed by William as he narrates versions of Billy Renfro's adventure tales suggests that William is addressing neither family nor acquaintances. Like the narrator in **"The Story of a Scar,"** William is speaking to an individual who both speaks and thinks along the same lines as he does, and thus we can assume that the "implied" listener is a trusted confidante. As we will see, William makes some confessions within the space of the narrative which bear this notion out.

The implications of audience are evidenced by the license William takes in presenting Billy's stories. He opens another tale:

> Neither is it true, as certain of his enemies have maintained, that Billy's left eye was lost during a rumble with that red-neck storekeep outside Limehouse, South Carolina. That eye, I now have reason to believe, was lost during domestic troubles. That is quite another story.

Again, the narrator invalidates the much more provocative tale and replaces it with a rhetorical substitute upon which he chooses not to elaborate. Hence, when he asserts, "I have this full account of the Limehouse difficulty," the listener must accept William's generic tale at face value, not as the story of how Billy lost his eye, but as another instance where Billy has escaped, however narrowly, from a situation which the narrator suggests is more indicative of Billy's madness than of his esprit de corps. The rhetorical approach William takes towards the tale underscores this notion:

> He entered the general store with the sole intention of buying a big orange soda. However, the owner of the joint, a die-hard white supremacist,

refused to execute the transaction. Being naturally suspicious of governmental intervention, Billy fell back on his own resources: He reached for the .22 he carried under his shirt for just such dalliances.

William's version of the tale removes the improvisatory quality Billy's idiom might have suggested. The events, though rendered comically, are colored by William's idiom which strips them of the underlying drama and recasts the setting of the tale as the scene of one of Billy's lies. Words like "transaction," "joint," and "dalliances," coupled with phrases like "die-hard white supremacist," and "governmental intervention," reflect the extent of William's comic intrusion.

William successfully maintains his obscurity as a character, largely through his ability to manipulate language. Moreover, it is his voice which overarches all the other voices in the story, and thus the reader must contend with him in an attempt to see the other characters in clear focus. Rhetorical master that he is, it is difficult to unmask William as a character more concerned with his own story than Billy's. Contrary to his own claims, William's use of Billy's tales serves to "make the case" of his own narrative intention. Billy is a foil for William, an alter ego of whom he would be rid. This is evidenced by William's careful description of their divergent paths, beginning in their adolescent years:

> He outgrew me from the start, perhaps because his father succumbed to alcohol before Billy was ten. And his mother, soon afterward made invalid by a stroke, let her son roam freely.

McPherson reverses here the perspective of **"Doc"** where, in heroic fashion, Doc is more man-child than boy. William's authorial control over Billy's history, here, serves to make Billy less of a hero than a hoodlum as William presents himself as the model youngster. In a fashion that suggests mirror opposites, William distances himself and his own history from Billy's life:

> While I completed school, he worked as the relay man on a garbage truck. While I attended church and learned social graces, he became more a loner, grew sullen, worked a tentative cynicism into his voice. The whites of his eyes reddened. He cultivated a process, dressed flashily, began socializing on a certain street corner sanctified by a tree that had once stood there.

Striking about this passage is that its rhythms, along with William's choice of details, suggest Billy's rapid decline. William recalls that "at sixteen," Billy "threw away his youth." Here, William reveals his innocence, for in many cultures, sixteen is an age where manhood rituals are performed and when many roles ascribed to manhood are assumed. What William describes as part of his own development has more to do with passive acceptance of social norms than with a movement towards manhood. Indeed, he intimates his own passivity as he states, "I accepted my name. Billy gloried in his, draining from it as much territory as the world would concede." This suggests that William portrays his own name as a symbol of inaction while Billy's life is couched in aggressive confrontations with the

world around him. The "glory" Billy finds in his name is indicative of the fullness of his life.

Innocent and naive as he is, William knows nothing of this. He describes a conversation with Billy in a Chicago bar where he gives his "best advice" and simultaneously shows how little he knows. "We are no longer young men," he tells Billy, "The foam has settled into the beer. I, myself no longer chase women, speak hotly, challenge opinions too far different from my own. I have learned it is to my advantage to get along. In short, Billy, I have become aware of complexity." This passive awareness of complexity comes to stand for William's definition of manhood, which, like his name, is more rhetorical than experiential. His ineptitude as a storyteller is evident, for he mistakes book sense—his impressive facility with language—for living. What distinguishes William, like the narrator in **"Scar,"** as a character is the fact that he becomes impotent. Billy's attitude toward the kind of life William suggests he try to attain is characterized by his response, "Bullshit!" a signifier for an untruth or preposterous idea.

As a character, then, William is another version of Ellison's Invisible Man. Like Ellison's narrator, William passively accepts his name. Moreover, William is more impressed by his rhetorical style than impressive, for what his speech, in all its eloquence, reveals is his innocence and the paucity of his own experience. When he sees Billy at the prison farm, he tells him that he is "making something" of his life. In a corner, another prisoner sings a work song which reflects William's state of existence, a call to which William responds: "Well, the load so heavy, I can hardly go, I can hardly go. . . . " William then talks about his life in college, attempting to

> communicate to him some sense of the broader options available to the man in possession of salable knowledge. [I] mapped out my future in blocks of years, stepladders of subgoals, ending with an affirmation of my ultimate ambition to settle into the good life in Los Angeles.

When Billy responds to this "text" by asking for a "hot sausage sandwich heavy on the mustard and a big orange soda," he shows his concern with the present. William, on the other hand, is locked into an existence informed only by the linear movement of time. His actions are based on a "map" of goals and subgoals projected toward future. Unlike Billy, who listens "only to the beating of his own heart," William's life is so future-oriented that he never begins living: His life is all ambition and no action. That Billy can hear only those callings that have to do with meeting his immediate needs suggests that he lives his life cyclically, untouched by history or progress. The song he sings exemplifies this: "I'm Wild Nigger Bill / From Red Pepper Hill / I never did die and I never will. . . . "

It is noteworthy that William posits a life in Los Angeles as one of his goals. This indicates that he desires to move west, to light out for the territory and achieve freedom from his life in the South. He continues to compare the respective natures of his and Billy's lives, piecing together the latter's life from "word-of-mouth" reports from family members, "bits of gossip from home folk." At one moment Billy is

> in New York, now in California, one month wounded in a Detroit hospital, another month married to a woman romanced during a repossession mission outside Baton Rouge.

Billy's life is movement, and in this regard he can be seen in the same light as Doc Craft and Big Boy Davis. His life is composed of the stuff that makes for storytelling, namely, living and moving.

William's life operates differently. He notes

> I moved westward, but only as far as Chicago, and settled in against this city's soul-killing winter winds. I purged from my speech all traces of the South and warmed myself by the fire of my thirty-year plan.

What is striking about this passage is that William, not having found employment in Los Angeles in the west, ends up in Chicago. This suggests that his life still operates within the machinery of ambition. He experiences Chicago's "soul-killing winter winds," and in order to survive, he begins to delude himself, erecting a caricature of a man energized by a "text" known as the "thirty year plan." He ceases to live in favor of dreaming. He erases all traces of his Southern heritage in order to begin "moving up" in the credit department of a Chicago department store.

After he meets his fiancée Chelseia, a "family-backed, efficiencyminded girl," he attempts to move closer to becoming a Chicago "native," not realizing that many Afro-Americans in Chicago originally migrated to the city from the South. His alienation is exemplified by his remarks:

> From time to time, trudging through the winter slush on Michigan, I would pause to explore a reflection of myself in a store window. By my fifth year in Chicago, I became satisfied that no one could have mistaken me for a refugee from the South.

Evidenced in this passage is the fact that William no longer possesses a legitimate sense of self: that is, he looks at himself and sees only a reflection. Moreover, it is significant that he looks in a store window, for this symbolizes his entrapment in the marketplace. In this regard he can, again, be compared to Ellison's Invisible Man, who feels that he has lived his invisibility "surrounded by mirrors of hard, distorting glass." Just as Ellison's narrator shuns any indication of his Southern background, declining the offer of pork chops and grits in a Harlem restaurant in favor of thick, acidic orange juice, William decides to accept the image in the store window as fact, playing a role that alienates him from his past and makes it impossible for him to see himself as he really is.

Billy's arrival in Chicago endangers William's illusion. Here, we can see another confluence in the narrative, for Billy, as William's double or alter ego, opposes in binary fashion the caricature that William has created. William is forced, through a confrontation with Billy, to confront his past. Whereas he can admire the singularity of his reflection, an image shaped by his innocence and ambition,

Billy's presence forces him to confront the flesh and bones of his life. Upon meeting Billy in the Chicago bar where Billy spins the story of his life (and deaths), William notices that Billy's suit is smeared with blood and dirt. Though he is disgusted by the picture Billy presents, what William fails to understand is that the "eerily green" stains represent the vitality and reality of Billy's life. The manmade fabric of the suit, which is black like an undertaker's, symbolizes the materialistic, hollow lifestyle of the uninitiated. The blood and dirt transform the suit, baptize it, and thus Billy lives even in "death," though William chooses to ignore this symbol.

Fittingly, Billy tells William the story of how he lost his eye, which, as he suggests, is also the story of how he dies and rises from the dead. As William listens in disbelief, Billy tells him,

> It was a hard-hearted woman down in Eufaula, Alabama, that done it, a widow-woman name of Miss Ruby Watson. I was laid up at her place, tired of runnin' the road for Mr. Floyd. She done root work, said she was gonna make me smart and set me up in business.

When Billy discovers that the "white pills" he has been taking have no effect on his intellect because they are nothing more than "jackrabbit shit," he confronts Miss Ruby. Having ignored all of Mr. Floyd's pleas for him to resume his job recovering defaulted autos, Billy soon realizes he is trapped in a delusion:

> She had me. She knowed it. I knowed it. She sat down on the bed and commenced to stroke my chest. She say, "Now ain't you a sight? Don't even know whichaway is up. But you my sweetmeat now, and there ain't a damn thing you can do about it."

In a move that represents his movement from innocence to insight, Billy confronts death.

> I knowed what I had to do. I gived the gun to her. I made her point it at my head. I told Miss Ruby, 'Me, I'm just dumb enough to believe it ain't even loaded. And if it is, it won't be the first time I been dead.'

Here Billy places his life in the hands of experience, knowing that however the scenario turns out, he will come away from it victorious for he has chosen to die on his own terms. This allows him to place his confidence in the cradle of his experience where he knows that his "death" will result in the creation of a newer, wiser self as his older, innocent self is slain.

Skillful storyteller that he is, Billy inserts a pause in order to allow the tale's suspense to achieve its full dramatic tension. Unaware of this technique, William's naiveté and impatience cause him to intrude on the narrative. In an attempt to provide the tale's ending, William says, "So you called her bluff, got your eye shot out, but proved you were a man." He is wrong, of course, because he does not understand the inner symbolism of the tale. Appropriately, Billy corrects William: "Naw, she pulled the trigger and killed me. That's how come I'm back on the road for Mr. Floyd today." Although William discounts the tale as a lie, in actuality, Billy has recounted his decision to choose freedom and reality over self-delusion and subservience. The tale is the representative anecdote of Billy's life as a "dead" man. Far from being a tale that illustrates Billy's macho inclinations, the tale presents his need to be free, to be able to move at his own whim and to live and die on his own terms. His decision to go back "on the road" for Mr. Floyd represents the fulfillment of his *Wanderlust,* not his subservience. It is Floyd who asks Billy to return during the latter's visit to Alabama, and although we question the ethics of Billy's employment, Floyd's act is significant because it reverses Southern race rituals. Billy's decision to return is based on his own needs not Floyd's. Floyd's business is a means for Billy, not an end. Were William a good listener, he would be transported by the tale since his situation entitles him, rather than empowers him, over his life. However, his adherence to the mythology of self he has created does not allow him to hear the tale's inner message: "Live life's terms but never accept them."

It is also interesting to note here the qualitative difference between Billy's tale and William's generic versions of Billy's adventures at the beginning of the story. Though it has a rough, comic quality, the tale, as Billy presents it, suggests the tragic lyricism and drama of the blues. In this sense, Billy does indeed rise from the dead, for inherent in his ability to tell a story is the process of regeneration. In relating his regeneration, his story is *regenerating,* for its relationship to the blues offers

> a language that connotes a world of transcience, instability, hard luck, brutalizing work, lost love, minimal security, and enduring human wit and resourcefulness in the face of . . . discouragements. Blues language enjoins one to accept hard luck, because without it there is 'no luck at all.'

Here we can draw parallels between Billy and Ellison's Trueblood. Though Billy is continually involved in repossessing defaulted cars from other blacks, he is valued by Mr. Floyd, who refers to him as "son." Like Trueblood, who tells Norton and the Invisible Man, "The nigguhs up at the school don't like me, but the white folks treats me fine," Billy exists both inside AND outside the tradition. Billy's skill as a storyteller makes him part of the blues tradition, yet his employment for Mr. Floyd places him outside of William's notion of literacy—which, in terms of his mode of freedom, makes Billy's life illegitimate. Moreover, Trueblood's assertion that "I ain't nobody but myself and ain't nothin I can do but let whatever is gonna happen, happen," squares directly with Billy's willingness to allow Mis Ruby to hold the .22 to his head. And just as Trueblood's despair induces him to sing the blues, Billy's remembrances of his life on the chain gang cause him to hum "snatches of songs, remembered from that time" which sustain him.

Finally, though, it is the manner in which William attempts to "package" Billy for his in-laws which makes Billy analogous to Trueblood. Just as the Invisible Man says of Trueblood and "his kind" that "We were trying to lift them up and they, like Trueblood, did everything it seemed to pull us down," William attempts to "lift" Billy

up by remaking him in one of his business suits and a pair of dark-blue sunshades.

The encounter that follows is the central incident of the story and chronicles the conjoining of Billy and William as parts of a whole. In the process, however, William's status as narrator of the story attempts to subvert Billy's presence in the scenario itself until William's authorial control makes his point of view ascendant. William's failure as a storyteller is marked by his inability to "make his case" for his desire to be considered apart from Billy. Rather than offering new insight, William's story of Billy's encounter with his in-laws is designed to explain the breaking of a family bond while simultaneously validating Billy's position. William begins this section of the story by immediately attempting to refute one of Billy's charges:

> It is certainly not true, though Billy maintains otherwise, that my in-laws and Chelseia ordered him out of their home. What happened that evening with the Raymonds is still fresh in my mind. They were civil to Billy, though a little bit wary about why he wore blue sunshades.

William's story, then, is precipitated by one of Billy's "lies." Throughout the story William attempts to set up his listeners (and the reader as well) to believe that everything that comes out of Billy's mouth is a lie. But, he misses the point. Billy's tales are not completely grounded in the truth, but Billy's skill in telling the tales makes them valuable. Moreover, because he has lived a "full" life—having learned the relationship between geography and sexual rhythms, the economics of migrant living, and the political assertiveness of bus-depot graffiti in various parts of the country—Billy's tales are praise-poems, the telling of which he has earned. William, by virtue of the static, deluded life he lives, is unable to comprehend the substance of Billy's "lies," concerned as he is with "proper" behavior, behavior more imagined than real.

Upon shaving, bathing, and dressing in one of William's business suits, Billy is "completely transformed." He resembles Ellison's Rinehart because of the sunshades which are meant to shield his bad eye from "inspection." Like the narrator in *Invisible Man,* William is the one who benefits from his cousin's disguise as "a publicity-shy banker." Such a ruse veils William's past as it attempts to transform Billy's. Under the fiction he creates around Billy's life, William is able to maintain his status as a "native" Chicagoan and thus remain in his in-laws good graces. Through Billy's invisibility, it is possible for William to maintain the pseudo-visibility he has attained and continue his self-deception. At first, the evening goes smoothly, with Billy and William successfully parrying off any of the Raymonds' inquiries into the former's past and present. However, it soon becomes evident that Mr. Raymond, a retired redcap forced, because of his race, to accept such employment even with two academic degrees, and Billy are "locked in [an] unholy union" which induces both to tell stories. Chelseia and her mother's discomfort, as Mr. Raymond commences to spin tales of his past, suggest that they, like William, are caught up in a "manufactured" image of their lives. The fact that Mrs. Raymond especially dislikes her husband's reminiscences denotes that, at one time, they, like William, were of lower circumstances and that, a good portion of their hard work to "achieve the good life" has been to erase all traces of their past. The "unhealthy chemical reaction" in Mr. Raymond, which William asserts is caused by Billy, is in actuality the older man's realization that it has been his life as a redcap, a life where he achieved a literacy far and above that exemplified by his two degrees, that has given his life its meaning. His relationship with Billy arises from his recognition of the kinship between men who have been forced to meet life's terms head-on while accepting themselves, affirming their existence. Thus they know the same redcap's escapades and share in the singing of a "salacious jingle."

The evening's pretense is finally destroyed when Billy, caught up in the excitement of finding a "kindred" spirit, removes the blue sunshades hiding his injured eye. Realizing that his imagined self is rapidly deflated as Billy's true self emerges, William attempts to "save the situation." After failing to convince Billy that they should go, William lies in an attempt to retain control of a worsening situation: "A red-neck down in South Carolina shot out Billy's eye. Billy is too proud to speak of it." It is too late, however, for Mrs. Raymond and Chelseia have already been repulsed by Billy's true appearance. Seeing this, Billy becomes enraged and takes measures by which he can regain control of his own sense of self and affirm his existence. He breaks the rhetorical kinship with William and through his ability as a storyteller, attempts to reconstruct a more legitimate relationship.

In relating these events, William's innocence and lack of awareness are evident. He claims that "The rest of the evening has been clouded by his lies" and that "Billy has maintained that I turned on him. The man is a notorious liar and likes to keep the family jumpy." We can assume that these remarks are directed at William's "implied" listener and that they are acceptable, as well as honorable, in the eyes and ears of his audience. But if we consider McPherson's relationship with the implied reader, William's remarks take on a different coloration. Rather than acting as the mere rendering of events making up a bad evening, William's story unveils him—makes him visible underneath the rhetorical screen his language creates. Hence, when Billy extricates himself from William's grasp—the grasp he has on both his body and his story—he is actually loosening himself from the constraints of the rhetorical kinship imposed upon him. When William lies about Billy's damaged eye and Billy responds with "Bullshit," William attempts to blame Billy for dissolving their family ties: "By this one word, and through his subsequent actions, Billy himself completely severed what was left of our family bond." But it is the rhetorical kinship that Billy severs, not the actual family relationship he and William share. As Billy strips off William's suit, tie, and shirt, exposing in the process all the scars acquired on his travels, he frees himself from the image imposed upon him by William's imprisonment within "the good life." When he boasts, "These here come from runnin' round the country. . . . And I'ma keep runnin till the pork chops get thicker and they give me two dollars more," Billy is actually asserting the intention to live his life around the ideal

of action, of movement. This is also an assertion of freedom for, as the scars suggest, freedom is won at great cost and borne with great pride. In this sense, William's plea for Billy to tell the truth is in fact a request for Billy to assume again the role he has created for him.

The story Billy subsequently tells of his adventures with Inner City Jones, where he lost his eye during the battle over a defaulted automobile, is valuable not only because of the truth it represents. It gains additional resonance because Billy's telling of the tale allows him to gain authorial control of his life. It is necessary for Billy to tell the tale, for the image he presents, stripped of William's suit, with the various scars in full view, must be suffused with a story to make his image clear in the minds of his audience. Knowing that he is "nobody but himself," Billy realizes that the costs of not telling his tale are greater than any he could incur from relating it. As he tells the tale, we see not only his ability to capture his audience's attention, as evident in his use of the glasses and silverware to set the scene, but also his code of honor as he declines the opportunity to "bad-talk" Inner City Jones's reputation as a marksman. In addition, Billy's tale shows him to be more detective than street killer: "I knowed that Earline, [Inner City Jones's] old lady, was up here in Harvey and he only felt safe with his head up under her dress. So I bought me a one-way bus ticket." Unlike William's version of Billy's tales, where they become "lies," here we can see Billy as a thinking, courageous individual capable of deductive logic. He closes off the tale by producing the proof of his conquest; the blood-stained keys to the Impala. As he produces them, he calmly states, "One of us knowed he had to die. . . . Next time it might be me." So spellbound is Billy's audience that they do not stop to think of Billy's tale as a lie; nor do they wonder if the keys Billy throws on the table will start the Impala he cites in his tale. The tale has achieved its desired effect: It has established Billy's true identity and substance. This is evident when Chelseia shouts at Billy, calling him a "common street nigger." Not only does she make a class distinction (which is, at root, more of an imagined reality than a fact); she strips away the evening's pretense as it exists in her mind and "names" Billy for who and what he is.

Delving into another McPherson story for a definition, we find the scale of the act of naming here. Looking to **"Elbow Room"** at the exchange between the narrator and Paul, a white man married to a black woman, we find Paul asking the question, "What's a nigger?" The narrator replies, "A descendant of Proteus, an expression of the highest form of freedom." This response, which creates a fresh definition, is useful for it describes both Billy and William. Again, the relationship between Billy, William, and Ellison's Rinehart is apparent. Though we must be careful not to take the similarities too far, Billy, as half of a whole, represents the freedom Rinehart's mobility allows while William, literate and articulate, represents the dilemma of Rinehart's existence; that is, he lacks a solid image that would allow him to live on his own terms rather than others' expectations. In the same manner that Invisible Man prepares to fight Hambro because he thinks it is expected of him, William fights a continuous battle with his southern heritage largely because he feels it is expected of him by people like the Raymonds. Thus, when Chelseia "names" Billy, she implicates William as well. Billy perceptively confirms this when he says, "And this here's my cousin, William." This, once and for all, links Billy and William in a legitimate kinship. As mentioned above, William, since he is now "one" with Billy, must choose to affirm or deny that bond. He chooses the latter option, again asking Billy to "tell the truth" in order to reestablish his own damaged image. When Billy laughs, choosing to affirm his own existence and, by implication, his kinship with William by shouting "God bless Mr. Floyd!" William knows that he must follow through on his choice by asking Billy to leave. The story ends with William's claim that he and Billy are still "tight." But to be able to say that, he must refute the "lie" that Billy is unwelcome in his home. William's pronouncement, "But it is not true, contrary to rumors circulating in my family, that Billy Renfro is unwelcome in my home," suggests that he is again addressing a listener, and we can assume that this explanation, like the others, is acceptable to that, listener. This last section underscores the implication that William is as "dead" as Billy, with the exception that he has no recourse to regeneration. Alienated from his family, with only his ambition, his "charted course," to placate him, William is more slave than freeman. Unlike the Invisible Man, who finds a "warm hole" where he discovers his identity and his voice, William settles in Chicago, "against the winter whippings of [the] City's winds," the symbol of his alienation.

"The Story of a Dead Man" explains the dialectics of invisibility which McPherson conceives in terms of "lies" and "truth." The relationship between these terms has to do with the dialectical distinction we can make between storytelling and testimony (as opposed to "testifying"). The difference lies in the regenerative powers inherent in the former, while the latter, depends for its success upon a "willing" audience. Indeed, a defendant cannot prove his innocence without an audience, a jury, or judge, willing to be taken in by the ability to manipulate facts, which is where William's talent lies. But this talent is also the source of his self-delusion. Billy, on the other hand, tells and retells the same story—the story of his death and rebirth—and in doing so, continually affirms his existence. His talent lies in his ability to tell his story to an unwilling audience and, by manipulating the tension of his tale, force his listener to accept his existence on the terms he himself sets. **"The Story of a Dead Man"** is unique among McPherson's stories in that it is concerned with the narrator's search for a name with which he can live. It accomplishes this in the guise of a family testimony, one which draws its power from language and rhetoric. What it suggests is that the careful reader can discover within the "exciting death" of storytelling an awareness of complexity that forms a complete vision. (pp. 565-77)

Herman Beavers, "I Yam What You Is and You Is What I Yam: Rhetorical Invisibility in James Alan McPherson's 'The Story of a Dead Man'," in Callaloo, *Vol. 9, No. 4, Fall, 1986, pp. 565-77.*

Edith Blicksilver (essay date Winter 1987-Summer 1988)

[*In the essay below, Blicksilver examines McPherson's depiction of interracial relationships in "Gold Coast," "Hue and Cry," and "Elbow Room."*]

During a question-and-answer session at Iowa State University in March 1980 after Ralph Ellison talked about "The Concept of Race in American Literature," a student asked if miscegenation was a necessary ingredient of racial integration. Ellison responded by saying:

> I don't think that any of us Americans wants to lose his ethnic identity. . . . The existence of such strong Negro-American influences in the society, the style, the way things are done, would indicate that there's never been the desire to lose that. . . . There are individual decisions which will be made by a few people. . . . There is enough of a hold of tradition, of ways of cooking, of ways of just relaxing, which comes right out of the family circle, to keep us in certain groups.

The individual decisions involving interracial relationships and marital concerns preoccupy modern blacks and figure prominently in three short stories of James Alan McPherson. **"Gold Coast," "Hue and Cry,"** and **"Elbow Room"** will be discussed in this paper through an analysis of the personality characteristics; motivations; actions and coping techniques of those involved; the influence of the geographical setting and historical period; parental reactions; society's acceptance or condemnation; and the outcome.

Because Ellison is a generation older than McPherson, their versions of black/white relationships were influenced by different young adult experiences, the former's taking place during the Depression and Second World War, the latter's during the 1960s civil rights movement. McPherson's background is essential because his works are semi-autobiographical. Born in Savannah, Georgia in 1943, the writer attended all-black Morris Brown College in Atlanta and Morgan State in Baltimore where he was chosen by a Harvard Law School recruiter for admission. Graduating in 1964, he never practiced law, choosing instead to become a writer and winning a *Reader's Digest* prize for his second story.

At Harvard, the setting for **"Gold Coast"** and **"Hue and Cry,"** the sensitive Southerner together with fellow blacks went through an adjustment period, frequently a debilitating struggle—among blacks, between whites and blacks, men and women, Northerners and Southerners, and poor and rich—for status, power and love. Later, while, ironically, recruiting for Harvard at a black southern college, McPherson describes talking to a student more insecure than he himself had been. Finally, losing patience, the writer asserted: "I went to a white law school and I survived it. . . . I'm still sane." But, the student, he continues, "sat looking at me, and his eyes were so close to accusation that I almost felt compelled to add, 'I think.' "

McPherson taught at the University of California at Santa Cruz, the University of Virginia, and now teaches creative writing at Iowa State, admitting that he experienced discomfort at the Charlottesville school where black men often are viewed as janitors or retainers. He felt like a trapped outsider, similar to some of the characters in his stories, only remaining in Virginia because of his former wife's urgings. Now single, his young daughter's education will be subsidized by a 1981 MacArthur Foundation grant. In 1961 McPherson became a contributing editor to *Atlantic* where a version of **"Gold Coast"** first appeared and won the best short story prize a year earlier. He was awarded the Pulitzer Prize in 1978 for *Elbow Room,* his second short story collection; the first, *Hue and Cry,* was published nine years before.

The historical period of all three works is the 1960s which McPherson calls "a crazy time."

> Opportunities seemed to materialize . . . and if you were lucky . . . you could become a doctor, a lawyer . . . an engineer. Achieving these things was easy if you applied yourself.
>
> But a very hard price was extracted . . . because certain institutional forces . . . threw together black peasants and white aristocrats . . . people who were peasants/frightened, threatened, and felt inferior, . . . there were idealists and opportunists, people who seemed to want to be exploited and people who delighted in exploiting them. Old identities were thrown off. . . . People from backgrounds like my own, those from the South, while content with the new opportunities, found themselves trying to make sense of the growing diversity of friendships . . . of the differences between their values and those of their parents . . . thinking of themselves in new and different ways. We never wanted to be 'white,' but we never wanted to be 'black' either. And . . . there was the feeling we could be whatever we wanted. But . . . unless we . . . accepted some provisional identity . . . for defining and stabilizing what it was we wanted to be . . . , this was an individual problem, and . . . one had to go inside one's self.

McPherson's experiences shaped many of his stories, and **"Gold Coast"** narrates a young man's maturing process during a summer job as a janitor similar to one the writer had in an apartment house near Harvard Square. Because Rob, the youthful protagonist, believes he is "gifted," his writing is going well, and he has "the urge to acquire . . . and youth besides . . . ," he finds himself a rich white girl to love. McPherson's tale deals in part with the tension between white and black, in its delineation of the course of the affair between the narrator and his girlfriend Jean.

Rob's youthful optimism is evident. He is ambitious, self-confident, dreaming of future success, "lulled by sweet anticipation of that time when his potential would suddenly be realized." He egotistically believes he can immortalize any of the tenants with the "magic" of his pen. Loving a white woman is an extension of his self-esteem.

Another janitor Sullivan, dislikes his choice of a white mistress because she is not a flower child and "liberal people will tolerate two interracial hippies more than they will an intelligent, serious-minded mixed couple." The former

liaison is dismissed because they are inferior folk deserving each other and the contempt of both races, but the latter proses a threat to racial purity. Sullivan, bigoted and hostile to those better off than himself, questions Robert about Jean's refined breeding and philosophizes that "the Colonel's Lady and Nelly O'Grady are sisters under the skin." The self-assured younger man replies: "that's why you have to maintain a distinction by marrying the Colonel's Lady." Rob's optimism reflects the changes in interpersonal contacts taking place, among young people, across race lines. These interactions became broader and deeper as individuals shared educational opportunities and traveled to liberated social climates. But provincial New England was not the setting in which their affair could flourish and survive.

The turmoil that Rob and Jean experience due to the intimidation from the community are overwhelming. At parties, blacks attempt to enchant Jean "with skillful dances and hip vocabulary, believing her to be community property," while she remains politely aloof. The affair ends after a subway incident where "one side of the car was black and tense and hating and the whites tense and hating on the other side. . . . " There was not enough room on either side for them to sit and they would not separate; and so they stood, holding on to a steel post "feeling all the eyes . . . ," and "there was nothing left to say."

An interracial couple creates a political and an emotional reaction, fostered by black consciousness and white racism, which makes it different from a normal love affair. Too many implications cannot be blocked out, and during the stressful subway incident communication and understanding are replaced by defeated, silent acceptance. Rob and Jean do not have an intense enough commitment to each other in order to challenge the critical value system of their New England environment. They are unable to find the strength to overcome society's judgmental hostility which destroys their love. They permit intolerance and aggressiveness to shatter their relationship, becoming victims of cultural arrogance.

Before these "social forces" disrupted their love affair, Rob pridefully internalizes looking back on the episode, that Jean "belonged to me and not to the race . . . I did not have to wear a beard or be especially hip or ultra-Ivy Leagueish. I did not have to smoke pot or supply her with it, or be for any other cause at all except myself." Rob's defensiveness is contrasted with his pity for and condescension toward Sullivan, the old, worn-out Irishman. But their relationship is different from that of the young black writer with his white girlfriend. Given the widespread historical attitude on the part of American society that blacks are inferior, it is not difficult to understand the complexity of Rob's reaction to his role in Jean's life. He faces a new situation for which his past has given him little guidance, so he charters new territory in exploring how to carry on this intimate contact. Internal stress results for both young people, but it is less difficult for a member of a dominant majority to adjust than for a sensitive individual from an oppressed minority. Jean's superior social and financial situation is an additional hurdle her janitor-lover faces.

Rob's illusions of instant success, his naive belief in his "boundless perception" and most importantly, his self-deception in trying to ignore his race are shattered. His fantasies that an interracial couple can find easy happiness are replaced by a maturing reality. As the narrator observes looking back on his younger self, "In those days I had forgotten that I was first of all a black . . . ." But after the relationship disintegrates, Rob's character growth is reflected by his changing attitude toward both Sullivan and Jean. He is more compassionate toward the old janitor who, although outwardly a failure is "well-read in history, philosophy, literature and law." With youthful resiliency, after "that desperate look had finally gone somewhere deep inside," Rob can love another girl, and at the end of the summer his values change. He abandons his superficial idea of happiness personified by a girl and a stereo. He shares a common bond of brotherhood with Sullivan. Both have suffered loss; he, Jean's love, the Irishman, his dog. When the young black man moves away, he places Jean's picture under some clothes in a trunk that he does not plan to open for quite some time. With the elderly man's fate awaiting him, Rob matures enough to realize that "nothing really matters except not being old and being alive and having potential to dream about, and not being alone."

McPherson's other stories **"Hue and Cry"** and **"Elbow Room"** also depict the dilemma confronting the displaced black intellectual during the 1960s in America, showing the tensions between brotherhood and separateness, between the emotional and the rational, especially where explosive interracial interactions are involved. He delineates minorities attracted to the power that whites symbolize and repelled by their racist record. Even lovers faced confrontations of bigoted injustice which vitiated American life, and nullified the attempts of those seeking to ignore or overcome ethnic barriers.

McPherson is not a revolutionary, however, and he deals with people and feelings, not masses nor slogans. His racially mixed couples, in particular, are drawn with sympathy and with respect for their suffering. Langston Hughes once wrote that "the relationships between mixed couples is always more graciously accepted by the viewers when related by a white author than by a Negro," but McPherson's artistic sensitivity will not offend readers of any color; the climate of opinion has changed.

The last two stories tell about affairs of black women with white men and the love relationship between Margot Payne and Eric Carney in **"Hue and Cry"** shows a male/female power struggle, also evident in Paul Frost's magnetic attraction for Virginia Valentine, in **"Elbow Room,"** resulting in a shaky marriage. All four young people fear entrapment and identity loss. McPherson's thematic development in these works is to show that some interracial couples are motivated to become lovers because it is a source of approval by their peer group; i.e., among so-called "hip" types and/or nonconformist liberals, much of whose behavior is a reaction or protest against anything associated with the conservative establishment. The affairs of Rob and Jean, that of Margot and Eric, and

the marriage of Paul and Virginia can be interpreted, in part, by exploring the individuality of each character.

Cleveland-born Margot, for example, is a studious non-conformist from early girlhood, who rebels against her mother's admonition to make her intelligence as imperceptible as possible because black men would resent it and her. She blames her family for teaching that life's greatest goal is smug security, and at her Ivy League college she decides to have a love affair with a New Hampshire Quaker idealist, clinging to him even after she admits that the relationship had become stagnant. Vulnerable Margot yearns to be loved as a woman and not as a symbolic moral issue. "I don't know," she says to Eric, "if I'm a person to you or an idea." After a stress-filled trip to his New Hampshire home, Margot tells her lover that "back there, I felt like a damn cause."

In Eric's case, McPherson implies that it is unlikely that he will marry Margot because his primary attraction to her is his desire to make a social contribution to better race relations. Margot senses his self-righteous attitude which adds an additional burden to the relationship. She realizes that this idealistic Quaker is trying to impress blacks with how liberal he is, and she resents being used to foster his missionary zeal. The young woman is too independent to be grateful, hardly a prideful attribute.

With so much potential, the girl starts losing her nerve due to social and parental condemnation. She no longer is able to summon that shrug of independent action which has set her above the cults and causes of campus life during the '60s when the events transpired. She drops out of school, dragged down in a tragic round-robin of mistakes and misfortunes such as sexual encounters, described in tones of sardonic understatement and controlled irony. Margot enjoys manipulating awe-struck black men such as Eric's roommate, Jerry. She taunts him when the young man boasts about his affair with an Anglo-Saxon: "Next time she calls, before you go running over, ask her to describe your face." Jerry becomes insulted because his girl is the liberated daughter of three generations of money invested in his car and in his clothes.

In the past, according to a study by Irving R. Stuart and Lawrence E. Abt entitled *Interracial Marriage,* black men married white women far more than white men married black women. The explanation is that the white woman "exchanges her superior class position over the black man for his personal traits, superior to those of white men available to her." However, because historically white men have had sexual access to black slave women without permanent commitments, they do not so often marry black women. In addition, because black men have been barred by law and by custom from intimate associates with white women, they find this relationship an exotic one and marriages result even though the female's class position and personality characteristics are inferior to available black women. In the case of Jerry, McPherson implies that the epitome of being a real "stud" is to show off a white mistress.

Margot believes that her affair with Eric is different from Jerry's indifferent liaisons with white women and that they will get married eventually. After all, Eric assures her that only people over thirty-five do not approve of their courtship. Slowly the affair disintegrates, and Margot loses her self-confidence where men are concerned. In a last attempt to find security, she accepts the devoted attention of a fellow black named Charles. Actually, Margot never appreciates his good qualities until he ceases to remain faithful and turns into a playboy. In desperation, she becomes another of Jerry's easy conquests, and the story ends with Margot begging Charles to marry her because she is spiritually wounded by Eric's final rejection. She was used as a source of private purgation by the white man, mistaking exploitation for love.

For both Eric and Paul, an interracial relationship represents a cleansing process. Paul is attracted to Virginia, in part, because "he felt the need to redeem the family": the narrator saw "dead Indians living in his eyes." Both idealistic men are Quakers and come from small towns in New Hampshire and Kansas with few black contacts. Both are rebelling against conservative middle-class families, who oppose the prospect of black daughters-in-law. When Eric tells his parents that he is bringing home "a special girl," his father chooses to go hunting, while his mother politely serves them tea, "close to tears."

McPherson explores what motivates a person of a particular culture to cross racial boundaries and have an affair or marry outside his group. Eric and Paul were brought up within a parochial social setting with parental prejudice instilled toward different ethnic groups, but after going to college, both young men became liberated during the 1960s and rejected the preconceived, stereotypical opinions of their families. They are motivated, in part, to love black women because of profound guilt feelings resulting from the physical exploitation which was historically characteristic of the sexual relationships between whites and blacks. They are seeking affection from a member of a former slave society to redress this abuse.

McPherson's gift for characterization and his mastery of dialogue are evident in **"Elbow Room"** as he describes Virginia's attempts to make the marriage work, sketching her personality more thoroughly than any of his other women with the exception of Margot by working hard on every nuance of her individuality. During the 1960s, as McPherson himself witnessed, blacks left southern cultural pockets moving north and west as did Virginia who

> had come out of Warren, Tennessee . . . on the crest of jailbreaking peasants. To people like her, imprisoned for generations, . . . the outside world seemed . . . full of sweet choices. Many could not cope with freedom. . . . Some committed suicide. Others, seeking safety, rushed into other prisons. But a few like Virginia rose and ranged far and wide in flight, like aristocratic eagles seeking high, free peaks on which to build their nests.

Virginia herself is exposed to different cultures as a Peace Corps volunteer, living in Ceylon, India, Kenya, Egypt, and Syria. Returning to America, she leaves the confines of provincial Tennessee and after marrying Paul in San Francisco, recreates the cosmopolitan environment in

their home that Virginia had experienced abroad, with friends who are Chicanos, Asians, French, Brazilians, and black and white Americans.

An interracial relationship invites attack from society, encouraging people to reveal their prejudices in a self-righteous manner. It is easier for Paul and Virginia to be accepted by friends in a cosmopolitan city than by parents in a small town because it doesn't threaten strangers who don't have to make commitments. On the other hand, adjustments are necessary when the members of this marriage share the home. Some families, McPherson observes, accept and love the young people while others merely tolerate an unchangeable situation.

Seeking parental acceptance of their union is difficult, and Paul's parents do not attend the wedding. Virginia's kinfolk, after failing to dissuade her, fly to San Francisco from Tennessee bringing country-cured hams and a wedding gift sewn by the bride's full-blooded Cherokee grandmother. Virginia's father with the facial features of an Indian, feels ill at ease during the reception. His face reveals "fear and pride and puzzlement" because he has assumed that "color was the highest bond," having come from a long line of family. Virginia, however, "has moved away from that small living room in which conventional opinion mattered."

Both families fear racial pollution, preferring ethnic purity. Fernando Henriques in *Children of Conflict* suggests that those hostile to miscegenation are influenced by the belief which originated when societies were divided into communities based upon self-sufficiency and isolation. To project the values of primeval hunters and food-gatherers into the modern world as a justification for racist theories is challenged by several of McPherson's characters.

Virginia, more worldly, forceful and self-confident than Margot, has a better chance of overcoming parental and group hostility because Paul wants to marry her, and the young woman, impressed with the patience and faith of the Indians, shows an outward display of strength that masks vulnerability. When she introduces Paul, she says, " '. . . meet my fiance, and if you don't like it you can go to hell!'," watching closely for reactions, with her dark eyes saying " 'I hurt easily.' " She has to convince herself that she is desirable, not secondary to a white woman.

Paul's father, as a good businessman, believes that "his son had made a bad investment that was bound to be corrected as soon as Virginia's stock declined." Unlike Eric, Paul courageously defies his family, and faces social slander, but he pays a price for his decision to marry the black woman. He cuts himself off from the company of most white males, denounces his father as "a moral coward . . . struggling and abysmally along, with large brown eyes desperately asking, 'Who am I?' " Since he is not socially sterile, Paul is aware of people's reactions, and giving up family ties is emotionally draining.

In a supermarket lot, a carload of children call Paul a nigger and an incident at a New Year's Eve Mass proves his loyalty. Virginia is wearing her usual mug's cap, popularized by movie gangsters in the forties, when a voice behind them breaks the church stillness: " 'Young man, if you're

too *drunk* to take your hat off in church get out! . . . ' "
The usually gentle Paul turns fiercely toward the old man
and retorts, " 'This is my wife. If you don't like what she's
wearing, that's tough!' " He then puts his arm around Virginia.

Finally, when both sets of parents learn that the young
wife is pregnant, they start making conciliatory gestures.
Her Tennessee folk propose treasured family names for
the baby; Paul's mother sends money for a bassinet and
hints that "more than European bloodlines ran in her
veins."

The trauma of Paul's father's refusal to acknowledge the
baby she will soon have provokes Virginia to speak freely
with the narrator about her own self-identity:

> I'm black. I've accepted myself as that. But
> didn't I make some elbow room though? She
> tapped her temple. . . . I mean up here! . . .
> When times get tough, *anybody* can pass for
> white. Niggers been doing that for centuries . . .
> But . . . wouldn't it of been something to be a
> nigger that could relate to white and black and
> everything else in the world out of a self as big
> as the world is?

Since Virginia feels that their relationship is contributing
to better race relations, her attitude solidifies the marriage.
But as the black partner, the young woman is more defensive because of the widespread historical attitude on the
part of the white society that negroes are inferior. However, the hostility from the outside world brings Virginia and
Paul closer together. They are individualists, not conform-
ists, able to cope with parental and community rejection.
McPherson implies that a person who doesn't have to depend upon kinship or group approval is more likely to get
involved in an interracial relationship than one who has
to depend upon familial and societal acceptance and conform to their thinking. A peripheral personality doesn't
need external reinforcement.

Margot feels that Eric is having the liaison because he is
committed to a liberal philosophy, and at first the affair
is an exotic one. But since the obstacles come from within
the relationship, it soon disintegrates, since neither person
has the courage or the strength to overcome these problems. As a result, the romantic involvement of Eric with
Margot and of Jean with Rob ended. Virginia has a better
chance of overcoming parental hostility because Paul has
married her, and the birth of a son helps heal the breach
between two sets of parents. Her search for a more inclusive, universal identity is emphasized at the story's conclusion when the narrator admonishes Virginia, "For the
sake of your child, don't be black. Be more of a classic
kind of nigger." The woman takes his advice and later
sends a picture of her new-born baby with the inscription,
"He will be a *classic* kind of nigger." The photo shows a
brown baby in his Kansas grandmother's arms; the grandfather looks serious; Paul, "defiant, has a familiar intensity
about his face"; Virginia "smiling triumphantly," is still
wearing her mug's cap. She never compromises with her
ideals, or with her unique personality. The narrator pays
tribute to her as "a magic woman," and this final scene

symbolizes McPherson's aspirations for greater interracial
harmony.

The author writes that the model he was depicting in
"Elbow Room" was epitomized by Albion Tourgee's argument in the *Plessy vs. Ferguson* case in 1896 interpreting
the Fourteenth Amendment. Its purpose was to "create a
new citizenship of the United States, embracing new
rights, privileges and immunities, . . . in a *new* manner
controlled by *new* authority, having a *new* scope and extent, depending on national authority for its existence and
looking to national power for its preservation." McPherson believes that Virginia and her baby embody the best
ideals of this representative American, which he states
"can be achieved with or without intermarriage, . . . a
product of culture and not of race." His people in **"Elbow
Room"** support the belief that "most of us are products
of much more complex cultural influences than we suppose" and McPherson agrees with Ellison that the identity
of the black American is "a blending of both cultures."

In all three of his stories, **"Gold Coast," "Hue and Cry,"**
and **"Elbow Room,"** McPherson describes these love relationships from the viewpoint of a black observer. In the
last narration, he plays the role of a family friend engaged
in a battle of his own to free himself of the "caste curtains"
that he is aware has resulted in "resegregating all imagination." A recurrent theme in his second tale deals with the

---

McPherson on being a writer:

[I am] a writer, a person who has to learn to live with contradictions, frustrations, and doubts. Still, I have [a] quote
that sustains me, . . . from a book called *The Tragic Sense
of Life*, by a Spanish philosopher named Miguel de Unamuno. In a chapter called "Don Quixote Today," Unamuno
asks, "How is it that among the words the English have borrowed from our language there is to be found this word *desperado*?" And he answers himself: "It is despair, and despair alone, that begets heroic hope, absurd hope, mad
hope."

I believe that the United States is complex enough to induce
that sort of despair that begets heroic hope. I believe that
if one can experience its diversity, touch a variety of its people, laugh at its craziness, distill wisdom from its tragedies,
and attempt to synthesize all this inside oneself without
going crazy, one will have earned the right to call oneself
"citizen of the United States," even though one is not quite
a lawyer, doctor, engineer, or accountant. If nothing else,
one will have learned a few new stories and, most important,
one will have begun on that necessary movement from contract to the next step, from province to the World's Fair,
from a hopeless person to a desperado. I wrote about my
first uncertain steps in this direction in *Elbow Room* because
I have benefited from all the contracts, I have exhausted all
the contracts, and at present it is the only new direction I
know.

*James Alan McPherson, in "On Becoming an American
Writer,* The Atlantic, *December, 1978.*

difficult options people have, with those choosing easy ones either pitied or hated because they betrayed loyalties, doomed to unhappy lives.

His story **"Elbow Room"** personifies what every character wanted: space enough to break free from a stereotyped life, a hollow role, a restraining sensibility. Like Hemingway, McPherson uses controlled dialogue to let his people speak eloquently for themselves, and his technique in handling introspection and psychological realism is similar to Kafka's. The tensions of American life produced by the psychic and spiritual alienation of interracial lovers and their attempts to find parental and community acceptance are some of the themes that vitalize these three memorable stories by a gifted contemporary writer, giving his works timeless, universal applications with whom the lonely and the exiled outsiders of all races, ethnic groups and classes can identify. (pp. 79-88)

> Edith Blicksilver, "Interracial Relationships in Three Short Stories by James Alan McPherson," in The CEA Critic, Vol. 50, Nos. 2-4, Winter, 1987-Summer, 1988, pp. 79-89.

Jon Wallace (essay date Spring 1988)

[*In the following essay, Wallace examines how the narrators in "The Story of a Dead Man," "The Story of a Scar," and "Just Enough for the City" use language to avoid intimacy with others.*]

"I'm black," declares Virginia Frost in the title story of James Alan McPherson's **Elbow Room:**

> "I've accepted myself as that. But didn't I make some elbow room though?" She tapped her temple with her forefinger. "I mean up *here!*" Then she laughed bitterly and sipped her tea. "When times get tough, *anybody* can pass for white. Niggers been doing *that* for *centuries,* so it ain't nothing new. But shit, wouldn't it of been something to be a nigger that could relate to white and black and everything else in the world out of a self as big as the world is?" She laughed. Then she said, "That would have been *some* nigger!"

As a seeker of personal space, of the elbow room she needs to develop herself and a sympathetic understanding of other human beings, Virginia represents one end of a psychological continuum within the book. At the opposite end stand other characters who also seek elbow room— but for antithetical reasons. My intention is to show that, unlike Virginia, who wants room to grow, the narrators of **"The Story of a Dead Man," "The Story of a Scar,"** and **"Just Enough for the City"** seek a space within which they can defend themselves against the claims of intimacy, human involvement, and personal history. The tool they use to accomplish this goal is language. Masters of what is primarily a white linguistic code, these narrators attempt to look out at the world from deep within the safety of conventional institutions and ideologies that implicitly justify their failure to see beyond them. In their mouths Standard English becomes a defensive weapon—a means of self-protection that, like Standard English in the mouths of defensive Whites, enables them to "hold the floor" at the expense of speakers of other codes (language varieties or dialects) who want, and often desperately need, to be heard. As a consequence, these characters avoid developing, or even considering, Virginia's admirable ideal of a self "as big as the world."

"It is not true," declares William, the narrator of **"The Story of a Dead Man,"** "that Billy Renfro was killed during that trouble in Houston." Thus begins a narrative designed to accomplish in fiction what the dramatic monologue accomplishes in poetry: unconscious self-revelation. The difference between most first-person fiction and the dramatic monologue, however, is that in the latter the identity of the audience is clear—and of course relevant to what the speaker is saying and why he is saying it. In **"The Story of a Dead Man"** McPherson does not identify William's audience, but he continually reminds us that William is speaking, or writing, to someone and that his motive is self-defense. Indeed, the narrative is William's response to stories told by Billy about his own heroic adventures on the road and to rumors about William's mistreatment of Billy. Both the stories and the rumors threaten William: the rumors for obvious reasons, the stories because they reveal, by implication, the staid pointlessness of William's very conventional life. "Neither is it true," William tells us in the second paragraph, "as certain of his enemies have maintained, that Billy's left eye was lost during a rumble with that red-neck storekeep outside Limehouse, South Carolina." At this point, William seems to be interested in establishing the truth about his cousin Billy. He says as much shortly thereafter: "I bother to refute these rumors because the man is my cousin, and I am honor-bound to love him as I know he really is." In this wonderfully rationalized construction, we discover William's underlying motive and the identity of the audience he is addressing. He speaks not of love here but of an obligation that requires love. He speaks also of Billy as "he really is." Given his "honor-bound to love him" construction, his casual fusing of love and obligation, we have to infer that William is both unable and unwilling to give us his wildly mythic cousin as "he really is"—that what we will get instead is a formal attempt to de-mythify Billy in the interests of William's very unmythical values.

And this is indeed what William proceeds to do. Thus, when he asserts at the end of the story that "it is not true, contrary to rumors circulating in my family, that Billy Renfro is unwelcome in my home," we appreciate the distinction between "not unwelcome" and "welcome"; and we know that William does also, for he is nothing if not a stickler for distinctions—a highly literate explainer resorting to the precisions of a standard code in an attempt to defend his bourgeois commitments, and a personal identity based on them, against the claims of the past and the present. His presumed audience is those who would not find anything the least objectionable in the candid but cautious fluency of the following lines:

> In contrast to [Billy], I moved westward [sic], but only as far as Chicago, and settled in against this city's soul-killing winter winds. I purged from my speech all traces of the South and warmed myself by the fire of my thirty-year plan. Employment was available in the credit

reference section of the Melrose Department Store, and there I established, though slowly, a reputation for efficiency and tact. Because I got along, I began moving up. In my second year in Chicago, I found and courted Chelseia Raymond, a family-backed, efficiency-minded girl. She was the kind of woman I needed to make my children safe. Her family loved me, and had the grace to overlook the fact that I had once been a poor migrant from the South. Third-generation Chicagoans, they nonetheless opened their hearts and home to me, as if I had been native to their city. With their backing, I settled into this rough-and-tumble city and learned to dodge all events detracting attention from the direction in which I had determined to move. From time to time, trudging through the winter slush on Michigan, I would pause to explore a reflection of myself in a store window. By my fifth year in Chicago, I became satisfied that no one could have mistaken me for a refugee from the South.

This was my situation when Billy Renfro came to visit.

Here the basic social and linguistic issues of the story are made clear. In the second sentence, William explicitly notes the relevance of language to identity, or at least to social success; moreover, his metaphor reveals how willingly he yielded his native dialect in order to succeed in Chicago—a sacrifice we can understand, even endorse, except, perhaps, in cases where such a sacrifice, made in the interests of "efficiency and tact," leads to a more costly sacrifice of human feeling.

That William has made such a sacrifice is implied throughout **"The Story of a Dead Man,"** more or less explicitly in the passages in which he attempts to justify his handling of Billy and implicitly in the language of the above paragraph. Consider, for example, the way William himself unknowingly modifies, at his own expense, the meaning of such honorific words as "loved," "grace," and "hearts." The context establishes the relationship between William and the Raymonds as a contingent and convenient one based on a mutual respect for efficiency, tact, and social status. "Loved," "grace," and "hearts" therefore mean something less here than they mean in most religious contexts—something significantly less spiritual and more commercial. It is a distinction easily missed in a paragraph in which the words seem to purr so naturally. But just as we can hear lines such as "let's not be so philosophical" without being aware of the enormous difference in meaning between the adjective in this sentence and the same word in, say, Plato, so we can easily miss the secularization of William's terms. To put the point another way, his words seem descriptive, but they are in fact argumentative: implicit predications intended to affirm the middle-class values that William and the Raymonds live by.

At the end of the paragraph, William returns to the identity issue—to acknowledge his determination "to dodge all events detracting attention from the direction in which I had determined to move." His narrative gives us every reason to believe that some of the events he dodged in-

volved love, grace, and matters of the heart in less commercial senses.

After establishing William as the voice of black middle-class propriety, McPherson goes on to dramatize the primary conflict of the story: William's struggle to demythify (which is to say, to kill, make into a dead man) Billy within a net of Standard English and the presuppositions it affirms. In reference to Billy's losing his eye in a rumble, William writes: "That eye, I now have reason to believe, was lost during domestic troubles." In the minds of most middle-class readers, especially those interested in efficiency and tact, a man who has a "reason to believe," who can make such a point in the form of a nonrestrictive clause and then follow it with alliterative and euphemistic phrases such as "during domestic troubles," is certainly going to seem more reliable than a man allegedly given to rumbling with red-neck storekeeps outside Limehouse, South Carolina. Such readers would also be inclined to accept William's conclusion that Billy was essentially nothing more than a liar. Here is a passage in which William seeks to justify this claim:

> "We are no longer young men," I said. "The foam has settled down into the beer. I, myself, no longer chase women, speak hotly, challenge opinions too far different from my own. I have learned it is to my advantage to get along. . . . In short, Billy, in my manhood I have become aware of complexity. You owe it to the family, and to the memory of your mother, to do the same."
>
> Billy swished his Scotch and drank it down, then rapped the glass on the table to alert the barmaid. When she looked, he pointed two fingers downward toward our glasses and kissed at her. Then, turning to focus his single, red-rimmed eye on my face, he said, "Bullshit!"
>
> He was dressed in the black gabardine suit of an undertaker. Dried purple-black blood streaked his coat sleeves, his black string tie, and the collar of the dirty white shirt he wore.
>
> "People change, Billy," I said.
>
> "Bullshit!" Billy Renfro said.
>
> I looked closely at him and saw a gangster. He was not the kind of man I wanted to meet my family. I glanced at my watch and sipped my drink. I listened to his stories.
>
> Billy spun his usual lies.

We do not know how many of Billy's stories are pure fiction and how many are authentic. The blood he carries on his clothes suggests that some of the violent ones must be based on fact, but it doesn't matter which. It doesn't even matter if Billy is all lies, as William believes—at least not as far as our reading of the story as a whole is concerned, because what distinguishes William and Billy is not their allegiance to truth but their relation to white middle-class values. As they stand, they are both partial men: two halves of a whole that would presumably add up to Virginia's "self as big as the world." One half, William, has defined himself in collective terms; the other, Billy, has defined himself in opposition to them. By so doing, each has exaggerated a truth: William the truth that we need to be *a part* of something, Billy that we need to be *apart*—individualized, to some extent alone. In a moral sense, then, they are equally limited. Linguistically, however, they are not, for William controls the power code: Standard American English, the "transparent" language of American industry and government, the means by which the middle- and upper-class do business and, at the same time, keep alternative realities or, more specifically, alternative stories from being heard as anything but lies.

In the last lines of the story, William hopes that he and Chelseia will one day be able to "reconstruct" Billy:

> I say it is just a matter of time. We are, after all, the same age. Yet I have already charted my course. I have settled into Chicago, against the winter whippings of this city's winds. He can do the same. But as things stand now, he is still someplace out there, with a single eye flickering over open roadways, in his careless search for an exciting death. Ah, *Billy!*

The last words recall the last words of another upholder of the ideological status quo: the narrator of Melville's "Bartleby," who was equally eloquent ("Ah, Bartleby! Ah, Humanity!") and equally determined to live a safe and easy life. In both stories, the outsider is abandoned not merely in favor of commercial interests, as a casual reading might suggest, but also in favor of spiritual security. Billy might not symbolize the existence of a Melvillian "organic ill," but he does represent a radical spiritual as well as social alternative to William's thirty-year plan. He represents not just a way of living but a dimension of the self that must, or so the story implies, be accommodated if human beings are ever to become fully human.

In **"The Story of a Scar"** we meet a man as pompous as, but even more presumptuous than, William:

> Since Dr. Wayland was late and there were no recent newsmagazines in the waiting room, I turned to the other patient and said: "As a concerned person, and as your brother, I ask you, without meaning to offend, how did you get that scar on the side of your face?"

The sentence reveals the narrator for what he is: a liar who uses language as a mask with which he attempts to protect himself by intimidating others. By demonstrating a fluent command of standard-to-formal English, he asserts what he presumes to be his superiority to most of his auditors: speakers of black dialect. Safely ensconced within it, he can look out upon a world of inferiors to whom, or so he believes, he owes nothing.

The quotation mark that precedes his utterance above draws the line between the private reality and public appearance. The narrator is interested in accumulating "information," preferably in print form, in isolation from others. Unable to find it, he resorts not to social intercourse but to interrogation. This form of discourse enables him to speak without involvement, risk, or concern. Contrary to his claim, therefore, he is not speaking as a brother, and he does intend to offend—in order to put his auditor on the defensive and so avoid the risks of intimacy. In

another formulation, he speaks as a detached reader of human texts:

> I studied her approvingly. Such women have a natural leaning toward the abstract expression of themselves. Their styles have private meanings, advertise secret distillations of their souls. Their figures, and their disfigurations, make meaningful statements. . . . Such craftsmen must be approached with subtlety if they are to be deciphered.

It is probably no coincidence that the narrator describes the woman as a "crafts*man*," thus missing, in language anyway, one of the most important facts about her. It is probably no coincidence, because although everything he says is true, he has neither the subtlety nor the sensitivity to "decipher" anyone's soul. And she knows it, as she knows his type: "I *knowed* you'd get back around to that," she says, when he asks again about her scar. "Black guys like you with them funny eyeglasses are a real trip. You got to know everything. You sit in corners and watch people." Unfazed, he continues to press for an answer. But shortly after she begins to talk about where she was when it happened and about the men she had been working with, the narrator interrupts what he calls "her tiresome ramblings" to demand "Which one of them cut you?"

> Her face flashed a wall of brown fire. "This here's *my* story!" she muttered, eyeing me up and down with suspicion. "You dudes cain't stand to hear the whole of anything. You want everything broke down in little pieces."

In a sense, she is wrong. The narrator isn't as interested in breaking things down as he is in discovering and imposing patterns on the world around him—patterns that suit *his* needs, *his* story about himself, and his relation to everyone else. Put another way, what he wants is the continual validation of the assumptions that confirm his presumed superiority. This becomes clear later when he again interrupts to answer his own question. While listening to the woman tell about her growing disenchantment with Billy Crawford, a bookish, Williamesque boyfriend, and her growing interest in a jive-talking newcomer to the post office named Teddy Johnson, whom she describes as "the last *true* son of the Great McDaddy," the narrator loses control:

> "Sister," I said quickly, overwhelmed suddenly by the burden of insight. "I *know* the man of whom you speak. There is no time for this gutter-patter and indirection. Please, for my sake and for your own, avoid stuffing the shoes of the small with mythic homilies. This man was a bum, a hustler and a small-time punk. He broke up your romance with Billy, then he lived off you, cheated on you, and cut you when you confronted him." So pathetic and gross seemed her elevation of the fellow that I abandoned all sense of caution. "Is your mind so *dead*," I continued, "did this switchblade slice so *deep*, do you have so little *respect* for yourself, or at least for the idea of *proportion* in this sad world, that you'd sit here and *praise* this brute!?"

What the narrator means by proportion is that quality of

coherence and meaning that *his* ideological presuppositions and stereotypes provide him—presuppositions and stereotypes that, among other things, identify him as superior intellectually and spiritually to practically everyone else. He himself is a more sophisticated Billy Crawford threatened by the physical (primarily sexual) power of the Great McDaddys of the world—and by earthy, voluptuous women who know what he is beneath his elaborate, carefully-articulated verbal shell. This is why he is so unnerved by her response. He tells us that while she looked at him through the smoke of her cigarette, he "watched her nervously, recognizing the evidence of past destructiveness, yet fearing the imminent occurrence of more. But it was not her temper or the potential strength of her fleshly arms that I feared." What he fears is her insight through his intellectual defenses into his frail, impotent heart.

For unspecified reasons, the narrator cannot, or will not, love. Language is his means of masking this fact, of keeping it from others and from himself. When the woman does finish the story, does reveal that it was Billy Crawford and not Teddy Johnson who knifed her, he is predictably unnerved. The situation is made worse by the fact that the woman then begins to speak to him as a "sister," as a human being in need:

> "This here's the third doctor I been to see. The first one stiched [sic] me up like a turkey and left this scar. The second one refused to touch me." She paused and wet her lips again. "This man fixed your nose for you," she said softly. "Do you think he could do somethin' about this scar?"

The narrator's subsequent behavior reveals him for what he is: a fearful wordman whose last refuge is print and abstract, impersonal rights—forms designed to compensate for the absence of human feeling:

> I searched the end table next to my couch for a newsmagazine, carefully avoiding her face. "Dr. Wyland is a skilled man," I told her. "Whenever he's not late. I think he may be able to do something for you."
>
> She sighed heavily and seemed to tremble. "I don't expect no miracle or nothin'," she said. "If he could just fix the part around my eye I wouldn't expect nothin' else. People say the rest don't look too bad."
>
> I clutched a random magazine and did not answer. Nor did I look at her. The flesh around my nose began to itch, and I looked toward the inner office door with the most extreme irritation building in me. . . . I resolved to put aside all notions of civility and go into the office before her, as was my right.

Needing desperately to escape the threat of intimacy, the narrator at first seeks protection behind a magazine. Then another idea occurs to him, a question that seems personal, that in fact can be personal, but that in context is merely another defensive tactic—the narrator's way of keeping his distance by reducing intimate discourse to mere form:

> And then I remembered the most important question, without which the entire exchange

would have been wasted. I turned to the woman, now drawn together in the red plastic chair, as if struggling to sleep in a cold bed. "Sister," I said, careful to maintain a casual air. "Sister . . . what is your name?"

For all interpretive purposes, the narrator of **"The Story of a Scar"** is the narrator of **"Just Enough for the City,"** who meets with various fundamentalist proselytizers, speculates on the nature of love, and concludes that just enough love for the city and the people therein is not very much—or much more than he is willing to give. Appropriately enough, he has an ear for language. Were it not for their accents, he tells us, he would not let the Germans into his house. Once in, however, they accomplish little, because he has nothing to give them but questions—to which he expects no answers; for he too is an interrogator trying to avoid self-revelation: "They both watch and wait for me to disclose myself. Backed into a corner, I have no choice but to shift their focus. 'Where do you get your money?' I ask them. 'Who finances your operation?' They go away." On this occasion, the narrator accomplishes his goal of self-defense through intimidation with relatively simple, factual questions. On other occasions, he resorts to elaborate conundrums designed to end uncomfortable discussions that he made possible by admitting fundamentalists into his apartment in the first place. By means of such elaborate verbosity he avoids living the basic truths that most of his visitors present. "Der simple problem," one German lady tells him, "is dat vee do not luff one anudder." Faced with such a simple but demanding fact, the narrator does what so many of McPherson's protagonists do so well, or at least so often: transform a spiritual or interpersonal issue into linguistic or aesthetic categories: "I agree with this. But I insist that they define for me the term."

Developing a simple definition of love, it turns out, is a goal the narrator has set for himself. Here is his first attempt:

> I think love must be the ability to suspend one's intelligence for the sake of something. At the basis of love therefore must live imagination. Instead of thinking always "I am I," to love one must be able to feelingly conjugate the verb *to be*. Intuition must be part of the circuitous pathway leading ultimately to love. I wish I could ask someone.

Within the story proper, the narrative of physical events, we see a narrator behaving in ways wholly at odds with his intellectual insights: intimidating people with his precise but distancing and at times baffling language. Together, his meditations on the theme of love, and his narrative of his human relations, reveal him to be a sensitive and intelligent but emotionally sterile man who knows what he should be but who cannot be it—despite the depth and apparent sincerity of his conclusions. "Love must be a going outward from the self," he writes, "from the most secret of safe positions. God is no more than the most secret place from which such emanations can be sent." The idea seems promising, thoroughly consistent with the speculations of, for example, Thomas Merton. His grammatical metaphor seems equally insightful:

If one is not too strict in his conjugation of the verb *to be,* he might wind up with a sense of living in the present. I believe that love exists at just that point when the first person singular moves into the plural estate: I am, you are, he is, she is, *we are.* . . . The saying of it requires a going out of oneself, of breath as well as confidence. Its image is of expansiveness, a taking roundly into and putting roundly out of oneself. Or perhaps another word should be used, one invented or one transported from another context: I am, you are, he is, she is, *we be.* . . . Or again, perhaps a beat of silence alone could best bear the weight of it, a silence suggesting the burden of subjectivity: I am, you are, he is, she is   they are. . . .

The possibilities proliferate, as defensive speculation always must, into a substitute for the experience speculated about; and the narrator's meditations become empty, idle, and destructive. Eventually he decides that he need not entertain proselytizers at all: "I am refusing these days to bow on my knees and cry holy." It is the beginning of the end. In response to the realization that he has seen deep into the eyes of a young, haunted woman, he is tempted to speak:

> I want to say, but do not dare to say, that I saw briefly in her face the shadow of a human soul.
>
> *I am.* . . .

Although still unable to conjugate feelingly the second-person singular, he nevertheless comes to realize that there is more to human experience than artful formulations. In an exchange with two ministers, he tells the story of a man who, "suspecting now that words were of little importance, he found himself watching gestures and facial expressions, listening to the rhythms of voices and not to the words spoken, for telltale insights into the true nature of reality. . . ." But like the man in his story, who later became "unable . . . to believe in any words" and who "retreated into a room, questioning even the character behind his own name," the narrator ends up isolated within a semantic universe that protects him against love by a wall of metaphor:

> Something breathes quickly against the cobwebs inside me. But because I fear what I feel is love, I turn my face away.
>
> *Tu es.* . . .
>
> I am becoming sufficient.

Read as correct French, *tu es* indicates that the narrator is once again attempting to conjugate the verb "to be"; read as incorrect Spanish (a second-person pronoun and a third-person verb), *tu es* indicates that the narrator cannot, or will not, "go outward from the most secret of safe positions," which in his case is not God, apparently, but his own fragile self: a matter of words contrived as defense. The disjunction expresses his inability to connect with the human world. In either interpretation, he is not really in the world of human relations; he is somewhere else, making use of what Joseph Chilton Pearce sees as a distinguishing characteristic of literate culture: an "infinite capacity for rationalization." It is just about all he has, and

is: words, words, words, spoken not to connect but to separate and protect a profoundly insufficient self.

At the conclusions of **"The Story of a Dead Man," "The Story of a Scar,"** and **"Just Enough for the City,"** McPherson leaves us with characters who might, but probably will not, break through the walls they have made to protect themselves against human involvement. Theirs is a problem that is inevitable in cultures—black or white—that value the individual as such. Within them, most sensitive human beings are alternately haunted and invigorated by the tension between the desire simply to be themselves in the narrow sense of "*apart* from the human community" and the desire to be *a part* of it, to connect with others in satisfying and yet necessarily self-effacing ways. Although this is a common problem inside and outside books, McPherson deepens our understanding of it by showing what a crucial role language can play as a means of protecting a self that is not "as big as the world" but as small—and as tenuous—as an ego. (pp. 17-26)

> *Jon Wallace, "The Politics of Style in Three Stories by James Alan McPherson," in* Modern Fiction Studies, *Vol. 34, No. 1, Spring, 1988, pp. 17-26.*

Jon Wallace   (essay date Fall 1988)

[In the essay below, Wallace discusses the narrator's moral and aesthetic struggle in "Elbow Room."]

As the epigraph to the title story of his Pulitzer Prize winning book *Elbow Room,* James Alan McPherson quotes a passage from *In the American Grain* in which William Carlos Williams declares that one challenge faced by American pioneers was to settle a new land without relying entirely on old values: "[Daniel] Boone's genius," says Williams, "was to recognize the difficulty as neither material nor political but one purely moral and aesthetic." Like Boone, McPherson recognizes the importance of moral and aesthetic problems: specifically, the moral and aesthetic problems of storytelling, which he considers a very serious business indeed. In fact, another quotation that would be equally useful as an introduction to **"Elbow Room"** is Joan Didion's simple but profound observation that "We tell ourselves stories in order to live." In much of McPherson's work and in Didion's essay, "story" can be read to refer simultaneously to fictional narratives and to ideological stories—myths which we use to order the world and define ourselves. Although such myths can be expressed in the form of a coherent series of assumptions about the nature of the world and persons (as in the world view of modern science), they generally take the form of dramatic mythical narratives (Genesis, for example) that serve as the bases of more abstract formulations. Hence the relevance of morality and aesthetics, for what McPherson implies in **"Elbow Room"** is that neither meaning nor identity should be considered material or political matters, that is, structures *necessarily* imposed upon us from without by external "realities." They should instead be recognized for what they always are: human creations whose validity can be measured not only by standards of realism and objective truth (if such truth is possible), but also by the sense of coherent purpose that they provide. Moreover, the plausibility of a given story or ideology is as much a matter of form as content. We don't live by a story simply because its theme or idea makes sense; we accept it because it appeals to us as a satisfying "new coherence" or dramatic structure. In short, all stories (all the myths that justify all abstract ideological values) are inventions, like fictional stories, that we live by because we find them both morally and aesthetically compelling.

All of which is to say that the protagonist of **"Elbow Room"** is neither Paul nor Virginia Frost, nor is the real story their struggle to live sanely and lovingly in a racist culture as a white man and black woman. The protagonist is the narrator, and the real story is about his struggle to find a form for their story—a form that will be, first, morally satisfying insofar as it will do justice to them as human beings seeking to define themselves in their own terms, and second, aesthetically satisfying insofar as it will engage and sustain our attention. The tempting alternative, one that the narrator succumbs to several times, is to explain—and exploit—them in terms appropriate to *his* story, not theirs.

McPherson dramatizes his narrator's moral and aesthetic struggle in both the frame and story-within-a-story of **"Elbow Room."** In the frame story, the narrator resists the conventional structures of an editor, who claims in his introduction that the

> *Narrator is unmanageable. Demonstrates a disregard for form bordering on the paranoid. Questioned closely, he declares himself the open enemy of conventional narrative categories. When pressed for reasons, narrator became shrill in insistence that 'borders,' 'structures,' 'frames,' 'order,' and even 'form' itself are regarded by him with the highest suspicion.*

The narrator's anti-establishment commitments are clear, arguing as he does for creative freedom from the conventional ideological constraints advocated by his editor. In their first exchange, the editor interrupts the narrator's discussion of a time when, after a short period of freedom (presumably in the sixties), "caste curtains" were again drawn in this country "resegregating all imaginations." During this time, the narrator tells us, he was obliged to go out in search of stories "to complete my sense of self." This search was often risky, due to the distrust that was then separating people:

> Yet not to do this was to default on my responsibility to narrate fully. There are stories that *must* be told, if only to be around when fresh dimensions are needed. But in the East, during that time, there was no thought of this. A narrator cannot function without new angles of vision. I needed new eyes, regeneration, fresh forms, and went hunting for them out in the territory.

> *A point of information. What has form to do with caste restrictions?*

> Everything.

> *You are saying you want to be white?*

A narrator needs as much access to the world as the advocates of that mythology.

> *You are ashamed then of being black?*

Only of not being nimble enough to dodge other people's straightjackets.

> *Are you not too much obsessed here with integration?*

I was cursed with a healthy imagination.

> *What have caste restrictions to do with imagination?*

Everything.

> *A point of information. What is your idea of personal freedom?*

Unrestricted access to new stories forming.

> *Have you paid strict attention to the forming of this present one?*

Once upon a time there was a wedding in San Francisco.

Insofar as he asserts the need for "new angles" and "new eyes," "fresh forms" and "unrestricted access to new stories forming," the narrator speaks as a literary subversive attempting to resist the editor's formal "straightjackets."

But once we leave the frame story and enter the story, or stories, of the wedding couple—Paul Frost and Virginia Valentine—we find the narrator becoming an editor in his turn, one who is interested primarily in form, not in people as creatures in time struggling to live sanely and lovingly. "Virginia I valued for her stock of stories," he writes. "I was suspicious of Paul Frost for claiming first right to these. They were a treasure I felt sure he would exploit." In these lines the narrator's moral and aesthetic interests clash. Good stories should be both somehow "moral" (purposive, idealistic) and aesthetic (dramatically engaging); but, McPherson would have us remember, so should story tellers. Indeed, the purpose of all good stories is to broaden and deepen awareness so that people can, among other things, learn to accept themselves and each other. As sensitive as the narrator is to his own sense of self, he nevertheless fails to "relate" to others without "intruding," as if he were literally "writing" them into *his* story. For example, after listening to Virginia talk about how Paul's father had refused to accept their marriage, the narrator confesses that "It was not my story, but I could not help intruding upon its materials. It seemed to me to lack perspective." He then proceeds to pontificate on the themes of time, media, and selfhood in a language hardly intended to express or encourage sympathetic understanding:

> "Time out here is different from time in the East. When we say 'Good afternoon' here, in the East people are saying 'Good night.' It's a matter of distance, not of values. Ideas that start in the East move very fast in media, but here the diversity tends to slow them down. Still, a mind needs media to reinforce a sense of self. There are no imaginations pure enough to be self-sustaining."

Angered by what he takes to be condescension, Paul declares: " 'I don't understand what you're talking about.' " We have been in such situations before in **Elbow Room:** a defensive protagonist attempting to order the world to his satisfaction, usually as a means of escaping its human entanglements. This seems to be the narrator's motive in **"Elbow Room,"** but we cannot be sure. What we do know is that he can be aesthetic to a fault, preoccupied with form at the expense of human involvement. His main goal seems to be to follow Paul and Virginia as an observer in order to make something artful out of them.

Shortly after the above exchange, the narrator again intrudes, this time as an interrogator. Pointing to an African mask on the wall of Paul and Virginia's apartment, he asks if Paul thinks it is beautiful. Paul says, " 'It's very nice. Ginny bought it from a trader in Ibadan. There's a good story behind it.' " The narrator presses the point, asking again if Paul thinks it is beautiful. Growing angry, Paul answers yes. The narrator then poses a problem:

> You are a dealer in art. You have extraordinary taste. But your shop is in a small town. You want to sell this mask by convincing your best customer it is beautiful and of interest to the eye. Every other dealer in town says it is ugly. How do you convince the customer and make a sale?

As theoretically useful as the question might be as a means of exploring racial differences, it is not an appropriate one, given the human context. Psychologically, Paul is hardly in a position to deal with such bewildering racial puzzles—a fact that the narrator understands but does not act upon: " 'You have enlisted in a psychological war,' " he tells Paul shortly before the latter orders him out of the apartment. "I left them alone with their dinner," he then adds, concluding the scene. "It was not my story. It was not ripe for telling until they had got it under better control."

Psychological war is everyone's story in **"Elbow Room."** What it involves at bottom is a struggle of self-creation in which individuals oppose the power of culture in an attempt to transcend its limited and limiting definitions. Immediately after the scene in Paul and Virginia's apartment, the editor interrupts, declaring that an

> *Analysis of this section is needed. It is too subtle and needs to be more clearly explained.*

I tried to enter his mind and failed.

Explain.

I had confronted him with color and he became white.

Unclear. Explain.

There was a public area of personality in which his 'I' existed. The nervous nature of this is the basis of what is miscalled arrogance. In reality it was the way his relationship with the world was structured. I attempted to challenge this structure by attacking its assumptions too directly and abruptly. He sensed the intrusion and reacted emotionally to protect his sense of form. He simply shut me out of his world.

Unclear. Explain.

I am I. I am we. You are.

Clarity is essential on this point. Explain.

Despite his detailed understanding of the personal and social implications of Paul's and Virginia's stories, the narrator eventually loses interest. After a conversation with Virginia in which she talks about her ideal of selfhood, he writes:

> Inside myself I suddenly felt a coolness as light as the morning mist against my skin. Then I realized that I was acting. I did not care about them and their problems any more. I did not think they had a story worth telling. I looked away from her and said, "Life is tough, all right."

With a cliche he writes them off, convinced that they and their child have essentially two choices: black isolation or self-destructive white compromise—entrapment within conventional social categories. His decision reveals the extent of *his* isolation—his essentially defensive commitment to aesthetic rather than moral values. Losing interest in Paul's and Virginia's ability to live "fresh forms," the narrator walks away in despair, "convinced there were no new stories in the world."

But Paul and Virginia, committed as they are to each other, and to ideals of selfhood that go beyond merely aesthetic form, succeed in proving him wrong. Broadened and deepened by her flight into the hearts of other countries, and other people, Virginia becomes "a magic woman" who could speak "with her whole presence in very complicated ways. She was unique. She was a classic kind of narrator." Virginia is also a woman capable of human intimacy and commitment—a trait evident in her relation to Paul, whom she resolves to protect against all psychological dangers. Paul himself is also magic, in his own subdued Kansas way. Willing, as the narrator notes, to confront "the hidden dimensions of his history" in order "to unstructure and flesh out his undefined 'I'," Paul marries Virginia, fathers a son, and eventually convinces his father to accept his family. More importantly, at least as far as the theme of the story is concerned, he constantly grapples with the issue of his identity, realizing that the question "Who am I?" can never be answered conclusively:

> And many times, watching him conceal his aloneness, I wanted to answer, "The abstract white man of mythic dimensions, if being that will make you whole again." But the story was still unfinished, and I did not want to intrude on its structure again. The chaos was his alone, as were the contents he was trying desperately to reclaim from an entrenched and determined form. But to his credit it must be said that, all during this time, I never once heard him say to Virginia, "I don't understand." For the stoic nature of this silence, considering the easy world waiting behind those words, one could not help but love him.

In the concluding lines of the story, the narrator describes his response to a photograph recently sent to him of Paul and Virginia, their baby, and Paul's parents. On the back of it are the words "He will be a *classic* kind of nigger." The editor intrudes to demand a clarification of this comment. "I would find that difficult to do," writes the narrator,

> It was from the beginning not my story. I lack the insight to narrate its complexities. But it may still be told. The mother is, after all, a country raconteur with cosmopolitan experience. The father sees clearly with both eyes. And when I called Kansas they had already left for the backwoods of Tennessee, where the baby has an odd assortment of relatives. I will wait. The mother is a bold woman. The father has a sense of how things should be. But while waiting, I will wager my reputation on the ambition, if not the strength, of the boy's story.

> *Comment is unclear. Explain. Explain.*

The narrator, himself partially transformed by Paul and Virginia's story, realizes that there is no explanation beyond the story of **"Elbow Room"** itself, beyond the texture of its language, images, tone, and syntax—in the feel of verbal formulations designed to make new eyes and new selves by modifying old forms, social and linguistic. Or, in terms of another metaphor, there is no explanation beyond the play of opposites that is the story: the editor and the narrator, the narrator and Paul, Paul and Virginia, male and female, and even the aesthetic and moral dimensions of stories that interact to generate a meaningful form. Paul? His son? Both? can become "classic" only by going beyond such antithetical classifications to a synthesis that subsumes them. Since such a synthesis does not yet exist, we cannot explain it, only sense it as a possibility somewhere beyond, or between, the lines of our current public and private stories—in a place beyond definitions, where there is room for everyone. (pp. 447-52)

> *Jon Wallace, "The Story Behind the Story in James Alan McPherson's 'Elbow Room',"* in Studies in Short Fiction, *Vol. 25, No. 4, Fall, 1988, pp. 447-52.*

FURTHER READING

Bibliography

Fikes, Robert, Jr. "The Works of an 'American' Writer: A James Alan McPherson Bibliography." *CLA Journal* XXII, No. 4 (June 1979): 415-23.

> Lists works by and about McPherson published before 1978.

Criticism

Christ, Ronald. Review of *Hue and Cry,* by James Alan McPherson. *Commonweal* XC, No. 21 (19 September 1969): 570-71.

> Faults McPherson's language in *Hue and Cry* as flat and awkward. The critic also states: "McPherson is a Negro writer who admittedly has tried to keep the question of race far in the background, and his stories show (and suffer from) this repression."

Jordan, Clive. "Malignant Growth." *New Statesman* (21 November 1969): 738-39.

> Brief review of *Hue and Cry* in which Jordan faults McPherson's verbosity but praises his characterization and dialogue.

Sullivan, Walter. "Where Have All the Flowers Gone?: The Short Story in Search of Itself." *The Sewanee Review* LXXVIII, No. 1 (Winter 1970): 530-42.

> Brief review in which Sullivan argues that McPherson's political views on racial issues compromise the literary qualities of *Hue and Cry.*

"Scenes before Themes." *The Times Literary Supplement* (25 December 1969): 1465.

> Praises the realistic depiction of urban life in *Elbow Room,* but states McPherson's "hip idiom" sometimes overpowers his themes.

Additional coverage of McPherson's life and career is contained in the following sources published by Gale Research: *Black Writers; Contemporary Authors,* **Vols. 25-28, rev. ed.;** *Contemporary Authors New Revision Series,* **Vol. 24;** *Contemporary Literary Criticism,* **Vol. 19;** *Dictionary of Literary Biography,* **Vol. 38; and** *Major 20th-Century Writers.*

Cornell Woolrich

1903-1968

(Full name Cornell George Hopley-Woolrich; also wrote under the pseudonyms William Irish and George Hopley) American novelist, short story writer, screenwriter, and autobiographer.

The following entry provides an overview of Woolrich's career.

INTRODUCTION

Woolrich is best remembered for the novels and short stories of mystery and suspense that he wrote from the 1930s to the 1960s. Many of Woolrich's works have been adapted for radio, television, and film productions, the most famous being Alfred Hitchcock's *Rear Window* (based on "It Had to Be Murder") and François Truffaut's adaptation of *The Bride Wore Black*. While critics—even some of his most ardent supporters—recognize Woolrich's often implausible plots, clichéd dialogue, and sometimes inelegant prose, they applaud his skill in creating suspenseful narratives and credit him along with Dashiell Hammett, Raymond Chandler, and James M. Cain for being one of the finest writers of "hard-boiled" crime fiction.

Woolrich was born in New York City but spent most of his childhood in Mexico as a result of his father's work as a civil engineer. The only child of an unhappy and short-lived marriage, Woolrich spent his adolescence primarily in New York City with his mother, with whom he also traveled in Europe. He entered Columbia University in 1921 and studied journalism for three years; an illness caused him to miss much of his junior year, and during his recovery he began writing fiction. Woolrich left school to write full time and, after producing a number of short stories, completed his first novel, *Cover Charge,* in 1926. Like each of his first six novels, *Cover Charge* is a romance set in the Roaring Twenties and mimics the style of F. Scott Fitzgerald's Jazz Age tales. His next novel, *Children of the Ritz,* won $10,000 in a contest sponsored by First National Pictures, which filmed the novel in 1929 and offered him a job as a screenwriter. From 1928 to early 1931 Woolrich worked on film scripts in addition to writing short stories and novels. While in Hollywood, Woolrich married Gloria Blackton, daughter of silent-film mogul J. Stuart Blackton. Their marriage was never consummated and ended in annulment after three months. Woolrich's biographer, Francis Nevins, has explained that Woolrich both idealized his wife to an excessive, platonic degree, and was consumed with self-loathing over his then promiscuous and clandestine homosexual activity. Woolrich moved back to New York where, as Nevins writes, "for the next quarter century he lived with his mother . . . trapped in a bizarre love-hate relationship which dominat-

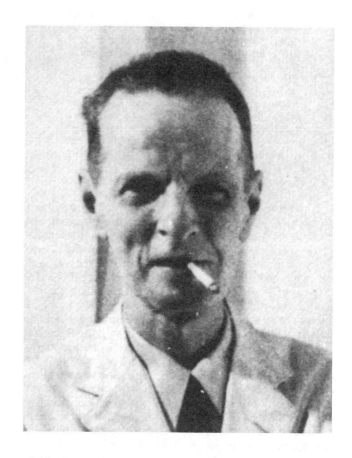

ed his external world" and was reflected in his fiction. Woolrich's subsequent life was marked by increasing emotional and physical deterioration; despite the financial wherewithal to do otherwise, he and his mother spent their last years together living among thieves, prostitutes, and other criminals in a rat-infested apartment house in Harlem. With his mother's death in 1957, Woolrich's own decay increased precipitously. After suffering years of alcoholism and the loss of a leg to an avoidable case of gangrene, Woolrich died in New York City in 1968.

Woolrich began writing the fiction for which he is famous in 1934. During the depression there was little demand for Woolrich's Jazz Age fiction, so he turned to such pulp crime magazines as *Black Mask, Detective Fiction Weekly,* and *Dime Detective* as a new market. His first publication in this genre is a story called "Death Sits in the Dentist's Chair." The story of a man's race to remove the cyanide a mad dentist hid in one of his fillings, it is characteristic of much of Woolrich's crime fiction in its depiction of random violence, bizarre coincidence, and suspense. Woolrich's literary universe developed in the numerous short stories he wrote over the next six years. In 1940 he published *The Bride Wore Black,* his first *roman noir* or

386

"black novel," a term French critics coined to describe the work of writers like Woolrich, Chandler, and Cain. Nevins has described this novel as "set in the grim *noir* universe of [Woolrich's] short fiction, its twin polestars being fate and chance." The novel, which chronicles a young woman's enigmatic and murderous exploits, is divided into five sections of three chapters each. Within each section the chapters are called "The Woman," followed by a chapter named for her current victim, and then one called "Post-Mortem on . . . " (her current victim). This structure, repeated five times, lends the narrative both a sense of fate—in that the victims are identified as such before they are introduced into the story—and an element of suspense—since the reader has no way of knowing if the woman will be stopped. *The Bride Wore Black* has proven to be Woolrich's most popular novel. Critical reaction at the time, however, was mixed; opinions ranged from displeasure with its self-conscious structure and sometimes illogical narrative, to favorable comparisons of Woolrich's narrative style with that of Hitchcock. Nevins has called Woolrich "the Poe of the twentieth century," and recent reevaluations of his work have concluded that he, along with Hammett, Chandler, and Cain, created the themes, characters, and imagery that inspired the cinematic style known as *film noir* and influenced the works of such writers as Ernest Hemingway and Albert Camus.

PRINCIPAL WORKS

Cover Charge   (novel)   1926
Children of the Ritz   (novel)   1927
Times Square   (novel)   1929
A Young Man's Heart   (novel)   1930
The Time of Her Life   (novel)   1931
Manhattan Love Song   (novel)   1932
The Bride Wore Black   (novel)   1940; also published as *Beware the Lady,* 1953
The Black Curtain   (novel)   1941
Black Alibi   (novel)   1942
Phantom Lady   (novel)   1942
The Black Angel   (novel)   1943
I Wouldn't Be in Your Shoes   (short stories)   1943; also published in abridged versions as *And So to Death,* 1944, and *Nightmare,* 1950
After-Dinner Story   (short stories)   1944; also published as *Six Times Death,* 1948
The Black Path of Fear   (novel)   1944
Deadline at Dawn   (novel)   1944
If I Should Die Before I Wake   (short stories)   1945
Night Has a Thousand Eyes   (novel)   1945
Borrowed Crime   (short stories)   1946
The Dancing Detective   (short stories)   1946
Waltz into Darkness   (novel)   1947
Dead Man Blues   (short stories)   1948
I Married a Dead Man   (novel)   1948
Rendezvous in Black   (novel)   1948
The Blue Ribbon   (short stories)   1949; also published as *Dilemma of the Dead Lady,* 1950
Fright   (novel)   1950

Savage Bride   (novel)   1950
Six Nights of Mystery   (short stories)   1950
Somebody on the Phone   (short stories)   1950; also published as *The Night I Died,* 1951, and *Deadly Night Call,* 1951
Strangler's Serenade   (novel)   1951
You'll Never See Me Again   (novel)   1951
Bluebeard's Seventh Wife   (short stories)   1952
Eyes That Watch You   (short stories)   1952
Nightmare   (short stories)   1956
Hotel Room   (novel)   1958
Violence   (short stories)   1958
Beyond the Night   (short stories)   1959
Death Is My Dancing Partner   (novel)   1959
**The Best of William Irish*   (short stories)   1960
The Doom Stone   (novel)   1960
The Dark Side of Love   (short stories)   1965
The Ten Faces of Cornell Woolrich   (short stories)   1965
Nightwebs   (short stories)   1971
Angels of Darkness   (short stories)   1978
The Fantastic Stories of Cornell Woolrich   (short stories) 1981
Rear Window, and Four Short Novels   (short stories) 1984
Blind Date with Death   (short stories)   1985
Darkness at Dawn   (short stories)   1985
Vampire's Honeymoon   (short stories)   1985
*Into the Night   (novel)   1987
Blues of a Lifetime: The Autobiography of Cornell Woolrich   (autobiography)   1991

*This novel, written during the 1960s but unfinished at the time of Woolrich's death, was completed by Lawrence Block.

CRITICISM

Cornell Woolrich   (essay date 1961-66)

[*In the following excerpt from his posthumously published autobiography,* Blues of a Lifetime, *originally written between 1961 and 1966, Woolrich describes his early development as a writer, beginning with his first novel,* Cover Charge.]

I think now it was a bad thing, from the short-range point of view, to have saved [*Cover Charge*], but a necessary thing in the long run, to ensure my future as a writer. It wasn't worth saving in itself, but if I hadn't saved it, I probably never would have written another. I would have remembered the fiasco of the first time, and there wouldn't have been enough encouragement to warrant my giving up an equal amount of time and effort a second time. In other words, though it did me no credit, was just an exercise rather than a finished product, I'm pretty sure I wouldn't have gone on to become a writer without it. To which the natural corollary immediately arises: Well, would that have been a loss? Who needed you? True, but everyone has to do something, everyone has to do the best he can. He's allowed that much, at least.

I started out with one line . . . Well, any writer does, any story or any book does. Then the line became a paragraph, the paragraph a page, the page a whole scene, the scene a whole chapter. But this stood alone, by itself, in the middle of nowhere. A scene without a story to go with it, in other words.

I wrote out from it in both directions, forward toward the ending and backward toward the beginning. Finally, I'd stretched it out forward as far as I could, and stretched it out backward as far as I could, and the thing was suddenly over, finished.

"So that's how you write a book!" I marveled, hardly able to believe it myself.

But the whole thing was still formless anyway; it had no plot progression, no dramatic unity, no structural discipline. There was a great deal of such writing being done at the time, it was called "slice-of-life," I think, and it deliberately avoided plot and structure. But the big difference between it and my own effort was this: these others had something to write about, at least. I didn't. They knew something about life, even if it was only one small segment, one infinitesimal microcosm of it, and they were writing about the part they knew. I knew nothing about any part of it, so therefore I was writing about something I knew nothing about.

What I was actually doing was, not writing autobiographically, which every beginner does and should, but writing objectively, which should come along only a good deal later. What saved it from being any worse than it was, was a facility with words, which probably had been latent in me all along.

But I came to realize later, as I grew a little, that it was far better to be short on words, scantily supplied, poor in them, so long as you could sprinkle the few you had over a damn good basic situation (which could carry you along by itself, almost without words), than to be able to work them into a rich weave, make them glitter, make them dance, range them into vivid descriptions and word pictures, and in the end have them covering nothing but a great big hole.

In one of my earlier clinkers, not the first but one that came soon afterward, on trying to reread it a few years later, I found out with the help of two spaced pencil marks that it had taken me a full one-and-a-half pages (and compact print and not unduly wide margins either) to describe a man riding up in an elevator from the ground floor to the third. Nothing happened that might have extenuated it; there was no knife fight, no pickpocket observed plying his trade. No one else was on the elevator with him. He just stood there and thought.

It could have been done in one four-part line that barely stretched all the way across the page, like this: "He got in, the car started; the car stopped at the third and he got out again."

But I know what the matter was. I knew I had nothing to

say, I knew I had to fill out two-hundred-odd pages to get it up to minimum book length, I was afraid I'd never make it, so I dragged out everything to unutterable length, just to fill all that empty white space with little black marks, no matter what the marks were or what they said. If I'd cut the thing down to appropriate size, I'd have had a medium-length short story there, but even that would have had the same defect: it would have been all about nothing at all. The real solution would have been not to let the damn thing be published at all, that would have been the best cure for it. But asking a young beginning author to deny himself publication is like asking a thirsty tongue-dangling pup to deny himself a drink of water.

I am dwelling on this first writing copy of mine at such great and unwarranted length, because I want to explain the defects inherent in it, and how I learned only later that they were defects and that I must try to avoid them. If there is one thing that is sure death to a writer it is, not having too hard a time of it, having too easy a time of it. That can stunt him, abort him, cripple him ineradicably. If he can get published without having to exercise self-discipline in his turn-out, he may never really learn how to write well at all. I was lucky, I got a second chance. I finally learned to do my job competently only in the mid-Thirties, after I'd already been hitting print steadily for eight years. It would have been a lot better if everything I'd done until then had been written in invisible ink and the reagent had been thrown away. If you can't write a thing well, don't write it at all; leave it unwritten, for somebody else to write. The world doesn't need stories that badly, it has too many already. (pp. 10-12)

Cornell Woolrich, "Remington Portable NC69411," in his Blues of a Lifetime: The Autobiography of Cornell Woolrich, *edited by Mark T. Bassett, Bowling Green State University Popular Press, 1991, pp. 3-30.*

Francis Lacassin   (essay date 1974)

[*In the following essay, originally published in 1974, Lacassin analyzes Woolrich's main thematic concerns and narrative devices.*]

They proclaimed him the master of suspense, the king of the thriller. And it's true.

It is an honor that any author of detective novels would envy. But it does not fully define the genius of Cornell Woolrich, alias William Irish. He was a narrator of tragic tales, a psychologist, a moralist, also a poet. . . . And as a painter, Woolrich was the impressionist of the detective novel.

He himself defined his work as a "form of subconscious self-expression." Undoubtedly, he would want to call his confession to imaginary crimes a kind of catharsis, an issuing forth of personal obsessions. That is why his work has pleased readers and set itself apart from the traditional detective story: because of its subjectivity, because of the animated gaze the author devotes to his characters. An inverted but convincing sincerity transforms the reader from spectator at an intellectual game into a repository of confidence. In other detective novels, the reader is entranced and keeps score. Here, he suffers and participates.

For Cornell Woolrich, the crime story is only an alibi, a simple skeletal framework, within whose interior he unfolds a vision of life filtered through his own sensibility. His is a vision of a world having for poles, love and death, and for governor, Destiny. It is a universe where the living mingle with phantoms of their desires and of their dreams, where a box of matches wedged in a door, an earring, a half-consumed cigarette, a ridiculous hat decides the termination of a life. A universe where mornings lounge in enthusiastic clarity, and twilights fall, implacable. (pp. 41-2)

[Woolrich's] first works (unknown in France) seem to be novels of love. He followed them with his detective novels—or rather with his tragic love stories. In such a manner one can characterize a work where affectivity (love and its derivatives: tenderness, hatred, jealousy, anguish, absence) assumes an uncustomary importance.

There, the detective never takes first place. The police officer is not very evident; sometimes not at all. He is represented by a car patroling in the distance (*Deadline at Dawn*), by a brief interrogation (*I Married a Dead Man*), by the registry of a complaint (*Waltz into Darkness*). In this last novel he intervenes a second time, when the lights are extinguished, the curtain fallen, the principal character dead. Once more he lives in the wings, knocking at a door that the author has closed, before writing the words "THE END."

Cornell Woolrich does not scorn the technical resources of the investigation. Without it, his narratives would be nothing but love stories disturbed by death. But he relies for its execution (sorting out miscellaneous clues, deductions, inquiries and examinations of witnesses) upon the interested principal—that person who everything indicates to be guilty (*Deadline at Dawn, The Black Curtain, "The Dog with the Wooden Leg"*)—or upon those who do reconnaissance for the victim, and not without reason: his wife (*The Black Angel*), or his friend and his mistress (*Phantom Lady*). Why such a strange choice of hero? Because of the dramatic and psychological richness offered by the ambiguity of this criminal/victim situation.

The investigation, conventional in method, but unusual because of the personality of the investigator, sees its inspiration radically modified. In other detective fiction, dramatic progress is marked by the discovery of elements that unlock the mystery concealing the truth; in Woolrich, one follows a psychological progress where the climax is servant to the analysis, as the mystery gives way to the anguish of the investigator.

The latter figure is no longer a salaried functionary searching for a criminal so that the law can retain its force; the investigation is not conducted out of professional conscience, to solve a mystery. The investigator is either a person who is struggling to save his own skin—or one of the relatives, who are attempting to prevent his execution. The investigation: elsewhere, it is a search for the truth; here, it is a race against death. The heightening and alleviation of anguish.

It is such anguish that the author causes the reader to share, no longer witness to a game, but co-responsible for a stake whose sincerity and gravity seize him, a cause that he makes his own. This identification of reader with character is skillfully accomplished by the author, thanks to three elements:

—the noble or pathetic character of the cause;
—the sympathetic personality of the victim-hero; and
—the use of suspense.

The hero is recruited from two categories. (1) Authentic victim unjustly accused of a crime that he did not commit, but whose circumstances accuse him of it (*Phantom Lady, The Black Angel*, "You'll Never See Me Again"). He is generally arrested, and the date of his execution fixed. It is necessary, between now and then, for a friend, a wife, or an adorable mistress to demonstrate, by means of a counter-investigation, his innocence. When Woolrich allows the hero some liberty, it is in order to cast a doubt on his innocence. Then, the condemned man struggles to postpone the deadline, to fend off some of his apprehension, and very much to preserve the confidence of those whom he loves (*The Black Curtain*, "The Dog with the Wooden Leg," *Deadline at Dawn*), always with the need to merit the love of others . . .

(2) If he is truly guilty, the hero has been driven to crime by a psychologically untenable situation. *Grief*: we witness, in this case (after an investigation points to a professional), the meticulous vengeance of the bride who has seen her groom killed in an accident at the church (*The Bride Wore Black*). *The feeling of injustice*: a husband kills the blackmailer who had made up love letters from his wife prior to their marriage ("The Earring").

They don't matter much—the degree of the hero's guilt, or other variables. From his entrance onto the scene, the reader is invited to sympathize with him. Before the reader has identified with him, some character is situated in such a way as to inspire tenderness or pity. *Adorable tenderness*: young ladies named "Angel Face" or "Smiles." Candid, fragile things, lent to sacrifice their lives to save conjugal bliss—or the life of the beloved. How could one fail to suffer, in anguish, their incursions into ambiguous milieus, where they expose themselves, decoys to a danger as terrible as it is unknown ("Dead Roses"), or to one that is truly fantastic (*Black Alibi, Night Has a Thousand Eyes*)?

Pathetic artifices often reinforce the personality of the hero in a manner that expands his affective resources. He is amnesiac, then restored by some shock to a life previously forgotten, and in which he is afraid of having committed a murder: "where?" and "when?" There is a moving quest to retrace his footsteps and prove his innocence to him (*The Black Curtain*). He is drugged, so that fear pushes him into an unnecessary crime ("Marihuana"). Blindness prevents the old negress of "The Hummingbird Comes Home" from discovering, by means of her son's cadaver, the vanity of her hope: he has not gone straight.

The blind man of "The Dog with the Wooden Leg," unbeknownst to his young daughter, begs in order to relieve their poverty. Profiting by his infirmity, some traffickers use the wooden leg of his dog, during their rounds, as a depository for drugs. Accused of complicity with them, the old man voluntarily throws himself into the hands of the gangsters, so as to unmask them and vindicate himself before his young daughter. It is a danger as terrible as it is invisible. Showing us this infirm old man—duped, swept off, sequestered, menaced—the author toys, not only with the nerves of the spectator, as in classical suspense, but also with his heart.

In this register, cruel and tender at the same time, Woolrich depicts the psychological and material encircling of an urchin, Buddy. One night, in the apartment where Buddy sleeps alone, he is besieged by his upstairs neighbors, whose crime he has betrayed: neither his parents nor the police had taken him seriously (**"Fire Escape"**).

Sometimes an atmosphere too black is brightened by a rare humor. There is the visit to the New York underworld by a young girl made up and dressed in her mother's clothes. She amuses herself, at the risk of her life, by duping some gangsters (**"Cinderella and the Mob"**). And, after a sojourn in New York, an old lady in a merry mood—in secret from her nephew—spends several nights disentangling the motives for an assassination committed in a museum, before her eyes (**"The Body in Grant's Tomb"**). [In a translator's note, Bassett adds: "Francis M. Nevins, Jr., has pointed out, in correspondence with me, that in the English-language version of **'The Body in Grant's Tomb,'** the murder is not committed before the old lady's eyes; she merely discovers the corpse."]

Yet, gay or sad, all are recognizable by a common denominator—love, in the less carnal sense of the term, that of the precept "Love one another." Love, or its absence, inspires their crime or their conflict. Love, or the sentiments that cause frustration to be born.

Compounded with culpability, or suffering over not meriting the love of others, in *I Married a Dead Man, Deadline at Dawn, The Black Curtain,* **"The Dog with the Wooden Leg."**

With incommunicability, or powerlessness in winning the love or the confidence of others, in **"Fire Escape,"** *Phantom Lady.* "He . . . let his hand trail over her shoulder as he passed her, in a parting accolade that expressed mutely but perfectly what it was intended to convey: mutual distress, sympathy without the power of helping one another, two people who were in the same boat" (*Deadline at Dawn*).

The absence, the brutal privation of love is evoked with a poetic obsession: "I see her every night. The smoke clears away and there she is. She sits next to me, and I buy her a drink. She comes with me into every one of these places." Or in an intimate snapshot, on the stroke of an arrest: "I ran back with them, and when I got there the door was standing open and the hallway beyond was empty. They hadn't waited; they were gone. I stood there in the open doorway, and the rolled-up pajamas dropped disconsolately to the floor at my feet and lay there" (*The Black Angel*).

Hatred and vengeance follow the destruction of love in *The Bride Wore Black.*

Solitude is for those forgetful of love, in *Deadline at Dawn,* **"Too Nice a Day to Die," "Marihuana."** "He stayed on awhile, hoping he'd have better luck after dark than during the daylight hours. Like a mendicant begging alms he stood there begging a donation of memories, but the obliviousness of those about him only increased rather than lessened" (*The Black Curtain*).

There is fear of the unknown, of the indefinable menace that love is powerless to exorcise: "He didn't tell Virginia any of it. What was there he could tell her? Only draw terrifying shadow outlines, without being able to fill in their meaning. A stranger on a street had pursued him. That was either too much or too little. He didn't know who the man was, nor what he wanted with him, nor even who it was that *he,* the one he wanted, was supposed to be" (*The Black Curtain*).

The fear of death is often masked by fear of the night: "You can't stop [the night] from coming back again. It's on its way even now. It goes around on a curve. The farther it gets, the nearer it gets" (*Night Has a Thousand Eyes*).

And, worst of all, "*The fear of losing the thing you love. The greatest fear there is*" (*I Married a Dead Man, The Black Angel*).

These, for the characters of Cornell Woolrich, are the forms of anguish, that feeling best suited for bringing into harmony all those who, at some moment or another in life, have surely felt it.

Then there is the last element necessary to seducing the reader and to his identification with a sympathetic hero whose cause he shares: suspense. Suspense—the means by which this art transports the anguish of an imaginary universe into the consciousness of the reader.

With Woolrich, suspense occupies the place reserved, in a traditional detective novel, for mystery, the monolithic obstacle destined to occupy the reader in solitude, and which, alone, the investigator manages to remove on the last page. In contrast, suspense requires the participation of the reader. By means of expert psychological gradations, the author provokes in the reader a tension analogous to that felt by the hero, followed by a brutal abatement. A slow crescendo is followed by brute failure. It is a technique founded on three essential artifices:

> —at the start, a serene situation in a placid setting, where, already insinuating itself, is the germ of some evil;

> —the author pretends to cast down his cards. He displays all the difficulties to be worked out by the hero, all the dangers to confront. It is a maneuver destined to make one fear for him, in anticipation: will he evade them? Among the favorite situations are those where a fragile creature—young girl, child, invalid—offers himself or herself as bait to an unknown criminal, in order to expose him. After the reader is invited to follow, the game taxes the author's ingenuity to thwart

his reader with an unfolding of events that set his nerves on end.

> —finally—a method dear to Woolrich—a deadline is fixed at the start, for proving the main character innocent, after which failure is penalized by death. The suspense is augmented by the menace of the time limit, more and more oppressive in measuring the fact that the reader is drawing close to a hero apparently incapable of surmounting his or her difficulties.

It is a diagram applied by the author of *Phantom Lady* to most situations in the detective novel. But his more dazzling demonstrations have been well executed, thanks to the subjects he prefers: substitutions of identity, the wait for an unknown or indefinable menace, an error of justice.

Whether known to the reader (*I Married a Dead Man*) or unknown to him (*Waltz into Darkness*), the substitution of identities puts onto the scene a woman, deserving or charming, who, from one blunder to the next, is unable to survive deceit and protect her security. In the former novel, the mechanism of degradation is put into movement in the course of a brilliant, fashionable soirée, through a gaffe of the heroine's: she is unaware that she is hearing the Barcarolle from *Tales of Hoffman,* which is, however, the favorite musical composition of the man whose widow she is pretending to be.

A paltry incident, hardly noticed in the euphoria of a fashionable dinner-party, provokes in *Night Has a Thousand Eyes*—a poetic novel bathed in occultism—Jean Reid's wait for the death of her father, predicted by a clairvoyant whose admonitions are infallible.

> It began in such a little way. A drop. . . . But not of water. A drop of hot consomme on a white evening frock, worn for the first time. There is no littler way in which a thing can begin than that. . . . But something has begun. Death has begun. Darkness has begun, there in the full jonquil-blaze of the dinner-table candles. Darkness. A spot no bigger at first than that spilled drop of consomme. Growing, steadily growing, by the days, by the weeks, by the months, until it has blotted out everything else. Until all is darkness. Until there is nothing *but* darkness. Darkness and fear and pain, doom and death.

The menace of a deadline also weighs heavily on *The Black Angel,* from the moment when the delightful young woman undertakes to prove that which the police have not succeeded in discovering: the innocence of the man of her life. Knowing that he will be executed "during the week of May sixteenth," she can not stop herself from beginning the struggle, with a cry of weariness: "I sank back against the seat. And all the way home the thought that rode with me was: 'I'm only twenty-two, and yet they're going to make me a widow in less than three months.'"

The deadline, measuring the period during which suspense will be exercised, can be remote, or quite near. In *Phantom Lady,* it is represented by the execution of Scott Henderson in the electric chair, victim of a miscarriage of justice. The lapse of time is 150 days, but everything happens during the last 15 days. There are false trails and in-

accessible witnesses. Finally located, these keep silent—after that, talking; then they die mysteriously before their testimony is recorded. Through this alternation between hope and defeat, the author carries off a successful tour de force, maintaining suspense throughout his tale, which is to say, for the final fifteen days "before the execution."

With *Deadline at Dawn,* Woolrich wanted to surpass himself, concentrating the anguish and the suspense in a single night, from ten o'clock to six in the morning. The workman, Quinn's electrician, has four hours in which to become an honest man again. To efface the traces of his burglary. To return the money that he has stolen. In setting out to do so, he discovers the still warm cadaver of his employer. Now he must guard himself against a miscarriage of justice, and exonerate himself in the eyes of the only person who understands: a dance hostess whose acquaintance he had made shortly before midnight. Thus is born an anguish whose gradient is measured by the chapter titles: [clock faces reading] "2:23," "4:19," "5:21." Finally, "5:45." Thanks to clues found at the scene of the crime, and with the help of the dance hostess—after all the errors along the way and the false trails—he manages to locate and tie up the guilty man, betraying him by a telephone call to the police.

In spite of this prodigy of psychological tension and dramatic conciseness, Woolrich manages to win only half his wager. Not because of the gross improbabilities, often pointed out [by detractors] for no apparent reason; they appear wrong upon first reading, and are absorbed into a certain poetic logic. Rather, because of the deadline's lacking some inexorability. Six in the morning: the hour to take the bus from New York into the country, which they will never have to leave. What would prevent them from taking it tomorrow? Bricky's argument, that the accursed city will deprive them of the courage of leaving if they miss the first bus, is poor indeed. And it is less poignant than Scott Henderson's situation. Legally condemned to death, his pardon refused, he will, inexorably, be executed at the appointed hour, if his innocence is not proven beforehand.

Classic suspense, as practiced by most authors of "thrillers"—and among whom Woolrich remains the virtuoso—utilizes a very short lapse of time, perhaps a minute. As in that scene where the ravishing Alberta, nicknamed "Angel Face," has instigated the arrival in her bedroom of the man she believes capable of having committed the crime of which her husband is accused (*The Black Angel*). The technique always consists of slowing down the dénouement—here, the death of the young woman. The appointed time, if brought near too soon, prohibits the introduction of false clues or connected events.

The role of restraint is played by an accumulation of details, which appear to be unavailing; they shrivel one's expectations and increase one's anguish, while underlining the prudence, meticulousness, and efficacy of the assassin. These details, these weighty expectations—supreme cleverness!—of the victim herself, encircle the reader, who is obliged to identify with her, and transform his nerves into violin strings.

> Suddenly the knob gave a warning flash, a coruscation, as its facets slowly began to revolve and

the light glanced off each successive one. He *had* been out there and he was coming in. It turned so slowly, and yet somehow so remorselessly, as though there were no power on earth could keep it from completing its appointed orbit. With not a forewarning sound to go with it. . . .

This blur, this new darkness against the old darkness, stood motionless for a while, then gradually started to shift over toward the bed. As it sidled in that direction the knob behind it came clear again, but that no longer held interest for me. . . . Thus the white plateau of the bed seemed to sidle forward and cut it off below the knees. . . .

Again it fell motionless and stood looking down at close range. Breathing was beginning to be audible, the strained, harsh breathing of slowly mounting, slowly unleashed rage. Deepening, thickening, struggling until it began to approach the catarrhal. My own had stopped, or seemed to have.

Tick, tick, tick—

Suddenly in the smoky dimness there was a flash midway down the vague form and close in against it. Oh, not a bright flash; the flicker of a tongue of ghostly gray flame. . . .

The silvery radiance slashed down and vanished, and there was the crunch of steel puncturing tight-packed layers of fabric; the bed quivered (*The Black Angel*).

The most magisterial demonstration of suspense, however, is found in **Phantom Lady.** With the privation of the writing, narrowness of the atmosphere, portrayal of secondary characters, dispassionate heightening and rigorousness of despair, and ingenuity of the failures that accumulate down to the final, unforeseeable reversal, this is the masterpiece of Cornell Woolrich. In a few pages he establishes an atmosphere and the particulars of a drama that would have required Balzac or Stendhal several chapters. The suspense begins even before the first line, thanks to the title of the opening chapter: "The Hundred and Fiftieth Day Before the Execution."

The threads of the plot are tied up before the drama has begun. In spite of the peaceful atmosphere, all is bound to one discordant note.

> The night was young, and so was he. But the night was sweet, and he was sour. . . . It was a shame, too, because it was all out of tune with everything around him. It was the one jarring note in the whole scene.
>
> It was an evening in May, at the get-together hour. The hour when half the town, under thirty, has slicked back its hair and given its billfold a refill and sauntered jauntily forth to keep *that date* . . .
>
> . . . The sky was rouge-red in the west, as though it was all dolled-up for a date itself, and it was using a couple of stars for diamond clips to hold up its evening-gown. . . . The air wasn't just air, it was aërated champagne, with a whiff

of Coty for good measure, and if you didn't watch out it went to your head. Or maybe your heart (*Phantom Lady*).

It is an intoxicating description that contradicts the prophetic chapter title: "The Hundred and Fiftieth Day Before the Execution." After that, it is the ninety-first day before the execution, the third day before the miscarriage of justice occurs. The inexorable countdown is recorded from one chapter to the next, as if to demonstrate the uselessness of struggling, the impossibility of making Destiny recant on a decision that has been kept in writing ever since.

Never has the weight of Destiny been so heavy as in *Phantom Lady,* unless in **"Too Nice a Day to Die,"** the cruel ballad of a solitary employee. On the verge of suicide, she delays her own execution for twenty-four hours. Never has she seen New York, the ravenous city, in such a sweet light. "The irregular picket-fence of tall building-tops around them on three sides in the distance looked trim and spruce and spotless as new paint in the sunshine. . . . Though [New York] had no honeysuckle vines and no balconies and no guitars, it was meant for love. For living and for love, and the two were inseparable; one didn't come without the other." Returning from a walk in the course of which she has found a fellow soul ready to unite his solitude with hers, the heroine is crushed to death by an automobile. Always, in Woolrich, there is the marriage of beauty and death, under the sign of fatalism.

Each initiative of his characters corresponds to a prophetic ending.

> So I wasn't going back, and oh, I wasn't going back, and no, I wasn't going back, and in between each recurrent resolve not to go back I'd see his face, Kirk's face, or think of him, or say his name down in my heart, and when nine o'clock on Saturday came I was back. . . . I was going into this place. . . . Mordaunt had told me to come back a second time after dark. . . . Now I was here, and the time for what I should have done and what I shouldn't have done was over; this was how I was going to do it (*The Black Angel*).

[In a translator's note, Bassett adds: "The passage that Lacassin cites [above] reads as follows: 'Pénétrer dans cette maison signifiait s'engager dans l'épreuve décisive y recontrer l'échec ou la victoire. Et une telle occasion ne se présenterait pas une seconde fois, c'était bien l'instant ou jamais de tenter sa chance. N'importe comment l'aventure touchait à sa fin. Cette nuit, cette heure, ce lieu avaient été marqués par le destin.' (My translation: 'To enter this house meant to take a decisive test and to know defeat or victory. And such an occasion does not come a second time. It was just that moment, or never to take one's chance. No matter how the adventure might draw to a close. This night, this hour, this place had been marked by destiny.') The fact that no comparable passage appears in the English text reveals that *Ange* (1953), published by Ditis (Paris) as part of the series 'Détective Club,' is not wholly true to the original text."]

Even when they think of escape, they obey the will of this

impenetrable power. "By fits and starts, by frightened spurts and equally frightened stops, some long, some short, they'd followed their destiny blindly" (***Waltz into Darkness***).

Unjust obstinance. It sometimes stirs, in the vanquished victim, a bitter sense of humor: "Well [I'm] to take part in an electrical experiment two and a half weeks from today. . . . I'll probably make every edition that day" (***Phantom Lady***).

In order to guard oneself better against Destiny, to escape from it, its characteristics are assigned to a place, or to a person. Thus the characters think of New York, the modern Babylon which has made them suffer:

> It's mean and bad and evil, and when you breathe too much of it for too long, it gets under your skin, it gets into you—and you're sunk, the city's got you. . . .
>
> There's a brain, something that thinks on its own, hanging over it. Watching you, playing with you, like a cat does a mouse. . . . There've been times I could almost feel the *pull* of it. Like when you're in swimming and an undertow gets you. You can't see anything, but you can feel the drag of it. . . . You can't break that by yourself (***Deadline at Dawn***).

Does a mouse have a chance of escaping the cat to whom it is a prisoner? Is it worth the pain of struggling against the blindness of fate to resist the ineluctable? A contrasting and poetic image, opposing the dissolution of sentiment to the solidity of matter, can allow one to believe in defeatism, to find fatalism delectable.

> Life was such a crazy thing, life was such a freak. A man was dead. A love was blasted into nothingness. But a cigarette still sent up smoke in a dish. And an ice cube still hovered unmelted in a highball glass. The things you wanted to last, they didn't; the things it didn't matter about, they hung on forever (***I Married a Dead Man***).

It is a simple process, with suspense destined to dramatize one's psychological progress. If the characters grow tender or resigned, it is only for a short while. Mediocre or washed up, fragile or despairing, tricked or frustrated, abused or disabused, they quickly exclaim against injustice and rebel against it. Sometimes with grandiloquence; sometimes in silence, armed with nothing other than their courage. Alone, they defy the power without a face, and they triumph over it. Alone? No. With the aid of love, represented by a woman ready to exchange her own life for that of the man she loves.

It is a primal combat. The true victory they don't win on the basis of error, egotism, injustice, or evil—but through themselves. Sublime, metamorphosed by the struggle, they attain, thanks to it, some of their lost values: purity, goodness, faith in life.

Even when the combat is finished tragically, through death, the characters reap some benefit from their effort. Jean Reid can not prevent the violent death of her father, written in the stars. His absence is compensated for by the recognition of love. She delivers herself from an anguish over life that her wealth has imposed on her. "Listen close," her father had said to her. "And tomorrow don't remember this. But remember it some other day. . . . [Being rich] means you'll have a hard time of it. It means you'll always be a little lonely. Reaching out, with no one there to clasp your hand. It means no one will ever love you. And if they do, you won't be able to tell if it's meant for you alone" (***Night Has a Thousand Eyes***).

The metamorphosis of the sinner, his redemption, figures even in ***Waltz into Darkness,*** the most despairing of Cornell Woolrich's novels. It is also his finest character study, a faithful transportation of *Manon Lescaut* into the materialistic and unromantic universe of the detective novel. For him alone could it succeed. The influence of the Abbé Prévost can be recognized on each page of this new tale of the destruction of a man by the woman he loves.

The setting: the same place where that distressed couple think to find peace. "It is to New Orleans that one must come, I often say to Manon, when one wants to taste the true sweetness of love. It is here that one loves without self-interest, without jealousy, without inconstancy" (*Manon Lescaut*).

The characters: he of French descent, Louis Durand, wealthy and esteemed merchant; she, Bonny, angelic and perverse, a trickster at cards, always in search of a generous lover. She fleeces him, betrays him, abandons him. He strips himself of everything in order to rejoin her—fortune, security, honor—and turns to crime, since it is the only means of protecting her.

The times gone by: Woolrich places his story in 1880, in order to maintain—through poetry now obsolete in its moods, sentiments, costumes—the greatest possible resemblance with the faded elegance of *Manon Lescaut.*

The End: love inflamed can believe that only death has defeated it. "I delayed, more than twenty-four hours, my lips pressed to the face and hands of my dear Manon," recounts Des Grieux (Prévost, *Manon Lescaut*). It is the kiss supreme, which Woolrich renders thus: "Their very souls seemed to flow together. To try to blend forever into one. Then, despairing, failed and were separated, and one slipped down into darkness and one remained in the light" (***Waltz into Darkness***).

The modern Des Grieux dies in place of his Manon, poisoned by her. This atrocious agony—her work—seizes Bonny's conscience, making her aware of the uselessness of her life, of the horror of her past. And when the police rap at the door, indifferent to the threat of punishment, she cries out: "Oh! Louis! Louis! I have loved you too late. Too late I have loved you." In finding love, even too late, she tells herself: "And this is my punishment" (***Waltz into Darkness***).

"Faces are masks, anyway," says one of the protagonists of ***Deadline at Dawn.*** It's true. Neither she nor her brothers in misfortune, once they have surmounted it, resemble their earlier image. Under the animated gaze of Cornell Woolrich, they have grown better, and have merited his sympathy, our sympathy. They have become conscious of their true personality. It was what their struggle revealed it to be. The author divines it for them, as if he were endowed with the third eye of Tibetan wisdom: the eye that sees inside of people.

Psychologist Cornell Woolrich has told of the anguish within the victim who is crushed by fatality. As moralist, he has written the novel of courage, of interdependence, and of strife.

As a painter of the varieties of anguish that love, or its absence, secretes, he does not make them the only object of his study. The observation of daily conduct, sensuality, and even the hypersensitivity of sympathetic but neuropathic characters have inspired him to abundant analyses.

There is no escape from the observation of the novelist: not one of the thousand daily details is useless to the dramatic progress, but a single one is enough to engender an atmosphere. Or to define a character, revealing through a single gesture an intimate preoccupation, his or her meticulousness, prudence, or modesty, in whatever way of life. Thus the fugitive and mysterious woman of *Phantom Lady* is intimidated by a luxurious restaurant and embarrassed by a hat that she has quit wearing: "The hat, which she had been carrying at arm's length beside her, she placed on the third chair of their table, and partly covered it with the edge of the cloth, possibly to protect it from stains."

To poeticize an atmosphere and cause us to appreciate its sweetness, he provides for himself an insect which has the power to reflect, like humans. "The perfume of the rosebushes was heavy on the June night, and sleepy little insects made a somnolent humming noise, as though they were talking in their sleep" (*I Married a Dead Man*).

A quickened sensibility, a certain poetic instinct, permits him, by the choice of a single adjective, to economize on several lines in order to introduce the reader into an atmosphere—for example, when he evokes the "lackadaisical gait" of a police car patrolling at random at the end of a night without incident (*Deadline at Dawn*), or when he wants to communicate his tenderness for the desolated interior of a dance-hostess used by life: "She struck a match, uncocked the jet, and a little circle of sluggish blue fire jumped into being. She placed a battered tin coffee-pot over this, readied for brewing from earlier in the day, when it had not been so much agony to move about." The flame is a symbol of happiness, her single glimmer rekindled. The word "sluggish" diminishes this symbol and signals the sorry state of a gas-ring, and therefore the poverty of her landlord.

A sole adjective, again, defines a poorly ventilated, dilapidated piece of property, inhabited by unpretentious and frustrated tenants: "Outside [his door he] found himself assailed by a delayed odor of cookery that must have taken several hours to creep up from the ground floor where it had originated at noon" (*The Black Curtain*). It is not just any odor, but an odor situated in space, in time, in the sensibility of the author.

All of his characters share with him an obsession with detail or an enervated sensuality. Sometimes in order to apologize for a disagreeable sensation, shaking hands with

an old man: "It was like clasping twigs" (*Night Has a Thousand Eyes*). Sometimes in order to measure their anguish, such as the hero of *The Black Curtain,* opening a door onto the unknown: "The knob felt cold and glibly elusive . . . The darkness of the interior lay as thick and palpable upon him as a drift of black feathers."

After smell and touch: taste. The architect of **"You'll Never See Me Again"** quarrels with Smiles, his wife, because she has baked him some biscuits that were "as hard as gravel, they tasted like lye." It is a premonitory sensation. Weeping, his wife runs out; soon, the husband is suspected of having killed her. Coming to exonerate himself before his in-laws, he is received in a living-room that appears to him to be "not restful." Questioning himself about this impression, he attributes it to the asymmetry of the room. Upon examining it, he discovers that one wall has been superadded in order to conceal a cadaver. From sensuality to hypersensitivity . . . Soon, it will be from hypersensitivity to the sixth sense.

The sensitivity is explainable, in certain cases, by an exceptional auditory acuity, stressed by memory or observation. Noises identified by the dying man, while his indifferent mistress dines:

> A busy little tinkering, ending with a tap against a cup rim: that meant she was stirring sugar into her coffee.
>
> A creak from the frame of a chair: that meant that she was leaning forward to drink it.
>
> A second creak: that meant that she had settled back after taking the first swallow.
>
> He could hear bread crust crackle, as she tore apart a roll (*Waltz into Darkness*).

This is a good example of analytical observation. But how can one explain the reaction of the heroine of *The Black Angel:* "a sluggish current of air, a displacement, had eddied toward and reached me"? Or that of the dance-hostess, detecting the presence of a cadaver in an unknown and obscure room, as soon as she opens the door: "The air changed subtly. There was someone in it besides themselves, yet there was no one in it. They say you can't smell death, at least not recent death. Yet there was a *stillness* in it, a presence in it that was more than just emptiness" (*Deadline at Dawn*).

Hypersensitivity, sixth sense, or message from the unconscious? The same woman, pursuing the unknown assassin into the interior of a building, identifies the apartment where this person lives with a single look at the door: "A swing around the turn, and there it was looming in front of her. Coffin-size. The door through which death had come home a little while before. It looked just like all the other doors here. But it wasn't. There was death pulsing from it, in unseen waves. She could almost feel them on her face, like a vibration" (*Deadline at Dawn*).

A closed door reveals to a pregnant Helen that her lover will not be coming back again: "Doors can express things. This one did. It was inert, lifeless; it didn't lead anywhere. It was not the beginning of anything, as a door should be. It was the end of something" (*I Married a Dead Man*).

These projections of the unconscious, which some tormented and neuropathic people effect on objects, emerge sooner or later as hallucinations. Each of Woolrich's novels contains an example of it. As though it were an assassin's dream in the expressionist cinema, the perceived image undergoes a cruel metamorphosis. Those drops of blood sketch a four-leafed clover. Or, on the other hand, a familiar gesture evokes blood spilt and not expiated. "It's the hand that holds out its coffee-cup across the breakfast-table in the mornings, to have the urn tipped over it. Bloody-red for a moment in fancy, then back again to pale as it should be. Or maybe, to the other, it's that other hand opposite one, that does the tipping of the urn" (*I Married a Dead Man*).

Cornell Woolrich never sacrifices analysis to plot, psychology to dramatic action. This touchstone categorizes him as being in the class of authors of "psycho-thrillers." He would be satisfied with that; to be occult is part of his personality, a not well-recognized facet of his talent. A great part of his work's success also rests on the quality of the writing.

He is also a poet.

The art of metaphor, the painting of sentiments, the identification of humanity with an ambient environment, the presence of nature, the vision of life filtered through his delicate sensibility—they merit him this title.

Moreover, he owes it to those short bits of sentences, printed in italics, that he sprinkles into each book, and certain of which are repeated three times in succession by the hero. Others, lancelike, are employed as a leitmotif in order to raise the level of anguish and tension, and assume an unexpected function: that of poetic incantation. They are verses detached from a secret poem, which one could reconstitute thus:

> She must have loved him.
> She must have.
> Yes, oh yes, she must have.
> She must have, all right!
>   (*The Black Angel*)

> And these words continued to beat the measure
> in her head, even to the moment
> where he gave her the kiss of welcome:
> Where and when?
> Where and when?
> Where and when?
>   (*I Married a Dead Man*)

> The handwriting of an unknown person.
> Of an unknown person. An unknown person.
>   (*Waltz into Darkness*)

> It was like train-wheels
> Going through her head:
> Though we've never seen you.
> Though we've never seen you.
> Though we've never seen you.
> Clicketty-clack,
> Stop and go back,
> You still have the time,
> Turn and go back,
> Too late to go back,
> Too late to go back,
>   (*I Married a Dead Man*)

> Chica chica boom boom.
> Chica chica boom boom.
> Maybe tonight, darling,
> Maybe tonight.
> Now I've got her.
> Now I've got her.
> Now I've got her. . . .
>   (*Phantom Lady*)

Instead of submitting to these incantations, certain characters prefer to abandon themselves to a lyrical feverishness. Therefore, the daughter of millionaire Reid says to the detective who has prevented her suicide:

> Home? . . . Death is waiting there. Death that hasn't died yet, and that death is the worst of all. Death is in bed there, in the room that used to belong to my father, with the covers up to its chin. And it hasn't moved all night, but still it hasn't slept, it's lain there awake, staring out before it. I know. I go in that room every morning. It'll turn that helpless look, those eyes, my way when I go in the door, saying, Help me, help me. I saw your face just now when you saw my eyes. You didn't think I did, but it was so clear to read. Such pain, such pity. And you're just a stranger I met last night. Then how do you think I feel, seeing those other eyes (*Night Has a Thousand Eyes*).

[In a translator's note, Bassett adds: "Lacassin's quotations from *Night Has a Thousand Eyes* in this paragraph indicate that the 1952 translation published by Denoël (Paris) as part of the series 'Oscar,' *Les Yeux de la nuit*, is not always faithful to Woolrich's text. At this point, instead of the original (which I have quoted), Lacassin quotes the following passage as Jean Reid's lament to Detective Shawn: 'Pour moi vous n'êtes qu'un passant. Vous vous êtes trouvé sur mon chemin et vous m'avez obligée à regarder les étoiles, alors que sans vous, j'en serais libérée depuis longtemps. Je ne sais pas si on doit remercier les gens pour ce genre de service . . . Arrêtez ces étoiles, là-haut, inspecteur. Voilà ce que vous pouvez faire! Mettez-leur les menottes . . . assommez-les à coups de matraque!' Here is my translation of the passage: 'To me you're merely a bystander. You found me in your way and you made me look at the stars. Whereas without you, I'd have been free for a long time. I don't know if one has to thank people for this kind of service . . . Arrest the stars up there, inspector. That's what you can do! Put them in handcuffs . . . beat them to death with your night-stick!'

It seems that considerable license has been taken by most, if not all, of Woolrich's French translators—although few passages may be as troublesome as that cited here. The issue is worth further study: French critics appear to have founded their (generally favorable) judgments of Woolrich upon impure texts. . . ."]

Metaphor, in the works of the author of *Phantom Lady*, knows multiple faces. It has an expressionistic function: like telescopic vision, it magnifies a detail entrusted to him alone, in order to summarize a situation, a state, an age. "His neck was like a slim sheaf of wires . . . His eyes were like rivets burning at white heat, eating their way inward through his skull" (*Night Has a Thousand Eyes*).

It permits economy in the description of a shabby night-club where one is assailed by "hailing, pelting two-quarter-time notes, like a stiff sandstorm hitting an accumulation of empty tin buckets, up there on the bandsmen's box" (*Deadline at Dawn*). It summarizes, all at once, a sentiment and its externalization: "Horror showed in her eyes" (**"Marihuana"**). It is the finishing touch supplied to an elegant atmosphere: Bonny sits down to breakfast "with a crisp little rustling" (*Waltz into Darkness*).

Woolrich also bends metaphor to more contrary objectives.

Humor: "A big red poker-chip on each cheek, as obvious as a pair of stop-lights, but whose effect was intended to be the opposite: go ahead" (**Phantom Lady**).

Despair: "Why not look inside the battered dog-eared valise under her bed back at the room at this moment? It didn't weigh much, but it was full. Full of stale dreams, that were no good now any more" (*Deadline at Dawn*). "She felt all shrivelled-up inside, and old; as though there were permanent wrinkles on her heart" (*I Married a Dead Man*).

Or, simply, a sensual image reinforced by an expressionistic trait: "A full-blown white rose; the perfume was almost like a bombshell in their faces" (*I Married a Dead Man*). From expressionism to the fantastic, by means of the surrealistic vision of a police car gliding into a calm and desperate night: "Then suddenly, without any warning sound, something white, shaped like an inverted boat, came drifting past on the dark tide of the night" (*Deadline at Dawn*).

The final use, more general, of metaphor: it enters into the composition of a symbol around which Woolrich orders most of his narratives. In **Phantom Lady** an orange and ridiculous hat, pumpkin-shaped symbol, is an eccentricity of the decisive and fugitive witness who wears it and who is the only hope of proving the innocence of him who is condemned to death.

Deadline at Dawn takes place beneath a symbol for lost time. A clock, that of the Paramount Theater tower—the only friend the dance-hostess has in New York—calls to mind lost and limited illusions, in conjunction with the passing of night, the freedom to hope.

A clairvoyant has predicted the date of millionnaire Reid's death (*Night Has a Thousand Eyes*). The symbol here is the stars. His fate, and the night—which measures the approach of his end—will be at the center of the anguish he shares with his daughter. The appearance of a pearl necklace, a stream of cars in the distant night, remind them at every moment of the haunting presence of the stars.

The poetry expresses itself through the color and the tonality that preside over the conception of each book as if, before writing it, Woolrich had chosen the color of the fabric from which to cut his story. Blue: *I Married a Dead Man;* Gray: **Deadline at Dawn;** blue print on gray: *Waltz into Darkness.* It is the color of the thoughts, the future, the sky, the characters, the scenery. Everything communes in the same monocolored osmosis. That which is the reigning tonality does not have an influence on the

symbolic value attached to the night: despair, solitude, inquietude; the morning, very pale, is the sign of happiness, hope, remission. Only twilight and dawn can, according to the color of the whole, oscillate between alleviation and melancholy.

The close of day, its dawning, light, shadow, night permit Woolrich to introduce nature again into the urban and dispassionate setting of the detective novel.

"In the morning the world was sweet just to look at from her window," he writes in *I Married a Dead Man.* He has painted admirable sunrises on his sets, however much deprived of romanticism.

> The light outside kept getting stronger. The blue started to seep out of it, and more and more white to ooze in. Then the white began turning a warm yellow, and that was daytime on, full strength. The occasional figures passing by outside the window cases became more numerous and more distinctly outlined. From blurred, anonymous silhouettes, they changed to three-dimensional pedestrians, complete and rounded, with separate shadows of their own that glided across the glass after them. Even the reversed lettering on the glass had a shadow of its own, now far behind it on the floor inside: CAFE . . .
>
> The unappreciated, disregarded miracle had happened once more; it was day again (*Night Has a Thousand Eyes*).

In a rare story that is neither gray nor blue, but purely black, he can not prevent himself from slipping in, like a false hope, the tableau of a particular dawn or twilight.

> That June day was slowly ebbing away at last, in velvety beauty. The twin towers of the Majestic Apartments were two-toned now, coral where they faced the imminent starting-point of night. The first star was already in the sky. It was like a young couple's diamond engagement-ring. Very small, but bright and clear with promise and with hope.
>
> New York. This was New York, on the evening of what was to have been the last day in the world—but wouldn't be now any more. It had been a lovely day, a nice day, too nice a day to die (**"Too Nice a Day to Die"**).

The poetry requires him, despite himself, to encounter his subject. It is thus that he can not restrain from playing a poetic note in what, elsewhere, would remain a banal household scene: "She threw a scent bottle, this time directly at him. He didn't swerve; it struck the wall just past his shoulder. A piece of glass nicked his cheek, and drops of sweet jasmine spattered his shoulder" (*Waltz into Darkness*).

In contrast to many novelists, Woolrich does not write in black and white, but in color. He succeeds at reserving for color a purely functional role: in order to denounce a vulgar taste or to create an obsession.

> It was a decorator's job, that outside room. Almost like a stage setting. Swell to look at, from the door like this, but no good for living in. Too

florid. It was flooded with this acutely vivid turquoise-blue color: upholstery, carpet, drapes, lamp shades. Either she or the decorator had a passion for it. Then all over, like flecks of blood, there were dabs of vermillion. . . . I could see a section of boudoir, and if the note in here was turquoise blue, the note in there was a sort of lush coral pink. It was drenched with it, even the satin-quilted walls (*The Black Angel*).

Alterations in color, craftily and economically, render the same occurrence as being separated by a lapse of time: "I sat there waiting for him, fawn swagger coat over my shoulders" (*Night Has a Thousand Eyes*). The sentence is repeated three times, changing in it only the color of the swagger coat: fawn, green, then black.

The author also yields to the desire to reproduce an effect of light that he must have observed in his own life. "[The color of the tile-topped stand] went down the chromatic scale, as shade after shade was drawn. Brilliant yellow to yellow green, to greenish blue, to indigo" (*The Black Curtain*).

A fascination with color is also experienced by his characters. The criminal/victim of ***Phantom Lady*** would never have returned to the prophetic bar "if the intermittent neon over it hadn't glowed on just then, as he was passing. It said 'Anselmo's' in geranium-red, and it dyed the whole sidewalk."

When Cornell Woolrich poises his pen to paint, it is most often due to an esthetic intention, in order to do the work of painting. His foremost quality is his sense of composition, as in this scene where color is forgotten in order to suggest the obsolete, passé, patined tone:

The place was stale with that stale smell that only old houses can attain. . . . On a center table there stood a platter of waxed fruits under a glass dome. Then there was a photograph with a crank handle protruding from the side and a great tulip-shaped horn rearing over it and threatening the middle of the room. Against a shield on the wall hung two mallards in high relief, complete with natural feathers, under convex glass. At the small of my back, until I dislodged it to find comfort, was a lumpy, battered mass that had once been a leather pillow (*The Black Angel*).

In this fashion he composes some still-lifes, over which weighs a feeling of absence that the color strains to support rather than to consume:

The room was a still life. . . .

A window haloed by setting sunlight, as if there were a brush fire burning just outside of it, kindling, with its glare, the ceiling and the opposite wall. The carpeting on the floor undulant and ridged in places, as if misplaced by someone's lurching footsteps, or even an actual bodily fall or two, and then allowed to remain that way thereafter. . . .

Dank bed . . . looking as if it had been untended for days. Graying linen receding from its skeleton on one side, overhanging it to trail the floor

on the other. A single shoe, a man's shoe, abandoned there beside it . . .

Forget-me-nots on pink wallpaper; wallpaper that had come from New York, wallpaper that had been asked for in a letter; "not too pink." There was a place where the plaster backing showed through in rabid scars (*Waltz into Darkness*).

His full measure he finds in living nature: both in the landscape and in the portrait. His vision of reality, his interpretation of color, and his manipulation of light, in order to modify the essence for the benefit of the sensation, make Cornell Woolrich the impressionist of the detective novel.

The house we live in is so pleasant in Caulfield. The bluegreen tint of its lawn, that always seems so freshly watered no matter what the time of day. The sparkling, aerated pinwheels of the sprinklers always turning, steadily turning; if you look at them closely enough they form rainbows before your eyes. The clean, sharp curve of the driveway. The dazzling whiteness of the porch-supports in the sun (*I Married a Dead Man*).

Here is a diurnal vision, to harmonize with the nocturnal vision of the same location, whose perspective has undergone a slight panoramic displacement:

In the light of the full-bodied moon the flower-garden at the back of the house was as bright as noon when she stepped out into it. The sanded paths that ran around it foursquare, and through it like an X, gleamed like snow, and her shadow glided along them azure against their whiteness. The little rock-pool in the center was polka-dotted with silver disks, and the wafers coalesced and separated again as if in motion, though they weren't (*I Married a Dead Man*).

These two visions have in common their perspective, their opposition being based on tones, in the alchemical role vested in light. Light does not clarify: it transposes, sometimes tints, sometimes shapes. They also have in common an interpretation of shadows that is rendered in blue and not in black. A blue shadow identifies the impressionist.

If the landscapes of Woolrich, often strewn with flowers, recall Monet, his numerous portraits of women make us think of Renoir, above all those in *Waltz into Darkness*, whose model lived in 1880, the epoch when impressionism was radiant.

The beauty of porcelain, but without its cold stillness, and a crumpled rose petal of a mouth.

. . . Her skin was that of a young girl, and her eyes were the innocent, trustful eyes of a child.

Tight-spun golden curls clung to her head like a field of daisies, rebelling all but successfully at the conventional coiffure she tried to impose upon them. They took to the ubiquitous psyche-knot at the back only with the aid of forceful pins, and at the front resisted the forehead-fringe altogether, fuming about like topaz sea-spray.

. . . Fitting tightly as a sheath fits a furled umbrella, [her dress] had a center panel, drawn and gathered toward the back to give the appearance of an apron or a bib superimposed upon the rest, and at the back puffed into a swollen protuberance of bows and folds . . .

A small hat of heliotrope straw, as flat as and no bigger than a man's palm, perched atop the golden curls, roguishly trying to reach down toward one eyebrow, the left, without there being enough of it to do so and still stay atop her head.

Amethyst-splinters twinkled in the tiny holes pierced through the lobes of her miniature and completely uncovered ears, and a slender ribbon of heliotrope velvet girded her throat. A parasol of heliotrope organdy, of scarcely greater diameter than a soup plate and of the consistency of mist, hovered aloft at the end of an elongated stick, like an errant violet halo (*Waltz into Darkness*).

Woolrich the painter does not always abandon himself to esthetic ends. In the course of a portrait, the novelist awakens and sets about manipulating the scenery, the light, the lighting, to suit some dramatic end. The scenery reflects the sentiments of the character. The waning light augments his solitude. The depopulation of the scene accompanies the depopulation of his soul.

The children began to hurry out of the park.

A random, homeward-bound nursemaid or two, wheeling her charges, followed after that, at intervals. The birds seemed to go too, or at least become voiceless. The sunlight itself started to withdraw from around him. The whole world was leaving the scene. The park became still, hushed . . .

Blue shadows, like tentatively clutching fingers, began a slow creep toward Townsend out from under the trees (*The Black Curtain*).

And behold the night, always inhospitable to the casualties of life. "They came out into the slumbering early-morning desolation . . . It was like walking through a massive, monolithic sepulchre. There was no one abroad, nothing that moved. Not even a cat scenting at a garbage-can. The city was a dead thing . . . stark and clammy, [and] it frightened them a little" (*Deadline at Dawn*).

But it appears in profile as an edifice symbolizing peace, and the empty streets again become reassuring: "[The house] was in a vicinity of eminent cleanliness and respectability. Trees lined the streets, and the streets were lifeless. . . . An occasional gas lamp-post twinkled. . . . A church steeple sliced like a stubby black knife upward against the brickdust-tinted sky" (*Waltz into Darkness*).

Variations in lighting either blacken or reduce the pressure of the atmosphere. Thus in *Deadline at Dawn,* we see the "direct lights out, and the figures on the floor moving about like rustling ghosts." On the other hand, less than a half-hour later, the hostess and her dance partner pause opposite a doorway "left open to the street, but with the perils of ingress ameliorated to some slight extent by a faltering lemon-pale backwash that came from deep within it."

Because of the rhythm of their dance, certain plays of light, observed from a moving vehicle, do not manage to dissipate, through a reassuring description, the menace that is posed to a landscape, and to promise peace.

Trees went by, dimly lit up from below, along their trunks, by the passing reflection of their headlight-wash, into a sort of ghostly incandescence. Then at times there weren't any trees, they fell back, and a plushy black evenness took their place—fields or meadows, she supposed—that smelled sweeter. Clover. It was beautiful country around here; too beautiful for anyone to be in such a hell of suffering in the midst of it (*I Married a Dead Man*).

The night ceasing to be the mirror of affectivity, the landscapes start to play the more subtle role of antithesis. Their sweetness, their beauty, contrasts with the distress of the character in order to accentuate it more.

The summer nights are so pleasant in Caulfield. They smell of heliotrope and jasmine, honeysuckle and clover. The stars are warm and friendly here, not cold and distant, as where I came from. . . . The breeze that stirs the curtains at the open windows is soft and gentle as a baby's kiss. And on it, if you listen, you can hear the rustling sound of the leafy trees turning over and going back to sleep again. The lamplight from within the houses falls upon the lawns outside and copperplates them in long swaths. . . . Oh, yes, the summer nights are pleasant in Caulfield.

But not for us (*I Married a Dead Man*).

The morning, habitually the promiser of hope, comes to its turn in this subtle game and becomes more sinister than the night.

Seeing the stars go out, and the dawn creep slowly toward her from the east, like an ugly gray pallor. She'd never wanted to see daybreak less, for at least the dark had covered her sorrows like a cloak but every moment of increasing light diluted it, until it had reached the vanishing-point, it was gone, there wasn't any more left (*I Married a Dead Man*).

And witness, returned, the familiar anguish.

To traverse these dramatic detours, moral or esthetic, the work of Woolrich returns to its first destination: that of relating anguish. But does the novel of anguish conceal its more secret preoccupations? Is there an obsession with death? Not a novel, not a short story of Woolrich's, fails to invoke it or make an appeal to ITS presence, to see a character hurling him- or herself before it. "She dressed faster than she ever had before. She had a date with death—in the oncoming pall of the blackout" ("**Dead Roses**"). Not one character seeks to flee it. On the contrary. "If you go back into that house again the doctor's name may not be Mordaunt the second time; the doctor's name may be death" (*The Black Angel*).

Through a projection of the unconscious, death becomes a figure personified: "death in high heels," "the morning snack of death." An invisible creature, but whose presence one can sense. "There was only silence in the room, waiting silence—and the three of them. There were three of them in the room now, where only two had first come in. Death was in the room with the two of them" (**"Marihuana"**).

Death personified. . . . In order to exorcise it? Or in order to submit to this fascination more fully? Beneath the horror that they display, the characters experience, in reality, a delectation for death, which is revealed in the ease with which they confront or provoke it, and in the complacency with which they contemplate its effects.

> She looked at his face, tried to reconstruct it, tried to fill it in. It was like reading a page on which the writing had already grown faded, blurred, distorted. It was like an ink-written page on which it has rained. Everything was still there yet, but everything had moved a little out of focus. The lines that had been facial characteristics were seams now. The mouth that had been either strong or weak, bitter or good-humored, was a gap now, a place where the face was open. The eyes that had been either kindly or cruel, wise or foolish, they were just glossy, lifeless insets now, like isinglass stuck into yellowish-gray dough.
>
> His hair was well-cared for and full of life and light yet, for it dies last (***Deadline at Dawn***).

Very revealing also is the strange alliance between the drop of blood and the drop of jasmine perfume, between the dying man and the angelic woman who has poisoned him, between death and beauty. "Dead. Strangled by a thing of beauty, a thing meant to give pleasure" (**"Wardrobe Trunk"**).

Sundays too beautiful to die, but where one dies all the same.

Crepuscular landscapes traversed by a festival of shadows and of lights, but where one of them kills the other.

Settings planted with honeysuckle, heliotrope, and jasmine, patrician houses guarded by the stars and which serve as jewel-box for the distress of a soul injured to death. Is it only in order to create suspense and anguish that Woolrich causes them to intertwine—beauty and death?

Behind them are divined the settings of Edgar Allan Poe: majestic houses devoured by fear and ruin, luxurious and suffocating gardens, sheets of water immobilized to poisoned tranquility.

These young women with smiles like angels, with "the eye that curls," dispatched by Cornell Woolrich into the arms of death, recall the girl-children that the author of "The Fall of the House of Usher" loved because they already bore the fatal mark.

Novel of anguish? Or novel of death?

Beyond its dramatic, esthetic, and poetic merits, the work of Cornell Woolrich owes perhaps part of the secret of its success to the ambiguous seduction that it works upon us. Beneath the mask of novel—novels are masks, after a fashion—is concealed a meditation, in elevated tones, on

Death. Death, adversary feared and beloved, evoked in the only universe where it is possible to contemplate it without damage: the universe of the detective novel. (pp. 43-73)

> *Francis Lacassin, "Cornell Woolrich: Psychologist, Poet, Painter, Moralist, An Essay," translated by Mark T. Bassett, in* Clues: A Journal of Detection, *Vol. 8, No. 2, Fall-Winter, 1987, pp. 41-78.*

Woolrich on literary inspiration:

I've had it happen in the damnedest places, as inconvenient as—as the high-spot of love—when you're *not* making love and are not in a position to. Then again when I've had everything set for it, it wouldn't come on. Once after days of exploratory bicycling, I found a deserted little cove along the coastline south of Biarritz that seemed to be just what I was looking for for the rest of that summer. I cycled down to it the next day with all my equipment, everything I needed, a shade for my eyes, *Gitanes,* a couple bottles of French beer (but always for *after,* never before). It was an ideal place for it; not a person in sight, not even a house, for miles around, the relaxing sand, the blue Biscay water, the warm, soothing breeze blowing from it. Nothing happened, not a word would come; I finally dozed off. It was *too* quiet, not enough background sound; it was like writing in a vacuum.

On the other hand, it hit me with such violent immediacy one night when I was coming home in a taxicab, that I didn't even have time to pay him off, hop out and get inside; I was afraid I'd choke it off or stillbirth it if I didn't give it its head immediately. So I kept him standing there at the door with his meter going while I scribbled away furiously on the back seat under the dim roof-light, using every scrap of paper I could fish out of my pockets. It turned what would have been a mere seventy-five-cent haul into about two-dollars-and-eighty-five cents worth of taxi-ride, but it was worth every nickel. And nickels were like half dollars to me in those days.

I remember he said to me, not very perceptively, when I finally opened the door to step out, "You're a writer, hunh, that what you are?"

Yes, I was a writer, hunh, that's what I was.

> *Cornell Woolrich, in his* Blues of a Lifetime: The Autobiography of Cornell Woolrich, *edited by Mark T. Bassett, Bowling Green State University Popular Press, 1991.*

Foster Hirsch (essay date 1981)

[Hirsch is an American educator and critic who has written extensively on film and filmmakers. In the following excerpt, Hirsch discusses the main characteristics of Woolrich's fiction and its affinities with film noir, *a name given to the dark, cynical, "hard-boiled" Hollywood movies made in the 1940s.]*

Cornell Woolrich . . . does not have the literary prestige of the hard-boiled quartet [Dashiell Hammett, Raymond Chandler, James M. Cain, and Horace McCoy]. The pulp base of Woolrich's style is less disguised than in the writing of the others, but Woolrich is a better storyteller than Hammett or Chandler and a master in building and sustaining tension.

Like other writers in the mystery-thriller field, Woolrich works within formulaic patterns. A Woolrich story begins typically in an ordinary and undramatic environment: a cafeteria, an office, a tenement, a city street at noon. Woolrich stresses the ordinariness of his urban settings and of his characters, his blue-collar workers, secretaries, housewives, clerks. He begins in a tone of exaggerated casualness, paying attention to seemingly small matters—to scraps of conversation, details of dress and behavior, to time—that are to figure importantly in the ensuing mystery. A dry, reportorial manner, in Woolrich's stories, is invariably a prelude to nightmare, as the seemingly everyday setting and the bland characters come quickly under attack.

A man has an argument with his wife and stalks out of the house for a night on the town. In a bar, he strikes up a conversation with a woman in an exaggerated hat who agrees to go with him to dinner and to the theatre, and then says good-bye without ever telling him her name. The man returns home to find his wife has been murdered. His one alibi—the one person standing between him and the gas chamber—is the phantom lady with the hat.

A little boy who tells tall stories happens, by chance (it is a stiflingly hot New York summer night and for relief he is on a fire escape), to see his upstairs neighbors commit a murder. When he tells his parents, they threaten to punish him for his lies. When he goes to the police, he is sent home. The neighbors find out about his "story," and when the boy is locked in his room by his irate father (his mother has been called to visit an ailing sister), the murderers close in on him.

A man confined to a wheelchair has little to do but peer across a courtyard into the windows of the facing buildings. What begins as a casual inspection of the comings and goings of his unsuspecting neighbors escalates to obsessive interest when the observer discovers a murder—a man across the way has done in his invalid wife, though how can this be proven? No one believes him, including his detective friend. He begins to deal directly with the murderer, who then tracks him down, an invalid alone in his apartment: the perfect victim.

A spoiled young man, despite his sister's pleas, is determined to run off with a floozy. When he calls at his fiancée's apartment, she is dead. Caught red-handed, the boy is sentenced to the chair. His sister, who is convinced of his innocence, sets out on a search for the murderer that takes her into a tough urban nightworld. When she discovers a link between the murdered girl and a nightclub, she applies for a job as a dancer. The gross entrepreneur goes wild over her, but when he finds out that she is a double-dealer, he orders his henchmen to finish her off.

These four archetypal Woolrich tales—*Phantom Lady,* **"The Boy Cried Wolf," "Rear Window,"** and **"Angel Face"** are expert variations on a formula. Innocent characters are accused of or in some way involved in a murder,

and saved at the last minute after a series of escalating catastrophes. The Woolrich world is a maze of wrong impressions as the author sets traps for his luckless protagonists and then watches as they fall into them. Filled with pitfalls and sudden violence, the landscape in Woolrich is the kind of place where a single wrong turn, a mere chance encounter, triggers a chain reaction in which one calamity follows another. Standing in the wings manipulating the movements of his players as though they were figures on a chessboard, Woolrich is a master contriver. His characters, more thinly conceived than those of his more illustrious hard-boiled predecessors, have no inner life, no history at all in fact apart from their immediate use to the author as pawns in his clever games.

Often Woolrich presents a story from the point of view of a criminal or an amateur avenging sleuth. The first person mode, with its necessarily limited perspective, increases the aura of claustrophobia and entrapment which hovers over all of Woolrich's work—Woolrich's characters seldom see the light, and are rarely prepared for what happens to them. As he operates above his near-sighted characters, watching them pinned and wriggling against their ghastly fates, Woolrich's humor is pitch black. An alcoholic and a recluse, Woolrich had a grim comic sense, a piercing irony, and a firm belief that the world was at best indifferent to its inhabitants, at worst an active conspirator against our well-being.

"Black," "night," and "death" appear with obsessive recurrence in Woolrich's titles: *The Bride Wore Black, The Black Curtain, Black Alibi, Rendezvous in Black, The Black Angel, Night Has a Thousand Eyes, Dead Man Blues, I Married a Dead Man.* Two recent collections of Woolrich stories are called *Nightwebs* and *Angels of Darkness.* Night, darkness, the menacing streets of the city at night, the city as a landscape of doom: these supply the inevitable *mise en scène* for Woolrich's taut stories of black deeds, sudden eruptions of foulness, grisly twists of fate. One of Woolrich's unfortunate protagonists suffers from amnesia; many of his characters are plagued by self-division, by conflicts between their rational daytime selves and their night-time alter egos, just as the typical Woolrich fable customarily begins in the ordered, daytime world before it plummets into darkness. The Woolrich canon is rife with visual and psychological doubleness, as day is contrasted with night and sanity teeters on the edge of darkness.

Woolrich's writing lacks Chandler's metaphoric frills and his characters are not as complex as Cain's, but he is a superb craftsman. The Woolrich style is colloquial and easy; it imitates the tone of his primarily working class characters. The opening of **"Angel Face"** conveys the author's rough-hewn, idiomatic quality:

> I had on my best hat and my warpaint when I dug into her bell. You've heard make-up called that a thousand times, but this is one time it rated it; it was just that—warpaint.
>
> I caught Ruby Rose reading at breakfast time— hers, not mine. Quarter to three in the afternoon. Breakfast was a pink soda-fountain mess, a tomato-and-lettuce, both untouched, and an

empty glass of Bromo Seltzer, which had evidently had first claim on her. There were a pair of swell ski slides under her eyes; she was reading Gladys Glad's beauty column to try to figure out how to get rid of them before she went out that night and got a couple more. A Negro maid had opened the door, and given me a yellowed optic.

"Yes ma'am, who do you wish to see?"

"I see her already," I said, "so skip the Morse code." I went in up to Ruby Rose's ten-yard line. "Wheeler's the name," I said. "Does it mean anything to you?"

"Should it?" She was dark and Salome-ish. She was mean. She was bad medicine.

The opening of **"Rear Window"** has the dry, matter-of-fact quality with which Woolrich typically begins his stories of crime and terror:

> I didn't know their last names. I'd never heard their voices. I didn't even know them by sight, strictly speaking, for their faces were too small to fill in with identifiable features at that distance. Yet I could have constructed a timetable of their comings and goings, their daily habits and activities. They were the rear-window dwellers around me.

Woolrich's scene-setting is precise and richly evocative of mood and atmosphere, as in this description of a bar in *The Black Angel:*

> The Oregon Bar . . . on Third above Forty-ninth, in the first half-hour after twelve that same night. It was deep and narrow, like an alcove piercing the building it was situated in. It was dark with a sort of colored darkness that was the tint of it. Although there were lights, and they were dusky orange, copper-rose, and other similar feverish tones, it was the darkness you were conscious of more than them; its overall cast was dimness, a confetti-like twilight.

Woolrich's stories often take place in a sickly, yellowish half-light. Inhabiting cramped, foul-smelling rooms in rundown hotels and tenements; hanging out in bars, all-night cafeterias and movie houses, many of his characters never seem to see the light of day.

Woolrich's manipulations of his puppet-like characters, his ironic detachment, his evident enjoyment in subjecting his characters as well as his readers to situations of ulcer-inducing tension, his deliberately narrow emotional range, his clipped vernacular dialogue, his dark city settings, link his methods to those of *film noir.* Woolrich was enormously popular in the forties, and though he continues to have a loyal following, he has not received his full recognition as a skillful popular artist (the best in his field, in fact), a writer with a distinct moral vision, dark and unsettling, and streaked with flashes of mordant comedy. (pp. 43-6)

> *Foster Hirsch, "The Literary Background: The Boys in the Back Room," in his* The Dark Side of the Screen: Film Noir, *1981. Reprint by Da Capo Press, 1983, pp. 23-52.*

Francis M. Nevins, Jr.   (essay date 1988)

> [*Nevins is an American attorney and educator who has written extensively on mystery fiction; considered the world's foremost expert on Woolrich's life and work, he serves as an advisor to the late author's estate. In the following excerpt from his biography* Cornell Woolrich: First You Dream, Then You Die, *Nevins analyzes the different kinds of stories Woolrich wrote and describes the thematically consistent fictional world he created in them.*]

[The *noir* world that Woolrich created in his fiction] first took shape in the pulp mystery magazines of the thirties, which published well over a hundred of his short stories and novelettes before the appearance of his first overt crime novel in 1940. The exact order in which these shorter works were written will never be known, but if we look at them more or less in the order of their publication, we sense a gradual movement from pulp to *noir.* The earlier the story, the more likely it is to stress pulp elements: one-dimensional macho protagonists, preposterous methods of murder (which are so common that I treat them as a distinctive type of tale), hordes of cardboard gangsters with predominantly Italian names, dialogue full of whiny insults, blistering fast action. Of all his pure pulpers the stories that have best survived the years are the nonstop action whizbangs like **"You Pays Your Nickel"** (1936), better known as **"Subway."**

But even in his earliest crime stories the pulp elements tend to be intermingled with aspects of *noir.* His first short mystery, **"Death Sits in the Dentist's Chair"** (1934), is a Bizarre Murder Method tale set among people so victimized by the Depression that they can't afford relief from agonizing toothaches. Worked into the climax but almost as a throwaway item is the protagonist's race against the clock to reach safety before he's killed by the poison that he let a psychotic dentist administer to him. Had Woolrich written the tale a few years later, this would have been the central theme, and we would have sweated and shuddered with the man for dozens of pages and thousands of words as his nightmare stretched out. In **"Walls That Hear You"** (1934), published two weeks after Woolrich's pulp debut, we find the first of his angels of vengeance, a harmless guy who turns into a fury as he hunts the madman who mutilated his kid brother. And in his third mystery tale, **"Preview of Death"** (1934), there's a primal Falling Beam sequence as the detective watches the shooting of a scene from a Civil War movie and suddenly the star is enveloped in flames and burns to death before his eyes. Nowhere near all of the early Woolrich stories contain seeds of *noir,* but many of them do. . . . Our goal here is to outline the features of the Woolrich world, the dark universe that worked itself pure from story to story over the fifteen years of his most intense creativity.

That universe is a trap, an incomprehensible place where beams happen to fall, and at the same time are toppled over by malevolent powers; a world ruled interchangeably by chance, fate and (to borrow a phrase from Mark Twain) God the malign thug. Three in one, echoing orthodox Catholic doctrine about the holy trinity. In stories like **"I Wouldn't Be in Your Shoes"** (1938) and **"The Light in** the Window" (1946) and in the novels *Night Has a Thousand Eyes* (1945) and *I Married a Dead Man* (1948) we are given two incompatible but mutually reinforcing accounts of the nature of the universe: (1) innocent lives are destroyed by a tightly knit pattern of events so dependent on multiple coincidence that some sadistic power beyond blind chance must be in control; (2) innocent lives are destroyed by a situation in which there are only two logical possibilities but neither makes sense or squares with what is known. This in a nutshell is Woolrich's metaphysics. The world of Hammett is a Victorian drawing room by comparison. Those commentators who wrote before *noir* became the standard descriptive term were not off the mark when they described the Woolrich type of fiction and film as paranoid thrillers.

In most of his work the metaphysical forces are kept in the background only, but the everyday world he portrays is just as terrifying and treacherous. The dominant economic reality, even well into the forties, is the Depression. The dominant political reality is a police force made up largely of sociopaths licensed to torture and kill, the earthly counterpart of the savage powers above. The prevailing emotional states are loneliness and fear. Events generally take place in the hours of darkness, with a sense of menace breathing out of every corner of the night. One of the keys to Woolrich's greatness is the unique word magic which makes this bleak cityscape come alive on the page and in our hearts.

Another, no less important key is his peculiar genius for creating situations perfectly consonant with the nature of his world. The Noir Cop story: a plainclothesman solves a murder or other crime but our interest is concentrated less on the plot than on the sadistic police procedure that is both routine and routinely accepted, even by its victims. The Clock Race story: the main character runs an unbearable and usually unwinnable marathon against the forces of time and death. The Waking Nightmare story: the protagonist comes to after a blackout—caused by amnesia, drugs, hypnosis or whatever—and then finds objective fragments from his bad dream all over and slowly becomes convinced that he did something horrible while out of himself. The Oscillation story: the viewpoint figure has built a tiny island of love and trust and friendship with another person only to see its foundations eaten away by suspicion—now rising, now falling, first rejected, then half believed, then suppressed only to rise again stronger than ever—that the other person is evil. The Headlong Through the Night story: we are plunged into the last hours of a hunted man as he flails desperately across the dark city to his doom. The Annihilation story: chance/fate/God has smiled, the protagonist (always a man) has found the one right woman, but suddenly she vanishes as if the universe had swallowed her up, and under such circumstances that he not only can't find her but can't establish that she ever existed. And most terrifying and personal of all, a kind of story to which I will not attach a name, where we are compelled to share the final hours and minutes of someone torn apart by the ultimate torture: knowing that he or she will die in a particularly awful way and at a particular moment. These situations, and variations on them, and others like them, are para-

digms of our position in the world as Woolrich sees it. What other writer created a milieu so worthy of the name *noir*?

We must surely count these among the building blocks that hold the Woolrich universe together. But what about the element which above all else made him a legend in his own lifetime? Woolrich is best known as the supreme master of suspense, whose words, like Hitchcock's images on film, keep us on the edge of our seats and gasping with fright. Certainly a good deal of his unsurpassed skill as a suspense writer is attributable to the nightmarish situations he conjured up and the power of his best prose—compulsively readable, vivid, highstrung almost to the point of hysteria, full of linguistic blunders that add to the sense of composition at white heat—to force us into the skins of the hunted and the doomed, living their agonies and dying a thousand small deaths with them. But suspense presupposes uncertainty. No matter how nightmarish the situation, how overwhelming the menace, how deep our empathy, if we know in advance that the protagonist will prevail, as we do for example in James Bond movies, then real suspense becomes impossible. This is one main reason Woolrich never used a series character guaranteed to return for more exploits. And if we know in advance that the protagonist will be destroyed, there likewise can be no real suspense but only the morbid fascination of watching an inevitable slide to doom, as in the crime novels of David Goodis. Woolrich was too canny a storyteller to stumble into this pitfall. If there is no assurance that a particular novel or story will end in triumph, neither can there be any that it will end in ruination. Despite his congenital pessimism he manages any number of times to squeeze out an upbeat resolution. In his oscillation stories, for example, sometimes the suspected person is innocent and the damning evidence the result of a frame-up or the sort of outlandish coincidence to which even in his pre-crime period he was prone; sometimes the suspect is indeed guilty; and occasionally, as in *Rashomon* [the 1951 film directed by Akira Kurosawa], neither the characters nor the reader ever learn the truth and we are thrown into the primordial chaos at the world's heart. A reader can never know in advance whether a particular Woolrich novel or story will be light or dark, *allègre* or *noir,* and this is yet another reason his work is so hauntingly suspenseful.

Of course, even though there are no *series* characters in Woolrich, there are *viewpoint* characters in each of his stories and novels. Typically these characters are trapped in living nightmares of one sort or another, and in a number of his tales, for example **"Johnny on the Spot"** (1936) and **"The Heavy Sugar"** (1937), he forces us to live unequivocally within his protagonists' skins. But in much of his finest work, even while exerting all his power to make us identify with his viewpoint character, he is also making it impossible for us to do so unambiguously. *He splits our reaction in two,* stripping his protagonists of moral authority, denying us the emotional luxury of total identification, portraying his viewpoint characters as at least psychologically warped and sometimes as totally despicable so that we are forced to pull away from complete union with the man or woman at the center of the storm and so that a part of us wants to see that person suffer. This is why Paul Stapp in **"Three O'Clock"** (1938) is presented as pathologically jealous to the point of planning murder, and why Robert Lamont in **"Men Must Die"/"Guillotine"** (1939) is a cold-blooded killer.

The other and more perverse side of this coin is that Woolrich also denies us the luxury of total disidentification with all sorts of sociopaths, especially those who wear badges. His Noir Cop stories are crammed with acts of police sadism, almost always committed or clearly endorsed by the detective protagonist. In his fifth published crime tale, **"The Body Upstairs"** (1935), the murdered woman's innocent husband is tortured with lighted cigarettes in a precinct station backroom until he makes a false confession, at which point the plainsclothesman narrator chews out the husband as a weakling who can't take a little pain! A few months later, in **"Dead on Her Feet"** (1935), the cop protagonist knows that the murdered woman's lover is not guilty but forces him to dance with her corpse until he cracks up. These fascist monstrosities are explicitly condemned almost never. One might defend Woolrich's approach by arguing that he was writing about institutionalized sadism as it looks from within, and couldn't violate that viewpoint for the sake of a stirring Frank Capra speech from a guy in a white hat. Leaving out such speechifying, leaving the moral outrage to us with no internal support from the stories except the objective horror of what is shown, does make his police tales stronger and more disturbing. But the voice of suspicion still whispers that this aspect of his fiction stems from a sadistic streak in Woolrich himself. Once again our reaction is split in two. In a very real sense this is the core of Woolrich's cunning and the secret of his power. *His most characteristic novels and stories are divided against themselves so as to evoke in us a divided response that mirrors his own self-division.* This I call the strategy of divided reaction. We shall encounter it in Woolrich again and again.

On at least one subject he might be expected not to split our allegiance, and that is love. Certainly his work tends to make us identify unambiguously with whoever is lonely, whoever is in love, or needs love, or has lost it. Woolrich longed for love as a dying man in the desert longs for water. He never found it. Probably he wouldn't have found it had he lived a hundred years. From its absence in his life springs much of the poignancy with which he portrayed its power, its joys and risks and pains, and much of the piercing sadness with which he described its loss. There is an unforgettable moment in the second chapter of the 1942 novel **Phantom Lady** when the morgue attendants are carrying out the body of Scott Henderson's wife. "Hands riveted to him, holding him there. The outer door closed muffledly. A little sachet came drifting out of the empty bedroom, seeming to whisper: 'Remember? Remember when I was your love? Remember?' " But even in this realm the rule of divided reaction holds true. Romantic that he was, yearn for love though he did, Woolrich knew in the depth of his soul that lovelessness could catapult a person over the edge, and several of his most famous novels are paradigms of divided reaction in which the protagonist—Julie in **The Bride Wore Black**, Alberta in **The Black Angel**, Johnny Marr in **Rendezvous in**

Black—destroys his or her own life and the innocent lives of countless others in a mad quest to save a loved one from death or avenge one who has already died.

Once and only once Woolrich will unite himself and us with his protagonist, and that is at the moment when he or she is face to face with the specter of Anahuac. On the brink of death it doesn't matter anymore what a person has done: saint or monster, sane or mad, Woolrich is with that person, becomes that person and makes us do the same. In the most powerful story he ever wrote, the 1938 **"Three O'Clock,"** we sit bound and gagged and paralyzed with the morally warped Stapp in his own basement while the time bomb he has set but can no longer reach ticks closer and closer to the moment of destruction, and Woolrich punctuates the unbearable suspense with religious language and imagery clearly echoing the story of the crucifixion of Jesus, whose agony likewise ended at three o'clock. In the brief electrocution scene of **"Three Kills for One"** (1942), the cold steel hood falls over the head of the murderer Gates and he whispers: "Helen, I love you" as the current begins to fry him. No character named Helen ever appears in the story. At the point of death we are forgiven much, and if we love we are forgiven everything.

The intense, feverish, irrational nature of the Woolrich world is mirrored not only in his strengths as a writer but in his faults as well. As a technical plot craftsman he is sloppy beyond endurance. Outlandish contrivances, outrageous coincidences, "surprise" developments that require us to suspend not only our disbelief but our knowledge of elementary real-world facts, chains of so-called reasoning that a two-year-old could pull apart—all these gaffes will be found in abundance and many more besides as we explore his novels and stories. But the principle of divided reaction operates here too. In his most powerful work these are not gaffes but functional elements that enable him to integrate contradiction and existential absurdity into his dark fabric. What careful craftsman could have written **"I Wouldn't Be in Your Shoes"** and *I Married A Dead Man,* where no conceivable explanation can account for events and we are faced with the irreducible senselessness of the universe? What meticulous researcher could have dreamed up the bone-freezing police procedures in Woolrich's Noir Cop stories? What routinely competent yarn-spinner would have dared to write a tale like Woolrich's **"Three Kills for One"** (1942) in which Eric Rogers carries on his fanatical crusade for three years without visible means of support, as if his rage to restore order to his world were all the food and drink he needed? Long before the Theater of the Absurd, Woolrich knew that an incomprehensible universe is best reflected in an incomprehensible story.

The same dichotomy prevails when we look at Woolrich's style. Judged in isolation, purely on its merits as prose, it's dreadful. No discipline or control, rampant emotional hysteria, a sprawling overabundance of words and phrases and clauses crying out to be cut, sentences without subjects or predicates or rhyme or reason, words that clearly do not mean what Woolrich guesses they mean—a complete catalogue of his literary offenses would be as thick as the one from Sears. In his article "Vertiginous Kitsch"

(*The Literary Review,* September 1985) critic Jerry Palmer says that Woolrich "is the best argument yet invented for speed-reading: his purple prose is so atrocious that normal word-by-word reading is painful. . . . [H]e is guilty of such abuses of the English language that it is a privilege to find them." The charge is not without justice, and many a Woolrich defender could provide supporting evidence in the form of Favorite Groaners from the canon. Palmer cites a description of sunlight on a windowpane as "God's own soapsuds." My own nomination is from Chapter Six of *The Black Curtain:* "His face was an unbaked cruller of rage." Palmer gives Woolrich top marks for devising nightmarish story situations but finds no redeeming value in his prose. "It takes a certain callus on the soul," he says, "consistently to come up with such gems." What he fails to see is that many (but by no means all) of the features of Woolrich's style that seem appalling when judged in isolation are functional in his doom-shrouded world, just like many (but by no means all) of his so-called plotting flubs. Without the sentences rushing out of control across the page like his hunted characters across the nightscape, without the manic emotionalism and indifference to grammatical niceties, the form and content of the Woolrich world would be at loggerheads. Take any of his most headlong passages and remove the signs of haste and white heat, recast the scene in cool calm controlled prose so that it sounds like John Collier, say, or Roald Dahl, and you will have gutted it. Between his style and his substance Woolrich achieved the perfect union that he never came within miles of in his private life.

No one can say how much of what lies at the core of his world was consciously intended and how much the unconscious product of his inner demons. Those who wish to be formalists, treating his work as a self-standing entity and refusing on principle to ask about its roots in his life, are free to do so. Those who want to trace back every distinctive element of his world into his twisted soul, attributing them to his loneliness, his paranoia, his Oedipus complex, his sadomasochistic streak, his homosexuality, his yearning for a father or God, are likewise free to take that approach. He was a chameleon, a man of smoke, a Rashomon figure. His life and work are riddles without solutions. (pp. 116-22)

Francis M. Nevins, Jr., in his Cornell Woolrich: First You Dream, Then You Die, *Warner Book, Inc., 1988, 613 p.*

Gary Indiana   (essay date May 1989)

[*In the following essay, Indiana assesses Woolrich's faults and merits as a writer.*]

The novel Cornell Woolrich never wrote concerns a highly strung, depressive, closeted homosexual alcoholic who lives with his mother for 30 years in a fleapit hotel apartment. The hero of this novel works in a business where most people are tough guys with firsthand experience—with women, work, petty criminals, the law. Their job is simple, even if it isn't easy. They manufacture suspense. Stories in which somebody gets knocked off and the wrong man gets fingered for the crime. Or somebody sees some-

body knock somebody off and can't convince anybody that it really happened. Or a whole slew of people buy the farm so nobody can tell what they know.

This is the book Woolrich didn't write. Many that he did write—25 novels, 23 short story collections—have recently resurfaced in endearingly gloomy-looking Ballantine Mystery editions: *The Black Angel, The Black Path of Fear, Black Alibi, Phantom Lady, Deadline at Dawn, Night Has a Thousand Eyes, I Married a Dead Man.* Written in the '40s, most of these suspense novels are expanded rewrites of stories he published a decade before. Woolrich also wrote some Fitzgeraldesque Jazz Age novels in the '20s, but his reputation rests on the *noir* thrillers, which sometimes appeared under the pseudonyms George Hopley and William Irish.

Despite their improbability and verbal excess, these books still exude the power of suspense. The inability to put them down is often accompanied by embarrassed disbelief that one is continuing to read them. The machinery is obvious and clanking, but it works. Woolrich's indefatigable talent for making the reader turn the pages is an industrial skill that may not be terribly enriching for anyone besides its owner.

Like Hollywood films, Woolrich's narratives exist primarily because they kill time. The vision is pitch black, but it is also patently unreal. For the fastidious reader, Woolrich's prose is full of irritations. The lyricism of his endless descriptive passages is deep purple, yet weirdly effective in creating an atmosphere. His plots are ridiculous, overdetermined by a corny fondness for "ironic twists." After a book's worth of detective work hunting down evidence that would free his condemned best friend, a good guy turns out to be the real killer. Having killed off a number of people she thinks were responsible for her husband's murder, a woman learns they were all innocent. A recovered amnesiac believes that he killed someone when he didn't know who he was, but then it turns out he only witnessed the crime, and then—and so forth.

The flaws in Woolrich are failures of realism, different from those of Chandler, Hammett, or Cain. It may be true that *The Big Sleep* makes no sense, that a large central hunk of *The Dain Curse* is unintelligible, that the train murder in *Double Indemnity* couldn't happen that way. But each of these books has a brevity of incident and a psychological clarity that ratifies the narrative. We trust the stories because they are well formed and set in a world we recognize. Woolrich never achieves this verisimilitude. He is profoundly uninterested in real human beings, actual social institutions, the complexity of adult relationships: an "imaginative writer," in the purest and worst sense.

Woolrich's florid style undoubtedly persuaded scores of pulp editors in the '30s that they were witnessing a class act: crime stories written in an overtly literary way. That much of Woolrich's word music was pathologically squandered on trivia (and generated because pulps paid by the word) didn't matter in a genre desperate for respectability. The crime novelists whose works have endured are stylists of a completely different sort. Chandler, Hammett, and Cain wrote the lean, abstemious sentences American literature has favored since Hemingway. This style has taken root as the American version of convincing exposition. Woolrich, whose sentences have accurately been termed elephantine, uses a much more sadistic technique to convince readers that something is really happening. He slows down the narration to a crawl and describes every nuance of the visual world in obsessive detail. One reason Woolrich's books were so readily bought by Hollywood must have been that nobody had to bother with a shooting script:

> In the light of the full-bodied moon the flower-garden at the back of the house was as bright as noon. . . . The sanded paths that ran around it foursquare, and through it like an X, gleamed like snow, and her shadow glided along them azure against their whiteness. The little rock-pool in the center was polka-dotted with silver disks. . . . (*I Married a Dead Man*)

The settings came camera-ready, and so did the characters.

> The beauty of her face was expressed in its proportions, in the width of her brow, in the wide spacing of her eyes, in their limpid candor, in the honesty and character already fully expressed in her chin. . . . There was no paint or other markings on her face. . . . Her hair, which was of the shade where dark blonde meets light brown, fell in soft disorder. . . . She had on a dress of dark cloth, without a single ornament. . . . (*Night Has a Thousand Eyes*)

That was a nice girl. Here is a floozy:

> A pair of artificial eyelashes, superimposed on her own with no regard for nature, stuck out all around her eyes like rays in a charcoal drawing of the sun. . . . Her hair was frizzy to the point of kinkiness. . . . She had a pair of untrue blue eyes, which probably deepened to green when she hated. (*Into the Night*)

Woolrich organizes his players into "decent" and "corrupt" characters by way of these irksome judgmental pictures. "Corruption" encompasses all forms of life outside the bourgeois family. A typical Woolrich story is set in motion by a rupture of the family order: a husband's infidelity in *The Black Angel,* the intrusion of a psychic's predictions into the blissful home life of an upper-class father and daughter in *Night Has a Thousand Eyes.* While Woolrich's decent people are frequently ruined by contact with corruption, it's fair to say that no one in any Woolrich novel has a discernible inner life until the corruption is wheeled into place. Once it is, the characters become carefully segregated responses to an escalating emergency, tricked out with little visual and verbal reminders that this one is a sympathetic decent female, that one a resolute protective male, someone else a paranoid obsessive concussion victim, and so on. Their lives before and after their encounters with suspense are insubstantial and static.

For Woolrich the quotidian lot of alienated work and sterile family life is a utopian promise, paradise the spiritually stunted heartland. In *Deadline at Dawn,* for instance, a hard-bitten taxi dancer and a desperate electrician bond when they discover they're both from Glen Falls, Iowa.

> But in the spring—! Oh I could skip it in the winter, in the fall, and even in the summer. But in the spring! Those pale pink things used to come out in the trees, and you'd walk down the street like through a whiff of Dorothy Ray's apple-blossom stuff.
>
> People that knew you from the time you were a kid, all up and down the line. People that took an interest in you. That stopped at the door with jellies if you were sick. That would gladly have lent you money, when you got a little older, if you happened to be broke . . .

Characteristically, Woolrich concludes this verbal glucose drip with a bitter indictment of city life. The boy next door, having at last met the girl next door in the Temple of Doom known as New York City, vows to return with her to wholesome Glen Falls. The process of ruination promises to reverse itself. But first they must solve a complicated murder the electrician will be wrongly blamed for when it's discovered the following day. They operate on blind intuition, between 1:30 and 6 in the morning. It's entirely possible to finish this book in roughly the same amount of time, and to instantly forget everything about the characters a minute later.

Woolrich's figures are not characters in the usual sense. He never created a Carmen Sternwood or a Terry Lennox, a Mildred Pierce or a Continental Op. None of his people has enough personality to seem remotely drawn from life. Rather, they are pathologies drawn from Woolrich: tics, obsessions, fears, exhaustions, and, always and everywhere, the kind of clinical depression usually treated with Thorazine, slogging from book to book with the demented persistence of a drunken vampire. The sustained unpleasantness of Woolrich's stories is itself a curious literary accomplishment, akin to the epic lubricity of de Sade. Suspense is to Woolrich as a beefy prong or a gaping snatch are to Sade: the real excuse for everything, the raison d'être of flimsy narrative. Readers will endure miles of Sade's philosophical divagations for a glimpse of the promised fuck-fest, and in Woolrich even a half-page description of a falling coffee cup is irradiated with "suspense."

If the "suspense substance" in Cain or Chandler is a subtle element of an unbroken narrative flow, in Woolrich it is brazen, as obviously manipulative as those dreadful process shots in Hitchcock. And, as with Hitchcock, one senses the willfulness of a practical joker who's learned to do several nasty, reliably effective things altogether too well. Woolrich's verbosity, his piling up of morbid surface details, his indifference to reality all provoke an alarming impression of the person behind the prose. (p. 26)

Woolrich's tireless articulation of fearfulness is significant in any archaeology of American popular culture. This culture is a monument to the confusion of talent with value and the celebration of energy over rationality. Woolrich had more talent than many writers who were better than he was. Because he could make anything seem like a workable plot by steering the most exaggerated male and female stereotypes through decors of heavy dread, he became a uranium mine of raw material for the film, radio, and television industries of the early Cold War.

The claustrophobia and hopelessness of Woolrich's narratives, his fondness for letting even the occasional happy ending glower with imminent repulsion and doom—characteristics determined by a lifelong morbidity, but also by the Depression—struck an especially resonant chord in the period when anticommunism was raised to a state religion. In the postwar era, Woolrich's evocation of the city as a malevolent power, a vortex where good people went bad, reflected a widespread yearning for a kinder, gentler America—an America where dope-peddling jigaboos and ethnic gangsters went to jail, and cops were free to pound a confession out of anybody. Where women simpered and cleaned while men acted strong and took care of business. Woolrich's books charted the absence of this great, good place; in them, the wrong people got worked over in the holding cells while psychopaths ranged freely in the peril-ridden streets. Woolrich laid claim to this geography of fear; he became the second-hand muse of a culture industry which told us then, as it tells us now, that everything is absolutely right and absolutely wrong. Since the script is basically his, perhaps this is a time when we can honor him. (p. 27)

> *Gary Indiana, "Man in the Shadows," in VLS, No. 74, May, 1989, pp. 26-7.*

FURTHER READING

Bibliography

Penzler, Otto. "Collecting Mystery Fiction: Cornell Woolrich." *The Armchair Detective* 19, No. 4 (Fall 1986): 388-95.
  Lists all books published under the Cornell Woolrich by-line; includes collectors' information on the value of first editions and lists the contents of Woolrich's short story collections, giving original publication data for the individual stories.

Biography

Malzberg, Barry N. "Woolrich." Afterword to *The Fantastic Stories of Cornell Woolrich,* edited by Charles G. Waugh and Martin H. Greenberg, pp. 329-34. Carbondale: Southern Illinois University Press, 1981.
  Reminiscence of Woolrich's last days.

Nevins, Francis M., Jr. Introduction to *Nightwebs,* edited by Francis M. Nevins, Jr., pp. ix-xxxiv. New York: Harper and Row, 1971.
  Description of Woolrich's life and work.

———. "The Poet of the Shadows: Cornell Woolrich." Introduction to *The Fantastic Stories of Cornell Woolrich,* edited by Charles G. Waugh and Martin H. Greenberg, pp. vii-xxvi. Carbondale: Southern Illinois University Press, 1981.
  Brief account of Woolrich's life and a discussion of his works and world view.

———. Introduction to *Darkness at Dawn,* edited by Francis M. Nevins, Jr. and Martin H. Greenberg, pp. ix-xv. Carbondale: Southern Illinois University Press, 1985.
  Account of Woolrich's life and career which focuses on his contribution to the *roman noir* and *film noir,* the subgenres of literature and film characterized by darkness, cynicism, and suspense.

———. *Cornell Woolrich: First You Dream, Then You Die.* New York: The Mysterious Press, 1988, 613 p.
  Focuses on Woolrich's early years and offers detailed analyses and descriptions of his works; also includes extensive bibliographical information on Woolrich's novels and short stories, detailed information on the films, television shows, and radio programs based on his works, and an annotated bibliography of secondary sources.

Criticism

Champlin, Charles. "Dark Fiction by an Invisible Author." *The Los Angeles Times Book Review* (2 January 1983): 1, 6.
  Brief, favorable discussion of Woolrich's merits as a writer.

Nevins, Francis M., Jr. "Cornell Woolrich on the Small Screen." *The Armchair Detective* 17, No. 2 (Spring 1984): 175-85.
  Discusses all the teleplay adaptations based on Woolrich's work, stating that "Woolrich's interaction with television begins in that prehistoric period when the networks were in their infancy and precious few Americans even owned sets." Includes a chronological list of casts, credits, and the stories upon which the shows were based.

———. "The Sound of Suspense: Cornell Woolrich on the Radio." *The Armchair Detective* 19, No. 4 (Fall 1986): 374-80, 382-87.
  Discusses the history of Woolrich adaptations on the radio; includes a list of casts, credits, radio stations, and source stories.

———. "Fade to Black: Cornell Woolrich on the Silver Screen, Part One." *The Armchair Detective* 20, No. 1 (Spring 1987): 39-51.
  Discusses all of the films made from Woolrich's novels and short stories from the beginning of his career to 1947.

———. "Fade to Black, Part Two: Cornell Woolrich in the Movies from 1947 to the Present." *The Armchair Detective* 20, No. 2 (Spring 1987): 160-75.
  Continuation of the above essay which includes a discussion of all foreign films based on Woolrich's work.

Rosenbaum, Jonathan. "Black Window: Cornell Woolrich." *Film Comment* 20, No. 5 (September/October 1984): 36-8.
  Introduction to Woolrich's life and work and a discussion of some of the major films based on his novels and short stories.

Ross, T. J. "Woolrich to Truffaut: *The Bride Wore Black.*" *New Orleans Review* 17, No. 4 (Winter 1990): 29-32.
  Analysis of François Truffaut's film version of *The Bride Wore Black* which focuses on the film's literary origins.

Sered, Jean. "The Dark Side." *The Armchair Detective* 22,

Nos. 2-3 (Spring-Summer 1989): 117-20, 121-28, 130-34; 240-58.

Two-part article which compares and contrasts the lives and works of Woolrich and Alfred Hitchcock.

Williams, Tony. "*Phantom Lady,* Cornell Woolrich, and the Masochistic Aesthetic." *CineAction,* Nos. 13-14 (Summer 1988): 56-63.

Discusses the psychoanalytic aspects of Woolrich's work and the film version of *Phantom Lady,* analyzing how his "subversive gender depictions" are tamed by Hollywood.

Additional coverage of Woolrich's life and career is contained in the following sources published by Gale Research: *Contemporary Authors,* **Vols. 13-14; and** *Contemporary Authors Permanent Series,* **Vol. 1.**

□ Contemporary
Literary Criticism
Indexes

Literary Criticism Series
Cumulative Author Index
Cumulative Nationality Index
Title Index, Volume 77

How to Use This Index

The main references

Calvino, Italo
1923-1985.....CLC 5, 8, 11, 22, 33, 39,
73; SSC 3

list all author entries in the following Gale Literary Criticism series:

CLC = Contemporary Literary Criticism
CLR = Children's Literature Review
CMLC = Classical and Medieval Literature Criticism
DC = Drama Criticism
LC = Literature Criticism from 1400 to 1800
NCLC = Nineteenth-Century Literature Criticism
PC = Poetry Criticism
SSC = Short Story Criticism
TCLC = Twentieth-Century Literary Criticism

The cross-references

See also CANR 23; CA 85-88;
obituary CA 116

list all author entries in the following Gale biographical and literary sources:

AAYA = Authors & Artists for Young Adults
AITN = Authors in the News
BLC = Black Literature Criticism
BW = Black Writers
CA = Contemporary Authors
CAAS = Contemporary Authors Autobiography Series
CABS = Contemporary Authors Bibliographical Series
CANR = Contemporary Authors New Revision Series
CAP = Contemporary Authors Permanent Series
CDALB = Concise Dictionary of American Literary Biography
CDBLB = Concise Dictionary of British Literary Biography
DLB = Dictionary of Literary Biography
DLBD = Dictionary of Literary Biography Documentary Series
DLBY = Dictionary of Literary Biography Yearbook
HW = Hispanic Writers
MAICYA = Major Authors and Illustrators for Children and Young Adults
MTCW = Major 20th-Century Writers
SAAS = Something about the Author Autobiography Series
SATA = Something about the Author
WLC = World Literature Criticism, 1500 to the Present
YABC = Yesterday's Authors of Books for Children

Antoninus, Brother
See Everson, William (Oliver)

Antonioni, Michelangelo   1912- . . . . . **CLC 20**
See also CA 73-76

Antschel, Paul   1920-1970. . . . . . **CLC 10, 19**
See also Celan, Paul
See also CA 85-88; CANR 33; MTCW

Anwar, Chairil   1922-1949   . . . . **TCLC 22**
See also CA 121

Apollinaire, Guillaume   . . . . **TCLC 3, 8**
See also Kostrowitzki, Wilhelm Apollinaris
de

Appelfeld, Aharon   1932- . . . . **CLC 23, 47**
See also CA 112; 133

Apple, Max (Isaac)   1941-. . . . . . . **CLC 9, 33**
See also CA 81-84; CANR 19; DLB 130

Appleman, Philip (Dean)   1926- . . . . . **CLC 51**
See also CA 13-16R; CANR 6, 29

Appleton, Lawrence
See Lovecraft, H(oward) P(hillips)

Apteryx
See Eliot, T(homas) S(tearns)

Apuleius, (Lucius Madaurensis)
125(?)-175(?) . . . . **CMLC 1**

Aquin, Hubert   1929-1977. . . . . **CLC 15**
See also CA 105; DLB 53

Aragon, Louis   1897-1982. . . . . . . **CLC 3, 22**
See also CA 69-72; 108; CANR 28;
DLB 72; MTCW

Arany, Janos   1817-1882. . . . . **NCLC 34**

Arbuthnot, John   1667-1735. . . . . **LC 1**
See also DLB 101

Archer, Herbert Winslow
See Mencken, H(enry) L(ouis)

Archer, Jeffrey (Howard)   1940- . . . . **CLC 28**
See also BEST 89:3; CA 77-80; CANR 22

Archer, Jules   1915- . . . . **CLC 12**
See also CA 9-12R; CANR 6; SAAS 5;
SATA 4

Archer, Lee
See Ellison, Harlan

Arden, John   1930- . . . . **CLC 6, 13, 15**
See also CA 13-16R; CAAS 4; CANR 31;
DLB 13; MTCW

Arenas, Reinaldo   1943-1990   . . . . **CLC 41**
See also CA 124; 128; 133; HW

Arendt, Hannah   1906-1975   . . . . **CLC 66**
See also CA 17-20R; 61-64; CANR 26;
MTCW

Aretino, Pietro   1492-1556   . . . . **LC 12**

Arguedas, Jose Maria
1911-1969   . . . . **CLC 10, 18**
See also CA 89-92; DLB 113; HW

Argueta, Manlio   1936- . . . . **CLC 31**
See also CA 131; HW

Ariosto, Ludovico   1474-1533. . . . . **LC 6**

Aristides
See Epstein, Joseph

Aristophanes
450B.C.-385B.C. . . . . **CMLC 4; DC 2**
See also DA

Arlt, Roberto (Godofredo Christophersen)
1900-1942   . . . . **TCLC 29**
See also CA 123; 131; HW

Armah, Ayi Kwei   1939-. . . . . **CLC 5, 33**
See also BLC 1; BW; CA 61-64; CANR 21;
DLB 117; MTCW

Armatrading, Joan   1950-. . . . . **CLC 17**
See also CA 114

Arnette, Robert
See Silverberg, Robert

Arnim, Achim von (Ludwig Joachim von
Arnim)   1781-1831   . . . . **NCLC 5**
See also DLB 90

Arnim, Bettina von   1785-1859. . . . **NCLC 38**
See also DLB 90

Arnold, Matthew
1822-1888   . . . . **NCLC 6, 29; PC 5**
See also CDBLB 1832-1890; DA; DLB 32,
57; WLC

Arnold, Thomas   1795-1842   . . . . . . **NCLC 18**
See also DLB 55

Arnow, Harriette (Louisa) Simpson
1908-1986. . . . . **CLC 2, 7, 18**
See also CA 9-12R; 118; CANR 14; DLB 6;
MTCW; SATA 42, 47

Arp, Hans
See Arp, Jean

Arp, Jean   1887-1966. . . . . **CLC 5**
See also CA 81-84; 25-28R

Arrabal
See Arrabal, Fernando

Arrabal, Fernando   1932- . . . **CLC 2, 9, 18, 58**
See also CA 9-12R; CANR 15

Arrick, Fran. **CLC 30**

Artaud, Antonin   1896-1948   . . . . . **TCLC 3, 36**
See also CA 104

Arthur, Ruth M(abel)   1905-1979. . . . **CLC 12**
See also CA 9-12R; 85-88; CANR 4;
SATA 7, 26

Artsybashev, Mikhail (Petrovich)
1878-1927   . . . . **TCLC 31**

Arundel, Honor (Morfydd)
1919-1973   . . . . **CLC 17**
See also CA 21-22; 41-44R; CAP 2;
SATA 4, 24

Asch, Sholem   1880-1957   . . . . **TCLC 3**
See also CA 105

Ash, Shalom
See Asch, Sholem

Ashbery, John (Lawrence)
1927- . . . . . **CLC 2, 3, 4, 6, 9, 13, 15, 25,
41, 77**
See also CA 5-8R; CANR 9, 37; DLB 5;
DLBY 81; MTCW

Ashdown, Clifford
See Freeman, R(ichard) Austin

Ashe, Gordon
See Creasey, John

Ashton-Warner, Sylvia (Constance)
1908-1984   . . . . **CLC 19**
See also CA 69-72; 112; CANR 29; MTCW

Asimov, Isaac
1920-1992   . . . . . . **CLC 1, 3, 9, 19, 26, 76**
See also BEST 90:2; CA 1-4R; 137;
CANR 2, 19, 36; CLR 12; DLB 8;
DLBY 92; MAICYA; MTCW; SATA 1,
26, 74

Astley, Thea (Beatrice May)
1925- . . . . **CLC 41**
See also CA 65-68; CANR 11

Aston, James
See White, T(erence) H(anbury)

Asturias, Miguel Angel
1899-1974   . . . . **CLC 3, 8, 13**
See also CA 25-28; 49-52; CANR 32;
CAP 2; DLB 113; HW; MTCW

Atares, Carlos Saura
See Saura (Atares), Carlos

Atheling, William
See Pound, Ezra (Weston Loomis)

Atheling, William, Jr.
See Blish, James (Benjamin)

Atherton, Gertrude (Franklin Horn)
1857-1948   . . . . **TCLC 2**
See also CA 104; DLB 9, 78

Atherton, Lucius
See Masters, Edgar Lee

Atkins, Jack
See Harris, Mark

Atticus
See Fleming, Ian (Lancaster)

Atwood, Margaret (Eleanor)
1939- . . . . **CLC 2, 3, 4, 8, 13, 15, 25, 44;
SSC 2**
See also BEST 89:2; CA 49-52; CANR 3,
24, 33; DA; DLB 53; MTCW; SATA 50;
WLC

Aubigny, Pierre d'
See Mencken, H(enry) L(ouis)

Aubin, Penelope   1685-1731(?). . . . . **LC 9**
See also DLB 39

Auchincloss, Louis (Stanton)
1917- . . . . **CLC 4, 6, 9, 18, 45**
See also CA 1-4R; CANR 6, 29; DLB 2;
DLBY 80; MTCW

Auden, W(ystan) H(ugh)
1907-1973   . . . . . **CLC 1, 2, 3, 4, 6, 9, 11,
14, 43; PC 1**
See also CA 9-12R; 45-48; CANR 5;
CDBLB 1914-1945; DA; DLB 10, 20;
MTCW; WLC

Audiberti, Jacques   1900-1965   . . . . . . **CLC 38**
See also CA 25-28R

Auel, Jean M(arie)   1936-. . . . . **CLC 31**
See also AAYA 7; BEST 90:4; CA 103;
CANR 21

Auerbach, Erich   1892-1957   . . . . **TCLC 43**
See also CA 118

Augier, Emile   1820-1889   . . . . **NCLC 31**

August, John
See De Voto, Bernard (Augustine)

Augustine, St.   354-430. . . . . **CMLC 6**

Aurelius
See Bourne, Randolph S(illiman)

Bierce, Ambrose (Gwinett)
1842-1914(?) . . . . . **TCLC 1, 7, 44; SSC 9**
See also CA 104; 139; CDALB 1865-1917;
DA; DLB 11, 12, 23, 71, 74; WLC

Billings, Josh
See Shaw, Henry Wheeler

Billington, Rachel 1942- . . . . **CLC 43**
See also AITN 2; CA 33-36R

Binyon, T(imothy) J(ohn) 1936- . . . . **CLC 34**
See also CA 111; CANR 28

Bioy Casares, Adolfo 1914- . . . . **CLC 4, 8, 13**
See also CA 29-32R; CANR 19; DLB 113;
HW; MTCW

Bird, C.
See Ellison, Harlan

Bird, Cordwainer
See Ellison, Harlan

Bird, Robert Montgomery
1806-1854 . . . . **NCLC 1**

Birney, (Alfred) Earle
1904- . . . . **CLC 1, 4, 6, 11**
See also CA 1-4R; CANR 5, 20; DLB 88;
MTCW

Bishop, Elizabeth
1911-1979 . . . . . **CLC 1, 4, 9, 13, 15, 32;**
PC 3
See also CA 5-8R; 89-92; CABS 2;
CANR 26; CDALB 1968-1988; DA;
DLB 5; MTCW; SATA 24

Bishop, John 1935- . . . . **CLC 10**
See also CA 105

Bissett, Bill 1939- . . . . **CLC 18**
See also CA 69-72; CANR 15; DLB 53;
MTCW

Bitov, Andrei (Georgievich) 1937- . . . **CLC 57**

Biyidi, Alexandre 1932-
See Beti, Mongo
See also BW; CA 114; 124; MTCW

Bjarme, Brynjolf
See Ibsen, Henrik (Johan)

Bjornson, Bjornstjerne (Martinius)
1832-1910 . . . . **TCLC 7, 37**
See also CA 104

Black, Robert
See Holdstock, Robert P.

Blackburn, Paul 1926-1971 . . . . . . **CLC 9, 43**
See also CA 81-84; 33-36R; CANR 34;
DLB 16; DLBY 81

Black Elk 1863-1950 . . . . **TCLC 33**

Black Hobart
See Sanders, (James) Ed(ward)

Blacklin, Malcolm
See Chambers, Aidan

Blackmore, R(ichard) D(oddridge)
1825-1900 . . . . **TCLC 27**
See also CA 120; DLB 18

Blackmur, R(ichard) P(almer)
1904-1965 . . . . **CLC 2, 24**
See also CA 11-12; 25-28R; CAP 1; DLB 63

Black Tarantula, The
See Acker, Kathy

Blackwood, Algernon (Henry)
1869-1951 . . . . **TCLC 5**
See also CA 105

Blackwood, Caroline 1931- . . . . **CLC 6, 9**
See also CA 85-88; CANR 32; DLB 14;
MTCW

Blade, Alexander
See Hamilton, Edmond; Silverberg, Robert

Blaga, Lucian 1895-1961 . . . . **CLC 75**

Blair, Eric (Arthur) 1903-1950
See Orwell, George
See also CA 104; 132; DA; MTCW;
SATA 29

Blais, Marie-Claire
1939- . . . . **CLC 2, 4, 6, 13, 22**
See also CA 21-24R; CAAS 4; CANR 38;
DLB 53; MTCW

Blaise, Clark 1940- . . . . **CLC 29**
See also AITN 2; CA 53-56; CAAS 3;
CANR 5; DLB 53

Blake, Nicholas
See Day Lewis, C(ecil)
See also DLB 77

Blake, William 1757-1827 . . . . **NCLC 13**
See also CDBLB 1789-1832; DA; DLB 93;
MAICYA; SATA 30; WLC

Blasco Ibanez, Vicente
1867-1928 . . . . **TCLC 12**
See also CA 110; 131; HW; MTCW

Blatty, William Peter 1928- . . . . **CLC 2**
See also CA 5-8R; CANR 9

Bleeck, Oliver
See Thomas, Ross (Elmore)

Blessing, Lee 1949- . . . . **CLC 54**

Blish, James (Benjamin)
1921-1975 . . . . **CLC 14**
See also CA 1-4R; 57-60; CANR 3; DLB 8;
MTCW; SATA 66

Bliss, Reginald
See Wells, H(erbert) G(eorge)

Blixen, Karen (Christentze Dinesen)
1885-1962
See Dinesen, Isak
See also CA 25-28; CANR 22; CAP 2;
MTCW; SATA 44

Bloch, Robert (Albert) 1917- . . . . **CLC 33**
See also CA 5-8R; CANR 5; DLB 44;
SATA 12

Blok, Alexander (Alexandrovich)
1880-1921 . . . . **TCLC 5**
See also CA 104

Blom, Jan
See Breytenbach, Breyten

Bloom, Harold 1930- . . . . **CLC 24**
See also CA 13-16R; CANR 39; DLB 67

Bloomfield, Aurelius
See Bourne, Randolph S(illiman)

Blount, Roy (Alton), Jr. 1941- . . . . . **CLC 38**
See also CA 53-56; CANR 10, 28; MTCW

Bloy, Leon 1846-1917 . . . . **TCLC 22**
See also CA 121; DLB 123

Blume, Judy (Sussman) 1938- . . . **CLC 12, 30**
See also AAYA 3; CA 29-32R; CANR 13,
37; CLR 2, 15; DLB 52; MAICYA;
MTCW; SATA 2, 31

Blunden, Edmund (Charles)
1896-1974 . . . . **CLC 2, 56**
See also CA 17-18; 45-48; CAP 2; DLB 20,
100; MTCW

Bly, Robert (Elwood)
1926- . . . . **CLC 1, 2, 5, 10, 15, 38**
See also CA 5-8R; CANR 41; DLB 5;
MTCW

Bobette
See Simenon, Georges (Jacques Christian)

Boccaccio, Giovanni 1313-1375
See also SSC 10

Bochco, Steven 1943- . . . . **CLC 35**
See also CA 124; 138

Bodenheim, Maxwell 1892-1954 . . . **TCLC 44**
See also CA 110; DLB 9, 45

Bodker, Cecil 1927- . . . . **CLC 21**
See also CA 73-76; CANR 13; CLR 23;
MAICYA; SATA 14

Boell, Heinrich (Theodor) 1917-1985
See Boll, Heinrich (Theodor)
See also CA 21-24R; 116; CANR 24; DA;
DLB 69; DLBY 85; MTCW

Bogan, Louise 1897-1970 . . . . . **CLC 4, 39, 46**
See also CA 73-76; 25-28R; CANR 33;
DLB 45; MTCW

Bogarde, Dirk . . . . **CLC 19**
See also Van Den Bogarde, Derek Jules
Gaspard Ulric Niven
See also DLB 14

Bogosian, Eric 1953- . . . . **CLC 45**
See also CA 138

Bograd, Larry 1953- . . . . **CLC 35**
See also CA 93-96; SATA 33

Boiardo, Matteo Maria 1441-1494 . . . . **LC 6**

Boileau-Despreaux, Nicolas
1636-1711 . . . . **LC 3**

Boland, Eavan 1944- . . . . **CLC 40, 67**
See also DLB 40

Boll, Heinrich (Theodor)
1917-1985 . . . **CLC 2, 3, 6, 9, 11, 15, 27,**
39, 72
See also Boell, Heinrich (Theodor)
See also DLB 69; DLBY 85; WLC

Bolt, Lee
See Faust, Frederick (Schiller)

Bolt, Robert (Oxton) 1924- . . . . **CLC 14**
See also CA 17-20R; CANR 35; DLB 13;
MTCW

Bomkauf
See Kaufman, Bob (Garnell)

Bonaventura . . . . **NCLC 35**
See also DLB 90

Bond, Edward 1934- . . . . **CLC 4, 6, 13, 23**
See also CA 25-28R; CANR 38; DLB 13;
MTCW

Bonham, Frank 1914-1989 . . . . **CLC 12**
See also AAYA 1; CA 9-12R; CANR 4, 36;
MAICYA; SAAS 3; SATA 1, 49, 62

Bonnefoy, Yves 1923- . . . . **CLC 9, 15, 58**
See also CA 85-88; CANR 33; MTCW

Cavanna, Betty .... **CLC 12**
See also Harrison, Elizabeth Cavanna
See also MAICYA; SAAS 4; SATA 1, 30

Caxton, William 1421(?)-1491(?)..... **LC 17**

Cayrol, Jean 1911- .... **CLC 11**
See also CA 89-92; DLB 83

Cela, Camilo Jose 1916-..... **CLC 4, 13, 59**
See also BEST 90:2; CA 21-24R; CAAS 10;
CANR 21, 32; DLBY 89; HW; MTCW

Celan, Paul .... **CLC 53**
See also Antschel, Paul
See also DLB 69

Celine, Louis-Ferdinand
.... **CLC 1, 3, 4, 7, 9, 15, 47**
See also Destouches, Louis-Ferdinand
See also DLB 72

Cellini, Benvenuto 1500-1571 .... **LC 7**

Cendrars, Blaise
See Sauser-Hall, Frederic

Cernuda (y Bidon), Luis
1902-1963 .... **CLC 54**
See also CA 131; 89-92; HW

Cervantes (Saavedra), Miguel de
1547-1616 .... **LC 6; SSC 12**
See also DA; WLC

Cesaire, Aime (Fernand) 1913- .. **CLC 19, 32**
See also BLC 1; BW; CA 65-68; CANR 24;
MTCW

Chabon, Michael 1965(?)- .... **CLC 55**
See also CA 139

Chabrol, Claude 1930- .... **CLC 16**
See also CA 110

Challans, Mary 1905-1983
See Renault, Mary
See also CA 81-84; 111; SATA 23, 36

Challis, George
See Faust, Frederick (Schiller)

Chambers, Aidan 1934- .... **CLC 35**
See also CA 25-28R; CANR 12, 31;
MAICYA; SAAS 12; SATA 1, 69

Chambers, James 1948-
See Cliff, Jimmy
See also CA 124

Chambers, Jessie
See Lawrence, D(avid) H(erbert Richards)

Chambers, Robert W. 1865-1933... **TCLC 41**

Chandler, Raymond (Thornton)
1888-1959 ....**TCLC 1, 7**
See also CA 104; 129; CDALB 1929-1941;
DLBD 6; MTCW

Chang, Jung 1952- .... **CLC 71**

Channing, William Ellery
1780-1842 .... **NCLC 17**
See also DLB 1, 59

Chaplin, Charles Spencer
1889-1977 .... **CLC 16**
See also Chaplin, Charlie
See also CA 81-84; 73-76

Chaplin, Charlie
See Chaplin, Charles Spencer
See also DLB 44

Chapman, George 1559(?)-1634...... **LC 22**
See also DLB 62, 121

Chapman, Graham 1941-1989 ..... **CLC 21**
See also Monty Python
See also CA 116; 129; CANR 35

Chapman, John Jay 1862-1933..... **TCLC 7**
See also CA 104

Chapman, Walker
See Silverberg, Robert

Chappell, Fred (Davis) 1936-....... **CLC 40**
See also CA 5-8R; CAAS 4; CANR 8, 33;
DLB 6, 105

Char, Rene(-Emile)
1907-1988 .... **CLC 9, 11, 14, 55**
See also CA 13-16R; 124; CANR 32;
MTCW

Charby, Jay
See Ellison, Harlan

Chardin, Pierre Teilhard de
See Teilhard de Chardin, (Marie Joseph)
Pierre

Charles I 1600-1649 .... **LC 13**

Charyn, Jerome 1937- .... **CLC 5, 8, 18**
See also CA 5-8R; CAAS 1; CANR 7;
DLBY 83; MTCW

Chase, Mary (Coyle) 1907-1981 ...... **DC 1**
See also CA 77-80; 105; SATA 17, 29

Chase, Mary Ellen 1887-1973....... **CLC 2**
See also CA 13-16; 41-44R; CAP 1;
SATA 10

Chase, Nicholas
See Hyde, Anthony

Chateaubriand, Francois Rene de
1768-1848 .... **NCLC 3**
See also DLB 119

Chatterje, Sarat Chandra 1876-1936(?)
See Chatterji, Saratchandra
See also CA 109

Chatterji, Bankim Chandra
1838-1894 .... **NCLC 19**

Chatterji, Saratchandra .... **TCLC 13**
See also Chatterje, Sarat Chandra

Chatterton, Thomas 1752-1770 .... **LC 3**
See also DLB 109

Chatwin, (Charles) Bruce
1940-1989 .... **CLC 28, 57, 59**
See also AAYA 4; BEST 90:1; CA 85-88;
127

Chaucer, Daniel
See Ford, Ford Madox

Chaucer, Geoffrey 1340(?)-1400 ..... **LC 17**
See also CDBLB Before 1660; DA

Chaviaras, Strates 1935-
See Haviaras, Stratis
See also CA 105

Chayefsky, Paddy .... **CLC 23**
See also Chayefsky, Sidney
See also DLB 7, 44; DLBY 81

Chayefsky, Sidney 1923-1981
See Chayefsky, Paddy
See also CA 9-12R; 104; CANR 18

Chedid, Andree 1920- .... **CLC 47**

Cheever, John
1912-1982 ..... **CLC 3, 7, 8, 11, 15, 25, 64; SSC 1**
See also CA 5-8R; 106; CABS 1; CANR 5,
27; CDALB 1941-1968; DA; DLB 2, 102;
DLBY 80, 82; MTCW; WLC

Cheever, Susan 1943-.......... **CLC 18, 48**
See also CA 103; CANR 27; DLBY 82

Chekhonte, Antosha
See Chekhov, Anton (Pavlovich)

Chekhov, Anton (Pavlovich)
1860-1904 ...... **TCLC 3, 10, 31; SSC 2**
See also CA 104; 124; DA; WLC

Chernyshevsky, Nikolay Gavrilovich
1828-1889 .... **NCLC 1**

Cherry, Carolyn Janice 1942-
See Cherryh, C. J.
See also CA 65-68; CANR 10

Cherryh, C. J. .... **CLC 35**
See also Cherry, Carolyn Janice
See also DLBY 80

Chesnutt, Charles W(addell)
1858-1932 .... **TCLC 5, 39; SSC 7**
See also BLC 1; BW; CA 106; 125; DLB 12,
50, 78; MTCW

Chester, Alfred 1929(?)-1971....... **CLC 49**
See also CA 33-36R; DLB 130

Chesterton, G(ilbert) K(eith)
1874-1936 .... **TCLC 1, 6; SSC 1**
See also CA 104; 132; CDBLB 1914-1945;
DLB 10, 19, 34, 70, 98; MTCW;
SATA 27

Chiang Pin-chin 1904-1986
See Ding Ling
See also CA 118

Ch'ien Chung-shu 1910-.......... **CLC 22**
See also CA 130; MTCW

Child, L. Maria
See Child, Lydia Maria

Child, Lydia Maria 1802-1880 .... **NCLC 6**
See also DLB 1, 74; SATA 67

Child, Mrs.
See Child, Lydia Maria

Child, Philip 1898-1978 .... **CLC 19, 68**
See also CA 13-14; CAP 1; SATA 47

Childress, Alice 1920-.......... **CLC 12, 15**
See also AAYA 8; BLC 1; BW; CA 45-48;
CANR 3, 27; CLR 14; DLB 7, 38;
MAICYA; MTCW; SATA 7, 48

Chislett, (Margaret) Anne 1943-.... **CLC 34**

Chitty, Thomas Willes 1926-....... **CLC 11**
See also Hinde, Thomas
See also CA 5-8R

Chomette, Rene Lucien 1898-1981 .. **CLC 20**
See also Clair, Rene
See also CA 103

Chopin, Kate .... **TCLC 5, 14; SSC 8**
See also Chopin, Katherine
See also CDALB 1865-1917; DA; DLB 12,
78

Chopin, Katherine 1851-1904
See Chopin, Kate
See also CA 104; 122

Chretien de Troyes
c. 12th cent. - .... **CMLC 10**

Collins, William 1721-1759 . . . . LC **4**
See also DLB 109

Colman, George
See Glassco, John

Colt, Winchester Remington
See Hubbard, L(afayette) Ron(ald)

Colter, Cyrus 1910- . . . . CLC **58**
See also BW; CA 65-68; CANR 10; DLB 33

Colton, James
See Hansen, Joseph

Colum, Padraic 1881-1972 . . . . CLC **28**
See also CA 73-76; 33-36R; CANR 35;
MAICYA; MTCW; SATA 15

Colvin, James
See Moorcock, Michael (John)

Colwin, Laurie (E.)
1944-1992 . . . . CLC **5, 13, 23**
See also CA 89-92; 139; CANR 20;
DLBY 80; MTCW

Comfort, Alex(ander) 1920- . . . . CLC **7**
See also CA 1-4R; CANR 1

Comfort, Montgomery
See Campbell, (John) Ramsey

Compton-Burnett, I(vy)
1884(?)-1969 . . . . . . CLC **1, 3, 10, 15, 34**
See also CA 1-4R; 25-28R; CANR 4;
DLB 36; MTCW

Comstock, Anthony 1844-1915 . . . . TCLC **13**
See also CA 110

Conan Doyle, Arthur
See Doyle, Arthur Conan

Conde, Maryse . . . . CLC **52**
See also Boucolon, Maryse

Condon, Richard (Thomas)
1915- . . . . CLC **4, 6, 8, 10, 45**
See also BEST 90:3; CA 1-4R; CAAS 1;
CANR 2, 23; MTCW

Congreve, William
1670-1729 . . . . LC **5, 21;** DC **2**
See also CDBLB 1660-1789; DA; DLB 39,
84; WLC

Connell, Evan S(helby), Jr.
1924- . . . . CLC **4, 6, 45**
See also AAYA 7; CA 1-4R; CAAS 2;
CANR 2, 39; DLB 2; DLBY 81; MTCW

Connelly, Marc(us Cook)
1890-1980 . . . . CLC **7**
See also CA 85-88; 102; CANR 30; DLB 7;
DLBY 80; SATA 25

Connor, Ralph . . . . TCLC **31**
See also Gordon, Charles William
See also DLB 92

Conrad, Joseph
1857-1924 . . . . . . TCLC **1, 6, 13, 25, 43;**
SSC **9**
See also CA 104; 131; CDBLB 1890-1914;
DA; DLB 10, 34, 98; MTCW; SATA 27;
WLC

Conrad, Robert Arnold
See Hart, Moss

Conroy, Pat 1945- . . . . CLC **30, 74**
See also AAYA 8; AITN 1; CA 85-88;
CANR 24; DLB 6; MTCW

Constant (de Rebecque), (Henri) Benjamin
1767-1830 . . . . NCLC **6**
See also DLB 119

Conybeare, Charles Augustus
See Eliot, T(homas) S(tearns)

Cook, Michael 1933- . . . . CLC **58**
See also CA 93-96; DLB 53

Cook, Robin 1940- . . . . CLC **14**
See also BEST 90:2; CA 108; 111;
CANR 41

Cook, Roy
See Silverberg, Robert

Cooke, Elizabeth 1948- . . . . CLC **55**
See also CA 129

Cooke, John Esten 1830-1886 . . . . . NCLC **5**
See also DLB 3

Cooke, John Estes
See Baum, L(yman) Frank

Cooke, M. E.
See Creasey, John

Cooke, Margaret
See Creasey, John

Cooney, Ray . . . . CLC **62**

Cooper, Henry St. John
See Creasey, John

Cooper, J. California . . . . CLC **56**
See also BW; CA 125

Cooper, James Fenimore
1789-1851 . . . . NCLC **1, 27**
See also CDALB 1640-1865; DLB 3;
SATA 19

Coover, Robert (Lowell)
1932- . . . . CLC **3, 7, 15, 32, 46**
See also CA 45-48; CANR 3, 37; DLB 2;
DLBY 81; MTCW

Copeland, Stewart (Armstrong)
1952- . . . . CLC **26**
See also Police, The

Coppard, A(lfred) E(dgar)
1878-1957 . . . . TCLC **5**
See also CA 114; YABC 1

Coppee, Francois 1842-1908 . . . . . . TCLC **25**

Coppola, Francis Ford 1939- . . . . CLC **16**
See also CA 77-80; CANR 40; DLB 44

Corcoran, Barbara 1911- . . . . CLC **17**
See also CA 21-24R; CAAS 2; CANR 11,
28; DLB 52; SATA 3

Cordelier, Maurice
See Giraudoux, (Hippolyte) Jean

Corman, Cid . . . . CLC **9**
See also Corman, Sidney
See also CAAS 2; DLB 5

Corman, Sidney 1924-
See Corman, Cid
See also CA 85-88

Cormier, Robert (Edmund)
1925- . . . . CLC **12, 30**
See also AAYA 3; CA 1-4R; CANR 5, 23;
CDALB 1968-1988; CLR 12; DA;
DLB 52; MAICYA; MTCW; SATA 10,
45

Corn, Alfred 1943- . . . . CLC **33**
See also CA 104; DLB 120; DLBY 80

Cornwell, David (John Moore)
1931- . . . . CLC **9, 15**
See also le Carre, John
See also CA 5-8R; CANR 13, 33; MTCW

Corrigan, Kevin . . . . CLC **55**

Corso, (Nunzio) Gregory 1930- . . . CLC **1, 11**
See also CA 5-8R; CANR 41; DLB 5,16;
MTCW

Cortazar, Julio
1914-1984 . . . . . CLC **2, 3, 5, 10, 13, 15,
33, 34;** SSC **7**
See also CA 21-24R; CANR 12, 32;
DLB 113; HW; MTCW

Corwin, Cecil
See Kornbluth, C(yril) M.

Cosic, Dobrica 1921- . . . . CLC **14**
See also CA 122; 138

Costain, Thomas B(ertram)
1885-1965 . . . . CLC **30**
See also CA 5-8R; 25-28R; DLB 9

Costantini, Humberto
1924(?)-1987 . . . . CLC **49**
See also CA 131; 122; HW

Costello, Elvis 1955- . . . . CLC **21**

Cotter, Joseph S. Sr.
See Cotter, Joseph Seamon Sr.

Cotter, Joseph Seamon Sr.
1861-1949 . . . . TCLC **28**
See also BLC 1; BW; CA 124; DLB 50

Coulton, James
See Hansen, Joseph

Couperus, Louis (Marie Anne)
1863-1923 . . . . TCLC **15**
See also CA 115

Court, Wesli
See Turco, Lewis (Putnam)

Courtenay, Bryce 1933- . . . . CLC **59**
See also CA 138

Courtney, Robert
See Ellison, Harlan

Cousteau, Jacques-Yves 1910- . . . . . . CLC **30**
See also CA 65-68; CANR 15; MTCW;
SATA 38

Coward, Noel (Peirce)
1899-1973 . . . . CLC **1, 9, 29, 51**
See also AITN 1; CA 17-18; 41-44R;
CANR 35; CAP 2; CDBLB 1914-1945;
DLB 10; MTCW

Cowley, Malcolm 1898-1989 . . . . CLC **39**
See also CA 5-8R; 128; CANR 3; DLB 4,
48; DLBY 81, 89; MTCW

Cowper, William 1731-1800 . . . . NCLC **8**
See also DLB 104, 109

Cox, William Trevor 1928- . . . CLC **9, 14, 71**
See also Trevor, William
See also CA 9-12R; CANR 4, 37; DLB 14;
MTCW

Cozzens, James Gould
1903-1978 . . . . CLC **1, 4, 11**
See also CA 9-12R; 81-84; CANR 19;
CDALB 1941-1968; DLB 9; DLBD 2;
DLBY 84; MTCW

Crabbe, George 1754-1832 . . . . NCLC **26**
See also DLB 93

Craig, A. A.
    See Anderson, Poul (William)

Craik, Dinah Maria (Mulock)
    1826-1887 .... NCLC **38**
    See also DLB 35; MAICYA; SATA 34

Cram, Ralph Adams 1863-1942 .... TCLC **45**

Crane, (Harold) Hart
    1899-1932 .... TCLC **2, 5; PC 3**
    See also CA 104; 127; CDALB 1917-1929;
    DA; DLB 4, 48; MTCW; WLC

Crane, R(onald) S(almon)
    1886-1967 .... CLC **27**
    See also CA 85-88; DLB 63

Crane, Stephen (Townley)
    1871-1900 ..... TCLC **11, 17, 32; SSC 7**
    See also CA 109; 140; CDALB 1865-1917;
    DA; DLB 12, 54, 78; WLC; YABC 2

Crase, Douglas 1944- .... CLC **58**
    See also CA 106

Craven, Margaret 1901-1980 ...... CLC **17**
    See also CA 103

Crawford, F(rancis) Marion
    1854-1909 .... TCLC **10**
    See also CA 107; DLB 71

Crawford, Isabella Valancy
    1850-1887 .... NCLC **12**
    See also DLB 92

Crayon, Geoffrey
    See Irving, Washington

Creasey, John 1908-1973 .... CLC **11**
    See also CA 5-8R; 41-44R; CANR 8;
    DLB 77; MTCW

Crebillon, Claude Prosper Jolyot de (fils)
    1707-1777 .... LC **1**

Credo
    See Creasey, John

Creeley, Robert (White)
    1926- .... CLC **1, 2, 4, 8, 11, 15, 36**
    See also CA 1-4R; CAAS 10; CANR 23;
    DLB 5, 16; MTCW

Crews, Harry (Eugene)
    1935- .... CLC **6, 23, 49**
    See also AITN 1; CA 25-28R; CANR 20;
    DLB 6; MTCW

Crichton, (John) Michael
    1942- .... CLC **2, 6, 54**
    See also AAYA 10; AITN 2; CA 25-28R;
    CANR 13, 40; DLBY 81; MTCW;
    SATA 9

Crispin, Edmund .... CLC **22**
    See also Montgomery, (Robert) Bruce
    See also DLB 87

Cristofer, Michael 1945(?)- .... CLC **28**
    See also CA 110; DLB 7

Croce, Benedetto 1866-1952 ...... TCLC **37**
    See also CA 120

Crockett, David 1786-1836 .... NCLC **8**
    See also DLB 3, 11

Crockett, Davy
    See Crockett, David

Croker, John Wilson 1780-1857 .. NCLC **10**
    See also DLB 110

Crommelynck, Fernand 1885-1970 .. CLC **75**
    See also CA 89-92

Cronin, A(rchibald) J(oseph)
    1896-1981 .... CLC **32**
    See also CA 1-4R; 102; CANR 5; SATA 25,
    47

Cross, Amanda
    See Heilbrun, Carolyn G(old)

Crothers, Rachel 1878(?)-1958 ..... TCLC **19**
    See also CA 113; DLB 7

Croves, Hal
    See Traven, B.

Crowfield, Christopher
    See Stowe, Harriet (Elizabeth) Beecher

Crowley, Aleister .... TCLC **7**
    See also Crowley, Edward Alexander

Crowley, Edward Alexander 1875-1947
    See Crowley, Aleister
    See also CA 104

Crowley, John 1942- .... CLC **57**
    See also CA 61-64; DLBY 82; SATA 65

Crud
    See Crumb, R(obert)

Crumarums
    See Crumb, R(obert)

Crumb, R(obert) 1943- .... CLC **17**
    See also CA 106

Crumbum
    See Crumb, R(obert)

Crumski
    See Crumb, R(obert)

Crum the Bum
    See Crumb, R(obert)

Crunk
    See Crumb, R(obert)

Crustt
    See Crumb, R(obert)

Cryer, Gretchen (Kiger) 1935- ...... CLC **21**
    See also CA 114; 123

Csath, Geza 1887-1919 .... TCLC **13**
    See also CA 111

Cudlip, David 1933- .... CLC **34**

Cullen, Countee 1903-1946 ..... TCLC **4, 37**
    See also BLC 1; BW; CA 108; 124;
    CDALB 1917-1929; DA; DLB 4, 48, 51;
    MTCW; SATA 18

Cum, R.
    See Crumb, R(obert)

Cummings, Bruce F(rederick) 1889-1919
    See Barbellion, W. N. P.
    See also CA 123

Cummings, E(dward) E(stlin)
    1894-1962 ..... CLC **1, 3, 8, 12, 15, 68;
    PC 5**
    See also CA 73-76; CANR 31;
    CDALB 1929-1941; DA; DLB 4, 48;
    MTCW; WLC 2

Cunha, Euclides (Rodrigues Pimenta) da
    1866-1909 .... TCLC **24**
    See also CA 123

Cunningham, E. V.
    See Fast, Howard (Melvin)

Cunningham, J(ames) V(incent)
    1911-1985 .... CLC **3, 31**
    See also CA 1-4R; 115; CANR 1; DLB 5

Cunningham, Julia (Woolfolk)
    1916- .... CLC **12**
    See also CA 9-12R; CANR 4, 19, 36;
    MAICYA; SAAS 2; SATA 1, 26

Cunningham, Michael 1952- .... CLC **34**
    See also CA 136

Cunninghame Graham, R(obert) B(ontine)
    1852-1936 .... TCLC **19**
    See also Graham, R(obert) B(ontine)
    Cunninghame
    See also CA 119; DLB 98

Currie, Ellen 19(?)- .... CLC **44**

Curtin, Philip
    See Lowndes, Marie Adelaide (Belloc)

Curtis, Price
    See Ellison, Harlan

Cutrate, Joe
    See Spiegelman, Art

Czaczkes, Shmuel Yosef
    See Agnon, S(hmuel) Y(osef Halevi)

D. P.
    See Wells, H(erbert) G(eorge)

Dabrowska, Maria (Szumska)
    1889-1965 .... CLC **15**
    See also CA 106

Dabydeen, David 1955- .... CLC **34**
    See also BW; CA 125

Dacey, Philip 1939- .... CLC **51**
    See also CA 37-40R; CAAS 17; CANR 14,
    32; DLB 105

Dagerman, Stig (Halvard)
    1923-1954 .... TCLC **17**
    See also CA 117

Dahl, Roald 1916-1990 .... CLC **1, 6, 18**
    See also CA 1-4R; 133; CANR 6, 32, 37;
    CLR 1, 7; MAICYA; MTCW; SATA 1,
    26, 73; SATA-Obit 65

Dahlberg, Edward 1900-1977 ... CLC **1, 7, 14**
    See also CA 9-12R; 69-72; CANR 31;
    DLB 48; MTCW

Dale, Colin .... TCLC **18**
    See also Lawrence, T(homas) E(dward)

Dale, George E.
    See Asimov, Isaac

Daly, Elizabeth 1878-1967 .... CLC **52**
    See also CA 23-24; 25-28R; CAP 2

Daly, Maureen 1921- .... CLC **17**
    See also AAYA 5; CANR 37; MAICYA;
    SAAS 1; SATA 2

Daniels, Brett
    See Adler, Renata

Dannay, Frederic 1905-1982 .... CLC **11**
    See also Queen, Ellery
    See also CA 1-4R; 107; CANR 1, 39;
    MTCW

D'Annunzio, Gabriele
    1863-1938 .... TCLC **6, 40**
    See also CA 104

d'Antibes, Germain
    See Simenon, Georges (Jacques Christian)

Danvers, Dennis 1947- .... CLC **70**

Danziger, Paula 1944- .... CLC **21**
    See also AAYA 4; CA 112; 115; CANR 37;
    CLR 20; MAICYA; SATA 30, 36, 63

Denis, Julio
See Cortazar, Julio

Denmark, Harrison
See Zelazny, Roger (Joseph)

Dennis, John 1658-1734 . . . . **LC 11**
See also DLB 101

Dennis, Nigel (Forbes) 1912-1989 . . . . **CLC 8**
See also CA 25-28R; 129; DLB 13, 15;
MTCW

De Palma, Brian (Russell) 1940- . . . . **CLC 20**
See also CA 109

De Quincey, Thomas 1785-1859 . . . **NCLC 4**
See also CDBLB 1789-1832; DLB 110

Deren, Eleanora 1908(?)-1961
See Deren, Maya
See also CA 111

Deren, Maya . . . . **CLC 16**
See also Deren, Eleanora

Derleth, August (William)
1909-1971 . . . . **CLC 31**
See also CA 1-4R; 29-32R; CANR 4;
DLB 9; SATA 5

de Routisie, Albert
See Aragon, Louis

Derrida, Jacques 1930- . . . . **CLC 24**
See also CA 124; 127

Derry Down Derry
See Lear, Edward

Dersonnes, Jacques
See Simenon, Georges (Jacques Christian)

Desai, Anita 1937- . . . . **CLC 19, 37**
See also CA 81-84; CANR 33; MTCW;
SATA 63

de Saint-Luc, Jean
See Glassco, John

de Saint Roman, Arnaud
See Aragon, Louis

Descartes, Rene 1596-1650 . . . . **LC 20**

De Sica, Vittorio 1901(?)-1974 . . . . . **CLC 20**
See also CA 117

Desnos, Robert 1900-1945 . . . . **TCLC 22**
See also CA 121

Destouches, Louis-Ferdinand
1894-1961 . . . . **CLC 9, 15**
See also Celine, Louis-Ferdinand
See also CA 85-88; CANR 28; MTCW

Deutsch, Babette 1895-1982 . . . . **CLC 18**
See also CA 1-4R; 108; CANR 4; DLB 45;
SATA 1, 33

Devenant, William 1606-1649 . . . . **LC 13**

Devkota, Laxmiprasad
1909-1959 . . . . **TCLC 23**
See also CA 123

De Voto, Bernard (Augustine)
1897-1955 . . . . **TCLC 29**
See also CA 113; DLB 9

De Vries, Peter
1910- . . . . **CLC 1, 2, 3, 7, 10, 28, 46**
See also CA 17-20R; CANR 41; DLB 6;
DLBY 82; MTCW

Dexter, Martin
See Faust, Frederick (Schiller)

Dexter, Pete 1943- . . . . **CLC 34, 55**
See also BEST 89:2; CA 127; 131; MTCW

Diamano, Silmang
See Senghor, Leopold Sedar

Diamond, Neil 1941- . . . . **CLC 30**
See also CA 108

di Bassetto, Corno
See Shaw, George Bernard

Dick, Philip K(indred)
1928-1982 . . . . **CLC 10, 30, 72**
See also CA 49-52; 106; CANR 2, 16;
DLB 8; MTCW

Dickens, Charles (John Huffam)
1812-1870 . . . . **NCLC 3, 8, 18, 26**
See also CDBLB 1832-1890; DA; DLB 21,
55, 70; MAICYA; SATA 15

Dickey, James (Lafayette)
1923- . . . . **CLC 1, 2, 4, 7, 10, 15, 47**
See also AITN 1, 2; CA 9-12R; CABS 2;
CANR 10; CDALB 1968-1988; DLB 5;
DLBD 7; DLBY 82; MTCW

Dickey, William 1928- . . . . **CLC 3, 28**
See also CA 9-12R; CANR 24; DLB 5

Dickinson, Charles 1951- . . . . **CLC 49**
See also CA 128

Dickinson, Emily (Elizabeth)
1830-1886 . . . . **NCLC 21; PC 1**
See also CDALB 1865-1917; DA; DLB 1;
SATA 29; WLC

Dickinson, Peter (Malcolm)
1927- . . . . **CLC 12, 35**
See also AAYA 9; CA 41-44R; CANR 31;
CLR 29; DLB 87; MAICYA; SATA 5, 62

Dickson, Carr
See Carr, John Dickson

Dickson, Carter
See Carr, John Dickson

Didion, Joan 1934- . . . . . **CLC 1, 3, 8, 14, 32**
See also AITN 1; CA 5-8R; CANR 14;
CDALB 1968-1988; DLB 2; DLBY 81,
86; MTCW

Dietrich, Robert
See Hunt, E(verette) Howard, Jr.

Dillard, Annie 1945- . . . . **CLC 9, 60**
See also AAYA 6; CA 49-52; CANR 3;
DLBY 80; MTCW; SATA 10

Dillard, R(ichard) H(enry) W(ilde)
1937- . . . . **CLC 5**
See also CA 21-24R; CAAS 7; CANR 10;
DLB 5

Dillon, Eilis 1920- . . . . **CLC 17**
See also CA 9-12R; CAAS 3; CANR 4, 38;
CLR 26; MAICYA; SATA 2, 74

Dimont, Penelope
See Mortimer, Penelope (Ruth)

Dinesen, Isak . . . . **CLC 10, 29; SSC 7**
See also Blixen, Karen (Christentze
Dinesen)

Ding Ling . . . . **CLC 68**
See also Chiang Pin-chin

Disch, Thomas M(ichael) 1940- . . . **CLC 7, 36**
See also CA 21-24R; CAAS 4; CANR 17,
36; CLR 18; DLB 8; MAICYA; MTCW;
SAAS 15; SATA 54

Disch, Tom
See Disch, Thomas M(ichael)

d'Isly, Georges
See Simenon, Georges (Jacques Christian)

Disraeli, Benjamin 1804-1881 . . **NCLC 2, 39**
See also DLB 21, 55

Ditcum, Steve
See Crumb, R(obert)

Dixon, Paige
See Corcoran, Barbara

Dixon, Stephen 1936- . . . . **CLC 52**
See also CA 89-92; CANR 17, 40; DLB 130

Doblin, Alfred . . . . **TCLC 13**
See also Doeblin, Alfred

Dobrolyubov, Nikolai Alexandrovich
1836-1861 . . . . **NCLC 5**

Dobyns, Stephen 1941- . . . . **CLC 37**
See also CA 45-48; CANR 2, 18

Doctorow, E(dgar) L(aurence)
1931- . . . . . **CLC 6, 11, 15, 18, 37, 44, 65**
See also AITN 2; BEST 89:3; CA 45-48;
CANR 2, 33; CDALB 1968-1988; DLB 2,
28; DLBY 80; MTCW

Dodgson, Charles Lutwidge 1832-1898
See Carroll, Lewis
See also CLR 2; DA; MAICYA; YABC 2

Doeblin, Alfred 1878-1957 . . . . **TCLC 13**
See also Doblin, Alfred
See also CA 110; DLB 66

Doerr, Harriet 1910- . . . . **CLC 34**
See also CA 117; 122

Domecq, H(onorio) Bustos
See Bioy Casares, Adolfo; Borges, Jorge
Luis

Domini, Rey
See Lorde, Audre (Geraldine)

Dominique
See Proust,
(Valentin-Louis-George-Eugene-)Marcel

Don, A
See Stephen, Leslie

Donaldson, Stephen R. 1947- . . . . . . **CLC 46**
See also CA 89-92; CANR 13

Donleavy, J(ames) P(atrick)
1926- . . . . **CLC 1, 4, 6, 10, 45**
See also AITN 2; CA 9-12R; CANR 24;
DLB 6; MTCW

Donne, John 1572-1631 . . . . **LC 10; PC 1**
See also CDBLB Before 1660; DA;
DLB 121; WLC

Donnell, David 1939(?)- . . . . **CLC 34**

Donoso (Yanez), Jose
1924- . . . . **CLC 4, 8, 11, 32**
See also CA 81-84; CANR 32; DLB 113;
HW; MTCW

Donovan, John 1928-1992 . . . . **CLC 35**
See also CA 97-100; 137; CLR 3;
MAICYA; SATA 29

Don Roberto
See Cunninghame Graham, R(obert)
B(ontine)

Doolittle, Hilda
1886-1961 . . . . **CLC 3, 8, 14, 31, 34, 73;
PC 5**
See also H. D.
See also CA 97-100; CANR 35; DA;
DLB 4, 45; MTCW; WLC

Ellis, Landon
See Ellison, Harlan

Ellis, Trey 1962- .... **CLC 55**

Ellison, Harlan 1934- .... **CLC 1, 13, 42**
See also CA 5-8R; CANR 5; DLB 8;
MTCW

Ellison, Ralph (Waldo)
1914- .... **CLC 1, 3, 11, 54**
See also BLC 1; BW; CA 9-12R; CANR 24;
CDALB 1941-1968; DA; DLB 2, 76;
MTCW; WLC

Ellmann, Lucy (Elizabeth) 1956-.... **CLC 61**
See also CA 128

Ellmann, Richard (David)
1918-1987 .... **CLC 50**
See also BEST 89:2; CA 1-4R; 122;
CANR 2, 28; DLB 103; DLBY 87;
MTCW

Elman, Richard 1934-............ **CLC 19**
See also CA 17-20R; CAAS 3

Elron
See Hubbard, L(afayette) Ron(ald)

Eluard, Paul.................. **TCLC 7, 41**
See also Grindel, Eugene

Elyot, Sir Thomas 1490(?)-1546 ..... **LC 11**

Elytis, Odysseus 1911-......... **CLC 15, 49**
See also CA 102; MTCW

Emecheta, (Florence Onye) Buchi
1944- .... **CLC 14, 48**
See also BLC 2; BW; CA 81-84; CANR 27;
DLB 117; MTCW; SATA 66

Emerson, Ralph Waldo
1803-1882 .... **NCLC 1, 38**
See also CDALB 1640-1865; DA; DLB 1,
59, 73; WLC

Eminescu, Mihail 1850-1889 ..... **NCLC 33**

Empson, William
1906-1984 .... **CLC 3, 8, 19, 33, 34**
See also CA 17-20R; 112; CANR 31;
DLB 20; MTCW

Enchi Fumiko (Ueda) 1905-1986.... **CLC 31**
See also CA 129; 121

Ende, Michael (Andreas Helmuth)
1929- .... **CLC 31**
See also CA 118; 124; CANR 36; CLR 14;
DLB 75; MAICYA; SATA 42, 61

Endo, Shusaku 1923- ..... **CLC 7, 14, 19, 54**
See also CA 29-32R; CANR 21; MTCW

Engel, Marian 1933-1985......... **CLC 36**
See also CA 25-28R; CANR 12; DLB 53

Engelhardt, Frederick
See Hubbard, L(afayette) Ron(ald)

Enright, D(ennis) J(oseph)
1920- .... **CLC 4, 8, 31**
See also CA 1-4R; CANR 1; DLB 27;
SATA 25

Enzensberger, Hans Magnus
1929-....................... **CLC 43**
See also CA 116; 119

Ephron, Nora 1941-.......... **CLC 17, 31**
See also AITN 2; CA 65-68; CANR 12, 39

Epsilon
See Betjeman, John

Epstein, Daniel Mark 1948-........ **CLC 7**
See also CA 49-52; CANR 2

Epstein, Jacob 1956- .... **CLC 19**
See also CA 114

Epstein, Joseph 1937-............ **CLC 39**
See also CA 112; 119

Epstein, Leslie 1938- .... **CLC 27**
See also CA 73-76; CAAS 12; CANR 23

Equiano, Olaudah 1745(?)-1797..... **LC 16**
See also BLC 2; DLB 37, 50

Erasmus, Desiderius 1469(?)-1536.... **LC 16**

Erdman, Paul E(mil) 1932- .... **CLC 25**
See also AITN 1; CA 61-64; CANR 13

Erdrich, Louise 1954-......... **CLC 39, 54**
See also AAYA 10; BEST 89:1; CA 114;
CANR 41; MTCW

Erenburg, Ilya (Grigoryevich)
See Ehrenburg, Ilya (Grigoryevich)

Erickson, Stephen Michael 1950-
See Erickson, Steve
See also CA 129

Erickson, Steve .... **CLC 64**
See also Erickson, Stephen Michael

Ericson, Walter
See Fast, Howard (Melvin)

Eriksson, Buntel
See Bergman, (Ernst) Ingmar

Eschenbach, Wolfram von
See Wolfram von Eschenbach

Eseki, Bruno
See Mphahlele, Ezekiel

Esenin, Sergei (Alexandrovich)
1895-1925 .... **TCLC 4**
See also CA 104

Eshleman, Clayton 1935-.......... **CLC 7**
See also CA 33-36R; CAAS 6; DLB 5

Espriella, Don Manuel Alvarez
See Southey, Robert

Espriu, Salvador 1913-1985........ **CLC 9**
See also CA 115

Espronceda, Jose de 1808-1842... **NCLC 39**

Esse, James
See Stephens, James

Esterbrook, Tom
See Hubbard, L(afayette) Ron(ald)

Estleman, Loren D. 1952- .... **CLC 48**
See also CA 85-88; CANR 27; MTCW

Evan, Evin
See Faust, Frederick (Schiller)

Evans, Evan
See Faust, Frederick (Schiller)

Evans, Marian
See Eliot, George

Evans, Mary Ann
See Eliot, George

Evarts, Esther
See Benson, Sally

Everett, Percival
See Everett, Percival L.

Everett, Percival L. 1956-......... **CLC 57**
See also CA 129

Everson, R(onald) G(ilmour)
1903- .... **CLC 27**
See also CA 17-20R; DLB 88

Everson, William (Oliver)
1912- .... **CLC 1, 5, 14**
See also CA 9-12R; CANR 20; DLB 5, 16;
MTCW

Evtushenko, Evgenii Aleksandrovich
See Yevtushenko, Yevgeny (Alexandrovich)

Ewart, Gavin (Buchanan)
1916- .... **CLC 13, 46**
See also CA 89-92; CANR 17; DLB 40;
MTCW

Ewers, Hanns Heinz 1871-1943 ... **TCLC 12**
See also CA 109

Ewing, Frederick R.
See Sturgeon, Theodore (Hamilton)

Exley, Frederick (Earl) 1929-.... **CLC 6, 11**
See also AITN 2; CA 81-84; 138; DLBY 81

Eynhardt, Guillermo
See Quiroga, Horacio (Sylvestre)

Ezekiel, Nissim 1924-............. **CLC 61**
See also CA 61-64

Ezekiel, Tish O'Dowd 1943-....... **CLC 34**
See also CA 129

Fagen, Donald 1948-............. **CLC 26**

Fainzilberg, Ilya Arnoldovich 1897-1937
See Ilf, Ilya
See also CA 120

Fair, Ronald L. 1932-............ **CLC 18**
See also BW; CA 69-72; CANR 25; DLB 33

Fairbairns, Zoe (Ann) 1948- .... **CLC 32**
See also CA 103; CANR 21

Falco, Gian
See Papini, Giovanni

Falconer, James
See Kirkup, James

Falconer, Kenneth
See Kornbluth, C(yril) M.

Falkland, Samuel
See Heijermans, Herman

Fallaci, Oriana 1930-............. **CLC 11**
See also CA 77-80; CANR 15; MTCW

Faludy, George 1913-............. **CLC 42**
See also CA 21-24R

Faludy, Gyoergy
See Faludy, George

Fanon, Frantz 1925-1961.......... **CLC 74**
See also BLC 2; BW; CA 116; 89-92

Fanshawe, Ann .... **LC 11**

Fante, John (Thomas) 1911-1983 ... **CLC 60**
See also CA 69-72; 109; CANR 23;
DLB 130; DLBY 83

Farah, Nuruddin 1945-............ **CLC 53**
See also BLC 2; CA 106; DLB 125

Fargue, Leon-Paul 1876(?)-1947 ... **TCLC 11**
See also CA 109

Farigoule, Louis
See Romains, Jules

Farina, Richard 1936(?)-1966 .... **CLC 9**
See also CA 81-84; 25-28R

Farley, Walter (Lorimer)
1915-1989 .... **CLC 17**
See also CA 17-20R; CANR 8, 29; DLB 22;
MAICYA; SATA 2, 43

Farmer, Philip Jose 1918- .... **CLC 1, 19**
See also CA 1-4R; CANR 4, 35; DLB 8;
MTCW

Farquhar, George 1677-1707 .... **LC 21**
See also DLB 84

Farrell, J(ames) G(ordon)
1935-1979 .... **CLC 6**
See also CA 73-76; 89-92; CANR 36;
DLB 14; MTCW

Farrell, James T(homas)
1904-1979 .... **CLC 1, 4, 8, 11, 66**
See also CA 5-8R; 89-92; CANR 9; DLB 4,
9, 86; DLBD 2; MTCW

Farren, Richard J.
See Betjeman, John

Farren, Richard M.
See Betjeman, John

Fassbinder, Rainer Werner
1946-1982 .... **CLC 20**
See also CA 93-96; 106; CANR 31

Fast, Howard (Melvin) 1914- ...... **CLC 23**
See also CA 1-4R; CANR 1, 33; DLB 9;
SATA 7

Faulcon, Robert
See Holdstock, Robert P.

Faulkner, William (Cuthbert)
1897-1962 .... **CLC 1, 3, 6, 8, 9, 11, 14,
18, 28, 52, 68; SSC 1**
See also AAYA 7; CA 81-84; CANR 33;
CDALB 1929-1941; DA; DLB 9, 11, 44,
102; DLBD 2; DLBY 86; MTCW; WLC

Fauset, Jessie Redmon
1884(?)-1961 .... **CLC 19, 54**
See also BLC 2; BW; CA 109; DLB 51

Faust, Frederick (Schiller)
1892-1944(?) .... **TCLC 49**
See also CA 108

Faust, Irvin 1924- .... **CLC 8**
See also CA 33-36R; CANR 28; DLB 2, 28;
DLBY 80

Fawkes, Guy
See Benchley, Robert (Charles)

Fearing, Kenneth (Flexner)
1902-1961 .... **CLC 51**
See also CA 93-96; DLB 9

Fecamps, Elise
See Creasey, John

Federman, Raymond 1928- ...... **CLC 6, 47**
See also CA 17-20R; CAAS 8; CANR 10;
DLBY 80

Federspiel, J(uerg) F. 1931- .... **CLC 42**

Feiffer, Jules (Ralph) 1929- .... **CLC 2, 8, 64**
See also AAYA 3; CA 17-20R; CANR 30;
DLB 7, 44; MTCW; SATA 8, 61

Feige, Hermann Albert Otto Maximilian
See Traven, B.

Fei-Kan, Li
See Li Fei-kan

Feinberg, David B. 1956- .... **CLC 59**
See also CA 135

Feinstein, Elaine 1930- .... **CLC 36**
See also CA 69-72; CAAS 1; CANR 31;
DLB 14, 40; MTCW

Feldman, Irving (Mordecai) 1928- .... **CLC 7**
See also CA 1-4R; CANR 1

Fellini, Federico 1920- .... **CLC 16**
See also CA 65-68; CANR 33

Felsen, Henry Gregor 1916- .... **CLC 17**
See also CA 1-4R; CANR 1; SAAS 2;
SATA 1

Fenton, James Martin 1949- .... **CLC 32**
See also CA 102; DLB 40

Ferber, Edna 1887-1968 .... **CLC 18**
See also AITN 1; CA 5-8R; 25-28R; DLB 9,
28, 86; MTCW; SATA 7

Ferguson, Helen
See Kavan, Anna

Ferguson, Samuel 1810-1886 ..... **NCLC 33**
See also DLB 32

Ferling, Lawrence
See Ferlinghetti, Lawrence (Monsanto)

Ferlinghetti, Lawrence (Monsanto)
1919(?)- .... **CLC 2, 6, 10, 27; PC 1**
See also CA 5-8R; CANR 3, 41;
CDALB 1941-1968; DLB 5, 16; MTCW

Fernandez, Vicente Garcia Huidobro
See Huidobro Fernandez, Vicente Garcia

Ferrer, Gabriel (Francisco Victor) Miro
See Miro (Ferrer), Gabriel (Francisco
Victor)

Ferrier, Susan (Edmonstone)
1782-1854 .... **NCLC 8**
See also DLB 116

Ferrigno, Robert 1948(?)- .... **CLC 65**
See also CA 140

Feuchtwanger, Lion 1884-1958 ..... **TCLC 3**
See also CA 104; DLB 66

Feydeau, Georges (Leon Jules Marie)
1862-1921 .... **TCLC 22**
See also CA 113

Ficino, Marsilio 1433-1499 .... **LC 12**

Fiedler, Leslie A(aron)
1917- .... **CLC 4, 13, 24**
See also CA 9-12R; CANR 7; DLB 28, 67;
MTCW

Field, Andrew 1938- .... **CLC 44**
See also CA 97-100; CANR 25

Field, Eugene 1850-1895 .... **NCLC 3**
See also DLB 23, 42; MAICYA; SATA 16

Field, Gans T.
See Wellman, Manly Wade

Field, Michael .... **TCLC 43**

Field, Peter
See Hobson, Laura Z(ametkin)

Fielding, Henry 1707-1754 .... **LC 1**
See also CDBLB 1660-1789; DA; DLB 39,
84, 101; WLC

Fielding, Sarah 1710-1768 .... **LC 1**
See also DLB 39

Fierstein, Harvey (Forbes) 1954- ... **CLC 33**
See also CA 123; 129

Figes, Eva 1932- .... **CLC 31**
See also CA 53-56; CANR 4; DLB 14

Finch, Robert (Duer Claydon)
1900- .... **CLC 18**
See also CA 57-60; CANR 9, 24; DLB 88

Findley, Timothy 1930- .... **CLC 27**
See also CA 25-28R; CANR 12; DLB 53

Fink, William
See Mencken, H(enry) L(ouis)

Firbank, Louis 1942-
See Reed, Lou
See also CA 117

Firbank, (Arthur Annesley) Ronald
1886-1926 .... **TCLC 1**
See also CA 104; DLB 36

Fisher, M(ary) F(rances) K(ennedy)
1908-1992 .... **CLC 76**
See also CA 77-80; 138

Fisher, Roy 1930- .... **CLC 25**
See also CA 81-84; CAAS 10; CANR 16;
DLB 40

Fisher, Rudolph 1897-1934 .... **TCLC 11**
See also BLC 2; BW; CA 107; 124; DLB 51,
102

Fisher, Vardis (Alvero) 1895-1968. ... **CLC 7**
See also CA 5-8R; 25-28R; DLB 9

Fiske, Tarleton
See Bloch, Robert (Albert)

Fitch, Clarke
See Sinclair, Upton (Beall)

Fitch, John IV
See Cormier, Robert (Edmund)

Fitgerald, Penelope 1916- .... **CLC 61**

Fitzgerald, Captain Hugh
See Baum, L(yman) Frank

FitzGerald, Edward 1809-1883 .... **NCLC 9**
See also DLB 32

Fitzgerald, F(rancis) Scott (Key)
1896-1940 .... **TCLC 1, 6, 14, 28; SSC 6**
See also AITN 1; CA 110; 123;
CDALB 1917-1929; DA; DLB 4, 9, 86;
DLBD 1; DLBY 81; MTCW; WLC

Fitzgerald, Penelope 1916-...... **CLC 19, 51**
See also CA 85-88; CAAS 10; DLB 14

Fitzgerald, Robert (Stuart)
1910-1985 .... **CLC 39**
See also CA 1-4R; 114; CANR 1; DLBY 80

FitzGerald, Robert D(avid)
1902-1987 .... **CLC 19**
See also CA 17-20R

Flanagan, Thomas (James Bonner)
1923- .... **CLC 25, 52**
See also CA 108; DLBY 80; MTCW

Flaubert, Gustave
1821-1880 ..... **NCLC 2, 10, 19; SSC 11**
See also DA; DLB 119; WLC

Flecker, (Herman) James Elroy
1884-1915 .... **TCLC 43**
See also CA 109; DLB 10, 19

Fleming, Ian (Lancaster)
1908-1964 .... **CLC 3, 30**
See also CA 5-8R; CDBLB 1945-1960;
DLB 87; MTCW; SATA 9

Fleming, Thomas (James) 1927- .... **CLC 37**
See also CA 5-8R; CANR 10; SATA 8

Fletcher, John Gould 1886-1950 . . . **TCLC 35**
See also CA 107; DLB 4, 45

Fleur, Paul
See Pohl, Frederik

Flooglebuckle, Al
See Spiegelman, Art

Flying Officer X
See Bates, H(erbert) E(rnest)

Fo, Dario 1926- . . . . **CLC 32**
See also CA 116; 128; MTCW

Fogarty, Jonathan Titulescu Esq.
See Farrell, James T(homas)

Folke, Will
See Bloch, Robert (Albert)

Follett, Ken(neth Martin) 1949- . . . . **CLC 18**
See also AAYA 6; BEST 89:4; CA 81-84;
CANR 13, 33; DLB 87; DLBY 81;
MTCW

Fontane, Theodor 1819-1898 . . . . . **NCLC 26**
See also DLB 129

Foote, Horton 1916- . . . . **CLC 51**
See also CA 73-76; CANR 34; DLB 26

Foote, Shelby 1916- . . . . **CLC 75**
See also CA 5-8R; CANR 3; DLB 2, 17

Forbes, Esther 1891-1967 . . . . **CLC 12**
See also CA 13-14; 25-28R; CAP 1;
CLR 27; DLB 22; MAICYA; SATA 2

Forche, Carolyn (Louise) 1950- . . . . . **CLC 25**
See also CA 109; 117; DLB 5

Ford, Elbur
See Hibbert, Eleanor Alice Burford

Ford, Ford Madox
1873-1939 . . . . **TCLC 1, 15, 39**
See also CA 104; 132; CDBLB 1914-1945;
DLB 34, 98; MTCW

Ford, John 1895-1973 . . . . **CLC 16**
See also CA 45-48

Ford, Richard 1944- . . . . **CLC 46**
See also CA 69-72; CANR 11

Ford, Webster
See Masters, Edgar Lee

Foreman, Richard 1937- . . . . **CLC 50**
See also CA 65-68; CANR 32

Forester, C(ecil) S(cott)
1899-1966 . . . . **CLC 35**
See also CA 73-76; 25-28R; SATA 13

Forez
See Mauriac, Francois (Charles)

Forman, James Douglas 1932- . . . . . . **CLC 21**
See also CA 9-12R; CANR 4, 19;
MAICYA; SATA 8, 70

Fornes, Maria Irene 1930- . . . . . . **CLC 39, 61**
See also CA 25-28R; CANR 28; DLB 7;
HW; MTCW

Forrest, Leon 1937- . . . . **CLC 4**
See also BW; CA 89-92; CAAS 7;
CANR 25; DLB 33

Forster, E(dward) M(organ)
1879-1970 . . . . **CLC 1, 2, 3, 4, 9, 10, 13,**
15, 22, 45, 77
See also AAYA 2; CA 13-14; 25-28R;
CAP 1; CDBLB 1914-1945; DA; DLB 34,
98; DLBD 10; MTCW; SATA 57; WLC

Forster, John 1812-1876 . . . . **NCLC 11**

Forsyth, Frederick 1938- . . . . . . **CLC 2, 5, 36**
See also BEST 89:4; CA 85-88; CANR 38;
DLB 87; MTCW

Forten, Charlotte L. . . . . **TCLC 16**
See also Grimke, Charlotte L(ottie) Forten
See also BLC 2; DLB 50

Foscolo, Ugo 1778-1827 . . . . **NCLC 8**

Fosse, Bob . . . . **CLC 20**
See also Fosse, Robert Louis

Fosse, Robert Louis 1927-1987
See Fosse, Bob
See also CA 110; 123

Foster, Stephen Collins
1826-1864 . . . . **NCLC 26**

Foucault, Michel
1926-1984 . . . . **CLC 31, 34, 69**
See also CA 105; 113; CANR 34; MTCW

Fouque, Friedrich (Heinrich Karl) de la Motte
1777-1843 . . . . **NCLC 2**
See also DLB 90

Fournier, Henri Alban 1886-1914
See Alain-Fournier
See also CA 104

Fournier, Pierre 1916- . . . . **CLC 11**
See also Gascar, Pierre
See also CA 89-92; CANR 16, 40

Fowles, John
1926- . . . . **CLC 1, 2, 3, 4, 6, 9, 10, 15, 33**
See also CA 5-8R; CANR 25; CDBLB 1960
to Present; DLB 14; MTCW; SATA 22

Fox, Paula 1923- . . . . **CLC 2, 8**
See also AAYA 3; CA 73-76; CANR 20,
36; CLR 1; DLB 52; MAICYA; MTCW;
SATA 17, 60

Fox, William Price (Jr.) 1926- . . . . . **CLC 22**
See also CA 17-20R; CANR 11; DLB 2;
DLBY 81

Foxe, John 1516(?)-1587 . . . . **LC 14**

Frame, Janet . . . . **CLC 2, 3, 6, 22, 66**
See also Clutha, Janet Paterson Frame

France, Anatole . . . . **TCLC 9**
See also Thibault, Jacques Anatole Francois
See also DLB 123

Francis, Claude 19(?)- . . . . **CLC 50**

Francis, Dick 1920- . . . . **CLC 2, 22, 42**
See also AAYA 5; BEST 89:3; CA 5-8R;
CANR 9; CDBLB 1960 to Present;
DLB 87; MTCW

Francis, Robert (Churchill)
1901-1987 . . . . **CLC 15**
See also CA 1-4R; 123; CANR 1

Frank, Anne(lies Marie)
1929-1945 . . . . **TCLC 17**
See also CA 113; 133; DA; MTCW;
SATA 42; WLC

Frank, Elizabeth 1945- . . . . **CLC 39**
See also CA 121; 126

Franklin, Benjamin
See Hasek, Jaroslav (Matej Frantisek)

Franklin, (Stella Maraia Sarah) Miles
1879-1954 . . . . **TCLC 7**
See also CA 104

Fraser, Antonia (Pakenham)
1932- . . . . **CLC 32**
See also CA 85-88; MTCW; SATA 32

Fraser, George MacDonald 1925- . . . . **CLC 7**
See also CA 45-48; CANR 2

Fraser, Sylvia 1935- . . . . **CLC 64**
See also CA 45-48; CANR 1, 16

Frayn, Michael 1933- . . . . . . **CLC 3, 7, 31, 47**
See also CA 5-8R; CANR 30; DLB 13, 14;
MTCW

Fraze, Candida (Merrill) 1945- . . . . . **CLC 50**
See also CA 126

Frazer, J(ames) G(eorge)
1854-1941 . . . . **TCLC 32**
See also CA 118

Frazer, Robert Caine
See Creasey, John

Frazer, Sir James George
See Frazer, J(ames) G(eorge)

Frazier, Ian 1951- . . . . **CLC 46**
See also CA 130

Frederic, Harold 1856-1898 . . . . . . **NCLC 10**
See also DLB 12, 23

Frederick, John
See Faust, Frederick (Schiller)

Frederick the Great 1712-1786 . . . . . . **LC 14**

Fredro, Aleksander 1793-1876 . . . . . **NCLC 8**

Freeling, Nicolas 1927- . . . . **CLC 38**
See also CA 49-52; CAAS 12; CANR 1, 17;
DLB 87

Freeman, Douglas Southall
1886-1953 . . . . **TCLC 11**
See also CA 109; DLB 17

Freeman, Judith 1946- . . . . **CLC 55**

Freeman, Mary Eleanor Wilkins
1852-1930 . . . . **TCLC 9; SSC 1**
See also CA 106; DLB 12, 78

Freeman, R(ichard) Austin
1862-1943 . . . . **TCLC 21**
See also CA 113; DLB 70

French, Marilyn 1929- . . . . . . **CLC 10, 18, 60**
See also CA 69-72; CANR 3, 31; MTCW

French, Paul
See Asimov, Isaac

Freneau, Philip Morin 1752-1832 . . **NCLC 1**
See also DLB 37, 43

Friedan, Betty (Naomi) 1921- . . . . . . **CLC 74**
See also CA 65-68; CANR 18; MTCW

Friedman, B(ernard) H(arper)
1926- . . . . **CLC 7**
See also CA 1-4R; CANR 3

Friedman, Bruce Jay 1930- . . . . **CLC 3, 5, 56**
See also CA 9-12R; CANR 25; DLB 2, 28

Friel, Brian 1929- . . . . **CLC 5, 42, 59**
See also CA 21-24R; CANR 33; DLB 13;
MTCW

Friis-Baastad, Babbis Ellinor
1921-1970 . . . . **CLC 12**
See also CA 17-20R; 134; SATA 7

Frisch, Max (Rudolf)
1911-1991 . . . **CLC 3, 9, 14, 18, 32, 44**
See also CA 85-88; 134; CANR 32;
DLB 69, 124; MTCW

Fromentin, Eugene (Samuel Auguste)
1820-1876 . . . . **NCLC 10**
See also DLB 123

Gawsworth, John
See Bates, H(erbert) E(rnest)

Gaye, Marvin (Penze) 1939-1984 . . . **CLC 26**
See also CA 112

Gebler, Carlo (Ernest) 1954- . . . . **CLC 39**
See also CA 119; 133

Gee, Maggie (Mary) 1948- . . . . **CLC 57**
See also CA 130

Gee, Maurice (Gough) 1931- . . . . **CLC 29**
See also CA 97-100; SATA 46

Gelbart, Larry (Simon) 1923- . . . **CLC 21, 61**
See also CA 73-76

Gelber, Jack 1932- . . . . **CLC 1, 6, 14**
See also CA 1-4R; CANR 2; DLB 7

Gellhorn, Martha Ellis 1908- . . . **CLC 14, 60**
See also CA 77-80; DLBY 82

Genet, Jean
1910-1986 . . . **CLC 1, 2, 5, 10, 14, 44, 46**
See also CA 13-16R; CANR 18; DLB 72;
DLBY 86; MTCW

Gent, Peter 1942- . . . . **CLC 29**
See also AITN 1; CA 89-92; DLBY 82

George, Jean Craighead 1919- . . . . . . **CLC 35**
See also AAYA 8; CA 5-8R; CANR 25;
CLR 1; DLB 52; MAICYA; SATA 2, 68

George, Stefan (Anton)
1868-1933 . . . . **TCLC 2, 14**
See also CA 104

Georges, Georges Martin
See Simenon, Georges (Jacques Christian)

Gerhardi, William Alexander
See Gerhardie, William Alexander

Gerhardie, William Alexander
1895-1977 . . . . **CLC 5**
See also CA 25-28R; 73-76; CANR 18;
DLB 36

Gerstler, Amy 1956- . . . . **CLC 70**

Gertler, T. . . . . **CLC 34**
See also CA 116; 121

Ghalib 1797-1869 . . . . **NCLC 39**

Ghelderode, Michel de
1898-1962 . . . . **CLC 6, 11**
See also CA 85-88; CANR 40

Ghiselin, Brewster 1903- . . . . **CLC 23**
See also CA 13-16R; CAAS 10; CANR 13

Ghose, Zulfikar 1935- . . . . **CLC 42**
See also CA 65-68

Ghosh, Amitav 1956- . . . . **CLC 44**

Giacosa, Giuseppe 1847-1906 . . . . . . **TCLC 7**
See also CA 104

Gibb, Lee
See Waterhouse, Keith (Spencer)

Gibbon, Lewis Grassic . . . . **TCLC 4**
See also Mitchell, James Leslie

Gibbons, Kaye 1960- . . . . **CLC 50**

Gibran, Kahlil 1883-1931 . . . . **TCLC 1, 9**
See also CA 104

Gibson, William 1914- . . . . **CLC 23**
See also CA 9-12R; CANR 9; DA; DLB 7;
SATA 66

Gibson, William (Ford) 1948- . . . **CLC 39, 63**
See also CA 126; 133

Gide, Andre (Paul Guillaume)
1869-1951 . . . . **TCLC 5, 12, 36**
See also CA 104; 124; DA; DLB 65;
MTCW; WLC

Gifford, Barry (Colby) 1946- . . . . **CLC 34**
See also CA 65-68; CANR 9, 30, 40

Gilbert, W(illiam) S(chwenck)
1836-1911 . . . . **TCLC 3**
See also CA 104; SATA 36

Gilbreth, Frank B., Jr. 1911- . . . . **CLC 17**
See also CA 9-12R; SATA 2

Gilchrist, Ellen 1935- . . . . **CLC 34, 48**
See also CA 113; 116; CANR 41; DLB 130;
MTCW

Giles, Molly 1942- . . . . **CLC 39**
See also CA 126

Gill, Patrick
See Creasey, John

Gilliam, Terry (Vance) 1940- . . . . **CLC 21**
See also Monty Python
See also CA 108; 113; CANR 35

Gillian, Jerry
See Gilliam, Terry (Vance)

Gilliatt, Penelope (Ann Douglass)
1932- . . . . **CLC 2, 10, 13, 53**
See also AITN 2; CA 13-16R; DLB 14

Gilman, Charlotte (Anna) Perkins (Stetson)
1860-1935 . . . . **TCLC 9, 37**
See also CA 106

Gilmour, David 1944- . . . . **CLC 35**
See also Pink Floyd
See also CA 138

Gilpin, William 1724-1804 . . . . **NCLC 30**

Gilray, J. D.
See Mencken, H(enry) L(ouis)

Gilroy, Frank D(aniel) 1925- . . . . **CLC 2**
See also CA 81-84; CANR 32; DLB 7

Ginsberg, Allen
1926- . . . . . **CLC 1, 2, 3, 4, 6, 13, 36, 69;
PC 4**
See also AITN 1; CA 1-4R; CANR 2, 41;
CDALB 1941-1968; DA; DLB 5, 16;
MTCW; WLC 3

Ginzburg, Natalia
1916-1991 . . . . **CLC 5, 11, 54, 70**
See also CA 85-88; 135; CANR 33; MTCW

Giono, Jean 1895-1970 . . . . **CLC 4, 11**
See also CA 45-48; 29-32R; CANR 2, 35;
DLB 72; MTCW

Giovanni, Nikki 1943- . . . . . **CLC 2, 4, 19, 64**
See also AITN 1; BLC 2; BW; CA 29-32R;
CAAS 6; CANR 18, 41; CLR 6; DA;
DLB 5, 41; MAICYA; MTCW; SATA 24

Giovene, Andrea 1904- . . . . **CLC 7**
See also CA 85-88

Gippius, Zinaida (Nikolayevna) 1869-1945
See Hippius, Zinaida
See also CA 106

Giraudoux, (Hippolyte) Jean
1882-1944 . . . . **TCLC 2, 7**
See also CA 104; DLB 65

Gironella, Jose Maria 1917- . . . . **CLC 11**
See also CA 101

Gissing, George (Robert)
1857-1903 . . . . **TCLC 3, 24, 47**
See also CA 105; DLB 18

Giurlani, Aldo
See Palazzeschi, Aldo

Gladkov, Fyodor (Vasilyevich)
1883-1958 . . . . **TCLC 27**

Glanville, Brian (Lester) 1931- . . . . . . **CLC 6**
See also CA 5-8R; CAAS 9; CANR 3;
DLB 15; SATA 42

Glasgow, Ellen (Anderson Gholson)
1873(?)-1945 . . . . **TCLC 2, 7**
See also CA 104; DLB 9, 12

Glassco, John 1909-1981 . . . . **CLC 9**
See also CA 13-16R; 102; CANR 15;
DLB 68

Glasscock, Amnesia
See Steinbeck, John (Ernst)

Glasser, Ronald J. 1940(?)- . . . . **CLC 37**

Glassman, Joyce
See Johnson, Joyce

Glendinning, Victoria 1937- . . . . **CLC 50**
See also CA 120; 127

Glissant, Edouard 1928- . . . . **CLC 10, 68**

Gloag, Julian 1930- . . . . **CLC 40**
See also AITN 1; CA 65-68; CANR 10

Gluck, Louise (Elisabeth)
1943- . . . . **CLC 7, 22, 44**
See also Glueck, Louise
See also CA 33-36R; CANR 40; DLB 5

Glueck, Louise . . . . **CLC 7, 22**
See also Gluck, Louise (Elisabeth)
See also DLB 5

Gobineau, Joseph Arthur (Comte) de
1816-1882 . . . . **NCLC 17**
See also DLB 123

Godard, Jean-Luc 1930- . . . . **CLC 20**
See also CA 93-96

Godden, (Margaret) Rumer 1907- . . . **CLC 53**
See also AAYA 6; CA 5-8R; CANR 4, 27,
36; CLR 20; MAICYA; SAAS 12;
SATA 3, 36

Godoy Alcayaga, Lucila 1889-1957
See Mistral, Gabriela
See also CA 104; 131; HW; MTCW

Godwin, Gail (Kathleen)
1937- . . . . **CLC 5, 8, 22, 31, 69**
See also CA 29-32R; CANR 15; DLB 6;
MTCW

Godwin, William 1756-1836 . . . . . . **NCLC 14**
See also CDBLB 1789-1832; DLB 39, 104

Goethe, Johann Wolfgang von
1749-1832 . . . . **NCLC 4, 22, 34; PC 5**
See also DA; DLB 94; WLC 3

Gogarty, Oliver St. John
1878-1957 . . . . **TCLC 15**
See also CA 109; DLB 15, 19

Gogol, Nikolai (Vasilyevich)
1809-1852 . . . . . **NCLC 5, 15, 31; DC 1;
SSC 4**

See also DA; WLC

Gold, Herbert 1924- . . . . **CLC 4, 7, 14, 42**
See also CA 9-12R; CANR 17; DLB 2;
DLBY 81

Goldbarth, Albert 1948-........ **CLC 5, 38**
See also CA 53-56; CANR 6, 40; DLB 120

Goldberg, Anatol 1910-1982 .... **CLC 34**
See also CA 131; 117

Goldemberg, Isaac 1945- .... **CLC 52**
See also CA 69-72; CAAS 12; CANR 11, 32; HW

Golden Silver
See Storm, Hyemeyohsts

Golding, William (Gerald)
1911- ..... **CLC 1, 2, 3, 8, 10, 17, 27, 58**
See also AAYA 5; CA 5-8R; CANR 13, 33; CDBLB 1945-1960; DA; DLB 15, 100; MTCW; WLC

Goldman, Emma 1869-1940 ...... **TCLC 13**
See also CA 110

Goldman, Francisco 1955-......... **CLC 76**

Goldman, William (W.) 1931-.... **CLC 1, 48**
See also CA 9-12R; CANR 29; DLB 44

Goldmann, Lucien 1913-1970 ...... **CLC 24**
See also CA 25-28; CAP 2

Goldoni, Carlo 1707-1793 .... **LC 4**

Goldsberry, Steven 1949-......... **CLC 34**
See also CA 131

Goldsmith, Oliver 1728-1774........ **LC 2**
See also CDBLB 1660-1789; DA; DLB 39, 89, 104, 109; SATA 26; WLC

Goldsmith, Peter
See Priestley, J(ohn) B(oynton)

Gombrowicz, Witold
1904-1969 .... **CLC 4, 7, 11, 49**
See also CA 19-20; 25-28R; CAP 2

Gomez de la Serna, Ramon
1888-1963 .... **CLC 9**
See also CA 116; HW

Goncharov, Ivan Alexandrovich
1812-1891 .... **NCLC 1**

Goncourt, Edmond (Louis Antoine Huot) de
1822-1896 .... **NCLC 7**
See also DLB 123

Goncourt, Jules (Alfred Huot) de
1830-1870 .... **NCLC 7**
See also DLB 123

Gontier, Fernande 19(?)- .... **CLC 50**

Goodman, Paul 1911-1972.... **CLC 1, 2, 4, 7**
See also CA 19-20; 37-40R; CANR 34; CAP 2; DLB 130; MTCW

Gordimer, Nadine
1923- .... **CLC 3, 5, 7, 10, 18, 33, 51, 70**
See also CA 5-8R; CANR 3, 28; DA; MTCW

Gordon, Adam Lindsay
1833-1870 .... **NCLC 21**

Gordon, Caroline
1895-1981 .... **CLC 6, 13, 29**
See also CA 11-12; 103; CANR 36; CAP 1; DLB 4, 9, 102; DLBY 81; MTCW

Gordon, Charles William 1860-1937
See Connor, Ralph
See also CA 109

Gordon, Mary (Catherine)
1949-..................... **CLC 13, 22**
See also CA 102; DLB 6; DLBY 81; MTCW

Gordon, Sol 1923-................. **CLC 26**
See also CA 53-56; CANR 4; SATA 11

Gordone, Charles 1925-......... **CLC 1, 4**
See also BW; CA 93-96; DLB 7; MTCW

Gorenko, Anna Andreevna
See Akhmatova, Anna

Gorky, Maxim.................... **TCLC 8**
See also Peshkov, Alexei Maximovich
See also WLC

Goryan, Sirak
See Saroyan, William

Gosse, Edmund (William)
1849-1928 .... **TCLC 28**
See also CA 117; DLB 57

Gotlieb, Phyllis Fay (Bloom)
1926-..................... **CLC 18**
See also CA 13-16R; CANR 7; DLB 88

Gottesman, S. D.
See Kornbluth, C(yril) M.; Pohl, Frederik

Gottfried von Strassburg
fl. c. 1210- .... **CMLC 10**

Gottschalk, Laura Riding
See Jackson, Laura (Riding)

Gould, Lois .... **CLC 4, 10**
See also CA 77-80; CANR 29; MTCW

Gourmont, Remy de 1858-1915.... **TCLC 17**
See also CA 109

Govier, Katherine 1948-......... **CLC 51**
See also CA 101; CANR 18, 40

Goyen, (Charles) William
1915-1983 .... **CLC 5, 8, 14, 40**
See also AITN 2; CA 5-8R; 110; CANR 6; DLB 2; DLBY 83

Goytisolo, Juan 1931- .... **CLC 5, 10, 23**
See also CA 85-88; CANR 32; HW; MTCW

Gozzi, (Conte) Carlo 1720-1806 .. **NCLC 23**

Grabbe, Christian Dietrich
1801-1836 .... **NCLC 2**

Grace, Patricia 1937-............ **CLC 56**

Gracian y Morales, Baltasar
1601-1658 .... **LC 15**

Gracq, Julien................ **CLC 11, 48**
See also Poirier, Louis
See also DLB 83

Grade, Chaim 1910-1982 .... **CLC 10**
See also CA 93-96; 107

Graduate of Oxford, A
See Ruskin, John

Graham, John
See Phillips, David Graham

Graham, Jorie 1951-............. **CLC 48**
See also CA 111; DLB 120

Graham, R(obert) B(ontine) Cunninghame
See Cunninghame Graham, R(obert) B(ontine)
See also DLB 98

Graham, Robert
See Haldeman, Joe (William)

Graham, Tom
See Lewis, (Harry) Sinclair

Graham, W(illiam) S(ydney)
1918-1986 .... **CLC 29**
See also CA 73-76; 118; DLB 20

Graham, Winston (Mawdsley)
1910- .... **CLC 23**
See also CA 49-52; CANR 2, 22; DLB 77

Grant, Skeeter
See Spiegelman, Art

Granville-Barker, Harley
1877-1946 .... **TCLC 2**
See also Barker, Harley Granville
See also CA 104

Grass, Guenter (Wilhelm)
1927-.. **CLC 1, 2, 4, 6, 11, 15, 22, 32, 49**
See also CA 13-16R; CANR 20; DA; DLB 75, 124; MTCW; WLC

Gratton, Thomas
See Hulme, T(homas) E(rnest)

Grau, Shirley Ann 1929-......... **CLC 4, 9**
See also CA 89-92; CANR 22; DLB 2; MTCW

Gravel, Fern
See Hall, James Norman

Graver, Elizabeth 1964-.......... **CLC 70**
See also CA 135

Graves, Richard Perceval 1945- .... **CLC 44**
See also CA 65-68; CANR 9, 26

Graves, Robert (von Ranke)
1895-1985 ..... **CLC 1, 2, 6, 11, 39, 44, 45; PC 6**
See also CA 5-8R; 117; CANR 5, 36; CDBLB 1914-1945; DLB 20, 100; DLBY 85; MTCW; SATA 45

Gray, Alasdair (James) 1934- ...... **CLC 41**
See also CA 126; MTCW

Gray, Amlin 1946- .... **CLC 29**
See also CA 138

Gray, Francine du Plessix 1930-.... **CLC 22**
See also BEST 90:3; CA 61-64; CAAS 2; CANR 11, 33; MTCW

Gray, John (Henry) 1866-1934 .... **TCLC 19**
See also CA 119

Gray, Simon (James Holliday)
1936-................. **CLC 9, 14, 36**
See also AITN 1; CA 21-24R; CAAS 3; CANR 32; DLB 13; MTCW

Gray, Spalding 1941- .... **CLC 49**
See also CA 128

Gray, Thomas 1716-1771 .... **LC 4; PC 2**
See also CDBLB 1660-1789; DA; DLB 109; WLC

Grayson, David
See Baker, Ray Stannard

Grayson, Richard (A.) 1951-....... **CLC 38**
See also CA 85-88; CANR 14, 31

Greeley, Andrew M(oran) 1928-.... **CLC 28**
See also CA 5-8R; CAAS 7; CANR 7; MTCW

Green, Brian
See Card, Orson Scott

Green, Hannah .... **CLC 3**
See also CA 73-76

Green, Hannah
See Greenberg, Joanne (Goldenberg)

Green, Henry.................... **CLC 2, 13**
See also Yorke, Henry Vincent
See also DLB 15

Green, Julian (Hartridge)
1900- .... **CLC 3, 11, 77**
See also CA 21-24R; CANR 33; DLB 4, 72;
MTCW

Green, Julien 1900-
See Green, Julian (Hartridge)

Green, Paul (Eliot) 1894-1981...... **CLC 25**
See also AITN 1; CA 5-8R; 103; CANR 3;
DLB 7, 9; DLBY 81

Greenberg, Ivan 1908-1973
See Rahv, Philip
See also CA 85-88

Greenberg, Joanne (Goldenberg)
1932- .... **CLC 7, 30**
See also CA 5-8R; CANR 14, 32; SATA 25

Greenberg, Richard 1959(?)- .... **CLC 57**
See also CA 138

Greene, Bette 1934- .... **CLC 30**
See also AAYA 7; CA 53-56; CANR 4;
CLR 2; MAICYA; SAAS 16; SATA 8

Greene, Gael .... **CLC 8**
See also CA 13-16R; CANR 10

Greene, Graham (Henry)
1904-1991 ... **CLC 1, 3, 6, 9, 14, 18, 27,**
37, 70, 72
See also AITN 2; CA 13-16R; 133;
CANR 35; CDBLB 1945-1960; DA;
DLB 13, 15, 77, 100; DLBY 91; MTCW;
SATA 20; WLC

Greer, Richard
See Silverberg, Robert

Greer, Richard
See Silverberg, Robert

Gregor, Arthur 1923- .... **CLC 9**
See also CA 25-28R; CAAS 10; CANR 11;
SATA 36

Gregor, Lee
See Pohl, Frederik

Gregory, Isabella Augusta (Persse)
1852-1932 .... **TCLC 1**
See also CA 104; DLB 10

Gregory, J. Dennis
See Williams, John A(lfred)

Grendon, Stephen
See Derleth, August (William)

Grenville, Kate 1950- .... **CLC 61**
See also CA 118

Grenville, Pelham
See Wodehouse, P(elham) G(renville)

Greve, Felix Paul (Berthold Friedrich)
1879-1948
See Grove, Frederick Philip
See also CA 104

Grey, Zane 1872-1939 .... **TCLC 6**
See also CA 104; 132; DLB 9; MTCW

Grieg, (Johan) Nordahl (Brun)
1902-1943 .... **TCLC 10**
See also CA 107

Grieve, C(hristopher) M(urray)
1892-1978 .... **CLC 11, 19**
See also MacDiarmid, Hugh
See also CA 5-8R; 85-88; CANR 33;
MTCW

Griffin, Gerald 1803-1840 .... **NCLC 7**

Griffin, John Howard 1920-1980.... **CLC 68**
See also AITN 1; CA 1-4R; 101; CANR 2

Griffin, Peter .... **CLC 39**

Griffiths, Trevor 1935- .... **CLC 13, 52**
See also CA 97-100; DLB 13

Grigson, Geoffrey (Edward Harvey)
1905-1985 .... **CLC 7, 39**
See also CA 25-28R; 118; CANR 20, 33;
DLB 27; MTCW

Grillparzer, Franz 1791-1872...... **NCLC 1**

Grimble, Reverend Charles James
See Eliot, T(homas) S(tearns)

Grimke, Charlotte L(ottie) Forten
1837(?)-1914
See Forten, Charlotte L.
See also BW; CA 117; 124

Grimm, Jacob Ludwig Karl
1785-1863 .... **NCLC 3**
See also DLB 90; MAICYA; SATA 22

Grimm, Wilhelm Karl 1786-1859 .. **NCLC 3**
See also DLB 90; MAICYA; SATA 22

Grimmelshausen, Johann Jakob Christoffel
von 1621-1676 .... **LC 6**

Grindel, Eugene 1895-1952
See Eluard, Paul
See also CA 104

Grossman, David .... **CLC 67**
See also CA 138

Grossman, Vasily (Semenovich)
1905-1964 .... **CLC 41**
See also CA 124; 130; MTCW

Grove, Frederick Philip .... **TCLC 4**
See also Greve, Felix Paul (Berthold
Friedrich)
See also DLB 92

Grubb
See Crumb, R(obert)

Grumbach, Doris (Isaac)
1918- .... **CLC 13, 22, 64**
See also CA 5-8R; CAAS 2; CANR 9

Grundtvig, Nicolai Frederik Severin
1783-1872 .... **NCLC 1**

Grunge
See Crumb, R(obert)

Grunwald, Lisa 1959- .... **CLC 44**
See also CA 120

Guare, John 1938- .... **CLC 8, 14, 29, 67**
See also CA 73-76; CANR 21; DLB 7;
MTCW

Gudjonsson, Halldor Kiljan 1902-
See Laxness, Halldor
See also CA 103

Guenter, Erich
See Eich, Guenter

Guest, Barbara 1920- .... **CLC 34**
See also CA 25-28R; CANR 11; DLB 5

Guest, Judith (Ann) 1936- .... **CLC 8, 30**
See also AAYA 7; CA 77-80; CANR 15;
MTCW

Guild, Nicholas M. 1944- .... **CLC 33**
See also CA 93-96

Guillemin, Jacques
See Sartre, Jean-Paul

Guillen, Jorge 1893-1984 .... **CLC 11**
See also CA 89-92; 112; DLB 108; HW

Guillen (y Batista), Nicolas (Cristobal)
1902-1989 .... **CLC 48**
See also BLC 2; BW; CA 116; 125; 129;
HW

Guillevic, (Eugene) 1907- .... **CLC 33**
See also CA 93-96

Guillois
See Desnos, Robert

Guiney, Louise Imogen
1861-1920 .... **TCLC 41**
See also DLB 54

Guiraldes, Ricardo (Guillermo)
1886-1927 .... **TCLC 39**
See also CA 131; HW; MTCW

Gunn, Bill .... **CLC 5**
See also Gunn, William Harrison
See also DLB 38

Gunn, Thom(son William)
1929- .... **CLC 3, 6, 18, 32**
See also CA 17-20R; CANR 9, 33;
CDBLB 1960 to Present; DLB 27;
MTCW

Gunn, William Harrison 1934(?)-1989
See Gunn, Bill
See also AITN 1; BW; CA 13-16R; 128;
CANR 12, 25

Gunnars, Kristjana 1948- .... **CLC 69**
See also CA 113; DLB 60

Gurganus, Allan 1947- .... **CLC 70**
See also BEST 90:1; CA 135

Gurney, A(lbert) R(amsdell), Jr.
1930- .... **CLC 32, 50, 54**
See also CA 77-80; CANR 32

Gurney, Ivor (Bertie) 1890-1937 ... **TCLC 33**

Gurney, Peter
See Gurney, A(lbert) R(amsdell), Jr.

Gustafson, Ralph (Barker) 1909- .... **CLC 36**
See also CA 21-24R; CANR 8; DLB 88

Gut, Gom
See Simenon, Georges (Jacques Christian)

Guthrie, A(lfred) B(ertram), Jr.
1901-1991 .... **CLC 23**
See also CA 57-60; 134; CANR 24; DLB 6;
SATA 62; SATA-Obit 67

Guthrie, Isobel
See Grieve, C(hristopher) M(urray)

Guthrie, Woodrow Wilson 1912-1967
See Guthrie, Woody
See also CA 113; 93-96

Guthrie, Woody .... **CLC 35**
See also Guthrie, Woodrow Wilson

Guy, Rosa (Cuthbert) 1928- .... **CLC 26**
See also AAYA 4; BW; CA 17-20R;
CANR 14, 34; CLR 13; DLB 33;
MAICYA; SATA 14, 62

Gwendolyn
See Bennett, (Enoch) Arnold

H. D. .... **CLC 3, 8, 14, 31, 34, 73; PC 5**
See also Doolittle, Hilda

Haavikko, Paavo Juhani
1931- .... **CLC 18, 34**
See also CA 106

Habbema, Koos
See Heijermans, Herman

Hacker, Marilyn   1942- ....**CLC 5, 9, 23, 72**
See also CA 77-80; DLB 120

Haggard, H(enry) Rider
1856-1925 ....**TCLC 11**
See also CA 108; DLB 70; SATA 16

Haig, Fenil
See Ford, Ford Madox

Haig-Brown, Roderick (Langmere)
1908-1976 ....**CLC 21**
See also CA 5-8R; 69-72; CANR 4, 38;
DLB 88; MAICYA; SATA 12

Hailey, Arthur   1920- ....**CLC 5**
See also AITN 2; BEST 90:3; CA 1-4R;
CANR 2, 36; DLB 88; DLBY 82; MTCW

Hailey, Elizabeth Forsythe   1938- ...**CLC 40**
See also CA 93-96; CAAS 1; CANR 15

Haines, John (Meade)   1924- ....**CLC 58**
See also CA 17-20R; CANR 13, 34; DLB 5

Haldeman, Joe (William)   1943- .....**CLC 61**
See also CA 53-56; CANR 6; DLB 8

Haley, Alex(ander Murray Palmer)
1921-1992 ....**CLC 8, 12, 76**
See also BLC 2; BW; CA 77-80; 136; DA;
DLB 38; MTCW

Haliburton, Thomas Chandler
1796-1865 ....**NCLC 15**
See also DLB 11, 99

Hall, Donald (Andrew, Jr.)
1928- ....**CLC 1, 13, 37, 59**
See also CA 5-8R; CAAS 7; CANR 2;
DLB 5; SATA 23

Hall, Frederic Sauser
See Sauser-Hall, Frederic

Hall, James
See Kuttner, Henry

Hall, James Norman   1887-1951 ...**TCLC 23**
See also CA 123; SATA 21

Hall, (Marguerite) Radclyffe
1886(?)-1943 ....**TCLC 12**
See also CA 110

Hall, Rodney   1935- ....**CLC 51**
See also CA 109

Halliday, Michael
See Creasey, John

Halpern, Daniel   1945- ....**CLC 14**
See also CA 33-36R

Hamburger, Michael (Peter Leopold)
1924- ....**CLC 5, 14**
See also CA 5-8R; CAAS 4; CANR 2;
DLB 27

Hamill, Pete   1935- ....**CLC 10**
See also CA 25-28R; CANR 18

Hamilton, Clive
See Lewis, C(live) S(taples)

Hamilton, Edmond   1904-1977 ......**CLC 1**
See also CA 1-4R; CANR 3; DLB 8

Hamilton, Eugene (Jacob) Lee
See Lee-Hamilton, Eugene (Jacob)

Hamilton, Franklin
See Silverberg, Robert

Hamilton, Gail
See Corcoran, Barbara

Hamilton, Mollie
See Kaye, M(ary) M(argaret)

Hamilton, (Anthony Walter) Patrick
1904-1962 ....**CLC 51**
See also CA 113; DLB 10

Hamilton, Virginia   1936- ....**CLC 26**
See also AAYA 2; BW; CA 25-28R;
CANR 20, 37; CLR 1, 11; DLB 33, 52;
MAICYA; MTCW; SATA 4, 56

Hammett, (Samuel) Dashiell
1894-1961 ....**CLC 3, 5, 10, 19, 47**
See also AITN 1; CA 81-84;
CDALB 1929-1941; DLBD 6; MTCW

Hammon, Jupiter   1711(?)-1800(?)..**NCLC 5**
See also BLC 2; DLB 31, 50

Hammond, Keith
See Kuttner, Henry

Hamner, Earl (Henry), Jr.   1923- ...**CLC 12**
See also AITN 2; CA 73-76; DLB 6

Hampton, Christopher (James)
1946- ....**CLC 4**
See also CA 25-28R; DLB 13; MTCW

Hamsun, Knut   1859-1952...**TCLC 2, 14, 49**
See also Pedersen, Knut

Handke, Peter   1942- ..**CLC 5, 8, 10, 15, 38**
See also CA 77-80; CANR 33; DLB 85,
124; MTCW

Hanley, James   1901-1985 ...**CLC 3, 5, 8, 13**
See also CA 73-76; 117; CANR 36; MTCW

Hannah, Barry   1942- ....**CLC 23, 38**
See also CA 108; 110; DLB 6; MTCW

Hannon, Ezra
See Hunter, Evan

Hansberry, Lorraine (Vivian)
1930-1965 ....**CLC 17, 62; DC 2**
See also BLC 2; BW; CA 109; 25-28R;
CABS 3; CDALB 1941-1968; DA;
DLB 7, 38; MTCW

Hansen, Joseph   1923- ....**CLC 38**
See also CA 29-32R; CAAS 17; CANR 16

Hansen, Martin A.   1909-1955 .....**TCLC 32**

Hanson, Kenneth O(stlin)   1922- ....**CLC 13**
See also CA 53-56; CANR 7

Hardwick, Elizabeth   1916- ....**CLC 13**
See also CA 5-8R; CANR 3, 32; DLB 6;
MTCW

Hardy, Thomas
1840-1928 .....**TCLC 4, 10, 18, 32, 48;
SSC 2**
See also CA 104; 123; CDBLB 1890-1914;
DA; DLB 18, 19; MTCW; WLC

Hare, David   1947- ....**CLC 29, 58**
See also CA 97-100; CANR 39; DLB 13;
MTCW

Harford, Henry
See Hudson, W(illiam) H(enry)

Hargrave, Leonie
See Disch, Thomas M(ichael)

Harlan, Louis R(udolph)   1922- .....**CLC 34**
See also CA 21-24R; CANR 25

Harling, Robert   1951(?)- ....**CLC 53**

Harmon, William (Ruth)   1938- .....**CLC 38**
See also CA 33-36R; CANR 14, 32, 35;
SATA 65

Harper, F. E. W.
See Harper, Frances Ellen Watkins

Harper, Frances E. W.
See Harper, Frances Ellen Watkins

Harper, Frances E. Watkins
See Harper, Frances Ellen Watkins

Harper, Frances Ellen
See Harper, Frances Ellen Watkins

Harper, Frances Ellen Watkins
1825-1911 ....**TCLC 14**
See also BLC 2; BW; CA 111; 125; DLB 50

Harper, Michael S(teven)   1938- ..**CLC 7, 22**
See also BW; CA 33-36R; CANR 24;
DLB 41

Harper, Mrs. F. E. W.
See Harper, Frances Ellen Watkins

Harris, Christie (Lucy) Irwin
1907- ....**CLC 12**
See also CA 5-8R; CANR 6; DLB 88;
MAICYA; SAAS 10; SATA 6, 74

Harris, Frank   1856(?)-1931 ....**TCLC 24**
See also CA 109

Harris, George Washington
1814-1869 ....**NCLC 23**
See also DLB 3, 11

Harris, Joel Chandler   1848-1908 ...**TCLC 2**
See also CA 104; 137; DLB 11, 23, 42, 78,
91; MAICYA; YABC 1

Harris, John (Wyndham Parkes Lucas)
Beynon   1903-1969 ....**CLC 19**
See also CA 102; 89-92

Harris, MacDonald
See Heiney, Donald (William)

Harris, Mark   1922- ....**CLC 19**
See also CA 5-8R; CAAS 3; CANR 2;
DLB 2; DLBY 80

Harris, (Theodore) Wilson   1921-....**CLC 25**
See also BW; CA 65-68; CAAS 16;
CANR 11, 27; DLB 117; MTCW

Harrison, Elizabeth Cavanna   1909-
See Cavanna, Betty
See also CA 9-12R; CANR 6, 27

Harrison, Harry (Max)   1925- ......**CLC 42**
See also CA 1-4R; CANR 5, 21; DLB 8;
SATA 4

Harrison, James (Thomas)   1937-
See Harrison, Jim
See also CA 13-16R; CANR 8

Harrison, Jim ....**CLC 6, 14, 33, 66**
See also Harrison, James (Thomas)
See also DLBY 82

Harrison, Kathryn   1961- ....**CLC 70**

Harrison, Tony   1937- ....**CLC 43**
See also CA 65-68; DLB 40; MTCW

Harriss, Will(ard Irvin)   1922- ......**CLC 34**
See also CA 111

Harson, Sley
See Ellison, Harlan

Hart, Ellis
See Ellison, Harlan

Hart, Josephine   1942(?)- ....**CLC 70**
See also CA 138

Hart, Moss   1904-1961 ....**CLC 66**
See also CA 109; 89-92; DLB 7

Harte, (Francis) Bret(t)
1836(?)-1902 . . . . . . **TCLC 1, 25; SSC 8**
See also CA 104; 140; CDALB 1865-1917;
DA; DLB 12, 64, 74, 79; SATA 26; WLC

Hartley, L(eslie) P(oles)
1895-1972 . . . . **CLC 2, 22**
See also CA 45-48; 37-40R; CANR 33;
DLB 15; MTCW

Hartman, Geoffrey H. 1929- . . . . **CLC 27**
See also CA 117; 125; DLB 67

Haruf, Kent 19(?)- . . . . **CLC 34**

Harwood, Ronald 1934- . . . . **CLC 32**
See also CA 1-4R; CANR 4; DLB 13

Hasek, Jaroslav (Matej Frantisek)
1883-1923 . . . . **TCLC 4**
See also CA 104; 129; MTCW

Hass, Robert 1941- . . . . **CLC 18, 39**
See also CA 111; CANR 30; DLB 105

Hastings, Hudson
See Kuttner, Henry

Hastings, Selina . . . . **CLC 44**

Hatteras, Amelia
See Mencken, H(enry) L(ouis)

Hatteras, Owen . . . . **TCLC 18**
See also Mencken, H(enry) L(ouis); Nathan,
George Jean

Hauptmann, Gerhart (Johann Robert)
1862-1946 . . . . **TCLC 4**
See also CA 104; DLB 66, 118

Havel, Vaclav 1936- . . . . **CLC 25, 58, 65**
See also CA 104; CANR 36; MTCW

Haviaras, Stratis . . . . **CLC 33**
See also Chaviaras, Strates

Hawes, Stephen 1475(?)-1523(?) . . . . . **LC 17**

Hawkes, John (Clendennin Burne, Jr.)
1925- . . . . . . **CLC 1, 2, 3, 4, 7, 9, 14, 15,
27, 49**
See also CA 1-4R; CANR 2; DLB 2, 7;
DLBY 80; MTCW

Hawking, S. W.
See Hawking, Stephen W(illiam)

Hawking, Stephen W(illiam)
1942- . . . . **CLC 63**
See also BEST 89:1; CA 126; 129

Hawthorne, Julian 1846-1934 . . . . . **TCLC 25**

Hawthorne, Nathaniel
1804-1864 . . . . **NCLC 39; SSC 3**
See also CDALB 1640-1865; DA; DLB 1,
74; WLC; YABC 2

Haxton, Josephine Ayres 1921- . . . . **CLC 73**
See also CA 115; CANR 41

Hayaseca y Eizaguirre, Jorge
See Echegaray (y Eizaguirre), Jose (Maria
Waldo)

Hayashi Fumiko 1904-1951 . . . . . . **TCLC 27**

Haycraft, Anna
See Ellis, Alice Thomas
See also CA 122

Hayden, Robert E(arl)
1913-1980 . . . . . . **CLC 5, 9, 14, 37; PC 6**
See also BLC 2; BW; CA 69-72; 97-100;
CABS 2; CANR 24; CDALB 1941-1968;
DA; DLB 5, 76; MTCW; SATA 19, 26

Hayford, J(oseph) E(phraim) Casely
See Casely-Hayford, J(oseph) E(phraim)

Hayman, Ronald 1932- . . . . **CLC 44**
See also CA 25-28R; CANR 18

Haywood, Eliza (Fowler)
1693(?)-1756 . . . . **LC 1**

Hazlitt, William 1778-1830 . . . . . . **NCLC 29**
See also DLB 110

Hazzard, Shirley 1931- . . . . **CLC 18**
See also CA 9-12R; CANR 4; DLBY 82;
MTCW

Head, Bessie 1937-1986 . . . . **CLC 25, 67**
See also BLC 2; BW; CA 29-32R; 119;
CANR 25; DLB 117; MTCW

Headon, (Nicky) Topper 1956(?)- . . . **CLC 30**
See also Clash, The

Heaney, Seamus (Justin)
1939- . . . . **CLC 5, 7, 14, 25, 37, 74**
See also CA 85-88; CANR 25;
CDBLB 1960 to Present; DLB 40;
MTCW

Hearn, (Patricio) Lafcadio (Tessima Carlos)
1850-1904 . . . . **TCLC 9**
See also CA 105; DLB 12, 78

Hearne, Vicki 1946- . . . . **CLC 56**
See also CA 139

Hearon, Shelby 1931- . . . . **CLC 63**
See also AITN 2; CA 25-28R; CANR 18

Heat-Moon, William Least . . . . **CLC 29**
See also Trogdon, William (Lewis)
See also AAYA 9

Hebert, Anne 1916- . . . . **CLC 4, 13, 29**
See also CA 85-88; DLB 68; MTCW

Hecht, Anthony (Evan)
1923- . . . . **CLC 8, 13, 19**
See also CA 9-12R; CANR 6; DLB 5

Hecht, Ben 1894-1964 . . . . **CLC 8**
See also CA 85-88; DLB 7, 9, 25, 26, 28, 86

Hedayat, Sadeq 1903-1951 . . . . **TCLC 21**
See also CA 120

Heidegger, Martin 1889-1976 . . . . . . **CLC 24**
See also CA 81-84; 65-68; CANR 34;
MTCW

Heidenstam, (Carl Gustaf) Verner von
1859-1940 . . . . **TCLC 5**
See also CA 104

Heifner, Jack 1946- . . . . **CLC 11**
See also CA 105

Heijermans, Herman 1864-1924 . . . **TCLC 24**
See also CA 123

Heilbrun, Carolyn G(old) 1926- . . . . . **CLC 25**
See also CA 45-48; CANR 1, 28

Heine, Heinrich 1797-1856 . . . . **NCLC 4**
See also DLB 90

Heinemann, Larry (Curtiss) 1944- . . **CLC 50**
See also CA 110; CANR 31; DLBD 9

Heiney, Donald (William) 1921- . . . . . **CLC 9**
See also CA 1-4R; CANR 3

Heinlein, Robert A(nson)
1907-1988 . . . . . . **CLC 1, 3, 8, 14, 26, 55**
See also CA 1-4R; 125; CANR 1, 20;
DLB 8; MAICYA; MTCW; SATA 9, 56,
69

Helforth, John
See Doolittle, Hilda

Hellenhofferu, Vojtech Kapristian z
See Hasek, Jaroslav (Matej Frantisek)

Heller, Joseph
1923- . . . . **CLC 1, 3, 5, 8, 11, 36, 63**
See also AITN 1; CA 5-8R; CABS 1;
CANR 8; DA; DLB 2, 28; DLBY 80;
MTCW; WLC

Hellman, Lillian (Florence)
1906-1984 . . . . . **CLC 2, 4, 8, 14, 18, 34,
44, 52; DC 1**
See also AITN 1, 2; CA 13-16R; 112;
CANR 33; DLB 7; DLBY 84; MTCW

Helprin, Mark 1947- . . . . . **CLC 7, 10, 22, 32**
See also CA 81-84; DLBY 85; MTCW

Helyar, Jane Penelope Josephine 1933-
See Poole, Josephine
See also CA 21-24R; CANR 10, 26

Hemans, Felicia 1793-1835 . . . . . . **NCLC 29**
See also DLB 96

Hemingway, Ernest (Miller)
1899-1961 . . . **CLC 1, 3, 6, 8, 10, 13, 19,
30, 34, 39, 41, 44, 50, 61; SSC 1**
See also CA 77-80; CANR 34;
CDALB 1917-1929; DA; DLB 4, 9, 102;
DLBD 1; DLBY 81, 87; MTCW; WLC

Hempel, Amy 1951- . . . . **CLC 39**
See also CA 118; 137

Henderson, F. C.
See Mencken, H(enry) L(ouis)

Henderson, Sylvia
See Ashton-Warner, Sylvia (Constance)

Henley, Beth . . . . **CLC 23**
See also Henley, Elizabeth Becker
See also CABS 3; DLBY 86

Henley, Elizabeth Becker 1952-
See Henley, Beth
See also CA 107; CANR 32; MTCW

Henley, William Ernest
1849-1903 . . . . **TCLC 8**
See also CA 105; DLB 19

Hennissart, Martha
See Lathen, Emma
See also CA 85-88

Henry, O. . . . . **TCLC 1, 19; SSC 5**
See also Porter, William Sydney
See also WLC

Henryson, Robert 1430(?)-1506(?) . . . . **LC 20**

Henry VIII 1491-1547 . . . . **LC 10**

Henschke, Alfred
See Klabund

Hentoff, Nat(han Irving) 1925- . . . . . **CLC 26**
See also AAYA 4; CA 1-4R; CAAS 6;
CANR 5, 25; CLR 1; MAICYA;
SATA 27, 42, 69

Heppenstall, (John) Rayner
1911-1981 . . . . **CLC 10**
See also CA 1-4R; 103; CANR 29

Herbert, Frank (Patrick)
1920-1986 . . . . **CLC 12, 23, 35, 44**
See also CA 53-56; 118; CANR 5; DLB 8;
MTCW; SATA 9, 37, 47

Herbert, George 1593-1633 . . . . **PC 4**
See also CDBLB Before 1660; DLB 126

Herbert, Zbigniew 1924- .... **CLC 9, 43**
  See also CA 89-92; CANR 36; MTCW

Herbst, Josephine (Frey)
  1897-1969 .... **CLC 34**
  See also CA 5-8R; 25-28R; DLB 9

Hergesheimer, Joseph
  1880-1954 .... **TCLC 11**
  See also CA 109; DLB 102, 9

Herlihy, James Leo 1927- .... **CLC 6**
  See also CA 1-4R; CANR 2

Hermogenes fl. c. 175- .... **CMLC 6**

Hernandez, Jose 1834-1886 ..... **NCLC 17**

Herrick, Robert 1591-1674 .... **LC 13**
  See also DA; DLB 126

Herriot, James .... **CLC 12**
  See also Wight, James Alfred
  See also AAYA 1; CANR 40

Herrmann, Dorothy 1941- .... **CLC 44**
  See also CA 107

Herrmann, Taffy
  See Herrmann, Dorothy

Hersey, John (Richard)
  1914-1993 .... **CLC 1, 2, 7, 9, 40**
  See also CA 17-20R; 140; CANR 33;
  DLB 6; MTCW; SATA 25

Herzen, Aleksandr Ivanovich
  1812-1870 .... **NCLC 10**

Herzl, Theodor 1860-1904 .... **TCLC 36**

Herzog, Werner 1942- .... **CLC 16**
  See also CA 89-92

Hesiod c. 8th cent. B.C.- .... **CMLC 5**

Hesse, Hermann
  1877-1962 ... **CLC 1, 2, 3, 6, 11, 17, 25,
                               69; SSC 9**
  See also CA 17-18; CAP 2; DA; DLB 66;
  MTCW; SATA 50; WLC

Hewes, Cady
  See De Voto, Bernard (Augustine)

Heyen, William 1940- .... **CLC 13, 18**
  See also CA 33-36R; CAAS 9; DLB 5

Heyerdahl, Thor 1914- .... **CLC 26**
  See also CA 5-8R; CANR 5, 22; MTCW;
  SATA 2, 52

Heym, Georg (Theodor Franz Arthur)
  1887-1912 .... **TCLC 9**
  See also CA 106

Heym, Stefan 1913- .... **CLC 41**
  See also CA 9-12R; CANR 4; DLB 69

Heyse, Paul (Johann Ludwig von)
  1830-1914 .... **TCLC 8**
  See also CA 104; DLB 129

Hibbert, Eleanor Alice Burford
  1906-1993 .... **CLC 7**
  See also BEST 90:4; CA 17-20R; CANR 9,
  28; SATA 2; SATA-Obit 74

Higgins, George V(incent)
  1939- ....**CLC 4, 7, 10, 18**
  See also CA 77-80; CAAS 5; CANR 17;
  DLB 2; DLBY 81; MTCW

Higginson, Thomas Wentworth
  1823-1911 .... **TCLC 36**
  See also DLB 1, 64

Highet, Helen
  See MacInnes, Helen (Clark)

Highsmith, (Mary) Patricia
  1921- ....**CLC 2, 4, 14, 42**
  See also CA 1-4R; CANR 1, 20; MTCW

Highwater, Jamake (Mamake)
  1942(?)- .... **CLC 12**
  See also AAYA 7; CA 65-68; CAAS 7;
  CANR 10, 34; CLR 17; DLB 52;
  DLBY 85; MAICYA; SATA 30, 32, 69

Hijuelos, Oscar 1951- .... **CLC 65**
  See also BEST 90:1; CA 123; HW

Hikmet, Nazim 1902-1963 .... **CLC 40**
  See also CA 93-96

Hildesheimer, Wolfgang
  1916-1991 .... **CLC 49**
  See also CA 101; 135; DLB 69, 124

Hill, Geoffrey (William)
  1932- ....**CLC 5, 8, 18, 45**
  See also CA 81-84; CANR 21;
  CDBLB 1960 to Present; DLB 40;
  MTCW

Hill, George Roy 1921- .... **CLC 26**
  See also CA 110; 122

Hill, Susan (Elizabeth) 1942- .... **CLC 4**
  See also CA 33-36R; CANR 29; DLB 14;
  MTCW

Hillerman, Tony 1925- .... **CLC 62**
  See also AAYA 6; BEST 89:1; CA 29-32R;
  CANR 21; SATA 6

Hillesum, Etty 1914-1943 .... **TCLC 49**
  See also CA 137

Hilliard, Noel (Harvey) 1929- ...... **CLC 15**
  See also CA 9-12R; CANR 7

Hillis, Rick 1956- .... **CLC 66**
  See also CA 134

Hilton, James 1900-1954 .... **TCLC 21**
  See also CA 108; DLB 34, 77; SATA 34

Himes, Chester (Bomar)
  1909-1984 .... **CLC 2, 4, 7, 18, 58**
  See also BLC 2; BW; CA 25-28R; 114;
  CANR 22; DLB 2, 76; MTCW

Hinde, Thomas .... **CLC 6, 11**
  See also Chitty, Thomas Willes

Hindin, Nathan
  See Bloch, Robert (Albert)

Hine, (William) Daryl 1936- .... **CLC 15**
  See also CA 1-4R; CAAS 15; CANR 1, 20;
  DLB 60

Hinkson, Katharine Tynan
  See Tynan, Katharine

Hinton, S(usan) E(loise) 1950- ..... **CLC 30**
  See also AAYA 2; CA 81-84; CANR 32;
  CLR 3, 23; DA; MAICYA; MTCW;
  SATA 19, 58

Hippius, Zinaida .... **TCLC 9**
  See also Gippius, Zinaida (Nikolayevna)

Hiraoka, Kimitake 1925-1970
  See Mishima, Yukio
  See also CA 97-100; 29-32R; MTCW

Hirsch, Edward 1950- .... **CLC 31, 50**
  See also CA 104; CANR 20; DLB 120

Hitchcock, Alfred (Joseph)
  1899-1980 .... **CLC 16**
  See also CA 97-100; SATA 24, 27

Hoagland, Edward 1932- .... **CLC 28**
  See also CA 1-4R; CANR 2, 31; DLB 6;
  SATA 51

Hoban, Russell (Conwell) 1925- .. **CLC 7, 25**
  See also CA 5-8R; CANR 23, 37; CLR 3;
  DLB 52; MAICYA; MTCW; SATA 1, 40

Hobbs, Perry
  See Blackmur, R(ichard) P(almer)

Hobson, Laura Z(ametkin)
  1900-1986 .... **CLC 7, 25**
  See also CA 17-20R; 118; DLB 28;
  SATA 52

Hochhuth, Rolf 1931- .... **CLC 4, 11, 18**
  See also CA 5-8R; CANR 33; DLB 124;
  MTCW

Hochman, Sandra 1936- .... **CLC 3, 8**
  See also CA 5-8R; DLB 5

Hochwaelder, Fritz 1911-1986 ...... **CLC 36**
  See also Hochwalder, Fritz
  See also CA 29-32R; 120; MTCW

Hochwalder, Fritz .... **CLC 36**
  See also Hochwaelder, Fritz

Hocking, Mary (Eunice) 1921- ..... **CLC 13**
  See also CA 101; CANR 18, 40

Hodgins, Jack 1938- .... **CLC 23**
  See also CA 93-96; DLB 60

Hodgson, William Hope
  1877(?)-1918 .... **TCLC 13**
  See also CA 111; DLB 70

Hoffman, Alice 1952- .... **CLC 51**
  See also CA 77-80; CANR 34; MTCW

Hoffman, Daniel (Gerard)
  1923- .... **CLC 6, 13, 23**
  See also CA 1-4R; CANR 4; DLB 5

Hoffman, Stanley 1944- .... **CLC 5**
  See also CA 77-80

Hoffman, William M(oses) 1939- ... **CLC 40**
  See also CA 57-60; CANR 11

Hoffmann, E(rnst) T(heodor) A(madeus)
  1776-1822 .... **NCLC 2**
  See also DLB 90; SATA 27

Hofmann, Gert 1931- .... **CLC 54**
  See also CA 128

Hofmannsthal, Hugo von
  1874-1929 .... **TCLC 11**
  See also CA 106; DLB 81, 118

Hogan, Linda 1947- .... **CLC 73**
  See also CA 120

Hogarth, Charles
  See Creasey, John

Hogg, James 1770-1835 .... **NCLC 4**
  See also DLB 93, 116

Holbach, Paul Henri Thiry Baron
  1723-1789 .... **LC 14**

Holberg, Ludvig 1684-1754 .... **LC 6**

Holden, Ursula 1921- .... **CLC 18**
  See also CA 101; CAAS 8; CANR 22

Holderlin, (Johann Christian) Friedrich
  1770-1843 .... **NCLC 16; PC 4**

Holdstock, Robert
  See Holdstock, Robert P.

Holdstock, Robert P. 1948- .... **CLC 39**
  See also CA 131

James, C(yril) L(ionel) R(obert)
1901-1989 . . . . **CLC 33**
See also BW; CA 117; 125; 128; DLB 125;
MTCW

James, Daniel (Lewis)   1911-1988
See Santiago, Danny
See also CA 125

James, Dynely
See Mayne, William (James Carter)

James, Henry
1843-1916 . . . . . **TCLC 2, 11, 24, 40, 47;**
SSC 8
See also CA 104; 132; CDALB 1865-1917;
DA; DLB 12, 71, 74; MTCW; WLC

James, Montague (Rhodes)
1862-1936 . . . . **TCLC 6**
See also CA 104

James, P. D. . . . . **CLC 18, 46**
See also White, Phyllis Dorothy James
See also BEST 90:2; CDBLB 1960 to
Present; DLB 87

James, Philip
See Moorcock, Michael (John)

James, William   1842-1910 . . . . . **TCLC 15, 32**
See also CA 109

James I   1394-1437 . . . . **LC 20**

Jami, Nur al-Din 'Abd al-Rahman
1414-1492 . . . . **LC 9**

Jandl, Ernst   1925- . . . . **CLC 34**

Janowitz, Tama   1957- . . . . **CLC 43**
See also CA 106

Jarrell, Randall
1914-1965 . . . . **CLC 1, 2, 6, 9, 13, 49**
See also CA 5-8R; 25-28R; CABS 2;
CANR 6, 34; CDALB 1941-1968; CLR 6;
DLB 48, 52; MAICYA; MTCW; SATA 7

Jarry, Alfred   1873-1907 . . . . **TCLC 2, 14**
See also CA 104

Jarvis, E. K.
See Bloch, Robert (Albert); Ellison, Harlan;
Silverberg, Robert

Jeake, Samuel, Jr.
See Aiken, Conrad (Potter)

Jean Paul   1763-1825 . . . . **NCLC 7**

Jeffers, (John) Robinson
1887-1962 . . . . **CLC 2, 3, 11, 15, 54**
See also CA 85-88; CANR 35;
CDALB 1917-1929; DA; DLB 45;
MTCW; WLC

Jefferson, Janet
See Mencken, H(enry) L(ouis)

Jefferson, Thomas   1743-1826 . . . . **NCLC 11**
See also CDALB 1640-1865; DLB 31

Jeffrey, Francis   1773-1850 . . . . **NCLC 33**
See also DLB 107

Jelakowitch, Ivan
See Heijermans, Herman

Jellicoe, (Patricia) Ann   1927- . . . . . . **CLC 27**
See also CA 85-88; DLB 13

Jen, Gish . . . . **CLC 70**
See also Jen, Lillian

Jen, Lillian   1956(?)-
See Jen, Gish
See also CA 135

Jenkins, (John) Robin   1912- . . . . **CLC 52**
See also CA 1-4R; CANR 1; DLB 14

Jennings, Elizabeth (Joan)
1926- . . . . **CLC 5, 14**
See also CA 61-64; CAAS 5; CANR 8, 39;
DLB 27; MTCW; SATA 66

Jennings, Waylon   1937- . . . . **CLC 21**

Jensen, Johannes V.   1873-1950 . . . . **TCLC 41**

Jensen, Laura (Linnea)   1948- . . . . . . **CLC 37**
See also CA 103

Jerome, Jerome K(lapka)
1859-1927 . . . . **TCLC 23**
See also CA 119; DLB 10, 34

Jerrold, Douglas William
1803-1857 . . . . **NCLC 2**

Jewett, (Theodora) Sarah Orne
1849-1909 . . . . **TCLC 1, 22; SSC 6**
See also CA 108; 127; DLB 12, 74;
SATA 15

Jewsbury, Geraldine (Endsor)
1812-1880 . . . . **NCLC 22**
See also DLB 21

Jhabvala, Ruth Prawer
1927- . . . . **CLC 4, 8, 29**
See also CA 1-4R; CANR 2, 29; MTCW

Jiles, Paulette   1943- . . . . **CLC 13, 58**
See also CA 101

Jimenez (Mantecon), Juan Ramon
1881-1958 . . . . **TCLC 4**
See also CA 104; 131; HW; MTCW

Jimenez, Ramon
See Jimenez (Mantecon), Juan Ramon

Jimenez Mantecon, Juan
See Jimenez (Mantecon), Juan Ramon

Joel, Billy . . . . **CLC 26**
See also Joel, William Martin

Joel, William Martin   1949-
See Joel, Billy
See also CA 108

John of the Cross, St.   1542-1591 . . . . **LC 18**

Johnson, B(ryan) S(tanley William)
1933-1973 . . . . **CLC 6, 9**
See also CA 9-12R; 53-56; CANR 9;
DLB 14, 40

Johnson, Charles (Richard)
1948- . . . . **CLC 7, 51, 65**
See also BLC 2; BW; CA 116; DLB 33

Johnson, Denis   1949- . . . . **CLC 52**
See also CA 117; 121; DLB 120

Johnson, Diane (Lain)
1934- . . . . **CLC 5, 13, 48**
See also CA 41-44R; CANR 17, 40;
DLBY 80; MTCW

Johnson, Eyvind (Olof Verner)
1900-1976 . . . . **CLC 14**
See also CA 73-76; 69-72; CANR 34

Johnson, J. R.
See James, C(yril) L(ionel) R(obert)

Johnson, James Weldon
1871-1938 . . . . **TCLC 3, 19**
See also BLC 2; BW; CA 104; 125;
CDALB 1917-1929; DLB 51; MTCW;
SATA 31

Johnson, Joyce   1935- . . . . **CLC 58**
See also CA 125; 129

Johnson, Lionel (Pigot)
1867-1902 . . . . **TCLC 19**
See also CA 117; DLB 19

Johnson, Mel
See Malzberg, Barry N(athaniel)

Johnson, Pamela Hansford
1912-1981 . . . . **CLC 1, 7, 27**
See also CA 1-4R; 104; CANR 2, 28;
DLB 15; MTCW

Johnson, Samuel   1709-1784 . . . . **LC 15**
See also CDBLB 1660-1789; DA; DLB 39,
95, 104; WLC

Johnson, Uwe
1934-1984 . . . . **CLC 5, 10, 15, 40**
See also CA 1-4R; 112; CANR 1, 39;
DLB 75; MTCW

Johnston, George (Benson)   1913- . . . **CLC 51**
See also CA 1-4R; CANR 5, 20; DLB 88

Johnston, Jennifer   1930- . . . . **CLC 7**
See also CA 85-88; DLB 14

Jolley, (Monica) Elizabeth   1923- . . . **CLC 46**
See also CA 127; CAAS 13

Jones, Arthur Llewellyn   1863-1947
See Machen, Arthur
See also CA 104

Jones, D(ouglas) G(ordon)   1929- . . . . **CLC 10**
See also CA 29-32R; CANR 13; DLB 53

Jones, David (Michael)
1895-1974 . . . . **CLC 2, 4, 7, 13, 42**
See also CA 9-12R; 53-56; CANR 28;
CDBLB 1945-1960; DLB 20, 100; MTCW

Jones, David Robert   1947-
See Bowie, David
See also CA 103

Jones, Diana Wynne   1934- . . . . **CLC 26**
See also CA 49-52; CANR 4, 26; CLR 23;
MAICYA; SAAS 7; SATA 9, 70

Jones, Edward P.   1951- . . . . **CLC 76**

Jones, Gayl   1949- . . . . **CLC 6, 9**
See also BLC 2; BW; CA 77-80; CANR 27;
DLB 33; MTCW

Jones, James   1921-1977 . . . . **CLC 1, 3, 10, 39**
See also AITN 1, 2; CA 1-4R; 69-72;
CANR 6; DLB 2; MTCW

Jones, John J.
See Lovecraft, H(oward) P(hillips)

Jones, LeRoi . . . . **CLC 1, 2, 3, 5, 10, 14**
See also Baraka, Amiri

Jones, Louis B. . . . . **CLC 65**

Jones, Madison (Percy, Jr.)   1925- . . . **CLC 4**
See also CA 13-16R; CAAS 11; CANR 7

Jones, Mervyn   1922- . . . . **CLC 10, 52**
See also CA 45-48; CAAS 5; CANR 1;
MTCW

Jones, Mick   1956(?)- . . . . **CLC 30**
See also Clash, The

Jones, Nettie (Pearl)   1941- . . . . **CLC 34**
See also CA 137

Jones, Preston   1936-1979 . . . . **CLC 10**
See also CA 73-76; 89-92; DLB 7

Jones, Robert F(rancis)   1934- . . . . . . **CLC 7**
See also CA 49-52; CANR 2

Kemal, Yashar 1923- . . . . **CLC 14, 29**
See also CA 89-92

Kemble, Fanny 1809-1893 . . . . **NCLC 18**
See also DLB 32

Kemelman, Harry 1908- . . . . **CLC 2**
See also AITN 1; CA 9-12R; CANR 6;
DLB 28

Kempe, Margery 1373(?)-1440(?) . . . . . **LC 6**

Kempis, Thomas a 1380-1471 . . . . **LC 11**

Kendall, Henry 1839-1882 . . . . **NCLC 12**

Keneally, Thomas (Michael)
1935- . . . . . . **CLC 5, 8, 10, 14, 19, 27, 43**
See also CA 85-88; CANR 10; MTCW

Kennedy, Adrienne (Lita) 1931- . . . . **CLC 66**
See also BLC 2; BW; CA 103; CABS 3;
CANR 26; DLB 38

Kennedy, John Pendleton
1795-1870 . . . . **NCLC 2**
See also DLB 3

Kennedy, Joseph Charles 1929- . . . . . **CLC 8**
See also Kennedy, X. J.
See also CA 1-4R; CANR 4, 30, 40;
SATA 14

Kennedy, William 1928- . . . **CLC 6, 28, 34, 53**
See also AAYA 1; CA 85-88; CANR 14,
31; DLBY 85; MTCW; SATA 57

Kennedy, X. J. . . . . **CLC 42**
See also Kennedy, Joseph Charles
See also CAAS 9; CLR 27; DLB 5

Kent, Kelvin
See Kuttner, Henry

Kenton, Maxwell
See Southern, Terry

Kenyon, Robert O.
See Kuttner, Henry

Kerouac, Jack . . . . . **CLC 1, 2, 3, 5, 14, 29, 61**
See also Kerouac, Jean-Louis Lebris de
See also CDALB 1941-1968; DLB 2, 16;
DLBD 3

Kerouac, Jean-Louis Lebris de 1922-1969
See Kerouac, Jack
See also AITN 1; CA 5-8R; 25-28R;
CANR 26; DA; MTCW; WLC

Kerr, Jean 1923- . . . . **CLC 22**
See also CA 5-8R; CANR 7

Kerr, M. E. . . . . **CLC 12, 35**
See also Meaker, Marijane (Agnes)
See also AAYA 2; CLR 29; SAAS 1

Kerr, Robert . . . . **CLC 55**

Kerrigan, (Thomas) Anthony
1918- . . . . **CLC 4, 6**
See also CA 49-52; CAAS 11; CANR 4

Kerry, Lois
See Duncan, Lois

Kesey, Ken (Elton)
1935- . . . . **CLC 1, 3, 6, 11, 46, 64**
See also CA 1-4R; CANR 22, 38;
CDALB 1968-1988; DA; DLB 2, 16;
MTCW; SATA 66; WLC

Kesselring, Joseph (Otto)
1902-1967 . . . . **CLC 45**

Kessler, Jascha (Frederick) 1929- . . . **CLC 4**
See also CA 17-20R; CANR 8

Kettelkamp, Larry (Dale) 1933- . . . . **CLC 12**
See also CA 29-32R; CANR 16; SAAS 3;
SATA 2

Keyber, Conny
See Fielding, Henry

Khayyam, Omar 1048-1131 . . . . . . **CMLC 11**

Kherdian, David 1931- . . . . **CLC 6, 9**
See also CA 21-24R; CAAS 2; CANR 39;
CLR 24; MAICYA; SATA 16, 74

Khlebnikov, Velimir . . . . **TCLC 20**
See also Khlebnikov, Viktor Vladimirovich

Khlebnikov, Viktor Vladimirovich 1885-1922
See Khlebnikov, Velimir
See also CA 117

Khodasevich, Vladislav (Felitsianovich)
1886-1939 . . . . **TCLC 15**
See also CA 115

Kielland, Alexander Lange
1849-1906 . . . . **TCLC 5**
See also CA 104

Kiely, Benedict 1919- . . . . **CLC 23, 43**
See also CA 1-4R; CANR 2; DLB 15

Kienzle, William X(avier) 1928- . . . . **CLC 25**
See also CA 93-96; CAAS 1; CANR 9, 31;
MTCW

Kierkegaard, Soeren 1813-1855 . . . **NCLC 34**

Kierkegaard, Soren 1813-1855 . . . . **NCLC 34**

Killens, John Oliver 1916-1987 . . . . . **CLC 10**
See also BW; CA 77-80; 123; CAAS 2;
CANR 26; DLB 33

Killigrew, Anne 1660-1685 . . . . **LC 4**
See also DLB 131

Kim
See Simenon, Georges (Jacques Christian)

Kincaid, Jamaica 1949- . . . . **CLC 43, 68**
See also BLC 2; BW; CA 125

King, Francis (Henry) 1923- . . . . . **CLC 8, 53**
See also CA 1-4R; CANR 1, 33; DLB 15;
MTCW

King, Stephen (Edwin)
1947- . . . . **CLC 12, 26, 37, 61**
See also AAYA 1; BEST 90:1; CA 61-64;
CANR 1, 30; DLBY 80; MTCW;
SATA 9, 55

King, Steve
See King, Stephen (Edwin)

Kingman, Lee . . . . **CLC 17**
See also Natti, (Mary) Lee
See also SAAS 3; SATA 1, 67

Kingsley, Charles 1819-1875 . . . . . **NCLC 35**
See also DLB 21, 32; YABC 2

Kingsley, Sidney 1906- . . . . **CLC 44**
See also CA 85-88; DLB 7

Kingsolver, Barbara 1955- . . . . **CLC 55**
See also CA 129; 134

Kingston, Maxine (Ting Ting) Hong
1940- . . . . **CLC 12, 19, 58**
See also AAYA 8; CA 69-72; CANR 13,
38; DLBY 80; MTCW; SATA 53

Kinnell, Galway
1927- . . . . **CLC 1, 2, 3, 5, 13, 29**
See also CA 9-12R; CANR 10, 34; DLB 5;
DLBY 87; MTCW

Kinsella, Thomas 1928- . . . . **CLC 4, 19**
See also CA 17-20R; CANR 15; DLB 27;
MTCW

Kinsella, W(illiam) P(atrick)
1935- . . . . **CLC 27, 43**
See also AAYA 7; CA 97-100; CAAS 7;
CANR 21, 35; MTCW

Kipling, (Joseph) Rudyard
1865-1936 . . . . **TCLC 8, 17; PC 3; SSC 5**
See also CA 105; 120; CANR 33;
CDBLB 1890-1914; DA; DLB 19, 34;
MAICYA; MTCW; WLC; YABC 2

Kirkup, James 1918- . . . . **CLC 1**
See also CA 1-4R; CAAS 4; CANR 2;
DLB 27; SATA 12

Kirkwood, James 1930(?)-1989 . . . . . . **CLC 9**
See also AITN 2; CA 1-4R; 128; CANR 6,
40

Kis, Danilo 1935-1989 . . . . **CLC 57**
See also CA 109; 118; 129; MTCW

Kivi, Aleksis 1834-1872 . . . . **NCLC 30**

Kizer, Carolyn (Ashley) 1925- . . . **CLC 15, 39**
See also CA 65-68; CAAS 5; CANR 24;
DLB 5

Klabund 1890-1928 . . . . **TCLC 44**
See also DLB 66

Klappert, Peter 1942- . . . . **CLC 57**
See also CA 33-36R; DLB 5

Klein, A(braham) M(oses)
1909-1972 . . . . **CLC 19**
See also CA 101; 37-40R; DLB 68

Klein, Norma 1938-1989 . . . . **CLC 30**
See also AAYA 2; CA 41-44R; 128;
CANR 15, 37; CLR 2, 19; MAICYA;
SAAS 1; SATA 7, 57

Klein, T(heodore) E(ibon) D(onald)
1947- . . . . **CLC 34**
See also CA 119

Kleist, Heinrich von 1777-1811 . . . . **NCLC 2**
See also DLB 90

Klima, Ivan 1931- . . . . **CLC 56**
See also CA 25-28R; CANR 17

Klimentov, Andrei Platonovich 1899-1951
See Platonov, Andrei
See also CA 108

Klinger, Friedrich Maximilian von
1752-1831 . . . . **NCLC 1**
See also DLB 94

Klopstock, Friedrich Gottlieb
1724-1803 . . . . **NCLC 11**
See also DLB 97

Knebel, Fletcher 1911-1993 . . . . **CLC 14**
See also AITN 1; CA 1-4R; 140; CAAS 3;
CANR 1, 36; SATA 36

Knickerbocker, Diedrich
See Irving, Washington

Knight, Etheridge 1931-1991 . . . . **CLC 40**
See also BLC 2; BW; CA 21-24R; 133;
CANR 23; DLB 41

Knight, Sarah Kemble 1666-1727 . . . . . **LC 7**
See also DLB 24

Knowles, John 1926- . . . . . . **CLC 1, 4, 10, 26**
See also AAYA 10; CA 17-20R; CANR 40;
CDALB 1968-1988; DA; DLB 6; MTCW;
SATA 8

Knox, Calvin M.
See Silverberg, Robert

Knye, Cassandra
See Disch, Thomas M(ichael)

Koch, C(hristopher) J(ohn) 1932- ... **CLC 42**
See also CA 127

Koch, Christopher
See Koch, C(hristopher) J(ohn)

Koch, Kenneth 1925- .... **CLC 5, 8, 44**
See also CA 1-4R; CANR 6, 36; DLB 5;
SATA 65

Kochanowski, Jan 1530-1584....... **LC 10**

Kock, Charles Paul de
1794-1871 .... **NCLC 16**

Koda Shigeyuki 1867-1947
See Rohan, Koda
See also CA 121

Koestler, Arthur
1905-1983 ...... **CLC 1, 3, 6, 8, 15, 33**
See also CA 1-4R; 109; CANR 1, 33;
CDBLB 1945-1960; DLBY 83; MTCW

Kohout, Pavel 1928-............. **CLC 13**
See also CA 45-48; CANR 3

Koizumi, Yakumo
See Hearn, (Patricio) Lafcadio (Tessima
Carlos)

Kolmar, Gertrud 1894-1943...... **TCLC 40**

Konrad, George
See Konrad, Gyoergy

Konrad, Gyoergy 1933- ...... **CLC 4, 10, 73**
See also CA 85-88

Konwicki, Tadeusz 1926-..... **CLC 8, 28, 54**
See also CA 101; CAAS 9; CANR 39;
MTCW

Kopit, Arthur (Lee) 1937- .... **CLC 1, 18, 33**
See also AITN 1; CA 81-84; CABS 3;
DLB 7; MTCW

Kops, Bernard 1926-............. **CLC 4**
See also CA 5-8R; DLB 13

Kornbluth, C(yril) M. 1923-1958.... **TCLC 8**
See also CA 105; DLB 8

Korolenko, V. G.
See Korolenko, Vladimir Galaktionovich

Korolenko, Vladimir
See Korolenko, Vladimir Galaktionovich

Korolenko, Vladimir G.
See Korolenko, Vladimir Galaktionovich

Korolenko, Vladimir Galaktionovich
1853-1921 .... **TCLC 22**
See also CA 121

Kosinski, Jerzy (Nikodem)
1933-1991 ... **CLC 1, 2, 3, 6, 10, 15, 53,
70**
See also CA 17-20R; 134; CANR 9; DLB 2;
DLBY 82; MTCW

Kostelanetz, Richard (Cory) 1940- .. **CLC 28**
See also CA 13-16R; CAAS 8; CANR 38

Kostrowitzki, Wilhelm Apollinaris de
1880-1918
See Apollinaire, Guillaume
See also CA 104

Kotlowitz, Robert 1924-........... **CLC 4**
See also CA 33-36R; CANR 36

Kotzebue, August (Friedrich Ferdinand) von
1761-1819 .... **NCLC 25**
See also DLB 94

Kotzwinkle, William 1938- ... **CLC 5, 14, 35**
See also CA 45-48; CANR 3; CLR 6;
MAICYA; SATA 24, 70

Kozol, Jonathan 1936-............ **CLC 17**
See also CA 61-64; CANR 16

Kozoll, Michael 1940(?)- .... **CLC 35**

Kramer, Kathryn 19(?)- .... **CLC 34**

Kramer, Larry 1935- .... **CLC 42**
See also CA 124; 126

Krasicki, Ignacy 1735-1801....... **NCLC 8**

Krasinski, Zygmunt 1812-1859 .... **NCLC 4**

Kraus, Karl 1874-1936........... **TCLC 5**
See also CA 104; DLB 118

Kreve (Mickevicius), Vincas
1882-1954 .... **TCLC 27**

Kristeva, Julia 1941- .... **CLC 77**

Kristofferson, Kris 1936-........... **CLC 26**
See also CA 104

Krizanc, John 1956-............. **CLC 57**

Krleza, Miroslav 1893-1981........ **CLC 8**
See also CA 97-100; 105

Kroetsch, Robert 1927- ...... **CLC 5, 23, 57**
See also CA 17-20R; CANR 8, 38; DLB 53;
MTCW

Kroetz, Franz
See Kroetz, Franz Xaver

Kroetz, Franz Xaver 1946- .... **CLC 41**
See also CA 130

Kroker, Arthur 1945-............ **CLC 77**

Kropotkin, Peter (Aleksieevich)
1842-1921 .... **TCLC 36**
See also CA 119

Krotkov, Yuri 1917-............. **CLC 19**
See also CA 102

Krumb
See Crumb, R(obert)

Krumgold, Joseph (Quincy)
1908-1980 .... **CLC 12**
See also CA 9-12R; 101; CANR 7;
MAICYA; SATA 1, 23, 48

Krumwitz
See Crumb, R(obert)

Krutch, Joseph Wood 1893-1970.... **CLC 24**
See also CA 1-4R; 25-28R; CANR 4;
DLB 63

Krutzch, Gus
See Eliot, T(homas) S(tearns)

Krylov, Ivan Andreevich
1768(?)-1844 .... **NCLC 1**

Kubin, Alfred 1877-1959 .... **TCLC 23**
See also CA 112; DLB 81

Kubrick, Stanley 1928-............ **CLC 16**
See also CA 81-84; CANR 33; DLB 26

Kumin, Maxine (Winokur)
1925- .... **CLC 5, 13, 28**
See also AITN 2; CA 1-4R; CAAS 8;
CANR 1, 21; DLB 5; MTCW; SATA 12

Kundera, Milan
1929- .... **CLC 4, 9, 19, 32, 68**
See also AAYA 2; CA 85-88; CANR 19;
MTCW

Kunitz, Stanley (Jasspon)
1905- .... **CLC 6, 11, 14**
See also CA 41-44R; CANR 26; DLB 48;
MTCW

Kunze, Reiner 1933-............. **CLC 10**
See also CA 93-96; DLB 75

Kuprin, Aleksandr Ivanovich
1870-1938 .... **TCLC 5**
See also CA 104

Kureishi, Hanif 1954(?)-........... **CLC 64**
See also CA 139

Kurosawa, Akira 1910-........... **CLC 16**
See also CA 101

Kuttner, Henry 1915-1958........ **TCLC 10**
See also CA 107; DLB 8

Kuzma, Greg 1944-.............. **CLC 7**
See also CA 33-36R

Kuzmin, Mikhail 1872(?)-1936 .... **TCLC 40**

Kyd, Thomas 1558-1594....... **LC 22; DC 3**
See also DLB 62

Kyprianos, Iossif
See Samarakis, Antonis

La Bruyere, Jean de 1645-1696...... **LC 17**

Lacan, Jacques (Marie Emile)
1901-1981 .... **CLC 75**
See also CA 121; 104

**Laclos, Pierre Ambroise Francois Choderlos
de** 1741-1803 .... **NCLC 4**

Lacolere, Francois
See Aragon, Louis

La Colere, Francois
See Aragon, Louis

La Deshabilleuse
See Simenon, Georges (Jacques Christian)

Lady Gregory
See Gregory, Isabella Augusta (Persse)

Lady of Quality, A
See Bagnold, Enid

**La Fayette, Marie (Madelaine Pioche de la
Vergne Comtes** 1634-1693....... **LC 2**

Lafayette, Rene
See Hubbard, L(afayette) Ron(ald)

Laforgue, Jules 1860-1887........ **NCLC 5**

Lagerkvist, Paer (Fabian)
1891-1974 .... **CLC 7, 10, 13, 54**
See also Lagerkvist, Par
See also CA 85-88; 49-52; MTCW

Lagerkvist, Par
See Lagerkvist, Paer (Fabian)
See also SSC 12

Lagerloef, Selma (Ottiliana Lovisa)
1858-1940 .... **TCLC 4, 36**
See also Lagerlof, Selma (Ottiliana Lovisa)
See also CA 108; CLR 7; SATA 15

Lagerlof, Selma (Ottiliana Lovisa)
See Lagerloef, Selma (Ottiliana Lovisa)
See also CLR 7; SATA 15

La Guma, (Justin) Alex(ander)
1925-1985 .... CLC 19
See also BW; CA 49-52; 118; CANR 25;
DLB 117; MTCW

Laidlaw, A. K.
See Grieve, C(hristopher) M(urray)

Lainez, Manuel Mujica
See Mujica Lainez, Manuel
See also HW

Lamartine, Alphonse (Marie Louis Prat) de
1790-1869 .... NCLC 11

Lamb, Charles 1775-1834........ NCLC 10
See also CDBLB 1789-1832; DA; DLB 93,
107; SATA 17; WLC

Lamb, Lady Caroline 1785-1828.. NCLC 38
See also DLB 116

Lamming, George (William)
1927- .... CLC 2, 4, 66
See also BLC 2; BW; CA 85-88; CANR 26;
DLB 125; MTCW

L'Amour, Louis (Dearborn)
1908-1988 .... CLC 25, 55
See also AITN 2; BEST 89:2; CA 1-4R;
125; CANR 3, 25, 40; DLBY 80; MTCW

Lampedusa, Giuseppe (Tomasi) di ... TCLC 13
See also Tomasi di Lampedusa, Giuseppe

Lampman, Archibald 1861-1899 .. NCLC 25
See also DLB 92

Lancaster, Bruce 1896-1963....... CLC 36
See also CA 9-10; CAP 1; SATA 9

Landau, Mark Alexandrovich
See Aldanov, Mark (Alexandrovich)

Landau-Aldanov, Mark Alexandrovich
See Aldanov, Mark (Alexandrovich)

Landis, John 1950-.............. CLC 26
See also CA 112; 122

Landolfi, Tommaso 1908-1979... CLC 11, 49
See also CA 127; 117

Landon, Letitia Elizabeth
1802-1838 .... NCLC 15
See also DLB 96

Landor, Walter Savage
1775-1864 .... NCLC 14
See also DLB 93, 107

Landwirth, Heinz 1927-
See Lind, Jakov
See also CA 9-12R; CANR 7

Lane, Patrick 1939- .... CLC 25
See also CA 97-100; DLB 53

Lang, Andrew 1844-1912........ TCLC 16
See also CA 114; 137; DLB 98; MAICYA;
SATA 16

Lang, Fritz 1890-1976 .... CLC 20
See also CA 77-80; 69-72; CANR 30

Lange, John
See Crichton, (John) Michael

Langer, Elinor 1939- .... CLC 34
See also CA 121

Langland, William 1330(?)-1400(?) ... LC 19
See also DA

Langstaff, Launcelot
See Irving, Washington

Lanier, Sidney 1842-1881 .... NCLC 6
See also DLB 64; MAICYA; SATA 18

Lanyer, Aemilia 1569-1645 .... LC 10

Lao Tzu .... CMLC 7

Lapine, James (Elliot) 1949- ...... CLC 39
See also CA 123; 130

Larbaud, Valery (Nicolas)
1881-1957 .... TCLC 9
See also CA 106

Lardner, Ring
See Lardner, Ring(gold) W(ilmer)

Lardner, Ring W., Jr.
See Lardner, Ring(gold) W(ilmer)

Lardner, Ring(gold) W(ilmer)
1885-1933 .... TCLC 2, 14
See also CA 104; 131; CDALB 1917-1929;
DLB 11, 25, 86; MTCW

Laredo, Betty
See Codrescu, Andrei

Larkin, Maia
See Wojciechowska, Maia (Teresa)

Larkin, Philip (Arthur)
1922-1985 ... CLC 3, 5, 8, 9, 13, 18, 33,
39, 64
See also CA 5-8R; 117; CANR 24;
CDBLB 1960 to Present; DLB 27;
MTCW

Larra (y Sanchez de Castro), Mariano Jose de
1809-1837 .... NCLC 17

Larsen, Eric 1941- .... CLC 55
See also CA 132

Larsen, Nella 1891-1964 .... CLC 37
See also BLC 2; BW; CA 125; DLB 51

Larson, Charles R(aymond) 1938-... CLC 31
See also CA 53-56; CANR 4

Latham, Jean Lee 1902-......... CLC 12
See also AITN 1; CA 5-8R; CANR 7;
MAICYA; SATA 2, 68

Latham, Mavis
See Clark, Mavis Thorpe

Lathen, Emma.................... CLC 2
See also Hennissart, Martha; Latsis, Mary
J(ane)

Lathrop, Francis
See Leiber, Fritz (Reuter, Jr.)

Latsis, Mary J(ane)
See Lathen, Emma
See also CA 85-88

Lattimore, Richmond (Alexander)
1906-1984 .... CLC 3
See also CA 1-4R; 112; CANR 1

Laughlin, James 1914-........... CLC 49
See also CA 21-24R; CANR 9; DLB 48

Laurence, (Jean) Margaret (Wemyss)
1926-1987 .. CLC 3, 6, 13, 50, 62; SSC 7
See also CA 5-8R; 121; CANR 33; DLB 53;
MTCW; SATA 50

Laurent, Antoine 1952- .... CLC 50

Lauscher, Hermann
See Hesse, Hermann

Lautreamont, Comte de
1846-1870 .... NCLC 12

Laverty, Donald
See Blish, James (Benjamin)

Lavin, Mary 1912-...... CLC 4, 18; SSC 4
See also CA 9-12R; CANR 33; DLB 15;
MTCW

Lavond, Paul Dennis
See Kornbluth, C(yril) M.; Pohl, Frederik

Lawler, Raymond Evenor 1922- .... CLC 58
See also CA 103

Lawrence, D(avid) H(erbert Richards)
1885-1930 ...... TCLC 2, 9, 16, 33, 48;
SSC 4
See also CA 104; 121; CDBLB 1914-1945;
DA; DLB 10, 19, 36, 98; MTCW; WLC

Lawrence, T(homas) E(dward)
1888-1935 .... TCLC 18
See also Dale, Colin
See also CA 115

Lawrence Of Arabia
See Lawrence, T(homas) E(dward)

Lawson, Henry (Archibald Hertzberg)
1867-1922 .... TCLC 27
See also CA 120

Lawton, Dennis
See Faust, Frederick (Schiller)

Laxness, Halldor.................. CLC 25
See also Gudjonsson, Halldor Kiljan

Layamon fl. c. 1200-............ CMLC 10

Laye, Camara 1928-1980........ CLC 4, 38
See also BLC 2; BW; CA 85-88; 97-100;
CANR 25; MTCW

Layton, Irving (Peter) 1912-..... CLC 2, 15
See also CA 1-4R; CANR 2, 33; DLB 88;
MTCW

Lazarus, Emma 1849-1887........ NCLC 8

Lazarus, Felix
See Cable, George Washington

Lazarus, Henry
See Slavitt, David R(ytman)

Lea, Joan
See Neufeld, John (Arthur)

Leacock, Stephen (Butler)
1869-1944 .... TCLC 2
See also CA 104; DLB 92

Lear, Edward 1812-1888 .... NCLC 3
See also CLR 1; DLB 32; MAICYA;
SATA 18

Lear, Norman (Milton) 1922- ...... CLC 12
See also CA 73-76

Leavis, F(rank) R(aymond)
1895-1978 .... CLC 24
See also CA 21-24R; 77-80; MTCW

Leavitt, David 1961-.............. CLC 34
See also CA 116; 122; DLB 130

Leblanc, Maurice (Marie Emile)
1864-1941 .... TCLC 49
See also CA 110

Lebowitz, Fran(ces Ann)
1951(?)- .... CLC 11, 36
See also CA 81-84; CANR 14; MTCW

le Carre, John .... CLC 3, 5, 9, 15, 28
See also Cornwell, David (John Moore)
See also BEST 89:4; CDBLB 1960 to
Present; DLB 87

Le Clezio, J(ean) M(arie) G(ustave)
1940- .... **CLC 31**
See also CA 116; 128; DLB 83

Leconte de Lisle, Charles-Marie-Rene
1818-1894 .... **NCLC 29**

Le Coq, Monsieur
See Simenon, Georges (Jacques Christian)

Leduc, Violette 1907-1972........ **CLC 22**
See also CA 13-14; 33-36R; CAP 1

Ledwidge, Francis 1887(?)-1917 ... **TCLC 23**
See also CA 123; DLB 20

Lee, Andrea 1953- .... **CLC 36**
See also BLC 2; BW; CA 125

Lee, Andrew
See Auchincloss, Louis (Stanton)

Lee, Don L........................ **CLC 2**
See also Madhubuti, Haki R.

Lee, George W(ashington)
1894-1976 .... **CLC 52**
See also BLC 2; BW; CA 125; DLB 51

Lee, (Nelle) Harper 1926- ...... **CLC 12, 60**
See also CA 13-16R; CDALB 1941-1968;
DA; DLB 6; MTCW; SATA 11; WLC

Lee, Julian
See Latham, Jean Lee

Lee, Lawrence 1903- .... **CLC 34**
See also CA 25-28R

Lee, Manfred B(ennington)
1905-1971 .... **CLC 11**
See also Queen, Ellery
See also CA 1-4R; 29-32R; CANR 2

Lee, Stan 1922-................... **CLC 17**
See also AAYA 5; CA 108; 111

Lee, Tanith 1947-................. **CLC 46**
See also CA 37-40R; SATA 8

Lee, Vernon...................... **TCLC 5**
See also Paget, Violet
See also DLB 57

Lee, William
See Burroughs, William S(eward)

Lee, Willy
See Burroughs, William S(eward)

Lee-Hamilton, Eugene (Jacob)
1845-1907 .... **TCLC 22**
See also CA 117

Leet, Judith 1935- .... **CLC 11**

Le Fanu, Joseph Sheridan
1814-1873 .... **NCLC 9**
See also DLB 21, 70

Leffland, Ella 1931- .... **CLC 19**
See also CA 29-32R; CANR 35; DLBY 84;
SATA 65

Leger, (Marie-Rene) Alexis Saint-Leger
1887-1975 .... **CLC 11**
See also Perse, St.-John
See also CA 13-16R; 61-64; MTCW

Leger, Saintleger
See Leger, (Marie-Rene) Alexis Saint-Leger

Le Guin, Ursula K(roeber)
1929- .... **CLC 8, 13, 22, 45, 71; SSC 12**
See also AAYA 9; AITN 1; CA 21-24R;
CANR 9, 32; CDALB 1968-1988; CLR 3,
28; DLB 8, 52; MAICYA; MTCW;
SATA 4, 52

Lehmann, Rosamond (Nina)
1901-1990 .... **CLC 5**
See also CA 77-80; 131; CANR 8; DLB 15

Leiber, Fritz (Reuter, Jr.)
1910-1992 .... **CLC 25**
See also CA 45-48; 139; CANR 2, 40;
DLB 8; MTCW; SATA 45;
SATA-Obit 73

Leimbach, Martha 1963-
See Leimbach, Marti
See also CA 130

Leimbach, Marti .... **CLC 65**
See also Leimbach, Martha

Leino, Eino .... **TCLC 24**
See also Loennbohm, Armas Eino Leopold

Leiris, Michel (Julien) 1901-1990... **CLC 61**
See also CA 119; 128; 132

Leithauser, Brad 1953-........... **CLC 27**
See also CA 107; CANR 27; DLB 120

Lelchuk, Alan 1938-.............. **CLC 5**
See also CA 45-48; CANR 1

Lem, Stanislaw 1921-........ **CLC 8, 15, 40**
See also CA 105; CAAS 1; CANR 32;
MTCW

Lemann, Nancy 1956-............. **CLC 39**
See also CA 118; 136

Lemonnier, (Antoine Louis) Camille
1844-1913 .... **TCLC 22**
See also CA 121

Lenau, Nikolaus 1802-1850 ...... **NCLC 16**

L'Engle, Madeleine (Camp Franklin)
1918- .... **CLC 12**
See also AAYA 1; AITN 2; CA 1-4R;
CANR 3, 21, 39; CLR 1, 14; DLB 52;
MAICYA; MTCW; SAAS 15; SATA 1,
27

Lengyel, Jozsef 1896-1975......... **CLC 7**
See also CA 85-88; 57-60

Lennon, John (Ono)
1940-1980 .... **CLC 12, 35**
See also CA 102

Lennox, Charlotte Ramsay
1729(?)-1804 .... **NCLC 23**
See also DLB 39

Lentricchia, Frank (Jr.) 1940-...... **CLC 34**
See also CA 25-28R; CANR 19

Lenz, Siegfried 1926-............. **CLC 27**
See also CA 89-92; DLB 75

Leonard, Elmore (John, Jr.)
1925- .... **CLC 28, 34, 71**
See also AITN 1; BEST 89:1, 90:4;
CA 81-84; CANR 12, 28; MTCW

Leonard, Hugh
See Byrne, John Keyes
See also DLB 13

Leopardi, (Conte) Giacomo (Talegardo
Francesco di Sales Save
1798-1837 .... **NCLC 22**

Le Reveler
See Artaud, Antonin

Lerman, Eleanor 1952-............ **CLC 9**
See also CA 85-88

Lerman, Rhoda 1936-............ **CLC 56**
See also CA 49-52

Lermontov, Mikhail Yuryevich
1814-1841 .... **NCLC 5**

Leroux, Gaston 1868-1927........ **TCLC 25**
See also CA 108; 136; SATA 65

Lesage, Alain-Rene 1668-1747....... **LC 2**

Leskov, Nikolai (Semyonovich)
1831-1895 .... **NCLC 25**

Lessing, Doris (May)
1919- .... **CLC 1, 2, 3, 6, 10, 15, 22, 40;
SSC 6**
See also CA 9-12R; CAAS 14; CANR 33;
CDBLB 1960 to Present; DA; DLB 15;
DLBY 85; MTCW

Lessing, Gotthold Ephraim
1729-1781 .... **LC 8**
See also DLB 97

Lester, Richard 1932-............. **CLC 20**

Lever, Charles (James)
1806-1872 .... **NCLC 23**
See also DLB 21

Leverson, Ada 1865(?)-1936(?) .... **TCLC 18**
See also Elaine
See also CA 117

Levertov, Denise
1923-.... **CLC 1, 2, 3, 5, 8, 15, 28, 66**
See also CA 1-4R; CANR 3, 29; DLB 5;
MTCW

Levi, Jonathan.................... **CLC 76**

Levi, Peter (Chad Tigar) 1931-..... **CLC 41**
See also CA 5-8R; CANR 34; DLB 40

Levi, Primo
1919-1987 .... **CLC 37, 50; SSC 12**
See also CA 13-16R; 122; CANR 12, 33;
MTCW

Levin, Ira 1929- .... **CLC 3, 6**
See also CA 21-24R; CANR 17; MTCW;
SATA 66

Levin, Meyer 1905-1981 .... **CLC 7**
See also AITN 1; CA 9-12R; 104;
CANR 15; DLB 9, 28; DLBY 81;
SATA 21, 27

Levine, Norman 1924-............ **CLC 54**
See also CA 73-76; CANR 14; DLB 88

Levine, Philip 1928-... **CLC 2, 4, 5, 9, 14, 33**
See also CA 9-12R; CANR 9, 37; DLB 5

Levinson, Deirdre 1931-.......... **CLC 49**
See also CA 73-76

Levi-Strauss, Claude 1908- .... **CLC 38**
See also CA 1-4R; CANR 6, 32; MTCW

Levitin, Sonia (Wolff) 1934- .... **CLC 17**
See also CA 29-32R; CANR 14, 32;
MAICYA; SAAS 2; SATA 4, 68

Levon, O. U.
See Kesey, Ken (Elton)

Lewes, George Henry
1817-1878 .... **NCLC 25**
See also DLB 55

Lewis, Alun 1915-1944........... **TCLC 3**
See also CA 104; DLB 20

Lewis, C. Day
See Day Lewis, C(ecil)

MacNeice, (Frederick) Louis
1907-1963 . . . . CLC 1, 4, 10, 53
See also CA 85-88; DLB 10, 20; MTCW

MacNeill, Dand
See Fraser, George MacDonald

Macpherson, (Jean) Jay 1931-. . . . . CLC 14
See also CA 5-8R; DLB 53

MacShane, Frank 1927-. . . . . CLC 39
See also CA 9-12R; CANR 3, 33; DLB 111

Macumber, Mari
See Sandoz, Mari(e Susette)

Madach, Imre 1823-1864. . . . . NCLC 19

Madden, (Jerry) David 1933- . . . . CLC 5, 15
See also CA 1-4R; CAAS 3; CANR 4;
DLB 6; MTCW

Maddern, Al(an)
See Ellison, Harlan

Madhubuti, Haki R.
1942- . . . . CLC 6, 73; PC 5
See also Lee, Don L.
See also BLC 2; BW; CA 73-76; CANR 24;
DLB 5, 41; DLBD 8

Madow, Pauline (Reichberg) . . . . CLC 1
See also CA 9-12R

Maepenn, Hugh
See Kuttner, Henry

Maepenn, K. H.
See Kuttner, Henry

Maeterlinck, Maurice 1862-1949 . . . TCLC 3
See also CA 104; 136; SATA 66

Maginn, William 1794-1842. . . . . . NCLC 8
See also DLB 110

Mahapatra, Jayanta 1928-. . . . . CLC 33
See also CA 73-76; CAAS 9; CANR 15, 33

Mahfouz, Naguib (Abdel Aziz Al-Sabilgi)
1911(?)-
See Mahfuz, Najib
See also BEST 89:2; CA 128; MTCW

Mahfuz, Najib. . . . . CLC 52, 55
See also Mahfouz, Naguib (Abdel Aziz
Al-Sabilgi)
See also DLBY 88

Mahon, Derek 1941-. . . . . CLC 27
See also CA 113; 128; DLB 40

Mailer, Norman
1923- . . . . . . CLC 1, 2, 3, 4, 5, 8, 11, 14,
28, 39, 74
See also AITN 2; CA 9-12R; CABS 1;
CANR 28; CDALB 1968-1988; DA;
DLB 2, 16, 28; DLBD 3; DLBY 80, 83;
MTCW

Maillet, Antonine 1929-. . . . . CLC 54
See also CA 115; 120; DLB 60

Mais, Roger 1905-1955 . . . . TCLC 8
See also BW; CA 105; 124; DLB 125;
MTCW

Maitland, Sara (Louise) 1950-. . . . . . CLC 49
See also CA 69-72; CANR 13

Major, Clarence 1936-. . . . . . . CLC 3, 19, 48
See also BLC 2; BW; CA 21-24R; CAAS 6;
CANR 13, 25; DLB 33

Major, Kevin (Gerald) 1949-. . . . . . . CLC 26
See also CA 97-100; CANR 21, 38;
CLR 11; DLB 60; MAICYA; SATA 32

Maki, James
See Ozu, Yasujiro

Malabaila, Damiano
See Levi, Primo

Malamud, Bernard
1914-1986 . . . . . CLC 1, 2, 3, 5, 8, 9, 11,
18, 27, 44
See also CA 5-8R; 118; CABS 1; CANR 28;
CDALB 1941-1968; DA; DLB 2, 28;
DLBY 80, 86; MTCW; WLC

Malcolm, Dan
See Silverberg, Robert

Malherbe, Francois de 1555-1628. . . . . LC 5

Mallarme, Stephane
1842-1898 . . . . NCLC 4; PC 4

Mallet-Joris, Francoise 1930-. . . . . . CLC 11
See also CA 65-68; CANR 17; DLB 83

Malley, Ern
See McAuley, James Phillip

Mallowan, Agatha Christie
See Christie, Agatha (Mary Clarissa)

Maloff, Saul 1922-. . . . . CLC 5
See also CA 33-36R

Malone, Louis
See MacNeice, (Frederick) Louis

Malone, Michael (Christopher)
1942-. . . . . CLC 43
See also CA 77-80; CANR 14, 32

Malory, (Sir) Thomas
1410(?)-1471(?) . . . . LC 11
See also CDBLB Before 1660; DA;
SATA 33, 59

Malouf, (George Joseph) David
1934- . . . . CLC 28
See also CA 124

Malraux, (Georges-)Andre
1901-1976 . . . . . . CLC 1, 4, 9, 13, 15, 57
See also CA 21-22; 69-72; CANR 34;
CAP 2; DLB 72; MTCW

Malzberg, Barry N(athaniel) 1939-. . . CLC 7
See also CA 61-64; CAAS 4; CANR 16;
DLB 8

Mamet, David (Alan)
1947-. . . . . CLC 9, 15, 34, 46
See also AAYA 3; CA 81-84; CABS 3;
CANR 15, 41; DLB 7; MTCW

Mamoulian, Rouben (Zachary)
1897-1987 . . . . CLC 16
See also CA 25-28R; 124

Mandelstam, Osip (Emilievich)
1891(?)-1938(?) . . . . TCLC 2, 6
See also CA 104

Mander, (Mary) Jane 1877-1949. . . TCLC 31

Mandiargues, Andre Pieyre de. . . . . . CLC 41
See also Pieyre de Mandiargues, Andre
See also DLB 83

Mandrake, Ethel Belle
See Thurman, Wallace (Henry)

Mangan, James Clarence
1803-1849 . . . . NCLC 27

Maniere, J.-E.
See Giraudoux, (Hippolyte) Jean

Manley, (Mary) Delariviere
1672(?)-1724 . . . . LC 1
See also DLB 39, 80

Mann, Abel
See Creasey, John

Mann, (Luiz) Heinrich 1871-1950. . . TCLC 9
See also CA 106; DLB 66

Mann, (Paul) Thomas
1875-1955 . . . TCLC 2, 8, 14, 21, 35, 44;
SSC 5
See also CA 104; 128; DA; DLB 66;
MTCW; WLC

Manning, David
See Faust, Frederick (Schiller)

Manning, Frederic 1887(?)-1935 . . . TCLC 25
See also CA 124

Manning, Olivia 1915-1980. . . . . . CLC 5, 19
See also CA 5-8R; 101; CANR 29; MTCW

Mano, D. Keith 1942- . . . . CLC 2, 10
See also CA 25-28R; CAAS 6; CANR 26;
DLB 6

Mansfield, Katherine. . . TCLC 2, 8, 39; SSC 9
See also Beauchamp, Kathleen Mansfield
See also WLC

Manso, Peter 1940-. . . . . CLC 39
See also CA 29-32R

Mantecon, Juan Jimenez
See Jimenez (Mantecon), Juan Ramon

Manton, Peter
See Creasey, John

Man Without a Spleen, A
See Chekhov, Anton (Pavlovich)

Manzoni, Alessandro 1785-1873 . . NCLC 29

Mapu, Abraham (ben Jekutiel)
1808-1867 . . . . NCLC 18

Mara, Sally
See Queneau, Raymond

Marat, Jean Paul 1743-1793. . . . . LC 10

Marcel, Gabriel Honore
1889-1973 . . . . CLC 15
See also CA 102; 45-48; MTCW

Marchbanks, Samuel
See Davies, (William) Robertson

Marchi, Giacomo
See Bassani, Giorgio

Margulies, Donald. . . . . CLC 76

Marie de France c. 12th cent. -. . . . CMLC 8

Marie de l'Incarnation 1599-1672. . . . LC 10

Mariner, Scott
See Pohl, Frederik

Marinetti, Filippo Tommaso
1876-1944 . . . . TCLC 10
See also CA 107; DLB 114

Marivaux, Pierre Carlet de Chamblain de
1688-1763 . . . . LC 4

Markandaya, Kamala . . . . CLC 8, 38
See also Taylor, Kamala (Purnaiya)

Markfield, Wallace 1926-. . . . . CLC 8
See also CA 69-72; CAAS 3; DLB 2, 28

Markham, Edwin 1852-1940 . . . . . . TCLC 47
See also DLB 54

Markham, Robert
See Amis, Kingsley (William)

Marks, J
See Highwater, Jamake (Mamake)

Marks-Highwater, J
See Highwater, Jamake (Mamake)

Markson, David M(errill) 1927- .... **CLC 67**
See also CA 49-52; CANR 1

Marley, Bob. . . . . **CLC 17**
See also Marley, Robert Nesta

Marley, Robert Nesta 1945-1981
See Marley, Bob
See also CA 107; 103

Marlowe, Christopher
1564-1593 . . . . **LC 22; DC 1**
See also CDBLB Before 1660; DA; DLB 62;
WLC

Marmontel, Jean-Francois
1723-1799 . . . . **LC 2**

Marquand, John P(hillips)
1893-1960 . . . . **CLC 2, 10**
See also CA 85-88; DLB 9, 102

Marquez, Gabriel (Jose) Garcia. . . . . . **CLC 68**
See also Garcia Marquez, Gabriel (Jose)

Marquis, Don(ald Robert Perry)
1878-1937 . . . . **TCLC 7**
See also CA 104; DLB 11, 25

Marric, J. J.
See Creasey, John

Marrow, Bernard
See Moore, Brian

Marryat, Frederick 1792-1848 . . . . **NCLC 3**
See also DLB 21

Marsden, James
See Creasey, John

Marsh, (Edith) Ngaio
1899-1982 . . . . **CLC 7, 53**
See also CA 9-12R; CANR 6; DLB 77;
MTCW

Marshall, Garry 1934- . . . . **CLC 17**
See also AAYA 3; CA 111; SATA 60

Marshall, Paule 1929- . . **CLC 27, 72; SSC 3**
See also BLC 3; BW; CA 77-80; CANR 25;
DLB 33; MTCW

Marsten, Richard
See Hunter, Evan

Martha, Henry
See Harris, Mark

Martin, Ken
See Hubbard, L(afayette) Ron(ald)

Martin, Richard
See Creasey, John

Martin, Steve 1945- . . . . **CLC 30**
See also CA 97-100; CANR 30; MTCW

Martin, Webber
See Silverberg, Robert

Martin du Gard, Roger
1881-1958 . . . . **TCLC 24**
See also CA 118; DLB 65

Martineau, Harriet 1802-1876. . . . **NCLC 26**
See also DLB 21, 55; YABC 2

Martines, Julia
See O'Faolain, Julia

Martinez, Jacinto Benavente y
See Benavente (y Martinez), Jacinto

Martinez Ruiz, Jose 1873-1967
See Azorin; Ruiz, Jose Martinez
See also CA 93-96; HW

Martinez Sierra, Gregorio
1881-1947 . . . . **TCLC 6**
See also CA 115

Martinez Sierra, Maria (de la O'LeJarraga)
1874-1974 . . . . **TCLC 6**
See also CA 115

Martinsen, Martin
See Follett, Ken(neth Martin)

Martinson, Harry (Edmund)
1904-1978 . . . . **CLC 14**
See also CA 77-80; CANR 34

Marut, Ret
See Traven, B.

Marut, Robert
See Traven, B.

Marvell, Andrew 1621-1678. . . . . **LC 4**
See also CDBLB 1660-1789; DA; DLB 131;
WLC

Marx, Karl (Heinrich)
1818-1883 . . . . **NCLC 17**
See also DLB 129

Masaoka Shiki. . . . . **TCLC 18**
See also Masaoka Tsunenori

Masaoka Tsunenori 1867-1902
See Masaoka Shiki
See also CA 117

Masefield, John (Edward)
1878-1967 . . . . **CLC 11, 47**
See also CA 19-20; 25-28R; CANR 33;
CAP 2; CDBLB 1890-1914; DLB 10;
MTCW; SATA 19

Maso, Carole 19(?)- . . . . **CLC 44**

Mason, Bobbie Ann
1940- . . . . **CLC 28, 43; SSC 4**
See also AAYA 5; CA 53-56; CANR 11,
31; DLBY 87; MTCW

Mason, Ernst
See Pohl, Frederik

Mason, Lee W.
See Malzberg, Barry N(athaniel)

Mason, Nick 1945- . . . . **CLC 35**
See also Pink Floyd

Mason, Tally
See Derleth, August (William)

Mass, William
See Gibson, William

Masters, Edgar Lee
1868-1950 . . . . **TCLC 2, 25; PC 1**
See also CA 104; 133; CDALB 1865-1917;
DA; DLB 54; MTCW

Masters, Hilary 1928- . . . . **CLC 48**
See also CA 25-28R; CANR 13

Mastrosimone, William 19(?)- . . . . . . **CLC 36**

Mathe, Albert
See Camus, Albert

Matheson, Richard Burton 1926- . . . **CLC 37**
See also CA 97-100; DLB 8, 44

Mathews, Harry 1930- . . . . **CLC 6, 52**
See also CA 21-24R; CAAS 6; CANR 18,
40

Mathias, Roland (Glyn) 1915- . . . . . . **CLC 45**
See also CA 97-100; CANR 19, 41; DLB 27

Matsuo Basho 1644-1694. . . . . **PC 3**

Mattheson, Rodney
See Creasey, John

Matthews, Greg 1949- . . . . **CLC 45**
See also CA 135

Matthews, William 1942- . . . . **CLC 40**
See also CA 29-32R; CANR 12; DLB 5

Matthias, John (Edward) 1941- . . . . . . **CLC 9**
See also CA 33-36R

Matthiessen, Peter
1927- . . . . **CLC 5, 7, 11, 32, 64**
See also AAYA 6; BEST 90:4; CA 9-12R;
CANR 21; DLB 6; MTCW; SATA 27

Maturin, Charles Robert
1780(?)-1824 . . . . **NCLC 6**

Matute (Ausejo), Ana Maria
1925- . . . . **CLC 11**
See also CA 89-92; MTCW

Maugham, W. S.
See Maugham, W(illiam) Somerset

Maugham, W(illiam) Somerset
1874-1965 . . . . **CLC 1, 11, 15, 67; SSC 8**
See also CA 5-8R; 25-28R; CANR 40;
CDBLB 1914-1945; DA; DLB 10, 36, 77,
100; MTCW; SATA 54; WLC

Maugham, William Somerset
See Maugham, W(illiam) Somerset

Maupassant, (Henri Rene Albert) Guy de
1850-1893 . . . . **NCLC 1; SSC 1**
See also DA; DLB 123; WLC

Maurhut, Richard
See Traven, B.

Mauriac, Claude 1914- . . . . **CLC 9**
See also CA 89-92; DLB 83

Mauriac, Francois (Charles)
1885-1970 . . . . **CLC 4, 9, 56**
See also CA 25-28; CAP 2; DLB 65;
MTCW

Mavor, Osborne Henry 1888-1951
See Bridie, James
See also CA 104

Maxwell, William (Keepers, Jr.)
1908- . . . . **CLC 19**
See also CA 93-96; DLBY 80

May, Elaine 1932- . . . . **CLC 16**
See also CA 124; DLB 44

Mayakovski, Vladimir (Vladimirovich)
1893-1930 . . . . **TCLC 4, 18**
See also CA 104

Mayhew, Henry 1812-1887 . . . . . . **NCLC 31**
See also DLB 18, 55

Maynard, Joyce 1953- . . . . **CLC 23**
See also CA 111; 129

Mayne, William (James Carter)
1928- . . . . **CLC 12**
See also CA 9-12R; CANR 37; CLR 25;
MAICYA; SAAS 11; SATA 6, 68

Mayo, Jim
See L'Amour, Louis (Dearborn)

Maysles, Albert 1926- . . . . **CLC 16**
See also CA 29-32R

Maysles, David 1932- . . . . **CLC 16**

Montagu, Elizabeth 1917- .... **NCLC 7**
See also CA 9-12R

Montagu, Mary (Pierrepont) Wortley
 1689-1762 .... **LC 9**
See also DLB 95, 101

Montagu, W. H.
See Coleridge, Samuel Taylor

Montague, John (Patrick)
 1929- .... **CLC 13, 46**
See also CA 9-12R; CANR 9; DLB 40;
MTCW

Montaigne, Michel (Eyquem) de
 1533-1592 .... **LC 8**
See also DA; WLC

Montale, Eugenio 1896-1981 ... **CLC 7, 9, 18**
See also CA 17-20R; 104; CANR 30;
DLB 114; MTCW

Montesquieu, Charles-Louis de Secondat
 1689-1755 .... **LC 7**

Montgomery, (Robert) Bruce 1921-1978
See Crispin, Edmund
See also CA 104

Montgomery, Marion H., Jr. 1925- .. **CLC 7**
See also AITN 1; CA 1-4R; CANR 3;
DLB 6

Montgomery, Max
See Davenport, Guy (Mattison, Jr.)

Montherlant, Henry (Milon) de
 1896-1972 .... **CLC 8, 19**
See also CA 85-88; 37-40R; DLB 72;
MTCW

Monty Python .... **CLC 21**
See also Chapman, Graham; Cleese, John
(Marwood); Gilliam, Terry (Vance); Idle,
Eric; Jones, Terence Graham Parry; Palin,
Michael (Edward)
See also AAYA 7

Moodie, Susanna (Strickland)
 1803-1885 .... **NCLC 14**
See also DLB 99

Mooney, Edward 1951- .... **CLC 25**
See also CA 130

Mooney, Ted
See Mooney, Edward

Moorcock, Michael (John)
 1939- .... **CLC 5, 27, 58**
See also CA 45-48; CAAS 5; CANR 2, 17,
38; DLB 14; MTCW

Moore, Brian
 1921- .... **CLC 1, 3, 5, 7, 8, 19, 32**
See also CA 1-4R; CANR 1, 25; MTCW

Moore, Edward
See Muir, Edwin

Moore, George Augustus
 1852-1933 .... **TCLC 7**
See also CA 104; DLB 10, 18, 57

Moore, Lorrie .... **CLC 39, 45, 68**
See also Moore, Marie Lorena

Moore, Marianne (Craig)
 1887-1972 ... **CLC 1, 2, 4, 8, 10, 13, 19,
47; PC 4**
See also CA 1-4R; 33-36R; CANR 3;
CDALB 1929-1941; DA; DLB 45;
DLBD 7; MTCW; SATA 20

Moore, Marie Lorena 1957-
See Moore, Lorrie
See also CA 116; CANR 39

Moore, Thomas 1779-1852 .... **NCLC 6**
See also DLB 96

Morand, Paul 1888-1976 .... **CLC 41**
See also CA 69-72; DLB 65

Morante, Elsa 1918-1985 .... **CLC 8, 47**
See also CA 85-88; 117; CANR 35; MTCW

Moravia, Alberto .... **CLC 2, 7, 11, 27, 46**
See also Pincherle, Alberto

More, Hannah 1745-1833 .... **NCLC 27**
See also DLB 107, 109, 116

More, Henry 1614-1687 .... **LC 9**
See also DLB 126

More, Sir Thomas 1478-1535 .... **LC 10**

Moreas, Jean .... **TCLC 18**
See also Papadiamantopoulos, Johannes

Morgan, Berry 1919- .... **CLC 6**
See also CA 49-52; DLB 6

Morgan, Claire
See Highsmith, (Mary) Patricia

Morgan, Edwin (George) 1920- ..... **CLC 31**
See also CA 5-8R; CANR 3; DLB 27

Morgan, (George) Frederick
 1922- .... **CLC 23**
See also CA 17-20R; CANR 21

Morgan, Harriet
See Mencken, H(enry) L(ouis)

Morgan, Jane
See Cooper, James Fenimore

Morgan, Janet 1945- .... **CLC 39**
See also CA 65-68

Morgan, Lady 1776(?)-1859 ...... **NCLC 29**
See also DLB 116

Morgan, Robin 1941- .... **CLC 2**
See also CA 69-72; CANR 29; MTCW

Morgan, Scott
See Kuttner, Henry

Morgan, Seth 1949(?)-1990 .... **CLC 65**
See also CA 132

Morgenstern, Christian
 1871-1914 .... **TCLC 8**
See also CA 105

Morgenstern, S.
See Goldman, William (W.)

Moricz, Zsigmond 1879-1942 ..... **TCLC 33**

Morike, Eduard (Friedrich)
 1804-1875 .... **NCLC 10**

Mori Ogai .... **TCLC 14**
See also Mori Rintaro

Mori Rintaro 1862-1922
See Mori Ogai
See also CA 110

Moritz, Karl Philipp 1756-1793 ...... **LC 2**
See also DLB 94

Morland, Peter Henry
See Faust, Frederick (Schiller)

Morren, Theophil
See Hofmannsthal, Hugo von

Morris, Bill 1952- .... **CLC 76**

Morris, Julian
See West, Morris L(anglo)

Morris, Steveland Judkins 1950(?)-
See Wonder, Stevie
See also CA 111

Morris, William 1834-1896 .... **NCLC 4**
See also CDBLB 1832-1890; DLB 18, 35, 57

Morris, Wright 1910- ... **CLC 1, 3, 7, 18, 37**
See also CA 9-12R; CANR 21; DLB 2;
DLBY 81; MTCW

Morrison, Chloe Anthony Wofford
See Morrison, Toni

Morrison, James Douglas 1943-1971
See Morrison, Jim
See also CA 73-76; CANR 40

Morrison, Jim .... **CLC 17**
See also Morrison, James Douglas

Morrison, Toni 1931- ..... **CLC 4, 10, 22, 55**
See also AAYA 1; BLC 3; BW; CA 29-32R;
CANR 27; CDALB 1968-1988; DA;
DLB 6, 33; DLBY 81; MTCW; SATA 57

Morrison, Van 1945- .... **CLC 21**
See also CA 116

Mortimer, John (Clifford)
 1923- .... **CLC 28, 43**
See also CA 13-16R; CANR 21;
CDBLB 1960 to Present; DLB 13;
MTCW

Mortimer, Penelope (Ruth) 1918- .... **CLC 5**
See also CA 57-60

Morton, Anthony
See Creasey, John

Mosher, Howard Frank .... **CLC 62**
See also CA 139

Mosley, Nicholas 1923- .... **CLC 43, 70**
See also CA 69-72; CANR 41; DLB 14

Moss, Howard
 1922-1987 .... **CLC 7, 14, 45, 50**
See also CA 1-4R; 123; CANR 1; DLB 5

Mossgiel, Rab
See Burns, Robert

Motion, Andrew 1952- .... **CLC 47**
See also DLB 40

Motley, Willard (Francis)
 1912-1965 .... **CLC 18**
See also BW; CA 117; 106; DLB 76

Mott, Michael (Charles Alston)
 1930- .... **CLC 15, 34**
See also CA 5-8R; CAAS 7; CANR 7, 29

Mowat, Farley (McGill) 1921- ..... **CLC 26**
See also AAYA 1; CA 1-4R; CANR 4, 24;
CLR 20; DLB 68; MAICYA; MTCW;
SATA 3, 55

Moyers, Bill 1934- .... **CLC 74**
See also AITN 2; CA 61-64; CANR 31

Mphahlele, Es'kia
See Mphahlele, Ezekiel
See also DLB 125

Mphahlele, Ezekiel 1919- .... **CLC 25**
See also Mphahlele, Es'kia
See also BLC 3; BW; CA 81-84; CANR 26

Mqhayi, S(amuel) E(dward) K(rune Loliwe)
 1875-1945 .... **TCLC 25**
See also BLC 3

Mr. Martin
See Burroughs, William S(eward)

Mrozek, Slawomir 1930- .... **CLC 3, 13**
See also CA 13-16R; CAAS 10; CANR 29;
MTCW

Mrs. Belloc-Lowndes
See Lowndes, Marie Adelaide (Belloc)

Mtwa, Percy (?)-................ **CLC 47**

Mueller, Lisel 1924-.......... **CLC 13, 51**
See also CA 93-96; DLB 105

Muir, Edwin 1887-1959 .... **TCLC 2**
See also CA 104; DLB 20, 100

Muir, John 1838-1914 .... **TCLC 28**

Mujica Lainez, Manuel
1910-1984 .... **CLC 31**
See also Lainez, Manuel Mujica
See also CA 81-84; 112; CANR 32; HW

Mukherjee, Bharati 1940- .... **CLC 53**
See also BEST 89:2; CA 107; DLB 60;
MTCW

Muldoon, Paul 1951- .... **CLC 32, 72**
See also CA 113; 129; DLB 40

Mulisch, Harry 1927-........... **CLC 42**
See also CA 9-12R; CANR 6, 26

Mull, Martin 1943-............. **CLC 17**
See also CA 105

Mulock, Dinah Maria
See Craik, Dinah Maria (Mulock)

Munford, Robert 1737(?)-1783 .... **LC 5**
See also DLB 31

Mungo, Raymond 1946-.......... **CLC 72**
See also CA 49-52; CANR 2

Munro, Alice
1931- .... **CLC 6, 10, 19, 50; SSC 3**
See also AITN 2; CA 33-36R; CANR 33;
DLB 53; MTCW; SATA 29

Munro, H(ector) H(ugh) 1870-1916
See Saki
See also CA 104; 130; CDBLB 1890-1914;
DA; DLB 34; MTCW; WLC

Murasaki, Lady................. **CMLC 1**

Murdoch, (Jean) Iris
1919- ...... **CLC 1, 2, 3, 4, 6, 8, 11, 15,
22, 31, 51**
See also CA 13-16R; CANR 8;
CDBLB 1960 to Present; DLB 14;
MTCW

Murphy, Richard 1927- .... **CLC 41**
See also CA 29-32R; DLB 40

Murphy, Sylvia 1937-............. **CLC 34**
See also CA 121

Murphy, Thomas (Bernard) 1935-... **CLC 51**
See also CA 101

Murray, Albert L. 1916- .... **CLC 73**
See also BW; CA 49-52; CANR 26; DLB 38

Murray, Les(lie) A(llan) 1938- ..... **CLC 40**
See also CA 21-24R; CANR 11, 27

Murry, J. Middleton
See Murry, John Middleton

Murry, John Middleton
1889-1957 .... **TCLC 16**
See also CA 118

Musgrave, Susan 1951- .... **CLC 13, 54**
See also CA 69-72

Musil, Robert (Edler von)
1880-1942 .... **TCLC 12**
See also CA 109; DLB 81, 124

Musset, (Louis Charles) Alfred de
1810-1857 .... **NCLC 7**

My Brother's Brother
See Chekhov, Anton (Pavlovich)

Myers, Walter Dean 1937- .... **CLC 35**
See also AAYA 4; BLC 3; BW; CA 33-36R;
CANR 20; CLR 4, 16; DLB 33;
MAICYA; SAAS 2; SATA 27, 41, 70, 71

Myers, Walter M.
See Myers, Walter Dean

Myles, Symon
See Follett, Ken(neth Martin)

Nabokov, Vladimir (Vladimirovich)
1899-1977 .... **CLC 1, 2, 3, 6, 8, 11, 15,
23, 44, 46, 64; SSC 11**
See also CA 5-8R; 69-72; CANR 20;
CDALB 1941-1968; DA; DLB 2;
DLBD 3; DLBY 80, 91; MTCW; WLC

Nagy, Laszlo 1925-1978........... **CLC 7**
See also CA 129; 112

Naipaul, Shiva(dhar Srinivasa)
1945-1985 .... **CLC 32, 39**
See also CA 110; 112; 116; CANR 33;
DLBY 85; MTCW

Naipaul, V(idiadhar) S(urajprasad)
1932-........ **CLC 4, 7, 9, 13, 18, 37**
See also CA 1-4R; CANR 1, 33;
CDBLB 1960 to Present; DLB 125;
DLBY 85; MTCW

Nakos, Lilika 1899(?)-............ **CLC 29**

Narayan, R(asipuram) K(rishnaswami)
1906-................ **CLC 7, 28, 47**
See also CA 81-84; CANR 33; MTCW;
SATA 62

Nash, (Fredric) Ogden 1902-1971 .. **CLC 23**
See also CA 13-14; 29-32R; CANR 34;
CAP 1; DLB 11; MAICYA; MTCW;
SATA 2, 46

Nathan, Daniel
See Dannay, Frederic

Nathan, George Jean 1882-1958 ... **TCLC 18**
See also Hatteras, Owen
See also CA 114

Natsume, Kinnosuke 1867-1916
See Natsume, Soseki
See also CA 104

Natsume, Soseki .... **TCLC 2, 10**
See also Natsume, Kinnosuke

Natti, (Mary) Lee 1919-
See Kingman, Lee
See also CA 5-8R; CANR 2

Naylor, Gloria 1950- .... **CLC 28, 52**
See also AAYA 6; BLC 3; BW; CA 107;
CANR 27; DA; MTCW

Neihardt, John Gneisenau
1881-1973 .... **CLC 32**
See also CA 13-14; CAP 1; DLB 9, 54

Nekrasov, Nikolai Alekseevich
1821-1878 .... **NCLC 11**

Nelligan, Emile 1879-1941....... **TCLC 14**
See also CA 114; DLB 92

Nelson, Willie 1933-............. **CLC 17**
See also CA 107

Nemerov, Howard (Stanley)
1920-1991 .... **CLC 2, 6, 9, 36**
See also CA 1-4R; 134; CABS 2; CANR 1,
27; DLB 6; DLBY 83; MTCW

Neruda, Pablo
1904-1973 .... **CLC 1, 2, 5, 7, 9, 28, 62;
PC 4**
See also CA 19-20; 45-48; CAP 2; DA; HW;
MTCW; WLC

Nerval, Gerard de 1808-1855...... **NCLC 1**

Nervo, (Jose) Amado (Ruiz de)
1870-1919 .... **TCLC 11**
See also CA 109; 131; HW

Nessi, Pio Baroja y
See Baroja (y Nessi), Pio

Neufeld, John (Arthur) 1938- ...... **CLC 17**
See also CA 25-28R; CANR 11, 37;
MAICYA; SAAS 3; SATA 6

Neville, Emily Cheney 1919-....... **CLC 12**
See also CA 5-8R; CANR 3, 37; MAICYA;
SAAS 2; SATA 1

Newbound, Bernard Slade 1930-
See Slade, Bernard
See also CA 81-84

Newby, P(ercy) H(oward)
1918- .... **CLC 2, 13**
See also CA 5-8R; CANR 32; DLB 15;
MTCW

Newlove, Donald 1928- .... **CLC 6**
See also CA 29-32R; CANR 25

Newlove, John (Herbert) 1938-..... **CLC 14**
See also CA 21-24R; CANR 9, 25

Newman, Charles 1938-.......... **CLC 2, 8**
See also CA 21-24R

Newman, Edwin (Harold) 1919- .... **CLC 14**
See also AITN 1; CA 69-72; CANR 5

Newman, John Henry
1801-1890 .... **NCLC 38**
See also DLB 18, 32, 55

Newton, Suzanne 1936-.......... **CLC 35**
See also CA 41-44R; CANR 14; SATA 5

Nexo, Martin Andersen
1869-1954 .... **TCLC 43**

Nezval, Vitezslav 1900-1958 ...... **TCLC 44**
See also CA 123

Ngema, Mbongeni 1955- .... **CLC 57**

Ngugi, James T(hiong'o)........ **CLC 3, 7, 13**
See also Ngugi wa Thiong'o

Ngugi wa Thiong'o 1938-.......... **CLC 36**
See also Ngugi, James T(hiong'o)
See also BLC 3; BW; CA 81-84; CANR 27;
MTCW

Nichol, B(arrie) P(hillip)
1944-1988 .... **CLC 18**
See also CA 53-56; DLB 53; SATA 66

Nichols, John (Treadwell) 1940-.... **CLC 38**
See also CA 9-12R; CAAS 2; CANR 6;
DLBY 82

Nichols, Peter (Richard)
1927-................ **CLC 5, 36, 65**
See also CA 104; CANR 33; DLB 13;
MTCW

Nicolas, F. R. E.
See Freeling, Nicolas

Niedecker, Lorine 1903-1970.... **CLC 10, 42**
See also CA 25-28; CAP 2; DLB 48

Nietzsche, Friedrich (Wilhelm)
1844-1900 .... **TCLC 10, 18**
See also CA 107; 121; DLB 129

Nievo, Ippolito 1831-1861 .... **NCLC 22**

Nightingale, Anne Redmon 1943-
See Redmon, Anne
See also CA 103

Nik.T.O.
See Annensky, Innokenty Fyodorovich

Nin, Anais
1903-1977 ..... **CLC 1, 4, 8, 11, 14, 60;
SSC 10**
See also AITN 2; CA 13-16R; 69-72;
CANR 22; DLB 2, 4; MTCW

Nissenson, Hugh 1933-.......... **CLC 4, 9**
See also CA 17-20R; CANR 27; DLB 28

Niven, Larry .... **CLC 8**
See also Niven, Laurence Van Cott
See also DLB 8

Niven, Laurence Van Cott 1938-
See Niven, Larry
See also CA 21-24R; CAAS 12; CANR 14;
MTCW

Nixon, Agnes Eckhardt 1927-...... **CLC 21**
See also CA 110

Nizan, Paul 1905-1940.......... **TCLC 40**
See also DLB 72

Nkosi, Lewis 1936-............... **CLC 45**
See also BLC 3; BW; CA 65-68; CANR 27

Nodier, (Jean) Charles (Emmanuel)
1780-1844 .... **NCLC 19**
See also DLB 119

Nolan, Christopher 1965-......... **CLC 58**
See also CA 111

Norden, Charles
See Durrell, Lawrence (George)

Nordhoff, Charles (Bernard)
1887-1947 .... **TCLC 23**
See also CA 108; DLB 9; SATA 23

Norfolk, Lawrence 1963-......... **CLC 76**

Norman, Marsha 1947- .... **CLC 28**
See also CA 105; CABS 3; CANR 41;
DLBY 84

Norris, Benjamin Franklin, Jr.
1870-1902 .... **TCLC 24**
See also Norris, Frank
See also CA 110

Norris, Frank
See Norris, Benjamin Franklin, Jr.
See also CDALB 1865-1917; DLB 12, 71

Norris, Leslie 1921-............. **CLC 14**
See also CA 11-12; CANR 14; CAP 1;
DLB 27

North, Andrew
See Norton, Andre

North, Captain George
See Stevenson, Robert Louis (Balfour)

North, Milou
See Erdrich, Louise

Northrup, B. A.
See Hubbard, L(afayette) Ron(ald)

North Staffs
See Hulme, T(homas) E(rnest)

Norton, Alice Mary
See Norton, Andre
See also MAICYA; SATA 1, 43

Norton, Andre 1912- .... **CLC 12**
See also Norton, Alice Mary
See also CA 1-4R; CANR 2, 31; DLB 8, 52;
MTCW

Norway, Nevil Shute 1899-1960
See Shute, Nevil
See also CA 102; 93-96

Norwid, Cyprian Kamil
1821-1883 .... **NCLC 17**

Nosille, Nabrah
See Ellison, Harlan

Nossack, Hans Erich 1901-1978 ..... **CLC 6**
See also CA 93-96; 85-88; DLB 69

Nosu, Chuji
See Ozu, Yasujiro

Nova, Craig 1945-.............. **CLC 7, 31**
See also CA 45-48; CANR 2

Novak, Joseph
See Kosinski, Jerzy (Nikodem)

Novalis 1772-1801 .... **NCLC 13**
See also DLB 90

Nowlan, Alden (Albert) 1933-1983 .. **CLC 15**
See also CA 9-12R; CANR 5; DLB 53

Noyes, Alfred 1880-1958 .... **TCLC 7**
See also CA 104; DLB 20

Nunn, Kem 19(?)-................ **CLC 34**

Nye, Robert 1939- .... **CLC 13, 42**
See also CA 33-36R; CANR 29; DLB 14;
MTCW; SATA 6

Nyro, Laura 1947- .... **CLC 17**

Oates, Joyce Carol
1938-..... **CLC 1, 2, 3, 6, 9, 11, 15, 19,
33, 52; SSC 6**
See also AITN 1; BEST 89:2; CA 5-8R;
CANR 25; CDALB 1968-1988; DA;
DLB 2, 5, 130; DLBY 81; MTCW; WLC

O'Brien, E. G.
See Clarke, Arthur C(harles)

O'Brien, Edna
1936- ... **CLC 3, 5, 8, 13, 36, 65; SSC 10**
See also CA 1-4R; CANR 6, 41;
CDBLB 1960 to Present; DLB 14;
MTCW

O'Brien, Fitz-James 1828-1862... **NCLC 21**
See also DLB 74

O'Brien, Flann....... CLC 1, 4, 5, 7, 10, 47
See also O Nuallain, Brian

O'Brien, Richard 1942-........... **CLC 17**
See also CA 124

O'Brien, Tim 1946-......... **CLC 7, 19, 40**
See also CA 85-88; CANR 40; DLBD 9;
DLBY 80

Obstfelder, Sigbjoern 1866-1900... **TCLC 23**
See also CA 123

O'Casey, Sean
1880-1964 .... **CLC 1, 5, 9, 11, 15**
See also CA 89-92; CDBLB 1914-1945;
DLB 10; MTCW

O'Cathasaigh, Sean
See O'Casey, Sean

Ochs, Phil 1940-1976............. **CLC 17**
See also CA 65-68

O'Connor, Edwin (Greene)
1918-1968 .... **CLC 14**
See also CA 93-96; 25-28R

O'Connor, (Mary) Flannery
1925-1964 ... **CLC 1, 2, 3, 6, 10, 13, 15,
21, 66; SSC 1**
See also AAYA 7; CA 1-4R; CANR 3, 41;
CDALB 1941-1968; DA; DLB 2;
DLBY 80; MTCW; WLC

O'Connor, Frank.......... CLC 23; SSC 5
See also O'Donovan, Michael John

O'Dell, Scott 1898-1989.......... **CLC 30**
See also AAYA 3; CA 61-64; 129;
CANR 12, 30; CLR 1, 16; DLB 52;
MAICYA; SATA 12, 60

Odets, Clifford 1906-1963 .... **CLC 2, 28**
See also CA 85-88; DLB 7, 26; MTCW

O'Doherty, Brian 1934-........... **CLC 76**
See also CA 105

O'Donnell, K. M.
See Malzberg, Barry N(athaniel)

O'Donnell, Lawrence
See Kuttner, Henry

O'Donovan, Michael John
1903-1966 .... **CLC 14**
See also O'Connor, Frank
See also CA 93-96

Oe, Kenzaburo 1935-.......... **CLC 10, 36**
See also CA 97-100; CANR 36; MTCW

O'Faolain, Julia 1932-....... **CLC 6, 19, 47**
See also CA 81-84; CAAS 2; CANR 12;
DLB 14; MTCW

O'Faolain, Sean
1900-1991 .... **CLC 1, 7, 14, 32, 70**
See also CA 61-64; 134; CANR 12;
DLB 15; MTCW

O'Flaherty, Liam
1896-1984 .... **CLC 5, 34; SSC 6**
See also CA 101; 113; CANR 35; DLB 36;
DLBY 84; MTCW

Ogilvy, Gavin
See Barrie, J(ames) M(atthew)

O'Grady, Standish James
1846-1928 .... **TCLC 5**
See also CA 104

O'Grady, Timothy 1951-.......... **CLC 59**
See also CA 138

O'Hara, Frank
1926-1966 .... **CLC 2, 5, 13**
See also CA 9-12R; 25-28R; CANR 33;
DLB 5, 16; MTCW

O'Hara, John (Henry)
1905-1970 .... **CLC 1, 2, 3, 6, 11, 42**
See also CA 5-8R; 25-28R; CANR 31;
CDALB 1929-1941; DLB 9, 86; DLBD 2;
MTCW

Parker, Robert B(rown) 1932- . . . . . . **CLC 27**
See also BEST 89:4; CA 49-52; CANR 1, 26; MTCW

Parkes, Lucas
See Harris, John (Wyndham Parkes Lucas) Beynon

Parkin, Frank 1940- . . . . **CLC 43**

Parkman, Francis, Jr.
1823-1893 . . . . **NCLC 12**
See also DLB 1, 30

Parks, Gordon (Alexander Buchanan)
1912- . . . . **CLC 1, 16**
See also AITN 2; BLC 3; BW; CA 41-44R; CANR 26; DLB 33; SATA 8

Parnell, Thomas 1679-1718 . . . . **LC 3**
See also DLB 94

Parra, Nicanor 1914- . . . . **CLC 2**
See also CA 85-88; CANR 32; HW; MTCW

Parrish, Mary Frances
See Fisher, M(ary) F(rances) K(ennedy)

Parson
See Coleridge, Samuel Taylor

Parson Lot
See Kingsley, Charles

Partridge, Anthony
See Oppenheim, E(dward) Phillips

Pascoli, Giovanni 1855-1912 . . . . . . **TCLC 45**

Pasolini, Pier Paolo
1922-1975 . . . . **CLC 20, 37**
See also CA 93-96; 61-64; DLB 128; MTCW

Pasquini
See Silone, Ignazio

Pastan, Linda (Olenik) 1932- . . . . . . **CLC 27**
See also CA 61-64; CANR 18, 40; DLB 5

Pasternak, Boris (Leonidovich)
1890-1960 . . . . . **CLC 7, 10, 18, 63; PC 6**
See also CA 127; 116; DA; MTCW; WLC

Patchen, Kenneth 1911-1972 . . . **CLC 1, 2, 18**
See also CA 1-4R; 33-36R; CANR 3, 35; DLB 16, 48; MTCW

Pater, Walter (Horatio)
1839-1894 . . . . **NCLC 7**
See also CDBLB 1832-1890; DLB 57

Paterson, A(ndrew) B(arton)
1864-1941 . . . . **TCLC 32**

Paterson, Katherine (Womeldorf)
1932- . . . . **CLC 12, 30**
See also AAYA 1; CA 21-24R; CANR 28; CLR 7; DLB 52; MAICYA; MTCW; SATA 13, 53

Patmore, Coventry Kersey Dighton
1823-1896 . . . . **NCLC 9**
See also DLB 35, 98

Paton, Alan (Stewart)
1903-1988 . . . . **CLC 4, 10, 25, 55**
See also CA 13-16; 125; CANR 22; CAP 1; DA; MTCW; SATA 11, 56; WLC

Paton Walsh, Gillian 1939-
See Walsh, Jill Paton
See also CANR 38; MAICYA; SAAS 3; SATA 4, 72

Paulding, James Kirke 1778-1860 . . **NCLC 2**
See also DLB 3, 59, 74

Paulin, Thomas Neilson 1949-
See Paulin, Tom
See also CA 123; 128

Paulin, Tom . . . . **CLC 37**
See also Paulin, Thomas Neilson
See also DLB 40

Paustovsky, Konstantin (Georgievich)
1892-1968 . . . . **CLC 40**
See also CA 93-96; 25-28R

Pavese, Cesare 1908-1950 . . . . **TCLC 3**
See also CA 104; DLB 128

Pavic, Milorad 1929- . . . . **CLC 60**
See also CA 136

Payne, Alan
See Jakes, John (William)

Paz, Gil
See Lugones, Leopoldo

Paz, Octavio
1914- . . . . . . **CLC 3, 4, 6, 10, 19, 51, 65; PC 1**
See also CA 73-76; CANR 32; DA; DLBY 90; HW; MTCW; WLC

Peacock, Molly 1947- . . . . **CLC 60**
See also CA 103; DLB 120

Peacock, Thomas Love
1785-1866 . . . . **NCLC 22**
See also DLB 96, 116

Peake, Mervyn 1911-1968 . . . . **CLC 7, 54**
See also CA 5-8R; 25-28R; CANR 3; DLB 15; MTCW; SATA 23

Pearce, Philippa . . . . **CLC 21**
See also Christie, (Ann) Philippa
See also CLR 9; MAICYA; SATA 1, 67

Pearl, Eric
See Elman, Richard

Pearson, T(homas) R(eid) 1956- . . . . **CLC 39**
See also CA 120; 130

Peck, John 1941- . . . . **CLC 3**
See also CA 49-52; CANR 3

Peck, Richard (Wayne) 1934- . . . . . . **CLC 21**
See also AAYA 1; CA 85-88; CANR 19, 38; MAICYA; SAAS 2; SATA 18, 55

Peck, Robert Newton 1928- . . . . **CLC 17**
See also AAYA 3; CA 81-84; CANR 31; DA; MAICYA; SAAS 1; SATA 21, 62

Peckinpah, (David) Sam(uel)
1925-1984 . . . . **CLC 20**
See also CA 109; 114

Pedersen, Knut 1859-1952
See Hamsun, Knut
See also CA 104; 119; MTCW

Peeslake, Gaffer
See Durrell, Lawrence (George)

Peguy, Charles Pierre
1873-1914 . . . . **TCLC 10**
See also CA 107

Pena, Ramon del Valle y
See Valle-Inclan, Ramon (Maria) del

Pendennis, Arthur Esquir
See Thackeray, William Makepeace

Pepys, Samuel 1633-1703 . . . . **LC 11**
See also CDBLB 1660-1789; DA; DLB 101; WLC

Percy, Walker
1916-1990 . . . **CLC 2, 3, 6, 8, 14, 18, 47, 65**
See also CA 1-4R; 131; CANR 1, 23; DLB 2; DLBY 80, 90; MTCW

Perec, Georges 1936-1982 . . . . **CLC 56**
See also DLB 83

Pereda (y Sanchez de Porrua), Jose Maria de
1833-1906 . . . . **TCLC 16**
See also CA 117

Pereda y Porrua, Jose Maria de
See Pereda (y Sanchez de Porrua), Jose Maria de

Peregoy, George Weems
See Mencken, H(enry) L(ouis)

Perelman, S(idney) J(oseph)
1904-1979 . . . **CLC 3, 5, 9, 15, 23, 44, 49**
See also AITN 1, 2; CA 73-76; 89-92; CANR 18; DLB 11, 44; MTCW

Peret, Benjamin 1899-1959 . . . . **TCLC 20**
See also CA 117

Peretz, Isaac Loeb 1851(?)-1915 . . . **TCLC 16**
See also CA 109

Peretz, Yitzkhok Leibush
See Peretz, Isaac Loeb

Perez Galdos, Benito 1843-1920 . . . **TCLC 27**
See also CA 125; HW

Perrault, Charles 1628-1703 . . . . **LC 2**
See also MAICYA; SATA 25

Perry, Brighton
See Sherwood, Robert E(mmet)

Perse, Saint-John
See Leger, (Marie-Rene) Alexis Saint-Leger

Perse, St.-John . . . . **CLC 4, 11, 46**
See also Leger, (Marie-Rene) Alexis Saint-Leger

Peseenz, Tulio F.
See Lopez y Fuentes, Gregorio

Pesetsky, Bette 1932- . . . . **CLC 28**
See also CA 133; DLB 130

Peshkov, Alexei Maximovich 1868-1936
See Gorky, Maxim
See also CA 105; DA

Pessoa, Fernando (Antonio Nogueira)
1888-1935 . . . . **TCLC 27**
See also CA 125

Peterkin, Julia Mood 1880-1961 . . . . **CLC 31**
See also CA 102; DLB 9

Peters, Joan K. 1945- . . . . **CLC 39**

Peters, Robert L(ouis) 1924- . . . . **CLC 7**
See also CA 13-16R; CAAS 8; DLB 105

Petofi, Sandor 1823-1849 . . . . **NCLC 21**

Petrakis, Harry Mark 1923- . . . . **CLC 3**
See also CA 9-12R; CANR 4, 30

Petrov, Evgeny . . . . **TCLC 21**
See also Kataev, Evgeny Petrovich

Petry, Ann (Lane) 1908- . . . . . . **CLC 1, 7, 18**
See also BW; CA 5-8R; CAAS 6; CANR 4; CLR 12; DLB 76; MAICYA; MTCW; SATA 5

Petursson, Halligrimur 1614-1674 . . . . **LC 8**

Philipson, Morris H. 1926- . . . . **CLC 53**
See also CA 1-4R; CANR 4

Raine, Craig 1944- . . . . CLC 32
See also CA 108; CANR 29; DLB 40

Raine, Kathleen (Jessie) 1908- . . . CLC 7, 45
See also CA 85-88; DLB 20; MTCW

Rainis, Janis 1865-1929 . . . . TCLC 29

Rakosi, Carl. . . . . CLC 47
See also Rawley, Callman
See also CAAS 5

Raleigh, Richard
See Lovecraft, H(oward) P(hillips)

Rallentando, H. P.
See Sayers, Dorothy L(eigh)

Ramal, Walter
See de la Mare, Walter (John)

Ramon, Juan
See Jimenez (Mantecon), Juan Ramon

Ramos, Graciliano 1892-1953 . . . . . TCLC 32

Rampersad, Arnold 1941-. . . . . CLC 44
See also CA 127; 133; DLB 111

Rampling, Anne
See Rice, Anne

Ramuz, Charles-Ferdinand
1878-1947 . . . . TCLC 33

Rand, Ayn 1905-1982. . . . . . . CLC 3, 30, 44
See also AAYA 10; CA 13-16R; 105;
CANR 27; DA; MTCW; WLC

Randall, Dudley (Felker) 1914- . . . . . . CLC 1
See also BLC 3; BW; CA 25-28R;
CANR 23; DLB 41

Randall, Robert
See Silverberg, Robert

Ranger, Ken
See Creasey, John

Ransom, John Crowe
1888-1974 . . . . CLC 2, 4, 5, 11, 24
See also CA 5-8R; 49-52; CANR 6, 34;
DLB 45, 63; MTCW

Rao, Raja 1909- . . . . CLC 25, 56
See also CA 73-76; MTCW

Raphael, Frederic (Michael)
1931- . . . . CLC 2, 14
See also CA 1-4R; CANR 1; DLB 14

Ratcliffe, James P.
See Mencken, H(enry) L(ouis)

Rathbone, Julian 1935- . . . . CLC 41
See also CA 101; CANR 34

Rattigan, Terence (Mervyn)
1911-1977 . . . . CLC 7
See also CA 85-88; 73-76;
CDBLB 1945-1960; DLB 13; MTCW

Ratushinskaya, Irina 1954- . . . . CLC 54
See also CA 129

Raven, Simon (Arthur Noel)
1927- . . . . CLC 14
See also CA 81-84

Rawley, Callman 1903-
See Rakosi, Carl
See also CA 21-24R; CANR 12, 32

Rawlings, Marjorie Kinnan
1896-1953 . . . . TCLC 4
See also CA 104; 137; DLB 9, 22, 102;
MAICYA; YABC 1

Ray, Satyajit 1921-1992. . . . . . . CLC 16, 76
See also CA 114; 137

Read, Herbert Edward 1893-1968. . . . CLC 4
See also CA 85-88; 25-28R; DLB 20

Read, Piers Paul 1941- . . . . . . CLC 4, 10, 25
See also CA 21-24R; CANR 38; DLB 14;
SATA 21

Reade, Charles 1814-1884 . . . . NCLC 2
See also DLB 21

Reade, Hamish
See Gray, Simon (James Holliday)

Reading, Peter 1946- . . . . CLC 47
See also CA 103; DLB 40

Reaney, James 1926- . . . . CLC 13
See also CA 41-44R; CAAS 15; DLB 68;
SATA 43

Rebreanu, Liviu 1885-1944 . . . . . . TCLC 28

Rechy, John (Francisco)
1934- . . . . CLC 1, 7, 14, 18
See also CA 5-8R; CAAS 4; CANR 6, 32;
DLB 122; DLBY 82; HW

Redcam, Tom 1870-1933 . . . . TCLC 25

Reddin, Keith. . . . . CLC 67

Redgrove, Peter (William)
1932- . . . . CLC 6, 41
See also CA 1-4R; CANR 3, 39; DLB 40

Redmon, Anne. . . . . CLC 22
See also Nightingale, Anne Redmon
See also DLBY 86

Reed, Eliot
See Ambler, Eric

Reed, Ishmael
1938- . . . . CLC 2, 3, 5, 6, 13, 32, 60
See also BLC 3; BW; CA 21-24R;
CANR 25; DLB 2, 5, 33; DLBD 8;
MTCW

Reed, John (Silas) 1887-1920 . . . . . . TCLC 9
See also CA 106

Reed, Lou. . . . . CLC 21
See also Firbank, Louis

Reeve, Clara 1729-1807 . . . . NCLC 19
See also DLB 39

Reid, Christopher (John) 1949-. . . . . CLC 33
See also CA 140; DLB 40

Reid, Desmond
See Moorcock, Michael (John)

Reid Banks, Lynne 1929-
See Banks, Lynne Reid
See also CA 1-4R; CANR 6, 22, 38;
CLR 24; MAICYA; SATA 22

Reilly, William K.
See Creasey, John

Reiner, Max
See Caldwell, (Janet Miriam) Taylor
(Holland)

Reis, Ricardo
See Pessoa, Fernando (Antonio Nogueira)

Remarque, Erich Maria
1898-1970 . . . . CLC 21
See also CA 77-80; 29-32R; DA; DLB 56;
MTCW

Remizov, A.
See Remizov, Aleksei (Mikhailovich)

Remizov, A. M.
See Remizov, Aleksei (Mikhailovich)

Remizov, Aleksei (Mikhailovich)
1877-1957 . . . . TCLC 27
See also CA 125; 133

Renan, Joseph Ernest
1823-1892 . . . . NCLC 26

Renard, Jules 1864-1910 . . . . TCLC 17
See also CA 117

Renault, Mary. . . . . CLC 3, 11, 17
See also Challans, Mary
See also DLBY 83

Rendell, Ruth (Barbara) 1930- . . CLC 28, 48
See also Vine, Barbara
See also CA 109; CANR 32; DLB 87;
MTCW

Renoir, Jean 1894-1979 . . . . CLC 20
See also CA 129; 85-88

Resnais, Alain 1922-. . . . . CLC 16

Reverdy, Pierre 1889-1960 . . . . CLC 53
See also CA 97-100; 89-92

Rexroth, Kenneth
1905-1982 . . . . . . CLC 1, 2, 6, 11, 22, 49
See also CA 5-8R; 107; CANR 14, 34;
CDALB 1941-1968; DLB 16, 48;
DLBY 82; MTCW

Reyes, Alfonso 1889-1959 . . . . TCLC 33
See also CA 131; HW

Reyes y Basoalto, Ricardo Eliecer Neftali
See Neruda, Pablo

Reymont, Wladyslaw (Stanislaw)
1868(?)-1925 . . . . TCLC 5
See also CA 104

Reynolds, Jonathan 1942- . . . . CLC 6, 38
See also CA 65-68; CANR 28

Reynolds, Joshua 1723-1792 . . . . LC 15
See also DLB 104

Reynolds, Michael Shane 1937- . . . . CLC 44
See also CA 65-68; CANR 9

Reznikoff, Charles 1894-1976 . . . . CLC 9
See also CA 33-36; 61-64; CAP 2; DLB 28,
45

Rezzori (d'Arezzo), Gregor von
1914- . . . . CLC 25
See also CA 122; 136

Rhine, Richard
See Silverstein, Alvin

R'hoone
See Balzac, Honore de

Rhys, Jean
1890(?)-1979 . . . . CLC 2, 4, 6, 14, 19, 51
See also CA 25-28R; 85-88; CANR 35;
CDBLB 1945-1960; DLB 36, 117; MTCW

Ribeiro, Darcy 1922- . . . . CLC 34
See also CA 33-36R

Ribeiro, Joao Ubaldo (Osorio Pimentel)
1941- . . . . CLC 10, 67
See also CA 81-84

Ribman, Ronald (Burt) 1932- . . . . CLC 7
See also CA 21-24R

Ricci, Nino 1959- . . . . CLC 70
See also CA 137

Rice, Anne 1941- . . . . CLC 41
See also AAYA 9; BEST 89:2; CA 65-68;
CANR 12, 36

Rice, Elmer (Leopold)
1892-1967 . . . . CLC 7, 49
See also CA 21-22; 25-28R; CAP 2; DLB 4,
7; MTCW

Rice, Tim 1944- . . . . CLC 21
See also CA 103

Rich, Adrienne (Cecile)
1929- . . . CLC 3, 6, 7, 11, 18, 36, 73, 76;
PC 5
See also CA 9-12R; CANR 20; DLB 5, 67;
MTCW

Rich, Barbara
See Graves, Robert (von Ranke)

Rich, Robert
See Trumbo, Dalton

Richards, David Adams 1950- . . . . . . CLC 59
See also CA 93-96; DLB 53

Richards, I(vor) A(rmstrong)
1893-1979 . . . . CLC 14, 24
See also CA 41-44R; 89-92; CANR 34;
DLB 27

Richardson, Anne
See Roiphe, Anne Richardson

Richardson, Dorothy Miller
1873-1957 . . . . TCLC 3
See also CA 104; DLB 36

Richardson, Ethel Florence (Lindesay)
1870-1946
See Richardson, Henry Handel
See also CA 105

Richardson, Henry Handel . . . . TCLC 4
See also Richardson, Ethel Florence
(Lindesay)

Richardson, Samuel 1689-1761 . . . . LC 1
See also CDBLB 1660-1789; DA; DLB 39;
WLC

Richler, Mordecai
1931- . . . . CLC 3, 5, 9, 13, 18, 46, 70
See also AITN 1; CA 65-68; CANR 31;
CLR 17; DLB 53; MAICYA; MTCW;
SATA 27, 44

Richter, Conrad (Michael)
1890-1968 . . . . CLC 30
See also CA 5-8R; 25-28R; CANR 23;
DLB 9; MTCW; SATA 3

Riddell, J. H. 1832-1906 . . . . TCLC 40

Riding, Laura . . . . CLC 3, 7
See also Jackson, Laura (Riding)

Riefenstahl, Berta Helene Amalia 1902-
See Riefenstahl, Leni
See also CA 108

Riefenstahl, Leni . . . . CLC 16
See also Riefenstahl, Berta Helene Amalia

Riffe, Ernest
See Bergman, (Ernst) Ingmar

Riley, Tex
See Creasey, John

Rilke, Rainer Maria
1875-1926 . . . . TCLC 1, 6, 19; PC 2
See also CA 104; 132; DLB 81; MTCW

Rimbaud, (Jean Nicolas) Arthur
1854-1891 . . . . NCLC 4, 35; PC 3
See also DA; WLC

Ringmaster, The
See Mencken, H(enry) L(ouis)

Ringwood, Gwen(dolyn Margaret) Pharis
1910-1984 . . . . CLC 48
See also CA 112; DLB 88

Rio, Michel 19(?)- . . . . CLC 43

Ritsos, Giannes
See Ritsos, Yannis

Ritsos, Yannis 1909-1990 . . . . . CLC 6, 13, 31
See also CA 77-80; 133; CANR 39; MTCW

Ritter, Erika 1948(?)- . . . . CLC 52

Rivera, Jose Eustasio 1889-1928 . . . TCLC 35
See also HW

Rivers, Conrad Kent 1933-1968 . . . . . . CLC 1
See also BW; CA 85-88; DLB 41

Rivers, Elfrida
See Bradley, Marion Zimmer

Riverside, John
See Heinlein, Robert A(nson)

Rizal, Jose 1861-1896 . . . . NCLC 27

Roa Bastos, Augusto (Antonio)
1917- . . . . CLC 45
See also CA 131; DLB 113; HW

Robbe-Grillet, Alain
1922- . . . . . . CLC 1, 2, 4, 6, 8, 10, 14, 43
See also CA 9-12R; CANR 33; DLB 83;
MTCW

Robbins, Harold 1916- . . . . CLC 5
See also CA 73-76; CANR 26; MTCW

Robbins, Thomas Eugene 1936-
See Robbins, Tom
See also CA 81-84; CANR 29; MTCW

Robbins, Tom . . . . CLC 9, 32, 64
See also Robbins, Thomas Eugene
See also BEST 90:3; DLBY 80

Robbins, Trina 1938- . . . . CLC 21
See also CA 128

Roberts, Charles G(eorge) D(ouglas)
1860-1943 . . . . TCLC 8
See also CA 105; DLB 92; SATA 29

Roberts, Kate 1891-1985 . . . . CLC 15
See also CA 107; 116

Roberts, Keith (John Kingston)
1935- . . . . CLC 14
See also CA 25-28R

Roberts, Kenneth (Lewis)
1885-1957 . . . . TCLC 23
See also CA 109; DLB 9

Roberts, Michele (B.) 1949- . . . . CLC 48
See also CA 115

Robertson, Ellis
See Ellison, Harlan; Silverberg, Robert

Robertson, Thomas William
1829-1871 . . . . NCLC 35

Robinson, Edwin Arlington
1869-1935 . . . . TCLC 5; PC 1
See also CA 104; 133; CDALB 1865-1917;
DA; DLB 54; MTCW

Robinson, Henry Crabb
1775-1867 . . . . NCLC 15
See also DLB 107

Robinson, Jill 1936- . . . . CLC 10
See also CA 102

Robinson, Kim Stanley 1952- . . . . . . CLC 34
See also CA 126

Robinson, Lloyd
See Silverberg, Robert

Robinson, Marilynne 1944- . . . . CLC 25
See also CA 116

Robinson, Smokey . . . . CLC 21
See also Robinson, William, Jr.

Robinson, William, Jr. 1940-
See Robinson, Smokey
See also CA 116

Robison, Mary 1949- . . . . CLC 42
See also CA 113; 116; DLB 130

Roddenberry, Eugene Wesley 1921-1991
See Roddenberry, Gene
See also CA 110; 135; CANR 37; SATA 45

Roddenberry, Gene . . . . CLC 17
See also Roddenberry, Eugene Wesley
See also AAYA 5; SATA-Obit 69

Rodgers, Mary 1931- . . . . CLC 12
See also CA 49-52; CANR 8; CLR 20;
MAICYA; SATA 8

Rodgers, W(illiam) R(obert)
1909-1969 . . . . CLC 7
See also CA 85-88; DLB 20

Rodman, Eric
See Silverberg, Robert

Rodman, Howard 1920(?)-1985 . . . . . CLC 65
See also CA 118

Rodman, Maia
See Wojciechowska, Maia (Teresa)

Rodriguez, Claudio 1934- . . . . CLC 10

Roelvaag, O(le) E(dvart)
1876-1931 . . . . TCLC 17
See also CA 117; DLB 9

Roethke, Theodore (Huebner)
1908-1963 . . . . . . CLC 1, 3, 8, 11, 19, 46
See also CA 81-84; CABS 2;
CDALB 1941-1968; DLB 5; MTCW

Rogers, Thomas Hunton 1927- . . . . . CLC 57
See also CA 89-92

Rogers, Will(iam Penn Adair)
1879-1935 . . . . TCLC 8
See also CA 105; DLB 11

Rogin, Gilbert 1929- . . . . CLC 18
See also CA 65-68; CANR 15

Rohan, Koda . . . . TCLC 22
See also Koda Shigeyuki

Rohmer, Eric . . . . CLC 16
See also Scherer, Jean-Marie Maurice

Rohmer, Sax . . . . TCLC 28
See also Ward, Arthur Henry Sarsfield
See also DLB 70

Roiphe, Anne Richardson 1935- . . . CLC 3, 9
See also CA 89-92; DLBY 80

**Rolfe, Frederick (William Serafino Austin
Lewis Mary)** 1860-1913 . . . . . . TCLC 12
See also CA 107; DLB 34

Rolland, Romain 1866-1944 . . . . . . TCLC 23
See also CA 118; DLB 65

Rolvaag, O(le) E(dvart)
See Roelvaag, O(le) E(dvart)

Romain Arnaud, Saint
See Aragon, Louis

Sahgal, Nayantara (Pandit) 1927-... **CLC 41**
See also CA 9-12R; CANR 11

Saint, H(arry) F. 1941- .... **CLC 50**
See also CA 127

St. Aubin de Teran, Lisa 1953-
See Teran, Lisa St. Aubin de
See also CA 118; 126

Sainte-Beuve, Charles Augustin
1804-1869 .... **NCLC 5**

Saint-Exupery, Antoine (Jean Baptiste Marie
Roger) de 1900-1944 .... **TCLC 2**
See also CA 108; 132; CLR 10; DLB 72;
MAICYA; MTCW; SATA 20; WLC

St. John, David
See Hunt, E(verette) Howard, Jr.

Saint-John Perse
See Leger, (Marie-Rene) Alexis Saint-Leger

Saintsbury, George (Edward Bateman)
1845-1933 .... **TCLC 31**
See also DLB 57

Sait Faik .... **TCLC 23**
See also Abasiyanik, Sait Faik

Saki .... **TCLC 3; SSC 12**
See also Munro, H(ector) H(ugh)

Salama, Hannu 1936- .... **CLC 18**

Salamanca, J(ack) R(ichard)
1922- .... **CLC 4, 15**
See also CA 25-28R

Sale, J. Kirkpatrick
See Sale, Kirkpatrick

Sale, Kirkpatrick 1937- .... **CLC 68**
See also CA 13-16R; CANR 10

Salinas (y Serrano), Pedro
1891(?)-1951 .... **TCLC 17**
See also CA 117

Salinger, J(erome) D(avid)
1919- .... **CLC 1, 3, 8, 12, 55, 56; SSC 2**
See also AAYA 2; CA 5-8R; CANR 39;
CDALB 1941-1968; CLR 18; DA;
DLB 2, 102; MAICYA; MTCW;
SATA 67; WLC

Salisbury, John
See Caute, David

Salter, James 1925- .... **CLC 7, 52, 59**
See also CA 73-76; DLB 130

Saltus, Edgar (Everton)
1855-1921 .... **TCLC 8**
See also CA 105

Saltykov, Mikhail Evgrafovich
1826-1889 .... **NCLC 16**

Samarakis, Antonis 1919- .... **CLC 5**
See also CA 25-28R; CAAS 16; CANR 36

Sanchez, Florencio 1875-1910..... **TCLC 37**
See also HW

Sanchez, Luis Rafael 1936- .... **CLC 23**
See also CA 128; HW

Sanchez, Sonia 1934- .... **CLC 5**
See also BLC 3; BW; CA 33-36R;
CANR 24; CLR 18; DLB 41; DLBD 8;
MAICYA; MTCW; SATA 22

Sand, George 1804-1876.......... **NCLC 2**
See also DA; DLB 119; WLC

Sandburg, Carl (August)
1878-1967 ... **CLC 1, 4, 10, 15, 35; PC 2**
See also CA 5-8R; 25-28R; CANR 35;
CDALB 1865-1917; DA; DLB 17, 54;
MAICYA; MTCW; SATA 8; WLC

Sandburg, Charles
See Sandburg, Carl (August)

Sandburg, Charles A.
See Sandburg, Carl (August)

Sanders, (James) Ed(ward) 1939- ... **CLC 53**
See also CA 13-16R; CANR 13; DLB 16

Sanders, Lawrence 1920-.......... **CLC 41**
See also BEST 89:4; CA 81-84; CANR 33;
MTCW

Sanders, Noah
See Blount, Roy (Alton), Jr.

Sanders, Winston P.
See Anderson, Poul (William)

Sandoz, Mari(e Susette)
1896-1966 .... **CLC 28**
See also CA 1-4R; 25-28R; CANR 17;
DLB 9; MTCW; SATA 5

Saner, Reg(inald Anthony) 1931- .... **CLC 9**
See also CA 65-68

Sannazaro, Jacopo 1456(?)-1530 ...... **LC 8**

Sansom, William 1912-1976....... **CLC 2, 6**
See also CA 5-8R; 65-68; MTCW

Santayana, George 1863-1952 ..... **TCLC 40**
See also CA 115; DLB 54, 71

Santiago, Danny .... **CLC 33**
See also James, Daniel (Lewis); James,
Daniel (Lewis)
See also DLB 122

Santmyer, Helen Hooven
1895-1986 .... **CLC 33**
See also CA 1-4R; 118; CANR 15, 33;
DLBY 84; MTCW

Santos, Bienvenido N(uqui) 1911-... **CLC 22**
See also CA 101; CANR 19

Sapper .... **TCLC 44**
See also McNeile, Herman Cyril

Sappho fl. 6th cent. B.C.-..... **CMLC 3; PC 5**

Sarduy, Severo 1937-.............. **CLC 6**
See also CA 89-92; DLB 113; HW

Sargeson, Frank 1903-1982 .... **CLC 31**
See also CA 25-28R; 106; CANR 38

Sarmiento, Felix Ruben Garcia 1867-1916
See Dario, Ruben
See also CA 104

Saroyan, William
1908-1981 ..... **CLC 1, 8, 10, 29, 34, 56**
See also CA 5-8R; 103; CANR 30; DA;
DLB 7, 9, 86; DLBY 81; MTCW;
SATA 23, 24; WLC

Sarraute, Nathalie
1900- .... **CLC 1, 2, 4, 8, 10, 31**
See also CA 9-12R; CANR 23; DLB 83;
MTCW

Sarton, (Eleanor) May
1912- .... **CLC 4, 14, 49**
See also CA 1-4R; CANR 1, 34; DLB 48;
DLBY 81; MTCW; SATA 36

Sartre, Jean-Paul
1905-1980 ... **CLC 1, 4, 7, 9, 13, 18, 24,
44, 50, 52; DC 3**
See also CA 9-12R; 97-100; CANR 21; DA;
DLB 72; MTCW; WLC

Sassoon, Siegfried (Lorraine)
1886-1967 .... **CLC 36**
See also CA 104; 25-28R; CANR 36;
DLB 20; MTCW

Satterfield, Charles
See Pohl, Frederik

Saul, John (W. III) 1942- .... **CLC 46**
See also AAYA 10; BEST 90:4; CA 81-84;
CANR 16, 40

Saunders, Caleb
See Heinlein, Robert A(nson)

Saura (Atares), Carlos 1932-....... **CLC 20**
See also CA 114; 131; HW

Sauser-Hall, Frederic 1887-1961.... **CLC 18**
See also CA 102; 93-96; CANR 36; MTCW

Saussure, Ferdinand de
1857-1913 .... **TCLC 49**

Savage, Catharine
See Brosman, Catharine Savage

Savage, Thomas 1915- .... **CLC 40**
See also CA 126; 132; CAAS 15

Savan, Glenn .... **CLC 50**

Saven, Glenn 19(?)- .... **CLC 50**

Sayers, Dorothy L(eigh)
1893-1957 .... **TCLC 2, 15**
See also CA 104; 119; CDBLB 1914-1945;
DLB 10, 36, 77, 100; MTCW

Sayers, Valerie 1952-............. **CLC 50**
See also CA 134

Sayles, John (Thomas)
1950- .... **CLC 7, 10, 14**
See also CA 57-60; CANR 41; DLB 44

Scammell, Michael .... **CLC 34**

Scannell, Vernon 1922- .... **CLC 49**
See also CA 5-8R; CANR 8, 24; DLB 27;
SATA 59

Scarlett, Susan
See Streatfeild, (Mary) Noel

Schaeffer, Susan Fromberg
1941- .... **CLC 6, 11, 22**
See also CA 49-52; CANR 18; DLB 28;
MTCW; SATA 22

Schary, Jill
See Robinson, Jill

Schell, Jonathan 1943-............ **CLC 35**
See also CA 73-76; CANR 12

Schelling, Friedrich Wilhelm Joseph von
1775-1854 .... **NCLC 30**
See also DLB 90

Scherer, Jean-Marie Maurice 1920-
See Rohmer, Eric
See also CA 110

Schevill, James (Erwin) 1920-....... **CLC 7**
See also CA 5-8R; CAAS 12

Schiller, Friedrich 1759-1805 .... **NCLC 39**
See also DLB 94

Schisgal, Murray (Joseph) 1926-..... **CLC 6**
See also CA 21-24R

Shackleton, C. C.
See Aldiss, Brian W(ilson)

Shacochis, Bob .... **CLC 39**
See also Shacochis, Robert G.

Shacochis, Robert G. 1951-
See Shacochis, Bob
See also CA 119; 124

Shaffer, Anthony (Joshua) 1926-.... **CLC 19**
See also CA 110; 116; DLB 13

Shaffer, Peter (Levin)
1926- .... **CLC 5, 14, 18, 37, 60**
See also CA 25-28R; CANR 25;
CDBLB 1960 to Present; DLB 13;
MTCW

Shakey, Bernard
See Young, Neil

Shalamov, Varlam (Tikhonovich)
1907(?)-1982 .... **CLC 18**
See also CA 129; 105

Shamlu, Ahmad 1925- .... **CLC 10**

Shammas, Anton 1951-........... **CLC 55**

Shange, Ntozake
1948- .... **CLC 8, 25, 38, 74; DC 3**
See also AAYA 9; BLC 3; BW; CA 85-88;
CABS 3; CANR 27; DLB 38; MTCW

Shanley, John Patrick 1950-....... **CLC 75**
See also CA 128; 133

Shapcott, Thomas William 1935- ... **CLC 38**
See also CA 69-72

Shapiro, Jane.................... **CLC 76**

Shapiro, Karl (Jay) 1913- .. **CLC 4, 8, 15, 53**
See also CA 1-4R; CAAS 6; CANR 1, 36;
DLB 48; MTCW

Sharp, William 1855-1905 .... **TCLC 39**

Sharpe, Thomas Ridley 1928-
See Sharpe, Tom
See also CA 114; 122

Sharpe, Tom.................... **CLC 36**
See also Sharpe, Thomas Ridley
See also DLB 14

Shaw, Bernard.................. **TCLC 45**
See also Shaw, George Bernard

Shaw, G. Bernard
See Shaw, George Bernard

Shaw, George Bernard
1856-1950 .... **TCLC 3, 9, 21**
See also Shaw, Bernard
See also CA 104; 128; CDBLB 1914-1945;
DA; DLB 10, 57; MTCW; WLC

Shaw, Henry Wheeler
1818-1885 .... **NCLC 15**
See also DLB 11

Shaw, Irwin 1913-1984...... **CLC 7, 23, 34**
See also AITN 1; CA 13-16R; 112;
CANR 21; CDALB 1941-1968; DLB 6,
102; DLBY 84; MTCW

Shaw, Robert 1927-1978 .... **CLC 5**
See also AITN 1; CA 1-4R; 81-84;
CANR 4; DLB 13, 14

Shaw, T. E.
See Lawrence, T(homas) E(dward)

Shawn, Wallace 1943- .... **CLC 41**
See also CA 112

Sheed, Wilfrid (John Joseph)
1930- .... **CLC 2, 4, 10, 53**
See also CA 65-68; CANR 30; DLB 6;
MTCW

Sheldon, Alice Hastings Bradley
1915(?)-1987
See Tiptree, James, Jr.
See also CA 108; 122; CANR 34; MTCW

Sheldon, John
See Bloch, Robert (Albert)

Shelley, Mary Wollstonecraft (Godwin)
1797-1851 .... **NCLC 14**
See also CDBLB 1789-1832; DA; DLB 110,
116; SATA 29; WLC

Shelley, Percy Bysshe
1792-1822 .... **NCLC 18**
See also CDBLB 1789-1832; DA; DLB 96,
110; WLC

Shepard, Jim 1956-.............. **CLC 36**
See also CA 137

Shepard, Lucius 19(?)-........... **CLC 34**
See also CA 128

Shepard, Sam
1943- .... **CLC 4, 6, 17, 34, 41, 44**
See also AAYA 1; CA 69-72; CABS 3;
CANR 22; DLB 7; MTCW

Shepherd, Michael
See Ludlum, Robert

Sherburne, Zoa (Morin) 1912-...... **CLC 30**
See also CA 1-4R; CANR 3, 37; MAICYA;
SATA 3

Sheridan, Frances 1724-1766........ **LC 7**
See also DLB 39, 84

Sheridan, Richard Brinsley
1751-1816 .... **NCLC 5; DC 1**
See also CDBLB 1660-1789; DA; DLB 89;
WLC

Sherman, Jonathan Marc.......... **CLC 55**

Sherman, Martin 1941(?)-......... **CLC 19**
See also CA 116; 123

Sherwin, Judith Johnson 1936-... **CLC 7, 15**
See also CA 25-28R; CANR 34

Sherwood, Robert E(mmet)
1896-1955 .... **TCLC 3**
See also CA 104; DLB 7, 26

Shiel, M(atthew) P(hipps)
1865-1947 .... **TCLC 8**
See also CA 106

Shiga, Naoya 1883-1971.......... **CLC 33**
See also CA 101; 33-36R

Shimazaki Haruki 1872-1943
See Shimazaki Toson
See also CA 105; 134

Shimazaki Toson................ **TCLC 5**
See also Shimazaki Haruki

Sholokhov, Mikhail (Aleksandrovich)
1905-1984 .... **CLC 7, 15**
See also CA 101; 112; MTCW; SATA 36

Shone, Patric
See Hanley, James

Shreve, Susan Richards 1939-...... **CLC 23**
See also CA 49-52; CAAS 5; CANR 5, 38;
MAICYA; SATA 41, 46

Shue, Larry 1946-1985........... **CLC 52**
See also CA 117

Shu-Jen, Chou 1881-1936
See Hsun, Lu
See also CA 104

Shulman, Alix Kates 1932- ...... **CLC 2, 10**
See also CA 29-32R; SATA 7

Shuster, Joe 1914- .... **CLC 21**

Shute, Nevil..................... **CLC 30**
See also Norway, Nevil Shute

Shuttle, Penelope (Diane) 1947- ..... **CLC 7**
See also CA 93-96; CANR 39; DLB 14, 40

Sidney, Mary 1561-1621 .... **LC 19**

Sidney, Sir Philip 1554-1586....... **LC 19**
See also CDBLB Before 1660; DA

Siegel, Jerome 1914- .... **CLC 21**
See also CA 116

Siegel, Jerry
See Siegel, Jerome

Sienkiewicz, Henryk (Adam Alexander Pius)
1846-1916 ....**TCLC 3**
See also CA 104; 134

Sierra, Gregorio Martinez
See Martinez Sierra, Gregorio

Sierra, Maria (de la O'LeJarraga) Martinez
See Martinez Sierra, Maria (de la
O'LeJarraga)

Sigal, Clancy 1926-............... **CLC 7**
See also CA 1-4R

Sigourney, Lydia Howard (Huntley)
1791-1865 .... **NCLC 21**
See also DLB 1, 42, 73

Siguenza y Gongora, Carlos de
1645-1700 .... **LC 8**

Sigurjonsson, Johann 1880-1919... **TCLC 27**

Sikelianos, Angelos 1884-1951 .... **TCLC 39**

Silkin, Jon 1930- .... **CLC 2, 6, 43**
See also CA 5-8R; CAAS 5; DLB 27

Silko, Leslie Marmon 1948- .... **CLC 23, 74**
See also CA 115; 122; DA

Sillanpaa, Frans Eemil 1888-1964... **CLC 19**
See also CA 129; 93-96; MTCW

Sillitoe, Alan
1928- .... **CLC 1, 3, 6, 10, 19, 57**
See also AITN 1; CA 9-12R; CAAS 2;
CANR 8, 26; CDBLB 1960 to Present;
DLB 14; MTCW; SATA 61

Silone, Ignazio 1900-1978 .... **CLC 4**
See also CA 25-28; 81-84; CANR 34;
CAP 2; MTCW

Silver, Joan Micklin 1935- .... **CLC 20**
See also CA 114; 121

Silver, Nicholas
See Faust, Frederick (Schiller)

Silverberg, Robert 1935- .... **CLC 7**
See also CA 1-4R; CAAS 3; CANR 1, 20,
36; DLB 8; MAICYA; MTCW; SATA 13

Silverstein, Alvin 1933- .... **CLC 17**
See also CA 49-52; CANR 2; CLR 25;
MAICYA; SATA 8, 69

Silverstein, Virginia B(arbara Opshelor)
1937- .... **CLC 17**
See also CA 49-52; CANR 2; CLR 25;
MAICYA; SATA 8, 69

Stead, Christina (Ellen)
1902-1983 . . . . **CLC 2, 5, 8, 32**
See also CA 13-16R; 109; CANR 33, 40;
MTCW

Stead, William Thomas
1849-1912 . . . . **TCLC 48**

Steele, Richard 1672-1729 . . . . **LC 18**
See also CDBLB 1660-1789; DLB 84, 101

Steele, Timothy (Reid) 1948- . . . . **CLC 45**
See also CA 93-96; CANR 16; DLB 120

Steffens, (Joseph) Lincoln
1866-1936 . . . . **TCLC 20**
See also CA 117

Stegner, Wallace (Earle) 1909- . . . **CLC 9, 49**
See also AITN 1; BEST 90:3; CA 1-4R;
CAAS 9; CANR 1, 21; DLB 9; MTCW

Stein, Gertrude
1874-1946 . . . . **TCLC 1, 6, 28, 48**
See also CA 104; 132; CDALB 1917-1929;
DA; DLB 4, 54, 86; MTCW; WLC

Steinbeck, John (Ernst)
1902-1968 . . . . . **CLC 1, 5, 9, 13, 21, 34,
45, 75; SSC 11**
See also CA 1-4R; 25-28R; CANR 1, 35;
CDALB 1929-1941; DA; DLB 7, 9;
DLBD 2; MTCW; SATA 9; WLC

Steinem, Gloria 1934- . . . . **CLC 63**
See also CA 53-56; CANR 28; MTCW

Steiner, George 1929- . . . . **CLC 24**
See also CA 73-76; CANR 31; DLB 67;
MTCW; SATA 62

Steiner, Rudolf 1861-1925 . . . . **TCLC 13**
See also CA 107

Stendhal 1783-1842 . . . . **NCLC 23**
See also DA; DLB 119; WLC

Stephen, Leslie 1832-1904 . . . . **TCLC 23**
See also CA 123; DLB 57

Stephen, Sir Leslie
See Stephen, Leslie

Stephen, Virginia
See Woolf, (Adeline) Virginia

Stephens, James 1882(?)-1950 . . . . . . **TCLC 4**
See also CA 104; DLB 19

Stephens, Reed
See Donaldson, Stephen R.

Steptoe, Lydia
See Barnes, Djuna

Sterchi, Beat 1949- . . . . **CLC 65**

Sterling, Brett
See Bradbury, Ray (Douglas); Hamilton,
Edmond

Sterling, Bruce 1954- . . . . **CLC 72**
See also CA 119

Sterling, George 1869-1926 . . . . **TCLC 20**
See also CA 117; DLB 54

Stern, Gerald 1925- . . . . **CLC 40**
See also CA 81-84; CANR 28; DLB 105

Stern, Richard (Gustave) 1928- . . . **CLC 4, 39**
See also CA 1-4R; CANR 1, 25; DLBY 87

Sternberg, Josef von 1894-1969 . . . . . **CLC 20**
See also CA 81-84

Sterne, Laurence 1713-1768 . . . . **LC 2**
See also CDBLB 1660-1789; DA; DLB 39;
WLC

Sternheim, (William Adolf) Carl
1878-1942 . . . . **TCLC 8**
See also CA 105; DLB 56, 118

Stevens, Mark 1951- . . . . **CLC 34**
See also CA 122

Stevens, Wallace
1879-1955 . . . . **TCLC 3, 12, 45; PC 6**
See also CA 104; 124; CDALB 1929-1941;
DA; DLB 54; MTCW; WLC

Stevenson, Anne (Katharine)
1933- . . . . **CLC 7, 33**
See also CA 17-20R; CAAS 9; CANR 9, 33;
DLB 40; MTCW

Stevenson, Robert Louis (Balfour)
1850-1894 . . . . **NCLC 5, 14; SSC 11**
See also CDBLB 1890-1914; CLR 10, 11;
DA; DLB 18, 57; MAICYA; WLC;
YABC 2

Stewart, J(ohn) I(nnes) M(ackintosh)
1906- . . . . **CLC 7, 14, 32**
See also CA 85-88; CAAS 3; MTCW

Stewart, Mary (Florence Elinor)
1916- . . . . **CLC 7, 35**
See also CA 1-4R; CANR 1; SATA 12

Stewart, Mary Rainbow
See Stewart, Mary (Florence Elinor)

Still, James 1906- . . . . **CLC 49**
See also CA 65-68; CAAS 17; CANR 10,
26; DLB 9; SATA 29

Sting
See Sumner, Gordon Matthew

Stirling, Arthur
See Sinclair, Upton (Beall)

Stitt, Milan 1941- . . . . **CLC 29**
See also CA 69-72

Stockton, Francis Richard 1834-1902
See Stockton, Frank R.
See also CA 108; 137; MAICYA; SATA 44

Stockton, Frank R. . . . . **TCLC 47**
See also Stockton, Francis Richard
See also DLB 42, 74; SATA 32

Stoddard, Charles
See Kuttner, Henry

Stoker, Abraham 1847-1912
See Stoker, Bram
See also CA 105; DA; SATA 29

Stoker, Bram . . . . **TCLC 8**
See also Stoker, Abraham
See also CDBLB 1890-1914; DLB 36, 70;
WLC

Stolz, Mary (Slattery) 1920- . . . . **CLC 12**
See also AAYA 8; AITN 1; CA 5-8R;
CANR 13, 41; MAICYA; SAAS 3;
SATA 10, 70, 71

Stone, Irving 1903-1989 . . . . **CLC 7**
See also AITN 1; CA 1-4R; 129; CAAS 3;
CANR 1, 23; MTCW; SATA 3;
SATA-Obit 64

Stone, Oliver 1946- . . . . **CLC 73**
See also CA 110

Stone, Robert (Anthony)
1937- . . . . **CLC 5, 23, 42**
See also CA 85-88; CANR 23; MTCW

Stone, Zachary
See Follett, Ken(neth Martin)

Stoppard, Tom
1937- . . . **CLC 1, 3, 4, 5, 8, 15, 29, 34, 63**
See also CA 81-84; CANR 39;
CDBLB 1960 to Present; DA; DLB 13;
DLBY 85; MTCW; WLC

Storey, David (Malcolm)
1933- . . . . **CLC 2, 4, 5, 8**
See also CA 81-84; CANR 36; DLB 13, 14;
MTCW

Storm, Hyemeyohsts 1935- . . . . **CLC 3**
See also CA 81-84

Storm, (Hans) Theodor (Woldsen)
1817-1888 . . . . **NCLC 1**

Storni, Alfonsina 1892-1938 . . . . **TCLC 5**
See also CA 104; 131; HW

Stout, Rex (Todhunter) 1886-1975 . . . **CLC 3**
See also AITN 2; CA 61-64

Stow, (Julian) Randolph 1935- . . **CLC 23, 48**
See also CA 13-16R; CANR 33; MTCW

Stowe, Harriet (Elizabeth) Beecher
1811-1896 . . . . **NCLC 3**
See also CDALB 1865-1917; DA; DLB 1,
12, 42, 74; MAICYA; WLC; YABC 1

Strachey, (Giles) Lytton
1880-1932 . . . . **TCLC 12**
See also CA 110; DLBD 10

Strand, Mark 1934- . . . . . . **CLC 6, 18, 41, 71**
See also CA 21-24R; CANR 40; DLB 5;
SATA 41

Straub, Peter (Francis) 1943- . . . . . . **CLC 28**
See also BEST 89:1; CA 85-88; CANR 28;
DLBY 84; MTCW

Strauss, Botho 1944- . . . . **CLC 22**
See also DLB 124

Streatfeild, (Mary) Noel
1895(?)-1986 . . . . **CLC 21**
See also CA 81-84; 120; CANR 31;
CLR 17; MAICYA; SATA 20, 48

Stribling, T(homas) S(igismund)
1881-1965 . . . . **CLC 23**
See also CA 107; DLB 9

Strindberg, (Johan) August
1849-1912 . . . . **TCLC 1, 8, 21, 47**
See also CA 104; 135; DA; WLC

Stringer, Arthur 1874-1950 . . . . **TCLC 37**
See also DLB 92

Stringer, David
See Roberts, Keith (John Kingston)

Strugatskii, Arkadii (Natanovich)
1925-1991 . . . . **CLC 27**
See also CA 106; 135

Strugatskii, Boris (Natanovich)
1933- . . . . **CLC 27**
See also CA 106

Strummer, Joe 1953(?)- . . . . **CLC 30**
See also Clash, The

Stuart, Don A.
See Campbell, John W(ood, Jr.)

Stuart, Ian
See MacLean, Alistair (Stuart)

Stuart, Jesse (Hilton)
1906-1984 . . . . **CLC 1, 8, 11, 14, 34**
See also CA 5-8R; 112; CANR 31; DLB 9,
48, 102; DLBY 84; SATA 2, 36

Warner, Sylvia Townsend
1893-1978 . . . . **CLC 7, 19**
See also CA 61-64; 77-80; CANR 16;
DLB 34; MTCW

Warren, Mercy Otis　1728-1814. . . **NCLC 13**
See also DLB 31

Warren, Robert Penn
1905-1989 . . .　**CLC 1, 4, 6, 8, 10, 13, 18,**
39, 53, 59; SSC 4
See also AITN 1; CA 13-16R; 129;
CANR 10; CDALB 1968-1988; DA;
DLB 2, 48; DLBY 80, 89; MTCW;
SATA 46, 63; WLC

Warshofsky, Isaac
See Singer, Isaac Bashevis

Warton, Thomas　1728-1790. . . . . **LC 15**
See also DLB 104, 109

Waruk, Kona
See Harris, (Theodore) Wilson

Warung, Price　1855-1911. . . . . **TCLC 45**

Warwick, Jarvis
See Garner, Hugh

Washington, Alex
See Harris, Mark

Washington, Booker T(aliaferro)
1856-1915 . . . . **TCLC 10**
See also BLC 3; BW; CA 114; 125;
SATA 28

Wassermann, (Karl) Jakob
1873-1934 . . . . **TCLC 6**
See also CA 104; DLB 66

Wasserstein, Wendy　1950-. . . . . . **CLC 32, 59**
See also CA 121; 129; CABS 3

Waterhouse, Keith (Spencer)
1929- . . . . **CLC 47**
See also CA 5-8R; CANR 38; DLB 13, 15;
MTCW

Waters, Roger　1944-. . . . . **CLC 35**
See also Pink Floyd

Watkins, Frances Ellen
See Harper, Frances Ellen Watkins

Watkins, Gerrold
See Malzberg, Barry N(athaniel)

Watkins, Paul　1964-. . . . . **CLC 55**
See also CA 132

Watkins, Vernon Phillips
1906-1967 . . . . **CLC 43**
See also CA 9-10; 25-28R; CAP 1; DLB 20

Watson, Irving S.
See Mencken, H(enry) L(ouis)

Watson, John H.
See Farmer, Philip Jose

Watson, Richard F.
See Silverberg, Robert

Waugh, Auberon (Alexander)　1939-. . **CLC 7**
See also CA 45-48; CANR 6, 22; DLB 14

Waugh, Evelyn (Arthur St. John)
1903-1966 . . .　**CLC 1, 3, 8, 13, 19, 27, 44**
See also CA 85-88; 25-28R; CANR 22;
CDBLB 1914-1945; DA; DLB 15;
MTCW; WLC

Waugh, Harriet　1944-. . . . . **CLC 6**
See also CA 85-88; CANR 22

Ways, C. R.
See Blount, Roy (Alton), Jr.

Waystaff, Simon
See Swift, Jonathan

Webb, (Martha) Beatrice (Potter)
1858-1943 . . . . **TCLC 22**
See also Potter, Beatrice
See also CA 117

Webb, Charles (Richard)　1939-. . . . . . **CLC 7**
See also CA 25-28R

Webb, James H(enry), Jr.　1946-. . . . **CLC 22**
See also CA 81-84

Webb, Mary (Gladys Meredith)
1881-1927 . . . . **TCLC 24**
See also CA 123; DLB 34

Webb, Mrs. Sidney
See Webb, (Martha) Beatrice (Potter)

Webb, Phyllis　1927-. . . . . **CLC 18**
See also CA 104; CANR 23; DLB 53

Webb, Sidney (James)
1859-1947 . . . . **TCLC 22**
See also CA 117

Webber, Andrew Lloyd. . . . . **CLC 21**
See also Lloyd Webber, Andrew

Weber, Lenora Mattingly
1895-1971 . . . . **CLC 12**
See also CA 19-20; 29-32R; CAP 1;
SATA 2, 26

Webster, John　1579(?)-1634(?) . . . . **DC 2**
See also CDBLB Before 1660; DA; DLB 58;
WLC

Webster, Noah　1758-1843 . . . . **NCLC 30**

Wedekind, (Benjamin) Frank(lin)
1864-1918 . . . . **TCLC 7**
See also CA 104; DLB 118

Weidman, Jerome　1913-. . . . . **CLC 7**
See also AITN 2; CA 1-4R; CANR 1;
DLB 28

Weil, Simone (Adolphine)
1909-1943 . . . . **TCLC 23**
See also CA 117

Weinstein, Nathan
See West, Nathanael

Weinstein, Nathan von Wallenstein
See West, Nathanael

Weir, Peter (Lindsay)　1944-. . . . . . . **CLC 20**
See also CA 113; 123

Weiss, Peter (Ulrich)
1916-1982 . . . . **CLC 3, 15, 51**
See also CA 45-48; 106; CANR 3; DLB 69;
124

Weiss, Theodore (Russell)
1916- . . . . **CLC 3, 8, 14**
See also CA 9-12R; CAAS 2; DLB 5

Welch, (Maurice) Denton
1915-1948 . . . . **TCLC 22**
See also CA 121

Welch, James　1940-. . . . . **CLC 6, 14, 52**
See also CA 85-88

Weldon, Fay
1933(?)- . . . . **CLC 6, 9, 11, 19, 36, 59**
See also CA 21-24R; CANR 16;
CDBLB 1960 to Present; DLB 14;
MTCW

Wellek, Rene　1903- . . . . **CLC 28**
See also CA 5-8R; CAAS 7; CANR 8;
DLB 63

Weller, Michael　1942-. . . . . **CLC 10, 53**
See also CA 85-88

Weller, Paul　1958-. . . . . **CLC 26**

Wellershoff, Dieter　1925-. . . . . **CLC 46**
See also CA 89-92; CANR 16, 37

Welles, (George) Orson
1915-1985 . . . . **CLC 20**
See also CA 93-96; 117

Wellman, Mac　1945- . . . . **CLC 65**

Wellman, Manly Wade　1903-1986 . . **CLC 49**
See also CA 1-4R; 118; CANR 6, 16;
SATA 6, 47

Wells, Carolyn　1869(?)-1942 . . . . . . **TCLC 35**
See also CA 113; DLB 11

Wells, H(erbert) G(eorge)
1866-1946 . . . . . . **TCLC 6, 12, 19; SSC 6**
See also CA 110; 121; CDBLB 1914-1945;
DA; DLB 34, 70; MTCW; SATA 20;
WLC

Wells, Rosemary　1943-. . . . . **CLC 12**
See also CA 85-88; CLR 16; MAICYA;
SAAS 1; SATA 18, 69

Welty, Eudora
1909- . . . . **CLC 1, 2, 5, 14, 22, 33; SSC 1**
See also CA 9-12R; CABS 1; CANR 32;
CDALB 1941-1968; DA; DLB 2, 102;
DLBY 87; MTCW; WLC

Wen I-to　1899-1946 . . . . **TCLC 28**

Wentworth, Robert
See Hamilton, Edmond

Werfel, Franz (V.)　1890-1945 . . . . . . **TCLC 8**
See also CA 104; DLB 81, 124

Wergeland, Henrik Arnold
1808-1845 . . . . **NCLC 5**

Wersba, Barbara　1932-. . . . . **CLC 30**
See also AAYA 2; CA 29-32R; CANR 16,
38; CLR 3; DLB 52; MAICYA; SAAS 2;
SATA 1, 58

Wertmueller, Lina　1928- . . . . **CLC 16**
See also CA 97-100; CANR 39

Wescott, Glenway　1901-1987. . . . . . . **CLC 13**
See also CA 13-16R; 121; CANR 23;
DLB 4, 9, 102

Wesker, Arnold　1932- . . . . **CLC 3, 5, 42**
See also CA 1-4R; CAAS 7; CANR 1, 33;
CDBLB 1960 to Present; DLB 13;
MTCW

Wesley, Richard (Errol)　1945-. . . . . . **CLC 7**
See also BW; CA 57-60; CANR 27; DLB 38

Wessel, Johan Herman　1742-1785 . . . . **LC 7**

West, Anthony (Panther)
1914-1987 . . . . **CLC 50**
See also CA 45-48; 124; CANR 3, 19;
DLB 15

West, C. P.
See Wodehouse, P(elham) G(renville)

West, (Mary) Jessamyn
1902-1984 . . . . **CLC 7, 17**
See also CA 9-12R; 112; CANR 27; DLB 6;
DLBY 84; MTCW; SATA 37

West, Morris L(anglo) 1916-..... **CLC 6, 33**
See also CA 5-8R; CANR 24; MTCW

West, Nathanael
1903-1940 .... **TCLC 1, 14, 44**
See also CA 104; 125; CDALB 1929-1941;
DLB 4, 9, 28; MTCW

West, Paul 1930- .... **CLC 7, 14**
See also CA 13-16R; CAAS 7; CANR 22;
DLB 14

West, Rebecca 1892-1983 .. **CLC 7, 9, 31, 50**
See also CA 5-8R; 109; CANR 19; DLB 36;
DLBY 83; MTCW

Westall, Robert (Atkinson) 1929-... **CLC 17**
See also CA 69-72; CANR 18; CLR 13;
MAICYA; SAAS 2; SATA 23, 69

Westlake, Donald E(dwin)
1933- .... **CLC 7, 33**
See also CA 17-20R; CAAS 13; CANR 16

Westmacott, Mary
See Christie, Agatha (Mary Clarissa)

Weston, Allen
See Norton, Andre

Wetcheek, J. L.
See Feuchtwanger, Lion

Wetering, Janwillem van de
See van de Wetering, Janwillem

Wetherell, Elizabeth
See Warner, Susan (Bogert)

Whalen, Philip 1923- .... **CLC 6, 29**
See also CA 9-12R; CANR 5, 39; DLB 16

Wharton, Edith (Newbold Jones)
1862-1937 .... **TCLC 3, 9, 27; SSC 6**
See also CA 104; 132; CDALB 1865-1917;
DA; DLB 4, 9, 12, 78; MTCW; WLC

Wharton, James
See Mencken, H(enry) L(ouis)

Wharton, William (a pseudonym)
.... **CLC 18, 37**
See also CA 93-96; DLBY 80

Wheatley (Peters), Phillis
1754(?)-1784 .... **LC 3; PC 3**
See also BLC 3; CDALB 1640-1865; DA;
DLB 31, 50; WLC

Wheelock, John Hall 1886-1978 .... **CLC 14**
See also CA 13-16R; 77-80; CANR 14;
DLB 45

White, E(lwyn) B(rooks)
1899-1985 .... **CLC 10, 34, 39**
See also AITN 2; CA 13-16R; 116;
CANR 16, 37; CLR 1, 21; DLB 11, 22;
MAICYA; MTCW; SATA 2, 29, 44

White, Edmund (Valentine III)
1940- .... **CLC 27**
See also AAYA 7; CA 45-48; CANR 3, 19,
36; MTCW

White, Patrick (Victor Martindale)
1912-1990 .. **CLC 3, 4, 5, 7, 9, 18, 65, 69**
See also CA 81-84; 132; MTCW

White, Phyllis Dorothy James 1920-
See James, P. D.
See also CA 21-24R; CANR 17; MTCW

White, T(erence) H(anbury)
1906-1964 .... **CLC 30**
See also CA 73-76; CANR 37; MAICYA;
SATA 12

White, Terence de Vere 1912-...... **CLC 49**
See also CA 49-52; CANR 3

White, Walter F(rancis)
1893-1955 .... **TCLC 15**
See also White, Walter
See also CA 115; 124; DLB 51

White, William Hale 1831-1913
See Rutherford, Mark
See also CA 121

Whitehead, E(dward) A(nthony)
1933- .... **CLC 5**
See also CA 65-68

Whitemore, Hugh (John) 1936-..... **CLC 37**
See also CA 132

Whitman, Sarah Helen (Power)
1803-1878 .... **NCLC 19**
See also DLB 1

Whitman, Walt(er)
1819-1892 .... **NCLC 4, 31; PC 3**
See also CDALB 1640-1865; DA; DLB 3,
64; SATA 20; WLC

Whitney, Phyllis A(yame) 1903-.... **CLC 42**
See also AITN 2; BEST 90:3; CA 1-4R;
CANR 3, 25, 38; MAICYA; SATA 1, 30

Whittemore, (Edward) Reed (Jr.)
1919- .... **CLC 4**
See also CA 9-12R; CAAS 8; CANR 4;
DLB 5

Whittier, John Greenleaf
1807-1892 .... **NCLC 8**
See also CDALB 1640-1865; DLB 1

Whittlebot, Hernia
See Coward, Noel (Peirce)

Wicker, Thomas Grey 1926-
See Wicker, Tom
See also CA 65-68; CANR 21

Wicker, Tom .... **CLC 7**
See also Wicker, Thomas Grey

Wideman, John Edgar
1941- .... **CLC 5, 34, 36, 67**
See also BLC 3; BW; CA 85-88; CANR 14;
DLB 33

Wiebe, Rudy (H.) 1934-...... **CLC 6, 11, 14**
See also CA 37-40R; DLB 60

Wieland, Christoph Martin
1733-1813 .... **NCLC 17**
See also DLB 97

Wieners, John 1934-.............. **CLC 7**
See also CA 13-16R; DLB 16

Wiesel, Elie(zer) 1928-..... **CLC 3, 5, 11, 37**
See also AAYA 7; AITN 1; CA 5-8R;
CAAS 4; CANR 8, 40; DA; DLB 83;
DLBY 87; MTCW; SATA 56

Wiggins, Marianne 1947-......... **CLC 57**
See also BEST 89:3; CA 130

Wight, James Alfred 1916-
See Herriot, James
See also CA 77-80; SATA 44, 55

Wilbur, Richard (Purdy)
1921- .... **CLC 3, 6, 9, 14, 53**
See also CA 1-4R; CABS 2; CANR 2, 29;
DA; DLB 5; MTCW; SATA 9

Wild, Peter 1940-............... **CLC 14**
See also CA 37-40R; DLB 5

Wilde, Oscar (Fingal O'Flahertie Wills)
1854(?)-1900 .... **TCLC 1, 8, 23, 41;**
SSC 11
See also CA 104; 119; CDBLB 1890-1914;
DA; DLB 10, 19, 34, 57; SATA 24; WLC

Wilder, Billy .... **CLC 20**
See also Wilder, Samuel
See also DLB 26

Wilder, Samuel 1906-
See Wilder, Billy
See also CA 89-92

Wilder, Thornton (Niven)
1897-1975 ..... **CLC 1, 5, 6, 10, 15, 35;**
DC 1
See also AITN 2; CA 13-16R; 61-64;
CANR 40; DA; DLB 4, 7, 9; MTCW;
WLC

Wilding, Michael 1942-........... **CLC 73**
See also CA 104; CANR 24

Wiley, Richard 1944-............. **CLC 44**
See also CA 121; 129

Wilhelm, Kate .... **CLC 7**
See also Wilhelm, Katie Gertrude
See also CAAS 5; DLB 8

Wilhelm, Katie Gertrude 1928-
See Wilhelm, Kate
See also CA 37-40R; CANR 17, 36; MTCW

Wilkins, Mary
See Freeman, Mary Eleanor Wilkins

Willard, Nancy 1936-........... **CLC 7, 37**
See also CA 89-92; CANR 10, 39; CLR 5;
DLB 5, 52; MAICYA; MTCW;
SATA 30, 37, 71

Williams, C(harles) K(enneth)
1936- .... **CLC 33, 56**
See also CA 37-40R; DLB 5

Williams, Charles
See Collier, James L(incoln)

Williams, Charles (Walter Stansby)
1886-1945 .... **TCLC 1, 11**
See also CA 104; DLB 100

Williams, (George) Emlyn
1905-1987 .... **CLC 15**
See also CA 104; 123; CANR 36; DLB 10,
77; MTCW

Williams, Hugo 1942-............. **CLC 42**
See also CA 17-20R; DLB 40

Williams, J. Walker
See Wodehouse, P(elham) G(renville)

Williams, John A(lfred) 1925-.... **CLC 5, 13**
See also BLC 3; BW; CA 53-56; CAAS 3;
CANR 6, 26; DLB 2, 33

Williams, Jonathan (Chamberlain)
1929- .... **CLC 13**
See also CA 9-12R; CAAS 12; CANR 8;
DLB 5

Williams, Joy 1944-............. **CLC 31**
See also CA 41-44R; CANR 22

Williams, Norman 1952- .... **CLC 39**
See also CA 118

Williams, Tennessee
    1911-1983 .... **CLC 1, 2, 5, 7, 8, 11, 15,**
                              19, 30, 39, 45, 71
    See also AITN 1, 2; CA 5-8R; 108;
      CABS 3; CANR 31; CDALB 1941-1968;
      DA; DLB 7; DLBD 4; DLBY 83;
      MTCW; WLC

Williams, Thomas (Alonzo)
    1926-1990 .... **CLC 14**
    See also CA 1-4R; 132; CANR 2

Williams, William C.
    See Williams, William Carlos

Williams, William Carlos
    1883-1963 ... **CLC 1, 2, 5, 9, 13, 22, 42,**
                                               67
    See also CA 89-92; CANR 34;
      CDALB 1917-1929; DA; DLB 4, 16, 54,
      86; MTCW

Williamson, David (Keith) 1942-.... **CLC 56**
    See also CA 103; CANR 41

Williamson, Jack................. **CLC 29**
    See also Williamson, John Stewart
    See also CAAS 8; DLB 8

Williamson, John Stewart 1908-
    See Williamson, Jack
    See also CA 17-20R; CANR 23

Willie, Frederick
    See Lovecraft, H(oward) P(hillips)

Willingham, Calder (Baynard, Jr.)
    1922- .... **CLC 5, 51**
    See also CA 5-8R; CANR 3; DLB 2, 44;
      MTCW

Willis, Charles
    See Clarke, Arthur C(harles)

Willy
    See Colette, (Sidonie-Gabrielle)

Willy, Colette
    See Colette, (Sidonie-Gabrielle)

Wilson, A(ndrew) N(orman) 1950- .. **CLC 33**
    See also CA 112; 122; DLB 14

Wilson, Angus (Frank Johnstone)
    1913-1991 .... **CLC 2, 3, 5, 25, 34**
    See also CA 5-8R; 134; CANR 21; DLB 15;
      MTCW

Wilson, August
    1945- .... **CLC 39, 50, 63; DC 2**
    See also BLC 3; BW; CA 115; 122; DA;
      MTCW

Wilson, Brian 1942- .... **CLC 12**

Wilson, Colin 1931- .... **CLC 3, 14**
    See also CA 1-4R; CAAS 5; CANR 1, 22,
      33; DLB 14; MTCW

Wilson, Dirk
    See Pohl, Frederik

Wilson, Edmund
    1895-1972 .... **CLC 1, 2, 3, 8, 24**
    See also CA 1-4R; 37-40R; CANR 1;
      DLB 63; MTCW

Wilson, Ethel Davis (Bryant)
    1888(?)-1980 .... **CLC 13**
    See also CA 102; DLB 68; MTCW

Wilson, John 1785-1854......... **NCLC 5**

Wilson, John (Anthony) Burgess
    1917- .... **CLC 8, 10, 13**
    See also Burgess, Anthony
    See also CA 1-4R; CANR 2; MTCW

Wilson, Lanford 1937-....... **CLC 7, 14, 36**
    See also CA 17-20R; CABS 3; DLB 7

Wilson, Robert M. 1944-........ **CLC 7, 9**
    See also CA 49-52; CANR 2, 41; MTCW

Wilson, Robert McLiam 1964- ..... **CLC 59**
    See also CA 132

Wilson, Sloan 1920- .... **CLC 32**
    See also CA 1-4R; CANR 1

Wilson, Snoo 1948-............... **CLC 33**
    See also CA 69-72

Wilson, William S(mith) 1932- ..... **CLC 49**
    See also CA 81-84

Winchilsea, Anne (Kingsmill) Finch Counte
    1661-1720 .... **LC 3**

Windham, Basil
    See Wodehouse, P(elham) G(renville)

Wingrove, David (John) 1954-...... **CLC 68**
    See also CA 133

Winters, Janet Lewis .... **CLC 41**
    See also Lewis, Janet
    See also DLBY 87

Winters, (Arthur) Yvor
    1900-1968 .... **CLC 4, 8, 32**
    See also CA 11-12; 25-28R; CAP 1;
      DLB 48; MTCW

Winterson, Jeanette 1959-........ **CLC 64**
    See also CA 136

Wiseman, Frederick 1930-........ **CLC 20**

Wister, Owen 1860-1938 .... **TCLC 21**
    See also CA 108; DLB 9, 78; SATA 62

Witkacy
    See Witkiewicz, Stanislaw Ignacy

Witkiewicz, Stanislaw Ignacy
    1885-1939 .... **TCLC 8**
    See also CA 105

Wittig, Monique 1935(?)-.......... **CLC 22**
    See also CA 116; 135; DLB 83

Wittlin, Jozef 1896-1976 .... **CLC 25**
    See also CA 49-52; 65-68; CANR 3

Wodehouse, P(elham) G(renville)
    1881-1975 ... **CLC 1, 2, 5, 10, 22; SSC 2**
    See also AITN 2; CA 45-48; 57-60;
      CANR 3, 33; CDBLB 1914-1945;
      DLB 34; MTCW; SATA 22

Woiwode, L.
    See Woiwode, Larry (Alfred)

Woiwode, Larry (Alfred) 1941-... **CLC 6, 10**
    See also CA 73-76; CANR 16; DLB 6

Wojciechowska, Maia (Teresa)
    1927- .... **CLC 26**
    See also AAYA 8; CA 9-12R; CANR 4, 41;
      CLR 1; MAICYA; SAAS 1; SATA 1, 28

Wolf, Christa 1929- .... **CLC 14, 29, 58**
    See also CA 85-88; DLB 75; MTCW

Wolfe, Gene (Rodman) 1931-...... **CLC 25**
    See also CA 57-60; CAAS 9; CANR 6, 32;
      DLB 8

Wolfe, George C. 1954- .... **CLC 49**

Wolfe, Thomas (Clayton)
    1900-1938 .... **TCLC 4, 13, 29**
    See also CA 104; 132; CDALB 1929-1941;
      DA; DLB 9, 102; DLBD 2; DLBY 85;
      MTCW; WLC

Wolfe, Thomas Kennerly, Jr. 1930-
    See Wolfe, Tom
    See also CA 13-16R; CANR 9, 33; MTCW

Wolfe, Tom .... **CLC 1, 2, 9, 15, 35, 51**
    See also Wolfe, Thomas Kennerly, Jr.
    See also AAYA 8; AITN 2; BEST 89:1

Wolff, Geoffrey (Ansell) 1937- ..... **CLC 41**
    See also CA 29-32R; CANR 29

Wolff, Sonia
    See Levitin, Sonia (Wolff)

Wolff, Tobias (Jonathan Ansell)
    1945- .... **CLC 39, 64**
    See also BEST 90:2; CA 114; 117; DLB 130

Wolfram von Eschenbach
    c. 1170-c. 1220 .... **CMLC 5**

Wolitzer, Hilma 1930-........... **CLC 17**
    See also CA 65-68; CANR 18, 40; SATA 31

Wollstonecraft, Mary 1759-1797...... **LC 5**
    See also CDBLB 1789-1832; DLB 39, 104

Wonder, Stevie .... **CLC 12**
    See also Morris, Steveland Judkins

Wong, Jade Snow 1922-........... **CLC 17**
    See also CA 109

Woodcott, Keith
    See Brunner, John (Kilian Houston)

Woodruff, Robert W.
    See Mencken, H(enry) L(ouis)

Woolf, (Adeline) Virginia
    1882-1941 .... **TCLC 1, 5, 20, 43; SSC 7**
    See also CA 104; 130; CDBLB 1914-1945;
      DA; DLB 36, 100; DLBD 10; MTCW;
      WLC

Woollcott, Alexander (Humphreys)
    1887-1943 .... **TCLC 5**
    See also CA 105; DLB 29

Woolrich, Cornell 1903-1968....... **CLC 77**
    See also Hopley-Woolrich, Cornell George

Wordsworth, Dorothy
    1771-1855 .... **NCLC 25**
    See also DLB 107

Wordsworth, William
    1770-1850 .... **NCLC 12, 38; PC 4**
    See also CDBLB 1789-1832; DA; DLB 93,
      107; WLC

Wouk, Herman 1915-......... **CLC 1, 9, 38**
    See also CA 5-8R; CANR 6, 33; DLBY 82;
      MTCW

Wright, Charles (Penzel, Jr.)
    1935- .... **CLC 6, 13, 28**
    See also CA 29-32R; CAAS 7; CANR 23,
      36; DLBY 82; MTCW

Wright, Charles Stevenson 1932- ... **CLC 49**
    See also BLC 3; BW; CA 9-12R; CANR 26;
      DLB 33

Wright, Jack R.
    See Harris, Mark

Wright, James (Arlington)
    1927-1980 ....**CLC 3, 5, 10, 28**
    See also AITN 2; CA 49-52; 97-100;
      CANR 4, 34; DLB 5; MTCW

CLC Cumulative Nationality Index

Nationality Index